a. 375

THE UNIVERSITY OF CHICAGO
ORIENTAL INSTITUTE PUBLICATIONS
VOLUME 105

THE UNIVERSITY OF CHICAGO
ORIENTAL INSTITUTE PUBLICATIONS
VOLUME 105

PREHISTORIC ARCHEOLOGY ALONG THE ZAGROS FLANKS

Edited by

LINDA S. BRAIDWOOD · ROBERT J. BRAIDWOOD

BRUCE HOWE · CHARLES A. REED

and PATTY JO WATSON

THE ORIENTAL INSTITUTE OF THE UNIVERSITY OF CHICAGO
CHICAGO · ILLINOIS

Library of Congress Catalog Card Number: 81-85896

ISBN: 0-918986-36-2
ISSN: 0069-3367

The Oriental Institute, Chicago

©1983 by The University of Chicago. All rights reserved
Published 1983. Printed in the United States of America

In memory of
three Arabian gentlemen
without whose enthusiasm, goodwill, and cooperation
the various activities of the Iraq-Jarmo Project
would never have prospered

DR. NAJI AL-ASIL
FUAD SAFAR
ABDULLAH SAID OSMAN AL-SUDANI

PREFACE

Another four years have gone by since the Introduction to this volume was written and the substantive editing of the various reports was completed. Our interested colleagues cannot feel more frustrated with the delay than we.

The Introduction, which follows, and the third chapter in our preliminary report of 1960, *Prehistoric Investigations in Iraqi Kurdistan* (SAOC 31), account for the general development of the Oriental Institute Prehistoric Project's activities in Iraq. We wish, however, once again to note the names of our field companions and also to thank those other individuals and institutions that aided our research efforts from the beginning. The Prehistoric Project of the Oriental Institute of the University of Chicago was first activated in early 1947.

From the original planning for our field campaigns onwards through the processing of the materials for publication we have had enthusiastic cooperation and support from the succession of directors of the Oriental Institute and from the chairmen of the Department of Anthropology of our university.

The field budget for the first season came primarily from the Oriental Institute, aided by a subvention from the Department of Anthropology for their graduate student grantee and by Robert Braidwood's release from academic duties. In the second and third seasons there were also grants from the American Philosophical Society, the American Schools of Oriental Research, and the Wenner-Gren Foundation for Anthropological Research; and the Oriental Institute and the Department of Anthropology participated as before. In 1954-55 the Department of Anthropology received the first of a series of substantial grants from the National Science Foundation for our fieldwork. And, from the beginning, we have appreciated warm interest and financial support from special friends of the Project.

We were most fortunate, from our start in Iraq in 1947, in that three officials of the Directorate General of Antiquities knew us and about our research interests. We had helped Seton Lloyd and the late Fuad Safar get their Hassuna site report published: Lloyd had once been an Oriental Institute field staff architect, and Safar and Taha Bakir (an epigrapher in the Directorate) had both been Oriental Institute graduate students. Through these three officials we came to know and greatly respect the late Dr. Naji al-Asil, the director general.

In the field we were also fortunate in having the late Abdullah Said Osman al-Sudani aid us as general foreman and then, later, as field superintendent. Abdullah had worked for the Oriental Institute since the Syrian Expedition's first field season in the ᶜAmuq in 1932. There was never a better foreman or a better field companion.

In Kirkuk, the town that served as the supply base for our field camp, we came to greatly depend on the openhearted helpfulness of the late Reverend Jefferson C. Glessner and his wife, Helen Glessner. Various officials of the Iraq Petroleum Company also aided us in many ways.

It has been our great fortune, overall, to have had a sequence of highly competent, interested, and sensitive field companions. These we name by the field seasons during which they served, giving their identifications as of that time (unless otherwise indicated, affiliations were with the University of Chicago):

1947-48

Faraj Basmachi (Iraq Directorate General of Antiquities representative)
Linda S. Braidwood (Oriental Institute)
Robert J. Braidwood (Oriental Institute and Department of Anthropology)
Charlotte M. Otten (Department of Anthropology grantee)

1950-51

Robert McC. Adams (Department of Anthropology grantee)
Fredrik Barth (Ethnographic Museum, Oslo, grantee)
Linda S. Braidwood (Oriental Institute)
Robert J. Braidwood (Oriental Institute and Department of Anthropology)
Vivian L. Broman [Morales] (Oriental Institute grantee)
Bruce Howe (Peabody Museum, Harvard University)
Sabri Shukri (Iraq Directorate General of Antiquities representative)
Elizabeth West [Fitzhugh] (Oriental Institute volunteer)
Herbert E. Wright, Jr. (Department of Geology, University of Minnesota)

Cornelius Hillen and Gustavus Swift, Jr. (Oriental Institute graduate students) served as part-time volunteers. Eleanor Swift also served as a volunteer.

PREFACE

1954-55

Patty Jo Anderson [Watson] (Department of Anthropology grantee)
Hussain Azzam (Iraq Directorate General of Antiquities representative)
Linda S. Braidwood (Oriental Institute)
Robert J. Braidwood (Oriental Institute and Department of Anthropology)
Vivian L. Broman [Morales] (Oriental Institute grantee)
Hans Helbaek (Danish National Museum)
Yusuf Mansur (Iraq Natural History Museum, Baghdad, representative)
Frederick R. Matson (Department of Anthropology, Pennsylvania State University)
Margaret Matson (Oriental Institute volunteer)
Charles A. Reed (Medical School faculty, University of Illinois)
Sabri Shukri (Iraq Directorate General of Antiquities representative)
Mayo Schreiber (Oriental Institute volunteer)
Beverly Schreiber (Oriental Institute volunteer)
Herbert E. Wright, Jr. (Department of Geology, University of Minnesota)
Rhea Wright (Oriental Institute volunteer)

For short periods, Mohammed Ali and Subhai Anwar also served as Iraq Directorate General of Antiquities representatives.

(The Braidwoods' daughter, Gretel, and son, Douglas, were in camp the first two seasons and Douglas also in the 1954-55 season. In the 1954-55 season the three Wright sons, Richard, Peter, and John, were also in the field camp.)

It is now over twenty-seven years since we left Jarmo for the last time, and our experience in completing these reports underlines the fact that the end of fieldwork is far from being the end of an archeological research project. The Introduction (page 1) mentions the names of authors in this volume who were not on any of the field staffs. One, Joseph R. Caldwell, an old student and warm friend (although, unfortunately, never our actual field companion), is no longer living. We list these additional contributors and their identification as of the time they made their reports (p.s. = professional staff; g.s. = graduate student):

James M. Adovasio (Department of Anthropology, University of Pittsburgh, p.s.)
Joseph R. Caldwell (Department of Anthropology, University of Georgia, p.s.)
Margaret Dittemore (Department of Anthropology, University of Chicago, g.s.)
Frank Hole (Department of Anthropology, University of Chicago, g.s.)
Joanne P. Laffer (Department of Anthropology, University of Illinois, g.s.)
Barbara Lawrence (Museum of Comparative Zoology, Harvard University, p.s.)
Hattula Moholy-Nagy (Department of Anthropology, University of Chicago, g.s.)
Hans R. Stampfli (Peabody Museum of Natural History, Yale University, postdoctoral fellow)
Priscilla F. Turnbull (Department of Zoology, Field Museum of Natural History, Chicago, p.s.)

The truly onerous task of editing the twenty-six manuscripts, including two that were jointly authored, as well as most of the design and production work for the text and tables, was in the highly capable hands of Heather L. Taylor, and we are most grateful to her. She bore the brunt of our own exasperation over delays with fortitude, humor, and understanding. She was assisted at various times by Pamela Bruton and Mary Evins (both graduate students) and by Paul Hoffman.

Aside from Broman Morales's fine pencil renderings of the clay figurines and objects, various illustrators were involved in preparing our drawings. Greta F. Blair made the excellent pen and ink drawings of the Karim Shahir flints and other artifacts. Valerie Clark and Nancy H. Flannery prepared many of the Jarmo illustrations. Shirley Jean Anderson, Mary Evins, and Paul Hoffman controlled the illustrative materials for publication.

We do hope that some day new archeological research may begin again in the Chemchemal valley. Our very best wishes to whoever undertakes it!

LINDA S. BRAIDWOOD
ROBERT J. BRAIDWOOD
BRUCE HOWE
CHARLES A. REED
PATTY JO WATSON

CHICAGO
September 1982

CONTENTS

INTRODUCTION, *Linda S. Braidwood, Robert J. Braidwood,* and *Bruce Howe* 1

1. KARIM SHAHIR, *Bruce Howe* 23
2. THE SITE OF JARMO AND ITS ARCHITECTURAL REMAINS, *Robert J. Braidwood* 155
3. THE JARMO STONE AND POTTERY VESSEL INDUSTRIES, *Robert McC. Adams* 209
4. THE JARMO CHIPPED STONE, *Frank Hole* 233
   Appendix. Additional Remarks on the Jarmo Obsidian, *Linda S. Braidwood* 285
5. JARMO ARTIFACTS OF PECKED AND GROUND STONE AND OF SHELL, *Hattula Moholy-Nagy* 289
6. JARMO WORKED BONE, *Patty Jo Watson* 347
7. JARMO FIGURINES AND OTHER CLAY OBJECTS, *Vivian Broman Morales* 369
   Appendix. Notes on the Textile and Basketry Impressions from Jarmo, *J.M. Adovasio* 425
8. THE JARMO DEAD, *Robert J. Braidwood* 427
9. THE FAUNA OF JARMO, WITH NOTES ON ANIMAL BONES FROM MATARRAH, THE ᶜAMUQ, AND KARIM SHAHIR, *Hans R. Stampfli* 431
10. THE DOGS OF JARMO, *Barbara Lawrence and Charles A. Reed* 485
11. BIRDS AND SMALL MAMMALS FROM JARMO, *Priscilla F. Turnbull* 495
12. A NOTE ON THE JARMO PLANT REMAINS, *Patty Jo Watson* 501
13. CLIMATIC CHANGE IN THE ZAGROS MOUNTAINS—REVISITED, *H.E. Wright, Jr.* 505
14. ARCHEOZOOLOGICAL STUDIES IN THE NEAR EAST: A SHORT HISTORY (1960-1980), *Charles A. Reed* . 511
15. JARMO CHRONOLOGY, *Robert J. Braidwood* 537
16. MISCELLANEOUS ANALYSES OF MATERIALS FROM JARMO, *Robert J. Braidwood* 541
17. THE SOUNDINGS AT BANAHILK, *Patty Jo Watson* 545
18. THE BANAHILK POTTER, *Frederick R. Matson* 615
19. THE FAUNAL REMAINS FROM BANAHILK, *Joanne P. Laffer* 629
20. THE POTTERY FROM THE SOUNDINGS AT GIRD ALI AGHA AND AL-KHAN, *Joseph R. Caldwell†* 649
    Appendix. The Nonceramic Yield from Ali Agha and al-Khan, *Editors* 669
21. THE SOUNDINGS AT M'LEFAAT, *Margaret Dittemore* 671
22. THE FAUNAL REMAINS FROM M'LEFAAT, *Priscilla F. Turnbull* 693

INTRODUCTION

Linda S. Braidwood, Robert J. Braidwood, and Bruce Howe

It is now almost a quarter of a century since the Oriental Institute's Iraq-Jarmo Prehistoric Project left the Chemchemal valley in northeastern Iraq. When we broke camp at Jarmo in June 1955, we did not realize then that we were leaving the valley for the last time.

There are a variety of reasons for the long-delayed appearance of these final reports, but to list the reasons as excuses would satisfy neither our readers nor ourselves. We did, at least, provide a reasonably full group of preliminary reports within four years after leaving the field. These preliminary reports were made by the various senior members of the field staff and appeared under the title of *Prehistoric Investigations in Iraqi Kurdistan* as volume 31 of the Oriental Institute's Studies in Ancient Oriental Civilization series, hereinafter referred to simply as SAOC 31.

The present volume includes the final reports on the artifactual and nonartifactual remains recovered from all of our sites save those within the paleolithic time range; these will be dealt with in a subsequent volume. What we shall treat here is the evidence acquired from the regular excavations at the sites of Karim Shahir and Jarmo in the Chemchemal valley (figs. 1, 2b) and from our brief soundings at the sites of M'lefaat, Ali Agha, al-Khan, and Banahilk, farther toward the northeast (figs. 1, 2a). The purpose of our reports on these sites is primarily to provide—insofar as is possible—an objective description of the materials exposed and recovered. These reports have been completed at various times over the last twenty years. This should be an advantage in that they were not done in a rush toward publication, but it has also inevitably resulted in an unevenness in presentation, especially in the currency of other work referred to and the degree to which interpretation has been attempted. Among other things, this situation reflects each author's individual interests, idiosyncracies, and priorities, and we have not attempted to homogenize these unevennesses editorially.

Furthermore, it will also be apparent that the authors of some of the following sections are not always people who were part of the field staff. Unfortunately, American universities seldom, if ever, have a corps of home-based professionally trained technicians or analysts available to aid in the analysis and presentation of field-acquired materials. Also, senior field personnel, once back home, are usually inundated with academic responsibilities. Our own solution to the problem has been to allow well-advanced and promising graduate students to undertake the analysis and presentation of some of the categories of artifacts or of small site soundings. The authors of certain sections of this volume—Adams, Broman Morales, and Watson—were junior members of the field staff, but Dittemore, Hole, Laffer, Moholy Nagy, Lawrence, and Turnbull unfortunately never saw the sites their materials came from, nor did Caldwell and Stampfli, both already at the postdoctoral level at the time they wrote.

In this introduction, we shall first include a few remarks on our field procedures and on the recording and processing of the materials recovered. Next, we turn to a very brief summary of how we viewed certain matters bearing on the appearance of an effective village-farming community way of life in southwestern Asia when SAOC 31 was written in 1959. To this summary, we add a few remarks on several of our subsequent papers indicating how our ideas gradually changed since SAOC 31 appeared. Reed and Wright do the same in sections of their own and Watson has updated Helbaek's ideas through direct correspondence with him. Next comes our brief assessment of what we take to be the more important points in the following reports and our remarks on what the evidence we recovered may suggest about the ways of life of the people who once lived on the sites we excavated. In conclusion, we offer a few modest observations on current theories concerning the beginnings of village-farming communities in southwestern Asia.

REMARKS ON PROCEDURES

We do not hesitate to suggest that our normal field procedures during the three field seasons, 1948-55, were well advanced over what RJB saw during his first Iraqi field season in 1930. In the same sense, we now realize the many inadequacies of our procedures during the earlier 1950s. It is not unreasonable to claim, however, that what is taken to

---

The manuscript for this chapter was essentially completed by 1978. Very few additions and only minor revisions have been made since that date.

be current excellence in field procedure is usually what is practiced at sites within the boundaries of the excavator's home country.[1] In such cases, much of the actual earth moving and even all of the field processing are likely to be done by students or intelligent amateurs who have at least some comprehension of the goals of culture-historical research and with whom the senior staff has no barrier either as to language or ethos. This is a type of situation which excavations by foreign archeologists in southwestern Asia do not normally achieve.

In our own case, we employed up to forty local workmen (when the excavations at both Jarmo and Karim Shahir were in work together) along with six to eight Shergati pickmen. The Shergatis are that guild of now third- and fourth-generation highly skilled archeological workmen who come from the town of Qalat Shergat (ancient Assur), where their forefathers were first trained by that site's German excavators in the period before World War I. Like our Egyptian field superintendent, Abdullah, the Shergatis were of course native Arabic speakers, but the locals were Kurds who had learned Arabic as army draftees. Their Arabic—and our own—was "basic" at best and we had no Kurdish whatsoever. They had little comprehension of our culture-historical goals in digging, and in the matter of Weltanschauung or ethos there was little common understanding.

The Shergatis' skill sometimes led to complications. Highly competent but also very proud, the Shergatis bitterly resented the sieves with which we began our excavation routine. For this reason, we tried restricting the use of sieves to situations where exceptionally rich floor debris was encountered, making frequent unannounced spot checks of our dumps, and assessing stiff fines on any careless pickman. Indeed, an advantage of the baksheesh system of rewards is that a fine (*jaiza*), if imposed, is also taken in good spirit. The number of individual kernels of carbonized grain, along with the number of minute microliths recovered, makes us firmly believe we lost little evidence which sieves could have saved. Further, the restriction of their use contributed much to the good morale we maintained with both the Shergatis and the locals. In addition, considering the relative toughness of the matrix we usually encountered, the use of sieves would have seriously slowed down our already slow pace of work (given the number of workmen our budgets would allow). Also, there would have been more general breakage in routinely forcing tough chunks of matrix through sieves.

We did not begin work with what is now known as an intensive surface survey. We did stake out our areas for exposure with respect to marked surface scatters of artifacts, but we also took topography, convenience for dumpage, and (in the case of Ali Agha) the presence of a cemetery into account.

No attempt was made to keep our exposures strictly rectilinear when interesting architectural features appeared. Because of the previous experience which Abdullah, the Shergatis, and we ourselves had had with clearing sun-dried mud-brick walling, we had no particular problem with the *tauf* (simple loaded mud) walls of Jarmo, once we were below the line of marked rainfall penetration (p. 156).

We worked without balks but took frequent level readings. Our section drawings were developed with the aid of these and the trench faces as we made the drawings of each level with a plane table and telescopic alidade.

Of the various new field procedures which have come into vogue since we dug, flotation for the reclamation of botanical materials (and of minute bones and even artifacts) fascinates us most. Nevertheless, we feel bound to wonder what would have happened to much of the lightly baked or sun-dried clay categories, for example, unless flotation had been very sparingly and cautiously used.

For purposes of assessing the proportion to the original universe from which a sampling of archeological material has been reclaimed, we believe there is value in listing the number of square meters of area exposed and the cubage of matrix removed (cf. Braidwood and Braidwood 1960, table I). While we naturally reject the purely mechanistic use of such figures (since accidental encounters of particularly rich or particularly poor yields can never be anticipated), areas and volumes exposed do hint at the relative values of generalizations from sites with very restricted exposures as against those with broader exposures.

For the Karim Shahir hilltop, the area of surface scatter totals about 6000 m^2. How much of this includes the original settlement and how much of the settlement was eroded away by the wadi are of course unknown. BH's exposures totaled almost 600 m^2, or about 10% of the hilltop. The area of the remaining settlement core exposed along the scarp edge itself (operation I) was about 400 m^2; the amount of matrix removed was 320 m^3. Certain other exposures were made (see p. 28), but these appear to have been outside the core area of occupation.

As to Jarmo, if we follow Wright's estimate (p. 155) that about one third of the original site had been eroded away by the wadi, we would estimate the area of the site as we first found it to be ca. 13,000 m^2. Our rechecking indicates that of this total, ca. 1,372 m^2, or 10%, were exposed in the near-surface levels. Only 1.2% exposure was made at the level of virgin soil, however. If the area presumably lost by erosion were taken into account, our upper level exposures would total only 7% of the original site. The amount of matrix removed in all our exposures totals ca. 2,290 m^3. Since there seems to have been some confusion over these data from Jarmo (see Renfrew, Dixon, and Cann 1966, p. 52), we provide the following tabulation:

INTRODUCTION

Operation and level*	Approximate areas and depths exposed		
	Area (m^2)	Depth (m)†	Volume (m^3)
J-I			
1 & 2	86	2.30	198
3	105	0.60	63
4 & 5	105	0.70	74
6 & 6a	105	0.40	42
6b-d	98	0.05	5
7	98	0.70	69
8 & 9	144‡	0.85	122
Total, J-I	--	5.60	573
J-II (incl. L1213 where pertinent)			
1	393‡	0.30	118
2	393	0.65	255
2fl.	393	0.25	98
3	393	0.30	118
4	201	0.45	90
5	201	0.65	131
6	95	1.05	100
Total, J-II	--	3.65	910
J-III	25‡	1.75	44
J-A (see fig. 57)	56‡	6.90	110
J-B, C, & D	36‡	1.00	36
HL1416	96‡	1.00	96
PQ14	18‡	3.50	63
150 2 × 2 m squares	604‡	average 0.75	453
Grand total	1,372		2,285

*For an explanation of operation/level designations, see pp. 158ff.

†Reference to the sections, e.g., figs. 37-38, 46-49, will show how the measurements between different floor levels vary, depending on where they are taken on any given vertical line.

‡These are the figures used in arriving at the area totals.

The excavations made at Ali Agha, Banahilk, al-Khan, and M'lefaat were only soundings, and thus—in conformance with the Iraqi government's antiquities law prevailing at that time—were very short-term affairs. Given the very limited time we had for the examination of each of these sites, our estimates of their original areas of occupation may be open to question. We list here the *apparent* site size, the approximate areas of our exposures, and the approximate amounts of matrix excavated:

Site	Total apparent area (m^2)	Total area exposed (m^2)	Percentage of apparent whole	Volume exposed (m^3)
Ali Agha	7,000?	(A & B) 35	0.5	34
Banahilk	13,000?	108	0.8	154
al-Khan	7,000?	15	0.2	23
M'lefaat	8,500?	(I & III) 38	0.4	40

At the time we worked, the Iraqi Directorate General of Antiquities required that a field register book of the artifactual yield be kept in duplicate, with one copy to go to the Iraq Museum. There was also at that time a division of the finds: first, unique objects were automatically registered and set aside for the Iraq Museum, then a half-and-half division of the remaining registered pieces was made between the Museum and the excavator. At the end of each of our three seasons, we felt we had received very fair treatment. The nonartifactual materials were directly assigned to us for laboratory study abroad. We were most fortunate, too, in that the Directorate General allowed all of the figurines of the 1954-55 season to be returned to Chicago for Broman Morales's study and postponed its selection of unique examples and the subsequent division of that season's material until after she had returned the whole collection to Baghdad.

Furthermore, as regards registration, the Directorate General, acting on behalf of the Iraq Museum, was at that time not interested in acquiring a full half share of the bulk categories of artifacts such as potsherds, flint or obsidian implements, and coarse ground-stone pieces. The Directorate was quite willing for us to make up small representative samples from these bulk categories for the Museum. Since all registered pieces were automatically required by the antiquities law to be treated within the division, we were not encouraged to register the artifacts of the bulk categories, and hence we did not do so. Instead, these artifacts of the bulk categories and, in addition, most of the very fragmentary pieces in some other categories were simply marked with their findspot designations. Therefore, in order to aid colleagues, either in Baghdad or Chicago, who may in the future work with the collections of the materials we recovered, we offer the following aid:

Karim Shahir. *Registered* objects were marked *K-* followed by a number in sequence (*K-1, K-2,* through *K-52*). *Unregistered* objects were marked in a code, in order to simplify the task of labeling in the bulk categories, thus:

Area	Depth (cm)	Code mark	Area	Depth (cm)	Code mark
Surface (sf)		K	Grid F	0-20	⊡
Operation I				20-30	—
The step	0-20	K II 0	Grids A, B, F, & extension cleanup	20-30	I
	0-40	K I 1	Grid G	0-20	≐
	40-90 (outer edge)	K I 0		20-30	=
	40-80	K I 2		30-40	≠
	40-90 (interior block)	K III 0		40-50	≠
	80-120	K I 3		50-60	✳
	120-160	K I 4		60-80	≡
	160-180	K I 5		80-100	≢
	Ochre pit	K I P		100-110	G 1
Grid A	0-20	⊡		110-120	G 2
	20-30	□		120-140	G 3
Grid B	0-20	K I B 1	The trench (tr)	0-30	J
	20-30	△	Operation II	0-20	II
Grid C	0-20	⊙	Operation III	0-20	C
	20-30	○		20-40	D
	30-40	⌀		40-60	N
	40-50	∞		60-80	M
	50-60	⦻		80-100	P
	60-80	O 1		100-300	III
	80-90	O 2	Operation IV	0-20	R
	90-100	O 3		20-30	T
	100-110	C 1		40-60	Y
	110-120	C 2		60-80	Z
	120-140	C 3		80-280	IV
	140-160	C 4	Operation V	0-20	•
	160-180	C 5		20-35	••
	180-380	C 6	Operation VI	0-20	VI
The extension (ext.)	0-20	⌐•	Operation VII	0-20	VII
			Operation VIII	0-20	VIII

Jarmo. *Registered* objects were marked *J-* for the 1948 season, *J2-* for the 1950-51 season, and *J3-* for the 1955 season, in each case followed by sequential numbers (e.g., *J2-134*). *Unregistered* objects were marked either directly as to findspot or by a code. For the *findspot* designations:

In the 1948 season, operation I was marked simply "J" with a level below, thus—
$$\frac{J}{3}$$

For the test squares A, B, C, and D, their letter with either the level or the depth (in cm) below it, thus—
$$\frac{J\text{-}B}{2} \quad \text{or} \quad \frac{J\text{-}B}{75}$$

In the 1950-51 season, the actual findspot was marked with the operation number above (with or without a preceding "J") and the level below, thus—
$$\frac{I}{6b} \quad \text{or} \quad \frac{J\text{-}I}{6b}$$

$$\frac{II}{3} \quad \text{or} \quad \frac{J\text{-}II}{3}$$

$$\frac{III}{1} \quad \text{or} \quad \frac{J\text{-}III}{1}$$

$$\frac{A}{IV\text{-}1} \quad \text{or} \quad \frac{J\text{-}A}{IV\text{-}1}$$

or a code (see p. 5) was used.

INTRODUCTION

In the 1955 season, the letters and figures of the 4 × 5 m coordinate grid system were used for each of the 2 × 2 m test squares, with the level or depth (in cm) marked below, thus—

K8
3

K21
175

For groups of the 2 × 2 m squares, where the depths were still shallow, we often labeled the groups together as a general area, thus—

HL1416
50

which should be read "squares in the area bounded by H14 to H16, L14 to L16 at depths of ca. 50 cm."

The Jarmo *code* for simplified marking, according to operation, is:

J-I (or simply "J")		J-II		J-III		J-A	
Level	Code	Level	Code	Level	Code	Level	Code
sf or dmp	⌒	sf or dmp	X	sf or dmp	V	sf or dmp	⌒
1	none	1	T	sf-1	∴	II-1	A1
2	none	1 East	E	1	1	II-4&5	A2
3	△	2	S			II-6&7	A3
4	none	2fl.	I			III	A4
5	none	3	□			III-1	A5
6	none	4	4			IV	A6
6a	A	5	W			IV-1	A7
6b	B	6	✛			IV-V	A8
6c	C					V	A9
7	Z						
7fl.	Z1						
8	O						
8fl.	O1 or 9						

NOTE: The symbols and abbreviations of the Jarmo code can be used to identify artifacts that came from the operations and levels indicated in the above tabulation. However, other excavation units exist that were *not coded*. The uncoded units indicated by "none" in the second column above, as well as other levels not referred to in this tabulation, can be directly located by their findspot designations.[2]

Code symbols used generally by us since the early seasons in the ᶜAmuq are:

  Surface ⌒ also *sf*
  Surface to first clear level ⌒-1 also *sf-1*
  Dump or matrix with lost context ▽ also *dmp*
  Floor ⊥ also *fl.*
  Pit or silo ⊕ also *pit*

The same general principles in labeling were used in marking the materials from the various soundings, thus:

  Ali Agha = AA, plus the operation, plus the level
  Banahilk = BH, plus the operation, plus the level
  al-Khan = EK, plus the operation, plus the level
  M'lefaat = ML, plus the operation, plus the level

The materials of the bulk categories were all marked individually, in the manner indicated above, then the whole yield from a unit findspot in such categories as heavy ground stone and pottery was put into a stout cloth sack. This was tied with a good-quality string, to which was attached a stout baggage label also marked with the findspot. Finer, more fragile materials were packaged in labeled boxes.

We cannot claim that the artifacts within each of the different categories received the same degree of exhaustive study when being processed for publication. Naturally, the finer ground stone and the figurines attracted our early attention. At the same time, however, these were the categories that we were required to divide with the Iraq Museum and they were thus not all available for study in the Chicago laboratory for a long period, unlike most of the bulk material. Perhaps this tends to equalize the matter. We are, however, conscious that certain groups of artifacts, such as the heavy coarse stone mortar and quern group, should have received much more attention than we gave them.

We are also conscious that our petrographic analyses are still inadequate and that certain smaller collections such as the marine shells remain unstudied. It is also hoped the time may come when reliable identification of the source areas of many minerals is possible.

In 1952, with impressions of our first two field seasons very fresh in her mind, LSB wrote a popular account of the expedition's work (L.S. Braidwood 1953), which gives a general picture of our field procedures.

RECAPITULATION OF PRELIMINARY WRITINGS

COMMENTS UPON REREADING SAOC 31

We see little point in a detailed repetition of the Prehistoric Project's general history through the time of the Iraqi field seasons or of our original conception of the Project's research goals. SAOC 31 does, we believe, adequately account for most of these, and its bibliography also cites our other papers which appeared up to 1960, although the SAOC 31 manuscripts were completed in 1959.

In retrospect, our general views as set forth in SAOC 31 probably can be taken as a summation of the ideas on the problem of the early appearance of the village-farming community way of life—at least in the trans-Euphrates portion of southwestern Asia—as these ideas had developed up to about 1959. With the exception of a brief note on Shimshara and the Soleckis' preliminary accounts of their earlier seasons at Shanidar and Zawi Chemi Shanidar, nothing, in fact, was in hand that related to the critical time range except the Prehistoric Project's materials. While it seemed clear to us (SAOC 31, p. 3) that there were other instances of the independent achievement of food production in other parts of the world, we certainly took the Near Eastern instance to have chronological precedence. Regarding the transition to food production and village-farming communities, we wrote (SAOC 31, p. 1) that

> on the upswing to the transition we note (1) a growing ability (and perhaps some motivation) for intensifying and localizing the exploitation of a given piece of terrain by food-collectors. . . .[3]

When SAOC 31 appeared, our earlier fascination with the "hilly flanks of the Fertile Crescent" as an environmental "nuclear habitat zone" within which the domestication of plants and animals appeared had become only slightly tempered. We wrote (SAOC 31, p. 13) that

> there is little doubt in our minds that the nuclear area for the appearance of the village-farming community in the Near and Middle East can—as a reasonable working hypothesis—already be taken to coincide with this zone. . . . Obviously, a major feature of the testing of an environment will be to discover the degree to which the present observable situation resembles, or is different from, the situation which obtained some eight or ten thousand years ago. Did the zone then, as it does now, naturally contain potentially domesticable plants and animals? We shall see that the available evidence suggests far greater similarity than difference.

However, in the field in the same year that SAOC 31 appeared, Wright was to begin his palynological work in Iran which brought new evidence suggesting that at least the climatic regime in our hilly flanks at the end of the Pleistocene was not that of the present!

Throughout SAOC 31, we noted that there were many regions from which evidence was then lacking:

> . . . we know as yet practically nothing of the earlier culture history of the zone of foothills and intermontane valleys in the Iranian, Syrian, and Turkish portions of the arc [p. 13].

And although Stuart Harris's surface finds at Urwell and Raseien (SAOC 31, p. 49) had prepared us for what might appear on the lower piedmont at Ali Kosh and Tamarkhan, we were clearly not even imagining what was yet to be found along the middle Euphrates at Mureybit and Abu Hureyra or in the Syrian desert at Kowm.

As to more specific points covered in SAOC 31 regarding the sites we excavated and their yields, we are still inclined to believe that Karim Shahir represents the remains of a short-term encampment (SAOC 31, p. 28). Had we returned to the Chemchemal valley in the later 1950s, we would not have resumed work at Karim Shahir; its very shallow deposit did not augur well for comprehensive architectural remains or for the recovery of contextually trustworthy nonartifactual or dating evidence. As already suggested in SAOC 31 (pp. 182-83), such sites as Turkaka and Qara Chiwar would have had our attention.

SAOC 31 (e.g., p. 39) also makes clear that when we left Jarmo in 1955, we realized that it had not been "adequately tested" and that a layer-cake simplicity of stratification was certainly not the case. Our earlier generalizations, based on the more restricted 1948 and 1950-51 exposures, were that "pottery appeared in the upper third of the deposit," that is, it seemed as if there might be pottery anywhere we dug within the uppermost levels and no pottery below that. The proposition for an absence of pottery in the lower levels quite clearly must still hold throughout Jarmo. However, by the end of the 1955 season we had acquired evidence that if we had made our exposures in certain other areas of the mound, we would have found no pottery even in the upper levels, although SAOC 31 (esp. p. 39 and fig. 6) then made the point only tentatively. We now know that the "upper third" generalization is vastly overgeneralized (to coin a phrase) and that the presence of pottery as a facile indicator of a late or "ceramic subphase" (or even a full "phase") as against an early or "preceramic subphase" (or even a full "phase") at Jarmo cannot—on present evidence—be maintained. There was, of course, a sequence through time in the occupation of Jarmo: we undoubtedly have a strong sampling for either end of this continuum but lack adequate evidence of its middle. For example, Adams's chart 2 (chap. 3) illustrates this particularly well with respect to certain stone vessel shapes.

In chapters 12, 13, and 14, Watson, Wright, and Reed give their own present reflections on the treatment given to the botanical, climatic, and faunal evidence in SAOC 31.

INTRODUCTION

SUMMARY OF IDEA CHANGES SINCE SAOC 31

Our surveys in Braidwood and Willey, eds., 1962*b* (esp. pp. 132-46, 330-59) and in Braidwood 1962 (pp. 115-26) were written after our 1959-60 work in the Kermanshah valley in Iran. In both of these surveys we seem to have felt increasingly unable to specify either the approximate beginning date for—or the duration of—our suggested range of incipience, seeing it "perhaps as the culmination of a longer range of unconscious manipulations of the potential domesticates" (see RJB and BH in Braidwood and Willey, eds., 1962*b*, p. 144). In that same volume (p. 337) we are very clear in that while incipience "was attained within a natural-habitat zone . . . we do not yet know the exact boundaries of this zone," and we noted also the very probable importance of physiographic and environmental diversity within the natural-habitat zone as the "settling-in" process proceeded.

By the time a short paper titled "Current Thoughts on the Beginnings of Food-Production in Southwestern Asia" (Braidwood and Braidwood 1969, pp. 149-55) appeared in the Dunand festschrift, we ourselves had already had two seasons at Çayönü (Çambel and Braidwood 1970). In addition, Suberde had been opened in Turkey; Ganj Dareh, Guran, Choga Mami, and Ali Kosh along the Zagros flanks were known; work had begun at Mureybit on the middle Euphrates; and the sites of the French colleagues and Beidha were being excavated in the Syro-Palestinian province. Furthermore, the implications of the palynological evidence acquired by van Zeist and Wright (1963) in the Iranian Zagros were beginning to appear. Jean Perrot's (1962) proposal that the Natufian was part of a long-continued level of intensified food collection in Palestine was taken into account, and it seemed equally clear to us that "villages without food production" had existed in the Near East. Further, we wrote (Braidwood and Braidwood 1969, p. 153) that

> any distinction between a level of intensified food collecting and of incipient plant and animal domestication may be more a matter of semantics than of reality.

In the earlier 1970s, RJB wrote three retrospective summary papers (Braidwood 1972, 1973, 1974)—the third almost a brief autobiography of the Prehistoric Project and of himself. Each of these papers reflects discussions which the three of us had about the implications of the considerably increased archeological activity—we even said "fashion"—concerning the problem of the origins of food production in southwestern Asia. Each paper also shows, among other things, our attempts to consider the full implications of the Wright-van Zeist palynological evidence (Wright 1968, 1970), but without declaring ourselves to be complete environmental determinists. We did not then and still do not think the sum total of available evidence warrants this position. At the same time, our fascination persisted with the problem of whether it was meaningful to think of an inchoate or incipient "level," *per se*, in the appearance of food production. RJB's (1972, pp. 317-18) formulation of our position was that

> the conceptualization of a level of incipient cultivation and domestication—as distinct from that of a terminal specialized hunting and collecting level—has always remained difficult, and the field identification of the incipient level has been even more difficult. As a heuristic device, the idea of a level of incipience may have convenience for us, but would have meant little to the people who were living in it, doubtless still by predominantly very specialized patterns of hunting and collecting.

In his 1973 paper, RJB wonders, in effect, whether sites such as Aşıklı, basal Ganj Dareh, and Suberde may represent either a very late phase of the general level of incipience or a markedly pre-Jarmo phase of the general level of effective village-farming communities.

In the most recent of our (far too many!) summary papers before the final reports appearing in this volume, RJB (1976, pp. 41-49) again attempted to make our general ideas current. The paper maintains a generally agnostic point of view (Braidwood 1976, p. 44):

> Exactly how domestication itself came about, I frankly do not know, nor have the several recent "explanations" seemed to me to make adequate use of the available evidence or to have respect for the lack of it. Wright, himself, perhaps quite naturally, has swung towards a degree of environmental determinism. My own (perhaps overly cautious!) tendency, given the *very restricted* number of sites and of exposures on them, for the incipient phase, is to patiently await more evidence.

Thus, since 1959 when the SAOC 31 manuscripts were completed, our main theoretical concerns appear to have been with the conceptualization of meanings for the still very restricted evidence of incipience or inchoateness—in other words, the actual transition from the end of the terminal hunting-collecting era to that of the primary village-farming communities. The Braidwoods and Reed recall a memorable luncheon with V. Gordon Childe in London in 1955, when we were enroute home from the last Jarmo season. Childe, with a sparkle in his eye, remarked that it would be exactly with the interpretation of the evidence for the transition that we would have our greatest difficulty.

It has always seemed to us much less difficult to conceptualize what was going on, when thinking about the evidence from an inventory such as Jarmo's. Perhaps we are wrong in this feeling. Perhaps it comes from our having lived during many field seasons either in or closely adjacent to simple present-day villages of the Near Eastern peasantry in the Zagros-Taurus hill country, and therefore perhaps we make too facile an assumption that life in a site such as Jarmo was very similar. Certainly, however, we have no illusions that we have ever observed a way of life which can conceivably be close to the one reflected by the Karim Shahir inventory. In any case, while inventories and exposures of the Jarmo type of settlement are by no means yet adequate for really broad-scale culture-historical interpretations, they do say more to us than the far too few excavations on sites of the Karim Shahir type. In the west, of course, the increasing number of Natufian and even Kebaran exposures makes the situation there somewhat clearer, but the processes of change there may also have been somewhat different.

ASSESSMENT OF THE PRESENT REPORTS
Karim Shahir

The assemblage found in the single prehistoric occupation of Karim Shahir points to an open-air hilltop encampment tending to be centered near the edge of a scarp but probably associated with small, shifting outliers. Here, at an unknown date, an undetermined number of individuals appear to have lived for some period of time, or come and gone over shorter periods, and carried on the routines of daily existence, which included the making of tools, constructing simple makeshift shelters, and preparing, cooking, and eating wild animals they had hunted and wild plants they had collected. Their sojourns here were probably seasonal or at least only periodical. The possibility of a single uninterrupted occupation of limited or longer duration cannot be excluded, but the apparent absence of well-developed more permanent sorts of dwelling structures argues against this interpretation. While there most likely were shelters of some sort here, they are not really demonstrable, and the only evidence for possible living emplacements and installations of the more temporary sort is the following:

1. An extensive and vaguely defined bed of field stones and stream pebbles at the edge of the scarp. These were somewhat closely set in one limited location and more widely scattered elsewhere, and all had been specially brought up to the otherwise silty hilltop site, suggesting the preparation of the area for some sort of shelters there.
2. Eleven small pits of varying size and depth and at least two shallow, broader depressions. The pits are presumed from their contents to have been fire or cooking pits. The depressions may have provided focal points or rudimentary circumscribed refuges or protection a little below the surrounding ground level for some sort of passing activity needing a shelter, although it is also possible that they were completely natural.
3. A deep pit that had a coating of red ochre over its bottom and yielded two small clay figurines suggesting stylized human or animal forms. The association of these elements points to some special function of a distinctly ceremonial nature, which might have been linked to structure or shelter.
4. Two lumps of heat-hardened ruddy tan clay, one with impressions of vegetable matter including a deep, straight groove (20 mm wide) evidently left by a stick or branch. These lumps hint at the existence of dwelling structures—perhaps wattle and daub—but their actual significance in this regard is very debatable (and perhaps should be entirely dismissed), coming as they did from a near-surface context in an eroding scarp-edge zone of the single prehistoric occupation horizon.

The ubiquitous remnants of a plentiful chipped stone industry, evidently manufactured on the spot, were found crammed in among the rocks—in particular large quantities of blade cores, blades and blade tools (both normal-sized and microlithic), with double-backed drills and numerous microlithic backed blades being the most carefully formed and outstanding types. There were moderate numbers of indifferent burins and of side, steep, and rounded scrapers, and a handful of poorly defined special forms such as denticulated, pointed, or obliquely truncated blades. Twenty-four unworked pieces, mostly blades, bore faint and limited traces of silica edge sheen. By far the most numerous single formal tool category of all was the one that comprised, for the most part, poorly made debased end scrapers on blades or flakes, both normal and microlithic. Most of these end scrapers appear to have been created by use and wear rather than by means of any deliberate retouch. There were also enormous numbers of nibbled, notched, or variously used blades and lesser quantities of undistinguished similarly marked flake tools, all displaying a mingled assortment of edge wear—several kinds on an edge—and thus doubtless multiple-use implements. Some of these pieces may have been scarred only by natural attrition in the ground. The sheer quantity of all these chipped tools and of the additional unworked and presumably featureless chipping debris found indicated a major set of activities at the site. It is assumed that these flint artifacts all belong to categories associated with various routine activities having to do with clothing, equipment, and the preparation and eating of wild foods. The backed and angled microlithic bladelets may perhaps be seen as possible components of composite forms hafted in wood or bone to serve as weapons.

Ground stone tools and ornaments constitute a numerically very minor but significant and characteristic element of the Karim Shahir assemblage. The principal types that make up the main part of this working kit of ground, pecked, and polished tools include numerous chipped and polished celts of both adze/hoe and axe forms, as well as two more fully ground celts of small, narrow chisel form; the group of fragmentary milling stones comprising a very few grinding stones (querns), boulder mortars, some used pebble pestles, extremely rare shaped and ground pestles, and a very limited number of hand rubbing stones (mullers); quite a few distinctive small grooved rubbing stones, seen as possible shaft straighteners or perhaps smoothers for soft stone ornaments; and numerous hammerstones. Completing the body of artifactual material that probably reflects, directly or indirectly, a considerable proportion of

INTRODUCTION

the activities and functions carried on at the encampment are a fragmentary decorated palette; a few striated and pecked pebbles perhaps used as anvils, whetstones, workstones, or polishers; some fragments of pierced pebbles possibly once attached to sticks as dibbles or maceheads; and an assortment of bits of red and yellow ochre, scanty and mostly unsatisfactory evidence of bitumen, and some obviously worn lumps of a distinctive heavy, iron-filled, cherty black rock, or lodestone.

The adze/hoe and axe forms imply soil working and woodworking or perhaps skin dressing. The blades with faint edge sheen and the milling stones imply the manipulation of plants (presumed to be wild in the absence of any contrary evidence), with both these categories rare and seemingly incipient here. On the other hand, the types and quantities of chipped stone tools suggest a strong continuing tradition of collecting and preparing materials according to long-standing practices and with long-familiar tools used in earlier horizons of a hunting and food-gathering existence. At the same time the limited typological range and debased technical aspects of a number of these artifacts, when compared to the technotypological variety and elegance of the preceding late upper paleolithic period, definitely imply partial abandonment of old forms and a shift toward newer usages. The chipped and polished celts, the fine double-backed drills, and the backed bladelets, together with the milling stones and pieces with edge sheen, perhaps signify the new more vital trends.

The ornaments found at Karim Shahir, primarily of ground stone, were perhaps made on the spot like the tools. They are present in very small numbers and are largely fragmentary. Included in this category are marble rings and so-called bracelets; a stone rod; simple, largely unshaped natural pebble pendants; well-shaped discoid, oval, or angular plaques and pendants made of marble or limestone, and pierced; some simple cylindrical tubular or barrel-shaped stone beads; and an outstanding form of biconical planoconvex stone bead with doubly pierced ends, possibly a plaque or button to be appliquéd. Present in extremely limited quantity are some small rectangular pierced shell plaques, some natural and virtually unshaped tiny shell beads, and a few badly preserved tubular beads of bird bone, as well as a small number of fragmentary tools suggesting awls and pins.

All these more finely finished ornaments and implements of stone, shell, and bone reflect some kind of a preoccupation with apparel and appearance and hint at the preparation and decoration of clothing or other equipment. Two tiny clay figurines and a fragmentary clay rod or stalklike object surely represent some manipulation and light baking of clay and when considered in conjunction with the pit faced with red ochre hint at some unknown ideas and ceremonial activity.

The animal bones recovered indicate a mode of life centered on the hunting of wild animals, with no evidence for domestication. Basing his opinion on a sampling of materials that was very small and poorly preserved, Stampfli reports that sheep and goat evidently made up virtually half of the kill. Boar, deer, gazelle, wild cattle, fox, wolf, marten, hare, and bird were each present in small quantities. All are types not unknown in the general region in historic times and are considered indigenous there in prehistoric times. It is not clear whether the predominance of sheep and goat represents only easy availability or else selective or seasonal hunting or even some further manipulation. The small sample permits no speculation about the possibility of age selection; only adult specimens of sheep and goat and of all the other species were represented. Restricted numbers of land-snail shells and rare fragments of freshwater clam shells, as well as some turtle bone (but no fish bones), attest to further possible items of diet from indigenous forms that are still extant. The widespread littering of the site with these fragmentary faunal remains, together with the presumed cooking and fire pits (in some instances containing obviously burned rocks and bones), indicates that the preparation, cooking, and eating of these foods took place repeatedly there. Examination of the scarce charcoal remains recovered showed the presence, probably nearby, of *Zelkova?*, a tree of the elm family, and, perhaps more distant, of *Tamarix*, a tree of stream valleys in semiarid regions, and possibly *Prosopis*, a mesquitelike dry grassland form. Doubtless because of the shallow deposit at Karim Shahir it was not possible to obtain any evidence of nuts, seeds, grains, and the like, although the rare grindstones, mortars, hand rubbing stones and pestles, and the pieces with edge sheen indicate the likely presence and preparation of such foodstuffs in a form one must assume was wild.

Karim Shahir was, then, a sizeable, active, and in all probability seasonal—or at least periodic—encampment of migratory hunters and collectors, of unknown number and time, who lived off wild animals (primarily sheep and goat, but also some boar, deer, gazelle, cattle, and smaller forms such as fox, wolf, marten, hare, turtle, birds, and molluscs) and wild plants (no evidence of specific edible plant materials was found, but the variety of milling stones and the trace of silica sheen on the edges of a very small handful of blades and flakes surely permit this assumption). These animals and plants were obtained in the immediate district and possibly further afield as well; the animals range from the gazelle, an open land species, to deer from forest areas, to sheep and goat from higher terrain. Even the severely restricted sample of tree and plant forms gives evidence of disparate and contrasting habitats—for example, dry grassland, semiarid stream valley, and perhaps parkland or forest. Some of these different areas may very likely have been a considerable distance from the Karim Shahir encampment.

Clothing, equipment, and shelter are barely hinted at—and, even so, only indirectly—by the scanty traces of tools such as awls and pins or needles, and ornaments such as beads, plaques, pendants, bracelets, and rings. Similarly, we have only the various pits, depressions, and the rocky scatter to indicate focal points for possible habitation. The tool kit was made up preponderantly of chipped stone implements—a blade industry marked by a limited variety of tool types—and a small number of chipped and polished celts suggesting hoeing, adzing, axing, or perhaps even skin-working enterprises. The entire artifactual component was evidently made on the spot out of locally available stone, bone, shell, and presumably wood, as well as other vegetable and animal materials now lost. There was not a trace of obsidian or any true and acceptable geometric microliths worthy of the name to be associated with the entire horizon. Evidence for the use of bitumen in the hafting of adze/hoes and perhaps certain other chipped stone tools lay in traces of this substance on some specimens and in suspiciously similar-looking dark crusty matter on certain pebbles. The use of bitumen here may imply familiarity with sparsely scattered natural seeps not only in the nearby region but also further afield to south and west (chap. 16). Finally, the lightly baked clay pieces (e.g., the figurines), the pit lined with red ochre, and a few ochre-smeared tools may reflect ritual procedures woven into the life at this campground.

Jarmo

In the years since 1959, when the preliminary reports of SAOC 31 were actually finished, we have noted a variety of points and problems of importance which—had excavation ever been resumed on the site—would have needed further attention. Certainly more survey, with respect to both ancient sites and the present situation in the same area, could improve on the bare essentials of population estimates and settlement patterns made by Braidwood and Reed (1957). That paper noted the presence of at least two Jarmo-like sites within less than 5 km of Jarmo itself; it also proposed that Jarmo might have had as many as twenty-five households, averaging about six people each. Thus a village population estimate of about 150 inhabitants was made. However, a more intensive study of the present situation in the Chemchemal valley, both as to the location of ancient sites and modern villages (assuming of course that the situation is not greatly changed from what it was in 1955!), would undoubtedly be rewarding. A caveat about any conclusions that might be drawn would be the very heavy degree of erosion that has taken place in the Chemchemal valley since Jarmo was occupied; many neighboring sites may have been completely eroded away.

Not only do we lack substantial evidence for the regional settlement pattern of the time of Jarmo (and of Karim Shahir) but also our attempt to recover the settlement plan of the village itself was not successful (pp. 158, 164). We did recover more or less comprehensible indications of some Jarmo house plans, and we appear to have at least one instance of separate houses built contiguously and without the use of party walls (p. 161). This might, of course, mean that there were many more than twenty-five households within the area we reckon to have been occupied. One cautionary note here follows from observance of the usual situation in modern villages: there are usually some unoccupied houses already slumping into ruin while other houses flourish nearby. In dealing with the remains of a long-extinct village, exquisitely detailed and broad exposures would be required in order to prove the exact simultaneity (or lack of it) of all the houses on one "level." Thus a simple count of all the house remains on any one "level" might lead to a very exaggerated population estimate.

We have no really good evidence that might help us specify the use to which the various rooms in a given house were put. Considering what has been observed in other recent exposures at sites such as Çayönü and Umm Dabaghiyah, the small size of many rooms in the Jarmo houses was not unusual; in fact, some small "rooms" may have been little more than storage bins.

Other outstanding architectural problems of detail remain. What, for example, is the meaning of the tough and blocky orange-buff silty clay zone (p. 155) and also of the gray to black ashy zone (p. 164)? The thick *tauf* wall in PQ14 (p. 165) certainly needs more attention, and a long trench to yield the stratigraphic profile between operations J-I and J-II would be most instructive; among other things, it might help to establish what went on in the now largely missing "middle" levels of the site.

An overall (not only architectural) concern is with what facilities the Jarmo people made for grain storage and the enfolding of animals. We did not encounter evidence of grain storage save for the appearance of three pits in J-I. Furthermore, since the inner surfaces of these J-I pits appeared to be untreated, their use for grain storage is questionable. The real significance of the fairly numerous Jarmo ovenlike features (p. 157) also still eludes us.

The meaning of the discontinuity in the appearance of pottery in different areas of the site (p. 155 and fig. 24) remains unclear, and we lack an explanation for Adams's "midden" (p. 215) in the western portion of J-II and westwards. It would be good, also, to know more of the uses to which the various stone and pottery vessels were put, and—in this connection as well as among others—we were unfortunate in not having encountered any very significant caches or "activity clusters" of artifacts.

The problem of how the use of pottery was first introduced to the Jarmo villagers remains open, and, although we reasonably suppose it to have been initially an introduction from without, was the later coarse pottery developed on the site itself? Adams is properly concerned with the "high esthetic achievement" which the stone vessels show and with the degree of specialization implied by the time-consuming craft by which such great numbers of stone vessels were produced.

The abundant chipped stone industry at Jarmo—both flint and obsidian—is predominantly a blade industry. Since all chipped stone work tends to be conservative and traditional, it is not surprising that many of the tool types in the Jarmo kit, types both obvious and not so obvious, are a repetition of those found in previous eras in the general region: borers, various scrapers on both blades and flakes, notched blades, fabricators, burins (rare at Jarmo and poor examples), backed bladelets (rare), geometric microliths but only triangles and trapezes (upper Jarmo levels), and, above all and in overwhelming numbers, blades and bladelets and their segmented fragments, used "as is." Undoubtedly, most of these last items served as all-purpose tools.

An outstanding feature of the Jarmo industry is its microlithic character. There are large flint tools throughout the levels and a limited number of obsidian blade fragments that are relatively small but still broader than 10 mm (our cutoff width for "microlithicness"). The flint and obsidian microliths *together*, however, make up at least 70% of the chipped stone tools in the J-I as well as the J-II levels (all blades and blade fragments are included in this estimate but not flakes unless retouched or heavily used). For the most part, it is the overwhelmingly microlithic character of the obsidian artifacts—from the earliest levels and from all the upper levels—and their abundance that ensure the industry's microlithic bias. If one ignores the obsidian component in the chipped stone category, taking only flint into consideration, the microlithic element of the industry decreases radically from the overall 70% to proportions that vary from 55% in J-I,8 to 33% in J-II,3, with an average of 51.1% in J-I,6 to 8, and 38% in J-II,1 to 6. However, one might speculate from the evidence in J-I,8—where the obsidian examples are the scarcest but the flint microliths are proportionately most abundant—that the Jarmo inhabitants had a desire and need for microliths and that this microlithic balance in the industry might have obtained even had obsidian not been available.

In addition to the traditional aspects of the tool kit that are mentioned above, there are also some new forms. Neat parallel-sided flint blade segments—for the most part unretouched—bearing "sickle sheen" are present in substantial numbers throughout all levels. (LSB feels disinclined to make much of the few blades and flakes with sheen found at Karim Shahir.) Obsidian, a material that had made an occasional rare appearance in earlier eras, was definitely appreciated by the Jarmo inhabitants, who used it for tools from the very earliest levels. A few new forms confined to obsidian appear in the earliest levels: "truncated obsidian blades and flakes," "pressure-flaked obsidian fabricators," and "thin sections" (side-blow blade-flakes). As Hole notes, the "truncated obsidian blades and flakes" are no longer in use by the time of the occupancies of the various levels in J-II. The "pressure-flaked obsidian fabricator," most common in the earliest levels, does seem to continue in use, though sparingly, in the later levels. "Thin sections" (side-blow blade-flakes) are present in minute quantities from the first. The idea is there, but the early examples are all extremely tiny and not retouched except for two or three dubious examples. Given our present exposures, it is only in the upper levels, from J-II,5 onwards, that one gets nicely retouched examples of this puzzling artifact, with the largest, most handsome, carefully retouched ones in J-II,3 and J-II,2.

As matters now stand, a new variation on the drill or borer shape was found only in the levels of J-II. This is the somewhat fiddle-shaped drill with a long narrow shaft (fig. 114:3-4,9).

Perhaps the most incomprehensible fact about the Jarmo chipped stone industry still remains the appearance and flourish of microlithic trapezes and triangles in both flint and obsidian. Present in the Palegawra Zarzian, they are missing at Karim Shahir and essentially absent from all but the very uppermost levels of Jarmo.

The sheer number of artifacts in the ground stone category at Jarmo is most impressive, especially as regards the smaller and more finely finished groups. We have, however, the uncomfortable feeling that we did not give enough attention to the fragmentary pieces in the coarser stone groups, such as mullers, querns, mortars, pestles, and hammerstones; broken pieces of these types were often found reused in stone foundations and were thus left in place until the architectural drawings were made, and hence not collected as part of the regular daily routine. The ground stone catalogue (pp. 302ff.) suggests that there were far fewer examples in these coarse groups in J-II than there were in J-I. The reason for this is not clear to us. Neither can we guess why there were more examples in the groups of smaller and more finely textured objects, such as the so-called bracelets, the rings, beads, and pendants, in J-II than in J-I. Given the restricted exposures and sample size on which judgment can be based, it would not be very meaningful to say that the deeper J-II levels represent "richer" households than do the deeper J-I levels. Further, we have no provable idea of the functions of many of the smaller, finer stone objects (chap. 5), such as the so-called bracelets, the small grooved stones, the small borers and/or pestles, the ground stone balls, and the so-called phallic objects. As in the case of the stone vessels, we may wonder about the degree of specialization of craftsmanship which the quantity in some of these finer ground stone object groups implies, and in this connection it would doubtless be useful if we knew much more than we do of the sources of the minerals involved.

The worked bone category (chap. 6) is well represented in the Jarmo yield, although most of the types are not extraordinary for this time range. The appearance of the phalangeal hafts is noted. We might wonder whether the function of the so-called spoons was exactly that of a spoon in our own sense. The shaft hole type of bone "point" or gouge is, to us, a new form, while the deer canine bead or pendant recalls Natufian examples.

The category of figurines and other clay objects makes up one of the most remarkable but indeed tantalizing groups of artifacts from Jarmo. It is particularly fortunate that Broman Morales had the two latter field seasons at the site, that she controlled the whole category from start to finish, and that she had the ability to make excellent pencil drawings of the pieces, which—along with a selection of photographs—add much to their clear presentation here. She was also able to study all of the pieces from the 1948 season in the Baghdad Museum and had full control in the field of the study and drawing of the 1950-51 season's figurines. As mentioned above (p. 3), she was allowed to bring all of the figurines from the shorter 1955 season back to Chicago for a short period of study, after which they were all returned to Baghdad for selection and division. Broman Morales handled all of the well over 5,000 pieces several times and the more comprehensible examples many times. She has also—with her understanding of how some of the many fragmentary parts fitted together and with her remarkable ability to test her ideas effectively with modeling clay—provided an exhaustive study of the whole category.

Naturally, it is her concern for the original meanings and use of the figurines that makes Broman Morales's task so difficult. She writes, for example (p. 392), that "for the cultural level exhibited at Jarmo, clay figurines can give almost the only clue to the intellectual life of the inhabitants, above and beyond the material life to be seen in their tools and architecture." Nevertheless, she adds, rather ruefully (p. 384), that "it is indeed remarkable how few definite conclusions can be drawn from the study of the human figurine category." The evidence of both their manufacture and their completely scattered occurrence throughout our available exposures suggests that their makers were not interested in the permanence of the figurines; it appears to have been the act of making them that was important. Broman Morales rejects the usual more generalized idea of fertility for the animals and in discussing the human females does not once speak of a "mother goddess."

The two groups called double-wing bases and stalks are also of particular interest, making up as they do a very early instance of the artistic attempt to delineate both human and animal forms in an abstract and, to us, incomplete way. The human-headed double-wing bases, which seem to appear only in the upper levels, cannot be identified as to the sex they represent.

A sufficient number of the figurine forms continue from the lowest to the uppermost levels in our various exposures to underline the homogeneity of the whole category, but there seems to be a proliferation of new forms in the upper levels.

There are a large number of small clay balls and some other geometric forms, some miniature vessellike pieces, and a few other miscellaneous forms in clay. On some of the clay balls there are incisions or fabric impressions, and the latter have been given special attention by Adovasio (chap. 7, Appendix).

Unfortunately, our Jarmo exposures yielded very little evidence of the physical types of the original inhabitants or of their burial practices. We can only suppose that the dead were normally buried in a cemetery outside the village.

Stampfli's study of the bulk of the animal bones indicates that the percentage of wild animals was higher than was our first estimate and that the percentage of juvenile animals was not high.

So far, the bones of domesticated pigs have appeared only in the broader upper level exposures; domesticated goats and probably domesticated sheep were already indicated in the lower level exposures and persisted throughout the sequence. Also, Lawrence and Reed found convincing evidence for large domesticated dogs at Jarmo. The *Bos* and *Equus* bones were identified as wild cattle and onager respectively, and Turnbull's study accounts for a few small and some additional larger mammalian forms. Many bones of really large animals may well have been left at the place of a kill, while the whole carcasses of smaller animals may have been brought back into the village itself from an adjoining but ecologically different niche. The matter of traditional choice and Reed's (Braidwood and Reed 1957, p. 23, n. 12) notion of the "culture filter" also enter. Thus the impression given by the the direct counting of bones from the site might well not represent the full environmental reality. It is interesting that from Palegawra through Jarmo times there is relatively little difference in the animal species represented by the bones.

In her recapitulating and updating of Helbaek's original study of the Jarmo plant material, Watson benefited by direct correspondence with Helbaek. She was also helped by new evidence from a variety of excavations subsequent to ours. Both wild and domesticated einkorn and emmer wheat were identified at Jarmo by Helbaek, and barley was indicated by wild two-row and apparently cultivated two-row forms. He also identified the field pea, the lentil, and the blue vetchling.

Wright's "revisitation" of his SAOC 31 paper reflects, of course, the results of the palynological investigations which he, van Zeist, and other workers undertook subsequent to our Iraqi field seasons (see Wright's references, chap. 13). This new research indicated that there was a cold, dry climate in southwestern Asia during the last glacial period. Obviously, the implications of this finding call for some rethinking of our original proposition that the "hilly flanks of the Fertile Crescent" were the "natural habitat zone." Our assumption had been that the wild cereals were available in the general region throughout the late Pleistocene (see also Wright 1960, p. 97). Wright's interpretation of the palynological evidence now suggests that the wild cereals could only have become established (east of the Euphrates, at least) after 14,000 B.P. or even later. Such a circumstance, which must have involved a relatively rapid appearance of new plant forms within the new climatic regime, must of course be taken into consideration when we theorize on the beginnings of cultivation in this area. We feel bound to take the implications of the Wright-van Zeist interpretations very seriously, although we sense some lack of palynological confirmation from the more southerly portions of the Levant. Most of all, we feel again the crucial lack of archeological evidence for the end phases of the upper paleolithic and the need for more and fuller inventories from the phases of the incipient or inchoate range of time.

In Reed's (chap. 14) retrospective summary of his earlier sections in SAOC 31, he concentrates mainly on the new techniques for the analyses of evidence which have appeared since 1960 and on the types of changes in interpretations which these analyses allow. With both his own "model" for speculations on early domestication and his conclusions based on the impressive group of symposium papers in the *Origins of Agriculture* (Reed 1977, pp. 543-67, 879-953) now in hand, Reed has not attempted to repeat many of the details of his position which are available in that volume.

INTRODUCTION

In our section on chronology, RJB has retained the opinion, as expressed in SAOC 31, that Jarmo flourished for several hundred years at about 6750 B.C. (Libby) and that the primary village-farming community era or level generally spanned the time range from ca. 9250 to 7750 B.P. (that is, ca. 7300-5800 B.C., Libby). Exasperatingly, the use made of radiocarbon age determinations increasingly appears to depend on the personal opinion of whoever is presenting a chronology. We all have our whimsies. Thus Hole (1977, table 2) labels each of the Jarmo determinations he selects as either "too old" or "too young," marks various of his Ali Kosh determinations as "OK" which *we* would consider too old, and also presents four Ganj Dareh determinations as of the later tenth millennium B.C. and one of the eleventh. Smith (1976*b*, p. 13) wisely writes concerning the Ganj Dareh situation that

> our early sondage in 1965 yielded several radiocarbon determinations that suggested that the basal level (E) dated to ca. 8500 B.C. and the latest levels to roughly 7000 B.C. This seemed reasonable in relation to other early village sites known in the Zagros of Iraq and Iran and in western Asia in general. This dating seemed further supported by radiocarbon determinations resulting from the 1967 season, when several charcoal samples from Levels B to D gave dates ranging between 7000-7300 B.C. However, four new samples collected from firepits in Level E in 1971 produced determinations averaging about 6500 B.C.—later than those in the stratigraphically younger levels above! It is clear that, just as in many other Neolithic sites of western Asia, some complicating factor which is still imperfectly understood is responsible for these contradictions.

Perhaps it is time that we admit that for southwestern Asiatic prehistory at present, the assessment of chronology on the grounds of radiocarbon age determinations alone does have more of whimsy than of science. The degree of comparability of the inventories available from a variety of sites within a general region (for which a chronological scheme is being attempted) must be given due respect. Such a "relative archeological chronology" can then serve to test the probable validity of "dates" within a wide scatter of radiocarbon age determinations.

Finally, as regards Jarmo, it is to our embarrassment that our section on miscellaneous analyses is so brief. At least there is a respectable selection of artifacts in the major categories in the Chicago sample at the Oriental Institute that is available for future analyses.

In sum, Jarmo appears to us to contain the remains of an early village-farming community of some 150 or more people—a permanent settlement of a size very well beyond that of the typical hunting-collecting band. BH takes the remains of Karim Shahir to suggest possibly only periodic or seasonal settlement.[4] At Jarmo we see no reason to doubt year-round settlement, probably for the duration of several centuries. Although at least two other sites (Kani Sur and Khora Namik, SAOC 31, p. 27) with surface indications of a Jarmo-type inventory are less than 10 km from Jarmo, no evidence for the general settlement pattern or of any "spatial hierarchy" of sites of the Chemchemal valley in the earlier seventh millennium B.C. is yet available. Although a thick *tauf* wall was encountered in a narrow search trench (p. 165), it still seems unlikely that the Zagros villages of this time were fortified in any way. Insofar as we have architectural evidence, it points exclusively to the proposition that the Jarmo people lived in rectilinear single-family units made up of several rooms.

There is at Jarmo not only secondary evidence of food production (artifacts such as sickle blades and milling stones may well *imply* it) but also substantial primary evidence: both the bones of domesticated animals and traces of domesticated plants were recovered. Houses do contain ovenlike structures and also hearths undoubtedly associated in some way with food preparation and perhaps also with warming the householders. Given Wright's evidence that the climatic trend in the area from cold, dry steppe conditions toward the present-day situation was not yet complete and also given the spells of bitter cold winter weather we ourselves experienced at Jarmo, the need for heat does call for serious consideration. Unfortunately, we have as yet no firm evidence of how grain was stored in bulk or of how the herds were sheltered. Certainly not all of the community's food was the result of farming; the bones of wild animals were more common than we had at first believed (p. 436), pistachio nuts and acorns were used, and Helbaek seems never to have specified that all of the identified legumes (p. 502) were necessarily domesticated. The very considerable bulk of land-snail shells was perhaps the most impressive reminder of the amount of food collection still being done by the Jarmo people.

There is no question but that there are some deposits within the exposures we made at Jarmo which do include the sherds of portable pottery vessels and some which do not. As stressed above, however, our first concern is that the matter not be oversimplified. While we ourselves originally thought that the upper third of the site had pottery and the lower two thirds did not, the results of the 1955 season showed the situation to be more complicated. Exactly what the solution to this problem may be must await further clearance at the site.

The second matter of interest regarding pottery is that where it was indeed encountered, the examples in the earlier pottery-bearing levels, although far fewer in number than those in the uppermost levels, were both technically and artistically of better workmanship (or preservation?) than those that were recovered from our near surface exposures. This must bear on the assumption that the invention of pottery vessels did certainly not take place at Jarmo.

Once the use of pottery vessels did become established at Jarmo, however, the number of units produced, as well as the variety of sizes and of profile types, increased markedly. Pottery vessels did not, however, lead to the displacement of stone vessels within the duration of Jarmo's occupation. Unfortunately, the generally friable nature of the pottery and the fact that we encountered no recognizable "activity clusters" or vessels that still had traces of their original contents leaves us with little basis upon which to suggest the particular purposes for which any particular profile type was made. Again with regard to the friability of the later Jarmo pottery, it is worth remarking that almost no potsherds were seen on the surface, a fact which doubtless prompted the first surveyors from the Directorate General of Antiquities to label the site as "mesolithic."

When it comes to the chipped stone industry—traditionally conservative—one especially wonders about its antecedents at Jarmo. It would be reasonable to expect that so old a tradition as the knapping of flint blade tools had a smoothly paced evolution. If this is correct, it underlines the discontinuities between the Palegawra, Karim Shahir, Jarmo, and Matarrah industries. The presently available materials particularly emphasize the fact that there are gaps in the record. It may possibly be that when more is known of Kani Sur and Khora Namik (see p. 13) or other comparable—but as yet not located—sites in the general area, the information from one or more of them may help solve this problem.

Aside from the types held in common with various earlier industries in the area, the few hints in the Jarmo industry that point in the direction of the Zarzian at Palegawra are the geometric microliths—specifically trapezes and triangles—found only in the uppermost levels at Jarmo and the neatly retouched and shaped end scrapers on blades. As regards Karim Shahir, perhaps the two types of Jarmo chipped stone artifacts that are most reminiscent of the Karim Shahir industry in particular are the rare, poorly made, ill-defined burins and the steep scrapers on core fragments (cf. figs. 17:1-2 and 120:7-9).

We are in a somewhat similar situation when we attempt to trace the Jarmo industry down through time. The undistinguished Ali Agha, Hassuna, and Matarrah chipped stone industries have little in common with the Jarmo industry. The only significant link between the chipped stone industries of Jarmo, Matarrah, and Ali Agha is the curious obsidian "thin section" (the side-blow blade-flake). On the other hand, the overall impression one gets from the small sampling of early material from Tell Shimshara (Mortensen 1970) is that it shares a tradition with Jarmo of neatly made blades, bladelets, and other tools (including well-retouched end scrapers on blades and a few trapezes). The Shimshara residents seem to have had more access to obsidian than the Jarmoans and were more generous in its use. Surprisingly, the side-blow blade-flake was apparently not a part of the Shimshara industry; however, another equally curious (its use or uses also unknown) obsidian artifact that is characteristic of the site is also characteristic of Çayönü. This is a type of backed blade, usually with both edges carefully backed by excellent pressure flaking (Mortensen 1970, figs. 25, 29, 36-37). A distinctive trait of most of the examples at Çayönü (Redman 1973, fig. 5:6-8) and also at Shimshara (Mortensen, pers. comm.) is the striations at and parallel to the edge on the surface below the retouch. Many of the Jarmo "pressure-flaked obsidian fabricators" would seem to be of this same type. This is perhaps not clearly evident, because these Jarmo examples are much smaller and more fragmentary and worn (probably due to reuse) than the Shimshara and Çayönü examples. In most of the Jarmo examples, however, where the surfaces are not too worn, the accompanying striations are in evidence.

These peculiar obsidian types seem to be missing so far in the Iranian Zagros; at present we can only say that these Iranian sites share with Jarmo the general tradition of neatly made blades and bladelets, as well as some of the better-known blade tool categories.

It is currently fashionable to picture the hunter-collectors as having been "the original affluent society" (e.g., Sahlins 1972) and to visualize the early food producers in a sort of full-time biblical "in the sweat of thy face shalt thou eat bread" image. Whatever the case may have been at Jarmo, the site's inhabitants certainly committed an impressive number of man-hours to activities other than simply producing food. It is perhaps in the stone vessels and in the other small ground-stone object categories that we see this best and in connection with them that the question of a degree of craft specialization must at least be posed. The number of figurines produced must also imply available time and so must the activities (whatever they actually were in detail) by which such materials as bitumen, obsidian, and ochre arrived at the site. One may also ponder over the amount of time doubtless spent in producing matting, basketry, and cloth and consider the probability of whole artifact classes in such perishable materials as hides and wood. The latter is implied at least by the stone tools which must have had hafts, including tools involved in the carpentry which went into the framing of roofs and doors and other details of house construction.

While it is clear that there are still serious gaps in the evidence for a general space-time continuum of culture-historical development in the Zagros flanks country, we know enough of the Jarmo inventory to see where it must fit in the general scheme. It did not immediately succeed the phase represented by Karim Shahir—the only other excavated site in the Chemchemal valley itself. Both the presence of obsidian with its implications of outside contact and Jarmo's various artifactual analogies with sites in higher intermontane valleys (Sarab, Guran) and sites along the piedmont (Tamarkhan, Ali Kosh) provide us with good reason to reject any suggestion that Jarmo lay in a cultural backwater.

Indeed, in a very broad sense, the Jarmo inventory appears to be part of the generalized assemblage which has appeared from as far south as the Khuzistan plain and thence to the northwest along the Zagros intermontane valleys and piedmont. At the moment, its northwesternmost available manifestation might be seen at Ali Agha if that site's inventory can be taken as the assemblage's latest aspect. Not only the degree of artifactual analogies within this generalized assemblage but also the instances of the use of such items as bitumen, marine shells, and obsidian underline the point that some form of trading network must have existed, binding all the settlements of this Zagros flanks and piedmont region into one loose culture area.

It is important to note in passing that the term "trade" must not be taken in an exaggerated sense, since the amount of obsidian that arrived at Jarmo each year must have been very small, contrary to Renfrew's original fantastic claim (Renfrew, Dixon, and Cann 1966, p. 52; but see LSB's appraisal of the bulk of obsidian that actually reached Jarmo, chap. 4, Appendix).

There are some hints that the Jarmo phase was not separated by too great a time from that of Hassuna and Matarrah (further exposures at a site such as Ali Agha, see below and chap. 20, would doubtless clarify the matter), although there appears to be no very direct continuum in the tradition of pottery making, and practically none in the case of chipped stone. There is a suggestion of a longer persistence of at least some ideas (the details of which elude us completely) expressed by the curious stone objects with cuplike projections on stalks (see p. 300) which also appear at Ali Kosh and in graves at Tell es-Sawwan.

In sum, we believe we are justified in assuming that the occupations of Karim Shahir and Jarmo both fell within the time range of about 11,000 to 8,500 years ago (Libby). The shift away from a cold and dry late Pleistocene climatic regime was already under way and it is likely that the floor of the Chemchemal valley was probably a green and gently rolling plain, not having the violently eroded topography which it shows today. Granting that the contextual uncertainty of small bits of charcoal is an issue at Karim Shahir, it is likely that the site's environment did include some trees (as did that of the Palegawra cave in the next valley; see SAOC 31, p. 59); and for Jarmo the case for trees is even stronger. There is, however, nothing in the available evidence from Karim Shahir, either primary or secondary, to allow us to confirm or deny Wright's proposition that the cereals must only recently have moved into the environment. For Jarmo, there is no question but that the cereals, certain legumes, and the early domesticated animals were all part of the scene.

The Soundings

None of the sites upon which we made our brief soundings in the autumn of 1954 were located on the Chemchemal valley plain. The environmental situation in the Diyana plain, where the Banahilk site was located, seemed not to be greatly different, although it was somewhat more remote and less easy of access from the piedmont. The other sites tested—M'lefaat, Ali Agha, and al-Khan—were really in situations at or closely adjacent to the piedmont plain and to major tributaries of the Tigris (SAOC 31, chaps. II and IV).

Generalizations based on the soundings, because of the very restricted time allotment and the limited exposures we were allowed to make, must remain modest. It should be clear from Dittemore's report (chap. 21) that further investigation of M'lefaat promises a considerable reward in new understandings of the era of incipience, even though we cannot at the moment specify whether this site might represent a phase somewhat before or somewhat after that of Karim Shahir. The soundings at both Ali Agha and al-Khan (chap. 20) were not sufficient to suggest that these particular sites would be the most fruitful places to expose a respectable portion of the post-Jarmo types of inventories which our brief tests sampled. As to Banahilk (chap. 17), the duration of the sounding was somewhat longer (eight days in total) than at any of the other sites we sounded. Although little architectural evidence was reclaimed, the Banahilk yield is otherwise a respectable one. Indeed, until more sites of the Halafian phase are excavated, Watson's contribution to our total understanding of the Halafian assemblage is important and may well—because of Banahilk's up-country location—remain so, even as more Halafian exposures come to be made on the piedmont and to the northwest and west.

At M'lefaat there were vague hints of the remains of what may have been roughly circular pit houses. Both the number and the workmanship of the coarse ground stone artifacts—querns, boulder mortars, and hand rubbing stones—were impressive, doubtless implying a fair degree of attention to vegetable foods. Also impressive was the highly microlithic character of the chipped stone industry. The bones recovered were of wild animals; our small sample did not include the bones of goats (really rough hill country being some distance away), but the remains of clams, crabs, and fish were well represented, which was no surprise with the Khazir River by the base of the mound.

Although the exposure at Ali Agha was relatively minute, Caldwell makes an excellent case for the importance of learning more of the inventory of the Ali Agha phase in our search for general culture-historical understandings. That site itself, as we remarked above, may not be the best place to do so. Our test pits encountered no trace of architecture, although we could not test the center of the mound because of the presence of a cemetery. It is with the pottery that the importance of the inventory is most clear, with its suggestion that the chronological position of the phase of Ali Agha must lie somewhere between those of Jarmo and Hassuna. The presence of a few examples of the Jarmo-type obsidian side-blow microliths, which occur again later at Matarrah, also underlines this point.

Our cleaning up of the face of the old tank-trap trench at al-Khan yielded little beyond a small study collection of potsherds of the Hassuna standard wares and the impression that the topographic-stratigraphic situation at the site is complicated. As with M'lefaat, immediately to the north, the location of al-Khan at what must always have been a natural crossing point of the Khazir River should make the site an interesting one. Our test, however, certainly did not prove the point.

Banahilk, situated just north of the Ruwanduz road and well on the way towards the final Zagros pass into present-day Iran, contained the remains of an evidently flourishing up-country settlement. First, this means that its Halafian ceramic yield must be taken into account in any general consideration of the possible interrelationships within the era of the developed village-farming communities (with their various early painted pottery styles) in western Iran, southern and eastern Turkey, and the upper Tigris drainage region of Iraq. Neither the repertoire of Halafian motifs nor that of pot profiles is as spectacular and varied, however, as was the case at Arpachiyah. To a fair degree, the importance of the Banahilk yield lies also with the availability of various artifacts in categories (other than pottery) of the still poorly known Halafian assemblage. To the evidence for the earlier animal domesticates, sheep, goat, and pig, Laffer now adds the identification of the bones of domestic cattle, which are indeed in greater frequency than those of pig. However, considerable quantities of snails were still being collected.

We trust that in the future the accounts of our brief soundings will be of use to colleagues who are considering the choice of new field excavations along the Iraqi Zagros. Given our own particular interests, we would certainly have wished to continue work at M'lefaat had we ourselves returned to the area.

THE BROADER PICTURE—THE APPEARANCE OF FOOD PRODUCTION IN SOUTHWESTERN ASIA RECONSIDERED

We shall not ourselves speculate on exactly *how* or *why* agriculture came to be adopted by the peoples of parts of southwestern Asia some time around ten thousand years ago. Within the last two years there have been searching studies dealing with the matter, most recently the impressive symposium volume, *Origins of Agriculture*, edited by Reed (1977b), with an important variety of papers by different authors. On the side of the currently popular population-pressure type of explanation is Cohen's *The Food Crisis in Prehistory* (1977). Philip E.L. Smith's little book, *Food Production and Its Consequences* (1976a), is a very useful shorter summary of how things stand at the moment in the matter of various types of explanations of agricultural origins. Smith himself, and various contributors to Reed's *Origins of Agriculture* symposium volume (Caldwell, Hassan, Harlan, Perrot, Redman, Reed, and Wright), have all had firsthand experience in southwestern Asia. Interpretations on more recent fieldwork are summarized in Jacques Cauvin's *Les premiers villages de Syrie-Palestine du IXème au VIIème millénaire avant J.C.* (1978), and Cauvin's interest goes well beyond the Syro-Palestinian region alone. A general textbook type of treatment of the later prehistoric and early historic periods in southwestern Asia is Charles L. Redman's *The Rise of Civilization* (1978). Thus we feel that almost anything we could say about matters of *how* and *why*—given the restrictions imposed by the available evidence—has already been said in the above volumes.

As we hinted in our recapitulations of our own earlier summarizing papers (pp. 6ff.), the critical problem in speculations on the issue of *how* and *why* food production began is the scarcity of really substantial exposures and evidence for the range of transition from the terminal upper paleolithic or Zarzian phase into and through the era of incipience. This same issue of scarce evidence is also critical for Redman's "threshold level" scheme (1977, p. 526) and for Reed's "adaptive cultural plateaux" (1977c, pp. 896-98). Further, when really adequate evidence of the range of transition is recovered, how will it relate to the palynological picture offered by Wright and van Zeist? Speculations on the basis of the Jarmo phase inventory and thereafter are not so troublesome—the Rubicon had already been crossed—but the nature of the progression from the phase or phases of Karim Shahir, Zawi Chemi Shanidar, and M'lefaat into that of Jarmo is still far from clear.

As matters stand at present, the sites worked by the Prehistoric Project in Iraq—once almost the only available examples of their particular time range—still make up an important part of the evidence available on the achievement of food production in the trans-Tigris portions of southwestern Asia. However, what seemed a very simple story to RJB in 1952—with only Jarmo and Karim Shahir to base it on—is now much more complex. The "hilly flanks of the Fertile Crescent" remains a region of considerable interest, but was it indeed a "natural habitat zone" for all of the potential domesticates some ten or twelve thousand years ago? Had it long been so or had it just become (and to what degree) a natural habitat zone? Wright's (1976, 1977) claims for Morocco as the late Pleistocene refuge for the wild cereals face some counterclaims—for example, the finding of *Triticum dicoccum* in the basal Kebaran deposits of Nahal Oren in Israel (Dennell 1973, p. 329) but evidently restricted to "three well-preserved grains"! There is an impressive series of radiocarbon determinations from Mureybit, well within the ninth millennium B.C., along with substantial evidence for wild cereals, and van Zeist (pers. comm.) now believes these could have grown around Mureybit itself. The middle Euphrates was certainly not part of our original "natural habitat zone."

We are not sufficiently informed on recent developments in the late prehistory of the Levant, beyond a general reading of the papers of the Dallas symposium (Wendorf and Marks, eds., 1975), and do not note anything that calls for specific comment in relation to the sites east of the Tigris. Nor can we think of anything useful to say of the evidence we know from Anatolia, the Aegean, or of the Soviet lands on either side of the Caspian, beyond a few obvious and general points of artifact comparison. The implications of Bordaz's (1973) thoughtful listing of early Anatolian radiocarbon determinations interest us regarding early sites there.

In both the introduction and the beginning of the last chapter of SAOC 31, we remarked that "the goal of understanding that we seek will not come within the lifetime of this expedition's staff." We all feel fine and expect to go on for some time, but we also stand by that remark. Few of the questions posed in the last chapter of SAOC 31 are as yet adequately answered. At the same time, we firmly believe significant contributions to knowledge have been outlined; the questions that can be put are now honed to a finer edge. Also, on a very personal level, we cherish the recollection of many fine field companions and many bright days on sites where people once lived and also developed a completely new way of life.

NOTES

1. Stampfli (p. 436) undoubtedly reflects this view in contrasting the restricted yield of small bone fragments recovered at Jarmo with the large Burgäschisee yield, even though he takes the latter to have been far less than the amount the site's inhabitants had once processed.

2. There were instances in certain architectural units in which closely layered floors—originally given submarkings ("a," "b," etc.)—proved to be ephemeral, and hence the material from these ephemeral floors was assimilated with the material from the main floors.

3. It was, incidentally, this notion of "settling-in" which was subsequently developed in Braidwood and Willey, eds., 1962a, pp. 331 ff., which Flannery (1969) eventually named the "broad spectrum revolution," and which Redman (1977, p. 526) and Reed (1977c, p. 896) have carried even further in their ideas about "threshold levels" and "adaptive cultural plateaux." We suppose our own ideas in the matter were first stimulated by reflection on Dorothy Garrod's (1953, p. 14) observation regarding the upper paleolithic that "the speeding-up of change and development which begins to show . . . is reflected . . . not only in the greater number of industries having enough individual character to be classified as distinct . . . but in their restrictions in space, since [cultural] evolution now starts to outstrip diffusion."

4. On this matter, LSB and RJB tend to be more impressed than is BH with the implications of the very considerable human effort required to transport the great quantity of large stream pebbles and rocks up onto the Karim Shahir surface, atop a natural rise composed entirely of fine-grained silt. Given this situation and the undoubtedly larger area of the original Karim Shahir settlement (now eroded away up to the present scarp), should not a somewhat stronger case for permanence also be an alternative suggestion for Karim Shahir?

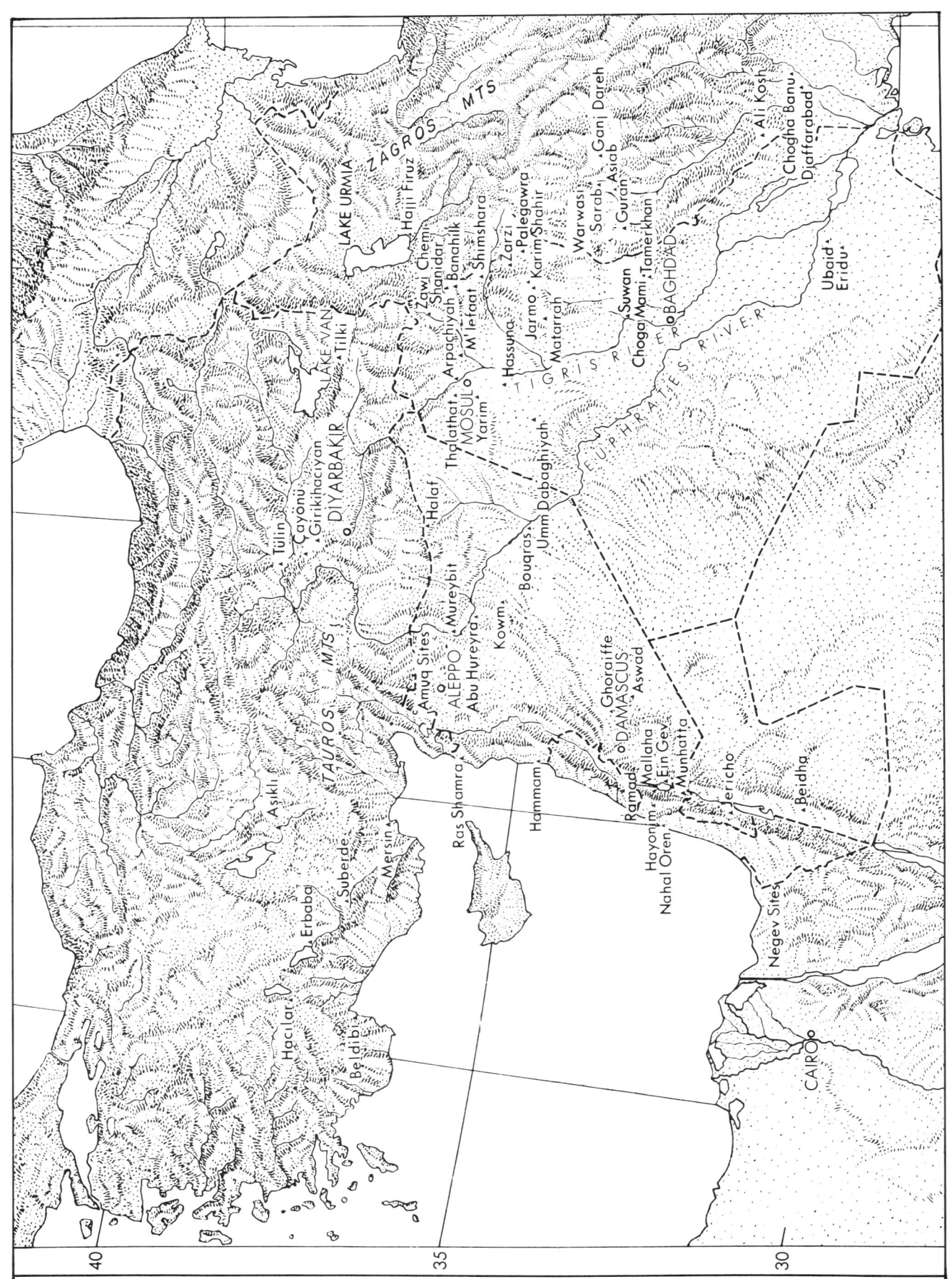

Fig. 1. Map of nearer southwestern Asia with a selection of early sites pertinent to the reports contained in this volume.

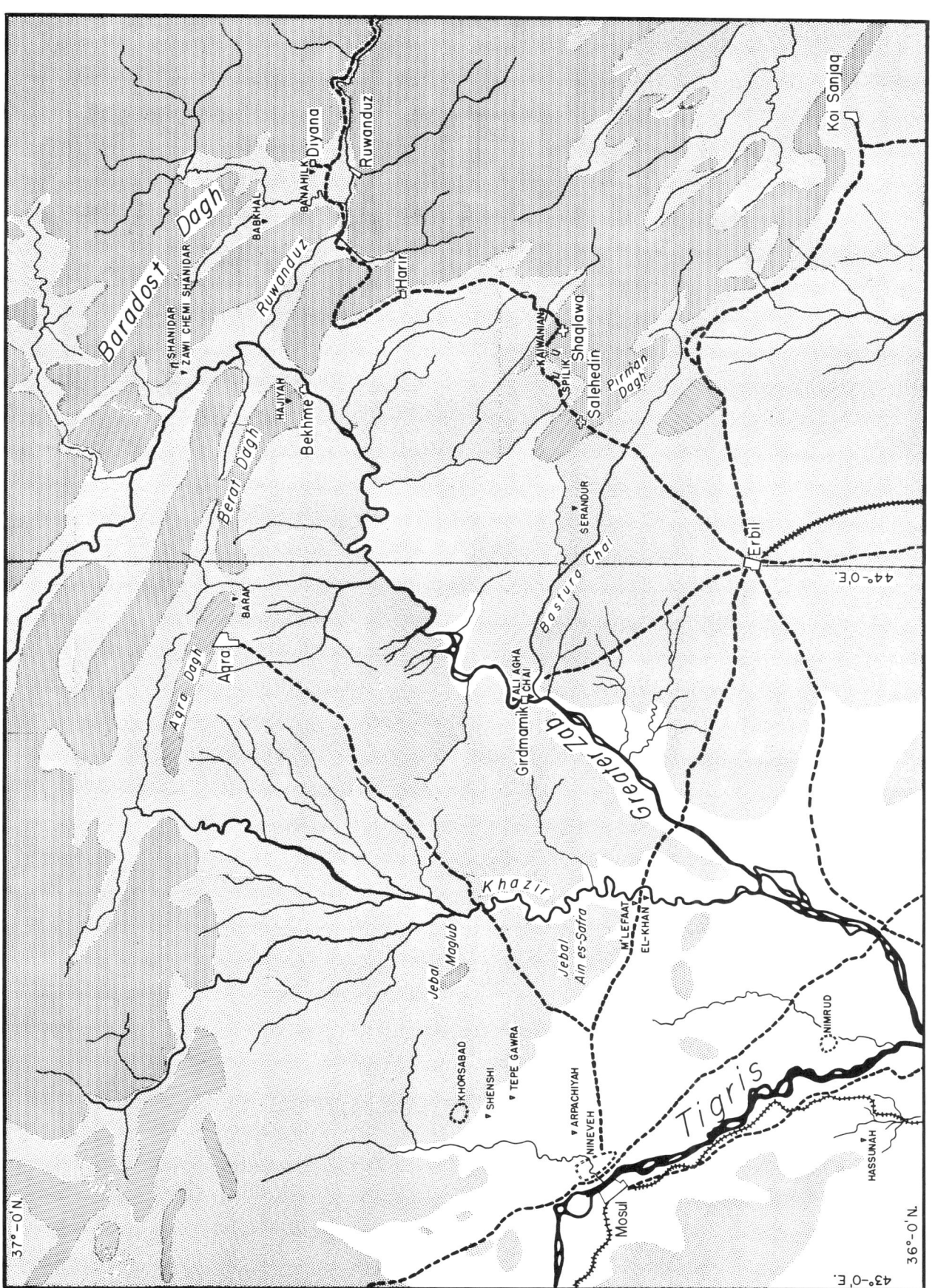

Fig. 2a. Map of sites in the Mosul-Ruwanduz region.

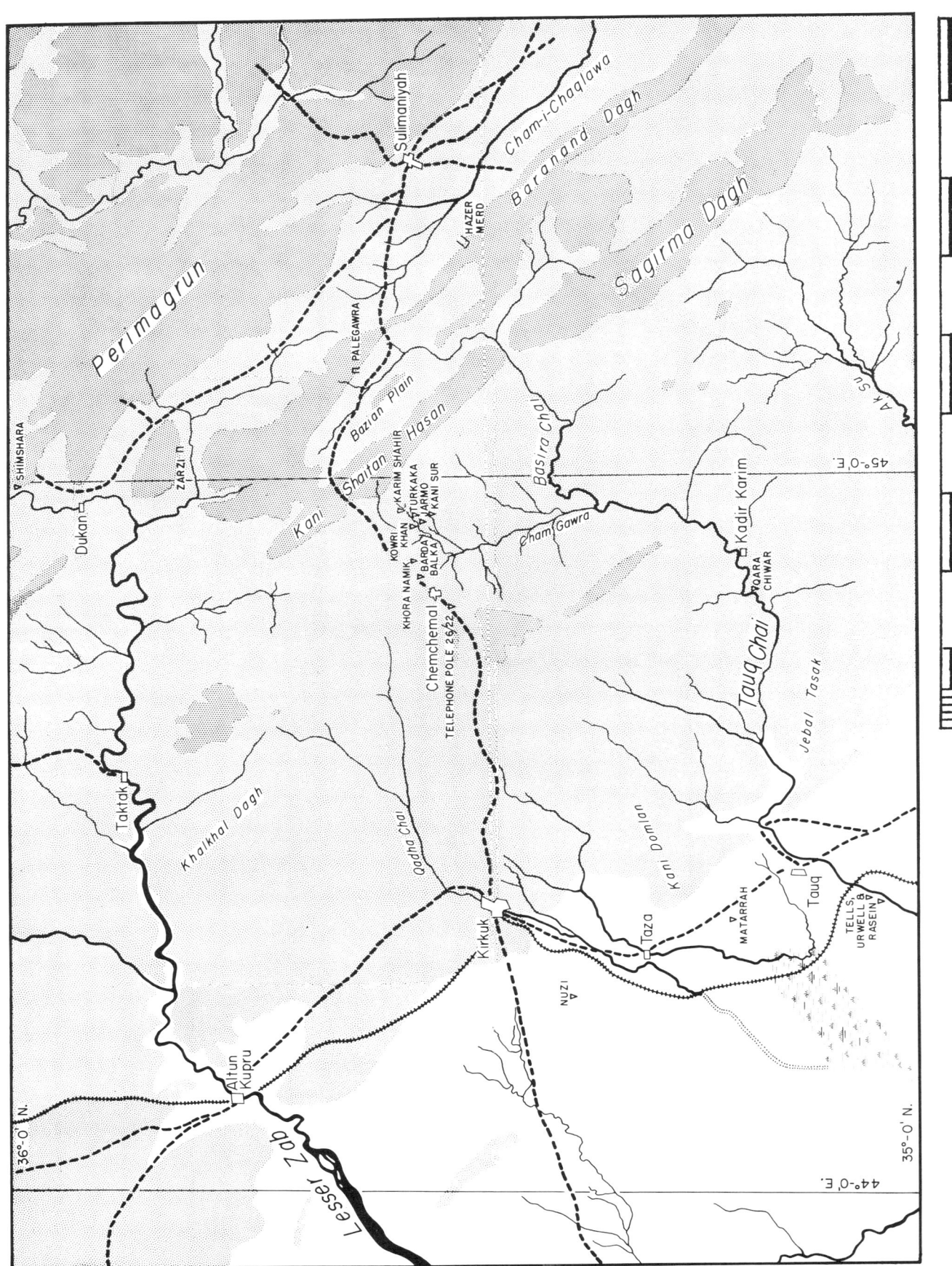

Fig. 2b. Map of sites in the Kirkuk-Sulimaniyah region.

REFERENCES

Bordaz, Jacques
- 1973 Current research in the Neolithic of south central Turkey: Suberde, Erbaba and their chronological implications. *American Journal of Archaeology* 77:282-88.

Braidwood, Linda S.
- 1953 *Digging beyond the Tigris.* New York: Henry Schuman.

Braidwood, Linda S., and Braidwood, Robert J.
- 1969 Current thoughts on the beginnings of food-production in southwestern Asia. In *Mélanges offerts à M. Maurice Dunand I, Mélanges de l'Université Saint-Joseph* (Beirut) 45:149-55.

Braidwood, Robert J.
- 1952 *The Near East and the foundations for civilization.* Eugene, Oreg.: Condon Lectures, Oregon State System of Higher Education.
- 1962 The earliest village communities of southwestern Asia reconsidered. In *Atti del VI Congresso internazionale delle scienze preistoriche e protostoriche*, vol. 1. Florence: Sansoni.
- 1972 Prehistoric investigations in southwestern Asia. *Proceedings of the American Philosophical Society* 116:310-20.
- 1973 The early village in southwestern Asia. *Journal of Near Eastern Studies* 32:34-39.
- 1974 The Iraq Jarmo Project. In *Archaeological researches in retrospect*, ed. Gordon R. Willey, pp. 59-83. Cambridge, Mass.: Winthrop.
- 1976 The background for Sumerian civilization in the Euphrates-Tigris-Karun drainage basin. In *The legacy of Sumer*, ed. Denise Schmandt-Besserat, pp. 41-49. Bibliotheca Mesopotamica, vol. 4. Malibu: Undena.

Braidwood, Robert J., and Braidwood, Linda S.
- 1960 *Excavations in the plain of Antioch I: the earlier assemblages, phases A-J.* Oriental Institute Publications, vol. 61. Chicago: University of Chicago Press.

Braidwood, Robert J., and Howe, Bruce
- 1962 Southwestern Asia beyond the lands of the Mediterranean littoral. In Braidwood and Willey, eds., 1962b, pp. 132-46.

Braidwood, Robert J.; Howe, Bruce; et al.
- 1960 *Prehistoric investigations in Iraqi Kurdistan.* Studies in Ancient Oriental Civilization [SAOC], no. 31. Chicago: University of Chicago Press.

Braidwood, Robert J., and Reed, Charles A.
- 1957 The achievement and early consequences of food-production: a consideration of the archeological and natural-historical evidence. In *Population studies: animal ecology and demography*, pp. 19-31. Cold Spring Harbor Symposia on Quantitative Biology, vol. 22. Cold Spring Harbor, L.I., N.Y.: Long Island Biological Assn.

Braidwood, Robert J., and Willey, Gordon R.
- 1962a Conclusions and afterthoughts. In Braidwood and Willey, eds., 1962b, pp. 330-59.
- 1962b (Eds.) *Courses toward urban life.* Chicago: Aldine.

Caldwell, Joseph R.
- 1977 Cultural evolution in the Old World and the New, leading to the beginnings and spread of agriculture. In Reed, ed., 1977b, pp. 77-88.

Cambel, Halet, and Braidwood, Robert J.
- 1970 An early farming village in Turkey. *Scientific American* 222 (3):50-56.

Cauvin, Jacques
- 1978 *Les premiers villages de Syrie-Palestine du IXème au VIIème millénaire avant J.C.* Collection de la Maison de l'Orient méditerranéen ancien, no. 4, série archéologique, 3. Lyons.

Cohen, Mark Nathan
- 1977 *The food crisis in prehistory.* New Haven: Yale University Press.

Dennell, R.W.
- 1973 The phylogenesis of *Triticum dicoccum:* a reconsideration. *Economic Botany* 27:329-31.

Flannery, Kent V.
- 1969 Origins and ecological effects of early domestication in Iran and the Near East. In *The domestication and exploitation of plants and animals*, ed. Peter J. Ucko and G.W. Dimbleby, pp. 73-100. Chicago: Aldine.

Garrod, Dorothy A.E.
- 1953 The relations between south-west Asia and Europe in the later Palaeolithic Age. *Journal of World History* 1:13-38.

Harlan, Jack R.
- 1977 The origins of cereal agriculture in the Old World. In Reed, ed., 1977b, pp. 357-83.

Hassan, Fekri A.
    1977   The dynamics of agricultural origins in Palestine: a theoretical model. In ibid., pp. 589-609.

Hole, Frank
    1977   *Studies in the archeological history of the Deh Luran plain: the excavation of Chagha Sefid.* Memoirs of the Museum of Anthropology, University of Michigan, no. 9. Ann Arbor.

Mortensen, Peder
    1970   *Tell Shimshara: the Hassuna Period.* Kongelige danske videnskabernes selskab, historisk-filosofiske skrifter, vol. 5 (2). Copenhagen: Munksgaard.

Perrot, Jean
    1962   Palestine-Syria-Cilicia. In Braidwood and Willey, eds., 1962b, pp. 147-64.
    1977   Abstract: the cultural processes leading to the origins of agriculture in the ancient Near East. In Reed, ed., 1977b, pp. 611-12.

Redman, Charles L.
    1973   Early village technology: a view through the microscope. *Paléorient* 1:249-61.
    1977   Man, domestication, and culture in southwestern Asia. In Reed, ed., 1977b, pp. 523-41.
    1978   *The rise of civilization.* San Francisco: W.H. Freeman.

Renfrew, Colin; Dixon, J.E.; and Cann, J.R.
    1966   Obsidian and early cultural contact in the Near East. *Proceedings of the Prehistoric Society* 32:30-72.

Reed, Charles A.
    1977a   A model for the origin of agriculture in the Near East. In Reed, ed., 1977b, pp. 543-67.
    1977b   (Ed.) *Origins of agriculture.* The Hague: Mouton.
    1977c   Origins of agriculture: discussion and some conclusions. In ibid., pp. 879-953.

Sahlins, Marshall
    1972   *Stone Age economics.* Chicago: Aldine.

SAOC 31
    1960   *Prehistoric investigations in Iraqi Kurdistan.* Robert J. Braidwood, Bruce Howe, et al. Studies in Ancient Oriental Civilization, no. 31. Chicago: University of Chicago Press.

Smith, Philip E.L.
    1976a   *Food production and its consequences.* Menlo Park, Calif.: Cummings.
    1976b   Reflections on four seasons of excavations at Tappeh Ganj Dareh. In *Proceedings of the IVth annual symposium on archaeological research in Iran*, ed. Firouz Bagherzadeh, pp. 11-22. Tehran: Iranian Centre for Archaeological Research.

Wendorf, Fred, and Marks, Anthony E.
    1975   (Eds.) *Problems in prehistory: North Africa and the Levant.* Dallas: Southern Methodist University Press.

Wright, H.E., Jr.
    1960   Climate and prehistoric man in the eastern Mediterranean. In SAOC 31, pp. 71-97.
    1968   Natural environment of early food production north of Mesopotamia. *Science* 161:334-39.
    1970   Environmental changes and the origin of agriculture in the Near East. *BioScience* 20:210-12.
    1976   The environmental setting for plant domestication in the Near East. *Science* 194:385-89.
    1977   Environmental change and the origin of agriculture in the Old and New Worlds. In Reed, ed., 1977b, pp. 281-318.

Zeist, Willem van, and Wright, H.E., Jr.
    1963   Preliminary pollen studies at Lake Zeribar, Zagros Mountains, southwestern Iran. *Science* 140:65-67.

1

KARIM SHAHIR
Bruce Howe

INTRODUCTION	25
THE EXCAVATIONS	27
General Description	27
The Assemblage	29
The Operations	29
Operation I	29
The Step	32
The Lateral Grid System and Extension	34
The Trench	38
Operations II to VIII	38
Geological Operations	41
THE NATURE OF THE LIVING FLOOR	42
DESCRIPTION AND ANALYSIS OF THE ASSEMBLAGE	43
Intrusive Materials	44
Materials Belonging to the Horizon	44
Lightly Baked Clay	44
Clay Rod	45
Clay Figurines	45
Hardened Clay with Impressions	45
Bone	46
Bone Tools	46
Bone Beads	47
Shell	47
Shell Plaques	47
Shell Beads	47
Ground and Pecked Stone	48
Ground Stone Bracelets and Rings	48
Ground Stone Plaques and Pendants	49
Ground Stone Beads	50
Ground Stone Rod	50
Grooved Rubbing Stones	51
Pierced Pebbles	53
Striated Pebbles	53
Used Discoid Pebbles	54
Chipped and Polished Celts	54
Boulder Mortars	60
Pestles	60
Palette	61

Grindstones (Querns)	62
Hand Rubbing Stones (Mullers)	62
Pieces with Flat Rubbed Surfaces	63
Hammerstones	64
Minerals	64
Artifacts Bearing Black Substance (Bitumen?)	64
Ochre and Ochre-bearing Pieces	66
Heavy Chert Pieces Containing Iron	66
Chipped Stone	67
Sheen-bearing Flint Pieces	67
Denticulated Blades and Flakes	69
Backed Blades	69
Fabricators	71
Drills	71
Miscellaneous Microliths	73
Unworked Triangular or Trapezoidal Segments of Blades	76
Microburins	77
Burins	77
Burin Spalls	79
End Scrapers	79
Side Scrapers	81
Steep Scrapers on Core Fragments	82
Rounded Scrapers	82
"Raclettes"	83
Blades with Obliquely Truncated Ends	84
Nibbled Blades and Flakes	84
Notched Blades	85
Notched Flakes	87
Used Blades and Blade Fragments	88
Used Flakes and Flake Fragments	89
Cores	89
Core Parts	94
Trimming Debris	97
Representative Cross Section of Stone Artifacts Deposited in Baghdad	98
Faunal and Floral Material	99
Fauna	99
Animal Bones	99
Shells	100
Flora	100
SUMMARY AND DISCUSSION	101
Traces of Settlement and Occupation	101
Artifactual Evidence	102
COMPARISONS	111
Zawi Chemi Shanidar, Layer B	112
Shanidar Cave, Layer B-1	114
Asiab	115
Ganj Dareh Tepe, Layer E	117
M'lefaat	118
Gird Chai	119
Ali Kosh, Bus Mordeh Phase	120

Mureybit	123
Abu Hureyra	126
Review of the Comparative Evidence	126
CONCLUSIONS	130
CATALOGUE OF ILLUSTRATIONS	133
LIST OF REGISTERED OBJECTS	151
REFERENCES	152

INTRODUCTION

One part of the Iraq-Jarmo Project's problem regarding the earliest appearance of the village-farming way of life was to try to find, by tracing the archeological evidence back through time, the very last phases of the hunting and collecting era or perhaps phases close to them that might represent some form of transition toward the food-producing stage. The goal was to gain some perspective on the phase being revealed at Jarmo and to obtain a body of comparative materials. It was hoped that these materials would include the technotypological and morphological traits of industries, perhaps evidence for dwellings and community living patterns, faunal and floral associations, and any other aspects of the record that might provide clues to the way of life of the inhabitants. Such data might then be matched against comparable evidence from different assemblages, from other sites in the same region or elsewhere, that perhaps reflected the same phase, or different heretofore unrecognized phases, in this era of transition. It was hypothesized that there might have been a somewhat long span of time within which the shift in life style from hunting and collecting to effective food production might have developed. The fieldwork was focused broadly for two reasons. First, it was hoped that samples might be obtained from several successive points of time within the span in question and that each of these points might reflect its own characteristic assemblage and associations. Second, it was thought that perspective might be gained by including, for working comparison, materials from near the earlier end of the transition era, when hunting and collecting probably predominated. The site of Karim Shahir seems to have provided an example of what was being sought; it may represent either a relatively early and perhaps even threshold phase or else a later and retarded such phase in the gradual cultural metamorphosis from the food-gathering to food-producing mode of life, and may also provide an archeological record of one way that this great development in human affairs may have manifested itself in one particular district of the foothill terrain in northeastern Iraq.

Karim Shahir is an open-air, shallow, one-period occupation site located near the summit of a high, grassy, flat-topped hill less than two kilometers upstream and east of Jarmo and lying about 850 m above sea level. Both these sites lie just east of Chemchemal in the province of Kirkuk. The site of Karim Shahir was brought to the Iraq-Jarmo expedition's attention soon after the personnel arrived in the area in the autumn of 1950. It was the practice to encourage those villagers who formed the expedition's work force, most of whom had occasion to walk widely over the land, to return to places where they had noticed particular concentrations of *chakmaktash*, the ubiquitous flints scattered throughout the area, and to collect for us whatever they saw at these spots. These limited, essentially "blind," surface collections gained us invaluable, time-saving first glimpses of potentially useful sites, because they usually revealed the simple presence or absence of flint, obsidian, ground stone, pottery, and other general categories of material culture. Knowledge of these facts, as well as some inkling of types, styles, and workmanship, enabled us to judge tentatively what archeological period or periods were represented and which places were worth exploring further with regard to our stated goals.

The introductory sampling from Karim Shahir indicated very sketchily the possibility that here was a one-period site whose material culture was characterized by worked flints, virtually no obsidian, and no pottery. The site was then

---

I am indebted to the American Schools of Oriental Research which made this enterprise possible by appointing me professor of the Baghdad School of the A.S.O.R. for the term 1950-51, and also to the American Philosophical Society which, by Grant No. 1269 from the Penrose Fund, provided support for travel and keep during the four-month spring season. Profound thanks are also due to my colleagues of the Iraq-Jarmo Project by whom I was greatly helped, stimulated, instructed, and encouraged both at the time of the fieldwork itself and during the overly long interval that has elapsed since. I am grateful, too, to the Iraqi authorities at every level for their understanding encouragement and good offices. My thanks also go to the various colleagues who identified specimens and gave guidance and advice in the interpretation of evidence; their contributions are acknowledged at appropriate places in the text.

The manuscript for this chapter was essentially completed by 1977. Very few additions and only minor revisions have been made since that date.

visited casually several times during the autumn by small parties of expedition staff to make further observations and to assemble surface collections. These visits resulted in somewhat larger and more expertly selected samplings than those acquired earlier, but the collecting was still unintensive and unmethodical.

A rough field classification made of all this introductory collection of surface material (over 5,100 pieces, including stone tools, cores, and trimming debris, as well as a little nonlithic material) strongly substantiated our earlier opinion that here was an aceramic, primarily flintworking, perhaps one-period, open-air occupation site. Moreover, on the one hand, the assemblage of chipped flint and ground stone artifacts was somewhat different— technically, typologically, and morphologically—from the assemblage that was coming to light during the excavations at the nearby settled village site of Jarmo; on the other hand, it was also different from the assemblages in the known late Upper Paleolithic levels of Zarzian tradition (e.g., at the not too distant rock shelter of Zarzi itself). At the same time, the Karim Shahir assemblage appeared to have certain typological traits in common with the assemblages of these other horizons. Thus, there was from the start a broad hint that Karim Shahir might well represent either (a) a phase within the transitional era that lay between a late phase of the food-collecting era as represented at Zarzi and an early phase of the food-producing era that was being revealed at Jarmo or (b) perhaps some outdoor seasonal or occupational variant of any one of these three eras.

The Karim Shahir material was only one of a number of provocative, possibly similar surface assemblages collected during the season in this same informal way by the workmen of the Iraq-Jarmo expedition from various open-air sites in the Chemchemal valley. The assemblages from these other sites are to be dealt with elsewhere at a future date. However, it appeared that Karim Shahir would be the most extensive and productive of all. After making preliminary assessments and comparisons and obtaining permission to excavate from the Directorate General of Antiquities of the Iraqi government, the work was carried out between March 14 and May 9, 1951, in a total of thirty-seven working days. These excavations were, in effect, a series of soundings, a number of which were expanded to expose further the traces of what turned out to be a single occupation horizon lying at, or close to, the present surface. These excavations of 1951 were the only ones conducted at Karim Shahir and produced the materials and observations upon which this report is based.

According to a decision taken by Dr. Naji al-Asil, Director General of Antiquities of Iraq, a representative cross section of all artifact categories from Karim Shahir was to be selected at the end of the season and deposited permanently in the Iraq Museum. Accordingly, a cross section of the assemblage, based upon field-sorted categories, was selected by the expedition's staff, inspected and approved by Dr. al-Asil himself, and then left in the Museum in Baghdad. Also, in compliance with the regulations then in force, one half of all registered objects from Karim Shahir, as well as unique specimens, went to the Iraq Museum (see disposition list of registered objects, p. 151). The other half of the registered objects and the remaining and greater part of the artifactual material were generously granted to the Iraq-Jarmo Project for removal to the Oriental Institute in Chicago where, by agreement, they are now permanently available for research purposes. This report takes into account all Karim Shahir materials except the representative cross section deposited in Baghdad, but the contents of that collection are briefly summarized in a supplementary statement (pp. 98-99).

The very poorly preserved and mainly fragmentary animal bones and teeth were granted in toto to the Oriental Institute and released by the Directorate for study. They had been roughly identified, sorted, and counted in the field by Fredrik Barth. As a one-time zoology and paleontology student (he had already then turned to social anthropology), he had agreed to undertake this informal preliminary field processing. He, incidentally, discarded only the most indeterminate and decomposed bits and splinters. Late in 1951 the roughly ordered lot was sent for more intensive study to Professor J. Wolfgang Amschler of the Institut für Tierzucht at the University of Vienna, where a cursory preliminary examination and a few general identifications were made. Professor Charles A. Reed, then of the College of Pharmacy, University of Illinois, also had the opportunity to review these materials with Amschler in 1954 and 1955. Unfortunately, Amschler died in 1956 before he could go further with this work. In subsequent shifts in the affairs of his laboratory the material was lost from sight for a considerable interval, during which time Reed, with the kind help of Miss Helly Kaluza at the Institute in Vienna, made attempts to have it located. Ultimately, a certain block of this material reached Reed at Yale University in the United States, where it was at last studied and described by Dr. Hans R. Stampfli of the Naturhistorisches Museum, Bern, Switzerland. This latest manifestation of the bone material provides the basis for the final report on bones from Karim Shahir by Stampfli, which is included with his consideration of Jarmo mammal remains in this volume (chap. 9). Certain data are excerpted from that report for the summary account of fauna in this present chapter. Nevertheless, since not all of the animal bones classified in the field by Barth reached the United States for study, it still seems worthwhile to continue noting some of the results of Barth's simple field identifications to supplement the Stampfli study. The sole accounting of the lost part of the material is to be found in SAOC 31, page 53. In any event, no large amount of organic material was ever uncovered in the Karim Shahir excavations because of the wretched conditions for preservation prevailing there; shallow, leached, and much weathered deposits containing calcareous concretions were the norm.

Molluscan remains were submitted to Dr. Joseph C. Bequaert, Museum of Comparative Zoology, Harvard University, in 1952. His identifications of the land and freshwater forms that made up over 99% of the Mollusca found at the site are included in this present report. Positive identification of the very small quantity of possible marine specimens among the molluscan artifacts was largely impossible because the shells had been cut down and their natural surfaces artificially defaced in prehistoric times. A few obvious examples of *Dentalium* were noted by Broman Morales and Howe but never confirmed by a specialist.

Ten charcoal specimens large enough for testing and recognition were identified by Professor E.S. Barghoorn, Harvard University, in 1952. A number of seed and other possible plant remains were collected but proved unsuitable for any useful study, according to Professor Hans Helbaek of the Danish National Museum. In any case, one must bear in mind that none of the samples from such a shallow occupation deposit is beyond suspicion of having been physically introduced, contaminated, or disturbed.

Whereas the results of the analyses of the aforementioned categories of faunal and floral remains are dealt with in the following text and in various chapters elsewhere in this volume, it must be pointed out that charcoal samples from Karim Shahir were never submitted for C^{14} determinations. Such tests were not undertaken for several reasons: the marked shallowness of the occupation horizon, the extremely disturbed, weathered, and limy concretion-filled state of the deposits, and the very poorly preserved, comminuted, and widely scattered condition of the little charcoal that there was, which dictated amalgamation of samples to obtain adequate bulk for testing purposes—an ultimately unsatisfactory situation. There were no concentrations of clearly marked pure black charcoal even though a number of fire pits containing heat-affected materials—rocks, bones, soil, and grayish deposits—were found. For the same reasons, the limited quantities of shell and bone were largely retained for identification and not submitted to C^{14} analyses. Indeed, the dangers latent in trying to date materials from such a shallow surface deposit were revealed when one lot of snail shells (notoriously unreliable as material for C^{14} determination) was assayed in 1952 in one of the dry carbon runs of those early days by Professor Willard Libby (then of the University of Chicago) and yielded a C^{14} determination of about 1500 B.C. (pers. comm. to R.J. Braidwood).

Tests for bitumen made on material that adhered to a very small number of stone artifacts from Karim Shahir were carried out in two different laboratories and gave only partly satisfactory results. In 1951 two samples were submitted to P.R. Ransford-Hannay, fields chemist in the chemical department of the Iraq Petroleum Company (IPC) at Kirkuk; one sample was reported to have traces of oil and the other to have traces of oil and bitumen (pers. comm. to R.J. Braidwood). In 1954 Dr. W.F. Foshag, Department of Geology, Smithsonian Institution, conducted tests on two other samples but could not state for certain that bitumen was present in either case (pers. comm. to Howe). With such inconclusive results our position regarding the use of bitumen at Karim Shahir is not clear, but the results do allow for assuming the presence of this substance on certain items as indicated later in this chapter.

Identification of various minerals and rocks that occurred in certain categories of stone artifacts and information about their properties were provided by Professors Robert Reuss of the Department of Geology, Tufts University; H.E. Wright, University of Minnesota, Minneapolis; and John Green and Ralph Marsden, together with various other members of the Department of Geology, University of Minnesota, Duluth.

The name Karim Shahir, according to Kurdish informants from the nearby village of Kani Sard, within whose bailiwick this locality lay, is given to the high hill on which the site was found. It apparently means "the wheat field of Karim," "the field of Karim," or "the place of Karim." Any further associations of the name have either been lost to history or not imparted to us. It was vaguely said that the summit plateau at Karim Shahir had in the not too distant past been tilled, but in 1951 the solidly grassed appearance of the place showed that there probably had been no very recent agricultural activity of any sort. Subsequently, however, excavations did reveal an overall disturbance due to plowing down to the usual depth of 10-15 cm. Erosion and redeposition due to natural slope wash was also noticeable on the distinctly inclined flat top of the hill. The erosion tended to extend over the northern and the redeposition over the southern parts of the southward-tilting plateau surface. Even more striking erosion was observed along the southern third of the eastern edge of the hilltop. There, a fresh-looking slumping scarp and long talus of earth betrayed active present-day erosion, as well as older long-term action by the seasonal stream, the Cham-Gawra, which ran ca. 40 m or more below. The occupation deposit was sharply truncated by this scarp, so that an unknown proportion of the site had been lost. Such were the conditions when work began. (See views, figs. 3-4, and contour map, fig. 5.)

THE EXCAVATIONS

General Description

A total of eight separate test excavations, labeled operations I-VIII, were laid out at widely scattered points on the hilltop plateau (see plot plan, fig. 7). The excavations originally cut as operations I, II, III, VI, and VIII were each expanded variously to follow occupation traces revealed by the initial excavations at those points. Operation I, situated along the eastern scarp where the most plentiful surface indications of occupation had been found, turned out to be the most rewarding locus and was expanded much more than the others by means of an extensive grid system. This operation produced the prime sample of this occupation site, both in quantity of material and evidence of living floors. The materials found in operation I and its extensions furnished the fundamental corpus of artifactual types, which have been analyzed by level and gross area, and with which materials from all other operations at the site were compared.

Unfortunately, when it was revealed that the occupation horizon was so close to the surface and so much of it was disturbed, it was considered unlikely that many precise observations on intact living floors or detailed associations could be made. Nevertheless, it will be seen that when virtually no other adulterations were found there, the site as revealed by operation I, with its meagre features but copious artifactual assemblage, may be taken as a reasonably reliable though imperfect example of one integral cultural unit or horizon.

The locations of operations II-VIII were chosen with some hope of finding additional traces of occupation, perhaps the same as or different from those found in operation I. In some cases, we were led to these locations by surface indications such as rock piles or other concentrations of rocks that indicated human activity. This was the case particularly in operations V, VI, and VIII, which were positioned along the eastern crest of the hill. In other instances, namely operations II and VII at the plateau's extreme western and northern limits respectively, we chose locations at arbitrary compass points, although a visible surface scatter of rocks reinforced our decision on the positioning of operation II. Finally, we tried to establish the living-floor boundaries at operation I not only by means of an extension northward and a trench westward but also by operations III and IV placed immediately west of operation I. In any event, none of the subsequent operations revealed as intensive a degree of occupation as operation I, although certain ones did yield some evidence of what was presumably the same prehistoric occupation and others also indicated that almost all parts of the hilltop had probably been used in one way or another through time.

Given the factors of limited available working time and the initially untrained work force, as well as the disturbed and fairly extended nature of this shallow, evidently one-period site, most of the excavation at Karim Shahir was carried out laterally and in arbitrary centimeter levels. Differences in soil texture and color were mostly subtle within a narrow range, with redeposited and original components indistinct from each other. For the most part, archeological materials were grossly lumped by trench or grid area, so that blocks of material were only broadly segregated by level and area. Less commonly, outstanding pieces were recorded according to their exact findspot, and the limited number of items found in and close to the few identifiable features such as pits were kept separate. Surface collecting continued sporadically as both staff and workmen had opportunities to walk over the hilltop plateau and its flanking slopes. Ultimately it became clear that no progressive shifts in typology or morphology were to be noted, either by depth or by area, within operation I or the other less productive operations. Thus, save for the very few obviously intrusive recent items recorded, the site assemblage has been considered as a single essentially uncontaminated cultural unit.

During the total of thirty-seven working days, the corps of workmen averaged 29 individuals daily, ranging from a minimum of 15 to a maximum of 39, depending upon attendance factors and excavation needs of the moment. At the start the force numbered ca. 20-25, swelled later to 30-35, and near the end rose to 35-39 men. Unskilled at first, the majority soon became proficient, attentive, and reliable.

After an initial period of training and close supervision of the workmen, the digging at Karim Shahir settled into the same general routines as those established for Jarmo (p. 2). Recognition of the various materials and detection of features by the pickmen were assured by those procedures. In particular, sieving through approximately ¼-in. or 6-mm mesh was carried out in unannounced spot checks of the sievers throughout the excavations. When one after another of these spot checks, each comprising five to ten sievefuls in sequence, produced virtually nothing of significance, we were put at ease about the thoroughness of the workmen. The repeatedly fruitless sieving clearly justified confidence in the overall procedures and vindicated the pickmen and earth carriers, who at first had been so indignant at this additional control over their performance.

As a final general observation about the site, one should note that the entire hilltop plateau from which surface collections were made was estimated to measure ca. 6,000 m². The total area of surface exposed by the excavations was ca. 600 m², representing roughly 10% of the plateau's surface. However, it should be remembered that the excavated surface of operation I and its extensions might possibly have represented a still larger proportion of the remnant occupation floor of this one-period site. Given the evident sterility of the northern third of the plateau, as suggested by the largely nonproductive operations VII and VIII, as well as the spotty and isolated nature of any indications of cultural activity in operations II, IV, and VI, it is thought that a good part of the 6,000 m² of hilltop may have been essentially unoccupied. Given also the insoluble problem as to what proportion of the original site had already been removed by natural erosion along the eastern edge (H.E. Wright has speculated on geomorphological grounds that perhaps one third may have been lost [pers. comm.]), one cannot arrive at a realistic estimate for the extreme outer limits or the degree of concentration of the remnant site, or for the horizontal extent and organization of the original occupation site. Moreover, most of the other operations were not located in positions that helped to solve these matters very effectively. One is, nevertheless, left to suppose on archeological evidence that the present core of the site's vestiges may lie within the southern half of the plateau, especially in a broad band along the eastern scarp edge, and that operation I (including its associated extension and trench), and to a lesser degree operations III and V nearby, sampled a good proportion of it, judging by the concentration of material and features revealed in them. One should also bear in mind that the scarp was in all likelihood not as high or as sharp at the time of occupation as now. Wright has estimated that the stream had cut down to only a moderate depth at that time (Wright 1952, p. 17) and that it has cut perhaps two thirds of its present depth since then (pers. comm.).

The Assemblage

The artifact assemblage recovered from the single occupation horizon at Karim Shahir, principally sampled in operation I, consists primarily of a large number of varied types of chipped stone tools as well as a very much more limited number of ground stone tools and articles of personal adornment. There are also a very few bone tools and simple bone and shell ornaments, and three lightly baked clay objects, at least two of which were recognizable figurines. These minor categories of bone, shell, and clay may originally have been present in greater quantity than that implied by the number recovered, but most of them probably succumbed, as did parts of the wild animal bone and shell debris, to weathering and other forms of deterioration in the shallow and superficial deposits of the site.

The chipped stone industry can unquestionably be characterized as a blade industry. As in the case of the ground stone categories noted below, the material for these tools—cherty flint, limestone, marble, schist, breccias, and other less common forms of raw material—came from a wealth of waterworn pebbles in nearby streams and in massive older conglomerates and gravel deposits, all of which had been derived from the materials of the mountainous hinterland. The industry includes a great many well-made flake and blade cores, the latter in especially striking quantity. There are also large classes of various types of simple scrapers on blades and flakes as well as notched, nibbled, or otherwise worked blades and flakes. Less common but still moderately plentiful and very characteristic categories include carefully worked drills or borers, backed blades, and, particularly, microlithic backed blades. Various simpler microlithic blade and flake tools created by use also occur. There are some simple forms of burins, but these are rare and usually poorly achieved or doubtful. Geometric microliths and the supposedly associated microburins are extremely rare; in fact, the presence of such a category at Karim Shahir is debatable.

A significant category is the chipped and polished celts, sometimes made of cherty flints but more often of numerous other types of relatively more fine-grained rocks. These include various igneous, sedimentary, and metamorphic rocks that were seemingly less resistant and more friable than flint and capable of being ground and polished. Roughly one third of the examples in this category are axe forms and the rest adze/hoe forms.

Other distinct simple ground and pecked stone tool forms have been identified, but they are few in number, very sparsely distributed, and mostly fragmentary: boulder mortars; grinding stones, querns, or metates; hand rubbing stones, mullers, or manos; pestles; maceheads or dibble weights; hammerstones; and a special characteristic sort of grooved rubbing stone invariably made of schist, with the groove worked across the grain.

The ornament category is a small one, composed primarily of some bracelets and smaller rings, most of which are made of white marble; a few bone, shell, and stone beads; and small, simple pendants and pierced plaques made usually of fine-grained stone but also occasionally of shell. All of these objects, except for the beads, are fragmentary.

The artifactual assemblage of the horizon has neither any pottery, in the strict sense, nor any obsidian. There is no sort of pebble chopper or chopping tool, but there are tools displaying obvious pebble form or traces of pebble cortex, namely the simple natural pebble pestles and small boulder mortars, the dibble weights or maceheads, the pebbles used as anvils or pounding and working stones, and the occasional celt, core, or gross primary flake or blade on which the pebble surface is still partly visible.

As evidenced by the bulk of the finds (which came from operation I), we may take it that most of this assemblage of artifacts was made and used on the spot. All were found amid masses of trimming debris, along with broken animal bones and shells, in intimate association with a rocky occupation floor interspersed with several depressions and pits filled with rocks and earth. Some of the earth, rocks, and bones were discolored by heat or fire.

It has been suggested that the more close-set portion of the rocky floor could have been made by packing rocks over the ground in order to keep from being overwhelmed by mud. Some proportion of the rocky scatter found on the hilltop could also be interpreted as the supply of selected rocks used for cooking in the fire pits and for toolmaking. Subsequent plowing and slope wash have disturbed much of this material. In any case, every piece must have been carried up by the occupants in prehistoric times to this site, located as it was at a high point with a commanding view of the countryside and resting upon massive and archeologically sterile deposits of silt.

The Operations

We may turn now to a more detailed report on the sequence and method of excavation carried out on the hilltop of Karim Shahir. Provided below for each operation (I-VIII) are the reasons for their positioning and the dimensions, excavation procedure, and yield.

Operation I

The greatest surface concentration of flint material appeared to extend over the southeastern quarter of the plateau, especially in an area near its eroding eastern edge. Thus, the first work in operation I was to cut a step, 20 m in length, along that segment of the margin of the scarp at this edge where the surface concentration of artifacts appeared densest (see plot plan, fig. 7). The step so cut permitted a clear view of a north-south section of the shallow, rocky, gray-brown occupation layer and showed the relation of that layer to the other deposits (see section, fig. 6). Had it not been for the presence of the rocks, it would have been almost impossible to distinguish this occupation layer from the disturbed overlying slope wash and plow zone deposits that were composed of virtually the same materials and thus similarly toned and textured. The step also provided an ample front from which to develop lateral expansion westward onto the plateau into whatever remained of the occupation horizon to be discovered behind this eroded edge. From this step, operation I was gradually expanded by a grid system of lettered squares (A-G), measuring 5 m on a side, that pushed both westward and northward to follow what was revealed of a closely packed fieldstone scatter, or "pavement," and other more sporadic stone scatters (see plot plan, fig. 7). In the northerly part of the area exposed by these grids and their extension, the occupation horizon proved to be lying at or close to the surface. Elsewhere to the west and south its rocky surface was found at a depth of ca. 20-25 cm or a little deeper, and the entire gray brown silty occupation deposit associated with the rocky layer was 25-40 cm thick. Nowhere was this deposit more than 50-60 cm below the present surface, except when a few deeper pits and depressions occurred (see section, fig. 6). Throughout much of this northern part, in grid A and the extension, the fact that the traces of occupation lay at or close to the present surface was evidently due to erosion of any overburden by slope wash on the surface of the plateau, which tilted down gently southward, fostering removal southward of any top soil from its northern portions. For the most part, excavations within the grid system simply scraped clean the fieldstone scatters. However, in the step and in the southerly grids C and G the excavations were in places taken to depths of 1.8 m, 3.8 m, and 1.4 m respectively, well down into the sterile silt, the natural top of which constituted the "Jarmo-B surface" of the geological scheme devised by Wright (1952). This deeper penetration was carried out in order to make certain that there were no features of earlier phases underlying those already found. With very few exceptions, only the smallest flint tools and trimming debris and the tinier shells and bits of bone, charcoal, and suspected bitumen were found at these lower depths, in small quantities and sparsely distributed. This minuscule material is typologically entirely comparable to the material found in the main part of the occupation layer and as such has been discounted as evidence of any separate horizons; it is considered to be simply the result of a natural downward migration of the smallest pieces from the single occupation layer. This displacement can be explained by the action of ground water, by expansion and contraction due to diurnal and seasonal temperature changes, by human trampling and digging, and by the presence of animal burrows and plant roots (animal runs and root holes were very much in evidence to considerable depths). Although excavated and initially studied according to its several separate 20-cm and 40-cm levels, this lower material was ultimately combined and considered with that from the main occupation horizon for convenience of treatment in this report.

In addition to this archeologically oriented complex of step, grids, extension, and trench in operation I, a long, narrow step trench was cut, for primarily geological reasons, from near the midpoint of grid C at right angles across the step and well down the talus into the silt formation (see plot plan, fig. 7). A second such narrow step trench and a pit were set separately further down the steep slope northeast of operation I and well down within the silt formation (see plot plan, fig. 7). These three geological probes were dug in order to have an unobstructed view of certain natural features in the sterile underpinnings of the site. The findings are briefly summarized later in this chapter.

Most of the artifacts, as well as virtually all of the few habitational features identified at the site of Karim Shahir, lay in operation I and its contiguous extension and trench. As already noted, the material culture includes a significant collection of chipped flint and ground stone tools, ornaments of stone, bone, and shell, a very few lightly baked clay objects and bone tools, and some animal bones, teeth, and mollusc shells. There are also very limited amounts of charcoal, seeds, and other floral remains and some traces of suspected bitumen. This assemblage was associated with an extensive rock scatter. These rocks were in part perhaps intact but in part disturbed, their chaotic distribution surely also the product of movement by slope wash and plowing of the original rock-laden site. In addition, at depths just below the rock scatter, there were found nine fire pits, as well as two (perhaps only one, with part displaced) shallow, debris-filled depressions suggesting either natural hollows, possible open-air living spaces, or (less possible) subsurface floors of a localized and ephemeral nature, and a single deep pit with a partial facing of red ochre at its base that might perhaps have ceremonial implications. The strictly artifactual components of the diverse cultural traces in operation I and comparable but much less extensive similar supporting material from the other seven soundings at the site (operations II-VIII) will be treated together, beginning on page 43.

Meanwhile, it is useful to describe here at greater length the work in operation I and its extensions, since it is upon the data obtained in this very productive portion of the excavations that the analyses and interpretation of the occupation horizon of Karim Shahir largely rest. We discuss each part of operation I as it developed, describing the site's features and the characteristics of its assemblage as they appeared. In addition to the initial 20 m long step, cut along the eastern edge of the site on a line 18° E of N, seven rectangular grid areas were excavated laterally from the step toward the west. These areas were lettered from north to south, grids A, B, and C being excavated contiguous to the step, and grids E, F, and G in turn contiguous west of them, with the space contiguous south for grids D and H left undug. The area of grid E was enlarged as an extension northward and northwestward from both the original basic grids F and A (see plot plan, fig. 7). Thenceforth, grid E and its extension were treated as a unit called *the extension*. In much of this extension the stone scatter and associated industry and living-floor debris lay at or near the surface and had been considerably disturbed by plowing in modern times. Elsewhere to southward the cultural traces lay presumably intact at a depth of 25-30 cm or below.

The heart of the most closely packed part of the rocky floor area was an amorphous zone along the eastern scarp edge (see plot plan, fig. 7, and views from the photographic tower, figs. 8-9). This pavementlike area was nearly 20 m long and some 2-8 m wide within grids A and B and the extension. It must be noted, however, that the sharply defined curved spaces devoid of rocks near the step edge in the areas of grids A and B and the ghost of an apparently stoneless straight line extending north-south (left to right) along the grid lines across the rocky area (figs. 8-9) were due to inadvertent removal of stones there by workmen before the archeological significance of the chaotic jumble of stream pebbles and coarse angular field stones became clear.

While the concentrated pavement could clearly be seen to extend irregularly to the north (fig. 7), the stone scatter as a whole was a more open and patchy affair, especially to the west and south (figs. 8-9, foreground). This scattered condition was perhaps the combined result of (a) some original scattered deposition left by the hunter-gatherers and in part still in situ, (b) subsequent disturbance by slopewash, and finally (c) plowing, the effect of the three processes being now indistinguishable. The rock scatter lay at some depth, where perhaps it was undisturbed, and also in zones of shallower deposits, where it surely was disturbed (see section, fig. 6). This rock scatter as a whole, with its associated cultural debris, was taken to constitute the chief manifestation of the occupation site. It was traced continuously west into the narrow trench, which led to operation III, and ended there just west of the grids on a line ca. 13-14 m west of the scarp edge (see plot plan, fig. 7). One may presume that the westward limits of the rocky area lay approximately along the same line under the sod north and south of the excavated point of observation in the trench. Thus, one has the impression that the occupation lay and its activities took place in a broad but vaguely defined area along the scarp and that it slacked off sharply west of this. A rocky band perhaps ca. 15 m wide was all that erosion of the scarp left us of this occupation area. It is further considered possible that little islands of a similar form of occupation may be represented by the rock clusters and by the scatters with associated artifacts and debris found at similar depths in most of the other operations dotted over the hilltop.

In the paramount exposed area represented by operation I, the plentiful artifacts and debris of flint and rarer ones of bone and shell, the broken animal bones and shells, and the traces of tiny charcoal specks and gray ash-tinted soil were all found widely disseminated through the rock scatter as well as immediately above and below it. No trace of postholes or walls or other specific hint of structure or shelter was detected in the course of the excavations.

The rock scatter, made up of angular field stones and rounded stream pebbles of flint and other rocks, many of which were cracked and discolored by fire or heat, was clearly an artificially accumulated cultural phenomenon on top of this high hill that otherwise was homogeneous, fine-grained, sterile water-laid silt, which had been deposited in massive amounts as a major geomorphological feature in the area. These rocks and stream pebbles, intended for the manufacture of artifacts, for filling fire pits, and perhaps for use in other living installations, were carried up there by the prehistoric inhabitants. Items found in and immediately under this rocky layer may be presumed to be essentially in situ wherever the surface of this layer lay under the 25-35 cm of deposit and thus safely below plow and superficial slope-wash action. Items found above this level were largely derived, but almost all came from nearby parts of the same single occupation layer.

Accordingly, the morphology and typology of the industry at this site, as evidenced predominantly by the materials recovered in operation I, had a unity throughout. At first, some particularly outstanding artifacts (including certain chipped and polished celts, ornaments of stone, bone, and shell, fragments of ground stone tools, and the few simple bone tools) were recorded precisely as to findspot. Later, when the fact that some of the material had been dislocated became apparent, it did not appear useful to be so precise. In any case, the disposition of these items did not seem to point to any revealing, rational pattern in relation to pits, areas of burned earth and rock, or any other possible prehistoric cultural locales or work spots. Thus, in this report, designations of provenience are in general given no more precisely than by grid or major excavation unit and by centimeter levels of depth en bloc within them. As far as the top 50-60 cm of deposits were concerned, there were no detectable variations or progressions in type or occurrence of artifact by area or by depth, and the size-sorted small items found below this level have, as we have said, been deemed part of the same cultural horizon. We decided to treat all the different groups in this corpus of artifacts, whether based on type or material, as categories within a single cultural unit.

It is this corpus of artifacts from operation I that is here described and interpreted as the characteristic industrial assemblage of the Karim Shahir occupation horizon. Since the horizon was considered to be internally undifferentiated and to be the same in all parts of the excavations, the operation I material is viewed as a reliable unit for comparison with assemblages from other sites. Therefore, the few artifacts and features found in operations II-VIII are simply assigned to the categories established for operation I. Archeological finds from operations III and V, the closest physically to operation I, are presumed to be contemporary with those of operation I and part of the same occupation. Those finds from operations II, IV, and VI-VIII, although typologically and morphologically comparable to the material of operation I but separated from it by considerable distances of uninvestigated terrain and so almost certainly contemporary, cannot be as surely related to the main site.

The sizeable representative cross section of operation I materials that was deposited in Baghdad has been noted separately in this report and treated according to the same typological system, with complete counts for each category. While not studied in as much detail as the main body of the materials brought to Chicago and not included in the tallying for this report, this representative selection is put on record so that it can be taken into account, if necessary, as part of the total yield from the horizon. It must also be noted that a number of registered pieces from this and other operations and now in Baghdad have been used to illustrate types in this report.

The Step

In a total of eleven working days the north-south step was dug for a distance of 20 m along the eroding eastern edge of the site. This work dealt first with slumping deposits that had broken away from their hilltop positions and were starting their move down the long slope. Thus, the upper and outer occupational deposits of sod, rocks, and silty earth laden with artifacts were greatly disturbed and could be removed in short order. This work was done mainly by excavating in a number of 40-cm levels. Each such level cut downward created both a higher section face and a broader step surface until, when the last cut was completed, the step displayed a section face ca. 1.8-1.9 m high and a platform 3.0-3.5 m wide, depending on the irregular conformation of the slope. When a full vertical cut had been opened up along the 20-m section line (the meter marking system having been started at the northern end), the major stratigraphy of the site became clear (see section, fig. 6). It may be described as follows:

(1) A top layer, 24-35 cm thick, of loosely packed brown humic material, was composed of surface humus as well as slope wash from northern parts of the site. It contained the disturbed soil from the 10-15 cm thick plow zone, an element that was virtually indistinguishable from the rest of the layer. This top layer contained a number of small rocks and numerous artifacts, as well as calcareous concretions.

(2) A second layer of dull gray-brown deposit was some 25-40 cm thick and conspicuously filled with small rocks (both rounded stream pebbles and angular field stones) and great quantities of artifacts. All this material, out of natural context on the top of this high silty hill, was taken as an indication of human occupation. This layer also displayed calcareous concretions throughout. Among these were close-set, short, thin, horizontal or slightly curved stringer zones of concretions which lay at intervals and undisturbed, often near the base (fig. 6). While the upper limit of this layer was in places quite localized and rather clearly defined at an average depth of about 30 cm, the lower limit appeared to be a vague transition into the layer below.

(3) Underlying these upper layers were tan silts, grayish tan on top but becoming increasingly pure tan below, which continued down to and below excavation limits. Some rocks and artifacts occurred in the very uppermost portions of this layer but gradually diminished in both size and quantity until sterile deposits were reached. The silt deposits also contained fairly evenly distributed calcareous concretions, which were detectable down to a level of 6.9 m. They diminished gradually in size with depth, progressing from small but still easily visible ones just above the base of excavations (fig. 6) but grading downward in increasingly smaller sizes until they were no longer detectable.

The rocky gray-brown zone proved to be the heart of the occupation horizon at Karim Shahir. In the area exposed by the step, and in the area of the grids adjacent on the west, the top of this rocky zone lay fairly uniformly at a depth of 25-35 cm below the surface. However, as excavations proceeded northward and northwestward into what was called the extension (grid E and its extension) and thus into an area slightly upslope from this original excavation area, the rocky gray-brown zone was found nearer to and virtually at the present surface. As already noted, this depth differential may well be the result of the slope-wash action that tended to denude northern sections of the hilltop and bury southern portions with silty earth containing occupational debris. Thus, in all likelihood, the topmost humic brown layer, wherever encountered, was a jumble of soil that had come from elsewhere in the occupation layer and had been redeposited and then disrupted again by plowing.

Additional occupation features uncovered in the step included remnants of a number of large and small pits evidently dug down to various depths below the rocky living floor as well as evidence of a broader, less defined depression—of debatable significance—in this floor. In most cases the upper portions of these features escaped detection; sometimes their presence was suspected but not clearly established amid the disturbed and slumping deposits of similarly toned and rock-laden material at the edge of the scarp. Once the worst of the surface slumping there had been cleared by removal of the 0-40 cm and 40-80 cm levels, some of these features became clearer in section. All contained some rocky rubble and an occasional artifact that came from the occupation floor. All save the broad depression and a large red-ochred pit near the north end contained enough obviously burned cracked rocks and bones and bits of orange and red soil to be labeled fire pits or hearths.

At the very start of digging, two clusters of field stones, cracked rocks, and some discolored earth and gray ashy deposit were found on the surface, one cluster located 1 m south of the north end and the other 3 m north of the south end of the step. These clusters may have been what was left of prehistoric fire pits, but they were too disturbed and superficial to be considered definite features. However, it was possible to establish the positions and rough dimensions of eight features that were definitely fire pits, as well as one vaguely outlined depression, at deeper levels during the latter half of clearance in the step (see section, fig. 6; plot plan, fig. 7).

All the fire pits were distinguished by concentrated quantities of field stones and fire-cracked rocks, by discolored and somewhat hardened earth, occasionally by lenses of grayish deposits, and, very rarely, by tiny charcoal specks. A few artifacts, animal bone fragments (some burned), and, more rarely, snail shells were at times found in or near the pits, but these categories were common throughout the site and no special clusters of artifacts were noted in association with these or other pits, with a few exceptions that we decided were fortuitous occurrences. These various features are described below in the order of their discovery.

At a depth of 25-45 cm, two shallow rock-filled pockets, each about 2 m in diameter, were located near the southern end of the step just east of the section line at the 14-16 m and 17-19 m marks. The pocket located at the latter point yielded a fragment of an incised stone.

At a depth of 60-80 cm, the remnants of a pit with a maximum diameter of 1.5 m were found with traces of fire-hardened earth and rocky dark earth down to a depth of 1.1 m. This feature appeared between the 13.5-15.0 m marks and was visible on the section line. Because it was well back from the eroding scarp edge and there was no indication of displacement, this pit may be taken as a typical example of the kind of fire pit dug at Karim Shahir. A flint core and some flakes were found in the fill.

At a depth of 0.8-1.0 m, near the north end of the step and visible on the section line between the 1-2 m marks, another rock cluster, approximately 1 m in diameter and marked by discolored ash-tinted and hardened earth, represented another fire pit.

Also at the north end, lying at depths of 0.9-1.4 m and 1.15-1.60 m, were two more pits, each of which was 1-1.5 m in diameter. They lay in positions well out from the section line and were probably considerably dislodged downward by slumping. Towards the south end, another similarly situated rock-filled pit, about 2 m in diameter, lay at a depth of 0.9-1.1 m between the 15.5-17.7 m marks.

At a depth of 1.4-1.5 m, near the center of the step at the 10-12 m marks and approximately 1 m east of the section line, was a large, shallow, relatively flat depression some 2 m in diameter. It contained thinly dispersed traces of dark gray-brown baked-claylike earth, fire-reddened earth with charcoal specks, snail shells and bone debris, and a few rocks and large pebbles, some of which bore a black crust, possibly bitumen. Fragments of a bone pin, grindstone, and hand rubbing stone were also found. Being in the outer part of the step, this depression may not have been entirely in its original place and may in fact constitute the slumped part of a zone similar in color that was found close by at a depth of 80-90 cm in the eastern half of grid C (see discussion under Grid C, p. 35). At first, the size and flatness of this feature, the relative thinness of its deposit, and the character of the few associated objects all suggested a living floor. However, in retrospect and after consideration of the somewhat similar flat, only sparsely littered, vaguely defined gray zone in the adjacent grid C, the two formations are now seen as possibly parts of a single large, slightly bowed, natural open-air basin or depression that retained a bit of litter either washed in during or after the occupation or else dropped there by inhabitants during the occupation. Indeed, no vestiges of any true floors at any depths were found elsewhere at the site.

Finally, the remains of what appeared to be the bottom of a large pit with some associated field stones, flint, bone debris (including a bead), discolored earth, and numerous flecks of charcoal were traced at the top of the 1.8-2.0 m level. Portions that were related were also detected in section directly above this, certainly at a depth of 1.4-1.6 m and possibly at 1 m. The surviving lowermost traces of this sizeable steep-sided pit, almost surely somewhat slumped and disturbed, lay in the outer part of the step, its estimated perimeter centered 1 m east of the section line close to the 4-m mark near the north end. The diameter of this shallowly basined bottom at the 1.8-m level measured ca. 3 m, aligned roughly between the 2.75-m and 5.90-m marks on the section. The very bottom of the basined area was carefully coated with bright red ochre on hard-packed soil. The coloring was compact near the center and both vestigial and fugitive near the periphery. A few fist-sized rocks, some tiny charcoal flecks, and, near the center, a small clay figurine rested on this ochre surface. Some of the numerous flints that were found in the fill above, presumably there by chance, bore traces of red ochre (p. 66).

The compact portion of the ochre-coated basin area was in a half-moon shape with a diameter of ca. 2 m, the rounded edge being near the outer lip of the step, the straight edge toward the section line. Fugitive traces of ochre completely surrounded the semilunar solid patch in a band 50 cm wide. While the red ochre may conceivably have been laid down originally in this semilunar form, the straight edge of the solid red bottom of the basin was so sharply defined that it strongly suggested that there had been a fissure and subsequent displacement in the deposits here and that roughly half the solid ochre surface of the presumably once-circular basin was thereby lost, probably left behind at some higher level under the rocky living floor and still unexcavated. (See also Grid C for evidence of still another possible fissure in the silt deposits that was probably due to slumping along the edge of the scarp.) Despite the slumped condition of its immediate surroundings, much of the red-ochre pit remained intact. There is every reason to believe that it depended from the main occupation horizon, which lay at a depth of ca. 25-40 cm, and may originally not have been more than 1 m deep.

It is noteworthy that the only two lightly baked clay objects found below ground at Karim Shahir were found in association with this red ochre pit: one stylized figurine (fig. 10:1a-b), which was found resting on the center of the bottom, as noted above, came from inside it; the other was found at a depth of 1 m just south of the south edge of the supposed upper traces of the pit.

Other outstanding finds in the step area besides the aforementioned items included a marble bracelet fragment, a fragmentary pierced shell plaque, two bone beads, two chipped and polished celts, a pebble pestle, a fire-reddened fragment of a grindstone, and a fragment of a small boulder mortar (all from the 0-40 cm level), as well as another celt, a marble bracelet fragment, a fragmentary pierced shell plaque, and one fragment of a hand rubbing stone and another from a grindstone (all from the 0.8-1.2 m level and below). In addition, there were some of the usual chipped flint artifacts, snail shells, and bone debris, most of which were concentrated in the top 80 cm, especially in the northern half of the step, and which evidently were loosely associated with the rocky floor in this slumped zone. Relatively sterile areas were noted between features and at the 1.2-1.6 m level in the northern half of the step. There was, in general, a great decrease in the number of finds in the 0.8-1.2 m level and below. Allowing for slumping along this scarp line, this last block of levels might conceivably be equated with the in situ deposits that immediately underlay the base of the occupation zone seen in section at a depth of ca. 60 cm.

The Lateral Grid System and Extension

Once the section face of the 20-m step front had been established, showing the position of the single rocky occupation horizon with its several dependent features, it remained to uncover an ample lateral exposure of this occupation layer that would extend westward from this section line. This was accomplished by excavating first the five 5-m² grids labeled A, B, C, F, and G, then the sizeable irregular extension running upslope north and northwest from grids A and F, and finally the trench on the west. All these contiguous lateral exposures in operation I totaled ca. 390 m² in area (see plot plan, fig. 7).

The lateral excavation cleared the shallow overburden of top soil, plow zone, and slope wash down to the rocky occupation layer. As noted above, this layer was found at, or close to, the present surface in part of grid A and in the extension, where it had been denuded of the shallow overburden. Elsewhere, to the south in grids B, C, G, and most of F, the occupation layer lay, presumably largely intact, protected under 25-35 cm of debris-laden slope wash from up hill.

With limited time available, the main effort was devoted simply to removing the overburden everywhere so that the rocky layer was clearly exposed, trying to establish its limits and character, collecting all possible cultural materials therefrom, and ultimately removing much of this layer. This sequence of work was done effectively within the top 50-60 cm of operation I. In fact, the excavations below the 50-60 cm level in operations I, III, and IV cast very little additional light on the character of this site. The step section had shown that the concentration of cultural materials was at and around the rocky layer and that a number of related pits and a depression extended below this layer to varying depths where associated artifacts were rare. Except for these deeper features, the deposits below ca. 50-60 cm were, in general, essentially sterile. Operation III (7.5 m west of operation I) and the trench connecting the two operations aimed to establish the western limits of the rocky living floor. It turned out that these limits lay not far beyond the western edges of the extension and grids F and G; there was little trace of occupation west of there. As far as we could determine, the people occupying the site evidently kept near the scarp edge.

A consideration of the assemblage and the detectable features in each part of the lateral extensions from the step and section in operation I showed that the site as a whole had an overriding uniformity. While there were a number of pockets in which materials generally seemed sparser, all areas of the rocky floor in every part of the excavation in operation I produced quantities of worked flints and much rarer specimens of ground stone, bone, and shell artifacts. This floor also produced a steady supply of broken animal bones that were much weathered, deteriorated, and fragmentary, and in some instances burned. There were also small bits of natural red and yellow ochre, sporadic specks of charcoal, and very rare hard shiny black particles of matter taken to be bitumen (see on pp. 27 and 55 the inconclusive findings of Ransford-Hannay regarding oil and bitumen; also see on pp. 27 and 64 the Foshag statement on the impossibility of establishing the presence of bitumen on the basis of any very small and heavily weathered piece). Here and there in the rocky floor there were areas where fire-discolored and cracked rocks and orange red earth occurred, indicating the presence of fire pits or shallow hearths. Concretionary calcareous nodules occurred in quantity.

With this general description of the character of the remains of cultural occupation at Karim Shahir we may proceed to more details about this evidence. Details are given by excavation unit and according to level and relative position therein.

Grid A.—The 0-20 cm level, located in humic brown soil comprising topsoil, plow zone, and redeposited slope wash, yielded quantities of rocks and worked flints throughout as well as some outstanding items: a fragment of a boulder mortar from the northwest quarter and a chipped and polished celt, a grooved rubbing stone, a marble bracelet fragment (fig. 10:16), two small fragmentary shell plaque ornaments, and a fragmentary bone point from the eastern half of the grid near the section line. In general, a smaller quantity of artifactual material came from the western side of grid A than from the eastern. A total of 1,183 artifacts, including the chipped stone categories, were found in this level.

The 20-40 cm level, incorporating the basal humic deposit and the top of the rocky gray-brown zone, yielded 879 artifacts. Most of the area of grid A at this level was filled by the close-set pavement of rocks that had been identified as the occupation floor. Two fragmentary shell plaques (one pierced), two fragmentary bone points, a pebble pestle, and a grooved rubbing stone came from the northeastern quarter, and two small shell plaques from the southern part.

Except for clearance of the rocky layer, no further excavating was done in grid A. It proved to be an area with materials that were average in quantity for the site and were found centered rather nearer to the scarp edge and step than to the west of it.

Grid B.—The 0-20 cm level here, composed of the same mixed humic brown topsoil as in grid A, yielded 1,815 artifacts including abundant flints, a bead, and a chipped and polished celt. A grindstone fragment lay in the southwestern quarter.

The 20-40 cm level, here too embracing the upper part of the rocky gray-brown layer, which contained the southernmost remnant of the close-set "pavement" area as well, yielded 1,239 artifacts, mainly great numbers of worked flints, including several fragments of backed bladelets. A complete double-pierced shell plaque came from the southeast quarter and a celt and a fragment of a small marble ring from the general grid area. There was somewhat more animal bone debris here than in grid A, including two heavy horn cores. In fact, a particularly marked concentration of occupational debris—artifacts, bones, and burned rocks and earth—was located around the junction of grids B, C, F, and G. This material is more fully described in the discussion of grids C and G (where digging proceeded through deeper levels); it was unfortunately not fully investigated within grid B because excavation there went only to a depth of ca. 40 cm and just into the top of the rocky layer. At any event, the plentiful quantities of bones and artifacts from this 20-40 cm level of grid B doubtless reflect the more concentrated numbers lying within this focal area. It must also be remembered that the yield from grid B may well have been affected by the inadvertent removal of rocks in the northeast and southeast areas early in the excavations, which left artificial gaps in the otherwise close-set rocky pavement that filled much of the northeastern part of this grid (see plot plan, fig. 7; fig. 9).

Grid C.—This area, and the part of grid G next to it on the west, proved very rich in materials and were exploited to a greater depth than other grids. As elsewhere, the derived and disturbed humic layer in the 0-20 cm level gave up its usual generous quota (here, over 1,500 accumulated artifacts). Furthermore, in grid C, as in A and B, most of the flints and other artifacts, together with animal bones, shells, and traces of hearths and fire pits, were closely associated with the rocky layer situated at a depth of ca. 30-40 cm. In fact, at the 30-40 cm and 40-50 cm levels there was again a very productive yield of materials largely concentrated around the junction of grids B, C, F, and G. In grid C this concentration also extended eastward toward the edge of the scarp and the section line. A pit was located and dug out in the eastern half of the grid on the section line (see further details under The Step, p. 33), and it is possible that another pit or even more underlay the concentration of materials noted at the junction point of the four grids, judging by the quantity of burned rocks, bits of bone, and little patches of fire-reddened earth uncovered thereabouts. The occupation floor within the 20-50 cm level of deposits in this grid yielded over 6,500 artifacts.

On the other hand, excavation below about the 50-cm level in grid C produced only very sporadic and very small flints, bones, and pieces of shell. With the exception of one pit and the possible exception of a discolored deep-lying depression zone to be noted below, the excavated parts of the underlying paler gray-tan silty deposit did not contain any real evidence for actual occupation there but only minor debris most probably displaced downward from the occupation layer. To this general overview of deposits and features, we now add details about specific finds, by level.

The 0-20 cm level produced abundant worked flints, two chipped and polished celts, and a marble bracelet fragment. Animal bones, on the contrary, were rare.

The 20-40 cm level revealed a rich sector of the rocky layer, the top of which lay here at 30-40 cm, marked by gray earth with calcareous concretions and sporadic patches of hard orange-red earth. A total of 5,694 artifacts were collected from these top two levels. In the northern half of the grid the level yielded many flints, including numerous backed bladelet fragments, five chipped and polished celts, a grooved rubbing stone, a pebble pestle, a fragmentary perforated stream pebble that was possibly a small mace or dibble weight fragment, a marble bracelet fragment, a fragment of a stone barrel bead, an elongated biconical stone bead with angled double end perforations (fig. 11:13), a double-pierced shell plaque fragment, and a fragmentary bone pin.

In the 40-50 cm level, 881 artifacts were found, primarily chipped flint. Notable finds included a grooved rubbing stone in the northwestern quarter and a chipped and polished celt and two fragmentary, long, narrow pebble pendants in the southwestern quarter. There were small patches of hard orange-red earth scattered here and there, and a bit of the suspected bitumen—hard and glossy black—came from the northeastern quarter. Moreover, careful scraping over much of the eastern and southern parts of the grid at a depth of ca. 40-50 cm showed no evidence of occupation such as pits or postholes, and almost the only rocks remaining at this level, except for those in the pit or pits, were isolated examples located toward the center of the grid.

In the 50-60 cm level there continued to be a reduction in the amount of flint, bone, shell, and rocks. There were 720 artifacts in this level. The silty deposit here was increasingly sterile and of a pale tan color.

As a rule, the 60-80 cm level and each of the three successive 20-cm levels down to the 140-160 cm point were, with one exceptional area, essentially sterile. Scattered widely in all of these levels were animal burrows filled with darker earth. In and near these burrows was found the greater part of the artifactual debris—small clusters of archeologically insignificant flint chips and bladelets, small pieces of bone and shell (including a possible dentalium bead), occasional flecks of charcoal, and bits of hard orange-red earth—all presumably displaced downward from the overlying occupation layer. A single bracelet fragment, round in cross section rather than the usual Karim Shahir oval, purportedly came from the 90-100 cm level, but in fact its origin was in doubt, since the fragment was suspected of having been brought in from outside by a workman in hopes of a bonus. (This item is discussed further on p. 48). Scraping at several levels in all quarters revealed no discoloration that would indicate any disturbance except the ubiquitous burrows. The various levels yielded artifacts in fairly consistent quantities, as follows: 60-80 cm, 519 pieces; 80-100 cm, 349 pieces; 100-120 cm, 289 pieces; and 120-140 cm, 168 pieces. However, as the one exception to this regularity, there occurred in the northeastern quarter of grid C, at a depth of ca. 80-90 cm, a virtually sterile gray zone—some 5-10 cm thick and spread over ca. 3 m^2 of the exposed area—that was in contrast to the tan deposits above and below it. No outstanding artifacts were found in it other than a few of the tiny nondescript bits of flint, bone, and shell common to these lower levels. Nothing like this gray zone was found elsewhere in grid C or in grid G. However, one must recall that in the step, immediately east of this gray zone in grid C, an equally noticeable gray zone containing somewhat more interesting artifactual debris was found. These two gray zones were aligned almost exactly east-west with each other and separated laterally by only the 1 m of evidently sterile deposit. Since the gray zone in the step area lay to the east, nearer the eroding scarp edge and some 50 cm lower than the similar zone in grid C, this displacement could be reasonably accounted for by the natural slumping and erosion along the scarp edge there. Such an assumption was strengthened by the fact that there was an unmistakable vertical fissure (filled with contrasting darker earth from overlying levels) at a depth of ca. 2 m in the north end of the 1-m trench that had been dug into the paler silty deposits along the eastern edge of grid C in this very area (see below). We may, then, provisionally link these two gray zones and view them as one.

In neither grid C nor the step was the gray deposit sufficiently different in color, clear-cut in outline, or compact nor was its associated artifact assemblage sufficiently densely distributed or numerous to be considered good evidence for an occupation floor. Neither area contained or lay under any detectable traces of deposit bands, other discoloration, or debris fill. Although it is possible that these low gray zones were parts of a very broad basin or depression related to the major occupation layer above, no intervening traces were found of any deposits, artifactually charged or discolored by fire, that might link them directly with the habitation floor. As far as could be determined, there was only clear silt at this depth, and the gray deposits themselves were vaguely defined and all but barren. Thus, we can only suggest that they might have been natural open-air depressions that gradually filled with slope wash and bits of artifactual debris during or after the occupation.

The 140-160 cm and 160-180 cm levels were excavated only in a 1-m wide strip along the east side of grid C contiguous to the step and section line. Although 112 artifacts, mostly very small flints, were found here, these levels furnished the same picture of essentially sterile tan silts penetrated only by animal burrows as that revealed in the levels above.

Next, in the northeast corner of grid C and within the same 1-m strip, a 1 × 3 m exploratory north-south trench was rapidly dug deeper into the tan silts along the step section line between the 10-m and 13-m marks. This trench went from the 180-cm level (here now dug down so that the north-south section was shared by both this part of grid C and the adjoining step area) to a depth of 3.8 m. It exposed only sterile tan silts that contained diminishing amounts and sizes of calcareous concretions, a phenomenon associated with the old pre-occupation exposed land surface, the "Jarmo-B (depositional) surface" (Wright 1952).

Also noted in the silts in the center of the north wall of the 1-m strip trench was the trace of a vertical fissure. It was visible at the 1.8-2.0 m level and below, and its slender wedge shape was set off from the surrounding tan silts by a slightly darker-toned fill from the occupation layer above. This crack and the suggestion of another in the horizontal plane running north-south across the red-ochre pit on the step to the north (p. 33) are clear witness to the slumping erosion at the scarp edge.

In addition to the archeological excavation in grid C that has just been described, a step trench for geological purposes was rapidly dug down from the 3.8-m level, starting at the south end of the 1-m strip trench noted above and running directly eastward, cutting across the step and down the steep slope (see Geological Operations, p. 41).

Grid F.—Grid F, like grids A and B and the extension, was excavated only down through the rocky layer. In grid F the lower limit of that floor lay at a depth of ca. 40 cm. This work comprised removal of the mixed overburden, clearance and removal of the floor, and collection of all artifacts and occupation debris. The horizontal scatter of rocks continued in diminishing quantity as far as the western edge of the grid (fig. 9). The western limit of the rock scatter was located just west of here in the trench (fig. 7).

The 0-20 cm level of grid F reached down just to the surface of the rocky layer. The digging yielded 1,866 artifacts, mainly good quantities of worked flint (including 6 backed bladelets and 4 borers), and in the southern half 2 chipped and polished celts and a marble bracelet fragment. Considerable quantities of flint, bone, and shell came from the eastern half of the grid, particularly in the southeastern quarter where the deposits formed part of the concentration of materials found around the junction of grids B, C, F, and G (see remarks under Grid C above).

In the 20-40 cm level encompassing the rocky layer, this concentration of materials continued in the same way; here 1,888 artifacts were found. Besides the bulk of worked flints from the grid as a whole (including 7 backed bladelets, 4 fabricators, and a small borer), there were 2 chipped and polished celts and a marble bracelet fragment from the southern half and 2 fragmentary bone points from the northwestern quarter of the grid.

Grid G.—This grid, with adjoining grid C on the east, proved to be one of the more productive areas of the occupation floor in operation I. In all, it yielded over 8,500 artifacts. The inconclusive traces of a pit or depression were found in the southeastern quarter at a depth of 80-90 cm. The scatter of stones making up the floor extended over the entire grid (fig. 9), pointing to the likelihood that this scatter and its associated occupational debris extended an unknown distance further south under the sod in a broad zone along and in from the scarp edge.

The 0-20 cm level lay completely within the disturbed zone. A good number of artifacts, predominantly worked flints, were found although they totaled only half of the quantity found at the same level in grid C.

The 20-40 cm level, yielding over 3,700 artifacts, contained the upper portion of the rocky living floor, the surface of which lay here in the 30-40 cm level (fig. 9) as in grid C. Besides the many worked flints in the grid area, there were items of special interest in the northeastern quarter (amid the rich concentration of materials noted under grid C above), namely, 4 chipped and polished celts (one with traces of what was probably bitumen remaining in crevices of the flake scars), a tiny marble ring fragment (fig. 10:12), a marble pendant fragment (fig. 11:2), a bone bead (fig. 10:7), a grooved rubbing stone, and a fragment of a hand rubbing stone. From the southeastern quarter came another hand rubbing stone fragment, a pierced stone fragment suggesting a macehead or dibble weight, a grooved barrel-shaped stone bead (fig. 11:12), and another biconical stone bead with angled double end perforations. The southwestern quarter at the 40-cm level was largely clear of stones, and scraping showed no traces of other occupational features.

The 40-50 cm level continued to produce rocks and occupational debris that included over 2,100 artifacts as well as fragmentary bone and shell in the central, northern, and eastern parts of the grid. This level and the one above it in this grid encompassed almost the entire living floor and its associated materials and contained over 5,800 artifacts. A fragmentary pierced stone pendant with a narrow groove came from the southeastern quarter of the grid. A fragment of a fully pecked and shaped pestle, an ornamented palette fragment (fig. 12:3), a green stone pendant, a bone bead, and a fragmentary stone bead were also found.

In the 50-60 cm level there was a sharp reduction in the occurrence of artifacts, bone, shell, and rocks, this level being to all intents and purposes below the occupation floor. Only 542 artifacts were found here. Worthy of note in the northwestern quarter were a marble bracelet fragment and another biconical elongated stone bead with angled double end perforations.

The 60-80 cm level contained virtually no rocks and was also comparatively unproductive, yielding only 637 artifacts. What there was came from the northern and eastern halves and included in particular a fragment of a perforated discoid marble plaque (fig. 11:8). There were sporadic traces of charcoal, small bits of red and yellow ochre, and another tiny, hard, glossy black fragment of supposed bitumen.

The 80-100 cm level was predominantly made up of clear tan silt in the northern and western halves, although there were the same sporadic charcoal specks and ochre bits as in the level above. In the southeastern quarter grayish discolorations, quite a few small flint chips, and some small snail shells and bone fragments were found. At a depth of 80-90 cm in this quarter there were also a grooved rubbing stone, a bone bead, part of a polished bone needle, some splinters of burned bone, and a number of snail shells. This cluster of material in the vicinity of discolorations and other debris may vaguely indicate a little open-air depression or else the bottom of a sizeable pit filled with otherwise sterile and characterless silty deposits. However, no traces of an outline or of any higher part of such a pit were detected.

In the 100-110 cm level there were several little clusters of very small flints, bits of bone, snail shells, charcoal, ochre, and possible bitumen. In this material was a total of 125 artifacts. Also, here and there in the deposits of the southern and eastern halves of the grid, grayish discoloration was noted—an interesting phenomenon when considered in conjunction with similar traces found especially in the southeastern quarter just above. The southwest and northeast quarters in particular produced numerous small flint chips and bladelet fragments, a few tiny backed, notched, and used pieces, bone fragments, snail shells, and minuscule charcoal and ochre bits. However, as in grid C, a good number of animal burrows were also evident, and much of this deep-lying small artifactual and material debris may be attributed to downward displacement conceivably linked with these burrows.

The 110-120 cm, 120-140 cm, and 140-160 cm levels also contained numerous animal burrows and produced the same sort of evidence but in diminishing amounts (including 327 very small artifacts).

A small perforated gastropod shell, probably a bead, came from the 110-120 cm level. In grid G, excavations stopped at the 160-cm level.

*The Extension.** —The irregular plot that was excavated toward the north and northwest from the step and the grid system in operation I was dug to trace out more of the rocky occupation floor revealed in the several grid areas. This extension contained some 200 m² and ran northwest for 20 m along the bluff edge. It was excavated in a single level 20 cm deep. By removing the topmost 20 cm of sod and silty deposit, much more of the floor was laid bare and a generous additional sampling from the site obtained. Over 30,000 artifacts were collected from the extension.

The removal of sod and superficial silty deposits was taken only far enough laterally to expose the western edges of the stone scatter and to confirm that it did indeed run east right to the brink of the scarp. In the extension, the rocky floor lay virtually at the surface and was, of course, disturbed by plowing and slope wash as in some of its other parts to the south. However, the extensiveness of the close-set rocky "pavement" that was traced in an unbroken band northwestward and northward along the bluff edge, away from the part that had already been laid bare in grids A and

---
* Abbreviated as *Ext.* in the tabulations.

B (figs. 7-8), suggests that perhaps here, in the strip of terrain lying close to the present brink of the precipitous eastern scarp, the rocky floor may have been left essentially in situ and undisturbed, perhaps partly because the prudent plowmen of later years were careful to keep their furrows at a safe distance from this precarious edge.

The 0-20 cm level was dug out as an undifferentiated unit. It not only contained the few centimeters of disturbed humus and topsoil but also penetrated well into the top centimeters of the rocky occupation floor so that, when the work was completed, the floor was clearly exposed. The plentiful artifacts and debris collected from this superficial level were also treated as a unit, since by then it was clear that the site was of only one period and virtually uncontaminated by other remains. Besides the considerable quantities of worked flint materials, the most noteworthy finds were 4 chipped and polished celts, 9 fragmentary pestles (7 pebble type, 2 pecked type), 5 grooved rubbing stones, 8 marble bracelet fragments, 2 stone beads (1 discoid [fig. 11:11] and 1 cylindrical in form), and 2 simple points worked on bone fragments. Very close to the surface at the westernmost angle of the extension a fragmentary iron horseshoe and a number of articulated vertebrae of sheep or goat were found. These obviously recent items, taken with the half-dozen small potsherds, a piece of glass, and 3 bits of obsidian reported elsewhere during operation I, are literally the only pieces of material easily recognized as later than, and unrelated to, the assemblage found in this operation—a remarkably clean record. The usual debris of fragmentary animal bones and snail shells and traces of fire were also found in the deposits of the extension.

A general cleanup of the rocky floor in grids A, B, and F and over much of the extension penetrated in places into the 20-30 cm level. This level yielded considerably more artifacts, including 2 bracelet fragments, a chipped and polished celt, 2 mortar fragments, and numerous worked flints, together with the usual bone and snail shell debris.

*The Trench**

Since the stone scatter of the rocky floor in grids F and G was found to be dispersed all the way to the western edge of excavations in operation I and since operations II and IV well to westward had not shown any convincing traces of the core area of the stone scatter, a trench was eventually dug west from this western edge of operation I, linking it to the exposure at operation III. It was hoped that the western limit of the stone scatter might thereby be established. This connecting trench, measuring 1 m wide and 7.5 m long, lay across the area of what would logically have been grid J and was aligned with the southern edges of grid F and operation III (fig. 7). It was cleared in a single level 20 cm thick down to the surface of the rocky layer, thus revealing that the western limit of the rocks was 3.2 m west of grid F on the northern edge of the trench and 4.8 m west of this on its southern edge. The outer limits of the rock scatter lay in a curvilinear diagonal between these two points. One could reasonably project the trend of the line northward to join the edge of the rock scatter exposed along the western edge of the extension and, with less assurance, southward for an unknown distance and perhaps roughly parallel to the scarp edge for an estimated core area of 700 m^2.

The 0-20 cm level in the trench included the overlying disturbed humic and topsoil deposit and the uppermost few centimeters of the rocky floor, also quite likely somewhat disturbed. Just over 1,000 artifacts were collected from this level. Besides an ample sampling of the chipped flint industry (including 3 backed bladelets), there were a chipped and polished celt, a grooved rubbing stone, and a fragmentary discoid stone plaque. One flake with faint traces of sheen along one edge was also found.

OPERATION II

Near the western brink of the plateau, operation II was begun on a day when a violent wind made work elsewhere impossible. It was laid out first as a 3 × 10 m excavation on the opposite side of the plateau from the main work area of operation I and was oriented so that it would be in west-east alignment with the 7- and 10-m lines of the grid system in operation I (fig. 7). This second operation was designed to uncover any traces of occupation, near the northern limits, of a sizeable surface scatter of angular and subangular field stones that were clearly visible in the southwestern quarter of the hilltop plateau. The work took place intermittently over a total of seven days. In a first effort, excavation went to a depth of 50 cm in 10- to 15-cm levels over an irregularly shaped zone, exposing the western end of the trench and extending irregularly along the entire north half of it for a total of ca. 15 m^2. The yield was negligible except toward the eastern end where a rock scatter and the edge of a rock-filled fire pit were exposed at a depth of ca. 15-20 cm at the base of the plow zone. The underlying silt was virtually sterile. The southern part of the originally contemplated trench was not further investigated. Later, in a second effort, an eastward extension was cut approximately as a 3 × 3 m square to expose the fire pit. This pit proved to be intact and was typical of its kind, measuring 2.4 × 2.6 m in diameter and 65 cm in depth and having steep sides and a basin-shaped bottom. It was filled with discolored rocks of various sizes closely packed in compact, stiff, reddish orange earth containing tiny charcoal specks.

Save for the fire pit and, in the superficial humic layer, scattered rocks and 152 largely nondescript artifacts—a few flints (including a backed bladelet, notched and variously used blades and flakes, and 2 pyramidal cores), a fragmentary obsidian end scraper, a bone bead, and modern glass (a blue bead and a clear bracelet fragment)— nothing of significance was found and operation II was abandoned. It appeared to have uncovered only isolated and mostly superficial and disturbed elements. Most of these were not particularly diagnostic, although they may possibly

---
* Abbreviated as *Tr.* in the tabulations.

be associated with similar elements found in the principal occupation. However, given the admixture of obsidian and recent glass and the shallow, isolated, and unrelated position of the whole, the area penetrated by operation II must remain unfixed in time and only tentatively linked to the main horizon on somewhat slim typological grounds.

OPERATION III

Laid out as a 3.0 × 7.5 m east-west excavation, operation III was dug westward from a line 17.5 m west of the 7-m and 10-m points in the 20-m long east scarp step (fig. 7). The operation was carried out intermittently over fifteen and a half days and was intended partly as a spot check on sparse surface indications there of a possible occupation remnant just below the turf. It was also hoped that the limits of the main occupation concentration definitely appearing nearer the scarp edge might be further defined. The excavation was dug in arbitrary 20-cm levels. First, deposits were removed to a depth of 60 cm throughout the operation. Next, the eastern and more productive half was dug to 1 m, and lastly, the easternmost meter of the operation was taken to a depth of 3.2 m. In the end, the western edge of the stone scatter proved to lie eastward of operation III and within the trench connecting operations I and III (see above).

The deposits uncovered in the course of this operation differed in certain ways from those in operation I. The humic and underlying silt deposits were not sharply differentiated in operation III but graded from one into the other within the 20-30 cm level. Also, it was in operation III that one could for the first time clearly observe that calcareous concretions occurred in the silt at the 35-45 cm level and that they were in evidence everywhere below that level to the bottom of our excavations in the operation and presumably below. As expected, in the uppermost 20-30 cm of deposit, both above and among the scattered field stones, there was the same significant concentration of vestiges of occupation, that is, a stone industry with bone and shell debris. For the most part, these vestiges lay within the humic deposit, the upper part of which was the disturbed plow zone and the base the least disturbed part resting directly upon the silt without an associated rock scatter. The assemblage occurred preponderantly in the eastern part of operation III toward the parts of the main occupation area that were being uncovered nearby in the grids to the east.

There was no distinctive rock scatter to be found in the area exposed by operation III, although a few isolated rocks were located here and there. This region appeared to be beyond the limits of the site's rocky floor. Although the topmost 20 cm of the area did yield over 3,600 pieces of artifactual debris, these pieces must be taken as mainly derived, being within the disturbed and displaced humic and topsoil layers.

Directly below the 0-20 cm level in operation III there was a sharp reduction in the number of finds; the silt was largely sterile save for the usual small items considered to have been displaced downward via rodent runs. These items were most noticeable in the southeast quarter to a depth of 1 m, but traces continued very sparsely to a depth of ca. 2.6 m. Considered in order of descending depth, the four 20-cm levels between 20 cm and 100 cm yielded 238, 146, 366, and 112 artifacts.

Also in this southeast quarter of the operation were isolated zones of occasional fragmentary snail shells, bones, and a few flints (mostly microlithic tools and debris) along with concretions of dark gray earth in the 40-60 cm and 60-80 cm levels and also at depths of 90 cm and 95-100 cm. Associated with this body of material were a fragment of what may possibly have been a small stone macehead or dibble weight at 60-80 cm and two of the familiar angular field stones at 90 cm. All these items in the southeast quarter at these levels may represent a zone of limited disturbance down from the presumed single occupation horizon near the surface. Such a disturbance might be either some natural size-sorted downward displacement of the predominantly smaller material or else a broad natural or artificial depression linked to the occupation horizon. The possibility of a depression is suggested by the dark concretions and the larger pieces, but no traces of any edges of such a formation were detected. One should consider, along with this vaguely attested feature, comparable traces of suspected depressions detected in operation I in the step at 1.4-1.5 m, in the northeastern quarter of grid C at 80-90 cm, and at various points in grid G at 80-100 cm.

For operation III as a whole, outstanding items included a fragment of a centrally pierced, angular, flat white marble plaque or pendant (fig. 11:3) at 0-20 cm and, associated with the rock scatter—here surely much disturbed—a marble bracelet fragment near the top of the 40-60 cm level (fig. 10:14), a number of microlithic tools (backed bladelets, microdrills, and a micro end scraper from 20-80 cm), and a few particles of shiny black material that looked as if it might be bitumen scattered through the 20-100 cm levels.

OPERATION IV

Another 3.0 × 7.5 m excavation, located in east-west alignment with operation III and 7.5 m west of it, became operation IV. It lay roughly midway between operations II and III (fig. 7). The work took place over a period of six and a half days. First, the entire area was excavated in 20-cm levels to a depth of 40 cm, then the eastern 4.25 m was dug downward in 20-cm levels to a depth of 1 m. The humic surface deposit, including the plow zone, was some 15-20 cm thick here and evidently superimposed directly upon the silt formation. The top of the concretion zone within the silt became visible at a depth of 30-40 cm.

Operation IV revealed very light traces of occupation with only rare scattered flint and bone debris. What little evidence there was came mainly from the topmost 20 cm of deposit (the humic layer) and just below and was seen primarily in the eastern half of the trench. This distribution may reflect an outlying occupation zone (perhaps the outermost) with respect to the major zone, which operation I indicated was probably concentrated around the area back of the scarp edge. Much more likely this is derived material. In any event, one should bear in mind that virtually all of what was found in the humic zone was disturbed and shifted to a degree (certainly laterally and probably also vertically).

Once again, below this 20-cm level lay the silt that was virtually sterile except for a few small pieces of flint and other debris. Again such artifactual material was preponderantly in the eastern half of the trench. These pieces included some snail shells in a small patch or zone in the 20-40 cm level and 169 small artifacts scattered through nearly a meter's thickness of deposit. The total amount of artifactual material involved in operation IV was 520 items (none particularly distinctive), fewer than in operation III, which was nearer the denser concentrations of operation I.

Operation V

Positioned near the plateau edge ca. 17 m north of the northern limits of the close-set rocky "pavement" in the extension of operation I, operation V was a 3 × 5 m excavation dug in alignment with the extension, with its long axis set roughly at right angles to the plateau's edge (fig. 7). The operation was dug intermittently over four days to test the occurrence of a considerable amount of flint debris and rock scatter visible in the sod in this sector near the edge of the plateau north of the main concentration. Initially, the digging went down to 20 cm in dark humic deposit. Then, in cleaning up and disengaging the partly disclosed stone scatter, an additional 15 cm of loose soil was removed to an overall depth of 35 cm below the surface here. The irregularly scattered stones at 20-30 cm thus uncovered were larger on the average than most in operation I and in general were scattered more openly rather than closely set in a "pavement." However, an irregular cluster of relatively close-set rocks lay in a roughly east-west axis that was visible out toward the middle of the operation. This grouping of stones was ca. 3.5 m long, some 30-40 cm wide in its western half, and 60 cm wide at the east end. This little rock scatter, being largely below 20 cm in depth, may represent a comparatively undisturbed portion of the occupation horizon.

Associated with this little spread of rocks in operation V and within the same general level were 2,636 flints, some snail shells, and a few ill-preserved bone fragments. Noteworthy finds in the topmost 20-25 cm of presumably disturbed deposit included a marble bracelet fragment, 2 fragmentary shell plaques, a tubular stone bead, 3 chipped and polished celts (1 with black adhesions taken to be possible traces of bitumen), a grooved rubbing stone, a shiny dark stream pebble of iron-heavy chert lodestone bearing a possible rubbing facet, and some small lumps of red and yellow ochre A few more flints were found at the base of excavations within the 30-35 cm level, close to the humus-silt contact zone. Materials from the uppermost 20 cm, largely within the plow zone, may be considered disturbed; those from the lower 15 cm in association with the rock scatter may be taken as largely undisturbed. The close typological and morphological similarity of this assemblage to that of operation I and the disposition and depth of the little scatter of rocks and its propinquity to the core area allow one to assume that these traces of occupation are contemporary with the main concentration found in the earlier operation.

Operation VI

Still another 3 × 5 m exploratory excavation with extensions, the whole labeled operation VI, was dug in four days on a northeast-southwest axis close to the eastern edge of the plateau ca. 27 m north of operation V (fig. 7). It was aimed at investigating the possible relationships to the main occupation of two groups of loose rocks that slumped over the brink of the plateau. Excavations were carried out in three 20-cm levels to a depth of 60 cm. The loosely knit humic plow zone was here a rich brown color and ca. 15 cm thick. The silt lay directly underneath and contained concretions from a depth of 25-30 cm to the base of the excavations.

No rock scatters and very little occupational debris were found save in the portion nearest the plateau edge. Consequently, a 20-cm level was dug eastward to the very rim of the plateau following the edge of the crest both north and south along the slumped rocky remnants visible there. It became clear that these rocky remnants lay in a block of slumped dark soil containing occupational debris and that this was the last vestige here of a more extensive deposit now lost to erosion. A total of 469 flints were found in operation VI. Incidentally, a considerable accumulation of archeologically rich but derived deposits lay on a flat of land down by the wadi bed at the foot of the high northeastern spur of the hill, and a fragmentary narrow pierced shell pendant was found on the surface of the spur's slope. These finds attest to the other end of the inevitable local erosion process.

Finds from operation VI included 2 hand rubbing stones, a grooved rubbing stone, a fragment of a stone rod (fig. 10:23), a marble bracelet fragment, a pebble pestle, a celt (fig. 13:4) and a flaked pebble fragment suggesting a possible rough-out for a chipped celt, a fragment of a barrel-shaped stone bead (fig. 11:10), and a possible bead of *Dentalium* shell—all from a depth of 0-20 cm. A bone bead came from 20-40 cm (fig. 10:5). A small group of snail shells, a single charcoal fragment, and a zone of darkened earth were noted at 40-60 cm within the silt. Once again, it is clear that the occupational debris here, although largely from disturbed superficial levels, is to be linked typologically and therefore culturally to that of the main concentration and that probably this debris represents what was once a separate but characteristic little outlier of the main occupation. However, it was too superficial, disturbed, and vestigial for us to be certain that it appeared in its original state. Furthermore, it is a fact that the cluster is both distant and detached from the major occupation focus and thus it must float in time and space. The artifacts it contained are the strongest evidence for association with the main horizon.

OPERATION VII

In a continuation of the effort to fix the limits and degree of the occupation on the plateau, operation VII became the northernmost of the tests. It was set some 45 m north of operation VI athwart a spur lying well north of the high point of the hill, in a sector where most of the land surface sloped down northward out of sight of most of the other operations (fig. 7).

In two days the 3 × 5 m operation was excavated in a single level to a depth of 20 cm. The excavation cut through the 10-15 cm humic and plow zone layer and into the top of the silt. It produced no significant evidence of occupation. A small zone of slightly darkened earth containing a few field stones lay at the humus-silt contact zone at a depth close to 20 cm in the northeast corner of the excavation, suggesting a possible shallow depression or superficial pit there. No further work was carried out at this locality.

OPERATION VIII

In a withdrawal south from the clearly unrewarding northern end of the hilltop, operation VIII was laid out at a point just over 10 m northeast of operation VI to include a partly visible rock pile there on the northeasterly spur of the plateau (fig. 7). Excavated in three days, the operation was originally 3 × 5 m in size but was extended eastward 2.5 m in an attempt to uncover further suspected rock scatters. It was dug only in a single level down to 20 cm, revealing the rock pile to this depth in the southwest corner and also a neighboring small rock-filled pit and a few surrounding widely scattered rocks. A moderate amount of occupational debris, including 705 artifacts, was also found, but virtually all of this material came from within the topmost 15-cm humic plow zone area. The more outstanding pieces included a grooved schist rubbing stone, a small marble bracelet fragment, a pale creamy greenish potsherd, and, in the eastern extension, several plain sherds. Although this assemblage quite probably included elements derived from another independent but unlocated outlier of the main occupation zone in the form of typologically characteristic artifacts, it was disturbed, derived, and far from intact, and mixed with remains of much later date.

GEOLOGICAL OPERATIONS

A final rapid digging effort during a three-day period at Karim Shahir had purely geological aims. The findings had no direct bearing on the investigation of the occupation site itself but added in a small way to the overall picture of the late Pleistocene-early Holocene geological sequence that was being developed for the district by H.E. Wright, Jr. (1952, 1960). The work at Karim Shahir involved trenching operations deep within the massive archeologically sterile silt that made up the hill on which the archeological site rested.

Starting from the deepest point of excavation in operation I, that is, the trench 3.8 m deep which had been cut down along the eastern edge of grid C, a step trench 1 m wide was rapidly cut in two days across the step of operation I and on down the steep slope (fig. 7). This step trench reached a point 11 m below the surface of the plateau, each step being approximately 1 m high. The trench was aimed at investigating not only the distribution of calcareous concretions in the silt but also the relatively dark greenish and gray deposits that were visible as a band on the slope well down within the silt. Many snail shells and flints were found in the course of digging through the silty deposit, all of which had of course been displaced by the erosion of the occupation horizon on the plateau above.

Natural calcareous concretions were found in situ. One group had not only developed in the primary silt beds themselves (the Jarmo silts) but also was disseminated uninterruptedly deep into those deposits, their great depth being a rough measure of the great age and longstanding existence of the old Jarmo-B surface of those silts. Another and less developed group had accumulated within the superficial humic layer and down through the thin underlying occupation deposit; these concretions had developed much later than the Jarmo-B surface and were found resting upon it. Because of the thinness of the combined humus and occupation deposits, the upper and later group of nodules penetrated the lower and earlier group and overlapped it. In effect, nodules extended within the Jarmo silt to a lower limit that was fixed at ca. 6.86-7.10 m below the surface of the Karim Shahir mound, or ca. 6.35-6.60 m below the level of the "Jarmo-B silt" surface. The approximate lower limit of easily visible concretions (see section, fig. 6, dot-dash line) was but an arbitrary point in a continuum down to this true lower limit. Indeed, the depth of this latter limit was itself determined somewhat arbitrarily, since the concretions graded down in size at these depths from minuscule forms to ones that were barely visible, and actually the little nodules probably extended further toward the base of the silts. They were only fleetingly distinguishable before everything dried out to uniform tones in the sun in the sectioning of successive fresh cuts in the step trench.

The concretions within the Jarmo silts relate to a late Pleistocene land surface, the Jarmo-B surface, and are discussed elsewhere by H.E. Wright, Jr. (1952, pp. 14-24). The later group of concretions is related to, and also occurs within, the archeological deposits at Karim Shahir, and the process producing the concretions in both kinds of deposits is one of the leaching and disintegrative destructive forces affecting archeological deposits and their contents.

As already noted, at Karim Shahir the cultural deposits are so thin that the two sets of concretions are often continuous. Well down within the silt deposit, at a depth of ca. 8.85 m below land surface, lay the top of an olive-green silt band 75 cm thick, which, in turn, rested upon a band of dark gray silt, some 60 cm thick, the top of which was ca. 9.6 m below land surface. This dark gray zone then graded imperceptibly downward through approximately the next 80 cm into the clean buff silt forming the mass of the hill.

The zone of dark gray silt with the overlying band of greenish deposit represents marshy land denoting an interlude of wet conditions in the area during the accumulation of the silt, perhaps a momentary directional swing or halting stage of the wadi. It contained remains of vegetation but has no archeological importance.

Two separate smaller soundings, a step trench 6 m long and a 1 × 1 m pit, were also rapidly cut into the silt well down the steep slope on the spur immediately adjacent to and northeast of operation I (fig. 7). These soundings also were probes made entirely for geological purposes and need not concern us further here.

THE NATURE OF THE LIVING FLOOR

The single occupation layer at Karim Shahir seems to have survived as a relatively concentrated scatter of stones intermingled with great quantities of living debris, spread about in a comparatively thin zone that is strikingly out of natural context atop the high hill formed by deposits of silt. All the stones must have been obtained from at least as far away as the stream beds below the hill and then carried up to the top. Most of the artifacts and debris would have been produced there on the spot.

We have described this concentration of rocks and debris as more thickly strewn toward the east, in the zones nearer the eastern scarp edge, than it was toward its western limits. The effective western edge of this rough arc of stony floor could be seen cutting diagonally across the middle of the trench on a line ca. 13-15 m west of the scarp edge (fig. 7). A similar true border may also exist along the west edge of the southern half of the extension to the north in operation I. The loose scatter of rocks and the limited artifactual material discovered in operation V to the north of this west edge may represent an integral part of the whole rocky floor or else a small isolated outlier, because the rock scatter is similar to the rocky floor and the assemblage found there has a typology and morphology that are identical to that of the assemblage found in operation I. While operation III revealed considerable related artifactual remains and some discoloration, it contained virtually no stone scatter.

In all of operation I, despite a sharp watch, no indications of specific building localities or features were detected either on the surface or at lower and largely undisturbed levels; there were no alignments, no specially built-up or worn pavements, no postholes or other evidence of any structure, permanent or temporary. This is not to say that these were not there at one time but only to suggest that continuous weathering, leaching, and slope wash as well as repeated plowing must have stirred the topsoil and obliterated any orderly trace of such features in situ in the upper centimeters of this shallow occupation deposit. Indeed, there was overall at the very surface a well-defined band of soil 10-15 cm thick that was looser and darker than the underlying soil—a band that was obviously a plow zone. The local villagers confirmed that the area had been plowed in recent years, and one presumes it had been plowed in earlier times as well. Thus, it is possible, indeed probable, that a good part of the stone scatter uncovered (figs. 8-9) is a jumble left by years of agricultural activity. Hence, virtually no significant artifact juxtapositions could be recorded.

At lower levels where presumably intact stretches of stone scatter and associated debris could be observed, repeated scraping failed to show any evidence of structures. There were, however, two sorts of solid evidence for occupation: (1) the close-set rocky floor (figs. 7-9) and (2) the several pits or depressions, large and small, displaying various similar characteristics.

Judging by its compact mosaiclike appearance, the extensive unbroken "pavement" containing close-set rocks near the eastern scarp edge cannot have been much disturbed, if at all, by plowing. It should be remembered when examining the photographs of this rock scatter that the relatively rockless appearance of the area immediately west of the section line and step was due to overzealous rock clearance by our workmen. Certainly at the eastern edge of the excavation some rocks were eliminated from the record in this way. Furthermore, the several neatly empty, oval-to-circular, rockless areas that abutted the close-set pavement areas (one at the northern edge of grid B, another at the northern edge of grid F, and perhaps another one or two in the extension) also surely represent inadvertent removals. The faint suggestion of a straight rockless line running north-south at the southern end of operation I between grids C and G can be explained in the same way. In actuality no such open-space features that could have been made purposefully in prehistoric times were found at the site.

The other evidence for occupation that can be depended upon as having remained in situ is the traces of eleven pits located down to various depths below the rocky occupation layer. These features were recorded in the areas of the step and grids C and G in operation I where the excavations penetrated well below the 40-50 cm level, while others doubtless exist under the unexcavated part of the rocky floor and scatter.

Nine of the pits lay in the area of the step that was cut at the edge of the scarp. Most of these had the same characteristic contents: some whole pebbles or field stones, some rocks cracked and discolored by heat, traces of discolored and partly baked earth, specks of charcoal, occasional very small lenses of ashy gray deposit, and a few stone artifacts, burned bone fragments, and snail shells. In sum, these pits, found down to depths of 1.0-1.6 m, may safely be classified as fire pits, used for camp fires or cooking at what must have been an essentially open-air site (see The Step, p. 32).

This series of pits on the step included two examples that seemed to be different from the others in that each extended over a somewhat larger and flatter area distinguished by vaguely defined patches of discolored earth. Each contained some artifactual litter and a few rocks. One of these features occurred approximately in the center of the step at a depth of 1.4-1.5 m. It lay ca. 1 m east of and out from the section line between the 10- and 12-m marks and may have slumped downward on the slope from its original position. Roughly oval, it measured some 2 m in diameter and was relatively flat rather than obviously basined in shape. It contained dark gray-brown claylike earth, reddened earth with specks of charcoal, some snail and bone debris, and rocks and large pebbles. Since it had no close-packed banded deposits in contrasting colors, it was not thought to represent a habitation floor, although its flatness and its associated artifacts—part of a bone needle or awl, a piece of a mortar or grindstone, and a fragmentary hand rubbing stone—might suggest the opposite interpretation. However, artifacts of the kind found in this pit, as well as fire-discolored earth, charcoal, and rocks, are equally characteristic of fire pits and the general litter at the site. It is also possible that these materials might have accumulated gradually in a broad, open, natural depression in the ground within the confines of the settlement area or might have been dropped or tossed there by the inhabitants during the clearance of some other spot. No evidence for shelter associated with this feature was found.

The other exception to the more obvious fire pits on the step was what appeared to be a wide pit situated near the north end between the 2.75 and 5.90 m marks. This pit was traced with some certainty from a depth of ca. 1.4-1.6 m down to the 1.8 m level. It also was considered to be in a slumped position and no longer in its original place, located as it was so near the silty slope. Its shallowly basined bottom was smeared with red ochre. Several artifacts, the most interesting of which were two small lightly baked clay figurines, were found in close association. These features give ceremonial connotations to this pit.

Traces of two more possible pits were found in the silts at a depth of ca. 80-100 cm in the eastern half of grids C and G. Neither of these features had any clear-cut outlines or contained any rocks; in both cases the evidence was a localized area of faint soil discoloration associated with considerable quantities of burned bone fragments, snail shells, specks of charcoal, and bits of reddened earth, together with little pockets of microlithic flintworking debris and a number of isolated single medium to small artifacts.

Finally, the probable presence of a major pit or pits below the base of the rock scatter at the junction of grids B, C, F, and G in operation I was indicated by a concentration of fire-reddened earth and cracked rocks and a striking quantity of artifacts and bones in that area.

On the whole, then, what remains of the shallow living floor, as revealed in operations I, III, and V, is a deposit, 20-30 cm thick, of close-set or scattered rocks and associated occupational debris, spread over several hundred square meters of a hilltop but concentrated particularly at its eastern edge. It is possible that we located the bounds of the greatest concentration of settlement, embracing an area of some 500-600 m^2, at a few points on the west and the north. We realize that an unknown proportion of the settlement has been lost to erosion on the east. The southern and some of the western bounds are still hidden under turf, unexcavated. Isolated outliers of limited size may also exist, hinted at by the remains found in operations II, V, VI, and VIII. Any superficial traces of structures or other installations, if they existed at all, have in all likelihood been obliterated by later plowing and slope wash; no such traces were found at intact levels below the turf. It is also likely that any deeper-lying evidence for structural installations was erased by the leaching and disintegration processes which created the widespread occurrence of calcareous concretions at the site. The only sure focal points of settlement found in situ were the scattered rock clusters, fire pits, and other depressions found at various depths below the living floor. There was no evidence of lower or earlier occupation; the artifactual assemblage appears to be a single typological and morphological unit without signs of internal change or significant outside contamination.

DESCRIPTION AND ANALYSIS OF THE ASSEMBLAGE

An inventory of finds, according to type and by area and level, is given for each operation. The inventory for operation I represents over 90% of the prehistoric materials from Karim Shahir and provides the basis for the characterization of the assemblage at this site. The yield from the outlying operations II-VIII, while reflecting essentially the same inventory, comprises very minor and subordinate samplings which add nothing to the main picture except the fact that this sort of settlement and its litter apparently left traces that were scattered outward in isolated clusters for a good many meters in all directions from the prime settlement locality, partly revealed in operation I.

The tabulations summarizing the quantities of these artifacts show clearly the uniformity of the assemblage for the site as a whole from start to finish. They also point up the fact that the main concentrations of finds occurred in the uppermost half meter of deposits, not only in the superficial layers displaced by slope wash and plowing but also in the largely undisturbed main occupation layer which was traced in operations I and V from the surface on the north to depths of 25-40/50 cm below the surface elsewhere. The tabulations give finds by 10- or 20-cm levels in most instances, but for the deeper and least productive levels in grids C and G of operation I and in operations III, IV, and VI such levels have sometimes been combined.

Intrusive Materials

Most of the few intrusive items at Karim Shahir came from the surface or no deeper than 20 cm and are in any case so disparate and rare as to be of no significance in the general assessment of the industrial assemblage there.

The undoubtedly recent pieces, which came only from the surface and from operations I, II, and VIII, were 2 bits of rusted iron (one a small fragmentary horseshoe), 4 fragments of weathered glass, and 4 blue-glazed wheel-made potsherds. The remaining pieces of pottery, which came from operations I and VIII, and which may be either modern or from a wide range of time extending back from recent to prehistoric times, were 2 tiny sherds of dull pink-buff handmade plain ware (the exterior color is similar to that of wares from the upper third of Jarmo, but the gritty, poorly baked, laminated paste of these sherds is unlike anything from that site), 5 creamy greenish wheel-made sherds, 4 sherds of reddish buff wheel-made wares with rim or base profile detail, and a handle.

There were two categories of artifacts that might reasonably be expected to belong within the horizon—obsidian and pieces of flint with edge sheen. However, the obsidian was so rare and so lacking in distinguishing characteristics that the 5 small fragments found singly at various depths and at widely scattered points may safely be classed as intrusive (see tabulation). On the other hand, the 24 pieces of flint with traces of sheen on their edges were classed with the artifacts from the main occupation horizon (pp. 67-69). Like the obsidian, these sheen-bearing pieces (18 blades and 6 flakes) were found at widely separated points, but they all came from within the broad band of concentrated materials that paralleled the eastern scarp in operations I and V. Fully half came from the surface or within the topmost level, but the rest were from deeper levels down to and including 40-50 cm. Although their comparative rarity and partly surface distribution argue against their having been an integral feature of the flint industry at this occupation site, the deeper distribution of many of these pieces and their association in these deposits with numerous fragments of grinding and pounding tools (all definitely considered part of the assemblage from the occupation horizon) lend considerable weight to arguments that they were an element in the tool kit and were used for the manipulation of plants.

A striking aspect of the total assemblage at Karim Shahir is the apparently virtually uncontaminated state of the archeological deposit, both on its surface and within its mass; later prehistoric admixtures were essentially absent and any sort of historic or modern artifacts or debris were extremely rare on this hilltop.

Obsidian

Depth (cm)	Operation and area	Description
Surface		Bladelet; both ends snapped off; wear shown as irregular nicks along both long edges
0-20	II	End scraper; well retouched on broken short blade end; wear across truncated end and along the two long sides; fresh, clear, translucent
20-30	I,B	Chip; tiny; clear with frosted surface
20-30	I,C	Flake; elongated, thick; some edge wear; opaque with frosted surface
90-100	I,C	Chip; tiny; from used microlithic blade; translucent with frosted surface

Materials Belonging to the Horizon

The enormous quantity of material that came from operation I provided a fully adequate basis for arriving at the details of the composition of the industry at this site. The material found in the 0-20 cm, 20-30 cm, 30-40 cm, and 40-50 cm levels of operation I formed the largest part of the sampling. The description and discussion of each category of artifact is based on the evidence found in these upper levels of operation I.

It has already been noted that levels below ca. 50 cm in operation I were not, except for the deposits in the pits, significantly productive, being below the level of the single occupation layer. Also, these lower levels furnished only an incomplete and misleading segment of the total inventory, including as they predominantly did only the smaller and microlithic sizes of some of the artifact categories and broken bits of debris which had worked their way downward from the occupation layer. Nevertheless, all this lower-level material under the living floor has been accounted for within the various categories below since it represents an integral part of the assemblage from this horizon. The only block of artifactual material not incorporated is the representative cross section that was selected and left behind in Baghdad at the end of the field season; that material has been recorded in a separate section (p. 98) in this report.

Lightly Baked Clay

Only 5 specimens of presumably lightly baked clay were found at Karim Shahir: a fragmentary rod, 2 small figurines that were virtually identical, and 2 hard discolored lumps of clay—one with possible plant or wood impressions.

Clay Rod

From the surface came a single clay rod fragment measuring 32 mm in length, with end diameters of 11 mm and 9 mm across the oval cross section (fig. 10:2). The hard, crackled surface, tan and gray color, and hard interior consistency all suggest that this piece may have been affected by heat or even fire baked. Whether it was subjected to heat accidentally or deliberately is arguable, but the shaping and the smoothing of the piece were deliberate. There is a faint trace of a flap of clay folded over at the tip end and pressed down to the surface of the rod. Although it lacks a base, its particular fabric, baked-looking surface, overall form, and the pressed flap feature suggest that it may be broadly comparable to the "stalk objects" found at Jarmo (pp. 386-87). Its surface position at Karim Shahir lessens its usefulness as a comparison.

Clay Figurines

Both of the lightly baked figurines of pinky gray clay were found in the slumping, disturbed step cut along the scarp edge. One (*K-5*) came from near the 6-m mark on the section line at a depth of 1 m just south of the southern periphery of the presumed upper levels of the red-ochre pit (opn. I,step, 0.8-1.2 m depth). The other (*K-30*) came from the bottom of this pit where, at a depth of 1.75-1.80 m, with some rocks, it rested on or very close to the film of red ochre that covered the bottom of the pit (opn. I,step, 1.8 m). Its carefully central position and the red ochre, to say nothing of the figurine itself, suggest a ceremonial use.

These two objects are very similar. Judging by the one intact specimen, they are apparently long-snouted, pointed-headed, armless creatures that stand well on flat or slightly concave bottoms steadied at either side by two rudimentary outspread lower limbs or "feet." They have cylindrical bodies and are roughly round in section. Each piece was apparently formed merely by pinching the soft, damp clay. No decoration or further art was applied to clarify any features.

The figurine found just outside the pit is nearly complete and measures 20 mm in height and 9-10 mm in diameter at its base. The tips of both its chin (snout?) and peaked head are missing. Its base is flat or very slightly concave with short, rounded projections or feet. The head is beveled or broken off behind, with a chin that sits high. This head may have been formed by folding over the platform top of the cylinder; possibly ears were intended as well.

The figurine found at the bottom of the red-ochre pit measures 18 mm in height and 8 mm in maximum diameter at its base (fig. 10:1a-b). It is complete save for a very limited loss of its surface under the right cheek. It is flat based and its feet are smaller than those on the other example. The head, which is shaped to a point in the rear, is larger in proportion to the body than in the other specimen. It is thought that perhaps the head was made separately and then smoothed on, as in the many specimens at Jarmo that seem to have been made on an assembly-line basis—for example, the "stalk objects" with tops that were pinched and twisted.

Despite the fact that these two Karim Shahir specimens are, according to Broman Morales (pers. comm.), distinctly different from any single piece found at Jarmo, it is curious that the closest comparisons in the material at Jarmo come from the later upper rather than the earlier lower levels. There is nothing in the limited exposure of the lower levels of Jarmo to suggest that the Karim Shahir forms were ancestral or related to them in any way. Nevertheless, the higher-level pieces at Jarmo are somewhat similar to the Karim Shahir forms; each has the pointed snout, and two are of the same general size with pointed head and flat base. These Jarmo specimens belong to the Jarmo figurine groups that were described as "double-wing-based objects" and "stalk objects." The two Karim Shahir specimens may be related typologically to the latter category. (For further comparison see pp. 385-87 and n. 9, p. 393).

Hardened Clay with Impressions

In operation I along the eastern scarp edge, in the very first few spadefuls of earth removed in the northern portion of the step (dug at 0-40 cm into loose and probably disturbed deposits), were two hard lumps of ruddy orange-buff clay with grayish patches. The larger, longer one (now lost) measured 55 × 38 × 27 mm and bore a groove that was rectilinear, broad, shallow, and gently rounded. This groove was 25-30 mm wide and 2-3 mm deep, and some faint striations were noticeable on its surface, as if the clay had originally been packed around a stick or other object with a linear surface structure and a curved surface or rounded angle. This lump also showed traces of plant impressions. The smaller lump, measuring 30 × 28 × 18 mm, is made of more sandy material and has no shaping or obvious impressions.

According to Matson (pers. comm.), these lumps were not made of clay like that found at Jarmo (situated only ca. 2 km from Karim Shahir on the same little stream). This observation would perhaps imply not only that two different time spans were involved but also that the material might not have come from near Jarmo or even the immediate Karim Shahir area. One might also logically suppose that an independent clay source could be accessible to the inhabitants of Karim Shahir. At all events, Matson considered that the clay did not appear to have been prepared in any way, that is, selected specially or sieved.

The above observations are noteworthy since these two lumps are the closest thing to evidence for the use of wattle and daub that was found at Karim Shahir. They are also the only artificially treated clay objects other than the two lightly baked clay figurines, the clay rod, and the obviously recent sherds. The objects in all these categories have been affected by heat, although in the case of the clay lumps this is only suggested by their hardness and coloring and there is no way of knowing whether they were placed near heat intentionally. No further information could be derived from the plant impressions visible on the surface of the larger piece.

BONE

There is every likelihood that much of the artificially shaped bone material at Karim Shahir has long since rotted away, judging by the small number of pieces found and by the generally weathered condition of the animal bone material. Certainly the bone artifacts are rare. Most are tools. A few are ornaments, namely beads.

Bone Tools

This category includes fragments of well-polished pins, bone splinters or fragments of whole bones with simple points worked to flat or beveled edges, and a simple tube made of a segment of bird long bone. Save for one piece found at the surface, all 9 fragments of bone artifacts were found well down in the deposits.

Bone Tools

Depth (cm)	Operation and area	Description
Surface		Shaped splinter; two probably naturally flat faces curved artificially into points (now broken) toward ends; sun bleached; incised striations especially at wider, base? end and on narrow sides there faintly worn zone of slight constriction across body near center, showing on upper face and sides but not on lower side (inner cancellous tissue of original bone); L. 24 mm, MAX. W. 5 mm; perhaps suggests crude toggle in detail and form; (fig. 10:8)
20-30	I,F	Awllike fragment (K-23); shaped to a conical point with tip broken off; well preserved, polished; circular section; L. 30 mm, MAX. W. 8 mm
20-30	I,G	Awllike splinter; short, stubby segment of pointed end; much defaced by weathering, but still retaining slight areas of polish and worked to neat point; comma-shaped cross section; L. 15 mm, MAX. W. 4-5 mm
20-30	I,F	Splinter fragment; broad, long, curved; striated and polished on outer face with slight bevel or smoothing, leaving diagonal striations that were cut on one edge of outer face; opposite edge bears splintering flakelike scars; MAX. L. 22 mm, MAX. W. 13 mm; although shaped and worked, piece too incomplete to reveal purpose; marks possibly made by gnawing of animals; (fig. 10:9)
30-40	I,C	Awllike or puncheonlike splinter fragment; worked into tapered point; concavo-convex cross section at broad broken-off end; traces of polishing especially at tip, but much defaced by weathering; MAX. L. 34 mm, W. 10 mm at broken base; (fig. 10:4)
30-40	I,C	Fragment of pin or point; mid-trunk parallel-sided segment; roughly circular in section; much defaced by weathering, but traces of polishing discernible on trunk; L. 21 mm, W. 4 mm in cross section
20-40	VI	Segment of small long bone (bird?); tapered, hollow; very defaced by weathering, but retaining traces of polish along shaft; MAX. L. 21 mm, DIA. 4-5 mm; possibly broken midsection of pointed tool or bead (but lacking obvious beveling at ends, which is characteristic of beads)
120-160	I,step	Segment of pin or point; parallel sided, truncated; dark brown, highly polished, probably burned; nearly circular in cross section; L. 10 mm, DIA. 4.5 mm; perhaps part of longer, pointed specimen of similar texture and color found in depression in same level (may be related to specimen described immediately below)
120-160	I,step	Broken pin (K-6); dark brown, highly polished, probably burned; broken at base end, pointed end intact; nearly circular in cross section; diameter greatest at broken end; L. 45 mm, MAX. DIA. 3 mm; most skillfully fashioned bone artifact found at Karim Shahir; associated with depression at 10-12 m marks (see fragment described immediately above); (fig. 10:3)

Bone Beads

The 5 bone beads are the slightly shaped segments of bird long bones, bearing one or more signs of preparation—beveling, incised striations, or sectioning—at their extremities (fig. 10:5-7). They were found at widely scattered spots and various depths. One of them came from one of the pits associated with the main occupation horizon. Another specimen came from quite low depths, well below the principal levels of occupation debris, and perhaps because of its small size found its way down there via animal burrows or by water and temperature action.

Bone Beads

Depth (cm)	Operation and area	Description
0-40	I,step	Complete bead (*K-16*); section of bird long bone with planoconvex cross section; striated and polished at ends, probably by cutting and truncation process; L. 28 mm, DIA. 6-8 mm
20-40	VI	Nearly complete bead; section of bird long bone; striated and polished, simple beveling at one end, partly destroyed beveling at other; small zone of slight narrowing or constriction from work or wear on surface near intact end; L. 21 mm, DIA. 4-5 mm; (fig. 10:5)
30-40	I,G	Incomplete bead; section of slender long bone (bird?), nearly circular in cross section; striated, polished along shaft; crudely beveled at one end probably by cutting and truncation process, broken at other end; entire surface much defaced by weathering; L. 32 mm, DIA. 8 mm; (fig. 10:7)
60-100	I,step	Complete bead (*K-7*); section of bird long bone, flattened tubular cross section; polished, striated along shaft; crudely beveled at both ends probably by truncation process; L. 25 mm, DIA. 3-7 mm
120-160	I,step, ochre pit	Complete bead (*K-8*); section of slender long bone (bird?), slightly flattened tubular cross section; striated, polished, and crudely beveled at ends probably by cutting and truncation process; L. 27 mm, DIA. 4-6 mm; (fig. 10:6)

SHELL

Shell Plaques

A total of 10 small, mostly fragmentary plaques worked out of shell were found. The material appears to come from sturdy specimens of freshwater clam shells (*Unio tigridis*) or from the sturdier parts of such specimens. Judging by the more complete examples, these plaques are either rectangular or square, do not exceed ca. 25 mm in maximum dimension, and may be centrally pierced either by a single hole or by two symmetrically aligned holes (fig. 10:10-11). These pieces are presumed to be objects of adornment for clothing or body or possibly equipment. They all came from a broad band of the occupation zone along the scarp edge in operations I and V and are considered contemporary with the single occupation horizon.

Shell Plaques

Depth (cm)	Operation and area	Description
0-20	I,step	Fragment (*K-1*); trace of single hole
0-20	I,A	2 fragments
0-20	V	Fragment
20-35	V	Fragment
20-40	I,step	Fragment (*K-4*); pierced in center; MAX. DIA. 25 mm; (fig. 10:11)
20-40	I,A	2 fragments: 1 nearly complete, small, square; 1 (*K-26*) pierced by single central hole and measuring L. 10 mm
20-40	I,B	Complete (*K-14*); pierced by two holes along center axis placed almost symmetrically near two opposing edges; 16 × 16 mm
20-40	I,C	Nearly complete (*K-13*); rectangular; pierced by two holes symmetrically placed along center axis near two opposing edges; 16 × 17 mm; (fig. 10:10)

Shell Beads

Of the 3 shell items that are presumed to be beads, 2 examples are simple (evidently virtually unworked) forms of *Dentalium* or some similar naturally tubular shell that lends itself to being used as a bead, and the third was a tiny, sturdy gastropod shell deliberately prepared by beveling and piercing on one face of the spiral form to permit stringing by means of this and the natural orifice. Two of these specimens lay at low depths, well below the main occupation levels, and probably came to be there because of water and temperature action or by way of animal burrows.

Shell Beads

Depth (cm)	Operation and area	Description
0-20	VI	Possible bead (*K-50*); segment of *Dentalium*; no evident traces of work except for opening at both ends; durable, white, relatively heavy; L. 21 mm, MAX. DIA. 5 mm; presence suggests possible cultural access to ocean shores, but specimen much more likely to be fossil from ancient marine formations in Zagros area
110-120	I,G	Nearly complete possible bead (*K-47*); small, squat, sturdy spiral gastropod, mottled dark gray; highly polished, perforated at one point on side, also beveled or planed off there; other aperture for stringing provided by natural orifice; MAX. L. 7 mm, MAX. DIA. 5 mm
120-140	I,C	Possible bead (*K-48*); segment of *Dentalium*; very sturdy, thick, relatively heavy, much polished down, leaving no original surface (unclear whether artificial or natural wear), open at both ends; L. 12 mm, MAX. DIA. 3 mm; probably fossil (see remarks for *K-50* above)

GROUND AND PECKED STONE

Ground Stone Bracelets and Rings

A total of 25 stone fragments fashioned into what for lack of more certain terms have been called bracelets or (in the case of smaller ones) rings were found at Karim Shahir. The largest and perhaps the medium-sized examples might reasonably be considered bracelets, but it would require some effort to fit them over most hands. The smallest are too small to be bracelets and might be rings, beads, some other ornament, or possibly children's effects. The rather unsymmetrical inner diameter (projected on fragments that are large enough to be measured) ranges from 73 mm to as small as 8 mm, with a number of examples clustering around 40-45 mm. All pieces are made of white marble or crystalline limestone, occasionally streaked or mottled with gray. Faint striations that are shallow but clearly discernible follow the curve of each piece, and there are also a few localized traces of short lines running across these striations. These characteristics may reflect some aspect of the manufacturing process, and one wonders if the grooved rubbing stones were used in this connection (p. 51). Nearly all pieces in the bracelet-ring category have a monotonously similar and unvarying oval cross section with, in about half of the cases, either a sharp or a subrounded carination at the exterior extreme. All are so made that the widest dimension of the cross section is horizontal and would have stood out at right angles to the outside part of the wrist or finger (fig. 10:13-21). Maximum thickness of the cross section ranges from 16 mm down to ca. 3 mm on the tiniest ringlike or beadlike specimen (fig. 10:12).

The general uniformity of cross section and, with one exception, the lack of decoration in this bracelet-ring category at Karim Shahir are in contrast to the greater variety in design and decoration of marble bracelets at Jarmo. The single exception is a fragment of what may be a small bracelet or large ring (*K-22*; opn. I,F, 20-30 cm). This piece is marked at one point by a series of very faintly incised lines in crude herringbone pattern between two parallel lines that cross the width on one face. There is another crude incised pattern—this one a single trapezoid—on the other face (fig. 10:21).

The rule of a horizontal oval cross section in bracelet fragments at Karim Shahir had been so overwhelmingly demonstrated that when, toward the end of the digging, one of the men produced a sizeable piece that was nearly circular in cross section (fig. 10:22), ostensibly from a depth of 90-100 cm in grid C well below the main concentration of the horizon, he was suspected of bringing it in from outside in the hopes of a bonus. Furthermore, the cross section of this fragment measured 8 × 9 mm, and its longest dimension was vertical—another seeming point of difference from the majority series at this site. Our suspicions were soon all but confirmed when another workman, in the course of the reconnaissance activity that we encouraged, brought in a collection from the nearby newly discovered site of Kani Sur. Among the pieces he submitted (later added to by further collections from the same site that showed its surface material to have much in common with specimens from numerous categories at Jarmo) were more bracelet fragments with a similar circular or nearly circular cross section.

Each site in the area appeared to have its own special undeviatingly uniform stone bracelet product. The shape of the cross section of these bracelets is suspected of being an idiosyncratic trait and is taken here as an example of a minor variation in manufacture by locality or through time. Such a trait is possibly to be expected in a material culture of any period, but it may perhaps be of particular diagnostic value for this early time within the limited region under consideration here. Within such a restricted zone this kind of special trait may help to characterize individual assemblages from specific sites and it may also be a reflection of each settlement's still rather separate and isolated cultural existence. In order to make this point, this untypical piece is illustrated here (fig. 10:22), despite its probable association with the separate and distinctive assemblage of nearby Kani Sur, not with Karim Shahir.

Ground Stone Bracelets and Rings

Depth (cm)	Operation and area	Cross section (mm)	Exterior carination	Remarks
Surface		9.0 × 5.0	X	
0-20	I,step	14.0 × 7.0	X	Bracelet (K-18)
0-40	I,step	9.0 × 4.0	--	
0-20	I,A	5.0 × 3.0	--	
0-20	I,C	6.5 × 4.5	--	
0-20	I,ext.	16.0 × 8.0	X	
0-20	I,ext.	7.0 × 4.0	--	
0-20	I,ext.	5.0 × 3.0	--	
0-20	I,ext.	12.0 × 5.0	X	Bracelet (K-39)
0-20	I,ext.	4.0 × 3.0	--	Ring (K-51)
0-20	I,F	13.0 × 7.0	X	Bracelet (K-15)
0-20	V	9.0 × 5.0	--	
0-20	VI	6.0 × 3.5	--	
0-20	VIII			
20-30	I,B	5.0 × 3.0	X	Ring (K-12)
20-30	I,F	10.0 × 5.0	X	Decorated bracelet (K-22)
20-30	I,A,B,F,ext.			
20-30	I,A,B,F,ext.			
20-40	I,G	12.0 × 6.0	--	
20-40	I,G	10.0 × 5.0	X	
20-40	I,G	8.0 × 4.0	--	Ring? (K-21)
20-40	I,G	3.0 × 1.5	X	Tiny ring (K-42)
40-60	III	8.0 × 5.0	X	Ring? (K-29)
40-80	I,step	9.0 × 4.0	X	Bracelet (K-3)
90-100	I,C	8.0 × 9.0	--	Suspect piece, bracelet

NOTE: All fragments.

Ground Stone Plaques and Pendants

Of 10 thin, flat, polished stone pieces, only 3 plaquelike fragments bear no trace of a pierced hole. Each of the remaining 7 fragments of similar kind have a hole (presumably for suspension) or a remnant portion of one. However, the 3 fragments that are unpierced but otherwise very similar to the others in appearance may well have been parts of pierced pieces. Those that are presumed to be pendants have a hole near an end or edge. When the hole is near the center, the piece is seen as a plaque or ornament designed to be attached to materials such as skins, textiles, or basketry. Most are of white marble or crystalline limestone, but 1 narrow, elongated piece is of slatelike hornfels and another is of chert, while 1 irregularly discoid piece is of fragile laminated limestone. None is very large. All are undecorated except for one fragment that bears three incised straight radiating lines on one face (fig. 11:9). Aside from the type represented by 2 elongated, narrow, teardrop-shaped pendants (fig. 11:1), the usual forms implied by the fragments are triangular, trapezoidal, lozenge-shaped, oval, or circular—all presumably centrally pierced (fig. 11:2-8). All but the laminated limestone piece (fig. 11:6) display careful workmanship, resulting in a smooth, even-surfaced face with faint incised striations and edges with small rubbing facets presumably formed by the shaping process. In nearly all cases the holes are the result of biconical borings made from each face.

Ground Stone Plaques and Pendants

Depth (cm)	Operation and area	Description
Surface	I,G	Plaque; probably originally discoid shaped; fragile laminated limestone; olive buff; pierced by biconical boring near presumed center of original piece, with possible trace of second hole on now-broken edge; smooth faces and edges, natural (waterworn?) but possibly worked in places; notching on other edge apparently from natural wear; MAX. DIA. 38 mm, TH. 3-4 mm; (fig. 11:6)
0-20	I,ext.	Plaque or pendant?; probably originally lozenge shaped; white marble; no trace of piercing; symmetrical, flattened, biconvex cross section; one face polished, other face dull; short, faint incised striations visible at right angles to and along one edge of polished face; small bevel with slight flaking along one edge of opposite face; no other signs of preparation or wear; symmetrical, uniformly smooth, and probably pierced for suspension or attachment when whole; MAX. TH. 5 mm; (fig. 11:4)

Ground Stone Plaques and Pendants—*Continued*

Depth (cm)	Operation and area	Description
0-20	I,G	Plaque (*K-28*); probably originally discoid shaped; crystalline limestone; buff; no trace of piercing; dark gray coating or patina covering one face, pitting on other face and rim; may be part of large, probably pierced, ornament, no thinner at rim than toward center; intact curved rim, with nearly perpendicular edge; (fig. 11:7)
0-20	III	Plaque or pendant?; probably originally angular, perhaps triangular; white marble; pierced by biconical boring near presumed center of original piece; (fig. 11:3)
0-40	I,step	Incised plaque (*K-2*); probably originally discoid; cream-colored marble; widely spaced, radiating, straight incised lines that maybe converged on some centrally placed point of original piece, here diverging toward thinner periphery and truncated by broken edges; where preserved, original edge zone smoothly worked and rounded; flat triangular cross section (fig. 11:9)
20-30	I,A	Plaque (*K-27*); probably originally angular, perhaps lozenge shaped; marble; pierced by twin holes near presumed center of original piece in symmetrical position; TH. 3 mm at center, slightly thinner at rounded edges; both faces smooth and well worked; (fig. 11:5)
30-40	I,G	Pendant (*K-35*); probably originally large and oval, elliptical, or possibly angular; white marble; flattened biconvex cross section; edges thin and rounded, but center mounded up so that TH. 11 mm, MAX. W. 39 mm, L. 50 mm; perforated near narrow end in central position; opposite end broken off; (fig. 11:2)
30-40	I,G	Pendant (*K-40*); probably originally shaped like long, narrow oval or teardrop, may be close to natural outline of stream pebble from which apparently fashioned; dark stone (probably "spotted slate" hornfels); pierced cylindrically at one end; smooth and sharply cut, with faint, roughly parallel incised striations running diagonally along one edge of long dimension, a few similar transverse ones across center of body near perforation, others paralleling long axis; beveled at pierced end; broken at end opposite perforation and split or spalled off on reverse, so that prepared face no longer there; oval in cross section; L. 37 mm, MAX. W. 12.5 mm; (fig. 11:1)
30-40	I,G	Pendant (*K-41*); probably originally shaped like long, narrow teardrop, may be close to original pebble in form; greenish streaked stone, probably chert; pierced at one end; faint incised striations and perhaps split on reverse face (since that face shows natural rough, flat cleavage plane); thin planoconvex cross section; L. 41 mm, W. 15 mm
60-80	I,G	Plaque (*K-46*); probably originally discoid; white marble; pierced by centrally located biconical boring, whose two segments lie on either side of an interior convexly bored zone; both flat faces moderately polished, showing numerous fine incised striations; edges shaped, perpendicular, and somewhat rounded with traces of beveling and rubbing; TH. 4 mm at center, but thinner at periphery; (fig. 11:8)

NOTE: All fragments.

Ground Stone Beads

Like the beads made of bone and of shell, the 9 stone beads were found in a wide variety of areas and depths. Each major type of stone bead is represented by one or more specimens found at depths of 20-30 cm and 30-40 cm, or below, thus well beneath the surface and definitely in the occupation horizon. A number of other stone beads, although from a depth of 0-20 cm and perfectly in keeping with horizon material, must also be considered as possibly surface material, since the surface was included in the excavation lots. Nevertheless, these are the simplest beads, while the two more elaborate forms—(1) the grooved and plain barrel-shaped beads (fig. 11:12) and (2) the biconical planoconvex beads with angled double end perforations (fig. 11:13)—were all well within the horizon levels and presumably uncompromised by surface disturbances or admixtures.

The stone beads are variously of marble, limestone, and serpentine. They are cylindrical, barrel shaped (fig. 11:10), discoid (fig. 11:11), or have a special long, biconical, planoconvex form with angled double end perforations (fig. 11:13). All are undecorated with the single exception of one barrel-shaped dark stone specimen that has a groove encircling its middle portion (fig. 11:12).

Ground Stone Rod

The single specimen in the stone rod category (fig. 10:23) was found in operation VI at a depth of 20-35 cm. It is a middle portion of a rodlike piece of tan sandstone composed of gritty medium-sized quartz grains or bits. This piece measures 12 mm in maximum length and 10 mm in diameter. It is oval to nearly circular in cross section and is

Ground Stone Beads

Depth (cm)	Operation and area	Description
0-20	I,B	Rough-out (*K-20*); white marble; discoid, with poorly centered perforation begun on one face; TH. 6-7 mm, DIA. 14-15 mm, BORE DPTH. 2-3 mm; (fig. 11:14)
0-20	VI	Fragment (*K-49*); longitudinal half of stubby tubular bead; white marble; gently barrel shaped; no decoration or outstanding characteristics save incised striations presumably from shaping process; L. 8 mm, CTR. DIA. 8.5 mm, END DIA. 8 mm; (fig. 11:10)
0-20	I,ext.	Complete bead (*K-52*); dark green to black stone, probably serpentine; stubby discoid shape; truncated flat ends, parallel sides both inside bore and on outside surface; L. 4 mm, W. 6 mm, BORE W. 3 mm; (fig. 11:11)
0-20	I,ext.	Complete bead (*K-33*); white limestone with reddish tinge due to concretionary adhesions; asymmetric, probably unfinished; cylindrical with parallel adjoining beveled facets running longitudinally along entire piece; unevenly truncated so that end faces not parallel; MAX. L. 5 mm, DIA. 6 mm
0-20	V	Nearly complete bead (*K-45*); white limestone; cylindrical, with relatively large straight bore, thin walled; two flat facets running length of cylinder; L. 9 mm, DIA. 7 mm
20-40	I,C	Complete bead (*K-11*); white marble; elongated, biconical, planoconvex; perforated not by single longitudinal bore on long axis but by twin holes at ends (i.e., a hole at each end of the piece and at each end of its plane face, the two end pairs joining to form an angled or curved diagonal perforation at each end of the piece); L. 28 mm, CTR. DIA. 9 mm, END DIA. 5-6 mm; flat face and twin end perforations suggest it was actually more likely a button or other applied ornament than a bead; (fig. 11:13)
30-40	I,G	Complete bead (*K-43*); white marble; elongated, biconical, planoconvex; twin end perforations (see remarks for *K-11* above); L. 23 mm, CTR. DIA. 8 mm, END DIA. 5-6 mm
30-40	I,G	Complete bead (*K-36*); green to black polished stone, probably serpentine and chlorite; tubular, gently barrel shaped; groove (nearly 2 mm deep), clean-cut but slightly askew and irregular around middle; slight bevel on inner face suggesting biconical boring; L. 17 mm, CTR. DIA. 12 mm, END DIA. 8-9 mm; (fig. 11:12)
30-40	I,C	Fragment (longitudinal half) of bead (*K-38*); dark stone, probably serpentine; tubular, barrel shaped, thick walled; straight bore; L. 16 mm, MAX. DIA. 15 mm

smooth and straight in outline. It appears to have been shaped artificially. With no further evidence on the piece itself and no comparable pieces in the ornament or clay rod categories, it cannot be further classified.

Grooved Rubbing Stones

Pebbles of schist or chlorite schist, a low-grade regional metamorphic rock, which has a distinctive greenish to gray fibrous and foliated appearance in these specimens, were evidently deliberately selected as material for some rubbing or friction operation or operations that needed or resulted in the formation of grooves. These grooves are straight, varied in width and depth, and usually curved symmetrically in cross section, although a few have a straight-sided V-shaped form. As suggested by R.L. and R.S. Solecki, the stones may have been used for shaft straightening; indeed, carefully backed and angle-ended microlithic bladelets were found at the site (1970, fig. 14:3-10), and these were perhaps involved in composite types of projectiles involving a shaft. Another possibility is that they may have been used in the polishing or grinding of beads, rings, bracelets, pendants, plaques, or other artifacts of stone, bone, shell, or wood, since some of these items were found at the site and some of their sizes and profiles tend to match those of the grooves.

Most of the 19 pieces recorded are fragmentary and to some degree artificially shaped. A sufficient number retain enough of the original form, both of the pebble itself and of the groove, to suggest what the shapes, special features, and dimensions of complete examples might have been. In most cases the stones tend to be an attenuated oval or pointed oval form, to have a mainly artificially shaped planoconvex cross section, and to have the groove or grooves on the convex face. One specimen bears a groove on both faces. One has a blunt-ended oval form and another is rounded to subrectangular. A fourth differs from the norm in having a biconvex cross section. The maximum length of the larger examples appears to have been ca. 70-80 mm (although one reached 87 mm), while that of the smaller ones was 55-60 mm. The shorter (cross) dimension in all cases varies proportionately around 40 mm. All these pebbles are easily held in the palm of the hand.

The ovoid form of this tool is perhaps the result of the natural fracturing properties of the schist but was further accentuated through appropriate shaping and smoothing, especially at the ends and along the sides of the long dimension. Shaping was evidently done by rubbing or polishing to form a smoothly curved or, in some cases, a faintly faceted or beveled surface for the convex groove-bearing face.

The grooves always run across the grain of the stone, lying across the shorter diameter of the oval and usually centered, judging by fragments that are large enough to reveal where they were located on the original piece. In the great majority of cases the grooves are broad, from 7 to 12 mm in width and averaging ca. 10 mm, but in 6 specimens the grooves are narrow, usually incipient V-shaped incisions, some of which are in conjunction with broad grooves. Thus, in this respect the group of grooved rubbing stones found at Karim Shahir is overwhelmingly like the commonest type (Type 1, Plain Transverse Grooved) at the not too distant site of Zawi Chemi Shanidar where much greater typological variety was reported. The 6 Karim Shahir examples with narrow V-shaped incisions resemble Type 5 (Narrow Transverse Grooved) at the other site (Solecki and Solecki 1970, p. 832).

Most grooves on the Karim Shahir pieces range in depth from 3 mm to 7-8 mm, are symmetrically curved in cross section, and usually are distinctly broader than they are deep. (In speculating about function, it is interesting to note that the breadths or thicknesses of all ornaments of *polished* stone documented from the site fall within these limits.) One rubbing stone specimen has a groove with a wide V-shaped cross section, the two flat sides ending in a deeply and sharply cut incision at the trough base (fig. 12:2). Another has a second sharp V-shaped groove cut into the curved trough line of the main groove. The other examples of V-shaped grooves are less distinct and shallower, with troughs that are less completely established, and perhaps are examples of incipient, less used, or uncompleted pieces.

All the trough surfaces are smooth, and the substance of the stone here has a compacted, rubbed—even polished—appearance. More detailed observations regarding this compacted state and especially the evidence for associated heat effects detected in the walls of such grooves have been reported in comparable artifacts found at Zawi Chemi Shanidar (Drew in Solecki and Solecki 1970, pp. 839-40). In those artifacts the compacted, heat-affected condition of the stone within the grooves is attributed theoretically to the heating for, and perhaps friction from, a shaft-straightening process.

A number of the stones bear, scattered on their convex surface, finely incised striations and more deeply incised lines of varying lengths, in addition to the main groove or grooves and the occasional faint rubbed facets previously noted. Some of the neater, more regularly spaced and pronounced incisions are perhaps to be seen as decoration (fig. 12:1); and the fainter, irregularly situated, more random striations and the flat facets are to be associated with the primary rubbing and shaping of the pebble. Unless otherwise noted, all the stones listed below have groove troughs that are curved in cross section.

Grooved Rubbing Stones

Depth (cm)	Operation and area	Description
Surface		Fragment; broad groove with very impacted shiny surface; another V-shaped incision at base of trough
0-20	I,ext.	4 fragments: 2 with broad groove; 2 with groove size unnoted
0-20	I,ext.	Largely complete example; original shape probably pointed broad oval; MAX. W. 47 mm (see remarks under 20-30, I,G, below); short, vertical, straight incised lines set with some regularity along one edge, maybe decorative; two parallel grooves—one broad and symmetrical (W. 10 mm, DPTH. 7 mm), other incipient; (fig. 12:1)
0-20	I,tr.	Fragment of pointed oval piece; broad groove
0-20	I,G	Fragment, uncharacterized
0-20	III	2 fragments: 1 with part of broad groove; 1 with striations only
0-20	V	Fragment; very broad groove, W. 12 mm, DPTH. 8 mm
0-20	VI	Fragment; straight-sided V-shaped groove, W. 7 mm, DPTH. 3 mm
20-30	I,A	Virtually complete (K-24); neatly finished and shaped all over; planoconvex cross section and subrectangular form (only such piece at site), gently convex ends, nearly parallel sides; L. 46 mm, W. 22 mm; moderately broad groove roughly centered on convex face, with rounded V-shaped cross section, W. 10 mm, DPTH. 6 mm
20-30	I,F	Fragment; broad groove
20-30	I,G	Complete (K-25); neatly finished and shaped symmetrical, broad oval (this and half of similar form from 0-20, I,ext., above are the only broad oval examples at site, where other oval specimens are more attenuated); thickly biconvex cross section, underface less bulgy than upper face; well shaped all over; all upper face smoothed or showing barely perceptible facets; L. 43 mm, W. 32 mm; broad, symmetrically curved groove, W. 10 mm, DPTH. 9 mm
20-35	V	Small fragment; made of especially scaly friable schistose rock; broad groove
30-40	I,C	Fragmentary, but evidently still serviceable, piece (K-31); roughly symmetrical pointed oval,

Grooved Rubbing Stones—*Continued*

Depth (cm)	Operation and area	Description
		the longest specimen found, L. 87 mm, W. 21 mm; upper face with broad V-shaped central groove, W. 10 mm, DPTH. 6 mm; upper face also has central longitudinal ridge or crest formed by intersection of two rather flat planes of similar size—one apparently artificially shaped, the other presumably natural or possibly accidentally fractured; (fig. 12:2)
30-40	I,C	Fragment; one face with shallow, incipient, broad groove, W. 9 mm, DPTH. 2.5 mm, the other face with similar groove
40-50	I,C	Fragment; poorly achieved, incipient, broad groove and several incipient V-shaped grooves or striations, all parallel to each other on prepared face

Pierced Pebbles

Four fragments of more or less shaped marble pebbles show evidence of being pierced; each has a trace of a straight bored hole. These objects may be parts of maceheads or of dibble or digging stick weights, judging by the shapes and sizes of the two larger, more comprehensible, fragments.

Pierced Pebbles

Depth (cm)	Operation and area	Description
Surface		Large fragment (ca. one third of original circumference); possibly part of dibble weight or macehead with slightly convex-sided cylindrical form; one end face flat, other lost by old break; perforation fairly straight, well made, but not centered in cylindrical mass; easily weathered soft granular marble; surface showing both natural pebble cortex and shaped areas; HT. 80 mm, W. 72 mm; period uncertain due to surface provenience, but piece's similarity to sizeable specimen from 20-30 cm (see below) implies its contemporaneity with main occupation horizon
20-30	I,G	Large fragment (*K-34*); wedge shaped; recognizable one third of pierced flattened spheroid; soft marble; original HT. 40 mm?, original DIA. 90 mm?; remnant of upper (exterior) face bearing small-scale fine striations in all directions, indicating artificial smoothing; well-centered, plumb, faintly biconical bore (CTR. DIA. 9 mm, END DIA. 11 mm and 12 mm), showing horizontal bands of striation but representing only part of original diameter and length
20-40	I,C	Small fragment; too small for original form to be projected; barest trace of bore visible
60-80	III	Small fragment; too small for original form to be projected; barest trace of bore visible

Striated Pebbles

A number of smooth stream-worn pebble fragments found among the artifactual debris during the excavations bear a distinctive overall gloss or polish, unlike the usual stream pebbles and field rocks of the area. These pebble fragments also have concentrated areas of small and fine but clear-cut striations, which appear on any or all faces and along some of the ridges and angles. Some of the fragments also have pecking and flaking marks. These stones may simply be abraded stream pebbles, but the gloss and the intensive character and focus of the wear strongly suggest that they were used as rubbers, whetstones, anvils, or some other sort of preparatory working stone. All but three of the specimens in this category are of dark fine-grained serpentine or serpentinite with white veining. The three exceptions are a big highly polished flake of gray marble shaped into an oval by crude peripheral flaking on one face, an olive-green stone with greasy-looking high polish, and a rectangular fragment of dark gray chert with less polish but with numerous striations at the rounded angles. Some thought was evidently given to the selection of these particular kinds of stones for the job at hand.

The most outstanding and heavily marked specimen is the large, oval, polished gray marble pebble flake. This piece measures 85 × 60 × 20 mm. One face, which is slightly convex pebble cortex, is much striated, scarified, and very smoothly polished; the bulbar face is rougher and unstriated, and its perimeter is marked by a nearly complete circuit of large irregular flake scars. It may have served as an anvil or other sort of work stone in its present form or else it was detached from a larger piece, flaked, and adapted for perhaps the same or other functions. The striations on this flake lie in all directions, and their lengths vary from ca. 3 m to 25 m, the majority being short.

From the summary that follows it may be seen that these pecked, glossy, striated pebble fragments were for the most part in close association with the rocky living floor.

Striated Pebbles

Depth (cm)	Surface	Operation and area							Total
		I							
		Step	B	C	Ext.	F	G	IV	
Surface	2								2
0-20		1*	--	--	1	1†	--	1	4
20-30		1‡	2	3	--	2	--	--	8
30-40		--	--	--	--	--	2	--	2
40-50		--	--	--	--	--	1	--	1
40-80		1	--	--	--	--	--	--	1
Total	2	3	2	3	1	3	3	1	18

NOTE: All fragments.
* Marked with red ochre.
† Olive green stone with greasy-looking high polish.
‡ Chipped marble oval.

Used Discoid Pebbles

Two flat discoid-to-ovoid pebbles bear signs of wear only on the periphery in the form of flake scars, pecking marks, and striations, but they lack both the faceted rubbing zones and the elongated shape associated with the so-called pestle pebbles and so have been classed separately. From the evidence of wear on their surfaces, it is assumed they were perhaps used as knapping tools, abraders, or other working stones in a combination of pounding, pecking, and rubbing actions.

Used Discoid Pebbles

Depth (cm)	Operation and area	Description
0-20	I,ext.	Complete; reddish limestone; thick symmetric oval; flaked at one end; 80 × 70 × 32 mm
0-20	I,ext.	Fragment of thin discoid pebble; ruddy tan chert; wear along rim consisting of small flaking scars, peck marks, and striations; ca. 80 × 60 × 12 mm

Chipped and Polished Celts

Chipped and polished celts were found intimately associated with the mass of the stone industry both on the surface and in the deposits that included the occupation horizon. A study of a selection of these pieces, kindly undertaken by Professor Robert Reuss, Department of Geology, Tufts University, elicited the striking fact that the raw materials used for this category at Karim Shahir seem to have been almost anything but the chert-flint-chalcedony group of rocks so commonly used in the rest of the chipped stone industry. There was evidently some sort of selection made in favor of a variety of relatively fine-grained rocks, including hornfels, shale, siltstone, quartzite, various breccias, and rocks that were unidentified but usually definitely not of the chert-flint-chalcedony group. Professor Reuss's identifications suggest further that the stones selected for making these celts were evidently more suitable in texture and other qualities for grinding and polishing—both necessary procedures in the making of a smooth bit surface and an even cutting edge—than the harder chert-flint-chalcedony rocks.

The 29 complete and 13 fragmentary celts that were found constitute, in the main, a single distinctive technotypological group. With the exception of one or two medium-to-large examples, they are medium to small in size, not at all burdensome, and, when hafted, must have been relatively lightweight tools. (See fig. 13:1-10.)

At Karim Shahir two main typological divisions of adze/hoe and axe forms have been established on the basis of the difference in the bit profile. These types have been subdivided according to the kind of shaping or working at the bit end. The gross shape of the great majority of celts at this site, whether axes or adze/hoes, does not vary greatly. They have a flattened ovoid or trapezoidal cross section and a rounded triangular or near-trapezoidal to oval silhouette. The celts generally have relatively narrow-arched butt ends and broader bit ends. Only a very few examples have almost straight bit and butt ends of nearly equal width, which produces a virtually parallel-sided form close to a rounded rectangle in overall shape. In other words, the sides leading from bit to butt ends are very rarely roughly parallel; usually their straight or slightly convex edges tend to converge. As a rule, the edges of the bits are gently convex. There are only 3 straight-edged examples, all adze/hoes (e.g., fig. 13:1,5). Most of the celts are broadest toward the bit end, but some convex-sided examples are widest nearer the middle.

In nearly half the cases the bits are ground on both faces, while some of the rest have a combination of grinding on one face and chipping on the other. The majority of these last (all adze/hoes) are chipped on both faces of the bit. It is not clear to what extent this flaking is primary shaping or subsequent wear or renewal. Further comments on evidence for other kinds of bit wear appear below.

The body surface on all these celts bears varying amounts of very irregular and rather coarse stepped, flat percussion flaking, whose rough appearance is probably a function of the kind of rock used. This flaking either covers or extensively invades both faces and has been applied mainly from each long edge and the butt. A few specimens display remnants of a natural pebble cortex area toward the interior of one face, and many bear traces of grinding or polishing there as if the principal process of grinding the bit had also incidentally affected the body. Some such ground faces are obviously superposed on the chipped surfaces; others appear to have preceded the chipping and to be invaded by it, perhaps in some process of wearing down, renewal, or readaptation of shape, bulk, or working edge. A number of isolated chips with ground surfaces were found, testifying to such procedures.

Traces of a thin, dark, crusty deposit suspected of being bitumen adhere to 8 of the adze/hoes. Such traces are found generally in crevices on the flaked area of the body away from the bit and, in some cases, closely approaching the bit. This material is black, dark gray, or sometimes dark brown gray. The one encrusted celt that was tested by P.R. Ransford-Hannay (p. 27), an adze/hoe from the 0-20 cm level in operation V, had dark material sandwiched between the celt surface and the superficial calcareous accretion, which proved to be traces of oil and bitumen. On the other hand, material seemingly identical in appearance that was encrusted on an artifact from the 30-40 cm level of operation I showed only traces of oil. However, it does not seem unreasonable to assume that at least the 8 dark-crusted adze/hoes had been hafted with the aid of bitumen and by extension that all other adze/hoes (and perhaps the axe and chisel forms as well?) had also been treated in this manner. Unfortunately, not only is the dark material hidden under the rock-hard calcareous accretions that often obscure much of the celts' flaked surfaces but also most of it becomes detached along with these accretions and rarely stays with a piece in ample enough quantity for testing after cleaning. These pieces and 2 adze/hoes with traces of red ochre, as well as the dilemma of inconclusive identification of the dark matter on other pieces, are also discussed elsewhere (pp. 27, 34, 64-66).

Furthermore, it should be pointed out that there is only very debatable evidence on these celts to suggest that they were used as axes, adzes, or hoes. The zone around the bit edge does not show, with any convincing regularity, signs of wear such as striations and small flake scars from soil abrasion that would imply use as hoes. Neither is there any sheen such as as might be found on adzes or any similar or other evidence that would indicate the celts might have been axes. Professor Arthur Jelinek inspected with the naked eye and a low-power magnifying glass more than two dozen examples of celts from Karim Shahir and found no suggestion of wear on the bit edge that would suggest action in soil. At the time, Professor Jelinek was engaged in a project involving flint artifacts from an American Indian site. He was examining their flake scars and striations due to soil wear that were clearly visible under low-power magnification and was well qualified to recognize easily such relatively small-scale but distinctive features. In the case of the Karim Shahir pieces, while there is some secondary, discontinuous, very small-scale edge nicking on the otherwise smooth bits of 4 adze/hoes and 1 axe, such nicking might logically be attributed to normal attrition in the ground at this shallow archeological site and not necessarily to any primeval action in stony soil or to any other human activity that would involve friction or percussion. In the absence of pronounced edge scarring, the possibility that these artifacts were used for the working of softer materials, such as skins and hides or reeds and rushes, is worth considering.

A number of celts, both the adze/hoe and axe (including chisel) types, show faint striations on the smooth ground areas of the bit and of the main body. These may well be related to the grinding or polishing action that shaped the celts. Four varieties of these fine striations, based on the direction in which they run and their location, have been identified:

1. Diagonal to the long axis of the celt and usually distributed only over the main body. This variety is common and is most often widely spread over the major body surface, extending back in from the bit area.
2. Askew in several random directions in relation to the long axis and distributed over the main body. Like those of type 1, these striations occur over the same inner surfaces, away from the bit edge, but are much less common.
3. Parallel to the bit edge, usually at the bit itself or near it but in some cases running inward. This variety is considerably more common on both bit and body edges than those running perpendicular to the bit edge (see type 4).
4. Perpendicular to the bit edge, on the bit itself or elsewhere.

On some celts no striations whatsoever are detectable under a low-power lens, either at the bit or running further inward. Natural cortex areas appear to be devoid of any kind of striation, which suggests that the phenomenon of striation is to be associated with artificial treatment or with the activity for which the stone was used. Varieties 1 and 2—the diagonal and the random askew forms that are noted mainly over the main body—may well be associated only with the preparation, shaping, and smoothing of the celts. Likewise, varieties 3 and 4—the parallel and the perpendicular striations—may also be associated with preparation of the tools, such as the process of smoothing the surface of the bit edge itself; on the other hand, being more often located on the bit edge area, varieties 3 and 4 may well be due to some special use as well.

Excluding the 3 registered celts in Baghdad, which are not available for evaluation, and 8 other celts that are either too fragmentary or too heavily flaked for use in this particular study, 31 celts (24 adze/hoes, 6 axes, 1 chisel form) display the following varieties of striation on one or both faces:

Location	Variety of striation	Adze/hoe	Axe	Chisel	Total
Bit area	Parallel	10	2	1	13
	Perpendicular	8	1	--	9
	Diagonal	2	1	--	3
Body area	Parallel	4	3	1	8
	Perpendicular	3	1	--	4
	Diagonal	12	3	--	15
	Askew random	6	3	--	9

In other words, since one can attribute the parallel and perpendicular striations on the bit edge either to preparation of the bit face or to tool action, the presence or absence of these particular puzzling phenomena can be of no help in establishing definite functions for these tools. Moreover, at low-power magnification no edge sheen or rounding was observed, and the possibility of such witness to the working of soft materials was not pursued. For lack of any clearer evidence regarding use, we distinguish the two major groups—adze/hoes and axes—on the basis of bit profiles alone. This broad typological subdivision of the celts is outlined below.

Adze/hoe type.—Celts with an asymmetrical bit profile are considered adze/hoes. The under face is flat, and the upper face rises from the bit on a line that may be concave, convex, or straight in profile. It is assumed that the implements may have been woodworking adzes or soil-working hoes, although they lack any clear diagnostic traces of edge wear such as striations, dulling, nicking, or polishing that may be surely ascribed to friction with soil, wood, or softer materials. This adze/hoe group has been further subdivided as follows:

Subtype with one concave or thinned face at bit. These examples have an asymmetrical planoconcave adzelike bit profile, formed by a flat underface and slightly concave rising upper face (fig. 13:1). The concave rising face is invariably flaked; the under face may be smooth or flaked.

Subtype with one convex protruding face at bit. These examples, all with a planoconvex bit profile, are of two kinds: (a) those on which the flat under face is often ground or made up of an original pebble surface and on which the rising upper or convex face mostly shows stepped flaking with heavy battering, perhaps from use (fig. 13:2); (b) those with both faces chipped at the bit (fig. 13:3-4), perhaps deliberately, perhaps as a result of wear.

Subtype with two straight faces fully ground at bit. These examples also have the characteristic asymmetrical bit profile. Both bit faces display a predominantly ground surface (either flat or faintly convex), although occasional isolated flake scars appear on either face at the edge (fig. 13:5-6). In no case is it clear whether these scars can be attributed to natural attrition or to use. In one case (fig. 13:7), a celt of this general subtype approaches the axe form (see below) as regards its bit profile.

Axe type.—Celts of the axe type have a fully ground bit, which has a symmetrical biconvex profile that may be variously thick or thin (fig. 13:8-10). The body may be completely or extensively flaked, sometimes with patches of grinding and polishing. Pebble cortex also may be visible here and there.

Chisel type.—Two specimens are small, almost entirely smoothed by grinding and polishing, and have an elongated, narrow, nearly parallel-sided silhouette and a symmetrical bit profile (fig. 12:8-9). These have been classified as chisels to distinguish them from the larger and broader flaked axes in the celt group. Furthermore, because of their distinctive traits, these two pieces might possibly be considered intrusive even though they are still relatively ancient items. However, while one did come from the top 20 cm, the other came from the 20-40 cm level, which is more closely associated with the main occupation horizon, and therefore both are treated as part of the assemblage.

The following tabulation of 33 classifiable celts includes 28 complete specimens and also the 5 fragmentary examples where enough remained of the whole to allow a characterization.

Chipped and Polished Celts

Depth (cm)	Operation and area	Description
ADZE/HOE TYPE WITH ONE CONCAVE OR THINNED FACE AT BIT		
Surface		Complete; fine-grained gray stone (not of chert-flint-chalcedony group), tan patination on one face; gouge-shaped planoconcave bit end, sides slightly converging toward butt, oval outline with bit slightly broader than butt; flaking all over both faces; no trace of dark encrustations; L. 61 mm, MAX. W. 35 mm
0-20	I,ext.	Complete; fine-grained mottled blue-gray siliceous rock, possibly siltstone or some type of volcanic rock with conchoidal fracture; gouge-shaped planoconcave bit end, slightly broader than narrow-arched butt end and with converging sides; flaking distributed over rising concave bit face, polish invaded by chipping on opposite bit face; polished and/or pebble cortex facet remnants scattered virtually from bit to butt on both faces (fig. 13:1); no calcareous crust or dark encrustation; L. 65 mm, MAX. W. 35 mm
20-30	I,F	Virtually complete; fine-grained tan-gray sedimentary rock with banded structure and conchoidal fracture (not of flint-chert-chalcedony group); gouge-shaped bit end, narrowly arched butt end, parallel sides; polished facet at bit on flatter face, other face masked by calcareous crust; remainder of butt flaked over one face, save for one small pebble cortex remnant on one edge, and probably flaked over face hidden by crust; traces of dark matter in crust; possible traces of red ochre on polished facet; L. 68 mm, MAX. W. 37 mm
40-80	I,step	Fragmentary; fine-grained blue-gray siliceous rock with conchoidal fracture; gouge-shaped concavoconvex bit end, slightly broader than butt end, with sides converging; surface nearly all chipped, one ground and polished facet present on flat under-face of bit toward one side, extending from there in irregular remnant ridge along body to truncation of break; traces of dark crust in flake scar crevices along one lateral edge on both faces, very close to bit region; L. undetermined, MAX. W. 35 mm
ADZE/HOE TYPE WITH ONE CONVEX PROTRUDING FACE AT BIT		
(a) Ground, Polished, or Natural Cortex Surface on Flat Bit Face; Chipped on Convex Opposing Face		
Surface		Complete; very fine-grained gray-tan quartzite; triangular, made on elongated, thick, planoconvex, spatulate flake, swelling on flat face suggesting percussion bulb at narrow butt end; grinding polish on bulbar face, broad flaking elsewhere—i.e., inward from one long edge over part of bulbar face and from all edges over all of convex nonbulbar face; no traces of dark crusts; L. 62 mm, MAX. W. 38 mm; single example which resembles planoconvex flake adze type at Mureybit
0-20	I,step	Complete (*K-19*); gray stone; elongated, triangular with gently converging sides, straight bit edge and blunt-arched butt; chipping over most of both faces, but remnants of ground, polished, or pebble cortex surfaces retained; no traces of dark crusts; L. 61 mm, MAX. W. 29 mm
0-20	V	Complete; fine-grained dark blue-gray banded siliceous rock; stubby, triangular outline; ground polished facets on both faces, but polishing largely removed from both faces by chipping across convex bit face and along sides and butt end; no dark crust; L. 50 mm, MAX. W. 35 mm
0-20	V	Virtually complete; fine-grained dark blue-gray stone (not of flint-chert-chalcedony group); near-rhomboidal shape with almost parallel sides; polishing across bit and part of body on plane face and discontinuously in central zone on convex face wherever flaking has not invaded; unmistakable traces of dark crust retained in crevices of flake scars along long edge and butt; L. 60 mm, MAX. W. 35 mm very close to bit; specimen tested for bitumen (IPC lab sample no. 14175)
20-30	I,C	Complete; very fine-grained mottled gray rock, tan patination in places; triangular outline; combination ground and polished and natural pebble surface on part of plane face, including bit area; predominantly chipped surface with central remnant of polished or pebble cortex surface on convex face; traces of dark crust; L. 68 mm, MAX. W. 37 mm
20-30	I,C	Complete; very fine-grained dark blue-gray streaked rock (not of chert-flint-chalcedony group); slightly tapering, elongated, ovoid outline with gently convex bit which is slightly broader than butt; ground polished surface on plane face at bit end and on most of area around bit end, extending back to butt in central area of plane face; chipping over all except for one small smoothed island on convex face and along both long edges of plane face; L. 69 mm, MAX. W. 31 mm
20-30	I,G	Nearly complete; fine-grained tan-gray rock; broken butt end; elongated, triangular outline; pebble cortex over much of both faces, only minor chipping—especially across convex bit face and along one long edge on both faces; traces of dark crust visible under calcareous crust near butt end on one face; L. 62 mm to broken end, MAX. W. 35 mm

Chipped and Polished Celts—*Continued*

Depth (cm)	Operation and area	Description
20-30	I,G	Complete; fine- to medium-grained dark gray hornfels; medium large; sides roughly parallel forming rounded rectangle; bit end nearly same width as butt end, both slightly convex in outline; plane face with ground polished surface extending back from bit nearly half total length, broad flaking over rest of plane face; nearly all convex face flaked save for irregular vestigial ground area near bit end (fig. 13:2), steep mounding of convex bit face—thickest in half toward bit end (12 mm near bit, 16 mm near center); no calcareous crust on convex chipped face, traces of dark crust under calcareous crust on plane face; L. 80 mm, MAX. W. 40 mm

(b) Both Bit Edge Faces Chipped

Depth (cm)	Operation and area	Description
Surface		Complete; fine-grained gray-tan stone (not of chert-flint-chalcedony group), patinated to yellow tan in spots; elongated, oval outline, nearly parallel long sides; chipping over most of both faces except for limited central remnants of natural cortex or of ground and polished surface; heavy battering scars and flaking on long edges; no traces of dark crust; L. 64 mm, MAX. W. 29 mm
Surface		Complete; fine-grained gray quartzite, tan patination; blunted, elongated, triangular outline with converging sides, bit broader than rounded butt; chipping over nearly all of both faces save for central ridge remnant, found on both faces, of pebble cortex or of ground polished surface; no traces of dark crust; L. 74 mm, MAX. W. near bit 39 mm
Surface		Nearly complete; very fine-grained green banded sedimentary rock (perhaps impure siltstone or mudstone), tan patination on one face; elongated oval outline but only slightly converging long edges; bit end defaced and incomplete, so celt category not entirely clear (probably convex steep-faced bit with flaking on both faces); chipping over most of both faces save for limited central zones of either pebble or polished surface; heavy battering and flaking on both long edges; no traces of dark crust; L. 70 mm, MAX. W. 34 mm
Surface		Complete; very fine grained rock (not of chert-flint-chalcedony group); narrow, elongated, triangular form, made on thin flake with probable bulb at butt end of flat, virtually unworked bulbar face; remnant of ground, polished surface toward bit end on broadly flaked upper face; small-scale bifacial flaking in very narrow peripheral zone on both long edges and on very thin bit of asymmetrical cross section; similar small flaking across butt on bulbar face; no traces of dark crust; L. 63 mm, MAX. W. 30 mm; perhaps pseudo-celt (lacks mass and prepared bit edge of usual Karim Shahir celts), classifiable as used flake but for trace of polished surface, continuous flaking on long edge, and elongated, triangular silhouette
0-20	I,A	Possibly complete; fine-grained gray-tan-banded bedded siliceous rock, with poor conchoidal fracture tending to horizontal parallel-line or laminated fracture; stubby, blunted triangular outline, converging sides, bit broader than rounded butt; somewhat disproportionately short length and irregular thick, steep aspect of bit end suggesting possibly rejuvenated specimen readapted on long butt-end fragment; chipping over nearly all of both faces save for remnant of ground, polished surface near one edge toward bit end on both faces; no dark crust traces; L. 53 mm, MAX. W. 32 mm
0-20	I,step	Complete (*K-17*); fine-grained gray rock with shallow conchoidal fracture (not of chert-flint-chalcedony group); stubby, blunted triangular outline, converging sides; broad bit and narrow, rounded butt; chipping over most of plane face along edges and at bit on both faces, but sizeable natural pebble cortex and ground surface present over center of convex face, and ground and polished remnant toward bit on other face; no dark crust; L. 64 mm, MAX. W. 42 mm
0-20	I,F	Complete; very fine-grained blue-gray bedded siliceous rock, probably quartzite, quartz-cemented quartz sandstone, or possibly bedded chert; very poor laminated fracture, strongly banded, horizontally bedded; tan patination; rhomboidal outline with butt and bit nearly equally broad, sides almost parallel; completely flaked over both faces; no dark crust traces; L. 82 mm, MAX. W. 47 mm; (fig. 13:3)
0-20	VI	Complete; breccia composed of very fine fragments of shale, mudstone, argillite, etc., but no chert-flint-chalcedony particles; gray, with tan patination on one face; medium large; asymmetric oval shape with convex bit edge and butt lines and slightly convex long sides; flaking over nearly all of both faces, but pebble cortex or ground polished remnants retained over center of convex face; no dark crust; L. 86 mm, MAX. W. 46 mm; (fig. 13:4)
40-50	I,C	Complete; fine-grained blue-gray quartzite, tan patination on one face; blunted, triangular outline with converging sides and with convex bit broader than rounded butt; chipping over nearly all of both faces save for central ridge remnants of ground and polished surfaces; dark deposit preserved under calcareous crust on one face; L. 64 mm, MAX. W. at bit 38 mm

Chipped and Polished Celts—Continued

Depth (cm)	Operation and area	Description
ADZE/HOE TYPE WITH TWO STRAIGHT FACES FULLY GROUND AT BIT		
20-30	I,C	Incomplete; fine-grained blue-gray siliceous rock; elongated, triangular shape with fully ground facet on both faces of medium-thick bit extending back irregularly onto main body nearly to butt; smooth surface invaded extensively by flaking from extant long edge and at butt; perhaps one longitudinal third of original mass carried off by break or by miscarried flaking along other long edge; no traces of dark crust; L. 58 mm, MAX. W. at bit end 25 mm
20-30	I,G	Complete; very fine-grained gray vesicular rock, probably volcanic, with tan-buff patination on one face; medium large; elongated, triangular shape with fully ground facet on both faces of bit and localized at thick bit (in profile, angles and proportions typologically approach axe category); rest of body broadly flaked, with some further secondary edge-flaking; no trace of dark crust; L. 83 mm, MAX. W. 40 mm; (fig. 13:5)
20-30	I,G	Complete; fine- to medium-grained gray rock, sedimentary or possibly hornfelsic; small; stubby, rounded triangular shape with fully ground bit facet on both faces forming fairly thin edge and extending back over nearly one half of main body on each face; flaking and extensive battering on long edges and butt on both faces; tiny traces of dark crust in flake scar crevices on each face; traces of red ochre on flatter face; L. 45 mm, MAX. W. 29 mm; (fig. 13:6)
30-40	I,C	Complete; very fine-grained brown-gray vesicular rock, probably volcanic; elongated, bluntly triangular shape with fully ground bit facet on both faces forming thin edge and extending slightly back onto main body; broad flaking covering rest of both faces; long edges gently convergent; no traces of dark deposit; L. 70 mm, MAX. W. near bit end 39 mm; (fig. 13:7)
AXE TYPE		
Surface		Complete; very fine-grained dark blue-gray rock (not of chert-flint-chalcedony group); medium-large with elongated, blunt, triangular outline, bit edge slightly wider than butt end; bit facets coming to medium-thick bit edge, rest of body broadly flaked on both faces except for vestige of further irregular polish on one face; no traces of dark crust; L. 86 mm, MAX. W. 45 mm; (fig. 13:8)
Surface		Complete; fine-grained blue-gray quartzite, tan patination; extensive bit facets forming thick edge; one bit face partially invaded by flaking, removing original corner angle there; rest of body broadly flaked bifacially save for central zone of pebble cortex surface on both faces; battering along both long edges; no traces of dark crust; L. 70 mm, MAX. W. 40 mm
0-20	I,C	Complete (K-9); fine-grained gray rock; bit facets forming medium-thick bit; flaking on both faces along both gently converging and slightly convex long edges and at much-thinned and strongly arched butt; no traces of dark crust; L. 55 mm, MAX. W. 33 mm
0-20	I,ext.	Complete; fine-grained gray rock (not of chert-flint-chalcedony group); tan patination; small, stubby, with extensive bit facets coming to thin edge; smoothed surfaces on both faces extending back over about two thirds the length, with flaking and battering along both long, gently converging edges and at butt; no traces of dark crust; L. 52 mm, MAX. W. 31 mm
0-20	I,F	Complete; gray breccia composed of fine-grained quartz sandstone fragments and perhaps some very fine-grained quartzite or chert fragments, all in compact clay matrix; possibly sedimentary or volcanic or combination of both; pale tan patination on one face; triangular shape with broad bit, narrow butt, and extensive bit facets forming thin edge; battering and flaking at butt and along both converging long edges and also invading central area near butt end; no traces of dark crust; L. 65 mm, MAX. W. 40 mm; (fig. 13:9)
0-40	I,step	Complete; very fine-grained gray rock, perhaps shale, mudstone, argillite, or altered volcanic rock (not of chert-flint-chalcedony group); tan patination; small, with stubby, subrectangular shape, slightly convex sides, bit and butt nearly same width; fully ground surface over most of both faces coming to thin bit edge; battering along both long edges toward butt end and over butt; thickest toward butt end; no traces of dark crust; L. 55 mm, MAX. W. 31 mm; battering and absence of overall flaking puts specimen closer to relatively unflaked types reported from Jarmo and M'lefaat (fig. 13:10)
20-30	I,A	Incomplete; fine-grained dark brown-gray rock; tan patination; butt end missing; parallel sided, probably subrectangular, with bit facets forming thin bit edge; ground surface extending somewhat up and onto mass of axe on both faces, although much of edges of long sides flaked; no traces of dark deposit; MAX. W. 35 mm
CHISEL TYPE		
0-20	I,C	Complete (K-10); fine-grained pale gray rock (not of chert-flint-chalcedony group); very small; very narrow and elongated, nearly parallel sided; thick oval cross section; some pebble

Chipped and Polished Celts—Continued

Depth (cm)	Operation and area	Description
		cortex and ground and polished surfaces retained on both sides of body; single bit facets on each face converging to form equiangular bit profile at one end; asymmetric pair of little facets on one face forming sort of bit edge at other end; no traces of dark deposit; L. 39 mm, W. 17 mm; possibly classifiable as chisel because of special shape and size; (fig. 12:8)
20-30	I,C	Complete (K-44); very fine-grained mottled gray rock (not of chert-flint-chalcedony group); tan patination on one face; rather small, narrow, elongated, parallel sided; thick oval cross section; ground over most of one face; pebble cortex and some ground areas on other face; peck marks and battering along one long edge and at butt; a few isolated flakes cut into smooth surfaces on both faces along other long edge; bit facets on each face converging to form equiangular bit profile; small-scale stepped flaking along one face of bit edge, truncating opposite bit-edge face; opposite bit-edge face with second larger, more invasive ground facet embracing truncated primary bit-edge facet; no traces of dark deposit; L. 54 mm, MAX. W. 24 mm; possibly classifiable as chisel because of special shape and size; (fig. 12:9)

Chips and fragments of chipped and polished celts.—The material from Karim Shahir included some unclassifiable celt fragments. Also, a limited quantity of flakes and chips that bore traces of having been very smoothly ground and polished were segregated on the assumption that they were either pieces broken during use or else by-products from the manufacture or readaptation of the chipped and polished celts found at the site.

There are 6 butt-end and 2 bit-end fragments of fine-grained gray stone of various sorts and various tones. One of the butt fragments is very large, with a breadth of 54 mm. The 17 flakes and chips of varying small sizes are of the same range of fine-grained stones in various tones of gray, gray green, and blue gray, except for three of reddish gray quartzite that took a high polish. These unclassifiable pieces came from the surface and various depths in operations I, III, V, VI, and VIII.

Boulder Mortars

Indications of boulder mortars at Karim Shahir show this to be a definite, though minor, category in the stone industry from the occupation horizon proper. As shown in the summary below, 6 fragments were found at various levels in operation I, and 2 more fragments came from the surface, well down the slope off to the south of the excavations. These 2 fragments and certain other flint artifacts found elsewhere on the lower slopes were doubtless separated from the site's deposits during erosion processes in the past.

Judging from the specimens available, small steeply basined depressions ca. 100 mm in diameter and perhaps 50-70 mm deep were developed into the body of selected cobbles and somewhat larger stones. The evidently limited occurrence of boulder mortars at the site is consistent with the similarly limited traces of pestles, both the natural used elongated pebble form and the artificially shaped type (see next section). These mortars and at least the natural pebble pestles may presumably be associated as paired working units for the preparation of seeds, nuts, and other wild plant material.

Boulder Mortars

| Depth (cm) | Surface | Operation and area | | | | Total |
		I,step	I,A	I,C	I,A,B,F,ext.	
Surface	2					2
0-20		--	1	--	--	1
0-40		1	--	--	--	1
20-30		--	--	--	2	2
40-50		--	--	1	--	1
40-80		1	--	--	--	1
Total	2	2	1	1	2	8

NOTE: All fragments.

Pestles

Shaped pestles.—Three fragments of well-made symmetrical pestles that have been shaped by pecking are too incomplete and do not constitute a large enough group to permit a reliable description of the type as a whole. At any rate, these fully shaped pieces appear to be much rarer at the site than the various natural pebbles probably used as pestles described in the next paragraph. Only one pecked pestle seems nearly complete. While two of the pieces come from the uppermost centimeters of the deposits and might therefore be intrusive, one comes from deep in the occupation layer. The fully pecked surface and careful artificial shaping of all three pieces suggest a stoneworking tradition that was later and more sophisticated than that reflected by much of the assemblage considered here; however, on the basis of the specimen from well within the undisturbed deposits, they are accorded a place among the ground stone artifacts belonging to the horizon proper.

Shaped Pestles

Depth (cm)	Operation and area	Description
0-20	I,ext.	Fragment (K-32) of working end of well-shaped pestle; somewhat granular gray limestone; oval cross section; pecked all over; flat working end separated from slightly diverging sides of shaft by roughly pecked curving interval; L. 60 mm, MAX. DIA. 42 mm
0-20	I,ext.	Nearly complete?; coarse limestone; pebble shaped, stumpy; nearly circular cross section; pecked at working end, flaked and battered at butt end; narrow longitudinal flake scars, probably partly due to fracturing properties of stone, possibly due to use as battering or pounding tool or perhaps as incipient core (compare somewhat similar flaking on certain natural pebble pestles [see next section]); DIA. 20 mm; (fig. 12:4)
40-80	I,step	Fragment of working end of large, shaped pestle; limestone; nearly circular cross section; profile marked by coarse flaking at butt end; slightly convex working end; DIA. ca. 40 mm; (fig. 12:5)

Natural pebble pestles.—Long, narrow stream pebbles were apparently selected for special use, primarily as pestles but perhaps for other purposes as well. They are distinctly worn at one narrow end, suggesting attrition due to pounding and grinding. Elsewhere on the shaft of the body they are striated, flaked, or otherwise worn, as if they had served variously as working stones (anvils, whetstones, abraders, or rubbers). Twelve specimens were found.

Natural Pebble Pestles

Depth (cm)	Operation and area	Description
0-20	I,A-G	Fragment; dark gray chert; oval to oval-rectangular cross section; pecking wear and flaking at both ends and striations on shaft; 75 × 45 mm
0-20	I,ext.	5 fragments: 3 tan chert, 1 red chert, 1 dark gray chert; all very small pieces; thick oval or oval-rectangular cross sections; pecking or wear at one end and striations or flake scars elsewhere
0-20	I,ext.	Fragment; gray limestone; narrow with small delicate proportions, subrectangular or oval cross section; some striations and peck marks and short, narrow, longitudinal flake scars around one end as though object was perhaps incipient core as well as pounding tool; 55 × 20 mm
0-20	I,ext.	Fragment like preceding piece, but dark tan sandstone; 55 × 23 mm
0-20	IV	Thick fragment; chert; oval to subrectangular cross section; pecking or wear at one end and striations or flake scars elsewhere
0-20	VI	Thin fragment; dark gray chert; planoconvex; high polish on parts of one face, battering and broad flake scars over one end on both faces; 55 × 50 mm
0-40	I,step	Elongated fragment; tan chert; wandlike; striations and rubbed flat facet near one end suggesting use as burnisher or rubber; striations and facet truncated by broad, irregular flake scars where original pebble was truncated; 53 × 15 mm
20-30	I,A	Thick fragment; chert; oval to subrectangular-oval cross section; pecking or wear at one end and striations or flakes elsewhere
20-30	I,C	Complete; red chert; long, narrow; small delicate shape; pecking and wear at one end; 60 × 20 mm

Palette

One fragment of what was thought to be a palette was found. It was so classified because of its absolutely flat grinding area and its raised and ornamented rim. It was found somewhat below the main concentration of other finds in the vicinity but within the vertical spread of the occupation horizon. Thus this piece may be accepted as an integral part of the stone industry, although its workmanship and relative sophistication perhaps hint at later periods.

Palette

Depth (cm)	Operation and area	Description
40-50	I,G	Fragment (*K-37*); warm gray sandstone; preserved segment of periphery slightly curved and marked by slightly bulging convex raised rim, which bears series of diagonal incisions along edge of upper and outer face resembling piecrust edge incisions; outer edge below rim curved sharply down to form neat, steep-sided edge; interior working surface completely horizontal, no indication of tilt or depression; fully and skillfully shaped overall, judging by visible top and sides; masking limy crust on lower face; no trace of any pigment; 80 × 60 × 23 mm, thickness seemingly constant throughout; (fig. 12:3)

Grindstones (Querns)

The 4 limited fragments of evidently somewhat large pieces forming this category are distinguished by grinding surfaces that are flat or very gently depressed, or markedly concave. All seem to have been made with a minimum of work on natural pebbles or angular field stone of coarse quality. The grinding surface is developed on only one face, and perhaps a little flaking appears elsewhere. It is noteworthy that all examples come from relatively deep levels and none are from the surface.

Grindstones (Querns)

Depth (cm)	Operation and area	Description
20-30	I,A,B,F,ext.	Fragment of tabular slab; limestone; smooth grinding surface worn flat on one face and either the natural or a naturally worn off, more irregular face on opposite side; 110 × 55 mm, TH. 25 mm
20-30	I,A,B,F,ext.	Fragment of slab; sandstone; gently concave grinding surface worn on one face; natural outer surface spalled off on lower face
40-80	I,step	Small fragment of notably concave quern; very crumbly reddened conglomerate rock, perhaps weakened by fire heating; original smooth, somewhat compacted inner grinding surface remaining and natural outer surface crumbled away; 60 × 70 mm
80-120	I,step, near center, just above gray deposit filling depression	Fragment; limestone; semilunar shape; upper face apparently fashioned artificially into nearly flat grinding-stone surface and covered by pitting and short striations in all directions; natural lower face, gently convex and mostly hidden by calcareous crust, but in one spot apparently retaining traces of dark deposit; edges of lower face crudely flaked around periphery to form steep-angled shelving inward; if close to true edge of piece, fragment probably about half size of original mass; planoconvex cross section; 120 × 120 × 50 mm

Hand Rubbing Stones (Mullers)

Stones of various shapes with signs of use as rubbing implements have been classed separately as hand rubbing stones because their artificially flat facets and their small size and light weight suggest they were easily manageable in the hand, in contrast to the items classed as grindstones, which seem to be fragments of larger stones. All are, of course, grainy-textured stone, mostly chert, a few sandstone or conglomerate, and one is of gneiss. All 23 specimens, only one of which is complete, seem to have had steep, nearly perpendicular sides and one or more virtually flat or slightly concave rubbing faces developed artificially on what was presumably a roughly symmetrical bun-shaped oval or cuboid-shaped mass. They have been subdivided on the basis of working surfaces and overall shape thus:

a. Flat rubbing surface on two opposed faces (fig. 12:6)
b. Flat rubbing surface on one face and slightly concave surface on opposite face
c. Flat rubbing surface on one face and a more or less natural steep convex surface on other face, forming a planoconvex shape
d. Flat rubbing surface on one or more faces, forming a cuboid (fig. 12:7)

Types *a* and *b* may be advanced forms of the most numerous category, type *c*. In other words, an additional rubbing face may have been developed on an originally convex face. The difference between the flat and the concave rubbing surface types may be ascribed to variations in function or in length and intensity of use.

The single specimen of the cuboid form, type *d*, may be an entirely different class of implement. It has generally smaller overall dimensions and may be a hammerstone as well as a rubber. Its rounded and roughened angles tend to give it a nearly spherical shape, but in any case the rubbing surfaces truncate the mass at one or more points. This specimen has two opposed flat rubbing faces. The cuboid type has been found at Jarmo, where it is part of a group called pecking and rubbing stones (p. 294). However, the rubbing stones at Karim Shahir are so fragmentary that it is difficult to compare them in form and size with their counterparts at other sites, although it looks as if the majority did not undergo much shaping except on the rubbing faces.

Frequency and provenience of the four types according to rubbing surface are to be found in the first tabulation below. The second tabulation records further details including significant dimensions of pieces, where possible. The only complete specimen is indicated under type *d*.

Hand Rubbing Stones (Mullers)

Depth (cm)	Type a	Type b	Type c	Type d	Total
Surface	--	1	--	--	1
0-20	1	--	6	--	7
20-30	2	--	6	--	8
30-40	2	--	2	1*	5
40-50	--	--	2	--	2
Total	5	1	16	1	23

Depth (cm)	Operation and area	No.	Stone	Dimensions (mm) Th.	L.	W.	Illustration
Type *a*							
0-20	I,ext.	1	Chert	50	115	90-100	--
20-30	I,A-G	1	Sandstone	40	--	100	--
20-30	I,G	1	Chert	45	120	70	Fig. 12:6
30-40	I,G	2	Sandstone	40	--	--	--
Type *b*							
Surface		1	Coarse conglomerate	38-45	--	115	--
Type *c*							
0-20	I,A,B,F,ext.	3	Chert	65	--	--	--
0-20	III	1	Chert	--	--	--	--
0-20	V	1	Chert	--	--	--	--
0-20	VIII	1	Chert	--	--	--	--
20-30	I,A-G	5	Chert	37-67	--	--	--
20-30	I,G	1	Sandstone	--	--	--	--
30-40	I,G	1	Conglomerate	65	--	--	--
30-40	I,G	1	Gneiss	30	--	--	--
40-50	I,C	1	Conglomerate	45	--	--	--
40-50	I,C	1	Chert	60	--	--	--
Type *d*							
30-40	I,G	1*	Chert	45	55	50	Fig. 12:7

*Complete piece.

Pieces with Flat Rubbed Surfaces

Eleven flakes and fragments of various types of rock bear portions of flat rubbed surfaces, as if they had been parts of larger worked milling pieces. However, they are too small for one to judge whether or not they are parts of grindstones or of hand rubbing stones.

These pieces are tabulated below according to the type of stone.

Pieces with Flat Rubbed Surfaces

Depth (cm)	Operation and area	Chert	Diorite	Granite	Quartzite	Sandstone	Total
0-20	I,ext.	--	1	--	--	--	1
0-20	VI	--	--	--	1	1	2
0-25	V	--	--	1	--	--	1
0-40	I,step	--	1	--	--	--	1
20-30	I,C	1	1	--	--	1	3
30-40	I,C	--	1	--	--	--	1
30-40	I,G	--	2	--	--	--	2
Total		1	6	1	1	2	11

Hammerstones

Included in the hammerstone category are stream-worn pebbles or field stones that range from medium-small to somewhat larger sizes. The few more complete specimens suggest original diameters of 50 mm to 70-80 mm, a size that would fill the palm of the hand. They are of various shapes but predominantly spheroid, all with signs of repeated heavy percussion and marked abrasion at one or more points. The points of percussion and repeated battering may be a face, one end, a flake scar ridge, or a prominence of the piece. The zones of peck marks and rather flat squamous flake scars or abrasion are localized and distinct. Because of all the battering it is difficult to determine the degree to which the form of these pieces is due to shaping, use, or natural formation. Thus, the category may, in part, contain examples whose proper classification is debatable. Most specimens are fragmentary, and all are of the chert-flint-chalcedony group of rocks, often of a particularly coarsely fracturing milky-blue variety. It must also be noted that in all likelihood this was a very numerous category, to judge by the quantities of flakes and fragments found with heavily battered surfaces. In the following tabulation, however, the quantities and distribution of only the complete or nearly complete examples are summarized, whereas the numerous battered fragmentary examples have been included in the discussion of used flakes and fragments (p. 89).

Hammerstones

Depth (cm)	Operation and area													
	I													
	Step	A	B	C	Ext.	F	G	Tr.	III	IV	V	VI	VIII	Total
0-20	--	1*	2	1	7(1*)	--	--	1	4	1	--	1	--	18
0-25	--	--	--	--	--	--	--	--	--	--	3	--	1	4
20-30	--	1	2	5	--	2	--	--	--	--	--	--	--	10
25-35	--	--	--	--	--	--	--	--	--	--	1	--	--	1
40-60	--	--	--	2(1*)	--	--	1	--	1	--	--	--	--	4
40-80	2	--	--	--	--	--	--	--	--	--	--	--	--	2
Total	2	2	4	8	7	2	1	1	5	1	4	1	1	39

*Complete piece.

Minerals

Artifacts Bearing Black Substance (Bitumen?)

Whereas tests on the dark crust adhering to one adze/hoe in the celt category revealed that it was bitumen (pp. 27, 55), which allows one to assume that celts found at Karim Shahir were in all probability hafted with the help of this substance, the situation is not so clear-cut in another small group of artifacts bearing a black crust. The group in question comprises pebble fragments and miscellaneous pieces of chipped flint. Judgment regarding the dark crusts found on these pieces must remain suspended, although there is a small amount of presumptive evidence (noted here below) that bitumen might once have adhered to these artifacts, too. This position was reached after various tests were conducted in 1954 by Dr. W.F. Foshag, Department of Geology, Smithsonian Institution, on the blackish stains suspected of being bitumen that were found on the edges of two flint blades from Karim Shahir.

Dr. Foshag (pers. comm.) found that chemical tests for both humus and manganese were negative. Definitive chemical tests for pitch or bitumen could not be carried out on these small pieces; such tests require that the sample be at least 0.5 gm in weight and that it be relatively pure material. Neither of these requirements could be met by the dark material from any one piece from Karim Shahir or by any of the rare free particles of such material found at the site. For the same reason both spectroscopic and x-ray examinations were also precluded. On the other hand, the test to prove the presence of and to remove the crust of calcium carbonate that frequently overlay the dark material removed that material as well, implying incidentally that the substance was mineral. Furthermore, Foshag pointed out that it is probable that bitumen of a very great age may have become completely free of any soluble or volatile components, leaving only some fixed carbon.

According to this information supplied by Foshag, it might then possibly be concluded that the dark substance covered by a calcareous crust on the two flint blades tested (and, by extension, on most other similarly encrusted pieces?) may perhaps be carbon. What we cannot say is that it is definitely bitumen, but neither can we say it was not at one time part of a substance considered to be bitumen. Although this matter is unresolved at present, the celts and the miscellaneous pieces displaying the blackish substance are here presented as a group. All the artifacts noted in this special category except the pebble fragments are included in the counts of their respective typological categories elsewhere in this chapter.

Celts bearing black substance.—All 8 specimens of the chipped and polished celts that have an adhering blackish film preserved under a calcareous crust fall within the adze/hoe category: 1 in the group of specimens with a bifacially flaked bit, 1 in the group with a bifacially ground bit, and 6 in the group with bits that have the flat face ground and the convex face flaked. In each instance the dark crust lay on the body of the celt but did not appear on the bit area, that is, the working zone. Here, again, the black material becomes detached with the crust when the crust is removed, either by hand or chemically. Following a single successful test for bitumen on one celt, one can feel reasonably certain that bitumen was used in the hafting of all these celts. There can be no such certainty about the use of bitumen for any purpose in the case of the pebbles and flints.

Pebbles bearing black substance.—Five pebble portions of limestone or chert bear a thin blackish encrustation on a limited part of their surface. This crusty formation is well developed in most cases and flakes off very easily. While limestone calcined in fire or extreme heat sometimes discolors and spalls off in crusts, the location of the black crust on the specimens under consideration here suggests they may be altered bitumen remnants on stones used as palettes or daubers. Some pieces have this distinct black crust on a flat surface as if they had been used as a palette or mixing stone; others have it on a stubby narrow end as if they had been used as daubers or pestles. As indicated below, all specimens were found well down in the deposits.

Pebbles Bearing Black Substance (Bitumen?)

Depth (cm)	Operation and area	Description
20-30	I	Pebble fragment; streaked olive-green chert, highly polished (sheen?) in places; remnant of blackish crust in depression at one narrow end, suggesting possible use as pestle or dauber for substance resembling bitumen.
60-80	I,C	Block of limestone; rounded, rectangular; on two faces, traces of blackish crust imperceptibly merging into burned black limestone zones, here maybe due to heating of block as palette for mixing bitumenlike pastes; L. 60 mm, W. 45 mm, TH. 50 mm
140-150	I,step, pit/depression near 10-m mark	Pebble fragment; limestone; apparently natural slight depression in center of one flat face near broken butt end, providing concave palettelike surface; thin, friable black crust disposed in irregular patches over this concave surface, at butt end extending in thinner film over part of an adjoining natural pebble surface at right angles to concave surface; heating by fire or calcining indicated by white and gray discoloration of limestone, i.e., crust perhaps due either to heating of limestone or to bitumen manipulation involving heat and leaving a coating; L. 80 mm, W. 75 mm, TH. 60 mm
140-150	I,step, pit/depression near 10-m mark	Small pebble fragment; limestone; one flat face thickly and thoroughly masked with black crust; L. 60 mm, W. 40 mm, TH. 25 mm
140-150	I,step, pit/depression near 10-m mark	Pebble fragment; calcined limestone; traces of black crust on two natural faces and on crest where they meet; one portion of wider flat face showing pronounced but easily rubbed-off traces of reddish color (red ochre or fire discoloration?); L. 95 mm, W. 55 mm

Miscellaneous flint pieces bearing black substance.—Traces of black crust were found on a very small number of flint pieces. These include blades, flakes, and fragments of blades and flakes, as well as a core fragment and a microlithic scraper.

Miscellaneous Flint Pieces Bearing Black Substance (Bitumen?)

Depth (cm)	Operation and area	Description
30-40	I	Core fragment; traces of black crust
40-50	I	Blade segment; black crust on notched (worn?) edge
100-180	I,step, ochre pit	Several used blades, flakes, and fragments: minute traces of black substance adhering to either face of each specimen, usually in association with (lying under) calcareous crust
100-180	I,step, ochre pit	Blade fragment; much black substance at one corner and along one edge of obverse (nonbulbar) face
60+	III	Microlithic end scraper; wear, notch, and black material along one nibbled edge

Ochre and Ochre-bearing Pieces

Items marked with red ochre.—A small number of flint artifacts, turtle bones, and a shell found in operation I retain some red ochre on their surfaces, preserved largely in and under the calcareous crust that formed on them after incorporation into the archeological deposit. All this material except for two celts came from the step, half the pieces coming from within or in close association with the pit near the north end whose bottom surface was covered by a thin layer of red ochre. All the pieces noted in this special category are included in the counts of their respective typological categories (stone, bone, or shell) elsewhere in this chapter.

Items Marked with Red Ochre

Depth (cm)	Operation and area	Description
0-20	I, step	1 striated pebble, 3 notched blades, and 1 used blade
20-40	I, step	1 used flake
40-60	I, step	3 fragments of turtle bone
180	I, step, ochre pit	2 notched blades, 3 used blades, 1 flake, 2 fragments of trimming debris, 1 snail shell
20-30	I, F	1 celt of adze/hoe type; possible faint traces of red ochre on smoothed area near bit on one face
20-30	I, G	1 celt of the adze/hoe type; clear traces of red ochre in crevices of flake scars on flatter, less convex, face (fig. 13:6)

Ochre lumps and discolored concretions.—There was some evidence for lumps of raw red and yellow ochre at the site. Small lumps, 5-25 mm in diameter, of a dense friable substance, looking like masses of fine-grained ochre, were found scattered singly or in little clusters randomly throughout the site. They vary in color from sulphur yellow to blood red, and some are intermediate tones of orange beige or buff. Some lumps have a combination of both the yellow and the red tints, which suggests discoloration by fire rather than the presence of any natural ochre deposit or the collecting of ochre pieces by the inhabitants. In general, the intensely colored red and yellow lumps are irregularly shaped and thus look much like the ordinary calcareous concretions found in great quantity at many levels. However, these purer red and yellow specimens are relatively rare. They are also sturdier, denser, and finer grained than the concretions. When rubbed on various surfaces they leave a definite colored smudge.

Besides the purer ochre lumps, a large number of earth-toned limy concretions were found, especially in the upper levels, and also at intervals throughout the excavations. The presumption is that these are all purely natural phenomena (see p. 41 for fuller discussion of these formations). A small number of the concretions are tawny orange or reddish and more are gray to dark gray, all differing from the commoner paler, more evenly tan-colored examples. Such variations from the norm were perhaps caused by fire or else by amalgamation of the surrounding discolored earth with the bodies of the concretions. Low-power microscopic examination of the surfaces of the grayer (ashy?) specimens—even the quite dark ones—failed to show any obvious charcoal-fragment components. Gray to dark gray concretions were frequently noticed in operations I, II, III (especially in levels of 60-80 cm just below the main rocky occupation layer), IV, and more rarely in the other operations as well.

The red, yellow, and orange lumps that were selected to be saved include not only a number apparently of pure ochre but also some that were more like the ochre-impregnated mass of concretionary nodules. Those concretions displaying dark gray or grayish hues were more numerous than the reddish and yellowish variety and were not saved.

Heavy Chert Pieces Containing Iron

Amid the occupational debris there occurred a number of pieces of a distinctive coal-black cherty rock containing enough natural iron components such as magnetite and hematite to make them noticeably heavier than other pebbles. Some of these heavy black pieces are slightly magnetic and are, in effect, lodestones. Many of the pieces have rounded cuboid or roughly spherical shapes with a diameter range of 30-50 mm, judging by examples that retain enough of the original piece to give reliable measurements. Most retain what appears to be a good part of their natural rather shiny and waterworn pebble cortex surface. A few, the cuboids, have flatter areas on several sides, which might suggest some artificial rubbing or wear. However, these areas (with some exceptions) bear no visible striations and therefore may more reasonably be considered the natural pebble cortex surface. The angles between such flatter surfaces, as well as some surfaces themselves, whether flat or convex, are often heavily battered, which is the basis for thinking these heavy lumps were used predominantly as hammerstones. Their weight and density would surely make them desirable for this purpose. Comparable battered ridges and flaked and flattened faces are found on similar subcuboid or spherically shaped pebbles of ordinary coarse chert of somewhat larger size; these are undoubtedly hammerstones. The combination of both flaked and flattened surfaces with battered ridges on a spheroid or rounded cuboid form appears so repeatedly that this must be accepted as an artifact type. Both the black "lodestones" and the similar coarse chert pieces are therefore viewed as percussion tools of some sort.

In addition to the heavy black stones there are three specimens of equally heavy dark brown stones. Their weight and color also imply iron content.

These various heavy stones, or fragments thereof, were found at different depths.

Heavy Chert Pieces Containing Iron

Depth (cm)	Operation and area	Description
Surface		Black stone fragment; clear striations and peck marks on very smooth, probably natural, pebble cortex face
Surface		Brown stone fragment; internal radial structure lines centered on surface depression, suggesting natural features of mineralized echinoid fossil or of a crystal or accretion; depression also possibly caused by hammering, polishing, or grinding
0-20	I,step	Black stone fragment
0-20	I,A	2 stone fragments (1 black, 1 brown)
0-20	I,ext.	7 black stone fragments (1 with striations and 1 with two opposed heavily battered faces)
0-20	I,F	Black stone fragment
20-30	I,step	Black stone fragment
20-30	I,A	Black stone fragment
20-30	I,G	Black stone fragment
20-30	I,A,B,F,ext.	Brown stone fragment
30-40	I,G	Black stone fragment
0-25	V	Black stone fragment

CHIPPED STONE

Sheen-bearing Flint Pieces

This class is neither large nor uniform, but all examples found happen to be pieces of flint from operations I and V along the broad eastern scarp zone. A greasy, silicalike sheen is clearly visible on these pieces in varying degrees of intensity, clarity of definition, extent of invasion from the edge, and distribution along the edge. Fully three quarters bear the sheen on one edge only, and the rest, including the single most symmetric and technically most skillfully made blade, bear it along both edges. Nearly half the pieces have sheen on both faces of the edge; the other half show it on only one face. One small fragment of a flake bears sheen not along an edge but over one entire very flat surface. The sheen in all cases withstands hydrochloric acid, water, and rubbing and seems to have developed, by whatever means, on the flint after its detachment from a core.

This category is made up of 24 specimens (12 fragmentary). Included are 18 well-struck, shapely blades, of which 6 are delicate and microlithic. Of the 6 flakes in the group, one is broad and large. Two of the above-mentioned pieces, one a fragmentary blade and the other a fragmentary flake, are actually poorly shaped small, irregular, thick-sectioned core fragments. The edges of all these pieces bear signs of notching, nibbling, nicking, flaking, and other scarring edge wear as well as the sheen. The sheen in most cases precedes, but in some cases follows, the various sorts of edge wear. The varied character of the edge flaking and the different locations of the sheen-bearing zones suggest that these pieces were multiple-use tools—tools of convenience or opportunity used for a number of different purposes rather than for one or two stereotyped functions. Of the 24 pieces, 14 are from lots that may include surface material redeposited either by slope wash from elsewhere in the site or by plowing, or else may be of true surface origin from a later date; whereas 10 are from lots from depths of 20-80 cm and thus well down in the site's deposit (see distribution by depths in tabulation below). It is to be noted also that no feature of any of these sheen-bearing pieces appears to predominate among surface and near-surface examples compared with those from deeper levels; the various characteristic features of the category are the same throughout all levels, and there is no evidence within this group for any technotypological subdivision by level or location that could provide a basis for cultural or chronological differentiation.

On present evidence, therefore, one might argue on the one hand that although somewhat less than half were found singly at deeper levels, the specimens in this category may once have been as numerous on the surface as lower down and so somewhat liable to the suspicion of being from a later time, at least in part. On the other hand, there is no gainsaying that the 24 sheen-bearing pieces found make up a larger group than any of the scarce and obviously intrusive categories such as obsidian, pottery, glass, and metal. Certainly most of the pieces did occur well within the occupation deposits.

It is generally assumed, and in part demonstrated, that sheen appears when stone has been used for manipulating vegetal matter. The presence in the site's assemblage of several kinds of milling stones, though limited in number, also points toward plant manipulation. Taken together, these facts strengthen acceptance of sheen-marked pieces as integral parts of the horizon's material culture. However, the pieces are at best a very tentative and incipient feature of the artifactual assemblage since they are indeed rare at the site. The sheen is mostly very limited and variable in both distribution and intensity, and the unstandardized morphology of the tools themselves suggests as well that their functions are not yet uniform. Thus, the category of artifacts with silicalike edge sheen may for the present be considered a very minor and undeveloped part of the stone industry of the Karim Shahir occupation site.

Below is a summary of quantities and distribution of pieces with edge sheen, followed by a more detailed breakdown according to shape and condition of edge.

Sheen-bearing Flint Pieces

Depth (cm)	Operation and area							Total
	I							
	Step	A	C	Ext.	G	Tr.	V	
0-20	3	--	--	8	--	2	--	13
0-25	--	--	--	--	--	--	1	1
20-30	--	1	2	--	--	--	--	3
20-40	2	--	--	--	--	--	--	2
30-40	--	--	--	--	1	--	--	1
40-50	--	--	1	--	--	--	--	1
40-80	3	--	--	--	--	--	--	3
Total	8	1	3	8	1	2	1	24

Depth (cm)	Operation and area	Description
Broad Irregular Flakes or Fragments		
0-20	I,step	Wide flake; narrow band of sheen along both faces of one half of one edge; edge worn
0-20	I,step	Fragment of wide flake; narrow band of sheen along both faces of one edge; nicked wear on edge
0-20	I,ext.	Small fragment; sheen covering one whole face
0-20	I,tr.	Flake; sheen on one face along one edge
20-30	I,C	Flake; sheen on one face along one edge
20-40	I,step	Fragment of core?; thick, angular, elongated; narrow zone of sheen along flake-scar face adjoining cortex face at right angles
Broad Blade Fragments		
0-20	I,ext.	3 blade portions, nicked and worn along both edges: 1 specimen with narrow band of sheen along both faces of one edge; 1 specimen with faint narrow zone of sheen along both faces of one edge; 1 specimen with distinct broader band of sheen 15 mm long in center of one edge, and limited traces in center of opposite face also
0-20	I,tr.	Blade portion; nicking on both edges, narrow band of sheen 10 mm long on nonbulbar face near center; opposite face hidden by crust
20-40	I,step	Blade portion; one edge with very faint narrow zone of sheen on bulbar face and limited continuous small squamous wear on nonbulbar face; opposite edge with even more limited wear and some discontinuous nicking on both faces
40-80	I,step	Blade portion; nicking and narrow band of faint sheen on both faces all along one edge; irregular nicking but no sheen along opposite edge
Notched Pieces		
30-40	I,G	Broad blade fragment (W. 20 mm); at one edge, faint narrow band of sheen on plain bulbar face; at same edge, steep squamous notching in incipient notches and some edge rounding on opposite face
40-50	I,C	Evenly shaped narrow blade; intermittent sheen remnants along both edges of bulbar face; also notching
Nicked and/or Worn Narrow Blades		
0-20	I,step	Nearly complete blade; finely made; scars parallel to long edges; edge nicking; narrow band of sheen on both faces along both edges

Sheen-bearing Flint Pieces—*Continued*

Depth (cm)	Operation and area	Description
0-20	I,ext.	Core-revival blade; nicking mainly on one edge; sheen in faint broad zone on nonbulbar face of this edge only
0-20	I,ext.	3 blade fragments, each with distinct trace of sheen along one edge on one face
0-25	V	Blade fragment; some nicking along one edge, with possible faint traces of sheen on nonbulbar face; heavier nicking (almost like notching) along other edge, with distinct narrow zone of sheen along ¾ of its nonbulbar face and possible faint traces of sheen on opposite face
20-30	I,A	Blade fragment; faint trace of sheen along one edge on one face
20-30	I,C	Midsection blade fragment; wear, nicking, and limited faint sheen down both long edges of nonbulbar face; rounded-off scars and limited sheen on bulbar face on one edge
40-80	I,step	2 blade fragments; each with nicking on both edges; each with narrow zone of sheen on both faces at one edge (distinct on one, faint on other)

Denticulated Blades and Flakes

There are very few denticulated pieces of the type frequently called *serrated blade* or *saw*. This category is firmly reserved for those pieces that display a more or less regular denticulated edge—a series of roughly equal-sized tooth-and-hollow serrations—achieved by a uniform repetitive method of flaking. Specimens that have any of the more irregular serrations of an uneven size and shape have been placed in the already large categories of notched blades and flakes. In actual fact, the types of serrated edges can be thought of as forming a continuum, with the denticulated category merging into the notched category.

These denticulated pieces are mostly blades, though a few flakes were found. The edge or part of an edge bears three or more evenly spaced, close-set, deeply gouged notches in series. These notches are often in the form of a single flake scar. The entire denticulated edge was in several cases subsequently subjected to wear which is manifested by small-scale nicking and battering in and between the hollows. There is no sheen on these pieces. The other edges often have notches or other flaking, too. There is the possibility that the entire form is the result of use and wear and was not deliberately prepared in any way; the serration is really very rudimentary and indistinct and not at all like what is seen in the sophisticated type of serrated tool associated with later neolithic assemblages, where longer zones of more clear-cut and uniform denticulation have been made by more standardized edge-flaking techniques. Of the total of 15 specimens, 6 came from the surface or the 0-20 cm level (fig. 14:1). The rest came from lower levels, presumably fairly well sealed off from surface mixture, though it is possible, in view of the slumping of deposits at the brink of the scarp, that the single specimen from a depth of 40-80 cm in the step (fig. 14:2) might once have lain nearer the surface.

Denticulated Blades and Flakes

Depth (cm)	Surface	Operation and area				III	Total
		I					
		Step	C	Ext.	G		
Surface	1*						1
0-20		--	--	5(1*,2†)	--	--	5
20-30		--	--	--	1	--	1
40-50		--	3(1*)	--	2	--	5
40-60		--	--	--	--	1	1
40-80		1	--	--	--	--	1
80-90		--	1	--	--	--	1
Total	1	1	4	5	3	1	15

*Flake.
†Microblade.

Backed Blades

Normal-sized.—Normal-sized backed blades do not constitute a large or standardized category of any importance. In this assemblage, blades over 10 mm wide are generally taken as normal sized, with one or two exceptions that are only slightly narrower. The 9 specimens in this category are partially backed blades or fragments too wide to be considered with the larger and more distinct category of microlithic backed bladelets, in which the specimens are markedly narrower.

The backing on these typologically unoutstanding and unstandardized specimens is not a true one made by concentrated stepped and squamous retouch from one or both faces along most of an edge to form a blunted back. Rather, it is steep squamous or stepped retouch on one edge and face and has usually been applied for a short distance only. The work has resulted in a truly blunted zone but one that is limited in extent. No other feature predominates; the traces of wear scattered elsewhere along the edges of specimens vary in position (tip, side, and base) and in type (from barely visible nibbling to deeper nicks, flaking, or heavy battering). Such nonuniformity implies variety in function.

Backed Blades, Normal-sized

Depth (cm)	Operation and area				
	I,step	I,C	I,ext.	I,G	Total
0-20	4	--	1	--	5
20-30	--	2	--	--	2
30-40	--	--	--	1	1
80-100	1	--	--	--	1
Total	5	2	1	1	9

Microlithic.—Microlithic backed bladelets make up a sizeable and well-defined group. Almost all are fragments (fig. 14:3-10). Only 4 complete specimens were found among the 415 examples, and their size suggests that the normal length for the category may be ca. 35-40 mm (fig. 14:3). They rarely exceed 5 mm in width. Each piece is characterized by fine, precise backing along one edge that has produced a sharp-angled blunt back whose surface lies nearly at right angles to the obverse (flaking) and reverse (bulbar) surface. Normally, this backing is formed by flaking mainly from the bulbar face. Furthermore, in about half of the bulbar end pieces found, the bulbar end has been left unbacked and forms a bulging unworked zone that probably represents nearly the original width of the bladelet (fig. 14:7); the rest have retouch that continues in a curve around the bulbar base.

On two thirds of the tip-end pieces found, the tip end bears a carefully worked rectilinear truncation. About two thirds of these truncations are diagonal, forming an obtuse angle with the line of the back portion (fig. 14:3,8-9); the remainder are nearly at right angles to the long axis (fig. 14:10). Backing continues onto this truncated zone where thickness has permitted it. The remaining third of tip-end pieces, involving a thin flint mass, have been left in a natural state without shaping and as a result have an elongated, tapering point.

Roughly 45% of the total number of specimens in this category bear delicate nibbled wear along one or both faces of the edge opposite the backed edge, and most of the remainder bear some other signs of wear there, with only a very few appearing unworn. About two fifths of all these nibbled and otherwise worn pieces have this wear on the reverse (bulbar) face and not on the obverse. Sometimes the wear on the truncated tip-end pieces is localized near the point.

Backed Bladelets, Microlithic

Depth (cm)	Surface	Operation and area														Total
		I														
		Step	A	B	C	Ext.	F	G	Tr.	II	III	IV	V	VI	VIII	
Surface	9															9
0-20		8(1*)	3	14	7	149	5	1	5(1*)	1	15	--	19	2	8	237
20-30		--	8	3	26	--	6	13	--	--	--	--	5	--	--	61
20-40		6	--	--	--	--	--	--	--	--	--	1	--	--	--	7
30-40		--	--	--	28	--	--	16	--	--	--	--	--	--	--	44
40-50		--	--	--	2	--	--	21	--	--	--	--	--	--	--	23
40-60		12(1*)	--	--	--	--	--	--	--	--	--	--	--	--	--	12
60-80		--	--	--	--	--	--	--	--	--	--	5	1	--	--	6
80+		10(1*)	--	--	--	--	--	--	--	--	6	--	--	--	--	16
Total	9	36	11	17	63	149	11	51	5	1	26	2	24	2	8	415

*Complete specimen.

Fabricators

Thick blades or fragments thereof, steeply retouched or battered along one or both of the long edges to a blunt, usually worn (and, more rarely, somewhat polished) point, make up this limited class. One specimen has this kind of retouch along alternate opposite faces; the rest have it entirely on the obverse (nonbulbar) face. The result is a sturdy artifact with a thickly planoconvex or polyhedral cross section (fig. 14:22-24). One or two of these tools are on rather broader blades than the others but have been left in the category due to their steep and bilateral retouch and characteristically polyhedral cross section.

The general term *fabricator*, long sanctioned by common usage, has been given to these tools for lack of a better term or any knowledge or reasonable hypothesis concerning the uses to which they may have been put. Their functions might have included drilling or flaking (in the case of battered pieces with steep, close-set scars), rubbing or burnishing (the polished pieces), or some other kind of piercing, friction, or percussion. Based on dimensions alone, without regard to function, artifacts of this class could be viewed as the largest in size of a more extended series which also includes normal-sized so-called drills on blades or bladelike flakes, as well as the microlithic and supermicrolithic drills on bladelets, described in the next sections. The fabricators are different from the drills, however, in that they have thicker, steeper cross sections and extensive edge retouch or wear set steeply or at low angles on either or both faces and long edges, which results in a larger and more bluntly pointed working end.

Complete specimens or tip ends of fabricators are rare among the material recovered; the majority of the 46 examples found were base or mid-trunk fragments. Length of the three complete specimens ranges from 65 mm to 90 mm.

Fabricators

Depth (cm)	Surface	Operation and area								
		I								
		Step	B	C	Ext.	F	G	V	VI	Total
Surface	11(2*)									11
0-20		3	1	--	4	--	1	--	1	10
20-30		--	4	7	--	4	2	1	--	18
30-40		--	--	1	--	--	2	--	--	3
40-50		--	--	2(1*)	--	--	1	--	--	3
60-80		1	--	--	--	--	--	--	--	1
Total	11	4	5	10	4	4	6	1	1	46

*Complete specimens.

Drills

Normal-sized.—This group is labeled *drills* on the supposition that tools of this form and size might quite logically have been applied to piercing, boring, and drilling operations. It comprises blades (and one flake) usually with steep retouch on both long edges converging to a comparatively sturdy little point (fig. 15:1-5). The retouch may in a few cases extend along most of each edge, but more commonly, especially on the broader pieces, it is confined to the region around the point and the larger remainder of the blade edges is left unworked. Retouch may be on either or both faces but is usually on the obverse (nonbulbar) face. In a few cases the retouch verges on the regular flat, squamous, almost pressure-flaking, variety, and may be found on the bulbar face at either the point or bulbar end. In some cases the broader pieces were given a pointed end by flanking a projection with notches and perhaps using the resulting formation as a drill-like point (fig. 15:5). In other cases a natural point seems to have been used directly, with no refining touches. Points may be blunt or sharp, depending upon the amount of wear or retouch there. Based on the 20 complete specimens from the total of 40 examples found, the normal drills appear to range in length from ca. 25 mm to ca. 65-70 mm. They are made on pieces 10 mm or more in width, with extensive or localized tip-end retouch.

Although achieved with a minimum of flaking, which is usually confined to the region of the working drill point, this normal-sized drill category may, by virtue of the drill-like point and the occasional instances of full steep retouching along most of the long edges, be viewed as part of the aforementioned continuum formed by tools that range from the larger fabricators to the smallest of the so-called supermicrolithic drills.

Microlithic.—This category of drill and the following supermicrolithic category are distinguished from the foregoing "normal-sized" category because all microlithic bladelet artifacts have been arbitrarily defined as those made on pieces less than 10 mm wide, and because the long parallel edges of tools in both the microlithic categories are

Normal-sized Drills

Depth (cm)	Surface	Operation and area										Total
		I										
		Step	A	B	C	Ext.	F	G	Tr.	III	V	
Surface	2*											2
0-20		4(2*)	2(1*)	3	2(1*)	3(1*)	3(1*)	1	1	1	1	21
20-30		--	2*	--	3(2*)	--	1*	3*	--	--	--	9
30-40		--	--	--	2*	--	--	--	--	--	--	2
40-50		--	--	--	1*	--	--	3	--	--	--	4
40-60		1*	--	--	--	--	--	--	--	--	--	1
80+		1	--	--	--	--	--	--	--	--	--	1
Total	2	6	4	3	8	3	4	7	1	1	1	40

*Complete specimens.

Microlithic Drills

Depth (cm)	Surface	Operation and area										Total
		I										
		Step	A	B	C	Ext.	F	G	III	IV	V	
Surface	1											1
0-20		1	--	1	1	15(3*)	2	--	8	--	--	28
20-30		--	2*	5(1*)	1*	--	--	5(1*)	--	--	2	15
20-40		2	--	--	--	--	--	--	--	1	--	3
30-40		--	--	--	3(1*)	--	--	3	--	--	--	6
40-50		--	--	--	--	--	--	3	--	--	--	3
40-60		1*	--	--	--	--	--	--	--	--	--	1
60-80		--	--	--	--	--	--	--	1	1	--	2
80+		1*	--	--	--	--	--	--	2	1	--	4
Total	1	5	2	6	5	15	2	11 6	11	3	2	63

*Complete specimens.

Supermicrolithic Drills

Depth (cm)	Operation and area							Total
	I,step	I,A	I,B	I,C	I,ext.	I,F	I,G	
0-20	2	1	1	--	12(2*)	--	--	16
20-30	--	--	--	--	--	2(1*)	3	5
20-40	2*	--	--	--	--	--	--	2
30-40	--	--	--	4(1*)	--	--	--	4
40-50	--	--	--	1	--	--	2(1*)	3
40-60	1*	--	--	--	--	--	--	1
Total	5	1	1	5	12	2	5	31

*Complete specimens.

steeply retouched for nearly their entire length, unlike most normal-sized drills whose edges have been left unworked or only partly worked.

The microlithic category is a very clear-cut and standardized one. On the typical specimen, all of both long edges and the point are thoroughly and steeply retouched. Of the 63 examples found, roughly one sixth are complete and suggest a length range of ca. 40-70 mm for the type. The class may, in a sense, be considered part of the microlithic sector of the size continuum comprising fabricators and so-called drills. Each microlithic specimen is made on a bladelet (one example from the surface is on a core revival, or crested, bladelet) and is considerably less than 1 cm in width. Although in 7 instances the retouch tends to be confined to the relatively thinner-bodied tip end where the flaking is apt to be more flat and shallow, it usually extends along much or all of the long dimension and is usually very steep, making parallel-sided, long, narrow tools with thick cross sections (fig. 15:6-7). In these respects these pieces resemble the even smaller supermicrolithic drills dealt with in the next section. This extensive steep retouch, almost like backing, was perhaps done to give strength to these otherwise delicate, narrow forms of blade tool, reducing each to its minimum mass in a more sturdily proportioned shape. Even so, the large number of fragments in both of these microlithic drill categories seems to indicate a high breakage rate for these fragile implements. (See section on normal-sized drills for a comparison of characteristics.)

Supermicrolithic.—This is a special category of microlithic bladelets that are very steeply retouched or backed along both long edges to form parallel sides and a fine drill-like point. These artifacts are the smallest of the series of so-called drills found at Karim Shahir and are remarkable in that they are almost needlelike. One quarter of the 31 examples have been found whole, and these specimens range from 30 mm to 45 mm in length. As a rule the width does not exceed 5 mm, and often the thickness is similar to the width, resulting in a thick planoconvex cross section. The steep retouch is apt to be much more extensive than that found in the other drill categories (fig. 15:8-10).

Miscellaneous Microliths

The great majority of the diverse types of tools grouped in this catchall category are made on microlithic blades or fragments thereof; only a few are on microlithic flakes, core fragments, or pieces too small to class. Each of the different forms is classified separately as a subtype.

The principal subtype is called, for lack of a better term, an *end scraper*. Only rarely have tools of this subtype been produced by what appears to be retouching; more commonly they seem to have been formed simply by use at one end of a bladelet, or more often a fragment of one. In the majority of cases, the flaking results in implements with *rectilinear-ended* (fig. 14:11) or *concave-ended* (fig. 14:12) working zones. More rarely, they are *convex-ended* (fig. 14:13) or *diagonal-ended* (fig. 14:14) pieces. Of the 13 specimens flaked at both ends and classified as *double-ended* scrapers, 2 are shaped on roughly diagonal lines producing a very elongated and somewhat trapezoidal form (fig. 14:15).

Aside from those concave forms described above as either deliberately retouched or worn to a concave working front, many of the concave-ended scrapers and a good number of the rectilinear ones are marked by a special combination of wear across the end in the form of one major distinctly concave flakelet scar, in the center or to one side, accompanied by a contiguous zone of additional small-scale wear. It appears as if this wear was caused by a combination of occurrences: first, sudden pressure at one point (either deliberate or fortuitous), which snapped off the blade segment leaving the concave flakelet scar, and then additional flaking of this broken end by use near its outer edges.

Many of these end scrapers on microlithic blades bear notching, edge retouch, or various forms of small-scale edge wear along the long dimension in addition to the end flaking. They have been classified, however, according to the main zone of preparation or wear at the ends.

The next largest subtype of miscellaneous microliths, though much smaller than the group of end scrapers on microlithic blades, comprises finely retouched or worn *scrapers on flakelets* including a few tiny core fragments that have had notches or scraper edges worked or worn into them at any opportune point along the edge by means of either steep or flat squamous nibbled retouch or wear, or a combination of these (fig. 14:16).

A third subtype, *pointed bladelets*, is a small one and includes bladelets or bladelet ends brought to a blunt point by small-scale squamous or nibbled retouch on both edges (fig. 14:17). This work may be on either or both faces, and some examples have been treated in this manner at the bulbar end.

At Karim Shahir, geometric microliths as a true category are unconvincing typologically and so are considered to be absent from the site. Nevertheless, for a complete accounting in the tabulation below, it has been necessary to include a separate subtype under the heading of *chance geometric microliths*. Only 4 isolated fragmentary examples—all doubtful as representatives of the geometrics category—were found. There are 2 doubtful lunates or imperfect scalene triangles as well as 1 possible triangle, all of which may be fragments of misshapen or incomplete backed bladelets (fig. 14:18-20). There is also a single small, angular flake, steeply retouched along two opposite diverging long edges, that has been classed as a doubtful trapezoid (fig. 14:21). It is quite obvious that these 4 examples are unique occurrences and that it is forcing the typological categories to put them into a separate group here.

Miscellaneous Microliths

Depth (cm)	Surface	Operation and area											Total
		I											
		Step	A	B	C	Ext.	F	G	Tr.	III	V	VI	
END SCRAPERS													
Rectilinear-ended													
Surface	29												29
0-20		--	1	8	3	41	5	--	3	10	--	--	71
20-30		--	8	3	19	--	5	12	--	--	3	--	50
20-40		4	--	--	--	--	--	--	--	--	--	--	4
30-40		--	--	--	4	--	--	1	--	--	--	--	5
40-60		--	--	--	2	--	--	8	--	--	--	--	10
60-80		--	--	--	--	--	--	--	--	--	--	--	0
80+		4	--	--	--	--	--	--	--	--	--	--	4
Total	29	8	9	11	28	41	10	21	3	10	3	0	173
Concave-ended													
Surface	3												3
0-20		1	1	3	2	24	3	--	--	--	--	--	34
20-30		--	1	--	3	--	--	--	--	--	--	--	4
20-40		3	--	--	--	--	--	--	--	--	--	--	3
30-40		--	--	--	--	--	--	--	--	--	--	--	0
40-60		--	--	--	--	--	--	--	--	--	--	--	0
60-80		--	--	--	--	--	--	--	--	--	--	--	0
80+		2	--	--	--	--	--	--	--	--	--	--	2
Total	3	6	2	3	5	24	3	0	0	0	0	0	46
Convex-ended													
Surface	6												6
0-20		1	1	1	--	5	--	--	--	--	--	--	8
20-30		--	--	--	1	--	1	1	--	--	--	--	3
20-40		--	--	--	--	--	--	--	--	--	--	--	0
30-40		--	--	--	1	--	--	--	--	--	--	--	1
40-60		--	--	--	--	--	--	--	--	--	--	--	0
60-80		--	--	--	--	--	--	--	--	--	--	--	0
80+		--	--	--	--	--	--	--	--	--	--	--	0
Total	6	1	1	1	2	5	1	1	0	0	0	0	18
Diagonal-ended													
Surface	5												5
0-20		1	2	--	2	14	--	1	--	4	1	--	25
20-30		--	--	2	5	--	2	1	--	--	4	--	14
20-40		--	--	--	--	--	--	--	--	--	--	--	0
30-40		--	--	--	2	--	--	--	--	--	--	--	2
40-60		--	--	--	--	--	--	--	--	--	--	--	0
60-80		--	--	--	--	--	--	--	--	--	--	--	0
80+		2	--	--	--	--	--	1	--	--	--	--	3
Total	5	3	2	2	9	14	2	3	0	4	5	0	49

Miscellaneous Microliths—*Continued*

Depth (cm)	Surface	Operation and area I Step	A	B	C	Ext.	F	G	Tr.	III	V	VI	Total
Double-ended													
Surface	3												3
0-20		--	1	2	--	1	1	--	--	--	--	--	5
20-30		--	--	1	2	--	--	1	--	--	--	--	4
20-40		1	--	--	--	--	--	--	--	--	--	--	1
30-40		--	--	--	--	--	--	--	--	--	--	--	0
40-60		--	--	--	--	--	--	--	--	--	--	--	0
60-80		--	--	--	--	--	--	--	--	--	--	--	0
80+		--	--	--	--	--	--	--	--	--	--	--	0
Total	3	1	1	3	2	1	1	1	0	0	0	0	13
SCRAPERS ON FLAKELETS													
Surface	--												0
0-20		--	3	2	1	9	1	--	--	--	--	--	16
20-30		--	--	--	--	--	--	--	--	--	--	--	0
20-40		--	--	--	--	--	--	--	--	--	--	--	0
30-40		--	--	--	--	--	--	2	--	--	--	--	2
40-60		--	--	--	1	--	--	2	--	--	--	--	3
60-80		--	--	--	--	--	--	--	--	--	--	--	0
80+		--	--	--	--	--	--	--	--	--	--	--	0
Total	0	0	3	2	2	9	1	4	0	0	0	0	21
POINTED BLADELETS													
Surface	--												0
0-20		--	--	--	--	1	1	--	1	1	3	1	8
20-30		--	--	--	2	--	--	--	--	--	--	--	2
20-40		--	--	--	--	--	--	--	--	--	--	--	0
30-40		--	--	--	5	--	--	3	--	--	--	--	8
40-60		--	--	--	4	--	--	2	--	--	--	--	6
60-80		1	--	--	--	--	--	--	--	--	--	--	1
80+		2	--	--	--	--	--	--	--	--	--	--	2
Total	0	3	0	0	11	1	1	5	1	1	3	1	27
CHANCE GEOMETRIC MICROLITHS													
Surface	--												0
0-20		--	1*	--	--	--	--	--	--	--	--	--	1
20-30		--	--	--	--	--	--	1†	--	--	1‡	--	2
20-40		--	--	--	--	--	--	--	--	--	--	--	0
30-40		--	--	--	--	--	--	--	--	--	--	--	0
40-60		--	--	--	--	--	--	--	--	--	--	--	0
60-80		--	--	--	1*	--	--	--	--	--	--	--	1
80+		--	--	--	--	--	--	--	--	--	--	--	0
Total	0	0	1	0	1	0	0	1	0	0	1	0	4

*Lunate?, scalene?
†Trapezoid?
‡Triangle?

Totals—Miscellaneous Microliths

Depth (cm)	End scrapers					Scrapers on flakelets	Pointed bladelets	Chance geometric microliths	Total
	Rectilinear-ended	Concave-ended	Convex-ended	Diagonal-ended	Double-ended				
Surface	29	3	6	5	3	--	--	--	46
0-20	71	34	8	25	5	16	8	1	168
20-30	50	4	3	14	4	--	2	2	79
20-40	4	3	--	--	1	--	--	--	8
30-40	5	--	1	2	--	2	8	--	18
40-60	10	--	--	--	--	3	6	--	19
60-80	--	--	--	--	--	--	1	1	2
80+	4	2	--	3	--	--	2	--	11
Total	173	46	18	49	13	21	27	4	351

Unworked Triangular or Trapezoidal Segments of Blades

In a generous but circumscribed sampling taken only from operation I, a number of small triangular or trapezoidal segments of blades or flakes were found that may represent, in descending order of likelihood, an

Unworked Triangular or Trapezoidal Segments of Blades

Depth (cm)	Operation and area								Total
	I,step	I,A	I,B	I,C	I,ext.	I,F	I,G	I,tr.	
Triangles									
0-20	--	3	1	4	34	4	1	--	47
20-30	--	1	1	4	--	4	2	--	12
20-40	--	--	--	--	--	--	--	--	0
30-40	--	--	--	7	--	--	--	--	7
40-60	3	--	--	--	--	--	--	--	3
80+	1	--	--	--	--	--	--	--	1
Total	4	4	2	15	34	8	3	0	70
Trapezoids									
0-20	2	--	3	3	19	3	--	2	32
20-30	--	1	1	1	--	2	2	--	7
20-40	3	--	--	--	--	--	--	--	3
30-40	--	--	--	--	--	--	2	--	2
40-60	1	--	--	--	--	--	--	--	1
80+	5	--	--	--	--	--	--	--	5
Total	11	1	4	4	19	5	4	2	50

Totals—Unworked Triangular or Trapezoidal Segments of Blades

Depth (cm)	Triangles	Trapezoids	Total
0-20	47	32	79
20-30	12	7	19
20-40	--	3	3
30-40	7	2	9
40-60	3	1	4
80+	1	5	6
Total	70	50	120

accidental or artificially imposed grouping, a by-product, or possibly even a type of implement in itself making up a distinctive class. The commoner form is a V-shaped wedge normally obtained by snapping off a piece across the width of a blade or narrow flake at an angle diagonal to each side, making a triangle whose two opposing long sides are simply diagonal fracture planes across the parent blade and whose base is part of one of the original edges of the parent piece. This base edge bears most of whatever retouch or wear there is on any one piece, such work ranging from notches to nibbled retouch to slight wear or battering from usage. This edge flaking may simply survive from the earlier full-blade stage of the evolution of the tool, or else it may have been added, entirely or in part, after the piece became the wedgelike segment. The converging fracture planes usually lack any signs of wear, although a few have edge wear, batter, or, rarely, even what appears to be slight retouch. By and large, however, the pieces remain unworked.

The form quite often differs from the normal triangular shape: when the surviving original edge of the parent piece is angular, or when the truncation scars are irregular or multiple (due perhaps to fracturing difficulties), or when the two diagonal truncation scars fail to converge, resulting in a trapezoid whose short edge is part of the original edge of the parent piece. Occasionally, there is only one truncation scar and much of the edge of the original end of the parent piece remains.

This category may well not be a deliberate product or by-product, but the frequent occurrence of its standard forms in the assemblage at many levels warrants recording it.

Microburins

Tools that are definitely microburins occur at Karim Shahir (fig. 15:11-13). Most of them are from the butt end of a blade or flake and thus have retained the bulb of percussion of the parent piece. Three pieces are from the tip end. Of the total of 30 pieces, 12 specimens clearly have the characteristic distinctly worked notch and diagonal truncation at this notch. In these cases the diagonal fracture plane has a fairly good, sometimes very clear-cut negative bulb of percussion—the characteristic conchoidal stigma and teardrop-shaped scar of the microburin blow. The remaining 18 specimens are of a poorer grade and do not display very convincing evidence of these classic features of microburins, yet overall they are distinctive enough as artifacts to be classified as examples of the category.

Microburins have been called the by-product of geometric microlith manufacture or, sometimes, the by-product of any manufacture involving the division of blades. As already noted, however, clear-cut geometric microliths are absent at Karim Shahir, and the only types found that might fit a divided blade category are (1) the diagonally or obliquely truncated blades, (2) the microlithic backed blades with straight or diagonal retouch across an end, and perhaps (3) some of the so-called end scrapers on microlithic blades.

Microburins

Depth (cm)	Operation and area							
	I							
	Step	C	Ext.	F	G	Tr.	V	Total
0-20	--	1	12	--	--	1	2	16
20-30	--	1	--	1	--	--	--	2
40-50	--	--	--	--	2	--	--	2
40-80	3	--	--	--	--	--	--	3
50-60	--	2	--	--	1	--	--	3
60-80	--	1	--	--	1	--	--	2
80+	2	--	--	--	--	--	--	2
Total	5	5	12	1	4	1	2	30

Burins

As a class, burins are definitely present at Karim Shahir, but they usually are not well made and rarely demonstrate a classic clarity of form. They are made on blades, blade fragments, flakes, and other pieces. Most of the 80 examples recorded are of normal size, and only 17 qualify as microlithic types because of the small size of the pieces used. There are 16 angle burins, that is, burins with the burin blow cutting at right angles across a worked edge (fig. 15:14-17), and 62 simple burins, those worked on the angles of broken blades and flakes (fig. 15:18-20). These two types are the common forms at Karim Shahir. Of the simple burins, 15 are miniature. Only 2 angle burins could be classed as microlithic (Noailles burins) and these are of poor quality (fig. 15:16-17).

Some of the specimens bear burin facets which encroach upon one or the other flat face of the parent piece, thus constituting a sort of flat or canted burin or "burin face plan" (fig. 15:15,20). This placement, however, is so rare at

Karim Shahir (11 cases) that it may be the result of accident rather than design. Several burins have multiple scars situated at one angle or else scars at several angles or at opposed angles (fig. 15:17-19). The burin scars on some pieces occur in combination with distinct and extensive notching or other retouch on the edges, including end scraper zones. Included in the series are 2 doubtful cases (chance burins), which have a long, narrow, flat-surfaced scar fortuitously resembling a burin scar but lacking the characteristic conchoidal fracture with concave surface.

Burins

Depth (cm)	Surface	Operation and area									Total
		I									
		Step	A	B	C	Ext.	F	G	V	VIII	
Angle Burins											
Surface	5										5
0-20		1	--	--	--	6	1	--	--	--	8
20-30		--	1	--	--	--	1	--	--	--	2
30-40		1	--	--	--	--	--	--	--	--	1
Total	5	2	1	0	0	6	2	0	0	0	16
Microlithic Angle Burins (Noailles)											
0-20		--	--	--	--	1	1	--	--	--	2
Total	0	0	0	0	0	1	1	0	0	0	2
Simple Burins											
Surface	6										6
0-20		1	--	--	1	5(1*)	--	1	2	2	12
20-30		--	--	6	12	--	6	3	--	--	27
30-40		--	--	--	4	--	--	1	--	--	5
40-50		--	--	--	2	--	--	3	--	--	5
50-60		--	--	--	3	--	--	--	--	--	3
60-80		--	--	--	1	--	--	2	--	--	3
Ochre pit		1*	--	--	--	--	--	--	--	--	1
Total	6	2	0	6	23	5	6	10	2	2	62

*Chance burin.

Totals—Burins

Depth (cm)	Angle burins	Microlithic angle burins (Noailles)	Simple burins	Total
Surface	5	--	6	11
0-20	8	2	12	22
20-30	2	--	27	29
30-40	1	--	5	6
40-50	--	--	5	5
50-60	--	--	3	3
60-80	--	--	3	3
Ochre pit	--	--	1	1
Total	16	2	62	80

Burin Spalls

A number of burin spalls were found, which tends to confirm the existence of burins at the site. The typically triangular or quadrilateral cross section and long, often twisted, bladeletlike form of the spalls indicate that they are by-products of burin making, having been struck off the edges of the parent piece. Some examples have a worn or retouched edge that is considered to have been an edge of the parent piece. Some opinion holds that this type of spall might even have been a tool in itself. Both large and small ones were found, the great majority being long, narrow bladelets and the rest more flakelike.

Burin Spalls

Depth (cm)	Operation and area								
	I								
	Step	A	B	C	Ext.	F	G	III	Total
0-20	1	1	--	--	14	--	--	2	18
20-30	--	1	3	11	--	5	8	--	28
30-40	--	--	--	5	--	--	3	--	8
40-50	--	--	--	1	--	--	2	--	3
50-60	--	--	--	--	--	--	2	--	2
80-180	--	--	--	--	--	--	1	--	1
Total	1	2	3	17	14	5	16	2	60

End Scrapers

End scrapers on blades.—This is a sizeable and rather banal category. Relatively few pieces are formed by unmistakable deliberate retouch or have the classic convex scraper front and neat shape. Most are formed by wear of varying type and degree (nearly half show only slight to moderate wear) on the ends of blades or bladelike flakes or often across the truncated ends of broken blades, including even the stubbiest end remnants. The edge flaking on the end ranges from slight and small-scale to heavy, concentrated, stepped, or squamous invasive scars. This variety suggests that there was a multiplicity of uses for the individual pieces and, possibly, a number of different activities to which the group as a whole may have been applied.

Many of these scraper edges are rectilinear or very slightly convex or concave or a combined form adhering simply to the line of the original break of the piece (fig. 16:1-3). A small number are distinctly concave, usually as a result of apparently intensive and concentrated wear focused at one working zone (fig. 16:4). Another small number are truly convex, often irregularly shaped and poorly flaked. They give the impression that this convexity, too, has not been deliberate but is derived from the original edge form. Many pieces are obviously multiple-use tools displaying a combination of wear or retouch at the scraper end, with the same sort of treatment, including notching, along one or both long edges; and frequently the evidence on these long edges is more developed and distinct than that found across the end.

Nearly one fourth of the examples are not flaked entirely across the end but only over a portion at one angle or side of the end (fig. 16:3,5). Such partial flaking, due perhaps to use only, produces either a rectilinear or concave front, rarely a convex one, and suggests intensive use at that one point. About one ninth of the entire category is composed of examples worked at the two opposite ends in any combination of all these types of retouch or wear (fig. 16:6-7).

There is also a type of break not treated separately here but mentioned in connection with this end-scraper-on-blade category. This type of break, noted frequently at Karim Shahir, produces a rectilinear potential working end or edge and is manifested by a fan-shaped series of related scars centering near the middle of the face of the broken end along the edge of the bulbar face, as if a single sharp blow or some degree of pressure had been intentionally applied on the bulbar face in order to break or snap off the blade at this point. Whether or not accidental, this little characteristic is of interest as a possible indication of a method or stage of production for this end-scraper category and for other categories of fragmentary blade tools. (See also the discussions of miscellaneous microliths and of unworked triangular or trapezoidal segments of blades.)

On the whole, the end-scraper-on-blade category includes pieces with a considerable technotypological range of working end; both form and edge flaking can vary greatly. We are here probably dealing with a catchall grouping of tools whose multipurpose functions are only dimly sensed. (In this connection, one should also consider the data on two possibly related categories—the end scrapers on flakes and the blades with obliquely retouched ends.)

End Scrapers on Blades

Depth (cm)	Surface	Operation and area														Total
		I														
		Step	A	B	C	Ext.	F	G	Tr.	II	III	IV	V	VI	VIII	

Partial or Slight Retouch or Wear at One End
Surface	100															100
0-20		1	2	1	8	19	2	2	1	1	18	4	--	1	1	61
20-30		--	1	5	2	--	3	3	--	--	--	--	--	--	--	14
20-40		4	--	--	--	--	--	--	--	--	5	--	--	--	--	9
30-40		--	--	--	9	--	--	11	--	--	--	--	--	--	--	20
40-50		--	--	--	4	--	--	8	--	--	--	--	--	--	--	12
50-180		2	--	--	4	--	--	5	--	--	--	--	--	--	--	11
Ochre pit		--	--	--	--	--	--	--	--	--	--	--	--	--	--	0
Total	100	7	3	6	27	19	5	29	1	1	23	4	0	1	1	227

Distinct Retouch or Wear at One End
Surface	11															11
0-20		6	5	4	8	35	9	2	3	3	19	4	1	1	2	102
20-30		--	7	7	27	--	6	7	--	--	--	--	--	--	--	54
20-40		5	--	--	--	--	--	--	--	--	6	--	--	--	--	11
30-40		--	--	--	2	--	--	3	--	--	--	--	--	--	--	5
40-50		--	--	--	2	--	--	--	--	--	--	--	--	--	--	2
50-180		6	--	--	8	--	--	6	--	--	--	--	--	--	--	20
Ochre pit		1	--	--	--	--	--	--	--	--	--	--	--	--	--	1
Total	11	18	12	11	47	35	15	18	3	3	25	4	1	1	2	206

Concave Retouch or Wear at One End
Surface	4															4
0-20		--	--	1	--	5	--	1	--	--	4	--	--	--	--	11
20-30		--	1	2	8	--	3	3	--	--	--	--	--	--	--	17
20-40		2	--	--	--	--	--	--	--	--	--	--	--	--	--	2
30-40		--	--	--	--	--	--	--	--	--	--	--	--	--	--	0
40-50		--	--	--	1	--	--	2	--	--	--	--	--	--	--	3
50-180		--	--	--	--	--	--	--	--	--	--	--	--	--	--	0
Ochre pit		--	--	--	--	--	--	--	--	--	--	--	--	--	--	0
Total	4	2	1	3	9	5	3	6	0	0	4	0	0	0	0	37

Retouch or Wear at Both Ends
Surface	9															9
0-20		1	1	1	2	8	3	2	--	--	7	2	--	--	--	27
20-30		--	--	--	5	--	1	4	--	--	--	--	--	--	--	10
20-40		1	--	--	--	--	--	--	--	--	1	--	--	--	--	2
30-40		--	--	--	3	--	--	--	--	--	--	--	--	--	--	3
40-50		--	--	--	2	--	--	1	--	--	--	--	--	--	--	3
50-180		--	--	--	1	--	--	--	--	--	--	--	--	--	--	1
Ochre pit		2	--	--	--	--	--	--	--	--	--	--	--	--	--	2
Total	9	4	1	1	13	8	4	7	0	0	8	2	0	0	0	57

Totals—End Scrapers on Blades

Depth (cm)	Partial or slight retouch or wear at one end	Distinct retouch or wear at one end	Concave retouch or wear at one end	Retouch or wear at both ends	Total
Surface	100	11	4	9	124
0-20	61	102	11	27	201
20-30	14	54	17	10	95
20-40	9	11	2	2	24
30-40	20	5	--	3	28
40-50	12	2	3	3	20
50-180	11	20	--	1	32
Ochre pit	--	1	--	2	3
Total	227	206	37	57	527

End scrapers on flakes.—This group is treated as a part of the major end-scraper category because each piece bears a strictly localized zone of edge retouch or wear, usually opposite the bulb if one is present, and on the narrow or short dimension of medium-to-small, often elongated or narrow flakes, flake fragments, or, more rarely, thicker core fragments. However, as in the end-scraper-on-blade category dealt with immediately above, the traces of use or workmanship are generally crude or minimal and the pieces irregularly shaped. Convex, concave, sinuous, or rectilinear forms, as well as double-ended working fronts, have been noted (fig. 16:8-12). (See also the general comments in the section on end scrapers on blades and in the section on blades with obliquely retouched ends.)

End Scrapers on Flakes

Depth (cm)	Surface	Operation and area														Total
		I														
		Step	A	B	C	Ext.	F	G	Tr.	II	III	IV	V	VI		
Surface	58															58
0-20		3	2	4	--	26	5	4	1	5	7	8	5	2		72
20-30		--	2	5	4	--	2	5	--	--	5	--	--	--		23
20-40		4	--	--	--	--	--	--	--	--	--	--	--	--		4
30-40		--	--	--	7	--	--	5	--	--	--	--	--	--		12
40-50		--	--	--	1	--	--	3	--	--	--	--	--	--		4
50-180		3	--	--	--	--	--	--	--	--	--	--	--	--		3
Ochre pit		2	--	--	--	--	--	--	--	--	--	--	--	--		2
Total	58	12	4	9	12	26	7	17	1	5	12	8	5	2		178

Side Scrapers

This group contains broad flakes or flake fragments, a few sturdy, thick-sectioned blades and bladelike flakes, and a number of relatively thick reused core fragments or trimming debris including core revival flakes, blades, and tablets. On all of these an appreciable portion of the edge of a long dimension has been worn or flaked by flat or steep squamous or stepped flaking into the semblance of a side scraper. These have straight or occasionally slightly convex or concave working edges (fig. 16:13-16). In nearly 15% of the cases, two of the edges have been worked, evidently because the shape and position of a second edge had fortuitously been found suitable for development (fig. 16:16). It is the clarity, extent, and concentration of wear or retouch that sets these tools off from less formally organized or exploited used flakes and blades with less or vaguer edge work and also distinguishes them from the notched-and-worn groups, which tend to show less formally organized but more intensive edge exploitation at relatively localized points than the side scrapers.

This side-scraper category is not, however, made up of pieces like the deliberately fashioned, well-achieved side scrapers, or "racloirs," of other periods and provinces of the stoneworking traditions. It is a miscellaneous and undistinguished group typologically at Karim Shahir, and the examples lack the classic combination of shapely form and continuous close-set stepped and squamous edge retouch on broad flakes. They appear to have come into existence in much the same manner as the end scrapers: by use or out of necessity, with a minimum of preliminary shaping, on debris that happened to be at hand. Also, there is often wear of one sort or another, ranging from slight to somewhat heavy, along the long edge opposite the so-called scraper edge, suggesting that these pieces were, like many others at the site, multipurpose tools.

A group of cores reused as scrapers is counted with the cores since they display neither sufficient retouch and wear nor regularity in the form and position of edge wear to warrant consideration separately. In any case most cores reused as scrapers approach the rounded scraper and not the side scraper in type.

Side Scrapers

Depth (cm)	Surface	Operation and area														Total
		I														
		Step	A	B	C	Ext.	F	G	Tr.	II	III	IV	V	VI	VIII	
Surface	21(3*)															21(3*)
0-20		13(2*)	4(2*)	4	4	54(10*)	8(1*)	5(2*)	3(1*)	1	7	3	1	7(1*)	1	115(19*)
20-30		--	9	17(1*)	19(5*)	--	14(4*)	6	--	--	5	--	--	--	--	70(10*)
20-40	9(2*)	--	--	--	--	--	--	--	--	--	--	--	--	--	--	9(2*)
30-40		--	--	--	4	--	--	6(1*)	--	--	--	--	--	--	--	10(1*)
40-50		--	--	--	2	--	--	--	--	--	--	--	--	--	--	2
50-80	4	--	--	--	1	--	--	--	--	--	--	--	--	--	--	5
Total	21(3*)	26(4*)	13(2*)	21(1*)	30(5*)	54(10*)	22(5*)	17(3*)	3(1*)	1	12	3	1	7(1*)	1	232(35*)

*Double-edged scrapers.

Steep Scrapers on Core Fragments

This very small group of scrapers seems related to other kinds of scrapers developed upon cores and core fragments, examples of which have been commented upon under Side Scrapers (above) and also under both Rounded Scrapers and Cores (below), but is somewhat more specialized in form and in the type and position of its edge wear than these other categories. The grouping of these pieces here may be subject to the criticism that they represent not reused cores but simply worked-down cores whose battered or worn edge zones along a flat platform are witness to unsuccessful final attempts at removing flakes. Nevertheless, the type, amount, and placement of this secondary edge flaking suggest repeated special use of these pieces at certain points.

The artifacts in this group seem to be the elongated or spatulate tip ends of pyramidal cores that have been either worked, revived, or broken off to a stubby remnant with a flat base and steep sides, ending in a peak or ridge. They are narrow oblong in plan. Often clearly truncated flaking scars of the core are traceable. Their overall mounded-up shape vividly recalls that of the old-fashioned tea cozy, and in the field we applied this label half-jokingly to this tool type. Wear or possibly rudimentary retouch is noticeable on the edges at one end and/or along the long dimension. There is certainly no clear secondary retouch that would have straightened out or regularized the working edge but rather a flaking from use that tended to leave intact the major edge irregularities produced by prior flake removal from the piece (fig. 17:1-2). As noted under Side Scrapers, full cores reused as scrapers have been dealt with under Cores.

It must be noted that the 26 specimens of steep scrapers on core fragments occurred primarily in the upper levels, as tabulated below.

Steep Scrapers on Core Fragments

Depth (cm)	Surface	Operation and area										Total
		I										
		Step	A	B	C	Ext.	F	Tr.	II	III	IV	
Surface	6											6
0-20		--	1	1	--	6	2	1	1	1	1	14
20-30		--	--	1	2	--	2	--	--	--	--	5
20-40		1	--	--	--	--	--	--	--	--	--	1
Total	6	1	1	2	2	6	4	1	1	1	1	26

Rounded Scrapers

This somewhat limited class comprises flakes, fragments, or the broken and revival parts of cores worked into either regular or irregular implements that have a partly circular or at least convex front. This shaping has been done either by wear or by continuous squamous, steep, stepped, or nibbled edge retouch. Where pieces bear this workmanship to only a limited extent along their periphery they are rendered simply convex; where the flaking is extensive the pieces become semicircular or discoid scrapers. Core tablets, core revival flakes, or similarly shaped portions of cores were easily adapted to a rounded shape; about half the category is made up of this sort of piece.

Only a few specimens are truly shapely and well retouched. These are the flat discoid scrapers on flakes, fragments, and core tablets and the steep, mounded semicircular scrapers on core fragments and on other kinds of thick fragments. The majority of pieces in this category bear slight edge retouch or, more commonly, wear and are apt to have irregular, somewhat sinuous edges following the original line of the piece; these are the convex scrapers.

The size of these rounded scrapers depends closely, of course, on the size of the flake or fragment used. Several are thumbnail size, that is, between 20 mm and 30 mm in diameter, whereas one large circular flake is 70 mm in diameter and bears extensive, clearly defined squamous retouch on nearly all of its periphery (fig. 17:5). The majority of pieces, ranging between 30 mm and 40 mm in diameter, are semicircular or convex scrapers displaying limited zones of steep squamous retouch or wear in a broad sinuous arc across one sector of a flake or fragment (fig. 17:3-4).

Rounded Scrapers

Depth (cm)	Surface	Operation and area										Total
		I										
		Step	A	B	C	Ext.	F	G	Tr.	III	IV	
Surface	16											16
0-20		2	1	1	--	9	2	5	1	1	2	24
20-30		--	4	4	11	--	5	4	--	--	--	28
20-40	4	--	--	--	--	--	--	--	--	--	--	4
30-40	--	--	--	--	2	--	--	2	--	--	--	4
40-50	1	--	--	--	3	--	--	2	--	--	--	6
60-80	1	--	--	--	--	--	--	--	--	--	--	1
Total	16	8	5	5	16	9	7	13	1	1	2	83

"Raclettes"

This is a very distinctive small group of flakes or fragments bearing rather uniform fine, small-scale nibbled retouch along substantial portions of their periphery (fig. 17:6). They lack the clear notching and the more extensive squamous retouch or signs of edge wear that would warrant placing them under other headings. They may perhaps be considered the flake counterpart, typologically and technically, of certain blades and bladelets with fine nibbled edge retouch within the groups described on pages 84-85. Indeed, their extreme rarity at Karim Shahir argues against isolating them from the general run of the nibbled blade and flake categories. Nevertheless, raclettes are set off by their specialized uniform fine edge flaking and are a distinctive artifact type recognized in prehistoric stoneworking assemblages from other continents. Their use is not known, although the uniform appearance of the tiny edge flaking suggests a single function.

This and all the following categories of artifacts in which differences in edge work are emphasized (e.g., raclettes or nibbled, notched, squamously flaked, or other used pieces) are nothing more than a groping attempt at classification based on variations in the types and disposition of gross edge flaking that may reflect the unknown functions of these pieces of flint. In some categories, the pieces bear many sorts of edge flaking and may have been multiple-use tools; in others (e.g., the raclettes), they show uniform traces of only one sort of work and may have been used for specialized work. Further analysis of micro edge wear might cast more light on functions and bring more order into classification.

Raclettes were found only in superficial levels.

"Raclettes"

Depth (cm)	Operation and area					Total
	I,step	I,C	I,ext.	I,F	I,G	
0-20	6	1	8	1	2	18
20-40	1	--	--	--	--	1
Total	7	1	8	1	2	19

Blades with Obliquely Truncated Ends

This comparatively small category might be considered a variant of the end scrapers in that the wear or retouch lies across one narrow end of the blades. It runs in an oblique line, however, forming a distinctly diagonal terminal working front. Wear or retouch occurs elsewhere on the edges of nearly every specimen in this category and may be in the form of notches or even scraperlike edges along the long dimension or at the opposite end from the primary terminal working edge. Flaking on the truncation is occasionally squamous but is more commonly nondescript nibbled or irregular wear on either or both faces (fig. 17:9-15). In nearly one half of the cases the terminal retouch or wear seems to follow the natural diagonal line of the blade edge and does not constitute a truncation in a true sense but rather a simple edge flaking (fig. 17:9,10,14). Three of the truly truncated pieces are retouched in a curvilinear convex manner. The function of these variable pieces is unknown, although multiple use seems possible. (For perhaps related microlithic specimens see Miscellaneous Microliths; compare also End Scrapers.)

Blades with Obliquely Truncated Ends

Depth (cm)	Surface	Operation and area									Total
		I						II	III	IV	
		Step	A	C	Ext.	F	G				
Surface	3										3
0-20		2	1	2	9	5	1	1	1	4	26
20-30		--	1	7	--	4	1	--	--	--	13
20-40		1	--	--	--	--	--	--	--	--	1
30-40		--	--	2	--	--	--	--	--	--	2
40-50		--	--	1	--	--	1	--	--	--	2
40-60		3	--	1	--	--	--	--	--	--	4
60-180		1	--	6	--	--	--	--	--	--	7
Ochre pit		1	--	--	--	--	--	--	--	--	1
Total	3	8	2	19	9	9	3	1	1	4	59

Nibbled Blades and Flakes

This large category comprises blades and microblades as well as flakes and fragments, all of which are marked more or less exclusively by a fine, very small-scale nibbled retouch or wear on either or both edges and faces (fig. 17:7-8). In general, blades outnumber flakes by about two to one, and microlithic blades are almost as frequent as normal-sized blades.

This class represents only some of the total number of pieces with nibbled edge flaking. It comprises only those pieces that show no significant development of distinctive edge features other than the nibbling. There are in the Karim Shahir assemblage many more pieces, both normal-sized and microlithic, that display edge nibbling, but because they also bear obviously notched or otherwise flaked edges or distinctive features such as backing, scraper zones, burin facets, and drill points, they have in this report been dealt with in their appropriate class. Again, the implication of multiple uses for each of these pieces is strong, in view of the different sorts of edge flaking, the specific shape, and the various adaptations to be noted on each tool. Microwear was not investigated, but such a study would certainly throw more light on this problem. Moreover, natural attrition or wear is not to be excluded as a factor, perhaps a major one, in the condition of the edge.

This group of nibbled pieces can be thought of as merging into a technotypological continuum with the nibbled pieces that are classified as "notched" and "used," since the different kinds of edge flaking are usually found jumbled together on most tools. One should also note that over half the nibbled category is composed of fragments and that it is likely that other forms of shaping, preparation, or wear existed on the now lost portions of these pieces.

Notched Blades

This large category comprises retouched or worn blades most of which bear pronounced and well-flaked notches. The remainder have broadly concave or sinuous flaked edges. The group includes specimens with fairly continuous edge retouch or wear ranging from steep and squamous in the large majority of cases (fig. 18:2-3,5) to rudimentary and finely nibbled (fig. 18:1,4,6-10). There are also specimens with limited discontinuous or even single zones of the same range of retouch or wear (fig. 18:11-15). This edge flaking is most often found on the obverse face alone but may also occur only on the reverse or bulbar face, often as a series of nibbled scars. The most outstanding feature of the category,

Nibbled Blades and Flakes

| Depth (cm) | Surface | Operation and area |||||||| II | III | IV | V | VI | VIII | Total |
| | | I |||||||| | | | | | | |
		Step	A	B	C	Ext.	F	G	Tr.							
Nibbled Blades and Microblades																
Surface	268															268
0-20		41	92	151	71	576	89	30	11	1	32	5	33	7	3	1,142
20-30		--	56	59	141	--	58	104	--	--	--	--	6	--	--	424
20-40		--	--	--	--	--	--	--	--	--	2	6	--	--	--	8
30-40		--	--	--	20	--	--	32	--	--	--	--	--	--	--	52
40-50		--	--	--	44	--	--	42	--	--	5	--	--	--	--	91
50-180		62	--	--	46	--	--	56	--	--	6	--	--	--	--	170
Ochre pit		5	--	--	--	--	--	--	--	--	--	--	--	--	--	5
Total	268	108	148	210	322	576	147	264	11	1	45	11	39	7	3	2,160
Nibbled Flakes and Microflakes																
Surface	67															67
0-20		16	72	91	27	301	25	14	9	2	53	4	25	17	2	658
20-30		--	12	31	65	--	36	35	--	--	--	--	10	--	--	189
20-40		24	--	--	--	--	--	--	--	--	4	3	--	1	--	32
30-40		--	--	--	15	--	--	14	--	--	--	--	--	--	--	29
40-50		--	--	--	16	--	--	31	--	--	7	--	--	--	--	54
50-180		17	--	--	21	--	--	15	--	--	6	--	--	--	--	59
Ochre pit		4	--	--	--	--	--	--	--	--	--	--	--	--	--	4
Total	67	61	84	122	144	301	61	109	9	2	70	7	35	18	2	1,092

Totals—Nibbled Blades and Flakes

Depth (cm)	Nibbled blades and microblades	Nibbled flakes and microflakes	Total
Surface	268	67	335
0-20	1,142	658	1,800
20-30	424	189	613
20-40	8	32	40
30-40	52	29	81
40-50	91	54	145
50-180	170	59	229
Ochre pit	5	4	9
Total	2,160	1,092	3,252

however, is the presence on over 90% of the pieces of one or more notches or scallops worked into the edge of each piece. These features may be deep or shallow, narrow or broad. Occasionally they may be multiple and close-set, producing a kind of denticulated effect (fig. 18:4,15), but more usually they are irregularly set at one or more points along either edge, sometimes producing a "strangled" or constricted shape when located exactly or nearly opposite each other (fig. 18:2-3). Some notches are merely the exploitation of an already existing concavity that was made perhaps by a prior blow or was inherent in the shape of the blade. Others are well-flaked, distinct notches cutting into the line of the edge (fig. 18:2-3,5). Still others are broad depressions marked by uniform fine nibbled edge flaking (fig. 18:12-14).

Such a variety of shapes and edge flaking is in all probability due to the different ways in which the blades were used; different processes would have employed or produced notches of all sorts in combination with sinuous or broadly concave edges. Experimentation by BH and LSB showed that at least one way of producing such notches and associated small-scale flaking was to saw a flake or blade back and forth across the shaft of a fresh long bone. After a few minutes, as the groove deepened, this action produced extensive flaking in a series of multiple notches on one or both faces. No retouch was involved in this experimental action, only edge wear, which was manifested by several sorts of flaking: nibbled, steep, stepped, and squamous, in all combinations. This finding strongly suggests not only that the general run of notched pieces were single- or multiple-use tools but also that they may have dulled quickly and been discarded in the course of whatever activity or activities in which they may have been employed. In fact, rapid wastage may help account for the great quantity of this kind of artifact found at the site. While finer forms of wear were not detected, microscopic study might show such wear and provide a more informed basis for classification.

Notched Blades

Depth (cm)	Surface	I Step	A	B	C	Ext.	F	G	Tr.	II	III	IV	V	VI	VIII	Total
Normal-sized																
Surface	257															257
0-20		234	74	93	85	716	102	45	59	4	30	--	34	26	17	1,519
20-30		--	89	101	306	--	141	145	--	--	--	--	6	--	--	788
20-40		92	--	--	--	--	--	--	--	--	4	8	--	3	--	107
30-40		--	--	--	108	--	--	90	--	--	--	--	--	--	--	198
40-50		--	--	--	84	--	--	65	--	--	--	--	--	--	--	149
40-60		111	--	--	23	--	--	19	--	--	2	1	--	1	--	157
60-80+		41	--	--	30	--	--	28	--	--	19	4	--	--	--	122
Ochre pit		39	--	--	--	--	--	--	--	--	--	--	--	--	--	39
Total	257	517	163	194	636	716	243	392	59	4	55	13	40	30	17	3,336
Microlithic																
Surface	122															122
0-20		38	43	76	49	533	45	15	22	--	--	--	10	3	7	841
20-30		--	53	78	167	--	67	154	--	--	--	--	3	--	--	522
20-40		45	--	--	--	--	--	--	--	--	--	8	--	--	--	53
30-40		--	--	--	73	--	--	28	--	--	--	--	--	--	--	101
40-50		--	--	--	10	--	--	60	--	--	--	--	--	--	--	70
40-60		34	--	--	16	--	--	5	--	--	--	5	--	--	--	60
60-80+		14	--	--	47	--	--	32	--	--	--	6	--	--	--	99
Ochre pit		10	--	--	--	--	--	--	--	--	--	--	--	--	--	10
Total	122	141	96	154	362	533	112	294	22	0	0	19	13	3	7	1,878

Totals—Notched Blades

Depth (cm)	Normal-sized	Microlithic	Total
Surface	257	122	379
0-20	1,519	841	2,360
20-30	788	522	1,310
20-40	107	53	160
30-40	198	101	299
40-50	149	70	219
40-60	157	60	217
60-80+	122	99	221
Ochre pit	39	10	49
Total	3,336	1,878	5,214

This category, as it stands now, is distinguished from others by its pronounced notches. The presence of a single deeply concave flake scar on the edge is not considered evidence for a true notch. If it were not for the notches, this category could be placed technically and typologically, on the basis of edge wears involved, in a continuum merging with blades in the "nibbled" or "used" categories or with some of the hollow or concave side scrapers.

Frequently the edge opposite the primary notched edge may be marked by wear, occasionally in the form of the heavy irregular nicking described under Used Blades (fig. 19:12). A few specimens seem smoothed by wear along the nibbled portions, so that the edges of scars are dulled. Again, such special features point to multiple uses in some cases and particular uses in others.

A sizeable microlithic subgroup has the same edge characteristics as the normal- and large-sized notched blades, although the microlithic blades that have one or two isolated notches are relatively more common than those that are multiple notched and continuously flaked (fig. 18:15).

Fragments of what were once obviously large, normal-sized, or microlithic notched blades have also been included in this class. The largest complete blades are nearly 100 mm long, but the great majority are 50-70 mm. The microlithic subgroup begins at a length of ca. 50-60 mm, that dimension being governed largely by the width of the blade (usually under 10 mm) and its delicacy. Blades are not regular nor do they have exactly parallel blade scars or edges in the larger sizes, whereas neatness and symmetry are more apparent in the microlithic group. The larger ones are apt to be thick sectioned. There were 23 specimens of both normal-sized and microlithic blades that had opposed simple notches near the base, possibly a hafting device, but only a few of these displayed any trace of wear or multiple flaking in these otherwise natural hollows or single flake scars. In any case, the function of such pieces is unknown, and any segregation of them into a little subdivision must be postponed until clearer evidence of hafting is obtained.

Notched Flakes

This group includes a few large flakes (35 × 60 mm to 40 × 70 mm), a majority of medium-sized flakes and fragments (30 × 50 mm), and a microlithic subgroup of whole or fragmentary examples (most with maximum dimensions of 10 × 20 mm, but some with less). Some flakes are bladelike or elongated, but because of their irregularity, proportions, and thickness they cannot be considered blades. Many are fragments, with or without the bulbar end, and there are a good number of notched core fragments or notched core revival flakes and tablets.

Notched Flakes

Depth (cm)	Surface	Operation and area														Total
		I														
		Step	A	B	C	Ext.	F	G	Tr.	II	III	IV	V	VI	VIII	
Surface	65															65
0-20		71	83	57	84	481	70	30	25	7	110	10	21	20	14	1,083
20-30		--	17	56	94	--	57	52	--	--	--	--	11	--	--	287
20-40		43	--	--	--	--	--	--	--	--	15	8	--	--	--	66
30-40		--	--	--	59	--	--	19	--	--	--	--	--	--	--	78
40-50		--	--	--	37	--	--	25	--	--	--	--	--	--	--	62
40-60		44	--	--	17	--	--	8	--	--	7	2	--	1	--	79
60-80+		8	--	--	22	--	--	14	--	--	10	--	--	--	--	54
Ochre pit		18	--	--	--	--	--	--	--	--	--	--	--	--	--	18
Total	65	184	100	113	313	481	127	148	25	7	142	20	32	21	14	1,792

Very few pieces in this class bear well-retouched multiple notches. Many bear a distinct and well-developed single notch and often have retouch or wear on the obverse (nonbulbar) face of the notch. The remainder have indifferent notches due to varying degrees of wear (fig. 19:1-3). Along with the notches, considerable amounts of various sorts of edge flaking are to be seen on the pieces in this group. The result is a class of very irregular and unstandardized-looking artifacts with miscellaneous edge wear (always including the distinctive notches). As in the case of the notched blades, the pieces seem to have been tools that perhaps came to have more than one function, that is, they were tools of opportunity and any flake or fragment at hand was apparently used for whatever job was to be done. Notching seems to have developed at any convenient point on the edge of a piece, and in cases where more distinct notching is seen it is likely that the piece was used long and hard there one or more times and then discarded.

The microlithic component—about one quarter of the group—is marked in numerous cases by steeply flaked notching on alternate opposite faces (fig. 19:4-5). As with the foregoing and other used categories to follow, no investigation was made of microwear. This subject requires study, as the information might well contribute much with regard to the basis on which these categories can be classified.

It must be emphasized that the gross character of the edge flaking is the basis for distinguishing between the notched flakes and other categories such as raclettes, side scrapers, and forms with nibbled wear or retouch on either face. On the notched flakes, the edge flaking is haphazardly executed and is a jumble of varying types, whereas the pieces in the other categories have edge flaking that is comparatively concentrated, distinctive, and standardized.

Used Blades and Blade Fragments

This category is very large. It brings together all normal-sized or microlithic blades, or fragments thereof, that bear even the slightest trace of one or more of a number of kinds of macroscopic wear, but it excludes blades with definite notches and other types of obvious special retouch or wear noted under previous headings. As in the case of the other types, this used class was not studied for evidence of microwear. Some two thirds of the specimens in the present category are small to microlithic in size, the rest being normal-sized examples varying from ca. 50 mm to 80-100 mm in length.

An attempt has been made here to distinguish between a number of forms of edge flaking which are to be found singly or in combination on pieces in this category. *Nicking* consists of deeply concave, sharply bitten-out, smallish edge scars, often on alternate opposite faces of the same edge (fig. 19:7-9). *Squamous* flake scars are invasive, broad, shallow, and irregular and may occur either on a large scale or on a very small, even microlithic, scale (fig. 19:6). *Nibbled* flake scars are tiny, usually rather uniformly sized, relatively steeply set flaking that is located close to the edge only and may be caused by some sort of light use or else by deliberate retouch (fig. 19:6,8). *Stepped* or *resolved* flake scars are a formation in which a series of overhanging squamous flake scars overlap, sometimes producing a steep face; this type may be combined with other types of flake scars and merge with them typologically. *Battering* is a localized, intensive, small-scale stepped or resolved flaking, on occasion ending in a gentle concavity or vague notch or at least a very dulled edge.

In addition to blades with the above forms of edge flaking, there are some 460 blades that were subjected to some unknown type of very heavy edge wear, which has left a series of pronounced deeply concave nicks, or "bites," often continuous, set either on alternate opposite faces or nearly at right angles to the blade's edge (fig. 19:11-12). When viewed end on, such an edge often has a tightly sinuous line. This sort of edge wear, which could have been produced either naturally or artificially, is to be seen as the foremost trait of the saw or saw-blade category from one of the upper paleolithic horizons at Yabrud in Syria, as described by Rust (1950, p. 45, pls. 49, 52). It is possible that all these forms of edge flaking described in connection with the catchall used blades category are partly marks of attrition due to natural pressures in the ground.

Careful comparison shows that the forms of edge wear in the present group are less intense, less concentrated at individual edge points, and less standardized than the edge wear seen in such categories as nibbled or notched pieces and various scrapers. However, while these used blades and fragments are marked by less distinct zones of the different edge wears, some of them may have been made by processes, and perhaps used in functions, no different from those involved in the more formal and standardized tools. The final form and disposition of the edge flaking—whether specialized or generalized, executed carefully or carelessly, limited or diffuse—are what form the basis of separation into the present groups. To summarize and emphasize, such flaking in the "used" category is more random and discontinuous, less uniform, and sparser than in the others, and it may have natural as well as artificial origins.

Used Blades and Blade Fragments

Depth (cm)	Surface	Operation and area														
		I														
		Step	A	B	C	Ext.	F	G	Tr.	II	III	IV	V	VI	VIII	Total
Surface	939															939
0-20		251	322	446	298	4,573	391	113	297	16	393	16	86	68	109	7,379
20-30		--	255	214	442	--	346	446	--	--	--	--	76	--	--	1,779
20-40		526	--	--	--	--	--	--	--	--	19	35	--	11	--	591
30-40		--	--	--	181	--	--	150	--	--	--	--	--	--	--	331
40-50		--	--	--	158	--	--	242	--	--	--	--	--	--	--	400
40-60		370	--	--	136	--	--	85	--	--	15	45	--	5	--	656
60-80+		167	--	--	290	--	--	243	--	--	143	20	--	--	--	863
Ochre pit		151	--	--	--	--	--	--	--	--	--	--	--	--	--	151
Total	939	1,465	577	660	1,505	4,573	737	1,279	297	16	570	116	162	84	109	13,089

Used Flakes and Flake Fragments

This is a motley and undistinguished assortment of irregularly shaped large and small flakes or, as in the majority of examples, fragments of flakes. Numerous thick and irregular core fragments, including minimal parts of revival flakes and tablets, small fragments of hammerstones, and cortex-bearing primary trimming flakes also occur. On each piece in this category, as in the preceding blade category, one or more of the edges is marked by sparse zones or isolated points of nicking or battering, or by small-scale squamous or stepped flake scars (fig. 19:10), or by the same sort of pronounced and continuous deeply gouged nicking probably due to heavy edge wear as seen in the used blades (fig. 19:13). Again, only pieces with sparse signs of such use, separately or in combination, but with no distinct notches or other special forms of edge preparation or wear have been included in this category, and any possible traces of microwear remain to be studied.

Used Flakes and Flake Fragments

Depth (cm)	Surface	Operation and area														Total
		I														
		Step	A	B	C	Ext.	F	G	Tr.	II	III	IV	V	VI	VIII	
Surface	947															947
0-20		122	187	351	274	3,304	325	107	226	24	397	29	129	48	57	5,580
20-30		--	125	128	337	--	256	167	--	--	--	--	52	--	--	1,065
20-40		254	--	--	--	--	--	--	--	--	44	41	--	1	--	340
30-40		--	--	--	161	--	--	125	--	--	--	--	--	--	--	286
40-50		--	--	--	156	--	--	201	--	--	--	--	--	--	--	357
50-60		--	--	--	69	--	--	42	--	--	--	--	--	--	--	111
40-60		202	--	--	--	--	--	--	--	--	16	37	--	1	--	256
60-80+		147	--	--	156	--	--	125	--	--	73	11	--	--	--	512
Ochre pit		80	--	--	--	--	--	--	--	--	--	--	--	--	--	80
Total	947	805	312	479	1,153	3,304	581	767	226	24	530	118	181	50	57	9,534

Cores

Over 1,600 cores were recovered from the excavations. They are an impressive indication of the considerable extent to which flintworking and toolmaking must have been pursued on the spot. As in the case of the limestone, marble, sandstone, and other fine-grained rocks used for making ground stone tools and ornaments, the primary source of stone for cores from which were struck the chipped stone flint implements at Karim Shahir also appears to have been the waterworn gravels in the area. These gravels were to be found not only in the widespread massive conglomerate deposits resting on the flat, high spurs of land in the valley but also in the great quantities of loose stone material lying in the then-existing stream beds and gullies of the surrounding valley region (Wright, pers. comm.; Wright 1952, p. 20). From these locations and perhaps more far-flung terrain the makers of the chipped stone tools evidently selected mainly waterworn pebbles or field stones of cherty flint—in the broad sense of the term that includes fine-grained variations resembling jasper and chalcedony as well as ordinary grades. The colors range from dull, entirely opaque tan or gray to banded or mottled brown, gray, red, and green, with a few somewhat translucent milky bluish-white pieces. As a rule the flint is of a good homogeneous quality that permitted blades, both normal and microlithic, and roughly uniform broad flakes to be struck. There are also somewhat coarser and brecciated forms. Some of the flint from which the chipped stone artifacts were made is of low quality with poor fracturing properties or else it is already fissured and shattered from natural causes, but this kind is relatively rare. The original size, proportions, and resulting portability of the pebbles that were selected to be carried up to the hilltop settlement may have been the controlling factors in the size of cores found in this assemblage; they rarely exceed 50-60 mm in length and often are nearer 40-50 mm. Naturally, however, what one finds is probably the exploited, exhausted, discarded, or mislaid cores or core remnants, reduced in size from their original state, from which somewhat larger blades and flakes would have already been removed. This seems likely when one compares the greater dimensions of some tools found with the smaller sizes of the general run of cores found.

A number of cores appear to have had the edges of their main striking platform used as scrapers, although they were apparently never given much deliberate retouch with this function in mind. Evidence of their reuse as scrapers is discussed elsewhere in more detail. The following subdivision of cores has been made on the basis of gross shaping and method of exploitation.

Pyramidal.—The predominant core type is a roughly circular and usually elongated pyramid. The neater blade or bladelet pyramidal cores, a few of which are nearly cigar-shaped in proportion, form 55-60% of this group. The remainder are cores that are more irregular but still pyramidal, although often more stubby in form, from which flakes or bladelike flakes (broader and less symmetrical than the blades) have been struck. These cores have a different form either by the maker's design, in the final stages of exploitation of the piece, or as a result of his lack of skill or some difficulty due to the core's diminishing proportions that made it unsuitable for knapping; possibly there were problems occasioned by the inherent quality of the chert itself.

Most of these pyramidal cores have been developed by the removal of blades or flakes in one direction along the periphery of a single flat striking platform which has usually been established by the truncation of one end of a pebble. This truncation has usually produced a single flake scar and a striking platform face at right angles or nearly right angles to the body of the core (fig. 20:1). In some cases, however, there are multiple scars on this platform surface (fig. 20:2), and there are also numerous cases of narrow-angled striking platforms in which the platform face forms an acute angle with the flaking face. Blades or flakes have normally been removed in a straight or convex line extending across only one face of such a truncated pebble (fig. 20:3-4). This, the largest subgroup, contains most of the narrow-angled striking platforms.

In the production of pyramidal cores the intention appears to have been to remove pieces along a bulging convex line around the entire pebble if possible. The ultimate stage was a complete oblong to conical pyramid with no pebble cortex remaining (figs. 20:5-6; 21:1-4). However, most of the pyramidal cores found represent stages in this process, being partial or semipyramidal and showing, in addition to the principal blade or flake removal surface, the following traits singly or in combination on the opposite or back face: (1) a pebble cortex remnant, (2) a face with a single broad flake facet or multiple flake facets, (3) a longitudinal zone of stubby flake scars aligned in one direction or two opposing directions along the length of the core at right angles to the trend of scars on the main removal surface, leaving a longitudinal ridge down the center or side of the back (fig. 20:2). The cortex-backed cores make up about half of the partial pyramidal cores, and the two flake-scarred types make up about a quarter each. In the case of the cores with right-angle back flaking it is theorized that this zone of right-angle scars may have been occasioned by attempts to shape the core originally, to remove cortex by superficial flaking, or to establish or restore a desired working shape in order to control the form of the product in the course of blade or flake removal. Indeed, an oblong pyramidal blade core apparently may have been what was usually wanted, and the right-angle flaking seems to have been a good method for simultaneously scaling off cortex and giving a controlled oblong optimum shape that would best yield the desired shape of blade.

In brief summary, then, one may say that in this major subdivision a few of the cores found have been exploited so skillfully that a slim cigar-shaped residual form has resulted, but the large majority are either elongated or squatty pyramids with peaks that are sharply pointed and spatulate or else broad, thick, and blunted, depending on the degree to which removals were prosecuted. On the other hand, a good number of cores found are still in an incipient stage of development, retaining much pebble cortex and displaying only a few blade or flake scars. Blades or flakes were usually removed from the smooth striking platform made by simple truncation of the pebble (forming pyramids that are circular, steep, and high, or steep, low, and squat, or planoconvex) but were also sometimes removed directly from an entire untruncated pebble. This incipient type thus constitutes in 91 cases a sort of pebble core. It is entirely possible that such cores were, in a good number of cases, preludes to the pyramidal types.

Many of the pyramidal cores bear combinations of fine parallel blade or bladelet scars and irregular broad or deep flake scars, perhaps evidence of some disruption in the removal series (fig. 20:6). The scars on the blade removal front of a good number of the fully pyramidal blade cores show that the last few strokes must have caused poor, irregular flakes, or else that these scars are merely the result of ineffectual battering over the previously successful blade-removal scars. However, the cores displaying these features have all been counted in the overall blade core category.

Bipolar.—A few cores bear evidence that at the time they were discarded, removals were being made from two striking platforms usually at opposite ends of a single flaking face (fig. 21:5-6) or, more rarely, at right angles or near right angles to each other on two faces (fig. 21:7). Cores exploited in this way have been called *bipolar*, while the variants bearing two groups of removal scars at right angles to each other are referred to as *crossed* bipolar cores.

Most of these bipolar cores are irregularly shaped and thick in cross section, although a very few are distinctly rectangular and relatively thin. In all likelihood, this bipolar group represents only a transient or a final stage in the exploitation of certain pebbles that would be unmanageable by normal methods for producing the optimum pyramidal specimens. Indeed, a number of the pyramidal cores resemble the bipolar cores in that they bear at their peaks evidence of small-scale removals in any direction on any surface broad enough to be exploited; some of them even suggest secondary use as scrapers. In other cases it is difficult to make an arbitrary division between true bipolar types and pyramidal types shaped by right-angle flake preparation. In general, most bipolar cores seem to represent one form of the last stage in the exploitation of a pyramidal core; by then the knapping might have been applied to any promising surface. Their small numbers suggest this interpretation and not that they were a consciously desired or developed type. In this category, as in others, the reduction in size and weight of the core may have been an unfavorable factor in the knapping process; as more and more blades or flakes were detached, the reduced mass may have had an adverse effect on the quality of the product.

Polyhedral/amorphous.—The small category of polyhedral or amorphous cores may either (1) represent a limited though deliberate departure from the major pyramidal form or else, more likely, (2) reflect (a) a lack of skill in establishing that form or (b) a persistence in using (in any promising direction) an originally pyramidal core down to its stub end or, finally, (c) an attempt to cope with a recalcitrant chert. In a number of cores in both this group and the pyramidal group, it appears that as the length was reduced the knapper tended to flake from the striking platform face itself, abandoning the remainder of the already established blade or flake removal surface and obtaining flakes wherever possible, thus producing a polyhedral/amorphous core. These cores are apt to be roughly spheroid or cuboid with quite irregular broad flake scars made by striking off pieces from three or more faces or directions (fig. 21:8).

Discoid.—The rare and atypical discoid cores found are generally made on what appear to be sizeable cortex-bearing, roughly circular, thick-bodied primary flakes from pebbles, or else they are made on the pebbles themselves. All of these pieces have had coarse irregular flakes removed from one or both faces in a radial fashion, and the edges often show wear in the form of battering and also some limited secondary flaking, as if they had been reused for scrapers (fig. 21:9). This is not a well-characterized category, and the few examples are poorly made.

There follows a combined overall summary of all core types found at Karim Shahir. They are classed according to gross form and method of exploitation as described above.

Cores

Depth (cm)	Surface	Step	A	B	C	Ext.	F	G	Tr.	II	III	IV	V	VI	VIII	Total
Fully Flaked Pyramidal																
Surface	25															25
0-20		9	14	6	4	68	12	8	2	1	9	4	5	3	3	148
20-30		--	4	8	9	--	6	5	--	--	--	--	--	--	--	32
20-35		--	--	--	--	--	--	--	--	--	--	--	--	--	--	0
20-40		2	--	--	--	--	--	--	--	--	2	--	--	--	--	4
30-40		--	--	--	4	--	--	6	--	--	--	--	--	--	--	10
40-50		--	--	--	1	--	--	6	--	--	--	--	--	--	--	7
40-60		4	--	--	--	--	--	--	--	--	1	--	--	--	--	5
50-60		--	--	--	1	--	--	1	--	--	--	--	--	--	--	2
60+		--	--	--	1	--	--	2	--	--	--	--	--	--	--	3
60-180+		3	--	--	--	--	--	--	--	--	--	--	--	--	--	3
Total	25	18	18	14	20	68	18	28	2	1	12	4	5	3	3	239
Partial Pyramidal, Cortex Back or Flake-Scarred Back																
Surface	77															77
0-20		59	35	30	15	265	36	17	9	1	29	10	2	11	6	525
20-30		--	13	23	62	--	23	13	--	--	--	--	--	--	--	134
20-35		--	--	--	--	--	--	--	--	--	--	--	3	--	--	3
20-40		23	--	--	--	--	--	--	--	--	1	--	--	--	--	24
30-40		--	--	--	12	--	--	16	--	--	--	--	--	--	--	28
40-50		--	--	--	12	--	--	12	--	--	--	--	--	--	--	24
40-60		12	--	--	--	--	--	--	--	--	6	--	--	--	--	18
50-60		--	--	--	8	--	--	1	--	--	--	--	--	--	--	9
60+		--	--	--	5	--	--	5	--	--	--	--	--	--	--	10
60-180+		4	--	--	--	--	--	--	--	--	--	--	--	--	--	4
Ochre pit		3	--	--	--	--	--	--	--	--	--	--	--	--	--	3
Total	77	101	48	53	114	265	59	64	9	1	36	10	5	11	6	859
Partial Pyramidal, Right-Angle-Flake-Scarred Back																
Surface	62															62
0-20		2	14	9	12	57	10	5	--	--	6	3	--	3	3	124
20-30		--	5	9	9	--	3	4	--	--	--	--	--	--	--	30
20-35		--	--	--	--	--	--	--	--	--	--	--	1	--	--	1

Cores—Continued

Depth (cm)	Surface	Operation and area														Total
		I														
		Step	A	B	C	Ext.	F	G	Tr.	II	III	IV	V	VI	VIII	
20-40		4	--	--	--	--	--	--	--	--	--	--	--	--	--	4
30-40		--	--	--	4	--	--	7	--	--	--	--	--	--	--	11
40-50		--	--	--	1	--	--	--	--	--	--	--	--	--	--	1
40-60		--	--	--	--	--	--	--	--	--	--	--	--	--	--	0
50-60		--	--	--	--	--	--	--	--	--	--	--	--	--	--	0
60+		--	--	--	--	--	--	1	--	--	--	--	--	--	--	1
60-180+		3	--	--	--	--	--	--	--	--	--	--	--	--	--	3
Total	62	9	19	18	26	57	13	17	0	0	6	3	1	3	3	237
Incipient, on Pebble																
Surface	5															5
0-20		1	4	4	6	27	3	2	2	--	9	--	--	1	--	59
20-30		--	2	7	6	--	1	1	--	--	--	--	--	--	--	17
20-35		--	--	--	--	--	--	--	--	--	--	--	1	--	--	1
20-40		--	--	--	--	--	--	--	--	--	--	--	--	--	--	0
30-40		--	--	--	--	--	--	2	--	--	--	--	--	--	--	2
40-50		--	--	--	5	--	--	--	--	--	--	--	--	--	--	5
40-60		1	--	--	--	--	--	--	--	--	--	--	--	--	--	1
50-60		--	--	--	--	--	--	--	--	--	--	--	--	--	--	0
60+		--	--	--	--	--	--	--	--	--	--	--	--	--	--	0
60-180+		1	--	--	--	--	--	--	--	--	--	--	--	--	--	1
Total	5	3	6	11	17	27	4	5	2	0	9	0	1	1	0	91
Bipolar																
Surface	5															5
0-20		5	6	--	2	20	2	1	--	--	4	--	3	--	--	43
20-30		--	--	6	7	--	1	1	--	--	--	--	--	--	--	15
20-35		--	--	--	--	--	--	--	--	--	--	--	1	--	--	1
20-40		1	--	--	--	--	--	--	--	--	--	--	--	--	--	1
30-40		--	--	--	1	--	--	--	--	--	--	--	--	--	--	1
40-50		--	--	--	1	--	--	--	--	--	--	--	--	--	--	1
40-60		4	--	--	--	--	--	--	--	--	1	--	--	--	--	5
50-60		--	--	--	--	--	--	--	--	--	--	--	--	--	--	0
60+		--	--	--	--	--	--	--	--	--	--	--	--	--	--	0
60-180+		--	--	--	--	--	--	--	--	--	--	--	--	--	--	0
Ochre pit		1	--	--	--	--	--	--	--	--	--	--	--	--	--	1
Total	5	11	6	6	11	20	3	2	0	0	5	0	4	0	0	73
Polyhedral/Amorphous																
Surface	22															22
0-20		1	6	5	2	31	7	2	1	--	4	--	--	2	--	61
20-30		--	5	7	13	--	4	2	--	--	--	--	--	--	--	31
20-35		--	--	--	--	--	--	--	--	--	--	--	--	--	--	0
20-40		--	--	--	--	--	--	--	--	--	--	--	--	--	--	0
30-40		--	--	--	3	--	--	5	--	--	--	--	--	--	--	8
40-50		--	--	--	1	--	--	2	--	--	--	--	--	--	--	3
40-60		2	--	--	--	--	--	--	--	--	1	--	--	--	--	3
50-60		--	--	--	1	--	--	--	--	--	--	--	--	--	--	1
60+		--	--	--	2	--	--	1	--	--	--	--	--	--	--	3
60-180+		--	--	--	--	--	--	--	--	--	--	--	--	--	--	0
Total	22	3	11	12	22	31	11	12	1	0	5	0	0	2	0	132

Cores—Continued

Depth (cm)	Surface	Operation and area														Total
		I														
		Step	A	B	C	Ext.	F	G	Tr.	II	III	IV	V	VI	VIII	
Discoid																
Surface	4															4
0-20		4	--	4	2	10	4	3	1	--	--	--	--	--	--	28
20-30		--	2	2	5	--	--	--	--	--	--	--	--	--	--	9
20-35		--	--	--	--	--	--	--	--	--	--	--	--	--	--	0
20-40		--	--	--	--	--	--	--	--	--	--	--	--	--	--	0
30-40		--	--	--	1	--	--	6	--	--	--	--	--	--	--	7
40-50		--	--	--	1	--	--	1	--	--	--	--	--	--	--	2
40-60		2	--	--	--	--	--	--	--	--	--	--	--	--	--	2
50-60		--	--	--	--	--	--	--	--	--	--	--	--	--	--	0
60+		--	--	--	--	--	--	--	--	--	--	--	--	--	--	0
60-180+		1	--	--	--	--	--	--	--	--	--	--	--	--	--	1
Total	4	7	2	6	9	10	4	10	1	0	0	0	0	0	0	53

Totals—Cores

Depth (cm)	Pyramidal			Incipient, on pebble	Bipolar	Polyhedral/ amorphous	Discoid	Total
	Fully flaked	Partial, cortex back or flake-scarred back	Partial, right-angle-flake-scarred back					
Surface	25	77	62	5	5	22	4	200
0-20	148	525	124	59	43	61	28	988
20-30	32	134	30	17	15	31	9	268
20-35	--	3	1	1	1	--	--	6
20-40	4	24	4	--	1	--	--	33
30-40	10	28	11	2	1	8	7	67
40-50	7	24	1	5	1	3	2	43
40-60	5	18	--	1	5	3	2	34
50-60	2	9	--	--	--	1	--	12
60+	3	10	1	--	--	3	--	17
60-180+	3	4	3	1	--	--	1	12
Ochre pit	--	3	--	--	1	--	--	4
Total	239	859	237	91	73	132	53	1,684

Cores reused as scrapers.—There is some evidence that a limited number of the cores already listed above were used as scrapers, although this is not demonstrable in a clear-cut way.

Besides the rather uniformly shaped core end fragments set apart as a group of steep scrapers formed by obvious reuse or retouch, ca. 15% of all cores show some debatable evidence that complete or virtually complete specimens were subsequently employed as implements per se in some manner that left definite signs of light to medium wear and heavier battering or even required some limited retouch at one or more points. It appears that certain protruding edges or sharp angles might have served as a convenient scraping edge. The most common site is the old striking platform edge, where a distinct concentration of small-scale retouch or wear cuts across the bases of the old flake- or blade-removal scars. More rarely, worn or retouched portions are to be found on the long dimension of the core along a flake- or blade-scar ridge. Also rare is secondary edge flaking at the tips of a spatulate or obtuse end of a core where the original core flaking has left either a broad, often concave, sharp, thin edge or a steep face rising from an edge or angle that was suitable for development as a scraper.

It has been difficult to draw a convincing line between the battering and intensely concentrated shattering of the flint edge due to unsuccessful flint removal and the edge flaking due to reuse. As a rule, however, if a specimen has batter scars that occur at angles that conform to the hollows, ridges, and general trend of the primary blade or flake scars and are irregularly located, and if it has a platform edge that remains scalloped, the tendency has been to consider it simply as a core. On the other hand, if the secondary scars are on a smaller scale, close to the edge, and concentrated in a regular, uninterrupted line, and if the platform edge profile is evened out rather than scalloped, the piece is regarded as a scraper.

Edge battering is normally considered to be associated with flake or blade removal and frequently coincides with the segments of the striking platform arc from which blades and flakes have been removed. It has not been noted on a cortex back or flake-scarred back segment of a core. Mostly, the observed battering coincides with stretches where flint is recalcitrant (i.e., where the piece bulges out or resists being broken off into long blade or flake forms), or the battering may flank, for short stretches, the place where blades have been cleanly removed, or it may appear in obvious association with failed attempts to lift off a blade or flake. In these cases it is considered that the cores were not reused as scrapers.

It is interesting to note that of all the core types found at Karim Shahir, only the incipient pyramidal cores on pebbles and the polyhedral/amorphous cores do not include specimens with traces of possible reuse as tools. Their pebblelike and thick spheroid or cuboid shapes evidently offer no suitable projections or edges for use as scrapers or other tools. Among pyramidal cores, the type of reuse, influenced probably by the shape of the core itself, seems to have been confined largely to edge wear at or near the spatulate butt end or along a longitudinal edge near it. Also, some core fragments classifiable as plunging flakes or bladelike flakes that carried away a tiny portion of the striking platform and a large part of the flaking face of the core (including all of the relatively bulky tip end) bear wear or retouch down one or both edges and faces of the long dimension, often near the old striking platform or bulbar end. Typologically these may be viewed as poorly developed side scrapers, concave scrapers, or at least reused pieces.

The following two tabulations summarize, for each core type, first, the positioning of and the frequency of examples with edge flaking and second, the incidence of traces of the kind of edge flaking that could be taken as evidence for the reuse of these cores and major core fragments as scrapers. These pieces have already been accounted for above as cores and are here simply observed from a different point of view without being counted a second time.

Cores Reused as Scrapers

	Pyramidal							
	Fully flaked	Partial, cortex back or flake-scarred back	Partial, right-angle-flake-scarred back	Incipient, on pebble	Bipolar	Polyhedral/ amorphous	Discoid	Total
Positioning of Edge Flaking								
(1) On edges of striking platform								
(a) Striking platform face	--	2	--	--	--	--	--	2
(b) Flaking face	21	56	4	--	6	--	3	90
(2) On long dimension	--	3	4	--	1	--	--	8
(3) On spatulate tip ends	1	7	2	--	--	--	--	10
(4) Combination of above	1*,1†	1	1†	--	--	--	--	4
Total	24	69	11	--	7	--	3	114
Incidence of Possible Reuse of Cores, Based on Spot Checks of Edge Flaking								
Total no. checked	115	491	110	--	38	--	26	
No. possibly reused	24	69	11	--	7	--	3	
Percentage reused	20.8	14.1	9.9	--	18.4	--	11.5	
Average Percentage of Cores Reused: ca. 14.95								

NOTE: Total count for this category of artifact is included under cores in summary tabulation on page 104.
*Combination of (2) and (3).
†Combination of (1b) and (3).

Core Parts

There is a sizeable miscellaneous group of core parts composed of pieces produced deliberately when reviving cores and of accidentally broken pieces. This group comprises *core revival tablets, flakes,* and *blades* that attest to the rejuvenation of the striking platform ends, flaking faces, and sides of cores of all kinds; *portions* that are relatively large, thick parts of recognizable but unclassifiable cores; and small, thick angular *fragments* too restricted in size and too amorphous to be classified other than as pieces presumed to be from cores.

Any examples bearing marked signs of readaptation as other tools or of reuse have been included under other appropriate headings elsewhere. Only those core parts with no sign of significant secondary working remain in this present group and are briefly characterized and listed below.

Core revival tablets.—These pieces are normally roughly discoid flakes knocked off to revive the striking platform face and edge. They have carried away all or a good part of the platform and of the adjacent truncated top ends of flake or blade scars on the platform's periphery. The face bearing these scars is generally at or close to right angles with the plane of the platform or truncation.

Core revival flakes.—These flakes usually bear a part of the striking platform surface and a part of the flaking face, with the striking platform portion often representing a lesser proportion of the whole. They have been struck, often at right angles, across the flake removal axis of the cores. Thus, the old striking edge along the rim of the platform is apt to have become a ridge or crest somewhere across the obverse face of the revival flake, dividing that face into two parts.

Core revival blades.—These pieces, also called *crested blades*, are sometimes considered to have been knocked off longitudinally along the crest of the striking edge formed at the junction of the flaking face and the striking platform. They have carried away roughly equal long, narrow portions of the striking platform and flaking face. It is possible that this may have been done to help revive the striking edge. On the other hand, these pieces may have been made by striking along the transversely flaked crest formed down the back or sides of certain partial pyramidal cores, those with right-angle-flake-scarred backs (fig. 20:2). In such cases the blade may have been struck off to start a new flaking point or face, to reshape a core, or to reduce the size of a crest at that point. Thus, all the blades made in these two ways are apt to have truncated scars at right angles to the central ridge, or crest, on either or both flanks of that ridge.

Core portions.—This category is made up of two sorts of pieces: some are rather like over-thick core tablets bearing truncated blade or flake scars on all or part of a cylindrical face and have one end constituting the striking platform and the other end truncated, or else both ends truncated; others consist of thick plunging flakes (those that carry off all, or a good part, of the core end opposite its striking platform because the shock wave from the detaching blow on the striking platform turned inward instead of outward) or other irregular bulky fragments that have carried away a major proportion of a core.

Core fragments.—This category comprises various thick angular fragments of cores too incomplete to classify by type of core or by any possible function. They also lack obvious signs of wear or retouch. They are amorphous, thick, multiscarred fragments or equally massive and amorphous flakes (primary, secondary, or tertiary) struck from pebbles in preparing a core, as well as parts of core masses or butt ends, perhaps carried away by a misplaced blow on the striking platform or elsewhere. Many are of poor-quality rock.

Core Parts

Depth (cm)	Surface	Operation and area														
		I														
		Step	A	B	C	Ext.	F	G	Tr.	II	III	IV	V	VI	VIII	Total
Core Revival Tablets																
Surface																0
0-20		2	7	8	1	51	9	2	3	--	7	1	6	7	3	107
20-30		--	5	12	18	--	9	5	--	--	--	--	--	--	--	49
20-40		4	--	--	--	--	--	--	--	--	4	--	--	--	--	8
30-40		--	--	--	5	--	1	--	--	--	--	--	--	--	--	6
40-50		--	--	--	2	--	5	--	--	--	--	--	--	--	--	7
40-60		--	--	--	--	--	--	--	--	--	--	--	--	--	--	0
50-60		--	--	--	1	--	1	--	--	--	--	--	--	--	--	2
60+		--	--	--	1	--	1	--	--	--	--	--	--	--	--	2
Ochre pit		--	--	--	--	--	--	--	--	--	--	--	--	--	--	0
Total	0	6	12	20	28	51	26	7	3	0	11	1	6	7	3	181
Core Revival Flakes																
Surface																0
0-20		7	2	17	3	57	2	2	3	--	8	2	7	8	3	121
20-30		--	9	12	22	--	21	11	--	--	--	--	4	--	--	79
20-40		2	--	--	--	--	--	--	--	--	3	--	--	--	--	5
30-40		--	--	--	6	--	--	14	--	--	--	--	--	--	--	20

Core Parts—Continued

Depth (cm)	Surface	I Step	A	B	C	Ext.	F	G	Tr.	II	III	IV	V	VI	VIII	Total
40-50	--	--	--	--	1	--	--	13	--	--	--	--	--	--	--	14
40-60	--	--	--	--	--	--	--	--	--	--	3	--	--	1	--	4
50-60	--	--	--	--	2	--	--	--	--	--	--	--	--	--	--	2
60+	--	2	--	--	3	--	--	3	--	--	1	--	--	--	--	9
Ochre pit	--	--	--	--	--	--	--	--	--	--	--	--	--	--	--	0
Total	0	11	11	29	37	57	23	43	3	0	15	2	11	9	3	254
Core Revival Blades																
Surface	99															99
0-20	--	5	--	10	2	34	4	--	3	--	7	--	6	8	4	83
20-30	--	--	6	9	31	--	26	21	--	--	--	--	1	--	--	94
20-40	--	7	--	--	--	--	--	--	--	--	1	--	--	--	--	8
30-40	--	--	--	--	14	--	--	17	--	--	--	--	--	--	--	31
40-50	--	--	--	--	4	--	--	17	--	--	--	--	--	--	--	21
40-60	--	--	--	--	--	--	--	--	--	--	1	--	--	--	--	1
50-60	--	--	--	--	--	--	--	--	--	--	--	--	--	--	--	0
60+	--	2	--	--	4	--	--	4	--	--	--	1	--	--	--	11
Ochre pit	--	--	--	--	--	--	--	--	--	--	--	--	--	--	--	0
Total	99	14	6	19	55	34	30	59	3	0	9	1	7	8	4	348
Core Portions and Fragments																
Surface	285															285
0-20	--	161	215	115	197	3,937	274	327	97	80	433	50	168	51	36	6,141
20-30	--	--	78	112	375	--	176	148	--	--	--	--	85	--	--	974
20-40	--	82	--	--	--	--	--	--	--	--	41	13	--	8	--	144
30-40	--	--	--	--	113	--	--	216	--	--	--	--	--	--	--	329
40-50	--	--	--	--	102	--	--	183	--	--	--	--	--	--	--	285
40-60	--	93	--	--	--	--	--	--	--	--	21	--	--	6	--	120
50-60	--	--	--	--	42	--	--	47	--	--	--	--	--	--	--	89
60+	--	67	--	--	99	--	--	82	--	--	26	1	--	--	--	275
Ochre pit	--	28	--	--	--	--	--	--	--	--	--	--	--	--	--	28
Total	285	431	293	227	928	3,937	450	1,003	97	80	521	64	253	65	36	8,670

Totals—Core Parts

Depth (cm)	Core revival tablets	Core revival flakes	Core revival blades	Core portions and fragments	Total
Surface	--	--	99	285	384
0-20	107	121	83	6,141	6,452
20-30	49	79	94	974	1,196
20-40	8	5	8	144	165
30-40	6	20	31	329	386
40-50	7	14	21	285	327
40-60	--	4	1	120	125
50-60	2	2	--	89	93
60+	2	9	11	275	297
Ochre pit	--	--	--	28	28
Total	181	254	348	8,670	9,453

Trimming Debris

This large and highly heterogeneous category is made up of whole and fragmentary pieces with virtually no signs of wear, use, or retouch visible to the naked eye. During careful classification of all chipped flint material from the site, these pieces were closely inspected by eye and finally relegated to this remnant category as being of no typological or functional significance. The group comprises such core-knapping debris as flakes and blades, both normal and microlithic, as well as insignificant essentially characterless fragments of these types and small bits of other stone debris such as hammerstones, firestones, and pebbles used as tools or as material for making tools. However, it must be emphasized that more finely nuanced realms of function and typology that would permit this body of trimming debris and tools to be largely absorbed into use categories already described would doubtless emerge if the specimens were to be submitted to microscopic analyses. Such analyses, of the sort that has been developed over the two decades since the Karim Shahir fieldwork and artifactual analysis were carried out, are aided by metallizers and colorizers to dramatize traces of action along edges and other working areas and have been described in several studies (e.g., Semenov 1964; Tringham et al. 1974; Odell et al. 1976). Ultimately, the entire trimming-debris category (with the exception of some 600 such pieces contained in the representative cross section of artifacts deposited in Baghdad) was discarded after the absence of any macroscopic edge wear was established and the final gross tallies of blades and flakes were recorded.

It is noteworthy that flakes and flake fragments in this debris outnumbered blades and their fragments by over three to one. Since on other grounds the industry at Karim Shahir was clearly a blade industry, the preponderance of presumably unused flake debris over blade debris suggests that blades were picked up and used (and so found their way into the large use categories of multipurpose "tools of opportunity") to a much greater extent than were the irregular flake and flake fragment debris counterparts.

With regard to any future microwear studies on the material from this site, it may be said that to counterbalance the possible gap in evidence caused by the discarding of the so-called trimming debris there remain on deposit at the Oriental Institute over 32,000 pieces of the various large use categories (heavy, normal, and slight wear; nibbling; notching). Since this body of material is as near as possible to a total collection of pieces representing these arbitrary segments of the artifactual record in the deposits excavated, it should provide an adequate sampling upon which to base any refined microscopic studies for wear and function.

Trimming Debris

Depth (cm)	Surface	Operation and area														Total
		I														
		Step	A	B	C	Ext.	F	G	Tr.	II	III	IV	V	VI	VIII	
Blades and Blade Fragments, Normal-sized																
Surface	20															20
0-20		368	4	4	15	389	32	4	27	3	109	1	162	17	61	1,196
20-30		--	15	69	506	--	85	225	--	--	--	--	14	--	--	914
20-40		45	--	--	--	--	--	--	--	--	8	3	1	--	--	57
30-40		--	--	--	107	--	--	108	--	--	--	--	--	--	--	215
40-50		--	--	--	53	--	--	54	--	--	--	--	--	--	--	107
40-60		55	--	--	--	--	--	--	--	--	8	1	--	3	--	67
50-60		--	--	--	29	--	--	30	--	--	--	--	--	--	--	59
60+		60	--	--	45	--	--	60	--	--	18	1	--	--	--	184
Ochre pit		25	--	--	--	--	--	--	--	--	--	--	--	--	--	25
Total	20	553	19	73	755	389	117	481	27	3	143	6	177	20	61	2,844
Blades and Blade Fragments, Microlithic																
Surface	35															35
0-20		170	6	44	34	1,288	61	9	37	--	169	2	115	8	71	2,014
20-30		--	17	55	72	--	99	207	--	--	--	--	55	--	--	505
20-40		19	--	--	--	--	--	--	--	--	--	4	--	5	--	28
30-40		--	--	--	151	--	--	42	--	--	--	--	--	--	--	193
40-50		--	--	--	11	--	--	173	--	--	--	--	--	--	--	184
40-60		32	--	--	--	--	--	--	--	--	3	5	--	1	--	41
50-60		--	--	--	63	--	--	52	--	--	--	--	--	--	--	115
60+		25	--	--	117	--	--	118	--	--	45	2	--	--	--	307
Ochre pit		20	--	--	--	--	--	--	--	--	--	--	--	--	--	20
Total	35	266	23	99	448	1,288	160	601	37	0	217	13	170	14	71	3,442

Trimming Debris—Continued

Depth (cm)	Surface	Operation and area														Total
		I														
		Step	A	B	C	Ext.	F	G	Tr.	II	III	IV	V	VI	VIII	
Flakes and Flake Fragments, Normal-sized																
Surface	186															186
0-20		680	264	239	330	3,534	425	131	172	6	390	33	324	68	107	6,703
20-30		--	85	181	887	--	348	467	--	--	--	--	110	--	--	2,078
20-40		300	--	--	--	--	--	--	--	--	64	5	--	4	--	373
30-40		--	--	--	352	--	--	369	--	--	--	--	--	--	--	721
40-50		--	--	--	147	--	--	245	--	--	--	--	--	--	--	392
40-60		273	--	--	--	--	--	--	--	--	39	3	--	2	--	317
50-60		--	--	--	81	--	--	48	--	--	--	--	--	--	--	129
60+		189	--	--	109	--	--	94	--	--	12	--	--	--	--	404
Ochre pit		66	--	--	--	--	--	--	--	--	--	--	--	--	--	66
Total	186	1,508	349	420	1,906	3,534	773	1,354	172	6	505	41	434	74	107	11,369
Flakes and Flake Fragments, Microlithic																
Surface	74															74
0-20		16	60	262	230	2,835	202	19	168	3	1,328	9	542	11	173	5,858
20-30		--	57	52	796	--	237	288	--	--	--	--	238	--	--	1,668
20-40		194	--	--	--	--	--	--	--	--	20	22	--	1	--	237
30-40		--	--	--	146	--	--	179	--	--	--	--	--	--	--	325
40-50		--	--	--	45	--	--	727	--	--	--	--	--	--	--	772
40-60		138	--	--	--	--	--	--	--	--	3	15	--	2	--	158
50-60		--	--	--	132	--	--	137	--	--	--	--	--	--	--	269
60+		154	--	--	371	--	--	439	--	--	90	8	--	--	--	1,062
Ochre pit		59	--	--	--	--	--	--	--	--	--	--	--	--	--	59
Total	74	561	117	314	1,720	2,835	439	1,789	168	3	1,441	54	780	14	173	10,482

Totals—Trimming Debris

Depth (cm)	Blades and blade fragments		Flakes and flake fragments		Total
	Normal-sized	Microlithic	Normal-sized	Microlithic	
Surface	20	35	186	74	315
0-20	1,196	2,014	6,703	5,858	15,771
20-30	914	505	2,078	1,668	5,165
20-40	57	28	373	237	695
30-40	215	193	721	325	1,454
40-50	107	184	392	772	1,455
40-60	67	41	317	158	583
50-60	59	115	129	269	572
60+	184	307	404	1,062	1,957
Ochre pit	25	20	66	59	170
Total	2,844	3,442	11,369	10,482	28,137

REPRESENTATIVE CROSS SECTION OF STONE ARTIFACTS DEPOSITED IN BAGHDAD

It must be remembered that this study is based solely upon the great bulk of material deposited in Chicago and the 52 special registered objects divided between the Iraq Museum in Baghdad and the Oriental Institute in Chicago. It omits consideration of 2,397 stone artifacts that were selected as a representative cross section of the stone industry in 1951 after the excavations were completed and have been kept in Baghdad since then, according to requirements of the

Iraqi Directorate of Antiquities. While this sample was selected according to the already quite workable preliminary typological categories decided upon toward the end of the field season at Karim Shahir, it could not later be subjected to the kind of final refining process that was applied to the greater body of material brought to Chicago. It has been necessary, therefore, to exclude the Baghdad samples from consideration in the final analyses. As may be seen when the figures given for the types in the limited Baghdad group are compared with the figures for the types reported in the main body of this study, the various smaller quantities in the cross section in Baghdad, which represent most of the major categories, not only are large enough to exemplify those categories effectively there but, at the same time, when subtracted from the total number of stone tools found, are small enough not to skew the study's morphological characterizations of the artifactual materials from the site.

The stone artifacts constituting this representative cross section in Baghdad are, with the exception of the pecked and worn hand rubbing stone, drawn entirely from the chipped stone categories. The selection was made in this way because this body of material was intended to complement the few selected special objects of ground and polished stone, bone, shell, and clay already represented in the Iraq Museum in Baghdad as its required share of registered unique objects. Thus, a spectrum of most of the major types of artifactual material from Karim Shahir is on file in Baghdad in a condensed and manageable form.

The items selected for this representative cross section came entirely from operation I and were drawn from all parts and most levels investigated in this operation. They are here summarized according to the preliminary field categories applicable in 1951. Fortunately, these categories coincide well with the final nomenclature used elsewhere in this report, lacking only more refined subdivision in some cases. Since the final study showed that there were no detectable typological or morphological shifts in the artifactual material, either within the stratigraphic sequence or in areal distribution in this single occupation horizon, the quantities for types in the representative cross section in Baghdad that were originally recorded by level and area are here amalgamated into totals.

Type	No.	Type	No.
Hand rubbing stones	1	Notched flakes, normal-sized and microlithic	90
Backed blades, normal-sized	3	Used blades, normal-sized and microlithic	525
Backed bladelets, microlithic	57	Used flakes, normal-sized and microlithic	473
Fabricators	3	Pyramidal cores, partial and fully flaked	76
Drills, normal-sized	6	Bipolar cores	6
Drills, microlithic and supermicrolithic	12	Polyhedral/amorphous cores	10
Burins	1	Discoid cores	7
End scrapers on blades and flakes	5	Core revival tablets	8
Side scrapers	17	Core revival flakes	19
Steep scrapers on core fragments	3	Core revival blades	15
Rounded scrapers	10	Core fragments and portions	47
Nibbled blades, normal-sized and microlithic	133	Trimming debris—blades, normal-sized and microlithic	208
Nibbled flakes, normal-sized and microlithic	62	Trimming debris—flakes, normal-sized and microlithic	405
Notched blades, normal-sized and microlithic	195	Total	2,397

Faunal and Floral Material

The faunal and floral material found at Karim Shahir was limited in quantity. The shallow deposits exposed to the elements on this hilltop and disturbed by plowing yielded remarkably little, much weathered, fragmentary bone and shell and also extremely little useful floral material. However, these finds do reveal certain information, which is briefly summarized here.

Fauna

Animal Bones

The study of the fragmentary animal bones from Karim Shahir was ultimately carried out by Dr. Hans R. Stampfli in combination with a study of animal bones from Jarmo and other sites (chap. 9). His findings on the Karim Shahir series are summarized here. On the basis of this study he found no evidence for the domestication of any species at Karim Shahir. In the case of the preponderant sheep and goat, while there was nothing to prove that they had *not* been domesticated, he judged, on balance, that it was improbable they had been. There were no indications of juvenile sheep, goat, pig, or other animals. Moreover, the bones were of the size of those of wild species. Stampfli concluded that the occupants of Karim Shahir were exclusively hunters.

Stampfli considered that about 47% of the 265 bones available to him were sheep and goat, while smaller percentages of other species were represented, as follows: 7.1%, wild boar; 7.1%, deer; 4.2%, gazelle; 3.5%, wild cattle; 3.5%, fox; 0.7%, hare; 10%, turtle, birds, and other forms. A final 17% remain unidentified. In ordering this material to try to account for the number of individual animals perhaps represented here, Stampfli was able to demonstrate that there were 19 individuals distributed among the different forms, so that sheep and goat were still the most numerous (9), with boar (3), gazelle (2), and fox (2), and the other species (1 each) giving very restricted but still significant and enlightening evidence. In one case, a single *Bos* bone was deemed to be intrusive and of modern origin because its color was unlike that of all the other bones found. This is quite conceivable in view of the shallowness of the deposit and the presence of several other intrusive materials at the site.

In addition to Stampfli's data, a little more information may be derived from Barth's initial, informal report on the original lot of 454 bones recorded for the site, which Barth had kept for study after processing them in the field (SAOC 31, p. 53). While definitely superseded by Stampfli's analysis, Barth's tentative preliminary listing is the only evidence now remaining about that part of the material, some 40% of which has been lost to sight. Thus it is worth emphasizing that Barth's original notes indicate there were a very few bones that suggested the presence of marten, wolf, and a canine, as well as numerous turtle bones, all of which simply reinforces Stampfli's conclusion that the hunting of wild forms prevailed at Karim Shahir. In other respects, Barth's type list agrees with Stampfli's.

Shells

Karim Shahir yielded a moderate quantity of shells, mainly those of several species of land snails. Most of this material was in fragmentary condition. It was scattered among the general debris; some pieces were found clustered together, and others occurred as isolated specimens. A very few samples of fragmentary freshwater clam shell were also found.

Land and Freshwater Shells*

Species	Operation							Total
	I	II	III	IV	V	VI	VIII	
Land snails								
Helix salomonica Naegele	15	4	6	3	1	2	1	32
Jaminia septemdentata triticea Rossm.	5	--	2	2	1	--	1	11
Helicella vestalis joppensis Roth	5	--	1	2	--	--	1	9
Helicella langloisiana	1	--	--	--	--	--	--	1
	26	4	9	7	2	2	3	53
Freshwater clams								
Unio tigridis Bourg?	1	--	--	--	1	--	--	2
Total								55

*Identified by Dr. Joseph C. Bequaert, Harvard University. Summary based on intact or identifiable fragmentary specimens.

The occasional much-defaced fragment that was inconclusively identified as marine shell also came to light. Most of the possible marine shells were taken to be items of ornament, probably fossil forms of *Dentalium* from rock formations in the area.

The shells occurred at virtually all levels down to the base of excavations, which varied according to locality from no more than 0.2-0.6 m to 1.0, 1.8, and 3.0 m in depth. The shells were in some cases dispersed well below the occupation horizon via numerous rodent holes. Nearly half (26) of these identified specimens came from the presumably undisturbed portions of the occupation layer at a depth of ca. 20-60 cm.

It is noteworthy that there is no evidence of fish.

FLORA

The only examples of flora that could be identified from Karim Shahir were found in ten of the larger charcoal specimens submitted to Professor Elso S. Barghoorn of Harvard University. His personal communications to Robert J. Braidwood furnish the basis for the following summary.

Barghoorn reported that the specimens were prepared with difficulty because they were excessively hard, brittle, fragile, and of an easily disintegrating consistency, probably due to their exposure to ground water and chemical processes in the soil for a long period.

Seven of the ten specimens are of the wood of *Zelkova*?, a tree of the Ulmaceae closely related to elm. These specimens conform in all respects to *Zelkova crenata*, a present inhabitant (reportedly now rare) of the wooded areas of Iraq, although there is a possibility that they are *Celtis*, a closely related genus. Two specimens are *Tamarix* sp. and one is the mesquitelike leguminous tree *Prosopis*. The absence of oak at Karim Shahir is curious but may be attributed perhaps to the statistics of sampling, although this seems doubtful in view of its abundance at nearby Jarmo and Palegawra. The occurrence of *Zelkova?* at Karim Shahir is notable since it is absent at the other two sites. *Tamarix* is a tree of river valleys in semiarid regions, but its ecology is not entirely clear. The occurrence of *Prosopis* here is interesting since, by analogy with the situation in southwestern United States and western South America, it seems to be a dry grassland tree perhaps forming scrub forests.

The materials studied came from combined lots collected in operation I. Five of the pieces of *Zelkova?* were from depths of 0-20 cm; specimens of *Prosopis, Zelkova?*, and *Tamarix* came from 20-100 cm; and one piece of *Tamarix* was found in the large, deep pit containing traces of red ochre near the north end of the step. It was also reported that the *Prosopis* specimen had much gum in its mass. One could therefore perhaps suspect it of being a recent intrusion at the site, like the few iron, glass, and pottery pieces and the single relatively fresh-looking *Bos* bone noted by Stampfli. On the other hand, the *Prosopis* came from well down in the deposits (though perhaps via rodent holes?). It is noteworthy, however, that *Prosopis* is reported present, though insignificant, in the Bus Mordeh phase of Ali Kosh, but in quantity in overlying later phases there, where Helbaek considers its pods were a grazing and fodder item and, perhaps, even a human diet item (Helbaek in Hole, Flannery, and Neely 1969, Appendix I, pp. 395-96 and table 3). Thus, the plant may have played some role in the diet at Karim Shahir. One cannot entirely dismiss the possibility, in a partly disturbed and so shallow a site, that all these different specimens of tree types making up this puzzling combination may be intrusive.

Otherwise, evidence for organic remains of such possible food items as nuts, seeds, and grains was not established. According to Dr. Hans Helbaek of the Danish National Museum, there was not enough such seed and plant material found at Karim Shahir for any exact determinations to be made or for any conclusions to be drawn about the presence or absence of either food collecting or cultivation. Given the poor state of preservation of the bone and shell materials at this shallow, one-period site, it is small wonder that plant materials did not survive.

SUMMARY AND DISCUSSION

There follows here a summary and discussion of the evidence found in the excavations at Karim Shahir, including the traces of settlement and occupation, the artifacts, and the faunal and floral materials, by which one can acquire some limited conception of the way of life at that time and place. The body of evidence, produced primarily by the extensive operation I adjacent to the scarp edge and also to a much lesser degree by operations II through VIII, is here treated as a unit.

Traces of Settlement and Occupation

Karim Shahir was a single-horizon open-air settlement located on an exposed hilltop, apparently mainly near the edge of a scarp and overlooking a wide sector of landscape, with what is today a seasonal stream visible some 40 m below. Today, the eastern edge of the site is being truncated by this scarp due to the erosive action of this stream. Thus, part of the original settlement area has been lost; Wright (pers. comm.) has estimated that perhaps one third of it is gone and also that at the time of occupation the stream, then presumably perennial, probably lay at only one third of the present vertical distance below the site. Moreover, repeated plowing and slope wash have disturbed and redeposited the topmost layers of soil. Weathering and leaching action and the formation of calcareous concretions have further affected the deposits. Nevertheless, what may be a generous sampling of the core occupation area was excavated in operation I.

The area that was exposed first revealed mainly a disorderly layer of field stones and river pebbles. Tracing the extent of this rocky scatter helped to delimit what remained of the heart of the habitation site, estimated at about 700 m^2. In other operations separate, smaller areas of rocky scatter and associated artifactual material and debris were found. Thus one envisages a vaguely defined, rather extensive major camping area concentrated along the scarp, with small isolated outliers dotted over the hilltop. Perhaps a surviving true nucleus is to be seen in the compact rocky pavementlike area, a 50-60 m^2 zone of presumably undisturbed stones, situated at or near the present scarp and providing an excellent lookout point over the district. These stones were not placed with any visible plan.

The "pavement" and the more openly scattered rocky area formed the surface of the 20-40 cm occupation deposit which lay at or just below the surface. Both areas were richly littered with artifactual and animal debris, including flint cores, chipped implements, used pieces, and trimming debris; much rarer ground and polished stone, bone, and shell artifacts; a handful of clay pieces; a considerable quantity of poorly preserved and fragmented animal bone material; a limited number of shells, principally those of land snails; and a widely but sparsely disseminated quantity of comminuted charcoal bits from which a few identifications of trees and shrubs have been made. All of this diverse debris attests to intensive living activity at this site.

Excavation also revealed a number of pits and depressions depending from the rocky layer to different depths. Some are taken to be fire or cooking pits, as they contained material discolored and cracked by fire—stones, burned animal bone, and occasionally flint debris.

Occasional broad discolored soil zones remotely suggested basins or floors rather than pits, but they were so limited in extent, so vaguely defined, and their deposits so thin that they do not seem to have been other than shallow depressions that became filled with small amounts of living-floor debris discarded in the course of daily activities and also brought down by slope wash. Nothing indicates whether or not they were ever covered.

In association with one deeper pit that was filled with debris-laden earth from the surrounding habitation and had a basined bottom carefully coated with red ochre were found the only two clay figures unearthed at the site. The conjunction of ochre and figurines here implies the likelihood of ceremonial activity.

These various pits and depressions, the rocky scatter and "pavement," and the associated debris are the only evidence of settlement installations noted, save for the two lumps of clay suspected of being associated with wattle-and-daub construction (p. 45). No formal trace of house floors, pit houses, postholes, walls, or other alignments were found despite scraping and a close watch for such structural features. Of course, there may have been some sort of ephemeral shelters or lean-tos such as might be found even in the most favored of fair weather sites. While permanent types of structures may possibly exist elsewhere at this extensive site and have not been revealed, due to the mischances of excavation or erosion, the evident lack of anything sturdier or more perennial must for now suggest that Karim Shahir was an encampment that was either used once for a relatively long time or else was occupied repeatedly for certain periods and remained unencumbered with "permanent" structures. Whether the site was truly a base camp or outlier, specialized or seasonal, cannot be determined from this line of evidence. Reason suggests it was a fair weather and therefore seasonal camp in this region of hard winters, while the area of occupation and amount of debris may imply that it was a more settled base camp. Certainly a convincing estimate of the number of inhabitants cannot be logically made from any line of evidence. In any case, perhaps not more than a few dozen individuals at a time can be pictured as occupying the site.

Artifactual Evidence

The following categories of artifacts at Karim Shahir have been selected to provide a trait list for the site. Such a list of elements enables one to characterize the typology and morphology of the particular assemblage here and to contrast it with the assemblages at other pertinent sites. By this step of comparison the various ways of life at the sites and their relationships may possibly be revealed. The only formal categories not included in this summary treatment are (a) artifacts bearing a black substance (bitumen?), (b) items marked with red ochre, (c) ochre fragments and discolored concretions, and (d) unclassifiable flakes and fragments with flat rubbed surfaces. The pieces in (a) and (b) are accounted for under their appropriate typological headings; items in (c) were not counted and in any case were probably mostly natural pieces; the bits of rubbed pieces in (d) were small, diagnostically useless fragments presumably from a variety of milling stones discussed under other headings.

For convenient reference, the following listing gives the pages of this chapter on which the various artifactual categories are described in detail. In some cases the page of the general section only is noted; in other cases reference is made to the page on which a specific typological group may be found.

Summary of Finds at Karim Shahir

Category and page number in text		Number of specimens
INTRUSIVE MATERIALS (p. 44)		
Metal		2
Glass		4
Pottery		15
Obsidian		5
Total intrusive materials		26
MATERIALS BELONGING TO THE HORIZON (p. 44)		
Lightly baked clay (p. 44)		
Rod	1	
Figurines	2	
Hardened clay with impressions	2	
Total lightly baked clay		5
Bone (p. 46)		
Tools	9	
Beads	5	
Total bone		14
Shell (p. 47)		
Plaques	10	
Beads	3	
Total shell		13

Summary of Finds at Karim Shahir—*Continued*

Category and page number in text	Number of specimens	
Ground and pecked stone (p. 48)		
Bracelets and rings (p. 48)	25	
Plaques and pendants (p. 49)	10	
Beads (p. 50)	9	
Rod (p. 50)	1	
Grooved rubbing stones (p. 51)	19	
Pierced pebbles (p. 53)	4	
Striated pebbles (p. 53)	18	
Used discoid pebbles (p. 54)	2	
Chipped and polished celts (p. 54)	42	
Boulder mortars (p. 60)	8	
Shaped pestles (p. 60)	3	
Natural pebble pestles (p. 61)	13	
Palette (p. 61)	1	
Grindstones (querns) (p. 62)	4	
Hand rubbing stones (mullers) (p. 62)	23	
Hammerstones (p. 64)	39	
Total ground and pecked stone		221
Minerals		
Heavy chert pieces containing iron (p. 66)	19	
Total minerals		19
Chipped stone (p. 67)		
Sheen-bearing flint pieces (p. 67)	24	
Denticulated blades and flakes (p. 69)	15	
Backed blades (p. 69)		
Normal-sized (p. 69)	9	
Microlithic (p. 70)	415	
Total backed blades	424	
Fabricators (p. 71)	46	
Drills (p. 71)		
Normal-sized (p. 71)	40	
Microlithic (p. 71)	63	
Supermicrolithic (p. 73)	31	
Total drills	134	
Miscellaneous microliths (p. 73)		
End scrapers on bladelets and flakelets (p. 73)	320	
Pointed bladelets (p. 73)	27	
Chance geometric microliths (p. 73)	4	
Total miscellaneous microliths	351	
Unworked triangular or trapezoidal segments of blades (p. 76)	120	
Microburins (p. 77)	30	
Burins (p. 77)	80	
Burin spalls (p. 79)	60	
Scrapers (p. 79)		
End scrapers on blades (p. 79)	527	
End scrapers on flakes (p. 81)	178	
Side scrapers (p. 81)	232	
Steep scrapers on core fragments (p. 82)	26	
Rounded scrapers (p. 82)	83	
Total scrapers	1,046	
"Raclettes" (p. 83)	19	
Blades with obliquely truncated ends (p. 84)	59	
Blades and flakes with edge flaking (p. 84)		
Nibbled blades and flakes (p. 84)	3,252	
Notched blades (p. 85)	5,214	
Notched flakes (p. 87)	1,792	
Used blades (p. 88)	13,089	
Used flakes (p. 89)	9,534	
Total blades and flakes with edge flaking	32,881	

Summary of Finds at Karim Shahir—*Continued*

Category and page number in text	Number of specimens	
Cores (p. 89)		
Fully flaked pyramidal (p. 90)	239	
Partial pyramidal, cortex back or flake-scarred back (p. 90)	859	
Partial pyramidal, right-angle-flake-scarred back (p. 90)	237	
Incipient, on pebble (p. 90)	91	
Bipolar (p. 90)	73	
Polyhedral/amorphous (p. 91)	132	
Discoid (p. 91)	53	
Total cores	1,684	
(Cores reused as scrapers: count included under cores, above)	(114)	
Core parts (p. 94)		
Core revival tablets	181	
Core revival flakes	254	
Core revival blades	348	
Core portions and fragments	8,670	
Total core parts	9,453	
Trimming debris (p. 97)		
Blades and blade fragments, normal-sized	2,844	
Blades and blade fragments, microlithic	3,442	
Flakes and flake fragments, normal-sized	11,369	
Flakes and flake fragments, microlithic	10,482	
Total trimming debris	28,137	
Total chipped stone		74,563
Total materials belonging to the horizon		74,835

NOTE: The counts for artifacts bearing black substance (bitumen?) and for ochre-bearing pieces are included under the appropriate typological headings.

The virtual absence of *intrusive materials* at Karim Shahir is striking. When they are present, they are clearly of relatively recent character. Most came from on or close below the disturbed surface. The modern iron and glass may pass without further comment. The small number of potsherds, ranging from indeterminate age to modern Islamic, are either small, poor, plain handmade pieces or else wheelmade specimens of plain or blue-glazed wares. The obsidian includes a fragmentary end scraper, a used bladelet, and undistinctive small flakes or chips. None of the few bits of obsidian, pottery, glass, and iron that came from below the 20-cm level are to be culturally associated with the overwhelming mass of artifactual remains from the single occupation horizon. While a very few other limited categories to be discussed in the following paragraphs may be liable to some suspicion of being intrusive, the pieces mentioned above may be dismissed with impunity.

We may now move on to the summary consideration of the *materials belonging to the horizon*. These items are so classified either because of their position in the deposits or because of their typological character, widespread distribution at the site, or great quantities. They total 74,835 pieces, involving clay, bone, shell, and stone artifacts.

Of the *lightly baked clay objects*, the deep-lying small figurines are the most outstanding, while the rodlike object and the amorphous clay lumps are not only from on or near the surface and thus possibly from disturbed deposits but are also somewhat characterless, providing little potential for insights or comparisons.

The almost identical *figurines* suggest stylized animal or human creatures and compare, in a general way, with certain figurines found in the upper levels of Jarmo. The somewhat unsophisticated style of manipulating the clay by pinching and smoothing of simply shaped small masses, the lightly baked technique of manufacture, and the broadly similar conception of the pieces at both sites strongly suggest a generally common tradition of thought and workmanship but do not at all suggest any degree of contemporaneity. In contrast to figurines and simply worked clay elsewhere, the pieces at Karim Shahir are a unique form and a type apart, but they do bear some degree of stylistic, technical, and conceptual relationship to the much larger and more fully documented sampling from nearby Jarmo and whatever separate horizons may be represented there. Certainly their association at Karim Shahir with a pit smeared with red ochre suggests a ceremonial element.

The *rod fragment* has the same lightly baked dull tan features as the figurines at this site and at Jarmo, although perhaps it is somewhat harder. Because it displays some faint evidence for a pressed-down, folded-over flap of clay at its intact rounded tip end, it can be broadly compared to the category of "stalk objects" at Jarmo. If, as appears likely, this rod fragment can be provisionally accepted as a part of the assemblage from the Karim Shahir horizon proper, it betokens still another form and category of clay working, probably on the same level of sophistication as the two figurines, and reinforces the impression of a vague traditional and technotypological link between the two sites without in any way imposing the idea of contemporaneity or direct cultural relationships. On other grounds, primarily the sharp contrasts in the technotypology of artifacts and the dissimilarity of habitation types and of the floral and faunal records, the horizons at the two sites are quite distinct from each other.

The two amorphous *clay lumps* may or may not be contemporaneous with the Karim Shahir horizon but, in any case, are a different order of clay object. They might be meaningless accidental lumps or fragments left by chance near a fire and preserved by baking. On the other hand, judging from the impressions of perhaps either wood or reeds left on the surface of one lump, they may more likely be samples of wattle-and-daub work connected with some form of structure. It should be emphasized, however, that the somewhat ruddy orange tint and the definitely harder, well-compacted fabric of the two pieces—when compared with the somewhat more crumbly quality and dull tan color of the figurines and rod fragment—combine to raise the suspicion that these lumps, while not definitely to be excluded from the Karim Shahir horizon, might be from a later horizon, and may be made of clay from other sources and part of other working traditions than the aforementioned pieces. Nevertheless, while they could be considered along with the more definitely intrusive objects, we deliberately retain them here as the only possible evidence for wattle-and-daub structure in the Karim Shahir horizon.

All in all, the clay objects found at this site were probably a rare category even at the time of occupation. Over time, due to weathering and the shallowness of the occupation deposit almost all have understandably been eliminated and those that are left are in poor condition. At all events, the modest early stages of clay manipulation and of the expression of ideas and needs in clay were evidently present at the time of this horizon.

For similar reasons, *bone objects* seem to have scarcely survived and surely have been left to us in unrepresentative numbers. Naturally, larger quantities of bone artifacts than the nine fragmentary bone tools and five beads were implied by the thousands of flints and numerous bone fragments found at the site. Some of the bone tools seem to have been simple awls made on long bones or long-bone splinters; others, much more carefully fashioned, strongly suggest pins or needles, although no pierced examples were found. Thus, insofar as a very narrowly confined sampling of bone tools can serve reliably to indicate the categories, Karim Shahir evidently had a limited range of simple bone tools. The so-called beads are, without exception, truncated segments of small, light long bones, presumably of birds, with differing degrees of faint beveling, cutting, or filing at the ends, which allow most of them to be classified as artificially prepared pieces of ornament. Like the bone tools, this category is a simple, widespread one in time and space with no special diagnostic characteristics at Karim Shahir. The tools point indirectly to the preparation and use of soft materials such as skin and wood and perhaps to the making of basketry or textiles at this site, while the beads imply a concern with personal adornment.

Shell pieces also survived in very limited quantity and are presumably entirely in the ornament category, either for adorning the body or for decorating clothing or equipment. They consist of parts of small pierced plaques and some plain beads made of various kinds of freshwater shells. Some marine forms may have been fossils. Thus, no assumptions can be made regarding any contemporary marine source.

Of the total number of stone tools, ornaments, and associated by-products (exclusive of cores, their parts, and trimming debris), only 0.48% are ground and pecked. The *ground stone ornaments* make up a very small but distinctive part of this ground and pecked group. The outstanding category consists of the fragments of white marble thought to be parts of bracelets and rings. All except one whose provenience is suspect are oval in cross section, and some have a sharp carination of the exterior edge; these two features are presumed to be diagnostic for the site, although the size varies. Most are severely uniform and simple, and all but one are unornamented and thereby in contrast to similar objects with some elaboration that were found at Jarmo (cf. fig. 135). Yet, like the clay figurines and rod, these finely worked marble ornaments suggest some degree of common tradition with Jarmo, but not necessarily a relationship in time.

Most of the fragmentary plaques and pendants are of white marble or crystalline limestone. Some of the specimens are pierced. Although many of the fragments have no holes, they are assumed to have been parts of pierced pieces. There is a variety of simple geometric forms, all unornamented, flat, and thin, with faint striations attesting to manufacture by abrasion. On the whole, these plain white marble plaques and pendants constitute a distinctive group; the Jarmo counterparts tend toward other forms, some of which are ornamented (cf. esp. figs. 136:25-27; 142:15,20).

The stone beads make up a somewhat more varied group than do the bracelets, rings, plaques, and pendants, but in general they are simple unornamented cylindrical or barrel-shaped forms made of creamy tan to white marble, limestone, steatite, and other workable stone. An exception, with no counterparts found elsewhere, is an elongated, biconical form with a planoconvex cross section and twin holes at each end that are angled from end to planar face, as if the form were designed for a button or plaquelike attachment to some object rather than for serial stringing as a bead.

The stone bracelets, rings, plaques, pendants, and beads are all simple forms made of selected workable softer stone, probably found in the prodigal assortment of stream gravels of the immediate district, and therefore these objects were presumably made on the spot. They may all have been body ornaments, although some may have been applied to skins, textiles, or basketry. They are all witness to considerable skill and sophistication in stoneworking and a certain preoccupation with ornamentation at this time.

The 221 *ground stone and used pebble tools* represent a very small proportion (0.48%) of the whole stone industry, but they include significant types such as celts; grindstones, mortars, and pestles; rubbing, striking, dressing, or anvil stones; and a palette. These may be taken as minor but distinctive diagnostic forms that are characteristic of this ground stone industry. Certain more expertly finished specimens (e.g., the ornamented palette fragment and a finely shaped carinated pestle end) might conceivably be suspected of being intrusive, belonging to a later period. However, there is no especially strong argument for this view, and these more elegantly shaped specimens may safely be included in this group. Certainly, considering the depths and well-separated positions of their findspots (one of the plain pestle fragments and the palette fragment came from a depth of 40-50 cm, which is comparable to the findspots of the several grindstone fragments and of the hand rubbing stones in levels associated with the rocky floor), these finer pieces are indeed fully consonant with the stone industry and acceptable as logical components of the occupational materials of a primitive living horizon of the sort revealed by the assemblage at Karim Shahir. Skillful grinding of stone ornaments does seem to have been a part of the technology.

Of these ground stone and used pebble implements the three most frequently occurring groups of tools are the hammerstones, the chipped and polished celts, and the hand rubbing stones or mullers, each category comprising whole examples as well as classifiable fragments.

Hammerstones most certainly were originally present in much greater quantity than is indicated by the small number recorded here, judging by the numerous fragments and small flakes of stones bearing similar heavily battered surfaces, but we have here confined ourselves to complete or virtually complete specimens which provide a standard of shape and size for the category. They evidently could be held in the hand and used to hit other hard materials. They are roughly cuboid or spherical in form, and the battered zones are extensively distributed on crests and faces, which implies that the position of the percussion point was occasionally shifted during use. In this way, an implement of repeatedly similar form, weight, and size (ca. 50-80 mm in diameter) was generally achieved. Most likely these implements were used to make the grinding, pounding, and rubbing tools and, perhaps, the cores, chipped stone tools, trimming debris, and other by-products found throughout the site. Thus, given the quantity of whole and fragmentary hammerstones, flint knapping (and perhaps other working in stone) seems to have been a major activity on the spot at Karim Shahir, especially if one also considers the many cores found there.

The presence of chipped and polished *celts*, another fairly common ground-stone form at the site, may indicate still other major activities. At Karim Shahir, they were on the whole a small and lightweight tool. They were invariably made of selected fine-grained rocks that were not of the flint-chert-chalcedony variety. The more usual adze/hoe form with its asymmetric bit profile and the less frequent axe form with a symmetric bit profile suggest, respectively, that there may have been considerable working of soil or wood and perhaps related chopping of brush or heavier wood. On the other hand, the type of rock selected and the generally small size and light weight of these tools seem inappropriate for efficient and strenuous action in soil or on wood and might more logically suggest use in preparing furs, skins, and the like. Two smaller narrow celts resembling chisels suggest different specialized activity. Most of the celts are a remarkably uniform oval to triangular shape, having a bifacially chipped surface with grinding and polishing at the bit end. Traces of bitumen coating over much of the body except for the ground bit zone were found only on the so-called adze/hoes. This chipped and polished celt type at Karim Shahir may well constitute a transitional form between the earlier stone-flaking traditions and subsequent technotypological phases involving increasing amounts of overall grinding and polishing on similar artifacts. Compare them, on the one hand, with the dissimilar smooth, faceted, and virtually unscarred celts from Jarmo (figs. 133-34) and M'lefaat (fig. 243:1-3) and, on the other hand, with the similar chipped and polished type reported from the upper level of prehistoric Zawi Chemi Shanidar (R.L. Solecki 1964).

At Karim Shahir there are three pieces that depart from the above norm. One exceptional relatively unflaked specimen of an axe form has a largely ground surface and a very few isolated flake scars but an overall shape like the others. Two further special exceptions are the much smaller, parallel-sided, bullet-shaped celts with narrow bits suggesting chisels; they display little or no surface flaking but rather more fully ground or natural pebble surfaces. On technotypological grounds these three pieces may or may not be part of the industry of the horizon proper, but their positions within excavated deposits argue that they are indeed proper to the horizon.

Hand rubbing stones (mullers) are present in sufficient quantity to suggest that the grinding of presumably wild grains, seeds, nuts, or similar plant foodstuffs was an important, if limited, activity at the site. However, a matching quantity of fragments of *grindstones (querns)* was not found, and the fragments are not large enough to indicate their original size and conformation. Those specimens of hand rubbing stones found appear to be planoconvex or flat-faced pieces of stone of easily manipulable sizes, and some evidence for the overall shaping of the specimen by flaking or pecking is recognizable in certain cases. The sampling includes pieces that suggest both oval planoconvex and subcuboid forms. Both the grindstone and hand rubbing stone types are present but only to a limited extent.

On the other hand, the quantities of fragments of *boulder mortars, shaped pestles,* and *natural pebble pestles* are very similar to those of the grinding and rubbing stones and fit well together as further evidence of the pounding and grinding of plant foodstuffs by a somewhat more ancient and primitive method than the use of querns and mullers. In the total absence of any direct evidence for grains or other remains of edible plants at the site, one should certainly not presume to speculate that the presence of these several forms of grinding and pounding tools would indicate anything more than the use of wild plants (nuts, seeds, perhaps some grasses and weeds, as well as various legumes).

A single fragment of a *palette* that is not basin shaped but flat surfaced with a simply incised raised rim or lip might also be associated with food preparation, although perhaps more reasonably with the processing of other materials such as pigments—even though no trace of any extraneous color matter is to be seen on the specimen. (A few small lumps of red and yellow ochre without signs of use were found at the site.)

The ornamentation and sure symmetry of the palette rim, the fine polish on the celt bits, the pecked and ground treatment and the skillful symmetrical carinated shaping of one of the pestles, the controlled curved surfaces of the grinding stone fragments, as well as the finer work on the various pieces of ornament, all reflect a considerable technical capacity for grinding and polishing stone at the time of occupation. However, the somewhat greater numbers of striated natural pebble pestles that were found perhaps indicate that those simpler pieces were still a commoner and more easily available tool for milling than the more carefully shaped specimens.

The uses of the remaining types of ground and pecked stone tools are less well understood. Among these types, the *used discoid pebbles* and the fragmentary *striated pebbles* bearing deeper scratches and peck marks at various points on the invariably shiny surfaces of their faces and edges suggest actions resembling those of anvils, strikers, whetstones, and the like, but to what precise ends these various actions were addressed cannot be guessed. The noticeable degree of polish on most of these pebble specimens also suggests buffing, rubbing, and burnishing of soft or fine-grained materials, and the fact that most of the pieces are of the same dark cherty veined rock implies a deliberate and rather careful selection of materials.

Other ubiquitous and distinctive categories of less well understood ground stone and used pebble artifacts are the grooved rubbing stones and the heavy chert pieces containing iron. Although there continues to be speculation on the purpose of the grooved rubbing stones and although the uses of the heavy, dark, cherty flint stones are completely unknown, it is noteworthy that in each of these two categories the particular stone material used seems to have been deliberately selected and to be so distinctive that it is a helpful diagnostic factor not only in assessing the similarity of site horizons but also in comparing the typology of these artifacts.

The *grooved rubbing stones* occurred widely at the site and are, with few exceptions, fragmentary but still sufficiently preserved to show what the type looked like when whole. They are generally elongated oval or subangular planoconvex pieces, invariably of dark gray to greenish fibrous laminated schist, presumably selected from nearby gravel beds or outcrops. The whole and the fragmentary specimens are all of a size small enough to have been held in the palm of the hand. On the convex surface of these pieces, always at right angles across the grain of the rock, usually one symmetrically concave or V-shaped groove has been cut or worn by rubbing, so that the surface of the resultant trough is polished and somewhat compacted and shows faint longitudinal striations as well. Studies on similar specimens from Zawi Chemi Shanidar show evidence that considerable heat was produced during the course of the work performed in these grooves (Drew in Solecki and Solecki 1970, pp. 839-40). At Karim Shahir the rounded grooves range from 7 to 12 mm in width, and the V-shaped grooves are narrower than that. In every case the grooves run across the short dimension, conforming to the Plain Transverse Grooved type and the Narrow Transverse Grooved type from Zawi Chemi Shanidar (Solecki and Solecki 1970, pp. 832-34, fig. 1*A-C* and fig. 1*H-I*, respectively). It is speculated by the Soleckis (1970) that these grooved pieces might have been shaft straighteners. It might also be possible that they were used as polishers for objects of stone or other materials. At Karim Shahir the absence of arrowheads or other projectile points that could have been set in shafts (save perhaps the backed and angled bladelets considered theoretically to be parts of composite forms of such projectiles) and the presence of ground stone bracelets, rings, beads, and other soft stone ornaments might argue for the latter interpretation, especially if one takes into account the compatible dimensions of the trough diameters and of the finished ornaments found. At any rate, the type crops up at many sites and from many time periods in the Near East, including neighboring Jarmo (fig. 131).

The *heavy chert pieces containing iron* are lodestones of very dark gray or black chert, mostly fragments. Enough complete specimens and fragments survive to indicate that these are in all likelihood pebbles that were naturally roughly spheroid or subcuboid. They were evidently specially selected from the streambeds or other gravel sources and then, without further work, used in some process of hammering, pecking, or rubbing that left bands of a rough abraded surface at their peaks or ridges and perhaps a smooth flattened area or two. The marked extra weight of each piece due to the iron content was likely a requirement for the unknown activity for which it was used, as was perhaps also the fine-grained texture, the compact material, and even the mineral content of the lodestone itself.

Lastly, the ground stone category includes fragmentary *pierced pebbles* of marble, limestone, or other relatively soft stone. All seem to be of medium size and thickness and to have been left in their natural overall shape or close to it. Projection of the exterior lines of the single almost complete specimen has suggested a diameter of ca. 90-100 mm and a height of 40-50 mm. In each case the trace of the perforation shows that it was positioned to pass as closely as possible through the center of the mass, and the diameter of the one measurable perforation is ca. 10 mm—enough, perhaps, for a slender stick or pole. The stones might reasonably have been attached to the end of a slim wooden stick as dibbles or maces. Alternatively, strung on thongs or fibrous cord they might have served still other purposes.

Of the grand total of stone artifacts—both chipped and ground—associated with the horizon, 99.52% (35,289 pieces) are *chipped stone* artifacts and their significantly interesting by-products. These figures do not include cores, core parts, and the presumably unused trimming debris. Within this enormous group of chipped stone artifacts the general typological categories may be tallied as follows:

Chipped Stone Tools

Category	No. of specimens	Percentage
Sheen-bearing flint pieces (blades, 18; flakes, 6)	24	0.07
Denticulated pieces (blades, 12; flakes, 3)	15	0.04
Backed blades (normal-sized, 9; microlithic, 415)	424	1.20
Perforating tools (fabricators, 46; normal-sized drills, 40; microlithic drills, 63; super-microlithic drills, 31)	180	0.51
Miscellaneous microliths (end scrapers, 320; pointed bladelets, 27; chance geometrics, 4)	351	0.99
Unworked blade segments (triangular, 70; trapezoidal, 50)	120	0.34
Microburins, 30; burins, 80; burin spalls, 60	170	0.48
Scrapers (end, 705; side, 232; steep, 26; rounded, 83)	1,046	2.94
"Raclettes" (19) and blades with obliquely truncated ends (59)	78	0.22
Nibbled pieces (blades, 2,160; flakes, 1,092)	3,252	9.21
Notched pieces (blades, 5,214; flakes, 1,792)	7,006	19.85
Used blades (13,089) and used flakes (9,534)	22,623	64.15
Total	35,289	100.00

This extensive body of chipped stone artifacts is marked by especially large quantities of *blades and flakes with different sorts of edge flaking*, as a glance at the tally list above shows. It must also be noted that the different forms of edge flaking are considered to be the result not of deliberate retouch and shaping but of various sorts of edge wear caused by actual use. Natural edge attrition may also account for an undetermined proportion. Commonly, several types of edge flaking appear on a given piece, and the predominant or outstanding type has determined the category to which the piece has been assigned. Clearly, this enormous series of over 32,000 pieces with different sorts of edge flaking represents multiple-use tools of convenience drawn from the freshly knapped sharp-edged blades and flakes lying about, easily and plentifully available at the settlement. This great variety of edge wear in which the types overlap suggests a multiplicity of actions, but, beyond stating that these may have included such activities as sawing, scraping, pounding, or smoothing of various hard or soft materials, no specific functions can be suggested. Experimenters have reported that various actions on various materials produce certain forms of edge flaking and edge wear, and investigations are progressing in the promising field of microanalysis of edges and their related surfaces. However, the material from Karim Shahir has been subjected to nothing more than inspection by the naked eye, and further study of the collection is indicated.

Blade pieces, subdivided on the basis of predominant edge phenomena into nibbled, notched, and less formalized flaking, all by use, are present in much greater numbers than their flake counterparts. In fact, when combined with all the end scrapers and the few other blade and bladelet categories such as backed bladelets, drills, and pointed blades, together with the denticulated and obliquely truncated blade or bladelet tools, they serve to fix this industry as a blade industry. Blades are both normal and microlithic in size in these major categories as well as in many of the smaller but more specialized and carefully shaped formal categories summarized below. Microlithic versions of the different types of blades with edge flaking generally are in a minority for the industry as a whole.

Of the more distinctively shaped tool types the scrapers, particularly the *end scrapers on blades and flakes*, followed by *side scrapers on flakes and fragments*, are the predominant groups. A few *rounded scrapers* and much rarer *steep scrapers* complete the group. This entire scraper category is characterized in the great majority of cases by implements shaped by use rather than by deliberate preparation. This situation is clearly evidenced by the poorly defined, often faint, traces of edge flaking. The edge flaking on the specimens in the sizeable end-scraper categories is particularly casual and undeveloped, in marked contrast to the workmanship in the exquisitely achieved drill and microlithic backed bladelet categories.

Microlithic backed bladelets are another notable group of artifacts used for an important but unknown activity. It has been suggested that they may have been part of some composite weapon or tool, perhaps harpoons or arrows, in a multiple hafting arrangement requiring many elements or replacements, and that the large number of pieces and their often fragmentary condition were occasioned by some destructive or attritional process. The regularity of the steeply retouched blunting or backing along one entire long edge of these bladelets and fragments shows that this type has been purposefully and painstakingly prepared and shaped. In many cases the careful backing continues uninterrupted across the bulbar end, providing the piece with a sturdy angled end. This is taken to be the base, while the naturally narrower or pointed opposite end is taken to be the working end largely because of small-scale traces of edge use on either face often found there. The careful backing of the bladelets and the angling off of the bases suggest attempts at strengthening and perhaps hafting of these fine pieces, although they might as logically suggest ways of dulling a tool for gripping directly in the hand, if the pieces themselves were not so tiny and apparently inappropriate for direct hand use. Whatever the use of such an artifact was, it probably involved a delicate and light action, as none of the edge flaking on the sharp edges is deep or extensive. The numerous broken bits attest to a fairly high rate of wastage and replacement, not surprising for so fragile a tool. An additional little category of *normal-sized backed blades* is an insignificant variant, more the product of classification by size and dimension in this study than of any special tool form or hypothetical function, and may safely be minimized in the consideration of the stone industry at this site.

Perforating tools (fabricators and several types of drills) form a significant but limited group. All are assumed to be some sort of drilling or piercing instrument used for another cluster of activities—perhaps for perforating skins, bone, wood, or stone. Most are on blades or bladelets, and the rest are on flakes or fragments of flakes. Classified primarily by size, they are all characterized by close-set, steep, clearly marked flaking along both edges of, and on one or both faces of, their working points. The *fabricators* are the largest and bluntest, with heavy, steep flaking continuing from the point down along their long edges. An occasional trace of polish or dulling overrides these edge flake-scar systems and suggests that these tools may sometimes have been used for some sort of smoothing operation on soft or fine-grained material. The *normal-sized drill* category contains subtypes made on the ends of blades, both narrow and broad, and on the ends of bladelike flakes. In the broader specimens, the drill point sometimes conspicuously protrudes from the body of the piece, like the French *mèche*. Both the *microlithic* and *supermicrolithic drills* are formed by steep retouch, almost like backing, that is applied painstakingly for most of the length of both long edges right up to and including the tip end of the working point. The resulting fragile double-backed implement is a straight, narrow, elegant piece of stoneworking.

Burins are a distinct but limited category that includes unelaborate forms such as the simple burins and the angle burins, most of which are here debased and not very clear-cut. Nevertheless, they are undoubtedly a component of the Karim Shahir stone industry and would have been used for whatever incising, grooving, or other cutting activity (presumably in bone and wood) was done in this horizon. The poorly defined forms of these burins suggest a reduced need or skill or else a shift to other kinds of implements for the same activity. Earlier prehistoric horizons were rich in very well made, distinct, and varied burin types, but in comparison there is a definite slump in the quality and quantity of burins at this juncture in the prehistoric record, which must betoken some radical change.

Our identification of these lackluster tools in the site's tool kit as burins was confirmed by the finding of a roughly matching number of incontrovertible *burin spalls*. Most spalls are bladeletlike and show the classic twisted thick-sectioned characteristics of this by-product, although a number are broader, more irregular flakelike pieces and therefore less obvious examples.

Microburins, often the special supposed by-product of the manufacturing of geometric microliths, are present, if not always in classic clear-cut form. In the absence of true geometrics at Karim Shahir (discussed below), microburins may perhaps be associated here with the making of obliquely truncated blades or other angled forms. The specimens found are flakes that range in size from very small to medium small, and a number are debatable representatives of the type. Here again there seems to have been a slump in skill, possibly due to the discontinuance of some activity related to a need that was no longer present or less strongly felt. Again, the less clear-cut specimens might thus reflect an early stage in the dying of a stone toolmaking tradition.

Since out of the myriads of specialized and generalized stone implements collected at Karim Shahir only four unconvincing specimens of what might be called geometric microliths were recorded (see *chance geometric microliths* [p. 73] and fig. 14:18-21), we have decided that a category of true geometric microliths does not exist in the assemblage here. This blank at Karim Shahir stands in contrast to the assemblages at some sites having a comparative interest, particularly Zawi Chemi Shanidar (upper levels), Jarmo (upper levels), and Mureybit (the Natufian level but not the succeeding phase II), all of which have various geometric microlithic forms.

The remaining *miscellaneous microliths* are mainly end scrapers by use made on microlithic blades and, in a few cases, small flakes. The scraper specimens recorded make up what is simply a classificatory microlithic extension of the even larger category of normal-sized end scrapers. A small subgroup of microlithic blades has pointed ends bearing delicate nibbled flaking or other faint traces of wear.

The *sheen-bearing flint blades and flakes* are just common enough and widely enough distributed by level and area to be taken seriously as a definite category in the horizon's industry and as an indication of some very limited special activity by the occupants of the site. The zones of sheen are too faint and too varied in width or position and the numbers of specimens too few to point to any one activity of any importance. Some experimenters have reported that flint used to cut grass, grain, or wood may acquire a sheen of one sort or another (Curwen 1930), but there is still considerable doubt and ignorance on the subject. One cannot, for instance, be sure what, if any, different characteristic sheens may arise from the cutting of reeds, grasses, or grains, or what role differences of season or soil chemistry might play here. Indeed, a number of apt but hardly prolonged experiments using flint on dry rushes, ripe grain, and other materials have either failed to produce any sheen whatsoever (LSB, pers. comm.) or else have yielded only a fugitive gloss that could be effaced by wiping (J. Harlan, pers. comm. to RJB). At Karim Shahir, when this sheen is considered in relation to the several small groups of grinding and pounding implements possibly used for processing of various plant materials, it reinforces our suspicion that these sheen-bearing pieces may have been used in the cutting of vegetation, living or dead, in a small-scale, unstandardized way at this early time.

A further miscellany of small but typologically distinctive implement categories such as denticulated blades, blades with obliquely truncated ends, and "raclettes" is not at all important numerically and perhaps has no great significance typologically, morphologically, or even functionally since the examples are so scarce and their character so poorly defined. Their use is problematical but would have been connected with some light type of work, to judge by the small scale of the flaking.

The *denticulated blades* are not at all uniform or well defined in overall form, and the denticulation, though somewhat regular, came about perhaps as much by accident or use as by any careful design. Certainly no sheen has been found in association with them. Because of their quantity and standardization, the *blades with obliquely truncated ends* are a more convincing group and may perhaps be viewed as a variant or extension of some end-scraper categories. All specimens have the same diagonal set and the same rudimentary quality of small-scale edge flaking at the ends. On some, the outline of the working end is perhaps more artificially shaped; on others, it is more natural and simply flaked a little by use.

The *"raclettes"* are also a minor type made on flakes and occasionally on blades. They are outstanding only because of their uniform regular small-scale nibbling, usually found in a single uninterrupted zone, and due to either preparation or use. In a way, raclettes are extensions of nibbled flakes and blades; except for their somewhat more formalized single zone, the edge flaking appears to be the same on this special type as on most of the nibbled pieces. The use to which they were put is not known.

A final form of chipped stone tool, a supposed by-product, is to be found in the group of *unworked triangular and trapezoidal blade segments*, selected as a sample from the yield of just one area, operation I, as tentative evidence of a suspected technotypological phenomenon possibly hitherto unnoted in the literature. The type appears to be quite widespread at the site. Nothing can be observed or reconstructed about these angular snapped-midsection fragments save that they exist in sufficient numbers and display enough similarity to suggest a link with some repeated stone tool use or manufacturing process that in nearly all cases involved pressure or percussion on blades.

The numerous *cores* at Karim Shahir are witness to intensive toolmaking on this hilltop and are demonstrable sources of the myriad chipped stone tools and by-products summarized above. Expressed as a percentage of the 35,000-odd chipped stone artifacts, cores constitute 4.5% of that industry, and when compared to the entire sum of 74,835 artifacts recorded at the site they represent 2.2% of the total.

While these cores (specifically stream pebbles, the most readily available source material) have been subdivided into several types for easier understanding and accounting, most of the variation appears to be logically explained as representing different stages in a single progressively exploitative process, one that developed in several ways with the aim of removing the maximum number of blades and flakes from any one core. Thus, various subvarieties of the so-called *pyramidal cores* represent stages in removing blades (the predominant form) or flakes from around a single striking platform along part, and eventually all, of the circumference of a pebble. The *bipolar cores*, with removals from opposing platforms, and their variant, the *crossed cores*, with removals at some angle to each other, are evidently a next stage in the fuller exploitation of a pyramidal core. *Polyhedral/amorphous cores* may be either the last stage of such an exploitative process during which blows removed flakes anywhere possible on all sides or else a deliberate overall exploitation of a core that was unsuitable for the pyramidal flaking technique. The very few *discoid cores* at Karim Shahir are evidently a distinct and anomalous type involving a different method of exploiting a round piece: in these, flakes were removed in an inward direction and radially over one or two opposite flattened faces. The almost equally scarce simple *incipient cores on pebbles* are stream pebbles from which so few isolated flakes were removed informally here and there that these pebbles fall well short of any of the other more fully styled core forms noted here, although it is conceivable that a good number on truncated pebble portions may have been starts on pyramidal forms that were early abandoned.

The single platform pyramidal core with its several presumed major subvarieties is by far the predominant form, making up virtually 80% of all cores found. Of this group, the partial pyramidal (either with cortex back or scarred back) forms 82%, and the completely achieved fully struck pyramidal cores, 18%. Of the remaining 20% of the whole series of cores, the polyhedral/amorphous make up 8%; the simple incipient cores on pebbles, 5%; bipolar and crossed cores, 4%; and the discoid cores, 3%. It seems clear that at Karim Shahir the pyramidal blade core was the usual desired form.

In addition, there are many *core fragments* and various core rejuvenation pieces including *core revival tablets*, *revival flakes*, and *revival blades*, all further testifying to an intensive exploitation of cores made from the stream pebbles laboriously carried up to this active habitation site. The vast quantities of *trimming debris* found are the expected consequence of all this stoneworking activity.

Faunal and floral remains at Karim Shahir are understandably in poor condition and relatively scarce. All are forms known in the general region in recent historical times. Stampfli could find evidence for only wild animals and he found no indication of juvenile individuals. Of the identifiable specimens, sheep and goat make up nearly half. A few examples each of wild boar, deer, gazelle, wild cattle, fox, and hare, and traces of turtle and bird form the balance. Barth's earlier tentative study of the somewhat larger quantity of the same sampling then available provides the same picture, with the further possible very limited indication of marten, wolf, and a canine. Bequaert identified four species of land snail, the geographically and historically widespread *Helix salomonica* Naegele constituting over half the total number of such snails, while freshwater clams are also present in very restricted quantity.

Floral remains are even scarcer than the faunal evidence. Helbaek obtained no positive determinations of seeds, nuts, or other such plant materials and thus could draw no conclusions as to the presence or absence of wild or domestic forms. However, using 10 samples of wood charcoal, Barghoorn was able to establish the probable presence of certain trees and shrubs at Karim Shahir. The majority are what he took to be almost certainly *Zelkova crenata*, and there are one or two specimens of *Tamarix* sp. and of *Prosopis*. Because of its physical state, the specimen of *Prosopis* is suspected of being intrusive. Indeed, in such a shallow occupation deposit the other samples of woody charcoal might to some extent be similarly suspect, but they are nevertheless presented here on face value as part of the evidence from this prehistoric horizon.

COMPARISONS

In reviewing the particular segment of prehistory in western Asia with which we are here concerned, we may ask ourselves what useful archeological materials are known to exist at present for comparison with the assemblage and features of such a settlement as Karim Shahir. What are the attributes and dating of such other sites and materials? To what degree, if any, does Karim Shahir have a counterpart elsewhere? Can one complement the patchy evidence from this site with any evidence from other sites and thereby place this one stage (or some group of related stages) in a certain band of prehistoric time and ultimately draw a clearer picture of Karim Shahir? At the present time there are but nine other sites in the area to which one can turn to place the material assemblage and related features revealed at Karim Shahir in their proper perspective. They lie at various widely scattered locations in three general districts where prehistoric investigations happen to have been made. Listed in a generally increasing order of distance from Karim Shahir, these sites are Zawi Chemi Shanidar, Shanidar Cave, M'lefaat, Gird Chai, and Ali Kosh in Iraq; Asiab and Ganj Dareh tepe in Iran; and Tell Abu Hureyra and Mureybit in Syria. They occur in a variety of topographic situations—mountain valley, foothills, and plain.

Each of these nine sites displays, to greater or lesser degree, a number of traits found in the Karim Shahir sample, and yet each also varies from that sample. No one of these sites, as a whole, is a convincingly close counterpart of the precise cultural horizon or phase exemplified by Karim Shahir. Each evidently represents, if not a distinctly different cultural phase, at least a variant in material culture, habitation forms, and food sources and thus represents a certain divergence from what has been exposed at Karim Shahir.

The implications of the similarities and differences of these sites are still not clearly understood. Shared or disparate characteristics may be reflected because of factors in geographical, ecological, or cultural province, because of relative chronological positions, or because of special habitational, occupational, or seasonal factors of way of life and subsistence, and these matters may be applicable individually or in combination. At some of these nine sites where it was possible to obtain C^{14} determinations in which one may have some confidence, dates seem to cluster broadly around 8000 B.C. However, the radioactive carbon data do not really solve the question of the relative chronology of these sites and the interrelationship of their revealed culture stages. Not only are they too widely spread in time but also there are still too many gaps and conflicts within the body of artifactual assemblages, in the structural traces, and in the faunal and floral record for us to accept the C^{14} determinations as simple guidelines. On the other hand, the determinations do perhaps help to strengthen the concept that, during a time span probably embracing some hundreds of years on either side of 8000 B.C., the kinds of settlements and living patterns exemplified by our particular nine sites were prevalent in this extended and geophysically varied area of the Near East.

An attempt is made here to compare the Karim Shahir data regarding habitation form, artifactual assemblage, food sources, and any possible further clues to the inhabitants' way of life with evidence from the nine other sites and then to weigh each sort of comparative evidence so as to arrive at a picture of the cultural horizons involved and a conception of their relationship in time. The evidence to be considered has been found at the following sites, here grouped according to general type of physical area. The distance from Karim Shahir is noted in each case.

Sites With Assemblages Relevant to Karim Shahir

Physiographic area	Site name and level	Type of site	Geographic location	Approximate distance from Karim Shahir
Central Zagros intermontane valley	Zawi Chemi Shanidar, layer B	Open-air, small, shallow settlement	Ca. 110 km NE of Mosul, Iraq	150 km NW
	Shanidar Cave, layer B-1	Cave	Ca. 4 km N of Zawi Chemi Shanidar	150 km NW
	Asiab	Open-air camp and midden	Ca. 5 km E of Kermanshah, Iran	250 km ESE
	Ganj Dareh Tepe, layer E	Initial occupation level in small mound	E of Kermanshah, Iran; 30 km E of Asiab	275 km ESE

Sites With Assemblages Relevant to Karim Shahir—*Continued*

Physiographic area	Site name and level	Type of site	Geographic location	Approximate distance from Karim Shahir
Central and southern Zagros lower foothills	M'lefaat	Small settlement	Ca. 30 km E of Mosul, Iraq	150 km NW
	Gird Chai	Small settlement	Ca. 25 km NE of M'lefaat	150 km NW
	Ali Kosh, Bus Mordeh phase	Initial occupation level in small mound	N. Khuzistan, Iran	450 km SE
Mesopotamian desert steppe plain	Tell Abu Hureyra, mesolithic settlement, NW corner	Initial occupation level in mound	On Euphrates River, 35 km ESE of Meskene, Syria	550 km W
	Mureybit, phases I and II	Earliest occupation levels in mound	On Euphrates River, just N of Meskene, Syria	600 km W

For purposes of comparison, it may again be emphasized that the excavations and the total assemblage and the observations therefrom amassed at Karim Shahir provide a strong sample of artifactual evidence and weak samples of structural—not to say architectural—traces and of faunal and floral remains. No C^{14} determinations proved possible at this shallow site despite collections of charcoal, bone, and shell. The surviving but poorly preserved faunal and floral material is inadequate for dating information, with much of both kinds lost or missing, but the lists of the few forms that were recorded are rather revealing as to the spectrum of what was available or preferred. Certainly, too, a considerable proportion (perhaps a third) of the original site has been lost due to stream erosion. With these caveats in mind it is still possible to point to some actual and inferred evidence regarding the cultural horizon at Karim Shahir. One may still sketch a picture of what probably existed and transpired there.

The evidence at Karim Shahir is contained in an extensive debris-crammed remnant scarp-edge area whose core zone (perhaps 73% excavated) is estimated to be some 700 m^2 in extent, probably with little outliers scattered widely beyond this core. The thin and shallow deposit of the core area and the seeming absence of any structures suggest a comparatively short-term encampment or, even more likely, a number of brief recurrent, perhaps seasonal, encampments. Furthermore, the considerable areal dimensions, the quantities of varied artifactual materials, and the few detected features of living style such as the fairly concentrated rock scatter and the numerous fire and cooking pits and depressions point toward a sizeable major type of occupation perhaps of the sort conceived of as a base camp. Indeed, it appears that this locality was used as a living center for hunting and collecting in the district. Whether this was continuous or periodic is not clear, although the exposed hilltop site obviously must have been less suited to winter conditions than to the more benign seasons of the balance of the year. All the animals that were brought to the site for butchering and cooking were wild. They were primarily, and perhaps significantly, sheep and goat, but there were also some wild boar, deer, gazelle, cattle, and a modicum of smaller forms such as fox, hare, and perhaps marten and wolf, as well as turtle and birds. Some land-snail shells were found, as well as a few freshwater clam shells, but no traces of fish were recorded. To some unmeasured but probably small degree, plant materials of unknown but almost certainly wild sorts only were collected and were processed by grinding and pounding tools, specimens of which, largely fragmentary, were found in very limited numbers. Also, a very small number of flint blades and flakes faintly marked by edge sheen point to cutting of grasses or other vegetation.

Most of the remaining (and greater) bulk of the assemblage consists of chipped stone artifacts made of flint, but not obsidian, in traditional, simple, but somewhat debased, forms, together with a few well-made microlithic backed types (that do not include geometrics), some chipped and polished celts with traces of bitumen, a very few simple bone tools, and very limited bone, shell, and polished stone ornaments. This more indestructible part of the assemblage may be related to the manipulation of animal carcasses and perhaps of wood, reeds, and other vegetable matter, and to the preparation and use of food, clothing, and other equipment related thereto, all perishable. With this very fragmentary picture of Karim Shahir in mind we may now proceed to a consideration of the sites selected for comparison.

ZAWI CHEMI SHANIDAR, LAYER B

Zawi Chemi Shanidar, layer B, is part of an inconspicuous prehistoric settlement site with a little overlying material of much later date (layer A) (R.L. Solecki 1964, 1971, pers. comm.). It lies 425 m above sea level on a low river terrace ca. 100 m from the banks of an upper reach of the Greater Zab River, which runs along the floor of a mountain valley in the Zagros range. The site extends over nearly 60,000 m^2 in an ovoid area measuring ca. 215 × 275 m. Excavations exposed ca. 250 m^2, or 0.42% of the suspected size of the settlement, and uncovered a maximum thickness of ca. 2 m of prehistoric deposit. A C^{14} determination (W-681) from this deposit is 10,870 ± 300 BP or 8920 BC (Deevey, Flint, and Rouse 1967, p. 200).

At the very base of the deposits there were several pits, including a large one cut into virgin soil and filled with rocks, animal bones, snail shells, charcoal, artifactual debris, and reddened earth. At one point elsewhere in the deposits, stones were set in a curved line reflecting a circular structure ca. 4 m in diameter, with traces of several rebuilding stages. This feature was made up of stream boulders, field stones, fragments of milling stones, and other sizeable stone artifacts, all of which might suggest foundations.

According to the excavator, the preponderantly impoverished and technically mediocre chipped stone industry associated with this prehistoric deposit (layer B) contains many multipurpose blades and flakes marked by various kinds of edge wear, especially notching and serration, and in some cases by edge flaking on alternate opposite faces. There are also a few poor end scrapers, some side and rounded scrapers on flakes, as well as borers that are either irregular and poorly made or more carefully made parallel-sided pieces. Minor forms include angle burins and backed blades. However, the site yielded outstanding microlithic components including over 300 small backed bladelets with angled bases, over 100 blunted backed lunates, a few double-backed microborers, and some small subtriangular points. Another particularly characteristic and common implement at Zawi Chemi Shanidar is the "spall tool"—a large, roughly elliptical or ovate flake form usually of quartzite or non-chert material struck from the surface of large stones, its naturally sharp cutting edge usually having been used without further preparation, perhaps as a skin dressing tool. An adze, a pick, and a few chopper forms are also reported. The large number of cores found run mostly to crude, incompletely exploited pebble flake cores, most with one striking platform but some with more, and there are also blade and bladelet cores from which the blade and microblade components have been struck. Obsidian is essentially absent, one single thick used blade being the only instance reported.

The ground and pecked stone industry is abundant and varied (R.L. Solecki 1964, 1971). It includes the following forms: sizeable heavy querns (trough querns, including those with shallower and those with deeper U-shaped or V-shaped trough; combination quern-mortars; flat querns; and bifacial varieties); a single boulder mortar; very plentiful hand rubbing stones with one or two flat or pitted working faces; numerous pestles (a deliberately pecked form and a natural elongated used pebble form); many hammerstones with heavy all-over battering (plain or pitted spheroid or discoid forms); and smaller cigar-shaped pecking and rubbing stones, some with beveling and wear at the ends. Over a dozen very distinctive grooved rubbing stones or abrading stones of chlorite were excavated (Solecki and Solecki 1970). They are classified into several subgroups according to the type and set of the groove upon the rock grain and according to whether the groove lies across the short or long dimension of the piece. Certain additional types of tools, including other "double-pitted" stones, a possible chisel, and rounded sandstone slabs were found at Zawi Chemi Shanidar. Of special interest are the chipped and polished celts which came preponderantly from the uppermost part of the prehistoric deposits. None were found below the 0.75-1.00 m level. A total of 76 whole or fragmentary examples were recovered, some 65 in the upper levels and the rest on the surface. They are shaped by chipping, with polishing confined to the bits, although a few have flaked bits. In addition, three or four celts that are more fully polished, though roughly, came from the surface. There are a few stone beads of simple cylindrical or discoid shape and a few simple pebble pendants and incised pebbles (R.S. Solecki 1963, p. 185, fig. 7). Lumps of lustrous hematite, or red ochre, occur. Flint pieces with edge sheen are rare (R.L. Solecki, pers. comm.).

The bone industry was abundant at all levels, with over 100 examples (R.L. Solecki 1964, pp. 408-9). The specimens range considerably in size and are mainly awls and point forms on long-bone fragments and condylar ends. About 50 smoothed and flat spatula-ended tools that have a working edge with a rounded outline and a shaft with transverse diagonal striations were found, as well as two bone chisel forms, a few perforated bone tools seen as rubbers or flakers, and numerous cut and used bones. A narrow, crescent-shaped, grooved bone haft was also found (Solecki and Solecki 1963). On a number of these bone tools there is, in places, some simple incised decoration including lines and notching as well as crosshatching, herringbone, and curvilinear incisions. There are also antler pieces with beveled ends, perhaps flakers. In the ornament category are beads made of small long-bone segments and pendants of pierced animal teeth as well as a flat, double-pierced, wing-shaped pendant.

No lightly baked clay objects were found at Zawi Chemi Shanidar, but a number of lumps of clay with vegetal impressions occurred (R.L. Solecki, pers. comm.).

The fauna reported on by Perkins (1960, 1964) are primarily (over 90%) wild sheep, goat, and red deer, and in the upper levels of layer B there was some evidence that has been construed as suggesting the probability of manipulation toward domestication of sheep. This suggestion is based on the preponderance of immature specimens of animals that were still morphologically wild. Other points of view have been expressed (see chap. 14, pp. 521-25). Wild boar, other species of deer, bear, and smaller forms (wolf, jackal, fox, marten, beaver, gerbil, rodents, birds) are reported. Scattered snail and freshwater clam shells and some fish and turtle remains suggest additional dietary items.

The roughly 2 m of accumulated prehistoric deposit and also perhaps the widespread surface indications, as well as the basal pits and the traces of circular structures, suggest some continuity and permanence and a considerable settlement of sorts, though perhaps not necessarily a full-fledged or even continuously occupied village.

The evidence from Zawi Chemi Shanidar cannot be directly compared with that from the obviously more transiently occupied Karim Shahir. The greater thickness of deposit and definite trace of a circular structure at the former site contrasts with the widespread shallow accumulation and lack of any evidence for constructions at the latter. The large numbers and variety of milling tools at Zawi Chemi Shanidar are also considerably at variance with the scanty yield of this kind of implement at Karim Shahir, although the presence of this category in both sites indicates a routine of plant food preparation. While only one boulder mortar was found at Zawi Chemi Shanidar—and that in doubtful context—they are present at Karim Shahir; in any case they are implied at both sites by pestles, both shaped and used pebble types. At Zawi Chemi Shanidar, as at Karim Shahir, in the absence of other indications it is presumed that only wild plant forms were treated. As regards animals, both sites depended on wild forms of their district. Perhaps domestication of sheep in the upper levels of layer B at Zawi Chemi Shanidar is hinted at by the tentative osteal evidence for selection for young animals. At all events, sheep and goat were in the great majority at both sites, with some variation between the sites in recorded percentages for certain of the remaining lesser forms (e.g., more deer at Zawi Chemi Shanidar, some gazelle at Karim Shahir).

It is exclusively in the upper levels of layer B at Zawi Chemi Shanidar, too, that the chipped and polished celts occur plentifully, in a version strikingly similar to that recorded for Karim Shahir, that is, displaying overall flaking with polish confined to the bits.

Indeed, while both the ground stone and the chipped stone industries at these sites are broadly very similar, there are some exceptions: the large number of milling stones (as opposed to their rare occurrence at Karim Shahir), the spall tools, or fleshers, certain adze, pick, and chopper forms, the small elongated beveled pecking and rubbing stones, and the microlithic lunates were present only at Zawi Chemi Shanidar. Marble rings and bracelets and perhaps boulder mortars (the last in slightly greater number than at Zawi Chemi Shanidar) were found at Karim Shahir. Percentages of occurrence may vary somewhat between the two sites but, aside from the special exceptions just noted, their tool kits as a whole and their technotypological caliber and range are strikingly similar. Each site has a few pieces with edge sheen. Each site also lacks obsidian. One gets the picture of quite similar little hunter-collector communities with certain differences: more or less permanent structures, slightly more sophisticated tool kit, increasing dependence on milling, and perhaps tentative animal domestication at Zawi Chemi Shanidar, as opposed to probably impermanent structures, an adherence to old tool types and ways, and full reliance on wild plant and animal forms at Karim Shahir. The apparently late entry of the chipped and polished celts into the picture at Zawi Chemi Shanidar seems significant in establishing a relatively later overall position for Karim Shahir, which seems in part contemporary with the later moments of the not too distant Zawi Chemi Shanidar settlement. Minor local variations in activities may be reflected in the special typological or quantitative features that were evident exclusively at one site or the other.

Shanidar Cave, Layer B-1

Shanidar Cave, layer B-1, contained shallow but significant remains of an occupation horizon that had many of the same characteristics as the horizon of layer B at Zawi Chemi Shanidar, which is located 4 km to the south down the valley of the Greater Zab. The cave lies 765 m above sea level and is ca. 365 m above and some 2.5 km away from the valley floor. For purposes of this study, one may assume that Shanidar Cave and Zawi Chemi Shanidar are the same distance from Karim Shahir. The artifactual assemblage in the cave layer is said to match—for the most part—that from Zawi Chemi Shanidar, both in general and in particular (R.S. Solecki 1964). For instance, there is mention of querns, mullers, mortars, grooved rubbing stones (Solecki and Solecki 1970; R.L. Solecki 1971), and many of the same types of chipped stone artifacts. A number of pieces of obsidian were found. There also occurred an alignment of stones in an arc reminiscent of the circular structure at Zawi Chemi Shanidar and, in one area, "pavements" of rough stone in association with hearths and numerous burials, mainly of children and infants. Linked with these burials were a straight grooved bone haft with a flint blade (without detectable trace of sheen) set in bitumenlike material at one end (Solecki and Solecki 1963), an oval pendant, plaque, or bead of cupreous mineral (malachite?) pierced at each end (R.S. Solecki 1969), beads of stone and shell and traces of basketry or matting impressions (R.S. Solecki 1968, p. 256), and an instance of a quern and muller laid on the feet of the skeleton of a young adult, with both the bones and the artifacts marked by red ochre (R.L. Solecki 1971, pp. 993-94). Whatever differences in relative quantities of artifacts there are between these two Shanidar sites are felt to be due perhaps to different seasons of occupation and vagaries of classification methods. In addition, at Shanidar Cave B-1, there is again some evidence for domestication of sheep in the great number of bones of immature individuals found. Both the Shanidar sites have the same range of wild animals, with heavy preponderance of sheep, goat, and red deer (Perkins 1960, 1964). A C^{14} determination (W-667) from Shanidar Cave B-1 of 10,600 ± 300 BP (Rubin and Alexander 1960, p. 183) or 8650 BC accords well with the ca. 8920 BC determination from the Zawi Chemi Shanidar prehistoric layer. On the whole, the body of evidence from layer B-1 not only supports and confirms the evidence from Zawi Chemi Shanidar but also adds considerably to a picture of the period.

Thus the evidence from Shanidar Cave, layer B-1, reflects the same general relationship to Karim Shahir as Zawi Chemi Shanidar, layer B. The cave layer has the same general chipped stone and bone industry but shows a comparatively greater number of milling stones, another permanent structure, and perhaps more carefully paved stone areas. It contains the same range of wild animal forms with emphasis on sheep and goat but, like Zawi Chemi Shanidar, hints at the possible but debatable domestication of sheep. The cave layer contributes the following additional evidence for potential insights into the way of life of the Zawi Chemi Shanidar horizon: human burials with clues about ritual, a cupreous mineral ornament, indications of obsidian, traces of matting or basketry, and yet another grooved bone haft, this one with a flint blade in place. Aside from the evidently similar wild animal diet and the tool kit of chipped stone and bone artifacts, all these things extend beyond the more restricted level of evidence at Karim Shahir, a simple encampment of hunters and collectors.

Asiab

Asiab is an open-air camp and midden covering the broad top of a low streamside eminence on the banks of the Kara Su, ca. 5 km east of Kermanshah, Iran. It is located ca. 1,330 m above sea level and ca. 250 km southeast of Karim Shahir. The two sites are in the same general intermontane valley zone, although Asiab is at a considerably higher elevation. The site was excavated during the 1959-60 season of the Oriental Institute's Joint Prehistoric Project program with the University of Tehran. Its yields have for the most part received only cursory preliminary attention (e.g., Braidwood, Howe, and Reed 1961).

Surface indications at Asiab suggested that the original site extended over an area of ca. 20,000 m^2. Test pits and trenches on the periphery and a sizeable excavation in the southern portion of the area that displayed significant surface scatter confirmed this view and also showed that most of the occupational deposits were probably in this southern half. The area of excavation totaled ca. 130 m^2, which represents ca. 0.6% of the estimated area of the site. The 2.5-3.0 m of deposit over virgin soil was made up of a chaotic jumble of animal bones (dismembered, broken, and partly burned), freshwater clam shells, coprolites, flintworking and other artifactual debris, rocks, and traces of fire and ash, as well as numerous debris-filled pits. There was one major change in color of soil to be seen about midway in the accumulated deposit: the upper portion was gray, the lower, tan gray. Thus, there may have been distinct earlier and later subdivisions in the cultural history of the site, but such a division is as yet unelucidated. There was also indication of later disturbance in the form of pits, bricks, and potsherds (largely of hard wheel-made wares including various plain and painted types). While these intrusions were confined mainly to the top 50-75 cm, some were also found in deeper levels.

At the very base of deposits in a 48 m^2 exposure was the vestige of a large shallow-basined oval excavation into virgin soil that suggested a refuse pit or possibly a man-made semisubterranean structure. By projecting from the uncovered portion, it was estimated that the diameters of this depression may have been ca. 8 m and 10 m. The quarter that was exposed had nearly perpendicular sides ca. 0.25-0.30 m deep. Just above but within the outline of this feature were two burials in the debris. One of the figures was flexed; the other was in an extended position and clearly sprinkled with red ochre. Also from within this low-level pit area came numerous animal bones.

In the deposits there were undoubtedly the remains of many small fire pits, cooking pits, and hearths. Such features were strongly hinted at throughout by the burned rocks, bones, and earth found helter-skelter everywhere but were otherwise virtually indistinguishable from the surrounding litter of relatively loosely packed, dry, uniformly gray-to-tan silt charged with stone tools, rocks, bones, shells, coprolites, and other debris. Most of these materials are considered contemporary with the principal prehistoric occupation, but some are from later periods, to judge by pottery found in upper levels.

Throughout the deposits a lithic industry prevailed that was evidently grossly undifferentiated from base to top, despite the possibility of a cultural division suggested by the major soil color change noted above. It should be remembered, however, that the impression of a single technotypological stone industry was obtained from field observations and from a preliminary tentative classification based on a sizeable sample of all the lithic material in one level in the heart of the deposits. Until further studies are made and reported, this generous interior sampling is the only impression we have available of the broad outlines of the industry at Asiab. The artifactual assemblage at Asiab is, then, in a tentative and preliminary way and subject to the above qualifications, assumed to be characterized by the categories described below

The blade and flake cores are predominantly those with a single platform, including both partially and fully flaked pyramidal cores, and there are some bipolar, discoid, and amorphous examples as well. There are numerous backed microlithic bladelets, both the angled and curved varieties; some drills on flakes and blades, including the microlithic double-backed variety; and a number of possible geometric microliths. Discoid or semilunate "fleshers" of easily flaked rock of poor quality recall the spall tools of Zawi Chemi Shanidar, although the two sorts are not typologically identical. There are numerous scrapers, including the end, side, rounded, and steep varieties, all of debased workmanship and probably largely formed by use alone, as well as poor-quality burins, distinct burin spalls, and microburins. Some diagonally truncated blades, pointed blades and bladelets, and steeply flaked blades are also present. Variously used blades and flakes with notched, nibbled, and other forms of edge flaking occur in great quantity. Blades and bladelets with edge sheen are definitely present but in limited numbers.

Stream pebbles and certain angular fragments of a local soft tabular rock with artificial striations, flaking, and peck marks are seen as working stones such as anvils, whetstones, or polishers for striking, dressing, rubbing, and the like. Milling stones are rare and those present are simple in form. Smaller palettelike forms, grooved rubbing stones, mullers or hand rubbing stones, and hammerstones were also found. There are no celts. The limited amount of obsidian found at various depths is suspected of being intrusive, probably introduced via the pottery-littered pits from a later period and related zones and also by way of the animal burrows, some very deep, found nearly everywhere. These few obsidian bits do not repeat or even reflect the characteristic typology found in the massive quantities of flintwork.

Bone tools such as awls and points were also found, but the examples are simple and fragmentary.

Although later prehistoric, historic, and other indeterminately aged sherds and some fragmentary pots were found scattered at various depths, most of the deposits at Asiab are aceramic and are tentatively taken to be of one period, with only limited but as yet unspecified subdivision likely. It must be emphasized that the aceramic qualification applies to formal, fully baked pottery only; actually, a considerable quantity of lightly baked clay material, largely fragmentary animal and human figurines and geometric forms, was found. This as yet unanalyzed material includes a small, crude face plaque with punctate decoration, numerous parts of little animal figurines, and geometric pieces in the form of little cones, disks, and pellets in the frequently encountered early clay working tradition that by now is well known from Zagros area sites.

Ornaments are simple and relatively rare at Asiab; the category comprises stone beads and pendants, a boar tusk pendant, bone beads, shell beads and plaques or pendants, and clay beads.

The faunal remains at Asiab are plentiful and have already been subjected to considerable preliminary examination. According to Bökönyi (1977), who has carried out the fullest study on this material, the commonest wild animal forms at this site in decreasing order of frequency are red deer, goat, pig, sheep, badger, red fox, hare, and cattle. In much more restricted numbers there are also gazelle, fallow deer, onager, lynx, leopard, jackal, wolf, hedgehog, rodent, and several species of bird. Tortoise remains are present in some quantity. A very large number of freshwater clam shells (*Unio tigridis* sp.) were found throughout, indicating that clams were a major article of food in a diet that was otherwise heavily based on wild mammalian species. Crab claws and the vertebrae of several kinds of fish also occurred. Land snails were present but not common.

Evidence of early attempts at goat domestication at Asiab has been presented by Bökönyi (1973, p. 71; 1976, p. 21; 1977, pp. 16-22), who based his opinion on characteristics of certain horn cores (1 whole and 2 fragments) and on the high ratio of bones of mature male individuals. It must be noted, however, that at this site—where later intrusive materials have been found in upper levels and elsewhere—such evidence may not prove conclusive. Judgment as to whether the goat had been domesticated at Asiab at such an early date should therefore be suspended until studies of all the evidence from the site as a complete entity have been carried out.

There are as yet no floral identifications, although a number of good samples of charcoal and seeds were collected. As with the faunal and artifactual evidence, the risk that more recent material has been intermingled, especially in upper levels, is considerable, judging by the indications of later pits as well as the numerous rodent holes and animal runs at various levels. For the present, one must assume that edible plants, if any, were wild.

Apparently, well-formed characteristic coprolites, probably both animal and human, were once present in great quantity and evidently had been well preserved for some period of time. However, since for the most part only the sediment-filled casts of the original material remain, no specific information about the contents of the coprolites is available.

A number of C^{14} determinations were made on samples from Asiab. According to information provided RJB by Professor H.T. Waterbolk in a letter of July 4, 1972, the Groningen laboratory (Naturkundig Laboratorium der Rijks Universiteit) gave a determination of 9755 ± 85 BP or 7805 BC on a charcoal sample (GrN-6413) taken from a depth of 1.65-1.70 m, a location that had been well sealed under a cluster of bones.

Three C^{14} determinations, based on assays of bone collagen from bone fragments of various unidentified animals, were made at the Institute of Geophysics of the University of California at Los Angeles (Protsch and Berger 1973). There is lack of agreement as to the validity of these assays (see Bökönyi, Braidwood, and Reed 1973; Solecki and Solecki 1974), and one is inclined to follow the principle of counterpoising suspect radiocarbon determinations with accepted "relative archeological chronology" (p. 537). A list of the California determinations follows:

Laboratory no.	Locus	C^{14} determination BP	Approximate date BC
UCLA-1714C	120-140 cm level	8700 ± 100	6750
UCLA-1714B	140-cm level	8900 ± 100	6950
UCLA-1714F	Below 140-cm level	9050 ± 300	7100

The most reasonable present choice is to focus on the Groningen determination, which would fix the earliest settlement of the site somewhere near 8000 B.C. or a little later.

At the present juncture, while identification and comparative study of both the faunal material and the artifactual assemblage are still in progress, all that can be said about Asiab is that it apparently is the site of what seems to have been essentially a one-period open-air camp and midden type of occupation of some duration, most likely seasonal in order to take optimum advantage of both the assorted wild game and freshwater clams in the area, the bones and shells of which were found throughout in great profusion. Any radical changes in the fauna within the exposed stratigraphic sequence are as yet unclear, and no radical changes in material culture have been detected anywhere at the site, although such changes in both kinds of material are possible and may yet be demonstrated after further study. The only traces of any structure or possible dwelling were the single large oval depression that was cut at the very base of the occupation—perhaps a refuse pit, judging by the very numerous animal bones it contained—and the many fire and cooking pits indicated throughout by the burned rocks, bones, and earth found everywhere, but which were otherwise completely undefined and unidentifiable as separate features. The two human burials, one with red ochre, within the precincts of the great oval pit are also of interest as indicators of habitation and cultural activity.

While the population of either site at any one time cannot be determined, in comparing the records from Karim Shahir and Asiab it may be said that a greater number of people probably passed through Asiab, judging by its accumulation of deposits and the greater amount of artifactual and faunal debris and even allowing for the better preservation there than at Karim Shahir. At both sites, with allowance made for a difference in altitude and terrain, there was reliance upon approximately the same spectrum of wild animals, with some tentative evidence at Asiab for domestic goat. Asiab has mostly deer, sheep, and goat, but significant quantities of wild boar, cattle, and less numerous gazelle, fallow deer, onager, leopard, and smaller forms including birds are also present, whereas at Karim Shahir the animals are primarily wild sheep and goat with some boar, deer, gazelle, and cattle, as well as smaller forms. Asiab is, in addition, a great freshwater clam-eating locale; it was evidently a seasonal center par excellence for this food, whereas Karim Shahir yielded only limited quantities of snail and clam shells. At any rate, both sites were occupied by migratory hunter-collectors with perhaps only temporary or repeatedly pitched ephemeral shelters that evidently left no trace. Both sites witnessed butchering, cooking, limited milling, and perhaps plant-cutting activities, and a great deal of flint knapping. The presence of lightly baked clay pieces at both Asiab and Karim Shahir provides another point of similarity. On the other hand, the definite presence of some sort of subterranean structure early in the span of occupation and the still moot status of animal domestication at Asiab, as opposed to the ostensible absence of these aspects at Karim Shahir, and also the presence of geometric microliths at Zawi Chemi and possibly Asiab but not Karim Shahir might all lend support to the suspicion that Asiab may be more akin to Zawi Chemi Shanidar. Also, there is absolute dating from C^{14} determinations from Asiab, and the most acceptable of these dates runs slightly later than those from Zawi Chemi Shanidar. On present evidence at least, the great amount of the same kind of predominantly undistinguished chipped stone artifactual material indicates a largely common way of life at these three Zagros sites, with no radical contrasts between any of them. Any difference in time at any of them might be of only a relatively small order. One must also bear in mind the possibility that the considerably higher altitude of Asiab may have been a deciding factor in the particular way of life possible there. One is increasingly left with the suspicion that there may have been several little variants of one general way of life dotted about the region during a single band of time around 8000 B.C.

Ganj Dareh Tepe, Layer E

The small, low mound of Ganj Dareh extends over 1,300 m^2, with nearly 8 m of deposits. It is located in a side valley ca. 5 km from the stream banks of the Gamas Ab in open rolling terrain some 37 km east of Kermanshah and thus only ca. 30 km east of Asiab. It is estimated to be ca. 1,350 m above sea level and some 275 km east-southeast of Karim Shahir, within the same intermontane valley zone but at a considerably higher altitude. Excavations to date have uncovered a sizeable area some 200 m^2, or 20% of the extent of the mound. Only about one third of this excavated area appears to involve layer E, the nonceramic basal prehistoric layer that is of interest to the present discussion (Smith 1968; 1972a,b; 1974; 1975; 1976; 1978).

This earliest occupation phase, layer E, was 0.5-1.0 m thick and rested on virgin soil. There was no evidence for solid architecture or even any impermanent structures, but at least 30 round or oval pits or basins dug into the virgin soil were found. Many of these were filled with rocks (some burned), others contained no rocks, and several had stratified deposits of ash, charcoal, and other signs of burning, indicating that they were used and reused as fire pits. One was partly edged by an arc of small up-ended stone slabs. These pits ranged from ca. 0.8-1.7 m in diameter and up to 0.5 m in depth. This basal complex was followed by a number of lenses of ash, clay, and stone, possibly indicating that occupation of layer E was intermittent.

The artifactual assemblage from layer E includes a chipped stone industry that is largely indistinguishable from the one found in succeeding layers, which suggests a continuum in the stoneworking tradition and perhaps accordingly in much of the way of life. This industry comprises backed and obliquely truncated blades and bladelets, end and side scrapers, numerous multipurpose pieces with special emphasis on notched and denticulated blades and flakes, and conical or cylindrical cores. The site thus yielded predominantly a blade industry combined with much formally undistinguished material, an assemblage that is in general limited and poor technotypologically. There are no proper geometric microliths, microburins, or arrowheads; no obsidian; no celt axes or adzes, fine ground stone bracelets, rings, or bowls; and no indication of any form of grinding or milling stones, although pieces with edge sheen and the type known as the grooved rubbing stone occur. Some lightly baked clay objects were found, mainly animal figurines but also human figurines and little geometric forms. A single potsherd of handmade punctate ware comes from this layer. There are also simple bone awls.

The C^{14} determinations for layer E include one sample (GaK-807) from a basal ash deposit, 10,400 ± 150 BP or 8450 BC (Kigoshi 1967, p. 61), and four from the pits averaging 6500 B.C. (Stuckenrath and Mielke 1973, pp. 398-99)—these four evidently being out of line with the other evidence from that lowermost occupation layer. This older determination is tolerably close to the ones adopted for Zawi Chemi Shanidar and Shanidar Cave B-1. Thus perhaps Ganj Dareh E should be placed with the Shanidar sites at the earlier end of any estimated period of time bracketing 8000 B.C. and Asiab nearer the later end. Yet the assemblages at Ganj Dareh E and Asiab seem very similar, and since both sites lie at the higher altitudes, they may be affected by factors of climate and ecology that impose a different way of life or, to all appearances, cause comparatively retarded situations.

Here at Ganj Dareh E, then, one again sees a chipped stone industry strikingly like those at Karim Shahir, Asiab, and Zawi Chemi Shanidar. Its continuation at Ganj Dareh into all overlying layers of considerably later periods is another indication of the conservatism and, as it were, the banality of such chipped stone components. Also present in layer E, as at all these other sites, are simple bone tools, grooved rubbing stones, a few pieces with edge sheen, and, with the exception of the Shanidar sites, lightly baked clay animal and human figurines and little geometric forms, reflecting traditions in common. Of more significance in layer E is the absence of milling stones, geometric microliths, obsidian, celts, and ground stone ornaments. The lack of celts and obsidian pairs up well with the record at Asiab, its near neighbor. One must, however, remember the very limited area that has been investigated so far in layer E, when attempting to assess whether the above traits were truly absent there.

M'LEFAAT

M'lefaat lies in open rolling country at the junction of the foothill and piedmont zones of northeastern Iraq at ca. 290 m above sea level. The site is located on the west bank of the Khazir River and immediately north of the Erbil-Mosul road, and it is ca. 150 km northwest of Karim Shahir. The two sites are thus separated from each other by a comparatively short distance and by several low ridges of an easily traversable portion of the foothill zone. Four days of testing opened up some 50 m² of a possible 9,000 m² of occupation area and produced over 1,700 artifacts. An examination of this material (SAOC 31, pp. 27-28, 50-52; this volume, chap. 21) has provided small but significant points of comparison for the present study.

At M'lefaat there is evidence of at least 1.5 m and perhaps up to 2 m of total accumulation of prehistoric deposit. Here a large ovoid pit that measured ca. 3.5 × 2.5 m was found. It had been dug in two stages, the later one partially superimposed on the earlier, with yet a subsequent enlargement. The signs of renovation and the amount of artifactual debris involved suggest that this structure was a pit house. At another point are traces of several other superimposed beds of artifact-bearing deposits that include flagstones and stone scatters; these beds measure several square meters in area and are seen as a succession of renovated dwelling floors.

The ground and polished stone industry at M'lefaat contains celts which have traces of chipping at the bits (perhaps from wear), boulder mortars and grinding stones, or querns, and some hand rubbing stones and pestles, as well as a number of rods, spheres, and pierced stones.

The chipped stone industry comprises well-made bladelets, perforators and reamers, a few microlithic backed bladelets, poorly made (and rare) burins, relatively large quantities of less outstanding forms such as various nibbled, notched, and used bladelets and flakes that were probably multiple purpose tools, and a few bladelet and flake cores. There are also some simple bone awls and beads and a number of lightly baked clay pieces including fragments of human figurines, rods, pellets, and beads. Since the very few pieces of obsidian were confined to the top 50 cm, this material may be intrusive. A very few impressions of matting were detected.

The remains of wild mammalian fauna are scanty at this site; they include gazelle, sheep, hare, wildcat, pig, red fox, large cattle, possibly wolf, and rodent. Also present are clam and crab shells and fish bones.

In sum, the relatively close similarity of the artifactual assemblages and of the wild fauna at M'lefaat and Karim Shahir argues for somewhat comparable functional patterns and way of life. Both yielded milling stones in some variety, a generalized and somewhat debased chipped stone industry, simple bone tools and beads, and lightly baked clay pieces. At both sites obsidian is extremely scarce. It is considered to be intrusive at Karim Shahir and quite probably at M'lefaat also. However, the celts at M'lefaat are closer in form to those of Jarmo and unlike those of both Karim Shahir and the upper part of layer B at Zawi Chemi Shanidar. M'lefaat has some of the same wild mammals found at Karim Shahir, but other species such as goat and deer are not recorded—their absence probably attributable to its open terrain and low altitude. Both sites have molluscs, but M'lefaat, on a river bank, also has crab and fish bones. The hunter-collectors who occupied these two sites may perhaps have had simple sheltering structures that were similar, but evidence of the nature of dwellings is available only at M'lefaat. There, the greater depth of deposit, the possible pit house, and the other living floors all indicate a greater duration and perhaps greater stability of occupation than at Karim Shahir, so that M'lefaat resembles Zawi Chemi Shanidar and perhaps Asiab more closely in this regard. It must be remembered, however, that the Karim Shahir site had been severely disturbed and partially obliterated and therefore traces of dwelling there may well have disappeared. One may tentatively assume only that M'lefaat and Karim Shahir were both small-scale settlements with limited simple structures—M'lefaat probably being a little more permanent and villagelike than the more camplike Karim Shahir—and that they were roughly equal in level of culture if not necessarily contemporary. While there is no indication of the absolute age (based on C^{14} determinations) of the deposits at either site, the broad technotypological characteristics of their artifactual industries, their faunal spectra, and their reflected simple ways of life are enough alike for the two sites to be considered roughly contemporaneous, especially in view of the relatively short distance and easy traversability of the intervening terrain. Nevertheless, it might be argued that at M'lefaat the round pit structure and the ground celts with bit flaking (albeit occasional and possibly accidental) suggest that this site is more closely related to basal Zawi Chemi Shanidar or to Jarmo respectively, thus providing archeological and technotypological arguments for an earlier or a later dating than that supposed for Karim Shahir. It is also possible, though less likely, that M'lefaat may have been a survival of an older way of life into later times.

GIRD CHAI

Gird Chai is situated on the Greater Zab River some 25 km northeast of M'lefaat and ca. 150 km northwest of Karim Shahir. It is in foothill country some 300 m above sea level. After an initial probe (SAOC 31, pp. 28, 54-55), the site was not investigated further since it proved to be highly disturbed and defaced throughout. The sounding was limited to several trenches totaling only 45 m^2 of exposure that at one point revealed 1.35 m of cultural deposits resting on sterile soil.

From the surface and from within the deposits came a chipped flint industry akin to the chipped flint industries at Karim Shahir and M'lefaat. There are blade and bladelet cores, flake cores, microlithic backed bladelets (both plain and angled), notched bladelets, and used pieces, as well as very rare burins. In addition, minor traces of obsidian are reported, but, given the site's very disturbed condition, obsidian may not be a credible component of the industry. The scanty ground stone component—a few milling stones and a few chipped and polished celts (which are closer to the predominantly chipped Karim Shahir sort than the more smoothly ground M'lefaat examples)—was found almost entirely on the surface. The interesting and significant point is that the celt type and the chipped stone industry type, together with the relative scarcity of milling stones in general, imply that the assemblage at Gird Chai is close in character to the one at Karim Shahir and that therefore Gird Chai may perhaps be closer in time to Karim Shahir than to M'lefaat. Thus there may have been similar communities and activities at these two sites during this supposed transitional period in this region.

The question as to whether Gird Chai had pits and large pit houses or other circular constructions like those at M'lefaat, Asiab, and Zawi Chemi Shanidar must be left unanswered. The much-disturbed state of the deposits here, involving numerous interpenetrating pits from a later time, precludes any deductions about the existence of floors, pits, or other structural features; they may be present but the situation is irretrievably confused by the later disturbances that are well documented by the later pottery found throughout the deposits.

On the other hand, the stone industry provides more rewarding evidence of shared traditions. The largely indistinguishable chipped stone assemblages at Gird Chai, M'lefaat, and Karim Shahir are also essentially similar to the chipped stone assemblages reported from Ganj Dareh E, Zawi Chemi Shanidar, and Asiab. The last two sites share the geometric microliths and the semicircular fleshers, or spall tools, and, along with M'lefaat, the ovoid or circular semisubterranean sort of structure. Thus, even making allowance for possible difference in dwelling types, for the presence of one or two implement types special to each site (such as the fleshers and the geometric microliths at Zawi Chemi Shanidar and Asiab and the chipped and polished celts in upper Zawi Chemi Shanidar and at Karim Shahir and Gird Chai), and for variation in incidence of certain categories (the milling stones), there is still a striking degree of shared artifactual tradition and presumably a primary dependence on wild animals and wild plants at all five of these intermontane and foothill sites of the central Zagros area. Here is a strong suggestion of a definable regional facies, a conservative though debased technotypological province of chipped stone tools with a few new backed and microlithic forms, and an entering wedge of various types of milling stones. Taken together, these tools from the five sites reflect not only common needs and functions perhaps still to be associated with a way of life strongly centered on the hunting of wild animals and collecting of wild plants but also certain common activities that would indicate the beginning of manipulation of the environment at other levels, during a period around 8000 B.C.

In a further step of comparative analysis and interpretation regarding the component parts of the assemblage at Karim Shahir and those of the possibly related six sites discussed above, one may consider evidence from three more sites that lie outside this central Zagros zone. These next three sites lie in or near the lower terrain of the more steppelike regions to the south and west. Here one finds chipped stone tools and ground stone milling tools that are similar to those at the seven sites already discussed. Moreover, the three more distant sites are associated with additional and markedly different influences involving more elaborate and fixed housing and settlement forms. Also, in one case (the Bus Mordeh phase of Ali Kosh), the diet sources and methods of processing involved domesticated animals and plants, while in the other cases (Mureybit and Abu Hureyra) they continued to involve full dependence on wild animal and plant forms. In essence, a conservative tradition of chipped stone tools and whatever routine daily needs it reflected seem here to have continued into another era. By observing such a persistence of a conservative chipped stone tool tradition into other living regimes, we may perhaps gain insight into the underlying character of the industry, as well as perspective on the concept that this part of the tool kit remained relatively unchanged technotypologically, in continuing response to numerous unchanged needs, even as the final phases of the Paleolithic gave way to the progressive transitional phases exemplified at the several more northerly central Zagros sites already reviewed above. The discussion of the following sites is intended to bring out these points.

Ali Kosh, Bus Mordeh Phase

The mound of Ali Kosh in northern Khuzistan lies in the Deh Luran plain, a southerly low-lying portion of the foothills zone situated at the margin of the desert-steppe (Hole, Flannery, and Neely 1969). The site is only ca. 170 m above sea level and is some 450 km southeast of Karim Shahir. The initial layer of the mound (zone C), resting on virgin soil, was named the Bus Mordeh phase. On the basis of architectural features and soils, this layer (with deposits ca. 2 m thick) was divided into an upper (C-1) and a lower (C-2) half. Some 40 m^2 of this horizon were exposed (only ca. 0.2% of the apparent area of the mound), revealing parts of an outdoor flintworking area, a pebble scatter or "pavement," and the rectangular walls of a building complex, all associated with artifactual and habitational debris (Hole, Flannery, and Neely 1969, figs. 5-9).

The open-air zone of scattered pebbles or rocks and gravel and the outdoor workshop area for flint knapping were the only traces of possible occupation spots that the Bus Mordeh phase and Karim Shahir had in common. The Bus Mordeh deposits also yielded a few clay lumps with mat impressions that might be paired off with the even more limited indication of such impressions at Karim Shahir (where a clay lump bearing impressions of wood or plant material was debatably associated with the prehistoric horizon). At both sites, these specimens might possibly be linked to wattle and daub or other structural components. Of quite another order were the building remnants found in both zones C-1 and C-2 of the Bus Mordeh phase (Hole, Flannery, and Neely 1969, pp. 33-40, figs. 6-9) in the form of mud-slab walls of definitely rectangular rooms that were either dwelling or storage areas. These rooms were usually ca. 2.0 × 2.5 m, had detectable indoor and outdoor aspects, entrance thresholds, and contiguous walls, and suggest small permanent buildings with courtyards. These architectural elements were more advanced than anything found at Karim Shahir and suggest similarity with a Jarmo-like stage of settlement.

Despite the contrasting architectural evidence, it is clear that the chipped stone industries of the Bus Mordeh and Karim Shahir horizons resemble one another quite closely in typology and morphology as well as in technological caliber. In comparing the two, allowance has had to be made for the somewhat different methods of classification and nomenclature applied to the industries of the two sites, especially with regard to the combining or splitting of certain categories. Nevertheless, with the help of the illustrative figures and text descriptions in the Ali Kosh site report (both of which are organized by presumed artifactual function) and the tables of numerical counts (organized by function and archeological-cultural phase), one can successfully match up types that are quite convincing counterparts in these two horizons (Hole, Flannery, and Neely 1969, pp. 76-105, figs. 24-41, tables 4-8).

Among the more than 40,000 pieces recovered from the Bus Mordeh levels, there are great quantities (over 23,000) of trimming debris, including various core fragments and revival parts, and equally plentiful (over 15,000) reportedly unused or slightly used blades and flakes. Of the 1,216 pieces considered to be well-characterized formal tool types, there are good numbers of notched blades and otherwise retouched or well-used blades, scrapers—both blade-end and rounded—nibbled bladelets, and various boring or drilling tools, including fabricators (reamers) and drills—both normal and microlithic. Also found were small numbers of double-backed drills, plain and angle-backed microlithic bladelets, pointed bladelets, and microlithic end scrapers. Burins are very scarce and rudimentary. There is an appropriate complement of pyramidal blade cores, comprising some specimens that are partially flaked and many that are fully flaked, including 159 very fine, small, elongated bladelet cores ("bullet cores"), as well as various pyramidal flake cores and a few cores each of the discoidal, partial pebble, and amorphous varieties. Also recorded are 42 plain blades with edge sheen, representing 3.4% of the formal tools. No geometric microliths were found. The Bus Mordeh deposits also yielded, in contrast to the foregoing tools, a single bifacially flaked foliate pointed piece that is unique at the sites under consideration here (and possibly even intrusive from overlying deposits at Ali Kosh which contained bifacially chipped flakes).

It is noteworthy that most of the types in this chipped stone industry continued upward in fairly similar relative quantities through the immediately succeeding Ali Kosh and Mohammad Jaffar phases, indicating a kindred typology and morphology in all three phases as well as reflecting a certain continuity in the use of these particular stone tools (Hole, Flannery, and Neely 1969, p. 91, table 5, fig. 32).

Both the Bus Mordeh and the Karim Shahir horizons have a few ground, pecked, and polished stone artifacts that may be broadly equated typologically if not exactly matched. The Bus Mordeh industry comprises rare grinding stones, slabs, or querns; hand rubbing stones, hand stones, or mullers, and pestles, both the pecked and shaped and the elongated natural use-pebble varieties (Hole, Flannery, and Neely 1969, pp. 170-88, figs. 70-78, tables 29-32). However, nearly all these milling stones are better made and more shapely than the fragmentary, simpler, more primitive forms found at Karim Shahir. There are also a few core or spherical pounders, or hammerstones, with traces of heavy battering and percussion. A few pebbles have traces of scarring, suggesting that they were used as various kinds of working stones. Lastly, perforated stones were found, but they were rare (Hole, Flannery, and Neely 1969, pp. 189-204, tables 33-34). On the other hand, grooved rubbing stones and celts were not found in the excavated part of the Bus Mordeh horizon.

Certain other types not found at Karim Shahir but appearing in the Bus Mordeh phase at Ali Kosh and in assemblages at other sites so far discussed in the present study (e.g., Asiab and Zawi Chemi Shanidar) include chipped limestone disks, pebble choppers, picks, and various shaped, elongated pebbles (Hole, Flannery, and Neely 1969, pp. 189-204; tables 33-39; figs. 80-81, 84, 88; pl. 32*f-h*).

The Bus Mordeh phase yielded only a few simple ornaments of stone, shell, or bone, such as beads, pendants, and plaques. The specimens include plain forms reminiscent of those at Karim Shahir, and some are polished. The bone and shell ornaments include boar tusk pendants like those from Asiab and also pierced small rectangular shell plaques, or "buttons," like the ones from Karim Shahir and Asiab. There are also small shell pendants (Hole, Flannery, and Neely 1969, pp. 232-44, figs. 100-101, tables 51-54).

The Bus Mordeh bone tool industry is simple like that of Karim Shahir, running primarily to awls or punches. One or two additional simple types of bone tool were found. These special types include pins, needles, and spatulate forms (Hole, Flannery, and Neely 1969, pp. 214-19, figs. 92-94, tables 43-44). They are isolated and rare instances, their rarity perhaps the result of chance factors of digging, poor preservation, or the limited extent of exposure. Better luck might conceivably have produced all these forms at Karim Shahir as well, enriching slightly the range of the shared bone tool kit.

Thus the fundamental similarity between the Bus Mordeh and Karim Shahir horizons seems to lie only in the simple outdoor flintworking and stone scatter areas, the plentiful and rather undistinguished chipped stone, the more restricted amount and variety of ground and polished stone artifacts, the simple bone tools, and, generally, the simple ornaments. In virtually nothing else is there any resemblance between the two horizons. In fact, the overriding impression given by the Bus Mordeh finds is that the phase represents a village settlement, a community that appears to have been permanent, with activities and a way of life therefore more like those of the earlier levels of Jarmo. It is certainly representative of a cultural phase distinctly different from (although not yet necessarily proved later than) the phase exposed at Karim Shahir and at the several somewhat comparable sites tentatively associated with it in this study. Additional Bus Mordeh finds, in quality and character suggesting later associations, are a few finely ground stone bowl fragments, perhaps intrusive from overlying layers (Hole, Flannery, and Neely 1969, p. 107, tables 9-10), a stone ball, and an elongated grooved "amulet" or phallic object (Hole, Flannery, and Neely 1969, pp. 200, 203; fig. 84; tables 36-37).

Also tending to be in line with the Jarmo assemblage, in view of their character, variety, and quantity, are the numerous lightly baked or unfired clay figurines in the Bus Mordeh levels. This category includes animal forms and also over 300 "cylinders" (rods or stalklike objects) with pinched, flared, punctate, or appliquéd ends, as well as a few geometric forms such as balls and lumps (Hole, Flannery, and Neely 1969, pp. 224-31; figs. 97, 99; tables 47-50). While the one clay rod from the surface of Karim Shahir does loosely match the general type of rod from the Bus Mordeh phase and Jarmo, the similarity of the small form with feet and a peaked head at Karim Shahir to specimens at Bus Mordeh or Jarmo is not close, strictly speaking, either in overall shape or smaller detail. Nevertheless, with allowance made for the very restricted size of the Bus Mordeh excavation area and the scanty sampling from Karim Shahir, the three groups of lightly baked clay objects (from Karim Shahir, Jarmo, and the Bus Mordeh phase) appear to be in a common tradition, one that is conservative like the chipped stone industry, and possibly understandably retains traits of form and methods of manufacture while being passed on through several otherwise changing successive cultural phases, without necessarily implying any association of ideas.

The fundamental difference between the Bus Mordeh and Karim Shahir horizons is further accentuated by the unmistakable presence of a limited amount of obsidian in the Bus Mordeh deposits. There are 347 pieces, primarily plain blades and trimming debris but also two cores, representing 0.9% of the total of the chipped stone industry (Hole, Flannery, and Neely 1969, table 8). In this respect, also, the Bus Mordeh phase is more in accord with Jarmo than with any of the sites lacking obsidian that are under study in this report.

In their nature and quantity, the Bus Mordeh faunal and floral remains show a marked affinity to the Jarmo end of the scale of cultural activity. The evidence from often quite considerable amounts of animal bone points to a great preponderance of sheep and goat (Hole, Flannery, and Neely 1969, pp. 262-330; tables 57, 59-60, 62-65, 67, 69, 72-75). There is also clear-cut evidence of some degree of domestication of very limited numbers of sheep and of a considerable number of goats. In addition, strong reliance continued on other wild animals such as a large quantity of gazelle, as well as some onager, aurochs, pig, red fox, gerbil, birds, turtle, lizard, and freshwater fish and molluscs. Enough plant remains were found (Helbaek in Hole, Flannery, and Neely 1969, Appendix I, pp. 383-405, table 3) to indicate the presence of domestic emmer wheat (*Triticum dicoccum*) in quantity, wild einkorn (*T. boeoticum*) and very rare domestic einkorn (*T. monococcum*), as well as plentiful wild two-row barley (*Hordeum spontaneum*) and some domestic naked six-row barley (*H. vulgare* var. *nudum*). Other wild plant forms, mainly grasses and a variety of legumes, including *Prosopis* pods, are reported as well. Here again, as in the case of the stone industry, the animals and plants of the Bus Mordeh phase continued to occur in the overlying Ali Kosh and Mohammad Jaffar phases, although there were some additions there. These other phases are of considerably later date and definitely represent cultures that were fully sedentary and food producing.

Although the resemblance of the Bus Mordeh phase to Jarmo rather than Karim Shahir is marked, it must be remembered that the faunal and floral evidence from Karim Shahir is so slim that one cannot identify any more outstanding sign of possible animal selection or manipulation at this site than the simple fact that there is a great preponderance of morphologically wild sheep and goat bones (perhaps only a seasonal hunting factor), compared with the number of bones of other definitely wild forms of mammal, bird, reptile, and mollusc found. Furthermore, the strictly floral evidence found at Karim Shahir can cast no light whatsoever on the presence or absence of wild or domestic food plants, although the fact that various milling stones and a few pieces with edge sheen were found permits the assumption that wild forms, at least, were handled.

The C^{14} determinations that have been published for the Bus Mordeh phase are as follows (Berger, Fergusson, and Libby 1965, p. 355; Buckley, Trautman, and Willis 1968, p. 290; cf. Hole, Flannery, and Neely 1969, p. 388, table 77):

Laboratory no.	Locus	C^{14} determination BP	Approximate date BC
I-1496	C-1, upper layer, near top	7380 ± 130	5430
I-1489	C-2, lower layer, base	7670 ± 170	5720
UCLA-750D	C-2, lower layer, inside house	9900 ± 200	7950

Within the limits of methodological and technical reliability, and after balancing the various factors that one assigns to this line of evidence (e.g., these samples came from depths affected by ground water—two from presumably outdoor localities and one from indoors—and were processed in two different laboratories), one accepts for the time being the excavator's decision to allow the dating to stand tentatively at the early end of the determined range at ca. 7500 to 6750 B.C. This would broadly equate the determinations for the Bus Mordeh phase with the similar but still moot "probable true general date of ca. 6750 B.C." based on the several determinations for Jarmo. On the other hand, the oldest approximate date of 7950 BC would also allow that phase to extend into older periods nearer the lower limits of the band of time to which Karim Shahir has tentatively been assigned, a chronological moment that might reasonably fit with the conservative debased chipped stone tool kit evidently shared by both the Karim Shahir and the Bus Mordeh horizons. However, considering all the available evidence—architectural, artifactual, faunal, floral, and chronological—as well as the apparent long-continuing conservatism of the lightly baked clay items, the simple bone tools, and the banal and debased chipped stone industry, all evidently embracing a wide time span, we are in favor of placing the Bus Mordeh horizon nearer the later end of the time range tentatively assigned above, well subsequent to the horizons of Karim Shahir and similar sites and closer to the time and cultural phase of Jarmo.

So far, then, our comparison of sites in the north-central Zagros has revealed that five of the six share an extensive catalogue of basic chipped stone tool types, some milling stones, simple bone tools, and, essentially, a lack of obsidian, all these to some extent reflecting shared activities and traditions. The single exception is Ganj Dareh, where, to date, evidently no milling stones have been found; nevertheless, that site has yielded all the other shared basic elements. Three of these same sites also contained an ovoid or circular structural form, and two of the three also yielded limited but debatable evidence for domestication—sheep in one case and goat in the other. However, the Bus Mordeh phase of Ali Kosh, while sharing with these five sites some of the more conservative surviving artifactual and wild faunal elements of the transitional period, differs significantly at least in having a rectangular dwelling type, obsidian, and more distinct evidence regarding animal and plant domestication. This horizon thereby constitutes a sample of a more evolved state of affairs in the transition from the relatively unanchored migrant hunting-collecting way of life to the fully settled food-producing regime. The C^{14} evidence from the Bus Mordeh phase indicates a broad enough time span to permit the horizon to be related to a later time as well, without having to grant priority to the earlier dating, which the excavators appear to favor. Adopting the later dating would still make the Bus Mordeh occupation (even divorced from the evidence provided by the record of the closely akin succeeding Ali Kosh and Mohammad Jaffar phases) one of the earlier instances of a settled village-farming community.

Moving now still further afield, we consider evidence from two early settlements that are located well westward of the eight sites in the Zagros area but are in part possibly broadly contemporaneous with them. These two sites, Tell Mureybit and Tell Abu Hureyra, lie out in the desert steppe zone but are set within a narrow band of riverine terrain that would have provided at the time of occupation, as now, more favorable conditions than other parts of the steppe. They happen to be within the territory now flooded by waters accumulating upstream from the new Tabka Dam on the middle Euphrates in Syria.

MUREYBIT

Mureybit, the larger of the two sites, is a mound on the left bank of the Euphrates River some 80-85 km east of Aleppo and just north of Meskene in northern Syria and is ca. 600 km west of Karim Shahir. It lies ca. 300 m above sea level in the desert steppe but in a relatively more favorable and restricted riverine locus within that regime. Excavations in 1964 and 1965 by Maurits van Loon (van Loon 1968) and during the period from 1971 to 1974 by Jacques Cauvin (J. Cauvin 1972; 1973a, b; 1974; 1979a, b) revealed ca. 8 m of deposits containing numerous stratified horizons of aceramic village settlement. We will deal with only the earliest three horizons since they are the only ones appropriate to our time span. These layers represented the lowest 4 m of the stratigraphic sequence in a series of partly overlapping deposits found in different parts of the mound.

These earliest horizons began with a limited exposure (35 m^2) of a bed resting on virgin soil composed of a little over 1 m of rather classic late Natufian deposit with, as yet, no indication of structures but with floorlike lenses, hearths, and pits (phase I-A). Over this was a thin (10-20 cm) epi-Natufian layer (phase I-B) containing a type of dwelling that consisted of a round semisubterranean structure of clay and exterior wood posts. Both phases I-A and I-B have a flint industry especially marked by microlithic bladelets, microborers, geometric microliths, various other scraping and cutting implements, and a few pieces with edge sheen. There are also some larger items in common such as grindstones, mortars, pestles, and a special local form of chipped adze. Very limited traces of obsidian occurred. However, small arrowheads appeared in the epi-Natufian. Only wild forms of animals were found, as well as only wild forms of plants.

The deposits of phase II (van Loon's original strata I-VIII), of which over 70 m^2 were exposed, immediately overlay phase I and, continuing upward, revealed several further occupation levels of settlement, the lower three marked by round houses in direct continuity with the preceding phase, I-B.

Other, higher levels of phase II had several versions of round houses. Also, in this phase as a whole, the composition of the chipped stone industry changed from that recorded in phase I. While continuing to be predominantly microlithic, the tool kit contained many fewer geometrics and backed bladelets and greatly increased numbers of microdrills and little arrowheads of several forms. There was a continuing component of the scraping and cutting tools and the chipped adzes. Again, there were a few pieces with edge sheen and a few obsidian blades. All of phase II was also aceramic and evidently an in situ development out of the preceding phase, with traits continuing as well as appearing and disappearing. It is this post-Natufian phase that constitutes a horizon of some interest in a comparison with Karim Shahir. Although studies on the site are still incomplete and preliminary, it appears that apart from the distinctive geometrics and arrowheads contributed by Natufian influences, the other types of chipped stone tools and the milling stones in phase II remain broadly the same throughout these levels, as do the flora and fauna.

Aside from the very significant presence at the stratigraphic base of the mound of a more or less classic Natufian industry—incidentally extending the Natufian well north and east of the hitherto known area—the initial sequence and assemblage at Mureybit suggest a fixed and developed small village occupation without animal domestication, plant cultivation, or pottery. However, the chipped flint and ground stone artifacts here are in part the same general sort as that found, for example, at Karim Shahir, Zawi Chemi Shanidar, Ganj Dareh, and probably Asiab, with the exception of a few tool types not found at Mureybit but special to each of these locales (e.g., the spall tools of Zawi Chemi Shanidar and the fleshers of Asiab). This shared part of the tool kit comprises borers (including the microlithic borers), microlithic backed bladelets, numerous end scrapers, some burins, and a limited number of blades with a trace of edge sheen. The other and distinctly Natufian portion of the tool kit comprises geometric microliths, including triangles and a high proportion of well-backed lunates, the special forms of arrowheads and large thick-tanged pieces, and the celtlike chipped adze/axes, or "erminettes." There is also a persistent trace of obsidian.

Save for the instances of Natufian occupation at the base of the occupational sequence at Mureybit and at nearby Abu Hureyra (see p. 126), which are at the easternmost and northernmost limits of the area in which the sites making up the province of the Natufian prehistoric tradition are distributed according to present knowledge, the sizeable group of well-documented Natufian and related sites in western Syria, Lebanon, Israel, and Jordan (i.e., the old physiocultural province of Syro-Palestine) are not considered here since they are clearly part of a distinct and separate cultural tradition and located in a different natural area. There, the response to certain unknown factors, perhaps partly the same as those applying within the Mesopotamian-Zagros area and perhaps at broadly the same range of time, did produce a quite different and rather uncomparable material culture and adaptation. This in itself is a provocative observation as it implies a mosaic of multiple types of response rather than any single linear one in these transitional times and places.

With certain exceptions to be noted, the horizons at Karim Shahir and Mureybit phase II share basically similar industries in chipped stone and ground stone. Moreover, while Mureybit II definitely displays a permanent architecture of round structures, in common with some early aceramic sites in the central Zagros foothills which have similar but simpler forms, this type of architecture is not demonstrable at Karim Shahir, Gird Chai, or Ganj Dareh E. Nevertheless, phase II is also clearly associated with an economy based on wild animals and plants, like virtually all of the Zagros sites (aside from the still moot evidence for animal domestication at Asiab and the Shanidar sites and the generally limited floral data at all these sites).

Let us review in more detail the evidence at Mureybit concerning cultural sequence, habitation type, artifactual remains, and faunal and floral records, and the general way of life reflected in this evidence. These facts are seen in a context of Natufian and other influences—call them Zagros or perhaps even some basic common forerunner—interplaying and overlapping near the presumed boundaries of these two cultural provinces.

It has already been noted that at Mureybit the rounded house forms of the epi-Natufian phase I-B evolved into the similar rounded forms of the aceramic phase II. (To date, no traces of this type of structure have been reported from the Natufian phase I-A.) They had a diameter range of ca. 2-4 m and were evidently semisubterranean, with prepared floors of clay combined variously with flagstones or with gravel, pebbles, and sand. Their low walls of prepared clay were stone-founded or -reinforced. In the epi-Natufian layer they showed imprints of wood stakes or poles on the exterior, but there has been no evidence as to type of roof covering. These structures at Mureybit displayed a sophistication in design and a quality of finish that surpasses anything reported so far from any other site in the Zagros mountain area. In addition, both Mureybit horizons had numerous outdoor pits (with a diameter range of 40-80 cm and depths to a maximum of 70 cm) that contained charcoal, ash, rocks, animal bone, and plant debris, clearly suggesting roasting, parching, or other forms of cooking. This is matched at the Zagros sites, though in a less richly filled version. The Mureybit phases had further (presumably outdoor) areas of gravels, sand, and compacted clay, hearth depressions, and miscellaneous occupational debris. These, too, can be found at one or another of the Zagros sites.

The evidence in both horizons at Mureybit points to numerous renovations and much rebuilding that undoubtedly represent many years of occupation of successive floors in a permanent settlement. This settlement was probably larger and had a longer duration than any associated with the Zagros sites studied here.

The following brief summary of the chipped stone industries of these earliest layers at Mureybit is drawn from M.-C. Cauvin's preliminary reports on phase I (M.-C. Cauvin in J. Cauvin 1972, pp. 108-9; 1979*b*) and from Skinner's preliminary analysis of the aceramic layers of phase II (Skinner 1968, pp. 282-88). Of the total studied, trimming debris and used pieces account for approximately 89%, typologically clear and distinct tools, 9%, and cores, 2%, matching closely the Karim Shahir proportions for similar categories of ca. 94%, 4%, and 2%, respectively.

At Mureybit the Natufian industry (phase I-A) came from the 1.0-1.2 m of deposits designated as phase I, which contained four occupation levels and appeared to be without significant detectable internal changes, as far as preliminary study of artifacts shows. It is a blade industry made up of many microliths (40% of the tools), including numerous geometrics (crescents, trapezoids, and triangles). According to the excavator, these geometrics represent 7-17% of the tools, depending on the level. There are also microborers, some microburins and backed bladelets, normal-sized borers, some end and side scrapers and burins, as well as various retouched and denticulated pieces. Plain blades with edge sheen occur, but very sparsely. A rather common and very characteristic tool here and in all succeeding layers at the site is the adze/axe, or erminette, a triangular-sectioned planoconvex flaked artifact usually made on a large heavy flake with a broad cutting edge at one end. The flat bulbar face of the flake has usually been left unflaked, and the piece has been shaped by flaking on the upper face alone. Virtually no obsidian was recovered from the lowermost levels, but a very little occurred higher up in the epi-Natufian level I-B. Also in the epi-Natufian level of phase I there were a very few arrowheads shaped by steep marginal retouch into bilaterally notched and tanged forms; here also microdrills increased in numbers, while among geometrics triangles and trapezes increased and lunates decreased.

The chipped stone industry of the aceramic phase II is also a blade industry (for example, 18% of the total number of pieces sampled in van Loon's stratum I), marked by a remnant of geometric microliths, but there is a strong continuing microlithic component, especially some backed bladelets and very great numbers of microborers. These, together with the varieties of normal-sized borers and the special form of supermicrolithic drill that the French call *mèche de foret* (with a centered, prominently protruding, long drill point steeply retouched on both its long edges), make up over 50% of the chipped stone tools in the sample studied. A sizeable representation of the adze type continues. In addition, there are modest quantities of end scrapers and burins and abundant arrowheads including a variety of tanged and laterally notched forms. Pieces with edge sheen continued to be very scarce in phase II, according to M.-C. Cauvin (see also van Loon's independent observation below). Obsidian, rare in phase I, makes up 0.9% of the industry in the sample of phase II studied. It must be emphasized that, for the most part, and excepting the microlithic types, the technological quality of the retouch and edge flaking of this industry at Mureybit is reported by the excavators to be unimpressive; much of the flaking is probably due to wear alone. This observation strikes a familiar note when one recalls similar characterizations for the chipped stone industry of the Zagros sites described above.

While there have as yet been no reports available about the ground stone industry in the phase I Natufian deposits at Mureybit, mention has been made of the presence of rare milling stones and a stone bowl fragment (M.-C. Cauvin 1979). For phase II, van Loon has noted some variety and quantity of milling stones (van Loon 1968, pp. 267-69, 279) as has Cauvin (J. Cauvin 1979*b*). The types recovered are querns, mortars, flat rubbing stones, pounders (including spheroids), and pestles made of natural cylindrical pebbles worn at the ends. As an indication of the scarcity and uneven distribution of some of these elements in the early phases, van Loon reports that the lowest and earliest occurrence together of querns and sheen-edged blades was in his stratum IV, somewhat above the beginnings of the aceramic deposits here (but see above for M.-C. and J. Cauvin's findings regarding both milling stones and sheen-bearing pieces). Three stone bowl fragments also came from phase II.

Bone artifacts, studied primarily by Stordeur (J. Cauvin 1972, pp. 108-9; 1979*b*), include awls and simple cylindrical beads made from segments of small long bones (bird?) from phase I, Natufian I-A; simple tools and a decorated pendant from the epi-Natufian I-B; and still numerous awls, some needles or pins, several polished pieces (polishers? spatulas?), and a trio of combing or carding implements (one long-toothed and two short-toothed) from the subsequent aceramic phase II. On the whole, both phases have a monotonously simple bone industry.

No lightly baked clay materials have been reported from either phase. However, one small fragmentary anthropomorphic limestone figurine from phase II suggests part of a torso from above the waist to the thighs (J. Cauvin 1973*a*, fig. 4). A small head of what the excavator called raw clay and possibly representing a human head is also recorded from phase II (J. Cauvin 1979*b*).

The wild fauna from phase I consists mainly of wild ass but also includes gazelle, large cattle, and fallow deer. There are also quantities of bird bones, fish bones, and freshwater molluscs (J. Cauvin 1972, 1973*b*, 1979*a*). Similarly, phase II had only wild fauna, including predominantly ass, cattle, and gazelle in nearly equal numbers, along with boar, fallow deer, wolf, hare, and some molluscs (van Loon 1968, p. 279; Ducos 1970, 1972).

The preliminary studies of van Zeist and Casparie on the flora of Mureybit (van Zeist and Casparie 1968; van Zeist 1970) indicate that wild grains were collected by the occupants. Among samples collected, only barley has so far been found in phase I. In phase II there is also wheat of a type known today in the Turkish foothills areas some 100-150 km to the north and east. It appeared abundantly at Mureybit more or less at the same time as increases in obsidian, the nearest sources for which are the Turkish highlands. Barley was recovered in limited quantity, and it is considered that this was collected from small wild stands that might reasonably be expected to have existed near the site. In addition, there are traces of other wild seed grasses, as well as legumes such as lentils and vetches, and pistachio. Wood reported from charcoal analyses includes poplar, tamarisk, and ash, all considered locally available then as now.

Evidence for absolute dating at Mureybit is diverse and may be summarized briefly as follows (J. Cauvin 1979*b*):

Phase	Laboratory no.	C^{14} determination BP	Approximate date BC
II	Lv-605	10,590 ± 170	8640
II	Lv-606	10,460 ± 200	8510
II	P-1217	10,215 ± 117	8265
II	P-1215	10,006 ± 96	8056
I-B	Lv-607	10,590 ± 140	8640
I-A	MC-733	10,030 ± 150	8080
I-A	MC-635	10,170 ± 200	8220
I-A	MC-674	10,090 ± 170	8150
I-A	MC-731	10,230 ± 170	8280
I-A	MC-732	10,230 ± 170	8280
I-A	MC-675	10,350 ± 150	8400

NOTE: The samples for phase I were taken from Cauvin's excavations and were treated in the Louvain laboratory (Gilot and Cauvin 1973) and in the Monaco laboratory (J. Cauvin 1979*b*). The samples for phase II were from van Loon's and Cauvin's excavations and were analyzed at the Louvain (Gilot and Cauvin 1973) and Pennsylvania laboratories (Stuckenrath and Lawn 1969, p. 151).

As Cauvin (1979*b*) has noted, the Louvain determinations for phases II and I-B are too old when compared with the Pennsylvania determinations, and they are similarly too old when compared with the Monaco determinations for phase I-A. He thus prefers the Pennsylvania determinations for phase II. He also notes that the phase I-A determinations are all from the upper level of that phase, since lower levels yielded no charcoal. Given these observations, Cauvin has established the following working scheme for the chronological sequence at Mureybit:

Phase II   8200-8000 B.C.
Phase I-B 8300-8200 B.C.
Phase I-A 8500-8300 B.C.

In sum, Mureybit was from the start and for quite a long period a not inconsiderable permanent aceramic settlement depending on hunting and gathering; studies so far have given no indication of any physiological changes in the animals or plants to suggest domestication or cultivation there. The distinctive and rather sophisticated rounded house forms and subsequent rectangular type seem unlike any indications found at Karim Shahir or any present evidence (the rudimentary rounded structures) from Zawi Chemi Shanidar, Asiab, or M'lefaat. Moreover, the presence of geometric microliths in the Natufian and epi-Natufian subphases, along with the first appearance of arrowheads in the latter subphase and an increase in their numbers in the succeeding phase II, distinguishes these phases from the horizon at Karim Shahir and all the other sites discussed in this report except Zawi Chemi Shanidar (where geometrics are recorded) and Asiab (where there are some possible examples). The apparent absence of lightly baked clay work (save for the single headlike clay lump) at Mureybit and the presence of some obsidian in phase I and phase II distinguish the assemblage at that site from the ones at Karim Shahir and most of the other Zagros sites under discussion. On the other hand, the general character of the rest of the chipped and the ground stone industries (e.g., the multiple-use pieces, the scrapers and burins, the microlithic components such as backed blades, bladelets, and drills, the faint indications of pieces with edge sheen, and the few milling stones), the simple bone industry, and the evident dependence on wild animals and plants all seem broadly akin in the two provinces. Put more specifically, the record from Zawi Chemi Shanidar is one in the Zagros group that accords fairly closely in several respects with the record from Mureybit: for example, the Zagros site has a chipped stone industry that is generally debased but includes microlithic components and geometric microlithic lunate forms; it has milling stones and round to oval semisubterranean structures (though a simple version) and evidently lacks lightly baked clay.

Abu Hureyra

Abu Hureyra, a low mound on the south bank of the Euphrates, is ca. 45-50 km downstream from Mureybit, some 550 km west of Karim Shahir, and lies perhaps a little under 300 m above sea level. It was briefly excavated in 1971 (Moore, Hillman, and Legge 1975). At the northwest corner of the mound there was evidence of a small so-called mesolithic settlement, characterized as Natufian, with ca. 1 m of accumulated deposit. Of this, ca. 49 m^2 were excavated. The basal settlement included evidence for pits, floors, hearths, and postholes cut into virgin soil, the ensemble suggesting semipermanent structures and the settlement seemingly considerably less elaborated and established than at Mureybit. The meter of deposit indicates a substantial period of occupation, probably intermittent but possibly continuous, on a regular basis.

A preliminary analysis of part of the artifactual material shows the presence of at least the following: backed blades and bladelets, numerous drills and microdrills, some geometric microliths including triangles and many lunates, and various kinds of ground stone milling tools in some quantity. No chipped flake adzes (erminettes) or obsidian were found. Bone tools are mostly simple awls, double-ended points, and a few needles. Ornaments include simple beads of stone, bone, and shell and some subcircular pear-shaped stone pendants.

The exclusively wild fauna comprises 65% gazelle, with a few examples each of a small equid (probably wild ass), sheep or goat, and hare making up the balance. Here again, as at Mureybit, there are traces of only morphologically wild plants, including mainly einkorn but also barley, rye, lentil, vetches, and a variety of seeds of grasses and other plants.

While no absolute age has been determined for this site, the general resemblances of its assemblage to that of the Natufian levels of nearby Mureybit are close. However, the absence of the erminette has been taken as an indication of a slightly earlier date. One may provisionally apply the same range of figures and tentatively suggest something a little prior to 8500 B.C. for this part of Abu Hureya.

In any attempt to compare such easternmost extensions of the Natufian tradition in the desert steppe area with anything in the transmesopotamian Zagros region, one might simply say that the same general level of cultural complexity obtained in both provinces; hunter-gatherers still lived in both regions, but in one area they were already beginning to change their way of life. Both groups lived off the wild animals and plants of their respective regions, but the people out on the steppe, having earlier absorbed influences from the neighboring Natufian province (as recorded at Mureybit) were already probably more fully sedentary, although some (at Abu Hureyra) were still semisedentary, while those in the Zagros region were largely migratory but in places semisedentary. In both regions the dwellings and artifact typology also varied locally in certain instances, with certain more advanced elements of habitation structure and tool kits out on the steppe, clearly drawn from the Natufian province. However, the basic tool kits in both areas were generally the same as far as the chipped stone and ground stone implements were concerned.

Review of the Comparative Evidence

Let us now review the cultural elements of this entire series of prehistoric sites in both the Zagros and the Euphrates areas.

The *chipped stone industry* is the single most outstanding cultural element shared by these ten different and geographically scattered occupation sites. Although there are individual variations in some respects, this industry has basically the same general typological characteristics at all these sites. Most of the artifacts are undistinguished in form. The uniformity prevailing among these sites has implications for similar functions and shared traditions. The shared elements at this series of sites are as follows:

1. It is primarily a blade industry, one that includes a distinct microlithic bladelet component and great quantities of multipurpose used and reused blades and flakes classified as used, nibbled, or notched according to their predominant edge features.

2. There are core types to match the large blade category, including various stages of blade and flake cores classified as to direction and degree of flaking. These pieces are generally of materials from demonstrable local sources—usually secondary stream pebbles but also primary nodular or tabular pieces from bedrock. The norm is a blade core with one, sometimes two, striking platforms.
3. Also included is a much more limited but characteristic body of the following specialized tool types:

   (a) A considerable number of elements of presumably composite tools or weapons, exactly shaped and neatly made, in the form of microlithic backed bladelets that usually have angled bases and used tip ends

   (b) A few backed blades or flakes, occasionally on larger blade forms

   (c) Rather plentiful piercing tools (borer or drill type) with worked and used points on blades, flakes, or fragments, which range in size from steeply backed microlithic forms (in quantity) up through retouched and used normal medium sizes to larger, thicker forms with blunting, edge wear, and occasional polishing or smoothing (these last are labeled fabricators or reamers according to different authors), and which were probably used for a variety of drilling, piercing, or stabbing functions on stone, bone, shell, wood, or skin

   (d) Quantities of casually made scraper forms, mostly end scrapers on blades or flakes, which are predominantly quite poorly formed and evidently the result of use and wear rather than any deliberate shaping by retouch, as well as a lesser number of elongated side and discoid or rounded scrapers, also formed by use (some with retouch shaping as well), and a few steep-fronted scrapers formed by use either on thick oblong core fragments or on reused cores

   (e) A very few burins scarcely to be dignified with a category designation but found just often enough in a number of typologically simple forms that they can be regarded as a real element in the tool kit, their presence at certain sites definitely corroborated by the presence of burin spalls there

   (f) A small miscellany of microlithic tools such as pointed or obliquely truncated bladelets or microlithic end scrapers

The two other characteristics that are generally applicable are (4) the occasional presence of unshaped blades or flakes with sheen along one or more edges and (5) the absence of obsidian (it is totally absent in some cases, virtually absent in others, and only a limited amount was found in the culturally comparable basal layers of the westernmost site, Mureybit, which lies within the Natufian province).

The *ground, pecked, and polished stone industry* found at these ten particular sites is in most cases relatively limited and includes a much smaller quantity of material than the chipped stone industry. It regularly includes the following types, often in fragmentary form:

1. Chipped and polished celts, occurring at several but not all sites (primarily Karim Shahir, upper levels of Zawi Chemi Shanidar, Gird Chai, and M'lefaat, all located in a distinctly circumscribed geographical district, although those from the first three are more flaked and thus perhaps more primitive in typology)
2. Boulder mortars
3. Grinding slabs, or querns, with flat or somewhat concave working surfaces
4. Hand rubbing stones, or mullers, of flat or planoconvex form with minimal shaping
5. Pestles either deliberately shaped by pecking and grinding (rare) or else (more commonly) minimally developed on selected natural elongated stream pebbles simply by having been used at the end, sometimes with numerous striations and incisions over the long axis, indicating double duty perhaps as an anvil or slicing surface
6. A few pebbles converted by deliberate pecking or grinding into pierced disks or spheres posssibly for use as dibbles, maces, clubs, or weights
7. The supposedly shaft-straightening grooved rubbing stones of schist or chlorite (most sites)

There is also a small but distinctive class of plain ornaments and personal adornments that are almost never decorated; these are virtually unshaped pebble pendants or ground and shaped pendants and plaques of various simple forms, as well as simple, usually cylindrical, barrel-shaped, or discoid stone beads. Curiously, the only site in the group under discussion here at which so-called bracelets and rings were found is Karim Shahir. These also occurred at closely neighboring Jarmo, which is of course of later date.

The *bone industry* almost never goes beyond simple awls and punches on shaft or condylar fragments of animal long bones, with a few surviving fragmentary examples of more shapely polished pins or needles and occasionally spatulate forms suggesting polishers or smoothers. Some comblike pieces from Mureybit seem exceptional at this stage. Also, as a common occurrence, there are a few bone ornaments in the form of simple tubular beads made from small long-bone (bird?) segments, as well as still rarer pierced plaques or pendants made of bone, tusks, or teeth.

A *shell industry* is sparsely represented (primarily at Karim Shahir, Zawi Chemi Shanidar, and Asiab) and consists entirely of ornaments such as beads, pendants, and little plaques or "buttons."

Lightly baked clay objects recovered in limited but consistent quantity at most sites (the prime exceptions being Zawi Chemi Shanidar, Mureybit I and II, and Abu Hureyra) include rather realistic animal figurines and human figurines more in the form of stylized abstractions (or occasionally a small plaque in the form of a "mask" or face). Rather more frequently, there are little plastic geometric forms such as pellets, cones, disks, and rods. A single small clay head (representing a human?) is reported from Mureybit, phase II. No true pottery of any kind has been found that can be convincingly associated with the early horizons here discussed, with the exception of a single as yet unexplained small piece from layer E at Ganj Dareh.

Types of dwelling are the last artifactual element reviewed here. There is no overall uniformity in the kind of habitation among the sites considered in the Zagros region nor are any structural remains there closely comparable to those at Mureybit in the middle Euphrates region. However, one may say that in both areas round to oval dwellings are a characteristic of the span of time, around 8000 B.C., that has been assigned to the transitional period under consideration. The Zagros area has the simpler, more primitive forms, while Mureybit, well to the west and within the Natufian province, contains more elaborately constructed and sophisticated forms. In addition, many fire pits, rubbish pits, and hearths occurred at all of these house-centered sites, presumably part of an equally significant open-air existence at such active dwelling clusters.

Of the Zagros sites, both Zawi Chemi Shanidar and M'lefaat have clear evidence for small-scale round to oval structures (2.5-4.0 m in diameter) defined by sizeable stones set in curves about floor areas or excavated depressions, suggesting semisubterranean dwellings. There is also evidence for limited renovations and successive floor levels, implying a certain continuity of occupation.

At Asiab one end of a large oval depression cut into virgin soil was uncovered. It had low vertical sides and a gently basined floor, but no other structural features were detected. However, it was crammed with living debris and contained two human burials lying at different levels. It is not clear whether the feature was a shelter with now-lost covering and walls or whether it was simply a large rubbish pile and pit intensely lived upon either intermittently or continuously. In any case, it is part of a habitation site, perhaps more camplike than the dwellings indicated for Zawi Chemi Shanidar or M'lefaat.

Karim Shahir was even more obviously a camp site, yielding no evidence for living structures but only rocky floors or scatters well littered with debris of wild animal bones and artifactual material. At the remaining Zagros sites, no evidence of anything that might be called dwellings has been found, although in the case of Shanidar Cave, habitation was inside the cave chamber.

Thus, for this area in general, one cannot speak of anything more elaborate than encampments or small settlements or clusters of rounded structures, and one cannot yet make a judgment as to whether any of these were truly permanently or only intermittently occupied.

At Mureybit, however, the house foundations reflected structures of such quality and durability and the succession of floors and renovations were so numerous as to imply prolonged continuity of occupation. Here was a true village with a marked degree of permanence. The evidence for habitation forms at Natufian Abu Hureyra is less decisive. The remains there are in part possibly contemporaneous with, or just predate, Mureybit, but it was only a small-scale, simple, possibly permanent (or more likely semipermanent) settlement that shared the same overall traditions and material culture as Mureybit.

The *fauna* in every case comprises wild forms, with sheep and goat often predominating. As to the two possible instances of manipulation toward domestication (at Zawi Chemi Shanidar, pp. 521-25, and Asiab, p. 116), both remain debatable.

As a general rule, then, the artifact assemblages from these ten different occupational deposits are marked by a simplicity of form, a lack of decoration, and a poverty of tool types and ornamental objects. The chipped stone industry displays a tremendous predominance of multipurpose tools formed through use alone on blades and flakes rather than any emphasis on tools that were distinctive, specialized, deliberately created, or carefully shaped; it is marked by debased scraper and burin forms and by two well-made microlithic forms (the angled and backed bladelets and the drills) and, at a few sites, geometrics. The ground and pecked stone industry appears to consist of the following categories: implements for the grinding and pounding of foodstuffs and possibly the knapping of flint; at several sites, tools resembling axes and adzes or hoes for working wood, soil, or perhaps skins; grooved rubbing stones perhaps for shaft straightening or some grinding processes; tools for use as weights, digging sticks, or weapons; a variety of working stones (anvils, whetstones, smoothers, etc.); and, finally, smaller, simpler articles of personal adornment. Small ornaments of bone or shell are also reported at some sites, and simple bone tools, only rarely ornamented, are the rule. Rudimentary lightly baked clay figurines and little geometric forms occur at a number of sites; perhaps they would have been found at most sites if preservation conditions had been better.

At some of the sites under consideration this whole conservative, stylistically simple, primitive cluster of artifactual material was found not only in one but in succeeding horizons as well, but in these later levels this typological cluster sometimes has combined with it additional features of ornament or changes in character of tools or a different proportion of certain artifactual elements, reflecting new living developments.

The basic cluster of artifacts as found in the presumably early part of the era of man's transition from food gatherer to food producer must surely reflect a specific series of uses. Thus, the chipped stone element may have focused mainly on the piercing, scraping, and cutting of various materials for food, equipment, and other living needs. The ground and pecked or polished elements were likely used primarily for hewing, hoeing, or scraping or for pounding, grinding, and further processing of foodstuffs and perhaps processing of clothing and equipment and secondarily for articles of ornamentation for body, dress, or equipment.

The continuation of this cluster of tools and ornaments into subsequent levels indicates the continuation of these fundamental and indispensable activities in a persisting tradition of human community existence. The presence or absence at different sites of such items as celts, spall tools, or fleshers, and geometric microliths may betoken new or different local developments. It is such newly introduced factors, including the major suspected ones of animal and plant domestication and perhaps certain initial house forms with associated innovative living arrangements, that may directly or indirectly have spurred artifactual changes and novelty. Nevertheless, despite such special items, the overall sameness of the bulk of the artifactual record is an impressive witness to continuity during this transitional era and reflects a sustained dependence on certain long-established activities thoughout this fairly protracted and still undefined interval of time around 8000 B.C. The nature of these activities is only dimly perceived and only partly provable, but their entrenched presence is strongly suspected. Most of the sites in question appear from their material records to have been still-archaic hunter-gatherer loci that contained only occasional observable hints or traces of new living arrangements or food manipulation. The assault on these obscurities continues on many fronts, but the results will be inconclusive for some time to come. The present evidence from our little series alone is certainly equivocal and fails to point clearly to any instance of undoubted settled food production.

At present, it can only be said that the tools of the chipped stone industry and also perhaps the tools of the innovative ground stone industry that continue into immediately subsequent phases survive as the indispensable components of life and its artifactual record, the chipped stone tools perhaps because they served certain persistent basic needs over this broad time range, the ground stone tools because newly established needs continued into later imes. Thus, on the one hand, in contemplating possible origins it is reasonable to suppose that one can trace the antecedents of the specific chipped stone tool types noted in our series of sites back to (1) the tools of the later Upper Paleolithic and then follow the development of these same types into (2) the tools of the terminal food-gathering era represented by the Zarzian, with its well-made and clear-cut backed blades, its normal and smaller-sized scraper types, its microliths (backed bladelets, geometric forms, and microburins), its burins and burin spalls, and its various types of edge flaking resulting in notched or nibbled pieces and other use scars. One can next trace this tool kit to (3) the technologically largely debased, monotonous, and typologically limited artifacts of the subsequent transitional era under consideration here (with ever-deteriorating stylistic traits occasioned by an increase in use over deliberate preparation of forms), as found at Karim Shahir and the other presumably broadly coeval Zagros and Euphrates sites. Finally, one can follow the changes in these industries into (4) the era strong in ground stone tools and ornaments and in obsidian, but weaker in chipped stone varieties, as represented by the inventories of such sites as Ali Kosh (Bus Mordeh phase), Jarmo, and Çayönü. Even in this early settled-village era the long-established tradition and basic types of the chipped stone industry persist as the least common denominator of artifacts and their associated activities and functions, whatever they may have been. It is the minority of more specialized surviving items such as backed bladelets, drills, burins, and geometrics (and their associated suspected but unknown functions) that appear and disappear in the sequence, representing particular activities that perhaps come and go and are of such outstanding interest.

On the other hand, turning now from the components that survive from the older periods, one may consider certain additional components engendered by new needs and activities. One immediately thinks of the innovation of milling tools, of the presumed domestication of animal and plants, of the probably related developments of a fixed sedentary life and its permanent architectural forms for both living and storage space. These new activities involve not only the gradual elaboration or specialization of pre-existing microlithic forms but also the phasing out or deterioration of such older forms as burins and various scrapers. There is also the phasing in of new forms, such as the various milling tools and also the celt axes and adze/hoes and, perhaps, the spall tools, or fleshers. Such shifts represent, in a way that is vague and only theoretically detectable and reconstructible, new functions and activities bound up in these new objects.

As regards the overall character of these habitation sites and their associated parts, the fashionable term "base camp" may be applied to sites such as Karim Shahir, whose remains and features may or may not record or reflect considerable population or duration along with the existence of impermanent structures or living arrangements (or even imply none). One notes ephemeral installations such as depressions or pits (with presumably associated perishable constructions in semisubterranean or surface combinations), fire pits and cooking pits containing debris affected by heat in various ways, plentiful chipped stone and ground stone in various stages of workmanship that incontrovertibly demonstrate on-the-spot craft activities, and hints of subsistence measures and food preparation involving wild animals and wild plants. There are other sites (Zawi Chemi Shanidar, M'lefaat, Ganj Dareh E, and perhaps Asiab and Abu Hureyra) that have enough depth of deposit, area of occupation, accompanying debris, and even traces of more fixed or permanent structures to suggest relatively longer periods or a greater number of repeated periods of settlement rather than a fleeting occupation. At the same time these five sites fall short of being the kind of settlement that represents a permanent, uninterrupted occupation or sedentary mode of living such as was found at Mureybit. All these different types of site still fit in a fully or partly migratory pattern of either camps of hunter-gatherers or little settlements of manipulators of incipient animal herds (but probably not yet of plants). The sort of protracted but still impermanent occupation site in some variety (e.g., Zawi Chemi Shanidar, M'lefaat, Ganj Dareh E, and perhaps Asiab and Abu Hureyra) and the type of settlement that is obviously more fixed yet still based on a hunter-gatherer economy (e.g., Mureybit), and also the simpler type of base camp (e.g., Karim Shahir) are *all* forerunners of the fuller sedentarism that accompanied domestication of animals and plants and the concurrent anchoring of a community to its locale. This can be said without any priority of cultural elements or chronological seniority having been clearly established as yet for any of these three kinds of occupation site. The degree of permanence varies by geographic district and indeed by individual site, and there may yet be intervening or variant stages to be discovered in this series. One must also bear in mind that while the sites may prove to be a sequential progression it is possible that if the C^{14} evidence were to prove reliable they might even all be broadly contemporaneous. Finally, it is interesting to note that at Ganj Dareh and Mureybit the basal layers were overlain by a succession of permanent communities that inherited artifactual, dwelling, and other cultural traditions from the preceding stages in increasingly structured and locale-bound conditions of existence.

CONCLUSIONS

On present evidence, the occupation at Karim Shahir seems to have been a camp of hunter-gatherers living on wild plants and animals (predominantly sheep and goats) and ranging fairly widely over the intermontane territory of one central Zagros district at ca. 850 m altitude. These people seem to have had access to a broad geographical range, including wooded, dry grassland, river valley, and semiarid tracts of land, as indicated by limited wood identifications. The faunal record reinforces this impression and adds higher mountain terrain as well. All these habitats are characteristic, here or there, of the central Zagros region today. While there is no absolute dating for the Karim Shahir archeological sampling, a revealing and distinctive assemblage has been found; it is characterized particularly by copious chipped stone tools in considerable variety (basic generalized debased forms, evidently persisting from earlier horizons, along with well-made more specialized microlithic forms), by rare pieces with edge sheen, by milling stones and a few other ground stone tools and simple ornaments, and by scanty ill-preserved remnants of simple bone, shell, and lightly baked clay items. This tool kit probably reflects responses both to continuing traditional uses and activities (as evidenced by most of the chipped stone categories) and to other, newly entering routines (as evidenced by the microliths and the ground stone elements, especially the various milling stones and celts).

A first step in putting Karim Shahir and other central Zagros sites into an integrated picture is to note that one especially diagnostic tool at Karim Shahir, the chipped and polished celt, is closely matched by numerous specimens confined to the upper level of Zawi Chemi Shanidar, a not too distant (150 km northwest), small, evidently rudimentary settlement at ca. 425 m altitude, with fixed rounded structures, a largely comparable artifactual and faunal record, and a C^{14} determination from its lower levels that dates the site to ca. 8900 B.C. This very characteristic celt form, distinctive enough and found at sites near enough to each other to be accepted as evidence for near contemporaneity, is an all but incontrovertible typological link. It follows that Karim Shahir not only was occupied somewhat later than the bulk of the Zawi Chemi Shanidar site but also was possibly an example of a retarded little hunter-gatherer occupation. More logical and likely, it may have been a seasonal encampment of individuals (temporarily specialized for hunting purposes, travelling light, perhaps making most of their limited equipment on the spot), conceivably a small social group normally lodged elsewhere in the district in a more fixed settlement with true dwelling structures and perhaps a fuller complement of tools that probably included a greater proportion of milling stones—all on the order of the more sedentary situation recorded at Zawi Chemi Shanidar.

In turn, Zawi Chemi has a roughly contemporaneous counterpart in nearby Shanidar Cave's layer B-1, where a C^{14} determination dates the assemblage to ca. 8600 B.C. This layer's artifactual and faunal assemblages and its traces of a rounded structure in a thin occupation deposit, all of which are closely comparable to those of Zawi Chemi, record a mode of existence that was similar to that at the other Shanidar site. Additional cultural items preserved in layer B-1 indicate a somewhat greater range of material goods for the horizon than has been indicated at either Karim Shahir or Zawi Chemi Shanidar. Also, the evidence clearly shows that cave shelter was another form of habitation roughly concomitant with the rudimentary rounded houselike structure and open-air encampment already noted. The still-debatable evidence of cultural manipulation of sheep at both Shanidar sites has also to be borne in mind.

In the same general central Zagros region, but at lower altitudes (300 m) and on the fringes of the piedmont zone, the site of M'lefaat shows rounded structures as at the Shanidar sites and an artifactual assemblage and list of wild fauna very like those of the aforementioned three intermontane sites. Only a few kilometers from M'lefaat and at about the same altitude lies Gird Chai, a heavily disturbed and therefore largely unrewarding site that nevertheless displays much of what is probably the same general artifactual assemblage, including the distinctive chipped and polished celt.

These five roughly comparable sites and assemblages within a radius of 150 km in the intermontane and piedmont zones of the central Zagros appear to form what might be considered a distinct cultural nucleus possibly dating to ca. 8900-8600 B.C. and perhaps continuing somewhat after that time. Also, the fact that all these five sites lack convincing traces of obsidian and any pottery whatsoever emphasizes that this hypothetical little cultural entity was probably quite locale-bound and isolated from more distant regions.

Two other comparable sites lie some 250-275 km southeast of the northern cluster. The midden campsite of Asiab and the limited exposure of some sort of simple settlement in the lowest horizon of Ganj Dareh are only 30 km apart and also in the intermontane zone but at ca. 1,300 m altitude, nearly twice that of the other group. Again there are the stone, bone, clay, and faunal assemblages in common, and again the noteworthy absence of obsidian and pottery. One site, Asiab, has an oval structure and debatable evidence for domestication of goat. The C^{14} determinations give dates of ca. 8400 B.C. in one sample at Ganj Dareh and ca. 7800 B.C. at Asiab. The first date accords reasonably with the indicated dating for the northern cluster; the second puts a lower limit on the entire complex of sites.

For these seven sites the faunal and artifactual assemblages are strikingly similar. Rounded structures (possibly representing fixed dwellings), cave occupancy, and open-air encampment are three compatible and seemingly broadly contemporaneous habitation styles. The sites are located in a topographical region of the central Zagros mountains that embraces intermontane and piedmont zones and extends over some 1,000 m in altitude and some 400 km in length. If we take the C^{14} determinations at face value, the sites of this hypothetical regional cultural entity appear to span a total of ca. 1,100 years covering a period both before and after 8000 B.C.

Admittedly, the artifactual evidence to date shows some individual differences by site. On the whole, though, there appear to be enough common denominators, both positive and negative, at all these sites and enough other features shared by two or more sites to weight the argument in favor of considering them part of a loosely knit, broadly contemporaneous but perhaps slowly evolving cultural group or province. While no two sites are exactly alike in their revealed archeological records, whatever apparently unreconcilable aspects there may be that work against grouping these sites together also work against placing them in some orderly chronological sequence. Thus, for example, geometric microliths appear at the earliest and the latest sites with a C^{14} determination (Zawi Chemi Shanidar and Asiab) but at no others; these same two sites are the only ones with possible cultural manipulation (albeit debatable) of one animal species, a different species in each case; a single site lacks milling stones (Ganj Dareh); two sites lack evidence for dwelling structures (Karim Shahir and Ganj Dareh, but excluding the heavily disturbed Gird Chai); two other sites have one distinctive ground stone category each that may point to certain ultimate relationships or common traditions with later horizons in the area (more fully polished celts at M'lefaat, ground marble bracelets/rings at Karim Shahir). However, these disparities and the individualistic artifactual variations between sites may in large part be explained as due to localized occupational or adaptive determinants, physical conditions, or fortunes of excavation. The greater number of striking and repeated similarities provides an overriding impression of general cultural unity, and the single broad band of shared traits signifies the same level of cultural complexity. Until further excavations at these or new sites give us more insight and additional evidence by which to subdivide this cluster, it appears that, on balance, lumping rather than splitting wins the day.

Indeed, this hypothetical cultural entity needs the data (structural, artifactual, faunal, and the C^{14} determinations) from all seven sites to fill out the picture. Starting in the intermontane zone with Karim Shahir (excavated spring 1951), this site supplied the initial evidence for the artifactual assemblage and the encampment way of life. More evidence accrued from Shanidar Cave (begun autumn 1951) and Zawi Chemi Shanidar (1956) for the presumption of cave habitation and settled dwelling clusters, confirmation of the artifactual assemblage, and the addition of several special artifact types; and there was also the possibility of cultural manipulation of sheep. The Shanidar sites also provided a terminus a quo for this hypothetical central Zagros cultural group. M'lefaat and Gird Chai (both 1954) reconfirmed the artifactual and faunal assemblages (and M'lefaat, the dwelling form), and these two sites, lying as they do on the edge of the piedmont zone, extended the horizon into lower altitudes. Subsequently, Asiab (1960) and Ganj Dareh (begun 1967) pushed the altitude to 1,300 m and the geographical extent southward in the intermontane zone and generally reconfirmed the artifactual and faunal assemblages. In addition, Asiab evidenced further special tools, an open-air shell midden, perhaps structural traces, and, possibly, domestic goat. Asiab also yielded a C^{14} determination that may give a terminus ad quem for this hypothetical cultural group, and at Ganj Dareh a C^{14} determination was obtained that fell within the dating span indicated for the northern cluster of sites.

This cultural stage, found through 1,000 m of altitude and over some 400 km of intermontane and piedmont terrain, may have lasted some 1,100 years. Such an extended period seems intolerably long when compared to the time spans of some other theoretical cultural eras during these early millennia in the Near East. However, this situation may have to stand until proven otherwise; so far, we lack any factually based sense of the speed, order, and directions in which cultural developments may have been taking place in the congeries of little communities that are assumed to represent this undoubted period of transition from hunting-gathering to new and different ways in the central Zagros region. Indeed, Mortensen long ago put forward the idea of such a tentative cultural group (based on Zawi Chemi Shanidar, Karim Shahir, and Asiab) in the course of developing his concept of an analogous but later cultural unity of village-farming sites in the Zagros area during the seventh and sixth millennia B.C. He even suggested that this younger group may prove to be derived from the older one, although he, and others, warned that there are probably as yet undiscovered intervening stages that might fit into the evident gap between the two (Mortensen 1964, pp. 33-34, 36).

Karim Shahir and the six other suggested central Zagros sites that appear to be of broadly similar date, character, and cultural complexity here render the service of strengthening the evidence and heightening our perceptions regarding such an earlier cultural group in that region during a period extending either side of 8000 B.C.

One further set of conclusions concerns observations made on the data from three sites outside the central Zagros region. Ali Kosh, lying at ca. 170 m altitude, is in the Khuzistani steppe zone some 450 km to the south, while the sites of Mureybit and Abu Hureyra at ca. 300 m altitude are riverine localities in the Syrian steppe zone some 600 km west.

Bus Mordeh, the basal layer and the earlier of two preceramic phases at Ali Kosh, appears on a number of counts to be later in date and more advanced in cultural stage than any of the central Zagros sites. For example, it has a C^{14} determination-based range of 7500-6750 B.C.; a rectangular house form, plentiful obsidian, and lightly baked clay items all more akin to Jarmo than to Karim Shahir; numerous milling stones; and ample clear evidence of domesticated plants and animals. However, the point of interest of this phase for this study is the unoutstanding chipped stone tool assemblage which greatly resembles those of all the central Zagros sites under consideration. The generally shared technotypological and morphological character of this stone industry, except for individual points of spot variation as noted earlier in this chapter (see Comparisons, pp. 111ff.), is taken to be an interesting reflection of conservatism and of the retention, in the Bus Mordeh phase, of tool types for some specific uses (as yet unknown) in what are likely to have been continuing basic ancient traditional routines in an already much changed world. The Bus Mordeh phase seems to have retained this part of the artifactual heritage from prior subhorizons or from a general cultural stage similar or related to that represented by the seven sites in the central Zagros.

On the other hand, and in a context of survival under strong outside influence, the aceramic horizons in Mureybit phases I-A, I-B, and lower II and at Abu Hureyra show that this more westerly group was primarily within the area of the separately and more westerly centered epi-Paleolithic Late Natufian cultural tradition (Mureybit I and Abu Hureyra). However, there was a subsequent shift, in the case of the occupation in Mureybit II, to what appears to be some particular local form of a basic technotypological tradition and artifactual assemblage which somewhat resembles the form known from the central Zagros but has elements retained from the powerfully influential earlier Natufian inroad. This shift, perhaps even a reversion as it were, may be tentatively documented by tallying how the traits in Mureybit I-A and I-B differ from those in Mureybit II. For phase I, the by now well-established Natufian characteristics of sophisticated round houses, milling stones, various geometric microliths and arrowheads, traces of obsidian and edge-sheen pieces, and the locally characteristic chipped planoconvex flake adzes (erminettes) are associated not only with special microlithic drills and backed blades but also with basic simple scrapers, burins, drills, and multipurpose tools familiar from the central Zagros. In phase II, the Natufian influence undergoes metamorphoses (geometrics gradually decrease in number; arrowheads increase; round houses, milling stones, and flake adzes continue; and obsidian and edge-sheen pieces are still rare but increasing), while the basic segment of the stone industry (banal scrapers, burins, multiuse pieces, and special microliths) persists as a technotypological series that has some resemblance to the central Zagros industry. That Mureybit I and II also have exclusively wild plants and a fauna that are of the same range as those in the central Zagros sites reinforces the impression that these Syrian steppe sites had the same general level of cultural complexity as the central Zagros group, save for traits that the Natufian influences had firmly imposed locally. The numerous C^{14} determinations for Mureybit I and II indicate time spans of 8500-8200 B.C. and 8200-8000 B.C. respectively, both being within the latter half of the somewhat longer span at present assigned to the central Zagros group. The Natufian sampling at Abu Hureyra essentially repeats the evidence from Mureybit I but has elements suggesting perhaps a slightly earlier moment and also suggesting encampment rather than more fixed settlement.

Thus, basal Mureybit I and II and the little settlement at Abu Hureyra are definitely part of a different and separate sophisticated Natufian province with a settled existence at the same time as the central Zagros sites were witnessing, on a simpler scale, the beginnings of various adaptations to more settled ways. However, at Mureybit, this advanced Natufian element appears to be intermingled with a way of life (represented by the basic chipped stone tools, the specialized microliths, the rare milling stones and edge-sheen pieces, and the wild fauna and flora) that corresponds broadly with the central Zagros tradition, though surely the evidently strong Natufian influence had already changed the Mureybit community radically and irreversibly.

In sum, two conclusions are offered here. (1) There is an argument for a hypothetical central Zagros intermontane-piedmont culture province of both shifting and semianchored hunter-gatherers who were in a state of transition toward being somewhat more settled, and possibly toward being incipient food producers, during a period extending either side of 8000 B.C. (2) Two instances are suggested in which the sort of characteristic chipped stone tool tradition associated with this transitional way of life (as noted, for example, in the central Zagros sites) seems to continue on into disparate phases (in two widely separated steppe zones) and thus are instructive examples of persisting conservative response to traditional needs and activities under otherwise radically changed conditions. These conclusions are offered not so much as developed working models but rather more as tentative accountings for the present scattered mass of incomplete, uneven evidence until such time as future analyses and fieldwork at these and new central Zagros sites undoubtedly reformulate the whole scene.

KARIM SHAHIR

CATALOGUE OF ILLUSTRATIONS (figs. 3-21)

FIGURE 3. AIR VIEW OF SITE

FIGURE 4. VIEW OF SCARP AND STREAM BED

FIGURE 5. CONTOUR MAP

FIGURE 6. NORTH-SOUTH SECTION

FIGURE 7. PLOT PLAN

FIGURE 8. ROCKY PAVEMENT IN GRID A AND THE EXTENSION

FIGURE 9. SCATTERED STONES IN GRIDS B, C, F, G

FIGURE 10. CLAY, BONE, SHELL, AND GROUND STONE OBJECTS
1. Clay figurine, from I,step,ochre pit, 180 cm (K-30) (a, drawings; b, photograph)
2. Clay rod, from I,sf
3. Bone pin frag., from I,step, 120-160 cm (K-6)
4. Bone awl frag., from I,C, 30-40 cm
5. Bone tubular bead, from VI, 20-40 cm
6. Bone tubular bead, from I,step,ochre pit, 180 cm (K-8)
7. Bone tubular bead?, from I,G, 30-40 cm
8. Worked bone frag., from I,sf
9. Worked bone frag., from I,F, 20-30 cm
10. Shell plaque frag., from I,C, 20-30 cm (K-13)
11. Shell plaque frag., from I,step, 20-40 cm (K-4)
12. Marble ring frag., from I,G, 20-30 cm (K-42)
13. Marble ring frag., from I,ext., 0-20 cm
14. Marble ring frag.?, from III, 40-60 cm (K-29)
15. Marble bracelet frag., from I,step, 0-40 cm
16. Marble bracelet frag., from I,A, 0-20 cm
17. Marble bracelet frag., from I,G, 20-30 cm
18. Marble bracelet frag., from I,G, 20-30 cm
19. Marble bracelet frag., from I,B, 0-20 cm (K-15)
20. Marble bracelet frag., from I,ext., 0-20 cm
21. Decorated marble bracelet frag., from I,F, 20-30 cm (K-22)
22. Marble bracelet frag., from I,C, 90-100 cm
23. Stone rod frag., from VI, 0-20 cm

FIGURE 11. GROUND STONE
1. Stone pendant frag., from I,G, 30-40 cm (K-40)
2. Marble pendant frag., from I,G, 30-40 cm (K-35)
3. Marble plaque frag., from III, 0-20 cm (K-28)
4. Marble plaque frag., from I,ext., 0-20 cm
5. Stone plaque frag., from I,A, 20-30 cm (K-27)
6. Stone plaque frag., from I,sf
7. Marble plaque frag., from I,G, 0-20 cm
8. Marble plaque frag., from I,G, 60-80 cm (K-46)
9. Incised limestone plaque frag., from I,step, 0-40 cm (K-2)
10. Stone bead frag., from VI, 0-20 cm (K-49)
11. Stone bead, from I,ext., 0-20 cm (K-52)
12. Stone bead, from I,G, 30-40 cm (K-36)
13. Stone bead, from I,C, 20-40 cm (K-11)
14. Stone bead rough-out, from I,B, 0-20 cm (K-20)

FIGURE 12. GROUND STONE
1. Grooved rubbing stone frag., from I,ext., 0-20 cm
2. Grooved rubbing stone frag., from I,C, 30-40 cm (K-31)
3. Palette frag., from I,G, 40-50 cm (K-37)
4. Pestle frag., from I,ext., 0-20 cm
5. Pestle frag., from I,step, 40-80 cm
6. Hand rubbing stone frag., from I,G, 20-30 cm
7. Hand rubbing stone, from I,G, 30-40 cm
8. Chisel type celt, from I,C, 0-20 cm (K-10)
9. Chisel type celt, from I,C, 20-30 cm (K-44)

FIGURE 13. CHIPPED AND POLISHED CELTS
1. Adze/hoe type, from I,ext., 0-20 cm
2. Adze/hoe type, from I,G, 20-30 cm
3. Adze/hoe type, from I,F, 0-20 cm
4. Adze/hoe type, from VI, 0-20 cm
5. Adze/hoe or axe type, from I,G, 20-30 cm
6. Adze/hoe type, from I,G, 20-30 cm
7. Adze/hoe type, from I,C, 30-40 cm
8. Axe type, from surface
9. Axe type, from I,F, 0-20 cm
10. Axe type, from I,step, 0-40 cm

FIGURE 14. CHIPPED STONE
1. Denticulated blade, from I,ext., 0-20 cm
2. Denticulated blade, from I,step, 40-80 cm
3. Backed bladelet, from I,step, 40-80 cm
4. Backed bladelet frag., from I,ext., 0-20 cm
5. Backed bladelet frag., from I,ext. 0-20 cm
6. Backed bladelet frag., from I,step, 0-20 cm
7. Backed bladelet frag., from I,B, 0-20 cm
8. Backed bladelet frag., from I,step, 0-20 cm
9. Backed bladelet frag., from V, 0-20 cm
10. Backed bladelet frag., from I,ext., 0-20 cm
11. Microlithic end scraper on blade, from I,ext., 0-20 cm
12. Microlithic end scraper on blade, from I,ext., 0-20 cm
13. Microlithic end scraper on blade, from I,ext., 0-20 cm
14. Microlithic end scraper on blade, from I,A, 0-20 cm
15. Microlithic end scraper on blade, from I,ext., 0-20 cm
16. Microlithic end scraper on flake, from I,B, 0-20 cm
17. Microlithic pointed bladelet, from I,ext., 0-20 cm
18. Chance geometric microlith (lunate?), from I,C, 60-80 cm
19. Chance geometric microlith (lunate?), from I,A, 0-20 cm
20. Chance geometric microlith (triangle?), from V, 20-35 cm
21. Chance geometric microlith (trapezoid?), from I,G, 20-30 cm
22. Fabricator, from V, 20-35 cm
23. Fabricator, from I,ext., 0-20 cm
24. Fabricator, from I,C, 30-50 cm

FIGURE 15. CHIPPED STONE
1. Normal-sized drill on blade, from I,G, 20-30 cm
2. Normal-sized drill on blade, from I,tr., 0-20 cm
3. Normal-sized drill on blade, from I,ext., 0-20 cm
4. Normal-sized drill on blade, from I,step,ochre pit, 80-180 cm
5. Normal-sized drill on flake, from I,C, 60-80 cm
6. Microlithic drill, from I,step, 160-180 cm
7. Microlithic drill, from I,step, 0-40 cm
8. Supermicrolithic drill, from I,C, 30-40 cm
9. Supermicrolithic drill, from I,ext., 0-20 cm
10. Supermicrolithic drill, from I,F, 20-30 cm
11. Microburin, from I,ext., 0-20 cm
12. Microburin, from I,ext., 0-20 cm
13. Microburin, from I,ext., 0-20 cm
14. Angle burin on blade, from I,F, 20-30 cm
15. Angle burin on flake, from I,G, 20-30 cm
16. Microlithic angle burin (Noailles) on blade, from I,ext., 0-20 cm

- *17* Microlithic angle burin (Noailles) on flake, from I,F, 0-20 cm
- *18* Simple burin on blade, from I,F, 20-30 cm
- *19* Simple burin on blade, from V, 0-20 cm
- *20* Simple burin on flake, from I,step, 40-90 cm

FIGURE 16. CHIPPED STONE
- *1* End scraper on blade, from I,ext., 0-20 cm
- *2* End scraper on blade, from I,ext., 0-20 cm
- *3* End scraper on blade, from I,A, 0-20 cm
- *4* End scraper on blade, from I,G, 20-30 cm
- *5* End scraper on blade, from I,tr., 0-20 cm
- *6* End scraper on blade, from I,ext., 0-20 cm
- *7* End scraper on blade, from I,F, 0-20 cm
- *8* End scraper on flake, from I,ext., 0-20 cm
- *9* End scraper on flake, from I,ext., 0-20 cm
- *10* End scraper on flake, from I,ext., 0-20 cm
- *11* End scraper on flake, from I,tr., 0-20 cm
- *12* End scraper on flake, from I,ext., 0-20 cm
- *13* Side scraper, from I,tr., 0-20 cm
- *14* Side scraper, from I,ext., 0-20 cm
- *15* Side scraper, from I,step, 40-80 cm
- *16* Side scraper, from I,ext., 0-20 cm

FIGURE 17. CHIPPED STONE
- *1* Steep core scraper, from I,tr., 0-20 cm
- *2* Steep core scraper, from I,ext., 0-20 cm
- *3* Rounded scraper, from I,ext., 0-20 cm
- *4* Rounded scraper, from I,G, 20-30 cm
- *5* Rounded scraper, from I,step, 40-90 cm
- *6* "Raclette," from I,step, 40-90 cm
- *7* Nibbled blade, from I,ext., 0-20 cm
- *8* Nibbled blade, from I,ext., 0-20 cm
- *9* Obliquely truncated blade, from I,ext., 0-20 cm
- *10* Obliquely truncated blade, from I,C, 20-30 cm
- *11* Obliquely truncated blade, from I,F, 0-20 cm
- *12* Obliquely truncated blade, from I,tr., 0-20 cm
- *13* Obliquely truncated blade, from I,ext., 0-20 cm
- *14* Obliquely truncated blade, from I,step, 40-80 cm
- *15* Obliquely truncated blade, from I,ext., 0-20 cm

FIGURE 18. CHIPPED STONE
- *1* Notched blade, from I,ext., 0-20 cm
- *2* Notched blade, from I,step, 40-90 cm
- *3* Notched blade, from I,ext., 0-20 cm
- *4* Notched blade, from I,step,ochre pit, 80-180 cm
- *5* Notched blade, from I,ext., 0-20 cm
- *6* Notched blade, from I,ext., 0-20 cm
- *7* Notched blade, from I,step, 40-80 cm
- *8* Notched blade, from I,F, 0-20 cm
- *9* Notched blade, from I,F, 0-20 cm
- *10* Notched blade, from I,ext., 0-20 cm
- *11* Notched blade, from I,ext., 0-20 cm
- *12* Notched blade, from I,step, 40-90 cm
- *13* Notched bladelet, from I,ext., 0-20 cm
- *14* Notched bladelet, from I,ext., 0-20 cm
- *15* Notched bladelet, from I,step, 40-90 cm

FIGURE 19. CHIPPED STONE
- *1* Notched flake, from I,F, 0-20 cm
- *2* Notched flake, from I,ext., 0-20 cm
- *3* Notched flake, from I,ext., 0-20 cm
- *4* Notched flakelet, from I,tr., 0-20 cm
- *5* Notched flakelet, from I,F, 0-20 cm
- *6* Used blade, from I,A, 0-20 cm
- *7* Used blade, from I,step, 40-90 cm
- *8* Used bladelet, from I,ext., 0-20 cm
- *9* Used bladelet, from I,ext., 0-20 cm
- *10* Used flake, from I,sf
- *11* Heavily used blade, from I,step 40-90 cm
- *12* Heavily used blade, from I,F, 0-20 cm
- *13* Heavily used flake, from I,ext., 0-20 cm

FIGURE 20. CHIPPED STONE
- *1* Partial pyramidal flake core, from I,ext., 0-20 cm
- *2* Partial pyramidal blade core, from I,F, 0-20 cm
- *3* Partial pyramidal flake core, from I,ext., 0-20 cm
- *4* Partial pyramidal blade core, from I,ext., 0-20 cm
- *5* Fully pyramidal flake core, from I,B, 0-20 cm
- *6* Fully pyramidal flake core, from I,ext., 0-20 cm

FIGURE 21. CHIPPED STONE
- *1* Fully pyramidal blade core, from I,ext., 0-20 cm
- *2* Fully pyramidal blade core, from I,step, 40-90 cm
- *3* Fully pyramidal blade core, from I,ext., 0-20 cm
- *4* Fully pyramidal blade core, from I,step, 40-90 cm
- *5* Bipolar core, from I,ext., 0-20 cm
- *6* Bipolar core, from I,ext., 0-20 cm
- *7* Crossed bipolar core, from I,F, 0-20 cm
- *8* Polyhedral/amorphous core, from I,ext., 0-20 cm
- *9* Discoid core, from I,B, 0-20 cm

Fig. 3. Air view of Karim Shahir, looking west. Site covers much of grassy hilltop immediately above erosion scarp. Excavations visible along top edge of scarp and on hilltop. (Flight courtesy of the Iraq Petroleum Company, Ltd.)

Fig. 4. Scarp and stream bed at Karim Shahir, looking north-northwest. Step cut along eroding scarp edge on skyline marked by figures of workmen. At lower right, stream bed of the Cham-Gawra, some 40 m below scarp edge.

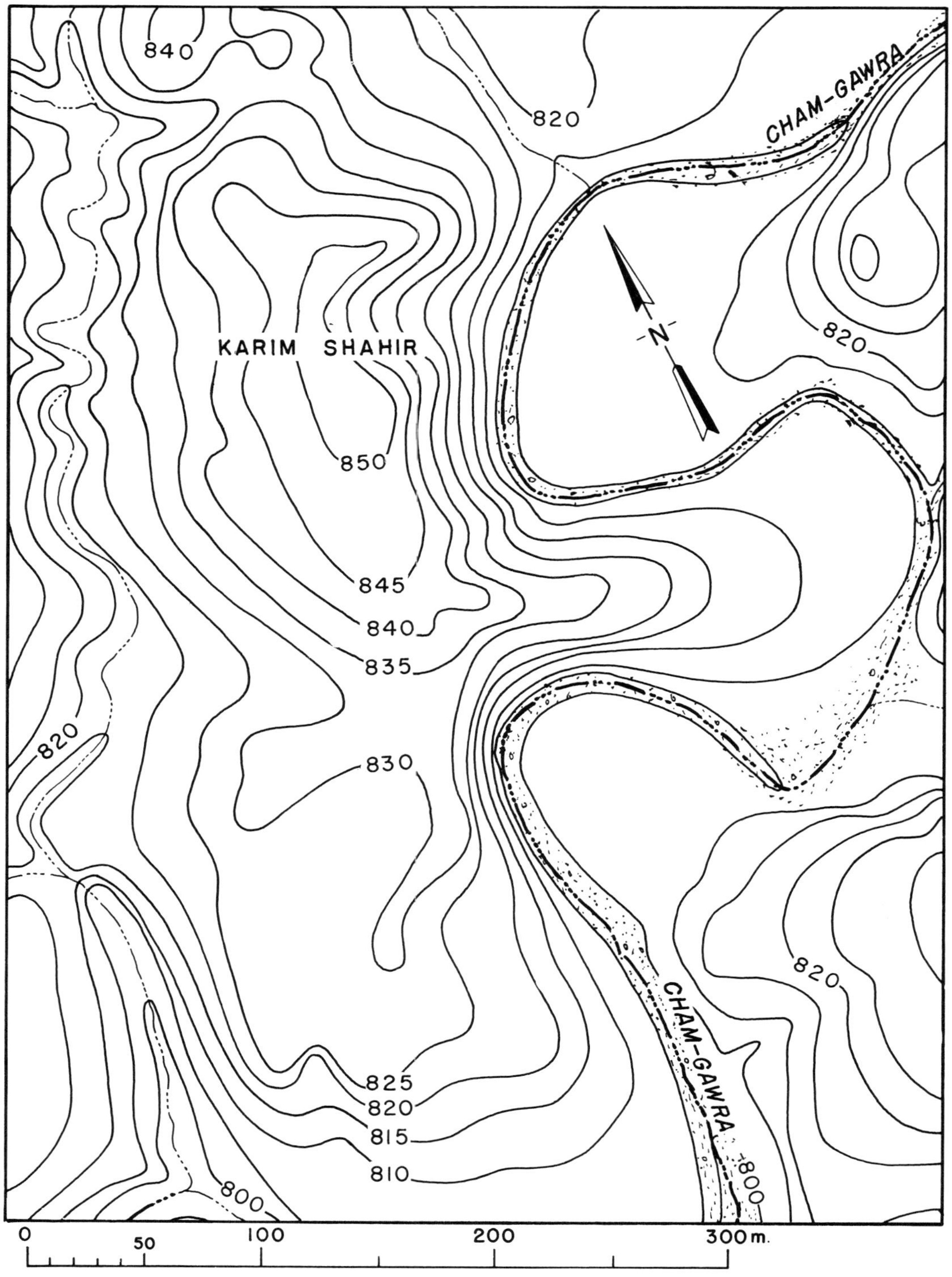

Fig. 5. Contour map showing character of locality of Karim Shahir. Extensive hilltop site is some 850 m above sea level on and inward from scarp steeply cut on east by Cham-Gawra.

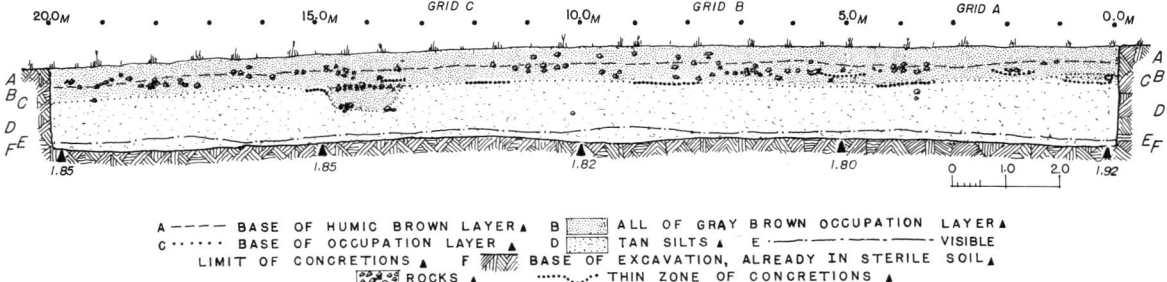

Fig. 6. North-south section at Karim Shahir, looking west, showing stratigraphic relationship of rocky floor, pits, and gray brown deposits of occupation horizon capping sterile tan silts.

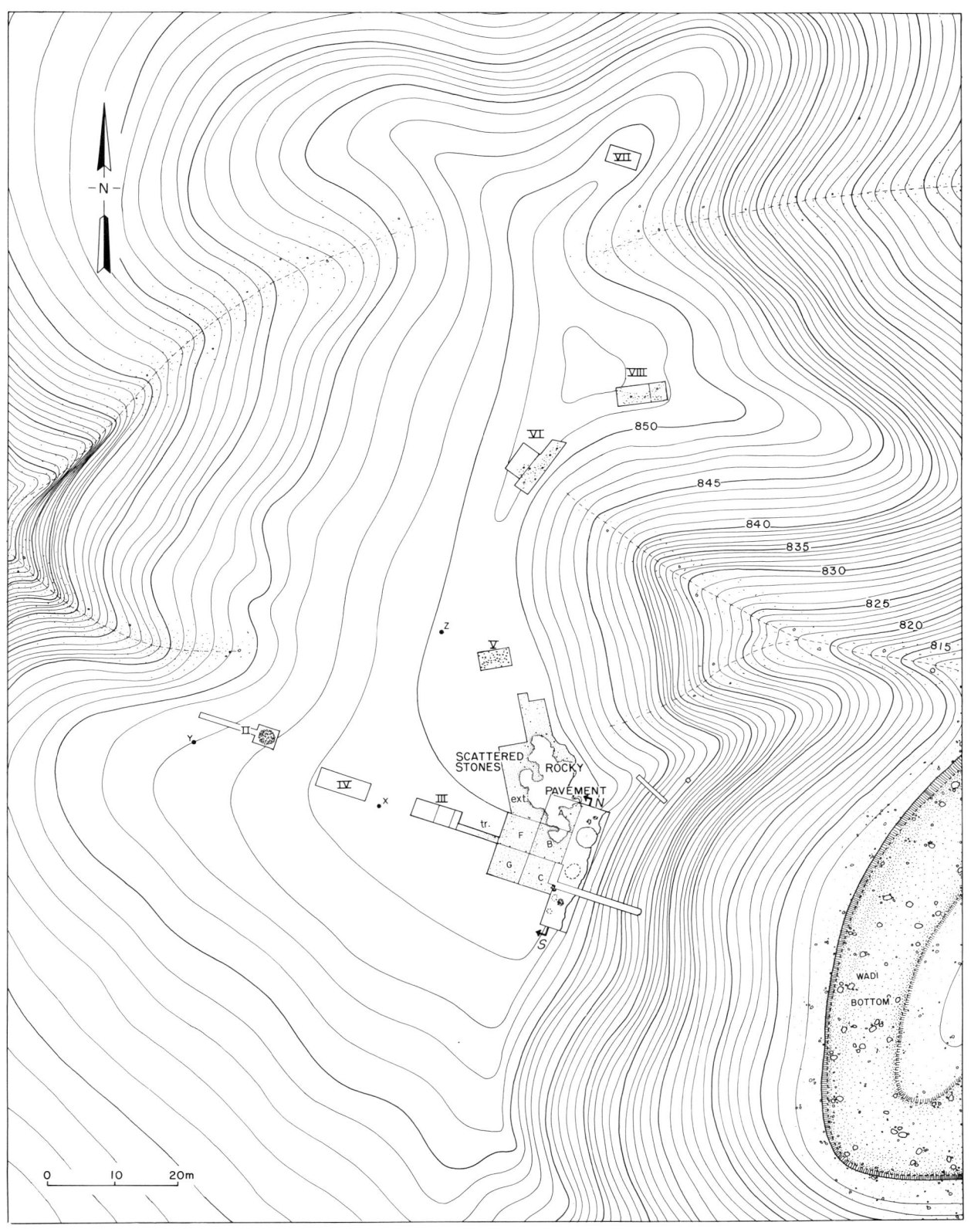

Fig. 7. Plot plan of Karim Shahir, showing location of excavation operations and principal features exposed: major operation I, including the 20-m north-south step and pits, the adjacent 5-m² grids A, B, C, F, G and the extension (ext.) with rocky "pavement" and stone scatter, and the trench (tr.); minor operations II-VIII; and three unlabeled geological exposures (2 trenches and 1 pit) cut in eroded face of scarp into underlying sterile silts.

Fig. 8. View east over operation I at Karim Shahir, showing central portion of exposed shallow occupation floor of scattered stones and close-set rocky "pavement." Grid A and the extension constitute most of view, with small parts of grids B and F appearing along right edge of picture. Upper half of photograph shows eastern edge of excavations, delimited to left by curving natural edge of scarp and to right by straight line of northern end of step.

Fig. 9. View east over operation I at Karim Shahir, showing southernmost part of exposed occupation floor with scattered stones. Grids F and G are in foreground, grids B and C in background, with straight edge of north-south step at top of picture. The turf later removed in the excavation of the extension appears along left side of view.

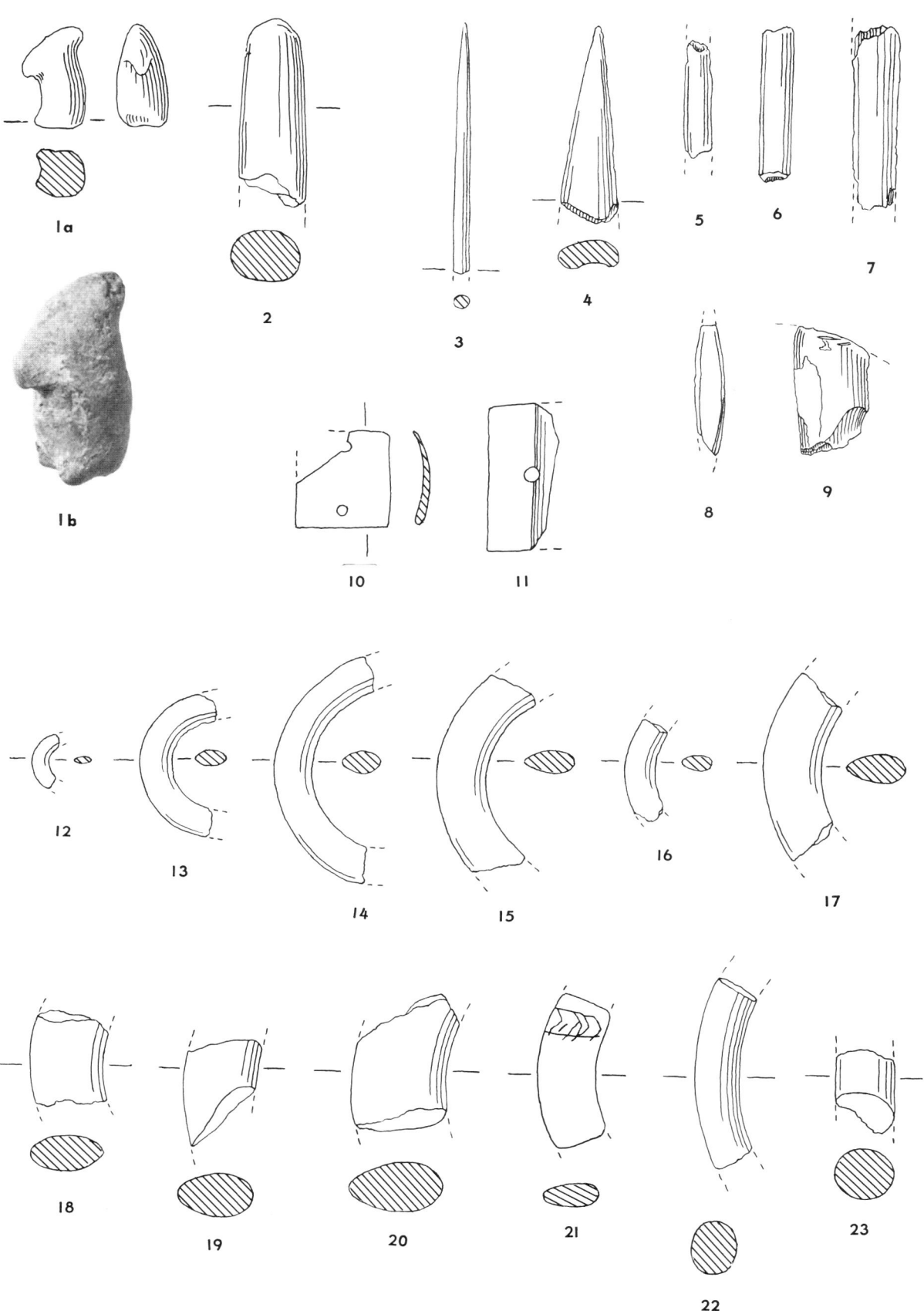

Fig. 10. Karim Shahir clay, bone, shell, and ground stone objects: lightly baked clay figurine, *1a,b*; lightly baked clay rod, *2*; bone pin or possible needle fragment, *3*; bone awl fragment, *4*; bone beads or bead rough-outs, *5-7*; worked bone fragments, *8-9*; fragmentary pierced shell plaques, *10-11*; marble bracelet or ring fragments, *12-22*; stone rod fragment, *23*. Scales 1:1, *1a,2-23*; 2:1, *1b*.

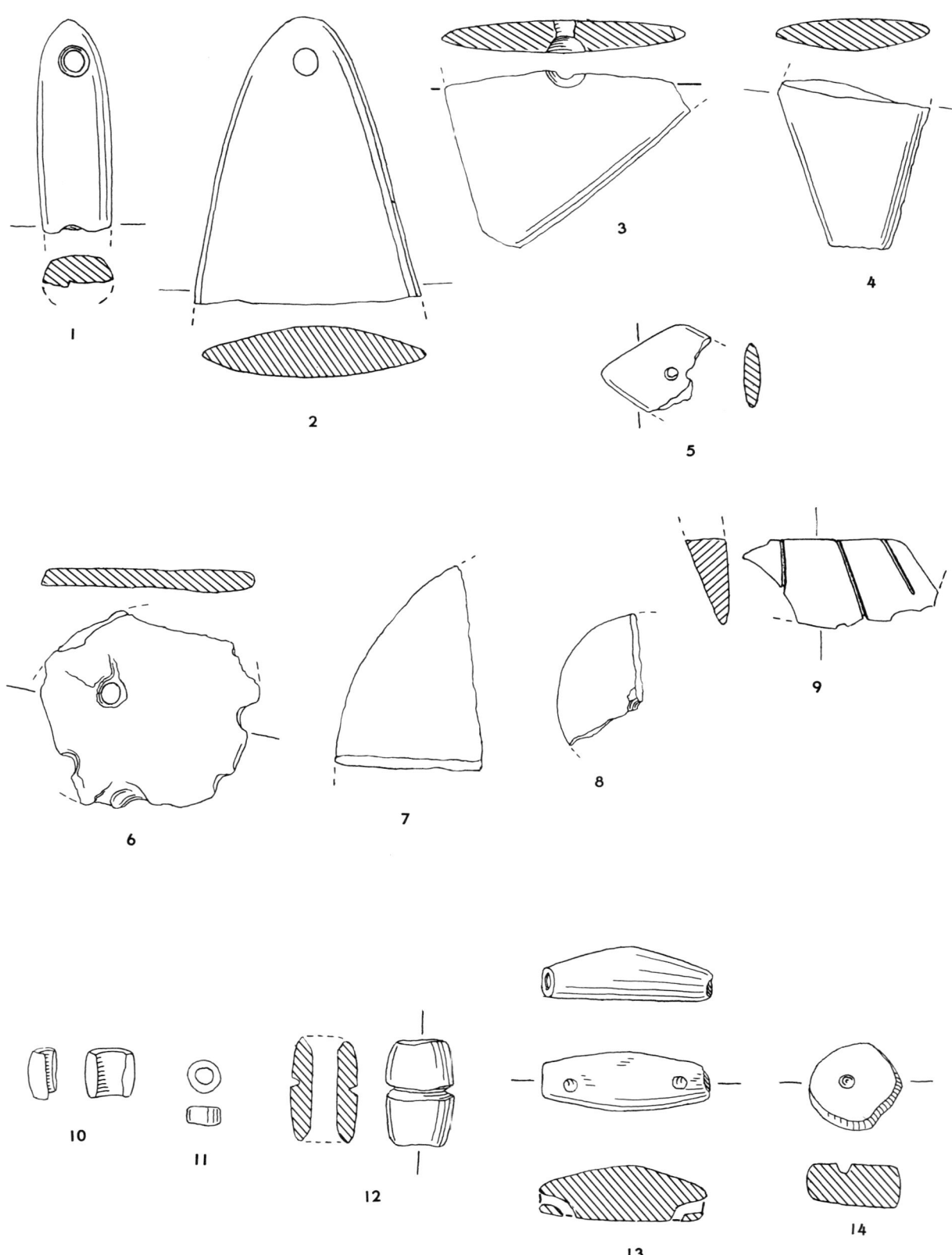

Fig. 11. Karim Shahir ground stone: fragmentary pendants, *1-2*; fragmentary plaques, *3-9*; beads, *10-13*; bead rough-out, *14*. Scale 1:1.

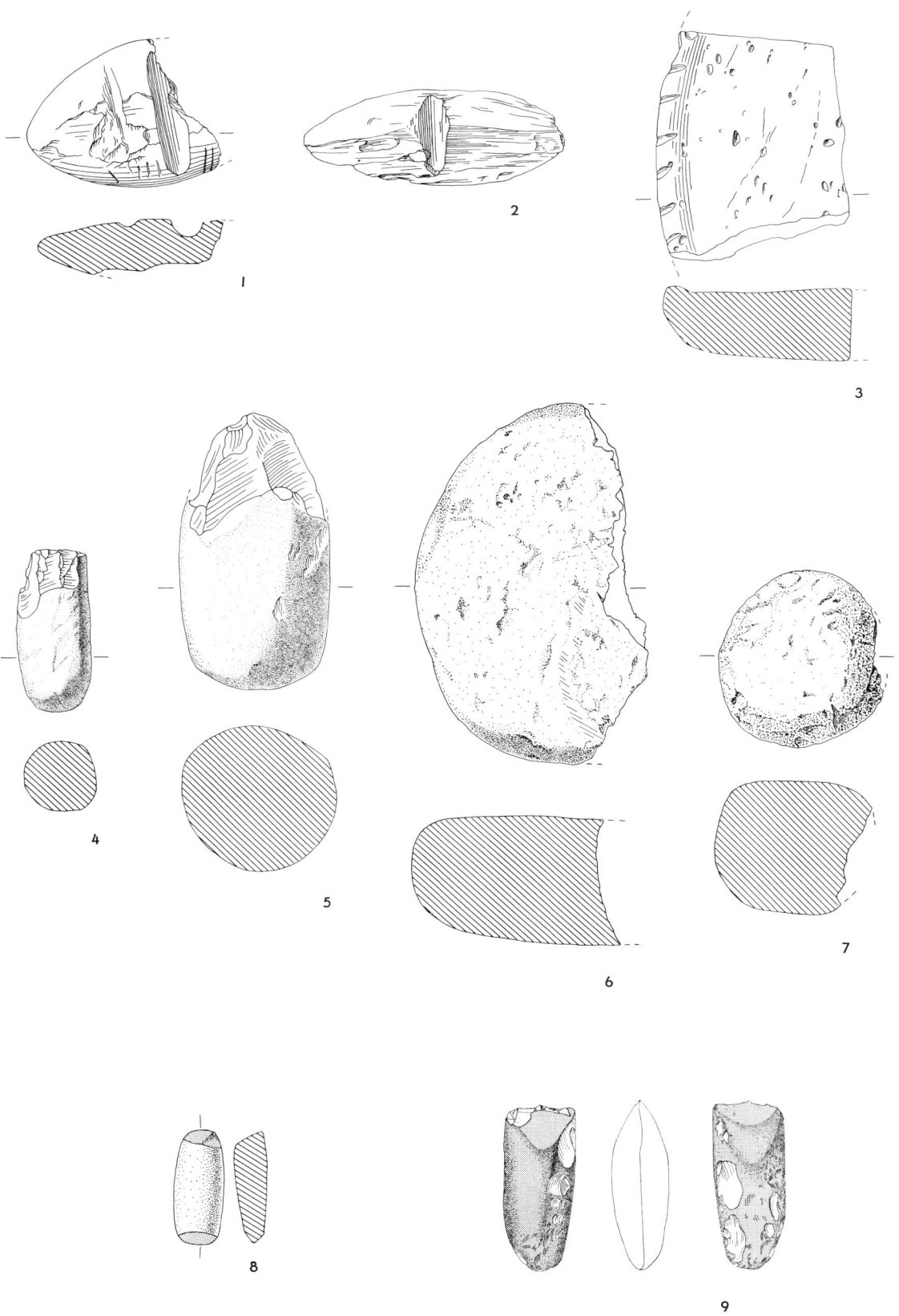

Fig. 12. Karim Shahir ground stone: fragmentary grooved rubbing stones, *1-2*; decorated palette fragment, *3*; fragmentary pestles, *4-5*; fragmentary hand rubbing stones or mullers, *6-7*; ground and polished chisels, *8-9*. Scale 1:2.

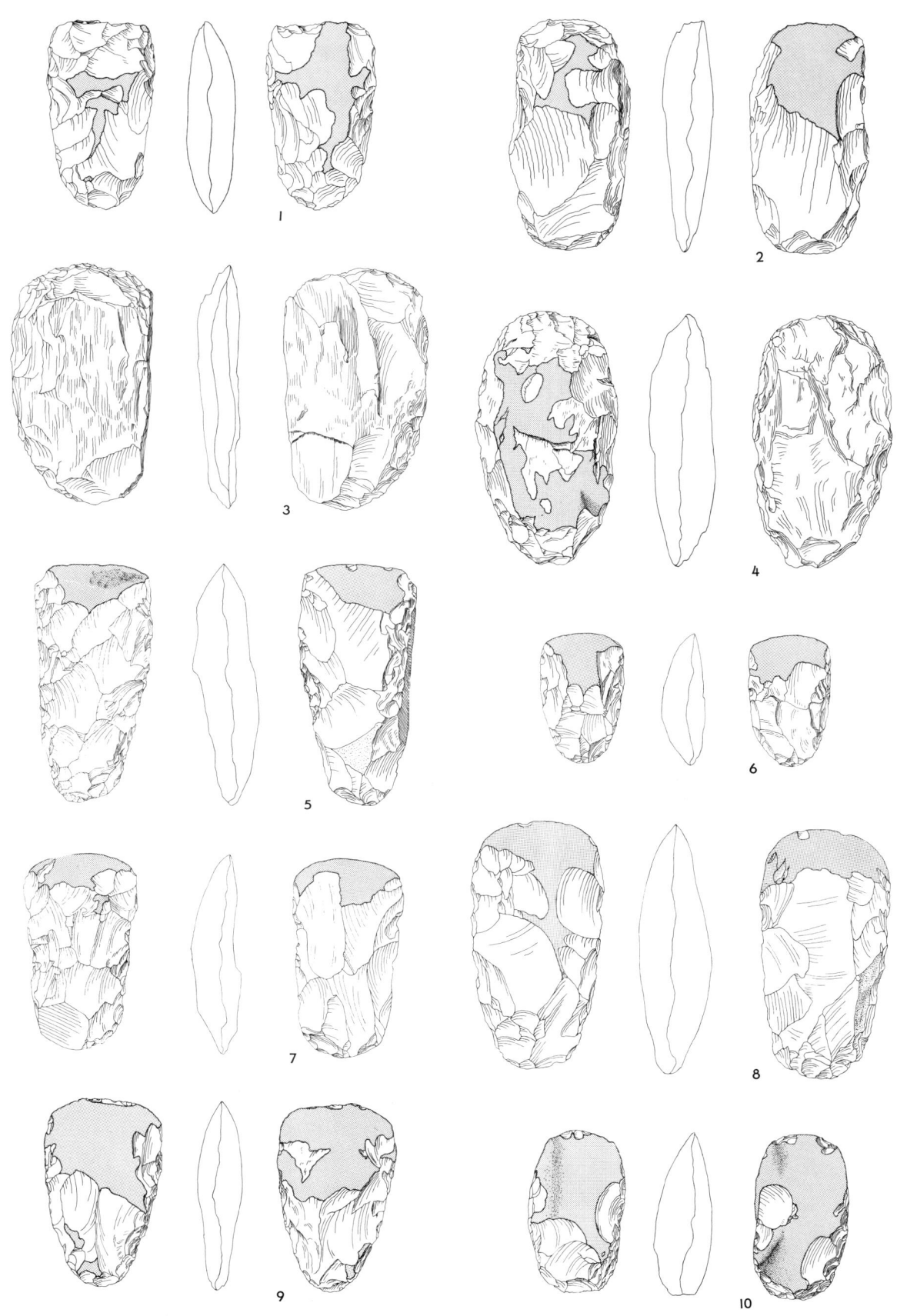

Fig. 13. Karim Shahir chipped and polished celts: adze/hoes, *1-4,6-7*; adze/hoe or axe, *5*; axes, *8-10*. Scale 1:2.

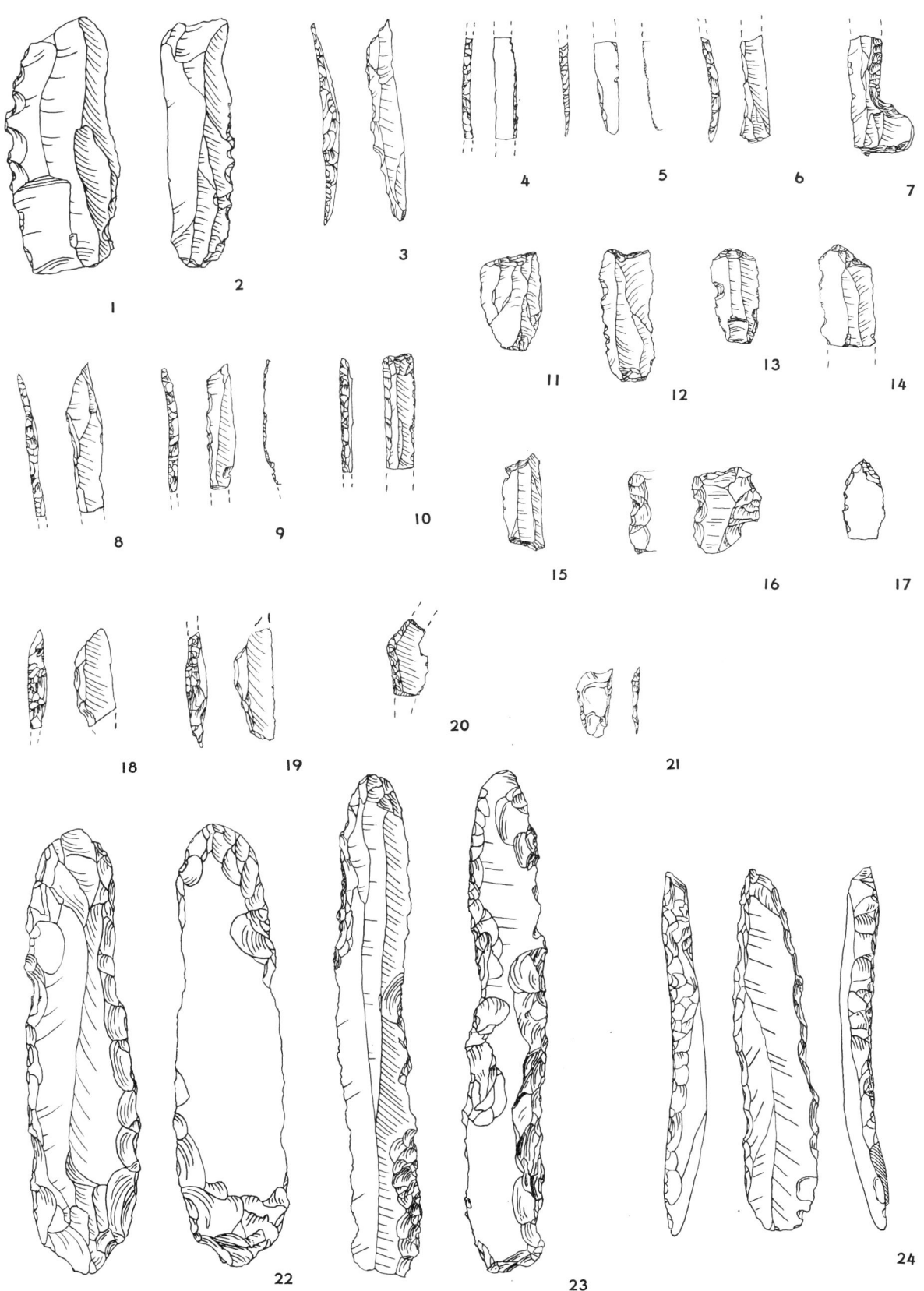

Fig. 14. Karim Shahir chipped stone: denticulated blades, *1-2*; microlithic backed bladelets, *3-10*; microlithic end scrapers, *11-16*; microlithic pointed bladelet, *17*; chance geometric microliths, *18-21*; fabricators, *22-24*. Scale 1:1.

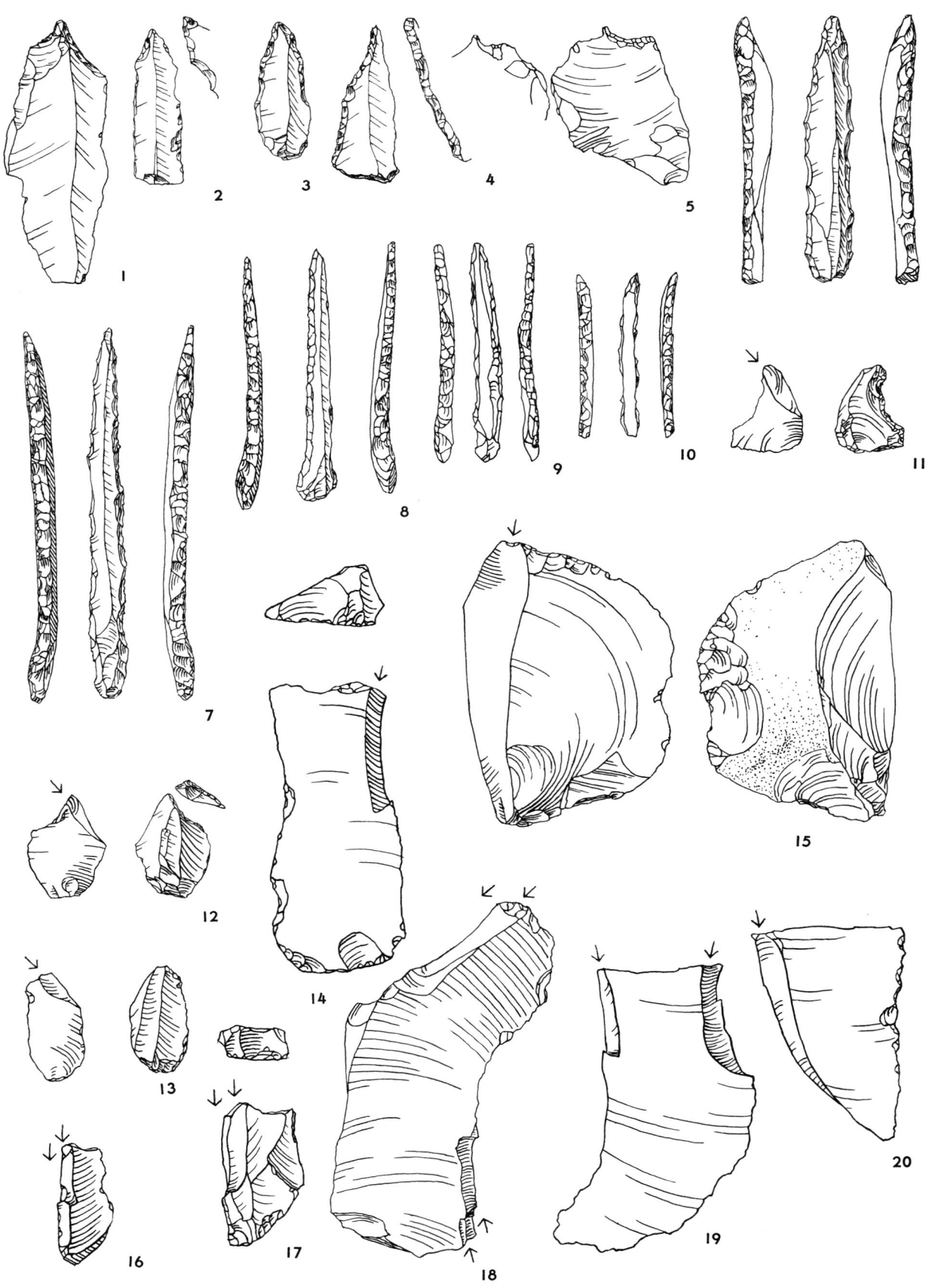

Fig. 15. Karim Shahir chipped stone: drills, normal-sized, *1-5*; drills, microlithic, *6-7*; drills, super-microlithic, *8-10*; microburins, *11-13*; burins, various, *14-20*. Scale 1:1.

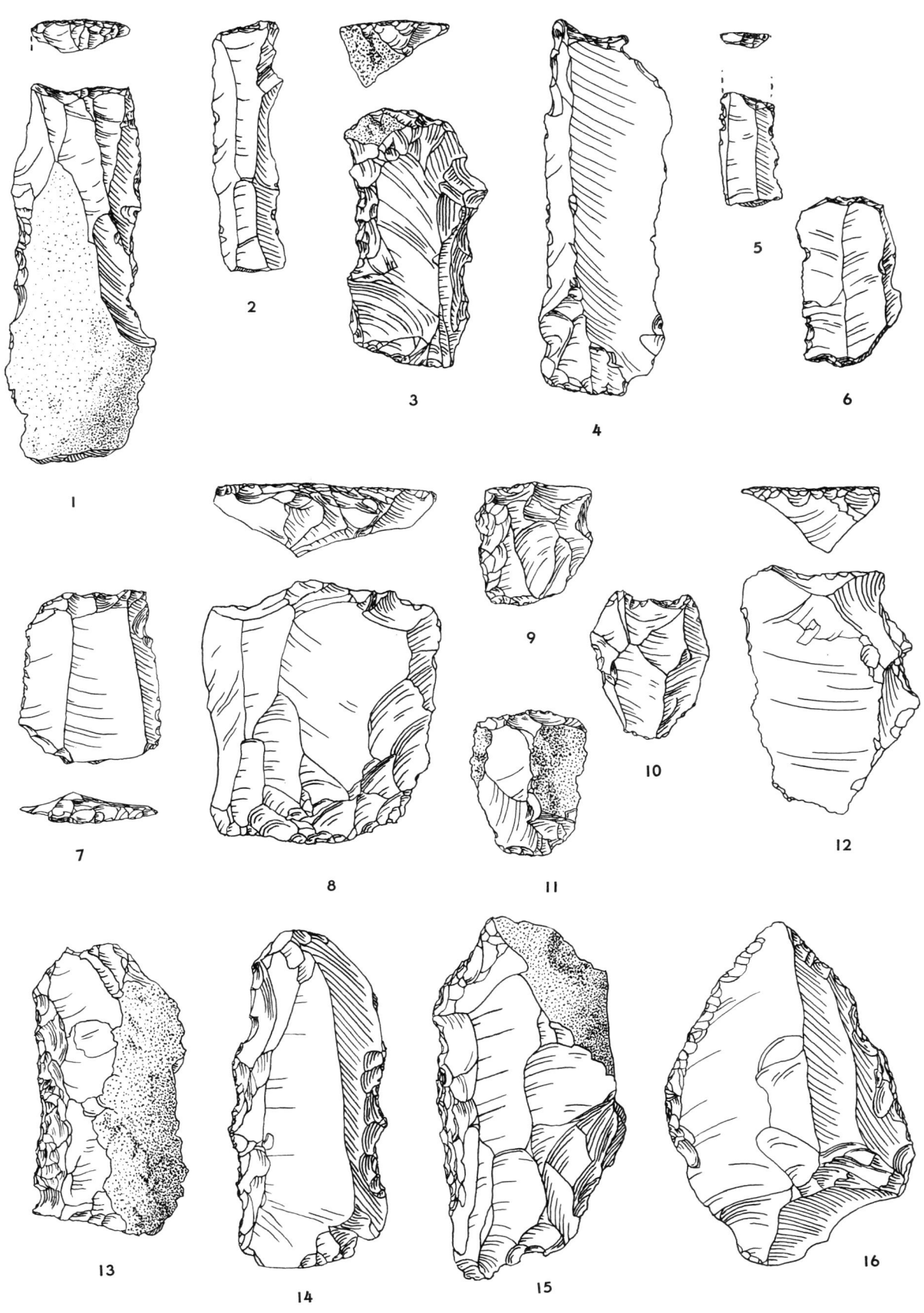

Fig. 16. Karim Shahir chipped stone: end scrapers on blades, *1-7*; end scrapers on flakes, *8-12*; side scrapers, *13-16*. Scale 1:1.

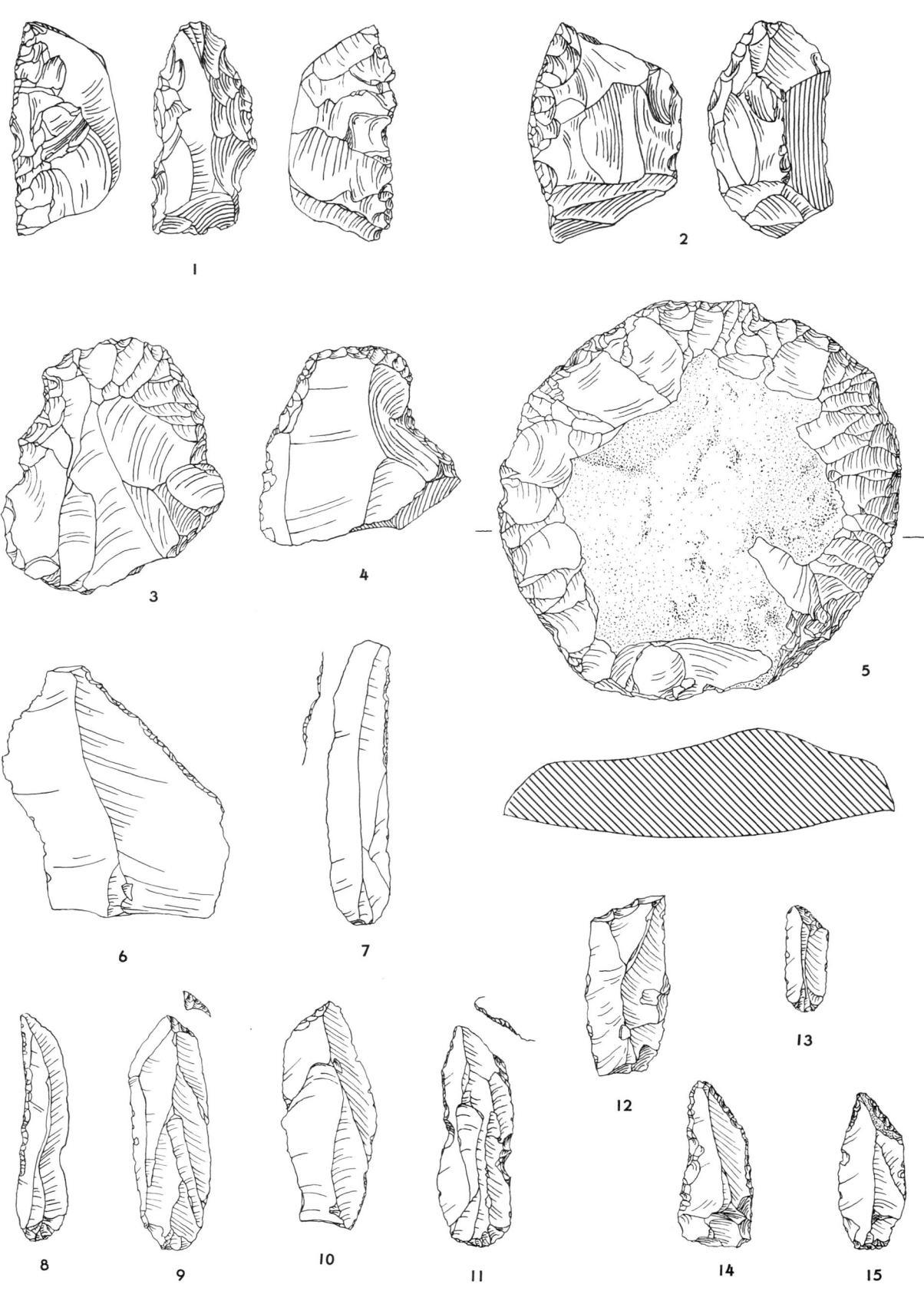

Fig. 17. Karim Shahir chipped stone: steep scrapers on core fragments, *1-2*; rounded scrapers, *3-5*; "raclette," *6*; nibbled blades, *7-8*; blades with obliquely truncated ends, *9-15*. Scale 1:1.

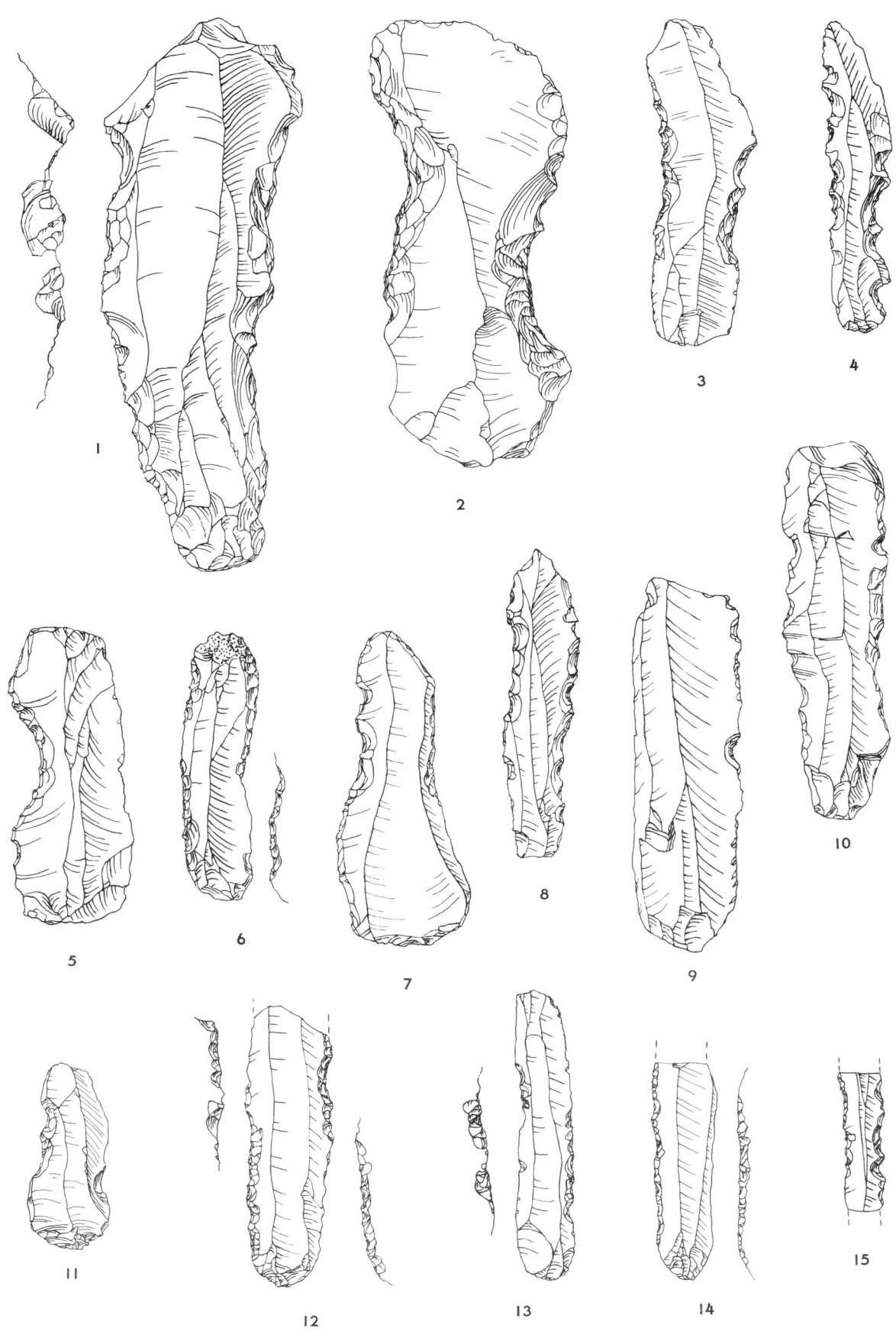

Fig. 18. Karim Shahir chipped stone: notched blades and bladelets, various, *1-15*. Scale 1:1.

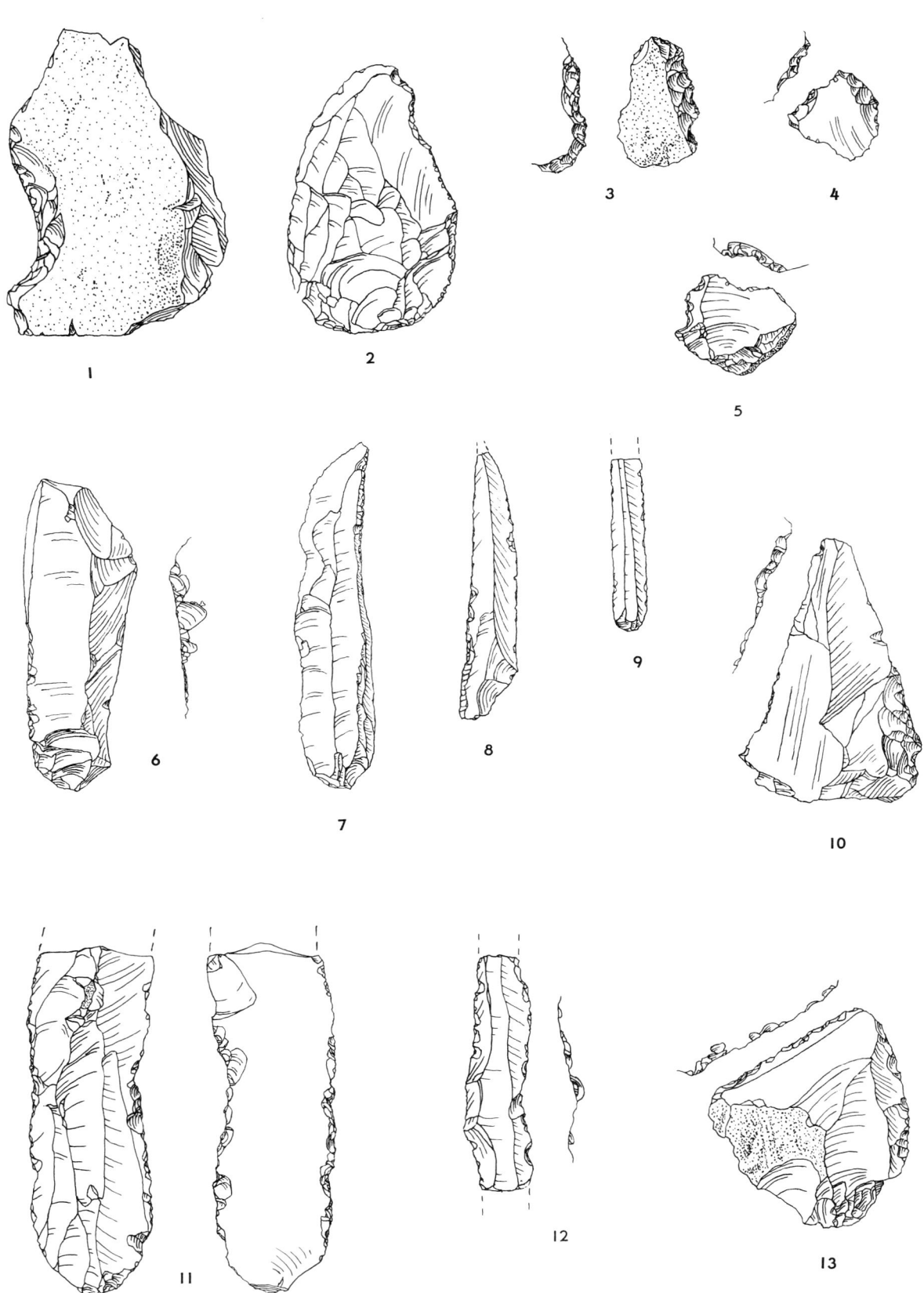

Fig. 19. Karim Shahir chipped stone: notched flakes, *1-5*; used blades, *6-9*; used flake, *10*; heavily used blades, *11-12*; heavily used flake, *13*. Scale 1:1.

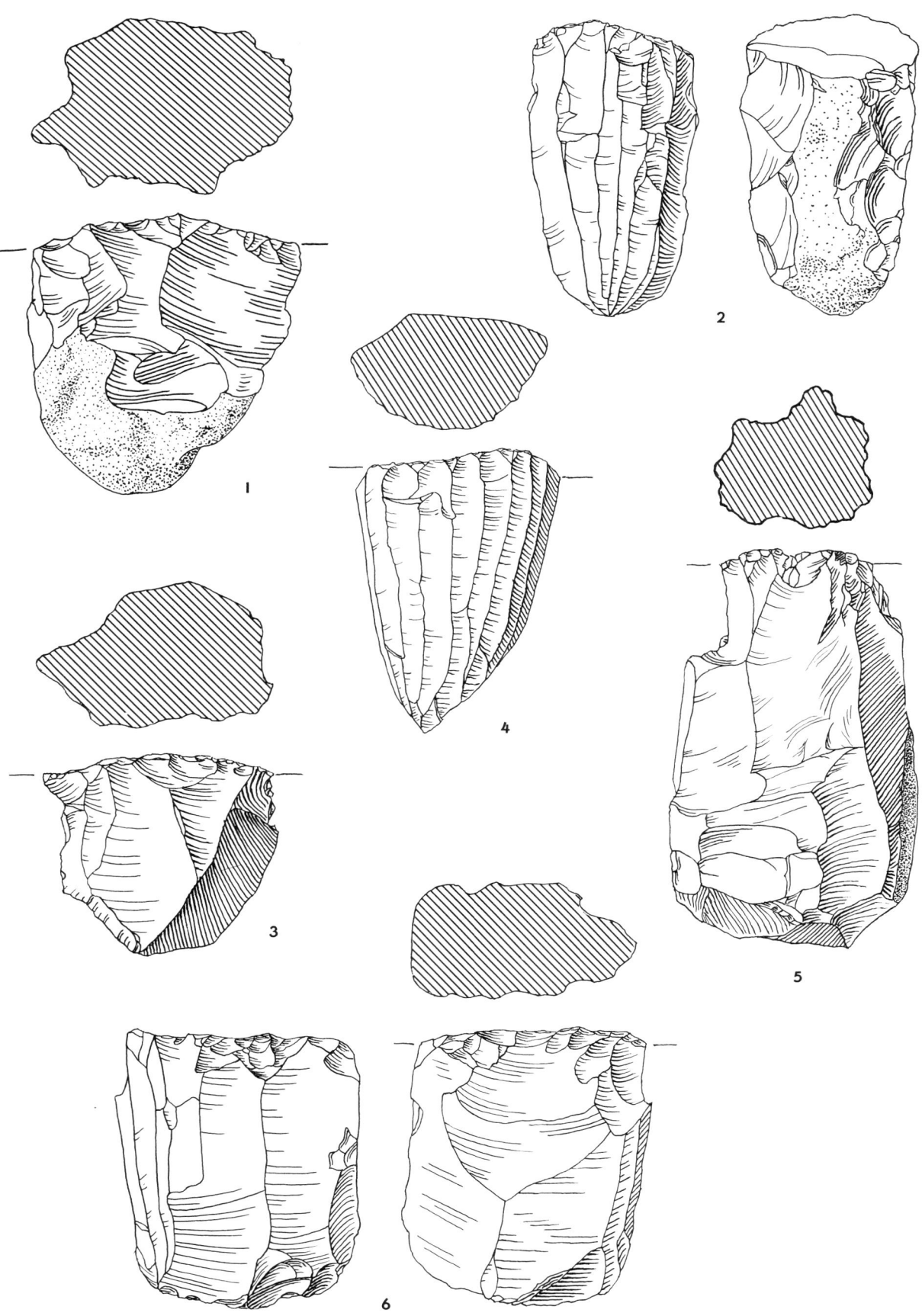

Fig. 20. Karim Shahir chipped stone: partial pyramidal flake cores, *1,3*; partial pyramidal blade cores, *2,4*; fully pyramidal flake cores, *5-6*. Scale 1:1.

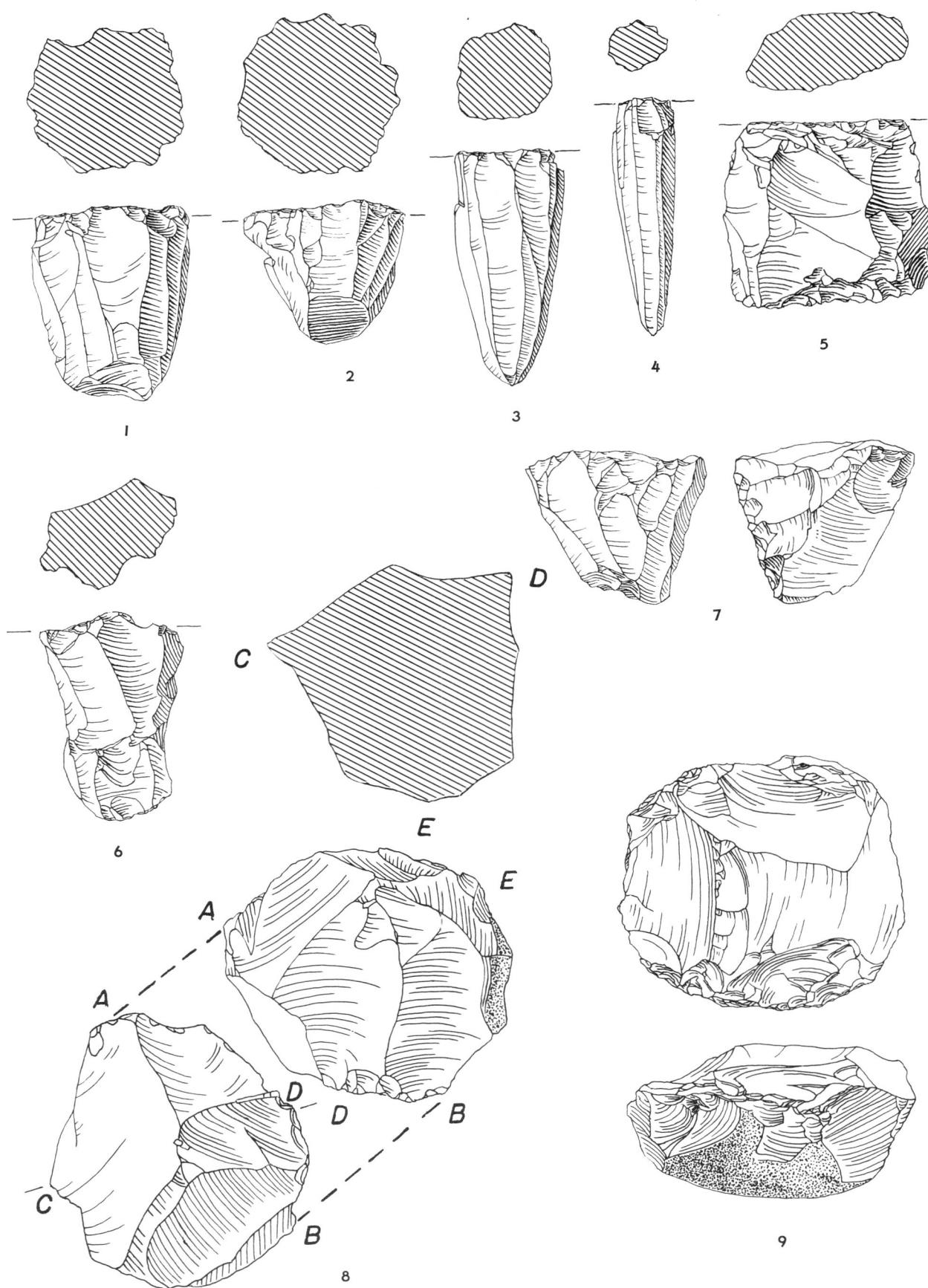

Fig. 21. Karim Shahir chipped stone: fully pyramidal blade cores, *1-4*; bipolar cores, *5-7*; polyhedral/amorphous core, *8*; discoid core, *9*. Scale 1:1

LIST OF REGISTERED OBJECTS*

Register number	Designation	Material	Operation and area	Depth (cm)	Disposition
K-1	Perforated angular plaque, frag.	Shell	I, step	Surface	Baghdad
K-2	Incised plaque, frag.	Limestone	I, step	0-40	Baghdad
K-3	Bracelet, frag.	Marble	I, step	40-80	Baghdad
K-4	Perforated angular plaque, frag.	Shell	I, step	20-40	Chicago
K-5	Lightly baked figurine, inc.	Clay	I, step	80-120	Baghdad
K-6	Pin or needle point, frag.	Bone	I, step	120-160	Chicago
K-7	Tubular bead	Bone	I, step	120-180	Baghdad
K-8	Tubular bead	Bone	I, step, ochre pit	180	Chicago
K-9	Chipped and polished celt, axe type	Limestone	I, C	0-20	Baghdad
K-10	Small polished celt, chisel? type	Limestone	I, C	0-20	Baghdad
K-11	Biconical planoconvex bead	Limestone	I, C	20-40	Chicago
K-12	Ring, frag.	Marble	I, B	20-30	Baghdad
K-13	Perforated angular plaque, inc.	Shell	I, C	20-30	Chicago
K-14	Perforated angular plaque	Shell	I, B	20-40	Baghdad
K-15	Bracelet, frag.	Marble	I, B	0-20	Chicago
K-16	Tubular bead	Bone	I, step	0-40	Baghdad
K-17	Chipped and polished celt, adze/hoe type	Sandstone	I, step	0-20	Chicago
K-18	Bracelet, frag.	Marble	I, step	0-20	Baghdad
K-19	Chipped and polished celt, adze/hoe type	Flint	I, step	0-40	Baghdad
K-20	Discoid bead rough-out	Marble	I, B	0-20	Chicago
K-21	Ring, frag.	Marble	I, G	20-30	Baghdad
K-22	Decorated bracelet, frag.	Marble	I, F	20-30	Baghdad
K-23	Awl point, frag.	Bone	I, F	20-30	Baghdad
K-24	Grooved rubbing stone, inc.	Dark stone	I, A	20-30	Baghdad
K-25	Grooved rubbing stone	Dark stone	I, G	20-30	Baghdad
K-26	Perforated angular plaque, inc.	Shell	I, A	20-30	Chicago
K-27	Perforated angular plaque, frag.	Limestone	I, A	20-30	Chicago
K-28	Perforated angular plaque, frag.	Marble	III	0-20	Chicago
K-29	Bracelet, frag.	Marble	III	40-60	Chicago
K-30	Lightly baked figurine	Clay	I, step, ochre pit	180	Chicago
K-31	Grooved rubbing stone, inc.	Dark stone	I, C	30-40	Chicago
K-32	Pestle, frag.	Limestone	I, ext.	0-20	Baghdad
K-33	Cylindrical bead	Marble	I, ext.	0-20	Baghdad
K-34	Dibble or macehead, frag.	Limestone	I, G	20-30	Chicago
K-35	Perforated oval plaque, frag.	Marble	I, G	30-40	Baghdad
K-36	Grooved barrel bead	Dark stone	I, G	30-40	Chicago
K-37	Decorated palette, frag.	Limestone	I, G	40-50	Chicago
K-38	Barrel bead, frag.	Stone	I, C	30-40	Baghdad
K-39	Bracelet, frag.	Marble	I, ext.	0-20	Baghdad
K-40	Elongated pebble pendant, frag.	Dark stone	I, G	30-40	Chicago
K-41	Elongated pebble pendant, inc.	Dark stone	I, G	30-40	Baghdad
K-42	Ring, frag.	Marble	I, G	20-30	Chicago
K-43	Biconical planoconvex bead	Limestone	I, G	50-60	Baghdad
K-44	Small polished celt, chisel? type	Limestone	I, C	20-30	Chicago
K-45	Tubular bead, inc.	Marble	V	0-20	Baghdad
K-46	Perforated circular plaque, frag.	Marble	I, G	60-80	Chicago
K-47	Perforated gastropod bead	Shell	I, G	110-120	Chicago
K-48	Tubular dentalium bead	Shell	I, G	120-140	Chicago
K-49	Barrel bead, frag.	Marble	VI	0-20	Chicago
K-50	Tubular dentalium bead	Shell	VI	0-20	Chicago
K-51	Ring, frag.	Marble	I, ext.	0-20	Baghdad
K-52	Cylindrical bead	Dark stone	I, ext.	0-20	Chicago

NOTE: frag. = fragment; inc. = incomplete.

*These 52 items entered in the register of special objects from Karim Shahir were recorded during the excavation and labeled K-1 through K-52 in order of discovery. They were divided at the end of the season between the Directorate of Antiquities in Baghdad and the Oriental Institute in Chicago. They have all been taken into account in the text of this chapter, and specimens from both the Baghdad and Chicago lots have been used for illustrations.

REFERENCES

Berger, Rainer; Fergusson, G.J.; and Libby, W.F.
    1965 UCLA radiocarbon dates IV. *Radiocarbon* 7:336-71.

Bökönyi, Sándor
    1973 Some problems of animal domestication in the Middle East. In *Domestikationsforschung und Geschichte der Haustiere*. ed. János Matolcsi, pp. 69-75. Budapest: Akadémiai Kiadó.
    1976 Development of early stock rearing in the Near East. *Nature* 264:19-23.
    1977 *The animal remains from four sites in the Kermanshah valley, Iran—Asiab, Sarab, Dehsavar and Siahbid: the faunal evolution, environmental changes and development of animal husbandry, VIII-III millennia B.C.* British Archaeological Reports, Supplementary Series, vol. 34. Oxford.

Bökönyi, Sándor; Braidwood, Robert J.; and Reed, Charles A.
    1973 Earliest animal domestication dated? *Science* 182:1161.

Braidwood, Robert J.; Howe, Bruce; and Reed, Charles A.
    1961 The Iranian Prehistoric Project. *Science* 133:2008-10.

Braidwood, Robert J.; Howe, Bruce; et al.
    1960 *Prehistoric investigations in Iraqi Kurdistan*. Studies in Ancient Oriental Civilization [SAOC], no. 31. Chicago: University of Chicago Press.

Buckley, James D.; Trautman, Milton A.; and Willis, Eric H.
    1968 Isotopes' radiocarbon measurements VI. *Radiocarbon* 10:246-94.

Cauvin, Jacques
    1972 Nouvelles fouilles à Tell Mureybet (Syrie): 1971-1972 rapport préliminaire. *Annales archéologiques arabes syriennes* 22:105-15.
    1973a Découverte sur l'Euphrate d'un village natoufien du IXe millénaire av. J.-C. à Mureybet (Syrie). *Comptes rendus hebdomadaires des séances de l'Académie des sciences*, ser. D 276:1985-87.
    1973b Les origines de la vie sedentaire: le village de Mureybet. *Recherche* 4 (39):1008-9.
    1974 Troisième campagne de fouilles à Tell Mureybet (Syrie) en 1973: rapport préliminaire. *Annales archéologiques arabes syriennes* 24:47-58.
    1979a Le Moyen Euphrate au VIIIe millénaire: Mureybet et Cheikh Hassan. In *Actes du Colloque "Le Moyen Euphrate, zone de contacts et d'échanges,"* ed. J.Cl. Margueron. Strasbourg.
    1979b Les fouilles de Mureybet (1971-1974) et leur signification pour les origines de la sédentarisation au Proche-Orient. In *Archeological reports from the Tabqa Dam Project—Euphrates Valley, Syria*, ed. David Noel Freedman, pp. 19-48. Annual of the American Schools of Oriental Research, vol. 44. Cambridge, Mass.

Cauvin, Marie-Claire
    1979 Du Natoufien sur l'Euphrate. In *Actes du Colloque "Le Moyen Euphrate, zone de contacts et d'échanges,"* ed. J.Cl. Margueron. Strasbourg.

Curwen, E. Cecil
    1930 Prehistoric flint sickles. *Antiquity* 4:179-86.

Deevey, Edward S.; Flint, Richard Foster; and Rouse, Irving
    1967 *Radiocarbon measurements: comprehensive index, 1950-1965*. New Haven, Conn.: American Journal of Science.

Ducos, Pierre
    1970 The Oriental Institute excavations at Mureybiṭ, Syria: preliminary report on the 1965 campaign, part IV: les restes d'Equidés. *Journal of Near Eastern Studies* 29:273-89.
    1972 The Oriental Institute excavations at Mureybiṭ, Syria: preliminary report on the 1965 campaign, part V: les restes des Bovidés. *Journal of Near Eastern Studies* 31:295-301.

Gilot, E., and Cauvin, J.
    1973 Datation par le carbone 14 du village natoufien et précéramique de Mureybet, sur l'Euphrate (Syrie). *Bulletin de la Société préhistorique française* 70:37-38.

Hole, Frank; Flannery, Kent V.; and Neely, James A.
    1969 *Prehistory and human ecology of the Deh Luran plain*. Memoirs of the Museum of Anthropology, University of Michigan, no. 1. Ann Arbor.

Kigoshi, Kunihiko
    1967 Gakushuin natural radiocarbon measurements VI. *Radiocarbon* 9:43-62.

Loon, Maurits van
    1968 The Oriental Institute excavations at Mureybiṭ, Syria: preliminary report on the 1965 campaign, pt. I: architecture and general finds. *Journal of Near Eastern Studies* 27:265-82.

Moore, A.M.T. (with contributions by Hillman, G.C., and Legge, A.J.)
1975 The excavation of Tell Abu Hureyra in Syria: a preliminary report. *Proceedings of the Prehistoric Society* 41:50-77.

Mortensen, Peder
1964 Additional remarks on the chronology of early village-farming communities in the Zagros area. *Sumer* 20:28-36.

Odell, George; Tringham, Ruth; Roberts, Michael; Voytek, Barbara; and Whitman, Anne
1976 Microwear analysis. *Journal of Field Archaeology* 3:239-40.

Perkins, Dexter, Jr.
1960 The faunal remains of Shanidar Cave and Zawi Chemi Shanidar: 1960 season. *Sumer* 16:77-78.
1964 Prehistoric fauna from Shanidar, Iraq. *Science* 144:1565-66.

Protsch, Reiner, and Berger, Rainer
1973 Earliest radiocarbon dates for domesticated animals. Ibid. 179:235-39.

Rubin, Meyer, and Alexander, Corrinne
1960 U.S. Geological Survey radiocarbon dates V. *American Journal of Science Radiocarbon Supplement* 2:129-85.

Rust, Alfred
1950 *Die Höhlenfunde von Jabrud (Syrien)*. Vor- und frühgeschichtliche Untersuchungen aus dem Schleswig-holst, Museum vorgeschichtlicher Altertümer in Schleswig, n.s., vol. 8. Neumünster: Karl Wachholtz.

SAOC 31
1960 *Prehistoric investigations in Iraqi Kurdistan*. Robert J. Braidwood, Bruce Howe, et al. Studies in Ancient Oriental Civilization, no. 31. Chicago: University of Chicago Press.

Semenov, S.A.
1964 *Prehistoric technology*. Trans. M.W. Thompson. London: Cory, Adams, and MacKay.

Skinner, James H.
1968 The Oriental Institute excavation at Mureybit, Syria: preliminary report on the 1965 campaign, pt. II: chipped stone finds. *Journal of Near Eastern Studies* 27:282-90.

Smith, Philip E.L.
1968 Ganj Dareh Tepe. *Iran* 6:158-60.
1972a Ganj Dareh Tepe. Ibid. 10:165-68.
1972b Prehistoric excavations at Ganj Dareh Tepe in 1967. In *Memorial volume of the Vth International Congress of Iranian Art and Archaeology: Tehran, Isfahan, Shiraz, 11th-18th April 1968*, vol. 1, ed. A. Tajvidi and M.Y. Kiani, pp. 183-93. [Tehran]: Ministry of Culture and Arts.
1974 Ganj Dareh Tepe. *Paléorient* 2:207-8.
1975 Ganj Dareh Tepe. *Iran* 13:178-80.
1976 Reflections on four seasons of excavations at Tappeh Ganj Dareh. In *Proceedings of the IVth Annual Symposium on Archaeological Research in Iran, 3rd-8th November 1975*, ed. Firouz Bagherzadeh, pp. 11-22. Tehran: Iranian Centre for Archaeological Research.
1978 An interim report on Ganj Dareh Tepe, Iran. *American Journal of Archaeology* 82:538-40.

Solecki, Ralph S.
1963 Prehistory in Shanidar valley, northern Iraq. *Science* 139:179-93.
1964 Shanidar Cave, a late Pleistocene site in northern Iraq. In *Report of the VIth International Congress on Quaternary, Warsaw 1961*, vol. 4, International Association on Quaternary Research, pp. 413-23. Łódź: Państwowe Wydawnictwo Naukowe.
1968 Cave archaeology in the Zagros Mountains. *Acta Archaeologica Carpathica* 10:245-59.
1969 A copper mineral pendant from northern Iraq. *Antiquity* 43:311-14.

Solecki, Ralph S., and Solecki, Rose L.
1963 Two bone hafts from northern Iraq. *Antiquity* 37:58-60.

Solecki, Rose L.
1964 Zawi Chemi Shanidar, a post-Pleistocene village site in northern Iraq. In *Report of the VIth International Congress on Quaternary, Warsaw 1961*, vol. 4, International Association on Quaternary Research, pp. 405-12. Łódź: Państwowe Wydawnictwo Naukowe.
1971 Milling tools and the Epi-paleolithic in the Near East. In *VIIIe Congrès INQUA, Paris 1969: études sur le Quaternaire dans le monde*, vol. 2, Union internationale pour l'étude du Quaternaire, pp. 989-94. [Paris.]

Solecki, Rose L., and Solecki, Ralph S.
1970 Grooved stones from Zawi Chemi Shanidar, a protoneolithic site in northern Iraq. *American Anthropologist*, n.s. 72:831-41.
1974 Shanidar Cave. *Science* 184:937.

Stuckenrath, Robert, Jr., and Lawn, Barbara
    1969 University of Pennsylvania radiocarbon dates XI. *Radiocarbon* 11:150-62.

Stuckenrath, Robert, and Mielke, James E.
    1973 Smithsonian Institution radiocarbon measurements VIII. *Radiocarbon* 15:388-424.

Tringham, Ruth; Cooper, Glenn; Odell, George; Voytek, Barbara; and Whitman, Anne
    1974 Experimentation in the formation of edge damage: a new approach to lithic analysis. *Journal of Field Archaeology* 1:171-96.

Wright, Herbert E., Jr.
    1952 The geological setting of four prehistoric sites in northeastern Iraq. *Bulletin of the American Schools of Oriental Research*, no. 128:11-24.
    1960 Climate and prehistoric man in the eastern Mediterranean. In SAOC 31, pp. 71-97.

Zeist, Willem van
    1970 The Oriental Institute excavations at Mureybiṭ, Syria: preliminary report on the 1965 campaign, part III: the paleobotany. *Journal of Near Eastern Studies* 29:167-76.

Zeist, Willem van, and Casparie, W.A.
    1968 Wild einkorn wheat and barley from Tell Mureybit in northern Syria. *Acta Botanica Neerlandica* 17:44-53.

2

THE SITE OF JARMO AND ITS ARCHITECTURAL REMAINS

Robert J. Braidwood

The location of the site of Jarmo and a description of its present-day general geographical and environmental circumstances are given in our preliminary report (SAOC 31, esp. p. 26 and fig. 3). Briefly, the site lies in the intermontane valley of Chemchemal, about an hour and a half's drive east of Kirkuk, its coordinates being about lat. 35°33′ N, long. 44°57′ E. Its elevation above sea level is ca. 800 m. It lies high on the south (left) bank of the Cham-Gawra wadi (fig. 22), which is no longer perennial although it does have occasional pools or springs that we were told remained through the hot summer.

In all probability, a figure of 1.3 hectares (3.2 acres) would be a maximum for the extant area of the site within which may lie the remains of buildings. The surface scatter of artifacts may be found over a larger area, perhaps 25% more. There is no way to reckon the original size of the Jarmo settlement; H.E. Wright believes about one third has been washed away on the north, northwest, and west by wadi erosion (figs. 24, 61). The greatest directly observed depth of deposit is slightly under 7 m (fig. 23). By combining the number of more or less clear "floor" lines in our step trench A (p. 164, figs. 57, 98) with those of the larger nearby exposure, J-II (figs. 24, 46), one could account for a total of sixteen "floors." It was clear, however, that some of these were more ephemeral than real as "floors," and that "floors" or "levels" generally were not invariably horizontal or continuous.[1]

It is therefore impossible, as things now stand, to equate a given "floor" or "level" in one Jarmo operation exactly with that of another. Our plans for further work at Jarmo, which were interrupted, included a full exposure of the area between J-I and J-II. Such an exposure, at depths below ca. 2 m (see p. 165, the GL513 area), doubtless would have allowed a directly observable linking of the floors or levels of I with II. At the moment, we have no observable linkage and can do no more than reckon the rough equivalences of levels, based on the apparent typological equivalences of their artifactual yields.

It has also not proved possible, without additional excavation, to give further explanation of other stratigraphic puzzles that our preliminary report has already introduced (SAOC 31, p. 39). These included a ca. 2-m surface layer of tough and blocky orange buff silty clay in the area about squares GL513, the even larger area of a pitching gray black ashy deposit that was not really adequately sectioned by the test squares and by the PQ14 trench (p. 165), and also several small areas of potsherd concentrations that appeared in certain of these test squares. We are still inclined to believe that the tough orange buff silty clay is a *tauf* disintegration product (see p. 165), weathered away from buildings that perhaps once stood on the now eroded northwest third of the mound. The gray black ashy zone may have been little more than a trash area within the village; we could point to such areas in nearby villages today. The prevailing winds at Jarmo came from the southwest; hence the position of the gray black ashy area would have been on the leeward side of the village, and the relative scarcity of architecture in the eastern test squares tends to fit this suggestion.

The areas of appreciable potsherd yields (i.e., more than five sherds in a 2 × 2 m square or its equivalent) included the uppermost levels of J-I to the depth of level 3, and especially the western portion of J-II to level 5 (fig. 24) and the test squares immediately to the west of it, extending into the GL513 series of squares. In these latter squares, the sherds lay upon a "floor" under the tough orange buff silty clay (p. 165). The other small areas of appreciable sherd yields lay about the HK2324 and WY1519 test squares (p. 165), but our notes show that another eleven of the test squares also yielded more than five potsherds each.

Some colleagues have been tempted, either through their interpretation of our preliminary reports or their own speculations, to visualize the "upper" and "lower" phases of Jarmo as having been quite separate and distinct. As an example, it has been easily assumed that the appearance of portable pottery vessels during the course of the site's occupation could serve as a horizon marker between two distinct phases or periods. My own interpretation of the totality of the available evidence at Jarmo has always led me to stress continuity rather than subdivision. Obviously, of course, the deeper levels (of which only restricted exposures and bulks of yield are available) did predate the higher

---

[1] The manuscript for this chapter was essentially completed by 1971. Very few additions and only minor revisions have been made since that date.

levels, but probably only in terms of some scores of years rather than many centuries. Unfortunately I cannot bring myself to rely on the available radiocarbon age determinations for any precision as to how long the site was occupied (see pp. 537f.).

GENERAL OBSERVATIONS ON THE BUILDING REMAINS

Our preliminary report (SAOC 31, pp. 40-43) contains a general description of the Jarmo architecture we exposed, but some repetition may not be amiss here. The conventions used on the drawings are indicated on figure 25; we generally followed the architectural routine and conventions applied earlier in the ʿAmuq publication (Braidwood and Braidwood 1960, pp. 27-28).

Building Materials and Primary Structural Features

The principal material used for wall building and for many secondary features appears without exception to have been hand-molded courses of clayey mud, known in Iraq today as *tauf*. The mix used today is plant tempered and of just enough fluidity so that a course some 12-15 cm in height may be formed vertically without slumping. Such a course is allowed to sun dry for several days before the next one is added. To all appearances, this was the technique used at Jarmo, although the courses were not so thick (10-12 cm). Wall thickness seems to have varied considerably, but probably averaged about 40 cm, and it seems likely that the thickness was greater near the floor than at the roof line, as is the case today. Obviously, only the stubs or lower courses of the Jarmo walls were preserved for us; none we found reached quite a meter in height.

In the lowermost levels the *tauf* itself seems to have served as the wall foundation material, but as time went on, the Jarmo people seem increasingly to have employed stone foundations under their *tauf* walls. These stone foundations were usually single courses of river-worn cobbles, especially of limestone. Each building site seems at least to have been smoothed and well cleared and perhaps the outline of the desired plan was trenched to a shallow depth to receive foundation stones when they were used. Door-socket stones, when they appeared with the traces of stone-founded buildings, were at the level of the rest of the foundation stones, making it doubtful that a stone foundation course was normally visible inside or outside a building unless we assume high door sills (of which we have so far found only one example, see p. 161). Due to the effects of rainfall penetration and leaching in the zone of the upper levels (SAOC 31, p. 40), which allowed little preservation of *tauf* or of unprepared floors, we almost invariably overdug our upper floors. For example, the stone foundations shown in figures 62 and 63 appear to be up in the air. In fact, the ground surfaces about these foundations are simply the arbitrary depth to which we dug in our clearances; the floor level pertaining to these foundations had already been removed when the photographs were taken. It was only by overdigging in the upper levels that we could adequately expose building plans at all.

Two general types of prepared floors can be accounted for, although it seems likely that many floors were simply the smoothed surface of the ground in whatever part of the village was selected for the construction of any new building. These latter unprepared floors tended to be compacted layers of earth, well mixed with charcoal flecks and general living trash, except for those in the upper levels where we could not adequately "feel" them with our light picks as we dug down. Artifacts, especially large ground stone pestles, boulder mortars, and querns tended to lie within these floor zones (except where the mortars and querns had been reused in subsequent stone foundations). Prepared floors, some of them composed of smoothed limestone cobbles or fist-sized nodules (fig. 66), appeared as partial pavements in a few of the upper-level clearances, and in one case, what seemed to be a portion of a well-laid flagstone floor was exposed (figs. 64-65). The far more usual type of prepared floor consisted of thin layers of reeds over which a thin layer of relatively clean clay had been puddled. These reed layers (Arabic *gussab*) were often spread over uneven surfaces and even over rolling surfaces (figs. 67, 95) but also were used on an already smoothed and level surface (fig. 68).

There is no clear evidence for roofing practice beyond the occasional appearance of semifired hunks of heavily plant-tempered clay which also retain the impressions of brushwood, sticks, or slender saplings. With no trace of wattle and daub walls, we assume that these hunks pertained to roofing. Given the lengths and breadths of the fairly intact rooms we exposed, it would seem that the framing of a Jarmo roof was probably little different from those of the modern Kurdish village houses near Jarmo. The roof span which the modern villager can manage depends on several factors. First, he must contend with the length-weight relationship of such timber as may be available for the ridgepole (beam) and his (and his neighbors') ability to mount these into place. Once in place, there is the question whether the ridgepole and the saplings (rafters) which rest on it are sufficiently strong to bear the weight of the mud-covered brush, reeds, or matting with which the roof is surfaced, especially when this mud surface is rain soaked or snow loaded. The pitch of such a roof must be very gentle at best, however; the mud is fairly fluid when it is applied and it must not run off in a rainstorm. Taken all together, these factors suggest why wide roof spans and broad rooms are not attempted by the ordinary modern villager. The use of a central column or two to support the ridgepole would allow broader spans, but today's villagers seldom use them and we found no trace of postholes or of probable stone column bases in the Jarmo houses. The widths of modern village houses with very low pitched roofs (fig. 69) seldom exceed 4 m. In some cases of modern houses, the top of the central wall of a pair of adjoining rooms may serve alone as the bearing for rafters, a ridgepole thus being unnecessary. The top of the central north-south wall in the south building of J-II,5 (fig. 51) may well have borne rafters.

It is especially clear in the case of J-II,5 (fig. 51) that the party-wall principle was not used. However, this may have had much more to do with providing space for rain to drip off the eaves than with a developing sense of private property. It is possible that a party wall was in use in the J-I,6b-7 building (see below, p. 159).

Even in the deeper levels of most of the traces of buildings we exposed, the positioning of doors was not always clear. As an example of our difficulties in interpretation, the stones of the southeast corner of the foundation in J-II,1 include a stone with a pivot-hole type of depression, as well as a short bit of foundation extending to the east in the form of an L (fig. 56). But since what we deal with can be no more than the remains of subfloor foundations, it would seem excessive to suggest a door, screened by a sort of vestibule. When doors occurred in the levels with well-preserved *tauf*, they were clearly evidenced, but not all rooms had obvious full-length doors (e.g., general plan of J-II,5, figs. 51, 70). Access to the smaller rooms or bins may have been through the roof, or, perhaps more likely, through waist-high creepholes (evidence for which was not preserved, but see Smith 1975, pl. III*b*, for a "porthole" door at Ganj Dareh). Probably the treatment of the recessed reveals of the door opening in J-II,6 (figs. 34-35) implies some form of wood frame door with pivot post, set into a subfloor stone pivot and held at the top by a stone object of the type we surmise may have been an upper pivot stone (figs. 35, 71). Figures 34, 35, and 72 show the probable window slot in J-II,6 and figure 35 also suggests the possible position of a creephole door into the northeast room. As to the supposed upper pivot stones, one of the two clearest examples was found near a door (see p. 162), but both were found associated with large limestone balls, as figure 71 shows, and we cannot comprehend the utility of the stone balls if the long pierced stones were really pivot stones. Patty Jo Watson's photograph (fig. 73) of a door in a contemporary Zagros village shows a forked stick, with double prongs embedded in the brick wall, serving as an upper doorpost pivot.

SECONDARY FEATURES

The two most common traces of secondary structural features clearly appear to have been associated in some way with fire, but we cannot offer a clear suggestion of original use for either type. The first, which we have called "baked-in-place basins," were encountered in the lower floors of both J-I and the step trench and hence appear to belong to the earlier levels of the Jarmo occupation. They seem to have been replaced subsequently, however, by the type of feature we have called "ovenlike," although one example where both types appear to have been in use occurs in J-I,6b (fig. 41).

The baked-in-place basins (figs. 26-29, 74-77) were little more than ovoid depressions in the floor. The sides and, in effect, the rims of these depressions had been coated with a heavily plant-tempered clayey mud and then burnished in a fairly continuous way. Later, either in the final process of their preparation or in their use, they were subjected to fire. In most cases, they were more or less filled with ashes, charcoal lenses, and stones, of which at least some were usually flat flags. Only one basin (figs. 75-76) showed that the burnished clay once covered its whole floor, while another was really little more than a shallow depression for carefully set flagstones (figs. 28, 77). It is inconceivable that these depressions can have been impermeable enough to hold liquids; hence they can hardly be true basins. They may, however, have served as simple roasting ovens, which could also explain the stones found in them. In addition, it may be noted that there were scattered groups of flagstones alone, just above virgin soil, in J-I,8-9 (figs. 39, 74, 78), as well as occasionally in other exposures. Their use as griddlestones can be suggested.

The ovenlike features are shown most clearly by the example in J-II,6 (figs. 34-35, 50, 72, 79-80, 84). The flooring of these features was ovoid in plan, with a scooplike apron in front (fig. 81), and consisted of a burnished and fire-hardened clay upper surface on a bed of clayey material highly tempered with fine gravelly bits and plant temper. It is evident that a well-smoothed floor surface was necessary for whatever use was made of these features, because once cracks appeared in the floor surface, a new bedding and surface appear to have been added (e.g., figs. 30, 82-83). Evidently the central portions of the surface tended to crack first, as the edges of the successive layers of surface were usually better preserved. The example in J-II,6 (e.g., figs. 34, 84) indicates that this type of feature was domed with *tauf*, and also shows how its chimney was framed within the wall against which the "oven" fronted and through which its fire door opened. Most but not all of the fire doors opened toward the west; some of them opened into what were probably open courtyards.

The purpose of these ovenlike features is not clear. Countering the obvious suggestion that they might have been for baking bread, Helbaek once suggested that both the still wild and the early domesticated forms of cereals, with tight-fitting glumes, could have been husked most easily by popping, and that this popping could have been done most easily on smoothed heated surfaces. The forms of the scooplike aprons and the slant of the floor surfaces upward toward the back would have facilitated both the removal of a fire set to heat the interior and the subsequent drawing out of grain thrown upon the hot floor surface to pop its husks. Harlan demonstrated, while experimenting with wild einkorn from near Çayönü in Turkey, that the husks of this grain may readily be removed by mortar and pestle (Harlan 1967), and he has never been persuaded that these ovens would necessarily have been used for popping. At present, we have no firm explanation for these ovenlike features.[2] Analogous floor features appeared at Matarrah (Braidwood, Braidwood, et al. 1952, p. 7); other rather well-preserved examples were cleared at Tepe Guran (Mortensen

1963, p. 111) and at Yarim tepe (Merpert and Munchaev 1973, p. 102). In the Tepe Guran case, the framing of the chimney is not apparent, and since carbonized grain was found in one example, drying or popping is favored. Certainly ovenlike features with fire-hardened inner surfaces became a fairly usual feature—for example, in Syro-Cilician (Braidwood and Braidwood 1960, p. 345) and Anatolian (Lloyd and Mellaart 1962, p. 36) sites—by the third millennium B.C., but the scooplike outer apron, whatever its utility, is gone.

Only two other types of feature might be included here, and neither may be "secondary" in any meaningful sense. The first would be the stall-like type of feature that appeared in J-I,8 (figs. 39, 86; see p. 159) and only possibly in J-II,1 and 2 (see p. 163). Both are considered in the discussion below, with their pertinent levels. The second feature would be the pits exposed in J-I,8 and J-I,2a. A section through the former is given (fig. 31) showing trash fill which undoubtedly accumulated subsequent to the pit's original use. The pits from J-I,2a (figs. 37-38, 43-44) when exposed were bell shaped in section and also trash filled. There is no explicit evidence of the original use of these pits.[3]

GENERAL PLANS

In effect, there is little to remark on here that is not better left until the architectural description pertaining to each excavation operation. The orientation of the Jarmo building foundations that have been excavated, including those exposed in the test squares, conforms reasonably closely to the points of the compass. Variations tend to fall to the west of north by as much as 15° or 20°. The plans (figs. 39-45, 50-56) show that almost all structures were essentially rectilinear and had several rooms.

Among the rooms we exposed, the southernmost group in J-II,5 (fig. 51) probably comes closest to being a complete unit plan. If the interrupted walls on the west belonged to open courtyards (although we suggest on p. 161 that the north "room" at least was probably roofed), then the total roofed area of this unit was only ca. 36 m^2. We had ourselves (Braidwood and Reed 1957, p. 26) once suggested—by analogy with modern dwellings in the Chemchemal valley—an average of six persons per housing unit. More recently some scholars—for example, Naroll (1962) and LeBlanc (1971)—using more varied ethnological information, have reckoned at least 10 m^2 per person for roofed structures, while Cook (1972) considers various possible figures. Certainly, if both the incomplete west enclosures were in fact roofed rooms, the total unit area would have been at least 60 m^2. Framing the roof ridge over the central east-west wall would have been structurally sound and could explain the buttress outside the north-south wall on the east.

We recorded very little in the way of specialized caches or groups of associated objects that might suggest the particular use of individual rooms. It is possible that very small rooms, found sometimes in groups, some of them adjacent to the ovenlike features, may have been storage bins with high-threshold creephole entrances. The ovenlike features themselves did not always have their fire doors opening into areas that we feel reasonably sure were open courts, but they usually had their domes within cramped quarters.

To our eye, there was hardly a trace of anything we could label as a building of specialized function (such as a "headman's house" or a "shrine"). We do not grasp the purpose of the grill-type plan of the central unit in J-II,5,[4] or of the stall-like structures in J-I,8 and J-II,1 and 2, and would be loath to make extravagant guesses about them. There is, indeed, a *tauf* wall of relatively monumental width sectioned in the PQ14 trench (p. 165 and fig. 60) that also remains to be explained, along with several other probably minor architectural imponderables that must simply await further clearances at Jarmo.

Any attempt to suggest the overall village plan, on the basis of our present information, would also be highly problematical. We cannot really say which building traces of operation J-I were contemporary with which ones in J-II, let alone which traces of foundation stones in the test squares or which buildings in J-I or J-II were in use at the same time. Even were we to assume 60 m^2 as an average unit size for uniformly oriented domestic structures, we have no idea of the density of structures over the surface of the original site (about one third of which is now eroded away) at any given moment of its occupation. One might repeat our attempt to assess structure density by way of air photos of nearby modern villages (Braidwood and Reed 1957, p. 26), making allowances for their random unit orientations, and by simulating this density scatter with cutout rectangles scaled to ca. 60 m^2 over a similarly scaled plot plan of Jarmo site, enlarged by about one third. The result might lead to a reasonably reliable *maximum* population figure, but one would still remain uncertain as to how the architecturally featureless areas (pp. 164f.) related to the site's overall structure density.

In the 1957 paper, we reckoned that Jarmo village probably numbered about 150 people. To arrive at a more precise figure, much more clearance would certainly be necessary. Even then, the problem of exact contemporaneity of habitation of all structures within a given level would remain. I have seen thriving contemporary villages in southwest Asia with from a quarter to a third of their mud-brick houses already roofless and slumping into abandoned ruin. It would be very difficult, indeed, for an archeologist to assess exact contemporaneity of occupation, were he or she to expose anything less than *all* of a similar instance from the seventh millennium B.C.

OPERATION J-I

Operation J-I (fig. 24) was first opened in the late spring of 1948 and was resumed and completed in the 1950-51 field season. The operation was located on the very westernmost corner of the upper mound surface proper.

The scarp, especially on the west, showed promising surface indications of occupation, and the slope of the scarp—both to the north and west—provided convenient dumpage areas (figs. 61, 87). The operation began with an exposure of ca. 8 × 10 m, was reduced at ca. 1.25 m depth, but still afforded an exposure that grew larger with depth because of the mound's slope. The area was thus ca. 9 × 16 m when virgin soil was reached at ca. 5.5 m below the upper surface at this point (ca. 7.25 m below the highest elevation on the mound; figs. 23, 37-38). However, for any given floor, the overall area exposed tended to have few if any intact architectural remains in a strip ca. 1.5 m wide immediately adjacent to the scarp. Furthermore, *tauf* walls were not well preserved until excavation had proceeded at least a meter and a half below the surface (p. 156).

To the best of our judgment, J-I yielded traces of at least nine and possibly ten significant phases of "architectural" activity (for some of these, the word *traces* should be emphasized!). There were perhaps double this many partial or ephemeral floor lines, especially if we had counted each of the multiple layered reed-bed "floors" separately (cf. p. 17, n. 2, and Jarmo code, p. 5). The plans and sections (figs. 37-45) account for the nine or ten successive architectural traces we judged to be most significant, i.e., 1, 2, 3, 4, 5, 6a-d, 7, and 8-9.

The deepest traces of occupation in the area of operation J-I rest on (and proceed into) virgin soil, and, although two different floors appear superimposed in some parts of the area, these probably imply no great time duration. However, the *tauf* wall in the southeast quarter of the area was built over a shallow pit and also overrode a corner of a baked-in-place depression. We have labeled the plan of this level as 8-9 although the sections show that the 8th may be as much as ca. 35 cm above the 9th in some places. On the south face of the J-I cut, a large pit appeared in section (fig. 31). It seemed to have been dug from the floor noted as 8th but was probably not completely filled even until the time of level 7. The portions of *tauf* walling in the south-southeast portion of the area, noted as belonging to the 8th floor, suggest little as to an overall building plan (figs. 39, 86). The floors of the stall-like alcoves yielded much ash and charcoal, and—in places—the normally buff-colored mud of the *tauf* was orange, suggesting some degree and duration of heat. The floor of the southeasternmost alcove yielded traces of irregular batches of reeds.

To the west and north of the *tauf* walling were two fragmentary portions of reed-bed flooring. The baked-in-place depressions (see p. 157), labeled A through F on the plan (fig. 39; see also figs. 26-29, 74), include some of the better-preserved examples of this type of feature yet available. In the center of the J-I area was a fair-sized fragment of mat impression, another portion of a baked-in-place depression, and some extended clumps of stones and flagstones in another area of ash and charcoal concentration (fig. 78). In fact, the group of flagstones in the center of the operation may have been within a very shallow pit, the exact margins of which we could not delineate. The yield of artifacts (especially of flint microliths) and of snail shells was relatively abundant here, but animal bones were relatively rare. It should be apparent from the sections that the pits and baked-in-place depressions were dug into virgin soil, while most of the other features described above rested on or closely above virgin soil.

The plan of the architectural traces of J-I at its 7th floor (figs. 40, 88) shows the earliest of several phases of what was probably a house (or two houses?). The portion of the area in the south and southeast remained unclear, but this lack of clarity may have been related to the large pit on the south (fig. 31), which undoubtedly had remained exposed until the *tauf* walling on the southwest was built over its filling. Again, the *tauf* walling along the west and northwest, adjacent to the scarp, was poorly preserved. The plan shown in figure 40 is of the exposure after almost all the various portions of several reed-bed floorings had been dug through, while figures 41-42 show later phases of the building. We provide a larger detail (fig. 32) of the floor of the southwest central room, with its scatter of antler, horn, bone, stone, and the flint blade elements of a curved sickle together with the traces of a higher reed bedding upon which they lay. It seems likely that the large southeast central room may have been an open court, as may the room at the northeast corner. During none of their phases did these rooms have traces of reed-bed flooring. Reed bedding did occur in the small west central room, which was considerably enlarged in the J-I,6b-d subphases. The east central complex suggests the plan of the original foundation of an ovenlike structure (figs. 41, 90). A second ovenlike structure, not well preserved in any phase, lies in the north central portion of the area. It was unclear why there were bits of reed bedding and stones within the foundation of the first example and a broken portion of a quern and a fragment of reed matting in the foundation of the second. One of our field sketches suggests that there was possibly a collapsed fire door on the east wall of the east central ovenlike structure. The rough boulder quern near the north margin of the J-I,7 area in the scarp-edge zone was not necessarily at its original level.

Whether the architectural traces of the 7th level suggest a single or two separate houses (ignoring the very incomplete southwesternmost room) would seem to depend on whether a house would have been provided with more than one ovenlike structure and on whether the party-wall principle obtained. It was not clear to us, when the exposure was made, whether the northernmost north-south wall (from which the northern ovenlike structure projected) was built at the same time as the east-west wall which it joins on the south.

The plan shown in figure 41, with the designation J-I,6b-d, shows the architectural situation between what we called 6a and 7 proper and assimilates the evidence for the existence of at least three ephemeral room-sized reed-bed floorings and some changes in position of *tauf* walling. The main wall on the west, while quite fragmentary as we recovered it, had been moved out toward the edge of the present scarp from its position in the 7th level. More room was also provided about the central ovenlike structure, to the east of which was a large area of ash and trash, including some bones and snail shells, as well as a fragment of baked-in-place flooring. It seems fairly likely that the fire door of the structure was to the east, through the *tauf* walling. We assume this partly on the basis of the generally comparable conformation of the remains of this structure to that in J-II,6, although the fire door of that example lay to the west. In part, also, as suggested above, we had the hint in our field sketches of a collapsed small doorhead in the *tauf* wall itself (fig. 90). At this level, the traces of the northern ovenlike structure were very fragmentary. Both in the southeast and northeast portions of the area, there were baked-in-place depressions. One rather large but incomplete example in the southeast had almost complete sections of its rim preserved and had been floored with carefully fitted flagstones (figs. 28, 77). Another good but also fragmentary example with burnished clay floor appeared in the northeast (figs. 75-76).

One very puzzling feature in the west central room was the presence of four east-west running cracks at right angles to the several layers of reed bedding. These cracks are faintly visible in the photograph (fig. 67) and are shown as broken lines in the plan (fig. 41). There were also stains of red ochre on some of the reed beddings, but with no comprehensible pattern.

Although floor 6a (figs. 42, 91) was incomplete especially on the south and southeast, the plan suggests a fair amount of revision from the original of the 7th. It also suggests that by now, at least, we may well have the traces of a single dwelling. Whether there was a broad door from the southwest to the main west room was unclear, as the *tauf* here was not in the best condition. A fragment of baked-in-place flooring at the east wall of the main west room did not suggest a full ovenlike structure.

Very few proper structural traces remained of floors 5, 4, 3, and 2. In addition to the disturbances caused by the digging of the two pits from J-I,2, there were doubtless other causes—imponderable now—for the lack of architecture and stratigraphic clarity in J-I,2-5. This part of the operation was partially exposed in the late spring of 1948. When we returned more than two years later, we found a fair amount of slumping and caving in of the operation margin in the southeast corner, which only added to the confusion. The only remaining portion of *tauf* walling rising from the floor of the level we called the 5th, in the south center of the plan (fig. 43), showed how it had been cut when the large bell-shaped pit was originally dug. The traces of the oblique *tauf* walling of the 4th level, on the same plan, tell us little. There is not much more to say about the traces of the 3rd level (fig. 44) or of a higher corner fragment of *tauf* (see dotted outline, fig. 44) that we counted as belonging to level 2a. (The pits must have been dug and refilled again before the building represented by this fragmentary corner was constructed.) Note (p. 427) that we judged that the skeletons in the southwest corner of the *tauf* wall fragment of the 3rd level had been crushed by a roof cave-in. In the photograph of skeleton J1-S3 (fig. 172:1), at the right and in the lower foreground, the very poor condition of the *tauf* walling here is evident. The only other architectural trace in the 3rd level was the fragmentary section of baked-in-place flooring in the north.

Figure 45 indicates all we recovered of the first and second levels in the J-I operation. Further, the sections (figs. 37-38) might well suggest that there is hardly enough difference in absolute elevation involved to make the distinction between the two levels meaningful. We considered the fragments of *tauf* and stone walling in the southeast and the portions of baked-in-place flooring in the center to pertain to the 2nd level. The larger ovoid piece of baked-in-place flooring is approximately the size and outline of one of the ovenlike structures. It is perhaps worth noting that this argues against any suggestion that the heavy stone foundations of the 1st level might be significantly later than the main Jarmo period. In our opinion, this possibility is most unlikely. It will also be seen that the general style and scale of the heavy stone foundations here (fig. 92) have their counterparts in the uppermost levels of J-II (see p. 163 and figs. 55-56). The shallow pit, which shows as a dark shadow across our photograph (fig. 92), and which cuts through the west portion of the baked-in-place flooring, was of recent origin.

OPERATION J-II

The J-II operation (fig. 24) was begun in the autumn of 1950 and carried on, as the weather allowed, through the late spring of 1951. The original exposure was 10 × 20 m, fronting on the present scarp at the north central and highest point of the mound. As work proceeded, it was soon expanded to the east, south, and west, and in the spring of 1955, two of that season's 2-m test squares (L12 and L13) were linked to it on its southwest edge. The total area thus exposed to the 3rd level was ca. 370 m^2, but cutting back on area began at the 4th level. The exposure at the 5th level totaled only ca. 200 m^2 and at the 6th level only ca. 90 m^2, with a depth of ca. 3.75 m below the surface. Given an elevation of 792.16 m for the base of the deepest floor in the adjacent operation A (see p. 164), there should still be a ca. 3.25 m depth yet unexposed in the J-II area.

Within the 3.75 m of excavated depth in J-II, we can point to at least eight successive "floors" which cover half or more of the areas exposed at the respective "floor" depths. We noted possibly another half dozen floors which were more restricted in area or ephemeral. On the other hand, it is difficult to make a case for even as many as four completely distinct architectural plans. Our section drawings of J-II (figs. 46-49) designate the following levels: 1, 1a (or 1fl.), 2, 2a (or 2fl.), 3, 4, 5, and 6. In the field, the yield of materials was recorded as being from J-II, levels 1, 1fl., 2, 2fl., 3, 4, 5, and 6. The major structural remains designated as 1 and 1fl. (fig. 56) are probably renovations of the large northern structure labeled 2 and 2fl. (fig. 55). The remains of a small building did appear in the 1955 extension in the southwest corner of the J-II exposure at the same general elevation as did fragmentary walls in the central portion which we designated as 3rd (figs. 36, 54), but a thoroughgoing floor (cf. fig. 47) did not link the two. Most of the wall fragments we designated as 4th appear to suggest a rebuilding of the same essential plan as the level called 5th. The 5th itself was a substantial architectural effort, and the traces of the 6th indicate a distinct plan for that level as well.

As we remarked previously (SAOC 31, p. 38), it is Wright's opinion that at least a third of the original site of Jarmo has been eroded away on the northwest by the wadi. Certainly we recovered very few, if any, traces of building suggesting completed architectural frontages against the present north scarp.

J-II,6 yielded not only the most complete instance of the ovenlike structure at Jarmo but also a high-silled door opening with recessed reveals and possibly a window or ventilation hole (figs. 34-35, 50, 72, 79-80, 84). The window, if it was indeed one, had been provided with a flat stone sill set only about 25 cm above the floor. The recessed jambs of the door opening presumably provided a more draft-free door closure, if we assume that the door itself was constructed and hung so as to fit snugly into the recesses. The ovenlike structure has already been described (p. 157). The two essentially complete rooms in the 6th level were very small and the remaining upper surface of the central portion of the *tauf* wall separating the two appeared to be worn smooth, which may suggest an approximately waist-high sill of a door or creephole. In this case, one could visualize that the small north room was little more than a storage bin, but if such were the case we found no trace of either its original contents or a door. It remains only to remark that we have little evidence to suggest whether the larger but incomplete west portion of the plan was originally part of a roofed room or part of a small open courtyard. The only hint that it might have been a courtyard might be the short bit of *tauf*—running northward to the west of the fire door of the ovenlike structure—which could have been meant to shield the fire door from the direct drafts that would have been likely in an open courtyard. Since we anticipated further seasons of work at Jarmo, we did not plumb below the floors in J-II,6. Presumably *gussab* beds lie directly below at least some of the floor surfaces here.

Superficially viewed, the plan of the level we recorded as the 5th (figs. 51, 70) would appear to suggest the remains of at least two and possibly three separate houses. But separation of the remaining wall and feature traces into three distinct although incomplete complexes of rooms (north, central, and south), each with an ovenlike structure opening westward, would undoubtedly be more apparent than real. Unhappily there are at Jarmo no set rules as yet for the identification of distinct house units within a large complex of contiguously arranged rooms. Not all *tauf* walls—let alone all exterior *tauf* walls—were stone founded. In this general level there appear to be two clear instances in which the party-wall principle was not followed. However, other explanations are also possible for these two instances and if the north room complex was indeed distinct from the central one only a party wall appears to separate the two. Even were we inclined to give much weight to differences in the absolute elevations of the floors, there are few such differences here—the floors of the central portion are perhaps no more than 25 cm higher than those of the north or south.

Given the above caveats, we proceed with our description of the 5th level in terms of south, central, and north room complexes purely for the sake of convenience. The south complex consists of the incomplete *tauf* wall traces of at least nine rooms (which lie about the intersection of our longitudinal and central transverse section lines; figs. 51, 70). Here, the larger of the two rooms on the west may have been an open courtyard, perhaps even provided with a bench of *tauf* on its south wall, and with the fire door of an ovenlike structure in its east wall (see p. 157). There is a hint of reed flooring for the northern of the two incomplete west rooms, which could suggest that it was a roofed room, rather than a second open courtyard. Reed flooring, although incomplete in several instances, also appeared in all the other rooms of the south complex except the one containing the ovenlike structure. Some of the reed floorings showed the same linear cracks (figs. 68, 93) noted in J-I (see p. 160). In the two relatively large east rooms an earlier transverse partition wall (or bench?) was subsequently moved south (cf. fig. 53 with fig. 51), but both of these partition walls were bedded upon (that is, laid over) the reed flooring, as was the fragmentary partition between the pair of north central rooms of this complex (fig. 93). The matter of circulation into and within the complex is characteristically unclear (p. 157); only one door was really well evidenced and this led into the southern corridorlike room. The three small (central to northwestern) "rooms" raise again the question of the possibility of bins with waist-high creephole doors. The *tauf* which we took to be that of the eastern exterior wall was very poorly preserved, but the position of what may have been the sill of an entrance door is suggested by two flat stones with reed bedding over them. Above this, only fallen *tauf* debris was found.

Immediately adjoining the southernmost wall of the south complex of rooms was a well-laid line of cobblestones. If this served as a wall foundation for a contemporary building still further to the south (no other trace of such a structure was encountered in our limited exposure), then the party-wall principle was clearly not in use here. Alternatively, however, it is possible that the line of cobblestones was added to the base of the southern wall of the south room complex itself as an exterior ground course and protection against rain splatter. We have exposed such features at Çayönü in Turkey.

The central complex of "rooms" (i.e., suggestions of enclosed spaces incompletely indicated by the remaining traces of *tauf* walling, stone foundations, and reed floorings) in the case of J-II,5 extends from ca. 3 m north of our central transverse section line to within about 1 m of the northern transverse section line (fig. 51). On the south, the separation of this complex from the south room complex is clearly marked in that both structures had walls of their own, at least toward the east. Here the party-wall principle was clearly not observed, again assuming that the two complexes were occupied contemporaneously, at least in part. (There is a somewhat complicating factor in that the south wall of the central complex appears to have taken on a new function in the plan revision we call the 4th level, see below.) There were also two high humps of reed-covered *tauf*, one cut by our longitudinal section line and the other, west of it, extending toward the west. Whether these were benches that flanked a southern *tauf* wall of the central complex was not clear.

In fact, the traces of this central "room" complex were exasperatingly incomplete, and we cannot be sure whether what we call the central and north complexes were indeed separate. If houses of this phase typically had only *one* ovenlike structure, then we would need to suggest here separate complexes that shared a party wall, but again only if we assume full contemporaneity. Whether this was strictly the case remains questionable, since the ovenlike structure of the central complex appears to have gone out of use when renovations were made to the west. Reeds were then bedded over the caved-in structure. The extant margins of this reed flooring may suggest the positions of light partition walls but no trace of such walls was found.

The most remarkable feature of the whole J-II,5 exposure was the curious grill-like floor plan of the east central room (or rooms?). In the nearly intact east room were five *tauf* humps or joistlike dividers (figs. 33, 51, 94) over which reeds had been bedded. An additional but fragmentary example of the same treatment appeared to the north of this room. The walls of both rooms appear to have been provided with substantial cobblestone foundations. As will be noted again (see below), a rectangle of cobblestones northwest of the heavy foundation between the two rooms appears to have been the elaborate sill foundation for a door; traces of the *tauf* jambs of this feature appeared in the 4th level.

The original reason for the grill-like plan eludes us. With reference to similar stone-built features at Çayönü (e.g., Braidwood, Cambel, et al. 1974), Professor Ezat O. Negahban of Tehran University told us that in the high Elburz region today villagers still construct low stone foundation joists, upon which they place saplings, brush, and finally, mud as flooring. The air spaces are said to make the floors less cold in winter. Jack R. Harlan, our colleague in agronomy, sees no reason to agree with the frequently offered suggestion that the room was originally intended to be a granary.

The relationship of the eastern line of cobblestones to the other traces of the north complex of rooms is not clear. The line appears to proceed northward from the large doorsill foundation which we are inclined to believe pertained to the central complex of rooms. One can even speculate that the boulder mortar just west of the sill foundation was a basal door socket that had shifted somewhat out of place and can suggest further that the pierced and decorated stone, found in the same relative position behind the northern door jamb in the 4th level, was an upper door socket (see p. 157 and below). The positions of doorways in the two reasonably intact small north rooms were not evidenced, possibly because the *tauf* wall butts were relatively low and high sills would not have remained. The fire door of the ovenlike structure of the west room presumably opened to the west, through a thin *tauf* wall. Reeds had been bedded against this structure, and a quern stood on end on the floor (fig. 95). There is little to be said of the stones to the north of these rooms. The easternmost clump seemed to be a trash pile and included stone bowl and pestle fragments. The cobbles cut by our longitudinal section line were probably foundation stones, and a higher course appeared in the same position at the 4th level. The cluster of flat flagstones on the west is too low for the general floors of the 5th-level room complexes but is also too high for the floors of the 6th level.

Finally, we can still offer no reasonable explanation for the ca. 2 m thickness of rather low-grade trash-filled *tauf* that ran west along the northern transverse section line and then made a right-angled corner to the north. As our sections show, this feature (wall? bench? L-shaped platform?) pertains only to this level, and it can scarcely be taken to hint at a fortification system adjacent to the mound edge, since the position of the present scarp is quite clearly due to erosion.

The architectural traces we recorded as J-II,4 were very incomplete (figs. 52, 96). Further, when the remains mapped for the 4th and 5th levels are superimposed (fig. 53), it is clear that the traces available from the 4th suggest mainly late renovations of the 5th. However, in addition to in-place wall renovation, there was evidently some revision as well. For example, the line of cobblestones suggesting the north wall of the more northerly of the two west rooms in the south room complex does not directly override its 5th-level counterpart, and the two are separated by some difference in elevation (fig. 46). The north wall of the northeast room of the south complex was moved northward to override the south wall of the room with the grill-like plan, and this latter room was also given a new transverse wall. The heavy rectangular sill foundation for a door opening in the northeast corner of the central room complex has already been mentioned. The door opening, which the *tauf* jambs allow, seems narrow for so large a foundation. To the north of the doorjamb, behind a transverse *tauf* wall (into which it could have been set originally, at about head height), lay one of the long round stones, pierced at one end, that we believe *may* have been upper doorpost sockets (see above and p. 157). Two fragments of hard-baked floors of what we presume were the ovenlike structures appeared to the west of the door opening, and there were fragments of reed-bedded floors in several parts of the exposure.

The architectural traces in J-II,3 (fig. 54) were exasperatingly fragmentary. The 1955 expansion of the exposure in the southwest, from squares L12 and L13, was essentially a superficial outlining of the edges of stone foundations, anticipating subsequent full clearance in later field seasons, which have never eventuated. These outlines may represent the overall size of a building, of which an eastern portion had already appeared in the southwest corner of the main exposure in 1951 (figs. 63, 81). However, save for the hard-baked floors of two ovenlike structures, we recovered no interior features or partition walls. (For the most part, the depth of this 3rd level below the surface was within the upper 1.5 m zone wherein *tauf* is not normally preserved.) The east-west cobblestone foundations near our central transverse section line presage a building which developed in J-II,2fl., although these lines of stone do not directly underbed those later foundations (figs. 46, 49).

There were two fragments of reed-bedded flooring and several poorly preserved runs of *tauf* walling in the central northeast part of the exposure (fig. 54). Two of these *tauf* wall fragments could conceivably have belonged to a very high phase of the 4th level (see fig. 53). Although their uppermost preserved traces were really too low in elevation for the mapping of J-II,2 and J-II,2fl., their positions are suggestive. If nothing else, they hint at a rough continuity in the positioning and orientation of the buildings of the 5th to 2nd levels.

There is probably no great lapse of time between the plans of the 2nd and the 2nd-floor levels, nor any great difference between these plans, which we show as one single plan (fig. 55; cf. also figs. 46, 49). The remaining stone foundations in the south (fig. 63) probably do not represent the total area of an original house, let alone much of its original circulation. The stones of the somewhat trapezoidal foundation on the southeast were quite high and probably pertain to a subsequent addition. The hard-baked floor of an ovenlike structure sloped characteristically downward toward the west and must have had its fire door through a wall on the west; this suggests that we missed at least one more room to the southwest.

The architectural traces in the central to northerly parts of the exposure were not very comprehensible to us. There was obviously one large east-west rectangular enclosure formed by cobblestone foundations, as well as a heavy inverted L-shaped cobblestone foundation complex. To the east of these ran two discontinuous pairs of parallel north-south stone foundations, and these appeared to have been provided with stone-founded cross-walls. On first impression, the result resembles bins or small stalls, but detailed study renders this suggestion very questionable. The general orientation and position of these foundation stones, the grill-like floor preparation of J-II,5 (fig. 51), and the fragments of parallel east-west cobblestone foundations in J-II,1 (fig. 56) all remain inexplicable to us.

It will be seen from figures 55 and 97 that there were several incomplete cobblestone wall foundations and pavements to the north of the inverted L-shaped foundation. The uppermost preserved J-II trace of a *tauf* wall, with both a right and an obtuse angle, appeared to the west of the inverted L-shaped foundation. We show, in outline (fig. 54), the position of the somewhat lower runs of *tauf*, mapped with J-II,3 (see above). Figure 55 also shows the position of a hard-baked floor for an ovenlike structure, with its characteristic slope toward the west. Adjacent to the *tauf* wall fragment on the west was a concentration of trash: small stones, bone, and snail shells.

The architectural traces we have called J-II,1 and 1fl. (fig. 62) represent, to the best of our judgment, the fragments of a building, parts of which may have had the same general plan as that of the 2nd and 2nd-floor levels. Figure 56 indicates that little trace of architecture occurred in the expanded southern part of J-II at this uppermost level, and both this plan and the sections (figs. 46-49) suggest varying elevations for the different traces encountered generally. The lines of cobblestones about the intersection of the central transverse and longitudinal section lines enclosed or enframed a larger area around the central cobblestone room foundation of the 2nd and 2nd-floor levels. It is conceivable that at least the southern portions of this cobblestone frame were added as an exterior ground course or as protection against rain splatter. Very little can be made of any other interior feature of this central area, save for a fragment of hard-baked flooring near the southeast corner of the cobblestone frame and more of the short transverse lines of cobbles along the east. Just west of these was a shallow pit grave. An irregular area of trash and snail shells lay to the west of our longitudinal section line and a concentration of animal bones to the southeast. Lines and clusters of cobbles occurred in the western extension and in the west and southwest parts of the main exposure, but none made any particular architectural sense to us.

We did indeed attempt to consolidate the mappings of J-II,1 and 1fl. with those of J-II,2 and 2fl., in order to suggest the possibility of a single plan with later renovations. However, the attempt had to be made with strict attention to the recorded elevations for the various traces (see figs. 46-49), and the result was, in our judgment, not trustworthy enough to illustrate, given the fragmentary nature of the remains.

SUBSIDIARY OPERATIONS

As suggested in the early pages of this section and as the plot plan (fig. 24) clearly shows, we undertook a variety of small test exposures at Jarmo. While the bulk of our yield in information came from the J-I and J-II operations, four test pits were dug in 1948. One of these was enlarged in 1951 and worked as a step trench. A 5-m square was also opened in the 1950-51 season. In the spring of 1955 we attempted—with no real success—to recover something of the whole village plan by means of a grid of 2-m squares.

THE J-A, B, C, D TEST SQUARES

During our month's testing operations in the spring of 1948, four 3 × 4 m test squares were opened, each to a depth of ca. 1 m, in an attempt to define the probable limits of positive architectural activity on the site (fig. 24). Squares B, C, and D yielded no architectural traces (save for presumably secondarily washed-in or rolled-in stones) and few artifacts, and we assumed that positive occupation—if it occurred at all in the areas these squares tested—must lie quite deep under the surface. Square A (later incorporated into the upper end of the step trench J-A) proved puzzling, as it exposed a tough and blocky brown buff soil with few artifacts.

THE STEP TRENCH, J-A

In March of 1951, we attempted to secure a complete section through the site, approximately at its greatest elevation and adjacent to the J-II operation, by means of a step trench expanding from J-A and projecting over the north scarp of the mound (figs. 24, 57, 98). Virgin soil appeared here at about 6.75 m below the surface at the scarp's edge. Unfortunately, the uppermost 2 m of the section consisted of the same tough and blocky brown buff soil already encountered in 1948 in the test square J-A (a matrix without floors or many artifacts) and subsequently encountered in the series of test pits of the area approximately bounded by squares GL513 (see below). The uppermost clearly observable floors and bits of *tauf* walling appeared at ca. 2.4 m below the surface, at an absolute elevation approximately equivalent to that of the 5th level in the nearby J-II. From this point on downward the section exposed by the step trench, J-A (fig. 57), shows at least nine reasonably well-marked floor lines and other more ephemeral traces of floor lines.

The step trench was ca. 3 m in width and was worked in five stages of "steps," of which the uppermost (number I) was ca. 1.8 m deep, and the rest (numbers II to V) were ca. 1.5 m deep each (see Braidwood and Braidwood 1960 for a general description of step trench operations as we have used them). As indicated above, the step trench was started, on the mound top at the scarp's edge, from the original 3 × 4 m test pit A, opened in the spring of 1948, and its sides were somewhat flared outward at its bottom in stage V. The floors (or general living surfaces) exposed had a tendency to pitch gently toward the south, into the mound, and some were fairly thick, dark in color, and rich in charcoal flecks. I am bound to wonder whether this southward sloping of the ancient surfaces implies that originally a mass of *tauf* buildings existed to the northeast-northwest of the present scarp and that the tough and blocky silty clay soil was derived from this mass by erosion before the wadi eroded away the whole northern portion of the mound. As noted above, there were few artifacts in the uppermost ca. 2 m, but thence downward the number of artifacts, snail shells, and bone fragments found was—if anything—above normal for Jarmo. However, we encountered only a few traces of *tauf* walling and only one baked-in-place depression (which shows on the section face; fig. 57).

THE J-III TEST SQUARE

Operation III, a 5 × 5 m square, was worked intermittently during the autumn of 1950 to a depth of ca. 1.75 m. It was laid out in the center of an area (fig. 24) where we had noted a relatively heavy surface concentration of flint. Almost immediately, we encountered a rather fine gray to blackish ashy material, light in weight but well consolidated, rich in artifacts but stratigraphically featureless to the depth we excavated. This ashy layer will be considered further (p. 165) but no section is shown of J-III because it yielded essentially nothing to delineate. The only exception was a formless mass of apparently normal silty earth (perhaps badly disintegrated *tauf*) that appeared at a depth of ca. 30 cm in the northeast corner of the square. The artifactual yield was noted as "surface to 1st" down to a depth of 1 m and was also recorded as to absolute depth. The 1st level was arbitrarily assumed to begin at a depth of 1 m, and this designation was continued to the depth of the test at ca. 1.75 m. Toward this depth, we began to note a few faint hints of orange buff soil, sloping toward the south and west, but the probing of these was left for our projected later field seasons.

The yield of figurine fragments and of clay balls, flint, and obsidian was much higher than normal for Jarmo in this square, perhaps because the matrix was so light and almost fluffy and hence very easy to work. Only one single potsherd (red surfaced) appeared, at a depth of ca. 60 cm, and we are inclined to view it as intrusive, given what we subsequently learned of the gray black ashy zone.

THE 2 × 2 METER TEST PIT SYSTEM

Our preliminary report (SAOC 31, p. 39) rather ruefully accounted for our "short-cut" attempt to expose the overall Jarmo village plan. I still believe the effort was worth trying; perhaps someday, on some other site, it may pay off in its intent. The plot plan (fig. 24) and the air view (fig. 61) show an overall 5 × 6 m grid, with 2 × 2 m test pits in 151 of the grid units. As this preliminary report suggested, we hoped—by extrapolation from one test-pit section to that of its neighbor—to be able to suggest a number of meaningful general sections through the original village as well as to expose the positions of most of the village's buildings, at least in the upper layers. We present here only the series of test-pit sections on the two longest central lines, the "K line" and the "19 line," to suggest that not a very great deal was learned, architecturally (figs. 58-59). The most impressive architecture revealed by the test pits was located in the region of HL1516 and a sketch plan of our preliminary exposure here is shown (figs. 36, 64-65, 99). Our intention was to pursue this group of buildings in later campaigns.

SAOC 31 (p. 39) gives a brief description of the approximately 2-m-deep uppermost layer of the tough and blocky orange buff to brown buff silty clay soil (apparently a *tauf* disintegration product; see p. 155 and above) in the northwest quadrant of the site (the area lying roughly about squares GL513; fig. 24). The illustrated test-pit sections (fig. 58; sections K7 to K13) show the occurrence of this *tauf* disintegration soil type as we observed it. In a few adjoining test pits we noted occasional concentrations of varvelike bands of fine silty clay (perhaps the traces of successively dried-out mud puddles that formed in depressions at some time not too long after the site was abandoned). We append Wright's explanation for these varves.[5] In several of the test pits (e.g., in the K7 to K9 region) there were scatters of potsherds at the base of the tough soil layer.

The test pits of the GL513 area exposed several other much more shallow (near surface) concentrations of potsherds, in addition to those mentioned above which were covered by the 2-m bed of tough brown soil. The GL513 complex was undoubtedly the westward extension of the potsherd-yielding region of J-II (see p. 214, chart 3). Two other marked near-surface concentrations appeared in the HK2324 and WY1519 regions. It will also be noted that there were potsherds in a few other squares (see fig. 24), as well as in the upper levels of J-I. The HK2324 and WY1519 regions were without apparent trace of meaningful architectural remains in our exposures.

The final general feature revealed by the test pits was a north-south zone, some 70 m in length, of the gray black ash deposit first encountered in test square J-III of 1950 (see above and fig. 24). Our most complete continuous section of this deposit was made by means of a trench 1 m wide and some 12 m long, running southwest from square Q14, through P14, to the edge of old J-II (figs. 60, 100). The section illustrated is of the southeastward face of this trench. It shows a succession of gray to black ash beds that pitch gently toward the southwest, interbedded with layers of red orange buff clayey soils. The color and texture of some of the layers possibly were the result of fire. These beds lay above a zone of tough brown buff soil that had the appearance of disintegrated *tauf*. This zone contained fewer artifacts than did the ash beds, but did include some ash lenses, floor lines, and odd stones, plus a short pavement of cobbles and a flagstone at one point. Toward its southwestern end, the trench encountered the lower portion of a wall of *tauf* that was about a meter thick and had an approximately east-west direction. From this wall another of equal thickness branched off to run north close to the northwestward face of our trench. The absolute level of the remaining upper portion of the wall was at ca. 797 m above sea level. This could be approximately the same absolute elevation as that of level 4 in J-II, although that operation had not been taken down to this depth in its southern end (cf. fig. 46).

The plan and details of a building with such substantial wall construction remains one of the major unfinished architectural challenges of Jarmo. Other problems are the subsequent stratigraphic history of this region of the site and the exact relationship of the gray black and red orange buff beds to the thick-walled building. With the exception of the broad wall-like mass of trash-filled *tauf* in the northwest corner of the north complex in J-II,5 (p. 162; fig. 51), the normal thickness of *tauf* walls at Jarmo appears to have been ca. 35 cm. Our section (fig. 60) indicates that the *tauf* walling in the PQ14 trench was overbedded by almost 2 m of soil, probably a *tauf* disintegration debris with random limestone concretions, as well as random stones, snail shells, bone, a few short ashy cleavage planes, and occasional artifacts. As was normal for the gray black ash deposit generally, there were no potsherds.

A few general remarks on the sections shown for the K line (fig. 58) and the 19 line (fig. 59) are in order. Limestone concretions normally did not appear at depths lower than ca. 1 m. Clusters of stones sometimes seemed to have no apparent association with a floor (e.g., in K9). The gray ash zone with some fragments of *tauf* material in K14 resembled that of the large gray black ashy area (see below) but must be localized as it appeared in none of the immediately surrounding test pits. More gray ash began to appear in the K line, southward from K19, and we had little doubt that the gray ash zones of about 80 cm and downward in K21, interbedded with orange yellow buff *tauf* disintegration product, pertained to the large gray black ashy area. The beds pitched gently southward, and at a depth of ca. 2.5-3.0 m there were random varves or mud flakes. A pair of horizontal cleavage planes with much broken snail shell appeared at ca. 3.75 m, and just below this (at an elevation of ca. 793.9 m) came a sterile blocky brown buff silty soil with limestone concretions. From K21 on southward, also, the soil immediately under the surface zone began to shift in color from a dark brown buff to an orange or orange gray buff. The large gray black ashy zone had its southernmost appearance in K25. Below clusters of varved mud flakes, the lower depths of K26 and K28 were sterile, with concretions.

For the 19 line, test pit D19 was taken to a depth of over 3 m in an attempt to ascertain whether buildings once stood in this part of the site (see pp. 163f. regarding test square B). We did not reach sterile soil but neither did we find clear traces of *tauf* walling. However, there were firm floor lines (dark cleavage planes and one clear bed of reeds) and the fill had the general appearance of disintegrated *tauf*. There was increasing indication of ashy gray material mixed with this in H19 and K19, and clear evidence in L19 that the large gray black ashy zone had been reached. Both in L19 (at a depth of ca. 1 m) and in M19 (at a depth of ca. 0.8 m) there was a thin scatter of rather flat orange-colored concretions. A few potsherds occurred in N19, to a depth of ca. 1.5 m, suggesting that this was probably the region of a subsequent depression in the gray black ashy zone. In P19, the gray black ash tended to have the form of lenses in an orange or even red orange buff soil, resembling that of the PQ14 section in color and texture. Concretions began to appear in the deepest portions of S19 and T19 as sterile soil was reached. In all probability, the materials in W19 were the result of subsequent surface wash.

I cannot resist the wry observation that had we restricted ourselves to only one or two small and strictly rectilinear exposures with well-plumbed margins, Jarmo probably would have appeared to be a much simpler affair!

NOTES

1. In general, we have used the term "floor" ("fl.") with reference to what we took to be an actual living surface within or immediately adjacent to a cluster of rooms that evidently pertained to one or more associated buildings. The use of the word "level" is somewhat more ambiguous, since it may sometimes denote simply a horizontal plane or elevation above sea level. By and large, however, our use of "level" tends to suggest the floor or floors, the associated remaining wall butts and secondary features, and the matrix or debris within which they appeared in a more or less horizontal plane or zone within one operation. In the Amuq volume (Braidwood and Braidwood 1960, p. 22), we remarked on our normal routine of excavation, as follows:

> Except in the step trenches, the floors were numbered serially as they appeared in a given operation, beginning with the first floor encountered below the surface-humus line. . . . In the strict sense, by "floor" we mean any line of compact earth (usually discolored), any layer of dark or grayish ash, any proper floor feature such as paving stones or pebbles, or even the general level at which architectural features (such as doorsills and sockets, hearths, bins, silos) indicated a floor. Such features usually were not more than *ca.* 10 cm. thick, although considerable variation was possible. Above such an observable line usually lay debris, in part accumulated by the leveling-off of the mud-brick walls of the building which referred to the particular floor, in part perhaps accumulated before the walls were leveled but after intense living activity had ceased. This debris varied in thickness from less than 20 cm. to over 2.0 m. Any surviving mud-brick wall butts remained within this debris layer.
>
> The routine for clearance in such a typical situation was ideally as follows. After the previous floor and some 10 cm. below it had been removed, the whole area was carefully scraped and swept. If new mud-brick wall butts showed in plan in the cleared area, their tracing began immediately; if not, the pickmen had to seek them as they dug. For this work, the pickmen used the type of light single-tined pick developed by Mr. Delougaz for wall-tracing in Iraq. Once the walls were discovered, the available plan was traced by simply picking along the walls. As one or more of the pickmen worked forward in narrow trenches tracing the walls, other, less experienced, pickmen removed the core of debris left in the center of the room. The pickmen working along the walls periodically went deep enough to expose the floor, but the general instructions were for them to remain 10 cm. (i.e., "a hand's breadth") above the floor line in the removal of debris. The pickmen removing the core of debris in the center of the room did not go below the depth set by the wall-tracers.
>
> The completion of this first step in the routine exposed the architectural plan to within *ca.* 10 cm. of its floor and saw the removal of the main bulk of debris. All materials encountered during the first step were marked as of *x* operation, plus the serial number of the floor or level: for example JK 3:6.
>
> The next step was to clear off the remaining 10 cm. above the floor proper and to expose whatever special features (e.g. hearths, benches, etc.) appeared on the floor. When this step was complete, the operation was ready for mapping and photography. The materials encountered during this step were marked as of *x* operation, plus the serial number of the floor or level with the specification "floor": for example JK 3:6 fl.

2. When we discussed the matter with Daniel Zohary in Chicago in February 1972, he pondered the possibility that these ovenlike features might have been used for the extraction of fat or of vegetable oils. This could help explain the undesirability of cracks in their floor surfaces.

3. Just what sort of facility the Jarmo people used for grain storage still eludes us. These pits, the small rooms or bins(?) included in such house plans as J-II,5 (p. 161), and the possibility of grain sacks or baskets have all been suggested, but there is no compelling evidence in the matter.

4. Even though we now have more elaborate examples at the site of Çayönü (Braidwood, Cambel, et al. 1971; Braidwood, Cambel, et al. 1974), the exact purpose of this grill type of construction still eludes us.

5. ["Varvelike bands" refers to laminations formed by gradations of silt, clay, sand, and grit grains which indicate that sorting action by water has taken place—running water in the case of sand and grit, quiet water in the case of silt and clay. Such laminae are preserved only when the area has remained undisturbed by the treading of feet. The step trench at Jarmo contained laminated earth that was more than 2 m deep. With 5-10 laminae per cm, the number of laminations deposited probably totaled 1,000 to 2,000. And overlying the 2 m of laminae in the step trench was a 1-2 m deposit of relatively barren earth, containing no hearth or ash layers, stone lines, snail lines, etc.

The following hypothesis is offered as an explanation for these laminations. After the village of Jarmo was abandoned, the roofs of the mud houses fell in but the walls remained partly standing, thereby creating for each room a depression bounded by collapsing walls. During the period of abandonment, rain wash carried earth from the disintegrating walls to the centers of the rooms, depositing it there in laminae of grit, sand, silt, and clay. After a time, the village was again inhabited. To prepare the site for new houses, remaining wall butts were knocked down to smooth out a living surface. In this manner, the laminated earth of the interim period was buried by the 1-2 m of barren, structureless soil.

There is evidence for the occurrence of this kind of process elsewhere in the area. About 2 miles southeast of the Tauq bridge on the Baghdad road, in connection with Jambour well no. 1 (actually the first oil well in Iraq), a camp of mud-brick houses was built in 1926. These buildings had mud-brick walls which supported roofs of wooden planks and corrugated steel topped with a mud cover. In 1927, both the well and the camp were abandoned; the wood and steel construction components were removed from the buildings and the site has remained untouched ever since. When I examined the site in 1955, the mud-brick wall butts stood to heights of 5-9 ft, enclosing rooms measuring 10-14 ft. Each room had a depression in the center, bounded by slopes of collapsed wall material leading up to the standing wall remnants. The center of one room was tested and found to have ca. 14 in. of laminated silt-clay-sand-grit sediment, which had accumulated during the 28-year period.—HEW, Jr.]

At the time he wrote, Wright suggested further testing of the Jarmo laminations, but since we did not return to Jarmo to continue fieldwork, this testing was never carried out.

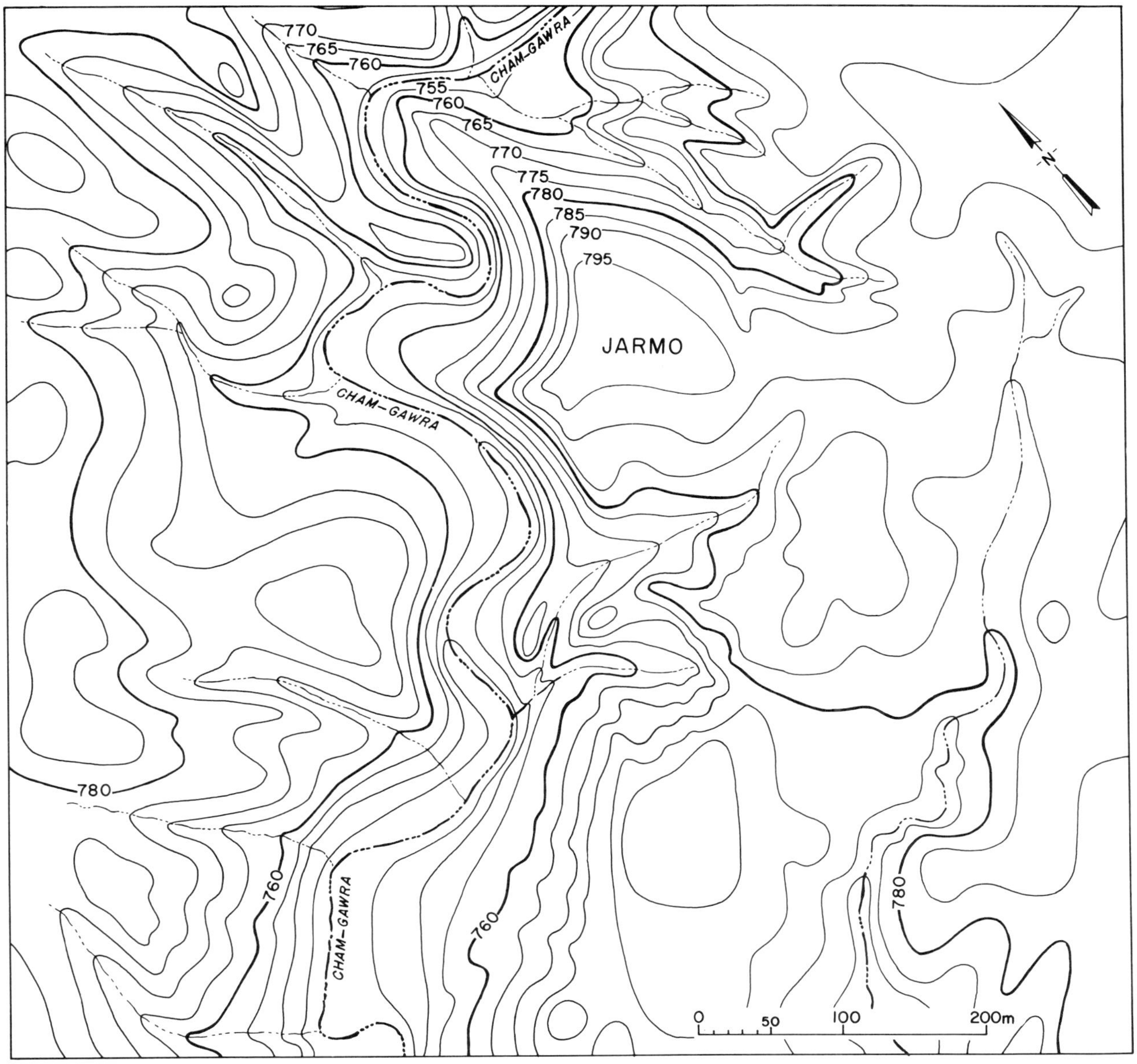

Fig. 22. The 64-hectare square about the site of Jarmo.

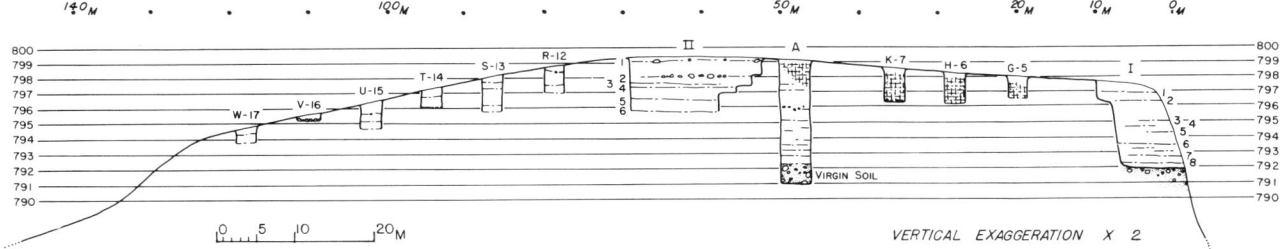

Fig. 23. Schematic east-west section of the Jarmo site (double vertical exaggeration). For the position of the section, see fig. 24.

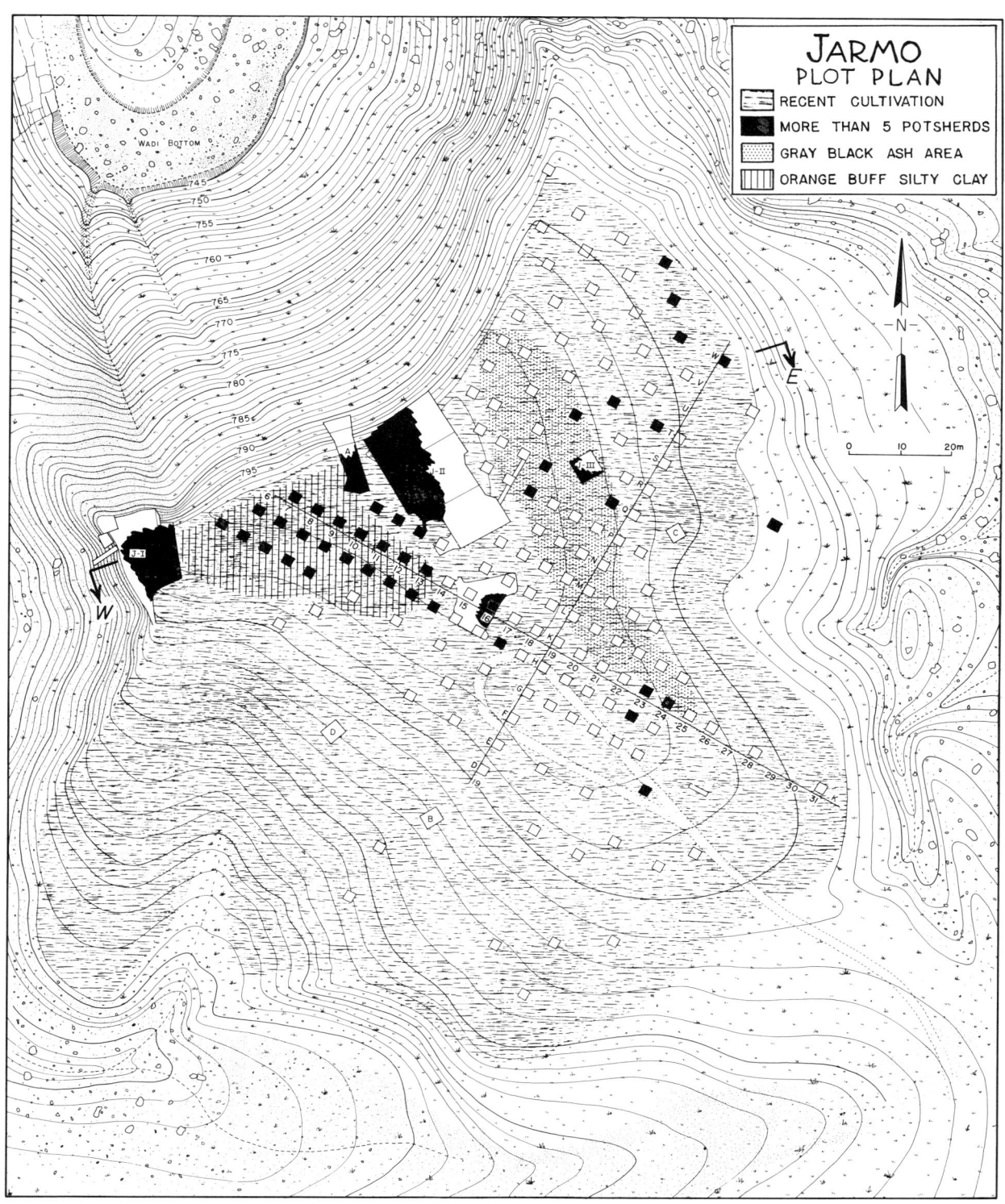

Fig. 24. Plot plan of the Jarmo site and operations, indicating areas of recent cultivation, potsherd concentrations, the gray black ash area, and the region of orange buff silty soil.

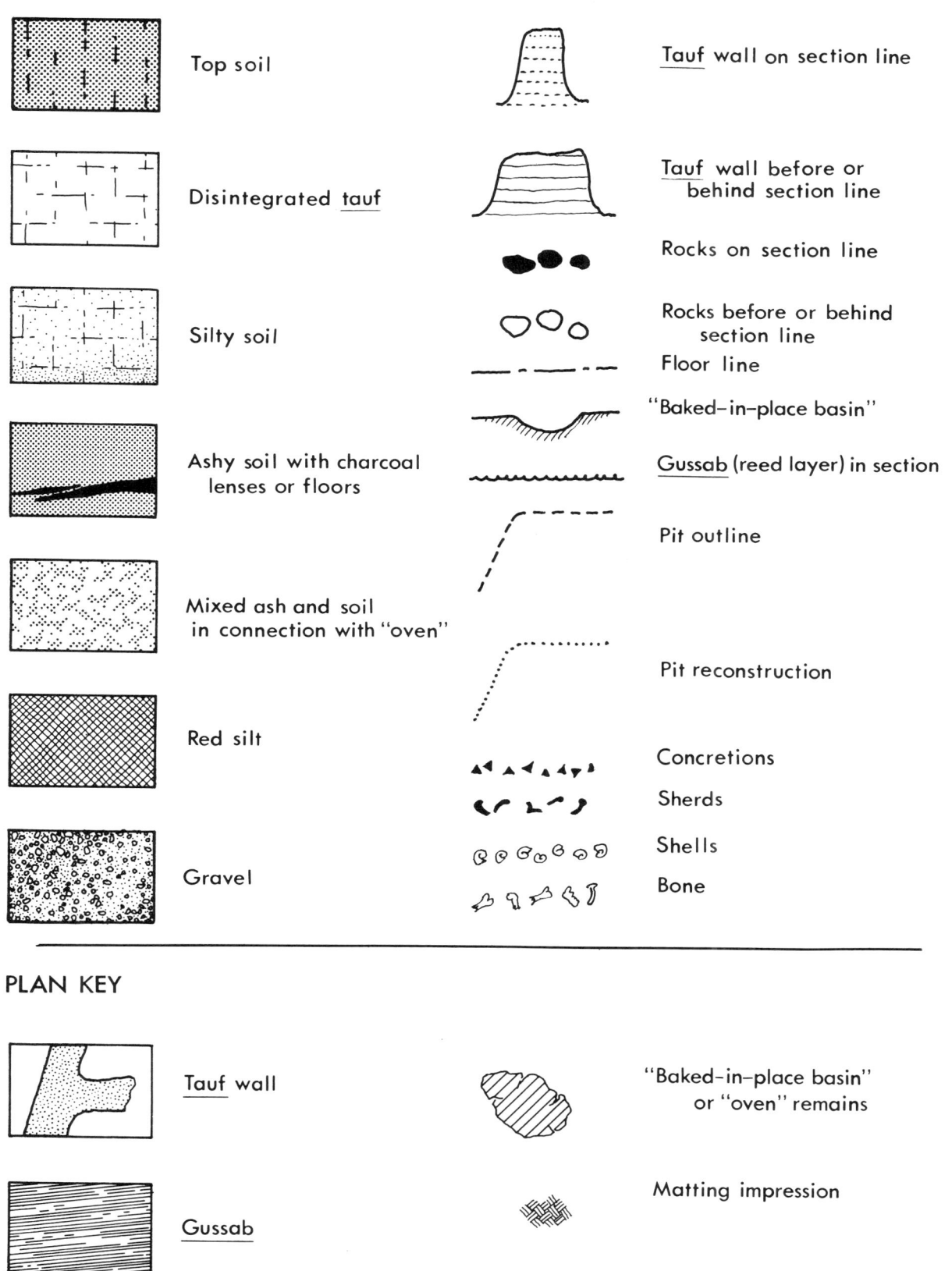

Fig. 25. Key to symbols used on the plans and sections.

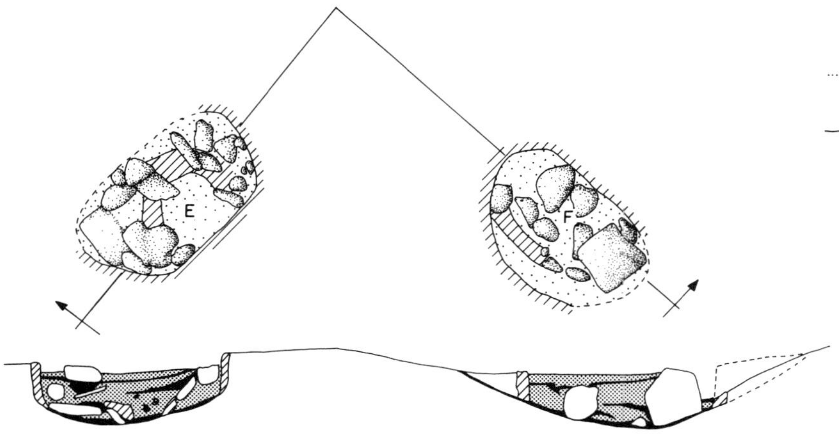

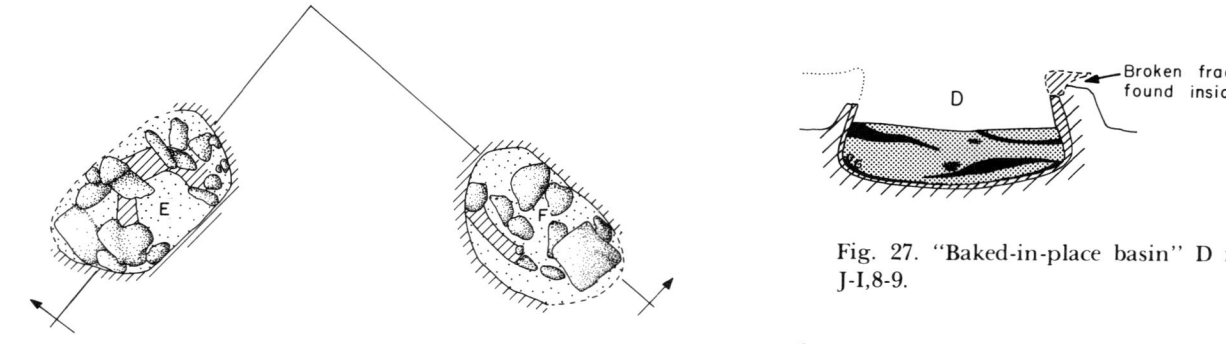

Fig. 26. "Baked-in-place basins" E and F in J-I,8-9. See also fig. 39, detail 4.

Fig. 27. "Baked-in-place basin" D in J-I,8-9.

Fig. 28. Section through "baked-in-place basin" with flagstones in J-I,6b.

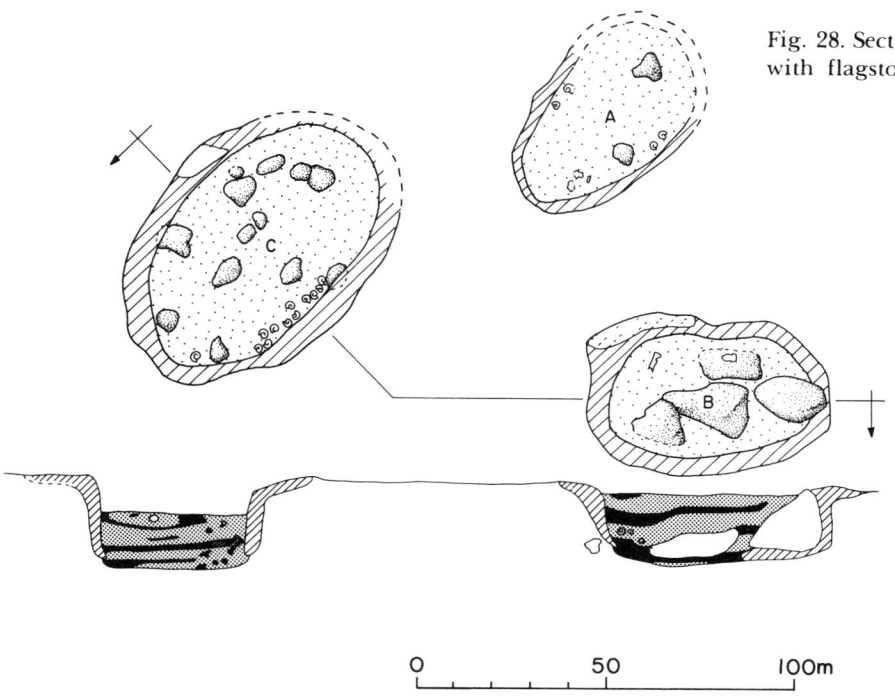

Fig. 29. "Baked-in-place basins" A, B, and C in J-I,8-9. See also fig. 39, detail 3.

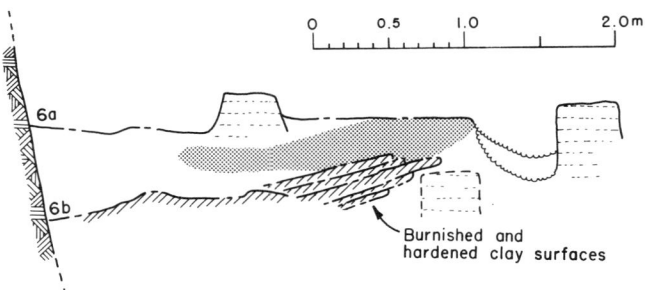

Fig. 30. Section through ovenlike surfaces in J-I,6b-c.

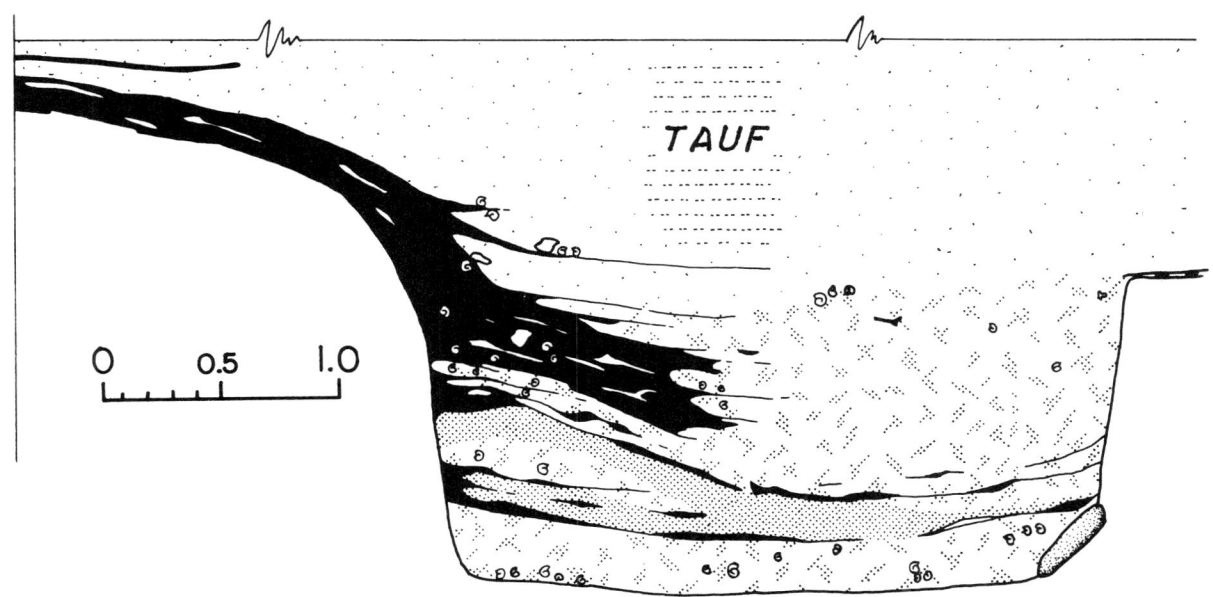

Fig. 31. Section through pit G in J-I,8. See also fig. 39, detail 1.

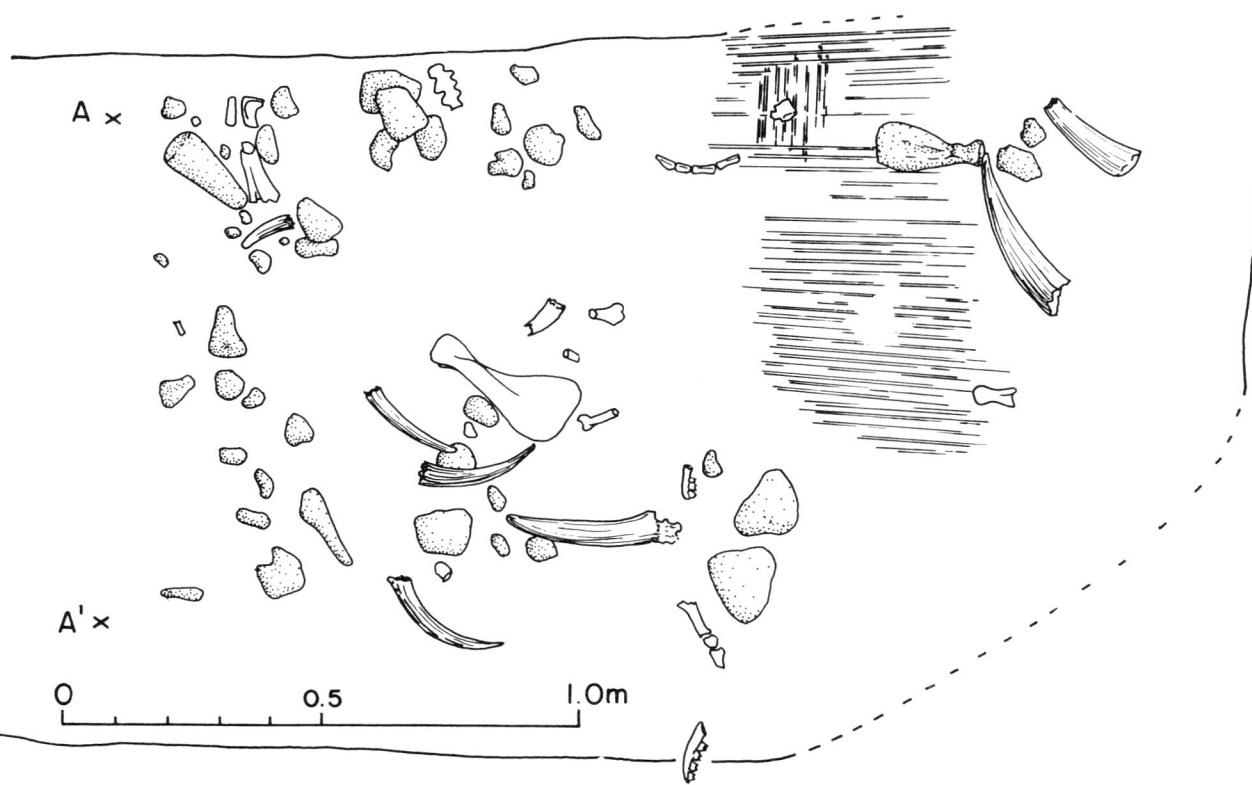

Fig. 32. Scatter of bones, horn cores, and artifacts on the floor of a room in J-I,7. See also fig. 40, detail A-A¹.

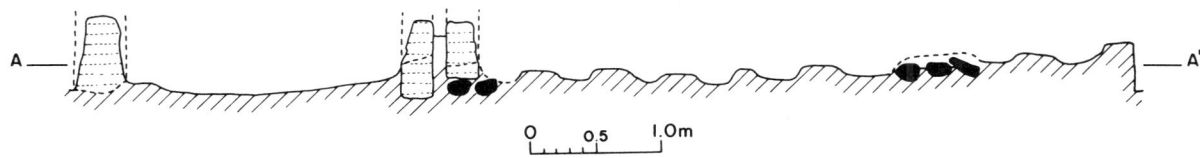

Fig. 33. Section through the grill-like floor and its adjoining room in J-II,5. See also fig. 51, detail A-A¹.

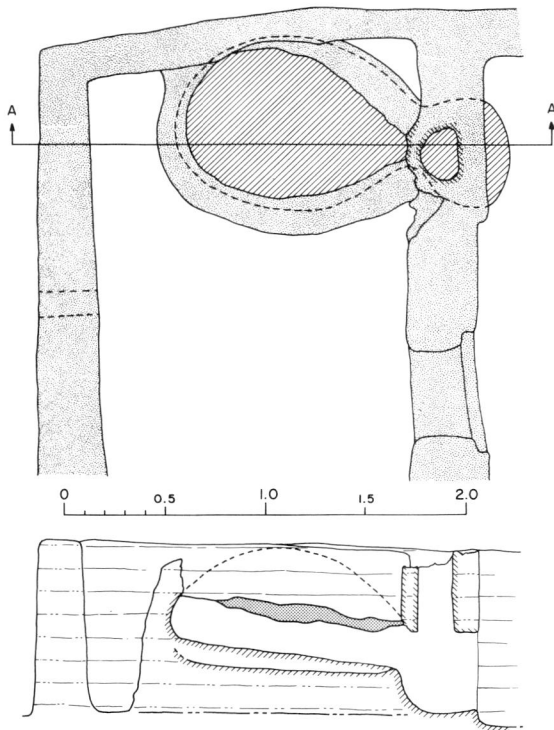

Fig. 35. Isometric sketch with partial restoration of the *tauf* remains in J-II,6.

Fig. 34. Plan of the ovenlike structure in J-II,6 and section at A-A¹. See also fig. 50.

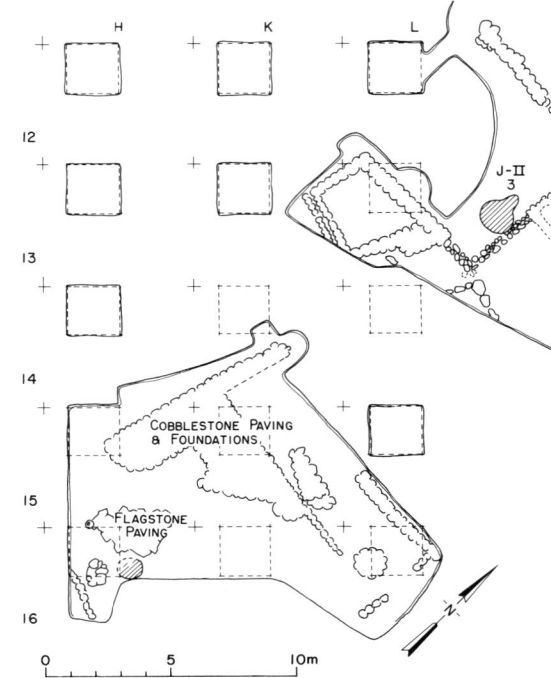

Fig. 36. Architectural traces first encountered in test squares of the HL1216 region, with subsequent exposures indicated.

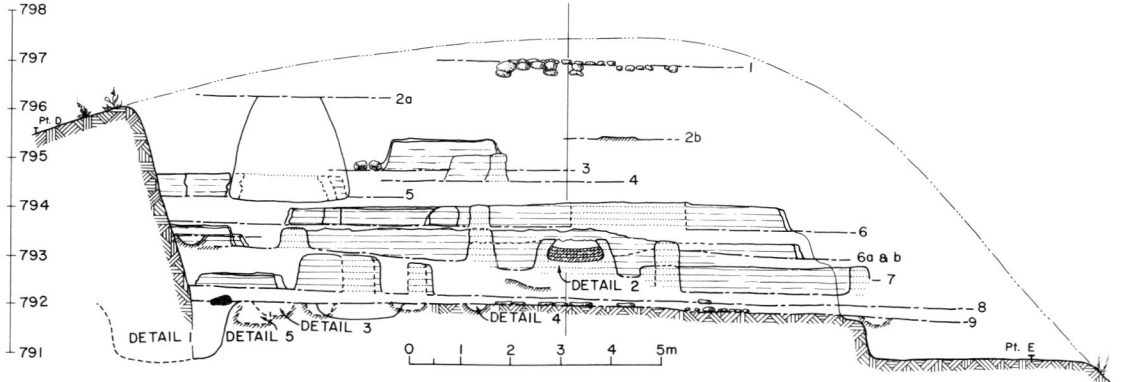

Fig. 37. South-north section through J-I, looking west.

Fig. 38. East-west section through J-I, looking south.

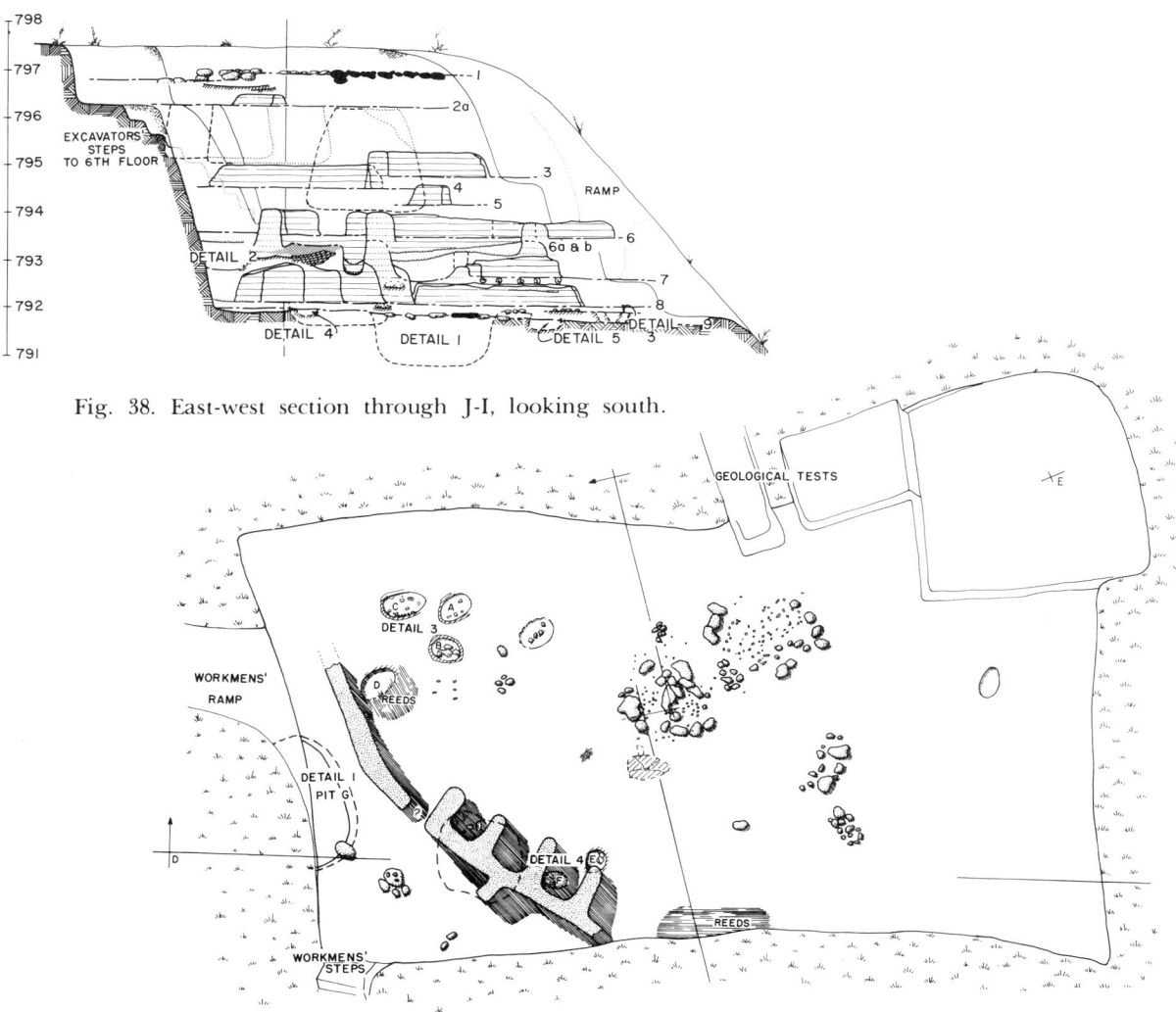

Fig. 39. J-I,8-9.

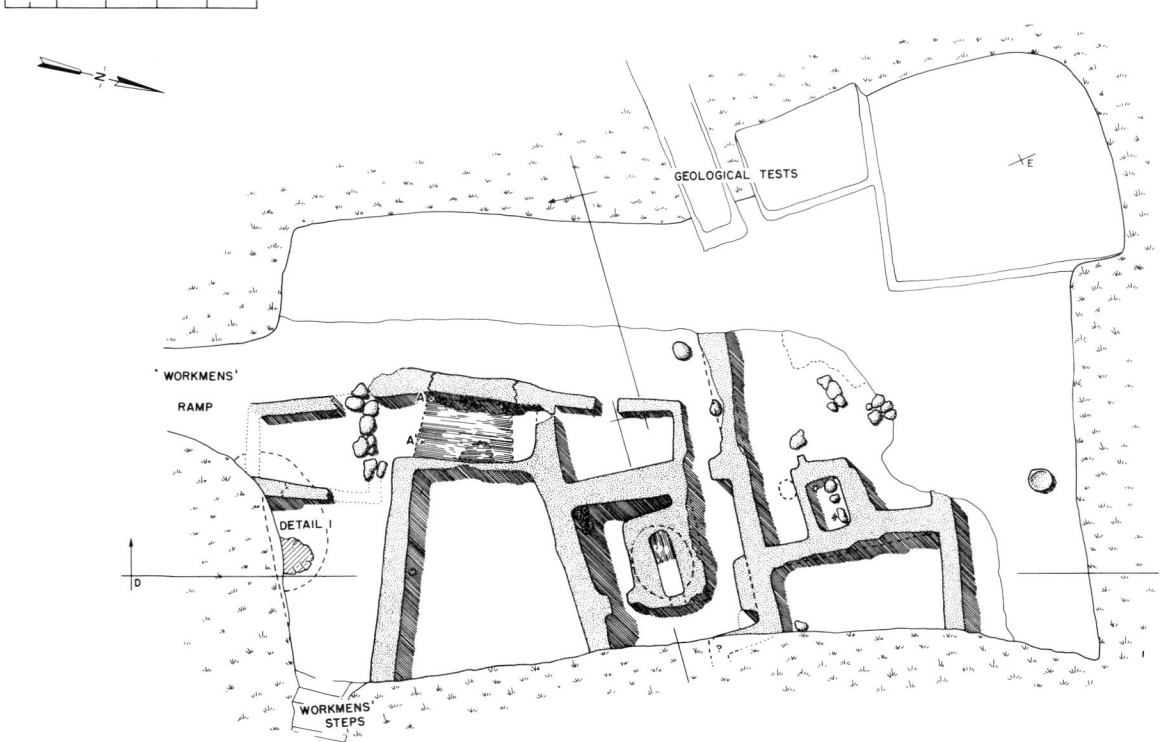

Fig. 40. J-I,7.

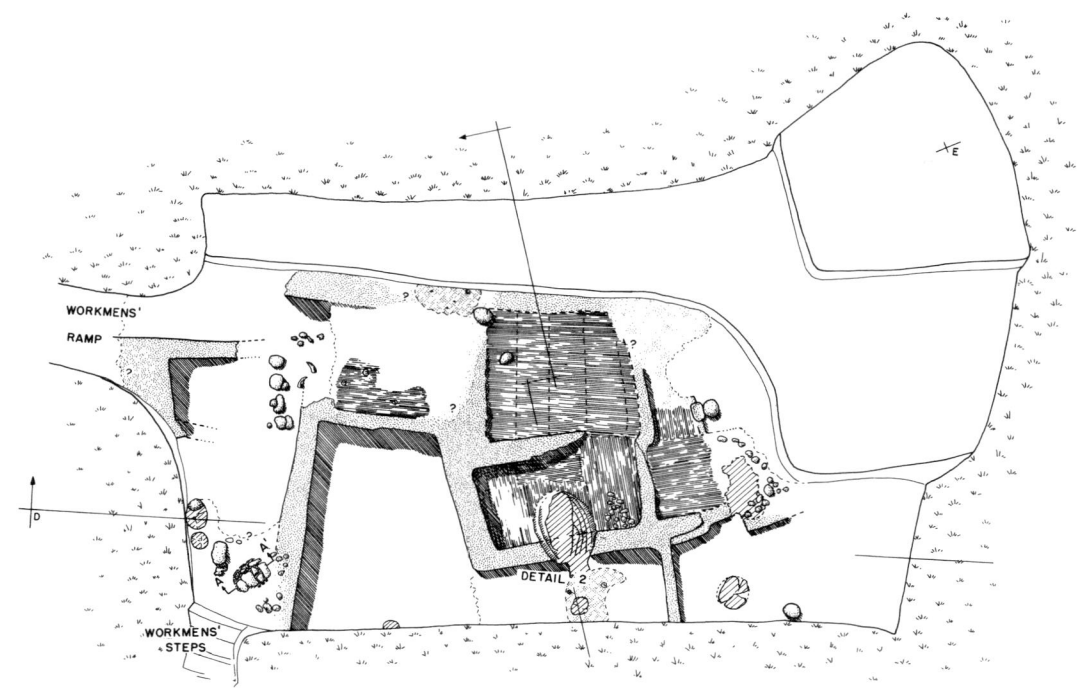

Fig. 41. J-I,6b-d.

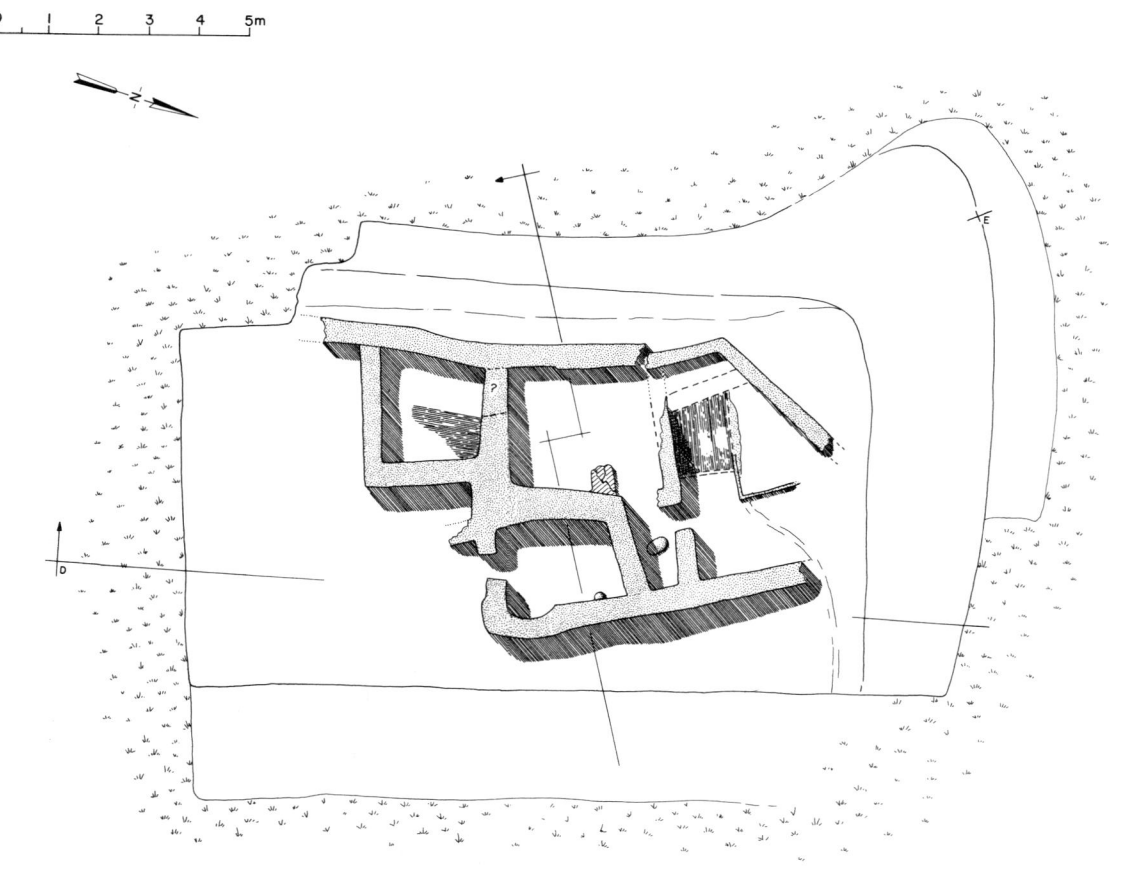

Fig. 42. J-I,6a.

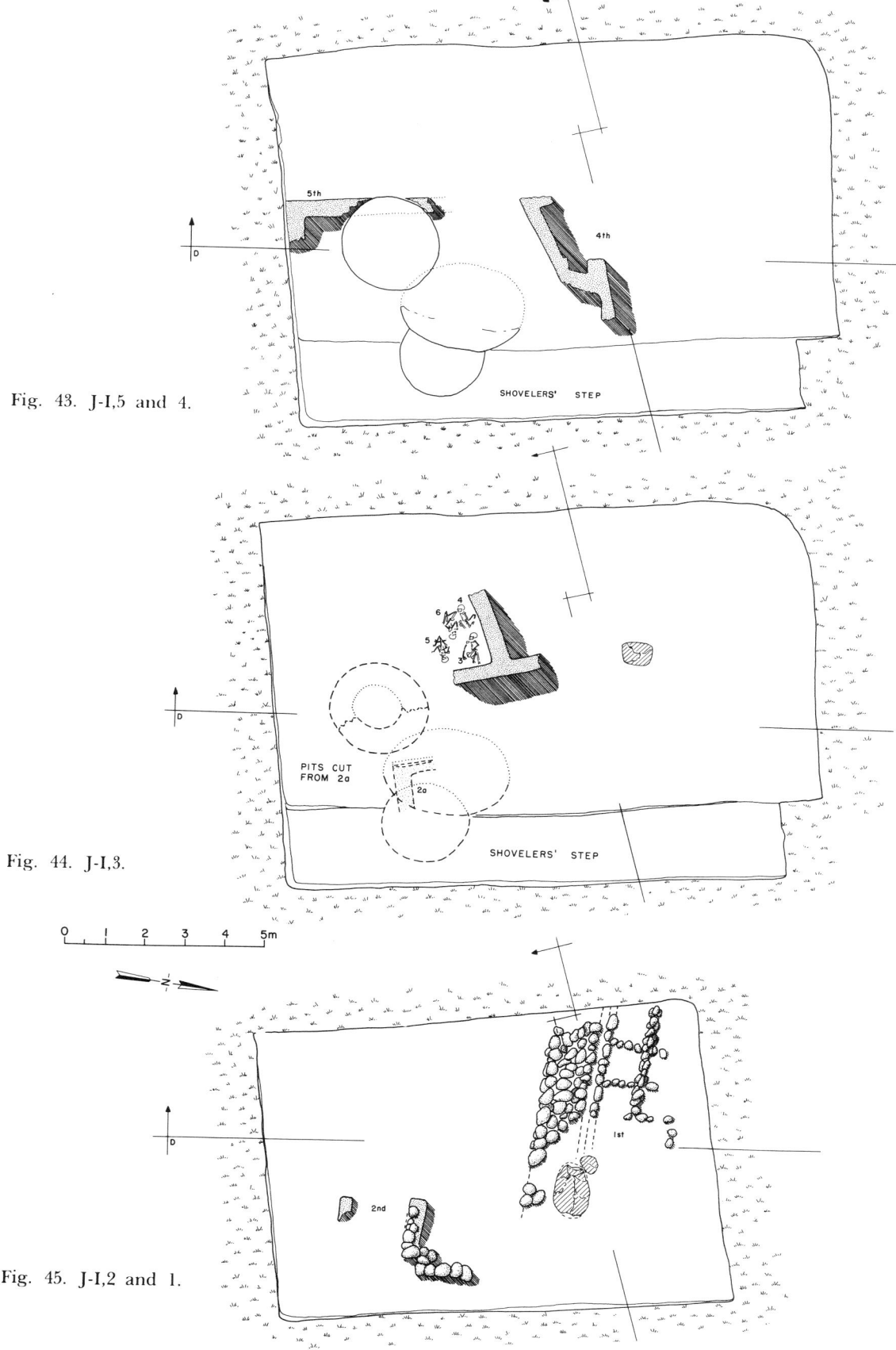

Fig. 43. J-I,5 and 4.

Fig. 44. J-I,3.

Fig. 45. J-I,2 and 1.

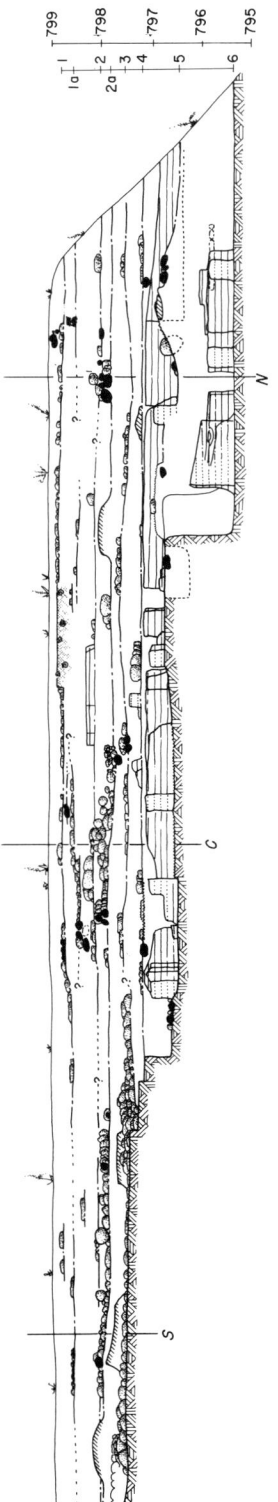

Fig. 46. South-north longitudinal section through J-II, looking west. Note: For figs. 46-50 the letters S, C, N, and L refer to the south, center, north, and longitudinal sections.

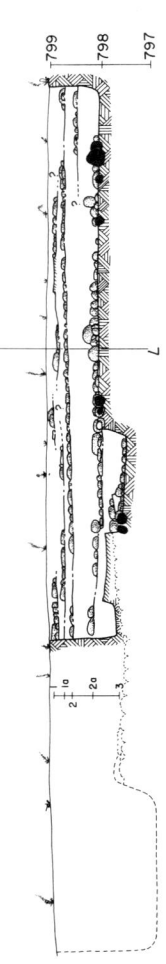

Fig. 47. Southern west-east transverse section through J-II, looking north.

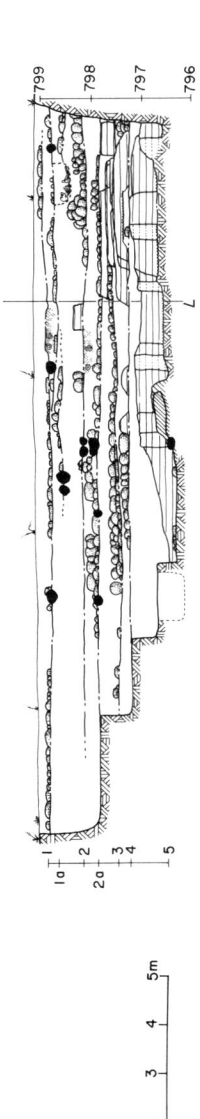

Fig. 48. Central west-east transverse section through J-II, looking north.

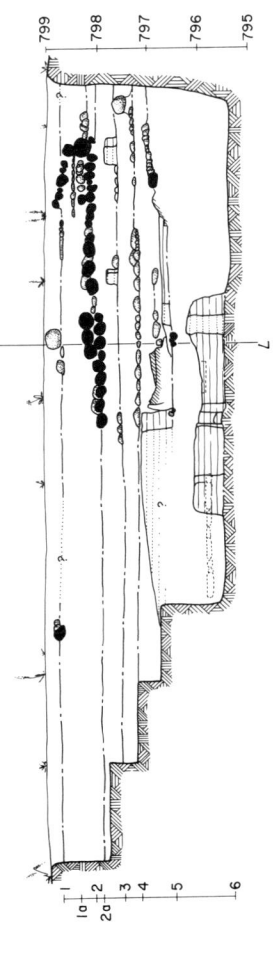

Fig. 49. Northern west-east transverse section through J-II, looking north.

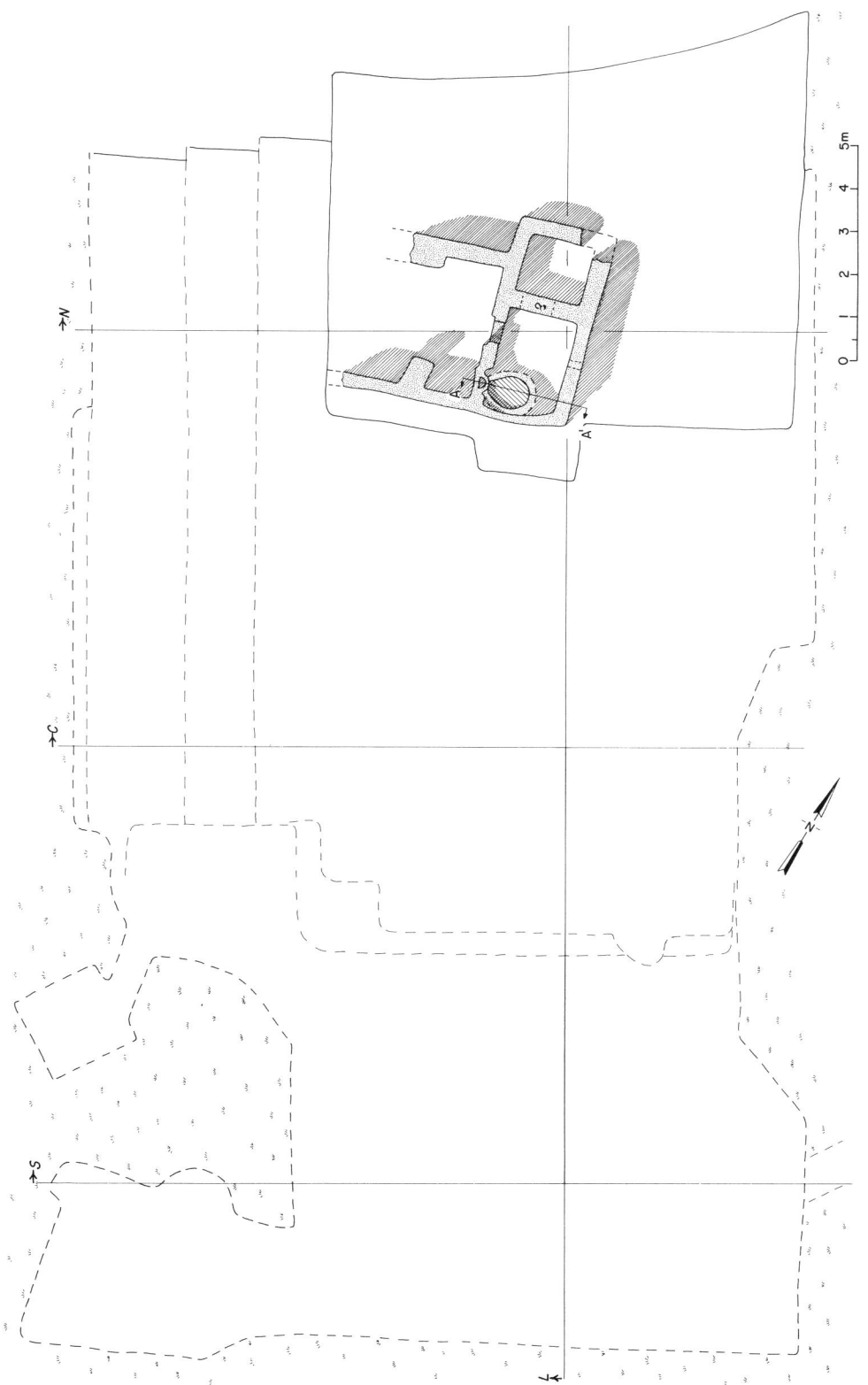

Fig. 50. J-II,6 exposure within the outline of the total J-II operation, shown in dotted line.

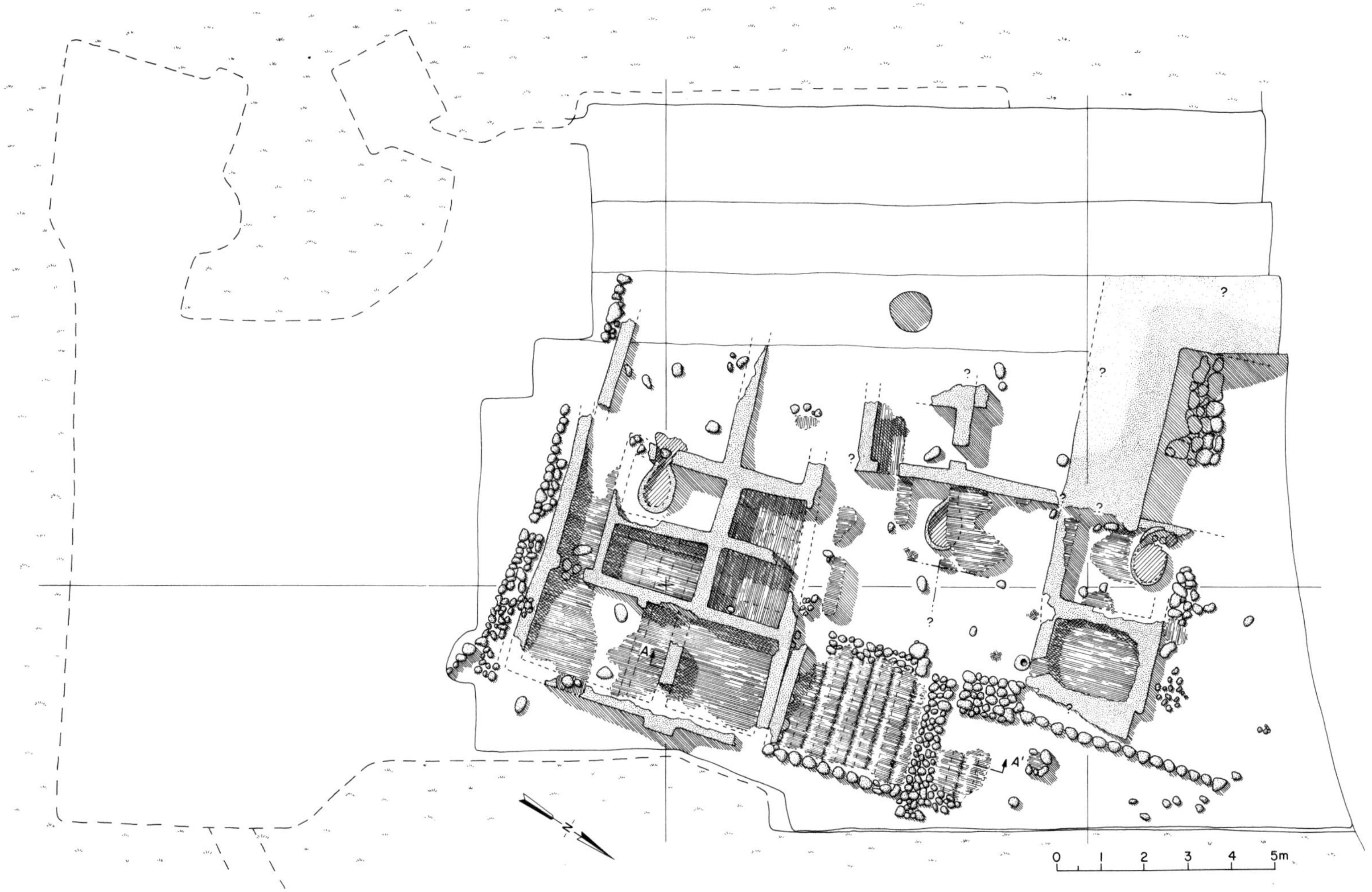

Fig. 51. J-II,5.

Fig. 52. J-II,4.

Fig. 53. Composite plan, J-II.5 and 4. The walls of level 4 are shaded.

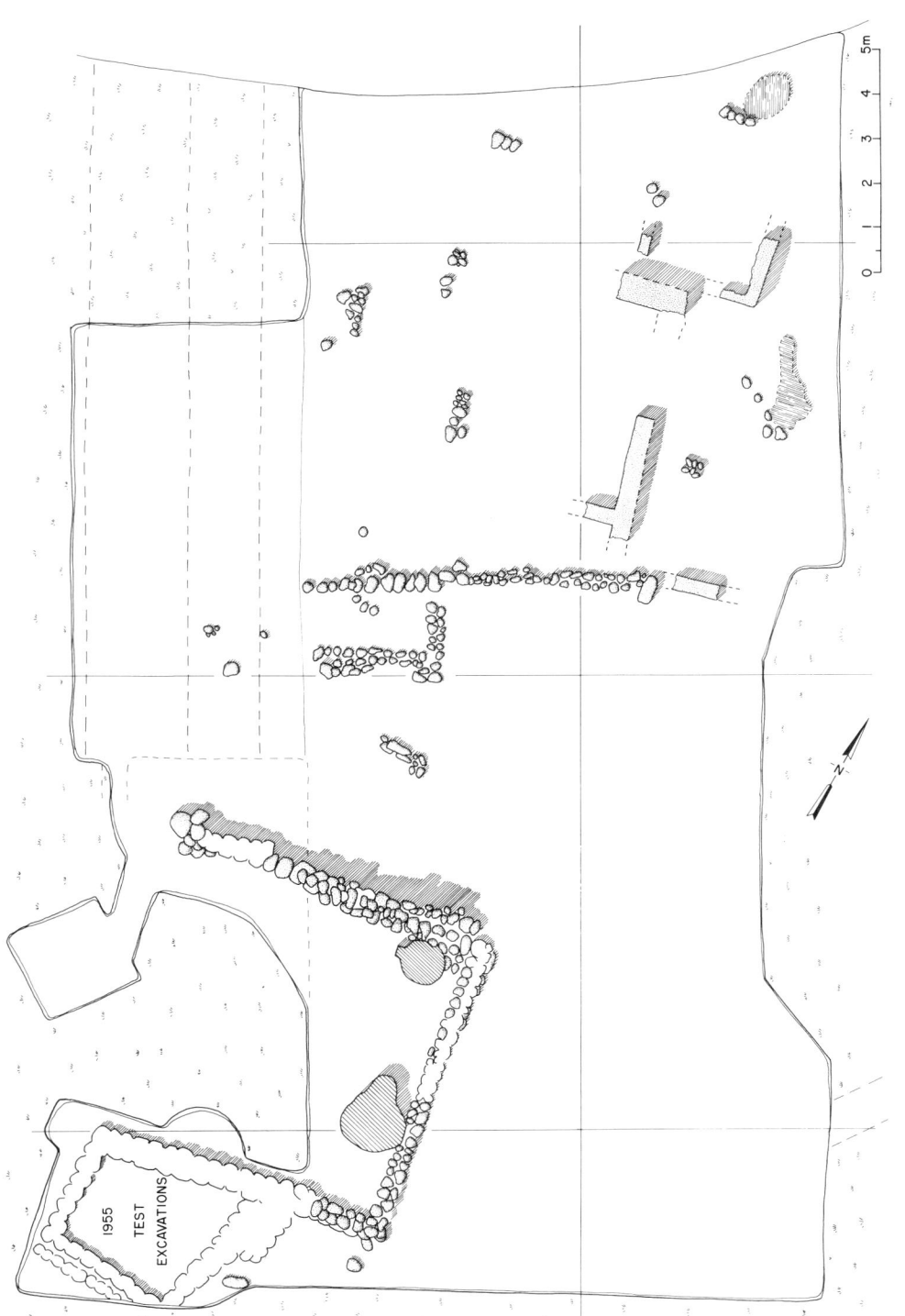

Fig. 54. J-II.3 and the exposures in the L12 and L13 area. See fig. 36.

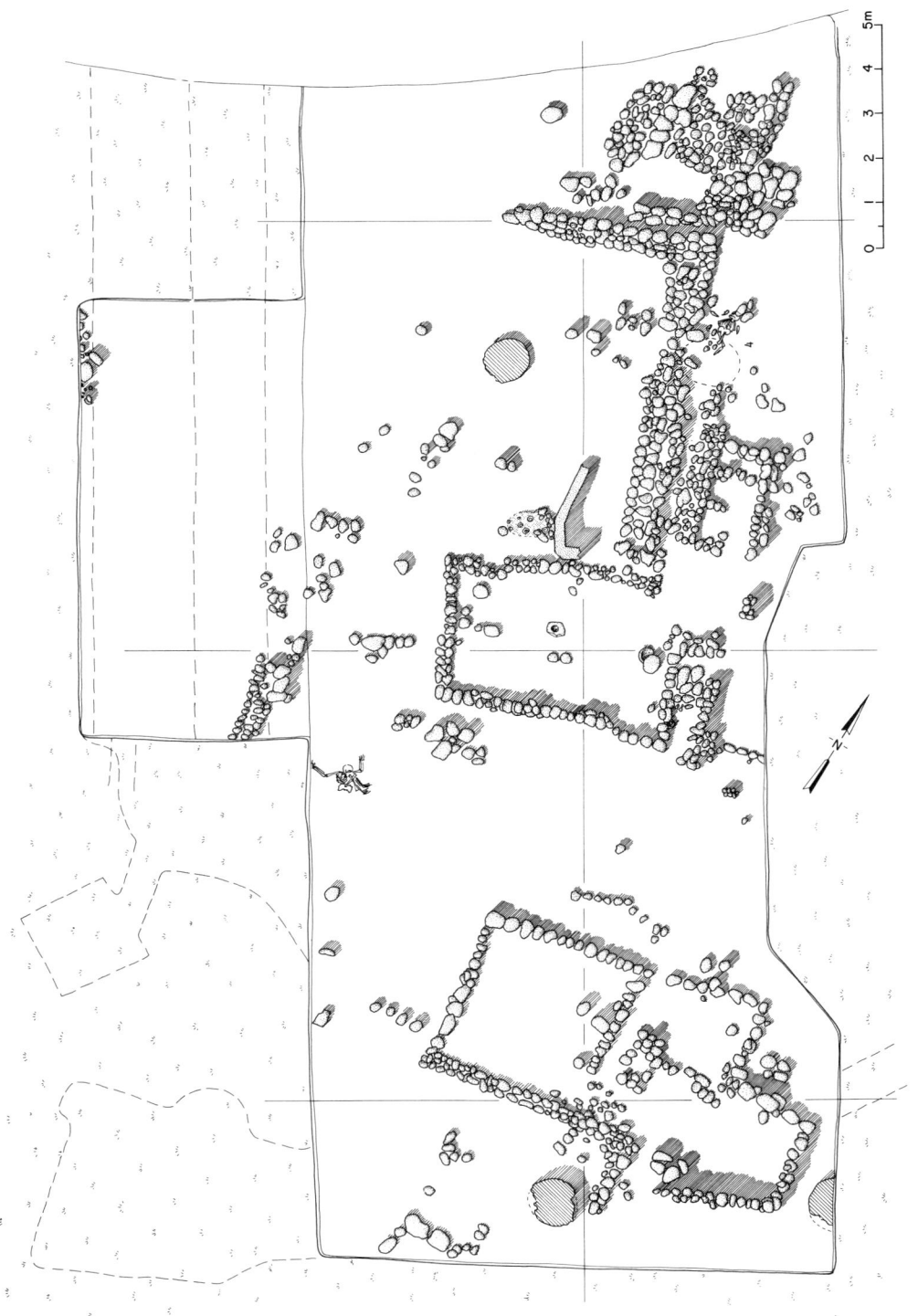

Fig. 55. J-II.2.

Fig. 56. J-II,1.

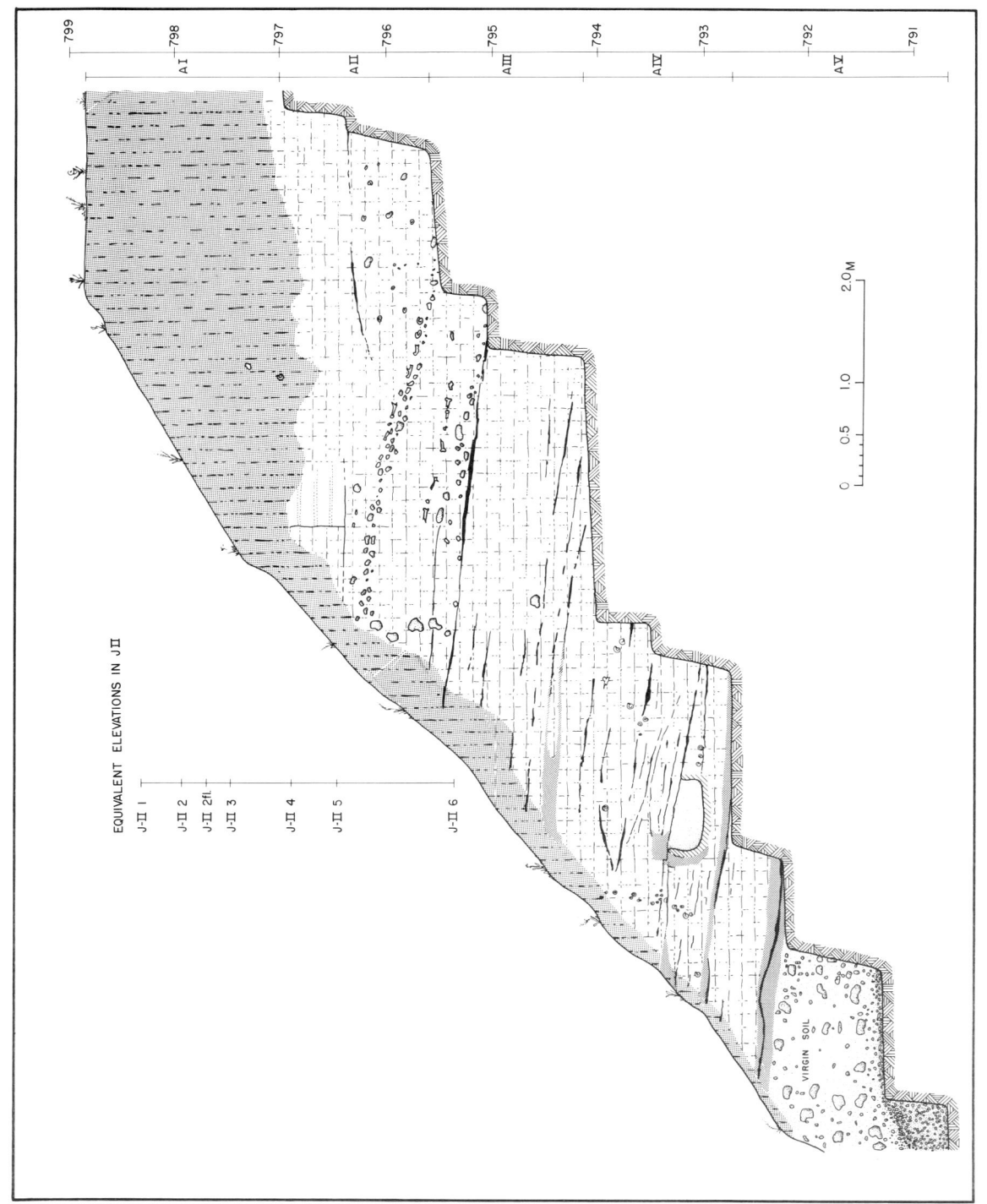

Fig. 57. Section along the east wall of the step trench J-A.

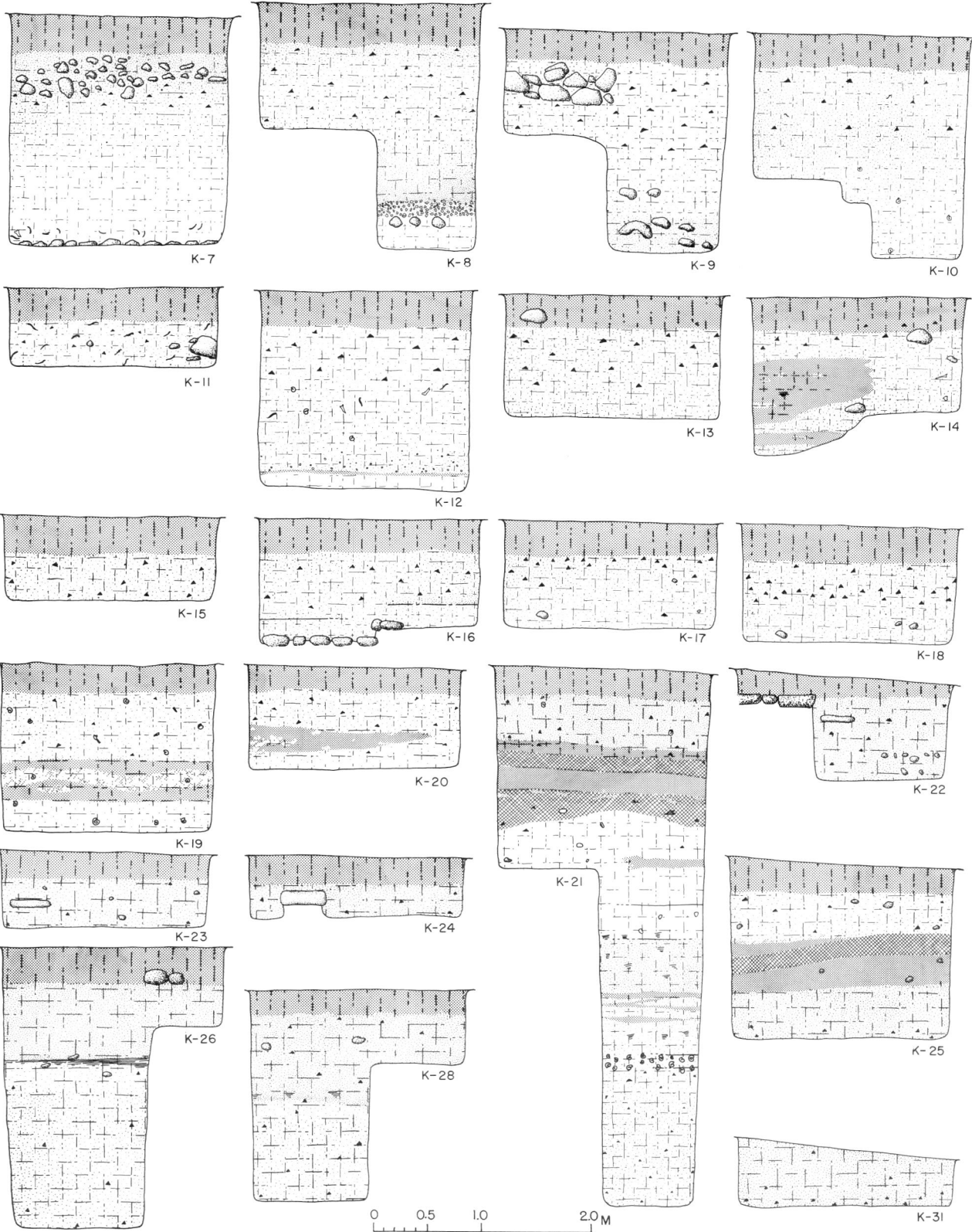

Fig. 58. Sections, looking east, in the succession of test squares along the K line. See fig. 24.

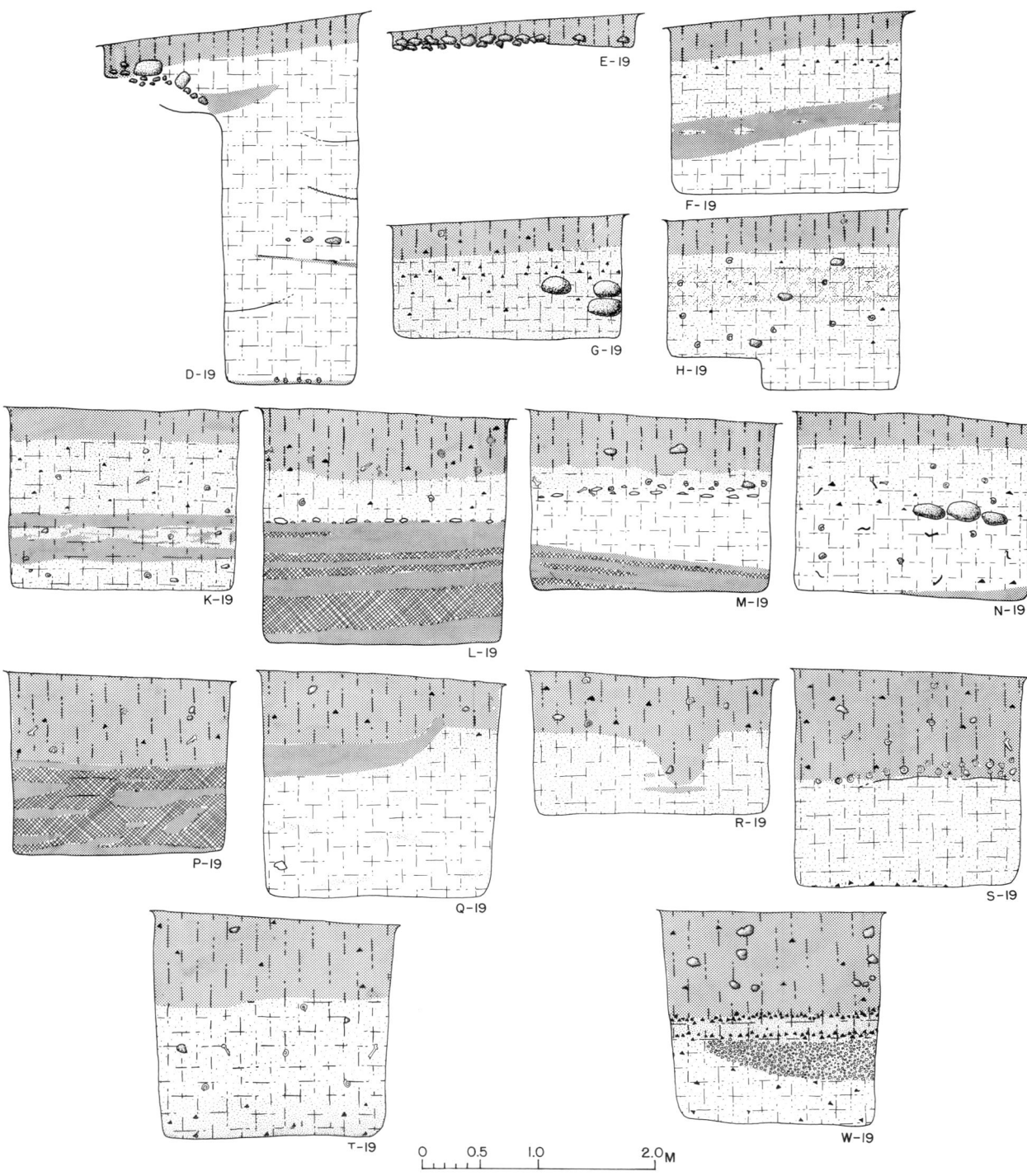

Fig. 59. Sections, looking east, in the succession of test squares along the 19 line. See fig. 24.

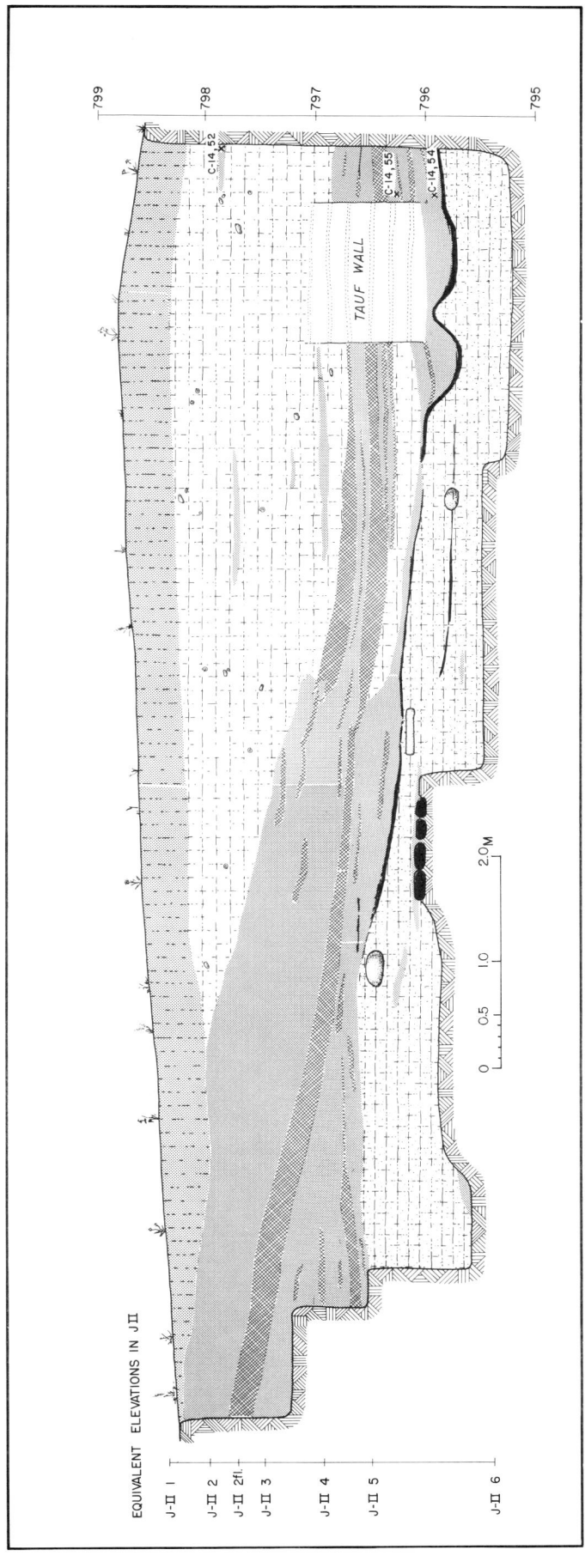

Fig. 60. Section along the southeast wall of the test trench, PQ14. See fig. 24.

Fig. 61. Air view of Jarmo in the spring of 1955, from the north. (Flight courtesy of the Iraq Petroleum Company, Ltd.)

Fig. 62. J-II,1, looking west.

Fig. 63. Southern section of J-II,2 and, on the right, a portion of the architecture of J-II,3. See also figs. 54-55, 81.

Fig. 64. Flagstone paving in H16. See fig. 36.

Fig. 65. Stone foundations and flooring in the HL15 region. See fig. 36.

Fig. 66. Floor of fist-sized limestone cobbles in test square V18.

Fig. 67. Traces of reed-layer floor in J-I,6a.

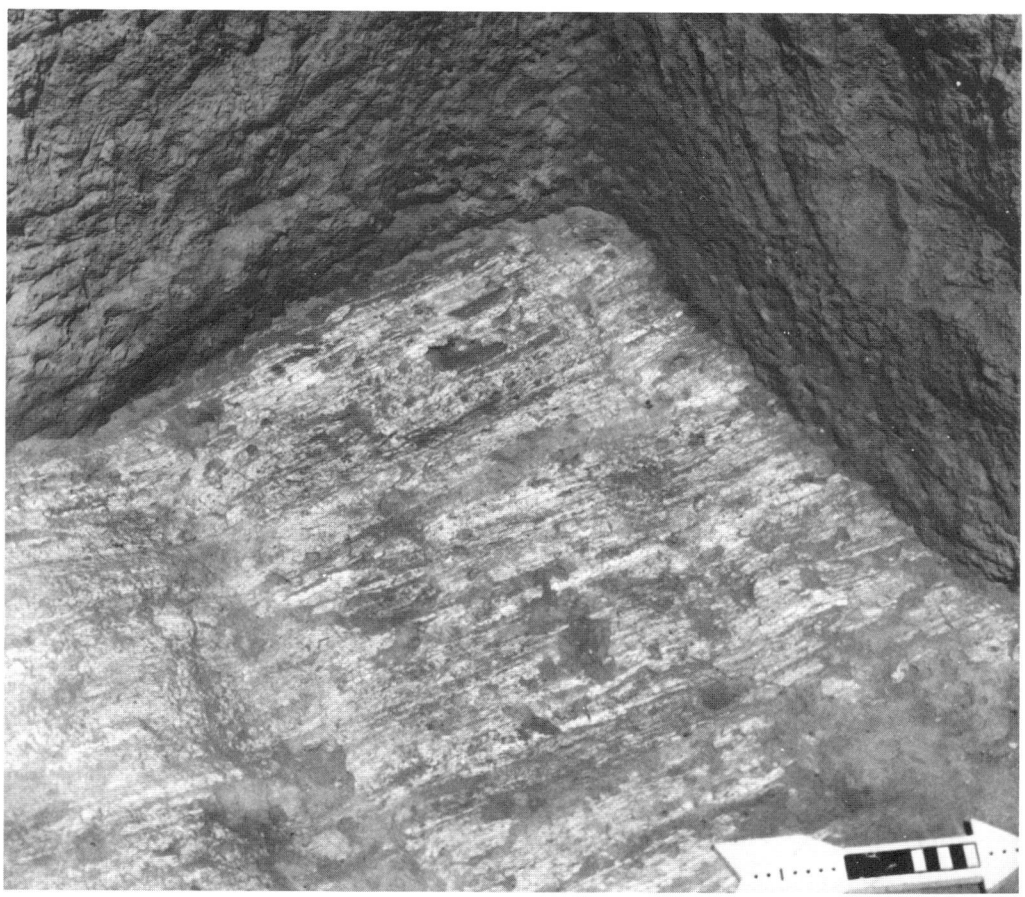

Fig. 68. Traces of reed-layer floor in J-II,5.

Fig. 69. Low gable roofs of houses in the village of Kani Sard, near Jarmo.

Fig. 70. J-II,5 exposure, looking northwest.

Fig. 71. Supposed upper door-pivot made of stone and a limestone ball from J-II,4. See also figs. 138:1; 140:12.

Fig. 72. Ovenlike remains in J-II,6, showing how the chimney was attached to the wall immediately behind the fire door. See also figs. 79-80. Possible window in the back wall and recessed reveal on the right jamb of the door can both be seen on the left.

Fig. 73. Upper door-pivot made of wood used in hinging a courtyard door in a contemporary village near Kermanshah, Iran. (Photograph by Patty Jo Watson.)

Fig. 74. Workman showing how clearing was being done around the "baked-in-place basin" features in J-I,8-9. (Actually the floor debris around the basins had already been removed when this photograph was made.)

Fig. 75. "Baked-in-place basin" in J-I,6b.

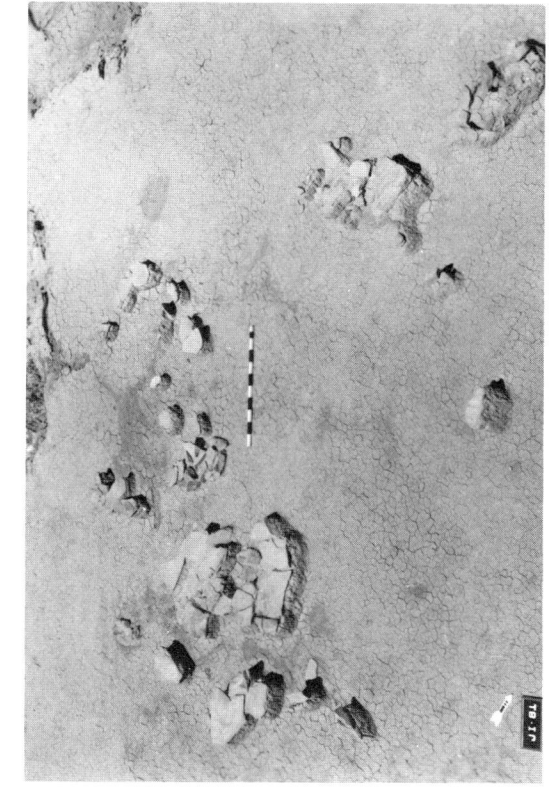

Fig. 76. Another view of the "baked-in-place basin" shown in fig. 75.

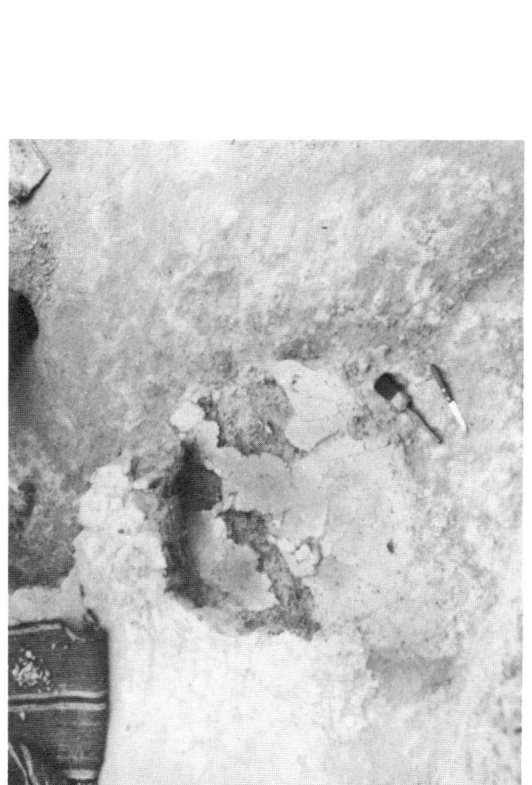

Fig. 77. Flagstone-floored basin in J-I,6b.

Fig. 78. Clusters of flagstone flooring in J-I,8-9.

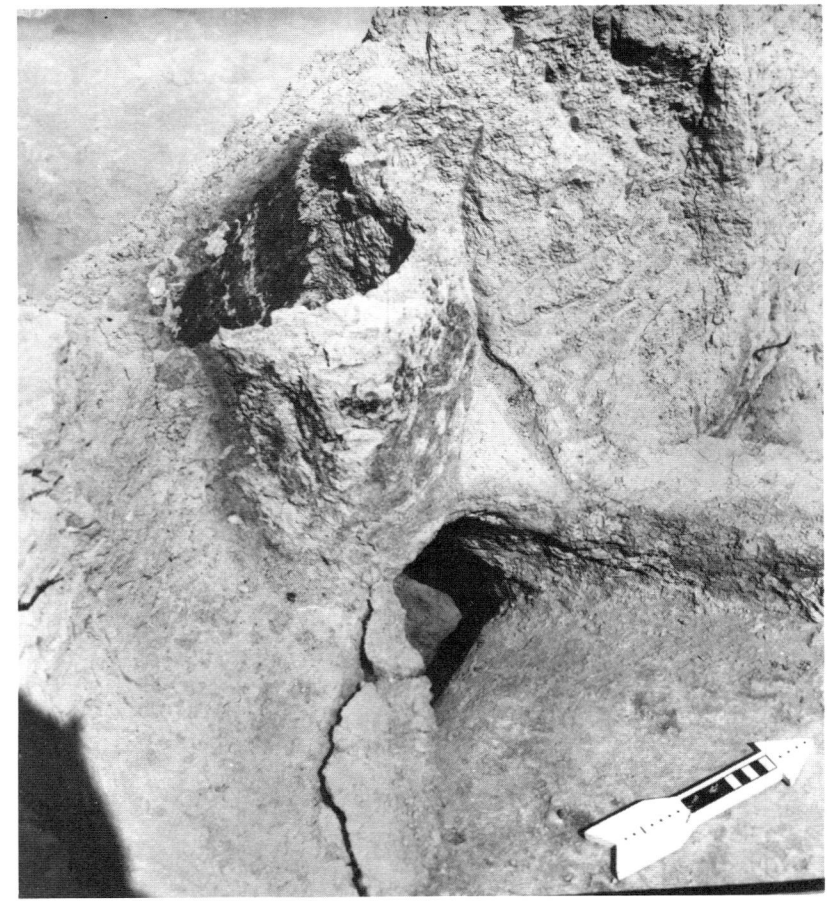

Fig. 79. Chimney remains over the fire door of the ovenlike feature in J-II,6.

Fig. 80. J-II,6, looking north, with the ovenlike feature in the foreground.

Fig. 81. Oven floors to the west of the foundations of J-II,2. On the right are portions of the stone foundations of J-II,3. See also figs. 54-55, 63.

Fig. 82. View showing the succession of renovations of the hardened clay floors of the ovenlike structure in J-I,6b-7. See also figs. 30, 40-41.

Fig. 83. Remains of an ovenlike feature in J-II,5, sectioned to show its floor renovations.

Fig. 84. View of the oven remains in J-II,6. See also figs. 34-35, 72, 79-80.

Fig. 85. An experimental fire made on an oven floor at Jarmo to see whether traces of bitumen might remain. None did.

Fig. 86. Stall-like *tauf* wall remains in J-I,8.

Fig. 87. Site of Jarmo viewed from the wadi bed on the west. J-I is situated at the highest point, on the upper left.

Fig. 88. J-I,7, with the scarp leading down into the wadi visible on the left.

Fig. 89. Four blades of a sickle, with bitumen adhesive remaining, found on the reed-layer floor in J-I,7. See also figs. 32, 40.

Fig. 90. *Tauf* walling of the ovenlike structure in J-I,6b-7. See also fig. 82.

Fig. 91. J-I,6, as it was first exposed in the spring of 1948.

Fig. 92. J-I,1.

Fig. 93. Reed-layer floors in J-II,5, with one of the curious linear cracks easily visible.

Fig. 94. Remains of the reed-layer floors over the grill-plan construction in the central portion of J-II,5. See also figs. 33, 51, 70.

Fig. 95. Reed layer in J-II,5 that presumably overrode the ovenlike feature (or its ruined remains) on the right.

Fig. 96. J-II,4, looking northwest.

Fig. 97. J-II,2 and 3, looking northwest. At this shallow depth, the moisture ghosts of walls (dark traces in upper center) did not prove traceable as *tauf* walls.

Fig. 98. View down into the step trench J-A.

Fig. 99. Foundations in the L13 region tentatively exposed in 1955. See also figs. 36, 54.

Fig. 100. View over the test trench PQ14, looking northeast.

REFERENCES

Braidwood, Robert J., and Braidwood, Linda S.
1960 *Excavations in the plain of Antioch I: the earlier assemblages, phases A-J*. Oriental Institute Publications, vol. 61. Chicago: University of Chicago Press.

Braidwood, Robert J.; Braidwood, Linda S.; Smith, James G.; and Leslie, Charles
1952 Matarrah: a southern variant of the Hassunan assemblage, excavated in 1948. *Journal of Near Eastern Studies* 11:1-75.

Braidwood, Robert J.; Cambel, Halet; Lawrence, Barbara; Redman, Charles L.; and Stewart, Robert B.
1974 Beginnings of village-farming communities in southeastern Turkey—1972. *Proceedings of the National Academy of Sciences of the United States of America* 71:568-72.

Braidwood, Robert J.; Cambel, Halet; Redman, Charles L.; and Watson, Patty Jo.
1971 Beginnings of village-farming communities in southeastern Turkey. Ibid. 68:1236-40.

Braidwood, Robert J.; Howe, Bruce; et al.
1960 *Prehistoric investigations in Iraqi Kurdistan*. Studies in Ancient Oriental Civilization [SAOC], no. 31. Chicago: University of Chicago Press.

Braidwood, Robert J., and Reed, Charles A.
1957 The achievement and early consequences of food-production: a consideration of the archeological and natural-historical evidence. In *Population studies: animal ecology and demography*, pp. 19-31. Cold Spring Harbor Symposia on Quantitative Biology, vol. 22. Cold Spring Harbor, L.I., N.Y.: Long Island Biological Assn.

Cook, Sherburne F.
1972 *Prehistoric demography*. Addison-Wesley Modular Publications, module 16. Reading, Mass.

Harlan, Jack R.
1967 A wild wheat harvest in Turkey. *Archaeology* 20:197-201.

LeBlanc, Steven
1971 An addition to Naroll's suggested floor area and settlement population relationship. *American Antiquity* 36:210-11.

Lloyd, Seton, and Mellaart, James
1962 *Beycesultan*. Vol. 1. Occasional Publications of the British Institute of Archaeology at Ankara, no. 6. London.

Merpert, N.Y., and Munchaev, R.M.
1973 Early agricultural settlements in the Sinjar plain, northern Iraq. *Iraq* 35:93-113.

Mortensen, Peder
1963 Early village-farming occupation. In Excavations at Tepe Guran, Luristan, Jørgen Meldgaard, Peder Mortensen, and Henrik Thrane, pp. 110-21. *Acta Archaeologica* 34:97-133.

Naroll, Raoul
1962 Floor area and settlement population. *American Antiquity* 27:587-89.

SAOC 31
1960 *Prehistoric investigations in Iraqi Kurdistan*. Robert J. Braidwood, Bruce Howe, et al. Studies in Ancient Oriental Civilization, no. 31. Chicago: University of Chicago Press.

Smith, Philip E.L.
1975 Ganj Dareh Tepe. *Iran* 13:178-80.

3

THE JARMO STONE AND POTTERY VESSEL INDUSTRIES
Robert McC. Adams

The brief sounding conducted at Jarmo in 1948 introduced the problem that is dealt with here at length: a hitherto unknown type of pottery appeared in the upper levels of a promising early village site that was preceramic in its lower levels but characterized throughout its occupation by a surprising abundance of stone vessels. During a full season of excavation in 1950-51, the intensive examination of Jarmo was pushed very much further, yielding the bulk of vessel fragments in proper stratigraphic context. But although the internal details of the pottery and stone vessel industries at Jarmo were becoming better known, their external relationships remained largely mysterious. Accordingly, there existed a basis for describing the new finds but not for incorporating them in the existing regional sequence or for reinterpreting the sequence in light of the new material.

Not until the 1954-55 field season were these deficiencies largely remedied. Additional soundings at Tell al-Khan and Gird Ali Agha provided comparative material, which helped to link the floating sequence at Jarmo with the previously accepted cultural and chronological fabric of sedentary village life that followed the transition from food gathering to food production in northern Mesopotamia. At the same time, new exposures at Jarmo and elsewhere provided an opportunity for technological study of the means and resources of the early potter soon after his craft had been introduced.

STONE VESSELS

Although the making of stone vessels was a normal concomitant of early village life throughout the Near East, there was at Jarmo a rare cultural emphasis on this industry that found expression not only in volume but also in quality of output. Many of the wide variety of shapes that are present are esthetically very fine, and the regularity of form, the high polish, and the extreme thinness that were frequently achieved reflect a high degree of craftsmanship.

While separate levels are never strictly comparable when only limited areas are exposed, there is no evidence of any significant change in the popularity of the stone vessel industry during the period of occupation of the site. The vessel fragments were fairly equally distributed through all operations and levels and indicate a continuing high rate of manufacture of stone vessels in spite of the very lengthy time that must have been required to produce each one. In all, 1,323 fragments were found during the 1948 and 1950-51 seasons, probably representing a minimum of 424 bowls. Considering the relatively small proportion of the volume of the mound that was excavated, this implies that a large number of vessels must have been in use simultaneously in every living unit.

Unlike the pottery, the stone vessel fragments did not seem to have any pattern of concentration of findspots, except that they seemed most numerous in and around the house architecture and least numerous in the area of a sherd midden located near the center of the site in the upper levels (chart 3 and p. 215). Nor was any greater concentration of stone vessels apparent in the vicinity of the large houses in level J-II,5 (see pp. 161ff.) than around the smaller houses of J-II,2 and 3, although in the J-II,5 houses the vessels were less fragmentary. Not a single wholly reconstructible vessel was recovered during the entire excavation, although several were nearly complete. Many fragments were pierced by repair holes, and in a few cases bitumen had been used to provide a watertight seal on repaired vessels.

Clearing caliche that adhered to fragments in the uppermost levels was a serious problem. Frequently this deposit was 5 mm or more thick and so hard that it could be removed only by prolonged chipping or grinding. Also, in some cases the vessel fragments had apparently been deformed by earth pressure, but in general the conditions of preservation below the top meter or so were very good.

For the most part, this chapter is a revised version of a paper submitted in partial fulfillment of the requirements for the Master of Arts degree in the Department of Anthropology, University of Chicago, in 1952. That thesis was essentially based on the findings of the second season at Jarmo in 1950-51, although I had an opportunity to utilize catalogues from the first season and to examine specimens collected in 1948 and deposited both in Baghdad and Chicago. My findings were believed to be consistent with those made during the final field season, in the opinion of the excavators who had the thesis available in the field, but my revision of it for publication has been made without access to specimens, notes, or illustrations made in 1954-55.

Rapid developments in the study of early villages over the past two decades have made obsolete an extensive comparative discussion that was included in the original thesis. This section has been eliminated since I have turned to other fields of study and am no longer conversant with the relevant literature.

Materials used include limestone, marble, and, to a lesser degree, sandstone. At all times the artisan seems to have been concerned with selecting materials that would make the finished product pleasing to the eye (fig. 110:2-3). Colorful red and orange mottled limestone or marble was frequently used in the lower levels, and in the upper levels a variety of white marble, parts of which are translucent, became quite common. Also in the upper levels, a banded effect was often achieved through the use of a light-colored marble with parallel streaks of a darker red or gray impurity. Most or all of the material for the vessels probably was obtained locally, principally (in the opinion of H.E. Wright, Jr.) from boulders lying in the wadi or strewn along the foot of the ridge several kilometers to the east.

Several incompletely or roughly finished examples suggest that the inside of each vessel was hollowed out by being ground with the edge of a small stone tool (e.g., a stone drill bit, p. 294), but the horizontally scored lines are in all cases too irregular to imply the use of a wheel. One fragment of an unfinished bowl from J-II,6 was roughly shaped and smoothed on the outside but only partly hollowed out. This suggests that first the outside was brought approximately to its final form by chipping or pecking, next the inside was hollowed out, and finally both surfaces were ground smooth. The outer surface of most vessels was more carefully finished than the inner one, although both surfaces of shallow plates and saucers were sometimes polished. Occasionally the artisan encountered a node of harder rock in the matrix he was working and left it as a slightly raised imperfection on the inside, but on the outside it was always carefully smoothed off.

It was not possible to exercise the same control over the fragments found during the 1948 season as was maintained over those recovered in 1950-51 because only a small selection of the 1948 finds could be retained for study. Most of the material excavated during the initial sounding came from the upper levels of J-I (levels 1-5) and fortunately these are paralleled by finds from J-II—the more extensive area opened on the crest of the mound during the 1950-51 season. While the excavations of the 1954-55 season sampled a wider area than had been investigated previously, they were relatively shallow for the most part and hence are also paralleled in the upper levels of J-II.

VARIETIES OF STONE VESSELS

In the field, stone vessel forms were classified into fifteen provisional types, lettered from A to O. With minor modifications, that classification is retained here for descriptive purposes, although in general each vessel is less a representative of some standardized type than a unique expression of the originality of its maker. This quality of individuality is not easily described, but it is perhaps the dominant characteristic of the industry as a whole. In the following listing the subjectively "most typical" illustrated example is the first given for each type.

Flat-bottomed Bowls with Flaring Sides

Type A (figs. 101:1-3; 110:6), generally, is a large and well-made bowl characterized by a curling or bead lip and frequently ground to extreme thinness. Occasionally the profile from base to junction with lip is almost straight (e.g., figs. 101:3; 110:7), but more often the side is gently flared and rounded. All examples of type A are circular in plan.

Type H (fig. 103:12) is a very small flowerpot-shaped cup or bowl with straight, flaring sides and a tapering rim. It is circular in plan.

Type L (fig. 102:9) is a poorly worked, thick-walled, noncircular vessel, with neither inner nor outer surface fully ground or polished. One example was found in association with a flat sandstone "lid."

Flat- or Round-bottomed Cups or Bowls with Rounded, More Vertical Sides

Type BC (figs. 101:4-5; 102:1-2,8,10-11; 103:1-4,6-7; 110:2-4), the most popular type, contains considerable variation. Some vessels are nearly hemispherical or subhemispherical (e.g., figs. 102:11; 103:4), but more frequently (as seen in section) there is greater curvature near the junction of bottom and side than elsewhere. Nevertheless, while the center of the bottom may be flat, the bottom and side always round into one another, so that, unlike the previous types, no clear line of demarcation between the two can be drawn. In addition, the sides flare out less and are more nearly vertical than in the previous category; some are even constricted at the lip into an unmistakably holemouth form (e.g., fig. 103:6). There is wide variation in size and thickness, but most are smaller than the bowls with flaring sides. A small minority are oval or rounded-rectangular in plan (fig. 102:8). Originally an attempt was made to divide type BC on the basis of differences in rim treatment, but there proved to be a continuous gradation from flattened through rounded to edged rims, often on a single vessel, and so any separation of type here would be artificial. In a few cases, a single shallow horizontal groove was incised on the outside of the vessel below the rim (e.g., fig. 102:1).

Type D (figs. 102:3-5; 103:5) is similar in every respect to type BC except for rim treatment. Characteristically, the rims are set off from the side either by a slight constriction, or by an outward curl, or by both (e.g., fig. 103:5). The rim is thus given the appearance of a tubular "bead," which is perhaps more resistant to breakage. All known examples are circular in plan.

Plates or Saucers with Circular Plan

Type F (figs. 103:10; 110:5) is a slightly carinated saucer with a flattened rim.

Type G (figs. 103:11,17; 110:1) is a small, smoothly rounded, rather deep saucer. The rim tapers almost to an edge, but, in the absence of a side, there is no other discontinuity in the smoothly rounded profile.

Type I (fig. 103:13) is a very small, shallow dish or saucer with a rounded bottom, flattened rim, and rudimentary vertical sides.

Type K (fig. 103:16) is a shallow dish similar to type G, except that the rim is rounded rather than tapered to an edge.

Type O (fig. 102:6) is a small, flat-bottomed dish with low, vertical sides and a flattened rim.

Carinated Bowls with Rounded Bottoms, Low Vertical Sides, and Circular Plan

Type E (figs. 103:14; 110:8) is a more or less sharply carinated, low bowl of small to medium size with a variety of rim treatments. Most frequently the profile at both shoulder and rim is crisp and sharp, and the latter is usually flattened. Since the side above the carination is roughly vertical, rim and shoulder diameters are about the same.

Type M (fig. 103:8) is a shallow bowl with a tapered, rounded rim. The full profile is not known.

Type N (fig. 103:9) is a large, thick-walled vessel with a flattened rim and only a slight shoulder.

CHANGES IN THE STONE VESSEL INDUSTRY

The total yield of stone vessel fragments from J-A, the step trench, was not sufficient to demonstrate any trends in the industry, and in J-I, on the edge of the mound, the lesser depth of deposit suggests that at best only an attenuated expression of the entire cultural sequence is available. Furthermore, although there is more material from the upper five levels of J-I than from the corresponding stages in the step trench, the J-I,1-5 levels were poorly manifested architecturally and stratigraphically imprecise.

A picture of strictly continuous quantitative changes in the stone vessel industry throughout the occupation of the site cannot be drawn from areas thus far exposed. Nevertheless, significant changes are discernible in size, form, and technique of manufacture, and thus possibly use, between the vessels in two successive sets of levels. The relevant bulks of material come from J-I,6-8 on the one hand and from J-II,1-6 on the other. Each of these groupings is distinct and

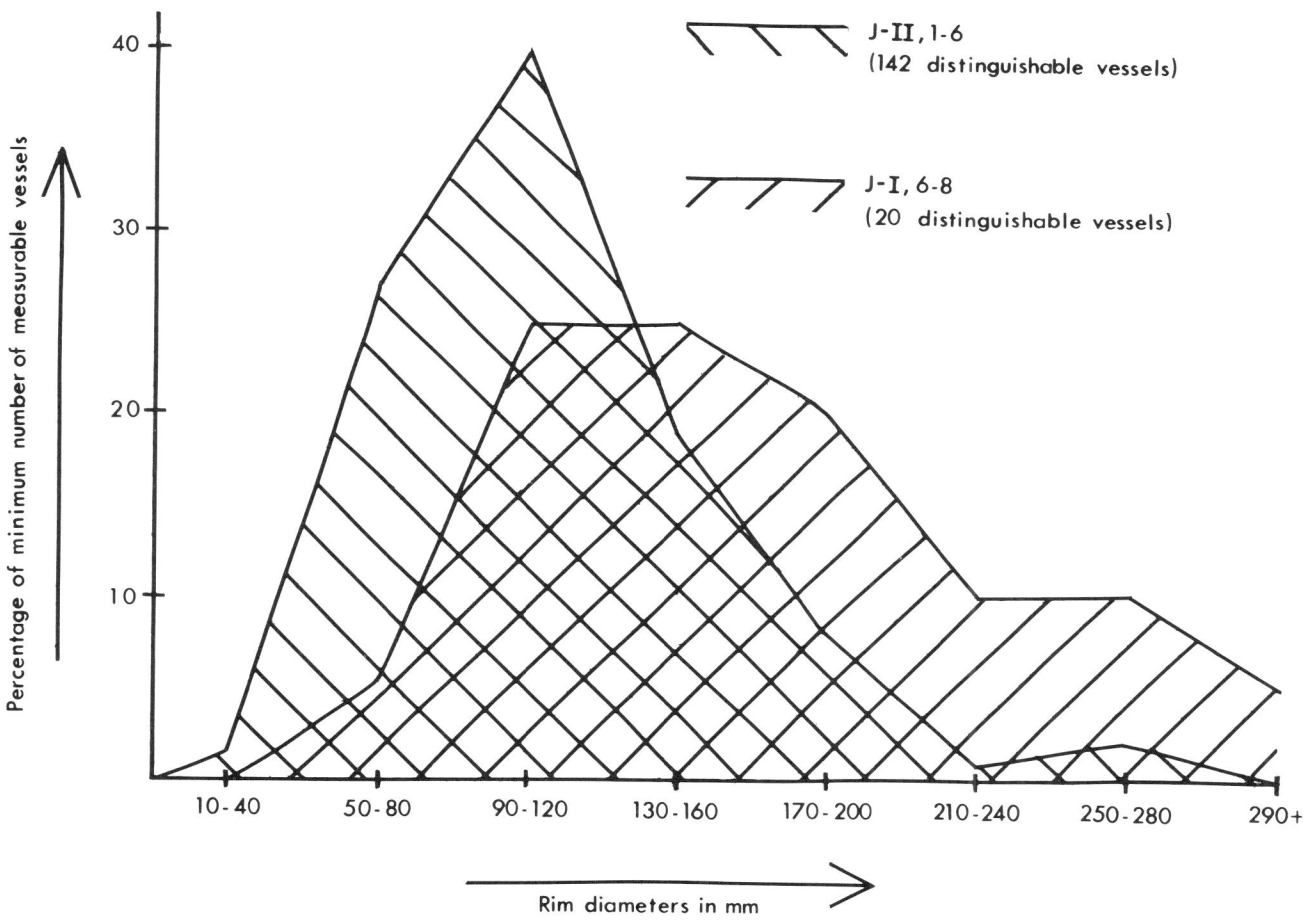

Chart 1. Distribution of rim diameters of Jarmo stone vessels in lower and upper levels (based on the 1950-51 season's yield).

Table 1.—Size of Rim Diameters of Jarmo Stone Vessels in Lower and Upper Levels
(Based on the 1950-51 Season's Yield)

Size (mm)	J-II,1 MNV	J-II,1 Ht	J-II,2 MNV	J-II,2 Ht	J-II,2fl. MNV	J-II,2fl. Ht	J-II,3 MNV	J-II,3 Ht	J-II,4 MNV	J-II,4 Ht	J-II,5 MNV	J-II,5 Ht	J-II,6 MNV	J-II,6 Ht	J-I,6 MNV	J-I,6 Ht	J-I,7 MNV	J-I,7 Ht	J-I,8 MNV	J-I,8 Ht
40 or less	--		--		--		--		--		2	24	--		--		--		--	
50	--		2	10	1	25	--		--		--		--		--		--		1	
60	3	27, 13	--		2	19, 14	1		--		--		--		--		--		--	
70	1		3	20	1	32	2	40, 15	--		2	35	1		--		--		--	
80	7	37, 32, 30, 24	1		4	75	1	37	2	38, 22	2		3		--		--		--	
90	2	32	2		1		--		3		--		1		--		--		--	
100	5	38, 18	4	26	--		2		3	60, 44	3	95, 74	3		--		--		1	
110	5	21	--		5	97, 20	1		4	42	2	67	2		--		--		--	
120	2	20	2	32	2		--		--		2		1		--		--		4	
130	--		2		1	75	--		--		2	100, 21	1		--		--		--	
140	4	135, 25	3	25	--		1	58	1		2	70	--		2	60	--		--	
150	--		2	43, 28	--		--		--		1		--		1	56	1		1	82
160	5	61	1		--		--		--		1		--		--		--		--	
170	2		--		1		--		--		--		1		--		--		--	
180	2		--		--		1		--		1		1		--		--		--	
190	--		1		--		--		--		--		--		--		--		--	
200	1		1		--		--		--		--		--		2		1		1	
220	1	60	--		--		--		--		--		--		--		1	71	1	
240	1		--		--		--		--		--		--		--		--		--	
260	2		--		--		--		--		--		--		--		--		1	
280	--		--		1	140	--		--		--		--		--		1		--	
290 or more	--		--		--		--		--		--		--		1		--		--	
Not round	1		--		1	41	--		1		5	63, 50	2	128	--		--		--	

NOTE: MNV = minimum number of vessels; Ht = height of vessel, when known.

quite homogeneous, and, on the limited evidence available, the material from J-II is consistent with that from the upper levels generally, while the material from the lower levels of J-I is consistent with that from the lowermost levels in the step trench.[1] Hence, it seems safe to conclude that the two groups of levels represent an early and a late subphase in the occupation of the mound. Although they are almost certainly separated by a transitional period—of unknown duration and inadequately explored—it is possible to deduce summary information from these two subphases about changes in the stone vessel industry from the beginning to the end of the occupation period.

Probably the most significant change is seen in vessel size (table 1 and chart 1). There appears to have been a decline in the popularity of large stone vessels as the occupation progressed. In the lower levels, 70% of the minimum number of vessels surviving in fragments large enough to be measured had a rim diameter in excess of 130 mm, and the large number of fragments that could not be measured exactly corroborated this assessment of size. In the upper levels, however, 69% of the minimum number of measurable vessel fragments had a diameter of less than 130 mm. The data about average vessel height in the upper levels are less adequate but do suggest that there was a corresponding reduction in this dimension as well (table 1).

It should be borne in mind that 120 mm is about the largest diameter that a vessel can have and still be comfortably grasped with one hand. Thus, on the basis of size distribution we can postulate that a whole new class of small and relatively shallow bowls and saucers came into existence during the later periods at Jarmo.

During the period of occupation, there was also a definite change in the degree of popularity of various forms of stone vessels. Decreasing rim diameter is reflected in the shift away from type A, with its flat base and flaring sides, toward type BC, relatively more rounded and vertical sided; the latter type is clearly easier to hold in the hand. The extent of the change is illustrated in chart 2.

Chart 2 records another, less well-documented development—the proliferation of previously unknown forms in the upper levels (types F through O). These occur only in small numbers, however, and types A through E remain the most popular; hence it seems possible that the greater variety recorded for the upper levels is partly a function of the larger area excavated.[2] Nevertheless, many of the new forms are shallow cups, plates, or saucers, and their appearance may thus be related to the above-mentioned trend in this direction even among the more popular types. It should also be observed that noncircular vessels (viz., oval or rounded-rectangular) appear only in the upper levels (see table 1, last row). These developments all suggest that the later phase of the occupation was a period of experimentation with form.

A number of important changes also occur in the materials used and in the quality of workmanship. In the first place, sandstone came into use in the upper levels, along with a softer variety of limestone, whereas marble was used almost exclusively in the lower levels. In the second place, although the best examples from J-II are as good as any from the earlier J-I levels, the quality of workmanship generally deteriorated. For example, the surfaces are not so often finely polished, the thickness of a part of a vessel can vary markedly, the average thickness is considerably greater,[3] and occasional irregularities of form are apparent. All these changes perhaps can be related to and explained by an assumed relaxed standard of craftsmanship. The sandstone and softer limestone, while less satisfactory in the finished product, would have been easier to work. The variations in thickness, the greater average thickness, the irregularities of form, and the omission of final polishing would also be the result of greater haste or carelessness.

POTTERY VESSELS

Pottery appeared at Jarmo only late in the site's occupation.[4] Sherds begin appearing at first in very small numbers, but they show a competence of technique that indicates that knowledge of the manufacture of pottery was already well advanced. In the uppermost levels the number of vessels in use expanded rapidly, but there is evidence of some discontinuity in the methods of preparation, and the later pottery is much less frequently decorated and in general more crudely made.

The provenience of the pottery recovered during the first two seasons is given in table 2. It will be noted that the overwhelming majority of the sherds came from small localized concentrations on the crest of the mound (fig. 24 and

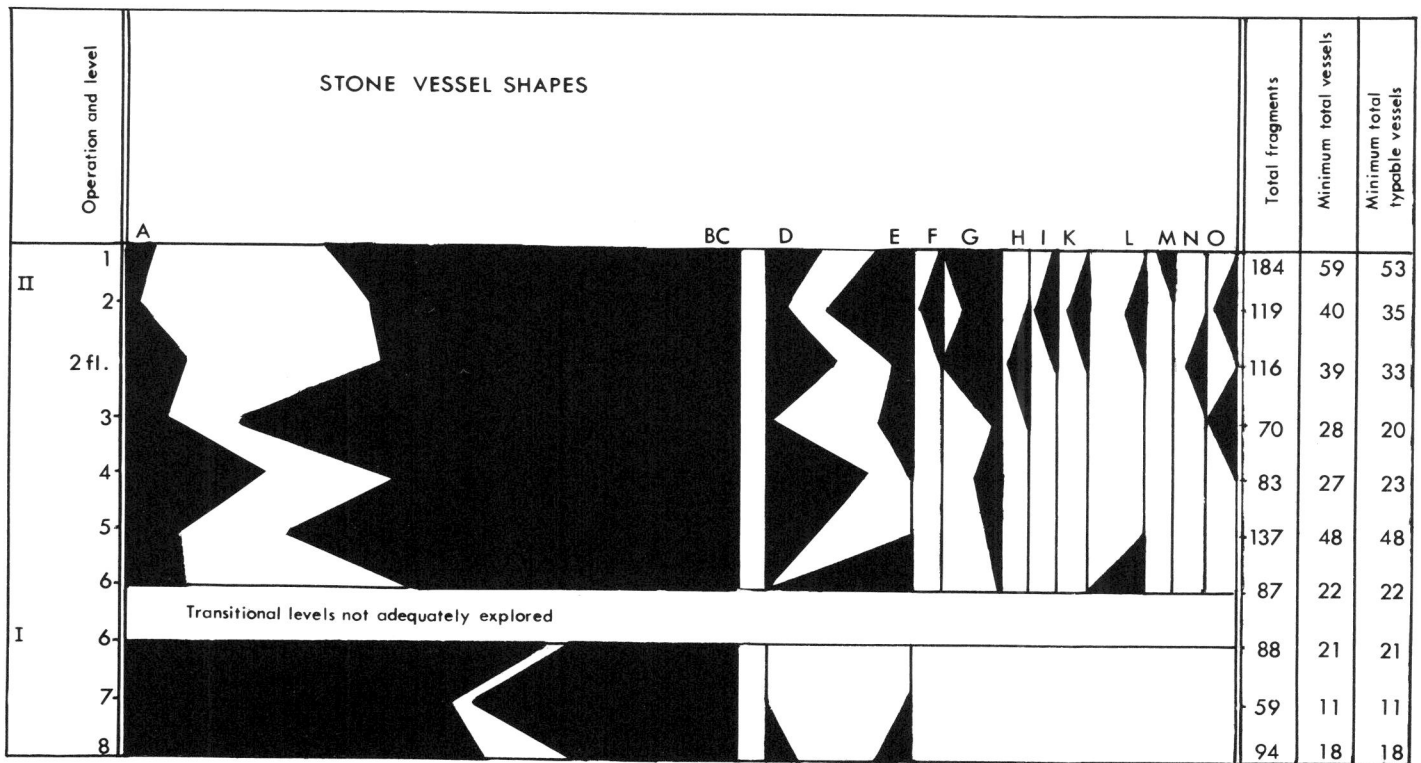

Chart 2. Distribution of Jarmo stone vessel shapes in lower and upper levels.

Table 2.—Jarmo Pottery: Proveniences and Sherd Counts (Seasons 1948 and 1950-51)

Levels within the operations[a]	Operations							Step trench (operation A)	
	I	II (a-h)[b]	II (l-n)[c]	III	B	C	D	Steps	
Surface	47	1,496	4,195	1	×	×	×	I	260
Surface-1				13					
1	10			1				II[d]	2
2		933	4,016						
2fl.	22	191	1,013					III	3[e]
3		71	25						
4	0	68							
5	0	65		Not excavated				IV	0
6	0	0							
7	0							V	0
8	0								

NOTE: × = small number.

[a] No attempt is made here to express chronological equivalences from one operation to another—e.g., it is most unlikely that level 3 in operation II was occupied at the same moment as was level 3 in operation I.

[b] Main operation, see chart 3.

[c] Extension into midden, see chart 3.

[d] This step and a part of the preceding one were dug very rapidly, in order to obtain a full profile of the mound, as our 1950-51 season's budget dwindled. In this process some sherds were undoubtedly lost. The two sherds listed were found near the mound edge, at an absolute elevation equivalent to that of J-II,5-6.

[e] These sherds came from the uppermost floor in this step, at about the same absolute elevation as J-II,6. They were less than 1.5 m from the edge of the mound but did not appear to be intrusive.

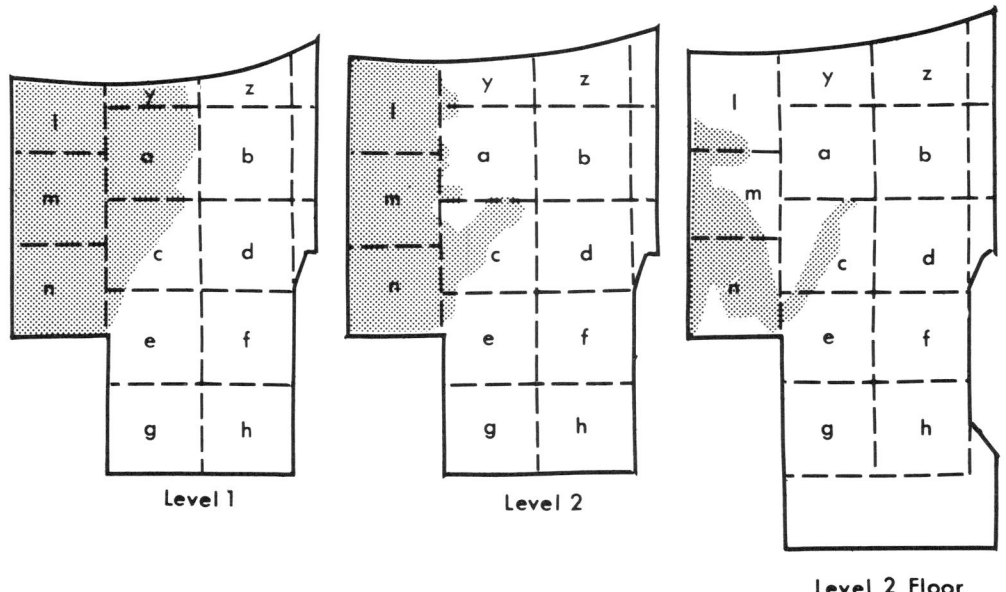

Chart 3. Potsherd "midden" in upper levels of operation II at Jarmo. Scale 1:400.

chart 3), as exemplified by J-II. Below the floor of level 2 in this operation, pottery was scattered fairly uniformly in and around the house architecture, as the stone vessels were; but in higher levels, although the sherds were far more numerous, they were confined almost exclusively to a relatively small part of the area excavated. This area of accumulation apparently had its center to the west of J-II and remained in use until the site was no longer occupied.

Identification of this area as a midden (chart 3) is, of course, tentative, but we are able to offer no more reasonable suggestion about its use. Within the so-called midden area pottery was very thickly scattered, but all other types of artifacts were quite rare. There was little or no recognizable house architecture (figs. 49, 55-56), nor was there evidence that pottery had been manufactured in this portion of the site, since ovens or kilns and fire pits were also completely absent. Furthermore, it was possible to completely restore only a single vessel (fig. 108:6) in spite of continuous efforts to match sherds from contiguous areas; hence, we believe that this was not primarily an area in which pottery vessels were used but rather a place to which they were carried after being broken elsewhere.

Like the stone vessel fragments, most of the pottery sherds were thickly coated with caliche in the uppermost levels. However, the encrustation generally could be easily removed while the sherds were still damp from the soil, and there is no evidence that its formation contributed to the widespread decomposition of surfaces characteristic of the later sherds. Surface deterioration apparently is to be attributed entirely to the low quality of the techniques and materials in use at the time of manufacture.

FABRIC AND SURFACE TREATMENT

Jarmo pottery can be grouped into two more or less distinct manifestations, primarily on the basis of changes in paste and decoration. As we have seen, the earlier manifestation is characterized by a much smaller volume of pottery and (in J-II) falls mainly within levels 3-5 inclusive. The later manifestation falls within the uppermost three levels, but we must stress that there is a considerable overlapping, mainly in J-II,3 and J-II,2fl., and thus no clear-cut stratigraphic distinction can be drawn.

We hesitate to call these manifestations separate wares because clear-cut distinctions in materials and methods of preparation are also difficult to draw; there is, in other words, evidence of continuity of tradition as well as evidence of difference. The fabric in both manifestations may be described as handmade, plant tempered, buff to orange buff in color, and frequently shows a darkened, unoxidized core on the break. Significant differences between the two may be more properly summarized after each has been described in detail.

Earlier Manifestation

Matson has summarized the results of his study of the pottery from J-II,3-5 as follows:

> The clay is very fine textured. Fresh breaks made with pliers show a relatively smooth fracture in some cases and a more mealy one in others. I am not convinced that this is a real distinction as sherds grade from one to the other.
>
> Both groups are tempered with a fine chaff that is up to 5 mm in length and about 1 mm in width, and the chaff shows fine longitudinal ridges. Some sherds show holes about 0.4 mm in diameter; some of these holes are completely round, while others are lunate or hemispherical. On fresh breaks of some sherds ash remains and carbonized material showed that these round holes were caused by seeds, ovoid in shape, 0.8 mm in length, 0.3-0.4 mm in width near the base, and tapering to a point. These looked like grass seeds and it is probable that the tempering material was grass, some of which had gone to seed so the heads of seed are concentrated in certain areas of the pottery. The term "grass" is a suggestion without necessarily botanical connotations; it is at least a bladed and ridged narrow leaf with a seed pod of the shape described.
>
> The sherds were sorted in terms of the abundance of chaff into two groups. The first, comprising 35 sherds, varied from almost no chaff to a moderate amount which was by no means dominant. The other group, numbering 44 sherds, contained more chaff; in some cases it was so closely packed that one wondered if the clay would really be workable and shapeable. In fact, in the heavily tempered group the surfaces were strongly marked with chaff. There do not seem to be any clear-cut differences between these two groups, but in general there was a tendency for the thinner-walled sherds (6-8 mm in thickness) to have less chaff than the thicker sherds. There are exceptions.
>
> The only diagnostic mineralogical characteristic of the clay was the presence of a small amount of mica—mostly muscovite but also a little biotite. The flakes were about 0.1-0.2 mm in diameter and could best be seen on the flat surfaces; in edge fractures the thin flakes would usually be seen on edge, since they tend to align themselves parallel to the worked faces of the vessels. An occasional lump of limestone or quartz occurred, but these were very sparse. This was apparently a natural clay deposit from the quiet reaches of back waters where only the fine clay remained in suspension and gradually settled out as the water sank in the field.
>
> Four sherds showed a considerable amount of very fine limestone well distributed through the clay. Although made from a different clay, they had the same general type of chaff temper as the others, and, according to Adams, are not distinguishable from the main group in terms of shape, color, or decoration. This group includes the one scratched and red-painted sherd examined [fig. 105:4]. A different clay was also represented by four sherds with burnished surfaces that tended to be more dark gray to gray brown in surface color. These sherds contained a few rounded pebbles of various types that were apparently included in the original clay. But Adams would isolate only one of these sherds in terms of color of painted decoration, and the clay difference may not be significant. Deposits can easily vary with depth or in different parts of the area mined due to water action (velocity of stream and amount of mud in it) at the time the clay was deposited.

The surface of most of the sherds from J-II,3-5 had some degree of burnish except for the thickest ones (12 mm and over); these could well have been basal pieces. The others were to a large extent rim sherds, and the burnishing marks were easily seen under the microscope. There had been surface scraping following the forming of the vessels, but later the surfaces appeared to have been rubbed when they were in a leather-hard condition or a little drier. In the latter case it would have been necessary to moisten the surface. The type of polishing tool could not be ascertained.

On some sherds there was definitely a slip, but on others of the burnished group the presence of a slip could not be definitely ascertained without the preparation of thin sections for microscopic study. The so-called self-slip is not impossible in some cases. In some cases the slip showed crazing, which suggests that it had had a higher degree of firing shrinkage than the body of the sherd because of its finer texture.

In color, the main trend was toward a very pale brown to pink shade in the oxidized areas. The burnished surfaces had a pale brown cast. Occasionally sherds were more pale yellow in color, probably because they were from areas in the kiln where reducing atmospheric conditions had existed and the iron in the clay did not have a chance to oxidize to the reddish ferric state. The color of the sherds gave evidence that they came from kilns (probably simple hearths) that had a reasonable degree of temperature control, since only in a very few cases was there any mottling. It is surprising how well oxidized such early pottery was. This indicates well-established firing techniques that perhaps preceded pottery making. There is no particular suggestion of open firing, such as is used in the southwestern United States today, although such a technique can result in quite uniformly fired pottery when skillfully used.

In summary, one type of clay seems to have been used. "Grass" chaff and seeds were used for temper in variable amounts. Many surfaces were burnished, and some have been slipped. Red-painted decoration appears with and without the burnish or slip. The coarser sherds tend to be unburnished but of the same fabric. This would seem to be a normal series from one pottery-making center. The degree of firing does not show much variation. The sample is too small to make far-reaching conclusions or deductions, but the paucity of sherds is in itself a significant factor.

In some respects, this description can be supplemented with quantitative data based on the entire sherd collection from J-II. It should be remembered, however, that although this operation was by far the largest excavated single area, the levels pertinent to the above description (3-5) yielded a total of only 204 sherds, probably representing no more than 35 vessels. Because of this small number, it would be meaningless to discuss the pottery from each level separately. Aside from the admixture of sherds more typical of the upper levels that becomes important in level 3, no significant differences were noted when such a separation was attempted.

Both paste and surface colors of the early pottery in J-II,3-5 range from orange buff to buff or gray buff, with a very rare somewhat redder sherd that might be classified as orange. Normally there is only minor variation in color from one part of the vessel to another and no significant difference between base and rim surface color. Eighty-five percent of all sherds from this manifestation have a surface color that is the same inside as outside, and the slight majority of the remainder whose outside surfaces appear redder probably is not significant. As Matson has indicated, this pottery must have been quite uniformly fired.

A study of core-darkening in these levels discloses that the amount of underfiring is roughly proportional to thickness. While 71% of the sherds that have more than half of their core areas darkened because of incomplete oxidation are over 10 mm thick, only 6% of those sherds that are not darkened at all are over 10 mm thick. But it should be pointed out that the correspondence is not complete; some quite thick sherds show no underfired cores, whereas some very thin ones do. Underfired cores appear in bases and rims about equally, reflecting their approximate uniformity in thickness and suggesting that heat and draft must have been quite uniformly applied in the kiln.

Pottery of J-II,3 and below is generally too hard and well compacted to be scratched with the fingernail and would be rated about 2.5 on the MOHS scale. Its friability is variable, depending mainly upon the amount of plant temper, but on the whole it is markedly less friable than the pottery encountered in later levels.

There is a variety of surface treatments on the earlier pottery vessels. Perhaps most important is burnishing, which had been applied to 135 sherds out of 204 from these levels. Fifty of the 69 unburnished sherds came from level 3; this high proportion reflects at least in part the fact that some of the pottery was more typical of later levels. Burnish seems to have been applied with fine strokes all over the outer surface of the vessel except for the bottom. Since burnish is most useful in reducing porosity when applied to the inside of a vessel, it is surprising to find that inside surfaces appear to be unburnished or very poorly burnished; perhaps traces of such treatment have more frequently worn away from the inside surfaces through use. On 6 sherds, all but one of them burnished, red slip was recognized in the field. However, the distinction between a thin slip and a wet-smoothed, burnished surface is sometimes difficult to make, and this identification cannot be regarded as certain for all of them. In any case, the slip, like the paint, was probably an aqueous suspension of ochre; a somewhat browner variant was used occasionally (e.g., fig. 105:10).

Sixty-five sherds, all but two of them in J-II,4 and 5, show traces of paint (fig. 111:1-5). It is evident that almost all were burnished afterward, since the burnish strokes go over the paint. In some cases (e.g., fig. 105:9) the vessel seems to have been burnished before the paint was completely dry, for the lines have been blurred by the burnishing. On several sherds (e.g., figs. 105:5,8; 111:2) thin, light scratches run underneath the painted lines. This feature was probably caused by two procedures: (1) a twig or some other relatively hard and inflexible object must have been used as a paint dauber and (2) the paint was sometimes applied while the clay was still wet enough to be easily scratched. Appearing also on one virtually complete vessel (fig. 105:12), which now, at least, shows no trace of paint, are similar scratches whose purpose is not clear; they seem too light to have been intended for decoration.

Painted patterns generally are simple and linear. Some appear to have been quite competently drawn (e.g., figs. 105:3-4,6-7; 111:3) but more often the lines consist simply of a row of blobs. Again, it is suggested that the coloring must have been applied with something like a twig which could absorb very little paint. With one exception (fig. 105:3) the patterns appear to be regular and continuous. To the extent that the blobs (e.g., on fig. 105:5,14) can accurately be described as crude beginning attempts to draw straight lines, the most common pattern appears to be continuous, roughly straight, diagonal lines extending from the rim or near the rim to the carination or to a point well down the side. Continuous patterns of horizontal bands and vertical lines also occur but not as often. Frequently seen is a thin band of paint along the top and outside of the rim. This band sometimes appears on the inside of the rim as well, but the inside surfaces bear no other decoration.

Plastic decoration of all forms is completely absent from pottery from these levels.

Aside from those fragments more typical of the later levels in that their fabric is softer and coarser, there were two clearly variant sherds in the lowest level containing pottery. One is a simple flaring rim that has apparently been overfired, for its paste and surface have a greenish cast and its outer surface is pockmarked, bloated, and somewhat vitrified. We need not be surprised at the phenomenon of vitrification in such an early context since, as Shepard has pointed out (1936, p. 399), this is due to fluxing impurities rather than to excessively high temperature; nevertheless, these impurities do not appear in the rest of the Jarmo pottery, and the sherd may be intrusive. Another sherd that may be intrusive is a fragment of a large, possibly hemispherical, bowl, whose outside is decorated with dull red bands of paint 30 mm wide. Neither the vessel's form, its decoration, nor the appearance of its paint have other parallels at Jarmo.

We have stressed that J-II,2fl. and J-II,3 show overlapping, to some extent forming a transitional period, and that some sherds from J-II,2fl. probably should be considered more closely related to the earlier manifestation than to the later. However, we have stressed further that although a distinction cannot be clearly drawn, 42 sherds, or about 22% of all the pottery in this level, seem to fall into this group (including those shown in fig. 107:5-7,9,11). Conversely, a number of sherds with paste and surface typical of the later manifestation were found in J-II,3-5, and they can best be described in terms of the analysis of the later manifestation to follow. Of the 71 sherds from J-II,3 in squares a to h, 21 are of this type, and so are all 25 sherds recovered from the corresponding level in the western extension (squares l-n). There is a single example (fig. 105:11) from an earlier level (J-II,4) of a vessel with fabric similar to the fabric characteristic of vessels from J-II,1-2fl.

Later Manifestation

Pottery in the uppermost three levels was also all handmade and primarily plant tempered, and, as in the lower levels, the tempering material consisted mainly of the blades and stalks of a plant resembling grass. But the material is generally more coarsely chopped and the tiny seeds seen in the earlier pottery are not present. The amount of temper, although highly variable, is usually very large, and chaff impressions are visible on almost all surfaces.

In addition to the organic temper, fine grains of limestone can be seen under 8.5× magnification to be scattered over the surfaces and in the body of many sherds. Fine grains of mica are also occasionally present. There is no evidence that either the limestone or the mica was intentionally added as temper, and since an occasional lump of rock up to 10 mm long and 3-5 mm wide was embedded in a vessel wall, it seems probable that the clay was used entirely without levigation.

The pot clay used in the uppermost three levels may also be characterized by its apparent relative lack of bonding material, for, although some sherds have been fired long enough for their organic temper to turn to ash and for their cores to oxidize completely, the pottery is uniformly very friable. All of the pottery typical of this manifestation can be scratched with a fingernail, and there is no evidence of any fusion.

As we have indicated, the color of paste and surfaces in the later manifestation varies within about the same limits as in the earlier, but the full range of variation is more often present on a single sherd, giving the impression that firing temperature and draft were less well controlled than they had once been. As in the earlier manifestation, there is no significant color difference between inner and outer vessel surfaces, or between bases and rims. However, there seems to be a gradual but perceptible shift from roughly equal amounts of orange buff and buff pottery in J-II,2fl. to a distinct predominance of orange buff as a paste and surface color in the uppermost level, while during this time orange sherds remain a variable but small minority. To the extent that greater redness is a measure of greater oxidation, this shift may indicate a gradual change in firing practices.

Further evidence bearing on this possibility is found by comparing the amount of core-darkening in the lower and upper levels. While only 34% of all sherds from J-II,3-5 show none of the darkening on the break which results from incomplete oxidation, this proportion increases to 39%, 52%, and 57% in J-II,2fl., J-II,2, and J-II,1, respectively. In other words, we can see again a trend in the later manifestation toward more complete oxidation during firing. At the same time, in contrast to the earlier manifestation, a higher proportion of bases than rims have dark cores. To a large extent this is probably due to the greater thickness near the base of most pottery vessels from the later manifestation.

Pottery of the uppermost three levels is characterized by a rarity of surface treatment. Aside from those sherds of J-II,2fl. that we have considered as survivals of the earlier manifestation, only 28 sherds (including those from the main operation as well as those from corresponding levels in the western extension) are slipped, painted, or burnished.

Twenty of these have a red slip, occasionally burnished, 2 are painted and burnished, and 6 bear traces of burnish only. The crosshatch pattern on the only large painted sherd found (fig. 109:22) is not known in the earlier manifestation. We do not believe, however, that the sherd is intrusive, because its fabric falls within the normal range for the uppermost three levels and its red brown paint is similar to that on a few earlier sherds (e.g., fig. 105:10).

Surface smoothing of most of the rest of the pottery was minimal, and most of the sherds are thick and somewhat irregular. Scraping, although demonstrable in a few instances, does not seem to have been done very frequently; wet-smoothing was more common, although this technique probably was used on less than 5% of the pottery.

Two examples of plastic decoration, the only ones found at Jarmo, were recovered from the uppermost level of the western extension (fig. 109:20,24). One, a crudely gouged meander, appears below a pot rim that is itself slightly serrated. The other is a surprisingly sophisticated "rope" in appliqué slightly below the rim of a bowl. Judging by the fabric in each case, neither sherd appears intrusive.

FORMS

Compared with the changes we have described in fabric and ornamentation, changes in form are far less important. While the small number of sherds found in J-II,3-5 obviously limits the significance of any generalizations about forms in the earlier manifestation, sufficient pottery was found in the later manifestation to make a quantitative treatment of form a useful adjunct to the usual description based solely on reference to drawings.

Earlier Manifestation

Of the vessels estimated to have been present in J-II,3-5 (35 at most) 19 are shown in figure 105, and these represent what is known at present about pottery shapes during this period. While definite conclusions are unwarranted, at least it can be said that in this initial period of the use of pottery at Jarmo, the vessel shapes, though simple, are quite varied. The flat-bottomed, shouldered bowl or pot that is characteristic of the upper levels also occurs in the J-II,3-5 levels (clear examples, although without bases, are shown in fig. 105:13,17-18; these examples are all from level 5). The fabric of one later example with a vertical but horizontally pierced lug handle (fig. 107:5) is more like that of pottery of the earlier manifestation, and many illustrated rim sherds may have been parts of shouldered vessels. But this form does not seem to have been predominant as it was in later times, for a number of shapes are found which are not present in the later manifestation. These include a low, flat-based, straight-sided, rounded-rectangular bowl (fig.105:10) and a tall, flat-based bowl with flaring rim but no carination (fig. 105:12). A minor variation in form that is apparently confined to the earlier manifestation is the "bead" rim (e.g., fig. 105:3,6,12,14). One bead rim (fig. 107:11) was found on a sherd of similar fabric from J-II,2fl. In level 2fl. only, there are two other forms, but each example is more closely related in paste and surface to pottery of the lower levels. The forms are a small, shallow, subhemispherical bowl (fig. 107:9) and a rim sherd from a pot that appears to have been slightly holemouthed (fig. 107:7). The pot has a vertical, horizontally pierced lug handle that is rather unusual in that it joins the vessel below the plane of the rim. The distribution of known rim diameters of vessels of this manifestation is given in chart 4.

Later Manifestation

The problem of analyzing pottery forms in the upper levels was more involved, as the forms were less amenable to directly descriptive treatment. In the first place, as will become evident, the shapes are characterized by a standardization and restraint that seem conducive to quantitative study only, and, in contrast with the earlier manifestation, there are sufficient sherds to validate at least a few generalizations obtained in this manner. Secondly, the very high friability of the later pottery reduces the amount of information that can be obtained solely from a description of wholly or partly reconstructed vessels. We were rarely able to fit together sherds broken in antiquity and succeeded in reconstructing the full profiles of only 8 vessels out of the 11,844 sherds found in these levels. Some factors that contributed to the low number of reconstructions are the absence of painted decoration (which usually acts as a guide in finding sherds that belong together), the generally rough and amorphous surface treatment, and the fact that little pottery was encountered that seemed to have been left by its users on the spot where it was broken.

Because of these circumstances, a method of study was devised that involved the measurement of every sherd that was in some respect diagnostic of vessel form.[5] Measurements were made of the diameters of every rim, base, and shoulder; the wall thickness at the base, at the shoulder, and at a point 5 mm below the rim, as well as at intermediate points; the heights from base to shoulder, shoulder to rim, and base to rim, both on sherds and on reconstructions where this was possible; and the angles between base and side and between upper and lower side at the shoulder. Also, rims were classified into a number of recurring forms. When tabulated, many of these measurements did not provide any significant or useful information, but a few did disclose apparently important regularities of form that would not otherwise have been recognized. It is upon the quantitative data thus obtained that the following analysis of form is primarily based.

Although a number of other shapes are present, the bulk of the pottery from these levels shows a considerable degree of uniformity. A flat-based, shouldered pot or deep bowl, frequently with vertical, pierced lug handles placed at the rim, is unquestionably the predominant form (e.g., figs. 106:1; 111:7). These features, however, appear on vessels of

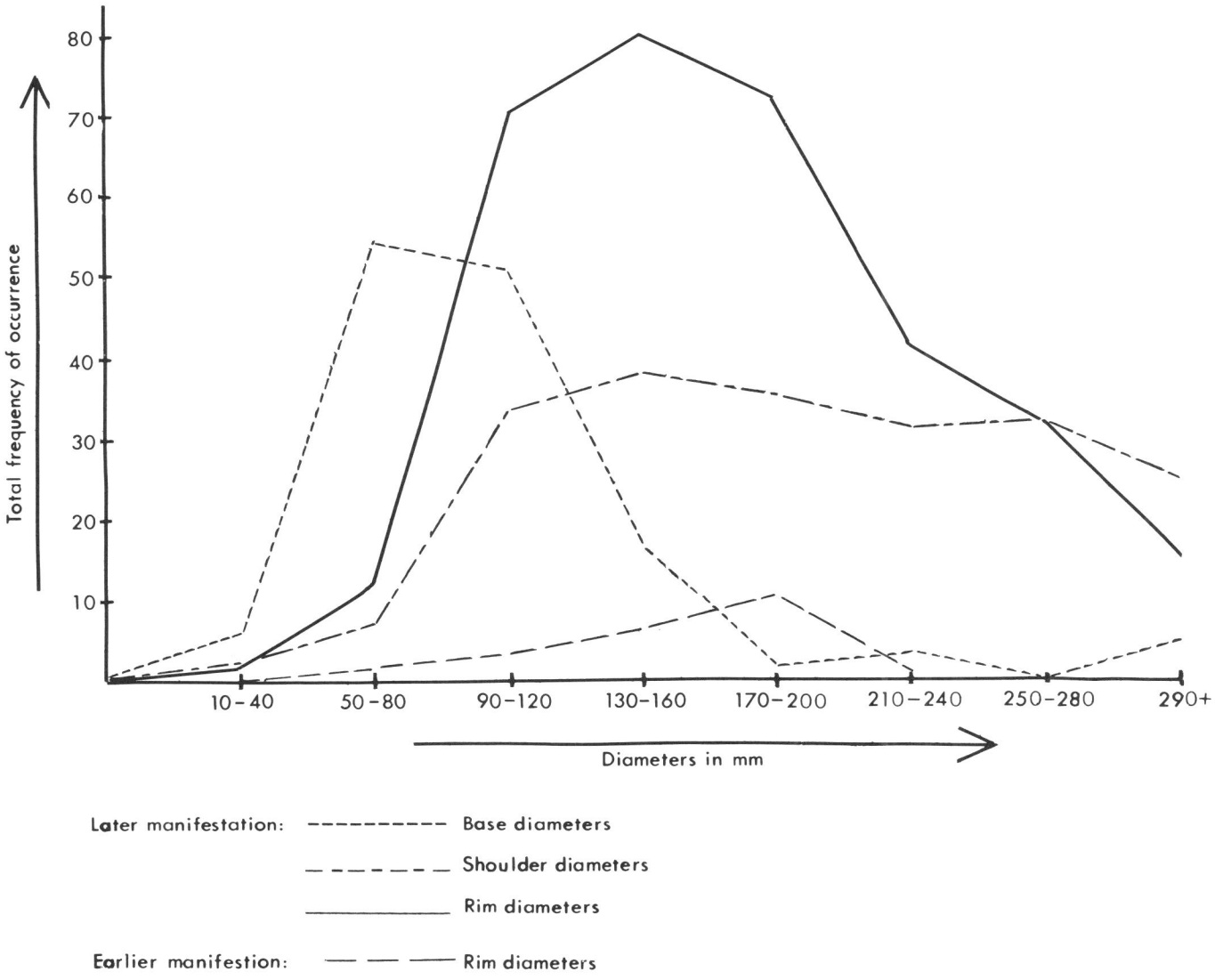

Chart 4. Distribution of base, shoulder, and rim diameters of Jarmo pottery vessels.

quite different sizes and proportions. Rim diameters range from less than 70 mm to more than 300 mm, and heights range from less than 40 mm to perhaps as much as 200 mm.

Below the shoulder, jars or pots and more open bowls[6] are indistinguishable. However, although the sides of bowls above the shoulder (which either flare or rise vertically) are of the same height above and below, such is not the case for vessels with more constricted rims. Here the upper portion, above the shoulder, is higher than the portion below it. This may be seen by comparing figure 109:7 with figure 109:9. If the neck of a vessel is constricted, the rim shows a uniform tendency to flare slightly and thus the vessel appears low collared rather than holemouthed. The designation "low-collared jar" is misleading, however, since the constriction at the neck is relatively slight. Bowl rims, too, frequently flare, although there are many exceptions. Both bowl and jar rims may be tapered to an edge or rounded and are always simple.

The distribution of diameters for all rim, shoulder, and base sherds—and thus, inferentially, for the original vessels as well—is given for pottery of the later manifestation in chart 4. It will be noted that the diameters of almost all bases fall in the range of 50-120 mm and that 80 or 90 mm is the size that occurs most frequently. Rim sherd diameters are somewhat more widely distributed; the maximum frequency of occurrence is reached at 130-160 mm, but the curve falls off sharply below 90 mm and rather more slowly above 200 mm. The diameters of vessels from which our shoulder sherds came were apparently still more variable; the distribution curve is essentially flat topped between

90 and 280 mm. The absence of two or more well-defined maxima on all of the distribution curves is noteworthy; it indicates an emphasis on vessels of general utility rather than specialized production of small and large pots for different uses.

One other aspect of these results is particularly significant. Almost all of the partially reconstructed vessels have vertical or flaring upper sides, and if an analysis of form were based on these alone, tall jars with constricted necks, such as have been described, would seem to have been a shape of very minor importance. But chart 4 shows that average shoulder diameter is considerably larger than average rim diameter among the "diagnostic" sherds from the upper levels of J-II that were intensively studied by form. This can only mean that vessels with constricted necks were actually quite numerous. The explanation for this apparent discrepancy must lie in the fact that sherds from tall vessels are more difficult to identify in sufficient quantity for profile reconstruction than sherds from short vessels. Thus, the quantitative data lead us to believe that large and tall jars or pots, as well as the more adequately illustrated deep bowls, formed a major subtype of later Jarmo pottery production. The wide variation of deep bowls is exemplified by figures 108:4 and 109:1, but we were able to reconstruct the full section of only one small example of the wide-mouthed jar (fig. 109:9). The rim sherds illustrated in figure 109:15,17,20 are probably from quite large pots.

As might be expected in view of its high friability, Jarmo pottery from the uppermost levels is generally quite thick. On the upper part of the vessel, thickness of the wall is directly proportional to rim diameter; in small vessels the upper wall is most frequently 4-6 mm thick, in medium-sized vessels it is 6-8 mm, and in large jars and shallow basins 8-10 mm. Although there is considerable overlapping, the ranges of thickness prevailing in the three groups are separate and distinct. Thickness of the base, however, is somewhat greater than the above figures and apparently less directly related to base diameter.

An important characteristic of later Jarmo pottery is the frequent use of handles. All of them are of one basic type: a vertical, pierced lug that is roughly triangular in cross section. They are of different sizes, corresponding for the most part to vessel size, but almost invariably they are placed at the rim (fig. 111:9). Some are flat topped (fig. 109:10); more frequently they rise above the plane of the rim at their outer extremity (fig. 109:15). In two cases the handle is pierced by two holes instead of one (fig. 108:10). On a majority the outer profile is roughly straight and vertical, but a few have a curvilinear or irregular profile (fig. 109:12). All the handles are well designed not only for carrying the vessel to which they are attached but also for hanging them, and we conceive the latter to have been their primary function.

Of the 1,273 rim sherds from the later manifestation in J-II, 112 (8.8%) have handles. This is a very high proportion in view of the friability and consequent small size of many of the rim sherds and suggests that most or all of the larger vessels, at least, had handles. While we were unable to reconstruct large enough portions of any vessel equipped with handles to demonstrate their spacing conclusively, we were able to reconstruct enough to infer that at most a pair of handles was the normal complement.

Other kinds of lugs are also present on these vessels but only in very small numbers. The most common type is a simple nipple lug immediately below the rim (fig. 109:16), but horizontally flattened lugs (figs. 108:11; 109:17), a T-shaped lug (fig. 109:23), and a nipple lug inside a crescent or oval (fig. 108:12) also appear.

The construction of shouldered bowls seems to have proceeded in two stages. Many shoulder sherds break in a characteristic pattern (fig. 109:25), indicating that the base and lower sides must have been modeled as a unit and allowed to dry before an upper structure was added.

The generalized bowl and jar shapes that have been discussed predominate throughout the later manifestation of pottery. During the three upper levels, this pottery shows no convincing evidence of seriational change. Moreover, obvious prototypes for these shapes can be found in the earlier manifestation (e.g., fig. 107:5, large pot; fig. 105:13, more open bowl), but the later examples are uniformly less well proportioned and more crudely finished.

Several other vessel shapes, however, are present in smaller numbers. The most significant of these is a very large, flat-bottomed oval bowl with flaring sides (figs. 108:13; 109:18) that is crudely made and closely resembles the Hassuna "husking tray," although it lacks the interior scoring characteristic of the latter. No example of this shape was found that could be reconstructed enough for its complete length or width to be measured, but in at least one case the width exceeded 300 mm (fig. 109:18). In height, most of the examples range from 90 to 120 mm, while base and side thicknesses are fairly uniform, between 15 and 20 mm. Generally the longer sides flare less than the ends and occasionally are almost vertical. The paste is even less well fired and more poorly fused than is usual in the later manifestation, and portability cannot have been a distinguishing feature of these vessels. Forty-eight sherds from bowls of this shallow oval type were identified in J-II.

Another type, which we have called a boat-shaped pot, is a large, rectangular vessel with a raised platform of solid clay in its center. The longer sides are almost vertical, but one end, at least, flares abruptly to form a sort of "prow." It is of unknown utility and apparently less numerous, being represented (in our collection) by one partially reconstructed vessel (figs. 109:21; 111:8) and possibly two sherds from others.

There were three examples, varying greatly in size, of a flat-bottomed, shoulderless bowl with slightly rounded sides (figs. 107:4; 109:8). Also found were one example of a low, flat-bottomed dish with flaring sides (fig. 108:14) and one neatly made "flowerpot" (figs. 108:6; 111:6). Two fragments of what were possibly pedestal bases were recovered (fig. 109:19), but neither can be identified with certainty.

Changes in the Pottery Vessel Industry

As has been remarked, some degree of relationship is implicit in the many resemblances in form and fabric between the earlier and later pottery. With respect to form, we have seen that the dominant shapes in the later manifestation occur also in the earlier, and the generally greater thickness and crudity of the later pottery may be less an independent difference between the two manifestations than a result of the high friability and low plasticity of the later paste. With respect to fabric, it has been shown that pottery of the later manifestation may be distinguished by (1) a greater amount of plant temper, more coarsely chopped, (2) relative rarity of "grass" seeds as tempering material, (3) inclusion, probably inadvertent, of a much greater amount of fine limestone and of a lesser amount of fine mica particles, and (4) markedly greater friability because of a relative lack of bonding material in the clay. When these elements are combined with a simultaneous sharp decline in the use of slip, burnish, and painted decoration, we must conclude that, in spite of the many important similarities, there is a considerable degree of discontinuity in the preparation tradition and not just a normal sequence of technical and stylistic changes.

A possible explanation for this discontinuity will be offered later; here it need only be noted that, with the exception of the trend toward more complete oxidation during firing characteristic of the later manifestation, all of the changes occur more or less simultaneously and do not indicate technical and artistic advancement but rather degeneration. At the same time, this apparent degeneration is accompanied by a very rapid increase in the use of pottery.

Relations Between the Jarmo Stone and Pottery Vessel Industries and Their Significance for Cultural Reconstruction

The decline in the use of stone vessels following the Jarmo period corresponds roughly with the large-scale introduction of well-fired pottery. One possible inference is, of course, that pottery replaced stone bowls since its plasticity, cheapness, and ease of manufacture would more than outweigh the disadvantage of its greater fragility. But the bulk of Jarmo pottery is of such inferior quality that the beginning of this broad trend is not easily seen during the period of the village's occupation. Since, however, the site reveals not only a well-documented series of changes in stone vessels but the introduction of pottery as well, it may be worthwhile to examine the extent to which the pattern of use of stone vessels was at least altered by the introduction of pottery.[7]

Since the size distribution of pottery vessels in the upper levels very closely parallels that of stone vessels in the lower levels (see charts 1 and 4), it might appear that pottery was directly replacing stone. There is a marked reduction, however, in the average size of stone vessels in the upper levels and no evidence for any reduction in the frequency of their occurrence. It would therefore be more accurate to state that while the decline in popularity of the larger stone vessels is perhaps related to the introduction of pottery, stone vessels continued to be made in undiminished numbers in spite of the new medium.

The use of poorer materials and the seeming decline of workmanship in the average stone bowl were perhaps also related to the appearance of pottery, but, again, it is not safe to conclude that the stone vessel industry as a whole retrogressed in the face of competition from pottery. There was simply a wider range of variation in workmanship, and not an absolute decline in the caliber of the best examples. The increased experimentation with form is further evidence of continuing interest in the stone vessel industry. Indeed, one would hardly expect a precipitate decline in the use of stone for receptacles as opposed to pottery (at the low level of technical competence shown in ceramic work at least in the upper levels, where the majority of the pottery comes from), since the stone was nonporous and hence useful for holding liquids, whereas the ceramic fabric was porous and would have been suitable for storing solid materials only.[8] This differentiation in function is not only to be inferred from differences in average size, shape, and porosity; it is also suggested by the presence on most of the pottery of lug handles for hanging, whereas apparently none of the stone vessels were designed to be hung. Finally, further evidence of different uses for vessels in the two materials may be found in the two characteristically different patterns of discarding the broken ones: pieces of stone were scattered both in and around the houses, while pottery sherds were confined mainly to a specialized midden.

We may summarize, then, by suggesting that the introduction of pottery was followed not by the completely competitive use of pottery and stone for all types of vessels but instead by some specialization of function. Although there is considerable overlapping, pottery was used somewhat more often for large pots and bowls, while stone was favored for small bowls, plates, saucers, and possibly cups.

Also involved in a discussion of the relation between pottery and stone vessels is the degree to which their respective modes of shape and ornamentation overlapped and influenced each other. We have indicated that open stone bowls with flat bottoms were largely replaced by counterparts in pottery, but there is no evidence that the former were simply copied in a new medium. The great majority of the pottery vessels are characterized by a distinct carination or shoulder that does not occur at all on flat-bottomed stone bowls. This feature does appear on stone vessels of type E, but these are decidedly round-bottomed forms with a very different rim treatment. Moreover, none of the stone vessels found thus far had been used as base rests or molds in the preparation of pottery, for their interiors are uniformly rounded (even those of the flat-based forms), whereas the pottery vessel bases were uniformly flat.

There are a few convincing, but to our view less important, similarities that may be noted. A rounded-rectangular pottery bowl (fig. 105:10) appears to be a direct copy of a stone vessel of type BC (e.g., fig. 102:8), while stone vessels of type H (e.g., fig. 103:12) are almost identical in profile with the single pottery "flowerpot" found (fig. 108:6).

The banded effect that the makers frequently tried to achieve in the ornamentation of stone bowls and saucers in the upper levels may possibly be related to the introduction of painted pottery, since the colors in the two mediums are often quite similar and since parallel lines suggestive of stripes are the most common painted motif. Without further exposure of intermediate levels at Jarmo, we cannot be sure whether the painting imitated the banded effect in the stone bowls or whether the stone was chosen to imitate the painting, since it is not clear which appeared first.

In any case, the kind of ornamentation found on pottery does not greatly enhance our understanding of the relationships between pottery and stone. In general, the minor comparisons we have made serve only to point up a basic dissimilarity between the pottery and stone vessel traditions. Since there seems every reason to believe that the independence of the two traditions transcends the limitations of their respective raw materials, it might be suggested that this independence implies the attention of different social groups to each—an emergent division of labor.

As an aid to general cultural reconstruction, several aspects of the stone vessel industry deserve further comment. In terms of the time and effort that must have gone into it, a flourishing stone vessel industry undoubtedly was a basic part of the Jarmo cultural tradition. While we do not deny that the origin of the industry, in the functional sense, is to be found in the basic utility of its products, it seems most conceivable that mere usefulness does not furnish an adequate explanation for the tremendous elaboration that the stone bowls underwent. This conclusion is not derived only from a consideration of the number of vessels simultaneously in use; it is also based on the uniformly high esthetic achievement, involving the visualization of stone as an essentially plastic medium, and the frequency of nonutilitarian embellishments, such as high polish and extreme thinness.

Three observations stem from a study of this industry. None conclusively affect a final interpretation of the entire body of material from Jarmo; rather, they suggest an approach that might with profit be explored in the ordering of the other categories of the Jarmo inventory and, indirectly, in the understanding of the prehistoric epoch which Jarmo represents.

In the first place, the very high development of this extremely time-consuming craft is surprising, by present standards, so soon after the initial utilization of domesticated plants and animals had become widespread. The Jarmo stone vessel industry furnishes evidence that a whole complex of new arts and customs could have followed rapidly upon—if, indeed, it did not actually precede—the establishment of a secure agricultural subsistence base.

Second, the manufacture of stone vessels of the quality and quantity found here demanded a level of skill that is more easily understood as the result of a considerable degree of specialization than merely as one of a number of products of members of the community at large. The almost total absence of poorly finished specimens might also be taken to support this view. Childe (1950, p. 11) and others have made a useful and important distinction between full- and part-time craft specialization as a measure of the developmental stage to which a society may be assigned. We do not mean to imply that the makers of stone bowls in this very early village context were already full-time craftsmen, divorced from a full and direct part in the subsistence process. However, this material at least serves as a reminder that a complex division of nonsubsistence functions within a community did not need to wait for the organization of crafts as full-time activities. It has been widely observed that the theoretical self-sufficiency and isolation of neolithic society was everywhere belied by some degree of intercourse and trade between groups. Perhaps we should also concede that the presumably simple division of labor (i.e., by sex and age only) that is thought to have been commonly associated with such a society is another abstraction that may never have been historically accurate.

Finally, it has been noted that the number of vessels present in different houses did not vary significantly. If supported by other evidence, this might be taken to suggest that social stratification was still very weakly developed.

We turn now to pottery with the same viewpoint of synthesis and reconstruction; the sudden appearance of a relatively highly developed ware at a time that corresponds roughly with level J-II,5 implies that the idea of portable pottery and probably also the technique of its manufacture were introduced from some outside source at that time. Many of the theoretically possible prerequisites for its independent development here are present; stone vessels, basketry, crude and lightly fired miniature clay vessels, and baked-in-place depressions or hearths all suggest possible points of departure. But we lack any evidence for the transitional steps that alone would make this local development a real possibility. Hence, we are led to assume a period of contact with some external stimulus which we are unable to identify even tentatively.

The nature of the borrowing process also remains obscure. Since sherds from probably no more than 35 vessels are present in the earlier manifestation (as seen in the still limited J-II,3-5 exposure), it is possible that all of the earlier pottery was actually imported. The differences that have been noted between the earlier and later fabric may support this view by suggesting a different origin for the clay from which the earlier vessels were made.[9] Yet it is also possible that pottery of both manifestations was produced locally from two different nearby sources of clay. The differences now known are not so great as to make this impossible, and it would certainly not be surprising if two demonstrably different techniques of pottery preparation depended on different local sources for their materials. In this case, we must suppose that the earliest potters carried with them to Jarmo the knowledge of an already well-established craft.

In spite of some searching in the surrounding Chemchemal valley, we could unearth no evidence for a nearby, contemporary, but more advanced sister village from which the pottery could easily have been carried. We are therefore inclined to favor the idea that the potters themselves might have immigrated; fragile vessels would obviously have been less easily transportable over distances than would their makers. But even if this were true, we can only speculate whether it is further evidence for the existence already at this early time of specialized craftsmen who exchanged their products for their means of subsistence in some rudimentary form of trade. The small number of vessels and the little skill and time required to produce them make it equally possible that the industry was associated with a simple sexual division of labor; in this case, its earliest practitioners at Jarmo may have been women from some distant village, perhaps brought back as wives by men engaged in trading for obsidian.

Whatever the explanation may be for the initial appearance of pottery, the rapid replacement of a few externally inspired prototypes by a certainly local manifestation of increasing importance is the central fact of the industry's existence at Jarmo. Work in the *pre*pottery levels has disclosed that the inhabitants of the site knew of the properties of fired and tempered clay (as shown by the baked-in-place depressions and hearths), made use of structures adaptable for kiln firing (as shown by the numerous ovens in some of the earliest levels), had developed a high level of craftsmanship (as shown by stone bowls and other artifacts), knew of and had need for rigid portable containers (as shown by stone bowls), and had sufficient leisure time and community interest (as shown by the emphasis placed on a host of suprasubsistence activities) to furnish extremely favorable conditions for the development of a new craft. It is hardly surprising that in the sequel indigenous pottery production expanded very rapidly.

It is significant, furthermore, that the new industry was adopted selectively and not slavishly; the technique of manufacture that was utilized when large-scale production began, as we have seen, was simpler and cruder than the techniques used for the earlier vessels. The people of Jarmo seem to have rejected many aspects of the pottery vessel industry as it was introduced to them and to have utilized instead inferior methods that in some way may have represented less of a departure from their prevailing level of handling clay in making other types of artifacts.

While the question of the origin of the pottery-making stimulus remains an interesting one, we are inclined not to regard "external influence" as the sole explanation for the adoption of pottery at Jarmo. Granting the diffusion of the industry from some outside source, our understanding of early village life will be most appreciably advanced by focusing attention instead on the complex of local conditions that led to its speedy acceptance. Moreover, Jarmo seems to have been sufficiently close in time to the initial center of development of pottery (if, indeed, there was a single center) for the technical and social changes accompanying its introduction to have proceeded along quite similar lines in both, and thus Jarmo may offer a reasonably close approximation to the initial process of pottery development. And we must stress that it is the *process*, rather than the precise locus, of the introduction of a new craft with which archeology can most profitably be concerned.

One particularly important feature of this process may be noted in conclusion—the rapidity with which the new trait was assimilated. The tremendously long, relatively static periods of human life prior to the neolithic revolution, coupled with observations of primitive groups today, have led many to equate resistance to change with primitive society in general. The circumstances surrounding the introduction of pottery at Jarmo remind us again that, relative to Jarmo's presumed lesser complexity, the rate of cultural change during the transitional period within which Jarmo falls must have been at least as great as any we have known since.

NOTES

1. The contemporaneity of the earliest occupation at the western edge of the mound (the J-I operation) with the earliest occupation at the center (in the step trench A) is supported by the finding of two fragments of a broken spindle whorl that fitted together, one from the basal level of each operation.

2. [The yield in stone bowl fragments from the spring excavations in 1955 is shown in the tabulation here.

The findspots were randomly scattered over most of the test squares at no great depth and with no appreciable concentration of types in any particular area. We assume that few examples could possibly be earlier than of the range of the upper levels of operation J-II. Thus, they do not appear to affect any of Adams's foregoing observations. Fig. 104 illustrates the examples now in Baghdad, including the two types (fig. 104:7-8) not seen earlier by Adams. With the exception of the large limestone bowl (fig. 104:13), which was far better finished than usual (cf. p. 292 and fig. 129:12), the pieces were normally white, yellowish white, gray, or sometimes variegated marble.—RJB]

Type	Number of fragments	Probable number of vessels	No. of diameters over 130 mm
A	13	12	7
BC	55	50	7
D?	2	2	--
E	8	8	--
G	17	15	3
H	3	3	--
K	7	7	1
L?	1	1	--
M	1	1	1
N	2	2	--
Bases	18	18	--
Misc. body	48	ca. 30	2+?
Fig. 104:7	1	1	--
Fig. 104:8	1	1	--

3. Particularly in the lower levels, a number of bowls were ground to such extreme thinness that they cannot ever have been very serviceable and may even have broken during manufacture (see the base of the specimen shown in fig. 101:1).

4. [Adams wrote before the 1954-55 field season, when it became clear that pottery was not uniformly encountered over all of the mound surface (see pp. 6 and 155).—RJB]

5. The attendant circumstances have also made it impossible to estimate the number of vessels from the J-II,1-2fl. levels, from which these sherds came. The following account presupposes that this number is fairly large, that is, that our generalizations are not unduly weighted by the presence of a disproportionate majority of sherds from a very small number of vessels. We can only say that constant supervision of the recovery of the pottery in the field and many months spent in handling it convince us that this presupposition is justified.

6. Although some of the vessels, including many of those drawn, could easily have been held in one hand, we have refrained from referring to them as cups. The term "cup" implies the use of the vessel for liquids, and the pottery of this manifestation is so poorly fired that, quite aside from its extremely high porosity, much of it crumbles in water. This matter of terminology may not be a very significant one since vessels of very small size are decidedly less common than they might appear to be in the drawings (see chart 4).

7. It must be admitted in connection with the introduction of pottery that on present evidence these postulated "effects" appear at least as old as their "cause." A study of table 1 and chart 2 discloses that the size and type distributions of stone vessels were essentially uniform for J-II,1-6. It will be recalled that no pottery was found in J-II,6. On the other hand, a few sherds were found in the step trench at about the elevation of J-II,6 (cf. table 2, n. *e*), and their absence in J-II,6 itself may have been a function of its reduced area. Only further excavation will show conclusively whether or not the introduction of pottery preceded (and thus, to some extent, may have "caused") the marked changes in the stone vessel industry. We consider this sequence of events to be inherently probable since the size and type distributions of stone vessels for the lower levels of J-I were also very uniform, indicating that the rate of change in stone vessels was very slow during much of the period prior to the first appearance of pottery.

8. There seems to have been some experimentation in the coating of pottery with bitumen. Six or eight sherds suggest this may have been tried on a small scale.

9. If the clay used for the two manifestations came from two widely separated beds, quantitative or qualitative differences ultimately may be detected through microscopic study of thin sections of sherds typical of the two manifestations.

REFERENCES

Childe, V. Gordon
    1950 The urban revolution. *Town Planning Review* 21:3-17.

Shepard, Anna O.
    1936 The technology of Pecos pottery. In *The pottery of Pecos*, vol. 2, pp. 389-587. New Haven, Conn.: Yale University Press.

CATALOGUE OF ILLUSTRATED STONE AND POTTERY VESSELS (figs. 101-11)

FIGURE 101. STONE BOWLS
   1 Type A, from J-I,7 (*J2-209*,* in Baghdad)
   2 Type A, from J-I,8 (*J2-292*, in Chicago)
   3 Type A, from J-I,6b (*J2-68* and *J2-78*, in Baghdad)
   4 Type BC, from J-I,6b (*J2-79*, in Chicago)
   5 Type BC, from J-I,6c

FIGURE 102. STONE BOWLS
   1 Type BC, from J-II,5 (*J2-392*, in Baghdad)
   2 Type BC, from J-II,5 (*J2-394*, in Chicago)
   3 Type D, from J-II,5 (*J2-384*, in Baghdad)
   4 Type D, from J-II,5
   5 Type D, from J-II,4 (*J2-308*, in Chicago)
   6 Type O, from J-II,3
   7 Type L, from J-II,5 (*J2-382*, in Chicago)
   8 Type BC, from J-II,5 (*J2-390*, in Chicago)
   9 Type L, from J-II,6 (*J2-413*, in Baghdad)
  10 Type BC, from J-II,4 (*J2-374*, in Chicago)
  11 Type BC, from J-II,5 (*J2-395*, in Baghdad)

FIGURE 103. STONE BOWLS
   1 Type BC, from J-II,2 (*J2-269*, in Baghdad)
   2 Type BC, from J-II,1 (*J2-129*, in Baghdad)
   3 Type BC, from J-II,1 (*J2-127*, in Chicago)
   4 Type BC, from J-II,1 (*J2-12*, in Baghdad)
   5 Type D, from J-II,1 (*J2-41*, in Baghdad)
   6 Type BC, from J-II,2fl. (*J2-297*, in Chicago)
   7 Type BC, from J-II,1 (*J2-112*, in Baghdad)
   8 Type M, from J-II,1 (*J2-42*, in Baghdad)
   9 Type N, from J-II,2fl.
  10 Type F, from J-II,2 (*J2-268*, in Chicago)
  11 Type G, from J-II,1 (*J2-105*, in Chicago)
  12 Type H, from J-II,2fl. (*J2-285*, in Chicago)
  13 Type I, from J-II,2
  14 Type E, from J-II,2 (*J2-194*, in Chicago)
  15 Type E, from J-II,2 (*J2-201*, in Chicago)
  16 Type K, from surface
  17 Type G, from J-III,1 (*J2-187*, in Chicago)

FIGURE 104. STONE BOWLS
   1 Type BC, from J-II,4W
   2 Type BC, from L13,2 (*J3-104*, in Baghdad)
   3 Type BC, from M18,1 (*J3-17*, in Baghdad)
   4 Type BC, from K14,2 (*J3-94*, in Baghdad)
   5 Type E, from H16,0.8m
   6 Type E, from RU1014,1 (*J3-102*, in Baghdad)
   7 Type x, from H14,2 [see n. 2, p. 223]
   8 Type x, from V12,3 (*J3-19*, in Baghdad) [see n. 2, p. 223]
   9 Type K, from VY1014,sf-1
  10 Type K, from J-II,5W
  11 Type G, from MQ1014,2
  12 Type E, from P15,sf-1 (*J3-21*, in Baghdad)
  13 Type N, from G15,1.4m

---

*Registration number.

THE JARMO STONE AND POTTERY VESSEL INDUSTRIES

FIGURE 105. POTTERY
1. From J-II,3
2. From J-II,3
3. From J-II,3 (*J2-356*, in Chicago)
4. From J-II,4 (*J2-358*, in Baghdad)
5. From J-II,4 (*J2-365*, in Chicago)
6. From J-II,4 (*J2-359*, in Chicago)
7. From J-II,4 (*J2-367*, in Baghdad)
8. From J-II,4 (*J2-366*, in Baghdad)
9. From J-II,4 (*J2-377*, in Chicago)
10. From J-II,4 (*J2-376*, in Chicago)
11. From J-II,4 (*J2-357*, in Baghdad)
12. From J-II,4 (*J2-378*, in Chicago)
13. From J-II,5 (*J2-387*, in Chicago)
14. From J-II,5
15. From J-II,5 (*J2-402*, in Baghdad)
16. From J-II,5 (*J2-379*, in Chicago)
17. From J-II,5
18. From J-II,5
19. From J-II,5 (*J2-386*, in Baghdad)

FIGURE 106. RESTORED POTTERY VESSEL FORMS

FIGURE 107. POTTERY
1. From J-II,2fl.
2. From J-II,2fl. (*J2-354*, in Chicago)
3. From J-II,2fl. (*J2-353*, in Chicago)
4. From J-II,2fl. (*J2-355*, in Baghdad)
5. From J-II,2fl. (*J2-346*, in Baghdad)
6. From J-II,2fl. (*J2-349*, in Chicago)
7. From J-II,2fl. (*J2-348*, in Chicago)
8. From J-II,2fl. (*J2-351*, in Chicago)
9. From J-II,2fl. (*J2-352*, in Chicago)
10. From J-II,2fl.
11. From J-II,2fl. (*J2-350*, in Chicago)

FIGURE 108. POTTERY
1. From J-II,2 (*J2-335*, in Baghdad)
2. From J-II,2
3. From J-II,2 (*J2-344*, in Baghdad)
4. From J-II,2 (*J2-336*, in Chicago)
5. From J-II,2 (*J2-338*, in Baghdad)
6. From J-II,2 (*J2-341*, in Chicago)
7. From J-II,2
8. From J-II,2 (*J2-340*, in Baghdad)
9. From J-II,2 (*J2-343*, in Baghdad)
10. From J-II,2 (*J2-342*, in Chicago)
11. From J-II,2
12. From J-II,2
13. From J-II,2 (*J2-337*, in Baghdad)
14. From J-II,2 (*J2-345*, in Chicago)

FIGURE 109. POTTERY
1. From J-II,1
2. From J-II,1
3. From J-II,1
4. From J-II,1
5. From J-II,1
6. From J-II,1
7. From J-II,1 (*J2-324*, in Chicago)
8. From J-II,1 (*J2-321*, in Baghdad)
9. From J-II,1 (*J2-322*, in Baghdad)
10. From J-II,1
11. From J-II,1
12. From J-II,1 (*J2-328*, in Baghdad)
13. From J-II,1 (*J2-331*, in Baghdad)
14. From J-II,1 (*J2-325*, in Chicago)
15. From J-II,1 (*J2-329*, in Baghdad)
16. From J-II,1
17. From J-II,1
18. From J-II,1 (*J2-326*, in Chicago)
19. From J-II,1
20. From J-II,1 (*J2-333*, in Baghdad)
21. From J-II,1 (*J2-330*, in Baghdad)
22. From J-II,1 (*J2-327*, in Baghdad)
23. From J-II,1
24. From J-II,1 (*J2-334*, in Chicago)
25. From J-II,1

FIGURE 110. STONE BOWLS
1. Type G, from J-II,1 (*J2-105*, in Chicago)
2. Type BC, from H24,pit (*J3-101*, in Chicago)
3. Type BC, from J-II,5
4. Type BC, from J-II,5 (*J2-394*, in Chicago)
5. Type F, from J-II,2 (*J2-268*, in Chicago)
6. Type A, from J-I,8 (*J2-292*, in Chicago)
7. Type A, from J-II,2fl. (*J2-285*, in Chicago)
8. Type E, from J-II,2 (*J2-201*, in Chicago)

FIGURE 111. POTTERY
1. Painted ware, from J-II,5 (*J2-386*, in Baghdad)
2. Painted ware, from J-II,4 (*J2-365*, in Chicago)
3. Painted ware, from J-II,4 (*J2-359*, in Chicago)
4. Painted ware, from J-II,5 (*J2-379*, in Chicago)
5. Painted ware, from J-II,5 (*J2-387*, in Chicago)
6. Simple ware, from J-II,2 (*J2-341*, in Chicago)
7. Simple ware, from J-II,1 (*J2-322*, in Baghdad)
8. Simple ware, from J-II,1 (*J2-330*, in Baghdad)
9. Red burnished ware, from J-II,2fl. (*J2-346*, in Baghdad)

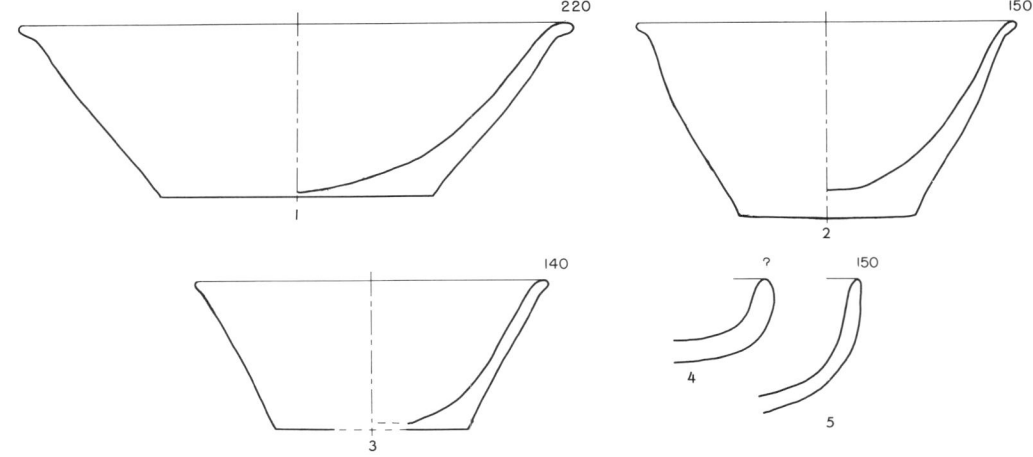

Fig. 101. Jarmo stone vessels: type A, *1-3*; type BC, *4-5*. (Rim diameters given in mm.)

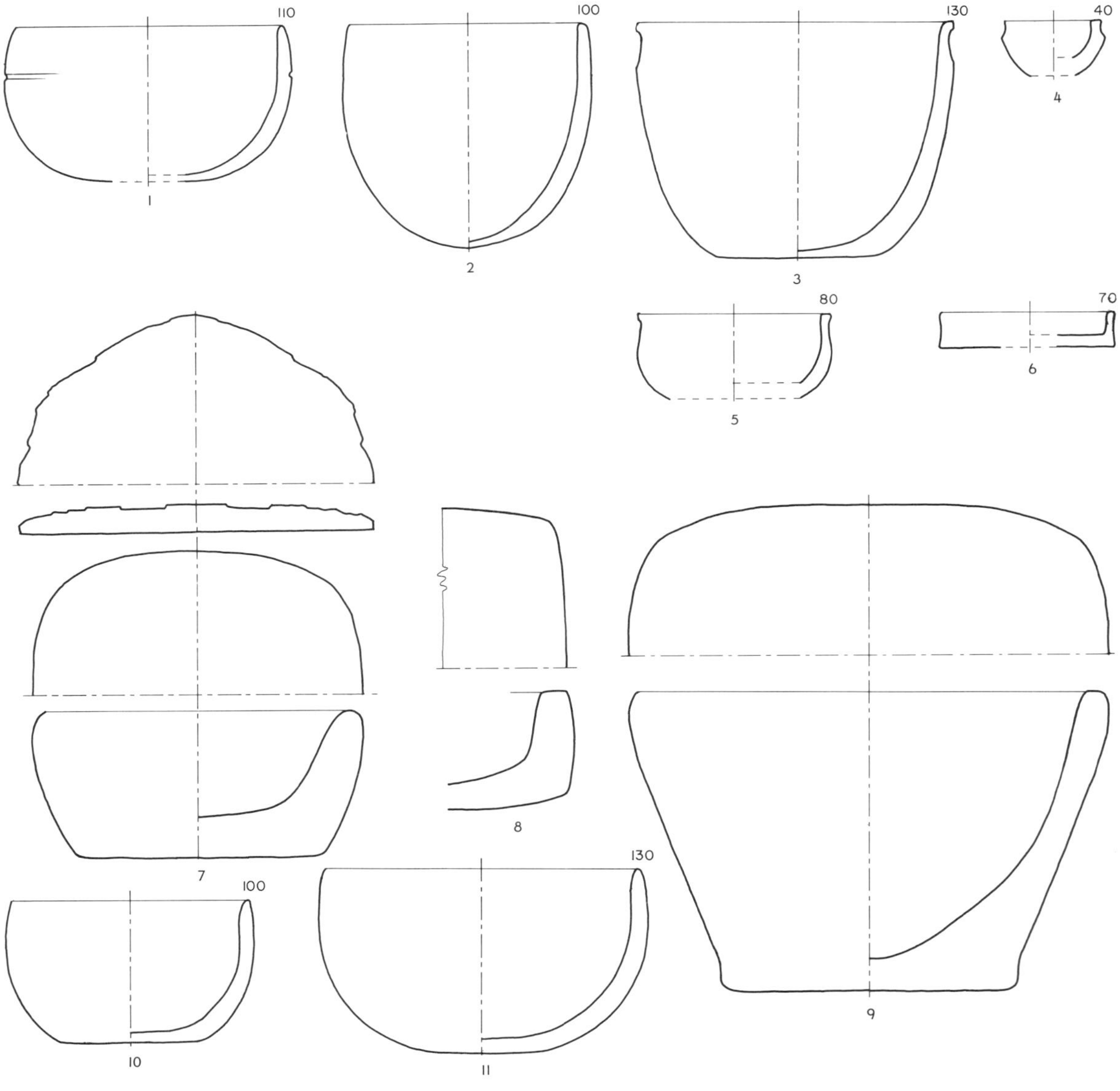

Fig. 102. Jarmo stone vessels: type BC, *1-2,8,10-11*; type D, *3-5*; type L, *7,9*; type O, *6*.

Fig. 103. Jarmo stone vessels: type BC, *1-4,6-7*; type D, *5*; type E, *14-15*; type F, *10*; type G, *11,17*; type H, *12*; type I, *13*; type K, *16*; type M, *8*; type N, *9*.

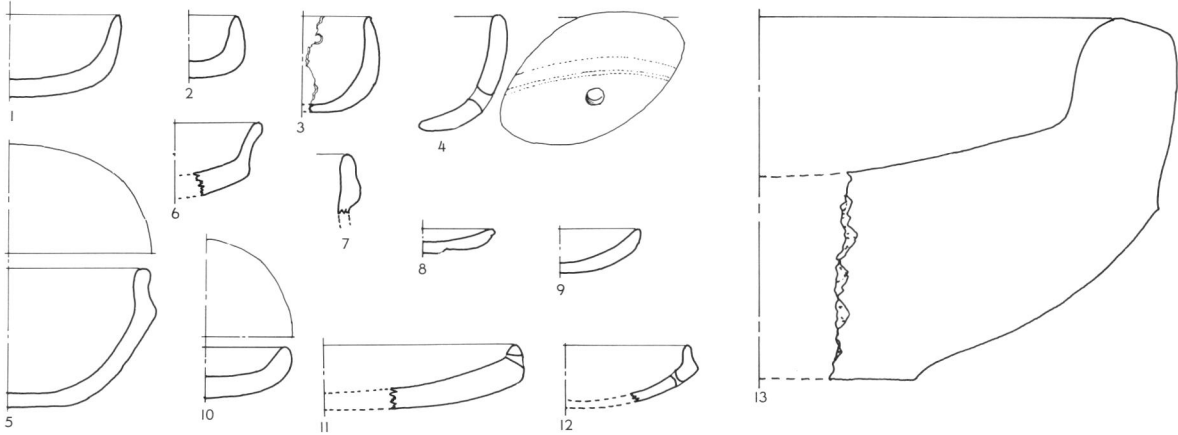

Fig. 104. Stone vessels recovered from the test squares at Jarmo in 1955 and now in Baghdad (see p. 223, n. 2).

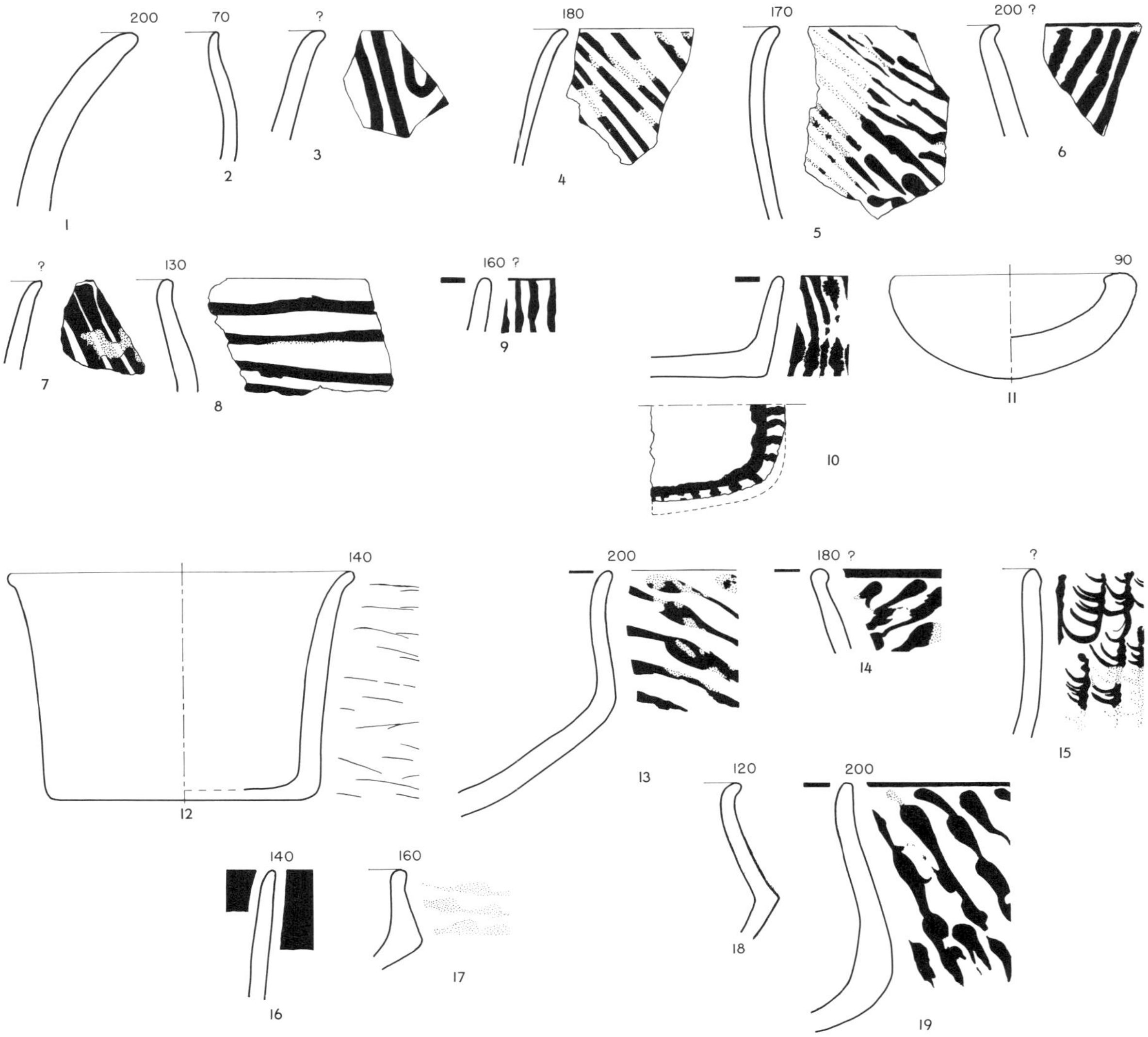

Fig. 105. Pottery from J-II,3-5.

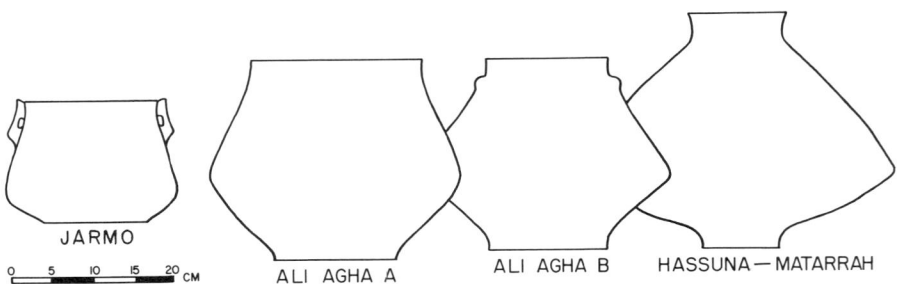

Fig. 106. Restored pottery vessel forms from Jarmo and other sites as compared by Joseph R. Caldwell.

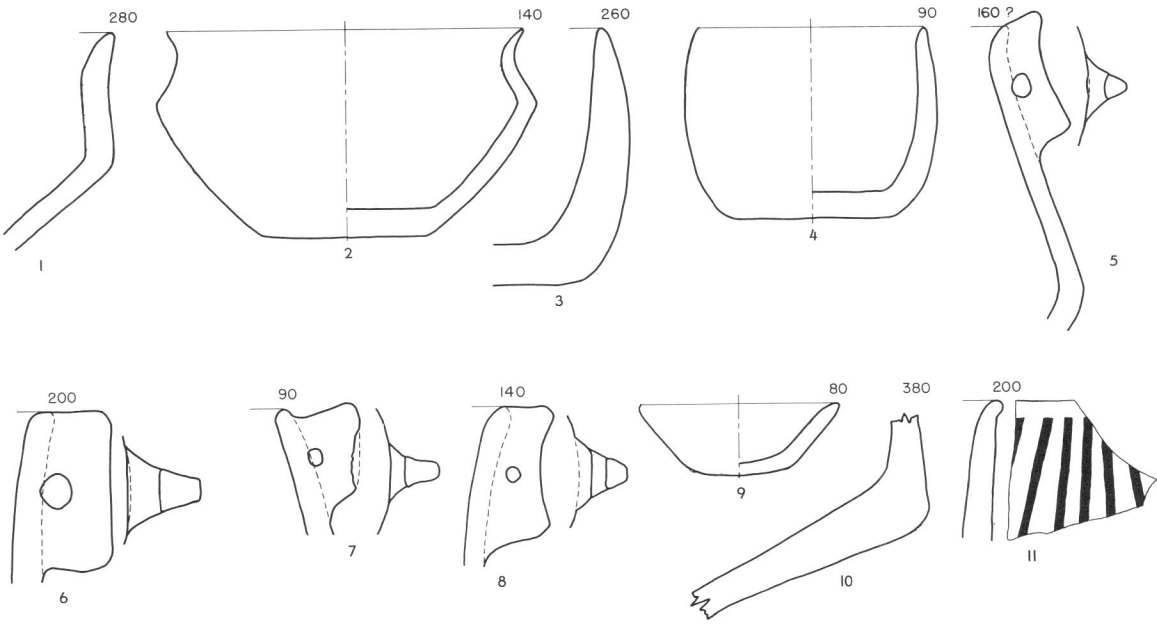

Fig. 107. Pottery from J-II,2fl.

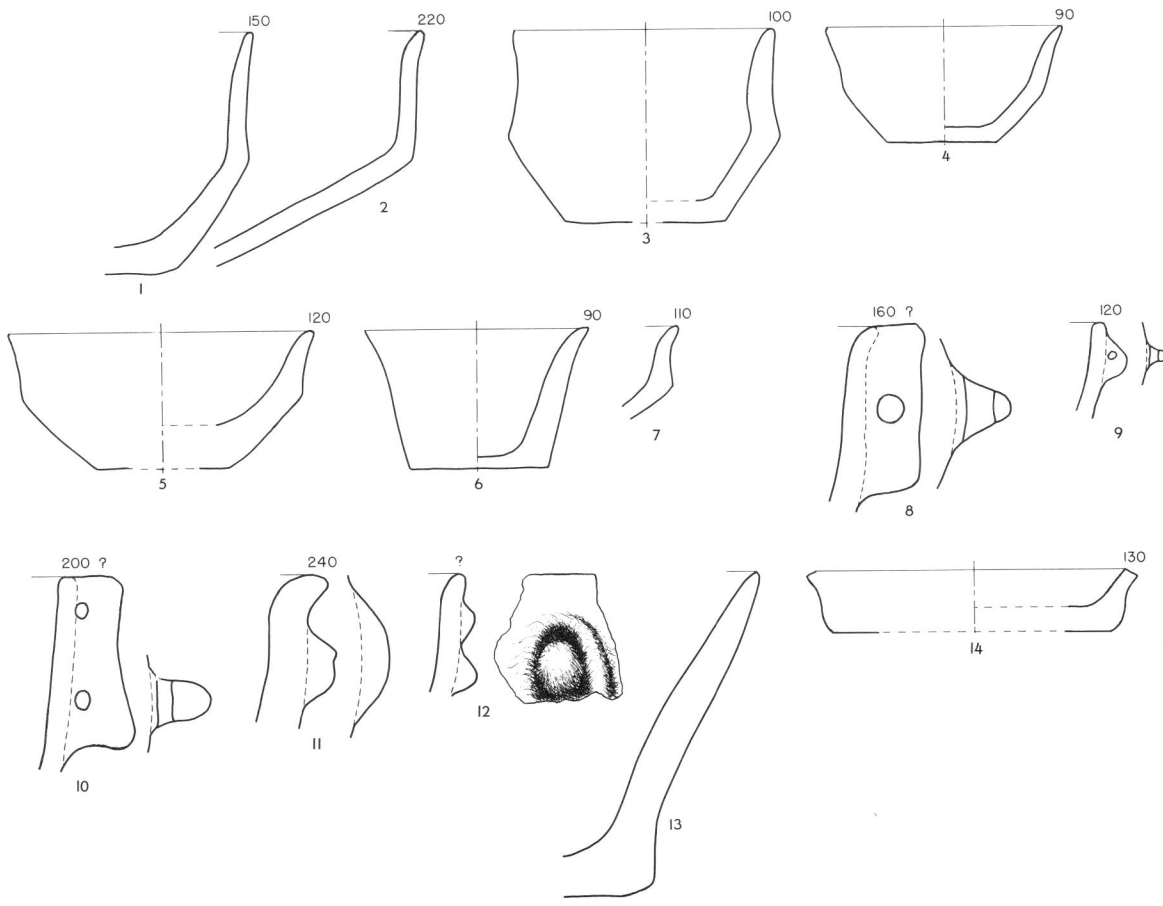

Fig. 108. Pottery from J-II,2.

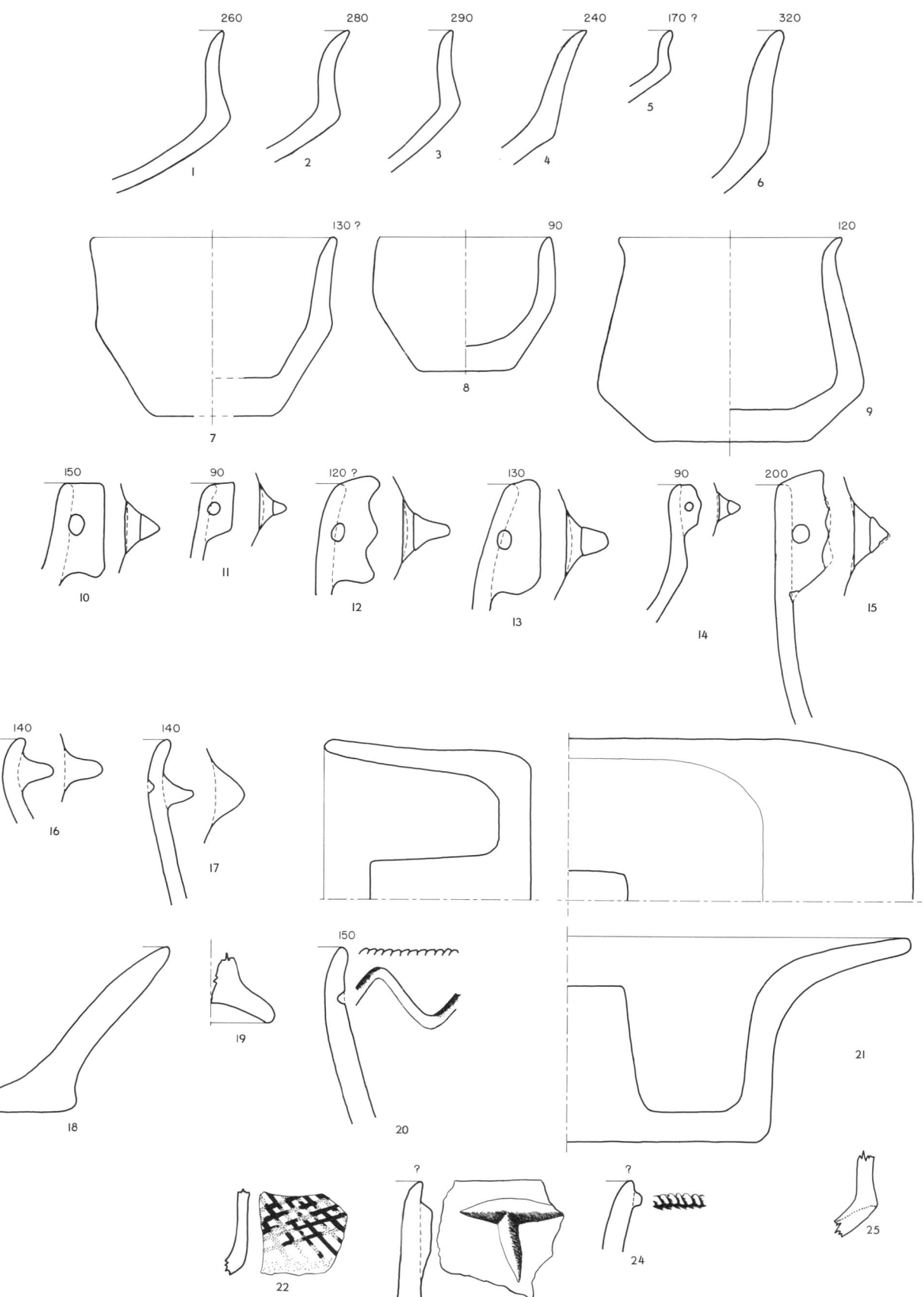

Fig. 109. Pottery from J-II,1.

Fig. 110. Jarmo stone vessels: type A, 6-7; type BC, 2-4; type E, 8; type F, 5; type G, 1. Scale ca. 3:4.

Fig. 111. Jarmo pottery: painted ware, *1-5*; simple ware, *6-8*; red burnished ware, *9*. Scales 1:3, *8*, ca. 3:5, *1-7,9*.

4

THE JARMO CHIPPED STONE
Frank Hole

INTRODUCTION	235
The Units of Analysis	235
TYPOLOGY AND DESCRIPTIVE TERMS	236
Terms Used in Description	236
General	236
Types of Chipping	236
DESCRIPTION OF CHIPPED STONE	237
Geometrics and "Other Microliths"	237
Types	237
Trapezes (fig. 112:1-12,14)	237
Triangles (fig. 112:13,15-16)	238
Crescents (fig. 112:17-18)	238
Diagonal-ended Bladelets (fig. 112:19-25)	238
Diagonal-ended and Backed Bladelets (fig. 112:26-28)	238
Backed Bladelets (fig. 112:29)	238
Discussion of Geometrics and "Other Microliths"	238
Piercing and Reaming Tools	239
Types	239
Shouldered Drills (figs. 113:16-22,25-27; 114:1-11)	239
Plain Drills (figs. 112:32-43; 113:1-9,11-12,14-15)	239
Pointed Pieces (figs. 114:15-21; 115:1-7,9)	239
Reamers or Fabricators (figs. 113:10,13,23-24,28; 114:12-14; 124:8-12,14-15,17)	241
Pressure-flaked Obsidian Fabricators (fig. 122:11-25)	241
Discussion of Piercing and Reaming Tools	241
Sickles	243
Types	243
Plain Sickles (figs. 115:8,10,12; 123:1-2)	243
Retouched Sickles (figs. 115:11,13-19; 116:1-4,7)	243
Discussion of Sickles	243
End Scrapers	244
Types	244
Blade, Round-ended Scrapers (figs. 118:9,14-22; 119:1,5-6,12,19)	244
Flake, Round-ended Scrapers (figs. 119:21-23; 120:1-12)	244
Flakes with Bulbar-end Retouch (fig. 121:4,9)	245
Blade, Miscellaneous-ended Scrapers (figs. 119:2-4,7-11,13-18,20)	245
Discussion of End Scrapers	245
"Other Scrapers"	245
Types	245

Denticulate Scrapers (fig. 121:1-3,5,7-8,12-13)	245
Notched Flakes (fig. 121:6,10)	245
Discussion of "Other Scrapers"	245
Miscellaneous Artifacts	247
Types	247
Thin Sections (figs. 122:1-10; 123:3-4)	247
Truncated Obsidian Blades and Flakes (fig. 122:26-40)	248
Burins (fig. 124:1-5,7)	249
Scaled Pieces (figs. 124:16; 125:1-7,12)	249
Microburins (fig. 124:6)	249
Discussion of Miscellaneous Artifacts	249
Retouched or Used Blades and Flakes	249
Types	249
Retouched or Used Blades (figs. 116:5-6,8-19; 117:1-8,11,13-17)	249
Retouched or Used Flakes (figs. 117:9-10,12; 118:1-8,13; 121:11)	251
Discussion of Retouched or Used Blades and Flakes	251
Residual Category	251
Types	251
Ground Pieces (figs. 124:13; 125:13)	251
Miscellaneous Backed Bladelets and Fragments (fig. 112:30-31)	251
Fragments of Piercing-Reaming Tools	253
Plain Blades and Blade Fragments (fig. 118:10-12)	253
Discussion of Plain Blades and Fragments	253
Chipping Debris	253
Types	254
Blade Cores (figs. 125:9-11,14-17; 126:7)	254
Flake Cores (fig. 126:1-3,5-6)	254
Core Fragments (figs. 125:8; 126:4)	254
Flakes without Retouch	254
Discussion of Chipping Debris	254
Discussion	257
Chronology	257
Uses of the Tools	257
The Nature of the Site	259
Levels Versus Phases	259
Comparisons with Other Sites	261
Concluding Remarks	262
Notes	262
Catalogue of Illustrated Chipped Stone	266
References	284

THE JARMO CHIPPED STONE

INTRODUCTION

The fundamental assumption on which this study is based is that chipped stone tools are a potentially valuable source of information about prehistoric ways of life and cultural practices. Stated simply, stone tools and the chips remaining from their manufacture can give us some insight into technological sophistication (craftsmanship), kinds of activities engaged in, and trade. Taken in conjunction with stratigraphic or other chronological information, stone tools can be made to yield information about changes in skills, activities, or trade, and, when dated in one context, they can also provide chronological information about contexts that cannot be dated independently. Other inferences can be made about areas of special activity within sites and even of social organization if the necessary correlative data on distribution and association are available. These are the principal ways in which studies of chipped stone can help archeologists with the general problem of reconstructing prehistoric ways of life. In the present study, chipped stone has suggested certain changes from the early levels to the latest and has given some clues about activities and some information about trade.

THE UNITS OF ANALYSIS

Both the interpretation and the basic description are done in the context of archeological units. The nature of the original problems and the excavations themselves suggested that I divide the areas excavated into two stratigraphic blocks, called here "lower Jarmo levels" and "upper Jarmo levels,"[1] which could be compared with one another but would still retain the distinct stratigraphy of the artifacts within these units by various building levels. There were two main excavation operations and many smaller ones (cf. fig. 24). The material analyzed here comes from operations J-I and J-II, but not all the material from either operation was used. To facilitate analysis, a block of stratigraphic levels from each operation was lumped and treated as a unit. The reasons for this lumping are outlined below.

J-I reached sterile soil on the western edge of the mound. Its levels 6, 7, and 8[2] are stratigraphically clear and aceramic. For the present interpretation, these levels are lumped together as "lower Jarmo levels" and represent one analytic unit. Above J-I,6 the relation of one level to another is ambiguous because of poorly preserved architectural traces. J-II, starting absolutely higher than J-I, was dug at the northern crest of the mound down to J-II,6, which at that spot was well above sterile soil. A step trench, operation A, immediately to the west of J-II, exposed the total depth of the mound. Presumably an absolute elevation in this step trench equivalent to J-II,6 would represent the same moment of time. Such an elevation in the step trench lies some three meters above sterile soil (see p. 164 and fig. 57). It must be noted that J-II,6 is not necessarily equivalent to J-I,6 in time. For convenience of interpretation, I chose to group together J-II,1-4 as representative of the ceramic occupation of the site, or "upper levels of Jarmo." (J-II,5 and 6 are included in the charts but are not assigned to either "upper" or "lower" levels.) It can safely be assumed here that the material in the "lower levels" is older than that in the "upper levels" of Jarmo; however, we do not know whether the "lower levels" represent the *earliest* occupation and "upper levels" the *latest* occupation, or just what interval separates the two.

Obviously, my use of two stratigraphically separate units for analysis presents problems by emphasizing the chronological extremes and completely ignoring the middle. Detailed studies, especially of change, are thus precluded for an indefinite segment of archeological time. It was precisely the indefiniteness of the middle ranges that led me to

---

This study was begun in 1958 as the basis of a Ph.D. dissertation on the Jarmo chipped stone artifacts. The work was interrupted by an archeological trip to Iran in 1959-60. Sarab was discovered and dug at this time; afterwards, its stone artifacts were included in the Ph.D. study, which was completed in 1961. Because this volume deals only with the archeological materials of the Iraqi sites, the Sarab analysis has been deleted. Since that time I have carried out excavations in Deh Luran, which have yielded voluminous new chipped stone material; therefore, the present version of this report reflects considerably more experience with chipped stone than the original version.

In order to understand the approach used here one must recall that in 1958 there had not yet been published any systematic studies of the total range of chipped stone from any site in the Zagros region. Accordingly, my first task was to establish a system by which the vast amount of data could be organized. In doing this I tried to serve two masters—description and interpretation. Describing the material provides a basis for comparative studies, and interpreting it can reveal the patterns of prehistoric activities in the perspective of time. The two processes are not necessarily compatible and required some compromise. The history of my decisions to change descriptive categories and methods of analysis over the years makes dull reading, but sufficient explanation will be given here to rationalize the final result.

The initial step was to develop a method of description that would enable me to set up a typology. Although many may disagree with both the descriptive system and the typology, it still remains, in its published version (Hole, Flannery, and Neely 1969), the only detailed study of all the chipped stone excavated from any site in the area. While I would do the analysis somewhat differently if I were starting anew, this model helps to achieve consistency—an advantage that perhaps outweighs any shortcomings it may have.

In developing a typology I was influenced most by discussions with Bruce Howe, Linda Braidwood, Jean Perrot, Hallam Movius, and Kent Flannery. The first three made many suggestions during the initial study in Chicago in 1958, and Movius gave me the opportunity to study European paleolithic types at the Abri Pataud in France. Suggestions from all of these people are incorporated in this report; however, the present result reflects work that Flannery and I subsequently did in Deh Luran. Although I received a great deal of help and sound advice from these people, I take full responsibility for the way I used it, and the conclusions can be considered mine.

As we gain experience, our ideas change. I no longer agree with many of the things I said in my earlier report and, as I mentioned previously, if I were starting this whole project again I would do it somewhat differently. However, since we cannot start anew each time we have another idea, it is important to present what we do have in as careful and useful a manner as possible. This I have tried to do.

[The manuscript for this chapter was essentially completed by 1973. Very few additions and only minor revisions have been made since that date.—EDS.]

use the extremes; had J-II reached sterile soil, there would have been no problem. But there is no way to get a stratigraphically clear-cut sample of the middle ranges of a size similar to J-I and J-II except by further excavation. Moreover, there is no way of telling now at which point, if any, the stratigraphic sequences of J-I and J-II overlap chronologically. For better or worse, we are still left with an analysis based on my best judgment in 1960-61.

TYPOLOGY AND DESCRIPTIVE TERMS

As I stated earlier, the description of the chipped stone was intended to organize a body of data in a form (1) that could be used to make comparisons between sites, so that it will be possible to say, for example, that trapezes are found at Jarmo but not at another site; (2) that will show chronological differences within the site; and (3) that can be used to make interpretations about prehistoric ways of life. In the absence of a suitable descriptive model, I chose to emphasize the differences that I could see; therefore, I described several types of tools, each with a number of variants. Some of the varieties helped in the subsequent analysis, but many did not. In the present report, therefore, I have eliminated many of the varieties of types simply by merging some groups. What remains is a simplified version of the first study, but it is more in line with the original intent. The present format is fairly similar to that of the Deh Luran report (Hole, Flannery, and Neely 1969).

The method of typing was to arrange the artifacts into groups that shared certain combinations of attributes (e.g., form, chipping technique, and size). The larger proportion of artifacts from a site can be typed, but there will nearly always be some examples that do not fit a type or for which the type cannot be determined because the piece is broken. These aberrant pieces are described here in a residual category.

In theory there is an almost infinite number of possible types, but even though archeologists may not agree on all details, there are some groups that they generally accept. For example, trapezes and blades are types that all archeologists will recognize. Numerous other categories, however, are not so universally recognized, and each archeologist may group them differently. What I have tried to do with such categories is to define them clearly and to use them consistently, so that the system of description remains constant, thus enabling one to make meaningful comparisons.

Terms Used in Description

General

Flint.—A series of cryptocrystalline quartzes, of which chert and chalcedony are two other varieties.

Obsidian.—A natural glass of volcanic origin.

Core.—A prepared lump of flint or obsidian from which flakes and blades were struck.

Flake.—Any piece of stone that was forcibly detached from a core. This is a very general category aimed at distinguishing waste material from tools.

Blade.—A flake that is parallel-sided and, when whole, at least twice as long as it is wide. It is relatively thin and has one or more ridges running the length of the piece. Crudely made blades are sometimes called "flake blades."

Bladelet.—A very small blade. The term is used here without any more precise denotation implied.

Microlith.—A small piece of chipped stone. Here the term "microlith" or "microlithic" is used to indicate small tools but not a type of tool. The term has been applied to the very small blades and flakes, especially of obsidian, that occur in great abundance in the Jarmo industry (SAOC 31, p. 45). Microliths occur alongside larger pieces in all chipped stone industries, and in general they can be considered the small end of a size continuum that includes large pieces as well.

Edge.—The portion of a blade that runs parallel to the axis. "Edge" is used here in the same locational, not functional, sense as "knife edge." "Primary edge" refers to one that has not been chipped. On flakes, edges are called "margins."

End.—The portion of a blade that is transverse to the axis. On most flakes the axis is not distinct, and, therefore, ends are considered to be at the bulb of percussion (see below) and opposite it.

Bulb of percussion.—A convex bulb on one end of a flake, at the point of conchoidal fracture, where it was struck from a core.

Bulbar surface (or face).—The surface on which the bulb of percussion is found. The bulbar face is plain, having no scars from previously struck flakes. It is also called the "reverse" or "ventral" side.

Upper surface.—The surface of a flake or blade that shows the scars of previously removed blades or flakes. It is opposite the bulbar face and is sometimes called the "obverse" or "dorsal" side.

Types of Chipping

Retouch.—The deliberate alteration of a primary blade or flake by a process of secondary chipping (see the various kinds of chipping described below). Tools are often, but not always, retouched. For example, plain blades, the most common type of tool at Jarmo, are not retouched. Except for plain blades, however, all the tools described here are retouched or used (see below).

Used.—Implements whose edges show chipping that was probably caused by use. On these examples the chipping tends to be localized along an edge, irregular, and relatively shallow. It is probably fruitless to try to distinguish retouch from use on many implements.

Squamous.—Retouch that consists of broad, shallow, and irregular flake scars. It is ordinarily used to shape the edges of scrapers.

Stepped.—Overhanging flake scars that occur in a series, producing a steep or semisteep face. This type of chipping, also called "resolved," merges typologically with steep and squamous retouch.

Steep.—Concentrated stepped and squamous chipping from one or both faces to produce an edge that is nearly perpendicular to the adjoining plain surface. This type of retouch is often called "backing" and is used to produce the blunt edge of a backed blade, to shape the end of a broken blade so that it becomes truncated, or to shape flakes into various forms of scrapers.

Nibbling.—Tiny, usually uniform flake scars occurring along an edge. Nibbling may be caused by use or by deliberate retouch.

Battering.—Concentrated stepped flaking on a small scale, usually producing a notch, or at least a very dull edge. Battering may result either from use or from deliberate retouch.

Nicking.—Deeply concave flake scars, often on alternate-opposite (upper and bulbar) faces of the same edge.

Crushing.—A dulled, pulverized edge produced by continuous pressure rather than a sharp blow.

Punch technique.—The use of a hard, pointed implement (a punch) to break a blade or flake. The technique results in a notch crushed into the point where the punch was set and a clean break across the remainder of the width of the piece.

DESCRIPTION OF CHIPPED STONE

An initial step in interpretation is to group the types[3] into categories that suggest similar uses for the tools so included. This grouping is based on simple inspection and my judgments about use.

Geometrics and "Other Microliths"

The six types included in this group[4] can be logically divided into two sets: the three geometric forms and the three types of retouched bladelets. The geometric forms were probably set transversely on the ends of arrow shafts, while the bladelets may have been arranged serially along the edges of shafts; hence, these tools relate specifically to hunting. The identification of these tools as arrowheads or barbs is based on both ethnographic and archeological sources (for a general reference see Clark 1963, figs. 13 and 14).

The bladelets are extremely small. For a comparison of the sizes of the various microliths, see table 3.

Table 3.—Percentage of Bladelets by Size Class

Type of bladelet	Level	Total number measured*	Size class (max. width)		
			Less than 4 mm	4-7 mm	7-10 mm
Backed† and diagonal-ended and backed	Upper	96	37%	51%	12%
	Lower	25	40%	56%	4%
Diagonal-ended	Upper	2	50%	50%	0%
	Lower	63	83%	17%	0%

* Totals for the two types of backed bladelets include measurable but broken examples that are counted in the residual category because their type could not be determined.

† All of the backed bladelets and the diagonal-ended bladelets are less than 10 mm wide. The highly standardized manufacture of the diagonal-ended bladelets is emphasized by the facts that they are typically narrower than the other two types and that their edges have not been artificially narrowed by backing.

Types

Trapezes (No. 1): 124 (flint, 25; obsidian, 99)

Trapezes are sections of blades or, rarely, flakes, broken and retouched so that the shape of the finished piece is trapezoidal.

In the prototype group consisting of 82 examples, the edges of the parent blade remain sharp, but the ends are retouched diagonally to the axis of the blade. The retouch is steep and was directed apparently indiscriminately from the bulbar side (fig. 112:1-2,4), rarely from the top (fig. 112:3,5), or in combination, that is, top on one edge and bottom on the other (fig. 112:6). In some cases the primary edge of the blade is nicked (fig. 112:7), and a few examples show retouch only part way across the ends (fig. 112:9). One trapeze was made on a flake (fig. 112:8). Specimens in this group can be considered finished examples of the ideal type.

A second group, 28 pieces, perhaps representing unfinished trapezes, has retouch on only one end (fig. 112:10-11), while the other end is simply broken to give the piece a trapezoidal shape.

The final group is composed of 14 examples whose two ends have been broken to give them a rough trapezoidal shape, often with a tang (fig. 112:12,14). These pieces are not retouched, and it seems likely that they were the roughed-out blanks from which the finished trapezes were made.

All but 4 examples occurred in J-II, levels 1, 2, 2fl., and 3; the 4 others were from J-I,7 and 8. Trapezes also occur at Sarab (one example, Hole 1961), Kuhbanen (Huckriede 1962, fig. 4), and in the Bayat phase in Deh Luran (one example, see Hole, Flannery, and Neely 1969, p. 77).

Triangles (No. 2): 12 (flint, 4; obsidian, 8)

Triangles form a small group similar to trapezes except that the retouched ends converge in an acute angle, leaving only one primary edge (fig. 112:13). This group is variable, including 2 relatively heavy pieces that have some chipping on their primary edge (fig. 112:15) and 2 that are flakes whose bulbar end is the apex of the triangle (fig. 112:16).

Triangles are closely related to and sometimes not distinguishable from trapezes and crescents.

Distribution is confined to J-II,1 and 2.

Crescents (No. 3): 6 (flint, 5; obsidian, 1)

Crescents are sections of blades or flakes broken and retouched so that the finished piece is crescent shaped. Three are made from blade sections and closely resemble the triangles and trapezes (fig. 112:17). Two are made from flakes that had both faces plain (fig. 112:18), and one was made from a flake that showed scars on the upper face.

Crescents were found in J-II, levels 1, 2fl., and 3, as well as in J-I,8. They have also been found at Zawi Chemi (R.L. Solecki 1964, p. 407) and Tepe Guran (Mortensen, pers. comm.) and in the Sabz phase in Deh Luran (Hole, Flannery, and Neely 1969, p. 77).

Diagonal-ended Bladelets (No. 4): 65 (flint, 25; obsidian, 40)

Diagonal-ended bladelets have retouch that is diagonal to the axis, across one end. The edges usually have no retouch. The overall shape is that of a scalene triangle, caused by the natural attenuation of the end which forms the apex of the triangle; the other end is snapped and subsequently retouched to produce a diagonal end (fig. 112:19-20) or rarely a concave end (fig. 112:24). The diagonal end is seldom made on the attenuation rather than on the bulbar end (fig. 112:21). Some examples have nibbling on the primary edges, usually near the attenuated end (fig. 112:22-23,25). A few pieces have traces of bitumen.

Distribution is confined to J-I,6-8, except for 2 examples from J-II,1-2. Similar pieces have been found in the Bus Mordeh, Ali Kosh, and Mohammad Jaffar phases in Deh Luran (Hole, Flannery, and Neely 1969, p. 77).

Diagonal-ended and Backed Bladelets (Nos. 5, 6): 17 (flint, 11; obsidian, 6)

Two varieties of bladelets are described here. The first group consists of 12 scalene triangles that have steep retouch on the "back" (fig. 112:26). On some of these there is also nibbling on the primary edge. Five pieces also have a sharp tip at the end opposite the diagonal that was formed by steep retouch on both edges (fig. 112:27). The 4 pieces in the second group have backing on the longest straight edge which merges with the diagonal in an acute angle (fig. 112:28).

Most of the bladelets were scattered in the upper part of J-II; 2 were in J-I,7 and 8. (Two other examples—fig. 112:26-27—are from J-I,3.) Others have been found at Zawi Chemi (R.L. Solecki 1964, p. 407), Karim Shahir (SAOC 31, p. 52), and Sarab (Hole 1961), and in the Bus Mordeh, Ali Kosh, and Mohammad Jaffar phases in Deh Luran (Hole, Flannery, and Neely 1969, p. 78).

Backed Bladelets (No. 7): 22 (flint, 11; obsidian, 11)

Backed bladelets are those on which the backed edge merges in an unbroken arc or line with one primary edge to produce a point. The "point" may be curved (fig. 112:29) or straight and may be tapered to a needlelike or a broader, blunter end.

Examples occurred mostly in the upper part of J-II, but one occurred in each of levels 6, 7, and 8 in J-I. Backed bladelets were also found at Zawi Chemi (R.L. Solecki 1964, p. 407), Karim Shahir (SAOC 31, p. 52), and Sarab (Hole 1961), and in the Bus Mordeh, Ali Kosh, and Mohammad Jaffar phases in Deh Luran (Hole, Flannery, and Neely 1969, p. 78).

DISCUSSION OF GEOMETRICS AND "OTHER MICROLITHS"

Inasmuch as the function of these artifacts is not seriously in question, this discussion will be limited to the chronological changes in the types and their implications concerning changes in patterns of hunting.

It is striking that of 142 geometric forms (trapezes, triangles, and crescents), 137 were found in J-II,1-3 and only 5 were found in earlier levels (1 in J-I,7 and 4 in J-I,8). This strongly suggests that the pieces found at the bottom of the lower levels are intrusive, and there are two other sound archeological reasons for thinking this. First, in the Deh Luran excavations geometrics do not antedate the appearance of pottery (Hole, Flannery, and Neely 1969, p. 77; unpublished data from Chagha Sefid). Second, the excavations at both Ali Kosh and Chagha Sefid showed that rodents, burrowing from the surface of the site 7-10 meters down to the lowest archeological strata, brought modern artifacts into prepottery contexts. One must expect similar rodent action in most sites.

Equally noteworthy is that only 2 of the diagonal-ended bladelets are found in later context than J-I,6. The distribution of geometrics and that of "other microliths" are thus quite limited and possibly mutually exclusive.

Inspection of table 4A also shows a peculiar fact: there are almost no geometrics and "other microliths" in the lower portion of J-II. The occurrence of a tool type in any particular stratum can depend on several things: (a) the kind of deposit (e.g., house, midden, workshop), (b) the quantity of artifacts recovered and the consequent probability that any particular type will be found, and (c) changes in the techniques of manufacture or in activities that would eliminate or add types as time passes. We do not have data that will permit us to assess the first two factors. Changes in chipping technique seem not to have been involved, nor is there substantial evidence for a change in hunting activities, although I initially suggested that the diagonal-ended bladelets might have been used on thrusting spears to hunt herd animals on the valley floor while the geometric forms might have been used with bows and arrows to hunt smaller, solitary game (Hole 1961, pp. 126-28). This hypothesis, which was based on the occurrence of different microlithic types with different animals, has not been supported by more recent evidence (Hole, Flannery, and Neely 1969, p. 77). Of course, bows and arrows could have been introduced with the geometrics, but we have no way to test this possibility. Either form could have been used with the bow.

A simple inspection of the number of tools in each level and especially of their percentages (table 4B) would lead one to think hunting was more important in the time range represented by the upper Jarmo levels, but judging by the information obtained from faunal remains, this contention is not justified.

When all the Jarmo levels are taken into consideration, we find that 67% of this group of tools were made of obsidian. Furthermore, while 60% of the geometrics and "other microliths" in the lower levels were made of obsidian, in the upper levels the percentage increased to 70%. This shows that obsidian was decidedly preferred for making these tools and that more of this imported material was available in the upper levels.

Piercing and Reaming Tools

Although there is considerable variety in the types included here, there seems little doubt that they served the purposes of piercing and reaming. The specific sizes and shapes of these tools probably relate to their use on different materials and for different specialized tasks.

Types

Shouldered Drills (No. 11): 110 (flint, 102; obsidian, 8)

Shouldered drills are blade sections which have bilateral steep retouch at one end. Ordinarily the edges of the remainder of the piece are unaltered, and the butt or shaft end of the piece is considerably wider than the shaft. The shaft may vary in length, but it is characteristically uniform in width throughout its length. Many pieces are whole and retain the bulbar end (figs. 113:16-22,25,27; 114:1,3,5,10). Some pieces have traces of grinding (concentric striations) on their tips showing that they were used to drill hard material (figs. 113:26; 114:2,6-7,11), and others have smoothly polished shafts (fig. 114:4). In some cases the drilling of holes of various sizes is indicated by zones of different diameter along the shaft (fig. 114:9,11). One example (fig. 114:8) had red ochre on the tip.

With the exception of 2 obsidian examples (J-I,6 and 7), all shouldered drills are confined to J-II.

Plain Drills (Nos. 8, 9): 209 (flint, 172; obsidian, 37)

Plain drills are made from blades, blade sections, and flakes by means of bilateral steep retouch that converges in a sharp point; the tips are all less than 5 mm in diameter. Typically the edges merge by means of a bilateral tapering (figs. 112:32-43; 113:1-2,6-8,11), although one edge may taper and the other remain straight (fig. 113:3-4). The flint blades usually have some primary edge remaining because the retouch is confined to the zone of tapering; in most of the obsidian examples the opposite is the case. Most of these drills are formed by retouch on the upper face; nearly as many are shaped by alternate-opposite retouch. A few pieces are double ended (fig. 113:5), and some have traces of grinding on the tip (fig. 113:9,12,14-15).

Plain drills appear throughout the upper and lower levels of Jarmo.

Pointed Pieces (Nos. 13, 14): 122 (flint, 112; obsidian, 10)

Pointed pieces are made from flakes (figs. 114:21; 115:1,4-7,9) and rarely from blades (figs. 114:15-20; 115:2-3). They have limited retouch at one end, forming a point or tip. These pieces are probably functionally equivalent to drills and awls, but they lack evidence of careful shaping and consequently are highly variable morphologically. A few tips show traces of grinding. All the examples made on flakes are flint.

Table 4.—Geometrics and "Other Microliths"

A. Stratigraphic Occurrence*

Operation and level	Geometrics				"Other microliths"				
	Trapezes	Triangles	Crescents	Diagonal-ended bladelets	Diagonal-ended and backed bladelets	Backed bladelets	Sub-total	Total
J-II,1	12	4	--	--	5	2	23	73
	40	3	1	1	--	5	50	
J-II,2	6	--	--	1	3	3	13	69
	46	5	--	--	3	2	56	
J-II,2fl.	6	--	3	--	--	1	10	19
	6	--	--	--	1	2	9	
J-II,3	--	--	1	--	1	2	4	9
	4	--	--	--	--	1	5	
J-II,4	--	--	--	--	--	1	1	1
	--	--	--	--	--	--	--	
J-II,5	--	--	--	--	1	--	1	2
	--	--	--	--	1	--	1	
J-II,6	--	--	--	--	--	--	--	0
	--	--	--	--	--	--	--	
J-I,6	--	--	--	1	--	--	1	5
	--	--	--	3	--	1	4	
J-I,7	--	--	--	5	--	1	6	11
	1	--	--	3	1	--	5	
J-I,8	1	--	1	18	1	1	22	57
	2	--	--	33	--	--	35	
Flint	25	4	5	25	11	11	81	
Obsidian	99	8	1	40	6	11	165	
Total	124	12	6	65	17	22	246	

B. Totals and Percentages to Total Retouched Tools

Operation and level	Total retouched tools	Geometrics		"Other microliths"	
		Total	%	Total	%
J-II,1	2,182	60	2.7	13	0.6
J-II,2	1,968	57	2.9	12	0.6
J-II,2fl.	1,029	15	1.5	4	0.4
J-II,3	822	5	0.6	4	0.5
J-II,4	526	--	--	1	0.2
J-II,5	798	--	--	2	0.3
J-II,6	612	--	--	--	--
J-I,6	757	--	--	5	0.7
J-I,7	695	1	0.1	10	1.4
J-I,8	1,173	4	0.3	53	4.5

*For each level: upper row = flint; lower row = obsidian.

Pointed pieces appear throughout the sequence.

Reamers or Fabricators (Nos. 10, 12, 38): 141 (flint, 110; obsidian, 31)

Relatively thick blades and thick elongated flakes are used to produce reamers or fabricators that usually have bilateral retouch. The retouch is often steep. The retouched edges are more or less parallel and never converge in a point; the ends are often blunted by retouch.

A number of varieties can be distinguished here for descriptive purposes, but there are no noteworthy chronological differences between them. One group consists of blade segments that have steep retouch along the whole of both edges. The bulbar end is intact and the other end is usually broken (fig. 113:10,13,23-24,28). Another group has intermittent, squamous, and often bifacial retouch along the two edges extending to the bulbar end (fig. 114:13-14). The retouch is generally predominant on one edge (fig. 114:12). The last group consists of relatively thick pieces, about equal in thickness and width, that have heavy steep, squamous, and stepped flaking over most of the edges, sometimes covering most of the surface. The flaking may be alternate-opposite. Some are triangular in section (fig. 124:8-10,12,14,17), and others more rectangular (fig. 124:11,15). All examples in the last group have blunt tips.

All varieties occur scattered throughout Jarmo. They are found also at Zawi Chemi (R.L. Solecki 1964, p. 407) and Sarab, except for the last group mentioned above (Hole 1961), and in the Bus Mordeh, Ali Kosh, and Mohammad Jaffar phases in Deh Luran (Hole, Flannery, and Neely 1969, p. 79).

Pressure-flaked Obsidian Fabricators (No. 34): 87

These rodlike pieces, all made of obsidian, have neat pressure flaking along one or both edges. The flaking is usually deep, leaving a serrated edge (fig. 122:18). On the smallest pieces the retouch is often steep (fig. 122:23). Some pieces are chipped only in spots, and the bulbar end is left intact (fig. 122:19). The following examples show the range of variation in chipping: both edges chipped on the bulbar face (fig. 122:17,19-20,23), one edge chipped on the bulbar face (fig. 122:11-12,21,24-25), both edges chipped—one on the upper and the other on the bulbar face—(fig. 122:13-14,22), and both edges chipped on the upper face (fig. 122:16,18). Some pieces show splintering on the ends as if they had been used as a punch (fig. 122:15).

By far the greatest number of pressure-flaked obsidian fabricators, 71 out of 87, occurred in the lower Jarmo levels.[5]

DISCUSSION OF PIERCING AND REAMING TOOLS

The two types of piercing and reaming tools that show the most careful chipping and, consequently, the most standardization, are also the best chronological indicators. Shouldered drills belong with the upper levels of Jarmo (only 2 examples out of 110 were found in the lower levels), and pressure-flaked obsidian fabricators were found principally in the lowermost levels (table 5A). The remainder of the types in this functional grouping show a more consistent distribution throughout the levels.

Perhaps the most interesting fact, however, is that drills, both plain and shouldered, are found in extraordinarily large quantities in J-II,6, as compared with all the levels in J-I. Taken together these two types make up 9.3% of the retouched tools of that stratum (table 5B). Note, too, that drills and fabricators are found in J-II,4-6 in numbers that are consistent with the area exposed, in contrast with the geometrics and "other microliths," which were absent or rare in the same levels. The evidence suggests that the nature of the site in J-II,4-6 was different from that in the uppermost and lowermost levels.

One advantage of making fine typological distinctions is illustrated by comparing the distribution of pressure-flaked obsidian fabricators with that of other fabricators that might have been considered in the same group, on the ground that they served the same purpose. Although the division into two types may not tell us anything about functional differences, it does give valuable information about changing preferences in materials. Obsidian was heavily favored for fabricators in the lower Jarmo levels.

The clearest instance of use is seen in shouldered drills, a type that I suggest was used principally for drilling beads. The bits frequently show traces of rotary grinding action in holes of small diameter. The tips of both the shouldered drills and the plain drills fit into a hole of 5 mm or less in diameter. It may be that the basic difference between plain and shouldered drills is that the latter were used longer and drilled deeper into the material being bored.

Pointed pieces should be considered tools that were used fortuitously and discarded without having been fashioned into standardized implements. Such tools would have served to prick holes or to engrave wood or bone.

The heavy retouch on the fabricators suggests that they were used either to ream out smaller drilled holes or else to drill and ream soft material such as wood. The pressure-flaked obsidian fabricators would have served well as rasps because of their regular ripple edges.

Most of the drills (88%) were made from flint, whereas half (52%) of the reamers and fabricators were made from obsidian. This choice suggests a functional difference. Obsidian is more brittle than flint and probably not as durable for drilling, especially when the bit may be subjected to horizontal as well as vertical pressure. Yet it can have a somewhat sharper edge and may be at least as suitable as flint for shaping wood.

Table 5.—Piercing-Reaming Tools

A. Stratigraphic Occurrence*

Operation and level	Shouldered drills	Plain drills	Pointed pieces	Reamers or fabricators	Pressure-flaked obsidian fabricators	Subtotal	Total
J-II,1	13 / 3	44 / 8	19 / 2	40 / 10	-- / 4	116 / 27	143
J-II,2	19 / 2	27 / 17	10 / 1	18 / 5	-- / 6	74 / 31	105
J-II,2fl.	16 / 2	16 / 4	10 / 2	13 / 1	-- / 2	55 / 11	66
J-II,3	4 / --	9 / 1	10 / --	9 / 2	-- / 2	32 / 5	37
J-II,4	6 / --	10 / 1	2 / 1	6 / 2	-- / --	24 / 4	28
J-II,5	13 / --	15 / --	4 / 1	7 / 5	-- / 2	39 / 8	47
J-II,6	30 / --	27 / --	9 / --	7 / 1	-- / --	73 / 1	74
J-I,6	-- / 1	12 / 2	22 / 1	2 / --	-- / 11	36 / 15	51
J-I,7	1 / --	5 / 1	7 / 1	4 / 2	-- / 22	17 / 26	43
J-I,8	-- / --	7 / 3	19 / 1	4 / 3	-- / 38	30 / 45	75
Flint	102	172	112	110	0	496	
Obsidian	8	37	10	31	87	173	
Total	110	209	122	141	87		669

B. Totals and Percentages to Total Retouched Tools

Total retouched tools	Shouldered drills Total	%	Plain drills Total	%	Pointed pieces Total	%	Reamers or fabricators Total	%	Pressure-flaked obsidian fabricators Total	%
2,182	16	0.7	52	2.4	21	1.0	50	2.3	4	0.2
1,968	21	1.1	44	2.2	11	0.6	23	1.2	6	0.3
1,029	18	1.7	20	1.9	12	1.2	14	1.4	2	0.2
822	4	0.5	10	1.2	10	1.2	11	1.3	2	0.2
526	6	1.1	11	2.1	3	0.6	8	1.5	--	--
798	13	1.6	15	1.9	5	0.6	12	1.5	2	0.3
612	30	4.9	27	4.4	9	1.5	8	1.3	--	--
757	1	0.1	14	1.8	23	3.0	2	0.3	11	1.5
695	1	0.1	6	0.9	8	1.2	6	0.9	22	3.2
1,173	--	--	10	0.9	20	1.7	7	0.6	38	3.2

*For each level: upper row = flint; lower row = obsidian.

Sickles

All of the flints described here[6] have a gloss on one or both edges which, according to recent studies made by Witthoft, "results from frictional fusion of flint and dehydration and fusion of opal to flint surfaces" (Witthoft 1967, p. 388). The opal derives from the cortex and fibers of the cereal grains that were reaped with the sickles. Although Witthoft's findings vary from the traditional view that sheen results from the polishing action of fine-grained silica on the flint, they fully substantiate the idea that gloss is produced during the cutting of cereal grains. Accordingly, there is no reason not to refer to these implements as sickles.

Reused sickles are not included in the following discussion on counts, since they have been dealt with in the section on retouched or used blades (see p. 249 and table 13A).

Types

Plain Sickles (No. 15): 447 (flint)

Plain sickles are blades, blade fragments, and elongated flakes that have a gloss or sheen on one or both edges but do not have retouch on either edge. There may be some nicking or irregular chipping, probably resulting from use (fig. 115:8,10,12).

Plain sickles occur throughout the sequence (table 6A).

Table 6.—Sickles

A. Stratigraphic Occurrence   B. Totals and Percentages to Total Retouched Tools

Operation and level	Plain sickles	Retouched sickles	Total*	Total retouched tools	Plain sickles Total	%	Retouched sickles Total	%
J-II,1	127	48	175	2,182	127	5.8	48	2.2
J-II,2	67	25	92	1,968	67	3.4	25	1.3
J-II,2fl.	35	14	49	1,029	35	3.4	14	1.4
J-II,3	37	17	54	822	37	4.5	17	2.1
J-II,4	14	10	24	526	14	2.7	10	1.9
J-II,5	26	13	39	798	26	3.3	13	1.6
J-II,6	7	3	10	612	7	1.1	3	0.5
J-I,6	34	14	48	757	34	4.5	14	1.8
J-I,7	50	15	65	695	50	7.2	15	2.2
J-I,8	50	13	63	1,173	50	4.3	13	1.1
Total	447	172	619					

*Totals of sickles do not include *reused* sickles; for the latter see table 13A.

Retouched Sickles (No. 16): 172 (flint)

Retouched sickles are a varied group, and it is difficult to determine whether subdivisions within it have any functional significance; however, there are chronological implications in the distribution of the varieties.

Sickles in the largest group (77 examples) have retouch along one whole edge of the bulbar face (fig. 115:13,16-19), and it is this edge that has the sheen. In some cases there is also chipping on the edge without sheen.

Those in the second largest group (46 examples) have edges that are smoothly rounded, presumably through prolonged use. With one exception these sickles are confined to J-II; moreover, most of them are made on a type of flint that is characteristic of J-II.[7]

Another group (38 examples) consists of miscellaneous irregular flakes and blades, a catchall category for those pieces that do not fit the other groupings (fig. 116:2-4,7). These are found throughout Jarmo.

Other varieties are sickles with retouch on both bulbar edges (6 examples; fig. 115:11,14-15) and truncated sickles (5 examples; fig. 116:1).

Retouched sickles have been found throughout the site, but the second largest group (except for 1 example) is limited to J-II.

Discussion of Sickles

The sickles reported here are all flint which, of course, shows sheen. Although obsidian blades, too, may have been used for sickles, no sheen was detected on their naturally shiny edges. If Witthoft (1967) is correct that opaline gloss accumulates on the original edge of a sickle through use, it should be possible to detect it on obsidian, perhaps by making microscopic thin sections. This has not been done, and it has not been possible for me to review the obsidian blades with this idea in mind.

It is likely that flint was preferred for sickles in any case. Though sharp, obsidian is more brittle than flint, and it may have proved less desirable. The data are not sufficient to support a final conclusion, but it has been found, as at Mersin, that although obsidian tools occurred in abundance, tools identified as sickles were made of local flint (Burkitt 1938, p. 107).

One might form a hypothesis that the frequency of occurrence of sickles would vary with the importance of agriculture and expect that this could be readily tested in a site such as Jarmo, where agriculture could have undergone some development.[8] This hypothesis is amply borne out in Deh Luran, where we have a 3,000-year sequence and detailed information on the agricultural history. There, sickles are found with gradually increasing frequency through the Bus Mordeh (3.4%), Ali Kosh (5.3%), and Mohammad Jaffar (7.6%) phases, and their numbers increase markedly in the Sabz phase (23.0%), when a new and more effective agriculture was practiced. By the Bayat phase (about 4000 B.C.) 42.4% of the chipped stone tools were sickles.

At Jarmo we find this is not the case. Sickles were found in similar frequencies throughout the site with no apparent trend through time, averaging 5.9%; the average for J-I is 6.7% and for J-II, 5.6% (table 6B). We might take these data to suggest that there was little, if any, change in the relative importance of agriculture at Jarmo.

The sickles do, however, show some differences between J-I and J-II in two respects. First, there is a tendency for the blades in J-II to be broader than those in J-I, although by far the majority of both groups fall between 10 and 20 mm in width (table 7). Such change as is visible in the J-II sickles probably resulted from the use of flint from a different source in J-II (see n. 7). This different flint, which was obvious in visual inspection, was rarely used in J-I. (However, the type of flint used in J-I continued to be used alongside the new material.) The group of retouched sickles whose edges are rounded and worn through use, most of which are made on the new flint, suggests the second difference between the sickles of J-I and J-II.

Table 7.—Percentage of Sickles by Size Class

Operation (all levels)	Total number measured*	Size class (maximum width)†					
		Less than 7 mm	10 mm	15 mm	20 mm	25 mm	Greater than 25 mm
J-II	397	0%	2%	41%	51%	5%	1%
J-I	217	0%	12%	60%	21%	6%	1%

*Includes reused sickles but does not include sickles that have an edge missing.
†The width of retouched sickles is less than the width of the primary blade.

END SCRAPERS

End scrapers of all kinds occur throughout Jarmo with no obvious trends in overall frequency or in the relative abundance of any of the types; thus they have little value as chronological indicators.

TYPES

Blade, Round-ended Scrapers (No. 20): 155 (flint, 146; obsidian, 9)

Round-ended scrapers made on blades have one or both ends convexly rounded, usually by steep retouch that extends to one or both of the edges (fig. 118:9,16-17,19,21). Some scraping ends are rounded smooth by prolonged use; these appear almost to have been ground and polished (figs. 118:14-15,20,22; 119:1,5). A few are double ended (figs. 118:18; 119:6,12,19). Eight of the 17 double-ended examples are made from obsidian, whereas only 1 of the remaining 138 was made from obsidian.

Round-ended scrapers made on blades have been found throughout the sequence.

Flake, Round-ended Scrapers (Nos. 25-27): 236 (flint, 234; obsidian, 2)

The largest group of round-ended scrapers made on flakes are probably functionally equivalent to those made on blades, although the range in thickness is much greater in the scrapers made on flakes. Thin ones look much like the blade scrapers (figs. 119:22-23; 120:1,4-5,11), but the extremely bulky ones are similar only in the shape of the retouched end (fig. 120:3,6). Many examples are worn through prolonged use (fig. 120:2).

Two subgroups are recognizable. The first, with 6 examples, is an oval-shaped, keeled scraper, sometimes made on a bladelet core (fig. 120:7-9). The best examples are readily distinguished, but some examples grade into round-ended scrapers or steep denticulate scrapers (fig. 120:10,12). Four examples were found in J-I,8, two in J-II,6, and one in J-II,5. The second group consists of 2 discoidal scrapers. These are flakes that have steep retouch around their entire periphery to produce a smooth convex edge (fig. 119:21). Both occur in J-I,6.

Aside from the restricted distribution of these two subgroups, round-ended scrapers made on flakes are distributed throughout the sequence.

Flakes with Bulbar-end Retouch (No. 32): 42 (flint, 39; obsidian, 3)

Flakes with secondary retouch on the bulbar end have a smooth edge suitable for scraping (fig. 121:4,9). They are thin in section and more or less crescentic or subround in plan. Many of these pieces resemble core tablets or core revival flakes, but they seem to have secondary retouch which smoothed the denticulate edges of the core platforms. Whatever their ultimate origin, these pieces could well have functioned as end scrapers. After studying materials from Sarab, where this type was very common, I separated these pieces from the round-ended scrapers made on flakes with which I had originally grouped them.

These tools are distributed throughout the sequence. They also occur at Sarab (Hole 1961) and in the Ali Kosh, Mohammad Jaffar, and Sabz phases in Deh Luran (Hole, Flannery, and Neely 1969, pp. 86-87).

Blade, Miscellaneous-ended Scrapers (Nos. 21-24): 469 (flint, 284; obsidian, 185)

Most of the miscellaneous-ended pieces could have resulted from use; they are not well made and do not conform to a clearly defined pattern.

Four varieties of miscellaneous-ended scrapers made on blades are included here. The scrapers in the largest and most uniform group have concave ends. These pieces were made by deliberately breaking the blade; in many cases the remaining concave-ended sections retain the bulb (fig. 119:2,8). Of the 105 examples, 64 are made from obsidian.

Another uniform group, with 53 examples of which 44 are obsidian, is made up of blades that have steep retouch diagonally across one end (fig. 119:11,17). Some have an asymmetrical tip produced by the intersection of two diagonals (fig. 119:16). Primary edges may have some nicking, nibbling, or squamous retouch. These pieces are always wider than the largest of the diagonal-ended microliths.

The third group, which is more diverse than the preceding two, contains 292 pieces, only 59 of which are obsidian. The artifacts in this group have horizontal (fig. 119:3-4,7,15), convex and concave diagonal (fig. 119:9,20), and notched (fig. 119:10) ends. A number of sickles were reused as end scrapers (fig. 119:13-14).

The fourth group consists of 19 pieces (18 obsidian) that have retouch on the bulbar face of one end. The retouch is squamous and often produces an irregular edge (fig. 119:18).

All four varieties are distributed throughout the sequence.

DISCUSSION OF END SCRAPERS

The lack of change in tools within this group suggests that the tasks for which they were used remained constant throughout the levels at Jarmo. The frequency distribution of the varieties within the group does fluctuate somewhat, however, and in addition, fewer scrapers appear, on the average, in the upper levels of J-II (table 8A,B).

End scrapers were probably used for a variety of tasks ranging from preparing skins to shaping wood. It is likely that many of the miscellaneous-ended scrapers made on blades were used on wood or bone, for they seem to be unsuited to scraping hides. Hide scrapers that are known ethnographically are usually rounded and have smooth edges, which would not tear the skins. We should note, however, that round-ended scrapers might also be used to shape wood. Müller-Beck's reconstruction of the technique of manufacturing wooden bowls with the scrapers is a good example (Müller-Beck 1965, figs. 288-89).

"OTHER SCRAPERS"

Included here are artifacts which are generally considered in archeological literature as scrapers, although they appear to be relatively crude and unstandardized as compared with end scrapers.

TYPES

Denticulate Scrapers (Nos. 28, 29): 918 (flint, 887; obsidian, 31)

Denticulate scrapers are made on thick flakes and chunks. Step flaking along the edge produces a rough, multinotched, or denticulate edge. Many of the chunks resemble very small one-directional flake cores (fig. 121:2). The retouch may be on all the edges (fig. 121:5) or on part of an edge or edges (fig. 121:1,3,7). Most examples have relatively steep retouch at the edges, although some, essentially similar to the others in quality of chipping and in the edge produced (fig. 121:8,12-13), have somewhat less steep retouch.

Denticulate scrapers are found at Jarmo throughout the sequence and also at Sarab (Hole 1961).

Notched Flakes (No. 30): 232 (flint, 228; obsidian, 4)

Notched flakes and fragments have a single notch worked into an edge by means of concentrated step flaking (fig. 121:6,10). Many of these notches could have resulted from use.

Notched flakes occurred throughout the sequence.

DISCUSSION OF "OTHER SCRAPERS"

Both types of "other scrapers" occurred throughout the site, although the quantities fluctuated considerably; in most cases, denticulate scrapers were at least three times as common (table 9A,B). It seems likely that notched flakes are

Table 8.—End Scrapers

A. Stratigraphic Occurrence*

Operation and level	Blades, round-ended	Flakes, round-ended	Flakes, retouched bulbar end	Blades, miscellaneous-ended	Subtotal	Total
J-II,1	23 2	21 1	3 1	52 26	99 30	129
J-II,2	14 2	15 --	5 --	46 61	80 63	143
J-II,2fl.	13 2	5 --	4 --	30 18	52 20	72
J-II,3	9 --	14 --	1 --	13 14	37 14	51
J-II,4	12 --	34 --	2 --	15 6	63 6	69
J-II,5	13 --	36 1	8 --	16 5	73 6	79
J-II,6	7 --	15 --	1 --	16 4	39 4	43
J-I,6	28 1	43 --	7 2	33 21	111 24	135
J-I,7	11 1	25 --	4 --	21 10	61 11	72
J-I,8	16 1	26 --	4 --	42 20	88 21	109
Flint	146	234	39	284	703	
Obsidian	9	2	3	185	199	
Total	155	236	42	469		902

B. Totals and Percentages to Total Retouched Tools

Operation and level	Total retouched tools	Blades, round-ended		Flakes, round-ended		Flakes, retouched bulbar end		Blades, miscellaneous-ended		All end scrapers	
		Total	%	Total	%	Total	%	Total	%	Total	%
J-II,1	2,182	25	1.1	22	1.0	4	0.2	78	3.6	129	5.9
J-II,2	1,968	16	0.8	15	0.8	5	0.3	107	5.4	143	7.3
J-II,2fl.	1,029	15	1.5	5	0.5	4	0.4	48	4.7	72	7.0
J-II,3	822	9	1.1	14	1.7	1	0.1	27	3.3	51	6.2
J-II,4	526	12	2.3	34	6.5	2	0.4	21	4.0	69	13.1
J-II,5	798	13	1.6	37	4.6	8	1.0	21	2.6	79	9.9
J-II,6	612	7	1.1	15	2.5	1	0.2	20	3.3	43	7.0
J-I,6	757	29	3.8	43	5.7	9	1.2	54	7.1	135	17.8
J-I,7	695	12	1.7	25	3.6	4	0.6	31	4.5	72	10.4
J-I,8	1,173	17	1.4	26	2.2	4	0.3	62	5.3	109	9.3

*For each level: upper row = flint; lower row = obsidian.

closely related in function to denticulate scrapers, and they may be nothing more than an extreme along a continuum. This is suggested by the ratios of notched flakes to denticulate scrapers, which did not fluctuate very much. Interestingly enough, the highest ratios of notched flakes to denticulate scrapers occur in the lower levels of Jarmo. This could be taken as an indication that more attention was paid to making tools consistently in the upper Jarmo levels.

These implements were most likely used in shaping wood since their rough edges would have been an advantage in such work.

Table 9.—"Other Scrapers"

	A. Stratigraphic Occurrence*				B. Totals and Percentages to Total Retouched Tools					C. Ratios
Operation and level	Denticulate scrapers	Notched flakes	Subtotal	Total	Total retouched tools	Denticulate scrapers Total	%	Notched flakes Total	%	Ratio of notched flakes to denticulate scrapers
J-II,1	177 / 10	47 / 3	224 / 13	237	2,182	187	8.6	50	2.3	1:3.7
J-II,2	124 / 4	29 / 1	153 / 5	158	1,968	128	6.5	30	1.5	1:4.3
J-II,2fl.	94 / 5	29 / --	123 / 5	128	1,029	99	9.6	29	2.8	1:3.4
J-II,3	96 / 2	17 / --	113 / 2	115	822	98	11.9	17	2.1	1:5.8
J-II,4	66 / 1	11 / --	77 / 1	78	526	67	12.7	11	2.1	1:6.1
J-II,5	95 / 2	22 / --	117 / 2	119	798	97	12.2	22	2.8	1:4.4
J-II,6	42 / --	6 / --	48 / --	48	612	42	6.9	6	1.0	1.7.0
J-I,6	77 / 4	27 / --	104 / 4	108	757	81	10.7	27	3.6	1:3.0
J-I,7	35 / 1	13 / --	48 / 1	49	695	36	5.2	13	1.9	1:2.8
J-I,8	81 / 2	27 / --	108 / 2	110	1,173	83	7.1	27	2.3	1:3.1
Flint	887	228	1,115							
Obsidian	31	4	35							
Total	918	232		1,150						

*For each level: upper row = flint; lower row = obsidian.

Miscellaneous Artifacts

Several types that cannot readily be grouped into functional categories are included here as miscellaneous artifacts (table 12A).

Types

Thin Sections (No. 33): 513 (all obsidian)

Thin sections (fig. 122:1-10) are horizontal sections of obsidian blades. They have been described as "side-blow flakes" (L.S. Braidwood 1961, p. 147 and fig. 1; SAOC 31, p. 45), but this label is misleading because, in fact, the pieces were produced by pressure directed either from the top or bottom of a blade near the point of its greatest thickness.[9] Figure 123:3 is an idealized schematic illustration giving various views of the thin section and showing its relation to the parent blade. The artifact drawings (fig. 122:1-10) are paired so that the upper portion shows the thin section in plan and the lower portion shows it in elevation.

The thin sections in the largest group (437 examples) are without secondary retouch (fig. 122:1). Many show crushing where the breaking force was applied (fig. 122:10); others have clean bulbs of percussion (fig. 122:5). Some have nibbling or limited retouch on their edges. Examples of this group are found throughout the sequence, although in much higher frequency in J-II (table 10).

The 54 examples of a second group have retouch on the edges directed from either the top or the bottom. To make these, the end of an obsidian blade was retouched, then the retouched end was removed as a thin section (fig. 122:2-3,6). Some of these superficially resemble backed bladelets.

A group of 16 were made in the same way except that half the end of the parent blade was retouched from the bottom and half from the top (fig. 122:4,8-9).

A final group of 6 have bilaterally retouched edges (fig. 122:7). This retouch occurred after the removal of a retouched end of the blade.

With the exception of one small, poor specimen in J-I,8, *retouched* thin sections are confined to the upper levels of Jarmo.

Truncated Obsidian Blades and Flakes (No. 35): 207

Truncated obsidian blades and flakes are characterized by being relatively small and by having steep retouch on one or more edges or ends. For descriptive purposes one can distinguish a number of varieties; aside from 2 examples found in J-II, all occur in J-I (table 11).

Table 10.—Stratigraphic Occurrence of Obsidian Thin Sections

Operation and level	No secondary retouch	Retouched top or bottom	Retouched top and bottom	Bilaterally retouched ends	Total
J-II,1	56	21	7	2	86
J-II,2	228	13	2	--	243
J-II,2fl.	64	8	2	1	75
J-II,3	48	8	1	1	58
J-II,4	7	2	2	--	11
J-II,5	15	2	--	2	19
J-II,6	--	--	--	--	0
J-I,6	11	--	--	--	11
J-I,7	5	--	--	--	5
J-I,8	3	--	2	--	5
Total	437	54	16	6	513

Table 11.—Stratigraphic Occurrence of Truncated Obsidian Blades and Flakes

Operation and level	Totally retouched	1-3 edges retouched	Deliberately broken ends	Bulbar segments with deliberately broken end	Total
J-II,1	--	--	--	1	1
J-II,2	--	--	--	--	0
J-II,2fl.	--	--	--	--	0
J-II,3	--	--	--	1	1
J-II,4	--	--	--	--	0
J-II,5	--	--	--	--	0
J-II,6	--	--	--	--	0
J-I,6	6	9	12	6	33
J-I,7	14	26	9	33	82
J-I,8	25	29	18	18	90
Total	45	64	39	59	207

There are 45 examples of retouched flake and blade fragments that are for the most part retouched around the entire circumference or edges; in a few examples, a short steep edge is not retouched. The retouch and deliberate breaking around the entire periphery of the piece produce a roughly discoidal object. Since the edges are rough, these pieces do not fit the usual conception of thumbnail scrapers, although they resemble them at first glance (fig. 122:31,36; cf. SAOC 31, pl. 18B, "scrapers"). The chipping is usually alternate-opposite (fig. 122:26,28). A few have a steeply broken edge that is not retouched (fig. 122:34). In J-I,7 the pieces made on blade sections are more likely to be rectangular than discoidal (fig. 122:32). One such piece, which may not have been completed, is shown in figure 122:35.

The 64 examples in the second group have retouch on fewer than four edges. There are blade sections with three edges chipped (fig. 122:29,40), two edges chipped (fig. 122:33), and one edge chipped (fig. 122:37).

Thirty-nine blade sections whose ends are deliberately broken (fig. 122:30) are included here as a group of probably unfinished artifacts.

The final group of 59 contains bulbar segments of blades that have one end deliberately broken, apparently by the punch technique (fig. 122:27,38-39). The chipping is identical to that found on many of the examples in the previous varieties.

Except for two examples mentioned above, figure 122:27 and 38, which are from J-II,1 and 3, truncated obsidian blades and flakes are confined to J-I.

Burins (No. 37): 30 (flint, 24; obsidian, 6)

Two basic varieties of burins, simple and angle, are distinguished here. Angle burins have an acute angle formed by the intersection of a truncated end and a burin blow (fig. 124:1-3). Simple burins have an acute angle formed by the intersection of a burin blow with a broken end of a blade or flake (fig. 124:4-5,7). In a few cases multiple burin blows were struck (fig. 124:1).

Burins were scattered throughout the sequence at Jarmo. They have also been found at Zawi Chemi (R.L. Solecki 1964, p. 407) and Sarab (Hole 1961) and in the Bus Mordeh, Ali Kosh, Mohammad Jaffar, and Sabz phases in Deh Luran (Hole, Flannery, and Neely 1969, p. 91).

Scaled Pieces (No. 39): 99 (flint, 74; obsidian, 25)

Scaled pieces are flakes and blades that show signs of localized, irregular, squamous spalling and shattering along their edges, often at opposite ends or sides, as if they had been used as punches. Thus, when the piece was used as a punch, small flakes spalled off both the end that was struck and the opposite end that was resting on the hard surface. The scaling is usually on the bulbar face (figs. 124:16; 125:1-7,12).

Scaled pieces appear throughout the sequence.

Microburins (No. 36): 4 (all flint)

Microburins are sometimes considered a by-product of the manufacture of geometrics, but in view of their rarity and their distribution at Jarmo it is hard to support this hypothesis. These artifacts are segments of blades that were notched and then broken through the notch. On the bulbar face occurs a teardrop-shaped scar where the broken portion was detached (fig. 124:6).

These pieces are probably not burins in the functional sense, nor are they equivalent in manufacturing technique to the burins described above.

The 4 examples were found in J-II,1 and 4, and in J-I,6. Microburins have also been found at Sarab (Hole 1961).

DISCUSSION OF MISCELLANEOUS ARTIFACTS

Two of the types, thin sections and truncated obsidian blades and flakes, show chronologically significant variation in frequency (table 12A). Most striking is that truncated pieces, except for the 2 illustrated examples from J-II (fig. 122:27,38), are confined to J-I. By contrast, thin sections occur mostly in J-II with relatively few examples below level 3; they are lacking in J-II,6. Examination of the percentages reveals that thin sections increase steadily through J-II,2 but drop off sharply in the uppermost level (table 12B).

The function of thin sections[10] and truncated pieces remains a question. Burins, which were found in very small numbers, were engraving tools. Scaled pieces were probably intermediary tools, like punches, which were splintered in use.

RETOUCHED OR USED BLADES AND FLAKES

Retouched or used blades and fragments were found in great numbers; retouched or used flakes, although common, were less numerous (table 13A).

TYPES

Retouched or Used Blades (No. 17): 4,928 (flint, 2,575; obsidian, 2,353)

Blades and broken segments of blades that have any retouch or chipping through use are included here.[11] The range of variation is great; there are pieces with steep retouch (fig. 116:5,9-10,15) and squamous retouch (figs. 116:8,11-14,16-19; 117:1-3), pieces with rough bifacial retouch along one edge (fig. 117:4,7), notched blades (figs. 116:6; 117:5-6,8,11,16-17), and pieces with more than one kind of retouch (fig. 117:13-14). Sickles whose shiny edges have been

Table 12.—Miscellaneous Artifacts

A. Stratigraphic Occurrence*

Operation and level	Thin sections	Truncated obsidian blades and flakes	Burins	Scaled pieces	Micro-burins	Subtotal	Total
J-II,1	-- / 86	-- / 1	7 / --	29 / 2	2 / --	38 / 89	127
J-II,2	-- / 243	-- / --	1 / --	10 / 2	-- / --	11 / 245	256
J-II,2fl.	-- / 75	-- / --	3 / --	6 / --	-- / --	9 / 75	84
J-II,3	-- / 58	-- / 1	3 / 1	3 / 2	-- / --	6 / 62	68
J-II,4	-- / 11	-- / --	-- / 1	1 / --	1 / --	2 / 12	14
J-II,5	-- / 19	-- / --	-- / 1	9 / 1	-- / --	9 / 21	30
J-II,6	-- / --	-- / --	-- / --	6 / --	-- / --	6 / --	6
J-I,6	-- / 11	-- / 33	4 / --	1 / 4	1 / --	6 / 48	54
J-I,7	-- / 5	-- / 82	2 / 3	1 / 5	-- / --	3 / 95	98
J-I,8	-- / 5	-- / 90	3 / 1	8 / 9	-- / --	11 / 105	116
Flint	513	--	23	74	4	101	
Obsidian		207	7	25	--	752	
Total	513	207	30	99	4		853

B. Totals and Percentages to Total Retouched Tools

Operation and level	Total retouched tools	Thin sections		Truncated obsidian blades and flakes		Burins		Scaled pieces		Micro-burins	
		Total	%	Total	%	Total	%	Total	%	Total	%
J-II,1	2,182	86	3.9	1	0.05	7	0.3	31	1.4	2	0.1
J-II,2	1,968	243	12.3	--	--	1	0.1	12	0.6	--	--
J-II,2fl.	1,029	75	7.3	--	--	3	0.3	6	0.6	--	--
J-II,3	822	58	7.1	1	0.1	4	0.5	5	0.6	--	--
J-II,4	526	11	2.1	--	--	1	0.2	1	0.2	1	0.2
J-II,5	798	19	2.4	--	--	1	0.1	10	1.3	--	--
J-II,6	612	--	--	--	--	--	--	6	1.0	--	--
J-I,6	757	11	1.5	33	4.4	4	0.5	5	0.7	1	0.1
J-I,7	695	5	0.7	82	11.8	5	0.7	6	0.9	--	--
J-I,8	1,173	5	0.4	90	7.7	4	0.3	17	1.4	--	--

*For each level: upper row = flint; lower row = obsidian.

nearly obliterated by chipping (fig. 117:15) are considered reused sickles and counted here (207 pieces); curiously enough, more than half were found in J-II,1 (table 13A).

Retouched or used blades occurred throughout the sequence.

Retouched or Used Flakes (Nos. 18, 31): 1,195 (flint, 1,062; obsidian, 133)

Retouched or used flakes is a category that includes flakes and fragments that have signs of retouch or chipping through use (figs. 117:9-10,12; 118:1-3,5-7,13; 121:11). A group within this category consists of flakes that have two or more notches. In numerous cases each notch was produced by a single blow directed from the bulbar face. The notches were not secondarily retouched (fig. 118:4,8).

Retouched or used flakes occurred throughout the sequence.

DISCUSSION OF RETOUCHED OR USED BLADES AND FLAKES

Together, these groups of implements make up the majority of the retouched artifacts in all levels except J-I,6, where they represent only 47% (table 13B). The percentages do not vary greatly throughout the site, however, and there is no trend toward greater or lesser use. There are other statistics, though, which do show a difference between the lower and upper levels of Jarmo.

The percentages of retouched or used blades in the total number of retouched tools increase sharply after J-I; whereas the average for J-I is 32.2% and the average for the upper levels (1-4) of J-II is 50.1%, indicating that relatively more of these tools were used in the upper levels of Jarmo. The reverse is true of the retouched and used flakes. In the lower levels they average 18.9% and in the upper levels 9.1%. Similarly, we find a difference in the ratio of retouched or used flakes to retouched or used blades. In the lower levels the average ratio is 1:1.9 and in the upper levels it is 1:5.6; the difference shows that the people of upper Jarmo used more blades than flakes for their incidental tasks.

In reading these statistics, one should remember that the relative amounts of these two tool types did not vary much. In the lower levels they accounted for 51.1% and in the upper levels for 59.2% of the retouched tools. This 8% difference is less than could account for all the variations described above.

For both tool types, flint accounted for the greater total; however, if we look at the ratios of flint to obsidian blades and flakes, we find some interesting differences in the levels (table 13A,B). In the lower levels, for each obsidian blade there was an average of 2.5 flint blades; in the upper levels, the average is 1.0 flint blade. If we look at flakes we find a similar difference between levels. In the lower levels, there is an average of 19.8 flints for each obsidian, whereas in the upper levels, there are 6.6 flints for each obsidian. Looked at in this way, we see a greater emphasis on the use of obsidian in the upper levels.

RESIDUAL CATEGORY

The residual category includes plain blades as well as various pieces of retouched flint and obsidian that could not be assigned to any of the well-defined types (table 14A). Plain blades are included here because they are not secondarily retouched tools even though they constitute a well-defined type. For purposes of computing percentages I have left plain blades out of the total of retouched tools because they are so numerous they swamp the percentages of all other types.

TYPES

Ground Pieces (Misc. No. 3): 62 (flint, 54; obsidian, 8)

These chipped flint and obsidian pieces show evidence of prolonged rubbing that has worn down or polished their edges, ridges, or faces. There is no apparent consistency in the group other than the attrition of their projecting surfaces. A blade with the ridges on the upper face completely obliterated is shown in figure 124:13, and a piece of obsidian shown in figure 125:13 has been ground to a nearly cylindrical shape.

Ground pieces occurred throughout the sequence.

Miscellaneous Backed Bladelets and Fragments (No. 7 and Misc. No. 1): 76 (flint, 36; obsidian, 40)

Miscellaneous pieces with backing (flint, 2; obsidian, 6) form too variable a group to be considered a type. They include 2 obsidian blades whose backing curves around the bulbar end onto the primary edge (fig. 112:31); 3 flakes, plain on both faces, with a straight-backed bulbar end and a convex primary edge (fig. 112:30); a blade that is double ended and double backed; and a blade that is backed and has steep retouch at the bulbar end.

The remaining 68 pieces are fragments of backed pieces that cannot be sorted into types; hence, although a count is given, these fragments are not used in the subsequent interpretations.

The few miscellaneous backed artifacts of obsidian came from J-II,1-3 and the 2 flint examples from J-I,8. The fragments of backed pieces were found in all levels in both operations except for J-II,4.

Table 13.—Retouched or Used Blades and Flakes

A. Stratigraphic Occurrence*

Operation and level	Reused sickles	Retouched or used blades	Retouched or used flakes	Subtotal	Total
J-II,1	131 / --	621 / 336	181 / 29	933 / 365	1,298
J-II,2	7 / --	443 / 549	111 / 35	561 / 584	1,145
J-II,2fl.	7 / --	284 / 225	85 / 10	376 / 235	611
J-II,3	1 / --	147 / 263	60 / 17	208 / 280	488
J-II,4	4 / --	81 / 176	47 / 4	132 / 180	312
J-II,5	8 / --	133 / 286	45 / 10	186 / 296	482
J-II,6	5 / --	89 / 293	42 / 2	136 / 295	431
J-I,6	4 / --	135 / 58	151 / 8	290 / 66	356
J-I,7	11 / --	189 / 70	77 / 10	277 / 80	357
J-I,8	29 / --	246 / 97	263 / 8	538 / 105	643
Flint	207	2,368	1,062	3,637	
Obsidian	--	2,353	133	2,486	
Total	207	4,721	1,195	6,123	

B. Totals and Percentages to Total Retouched Tools

Total retouched tools	Retouched or used blades Total	%	Retouched or used flakes Total	%	Total retouched or used blades and flakes Total	%
2,182	1,088	49.9	210	9.6	1,298	59.5
1,968	999	50.8	146	7.4	1,145	58.2
1,029	516	50.1	95	9.2	611	59.4
822	411	50.0	77	9.4	488	59.4
526	261	49.6	51	9.7	312	59.3
798	427	53.5	55	6.9	482	60.4
612	387	63.2	44	7.2	431	70.4
757	197	26.0	159	21.0	356	47.0
695	270	38.8	87	12.5	357	51.4
1,173	372	31.7	271	23.1	643	54.8

C. Ratios

Ratio of flakes to blades	Ratio of obsidian blades to flint blades	Ratio of obsidian flakes to flint flakes
1:5.2	1:1.8	1:6.2
1:6.8	1:0.8	1:3.2
1:5.4	1:1.3	1:8.5
1:5.3	1:0.6	1:3.5
1:5.1	1:0.5	1:11.8
1:7.8	1:0.5	1:4.5
1:8.8	1:0.3	1:21.0
1:1.2	1:2.3	1:18.9
1:3.1	1:2.7	1:7.7
1:1.4	1:2.5	1:32.9

NOTE: "Plain blades" and "flakes without retouch" are not included but are to be found in tables 14 and 15.
*For each level: upper row = flint; lower row = obsidian.

Fragments of Piercing-Reaming Tools (Misc. No. 2): 184 (flint, 176; obsidian, 8)

The fragments of piercing-reaming tools included here have retouch similar to that found on the various types of piercing-reaming tools, but they are too small to permit identification of specific types. They were found throughout the excavations.

Plain Blades and Blade Fragments (No. 19): 44,556 (flint, 13,121; obsidian, 31,435)

Plain blades are those that have no deliberate retouch or evidence of extensive use, although the edges may have irregular chips and nicks (fig. 118:10-12). The obsidian blades and fragments are mainly microlithic (i.e., less than 10 mm in width).

Plain blades were found throughout the sequence (table 14A).

DISCUSSION OF PLAIN BLADES AND FRAGMENTS

Plain blades are highly standardized and found in great numbers (averaging about three times as many as the retouched stone artifacts); these characteristics argue for their use as tools in their own right. Certainly the blades would have been useful for almost any cutting operation. It is not unreasonable to assume that because they were easy to make they were used once or twice and then discarded for a cleaner or sharper blade.

As one moves from the lower to the upper levels of Jarmo, there is a slight increase in plain blades compared with other tool types, but the figures fluctuate and their meaning is not clear. The pattern of increase/decrease appears to be the same as that for retouched tools.

One can also see some differences in the proportions of obsidian and flint among plain blades. The smallest proportion of obsidian occurred in J-I,7 and 8 (table 14B).

Table 14.—Artifacts in Residual Category

A. Stratigraphic Occurrence*

B. Ratios (Plain Blades)

Operation and level	Ground pieces	Miscellaneous backed bladelets and fragments	Fragments of piercing-reaming tools	Subtotal	Total	Plain blades	Total	Total retouched tools	Ratio of retouched tools to plain blades	Ratio of flint to obsidian
J-II,1	12 --	7 14	57 2	76 16	92	3,176 8,339	11,515	2,182	1:5.3	1:2.6
J-II,2	5 1	6 12	28 2	39 15	54	2,250 6,313	8,563	1,968	1:4.4	1:2.8
J-II,2fl.	6 1	3 2	11 1	20 4	24	1,086 4,020	5,106	1,029	1:5.0	1:3.7
J-II,3	10 1	1 6	29 3	40 10	50	837 2,926	3,763	822	1:4.6	1:3.5
J-II,4	3 2	-- --	6 --	9 2	11	522 1,411	1,933	526	1:3.7	1:2.7
J-II,5	5 --	1 2	10 --	16 2	18	537 2,692	3,229	798	1:4.0	1:5.0
J-II,6	2 1	3 --	12 --	17 1	18	330 1,168	1,498	612	1:2.4	1:3.5
J-I,6	3 --	8 2	4 --	15 2	17	695 1,729	2,424	757	1:3.2	1:2.5
J-I,7	3 1	2 --	6 --	11 1	12	838 1,253	2,091	695	1:3.0	1:1.5
J-I,8	5 1	5 2	13 --	23 3	26	2,850 1,584	4,434	1,173	1:3.8	1:0.6
Flint Obsidian	54 8	36 40	176 8	266 56		13,121 31,435				
Total	62	76	184	322		44,556				

*For each level: upper row = flint; lower row = obsidian.

CHIPPING DEBRIS

During the study of chipped stone all types were separated into flint and obsidian. None of the notes available to me at the time of the final writing of this report in 1973, however, give any breakdown by flint and obsidian for cores and core fragments. For this reason only the total counts are given; it is my recollection that there were few, if any, obsidian cores and fragments.[12]

Types

Blade Cores (Misc. No. 4): 49 (all flint)

Blade cores are usually pyramidal in shape with an oval or round striking platform at right angles to the axis of the core. In most examples, blades were struck from only part of the perimeter of the platform (figs. 125:11; 126:7), although a few are completely chipped (fig. 125:9-10,14-16). Three cores are double ended (fig. 125:17).

The only hint of a chronological difference in the distribution of the varieties is that 6 examples that are as wide at the base as at the platform were found in J-I. The remainder of the blade cores were found throughout the sequence (table 15).

Flake Cores (Misc. No. 5): 414 (all flint)

Flake cores may be pyramidal, spheroid, or chunky. The most common variety has flakes struck from one platform. The platform may be faceted or nonfaceted (fig. 126:2-3). The flakes may have been struck from the entire periphery of the platform or only a part (fig. 126:1).

A second group consists of 100 examples that have two (nonopposed) or more platforms. The platforms are usually small and have only a few flakes removed from them (fig. 126:5).

Four flake cores are double ended, and 7 are discoidal. The peripheral edge of the disk type is the platform; the flaking is from the edge toward the center, and since it is usually alternate-opposite, it leaves a sinuous edge (fig. 126:6).

Flake cores are distributed throughout the sequence.

Core Fragments (Misc. No. 6): 967 (all flint)

Two broad varieties of core fragments were distinguished: those from blade cores (55) and those from flake cores (912).

Blade core fragments include core faces or plunging flakes (fig. 126:4), resulting from the removal (purposeful or accidental) of the side of the core from which blades had been struck, and tablets (fig. 125:8), which are platforms that were removed from the top of the core.

The larger group of flake core fragments is highly variable and consists of chunks produced, most likely, during the initial trimming of cores.

Core fragments are, of course, chipping debris in the same sense that plain flakes or debitage are. The only advantage in distinguishing them is that their distribution may indicate when and where chipping of flint was taking place.

Core fragments are distributed throughout the sequence.

Flakes Without Retouch (Misc. No. 7): 50,334 (flint, 41,042; obsidian, 9,292)

Unlike blades, these unretouched flakes are not shaped to do a particular job and can be considered waste chips from the manufacture of cores and tools. They are often called "debitage."

Debitage occurs throughout the sequence.

Discussion of Chipping Debris

Although chipping debris constitutes a large percentage of the total stone in each level (42%-60%), it is still not certain that primary chipping was done in any of the areas that were excavated. Taking the manufacture of blades as an example, we find that in only one or two levels is there even a remote possibility that the number of cores is sufficient to account for the number of plain blades (see table 16), let alone the number of all the tools made on blades. The range is 66 plain flint blades per flint blade core in J-II,6 to 1,086 plain flint blades per flint core in J-II,2fl. There is considerable variation in this ratio of plain flint blades to flint blade cores; in the other levels it ranges from 139 to 529 per core.[13] On the face of it, one might assume that blades were not made in the areas excavated, but there is the possibility that cores were removed from the area, perhaps to be used as tools in their own right in some other place on the site. This is a question that cannot be resolved with the present data, but a comparison with our findings at Ali Kosh is instructive.

In the three phases at Ali Kosh, where the blades were typically smaller than those at Jarmo, the numbers of plain blades per core in the Mohammad Jaffar, Ali Kosh, and Bus Mordeh phases were 43, 45, and 67, respectively. The sample sizes at Ali Kosh were also much larger—10,516 for Mohammad Jaffar, 9,789 for Ali Kosh, and 15,085 for Bus Mordeh. The case for chipping having been done on the spot at Ali Kosh is thus more secure. In fact, at one locality in

Table 15.—Stratigraphic Occurrence of Chipping Debris

Operation and level	Flint blade cores*	Flint flake cores*	Flint core fragments*	Flakes without retouch†	Subtotal†	Total
J-II,1	6	92	226	6,755 3,079	7,079 3,079	10,158
J-II,2	5	50	54	8,045 2,440	8,154 2,440	10,594
J-II,2fl.	1	47	119	4,282 878	4,449 878	5,327
J-II,3	5	54	88	3,872 782	4,019 782	4,801
J-II,4	2	28	71	3,268 285	3,369 285	3,654
J-II,5	3	54	103	4,227 487	4,387 487	4,874
J-II,6	5	21	83	1,661 510	1,770 510	2,280
J-I,6	5	28	64	2,711 182	2,808 182	2,990
J-I,7	2	22	59	2,324 114	2,407 114	2,521
J-I,8	15	18	100	3,897 535	4,030 535	4,565
Flint Obsidian	49	414	967	41,042 9,292	42,469 9,292	
Total	49	414	967	50,334		51,764

*Obsidian core and core fragments not included; see n. 12.
†For each level: upper row = flint; lower row = obsidian.

Table 16.—Selected Ratios and Percentages of Chipped Stone

Operation and level	Total all chipped stone	Ratio of blade cores to plain blades (flint)	% all plain blades to all chipped stone	% all chipping debris to all chipped stone
J-II,1	23,947	1:529	48.1	42.4
J-II,2	21,179	1:450	40.4	50.0
J-II,2fl.	11,486	1:1,086	44.5	46.4
J-II,3	9,436	1:167	39.9	50.9
J-II,4	6,124	1:261	31.6	59.7
J-II,5	8,919	1:179	36.2	54.7
J-II,6	4,408	1:66	34.0	51.7
J-I,6	6,188	1:139	39.2	48.3
J-I,7	5,319	1:419	39.3	47.4
J-I,8	10,198	1:190	43.5	44.8
Total	107,204			

the Bus Mordeh phase, we did find a clear example of chipping with the nodules of flint, cores, blades, and chipping debris all in situ.

At Ali Kosh, although obsidian cores were not numerous, the number of blades per core was 91 in the Bus Mordeh phase, 128 in the Ali Kosh phase, and 59 in the Mohammad Jaffar phase.

Table 17.—Artifacts Whose Stratigraphic Occurrence Has Chronological Significance: Totals and Their Percentage to Total of Retouched Tools

Operation and level	Total retouched tools	Total obsidian*	Geometrics Total	Geometrics %	"Other microliths" Total	"Other microliths" %	Shouldered drills Total	Shouldered drills %	Pressure-flaked obsidian fabricators Total	Pressure-flaked obsidian fabricators %	Retouched sickles Total	Retouched sickles %	Round-ended flake scrapers Total	Round-ended flake scrapers %	Obsidian thin sections Total	Obsidian thin sections %	Truncated obsidian blades and flakes Total	Truncated obsidian blades and flakes %
J-II,1	2,182	12,008	60	2.7	13	0.6	16	0.7	4	0.2	48	2.2	22	1.0	86	3.9	1	0.05
J-II,2	1,968	9,752	57	2.9	12	0.6	21	1.1	6	0.3	25	1.3	15	0.8	243	12.3	--	--
J-II,2fl.	1,029	5,257	15	1.5	4	0.4	18	1.7	2	0.2	14	1.4	5	0.5	75	7.3	--	--
J-II,3	822	4,086	5	0.6	4	0.5	4	0.5	2	0.2	17	2.1	14	1.7	58	7.1	1	0.1
J-II,4	526	1,901	--	--	1	0.2	6	1.1	--	--	10	1.9	34	6.5	11	2.1	--	--
J-II,5	798	3,515	--	--	2	0.3	13	1.6	2	0.3	13	1.6	37	4.6	19	2.4	--	--
J-II,6	612	1,979	--	--	--	--	30	4.9	--	--	3	0.5	15	2.5	--	--	--	--
J-I,6	757	2,074	--	--	5	0.7	1	0.1	11	1.5	14	1.8	43	5.7	11	1.5	33	4.4
J-I,7	695	1,586	1	0.1	10	1.4	1	0.1	22	3.2	15	2.2	25	3.6	5	0.7	82	11.8
J-I,8	1,173	2,435	4	0.3	53	4.5	--	--	38	3.2	13	1.1	26	2.2	5	0.4	90	7.7

Table 18.—Percentage of Obsidian in Various Tool Categories

Operation and level	Total all chipped stone*	Total obsidian*	% obsidian to all chipped stone	Total all plain blades	Total obsidian plain blades	% obsidian plain blades to all plain blades	Total all plain flakes	Total obsidian plain flakes	% obsidian plain flakes to all plain flakes
J-II,1	23,947	12,008	50.1	11,515	8,339	72.4	9,834	3,079	31.3
J-II,2	21,179	9,752	46.0	8,563	6,313	73.7	10,485	2,440	23.3
J-II,2fl.	11,486	5,257	45.8	5,106	4,020	78.7	5,160	878	17.0
J-II,3	9,436	4,086	43.3	3,763	2,926	77.8	4,654	782	16.8
J-II,4	6,124	1,901	31.0	1,933	1,411	73.0	3,553	285	8.0
J-II,5	8,919	3,515	39.4	3,229	2,692	83.4	4,714	487	10.3
J-II,6	4,408	1,979	44.9	1,498	1,168	78.0	2,171	510	23.5
J-I,6	6,188	2,074	33.5	2,424	1,729	71.3	2,893	182	6.3
J-I,7	5,319	1,586	29.8	2,091	1,253	59.9	2,438	114	4.7
J-I,8	10,198	2,435	23.9	4,434	1,584	35.7	4,432	535	12.1

*See note 12.

DISCUSSION

In the following pages, I attempt to present the information obtained from the chipped stone industry that has particular bearing on the nature of the site of Jarmo.

CHRONOLOGY

There are two main sources of chronological information in the data: the presence or absence of certain kinds of artifacts in various levels and the changes in percentages of tools or of type of raw material (flint or obsidian). Tables 17 and 18 present these data.

The distribution of three types, geometrics, shouldered drills, and a variety of retouched sickles (see p. 243), strongly suggests that they are restricted to upper levels. In each case at least one example was found in J-I, but these could easily have been introduced into the lower portion of the site through natural disturbance. The same may be said for truncated obsidian blades and flakes which, except for two examples, are confined to the lower levels.

Two varieties of flake, round-ended scrapers are found only in J-II,5 and 6 and in J-I; this at least suggests that they are typical of the lower rather than upper levels of Jarmo.

The remainder of the significant tool groups have distributions that can be analyzed chronologically if we compare their percentages rather than quantities. "Other microliths," as a group, are much more abundant in the lower than in the upper levels. In fact, in J-I,7 and 8 they may have had their last moments of real popularity, for these tools always occur in much smaller percentages in the later levels. The same is true of pressure-flaked obsidian fabricators. The reverse situation is found with the thin sections; their maximum popularity occurs in J-II,2. The percentages steadily rise from J-I,8 to J-II,2 and then decline again. It is somewhat puzzling that no thin sections were found in J-II,6.

In summary, a few types or varieties give evidence of chronologically significant differences in the tool kit. It is not possible to designate a definite break in the sequence, but it seems evident that the overall yield of J-I is different from that of J-II and that the lowermost and uppermost levels of Jarmo, as now known, show the greatest divergence.

Additional information from data not included in this report ought to be mentioned here. My first study of the chipped stone included all the material from J-I as well as from J-II, although, as explained previously, I chose to omit the data from the upper levels of J-I because the relation of one level to another was ambiguous. However, certain features in the occurrence of some types lend further support to the above conclusions.

No diagonal-ended bladelets occurred above J-I,5; a crude trapeze came from J-I,5, but all the others were from the surface of that operation; a few examples of varieties of truncated obsidian blades and flakes (but no completely retouched examples) were found in J-I,3a and 5; thin sections were commonest in the upper part of J-I. Finally, a rapid examination of the sickles and plain blades showed that none of the flint from the new source (see p. 243) occurred lower than J-I,3 and most of it was found in the surface stratum. Compared with the lower levels, there was relatively little chipped stone above J-I,6.

Other statistics, interestingly enough, show the increase in use of obsidian throughout the site (table 18). The proportion of obsidian in the totals begins with a low of 23.9% in J-I,8 and rises to 50.1% in J-II,1. There are some fluctuations, but a tendency toward increased use of the material in later times seems clear. The use of obsidian for making plain blades is a different matter, however. With these artifacts there is a rapid rise from 35.7% in J-I,8 to 71.3% in J-I,6; thereafter, the percentages fluctuate. By combining the levels we find that 51% of the blades in J-I and 75.4% in J-II were obsidian. Plain flakes were much the same except that less obsidian was expended on these artifacts. The proportion of obsidian used in J-I was 8.5% and in J-II it was 20.8%. Thus, in the various ways we can examine the data on the use of obsidian as compared with flint, it is clear that proportionally much more obsidian was used in J-II than in J-I and that it was most commonly used in the making of plain blades.

We can obviously use these data to indicate chronological differences in the site, and if we were to excavate a portion of Jarmo that was not directly related by stratigraphy to either J-I or J-II, we might be able to identify its relation by observing the presence or absence of certain tools or the percentages of obsidian with respect to the total number of chipped stone pieces.

USES OF THE TOOLS

There are three principal ways to determine the uses to which tools were put: analogy, experimentation, and analysis of traces of wear. Most determinations of use depend on analogy and are self-evident in cases of tools such as arrowheads. Similar analogy allows us to state that scrapers are used in preparing hides, shredding plant fibers, and working wood. We may also combine experimentation with the use of analogy in more ambiguous instances. For example, Witthoft (1967, p. 388) has observed gloss on iron sickles used in the harvesting of grain, and a number of workers have tried to induce sheen on flint blades by harvesting fields with primitive-style sickles. These experiments have given inconclusive results, but most archeologists assume in the absence of contrary evidence that glossy flints were used in the harvesting of cereal grains. In the course of this study I determined through experiments that the grinding observed on many drills could be produced by boring in hard material; therefore the use of the shouldered tools with ground bits seems clear-cut. These and similar identifications of use are readily accepted.

More difficult problems arise, however, when we try to determine the use of objects that have no analogues in modern use and that show no obvious traces of wear. It should be remarked parenthetically here that studies of wear under high magnification are now being made, with interesting preliminary results. Such techniques were not available at the time of this study and, in any case, may not be very useful for many artifacts. How, for example, are we to determine the use of thin sections? Their distinguishing characteristics are their shapes (which are somewhat geometric) and the deliberately sharpened tips that are found on some examples. Depending on which characteristic is emphasized, one might say that these artifacts are tips for projectile points or small drills. Neither of these suggestions seems reasonable, because thin sections exhibit considerable variation in size and shape (which the other geometrics do not), they are made by a different process from the other geometrics, and there are no similar tools known to be in use today as projectile tips. Moreover, there is no trace of grinding on the tips, and obsidian is not a very good material from which to make drills because it is brittle and the sharp edges wear quickly. We are left, therefore, with a problem which we cannot solve immediately. The same is true of the truncated obsidian blades and flakes. Both of these types are highly characteristic of the Jarmo industry in general and occur in quantities large enough that they are not likely to be accidental, but we have no obvious explanation for their use.

Other problems in interpretation arise when tools are made for more than one use. The various scrapers provide a case in point. End scrapers were probably used on hides, but we have seen that, as Müller-Beck has shown (1965), they might also have been used on wood. They may also have been used as knives for skinning, a task for which they are well suited since they work the skin free from the flesh without cutting or tearing. From my own experiments I can testify that end scrapers work very well for this purpose.

In cases like these and with tools like awls or drills, we will often have to be content to say that there is a series of uses to which they may have been put. Only rarely is it possible to specify exactly what was being hunted with the projectile points, what an end scraper was used for, or what kind of material was drilled with a particular tool. The information that would make it possible to specify these things is the co-occurrence of the animals hunted, the hide scraped, or the bead drilled with these tools. Occasionally projectiles are found in bones, but much more commonly we know for certain only what animals were hunted, not the specific projectile used. However, if the geometrics were projectile tips and if they are found in the same context as caprid bones, for example, we can deduce that they were used to hunt goats. Accordingly, I suggested that the diagonal-ended microliths had been used to hunt onagers (Hole 1961, pp. 126-28)—a judgment based on preliminary studies of the fauna, which indicated a higher proportion of onager during the occupation of the lower part of Jarmo than during the occupation of the upper part of the site. My assumption then was that the goats and sheep were domesticated and not subject to the hunt. Stampfli's final study of the Jarmo bones (see chap. 9) now makes it clear that onagers were hunted during the time of the lower levels and only rarely during that of the upper levels, and so it still seems likely that the microliths were used to hunt these animals; however, they may also have been used to hunt goats and sheep, which were apparently not all domesticated at that time (see p. 454).

It should be emphasized again that the above argument depends on the premise that microliths were projectile elements. This premise is reinforced by the finding of such flints in their original shafts in a few archeological sites and by the absence of any other type of tool in the site that appears, by analogy, to have been used as a projectile point. These observations, added to the fact that hunting of wild animals was practiced at Jarmo, make it a near certainty that the geometrics and microliths were used in hunting. What remains in doubt is whether spears, harpoons, or arrows were used, since any of these projectiles could have been set with barbs made of either geometrics or other microliths.

This example shows the value of relating associated data to particular tools. This procedure was also followed in the case of the shouldered drills, which were probably used to drill beads (Hole 1961). Since the preliminary study of ground stone showed an increase in the occurrence of beads in the upper levels, where shouldered drills also showed an increase (cf. table 5A), and since the bits proved to fit into the holes in the beads, it seems clear that the drills had been used in the manufacture of the beads. Other relationships can no doubt be established through the final studies of other artifacts that are now available.

There is, however, another way to proceed toward interpretation of the use of tools. If we possess full information about the economy of a prehistoric people, we can then try to determine what tasks must have been carried out. For example, if we know the people were agriculturalists, then we know that they must have had a way to prepare the soil for planting, methods for reaping and grinding the grains, and finally utensils to cook and serve food in. We might also expect the people to have had storage containers. Of course, not all tasks would have been carried out with chipped stone tools, but an archeologist working with the full range of data would probably be able to find artifacts that were used for at least some of them. For example, digging sticks or hoes would be needed to prepare the soil. Neither type of instrument would require chipped stone, but celts or hoes or digging-stick weights might be found. Cutting the grain would require sharp knives, or sickles. But cutting the stalks is only part of the process of making cereal ready for use. It must also be threshed. Today, Near Eastern villagers commonly use one of two methods: either they beat or trample the grain, or they attempt to chop the chaff from the heads. The beating method would not require chipped stone but the other might. Today, villagers use threshing sleds whose flat beds are set with bits of either flint or iron, or they use sleds that have rollers set with hoe-shaped cutters. Today, these cutters are iron but they could also be made of flint. I have never examined a threshing sled, or *tribulum*, to see how the flints wear when they have been dragged across the grain, but it seems likely that the pattern of wear would be recognizable and distinct from that found on reaping sickles. A problem in linking glossy flints with the *tribulum*, however, is the fact that such devices are usually drawn by animal rather than human power; in fact, they may be beyond the capabilities of humans to pull. If this were the case, we could probably eliminate further consideration of the *tribulum* and related devices as far as Jarmo is concerned. This is a question that zoologists and ethnologists can help with, and it again illustrates the interaction of participants in various fields and the necessity of considering all aspects of the problem.

Once the grain has been threshed, it must be winnowed, a task probably carried out at Jarmo with baskets or trays. Then the grain must be ground to ready it for eating. Again, chipped stone tools are not necessary except for blades to cut the saplings or reeds for the baskets. Afterward, the ground grain must be put into some container for storage, soaking, or cooking. Baskets as well as pottery were probably used for these tasks, but we might also consider the possible use of wooden and stone vessels. We have already noted that various types of chipped stone tools—drills, pressure-flaked obsidian rasps and scrapers, and adzes—could have been used in the making of wooden objects. How, then, were stone bowls made? They were ultimately ground carefully and polished, but we do not have much information on the procedure for initially roughing them out. Perhaps some chipped stone was used, but it is more likely that ground stone served as large drills and polishers.

After their food was prepared, the people of Jarmo may have eaten it with their fingers, but we know that at least some bone utensils were present at the site, and there is a possibility that wooden spoons were also used. Bone and wood tools had to be shaped and here again we find that flint knives, scrapers, and spokeshaves (notched flakes and blades) would have been employed.

This discussion has been presented more as an example of the ways in which we can make inferences about the uses of chipped stone tools than as a definitive account of how the tools found at Jarmo were actually employed. Such reconstructions are reasonable for the Jarmo data, but clearly they do not exhaust the limits of what might be done with data collected under different conditions.

A number of archeologists today are working with statistical methods for relating artifacts to activities. They use tests of covariance together with very precise information about the nature of the deposits in which the tools are found. For these purposes it is necessary to have many more controls over the data than we presently have over data from any site in the Near East of which I am aware. In the future, however, with these techniques in mind we should be able to gather more suitable data and to extend the range of our interpretations accordingly.

The Nature of the Site

Jarmo is a complex site, and it is not possible for me to say a great deal about its internal structure—the nature of the deposits, rate of deposition, and so on—from a study of the chipped stone alone, but there is some information that may help in the overall interpretation of the site.

I have already mentioned some tools that have limited distribution chronologically. These data do not indicate an obvious point at which to divide the site, but the differences between the lower and upper levels of Jarmo and those within the upper levels need to be examined along with all the other relevant data. In these data there is at least a hint of some changes in activities, which it may be possible to specify when the various lines of evidence have been compiled.

It is interesting to see how the percentages of all chipped stone vary from one level to another (table 19). Assuming equivalence of the levels, each should contain 10% of the total chipped stone, but this is not the case; J-II,1 and 2 together contain about 53% of the stone, and the lower levels of J-I contain only 20%. In part this is related to the volume excavated in each level.[14] Table 20 shows that 79% of the volume occurs in J-II and that 80% of the total amount of chipped stone is from these levels. More precise calculations show, however, that although J-II,1,2, and 2fl. account for about 41% of the volume, they have 53% of the flint. Thus the grouped figures for J-I and J-II are misleading and fail to point up the differences in the upper levels of J-II. Two possible explanations come to mind: the deposits in the upper levels of J-II are of a different character from those in the remainder of the site, or erosion and deflation of the upper surface has concentrated more chipped stone than would be normal in these layers.

Levels Versus Phases

The yield from Jarmo has been recorded by stratigraphic levels, and these have formed the framework for my observations. It is clear from the previous discussions and from examination of the tables, plans, and sections that the levels are unequal in size, quantity of material, and content. Levels embrace indeterminate amounts of time and have no implicit distinctiveness as far as their assemblages are concerned; that is, it may be the case that each level is "culturally" distinct, or that any combination of levels is distinct, or that they are homogeneous with respect to the artifacts that they contain. Jarmo has been treated as an essentially one-period site. I take this to mean that it contains no remarkable differences throughout its duration. There is nothing in my study of the chipped stone tools that makes this assertion necessarily incorrect; it depends on the definition one gives to "remarkable" or whatever adjectives one chooses to use. Everyone who has examined the artifacts recognizes that there are differences between the lower and

Table 19.—Summary of Chipped Stone by Groups

Operation and level	Retouched tools								Other chipped stone			
	Geometrics and "other microliths"	Piercing-reaming tools	Sickles	End scrapers	Other scrapers	Miscellaneous artifacts	Retouched or used blades and flakes	Total retouched tools	Residual category	Plain blades	Chipping debris	Total chipped stone
J-II,1	73 (29.7)	143 (21.4)	175 (28.3)	129 (14.3)	237 (20.6)	127 (14.9)	1,298 (21.2)	2,182 (20.7)	92 (28.6)	11,515 (25.8)	10,158 (19.6)	23,947 (22.3)
J-II,2	69 (28.0)	105 (15.7)	92 (14.9)	143 (15.9)	158 (13.7)	256 (30.0)	1,145 (18.7)	1,968 (18.6)	54 (16.8)	8,563 (19.2)	10,594 (20.5)	21,179 (19.8)
J-II,2fl.	19 (7.7)	66 (9.9)	49 (7.9)	72 (8.0)	128 (11.0)	84 (9.8)	611 (10.0)	1,029 (9.7)	24 (7.5)	5,106 (11.5)	5,327 (10.3)	11,486 (10.7)
J-II,3	9 (3.7)	37 (5.5)	54 (8.7)	51 (5.7)	115 (10.0)	68 (8.0)	488 (8.0)	822 (7.8)	50 (15.5)	3,763 (8.4)	4,801 (9.3)	9,436 (8.8)
J-II,4	1 (0.4)	28 (4.2)	24 (3.9)	69 (7.6)	78 (6.8)	14 (1.6)	312 (5.1)	526 (5.0)	11 (3.4)	1,933 (4.3)	3,654 (7.1)	6,124 (5.7)
J-II,5	2 (0.8)	47 (7.0)	39 (6.3)	79 (8.8)	119 (10.3)	30 (3.5)	482 (7.9)	798 (7.6)	18 (5.6)	3,229 (7.2)	4,874 (9.4)	8,919 (8.3)
J-II,6	-- --	74 (11.1)	10 (1.6)	43 (4.8)	48 (4.2)	6 (0.7)	431 (7.0)	612 (5.8)	18 (5.6)	1,498 (3.4)	2,280 (4.4)	4,408 (4.1)
J-I,6	5 (2.0)	51 (7.6)	48 (7.8)	135 (15.0)	108 (9.4)	54 (6.3)	356 (5.8)	757 (7.2)	17 (5.3)	2,424 (5.4)	2,990 (5.8)	6,188 (5.8)
J-I,7	11 (4.5)	43 (6.4)	65 (10.5)	72 (8.0)	49 (4.3)	98 (11.5)	357 (5.8)	695 (6.6)	12 (3.7)	2,091 (4.7)	2,521 (4.9)	5,319 (5.0)
J-I,8	57 (23.2)	75 (11.2)	63 (10.2)	109 (12.1)	110 (9.6)	116 (13.6)	643 (10.5)	1,173 (11.1)	26 (8.1)	4,434 (10.0)	4,565 (8.8)	10,198 (9.5)
Total	246	669	619	902	1,150	853	6,123	10,582	322	44,556	51,764	107,204

NOTE: Figures in parentheses indicate percentages.

Table 20.—Quantities of Chipped Stone in Relation to Volume of Site Excavated

Operation and level	Excavated volume		Chipped stone	
	Total volume (m³)	% of total volume excavated	Total number recovered	% of total number
J-II,1	ca. 118	10.3	23,947	22.3
J-II,2	ca. 256	22.3	21,179	19.8
J-II,2fl.	ca. 98	8.5	11,486	10.7
J-II,3	ca. 118	10.3	9,436	8.8
J-II,4	ca. 90	7.8	6,124	5.7
J-II,5	ca. 131	11.4	8,919	8.3
J-II,6	ca. 100	8.7	4,408	4.1
J-I,6	ca. 47	4.1	6,188	5.8
J-I,7	ca. 69	6.0	5,319	5.0
J-I,8	ca. 122	10.6	10,198	9.5
Total	ca. 1,149	100.0	107,204	100.0

upper levels; however, if one were to depend solely on the chipped stone evidence, it is abundantly clear that there is no sharp line of demarcation at which one can divide the site. In a trial division I would treat J-I,6,7, and 8 collectively and separate the levels in J-II with little or no pottery (J-II,3,4,5, and 6) from those in that operation that do have pottery (J-II,1,2, and 2fl.).[15] By tabulating the incidence of different types of artifacts and features (for example, stone bowls, grinding stones, animal bones, architecture—in short, all the evidence one has), it will be possible to see if these divisions actually can be identified as separate units. If they can, then a term such as phase or subphase might be applied to each group of levels that has a sufficiently distinctive assemblage.

This is the practice we followed in Deh Luran. We were able to relate all the evidence from Ali Kosh and see where there were definable changes, which enabled us to be more precise in comparing the subunits among other sites. And by emphasizing change, we gain some appreciation of rates of change and of the things that were changing, thereby reaching a better understanding of the nature of the material with which we are working.

Comparisons with Other Sites

Jarmo still stands as a unique site among others of its age in southwestern Asia; however, it has close counterparts at Sarab, Guran, and Ali Kosh. In the type descriptions I have already indicated at which of these sites similar tools occurred. It is sufficient to say that no other site has an identical assemblage of chipped stone and then to add some general remarks about the various assemblages at other sites.

In my earlier study, a detailed comparison showed that Jarmo has much more variety in its chipped stone than Sarab has. I concluded that this was an indication that more varied activities were carried out at Jarmo, but final word on the Sarab materials must await its publication by our colleagues at the Royal Ontario Museum in Toronto.

The chipped stone from Tepe Guran has not yet been described in detail, and so we cannot compare this site with Jarmo except in general terms. Mortensen reports (1963, pp. 118-19),

> The flint and obsidian industries at Guran were based on flakes and blades some of which may be characterized as microlithic. Conical micro-blade cores were numerous, but only a few genuine microliths (lancets and trapezes) occurred. It was surprising to see that more than 80% of the pieces had not been retouched. . . . Compared with obsidian, flint dominated in all levels, amounting to an average of 90-95% of the material. The most common tools were blades with gloss along the edge, . . . end-of-blade scrapers, borers, and a large number of retouched and notched blades.

The situation appears very similar to that at Sarab. The pottery at Guran shows some changes which make the subdivisions of that site comparable to Jarmo, Sarab, and Ali Kosh. Mortensen's chart (1963, fig. 22) shows this very well; the final report may make it possible to compare contemporary units in all of the sites in some detail.

The remaining site to which Jarmo might be compared closely is Ali Kosh, which has been divided into three phases—the Bus Mordeh and Ali Kosh phases, which are preceramic, and the Mohammad Jaffar phase, which has pottery. Chronologically, the Ali Kosh and Mohammad Jaffar phases are probably approximately contemporary with the lower and upper levels of Jarmo respectively. And in apparent parallel with Jarmo, but in contrast to Guran, pottery appears abruptly, leaving in question whether an earlier ceramic phase may have been missed. The types of tools found in the phases of Ali Kosh closely resemble those at Jarmo, the chief exception being that geometrics do not occur. The other microlithic forms, however—as well as a type not found at Jarmo, nibbled bladelets—appear in higher frequencies. In the Ali Kosh phase (see table 21), 8.3% of the total number of retouched tools were microliths as

Table 21.—Ali Kosh Chipped Stone Tool Groups

Phase	Total retouched tools*	Main tool groups compared with total retouched tools										Plain blades compared with total chipped stone	
		Microliths		Piercing-reaming tools		Sickles		End scrapers		Retouched and used blades and flakes			
		Total	%	Total	%	Total	%	Total	%	Total	%	Total	%
Mohammad Jaffar	1,574	211	13.4	109	6.9	121	7.7	56	3.6	1,077	68.4	10,516	44.0
Ali Kosh	2,067	171	8.3	113	5.5	114	5.5	125	6.0	1,544	74.7	9,789	42.1
Bus Mordeh	1,213	161	13.3	138	11.4	42	3.4	125	10.3	747	61.6	15,082	37.6

SOURCE: Data from Hole, Flannery, and Neely 1969, table 5.
*Figures in this column do not include the 8 "one-of-a-kind" tools which were included in the original table as Miscellaneous Tools.

were 13.4% in the Mohammad Jaffar phase; both figures are considerably higher than any at Jarmo (tables 4B and 19).[16] Piercing-reaming tools are relatively more abundant in Ali Kosh, but the percentages of sickles and end scrapers are lower than those observed at Jarmo (tables 5B, 6B, 8B, and 19). In the various phases at Ali Kosh, retouched or used blades and flakes occur in higher percentages than at Jarmo but plain blades occur in about the same proportions (tables 13B, 14B, and 19).

These figures probably say more about the tasks being carried out at Ali Kosh than they do about chronology; in other words, direct comparisons between sites without taking into account the relevant data on subsistence and daily activities are probably meaningless.

It has been reported that a number of other sites have material like that from Jarmo, but at this writing there are no publications that we can use for comparative purposes.

At the moment, therefore, it seems that the most important procedure is to describe each of the villages fully to try to determine as much about them as possible. In this way we can approach the nature of the assemblages in their own contexts. From this kind of study we may then be able to determine which artifacts lend themselves to making comparisons between sites and which pertain only to local situations. Perhaps when we have enough illustrations and descriptions, it may be possible to make such comparisons of techniques of chipping, but it is premature to attempt this now.

CONCLUDING REMARKS

This report is a description of the chipped stone from two operations at Jarmo (table 22). All of the stone from J-II—except that found on the surface—and the stone from J-I, 6, 7, and 8 has been ordered into types and presented in tables that show quantities and percentages. A great deal more chipped stone has been found at Jarmo, some of which I examined in my initial study but which was never given a final treatment, and some of which was only looked at superficially. In the latter category is all the chipped stone from the final season's work at Jarmo, when a series of squares was opened. I chose to give a full treatment to the material reported here for the reason that it represented two stratigraphic sequences that gave promise of including both the lower and upper portions of the site. There is perhaps a middle range of material relevant to an analysis of the chipped stone, but if it occurred in J-I it was represented by very little material. Since there is presently no way to relate the two main operations stratigraphically, we are uncertain about the degree to which the upper and lower levels are different. We do not know, for example, that there is not a gradation in types between the lower and upper levels that is obscured by my focusing on the stratigraphic extremes. In any event, it is clear that differences exist between the early and late levels in the site.

Since I first began work on this material, a number of new ways to treat archeological data statistically have come into use. Such techniques are most useful when the excavations are organized to obtain the necessary data on the association of artifacts with fine changes in stratigraphy and architecture. Statistical techniques are also more useful when broad areas of sites have been dug. Since neither of these conditions pertains to the present excavation, it is fruitless to push statistical interpretation too far. What I have tried to do is present the data in a consistent way, following the pattern used in the Deh Luran reports.

NOTES

1. The use of the phrases "lower Jarmo levels" and "upper Jarmo levels" replaces my former "Units X and Y" respectively and references to "lower" and "upper" Jarmo. The change to a more cumbersome terminology is to eliminate the implication that the lower levels of Jarmo are necessarily of a different period or culture from the upper levels.

2. For the nomenclature on context, see p. 166, n. 1.

3. In my original manuscript (Hole 1961) the types of

Table 22.—Summary of Chipped Stone by Types

	J-II,1	J-II,2	J-II,2fl.	J-II,3	J-II,4	J-II,5	J-II,6	J-I,6	J-I,7	J-I,8	Total
Geometrics and "Other Microliths"											
Trapezes	52	52	12	4	--	--	--	--	1	3	124
Triangles	7	5	--	--	--	--	--	--	--	--	12
Crescents	1	--	3	1	--	--	--	--	--	1	6
Diagonal-ended bladelets	1	1	--	--	--	--	--	4	8	51	65
Diagonal-ended and backed bladelets	5	6	1	1	--	2	--	--	1	1	17
Backed bladelets	7	5	3	3	1	--	--	1	1	1	22
Piercing-Reaming Tools											
Shouldered drills	16	21	18	4	6	13	30	1	1	--	110
Plain drills	52	44	20	10	11	15	27	14	6	10	209
Pointed pieces	21	11	12	10	3	5	9	23	8	20	122
Reamers or fabricators	50	23	14	11	8	12	8	2	6	7	141
Pressure-flaked obsidian fabricators	4	6	2	2	--	2	--	11	22	38	87
Sickles											
Plain sickles	127	67	35	37	14	26	7	34	50	50	447
Retouched sickles	48	25	14	17	10	13	3	14	15	13	172
End Scrapers											
Blade, round-ended	25	16	15	9	12	13	7	29	12	17	155
Flake, round-ended	22	15	5	14	34	37	15	43	25	26	236
Flakes with bulbar-end retouch	4	5	4	1	2	8	1	9	4	4	42
Blade, miscellaneous-ended	78	107	48	27	21	21	20	54	31	62	469
"Other Scrapers"											
Denticulate scrapers	187	128	99	98	67	97	42	81	36	83	918
Notched flakes	50	30	29	17	11	22	6	27	13	27	232
Retouched or Used Pieces											
Retouched or used blades (including reused sickles)	1,088	999	516	411	261	427	387	197	270	372	4,928
Retouched or used flakes	210	146	95	77	51	55	44	159	87	271	1,195
Miscellaneous Artifacts											
Thin sections	86	243	75	58	11	19	--	11	5	5	513
Truncated obsidian blades and flakes	1	--	--	1	--	--	--	33	82	90	207
Burins	7	1	3	4	1	1	--	4	5	4	30
Scaled pieces	31	12	6	5	1	10	6	5	6	17	99
Microburins	2	--	--	--	1	--	--	1	--	--	4
Residual Category											
Ground pieces	12	6	7	11	5	5	3	3	4	6	62
Miscellaneous backed fragments	21	18	5	7	--	3	3	10	2	7	76
Fragments of piercing-reaming tools	59	30	12	32	6	10	12	4	6	13	184
Plain blades	11,515	8,563	5,106	3,763	1,933	3,229	1,498	2,424	2,091	4,434	44,556
Chipping Debris											
Flint blade cores	6	5	1	5	2	3	5	5	2	15	49
Flint flake cores	92	50	47	54	28	54	21	28	22	18	414
Flint core fragments	226	54	119	88	71	103	83	64	59	100	967
Plain flakes, flint and obsidian	9,834	10,485	5,160	4,654	3,553	4,714	2,171	2,893	2,438	4,432	50,334
Totals											
Retouched tools	2,182	1,968	1,029	822	526	798	612	757	695	1,173	10,562
Residual category	92	54	24	50	11	18	18	17	12	26	322
Plain blades	11,515	8,563	5,106	3,763	1,933	3,229	1,498	2,424	2,091	4,434	44,556
Chipping debris	10,158	10,594	5,327	4,801	3,654	4,874	2,280	2,990	2,521	4,565	51,764
Total chipped stone	23,947	21,179	11,486	9,436	6,124	8,919	4,408	6,188	5,319	10,198	107,204

tools were given descriptive labels and numbers ranging from 1 to 39 with some types each having several varieties. In this report the numbering system has been discarded in favor of descriptive terms, and the numbers following these terms refer to the earlier system; several of the types have been reconsidered and combined.

4. "Other microliths" refers to specially retouched bladelets that are typologically distinct from the large numbers of other bladelets. The latter are not divided by size and are counted as plain blades and used blades along with the larger examples.

5. [A number of these fragmentary artifacts recall the double- (and single-) backed blade tools of Çayönü (Redman 1973, p. 258) and Shimshara (Mortensen 1970, p. 43). They have the same type of regular, abrupt, scale-shaped retouch along the edges—less often along one edge only—and, in many cases, the long linear striations along the edge, directly below the pressure flaking on the opposite surface, that are characteristic of the Cayönü examples. (In fig. 122, nos. 11 and 13-21 have striations. Written communication from Peder Mortensen confirms the fact that the Shimshara examples have the same striations. He also agrees that the striations are probably not the result of wear but might possibly have been made by the toolmaker as an easy way to provide the necessary secure purchase for the pressure-flaking tool.) These artifacts tend to be much smaller at Jarmo since obsidian was scarcer there than at Cayönü or Shimshara. There are other differences: the retouch is less steep on the Jarmo examples (ca. 60°-85°) and the retouch is typically on the bulbar surface rather than on the dorsal surface.—LSB]

6. [A four-element sickle-shaped implement was found in J-I,7 in the northwest room (figs. 32; 76; 123:1-2). Most of the surface areas of the three flint blades and the one blade segment (save for their cutting edges) were still covered with bitumen. No traces of the haft—presumably of wood—remained. The sickle was found lying on a reed flooring, and some bits of reed flooring existed above it as well. Only the impressions of the reeds and the white ghosts of their opal skeletons remained.

The working edge of each element was somewhat irregular and worn by use and had traces of sheen; the second edge of each flint showed no signs of use.

Figure 123:2 is a drawing of the reverse side of the aspect visible in the photograph (fig. 123:1), taken when the object was first uncovered. As drawn, reading from left to right, the elements encountered in the drawing are:
(1) A roughly shaped flakelike blade of coarse tan chert, 68 × 22 × 10 mm, bulbar side up, oriented with distal end to the left and fairly broad plain striking platform at right. There is rough steep retouch at the back edge, beginning at the striking platform and petering out towards the distal end.
(2) A roughly shaped blade of coarse light green chert, 74 × 26 × 10 mm, with the dorsal surface up, the broad, plain striking platform at the left, and distal end at the right. The back edge was not retouched; here, the natural blade shape provided a thick, steep back.
(3) A roughly shaped flakelike blade of coarse light green chert, 83 × 18 × 11 mm, with the bulbar surface up, distal end at left, and broad, plain striking platform at the right. The back edge was not retouched.
(4) A midsection of a regularly shaped blade of a smooth, homogeneous, honey-colored chert, 35 × 14 × 3 mm, dorsal side up. Both ends have been snapped at right angles to the long axis. Two large chips were removed from the back of the segment at the left (where it touched the preceding blade) to round off the edge and at the same time make a steeper back.

This is the only retouch. Although this element was almost hidden by the bitumen, its working edge has sheen and is slightly worn by use.

The first and fourth elements had their backs retouched in the same position—in from the end—presumably to make them fit into the general curve of the shaft. The placing of the elements—alternating bulbar side, then dorsal side up—may perhaps have been purposeful as an aid in keeping the elements more securely in place. It is a bit odd that only one of the four elements was made from a relatively slender, regularly shaped blade, for the majority of blades and blade fragments with sheen found in the general excavations throughout the levels are slender (between 10-15 mm in width) and neat (see figs. 115:8,10-19; 116:1-4,7). Only figure 116:3 of the illustrated examples is a comparable flakelike blade, though smaller in size, with broad, plain striking platform (located at the lower side of fig. 116:3). The striking platform extends over almost the entire width.—LSB]

7. When I began sorting the Jarmo flints, a difference in material used for blades in the upper Jarmo levels was apparent visually. I have not seen this material for nearly ten years and have no petrographic analyses to support my impression, so I cannot be more precise than to say that at the time I did the sorting it seemed to me the "new" source produced larger blades but that their edges were "softer" and resulted in the rounded edges described for sickles. Experiments should be made to determine whether the flint was heat treated; its light buff gray color suggests this possibility to me in retrospect.

8. While this hypothesis stands as stated, it should be noted that there is good evidence of the reaping of wild grains at sites antedating the certain appearance of agriculture. Nevertheless, as agriculture came to dominate subsistence, sickles became more common relative to other (e.g., hunting) tools.

9. [It was our good fortune to have Harriet Blitzer take some of the Jarmo thin sections to Don Crabtree during his 1974 summer flintknapping session at Dierks Lake. He was able to duplicate them, and the students also learned to make them. The photograph (fig. 123:4) shows, in sequence, a few very broad thin sections made during the summer session. Although they are larger than the typical Jarmo thin sections (which were made from narrower blades), they are helpful in illustrating the relation of the thin sections to the parent blade. A brief account by Blitzer follows:

> The implements used by Crabtree to duplicate the blade sections were: a small hammerstone of limestone, a wooden stick with a rounded end, and an obsidian blade. The wooden stick was placed upright between the knees of the seated knapper (the rounded end to serve as an anvil) and the ventral side of the blade was held directly over the rounded end and almost perpendicular to it. By striking the center of the dorsal surface of the blade with the hammer, a section of the blade—similar to those examples from the Jarmo assemblage—was removed. By moving the blade along the anvil and delivering a percussion blow at each point desired, a complete blade could be sectioned into many small fragments of desired thickness. The process was easily and swiftly carried out, and by directing the angle of the hammerstone blow and the angle of the original blade as it rested on the anvil, the oblique angle of the thin sections was regulated. Mr. Crabtree surmised that these thin sections would make excellent all-purpose tools.

Perhaps the thin sections could also be made by pressure but Crabtree found this an easy way to produce them.—LSB]

10. [The use of this artifact is indeed puzzling; it may well have been a multipurpose tool as suggested by Crabtree. In addition to Hole's remarks, we would add that most of the

pieces show signs of use at one or both extremities—whether a blunt point or a narrow chiselike edge—but that the signs of use in many cases only become obvious if one uses a 10× hand lens or microscope (not available to Hole at the time of the study).—LSB]

11. Determining whether a piece has been used is a matter of judgment because under sufficient magnification the edge of almost any flint shows some nicking. A great deal of minor nicking of edges occurs when flints are handled in analysis and especially during shipping. Therefore, used pieces are those that show chipping concentrated along one or more portions of an edge. A low-power (ca. 2×) illuminated magnifier was used in studying all the chipped stone. After a great deal of trial and error in setting up arbitrary divisions I concluded that only the minimal separation of "plain" from "used" could be achieved consistently. And a glance at table 13B will show that the used pieces as distinguished here do give us useful chronological information at Jarmo.

12. [As far as it is possible to check, the quantities given in Hole's count for blade cores, flake cores, and core fragments (see p. 254 and table 15) are only for flint examples. The obsidian cores and core fragments, although sorted out by him, were inadvertently overlooked in the final count. The following is at best a tentative count, relatively accurate for the obsidian cores and for the obsidian blade core fragments from J-II,2fl., J-II,5, and J-I,8, but definitely on the low side for the obsidian core fragments from all the other levels. Over the years, many of the core fragments inadvertently have been put into wrong boxes and will only reappear with further detailed study. (Preliminary notes made in the field give a greater number of obsidian blade core fragments for each level than are given here.)

There are relatively few whole obsidian blade cores, only 19 in all. They are cylindrical or pyramidal and all bear signs of subsequent use. Examples were found in J-II,1 (8), J-II,2 (1), J-II,2fl. (1), J-II,3 (1), J-II,4 (1), J-II,5 (1), J-I,6 (1), J-I,7 (2), and J-I,8 (3). There are also 2 small amorphous obsidian flake cores, 1 from J-II,1 and the other from J-I,6. The 223 obsidian blade core fragments and parts—core fronts, core tablets and platform edges, core rounds or cross sections, and crested blade fragments—show considerable wear. These blade core fragments came from J-II,1 (43), J-II,2 (50), J-II,2fl. (23), J-II,3 (21), J-II,4 (15), J-II,5 (24), J-II,6 (8), J-I,6 (6), J-I,7 (14), and J-I,8 (19). The majority of obsidian core fragments would seem to have been made after the blade core had been relatively exhausted.

Although obsidian became more plentiful in the upper levels, it was still prized. Not only were the small stubby complete cores themselves used as implements, but the habit begun in earliest Jarmo of breaking the obsidian cores into horizontal sections and using these for scrapers persisted throughout the occupation of the site.

In keeping with the overwhelmingly microlithic character of the obsidian blades (usually much narrower than 10 mm), it is not surprising that the blade cores and blade core fragments all pertain to minute bladelets. There was, however, a small macrolithic obsidian component—smallish blade fragments but broader than 10 mm—scattered throughout the levels with no discernible pattern. (In J-I,8 the macrolithic component is less than 4%, in J-II,5 it is ca. 16%, and in J-II,2fl. it is ca. 14%. These are the only levels in which detailed measurements have been made.)

Since none of the obsidian cores or fragments have facets corresponding to the broader blades, it seems likely that at least some of the obsidian nodules were first used for producing larger blades, and then the same cores were used for making microlithic bladelets.

The above counts for obsidian cores and core fragments have not been inserted into Hole's tables (see especially tables 15 and 18), since we are not sure how closely the figures would conform with his original studies. However, since the numbers are relatively small compared to the total number of artifacts, they actually do little to change Hole's overall computations. In table 16, where he gives the percentage of *all* plain blades to *all* chipped stone, the inclusion of the obsidian cores and core fragments in the chipped stone total would decrease the percentage only slightly in each level, ranging from 0.2% to 0.05%, with an average decrease of 0.09%. By including the obsidian cores and fragments in the total of the chipping debris as well as in the total of all chipped stone, there would be a slight increase in assessing the percentage of the former to the latter; this increase ranges from 0.07% to 0.2%, with a mean change of 0.1%.

In table 18, if the obsidian cores and core fragments were added to the totals of the "all chipped stone" column and to the "total obsidian" column, the percentage of obsidian to all chipped stone in column 3 would be increased only slightly, ranging from a 0.09% to 0.2% increase for the various levels, with a mean increase of 0.1%.—LSB]

13. [There is a question in our minds as to how meaningful this ratio of flint cores to flint blades is. The "plain blades" count used here mainly covers flint blade fragments or purposeful segments, and relatively few whole blades. We simply do not know at this point whether there is a consistent ratio of flint blades to flint blade fragments and segments throughout the Jarmo levels. Then we would question the omission of "retouched blades" and the specialized blade tools (again these would be predominantly blade fragments and/or segments) from the count. For example, if the above categories were included, the ratio of flint blade cores to flint blade fragments and segments and blades in J-II,6 would be 1:106 (vs. the present 1:66); the ratio for J-II,2fl. would be 1:1,534 (vs. 1:1,086) blade fragments and/or segments and blades. And other factors enter in (even aside from the ever-present one of accident of finds). In the one level, J-I,8, where recent reanalysis of the chipped stone has made a more detailed account available, the sum of all flint blades and blade fragments and/or segments, including retouched blades and normally recognizable tool types is ca. 3,300. Of these, ca. $^1/_{10}$ are whole blades and the remainder are blade fragments and/or segments; furthermore, ca. $^2/_3$ of the total number are microliths (i.e., 10 mm or less in width). Since the flint cores preserved from J-I,8 are all microlithic, it would seem only reasonable to restrict the ratio of flint microlithic cores to *micro* flint blade fragments, segments, and blades, and retouched and recognizable blade tools. This would give us a ratio of ca. 1:169 (vs. the 1:190 shown on table 16). But then if we also include some of the larger fragments of micro blade cores, which obviously represent additional blade cores, we would get a ratio of ca. 110 micro blades and blade fragments and segments to 1 core. Perhaps 10 of these represent whole bladelets and 100 represent mainly proximal (bulbar) sections, but also mid- and distal sections.

Ratios aside, there was actually nothing in J-I,8 to suggest a chipping area. We would diffidently suggest that the reason so many cores and core fragments appeared in this area is that they made excellent, sturdy tools; most of them show signs of use.—LSB]

14. In the units under consideration, the volume excavated is: J-II,1 = ca. 118 m^3, J-II,2 = ca. 256 m^3, J-II,2fl. = ca. 98 m^3, J-II,3 = ca. 118 m^3, J-II,4 = ca. 90 m^3, J-II,5 = ca. 131 m^3, J-II,6

= ca. 100 m³, J-I,6 = ca. 47 m³, J-I,7 = ca. 69 m³, J-I,8 = ca. 122 m³.

15. In fact, only J-II,6 has no pottery at all. According to Adams's analysis only 204 sherds came from J-II,3-5, while more than 12,000 came from J-II,1,2, and 2fl.

16. [We are not completely convinced that this distinction would hold, were Hole to study the Jarmo chipped stone now after having handled the Deh Luran material. As one moves from the Levant eastwards in the Near East, the early village chipped stone tool kits seem to become ever more simple as far as recognizable tool types are concerned. Used blades (Hole's "plain" blades) become more and more predominant. They are definitely tools but a disappointment to the archeologist since at this point it is still not possible to distinguish and adequately describe the various types of wear patterns in a way that has meaning for other archeologists.

In the Jarmo materials, Hole found a certain number of describable chipped stone tool types; when he later dealt with the Deh Luran chipped stone, he found fewer describable types and we suspect that he naturally worked hard to discover more types. In so doing, he must have discovered the "nibbled" microlithic bladelet type that is the predominant microlithic type tool in the Bus Mordeh, Ali Kosh, and Mohammad Jaffar phases. We further suspect that were he to reexamine the Jarmo material in the light of Deh Luran, he would also find the same nibbled bladelet type predominating.

Jane MacRae, presently doing detailed work on the chipped stone of J-I,8, reports nibbled microlithic bladelets (mainly blade fragments and/or segments) as a definite type in both flint (ca. 183) and obsidian (ca. 720). In Hole's tables, J-I,8 has the highest percentage of geometrics and "other microliths" to retouched tools of all the levels—4.9% (the percentages for all the levels range from 0 to 4.9%, with an average of 1.7%). By adding MacRae's nibbled bladelets, the percentage in J-I,8 shoots up to 46.4%. Granted that Hole might well cut down significantly on the number that he would put into his "nibbled" bladelet classification, it still seems likely that now he would also include a substantial "nibbled" bladelet category for Jarmo.

It would be interesting to know whether, in fact, the overall character (this would include the "plain" blades) of the Deh Luran chipped stone in the Bus Mordeh, Ali Kosh, and Mohammad Jaffar phases is more microlithic or less microlithic than the chipped stone of Jarmo.—LSB]

CATALOGUE OF ILLUSTRATED CHIPPED STONE (figs. 112-26)

FIGURE 112. MICROLITHS AND PLAIN DRILLS
1 Trapeze (flint), from J-II,2fl.
2 Trapeze (obsidian), from J-II,1
3 Trapeze (obsidian), from J-II,1
4 Trapeze (flint), from J-II,1
5 Trapeze (obsidian), from J-II,1
6 Trapeze (obsidian), from J-II,1
7 Trapeze (flint), from J-II,1
8 Trapeze (flint), from J-I,8
9 Trapeze (flint), from J-II,1
10 Trapeze (obsidian), from J-II,2
11 Trapeze (obsidian), from J-II,1
12 Trapeze (flint), from J-II,1
13 Triangle (obsidian), from J-II,2
14 Trapeze (obsidian), from J-II,2
15 Triangle (obsidian), from J-II,2
16 Triangle (flint), from J-II,1
17 Crescent (flint), from J-II,3
18 Crescent (obsidian), from J-II,1
19 Diagonal-ended bladelet (obsidian), from J-II,1
20 Diagonal-ended bladelet (obsidian), from J-II,2
21 Diagonal-ended bladelet (flint), from J-I,8
22 Diagonal-ended bladelet (flint) from J-I,8
23 Diagonal-ended bladelet (flint), from J-I,8
24 Diagonal-ended bladelet (flint), from J-I,8fl.
25 Diagonal-ended bladelet (flint), from J-I,8
26 Diagonal-ended and backed bladelet (flint), from J-I,3
27 Diagonal-ended and backed bladelet (flint), from J-I,3
28 Diagonal-ended and backed bladelet (flint), from J-I,8fl.
29 Backed bladelet (obsidian), from J-II,2
30 Miscellaneous backed flake (flint)
31 Miscellaneous backed bladelet (obsidian), from J-II,2
32 Plain drill (flint), from J-II,2
33 Plain drill (obsidian), from J-II,1
34 Plain drill (flint), from J-II,1
35 Plain drill (flint), from J-II,6
36 Plain drill (flint), from J-II,6
37 Plain drill (obsidian), from J-II,1
38 Plain drill (obsidian), from J-II,3
39 Plain drill (flint), from J-II,2
40 Plain drill (flint), from J-II
41 Plain drill (flint), from J-II,1
42 Plain drill (flint), from J-II,1
43 Plain drill (flint), from J-II,1

FIGURE 113. DRILLS AND REAMERS
1 Plain drill (flint), from J-II,3
2 Plain drill (flint), from J-II,2fl.
3 Plain drill (flint), from J-II,2
4 Plain drill (flint), from J-II,1
5 Plain drill (flint), from J-II,5
6 Plain drill (obsidian), from J-II,2
7 Plain drill (obsidian)
8 Plain drill (obsidian), from J-II,2fl.
9 Plain drill (flint), from J-II,6
10 Reamer or fabricator (flint), from J-II,1
11 Plain drill (flint), from J-II,1
12 Plain drill (flint), from J-II,1
13 Reamer or fabricator (flint), from J-II,1
14 Plain drill (flint), from J-II,1
15 Plain drill (flint), from J-II,6
16 Shouldered drill (obsidian), from J-I,6
17 Shouldered drill (flint), from J-II,2
18 Shouldered drill (flint), from J-II,1
19 Shouldered drill (flint), from J-II,2
20 Shouldered drill (flint), from J-II,2fl.
21 Shouldered drill (flint), from J-II,6
22 Shouldered drill (flint), from J-II,2
23 Reamer or fabricator (flint), from J-II,2fl.
24 Reamer or fabricator (flint), from J-II,4
25 Shouldered drill (obsidian), from J-II,2
26 Shouldered drill (obsidian), from J-II,2
27 Shouldered drill (flint), from J-II,2
28 Reamer or fabricator (flint), from J-II,1

FIGURE 114. DRILLS, REAMERS, POINTED PIECES
1 Shouldered drill (flint), from J-II,1
2 Shouldered drill (flint)
3 Shouldered drill (flint), from J-II,5
4 Shouldered drill (flint), from J-II,4
5 Shouldered drill (flint), from J-II,1

6 Shouldered drill (flint), from J-II,2fl.
7 Shouldered drill (flint), from J-II,6
8 Shouldered drill (flint), from J-I,7
9 Shouldered drill (flint), from J-II,6
10 Shouldered drill (flint), from J-II,2fl.
11 Shouldered drill (flint), from J-II,2fl.
12 Reamer or fabricator (flint), from J-II,1
13 Reamer or fabricator (flint), from J-II,1
14 Reamer or fabricator (obsidian), from J-II,1E
15 Pointed piece (flint), from J-II,1
16 Pointed piece (flint), from J-II,2
17 Pointed piece (flint), from J-II,1
18 Pointed piece (flint), from J-II,1
19 Pointed piece (flint), from J-II,1
20 Pointed piece (flint), from J-II,1
21 Pointed piece (flint), from J-II,1

FIGURE 115. POINTED PIECES AND SICKLES
1 Pointed piece (flint), from J-II,6
2 Pointed piece (obsidian), from J-II,1
3 Pointed piece (flint), from J-II,2fl.
4 Pointed piece (flint), from J-II,2fl.
5 Pointed piece (flint), from J-II,2fl.
6 Pointed piece (flint), from J-I,6b
7 Pointed piece (flint), from J-II,1
8 Plain sickle (flint), from J-II,2fl.
9 Pointed piece (flint), from J-II,6
10 Plain sickle (flint), from J-II,2
11 Retouched sickle (flint), from J-II,6
12 Plain sickle (flint), from J-II,2
13 Retouched sickle (flint), from J-II,2fl.
14 Retouched sickle (flint), from J-II,5
15 Retouched sickle (flint), from J-II,5
16 Retouched sickle (flint), from J-I,8fl.
17 Retouched sickle (flint), from J-II,2
18 Retouched sickle (flint), from J-I,8
19 Retouched sickle (flint), from J-II,1

FIGURE 116. SICKLES AND BLADES
1 Retouched sickle (flint), from J-II,1
2 Retouched sickle (flint), from J-II,6
3 Retouched sickle (flint), from J-I,8
4 Retouched sickle (flint), from J-I,8
5 Retouched or used blade (obsidian), from J-II,1
6 Retouched or used blade (obsidian), from J-II,1
7 Retouched sickle (flint), from J-I,8
8 Retouched or used blade (flint), from J-II,1
9 Retouched or used blade (flint), from J-II,1E
10 Retouched or used blade (obsidian), from J-II,1
11 Retouched or used blade (obsidian), from J-II,1
12 Retouched or used blade (obsidian), from J-II,1
13 Retouched or used blade (obsidian), from J-II,1
14 Retouched or used blade (flint), from J-II,1
15 Retouched or used blade (flint), from J-I,6a
16 Retouched or used blade (flint), from J-II,1
17 Retouched or used blade (flint), from J-II,1
18 Retouched or used blade (flint), from J-II,1
19 Retouched or used blade (flint), from J-II,1

FIGURE 117. RETOUCHED OR USED BLADES AND FLAKES
1 Retouched or used blade (flint), from J-II,1
2 Retouched or used blade (flint), from J-II,1
3 Retouched or used blade (flint), from J-II,1
4 Retouched or used blade (flint), from J-II,1
5 Retouched or used blade (flint), from J-II,1
6 Retouched or used blade (flint), from J-II,1
7 Retouched or used blade (flint), from J-II,1
8 Retouched or used blade (flint), from J-II,1
9 Retouched or used flake (flint), from J-II,3
10 Retouched or used flake (flint), from J-II,3
11 Retouched or used blade (flint), from J-II,1
12 Retouched or used flake (flint), from J-II,3
13 Retouched or used blade (flint), from J-II,1
14 Retouched or used blade (flint), from J-II,1
15 Retouched or used blade (flint), from J-II,1
16 Retouched or used blade (obsidian), from J-II,1
17 Retouched or used blade (flint), from J-II,1

FIGURE 118. FLAKES, BLADES, SCRAPERS
1 Retouched or used flake (flint), from J-II,1
2 Retouched or used flake (flint), from J-II,1
3 Retouched or used flake (obsidian), from J-II,1
4 Retouched or used flake (flint), from J-II,1
5 Retouched or used flake (flint), from J-II,1
6 Retouched or used flake (flint), from J-II,1
7 Retouched or used flake (flint), from J-II,1
8 Retouched or used flake (flint), from J-II,1
9 Blade, round-ended scraper (flint), from J-II,4
10 Plain blade (flint), from J-II,1E
11 Plain blade (flint), from J-II,2
12 Plain blade (flint), from J-II,1
13 Retouched or used flake (flint), from J-II,1
14 Blade, round-ended scraper (flint), from J-I,8
15 Blade, round-ended scraper (flint), from J-II,3
16 Blade, round-ended scraper (flint), from J-I,6
17 Blade, round-ended scraper (flint), from J-II,1
18 Blade, double-ended scraper (flint), from J-I,7
19 Blade, round-ended scraper (flint), from J-I,8
20 Blade, round-ended scraper (flint), from J-I,6
21 Blade, round-ended scraper (flint), from J-II,1
22 Blade, round-ended scraper (flint), from J-I,6c

FIGURE 119. SCRAPERS
1 Blade, round-ended scraper (flint), from J-II,1
2 Blade, miscellaneous-ended scraper (flint), from J-II,1
3 Blade, miscellaneous-ended scraper (flint), from J-II,3
4 Blade, miscellaneous-ended scraper (flint), from J-II,1
5 Blade, round-ended scraper (flint), from J-I,6
6 Blade, double-ended scraper (flint), from J-II,1
7 Blade, miscellaneous-ended scraper (flint), from J-II,5
8 Blade, miscellaneous-ended scraper (flint), from J-II,1
9 Blade, miscellaneous-ended scraper (flint), from J-II,1
10 Blade, miscellaneous-ended scraper (flint), from J-II,3
11 Blade, miscellaneous-ended scraper (flint), from J-II,1
12 Blade, double-ended scraper (flint), from J-I,7
13 Blade, miscellaneous-ended scraper (flint), from J-II,1
14 Blade, miscellaneous-ended scraper (flint), from J-I,6b
15 Blade, miscellaneous-ended scraper (flint), from J-II,1
16 Blade, miscellaneous-ended scraper (obsidian), from J-I,6
17 Blade, miscellaneous-ended scraper (obsidian), from J-I,6c
18 Blade, miscellaneous-ended scraper (obsidian), from J-II,1
19 Blade, double-ended scraper (flint), from J-I,8
20 Blade, miscellaneous-ended scraper (flint), from J-II,1
21 Flake, round-ended scraper (flint), from J-I,6c
22 Flake, round-ended scraper (flint), from J-II,1
23 Flake, round-ended scraper (flint), from J-I,8

FIGURE 120. SCRAPERS
1 Flake, round-ended scraper (flint), from J-I,6
2 Flake, round-ended scraper (flint), from J-I,8
3 Flake, round-ended scraper (flint), from J-I,8
4 Flake, round-ended scraper (flint), from J-I,7

5 Flake, round-ended scraper (flint), from J-I,6
   6 Flake, round-ended scraper (flint), from J-I,6
   7 Round-ended scraper (flint), from J-I,8
   8 Round-ended scraper (flint), from J-II,5
   9 Round-ended scraper (flint), from J-II,6
  10 Round-ended scraper (flint), from J-I,8fl
  11 Flake, round-ended scraper (flint), from J-I,8
  12 Round-ended scraper (flint), from J-I,8fl

FIGURE 121. SCRAPERS AND FLAKES
   1 Denticulate scraper (flint), from J-I,8
   2 Denticulate scraper (flint), from J-II,5
   3 Denticulate scraper (flint), from J-I,8fl
   4 Flake, bulbar-end retouch (flint), from J-II,3
   5 Denticulate scraper (flint), from J-I,8
   6 Notched flake (flint), from J-I,7
   7 Denticulate scraper (flint), from J-I,8fl
   8 Denticulate scraper (flint), from J-I,8fl
   9 Flake, bulbar-end retouch (flint), from J-II,2fl
  10 Notched flake (flint), from J-I,8
  11 Retouched or used flake (flint), from J-II,1
  12 Denticulate scraper (flint), from J-I,8
  13 Denticulate scraper (flint), from J-I,8

FIGURE 122. OBSIDIAN THIN SECTIONS, FABRICATORS, BLADES AND FLAKES
   1 Thin section (obsidian), from J-II,1
   2 Thin section (obsidian), from J-II,3
   3 Thin section (obsidian), from J-II,1
   4 Thin section (obsidian), from J-II
   5 Thin section (obsidian), from J-I,3
   6 Thin section (obsidian), from J-II,2
   7 Thin section (obsidian), from J-II
   8 Thin section (obsidian), from J-II,1
   9 Thin section (obsidian), from J-II,3
  10 Thin section (obsidian)
  11 Fabricator (obsidian), from J-I,7
  12 Fabricator (obsidian), from J-I,6
  13 Fabricator (obsidian), from J-I,8
  14 Fabricator (obsidian), from J-I,7
  15 Fabricator (obsidian), from J-II,2
  16 Fabricator (obsidian), from J-II,3
  17 Fabricator (obsidian), from J-I,7
  18 Fabricator (obsidian), from J-II,5
  19 Fabricator (obsidian), from J-II,2
  20 Fabricator (obsidian), from J-I,6b
  21 Fabricator (obsidian), from J-I,7
  22 Fabricator (obsidian), from J-I,7
  23 Fabricator (obsidian), from J-I,7
  24 Fabricator (obsidian), from J-II,1
  25 Fabricator (obsidian), from J-I,7
  26 Truncated blades and flakes (obsidian), from J-I,8
  27 Truncated blades and flakes (obsidian), from J-II,1
  28 Truncated blades and flakes (obsidian), from J-I,8
  29 Truncated blades and flakes (obsidian), from J-I,8fl
  30 Truncated blades and flakes (obsidian), from J-I,8
  31 Truncated blades and flakes (obsidian), from J-I,7
  32 Truncated blades and flakes (obsidian), from J-I,7fl
  33 Truncated blades and flakes (obsidian), from J-I,7fl
  34 Truncated blades and flakes (obsidian), from J-I,8
  35 Truncated blades and flakes (obsidian), from J-I,7fl
  36 Truncated blades and flakes (obsidian), from J-I,8fl
  37 Truncated blades and flakes (obsidian), from J-I,8
  38 Truncated blades and flakes (obsidian), from J-II,3
  39 Truncated blades and flakes (obsidian), from J-I,7fl
  40 Truncated blades and flakes (obsidian), from J-I,7

FIGURE 123. SICKLE AND THIN SECTIONS
   1 Photograph of four-element sickle found in J-I,7, northwest room
   2 Sketch of the sickle in fig. 123:1
   3 Schematic sketch of obsidian "thin section" and parent blade
   4 Photograph of modern duplication of obsidian "thin sections"

FIGURE 124. MISCELLANEOUS
   1 Burin (flint), from J-II,2fl
   2 Burin (flint), from J-II,1
   3 Burin (obsidian), from J-II,4
   4 Burin (obsidian), from J-I,7
   5 Burin (obsidian), from J-II,1
   6 Microburin (obsidian), from J-II,1
   7 Burin (obsidian), from J-I,8
   8 Reamer or fabricator (flint), from J-II,1
   9 Reamer or fabricator (flint)
  10 Reamer or fabricator (flint), from J-II,2
  11 Reamer or fabricator (flint), from J-II,4
  12 Reamer or fabricator (obsidian), from J-II,5
  13 Chipped and ground piece (flint), from J-II,2fl
  14 Reamer or fabricator (flint), from J-II,1
  15 Reamer or fabricator (flint), from J-II,6
  16 Scaled piece (flint), from J-I,8
  17 Reamer or fabricator (flint), from J-II,1

FIGURE 125. MISCELLANEOUS
   1 Scaled piece (flint), from J-II,6
   2 Scaled piece (flint), from J-II,1
   3 Scaled piece (flint), from J-II,1
   4 Scaled piece (obsidian), from J-II,5
   5 Scaled piece (flint), from J-I,8
   6 Scaled piece (obsidian), from J-I,6c
   7 Scaled piece (obsidian), from J-I,8
   8 Core tablet (flint), from J-I,8fl
   9 Blade core (flint), from J-I,8
  10 Blade core (flint), from J-I,8fl
  11 Blade core (flint), from J-II,6
  12 Scaled piece (obsidian), from J-I,7
  13 Chipped and ground piece (obsidian), from J-I,7
  14 Blade core (flint), from J-I,7
  15 Blade core (flint), from J-II,6
  16 Blade core (flint), from J-I,7
  17 Blade core (flint), from J-I,8

FIGURE 126. MISCELLANEOUS
   1 Flake core (flint), from J-II,3
   2 Flake core (flint), from J-II,1
   3 Flake core (flint), from J-II,1
   4 Blade core fragment, plunging flake (flint), from J-I,6
   5 Flake core (flint), from J-II,1
   6 Flake core (flint), from J-II,1
   7 Blade core (flint), from J-II,2

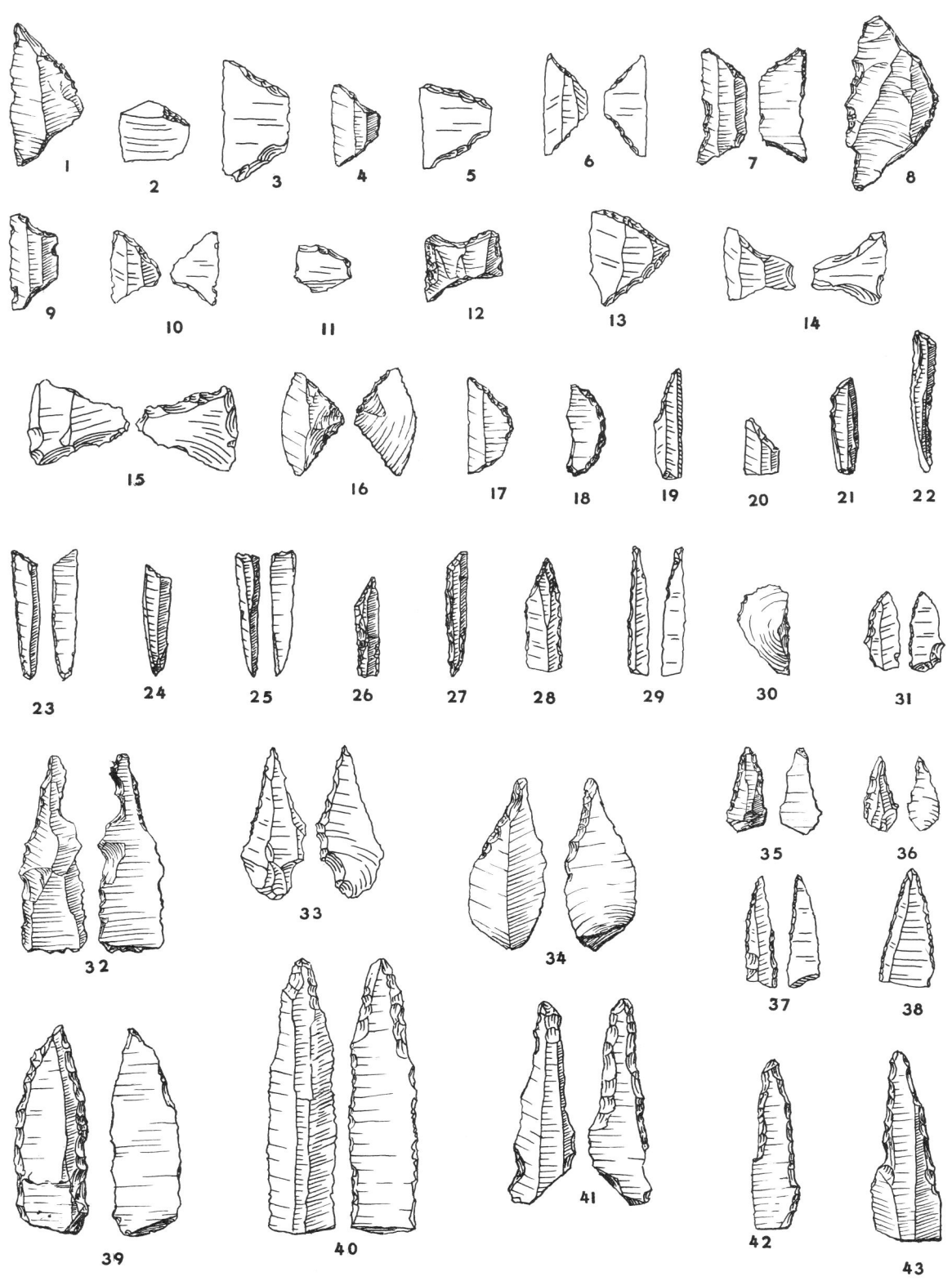

Fig. 112. Jarmo chipped stone: trapezes, *1-12,14*; triangles, *13,15-16*; crescents, *17-18*; diagonal-ended bladelets, *19-25*; diagonal-ended and backed bladelets, *26-28*; backed bladelet, *29*; miscellaneous backed flake and bladelet, *30-31*; plain drills, *32-43*. Black dot denotes obsidian. Scale 1:1.

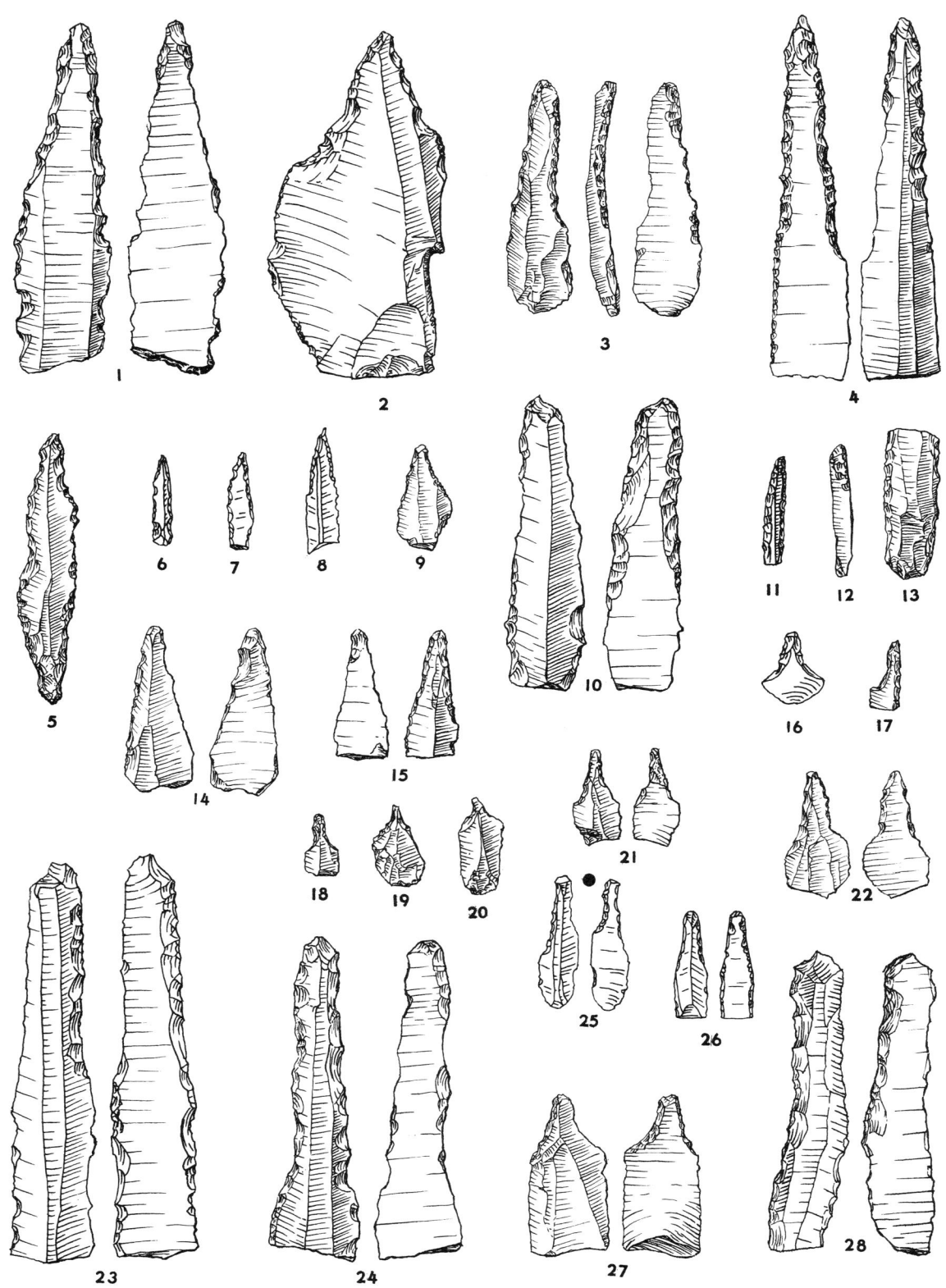

Fig. 113. Jarmo chipped stone: plain drills, *1-9,11-12,14-15*; shouldered drills, *16-22,25-27*; reamers or fabricators, *10,13,23-24,28*. Black dot denotes obsidian. Scale 1:1.

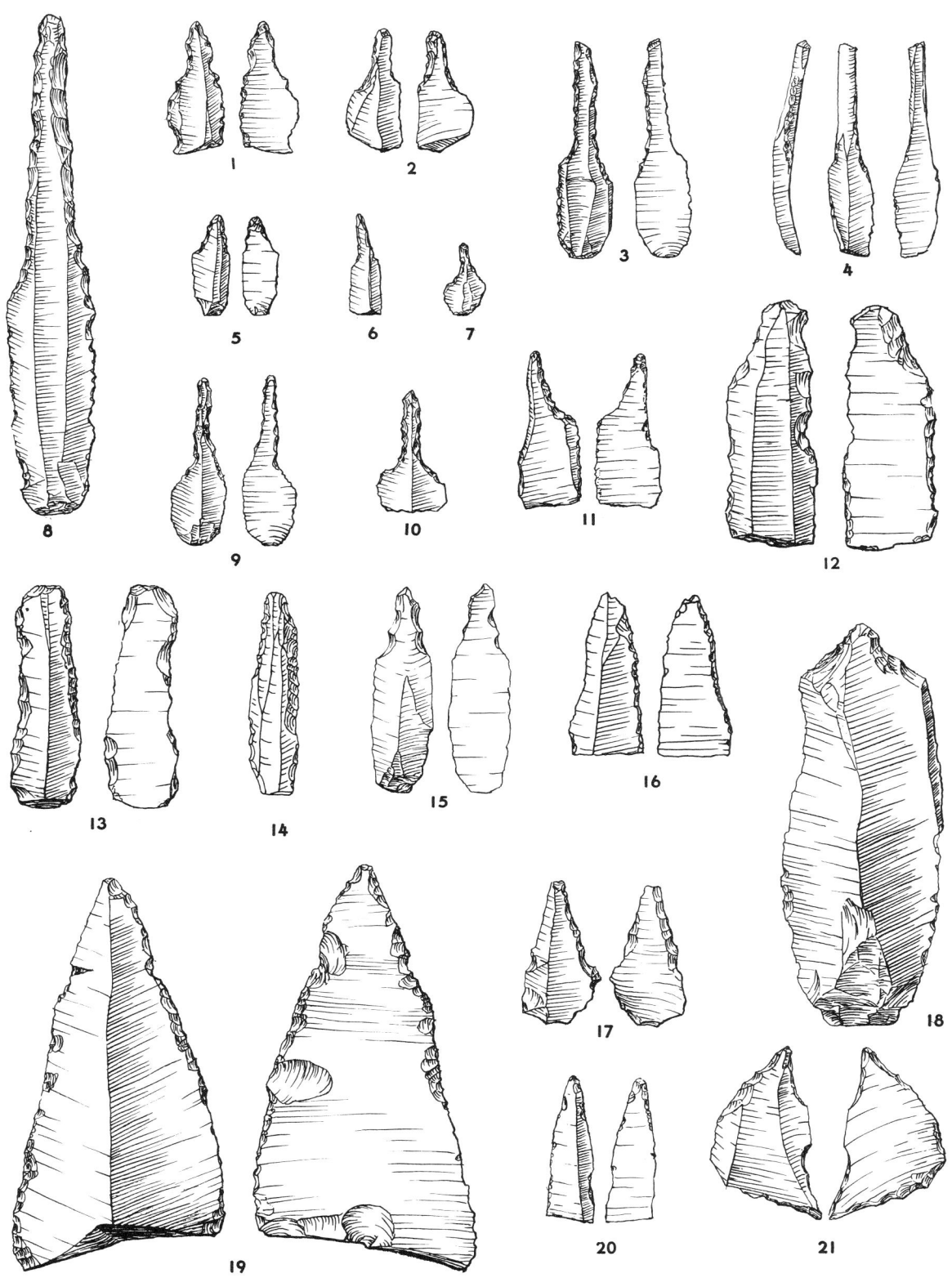

Fig. 114. Jarmo chipped stone: shouldered drills, *1-11*; reamers or fabricators, *12-14*; pointed pieces, *15-21*. Black dot denotes obsidian. Scale 1:1.

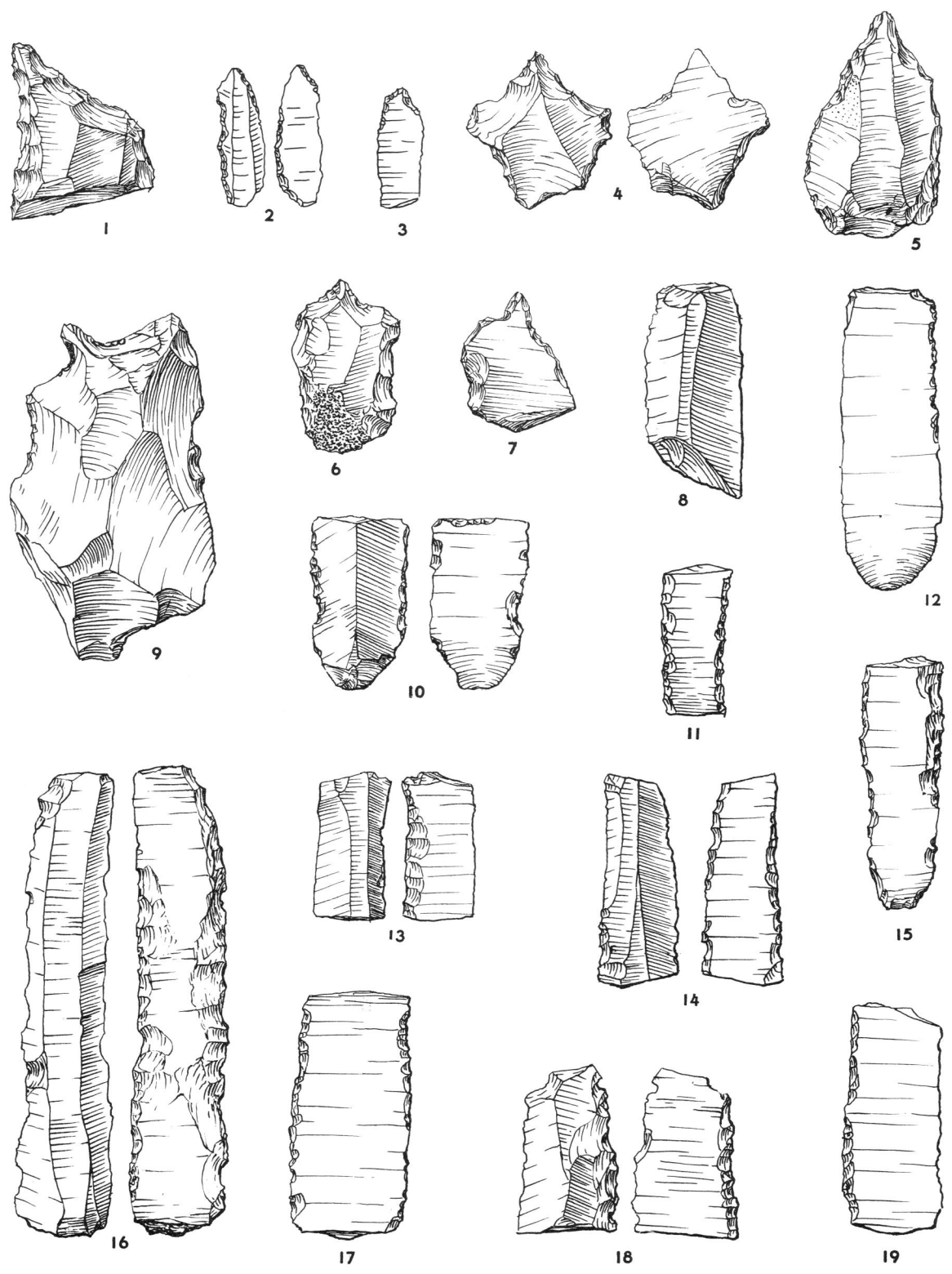

Fig. 115. Jarmo chipped stone: pointed pieces, *1-7,9*; plain sickles, *8,10,12*; retouched sickles, *11,13-19*. Black dot denotes obsidian. Scale 1:1.

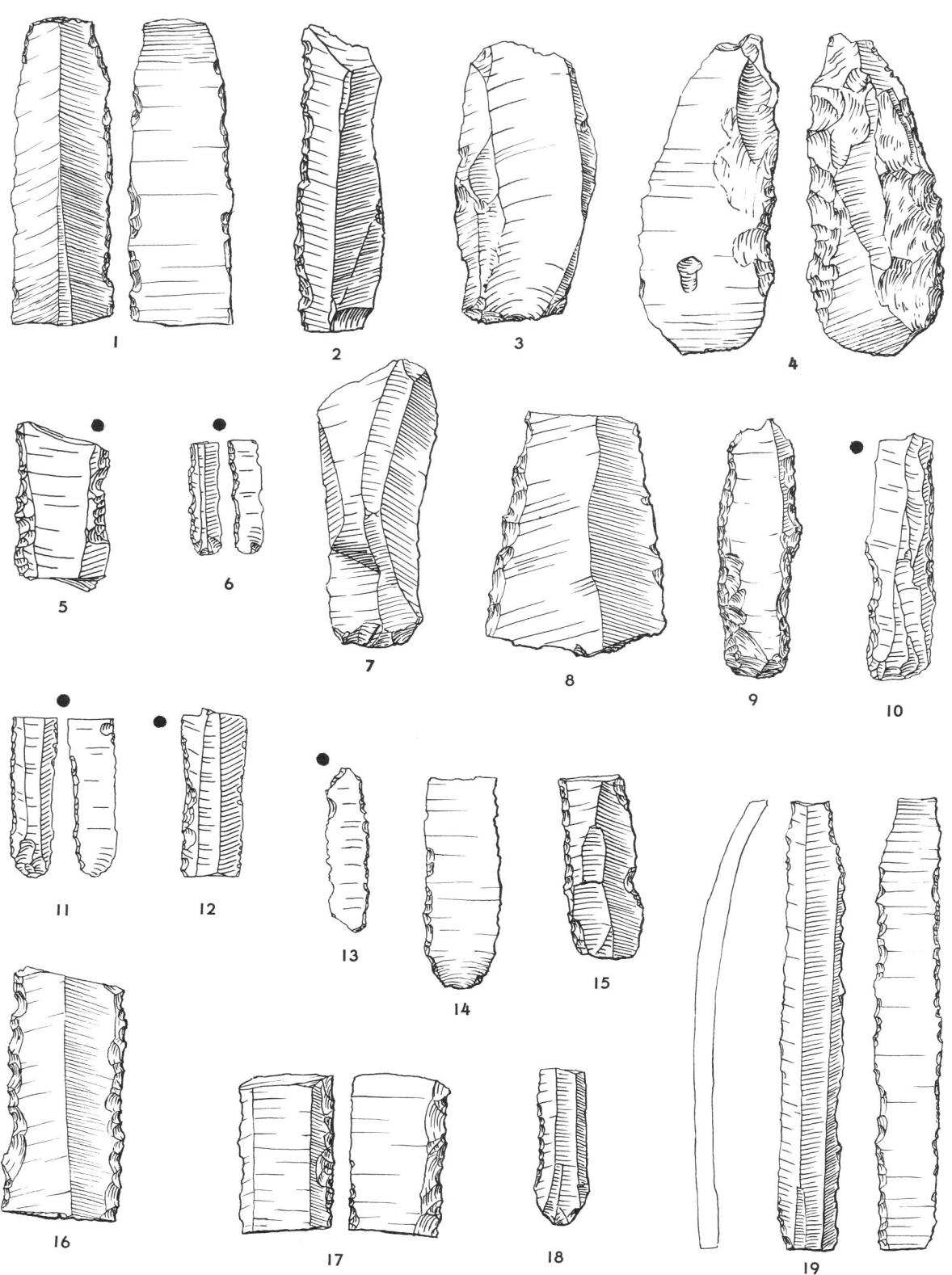

Fig. 116. Jarmo chipped stone: retouched sickles, *1-4,7*; retouched or used blades, *5-6,8-19*. Black dot denotes obsidian. Scale 1:1.

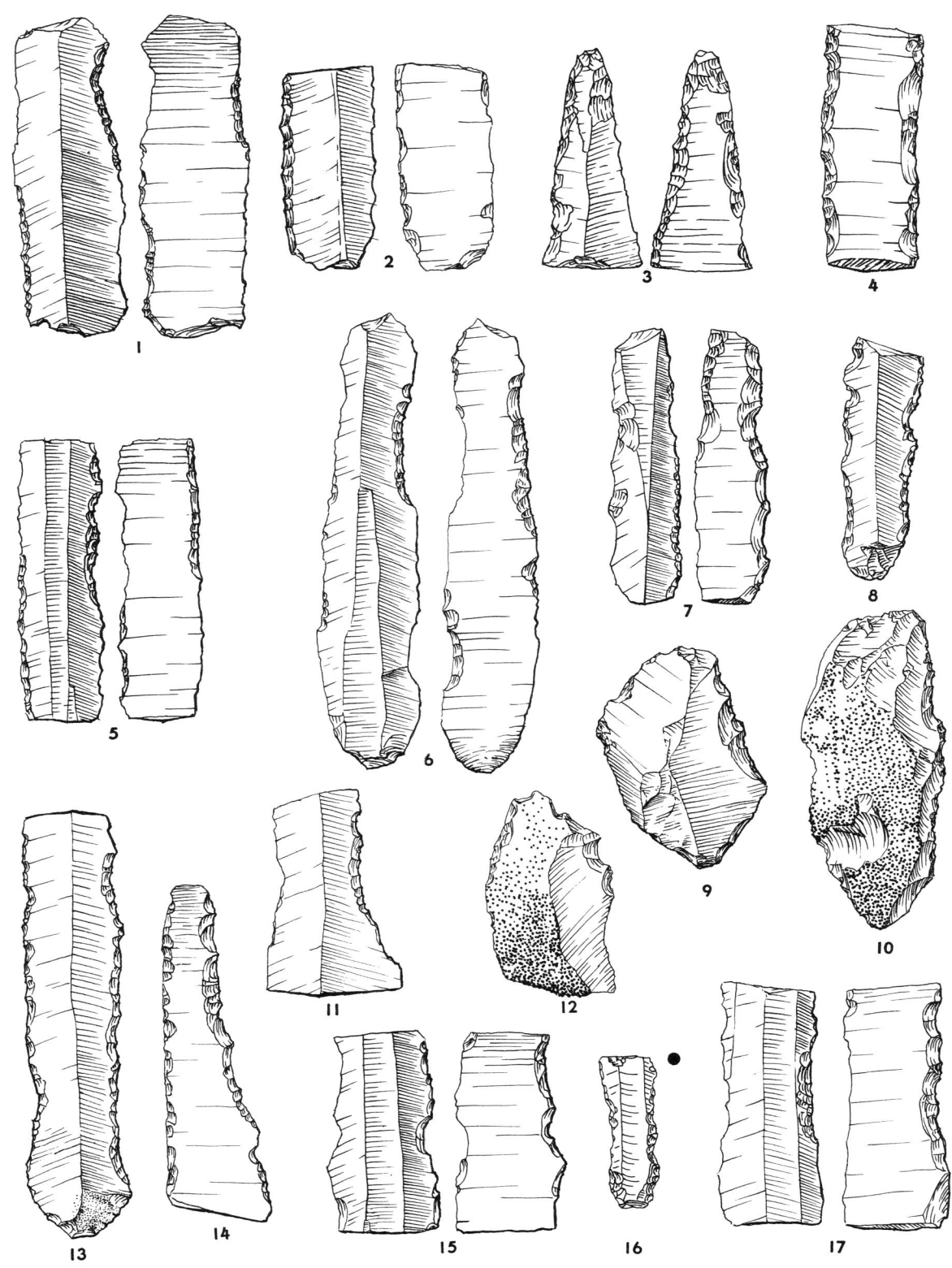

Fig. 117. Jarmo chipped stone: retouched or used blades, *1-8,11,13-17*; retouched or used flakes, *9-10,12*. Black dot denotes obsidian. Scale 1:1.

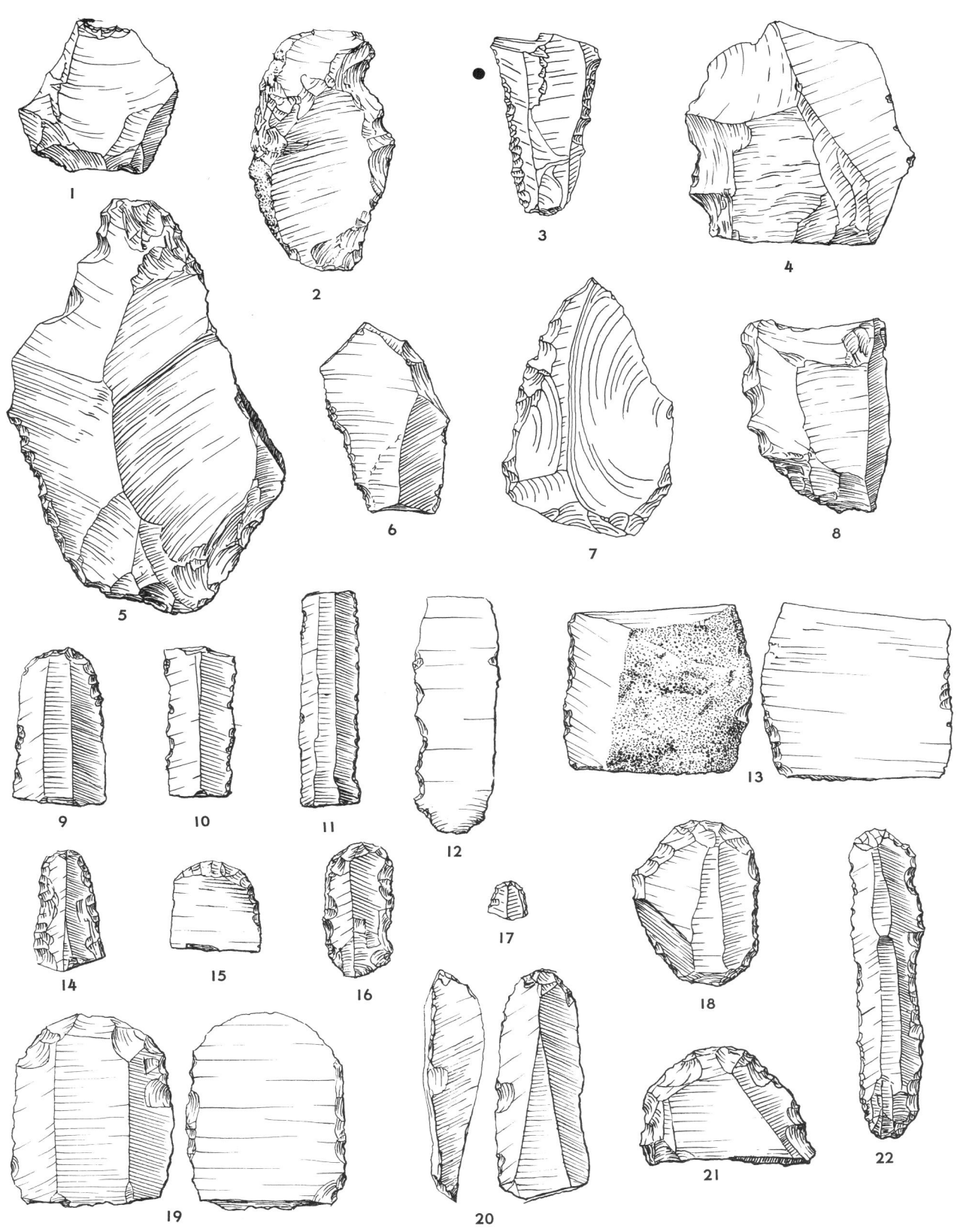

Fig. 118. Jarmo chipped stone: retouched or used flakes, *1-8,13*; plain blades, *10-12*; blade, round-ended scrapers, *9,14-17,19-22*; blade, double-ended scraper, *18*. Black dot denotes obsidian. Scale 1:1.

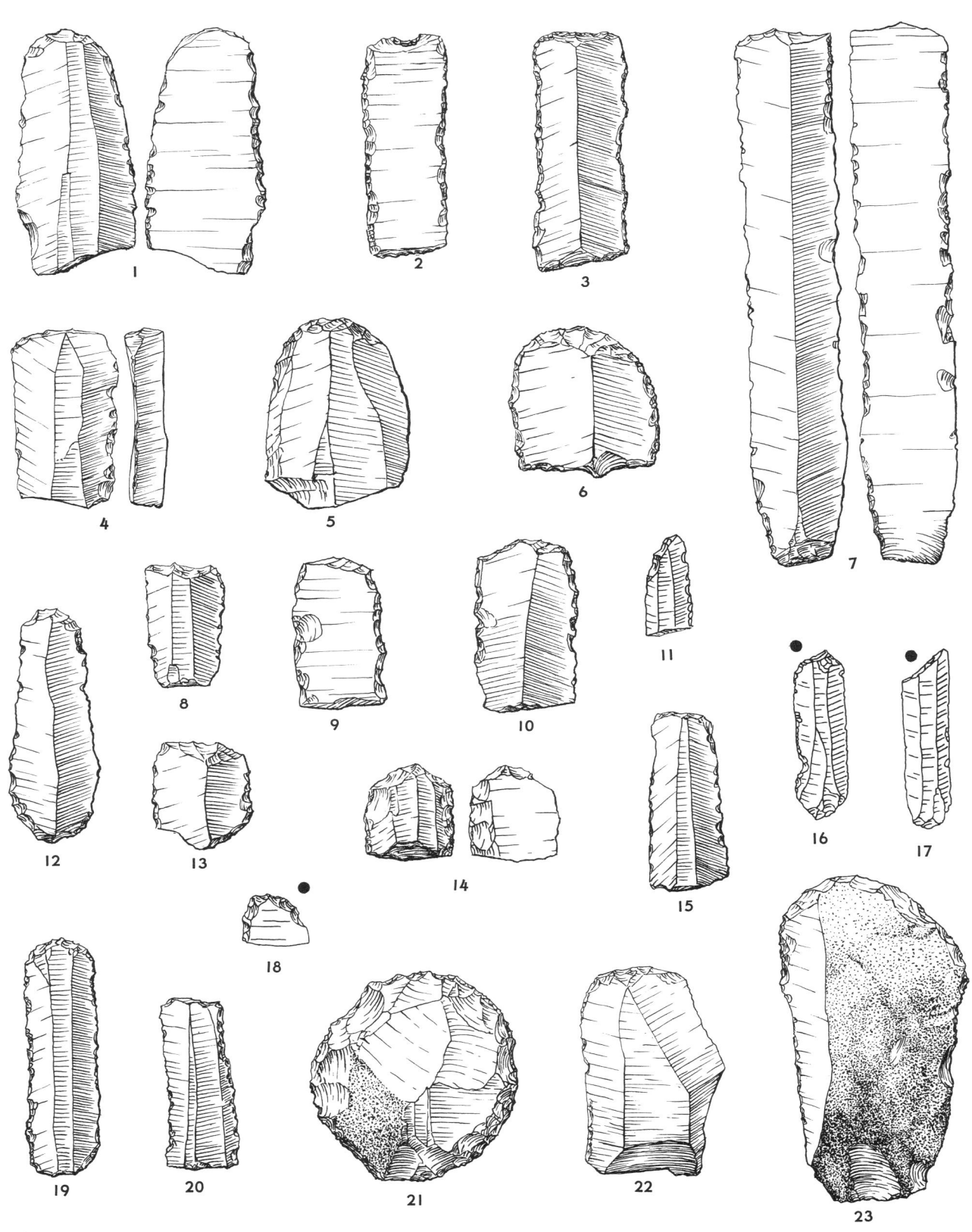

Fig. 119. Jarmo chipped stone: blade, round-ended scrapers, *1,5*; blade, miscellaneous-ended scrapers, *2-4,7-11,13-18,20*; blade, double-ended scrapers, *6,12,19*; flake, round-ended scrapers, *21-23*. Black dot denotes obsidian. Scale 1:1.

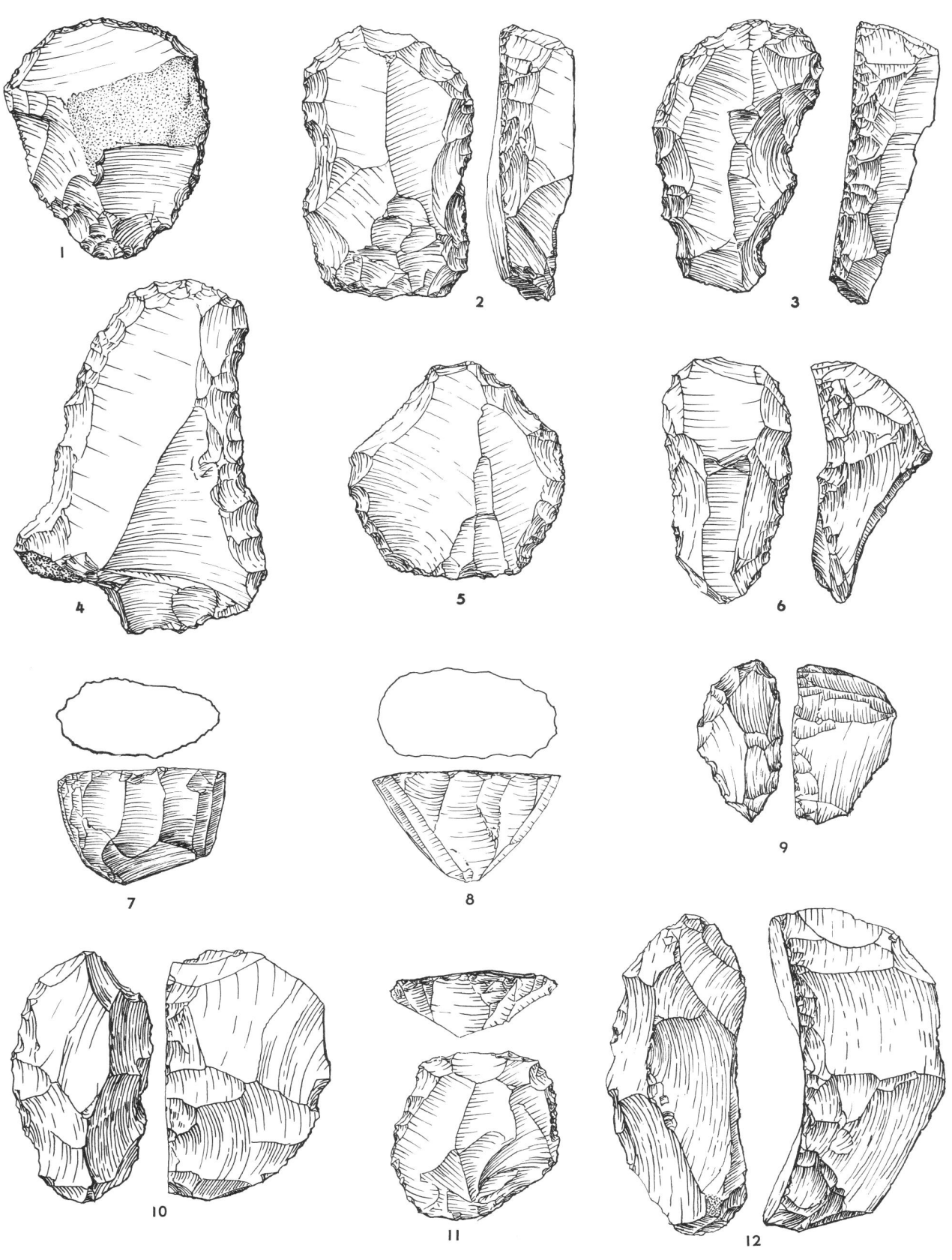

Fig. 120. Jarmo chipped stone: flake, round-ended scrapers, *1-6,11*; round-ended scrapers, *7-10,12*. All flint. Scale 1:1.

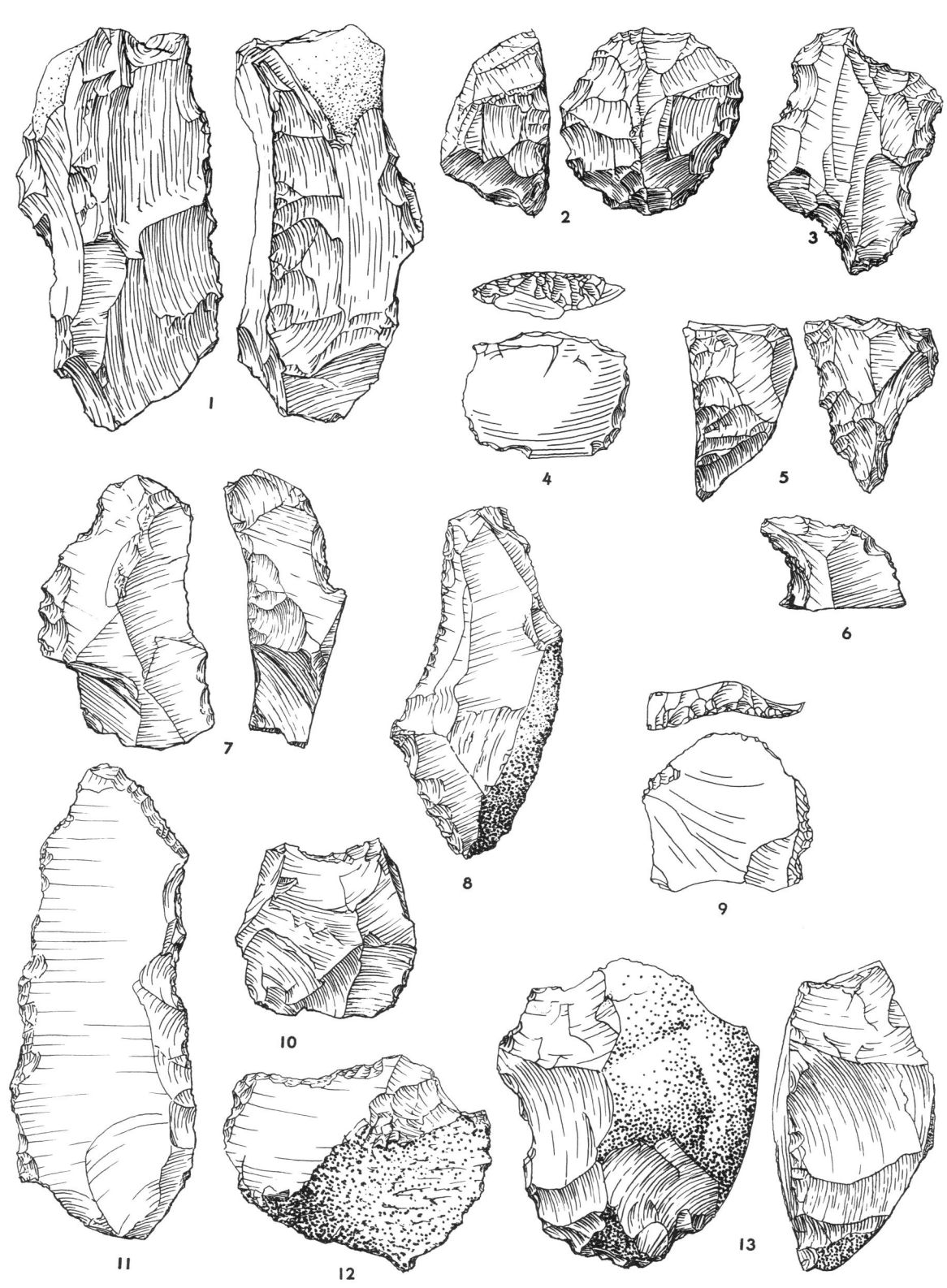

Fig. 121. Jarmo chipped stone: denticulate scrapers, *1-3,5,7-8,12-13*; flakes, bulbar-end retouch, *4,9*; notched flakes, *6,10*; retouched or used flake, *11*. All flint. Scale 1:1.

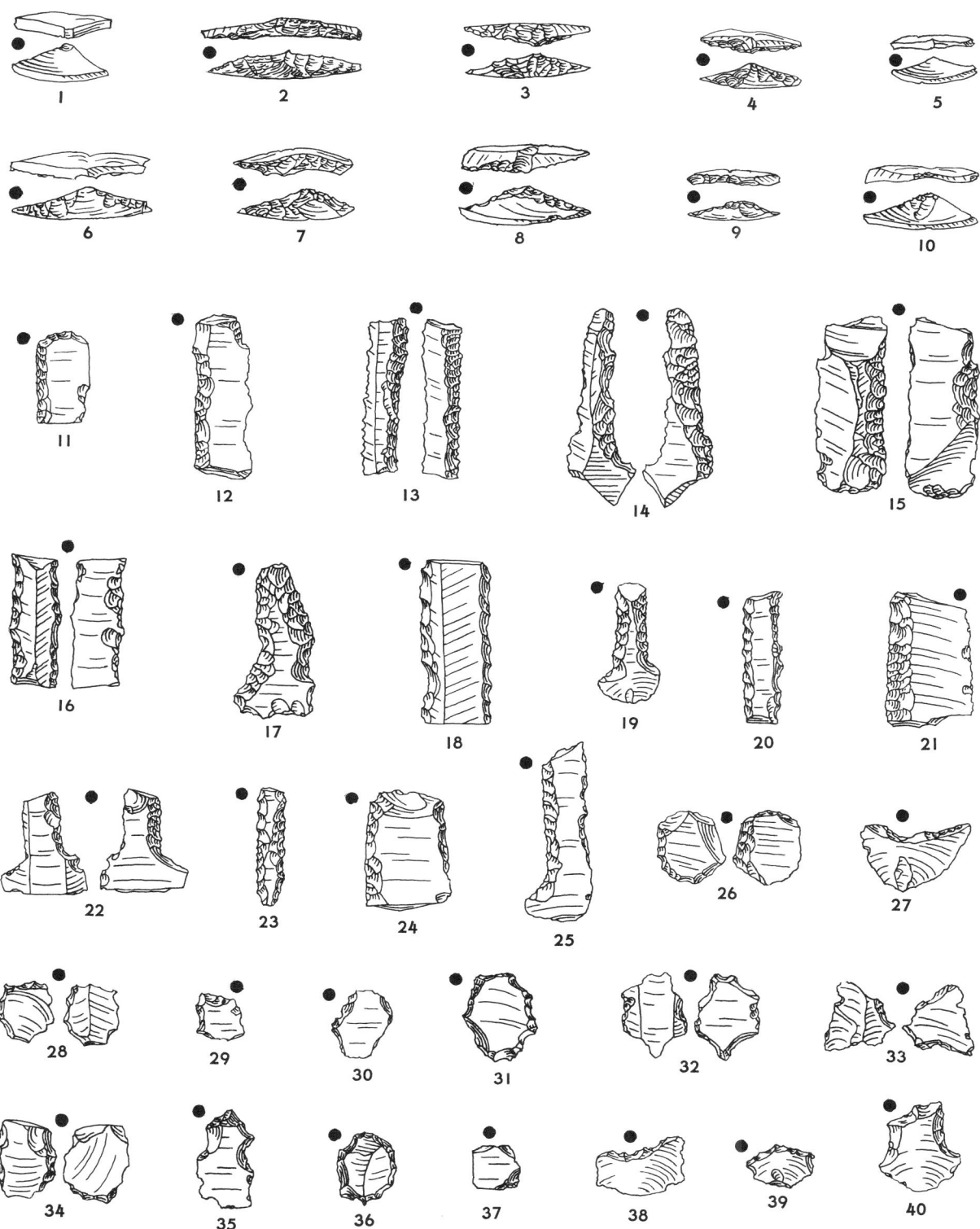

Fig. 122. Jarmo chipped stone: thin sections, *1-10*; pressure-flaked obsidian fabricators, *11-25*; truncated obsidian blades and flakes, *26-40*. All obsidian. Scale 1:1.

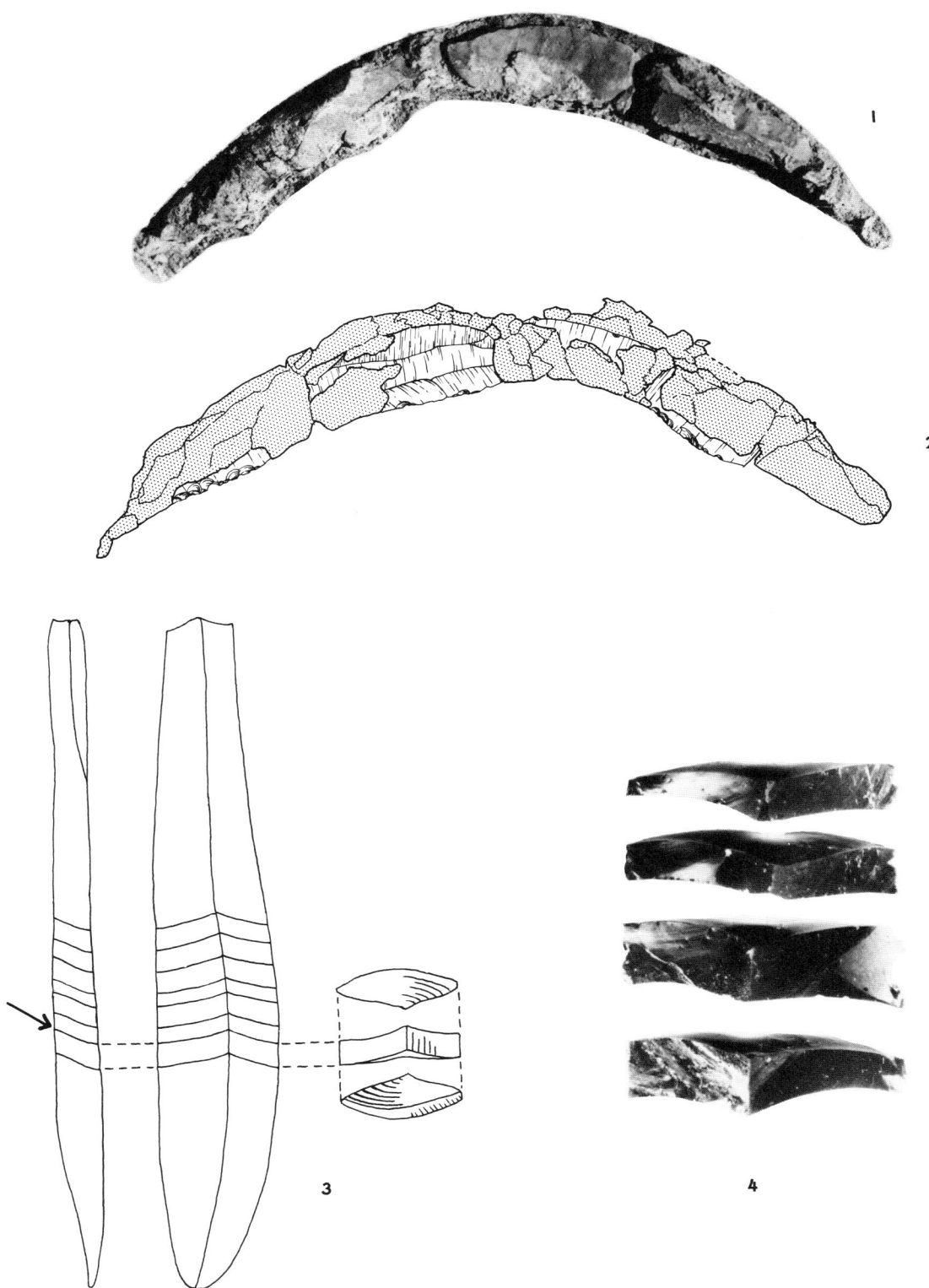

Fig. 123. Jarmo chipped stone: *1*, photograph of four-element sickle found in J-I,7, northwest room; *2*, sketch of same sickle; *3*, schematic sketch of an obsidian "thin section" (*right*) and the blade from which it was struck (*left and center*); *4*, modern duplication of obsidian "thin sections." Scale 1:2, *1-2*. In no. *3*, the sketches at the left and center are, respectively, the side and plan views of the parent blade. In the side view, the arrow indicates the direction in which force was applied on the center ridge of the blade (using Crabtree's method of manufacture, see p. 264 n. 9). To the right in no. *3* are three views of the "thin section": the bottom one shows the face with the negative bulb of force at the ridge where the blow was applied; the top view bears a positive bulb of force.

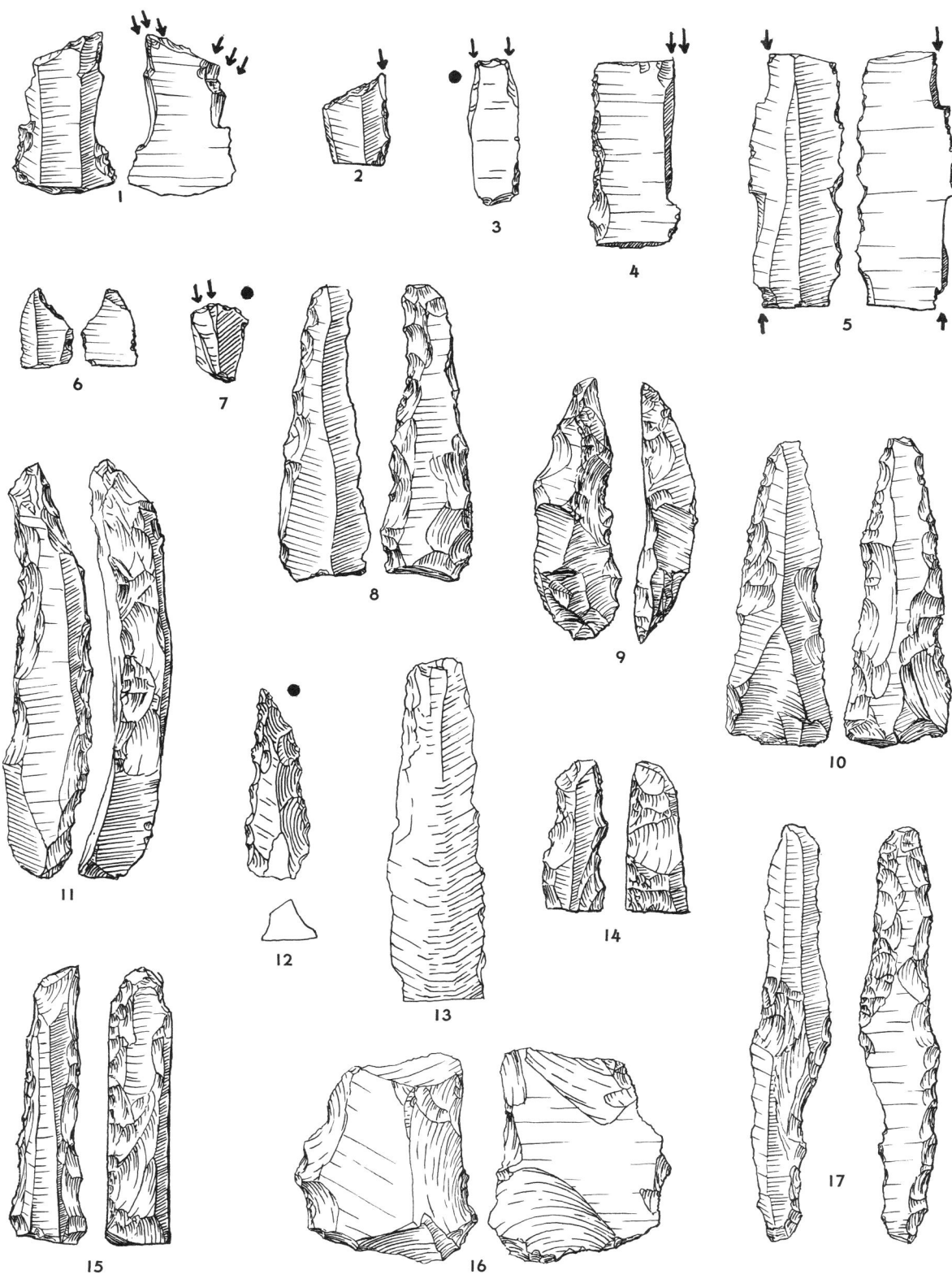

Fig. 124. Jarmo chipped stone: burins, *1-5,7*; microburin, *6*; reamers or fabricators, *8-12,14-15,17*; chipped and ground piece, *13*; scaled piece, *16*. Black dot denotes obsidian. Scale 1:1.

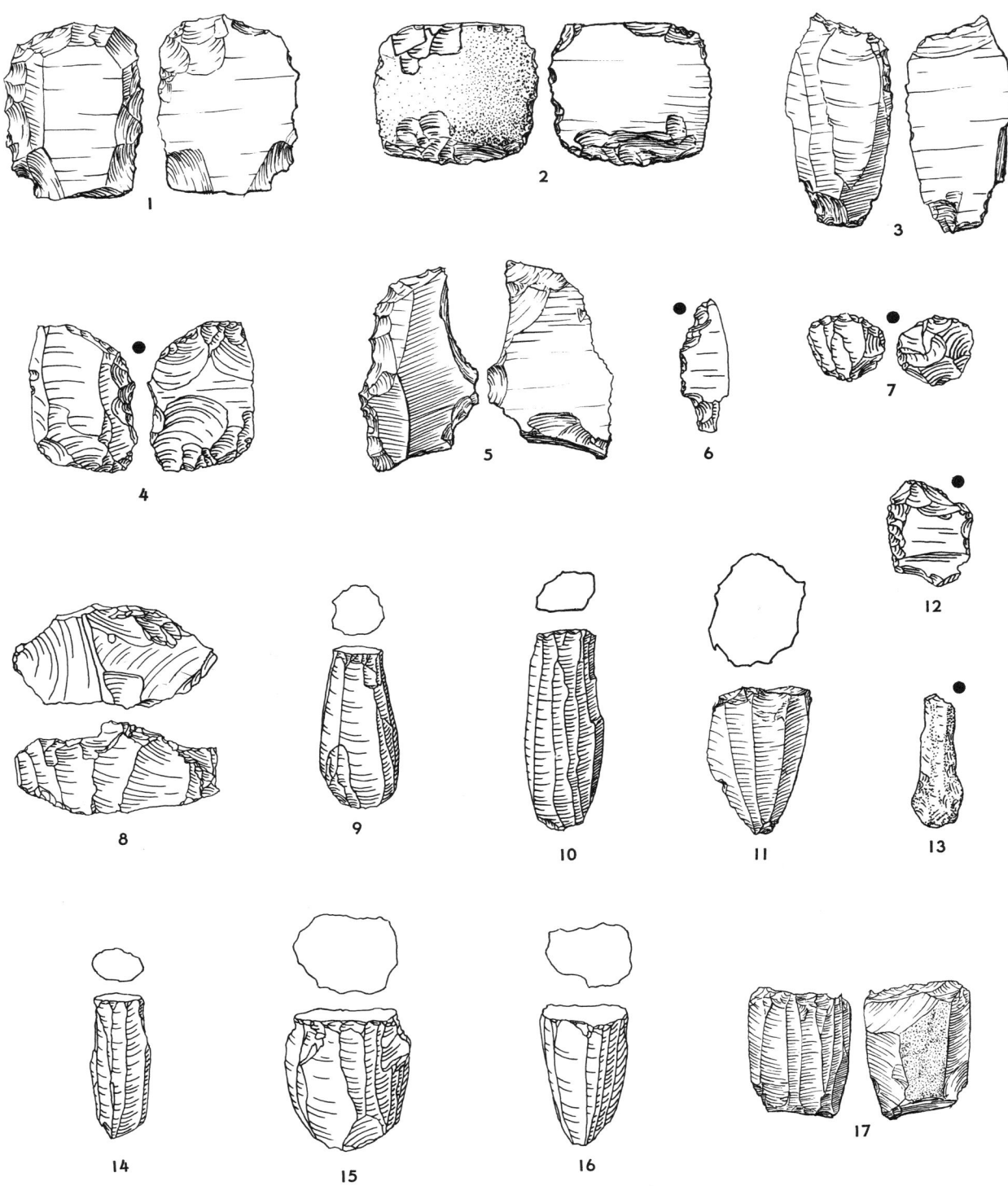

Fig. 125. Jarmo chipped stone: scaled pieces, *1-7,12*; core tablet, *8*; blade cores, *9-11,14-17*; chipped and ground obsidian, *13*. Black dot denotes obsidian. Scale 1:1.

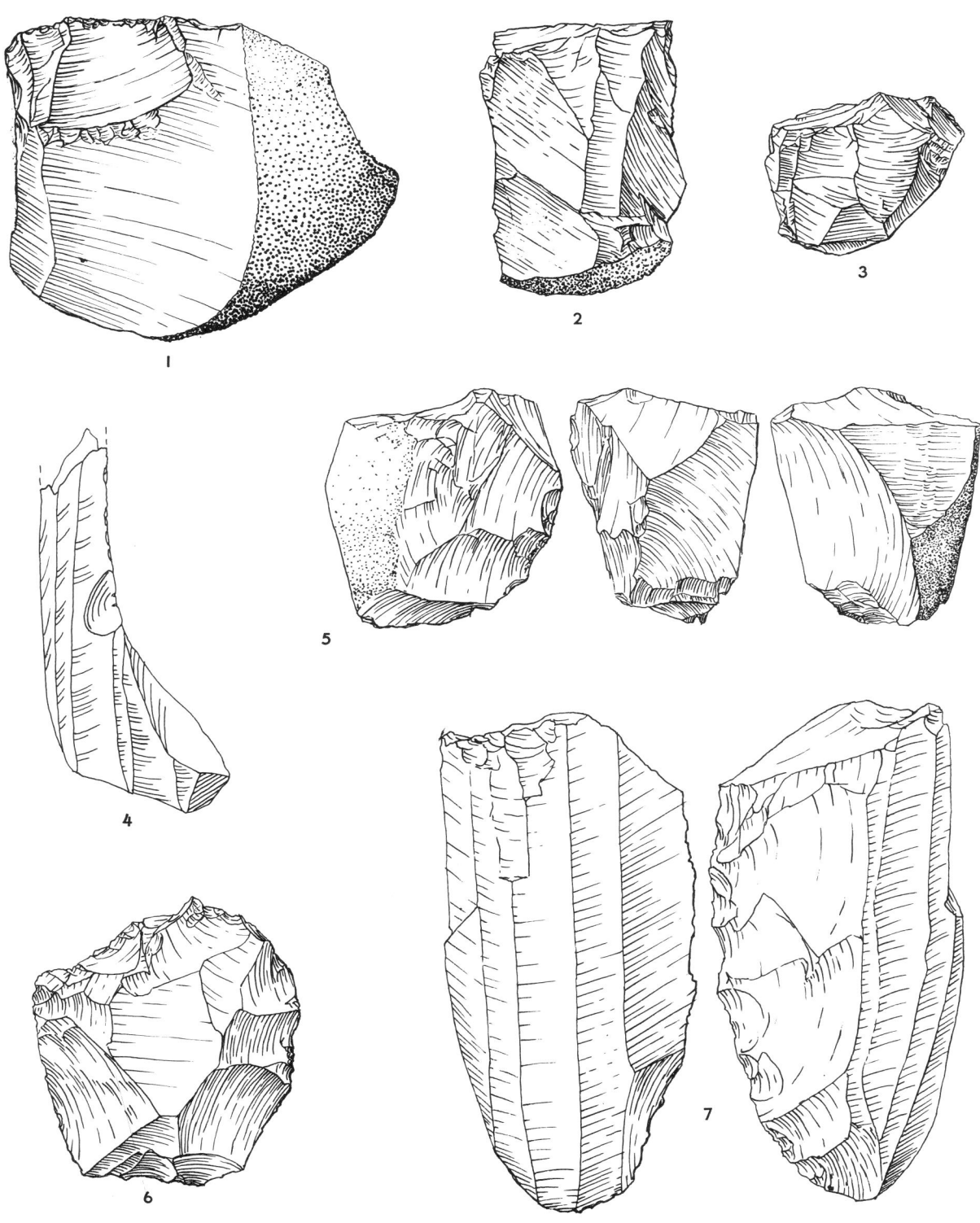

Fig. 126. Jarmo chipped stone: blade core, 7; flake cores, *1-3,5-6*; blade core fragment, plunging flake, *4*. All flint. Scale 1:1.

REFERENCES

Braidwood, Linda S.
1961 The general appearance of obsidian in southwestern Asia and the microlithic side-blow blade-flake in obsidian. In *Bericht über den V. internationalen Kongress für Vor- und Frühgeschichte: Hamburg: von 24. bis 30. August 1958*, ed. Gerhard Bersu, pp. 142-47. Berlin: Verlag Gebr. Mann.

Braidwood, Robert J.; Howe, Bruce; et al.
1960 *Prehistoric investigations in Iraqi Kurdistan.* Studies in Ancient Oriental Civilization [SAOC], no. 31. Chicago: University of Chicago Press.

Burkitt, Miles
1938 A note on a stone age industry of pre-Tell Halaf age. *Annals of Archaeology and Anthropology* 25:106-9.

Clark, J.G.D.
1963 Neolithic bows from Somerset, England, and the prehistory of archery in north-western Europe. *Proceedings of the Prehistoric Society* 29:50-98.

Hole, Frank
1961 Chipped stone analysis and the early village-farming community. Ph.D. diss., University of Chicago.

Hole, Frank; Flannery, Kent V.; and Neely, James A.
1969 *Prehistory and human ecology of the Deh Luran plain.* Memoirs of the Museum of Anthropology, University of Michigan, no. 1. Ann Arbor.

Huckriede, Reinhold
1962 Jung-Quartär und End-Mesolithikum in der Provinz Kerman (Iran). *Eiszeitalter und Gegenwart* 12:25-42.

Mortensen, Peder
1963 Early village-farming occupation. In Excavations at Tepe Guran, Luristan, Jørgen Meldgaard, Peder Mortensen, and Henrik Thrane, pp. 110-21. *Acta Archaeologica* 34:97-133.
1970 *Tell Shimshara: the Hassuna period.* Kongelige danske videnskabernes selskab, historisk-filosofiske skrifter 5 (2). Copenhagen: Munksgaard.

Müller-Beck, Hansjürgen
1965 *Seeberg, Burgäschisee-Süd.* Pt. 5. *Holzgeräte und Holzbearbeitung.* Acta Bernensia, vol. 2. Bern: Stämpfli.

Redman, Charles L.
1973 Early village technology: a view through the microscope. *Paléorient* 1:249-61.

SAOC 31
1960 *Prehistoric investigations in Iraqi Kurdistan.* Robert J. Braidwood, Bruce Howe, et al. Studies in Ancient Oriental Civilization, no. 31. Chicago: University of Chicago Press.

Solecki, Rose Lilien
1964 Zawi Chemi Shanidar, a post-Pleistocene village site in northern Iraq. In *Report of the VIth International Congress on Quaternary, Warsaw 1961*, vol. 4, International Association on Quaternary Research, pp. 405-12. Łódź: Państwowe Wydawnictwo Naukowe.

Witthoft, John
1967 Glazed polish on flint tools. *American Antiquity* 32:383-88.

APPENDIX

ADDITIONAL REMARKS ON THE JARMO OBSIDIAN

Linda S. Braidwood

Because Jarmo obsidian has figured prominently since 1966 in discussions on obsidian (Renfrew, Dixon, and Cann 1966, 1968; Renfrew 1969, 1977; G.A. Wright 1969), it seemed best to provide more detailed information than has been provided in Hole's treatment of the chipped stone, which was written in 1961.

As mentioned on page 2, there has been some confusion on Renfrew's part as to how much of Jarmo has been excavated. We still do not comprehend how he arrived at the estimate that 1/25 of the total settlement has been uncovered (Renfrew, Dixon, and Cann 1966, p. 52).[1] He has, however, made it clear how he arrived at his original and astounding calculation that 4 *tons* of obsidian had been imported into Jarmo during the habitation of the site (Renfrew 1969, p. 432). He explains that he based his estimate of the weight of the individual Jarmo obsidian artifacts (at that time still unseen by him) on his firsthand knowledge of the obsidian "flake industry" of Saliagos, which consisted of large artifacts weighing 4 kg per 1,000 pieces.

After a visit to Chicago, where he was able to see for himself the minuteness of Jarmo obsidian artifacts, Renfrew published a new calculation for the Jarmo obsidian (1969, pp. 431-33) based on his weighing of one small box of Jarmo obsidian from J-I,7 containing over 3,000 microlithic blade fragments. His estimate was 0.2 gm per item—200 gm per 1,000 pieces—a much more realistic weight but based on a minute and biased sample of only microlithic blade fragments. In the same article, he assessed the total weight of obsidian brought to Jarmo during the life of the settlement as being 196 kg. (This figure is certainly much closer to the mark and we would not quarrel with it as a rough guess.)

In a more recent publication (Renfrew 1977, p. 296), however, he notes that the mean weight of "waste fragments" (he includes unretouched blades in this category) at Chagha Sefid, a site considerably further from obsidian sources than Jarmo, was 0.85 gm and so was more comparable to the weight of the obsidian at Çayönü, a site "much nearer to the natural sources,"[2] than to that of the Jarmo obsidian. As a result, Renfrew questioned his estimate of 0.2 gm per obsidian item, based on the sample he had weighed in Chicago, and stated he would now "await the publication in the Jarmo report of the full data" (Renfrew 1977, p. 296).

Unfortunately, for lack of time we are not able to meet his full data request, but we have been able to gather at least some pertinent information from several levels. The histograms on page 286 and the tabulation on page 288 give detailed information for levels J-II,5 and J-II,2fl. The histograms illustrate the widths of unretouched blades and fragments used in the two levels. Curiously, there seems to be a very slight tendency toward narrower blade widths in J-II,2fl. (where greater use was made of obsidian relative to flint) than in J-II,5; the mean width was 7 mm in J-II,2fl. and 8 mm in J-II,5. At present we do not have the exact details on J-II,8 blade widths for constructing a similar tabulation, but there is enough evidence in hand to indicate a much greater emphasis on the microlithic character of the blades; ca. 96% of the unretouched blades and blade fragments are in the 2-10 mm width range (as compared with ca. 84% in J-II,5 and ca. 86% in J-II,2fl.) and the mean width is probably 6 mm.

As can be seen in the tabulation on page 288, which gives various details on quantities and weights of obsidian used in J-II,5 and J-II,2fl., the average weight of each piece of obsidian in J-II,5 is 0.34 gm as against 0.30 gm for each item in J-II,2fl. For the time range of J-I,8 and J-I,8fl., when obsidian seems to have been relatively scarce, the average weight of each whole or fragmentary obsidian artifact is 0.25 gm (based on a sample of 2,267 pieces weighing 565 gm; the heaviest artifacts are two core fragments of 6.5 and 6.1 gm each; the average weight of all the *unretouched* blades and blade fragments would be ca. 0.19 gm).[3]

In an attempt to arrive at a reasonably accurate assessment of the amount of obsidian arriving at Jarmo in *one year*, we felt the best example to take would be the J-II,5 exposure whose architecture seems to indicate about 2½ households. The total depth of deposit in Jarmo is ca. 7 m; the depth of level J-II,5 is ca. 0.65 m. If we assume a 300-year duration for all of Jarmo (see p. 537), this would allow about 25 years for J-II,5 (not an overly long duration for dwellings of the type indicated there). And if one accepts the estimate of 25 households (see p. 10), J-II,5 would have covered an area ten times as great as that excavated.

The total weight of 3,663 obsidian pieces from J-II,5 is 1,228.2 gm, an average of 0.335 gm per item. Allowing for

---

The manuscript for this appendix was essentially completed by 1978. Very few additions and only minor revisions have been made since that date.

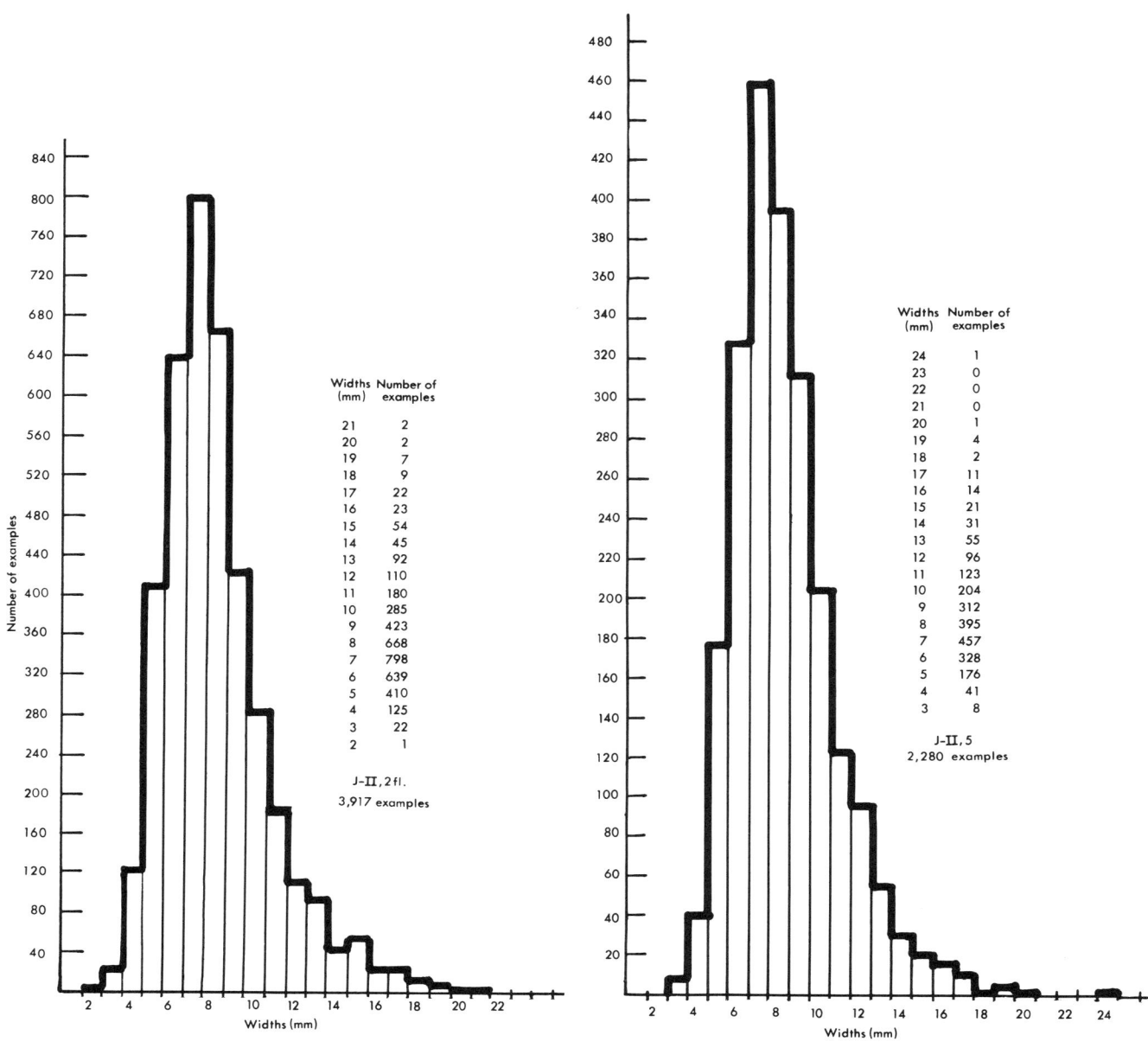

Widths of *unretouched* blades and blade fragments from J-II,2fl. and J-II,5.
Note: Left histogram is based on 3,917 examples and right histogram is based on only 2,280 examples.

the J-II,5 obsidian examples in the Baghdad Museum, the small number of obsidian artifacts that escaped the eagle eyes of our workers, and the tiny chips that would have been left in the chipping areas,[4] we would tend toward an overall figure of 1,500 gm as reasonable for the 2½ households in J-II,5 over a period of about 25 years. If we then reckon that 25 households would use ca. 15,000 gm in 25 years, this would mean that less than 1 kilo of obsidian would have been available per year for all of the 25 households together. This is indeed an extremely rough estimate, based on only one level and on not as large a sample as one would like to have. But even if one does a certain amount of figure manipulation—for example, increases the number of assumed households in the village and decreases the number of years to be assigned to level J-II,5—in the end it is an inescapable fact that the weight of obsidian used at Jarmo in any one year must have been extremely low.

It seems quite clear that not as much obsidian was available to the earliest settlers at Jarmo as to their descendants (see p. 257 and table 18). It is also evident that the early Jarmoan idiosyncratic preference for extremely small tools in obsidian continued even when more obsidian was available; there was very little change in tool size over the years. In general, in such a conservative occupation as stone knapping, it would seem most likely to us that tool size preference would be more pertinent than availability of material. In our minds this would explain the greater size of the obsidian implements not only at Chagha Sefid and other parts of the Iranian Zagros but also at Çayönü.

NOTES

1. Speaking specifically of obsidian, Renfrew says, "The 40,000 pieces recovered at Jarmo come from an excavated area of about one twenty-fifth of the total settlement [SAOC 31, p. 39] . . . some 4 tons of obsidian altogether" (Renfrew, Dixon, and Cann 1966, p. 52). Actually, the total number of obsidian pieces recovered at Jarmo would have been closer to 60,000; Hole makes it clear that his study deals with the major portion of the chipped stone finds but not the entire bulk.

2. Renfrew's statement (1977, p. 296) that the Çayönü "average for phase 4 (1.2 gms) is greatly exceeded by that for phase 5 (3.8 gms)" is, unfortunately, a misreading of Redman (1973, p. 719). What Redman actually gives is just the reverse—the average weight of each obsidian piece at Çayönü in subphase 4 is 3.8 gm, in subphase 5, 1.2 gm.

3. We have even less information for J-II,2, but it is nevertheless revealing. We find that 9,752 pieces of obsidian weigh 2,656.2 gm, giving us an average of 0.27 gm for each item. The heaviest obsidian artifact in J-II,2 is a flake weighing 16.6 gm.

4. At a time when it was incorrectly assumed that there were no obsidian cores or core fragments at Jarmo, Gary Wright (1969, p. 35) suggested that the obsidian was brought into Jarmo as blades. This, however, makes no sense at all unless each tiny bladelet could have been individually wrapped in leather, grasses, or other soft material, for obsidian is extremely fragile and also dulls easily. Obsidian was certainly chipped on the site, but it is not the sort of job that one would choose to perform near a habitation site, for the splinters are extremely sharp. Since only occasional bits of cortex are found on the Jarmo obsidian artifacts, we would imagine that the obsidian came to Jarmo in nodules conveniently sized for the carrier and with most of the cortex already chipped away. Incidentally, we were fortunate to happen upon one area at Jarmo (E28,1, corresponding to one of the upper levels at the site) that was reminiscent of a possible obsidian chipping area. It contained an unusually large number of small flakes and chips and a few core fragments, in addition to bladelet fragments of obsidian and—in addition—miscellaneous bits of flint.

Weights of Obsidian Artifacts from J-II,2fl. and J-II,5

Type of artifact	Obsidian from J-II,2fl. (Weight of 5,468 artifacts = 1,658.06 gm Average weight per piece = 0.303 gm)					Obsidian from J-II,5 (Weight of 3,663 artifacts = 1,228.20 gm Average weight per piece = 0.335 gm)				
	No. in sample	Total weight	Weight/item	Average weight	Heaviest item	No. in sample	Total weight	Weight/item	Average weight	Heaviest item
Unretouched blades and fragments										
2-10 mm widths	3,371	724.1	0.21	0.27	1.1	1,921	451.9	0.24	0.31	0.6
11-21 mm widths	546	352.7	0.65		2.6	390	255.0	0.65		7.0
Retouched and/or heavily used blades and fragments	341	167.3	0.50		6.4	320	179.4	0.56		2.5
Unretouched flakes	863	297.3	0.30	0.39	5.3	489	190.2	0.39	0.41	6.0
Retouched and/or heavily used flakes	14	42.5	3.00		7.5	14	14.5	1.04		2.9
Cores and core fragments	23	32.0	1.40		7.1	24	31.3	1.30		8.0

The 310 artifacts not itemized above (weight = 42.16 gm, averaging 0.136 gm each) include ca. 250 extremely fragmentary blade bits averaging 0.14 gm each, 2 whole blades averaging 0.75 gm, and ca. 50 chips averaging 0.13 gm each.

The 505 artifacts not itemized above (weight = 105.9 gm, averaging 0.21 gm each) include ca. 350 blade fragments (unsorted for width) averaging 0.27 gm each and ca. 150 extremely fragmentary blade bits averaging ca. 0.07 gm each.

NOTE: All of the unretouched blades and blade fragments have been used; the great majority of the unretouched flakes have also been used. All weights are in grams.

REFERENCES

Braidwood, Robert J.; Howe, Bruce; et al.
    1960   SAOC 31 (see below).

Redman, Charles L.
    1973   Multivariate approach to understanding changes in an early farming community in southeast Anatolia. In *The explanation of culture change*, ed. Colin Renfrew, pp. 717-24. London: Duckworth.

Renfrew, Colin
    1969   The sources and supply of the Deh Luran obsidian. In *Prehistory and human ecology of the Deh Luran plain*, Frank Hole, Kent V. Flannery, and James A. Neely, pp. 429-33. Memoirs of the Museum of Anthropology, University of Michigan, no. 1. Ann Arbor.
    1977   The later obsidian of Deh Luran: the evidence of Chagha Sefid. In *Studies in the archeological history of the Deh Luran plain: the excavation of Chagha Sefid*, Frank Hole, pp. 289-311. Memoirs of the Museum of Anthropology, University of Michigan, no. 9. Ann Arbor.

Renfrew, Colin; Dixon, J.E.; and Cann, J.R.
    1966   Obsidian and early cultural contact in the Near East. *Proceedings of the Prehistoric Society* 32:30-72.
    1968   Further analysis of Near Eastern obsidians. Ibid. 34:319-31.

SAOC 31
    1960   *Prehistoric investigations in Iraqi Kurdistan*. Robert J. Braidwood, Bruce Howe, et al. Studies in Ancient Oriental Civilization, no. 31. Chicago: University of Chicago Press.

Wright, Gary A.
    1969   *Obsidian analyses and prehistoric Near Eastern trade: 7500 to 3500 B.C.* Anthropological Papers of the Museum of Anthropology, University of Michigan, no. 37. Ann Arbor.

5

JARMO ARTIFACTS OF PECKED AND GROUND STONE AND OF SHELL

Hattula Moholy-Nagy

INTRODUCTION	290
ARTIFACTS OF PECKED AND GROUND STONE	290
Mullers (figs. 127:1-3; 139:1-2)	290
Querns (figs. 127:4-7; 128:1-2; 139:3-6; 140:10)	291
Pecked and Ground Slabs (fig. 128:3-6)	291
Utilized Cobbles (fig. 128:7-8)	291
Pestles (figs. 128:9-11; 129:1-2; 139:7)	291
Pestle-Hammerstones (fig. 129:3-10)	292
Hammerstones (figs. 129:11; 141:1)	292
Mortars (figs. 129:12-18; 130:1; 139:8-12)	292
Palettes or Pigment-Grinding Stones (figs. 130:2-5; 140:1)	293
Disks with Pecked Depressions (fig. 130:6-8)	293
Retouchers (fig. 131:1-4)	293
Rubbing and Polishing Stones and Whetstones (figs. 130:9-12; 131:5-11; 140:2)	293
Pecking and Rubbing Stones (figs. 130:13-14; 140:3; 141:3)	294
Grooved Stones (figs. 131:12-14; 140:7)	294
Whorls (figs. 131:15-18; 140:6)	294
Digging-Stick Weights or Maceheads (figs. 132:1-6,8; 140:4-5)	294
Large Drill Bits (figs. 132:7; 140:8)	294
Small Borers and/or Small Pestles (figs. 133:1-13; 140:14-17)	295
Curved and Humped Objects (fig. 133:14-15)	295
Celts and Chisels (figs. 134:1-9; 141:7-15)	295
Doorpost Pivot Stones (figs. 138:1,3; 140:11-13)	296
Unfinished Round Stone Blanks (figs. 132:9; 138:2)	296
Bracelets and Rings (figs. 135:1-24; 142:21-25,28-29)	296
Beads (figs. 136:1-18; 142:1-13)	297
Pendants (figs. 136:20-29; 142:15-18,20)	299
Broad, Flat Rings (fig. 137:1)	299
Ground Stone Balls (figs. 137:2-4; 141:2,4-6)	299
Phallic Objects (figs. 137:5-8; 140:18-20; 142:32)	300
Miscellaneous Stone Artifacts (figs. 137:9-11; 138:4-6; 140:10; 142:26-27,30-31)	300
ARTIFACTS OF SHELL (figs. 138:7-13; 142:14,19)	301
CATALOGUE OF GROUND STONE AND SHELL ARTIFACTS	302
REFERENCES	346

INTRODUCTION

This paper is a classification and description of stone artifacts of the nonchipped categories from Jarmo, based mainly on a study of the archeological materials in Chicago, that is, those apportioned to the Iraq-Jarmo Project in the division of finds with the Directorate General of Antiquities of Iraq. Furthermore, by means of photographs, drawings, the expedition's register of artifacts, and field notes kept on artifacts by Linda Braidwood and others of the field staff, it was possible to include information on the artifacts and objects that remained in the Iraq Museum.

At Jarmo, several methods of working stone other than chipping were in use (chap. 4): pecking; sawing, probably exclusively with a rigid saw; polishing; incising, grooving, and carving; drilling and reaming to perforate an artifact or to remove portions of it. Most drilling was done with a solid drill of stone or other substance, but occasionally it was done with a hollow drill bit of a material that has since perished. There was a considerable amount of reworking and reusing of broken artifacts.

In general, the pecked and ground stone artifacts are competently made, and many are esthetically pleasing to us. The large quantity of these artifacts and fragments excavated (besides hundreds of sherds of ground stone vessels [pp. 209-13]) and the considerable variety of forms attest to a strong and perhaps long-established cultural interest in working stone as well as to a demand for such products.

A variety of materials was used. In the 1950s, Mrs. Hans Ramberg, then of the University of Chicago's Department of Geology, made the petrographic identifications of the early ʿAmuq ground stone artifacts (Braidwood and Braidwood 1960). She then examined most of the Jarmo ground stone (save the beads and pendants) then available to her in Chicago. A list of the different types of minerals, with the abbreviations used in our ground stone catalogue, appears on page 302. In the opinion of the project's geologist, Herbert E. Wright, Jr., most of the raw materials are of local origin (SAOC 31, p. 48). The obsidian used for two pendants, however, was imported, probably from Lake Van (G. Wright 1969, p. 22), and it is also possible that some of the stones used for beads, most of which are yet to be identified, also came from a distance. The possible presence of turquoise, which, according to present knowledge, could only have come from the Negev or Sinai or from Afghanistan (G. Wright 1969, pp. 59-60), still awaits confirmation by an expert. The freshwater mussel shells were presumably locally available; the marine shells must have been imported. I have no information on the origins of the fossil marine shells.

Two functional groups appear to be unusually well represented among the Jarmo ground stone artifacts: (a) tools for making other artifacts and (b) ornaments. The quantity and variety of well-made tools point to specialization in production as well as in products, and of course imply a certain amount of time available in which to develop such artifacts and use them. The large quantity of ornaments such as bracelets, beads, and pendants that was recovered also seems remarkable in that none of these articles came from burials, which on other sites are often the main source of such artifacts. Particularly noteworthy is the number of unfinished bracelets and beads. Perhaps there were special workshops for ground stone artifact production.

The quality, quantity, and variety of pecked and ground stone artifacts and the probable presence of different kinds of specialized manufacturing tools all suggest craft specialists, perhaps even full-time professionals.

For whom were these craftsmen producing? On the one hand, ornaments can sometimes be indicators of a stratified social structure. On the other hand, they are favorite trade items. At the time of Jarmo, certain varieties of stone bracelets and flat-sectioned stone beads were widely distributed throughout the Near East, over an area extending from central Anatolia to western Iran. While supplying local demands, Jarmo craftsmen may also have produced for export.

Imported materials such as obsidian and perhaps turquoise came to Jarmo by well-organized long-distance trade. (Unfortunately, almost nothing is known at present about these early traders or their methods of operation.) Casual contacts, however, perhaps brought about by nomadism or transhumance may also have been marked by exchanges, and such contacts perhaps accounted for the rare appearance of marine shells at Jarmo.

ARTIFACTS OF PECKED AND GROUND STONE*

Mullers (figs. 127:1-3; 139:1-2)

Mullers (handstones, manos, riders) are ground stone artifacts that are reasonably assumed to have been used for the grinding of materials (especially foodstuffs?) on querns. Such tools are small enough to have been manipulated

---

The manuscript for this chapter was essentially completed by 1970. Very few additions and only minor revisions have been made since that date.—EDS.

*A glance at the catalogue (see pp. 302ff.) definitely gives the impression that there were far larger numbers of the heavier coarse stone artifacts (such as mullers, querns, and hammerstones) recovered from operation J-I than from operation J-II. In fact, many of the J-I examples catalogued are fragments found in the first field season (1948). Given the short duration of that campaign, we asked for and were given permission (by the Directorate General of Antiquities) to bring back a large quantity of coarse stone fragments to Chicago: this is what the catalogue reflects. In the subsequent seasons we were (doubtless unfortunately) much more selective in what we brought back to Chicago and Moholy-Nagy had fewer examples available for her synthesis.—EDS.

with one hand although they were doubtless normally used—in a backwards-forwards motion—with two hands. Even considering the probable size of the largest mullers before they were broken, the incomplete examples in our series undoubtedly represented artifacts that did not exceed 220 mm in maximum dimension. The examples are flattened in section and have at least one smoothed and ground or pecked and ground surface, which is usually, but not invariably, convex to some degree along at least one axis. There is also some degree of edge shaping.

Of the 41 mullers and fragments in Chicago, 27 have predominantly unifacial signs of use (fig. 127:1-2) and 14 have predominantly bifacial wear (figs. 127:3; 139:1-2). Three of this second group are flat, broad fragments, which might not have been parts of mullers but rather parts of pecked and ground slabs (see below), that is, they may have served as nether stones. The range of size of complete examples as available in Chicago is: length, 104-178 mm; width, 90-147 mm; thickness, 24-59 mm.

Most of the mullers in the Chicago sample are of various kinds of limestone, but 5 were of chert or chalcedony and 3 were not identified.

The chert and lime conglomerate mullers may have been large pebbles, perhaps from the stream that ran below the site. Some of the mullers, particularly those of impure limestone containing grains of sand and clay, seem to have been made on slablike chunks of rock—a kind of rock that appears to have a natural tendency to break into slabs.

The method of shaping the edges of the mullers depended on the kind of stone used; chert mullers are chipped (fig. 127:2), while most of the limestone examples are pecked and ground and a few appear to have finger grips pecked into the sides (fig. 127:1).

The working surface or surfaces of a muller resulted from a combination of preliminary shaping and roughening, use on a quern, and periodic pecking to restore the grinding efficiency. Mullers were held flat against the quern's grinding surface during use and the direction of movement was along the long axis of the quern.

Secondary modification of mullers includes signs of use (on all), burning (on 1 complete muller and on 9 fragments), and reworking (the broken edge of 1 end fragment was apparently smoothed down and the stone put to further use).

Querns (figs. 127:4-7; 128:1-2; 139:3-6; 140:10)

Querns (saddle querns, metates) are the relatively large ground stone artifacts considered to have been used as the nether element of the milling-grinding apparatus, of which the mullers were the upper element. The working surfaces of the querns tended to be smooth and to some degree concave. There were some examples on which the working surfaces appear to have been "sharpened" by re-pecking (Bartlett 1933, p. 4).

Unfortunately, not many of the Chicago samples were complete (most of the complete samples being in Baghdad), and I was thus not able to directly control the whole series, but it is clear that there is a considerable variety of forms. This variety may, at least in part, be merely a function of the length, breadth, thickness, and hardness of the pieces of stone that were randomly available (presumably boulders from the stream below the site). There are also degrees of difference in the amount of concavity of the working surfaces, some of which are also provided with secondary (mortarlike) depressions. Characteristically, the Jarmo querns have relatively shallow grinding surfaces; in most cases, the long axis is only slightly concave and the short axis is sometimes flat or even slightly convex. The mullers have this same tendency toward having flat working surfaces.

Pecked and Ground Slabs (fig. 128:3-6)

Pecked and ground slabs are artifacts the surfaces of which were evidently utilized for both grinding and cracking of such materials as coloring matter and nuts. Their grinding surfaces tend to be convex (in a few cases almost flat); they are wider than the items we classify as mullers, and shorter than our querns. Some fragments listed under mullers might equally well be classified in this group. The working surfaces are prepared by pecking, then generally smoothed, especially in the center of the working face.

The slabs are of the same kinds of stone as the querns and were probably manufactured by the same techniques. Shaping of the edges generally seems to have depended on the kind of stone used, and in no case is it extensive. The edges of the slabs of chert appear to be unmodified, but the edges of the limestone examples are ground to some extent.

Several examples show traces of what appears to be ochre on their working surfaces.

Utilized Cobbles (fig. 128:7-8)

Utilized cobbles are large, rounded, probably waterworn stones. They are essentially unworked, but exhibit marks of grinding, pecking, or pounding, or they may bear scratches or cuts, or a combination of these marks of use. They probably served a number of different purposes—as hammerstones, rubbing stones, or perhaps as anvils in artifact manufacture. They may all have come from the stream below Jarmo.

Pestles (figs. 128:9-11; 129:1-2; 139:7)

Pestles, as the term implies, are elongated, unusually well-made artifacts that have straight sides usually tapering toward one end, flattened to rounded ends, and approximately round cross sections. They were normally finished by overall grinding.

These artifacts were shaped by pecking, the marks of which were then practically obliterated by careful grinding. Presumably they were used to mash and grind substances in the mortars to be described below. Their size, weight, and hardness would have made them very useful as crushers when used with either one or both hands. Thus, they are distinguished from the miniature "pestlelike" forms we describe later (p. 295).

The size range of the group that appears to be most characteristic is illustrated (fig. 128:9-11). The incomplete examples in the catalogue (pp. 305-6) conform to this size range. Other artifacts that also may well have had the function of pestles appear in our next category.

Pestle-Hammerstones (fig. 129:3-10)

Pestle-hammerstones are ground stone artifacts of forms and sizes that fall midway on a spectrum, one end of which is represented by the more formal pestles (see preceding section) and the other by the essentially spherical stones that we take without qualification to be hammerstones (see next section). Cross sections of pestle-hammerstones are usually rounded to rectangular or even trapezoidal. Some of these objects appear to be battered or unfinished pestles (fig. 129:3-4). A few appear to have been finished as if they were intended to be double-ended pestles (fig. 129:6-7; and fig. 129:8, a battered example). There are also several examples of what seem simply to have been selected waterworn pebbles battered from use.

One odd form (fig. 129:10), pestlelike in profile, but thin ovoid in section and rather light in weight, is of uncertain utility.

Some of these objects were doubtless used with mortars; some show clear traces of battering as well as of grinding (as if they had been utilized both as pestles and as hammerstones). Some seem too light in weight to have been effective pestles but do show battering. One fragment has traces of red pigment, perhaps ochre, on the pecked edges and on both of two remaining faces. Another example seems to be a broken pestle, trimmed as if for use as a cleaver (fig. 129:5).

Hammerstones (figs. 129:11; 141:1)

Hammerstones are taken to be represented by a rather large category of more or less well-pecked spherical or subspherical artifacts. The group may well intergrade into our pecking and rubbing stones category (p. 294), and indeed their original utility is not completely clear to us. The majority of the Chicago examples (details of the Baghdad examples of this category were not available for this study) are of hard varieties of chert or chalcedony and range in size from slightly smaller than golf balls to slightly larger than tennis balls.

It is curious that the findspots for hammerstones appear to be concentrated in or near J-I. Were it not for H.E. Wright's opinion (p. 155) that much of the northern and northwestern portions of the mound are now eroded well back from their original position, it would be tempting to suggest that these objects were sling missiles, ready at hand for the defence of the mound slope. It is to be noted that, when possible, the weights of these objects have been supplied in the catalogue.

There are also several rather larger and well-rounded balls of limestone, about the size of a grapefruit, which were probably not hammerstones in the normal sense. Figure 140:10 shows such a ball on a quern, but it was actually found adjacent to and not on the quern. One or two other larger limestone balls were found next to querns, but we note (p. 157) that others were also found adjacent to upper doorpost pivot stones.

Mortars (figs. 129:12-18; 130:1; 139:8-12)

Mortars are large, heavy, bowllike artifacts with smoothed interiors. They were probably used, in combination with the large pestles described previously, to break up and grind foodstuffs and perhaps other substances as well. Unlike the back-and-forth motion of a muller on a quern, the action of a pestle in a mortar would presumably have been either percussive or rotary. Mortars and mortar fragments were very often found reused in stone wall foundations. Some "mortars" may have been reused as doorpost pivot stones (see p. 296).

The Jarmo examples considered to be mortars vary in size, in shape, and in the attention (or lack of it) given to finishing their exteriors. Some examples would doubtless have been considered stone bowls if the quality of workmanship of the Jarmo series in that category had not been so high. In general, even the most finished of the examples we present here as mortars are relatively much thicker walled than are the Jarmo stone bowls, and the mortars tend to have been made of limestone. Figure 129:12 is a well-finished example with a broad, smoothed lip treatment. Another relatively well finished example (fig. 129:13) is one of several instances with a shallow secondary depression inside. Figure 129:14 is of a well-finished example on the smaller end of the size range. The interior depressions are usually round but in rare instances are ovoid (fig. 129:15).

The more usual examples of Jarmo mortars, of which there are a number (many of them fragmentary), were of the thick-walled variety, with the depression simply worked into one side of a limestone boulder. There is one such boulder with five more or less distinct depressions (fig. 129:16). Mortars whose bottoms have been broken through, presumably by use, occasionally appear (fig. 130:1). Hayden (1969), considering Mexican mortars with open bottoms, suggests that their openings may have been intentional.

Palettes or Pigment-Grinding Stones (figs. 130:2-5; 140:1)

Palettes or pigment-grinding stones are medium-sized flat pieces of relatively fine-grained stone that show some hollowing on one or two faces. They presumably were used as nether stones in the grinding of mineral materials into powder form. The artifactual type we refer to as palettes is usually rectangular with straight sides and ends (figs. 130:2-3; 140:1). They were carefully made with all surfaces ground and no peck marks visible. There are, however, less carefully made examples which show more pecking than grinding and which are not necessarily rectilinear in form.

In this category, we also include certain paint-preparing? stones unifacially used, with roughly shaped edges. These examples carry traces of red pigment. The object in figure 130:4, especially, has a neat round depression on one face, with red pigment traces around but not in it. Perhaps its maker's original intention was to produce a bracelet (see pp. 296f.). Striations show very clearly on the surface of this stone; they run in various directions on the working face but predominantly across it. They are mostly diagonal in the depression. On the reverse face, a few concentric striations occur along the perimeter. The center of this face is polished.

Disks with Pecked Depressions (fig. 130:6-8)

Disks with pecked depressions are objects of problematical use. Only one is complete (fig. 130:6). All have a round depression in the center of both faces. There are examples in which the depressions meet, forming an irregular, rounded perforation. Most are minimally worked pebbles of a white or gray marblelike stone. One example bears traces of red pigment over one face, except within the depression; this recalls the object with the depression on one side only in the previous group, palettes (fig. 130:4). There are also transversely broken examples, which retain traces of a surface crust of dark material (bitumen?).

It is again possible to speculate that these objects may simply represent the first step in the preparation of bracelets or rings (pp. 296f.), perhaps unfinished or broken due to the unfortunate choice of a recalcitrant stone.

Retouchers (fig. 131:1-4)

Retouchers are smooth, flat pieces of stone that fit comfortably in one hand and may have been used for retouching flint or obsidian artifacts. One (fig. 131:1) appears to be a reworked fragment of a limestone vessel. Other examples are pebbles, probably all waterworn. The smooth surfaces and comfortable shapes of these pebbles first led to their classification as polishing stones. Reexamination of their pocked faces and ends suggests that they resemble artifacts Semenov has identified as pressure-retouching tools used in knapping (1964, figs. 14:1-4; 15:1-3). Our examples tend to intergrade with some of the polishing stones described in the next section, which are of the same shapes and materials and have pecking around the edges.

On the retouchers, pocking is concentrated toward the ends and edges but sometimes occurs in the center of the faces as well. In addition to pocking, the faces of the retouchers also bear numerous fine scratches, sometimes parallel to each other, sometimes not. Such signs of use are usually bifacial. The squared edges of the sides on one example (fig. 131:3) are the result of intentional grinding. Otherwise the pebbles do not appear to have been artificially shaped.

Rubbing and Polishing Stones and Whetstones (figs. 130:9-12; 131:5-11; 140:2)

Rubbing stones are artifacts considered too small to serve as mullers. Over half have one or both surfaces flattened and smoothed (fig. 131:5-9). Most examples are of impure limestone but one (fig. 131:9) is of highly vesicular lava. A few rubbing stones show traces of a red mineral pigment (ochre?). There are, of course, other stones that are very similar to these but lack obviously worn surfaces. They may or may not have been used as rubbing stones, and form part of a rather large group of possibly utilized slabs of impure limestone or sandstone (see, e.g., the possible griddle stones [p. 157]).

Polishing stones consist of smooth, fine-grained, waterworn stones that show signs of use in the form of faint parallel transverse striations, scratches, wear facets, or pecked edges (figs. 130:10; 131:8). The characteristic that distinguishes them most clearly from our rubbing stone group, however, is their shiny surfaces. Presumably, they were used for finer finishing work.

Whetstones are rough-grained stones with one or more faces that are smoothed flat or slightly concave, which suggests their use in the sharpening of stone, bone, and shell artifacts (figs. 130:11-12; 131:10-11). The largest example (fig. 130:12) is a waterworn slab, probably of impure limestone, with a flat back. Part of the face is smoothly concave and within this area are four narrow transverse grooves suggesting that pointed tools such as needles, awls, or flakers may have been sharpened on this stone.

In all, some 71 examples of the type we call rubbing stones were found, as well as 10 examples of the polishing stone type and 14 examples of our so-called whetstone group. There were, of course, many more small and relatively flat bits of stone that showed traces of utilization but that we made no attempt to classify.

One further type is appended here—a curious knob-handled form (figs. 130:9; 140:2) that suggests a squat pestle, rubber, smoother, or pounder, although no evidence of any such usage can be deduced through examination of an incomplete Chicago example.

Pecking and Rubbing Stones (figs. 130:13-14; 140:3; 141:3)

Pecking and rubbing stones consist of roundish or relatively cubical stones whose degree of flat-sidedness evidently depended on the extent of utilization. The surfaces suggest that these were multipurpose tools. All were originally pecked all over. The quality of pecking varies from coarse to fine, maybe depending partly on the amount of use and perhaps partly on the shaping of a more efficient grinding surface.

Of the 9 Chicago specimens, all but one (which is of very hard stone) show grinding or polishing on one or more faces. In examples that had grinding on each of the faces, two opposing or three adjacent faces show more use than the others. The polished surface on one face of figure 130:14 bears a number of parallel striations indicating that the stone was rubbed in various directions with a back-and-forth, rather than rotary, motion. (The weights of the intact Chicago examples are given in the catalogue at the end of this chapter.)

Grooved Stones (figs. 131:12-14; 140:7)

Grooved stones are elongated pebbles with planoconvex cross sections. A marked groove runs across the convex face approximately at the center, while the opposite face is flat and quite smooth. The grooves tend to be more polished than the rest of the artifact and may exhibit faint, parallel, lengthwise striations along their entire length. These characteristics, plus the lack of end wear (on those pieces that have their ends intact), indicate that the grooves were not intended for hafting but rather served for shaping and polishing long, round-sectioned objects. Rose and Ralph Solecki (1970) have given detailed attention to the proposition that these objects may have been arrowshaft straighteners.

Whorls (figs. 131:15-18; 140:6)

Whorls are small perforated stone disks. Cursory experimentation suggests that they would have made excellent flywheels, perhaps for use with drills as much as for spindles. Jarmo does yield evidence of the spinning of thread (see pp. 389, 425). The perimeters of some examples appear to have been unmodified (e.g., fig. 131:15; half of this example was found in J-I,8-9, the other half in J-A,IV; see p. 223, n. 1). The perimeters of other examples were ground (fig. 131:16) or battered (fig. 131:17). All perforations were biconically drilled and subsequently widened by reaming. The soft stones clearly show concentric striations within the bores. There are instances in which the perforations do not meet (e.g., fig. 131:17). They are simply assumed to be unfinished whorls.

There are also examples of round to oval disks, generally ground all over (e.g., fig. 131:18), with flaked and ground or simply ground edges. Some of these may also be unfinished whorls, although some may equally well have served simply as scrapers. We have tabulated these unperforated disks separately in the catalogue.

Digging-Stick Weights or Maceheads (figs. 132:1-6,8; 140:4-5)

Objects classified as digging-stick weights or maceheads are subspherical, centrally perforated stones. All were shaped by pecking and then were completely ground; all have wide, reamed, biconical perforations or the beginnings thereof. There are differences in the quality of workmanship. The more crude examples have usually been classified as digging-stick weights while the finer ones are thought to have been maceheads. I can present no evidence either for or against such assumptions of use for the round perforated stones from Jarmo. Their most obvious morphological characteristic is that they form a continuum, from large, crudely formed "digging-stick weights" (e.g., fig. 132:1) to smaller, well-shaped, carinated, collared, and polished "maceheads" (fig. 132:4,6).

Of the coarser or digging-stick weight variety there are both completely perforated stones and another type that has a pecked depression at either end instead of a finished perforation—presumably unfinished examples in which the perforation was started by pecking before drilling was begun. It is, of course, conceivable that these incompletely perforated objects may have had some other function. An unusual completely polished example (fig. 132:3) has a deep depression drilled into each end and traces of pecking left on the margins of the drill holes. Not all the examples in this larger, coarser variety are round; there is at least one that is clearly oval.

The smaller and more carefully shaped and finished (macehead?) variety appears generally to have been made of relatively softer and finer-grained stone. Illustrated are examples with sections that are biconical, elongated ovoid, squat ovoid, and slightly collared in profile (fig. 132:4,5,8, and 6, respectively).

Large Drill Bits (figs. 132:7; 140:8)

Large drill bits are quite flattened spheroids of ground stone with waisted opposite edges. The example in the Chicago collection was made of hard, granular, greenish stone (probably indurated sandstone). The faces of these objects show concentric striations and, as already noted in the field, the curvature of the faces fits snugly within the curvature of broken bracelet blanks (e.g., fig. 135:20). We have noted similar objects described as "vase borers" from Late Predynastic-Old Kingdom contexts in Egypt (Petrie 1902, pl. III; 1917, p. 45, pl. LII). (Indeed, Nicholas Millet, at the time a graduate student in Egyptology and docent in the Oriental Institute, once simulated such a bitlike object of sandstone, mounted it in a forked wooden shaft, as shown in fig. 140:9, provided a bow, and, with the aid of a class of school children, bored through a slab of coarse marble.)

Small Borers and/or Small Pestles (figs. 133:1-13; 140:14-17)

Small borers and/or small pestles make up an especially puzzling group of artifacts. In form they are all small, elongated, and fairly slender, with one end—here called the tip—more pointed than the other end—called the butt or base. What makes them so difficult to classify is that their forms intergrade and the traces of use they exhibit do not readily correlate with the forms. For instance, most of the slender examples have some complete transverse parallel striations extending partway along their lengths from the tip end. Most of the thick examples have flat bases with battered perimeters, similar to the artifacts called pestle-hammerstones (see p. 292). However, a few slender examples show no tip striations (under a 10× hand lens), while concentric striations—in combination with battered perimeters or with smoothly rounded butts or bases—occur on some thick examples.

The following three or four subtypes, then, tend to intergrade. The first, subtype *a*, consists of long, slender borers, none of which has a diameter greater than 25% of the length. In profile, the long edges are nearly parallel to each other or very slightly convex. The tip usually shows transverse striations indicating possible use as a drill or awl; the butt may be irregular or flat. The flat butt of one such borer was notched with short, vertical grooves (fig. 133:2), perhaps an indication that the borers were hafted. One example showed signs of use at both ends and was ground flat at the midpoint on two opposing sides—perhaps for hafting (fig. 133:3).

The second subtype (*b*) consists of small pestlelike artifacts that are usually thicker than the objects of the above subtype and often more conical in plan (fig. 133:5). In figure 133:6-10 we illustrate the general size and profile range of this and the next subtype together. The basal perimeters may show wear (grinding or battering) and some are extremely battered. The edges of one of these pestlelike objects show use and its flat base has a small pit drilled in the center. Another example may have been used in a double-ended sense and is waisted (fig. 133:11), suggesting that it—and perhaps all of the others of this subtype—was used without a haft.

The third or borer-pestle subtype (*c*) consists of artifacts resembling the small pestles in form and basal usage but showing the same kind of transverse striations at the tips as the long borers. In addition, one has a few vertical flakes removed from the base, perhaps for hafting purposes (fig. 133:12). The Chicago sample has one or two examples with a chip removed from the tip end, bringing to mind another possible use—or reuse—as tools for pressure flaking flint implements.

A possible fourth subtype (*d*) consists of tools that were apparently borers—elongated triangular in plan and flat in section, and all evidently reworked by grinding and polishing the sherds of stone vessels (fig. 133:13). Striations at the tip are not as clear as on other varieties of borers. Borers made from sherds fit more comfortably in the hand and may have been used unhafted as awls as well as borers or drills.

Curved and Humped Objects (fig. 133:14-15)

Curved and humped objects are short, well-shaped artifacts that are curved in profile and round in section, perhaps reworked from fragments of stone rings and bracelets. The outer edge curves more than the inner one, giving these objects a humped appearance. All show marked transverse striations at their ends, perhaps the result of usage. They may have been hafted tools; one of them (fig. 133:15) has a ground facet at one corner of the butt that could have facilitated hafting. On the other hand, the marked curvatures and fine workmanship suggest that these objects may have had some ornamental function.

Celts and Chisels (figs. 134:1-9; 141:7-15)

Typically, the Jarmo celts and chisels are pecked or ground, with a transverse cutting edge at one end—the bit. The other or butt end has been rounded, squared, or irregularly blunted, or left more or less in the form of the original nodule. The rest of the artifact may or may not have been treated by pecking or grinding. On the other hand, the bit bevel was shaped by grinding and may even show polish. By and large, the nodules utilized appear to be elongated pebbles (small finger size to fist size), probably selected from the streamside. In the examples recovered from Jarmo, these artifacts have much diversity in size and form. A clearly defined adze type of bit bevel rarely occurs, and the line of the top edge of the bevel is usually poorly defined (our terminology follows that of Braidwood and Braidwood 1960, pp. 41ff.). There is only one possible instance of residual lengthwise grooves (sometimes seen on celts) that appear to indicate the preparation of more than one tool from a given flat nodule.

One group is of relatively small and also relatively parallel-sided celts (fig. 134:1-5), which presumably were hafted like modern chisels. In this group, the breadth of the bit tends to be less than the breadth of the face of the tool. In one specimen—a rather large one for this group—the bit has been broken (fig. 134:5).

There are a few examples of a relatively long but narrow type with a quite narrow bit (fig. 134:6). These celts are of dark fine-grained stone and some may have been produced from sherds of stone vessels.

The most numerous group of celts consists of examples whose bit is formed on the broad base of a somewhat flattened conical nodule (fig. 134:7-9). It can be noted that one of the illustrated examples (fig. 134:9) has a bit with a somewhat curved edge, an unusual characteristic that may mean that the bit was designed as a gouge.

Finally there are a few rare celts, produced on flintlike nodules, that show traces of chipping done as a preparatory step before the bit was ground and polished. This is characteristic of the preparation of celts at Karim Shahir (cf. fig. 13).

Fine nicking and chipping of the bit edge, presumably from use, is common on Jarmo celts and chisels. Almost all artifacts of this category examined in Chicago had uneven or battered butt ends; well-preserved examples of neatly finished butts are exceptional. I believe the condition of these butts suggests that the celts were always used in a haft, and perhaps it was not considered absolutely necessary to finish the butt. However, it has also been suggested by others that irregular butts may be the result of hammering the unhafted implement with a mallet or hammerstone. Present evidence, however, does favor hafting. Traces of bitumen were noted on the butt ends of two of the larger celts in the Baghdad collection. Comfortable bone hafts of various sizes that would have fit the chisels and some of the smaller celts occurred in the excavations and are described with other Jarmo bone artifacts (pp. 347f.).

Reworking and reuse are usual. Several larger celts were heavily pecked at both ends, perhaps for reuse as hammerstones or as a result of such reuse (fig. 134:7).

A diversity of function probably partly accounts for the diversity of forms and sizes of the celts and chisels. The small ones were probably used for carving wood and perhaps bone. The purpose and mode of use of the larger celts are somewhat more obscure. Larger celt bits are sometimes slightly off-center, although almost never to the extent found in an unequivocal adzelike bit.

Examination of the bits for use-striations with a 10× hand lens following suggestions by Semenov (1964, pp. 122-23, figs. 58-64) did not result in any definitive information. Ideally, a binocular microscope with special lighting should have been used for this purpose. Until a thorough study can be carried out, we are left with the possibility that the larger celts may have been used as choppers (i.e., axes or hatchets) to clear land and to get material for what must have been a flourishing industry in wood. Although adze bits can imply planing or the preparation of squared boards of wood, there is no firm evidence that any such procedures were carried out. Further, none of the celts show "scour-grooving" (Sonnenfeld 1962) and thus were probably never used as hoes.

Doorpost Pivot Stones (figs. 138:1,3; 140:11-13)

Doorpost pivot stones are heavy stone artifacts some of which *may* have been used as the upper element (figs. 138:1; 140:1,12) of a system for hanging the doors of houses, and others *certainly* were used as the lower element (figs. 138:3; 140:13). The suggestion follows from observation of such a system in more remote peasant houses in the Zagros region today, although the upper element is now a heavy forked branch of oak, with the spread ends of the fork embedded horizontally and almost fully into the wall (fig. 73). The still exposed crotch section of the fork receives the upper end of the doorpost, and a stone pivot (or, sometimes, simply a mudlined hole) receives the lower end. These contemporary village doors have a wooden frame of which the upright post is part, and the frame is covered with matting, flattened kerosene tins, or corrugated iron. The excavator has thus suggested that some of the multiroomed *tauf* houses at Jarmo may have had similar door constructions with a mat, skin, or cloth-covered frame mounted on a pivot post. If the suggestion is valid, the upper end of the doorpost would sometimes have been held by a long perforated stone embedded into the house wall, while the lower end turned in a pivot socket of stone. Some of the upper doorpost holders at Jarmo may also, of course, have been of wood.

The difficulty with this suggestion, of course, is that no walls at Jarmo were preserved to such a height that the upper element could be found in place. In two cases (see p. 157) there is also the curious association of the supposed upper pivot-post holders with large limestone balls (see p. 300). As to the lower pivot stones, several were found adjacent to door openings.

Several complete or almost complete examples of the supposed upper element were found. The most remarkable is a large, naturally elongated, beige-colored boulder, probably of limestone and approximately planoconvex in cross section (figs. 138:1; 140:12). One end is missing. The other end is rounded, has a wide biconical perforation, and is decorated with five vertical flutes. There are peck marks and scratches in the perforation, especially at the perimeter, lengthwise striations in the flutes, and some polish and peck marks on the convex face. The plane face shows lengthwise striations from grinding and large patches of roughness (use? reuse?). The perforation was probably made by pecking and reaming rather than by drilling.

The examples that we suggest might be lower pivot stones are large, unmodified chunks of limestone with a shallow, round depression on one face (figs. 138:3; 140:13). The possibility remains that some of the artifacts we have already classified as boulder mortars were actually reused as lower pivot stones.

Unfinished Round Stone Blanks (figs. 132:9; 138:2)

Unfinished round stone blanks that were perhaps intended for stone bowls or for bracelets (see next section) may be represented in the Chicago sample. Each object is round, approximately subhemispherical to cylindrical in section, and quite evidently unfinished. The first example (fig. 132:9), probably of limestone, was pecked into shape and shows little or no grinding. The second (fig. 138:2), of soft banded stone, perhaps alabaster or calcite, is lightly ground all over and has a flat base.

Bracelets and Rings (figs. 135:1-24; 142:21-25,28-29)

Bracelets and rings make up a large category of well-finished circular stone artifacts which appeared throughout the sequence. Although no complete or fully reconstructible examples were recovered, there is no reason to doubt that both the bracelets and rings were closed circles (see fig. 135:1). Bracelets and rings of stone, bone, and ivory seem, in fact, to have been the only such ornaments preserved to us from the ancient Near East until metals came into use. Although some of the so-called bracelets and some of the supposed (finger?) rings were probably used as such, other artifacts of this category could very well have had other ornamental uses, perhaps as ring pendants, hair ornaments, ear ornaments, sew-on ornaments, clothing fasteners or toggle loops, and so on.

My tendency is to consider all of these artifacts with an *inner* diameter of over 25 mm as bracelets and those with an inner diameter less than this as rings. Further subdivision within the whole category is made on the basis of the shape of the transverse sections of the artifacts, as follows:

   a. Bracelets with elongated planoconvex or lens-shaped cross sections in which the thickness is less than half of the width (30 examples; e.g., fig. 135:2).
   b. Bracelets with planoconvex, oval, or round cross sections in which the thickness approaches the width or exceeds it (242 examples; e.g., fig. 135:5). This is by far the most common variety of Jarmo bracelet.
   c. Bracelets with grooved and massive cross sections, decorated on the exterior with narrow, diagonal parallel grooves—"rope" motifs and "braided" motifs (6 examples; e.g., fig. 135:9).
   d. Bracelets decorated with circumferential grooves, either single (e.g., fig. 135:11) or double (e.g., fig. 135:15), totalling 12 examples.
   e. Rings, variable in cross section perhaps according to the small size of the inner diameter (5 examples; e.g., fig. 135:17-19). (Rings are rare in stone but quite common in bone.)
   f. Bracelets with cross sections that are approximately diamond- or kite-shaped, rounded on the exterior but with a well-defined angle on the inside (18 examples; fig. 135:20-23). The interior angle, as well as the size, suggests that these fragments may be unfinished bracelets that were broken in the process of manufacture. These pieces should be considered in relation to other apparently unfinished artifacts already noted elsewhere (e.g., figs. 130:6-8; 132:9; 138:2) and in relation to the artifact that we have suggested may be a bit from a drill (fig. 132:7). We also consider as belonging to the same group certain irregular cross sections that are doubtless also examples of the bracelet category but that were accidentally broken in the process of preparation (e.g., fig. 135:16). It is conceivable that the fragment in figure 135:24 is from a broken bracelet that was in the process of being sectioned for the making of beads.

Of the 316 ring and bracelet fragments, 228 are of white stone, quite probably marble. A few were identified as such, and the others appear to be the same by gross comparison. Eleven fragments are of gray stone, probably marble and perhaps discolored by fire; 5 are of a streaky blue gray stone; and 2 are of gray-veined stone, probably marble. A softer, unidentified stone, probably limestone, was used for 7 other fragments (2 tan, 1 pinkish, 1 yellow and red, 1 black and white, 1 red, and 1 dark brown). It should be noted that of the 53 fragments found in the 1954-55 test squares 16 were of colored stone—an unusually large proportion.

The reworking of fragments was fairly common. In the Chicago sample, it was observed on 33 fragments in the form of traces of grinding on one or both ends, incomplete or complete perforations of fragments near one end, or shallow transverse incisions or deeper grooves, some running completely around the fragment. The perforations may represent attempts to mend broken pieces or to make them still useful by joining them with cord or thongs, segmented-bracelet fashion. The incisions, grooves, and notches may be attempts to refashion the fragments into other artifacts such as short borers, beads, or naillike objects. Almost all of the reworked fragments are of the *b* type.

Beads (figs. 136:1-18; 142:1-13)

Beads are here defined as small objects that are perforated so that they can be strung and are small enough to be worn in numbers—and thus cannot reasonably be assigned to any other category. Beads were found in quantity at Jarmo and show great diversity in form, size, and material. As a starting point in classifying them I have used the system suggested by Beck (1928).

In brief, Beck's basic system combines the following formal modes:

> Profile
>   *A*. cylinder
>   *B*. barrel
>   *C*. biconical
> Relative length
>   *1*. short (shorter than diameter or width)
>   *2*. long (equal to or longer than diameter or width)
> Cross section
>   *a*. flattened (thickness less than width)
>   *b*. round (thickness equal to or almost equal to width)

Whether the ends of the beads, as seen in profile, were parallel to each other might also be considered a varietal mode, but this was not included in my classification. Except in the case of disk beads, where most ends are parallel, the ends of Jarmo beads tend to be somewhat irregular. A total of 124 beads were available for classification and study in the Chicago sample and 58 more were studied by the use of field sketches and notes describing specimens in the Baghdad sample.

Twelve varieties were noted (including a long type with a collar at each end, for which I use the notation *B2b2*), as follows:

A1a	Short flattened cylinder beads (disk beads). Very rare in stone (fig. 136:1).
A1b	Short round cylinder beads (disk beads). The most common bead variety (fig. 136:2). One unique example (fig. 136:3) is a disk bead into which a V-shaped boring from one side was unsuccessfully attempted.
A2a	Long flattened cylinder beads. Very rare at Jarmo.
A2b	Long round cylinder beads. A fairly numerous group (fig. 136:4). One unusual example was decorated with a spiral incision.
B1a	Short flattened barrel beads. Rare (fig. 136:5).
B1b	Short rounded barrel beads (fig. 136:6).
B2a	Long flattened barrel beads (fig. 136:7).
B2a2	Long flattened barrel beads with collars (figs. 136:18; 142:9).
B2b	Long rounded barrel beads. Fairly common (fig. 136:8).
B2b2	Long rounded barrel bead, low collar at each end. Only 1 example (fig. 136:9).
C1a	Short flattened biconical beads. Only 2 examples.
C2a	Long flattened biconical beads. Rare (fig. 136:10).
D	A group added to include beads of miscellaneous shapes, unfinished beads, and reworked beads (fig. 136:11-17). One, a rounded conical form of white stone (fig. 136:11), perhaps imitates a bead of fossilized univalve shell. For the most part, the unfinished beads are roughly blocked-out blanks of stone resembling the finished beads described above (fig. 136:12-14). Four have incomplete perforations started from one or both faces or ends (fig. 136:15-17). Reworked beads are beads that appear to have once been whole but have been broken while being perforated; the holes were irreparably botched.

We might note, in passing, that the simpler bead forms were also copied in clay. There is also a curious roughly octagonal blank (for a bead?) that is made of lead (fig. 136:19; see p. 542).

On the basis of findings obtained from the present exposures, which are admittedly inadequate, we might surmise that short cylinders and barrel beads were made earlier in the life of the village than long ones, that round-sectioned beads may occur earlier than flat-sectioned ones, and that beads with collars and biconical profiles may appear quite late in the sequence.

So far, it has not been possible to secure detailed petrographic analyses of the materials from which the Jarmo beads were made. Accordingly, the color has been noted because it may provide some hint of the stone used. In my opinion, most of the beads in the Chicago sample are of marble, usually opaque white, but also gray, pink, red and white, and red and cream in color. Opaque brown-and-tan beads are probably of limestone, while black ones seem to be serpentine or chlorite. Green beads (from light to dark in shade) resemble the stones used for some of the Jarmo celts that were identified as chlorite. Light aquamarine beads look very much like turquoise. If they are, they would be yet another indication of long distance trade at Jarmo, for the nearest known sources are in Afghanistan and in the Negev and Sinai (G. Wright 1969, pp. 59-60). Clear, colorless beads and fragments may be calcite, while the translucent red orange stone concentrated in J-II is probably carnelian. Much of the material, then, may be of local origin. Small pebbles of translucent, brightly colored stone may have come from the stream below Jarmo. There are various small, rough, unworked varicolored waterworn pebbles, which reinforces the impression that there was a home production of Jarmo beads. Only a few undoubtedly modern beads and bead fragments were found and these were from surface or near surface context.

The broken or unfinished beads, especially, permit some conjectures about manufacturing procedures. From the evidence at hand, it appears that a craftsman first blocked out the bead by sawing it, or by grinding it against a coarse-grained stone. The perimeters of disk beads were often chipped into shape (fig. 136:13). On long beads, a flat surface was formed at each end and the bead blank was then perforated using a solid drill. Long beads were evidently always biconically perforated (fig. 136:16), but some of the short beads may have been drilled through from only one face (fig. 136:15). After being perforated, the bead was then ground into final shape and polished. The great symmetry of the short cylinder beads (disk beads) and the occurrence of three unperforated blanks of identical dimensions in J-II suggest that several such beads were strung together and then shaped against an abrading stone. Another alternative is suggested by the apparently hollow-drilled decoration seen on a stone pendant (p. 299).

Another interesting feature of some of the Jarmo beads is the nearly straight and smooth perforation. This feature might be due to an extremely careful reaming after the bead was perforated from both sides. It might also be the result of cutting into segments a very long bead that had already been perforated. Although there is no direct evidence for such a method, nor am I clear about how and with what the Jarmo craftsmen sawed stone, it is a possibility.

The smallest perforations to be seen on the Jarmo beads are approximately 1 mm in diameter. At present, it appears that none of the drill-like artifacts of chipped or ground stone found at Jarmo could have been used to make such small perforations although some of them could have been used to make perforations as small as 3 mm. Haury

(1931) suggests a method of perforating stone beads with a drill of thorn mounted in the end of a stick, which would be rotated between the hands and used in combination with an abrasive of fine sand and water. Experimenting with the method, Haury was able to make perforations as small in diameter as 0.94 mm. It is possible that a similar method was used to perforate the smallest and shortest of the Jarmo beads.

Pendants (figs. 136:20-29; 142:15-18,20)

Pendants are so classified if they were perforated so as to hang more or less asymmetrically, if they are small enough to have conceivably been worn as ornaments, and if they appear to have had no other purpose. The category consists of three varieties, according to the amount of modification exhibited:

 a. Pendants with simple forms (figs. 136:20-22; 142:18) consisting of selected and usually modified pebbles, either elongated or squat in shape, with an overall polish and a more or less biconically drilled perforation near one end. Figures 136:22 and 142:18 show a form that recalls beads of pierced deer canine teeth (cf. e.g., Garrod and Bate 1937, p. 40 and pl.XII, fig. 2:2). There are also reworked stone vessel sherds with either one or two perforations (figs. 136:23,26; 142:16). One large probable pendant, a stone bowl sherd, has been worked on all surfaces and has three perforations (figs. 136:27; 142:20). A small fragment of ground and drilled obsidian may represent a pendant, and another fragment of similar form appears to be a gray chalcedony concretion, unworked except for the perforation. Pendants of the *a* variety exhibit considerable diversity, but the most popular form seems to have been the elongated oval with a perforation near one end (e.g., fig. 136:21). A sugarloaf-shaped form of polished clear crystal has an incipient borehole in its base, as well as a normal perforation through the top (fig. 136:20).
 b. These are pendants with more elaborate forms and with carving, incised decoration, or other extensive working. One incomplete example is of a truncated elongated triangle decorated on one surface with a design resembling a face. The design is composed of two eyelike elements consisting of a circular groove with a small pit in the center and two tiny biconically drilled perforations between them (figs. 136:25; 142:15). The circular grooves are interesting. They appear to have been made either with a hollow drill or with some device that would serve as an engraving compass. The small pit in the center was made either with a small-diametered solid drill or with the point of the compass. If the hollow drill was indeed used, as seems most likely, this pendant shows the clearest evidence of hollow-drilling of the Jarmo ground stone objects, although some of the smaller disk beads, phallic objects, and miscellaneous stone objects may also have been made by this technique. Another remarkable pendant, plaquelike in form and almost complete, carries an incised design of parallel and crosshatched lines on one face (fig. 136:29). Two of the *b* variety pendants are carefully carved on all surfaces and might be described as foot shaped. The more complete example is a particularly fine piece of workmanship (figs. 136:28; 142:17).
 c. This variety accounts for a few unfinished pendants that were made primarily from naturally smooth pebbles and had incomplete perforations.

Pendants were made predominantly of fine-grained limestone or marble. A few examples of ground obsidian appeared and at least one example of a heavy mineral (hematite or limonite). There were other types of stone used, none of which have yet been positively identified. The pendants were usually ground and/or polished all over and have no visible marks of preliminary shaping. All completed perforations were biconically drilled and carefully reamed out.

Broad, Flat Rings (fig. 137:1)

Broad, flat rings are rather enigmatic objects, made more so by the circumstance that all known examples are incomplete. They are well made and their purpose may have been ornamental. It is assumed that the original form was a large, broad ring that was thin in cross section and had a tapering outer edge. In the larger fragments it can be seen that the central perforation is off-center. One small fragment has two conical perforations set next to each other parallel to the broken edge, made perhaps for suspension but more probably as mend holes. Another larger fragment has two biconical perforations; one is located near a break, which has been reground, and the other is at the point of another break (fig. 137:1). One fragment is unusual in having a secondarily chipped perimeter, while all of the others have smoothly ground perimeters.

These rings appear to be of either limestone or marble, with one exception that is possibly serpentine. These rings were well shaped by overall grinding and possibly all of them were once polished. In the absence of complete examples it is difficult to assess the purpose of the central perforations.

Ground Stone Balls (figs. 137:2-4; 141:2,4-6)

The stone ball category is made up of numerous smoothly ground stone spheres that are quite in contrast to the round hammerstones described earlier in this chapter (p. 292). The balls are predominantly of marble or limestone, although several were of chlorite and chlorite-ochre. Care appears to have been taken to give these artifacts nearly perfect symmetry (fig. 141:2,4-6). The surfaces were shaped by grinding and three fourths of the examples in Chicago show high polish; in fact all of these ground spheres were probably finished by polishing. The diameters of the some 60 measured examples range from 12.5 mm to over 62.0 mm.

Almost half of the examples in Chicago have been somewhat battered subsequent to shaping and polishing. One possibly unique example of a spheroid shape, with a diameter of 43.5 mm, has been severely battered on one face, which was then used for grinding with a back-and-forth motion (fig. 137:3). This sphere shows clear traces of red pigment, perhaps ochre on the battered face as well as on the face opposite. The pigment traces, plus the evidence of back-and-forth grinding, suggest that this sphere, at least, might have been used as a handstone on the palettes and paint-preparing stones already described (p. 293), and there are a few other examples that show evidence of secondary grinding and traces of pigment. In the case of the three spheres of chlorite-ochre the mineral substance itself readily rubs off on paper. But even if we can attribute the battering and grinding marks on the larger balls to use of these stones in the preparation of mineral pigments, we are still left with the problem of explaining their carefully shaped and polished surfaces. Perhaps these attributes were functional, or perhaps even the result of mode of use. Spheres of smaller diameter are identical to the larger ones in all respects, except that they show no obvious signs of use. A shallow pit about 4 mm in diameter was drilled into one small smooth sphere (fig. 137:4). Stimulated by Korfmann's article (1973) on ancient slings and sling missiles, we have recorded in the catalogue at the end of this chapter the weights of the reasonably complete examples in the Chicago sample.

Phallic Objects (figs. 137:5-8; 140:18-20; 142:32)

Included here as phallic objects are well-finished sculptured forms that appear to represent the head of the human penis and on which, according to medical opinion, circumcision may be represented (SAOC 31, p. 46). Unfortunately none of the objects is absolutely intact; all show considerable battering and only two of the stone examples are complete enough to make the other fragments comprehensible (figs. 137:5-6; 140:18,20). The examples in stone are evidently all of marble; the form also appears in clay (p. 383 and fig. 162:3).

The base (or proximal end) of the form is finished in a curious manner, with a round hole drilled to some depth in the natural location of the urethral tube. Below this, there is a cup-shaped depression (figs. 137:5-6; 140:20) which "could be accounted for as the cavity formed by the terminations of the corpora cavernosa" (SAOC 31, p. 46).

It is also noteworthy that in each example whose head (or distal end) is preserved, there are clear traces of battering in that area.

Another possibly phallic representation, but formed of a probably natural concretion of coarse limestone (and from a near surface context), was provided only with a pair of grooves to indicate the head (figs. 137:8; 140:19).

We also include in this group, without implying that they may be phallic representations, a pair of fragments of enigmatic objects that have cuplike projections at right angles to long stalklike tangs (figs. 137:7; 142:32). This kind of object is now known, in its intact form, from graves at Tell es-Sawwan (al-Wailly and Abu es-Soof 1965, fig. 66, center) and at Ali Kosh (Hole, Flannery, and Neely 1969, fig. 87a and pl. 38a). Again, the material is apparently marble and the careful attention to the sculpturing and finishing of the form is much like that of the above mentioned phallic objects.

Miscellaneous Stone Artifacts (figs. 137:9-11; 138:4-6; 140:10; 142:26-27,30-31)

Miscellaneous stone artifacts are those that are either unique or those that I cannot assign to any of the previously described types. Most of these artifacts defy classification simply because they are incomplete. What follows is a much abbreviated notation of some 40 of the more comprehensible forms, without suggestion as to original use.

There is a group of 10 curved naillike objects, perhaps fashioned of broken bracelet fragments, usually made of marble. They have been carefully ground into shape and probably also have been polished. In their most completely finished form, these "nails" have heads and the opposite end is tapered to a point (figs. 137:10; 142:31). Whether from manufacture or use, most of these artifacts have concentric (transverse) striations on their surfaces.

Another small stone object is a fragment of a spoonlike form (figs. 137:9; 142:26) made of what appears to be fire-darkened marble. Spoonlike objects are more common in bone (see pp. 353f.). There is also a white marble stud or stamp-shaped artifact (fig. 137:11) that is similar to objects found in some quantity at Tepe Sarab, usually in clay. At Sarab we tended to consider them to be labrets. Finally, we note 4 other finely worked but enigmatic stone objects: a gray stone artifact of roughly conical form that has a concave base with a notched edge (fig. 138:5), 2 small somewhat pestlelike or stalklike objects of limestone? and marble (figs. 138:6; 142:30), and a fragment of what appears to have been a vastly oversized bracelet (figs. 138:4; 142:27).

Of the larger and coarser miscellaneous artifacts of stone—either those that are too fragmentary to suggest their original form or those of enigmatic utility—we illustrate only one example. This object is one of several exceptionally large pecked and partially ground limestone balls that have a diameter range of from ca. 100 to 150 mm (fig. 140:10, on quern). Two of these balls were noted near the so-called doorpost pivot stones (see p. 296).

Some 170 examples of unworked stone were returned to Chicago for mineralogical identification, but this study has yet to be made.

ARTIFACTS OF SHELL (figs. 138:7-13; 142:14,19)

Artifacts of shell, including those made of recent or of fossil shells, the unworked casts of fossil shells (e.g., fig. 138:12), and objects that are either unfinished artifacts of shell (fig. 138:13) or apparently utilized shell fragments were all evidenced at Jarmo, but in relatively modest quantity.

Beads were the most common type of shell artifact. Of the beads of this material in Chicago, at least three appear to be made from marine shells, such as the *Dentalium* (fig. 138:10). The spires of small fossil univalves (resembling the genus *Oliva*) were removed so that the shells could be strung as beads (figs. 138:7; 142:14). Simple disk beads (short cylinders, variety *A1b*) of freshwater mussel shell were fairly common. Unfortunately, we have not yet secured a thoroughgoing series of identifications of the shell remains, either fossil or modern.

Shell pendants, evidently all of freshwater mussel shell, included a curious pierced plaquelike object with several drillings (fig. 138:8) and a simple inverted triangle with double drill holes (figs. 138:9; 142:19). One fragment of a perhaps otherwise unaltered mussel shell had been drilled (fig. 138:11) and may have served as a pendant.

At least two fossil castings of rather large shells were encountered (see fig. 138:12). Presumably these had no utility but had simply been brought into the village by someone curious about their spiraliform appearance.

Along with the very considerable quantities of land snail shells (*Helix salomonica*) that the excavations at Jarmo yielded, there were occasional unaltered mussel shells. These were in such relatively small numbers that we are not inclined to assume that the mussels (*Unio tigridis*) formed an important part of the human diet at Jarmo. As well as being raw material for such artifacts as beads and pendants, these mussel shells may well have served in their unaltered form as scoops, scrapers, or spoons.

CATALOGUE OF GROUND STONE AND SHELL ARTIFACTS (figs. 127-42)

ABBREVIATIONS

Measurements

L/gD = length or greatest diameter or (in the case of bowllike, disklike, and subspherical objects) height of vertical axis, in millimeters

W/gD = width or (in the case of bowllike, disklike, and subspherical objects) greatest diameter, in millimeters

Th/Wt = thickness in millimeters or (in the case of hammerstones, pecking and rubbing stones, and ground stone balls) weight in grams

NOTE: Numbers in parentheses indicate the greatest available measurement when an object is incomplete. Only the thickness may be given if there is little or nothing left of the sides.

Minerals

alabas	= alabaster
bt grnst	= biotitic greenstone
calc	= calcite
cal lmst	= calcareous limestone
ch/cdy	= chert or chalcedony
chl och	= chlorite and ochre
chl	= chlorite
cryst	= crystal
diab	= diabase
grn neph	= green nephrite
grnst	= greenstone
hemat	= hematite
hrn sch	= hornblende schist
lmst	= limestone
lmst chalc	= limestone with chalcedony
lmst cong	= limestone conglomerate
lmst sa/cl	= limestone with sand or clay
low metam	= low metamorphic rock
obsid	= obsidian
sandst	= sandstone
serp	= serpentine
steat	= steatite
trav flnt	= travertine with flint
ves lav	= vesicular lava
unident	= not identified

Mineral Colors

blk/wh	= black and white
blu/grn	= blue to green
blu/gry	= blue to gray
dk grn	= dark green
dk gry	= dark gray
gry/grn	= gray to green
gry/wh	= gray to white
red/orn	= red to orange
red/wh	= red to white
red/yl	= red to yellow

Remarks

inc	= incomplete
inc?	= probably incomplete
comp	= complete
comp?	= nearly complete
rewkd	= reworked
bif	= bifacially worked
unif	= unifacially worked
fi	= traces of fire
frag	= fragment
transl	= translucent
transp	= transparent
(B)	= Baghdad (Iraqi National Museum)
(C)	= Chicago (Oriental Institute Museum)

Register number is italicized.

PECKED AND GROUND STONE ARTIFACTS*

Context	Figure no.	Measurements			Mineral	Remarks
		L/gD (mm)	W/gD (mm)	Th/Wt (mm/gm)		
Mullers						
J-I,dmp	139:1	100	--	--	unident	comp; bif; worked edges; (B)
J-I,1-2	--	(140)	136	33	trav flnt	inc; unif; (C)
J-I,1-2	--	(82)	118	40	trav flnt	inc; unif; (C)
J-I,1-2	--	--	--	49	trav flnt	inc; unif; fi; (C)
J-I,1-2	--	(60)	144	44	trav flnt	inc; unif; (C)
J-I,2-3	--	(91)	124	38	trav flnt	inc; unif; both faces pecked; rough edges; (C)
J-I,2-3	--	(146)	111	55	lmst sa/cl	inc; unif; (C)
J-I,2-3	--	(62)	132	36	trav flnt	inc; unif; fi; (C)
J-I,2-3	--	--	--	37	trav flnt	inc; unif; fi; (C)
J-I,2-3	--	(75)	108	31	lmst chalc	inc; bif; rough edges; fi; (C)
J-I,2-3	--	166	110	34	lmst chalc	comp; bif; roughly shaped sides; (C)
J-I,2-3	--	--	--	28	unident	inc; bif; (C)
J-I,3	--	81	55	--	unident	*J-36*; comp; bif; (B)
J-I,3	--	(156)	132	34	trav flnt	comp?; unif; rounded edges, flat section; (C)
J-I,3	--	144	117	36	trav flnt	comp; unif; pecked sides; (C)
J-I,3	--	(71)	94	42	trav flnt	inc; unif; top pecked and ground; (C)
J-I,3	--	--	--	36	trav flnt	inc; unif; rough sides; (C)
J-I,3	--	--	--	30	lmst sa/cl	inc; bif; fi; (C)
J-I,3	--	--	--	34	lmst sa/cl	inc; bif; (C)

---

*See footnote on page 290 regarding the listing in the catalogue of a far larger number of examples of heavier artifacts, such as mullers, querns, and hammerstones, from J-I than from J-II.

Context	Figure no.	L/gD (mm)	W/gD (mm)	Th/Wt (mm/gm)	Mineral	Remarks
Mullers—Continued						
J-I,3	--	--	--	34	lmst sa/cl	inc; bif; fi; (C)
J-I,4-5	--	--	--	--	unident	inc; bif?; muller?; (B)
J-I,5	--	178	(80)	38	lmst cong	inc; unif; rough sides; (C)
J-I,5	--	(77)	137	38	lmst cong	inc; unif; rough sides; (C)
J-I,5	--	158	98	50	ch/cdy	comp; unif; rough sides; red pigment traces top and end; (C)
J-I,5	127:2	174	127	47	ch/cdy	comp; unif; irregular, wide; (C)
J-I,5	--	(118)	100	31	lmst sa/cl	rewkd; unif; pecked edges, top slightly ground; edge depression; (C)
J-I,5	--	--	--	31	lmst sa/cl	inc; unif; (C)
J-I,5	--	--	--	29	lmst sa/cl	inc; unif; rounded edge; fi; (C)
J-I,5	--	104	103	39	ch/cdy	comp; unif; some top use, irregular plan; (C)
J-I,5	--	--	--	28	lmst cong	inc; bif; rough edges; fi?; (C)
J-I,5-6,pit	--	--	--	31	lmst sa/cl	inc; unif; fi; (C)
J-I,6c	--	--	125?	--	chert?	inc; flat surfaces, wedgelike section; (B)
J-I,6	127:1	143	103	43	trav flnt	comp; unif; finger grips; (C)
J-I,6	--	133	110	59	ch/cdy	comp?; unif; ovoid plan; pecked edges and faces; (C)
J-I,6	--	(112)	140	30	lmst cong	inc; bif; (C)
J-I,6	127:3	122	100	35	unident	comp; bif; fi; (C)
J-I,6	--	(87)	112	24	lmst sa/cl	inc; bif; rough edges; (C)
J-I,6	--	--	--	28	marble	inc; bif; one end battered; (C)
J-I,7	--	--	--	--	unident	comp; bif; worked edges; (B)
J-I,7	--	110	--	--	unident	comp; bif; muller?; (B)
J-I,7	139:2	110?	--	--	unident	comp; bif; (B)
J-I,7	--	(69)	115	56	lmst cong	inc; unif; rough sides; (C)
J-I,7	--	--	--	59	lmst	inc; unif; pecked sides; (C)
J-II,W,sf-3	--	149	90	45	trav flnt	comp; unif; pecked all over; (C)
J-II,3	--	100	--	--	trav flnt	comp; (B)
J-D,sf-1	--	(77)	101	54	trav flnt	inc; unif; rounded edges; (C)
GL1519,1	--	120?	--	--	unident	comp; round oblate form; (B)
GL1519,1	--	130?	--	--	unident	comp; (B)
K7,2	--	160	--	--	unident	comp; (B)
Querns						
J-I,1-2	--	(120)	(150)	37	trav flnt	inc; (C)
J-I,1-2	--	--	--	90	lmst sa/cl	inc; (C)
J-I,2-3	--	(178)	(150)	67	trav flnt	inc; (C)
J-I,2-3	--	--	--	46	lmst sa/cl	inc; fi; (C)
J-I,2-3	--	--	--	54	lmst sa/cl	inc; fi; (C)
J-I,2-3	--	(156)	111	28	lmst sa/cl	inc; (C)
J-I,2-3	--	(140)	111	56	lmst sa/cl	inc; (C)
J-I,2-3	--	(160)	140	100	trav flnt	inc; fi; (C)
J-I,2-3	--	--	--	51	trav flnt	inc; (C)
J-I,2-3	--	--	--	40	lmst sa/cl	inc; (C)
J-I,2-3	--	--	--	71	lmst sa/cl?	inc; heavily reworked bottom frag?; (C)
J-I,2-3	--	--	--	55	ch/cdy	inc; fi; (C)
J-I,3	--	--	--	52	lmst cong	inc; (C)
J-I,3	--	--	--	61	lmst sa/cl	inc; (C)
J-I,3	--	--	--	57	lmst chalc	inc; (C)
J-I,3	--	--	--	36	lmst sa/cl	inc; (C)
J-I,3	--	--	--	50	trav flnt	inc; fi; (C)
J-I,3	--	--	--	49	trav flnt	inc; (C)
J-I,3	--	--	--	42	trav flnt	inc; (C)
J-I,3	--	--	--	38	lmst sa/cl	inc; (C)
J-I,3	--	--	--	30	lmst chalc	inc; (C)
J-I,3	--	--	--	47	trav flnt	inc; (C)

Context	Figure no.	Measurements			Mineral	Remarks
		L/gD (mm)	W/gD (mm)	Th/Wt (mm/gm)		
Querns—*Continued*						
J-I,3	--	--	--	24	trav flnt	inc; ochre traces on face; (C)
J-I,3	--	(131)	(123)	34	lmst chalc	inc; (C)
J-I,3	--	--	--	43	lmst cong	inc; (C)
J-I,3	128:1; 139:6	(383)	350	130	lmst	comp?; (C)
J-I,3	127:7	(480)	245	105	lmst chalc	inc; (C)
J-I,3	127:6	(335)	310	98	lmst	inc; (C)
J-I,3	--	--	--	85	trav flnt	inc; (C)
J-I,3	--	(139)	(91)	33	trav flnt	inc; (C)
J-I,3	--	--	--	60	sandst	inc; polished face; (C)
J-I,3	--	--	--	--	unident	inc; (B)
J-I,3a	--	--	--	--	unident	inc; ochre traces?; (B)
J-I,3,pit	--	--	--	--	unident	inc; (B)
J-I,4-5	--	--	--	62	lmst chalc	inc; well-shaped edge; (C)
J-I,4-5	--	--	--	29	trav flnt	inc; (C)
J-I,4-5	--	--	--	32	lmst chalc	inc; (C)
J-I,4-5	--	--	--	32	lmst chalc	inc; (C)
J-I,5	--	(300)	169	100	lmst sa/cl	inc; (C)
J-I,5	--	--	--	35	lmst chalc	inc; (C)
J-I,5	--	--	--	39	lmst sa/cl	inc; (C)
J-I,5	--	(122)	152	55	trav flnt	inc; (C)
J-I,5	--	--	--	36	trav flnt	inc; (C)
J-I,5	--	--	--	24	lmst sa/cl	inc; (C)
J-I,5	--	252	(146)	60	lmst chalc?	inc; (C)
J-I,5	--	--	--	--	lmst sa/cl	inc; (C)
J-I,5	--	(161)	(174)	125	lmst cong	inc; (C)
J-I,5	--	--	--	--	unident	inc; (B)
J-I,6	--	--	--	37	lmst	inc; (C)
J-I,6	--	--	--	37	lmst chalc	inc; fi; (C)
J-I,6	--	(103)	157	52	lmst sa/cl	inc; (C)
J-I,6	--	(113)	(86)	30	lmst cong	inc; (C)
J-I,6	128:2; 139:4	586	375	187	lmst	comp; double depression; center of underside polished; (C)
J-I,6	--	400	(160)	240	ch/cdy	inc; (C)
J-I,6	--	350	199	97	lmst chalc	comp; (C)
J-I,7	--	--	--	--	unident	inc; quern?; (B)
J-I,7	--	(350)	--	--	unident	inc; (B)
J-I,8	--	--	--	--	unident	comp; small quern?; (B)
J-I,8fl.	139:3	(290)	--	--	unident	inc; (B)
J-II,W,sf-3	140:10	550	220	--	unident	comp; two secondary depressions; unique; (B)
J-II,W,sf-3	--	(380)	--	--	unident	inc; (B)
J-II,W,sf-3	--	(400)	--	--	unident	inc; (B)
J-II,1	139:5	370	225	62	unident	J2-223; comp; (B)
J-II,1	--	340?	--	--	unident	comp; (B)
J-II,2fl.	127:5	453	290	190	unident	comp; slanted grinding surface; (B)
J-II,4	--	(308)	--	--	unident	inc; (B)
J-II,5	127:4	448	190	52	lmst sa/cl?	comp; smooth underside, worked?; (C)
J-A,sf-1	--	--	--	38	trav flnt	inc; very weathered; (C)
J-B,sf-1	--	(237)	(183)	85	trav flnt	inc; (C)
J-B,sf-1	--	--	--	40	trav flnt	inc; (C)
J-B,sf-1	--	--	--	28	lmst sa/cl	inc; fi?; (C)
J-B,sf-1	--	--	--	50	lmst sa/cl	inc; smooth underside, use-friction?; (C)
J-B,1-2	--	(117)	(101)	42	unident	inc; (C)
J-B,1-2	--	--	--	31	trav flnt	inc; (C)
J-B,1-2	--	--	--	31	trav flnt	inc; (C)
Pecked and Ground Slabs						
J-I,dmp	--	(320)	--	--	unident	comp?; (B)

Context	Figure no.	L/gD (mm)	W/gD (mm)	Th/Wt (mm/gm)	Mineral	Remarks
Pecked and Ground Slabs—*Continued*						
J-I,3	--	--	--	--	unident	inc; worn boulder frag; (B)
J-I,3	--	212	165	89	trav flnt	comp?; unmodified; (C)
J-I,3a	--	125	--	--	unident	comp?; artifact?; (B)
J-I,5	128:5	234	145	74	ch/cdy	comp; bif; (C)
J-I,5	--	(145)	(115)	47	lmst sa/cl	inc; probably unmodified; ochre on face?; (C)
J-I,5	--	--	--	24	lmst sa/cl	inc; small; muller frag?; (C)
J-I,5	128:3	260	(145)	65	lmst	inc; finely pecked shallow depression; (C)
J-I,6	--	225	220	45	lmst sa/cl?	comp; bif; brown stain on face; fi?; (C)
J-I,8	128:4	205?	90	35	lmst chalc	rewkd; bif; (C)
J-II,2fl.	128:6	240?	160?	88?	unident	comp; unif; ochre traces on face; (B)
J-II,5	--	--	275?	--	unident	comp; unif; slab?, large disk; chipped circumference; (B)
HK16,sf-1	--	--	--	--	unident	comp?; (B)
PQ14,3	--	232	--	--	unident	comp; slab; one face with round shallow mortar depression, other convex and ground; (B)
Utilized Cobbles						
J-I,1-2	--	184	107	54	serp	comp; faint multidirectional scratches on both faces, peck marks in middle of both faces; anvil?; (C)
J-I,2-3	--	74	63	35	marble	comp; artifact?; (C)
J-I,2-3	--	80	(57)	37	unident	inc; polish and multidirectional scratches on one face; (C)
J-I,2-3	--	92	73	40	lmst	rewkd; battered ends, surface scratches, bifacially flaked long edge showing slight smoothing; (C)
J-I,3	--	(129)	61	54	lmst	inc; end battered; fi; (C)
J-I,3	--	(38)	--	--	lmst	inc; peck marks and faint transverse scratches; fi; (C)
J-I,3	--	(25)	--	--	lmst	inc; part of above?; (C)
J-I,3-4	--	178	--	--	dark stone	J-45; comp; peck marks, especially at ends; (B)
J-I,5	--	(56)	--	--	marble	inc; pecked face with some grinding and short transverse scratches; (C)
J-I,5	128:8	109	86	56	marble	comp; short white transverse scratches on both faces, some grinding; anvil; (C)
J-I,6	128:7	95	90	70	marble	comp; battered ends with ochre traces, transverse striations on larger surfaces, some grinding; (C)
J-I,6	--	114	96	61	marble	comp?; some grinding of all faces, multidirectional scratches; ochre traces; (C)
J-I,6	--	(48)	42	33	lmst	inc; broken, battered; (C)
J-I,8	--	90	45	27	lmst	comp; overall grinding, peck marks, battering; (C)
GL1519,1	--	150?	--	--	dark stone	comp; peck marks, especially at ends; (B)
Pestles						
J-I,sf	--	132	69	--	trav flnt	comp; (C)
J-I,dmp	--	170	--	--	unident	comp; (B)
J-I,1-2	--	166	64	--	lmst sa/cl	comp; fi; (C)
J-I,2	--	--	--	--	lmst sa/cl	inc; artifact frag?; (C)
J-I,2-3	--	(109)	69	--	lmst sa/cl	inc; (C)
J-I,2-3	--	(71)	69	--	lmst sa/cl	inc; (C)
J-I,2-3	--	107	58	--	lmst sa/cl	rewkd; (C)
J-I,2-3	--	--	70?	--	trav flnt	inc; (C)
J-I,2-3	--	(108)	--	--	unident	inc; (B)

		Measurements				
Context	Figure no.	L/gD (mm)	W/gD (mm)	Th/Wt (mm/gm)	Mineral	Remarks
Pestles—*Continued*						
J-I,3	--	(97)	57	--	diab	inc; (C)
J-I,3	--	(67)	69	--	lmst sa/cl	inc; flat end, broken, reused; fi; (C)
J-I,3	--	(41)	57	--	lmst	inc; (C)
J-I,3	--	--	--	--	unident	comp; (B)
J-I,3	--	--	--	--	unident	inc; pestle?; (B)
J-I,3a	--	200?	--	--	unident	comp; pestle?; (B)
J-I,3-4	128:11; 139:7	178	80	--	unident	J-45; comp; (B)
J-I,7	129:1	(195)	82	--	unident	inc; (C)
J-II,W,sf-3	--	200	--	--	unident	comp; battered base; (B)
J-II,1	128:9	110	52	--	unident	J2-227; comp; (B)
J-II,1	--	154	--	--	unident	comp?; (B)
J-II,1	--	164	61	--	lmst sa/cl?	comp; fi?; (C)
J-II,2fl.	129:2	184	76	--	unident	comp; unusual base; (B)
J-II,5	--	160	--	--	unident	rewkd; section flattened, base battered; blackened; (B)
J-II,6	128:10	173	58	--	lmst sa/cl?	comp; (C)
J-B,1-2	--	--	60?	--	lmst cong	inc; (C)
J-D,1fl.	--	(75)	(40)	--	blk schistlike	inc; (C)
GL2024,3	--	(93)	53	--	lmst sa/cl	inc; (C)
K line,1	--	--	43?	--	unident	comp?; (B)
Pestle-Hammerstones						
J-I,sf	--	88	45	44	lmst cong?	comp; edge of end battered, square cross section; (C)
J-I,sf	--	104	52	50	lmst chalc	comp; edge of end battered, square cross section; (C)
J-I,1-2	129:4	(158)	65	43	lmst chalc	comp?; (C)
J-I,3a	129:5	119	69	49	lmst sa/cl	comp?; side reground; (C)
J-I,3,pit 2	--	--	--	--	unident	comp?; base chipped; (B)
J-I,4	--	93	45	--	unident	J-62; comp; (B)
J-I,4-5	--	(39)	50	--	hrn sch	inc; one face pecked, others polished; (C)
J-I,4-5	--	(157)	79	57	lmst	inc; battered top; brown stained face; (C)
J-I,5	129:8	106	40	40	unident	comp; (C)
J-I,5	--	--	--	--	lmst sa/cl	rewkd; one end smoothed, other rounded and battered; slight pecking all over, fi; (C)
J-I,5	--	--	--	--	unident	comp?; slightly tapered; (B)
J-I,5	--	256	91	60	lmst?	comp; battered; fi (charred end); (C)
J-I,5	--	(105)	72	37	lmst sa/cl	inc; battered end; (C)
J-I,5	--	(116)	57	49	lmst sa/cl	inc; battered end; (C)
J-I,5	--	(105)	70	53	lmst sa/cl	inc; battered end; (C)
J-I,5	--	156	64	48	lmst	comp?; battered ends; (C)
J-I,5	--	177	81	55	lmst sa/cl	comp; irregular ends; (C)
J-I,5	--	(149)	70	(30)	lmst sa/cl?	inc; rounded, pecked end; fi; (C)
J-I,5	--	163	80	68	lmst chalc?	comp; overall pecking, sides polished, battered end; fi?; (C)
J-I,6	129:3	(149)	69	54	unident	comp?; (C)
J-I,6	--	148	62	62	lmst sa/cl	comp; one end smoothed, other rounded; battered; (C)
J-I,6	--	149	69	54	unident	comp; oblong cross section; (C)
J-I,7	--	94	54	(44)	lmst chalc	inc; trapezoidal cross section; battered face and end-edge; ochre traces; (C)
J-I,8	129:9	94	47	28	lmst chalc	comp; slightly waisted; faces polished, battered end-edge; (C)
J-II,1	--	116	56	50	lmst chalc?	comp; square cross section; battered end-edge; (C)
J-II,1	129:6	141	64	--	unident	J2-224; comp; (B)
J-II,1	--	100?	--	--	unident	comp; (B)
J-II,1	129:10	153	57	24	sandst	comp?; flattened cross section, flared base; (C)
J-II,2fl.	--	164	78	76	lmst chalc?	comp; square cross section; (C)

		Measurements				
Context	Figure no.	L/gD (mm)	W/gD (mm)	Th/Wt (mm/gm)	Mineral	Remarks
Pestle-Hammerstones—*Continued*						
J-II,2fl.	129:7	110	60	--	unident	comp; (B)
J-II,6	--	90?	--	--	unident	comp; (B)
Hammerstones				(gm)		
J-I,sf	--	61	73	493	unident	comp; (C)
J-I,sf	--	51	55	203	unident	comp; (C)
J-I,sf	--	48	56	179	unident	comp; (C)
J-I,1-2	--	53	65	292	lmst	comp; (C)
J-I,1-2	--	46	53	167	lmst	comp; (C)
J-I,2	--	47	55	182	ch/cdy	comp; (C)
J-I,2-3	--	48	56	202	ch/cdy	comp; (C)
J-I,2-3	--	53	67	337	ch/cdy	comp; irregular; (C)
J-I,2-3	--	45	56	198	ch/cdy	comp; (C)
J-I,2-3	--	49	58	202	ch/cdy	comp; (C)
J-I,2-3	--	50	55	213	ch/cdy	comp; (C)
J-I,2-3	141:1	59	64	317	ch/cdy	comp; (C)
J-I,3	--	34	56	132	ch/cdy	inc (ca. half); reused; (C)
J-I,3	--	--	(42)	--	lmst cong	inc; (C)
J-I,3	--	54	59	245	chert	comp; (C)
J-I,3	--	36	45	106	marble	comp; (C)
J-I,3,pit 2	--	49	54	204	ch/cdy	comp; (C)
J-I,3,pit 2	--	45	48	136	ch/cdy	comp; (C)
J-I,3,pit 2	--	43	70	255	ch/cdy	inc (ca. half); reused; (C)
J-I,3a	--	--	(95?)	--	ch/cdy	inc; (C)
J-I,3a	--	42	65	223	ch/cdy	comp; (C)
J-I,3a	--	51	62	257	lmst cong	comp; (C)
J-I,3a	129:11	63	73	396	ch/cdy	comp; (C)
J-I,3a	--	34	--	163	ch/cdy	comp; irregular, roughly squared; (C)
J-I,3a	--	48	66	265	marble	comp; (C)
J-I,3a	--	42	60	193	marble	comp; irregular; (C)
J-I,3a	--	39	61	158	ch/cdy	comp?; reused; (C)
J-I,3a	--	33	51	122	lmst	comp; (C)
J-I,3a	--	35	70	183	ch/cdy	comp?; reused; (C)
J-I,3a	--	30	62	154	ch/cdy	comp?; reused; (C)
J-I,3a	--	35	57	155	ch/cdy	comp?; reused; (C)
J-I,3a	--	--	(58)	--	marble	comp?; (C)
J-I,4-5	--	30	65	166	ch/cdy	comp?; reused; (C)
J-I,5	--	39	54	149	ch/cdy	comp?; reused; (C)
J-I,5	--	30	54	100	ch/cdy	comp?; reused; (C)
J-I,5	--	27	54	118	ch/cdy	comp?; reused; (C)
J-I,5	--	--	50	163	ch/cdy	comp; (C)
J-I,5	--	61	66	306	ch/cdy	comp; (C)
J-I,5	--	60	67	346	ch/cdy	comp; (C)
J-I,6	--	34	46	98	marble	comp; (C)
J-I,6	--	--	43	103	chert?	comp; (C)
J-I,6	--	57	68	325	lmst cong	comp; (C)
J-I,6	--	42	56	133	lmst cong	comp; (C)
J-I,6	--	45	56	184	ch/cdy	comp; (C)
J-I,6	--	--	(51)	125	lmst cong	inc; roughly squared to 47 mm; (C)
J-I,6	--	38	62	209	ch/cdy	comp?; reused; (C)
J-I,6c	--	--	42	93	unident	comp; (C)
J-I,7	--	40	44	105	chert	comp; (C)
J-B,sf-1	--	--	(63)	--	ch/cdy	inc; (C)
J-B,sf-1	--	44	50	152	ch/cdy	comp; (C)
J-B,sf-1	--	37	60	171	ch/cdy	inc; reused; (C)
J-B,sf-1	--	--	(50)	--	ch/cdy	inc; (C)
J-B,sf-1	--	28	34	38	lmst	comp; (C)
J-B,sf-1	--	--	(84)	--	lmst	inc; (C)
J-B,1-2	--	--	55	127	ch/cdy	comp; (C)

Context	Figure no.	Measurements			Mineral	Remarks
		L/gD (mm)	W/gD (mm)	Th/Wt (mm/gm)		
Hammerstones—*Continued*						
J-B,1-2	--	41	48	128	ch/cdy	comp; (C)
J-B,1-2	--	32	77	225	ch/cdy	inc; reused?; (C)
J-D,sf-1	--	54	60	259	ch/cdy	comp; (C)
GL1014,2	--	52	56	215	unident	comp; (C)
GL2024,2	--	41	49	130	unident	comp; (C)
Mortars				*(mm)*		
J-I,dmp	129:18; 139:12	195	300	135	unident	inc; (B)
J-I,3	--	--	--	--	sandst	inc; rim thickness, 58 mm; (C)
J-I,3	--	--	310?	--	lmst sa/cl	inc; shallow rim frag; (C)
J-I,3	--	--	--	--	lmst sa/cl	inc; part of above?; (C)
J-I,3	--	--	--	--	lmst sa/cl	inc; rim thickness, 34 mm; (C)
J-I,5	--	--	290?	--	lmst sa/cl	inc; fi?; (C)
J-I,6	--	--	350?	--	lmst sa/cl	inc; (C)
J-I,6	--	125	(206)	--	trav flnt	inc; pecked all over; deep secondary depression; (C)
J-I,6	130:1	105	333	--	trav flnt	inc; (C)
J-I,7	--	--	115	--	unident	comp; opposing mortar depressions, rounded rectangular plan; (B)
J-I,8fl.	--	--	320?	--	unident	comp?; base broken through, flat, slab-like; (B)
J-II,W,sf-3	--	--	--	--	lmst sa/cl?	inc; small frag; fi?; (C)
J-II,1	--	--	280?	--	unident	comp?; base broken through; (B)
J-II,1	129:12	135?	300?	--	lmst sa/cl?	inc; rim thickness, 18 mm; (C)
J-II,2	129:13; 139:9	128	310	--	trav flnt?	comp?; secondary depression; (C)
J-II,2	129:16; 139:10	--	370?	--	lmst?	comp; unusual, 5 mortar depressions; (B)
J-II,2fl.	129:14; 139:11	105	146	--	lmst?	comp; small; (C)
J-II,2fl.	129:17	150?	250?	--	unident	comp; (B)
J-II,5	139:8	--	260?	--	unident	comp; (B)
J-II,5	--	--	98	--	unident	J2-399; comp; roughly finished pebble mortar; (B)
J-A,sf-1	--	--	(310)	--	trav flnt	inc; (C)
J-D,sf-1m	--	--	(310)	--	trav flnt	inc; (C)
G15	--	--	--	--	unident	inc; flat base, straight walls, unusual; (B)
H16,sf-1	--	--	320?	--	unident	inc; irregular rim; (C)
H17	--	153	(300)	--	lmst?	inc; ovoid plan, incipient secondary depression; (C)
H17	--	--	350?	--	unident	inc; oval plan; much battered; (B)
K9	--	--	255	--	unident	inc; (B)
HK16,sf-1	--	--	--	--	unident	comp; (B)
HK16,sf-1	--	--	--	--	unident	comp; base broken through; (B)
HK16,sf-1	129:15	112	270	--	trav flnt?	comp; rounded rectangular plan; (C)
L11	--	--	347	--	unident	comp; base broken through; (B)
PQ14	--	--	270	--	lmst?	inc; (C)
Palettes or Pigment-Grinding Stones						
J-I,3	--	--	--	43	lmst sa/cl	inc; heavy use, broken through, lengthwise striations; (C)
J-I,3	--	--	--	39	lmst sa/cl	inc; paint on one face; (C)
J-I,3a	--	--	--	--	unident	inc; squared rim; (B)
J-I,6	130:5	(145)	150	23	lmst sa/cl	J-16; inc; edge probably shaped; paint on upper face; (C)
J-I,6a	--	120	--	--	unident	comp; crude, square; (B)
J-II,3	130:3; 140:1	197	119	25	lmst sa/cl?	J2-298; comp; irregular base; lengthwise striations; (C)
J-II,4	--	205	168	35	lmst sa/cl	J2-319; comp?; crude, oval, slight depression on one end with red pigment traces; (B)
J-II,5	--	(260)	--	--	unident	inc; squared corner, large; palette?; (B)
J-II,5	130:4	112	99	27	lmst?	comp; round depression, 40 × 40 mm; paint on one face except in depression; (C)

Context	Figure no.	Measurements			Mineral	Remarks
		L/gD (mm)	W/gD (mm)	Th/Wt (mm/gm)		

Context	Figure no.	L/gD (mm)	W/gD (mm)	Th/Wt (mm/gm)	Mineral	Remarks
Palettes or Pigment-Grinding Stones—Continued						
J-II,6	130:2	188	141	28	lmst sa/cl?	J2-6; comp; fine example; worn through; paint on one face; (C)
M18,3	--	(88)	129	36	lmst sa/cl?	inc; pecked all over; unfinished; (C)
Disks with Pecked Depressions						
J-I,sf	--	17	--	--	unident	inc; perforated, ground perimeter; (C)
J-I,6	--	25	96	--	unident	inc; pecked all over; (C)
J-I,6	--	15	80?	--	unident	inc; pecked all over; paint on one face except in depression; (C)
J-II,1E	130:8	28	105	--	unident	inc; black crust on one face; (C)
J-II,1	130:7	13	65?	--	unident	inc; perforated; (C)
J-II,4	130:6	28	110	--	unident	comp; ground perimeter; (C)
Retouchers						
J-I,1-2	--	68	58	16	grnst	comp; center of faces used; (C)
J-I,8	131:3	(50)	(35)	9	serp	inc?; one end battered, pocked; (C)
J-I,8fl.	131:1	78	35	12	lmst?	comp; both ends pocked; (C)
J-II,2	--	100	25	--	unident	comp; one end used?; (B)
D19,5	131:4	70	23	10	lmst?	comp; both ends roughened, faces striated; fi?; (C)
RU1014,1	131:2	82	49	13	serp?	comp; both faces pecked around edges; (C)
Rubbing Stones (R), Polishing Stones (P), and Whetstones (W)						
J-I,sf-1	--	44	37	13	grnst	P; comp; bif; pecked edges; (C)
J-I,1-2	131:5	96	70	27	trav flnt	R; comp; unif?; uneven face; (C)
J-I,1-2	--	86	72	24	lmst cong	R; comp; unif?; (C)
J-I,1-2	--	(110)	58	25	lmst sa/cl	R?; inc; unif?; fi; (C)
J-I,1-2	--	63	--	--	lmst sa/cl	R?; inc; bif?; (C)
J-I,1-2	130:10	190	105	45	unident	P; comp; bif; fine striations; (C)
J-I,1-2	--	--	--	--	pumice?	R?; comp?; oval, thin; (B)
J-I,1-2	--	53	--	--	unident	R?; comp?; oval, flat pebble; (B)
J-I,2-3	--	(70)	45	28	lmst	R?; inc; bif?; (C)
J-I,2-3	--	(95)	58	18	lmst sa/cl	R?; inc; bif? unif?; split pebble; fi; (C)
J-I,2-3	--	100	80	18	lmst sa/cl	R; comp; bif?; center of one face pecked (C)
J-I,2-3	--	73	--	--	unident	W?; inc; planoconvex cross section; (B)
J-I,2-3	--	--	55	--	unident	R?; comp; round, flat stone; (B)
J-I,2-3	--	--	51	--	unident	R?; comp; round, flat pebble; (B)
J-I,2-3	--	--	50	--	flint?	P?; comp; faceted nodule; (B)
J-I,3	--	(58)	--	--	slate	R?; inc; unif?; (C)
J-I,3	--	(78)	30	18	lmst	R; inc; bif?; fi; (C)
J-I,3	--	(95)	110	30	lmst	R; inc; unif; (C)
J-I,3	--	(120)	70	25	lmst sa/cl	R?; inc; bif?; (C)
J-I,3	--	101	68	37	lmst sa/cl	R; comp; unif; (C)
J-I,3	--	29	--	--	lmst sa/cl	R?; inc; unif?; (C)
J-I,3	--	(102)	40	21	lmst sa/cl	R; inc; bif; thin pebble; (C)
J-I,3	--	(130)	78	17	lmst sa/cl	R; inc; bif?; fi on one end; split pebble; (C)
J-I,3	--	145	63	17	lmst sa/cl	R?; comp; unif?; (C)
J-I,3	--	(67)	60	28	lmst sa/cl	R; inc; unif; long pebble; (C)
J-I,3	--	(38)	--	--	lmst sa/cl	R; inc; unif; pebble end; (C)
J-I,3	--	--	--	--	lmst	W; inc; fi; (C)
J-I,3	--	--	72	--	unident	J-38; R; comp; (B)
J-I,3,pit 2	130:11	(118)	(93)	40	lmst sa/cl	W; inc; one face used; (C)
J-I,3,pit 2	131:6	68	43	18	lmst cong	R; comp; bif; pecked all over, center faces smoothed; (C)
J-I,3,pit 2	--	41	--	--	unident	R?; comp; oval, flat; (B)
J-I,3,pit 2	--	65	--	--	unident	R?; comp; oval, flat; (B)
J-I,3a	--	--	55	--	unident	R; comp; round, slightly faceted; (B)
J-I,3a	--	--	100?	--	unident	R?; inc; flattened discoid; (B)
J-I,3a	--	--	43	--	unident	R; comp; round, faceted; (B)

Context	Figure no.	L/gD (mm)	W/gD (mm)	Th/Wt (mm/gm)	Mineral	Remarks
Rubbing Stones, Polishing Stones, and Whetstones—*Continued*						
J-I,3a	--	--	--	--	unident	R; comp; round, faceted; (B)
J-I,3a	--	75	--	--	unident	R; comp; squarish; (B)
J-I,3-4	--	(63)	48	18	grnst	P; inc; (C)
J-I,4-5	--	63	57	20	marble	R?; comp; unif?; (C)
J-I,4-5	--	170	75	24	lmst sa/cl	R?; comp; unif?; split pebble; (C)
J-I,4-5	--	121	45	20	hrn sch	P; comp; edges pecked; (C)
J-I,4-5	131:10	(73)	47	15	lmst sa/cl	W; inc; (C)
J-I,4-5	--	--	55?	--	unident	R; comp; round; (B)
J-I,4-5	--	--	60?	--	unident	R; comp; round; (B)
J-I,4-5	--	105	--	--	unident	W?; inc; tapered plan; one face smoothed; (B)
J-I,5	--	88	82	24	lmst sa/cl	R?; comp; bif?; (C)
J-I,5	--	81	73	19	lmst sa/cl	R; comp; bif; one end squared off; (C)
J-I,5	--	(59)	69	22	lmst sa/cl	R; inc; bif?; (C)
J-I,5	--	119	101	36	lmst sa/cl?	R; comp; unif; (C)
J-I,6	--	71	60	25	lmst sa/cl	R; comp; unif; (C)
J-I,6	--	39	--	--	lmst	R?; inc; bif?; ochre? on one face; (C)
J-I,6	--	91	83	27	lmst sa/cl	R?; comp; bif?; ochre? on one face; (C)
J-I,6	--	--	--	20	lmst sa/cl	R; inc; unif; (C)
J-I,6	--	70	60	20	lmst	R; comp; bif; battered perimeter; ochre on one face; (C)
J-I,6	--	(66)	67	22	hrn sch	P; inc; bif; battered edges; (C)
J-I,6	--	--	--	--	pumice?	R; inc; (B)
J-I,6	--	--	--	--	unident	W?; comp; elongate, narrow, planoconvex cross section; (B)
J-I,6c	--	--	--	--	black	P and retoucher?; comp; flat cross section; (B)
J-I,6c	--	120	--	--	unident	W?; comp; elongate, narrow, planoconvex cross section; (B)
J-I,7	--	--	--	--	unident	R?; comp; long, flat, rounded rectangular pebble; (B)
J-I,7	--	--	--	--	black	P; comp; flat cross section; retoucher?; (B)
J-II,sf	--	85	--	--	lava	R; comp; squarish; (B)
J-II,1	--	(90)	--	--	lmst?	R; inc; unif; (C)
J-II,2	--	--	--	12	lmst sa/cl?	R; inc; bif?; small; (C)
J-II,2	--	80	--	--	unident	W?; comp; square, shaped edges; (B)
J-II,2fl.	--	130	--	--	unident	W?; elongate trapezoid, shaped edges; (B)
J-II,3	131:7	96	81	27	lmst cong?	R; comp; bif; (C)
J-II,4	130:12	140	130	28	lmst. sa/cl?	W; comp; concave face, 4 narrow grooves; (C)
J-II,4	130:9	106	117	97	unident	J2-317; unclassified; comp; (B)
J-II,4	--	60	--	--	unident	W?; comp; square, shaped edges; (B)
J-II,5	--	120?	--	--	unident	R; comp; long oblong; one end battered?; (B)
J-II,5	--	(42)	15	4	lmst sa/cl?	W; inc; rectangular; 4 faces used?; fi; (C)
J-II,6	--	120	--	--	unident	unclassified; comp; constricted handle; pecked; pestlelike; (B)
J-A,sf-1	--	100	75	18	lmst sa/cl	R; comp; bif; roughly shaped edges; (C)
J-B,sf-1	--	105	81	25	lmst cong	R; comp?; unif; (C)
J-B,sf-1	--	(63)	90	18	lmst sa/cl	R?; inc; bif?; (C)
J-B,sf-1	--	83	(52)	33	lmst sa/cl	R; inc; unif; (C)
J-B,sf-1	--	(55)	62	9	lmst sa/cl	R; inc; bif?; split pebble; (C)
J-B,sf-1	--	78	68	24	lmst	R?; comp; bif?; (C)
J-B,sf-1	--	145	115	53	lmst	R; comp; unif?; large; mullerlike pebble; (C)
J-B,1-2	--	--	--	29	lmst sa/cl	R; inc; unif; (C)
J-B,1-2	--	--	--	25	trav flnt	R; inc; unif; (C)
CF1519,3	--	--	25	12	chert?	P; comp; polished all over; small, round pebble; ochre on flat base; (C)
G20,2	131:11	(73)	25	30	lmst sa/cl?	W; inc; rectangular; 3 faces used; (C)

Context	Figure no.	Measurements			Mineral	Remarks
		L/gD (mm)	W/gD (mm)	Th/Wt (mm/gm)		

Rubbing Stones, Polishing Stones, and Whetstones—*Continued*

Context	Figure no.	L/gD (mm)	W/gD (mm)	Th/Wt (mm/gm)	Mineral	Remarks
G27,2	--	--	--	--	unident	R?; comp?; rounded square; (B)
GL1014,sf-1	--	68	50	28	lmst cong?	R?; comp; bif?; pecked edges; (C)
GL1519,1	--	50	35	--	chert?	P; comp; ground all over, polished areas around middle, some pecking (with ochre in pits); (C)
GL1519,2	131:8	68	65	20	serp?	P; comp; bif; battered thick edge, pecked faces; (C)
H11,3	--	102	33	22	serp?	R; comp; unif?; transverse striations; (C)
H15	--	105	--	--	unident	W?; comp; rectangular plaque, worked edges; (B)
H17,sf-1	--	78	50	14	lmst cong?	R; comp; bif; rectangular; (C)
M17,2	131:9	--	82	17	ves lav	R; comp; bif; disk; (C)
N18,5	--	(63)	44	24	lmst sa/cl?	R; inc; bif; long pebble, 2 notches on end; fi?; (C)
R14,3	140:2	54	45	--	unident	J3-33; unclassified; comp; knobbed, round; pitted gray stone; (B)
VY1014,4	--	115	81	25	pumice?	R; comp; bif?; oval; worked edges; (C)

Pecking and Rubbing Stones

Context	Figure no.	L/gD (mm)	W/gD (mm)	Th/Wt (gm)	Mineral	Remarks
J-I,2-3	141:3	43	52	172	lmst cong	comp; roughly squared to 48 mm; (C)
J-I,3	--	(58)	--	--	grnst	inc; (C)
J-I,3a	140:3	42	72	364	lmst cong	comp; (C)
J-I,5	--	52	82	482	lmst cong	comp; (C)
J-I,5	--	50	45	175	diab	comp; (C)
J-I,6	130:13	47	62	311	bt grnst	comp; parallel striations; (C)
J-I,6	130:14	34	41	98	diab	comp; roughly squared to 38 mm; (C)
J-I,7	--	33	40	88	diab?	comp; roughly squared to 37 mm; (C)
J-I,7	--	25	--	--	unident	comp; (B)
J-I,8	--	35	--	--	unident	comp; (B)
J-II,1	--	44	54	213	diab?	comp; roughly squared to 48 mm; (C)
J-II,1	--	40	--	--	unident	comp; (B)

Grooved Stones

Context	Figure no.	L/gD (mm)	W/gD (mm)	Th/Wt (mm)	Mineral	Remarks
J-I,dmp	--	58	--	--	schist?	inc; (B)
J-I,7	--	57	--	--	schist?	inc; (B)
J-I,8fl.	--	(74)	(21)	26	schist?	inc; (C)
J-II,1	131:13	90	(56)	19	hrn sch?	J2-28; inc; (C)
J-D,sf-1m	--	--	--	14	serp	inc; (C)
G20,2	131:14; 140:7	74	56	29	unident	J3-23; comp; (B)
PQ14,1	131:12	53	30	14	schist?	comp; (C)

Whorls

Context	Figure no.	L/gD (mm)	W/gD (mm)	Th/Wt (mm)	Mineral	Remarks
J-I,sf-1	--	--	68	--	unident	J-7; comp; incomplete perforations; (B)
J-I,6c	131:17	11	45	--	lmst	comp; (C)
J-I,6c	--	6	60	--	lmst sa/cl	comp; edges chipped; (C)
J-I,6	--	(12)	70?	--	lmst	inc; edges ground and battered; (C)
J-I,8-9	131:15	(8)	56	--	lmst sa/cl?	comp?; edges unmodified? (see p. 294 and J-A,IV, below); fi; (C)
J-II,2	140:6	--	42	--	unident	J2-246; inc; (B)
J-A,IV	131:16	8	88	--	lmst sa/cl	comp; edges ground; (C)
J-A,IV	--	(8)	56	--	lmst sa/cl?	comp?; edges unmodified? (see p. 294 and J-I,8-9, above); fi; (C)
K14,2	--	--	80	--	unident	J3-94; comp; vessel sherd, rewkd; oval; off-center perforation; whorl?; (B)
K21,2	--	9	56	--	lmst sa/cl	J3-93; comp; edges ground?; (C)

Unperforated Disks

Context	Figure no.	L/gD (mm)	W/gD (mm)	Th/Wt (mm)	Mineral	Remarks
J-I,1-2	--	7	70?	--	lmst sa/cl	inc; only edges ground; (C)
J-I,1-2	--	7	49	--	lmst sa/cl	comp; oval (breadth, 36 mm); (C)
J-I,3-4	--	--	50	--	unident	J-52; comp; (B)
J-I,6	--	9	54	--	lmst sa/cl	comp; oval (breadth, 43 mm); (C)

		Measurements				
Context	Figure no.	L/gD (mm)	W/gD (mm)	Th/Wt (mm/gm)	Mineral	Remarks
Unperforated Disks—Continued						
J-I,6	--	5	55	--	cal lmst	comp; (C)
J-I,7	--	10	46	--	lmst sa/cl	comp; oval (breadth, 37 mm); (C)
J-I,8	131:18	15	68	--	cal lmst	comp; (C)
J-II,6	--	--	90?	--	unident	comp; (B)
Digging-Stick Weights or Maceheads						
J-sf	--	115	--	--	unident	comp; pecked only; (B)
J-I,dmp	132:2	60	95	--	marble?	J2-44; comp; unfinished?; one side stained; (C)
J-I,3	--	82	--	--	unident	J-35; comp; polished; (B)
J-I,5	--	100?	--	--	unident	comp; ground and polished; (B)
J-I,6	--	60	117	--	marble	comp; unfinished?; (C)
J-I,6	132:3	40	95	--	marble	comp; (C)
J-II,W,sf-3	--	50	110?	--	marble?	inc; vertical and diagonal reaming in perforation; (C)
J-II,1	--	75	(140)	--	unident	inc; ground; (B)
J-II,2	132:5	62	(77)	--	marble?	J2-220; inc; all-over polish; (C)
J-II,2	132:4	50	72	--	marble?	J2-239; comp; battered side; (C)
J-II,4	132:8; 140:4	47	72	--	unident	J2-318; comp; (B)
J-II,5	132:6; 140:5	40	78	--	unident	J2-398; inc; carinated, ends collared; (B)
J-II,6	132:1	50	90	--	marble?	comp; (C)
N18,5	--	41	63	--	unident	comp; slightly carinated; (B)
Large Drill Bits						
J-I,2-3	--	--	--	--	unident	comp; similar to J3-29 (below); (B)
M20,2	--	65	--	--	unident	comp; similar to J3-29 (below); (B)
MQ1519,sf-1	132:7; 140:8	76	62	34	sandst?	J3-29; comp; (C)
Small Borers and/or Small Pestles (Note: The forms of subtypes a-d under Remarks are described on p. 295)						
J-I,sf	--	(29)	21	--	lmst?	b; inc; (C)
J-I,dmp	133:1	66	8	--	lmst?	J2-56; a; comp; transverse striations; (C)
J-I,sf-1	--	82	--	--	unident	J-6; b?; comp; (B)
J-I,1-2	--	(55)	25	--	lmst sa/cl	c; inc; battered, transverse striations; (C)
J-I,3	--	(39)	--	--	unident	J-13; c?; inc; (B)
J-I,3	133:7	49	18	--	unident	J-21; b?; comp; (B)
J-I,3	--	49	--	--	unident	J-40; b?; comp; (B)
J-I,3a	133:10	108	31	--	unident	J-59; b?; comp; (B)
J-I,3a	--	67	10	--	unident	J-63; a?; comp; (B)
J-I,3-4	--	82	19	--	unident	J-53; c?; comp; (B)
J-I,6	--	20	7	--	lmst?	d; comp; transverse striations; (C)
J-I,6	--	25	13	--	lmst?	d; comp; (C)
J-I,7	--	23	12	--	lmst?	d; comp; transverse and diagonal striations; (C)
J-I,7	--	38	--	--	unident	J2-212; d; comp; rewkd vessel rim sherd; (B)
J-I,8fl.	133:13	39	11	--	lmst?	d; comp; transverse striations?; (C)
J-II,1	133:11	43	17	--	marble?	b; comp; fi; (C)
J-II,1	133:2	(36)	10	--	lmst?	J2-294; a; inc; (C)
J-II,1	133:9; 140:17	74	25	--	unident	J2-25; b?; comp; (B)
J-II,2	--	(24)	14	--	lmst?	b; inc; (C)
J-II,2	133:8; 140:16	70	21	--	marble	J2-235; c; comp; perimeter battered; ground?; (C)
J-II,2fl.	--	(40)	13	--	marble?	a; inc; (C)
J-II,2fl.	--	(27)	16	--	marble?	a; inc; (C)
J-II,2fl.	133:6; 140:14	35	19	--	marble?	J2-273; c; comp; perimeter battered; striated; (C)
J-II,3	133:3	56	14	--	marble?	a; comp; (C)
J-II,3	--	43	13	--	marble?	c; comp; bases ground, tip striated; (C)
J-II,4	--	47	19	--	marble?	c; comp; base battered; (C)
J-II,5	--	(29)	14	--	marble?	a; inc; (C)
J-II,5	--	(31)	10	--	lmst?	b?; inc; parallel vertical striations; (C)

Context	Figure no.	Measurements			Mineral	Remarks
		L/gD (mm)	W/gD (mm)	Th/Wt (mm/gm)		
Small Borers and/or Small Pestles—*Continued*						
J-II,5	--	(46)	9	--	marble?	*a*; inc; (C)
J-II,5	--	(29)	18	--	marble?	*b*; inc; (C)
J-II,5	133:12	47	15	--	lmst?	*c*; comp; (C)
J-II,6	--	(32)	15	--	marble?	*a*; inc; (C)
J-II,6	140:15	42	14	--	marble	*a*?; comp; (B)
J-III,sf-1	--	(19)	--	--	unident	*J2-90*; *b*?; inc; (B)
J-A,3m	--	(47)	27	--	lmst	*b*; inc; fi?; (C)
J-D,1fl.	133:5	(56)	29	--	marble	*b*; inc; broken and reused?; (C)
CF2024,1	--	(20)	17	--	marble?	*b*?; inc; (C)
GL1014,2	--	(50)	17	--	marble?	*b*; inc; (C)
K18,1	--	(42)	21	--	marble?	*b*; inc; (C)
N18,4	133:4	(56)	21	--	lmst	*J3-28*; *a*; inc; battered break on top; (C)
N18,4	--	59	--	--	unident	*J3-25*; *b*?; comp; (B)
P16,sf-1	--	--	--	--	unident	*a*?; inc; (B)
W11,1	--	(50)	21	--	marble?	*b*; inc; small pit drilled into base; fi?: (C)
L19,sf-1	--	(40)	17	--	marble?	*b*; inc; (C)
Curved and Humped Objects						
J-I,8	133:14	(30)	8	--	marble?	inc; (C)
J-I,8fl.	--	(19)	9	--	marble	inc; (C)
J-II,6	133:15	22	9	--	marble?	comp; (C)
GL59,sf-1	--	32	9	--	marble?	comp; (C)
Celts and Chisels						
J-I,sf	--	(57)	20	11	unident	inc; chipped and ground; (C)
J-I,sf	--	(47)	26	14	chl	inc; (C)
J-I,sf	--	59	27	10	chl	comp; chipped and ground; (C)
J-I,sf	--	84	58	38	unident	comp; pounder, reused; (C)
J-I,sf	--	58	33	22	chl	comp; (C)
J-I,sf	--	(71)	43	23	serp	inc; badly battered; (C)
J-I,sf	--	79	40	34	unident	comp; (C)
J-I,sf	--	(48)	39	17	unident	inc; rewkd?; (C)
J-I,sf	--	76	56	19	unident	comp; unfinished?; (C)
J-I,sf	--	38	21	15	chl?	comp; (C)
J-I,sf	--	28	20	9	grn neph	comp; straight edge, faceted; (C)
J-I,sf-1	--	85	40	--	unident	*J-11*; inc; rewkd bit; (B)
J-I,1-2	--	--	--	--	unident	comp?; adzelike; (B)
J-I,3	--	62	41	--	unident	*J-12*; comp; (B)
J-I,3	--	46	19	12	unident	comp; rewkd, chipped and ground; (C)
J-I,3	--	(26)	22	15	unident	inc; (C)
J-I,3	--	(27)	23	16	chl	inc; (C)
J-I,3	--	(23)	17	15	unident	inc; faceted sides unfinished; (C)
J-I,3a	--	--	--	--	unident	comp?; (B)
J-I,3-4	--	65	52	--	unident	*J-51*; comp; (B)
J-I,7	--	58	--	--	unident	comp; (B)
J-I,8	134:6	66	17	9	unident	comp; all-over grinding; possibly rewkd vessel sherd; chisel; (B)
J-I,8	141:12	67	8?	--	unident	*J2-283*; comp; chisel (same as above); (B)
J-I,8	--	(21)	(10)	7	unident	inc; (C)
J-I,8fl.	--	67	45	20	unident	comp; chipped and ground, unfinished; (C)
J-I,8fl.	--	48	40	8	unident	*J2-315*; comp?; (B)
J-II,W,sf-3	141:15	83	44	35	unident	comp; adze?; (C)
J-II,W,sf-3	--	--	--	--	unident	comp; bitumen traces on butt; (B)
J-II,1	134:5	(78)	31	24	unident	*J2-17*; inc; (B)
J-II,1	--	104	58	31	unident	*J2-27*; comp; rewkd?, bit end rough; (B)
J-II,1	--	75	39	24	unident	*J2-37*; comp; reused as pounder; (B)
J-II,1	--	35	33	8	unident	*J2-43*; comp; (B)
J-II,1	--	(37)	21	13	unident	*J2-46*; inc; (B)
J-II,1	134:9	60	36	21	unident	*J2-102*; comp; (B)
J-II,1	--	32	28	9	unident	*J2-160*; comp; (B)

314 PREHISTORIC ARCHEOLOGY ALONG THE ZAGROS FLANKS

Context	Figure no.	Measurements			Mineral	Remarks
		L/gD (mm)	W/gD (mm)	Th/Wt (mm/gm)		
Celts and Chisels—Continued						
J-II,1	--	47	41	16	unident	J2-176; comp; (B)
J-II,1	--	48	22	15	unident	comp; chipped only; (C)
J-II,1	--	101	56	30	unident	J2-35; comp; somewhat adzelike; (C)
J-II,1	--	79	53	30	unident	J2-225; comp; reused as pounder; (C)
J-II,1	--	91	55	29	unident	J2-135; comp; reused as pounder; (C)
J-II,1	134:8	40	38	17	unident	J2-94; comp; (C)
J-II,1	141:9	43	27	13	serp?	J2-36; comp; chipped and ground; (C)
J-II,1	--	(21)	19	9	flint?	inc; unfinished; (C)
J-II,2	--	38	17	13	chl?	J2-199; comp; chipped and ground; (C)
J-II,2	--	72	41	24	unident	J2-205; comp; battered; (C)
J-II,2	--	74	43	26	unident	J2-208; comp; (C)
J-II,2	--	(34)	24	15	unident	inc; small frag; celt?; (C)
J-II,2	134:1	26	10	8	unident	J2-202; comp; (C)
J-II,2	--	33	16	15	chert?	J2-272; comp; (C)
J-II,2	141:7	57	35	19	serp?	J2-191; comp; (C)
J-II,2	134:7	27	22	8	chl?	J2-262; comp; (C)
J-II,2fl.	134:4	42	18	13	unident	J2-296; comp; (C)
J-II,2fl.	--	36	14	9	unident	J2-284; comp; (B)
J-II,3?	141:13	(68)	45	25	unident	inc; transverse groove, bit and butt battered; (C)
J-II,3	--	46	(28)	14	unident	inc; (C)
J-II,3	--	55	29	17	unident	comp; battered, rewkd; (C)
J-II,4	--	24	12	4	unident	comp; small, crude; (C)
J-II,5	--	(44)	16	16	chert?	inc; (C)
J-II,5	--	33	20	10	unident	comp; crude, rewkd?; (C)
J-II,6	141:8	40	43	17	unident	comp; (C)
J-III,sf-1	--	(69)	51	27	unident	inc; (C)
J-III,sf-1	--	43	39	19	unident	comp?; (C)
J-III,sf-1	--	(84)	41	34	unident	J2-113; comp?; (B)
J-III,sf-1	134:3	32	17	9	unident	J2-125; comp; (B)
J-A,IV	--	44	34	14	unident	comp; chipped and ground; battered butt; (C)
GL1014,sf-1	--	(29)	(23)	12	unident	inc; (C)
GL1519,3	--	43	25	12	chl	comp; (C)
H19,2	--	42	17	12	unident	comp; (C)
K14,1	--	(81)	45	21	unident	inc?; unfinished?; (C)
K21,7	--	--	--	--	unident	comp; (B)
L21,2	--	--	--	--	unident	comp; rounded chisel end; (B)
M16,sf	--	35	17	18	unident	comp; (C)
M17,3	--	--	--	--	unident	comp; (B)
MQ1519,1	--	(70)	42	33	unident	inc; adze?; (C)
MQ1519,2	--	200?	--	--	unident	comp?; unusually large; (B)
N17,4	--	48	33	13	marble?	comp; polished; adze?; (C)
P17,3	--	32	22	9	unident	J3-35; comp; (C)
PQ14,4	141:10	31	17	8	unident	comp; V-shaped diagonal groove on each face; (C)
Q15,3	--	--	--	--	unident	comp; (B)
RU1014,sf-1	141:14	73	32	18	unident	J3-26; comp; dull, patinated?; chipped but only slightly ground; unfinished?; (C)
RU1014,sf-1	--	--	--	--	unident	inc; (B)
RU1014,2	--	--	--	--	unident	inc; (B)
RU1014,4	--	(79)	62	32	unident	inc; butt repecked; (C)
RU1519,3	--	64	26	11	unident	comp; (C)
S15,sf-1	--	--	--	--	unident	comp; (B)
T12,sf-1	--	32	24	14	unident	J3-27; comp; (B)
T16,4	134:2; 141:11	26	10	8	dk grn	comp; (C)
Doorpost Pivot Stones						
J-II,1	--	253	96	99	sandst?	J2-221; comp; upper unit; (B)

Context	Figure no.	Measurements			Mineral	Remarks
		L/gD (mm)	W/gD (mm)	Th/Wt (mm/gm)		
Doorpost Pivot Stones—*Continued*						
J-II,2fl.	138:3; 140:13	420	--	125	lmst?	comp; slablike; lower unit; (B)
J-II,4	138:1; 140:12	(420)	130	72	lmst?	J2-375; comp?; upper unit; (C)
HK16,2	--	330	--	185	lmst?	comp; lower unit?; (B)
K16,1	140:11	381	154	120	lmst?	comp; upper unit; (B)
Unfinished Round Stone Blanks						
GL1519,sf-1	132:9	73	139	--	lmst	comp; pecked; (C)
MQ1519,sf-1	138:2	59	108	--	alabas	comp; ground; (C)

Context	Figure no.	Inner diameter (mm)	Width (mm)	Mineral*	Remarks
Bracelets and Rings (Note: The types *a-f* under Remarks are described on p. 297.)					
J-I,dmp	--	70	6	unident	*b*; inc; (C)
J-I,dmp	--	50	12	unident	*b*; inc; (C)
J-I,dmp	--	50	13	unident	*b*; inc; (C)
J-I,dmp	--	50	14	unident	*b*; inc; (C)
J-I,sf	--	40	11	unident	*b*; inc; (C)
J-I,sf	--	70	11	unident	*b*; inc; (C)
J-I,sf	--	40	11	gray	*b*; inc; one end ground; (C)
J-I,sf	--	80	12	unident	*b*; inc; partial perforation; (C)
J-I,sf	--	70	14	unident	*b*; inc; one end ground; (C)
J-I,sf	--	80	14	unident	*b*; inc; (C)
J-I,sf	--	80	16	unident	*f*; inc; (C)
J-I,sf	135:20	--	22	unident	*f*; inc; outer diameter, ca. 100 mm; (C)
J-I,sf-1	--	70	7	gray	*b*; inc; (C)
J-I,sf-1	--	40	10	unident	*b*; inc; (C)
J-I,sf-1	--	100	10	unident	*b*; inc; (C)
J-I,sf-1	135:22	50	18	unident	*f*; inc; unfinished; (C)
J-I,sf-1	--	--	--	unident	J-9; *b*; inc; (B)
J-I,2	--	60	17	unident	*b*; inc; (C)
J-I,2	--	70	8	unident	*b*; inc; (C)
J-I,2	--	--	--	unident	*a*; inc; broken at mend hole; (B)
J-I,3	--	70	9	unident	*b*; inc; (C)
J-I,3	--	70	10	unident	*b*; inc; (C)
J-I,3	--	50	11	unident	*b*; inc; (C)
J-I,3	--	70	13	unident	*b*; inc; (C)
J-I,3	--	--	14	unident	*b*; inc; both ends ground; (C)
J-I,3	135:4; 142:23	70	14	unident	J2-53; *b*; (C)
J-I,3	--	80	16	gray	*b*; inc; (C)
J-I,3	--	--	22	unident	J-20; unclassified; inc; long, thin, rectangular section, somewhat bowed; (B)
J-I,3	--	--	19	unident	J-23; *b*?; inc; (B)
J-I,3,pit 2	--	--	--	unident	*b*; inc; (B)
J-I,3,pit 2	--	--	--	unident	*b*; inc; (B)
J-I,3?	--	--	--	unident	*b*?; inc; planoconvex; (B)
J-I,3-4	--	50	13	unident	*b*; inc; (C)
J-I,4	--	60	6	unident	*b*; inc; (C)
J-I,4	--	--	8	unident	*b*; inc; (C)
J-I,4	--	--	19	unident	J-67; *d*; inc; rewkd end, 2 probable mend holes near it; (B)
J-I,4	--	--	--	unident	*b*; inc; (B)
J-I,5	--	50	9	unident	*b*; inc; (C)
J-I,5	--	--	9	unident	*b*; inc; (C)
J-I,5	--	80	9	unident	*b*; inc; (C)

*With few exceptions, the material used for these objects appears to be a whitish-colored marble; in a few cases, other colors are noted.

Context	Figure no.	Inner diameter (mm)	Width (mm)	Mineral	Remarks
Bracelets and Rings—*Continued*					
J-I,5	--	80	10	unident	*b*; inc; (C)
J-I,5	--	70	11	unident	*b*; inc; (C)
J-I,5	--	90	12	unident	*b*; inc; (C)
J-I,6	--	60	22	unident	*a*; inc; (C)
J-I,6	--	40	7	gray	*b*; inc; (C)
J-I,6	--	70	7	unident	*b*; inc; (C)
J-I,6	--	50	8	unident	*b*; inc; (C)
J-I,6	--	60	8	unident	*b*; inc; (C)
J-I,6	--	50	9	unident	*b*; inc; (C)
J-I,6	135:24	70	9	unident	*b*; inc; incised, both ends ground, sectioned for beads?; (C)
J-I,6	--	80	10	unident	*b*; inc; both ends ground; (C)
J-I,6	--	80	11	unident	*b*; inc; both ends ground, incised; (C)
J-I,6	--	60	13	unident	*J2-76*; *b*; inc; (C)
J-I,6	135:14	60	13	unident	*d*?; inc; (C)
J-I,6	135:17	20	2	unident	*e*; inc; (C)
J-I,6	135:18	20	8	unident	*e*; inc; (C)
J-I,6	--	--	--	unident	*b*; inc; (B)
J-I,6	--	--	--	unident	*a*?; inc; 2 frags fitting together, perforations either side of break, elliptical cross section; (B)
J-I,6a	--	20?	6	unident	*J2-74*; *e*; inc; (B)
J-I,7	--	25	9	unident	*b*; inc; one end ground; (C)
J-I,7	--	--	12	unident	*b*; inc; both ends ground; (C)
J-I,7	--	19	9	unident	*d*; inc; (C)
J-I,7fl.	--	100	7	gray	*b*; inc; (C)
J-I,8	135:8	70	6	unident	*b*; inc; (C)
J-I,8	--	100	7	unident	*b*; inc; (C)
J-I,8	--	40	8	unident	*b*; inc; both ends ground; (C)
J-I,8	--	40	10	unident	*b*; inc; (C)
J-I,8	--	80	10	unident	*b*; inc; one end ground; (C)
J-I,8	--	80	11	unident	*b*; inc; incised; (C)
J-I,8	--	70	12	unident	*b*; inc; (C)
J-I,8	--	--	16	unident	*f*; inc; outer diameter, 80 mm; (C)
J-I,8	142:21	--	24	unident	*f*; inc; outer diameter, 90 mm; (C)
J-I,8	--	--	28	unident	*f*; inc; outer diameter, 130 mm; (C)
J-I,8fl.	135:15; 142:25	--	20	unident	*J2-314*; *d*; inc; (B)
J-II,sf	--	100	6	unident	*b*; inc; (C)
J-II,sf	--	70	6	unident	*J2-3*; *b*; inc; (C)
J-II,sf	--	70	7	unident	*b*; inc; (C)
J-II,sf	--	80	7	unident	*b*; inc; (C)
J-II,sf	--	--	9	unident	*b*; inc; one end ground, partial perforation; (C)
J-II,sf	--	60	9	unident	*b*; inc; (C)
J-II,sf	--	90	10	unident	*b*; inc; (C)
J-II,sf	--	60	12	unident	*b*; inc; (C)
J-II,sf	--	60	12	unident	*b*; inc; (C)
J-II,sf	--	60	13	unident	*b*; inc; (C)
J-II,sf	--	--	16	unident	*b*; inc; one end ground; (C)
J-II,sf	--	80	21	unident	*J2-1*; *a*; inc; (B)
J-II,sf	--	100	9	unident	*J2-2*; *b*; inc; (B)
J-II,W,sf-3	--	50	9	unident	*b*; inc; one end ground; (C)
J-II,W,sf-3	--	80	14	unident	*b*; inc; (C)
J-II,W,sf-3	--	80	17	unident	*b*; inc; both ends ground; (C)
J-II,W,sf-3	--	--	--	unident	*b*; inc; (B)
J-II,W,sf-3	--	--	--	unident	*b*; inc; (B)
J-II,W,sf-3	--	30?	--	unident	*f*; inc; (B)
J-II,1	--	70	10	unident	*J2-15*; *b*; inc; one end ground; sectioned for beads?; (B)
J-II,1	--	70	9	unident	*J2-19*; *b*; inc; (B)

Context	Figure no.	Inner diameter (mm)	Width (mm)	Mineral	Remarks
Bracelets and Rings—*Continued*					
J-II,1	--	50	8	unident	J2-20; b; inc; (B)
J-II,1	--	60	16	unident	J2-39; f; inc; (B)
J-II,1	--	80	14	unident	J2-81; b; inc; (B)
J-II,1	--	40	18	unident	J2-121; b; inc; (B)
J-II,1	142:29	60	10	unident	J2-134; c; inc; (B)
J-II,1	--	60	8	unident	J2-139; a; inc; (C)
J-II,1	--	50	18	unident	a; inc; (C)
J-II,1	--	80	18	unident	a; inc; (C)
J-II,1	--	--	--	unident	b; inc; (C)
J-II,1	135:6	70	6	unident	b; inc; (C)
J-II,1	--	--	7	unident	b; inc; (C)
J-II,1	--	40	7	unident	b; inc; (C)
J-II,1	--	40	7	unident	b; inc; (C)
J-II,1	--	70	7	unident	b; inc; (C)
J-II,1	--	70	7	unident	b; inc; (C)
J-II,1	--	--	7	unident	b; inc; (C)
J-II,1	--	50	7	unident	b; inc; (C)
J-II,1	--	60	7	unident	b; inc; (C)
J-II,1	--	70	7	unident	b; inc; (C)
J-II,1	--	80	7	unident	b; inc; (C)
J-II,1	--	70	8	unident	b; inc; (C)
J-II,1	--	80	8	unident	J2-16; b; inc; (C)
J-II,1	--	80	8	unident	b; inc; (C)
J-II,1	--	60	8	unident	b; inc; (C)
J-II,1	--	70	8	unident	b; inc; (C)
J-II,1	--	70	8	unident	b; inc; (C)
J-II,1	--	40	9	unident	b; inc; (C)
J-II,1	--	70	9	unident	b; inc; (C)
J-II,1	--	90	9	unident	b; inc; incised; (C)
J-II,1	--	60	10	unident	b; inc; (C)
J-II,1	--	70	10	unident	b; inc; (C)
J-II,1	--	80	10	unident	b; inc; (C)
J-II,1	--	50	10	unident	b; inc; (C)
J-II,1	--	70	10	unident	b; inc; (C)
J-II,1	--	70	11	unident	b; inc; (C)
J-II,1	--	90	11	unident	b; inc; one end ground; (C)
J-II,1	--	70	12	unident	b; inc; (C)
J-II,1	--	--	13	unident	b; inc; (C)
J-II,1	--	80	13	unident	b; inc; (C)
J-II,1	--	110	16	unident	b; inc; (C)
J-II,1	135:9	80	12	unident	J2-73; c; inc; (C)
J-II,1	--	100	19	unident	d; inc; (C)
J-II,1	135:12	100	20	unident	d; inc; (C)
J-II,1	--	60	16	unident	J2-167; f; inc; (C)
J-II,2	--	80	17	unident	a; inc; (C)
J-II,2	--	70	22	unident	a; inc; (C)
J-II,2	135:3; 142:22	70	23	unident	a; inc; (C)
J-II,2	--	80	6	unident	b; inc; (C)
J-II,2	--	100	6	unident	b; inc; (C)
J-II,2	--	50	7	unident	b; inc; (C)
J-II,2	--	70	7	unident	b; inc; (C)
J-II,2	--	60	7	unident	b; inc; (C)
J-II,2	--	60	8	unident	b; inc; (C)
J-II,2	--	60	8	unident	b; inc; (C)
J-II,2	--	70	8	unident	b; inc; (C)
J-II,2	--	50	9	unident	b; inc; (C)
J-II,2	--	80	9	unident	b; inc; one end ground; (C)
J-II,2	--	60	9	unident	b; inc; (C)
J-II,2	--	70	10	unident	b; inc; (C)

Context	Figure no.	Inner diameter (mm)	Width (mm)	Mineral	Remarks
Bracelets and Rings—*Continued*					
J-II,2	--	70	10	unident	*b*; inc; (C)
J-II,2	--	70	14	unident	*b*; inc; (C)
J-II,2	--	90	20	unident	J2-256; *a*; inc; mend hole or rewkd into pendant?; (B)
J-II,2fl.	--	60	6	unident	*b*; inc; (C)
J-II,2fl.	--	60	7	unident	*b*; inc; (C)
J-II,2fl.	--	70	7	unident	*b*; inc; (C)
J-II,2fl.	--	70	7	unident	*b*; inc; (C)
J-II,2fl.	--	50	7	unident	*b*; inc; (C)
J-II,2fl.	--	60	9	unident	*b*; inc; (C)
J-II,2fl.	--	70	9	unident	*b*; inc; (C)
J-II,2fl.	--	80	10	unident	*b*; inc; (C)
J-II,2fl.	--	60	10	unident	*b*; inc; (C)
J-II,2fl.	135:11; 142:24	40	9	unident	J2-290; *d*; inc; (C)
J-II,2fl.	--	--	15	unident	*f*; inc; greatest outer diameter, 90 mm; (C)
J-II,3	--	70	17	unident	*a*; inc; (C)
J-II,3	--	70	18	unident	*a*; inc; (C)
J-II,3	--	80	6	unident	*b*; inc; (C)
J-II,3	--	70	7	unident	*b*; inc; (C)
J-II,3	--	--	8	unident	*b*; inc; (C)
J-II,3	--	50	9	unident	*b*; inc; (C)
J-II,3	--	--	9	unident	*b*; inc; (C)
J-II,3	--	80	9	unident	*b*; inc; (C)
J-II,3	--	80	10	unident	*b*; inc; (C)
J-II,3	--	100	9	unident	*b*; inc; (C)
J-II,3	--	60	11	unident	*b*; inc; (C)
J-II,4	--	70	14	unident	*a*; inc; (C)
J-II,4	--	70	8	unident	*b*; inc; (C)
J-II,5	135:7	70	9	unident	*b*; inc; (C)
J-II,5	--	70	9	unident	*b*; inc; (C)
J-II,5	--	70	10	unident	*b*; inc; (C)
J-II,5	--	70	10	unident	*b*; inc; (C)
J-II,5	--	80	10	unident	*b*; inc; (C)
J-II,5	--	60	13	unident	*b*; inc; (C)
J-II,5	--	60	9	tan	J2-406; *d*; inc; unfinished; concave; (C)
J-II,5	--	70	15	unident	*f*; inc; (C)
J-II,6	--	--	10	unident	*b*; inc; both ends ground; (C)
J-II,6	--	120	12	unident	*b*; inc; notched; (C)
J-III,sf	--	60	9	unident	*b*; inc; (C)
J-III,sf	--	70	10	unident	*b*; inc; (C)
J-III,sf-1	--	70	18	tan	J2-124; *a*; inc; (C)
J-III,sf-1	--	60	13	unident	*a*; inc; (C)
J-III,sf-1	--	--	9	unident	*b*; inc; one end ground; (C)
J-III,sf-1	--	60	10	gray	*b*; inc; (C)
J-III,sf-1	--	60	12	unident	J2-114; *b*; inc; (C)
J-III,sf-1	--	80	12	unident	*b*; inc; one end ground; (C)
J-III,sf-1	--	70	13	unident	*b*; inc; (C)
J-III,sf-1	--	70	10	unident	J2-91; *c*; inc; (C)
J-III,sf-1	--	60	11	unident	J2-87; *f*; inc; (C)
J-A,sf-1	--	60	6	unident	*b*; inc; one end ground; (C)
J-A,3m	--	90	5	unident	*b*; inc; (C)
J-A,3m	--	90	7	unident	*b*; inc; (C)
J-A,3m	--	60	8	unident	*b*; inc; (C)
J-A,3m	--	70	8	unident	*b*; inc; (C)
J-A,3m	--	70	8	unident	*b*; inc; (C)
J-A,3m	--	70	8	unident	*b*; inc; (C)
J-A,3m	--	70	9	unident	*b*; inc; (C)
J-A,3m	--	70	9	unident	*b*; inc; (C)
J-A,3m	--	90	10	unident	*b*; inc; (C)

Context	Figure no.	Inner diameter (mm)	Width (mm)	Mineral	Remarks
Bracelets and Rings—Continued					
J-A,3m	--	40	12	unident	*b*; inc; (C)
J-A,3m	--	100	13	unident	*b*; inc; (C)
J-A,3m	--	80	16	unident	*b*; inc; (C)
J-A,3m	135:23	70	16	unident	*f*; inc; unfinished; (C)
J-A,III	--	80	7	unident	*b*; inc; (C)
J-A,III	--	90	9	unident	*b*; inc; (C)
J-A,III-1	--	80	31	unident	*a*; inc; (C)
J-A,III-1	--	50	10	unident	*b*; inc; (C)
J-A,III-1	--	--	7	unident	*b*; inc; grooved; (C)
J-A,III-1	--	70	12	unident	*b*; inc; (C)
J-A,III-1	135:10; 142:28	50	13	unident	J2-312; *c*; inc; herringbone incisions; (B)
J-C,sf-1	--	--	--	unident	unclassified; inc; T-shaped cross section; (B)
J-C,sf-1	--	25	20	blu/gry	*a*; inc; (C)
J-C,sf-1	--	70	12	blu/gry	*b*; inc; (C)
J-D,1fl.	--	40	--	pink	*a*; inc; (C)
CF1519,sf-1	--	80	26	blu/gry	*a*; inc; (C)
CF1519,sf-1	--	80	--	unident	*b*; inc; (C)
CF2024,sf-1	--	60	9	unident	*b*; inc; (C)
CF2024,sf-1	--	60	9	unident	*b*; inc; perforated; (C)
CF2529,1	135:16	30	16	red/yl	*f*; inc; (C)
CF2529,2	--	60	9	unident	*b*; inc; (C)
F17,1	135:2	30	31	blu/gry	*a*; inc; (C)
GL1014,2	--	90	11	unident	*b*; inc; (C)
GL1014,2	--	--	--	unident	*b*?; inc; (B)
GL1014,3	--	70	8	unident	*b*; inc; (C)
GL1519,sf-1	135:5	70	8	unident	*b*; inc; (C)
GL1519,sf-1	--	70	8	unident	*b*; inc; (C)
GL1519,2	--	70	11	unident	*b*; inc; (C)
GL1519,3	--	60	7	unident	*b*; inc; (C)
GL1519,3	--	70	16	gray	*f*; inc; (C)
GL1519,5	--	70	8	unident	*b*; inc; (C)
GL2024,1	--	--	--	unident	*d*; inc; (B)
GL2024,1	--	30	21	blk/wh	*a*; inc; (C)
GL2024,2	--	50	8	unident	*b*; inc; (C)
GL2024,3	--	60	7	unident	*b*; inc; (C)
GL2024,3	--	70	8	unident	*b*; inc; (C)
GL2024,3	--	35	8	blu/gry/wh	*d*; inc; unfinished; concave; (C)
GL2024,3	--	18	6	gray	*e*; inc; (C)
H16,sf-1	--	70	9	unident	*b*; inc; (C)
H16,sf-1	--	70	10	unident	*b*; inc; (C)
H21,2	--	30	28	unident	J3-34; *a*; inc; (C)
K12,3	--	80	17	unident	*a*; inc; (C)
K19,2	--	50	7	unident	*b*; inc; (C)
K25,2	--	--	--	unident	*a*?; inc; (B)
L24,1	--	20	34	red	*a*; inc; (C)
M17,2	--	--	--	unident	*b*?; inc; narrow encircling incision; probably rewkd; (B)
M18,1	--	--	--	unident	*b*; inc; (B)
M18,2	--	--	--	unident	*b*; inc; (C)
M20,sf-1	--	80	14	unident	*f*; inc; perforated; (C)
M20,2	--	--	--	unident	*b*; inc; (B)
MQ1014,3	--	--	--	unident	*b*; inc; (B)
MQ1519,sf	--	--	--	unident	*b*?; inc; (B)
MQ1519,sf-1	--	--	--	unident	*b*; inc; (B)
MQ1519,1	--	--	--	unident	*b*?; inc; (B)
MQ1519,1	--	--	--	unident	*b*?; inc; (B)
MQ1519,1	--	--	--	unident	*b*?; inc; (B)
MQ1519,1	--	--	--	unident	*b*; inc; (B)
MQ1519,2	--	--	--	unident	*b*; inc; (B)

Context	Figure no.	Inner diameter (mm)	Width (mm)	Mineral	Remarks
Bracelets and Rings—Continued					
MQ1519,2	--	--	--	unident	b; inc; (B)
MQ1519,2	--	--	--	unident	b?; inc; (B)
MQ1519,2	--	--	--	unident	c; inc; (B)
MQ1519,3	--	--	--	unident	b; inc; (B)
MQ1519,3	--	--	--	unident	b; inc; (B)
MQ2024,sf-1	--	30	11	gray	b; inc; (C)
MQ2024,2	--	60	7	unident	b; inc; (C)
N18,1	135:19	15	10	unident	e; inc; (C)
N18,3	--	--	--	unident	unclassified; inc; triangular cross section; reused as scraper?; (B)
N18,4	--	--	--	unident	b?; inc; (B)
P19,3	135:13	90	26	pink tan	J3-39; d; inc; (B)
PQ14	--	110	8	unident	b; inc; one end ground; (C)
PQ14	--	70	9	unident	b; inc; (C)
Q15,2	--	--	--	unident	d; inc; (B)
RU1014,sf-1	--	--	--	unident	b?; inc; (B)
RU1014,sf-1	--	--	--	unident	b; inc; (B)
RU1014,sf-1	--	--	--	unident	b; inc; (B)
RU1014,1	--	--	--	unident	b; inc; (B)
RU1014,1	--	--	--	unident	b; inc; (B)
RU1014,1	--	--	--	unident	b; inc; (B)
RU1014,1	--	--	--	unident	b; inc; (B)
RU1014,1	--	--	--	unident	b; inc; (B)
RU1519,sf-1	--	70	16	unident	a; inc; (C)
RU1519,sf-1	--	50	6	unident	b; inc; one end ground; (C)
RU1519,sf-1	--	70	8	unident	b; inc; (C)
RU1519,sf-1	--	35	6	gray	b; inc; both ends ground; (C)
RU1519,sf-1	135:21	90	18	gray	f; inc; (C)
RU1519,1	--	80	7	unident	b; inc; (C)
RU1519,1	--	70	11	unident	b; inc; (C)
RU1519,2	--	80	10	unident	b; inc; (C)
RU1519,2	--	80	13	unident	b; inc; (C)
RU1519,3	--	40	5	unident	b; inc; (C)
RU1519,3	--	40	11	gray	b; inc; (C)
RU1519,5	--	60	10	unident	b; inc; incised; (C)
T14,2	--	90	8	gray	b; inc; (C)
T16,sf-1	--	35	29	brown	a; inc; (C)
V14,3	--	80	12	gray	c; inc; (C)
VY1014,sf-1	--	60	14	tan	a; inc; (C)
VY1014,sf-1	--	40	6	unident	b; inc; both ends ground; (C)
VY1014,sf-1	--	90	9	unident	b; inc; one end ground; (C)
VY1519,sf-1	--	70	11	unident	b; inc; (C)
XL19,sf-1	--	30	15	unident	a; inc; (C)
XL19,1	--	--	--	unident	b; inc; (B)
XL19,1	--	--	--	unident	b?; inc; (B)
XL19,1	--	--	--	unident	f; inc; (B)
XL19,1	--	ca. 30	--	unident	b?; inc; (B)

		Measurements				
Context	Figure no.	L/gD (mm)	W/gD (mm)	Th/Wt (mm/gm)	Mineral*	Remarks
Beads (Note: The formulae given refer to Beck's system for the classification of bead forms under Remarks; see p. 297.)						
J-sf	--	1	--	--	aqua	A1b; inc; glazed; modern?; (C)
J-sf	--	2	--	--	aqua	A1b; inc; glazed; modern?; (C)
J-sf	--	5	--	--	aqua	B1a; inc; glazed; modern?; (C)
J-sf	--	--	--	--	--	D; comp; (B)

*In lieu of mineralogical identifications, the colors of the stones are noted; in many cases, the beads were of marble (see p. 298).

JARMO ARTIFACTS OF PECKED AND GROUND STONE AND OF SHELL

Context	Figure no.	Measurements			Mineral	Remarks
		L/gD (mm)	W/gD (mm)	Th/Wt (mm/gm)		
Beads—Continued						
J-I,sf	136:12; 142:12	11	13	7	green	*C1a*; comp; faceted, unperforated; (C)
J-I,dmp	--	16	--	--	black	*B2a*; inc; (C)
J-I,sf-1	--	--	7	--	green	*J-10*; *A1b*; comp; (B)
J-I,1-2	--	--	--	--	black	*B2?*; inc; highly polished; (B)
J-I,3	--	5	7	--	marble?	*B2*; comp; approximately hexagonal; (B)
J-I,3	--	21	--	--	white	*J-24*; *B2b*; comp; (B)
J-I,3	--	--	14	--	gry/wh	*J-34*; *A1b*; comp; (B)
J-I,3	--	--	7	--	red	*J2-52*; *A1b*; comp; (B)
J-I,3	--	3	10	--	white	*A1b*; comp; chipped edges, unperforated; (C)
J-I,3?	--	--	--	--	blue	*A2?*; inc; (B)
J-I,3,pit 2	142:5	29	20	--	white	*J-80*; *B2a2*; comp; ovoid cross section; (B)
J-I,3-4	--	--	5	--	gray	*J-54*; *A1b*; comp; (B)
J-I,3-4	--	--	10	--	white	*J-55*; *A1b*; comp; (B)
J-I,4	--	2	5	--	dk grn	*A1b*; comp; (C)
J-I,4	--	3	20	--	white	*A1b*; inc; (C)
J-I,6	--	7	9	--	green	*B1a*; comp; (C)
J-I,6	--	16	--	--	white	*J-71*; *A2b*; comp; (B)
J-I,6a	--	--	22	--	marble?	*J2-62*; *D*; comp; oblate sphere; (B)
J-I,6c	--	--	5	--	orange	*J2-177*; *A1b*; comp; (B)
J-I,6c	136:2; 142:1	1	6	--	black	*J2-178*; *A1b*; comp; (C)
J-I,7	136:1; 142:7	3	8	4	green	*J2-217*; *A1a*; comp; (C)
J-I,7	--	21	--	--	green	*J2-214*; *B2a*; comp; (B)
J-I,7	--	13	--	--	--	*B2?*; inc; (B)
J-I,7	--	25	--	--	white	*J-25*; *D*; comp?; possible bead blank; (B)
J-I,8	--	--	6	--	dk gry	*J2-280*; *A1b*; comp; (B)
J-I,8	--	3	5	--	red/orn	*A1b*; comp; (C)
J-I,8	--	5	9	--	tan	*J2-288*; *B1b*; comp; (C)
J-I,8fl.	--	12	4	--	white	*A2b*; comp; (C)
J-II,sf	--	2	6	--	white	*J2-10*; *A1b*; inc; (C)
J-II,sf	--	5	8	--	black	*J2-47*; *A1b*; comp; (C)
J-II,sf	--	15	5	--	brown	*J2-4*; *A2b*; comp; (C)
J-II,sf	--	18	7	--	gray	*A2b*; comp; (C)
J-II,sf	--	--	15	--	marble?	*J2-29*; *A1b*; comp; (B)
J-II,W,sf-3	--	--	--	--	--	*A1b*; comp; (B)
J-II,W,sf-3	--	4	2	--	white	*D* (*A1a?*); comp; lopsided, unperforated; (C)
J-II,1	--	3	4	--	aqua	*J2-130*; *A1b*; comp; (C)
J-II,1	--	1	5	--	black	*J2-146*; *A1b*; comp; (C)
J-II,1	--	2	5	--	red/orn	*J2-111*; *A1b*; comp; (C)
J-II,1	--	3	8	--	white	*J2-181*; *B1b*; comp; (C)
J-II,1	136:6; 142:2	5	9	--	white	*J2-133*; *B1b*; comp; (C)
J-II,1	--	2	8	--	white	*J2-142*; *B1b*; comp; (C)
J-II,1	136:7; 142:4	24	18	8	white	*J2-148*; *B2a*; comp; (C)
J-II,1	--	15	--	--	black	*B2a*; inc; (C)
J-II,1	--	15	10	--	black	*J2-120*; *B2b*; comp; (C)
J-II,1	--	16	13	--	black	*J2-119*; *B2b*; comp; (C)
J-II,1	136:11	13	12	--	white	*D*; comp; hollow conical, imitation fossil?; (C)
J-II,1	--	20	8	4	red/wh	*D* (*B2a?*); comp; (C)
J-II,1	--	2	10	--	white	*D* (*A1b?*); comp; incomplete perforation; (C)
J-II,1	--	17	11	--	blk/wh	*D* (*B2b*); inc; (C)
J-II,1	--	26	--	--	dk gry	*J2-21*; *B2b*; comp; (B)
J-II,1	136:3	4	12	--	white	*J2-14*; *A1b*; comp; broken V-drilling; (B)
J-II,1	--	--	9	--	lmst?	*J2-48*; *B1b*; comp; (B)
J-II,1	--	3	8	--	marble?	*J2-51*; *A1b*; inc; (B)
J-II,1	--	--	6	--	marble?	*J2-82*; *A1b*; comp; (B)
J-II,1	--	12	14	5	aqua	*J2-136*; *C1a*; inc; (B)
J-II,1	--	5	12	--	gry/wh	*J2-140*; *A1b?*; comp; nonparallel ends, off-center perforation; (B)

Context	Figure no.	L/gD (mm)	W/gD (mm)	Th/Wt (mm/gm)	Mineral	Remarks
Beads—*Continued*						
J-II,1	--	2	6	--	marble?	*J2-161*; *A1b*; comp; (B)
J-II,1	--	3	5	--	orange, carnelian?	*J2-175*; *B1b*; comp; marked carination; (B)
J-II,2	--	7	5	--	dk gry	*J2-195*; *A2b*; comp; (B)
J-II,2	--	15	--	5	black	*J2-198*; *C2a?*; inc; polished; (B)
J-II,2	--	2	5	--	dk gry	*J2-203*; *A1b*; comp; (B)
J-II,2	--	9	7	--	black	*J2-219*; *D (B2b)*; inc; break reground; (B)
J-II,2	--	3	5	--	green	*J2-241*; *A1b*; comp; (B)
J-II,2	--	4	6	--	--	*J2-242*; *B1a*; comp; (B)
J-II,2	--	9	15	--	marble?	*J2-266*; *A1b*; comp; (B)
J-II,2	--	2	4	--	aqua	*A1b*; inc; (C)
J-II,2	--	1	6	--	white	*A1b*; comp; (C)
J-II,2	--	2	6	--	white	*J2-211*; *A1b*; comp; (C)
J-II,2	--	20	5	--	dk gry	*J2-230*; *A2b*; comp; (C)
J-II,2	--	33	10	--	gray	*J2-250*; *A2b*; comp; (C)
J-II,2	--	2	5	--	red	*J2-216*; *B1b*; comp; (C)
J-II,2	--	4	5	--	red	*J2-229*; *B1b*; comp; (C)
J-II,2	--	6	--	--	orange	*B2b*; inc; (C)
J-II,2	--	15	9	--	gray	*J2-238*; *B2b*; comp; (C)
J-II,2	136:10; 142:6	18	17	5	green	*J2-267*; *C2a*; comp; (C)
J-II,2	136:17	22	12	7	quartzite?	*D (B2a)*; comp; incomplete perforation; (C)
J-II,2	136:16; 142:13	20	15	--	red/wh	*D (B2a?)*; comp; incomplete perforations; (C)
J-II,2	--	3	16	--	white	*D (A1b?)*; comp; chipped edges; (C)
J-II,2	136:13	2	9	--	white	*D (A1b?)*; inc; unperforated; (C)
J-II,2	--	2	9	--	white	*D (A1b?)*; inc; unperforated; (C)
J-II,2	--	2	9	--	white	*D (A1b?)*; inc; unperforated; (C)
J-II,2	--	15	--	--	red/orn	*D (B?)*; inc; pebble frag; (C)
J-II,2	136:18; 142:9	34	(16)	5	red/wh	*J2-234*; *D (B2a2)*; inc; terminal collars?; (C)
J-II,2fl.	--	3	8	--	white	*A1b*; comp; (C)
J-II,2fl.	--	17	6	--	dk gry	*A2b*; comp; (C)
J-II,2fl.	--	8	6	--	red/orn	*J2-289*; *B2b*; comp; (C)
J-II,2fl.	--	3	15	--	white	*D (A1b?)*; comp; ground all over; (C)
J-II,2fl.	--	8	7	7	pinkish	*D (A1? B1?)*; comp; (C)
J-II,2fl.	--	9	6	5	red/orn	*D (B1a?)*; comp; (C)
J-II,2fl.	--	20	--	--	red/orn	*D?*; inc; (C)
J-II,2fl.	--	--	10	--	--	*A1b*; comp; (B)
J-II,3	--	--	8	--	--	*A1a*; comp; (B)
J-II,3	--	10	8	--	orange	*J2-300*; *B2b*; comp; (B)
J-II,3	--	2	5	--	black	*A1b*; comp; (C)
J-II,3	--	19	5	--	black	*A2b*; comp; (C)
J-II,3	--	3	4	--	white	*B1b*; comp; (C)
J-II,3	--	3	7	--	green	*B1b*; comp; (C)
J-II,3	--	8	7	--	black	*B2a*; comp; (C)
J-II,3	--	8	--	--	olive	*B2b*; inc; (C)
J-II,4	--	1	5	--	white	*A1b*; comp; (C)
J-II,4	--	1	5	--	white	*A1b*; comp; (C)
J-II,4	--	6	12	--	white	*A1b*; comp; (C)
J-II,4	--	--	--	--	gray	*B2a*; inc; (C)
J-II,4	--	7	--	--	violet	*B2a*; inc; transp; (C)
J-II,4	--	5	--	--	red	*B2b*; inc; transl; (C)
J-II,4	--	12	--	--	brown	*B2b*; inc; transl; (C)
J-II,4	--	8	7	--	gray	*B2b*; comp; (C)
J-II,4	136:14	13	14	9	brown	*D (C2a?)*; inc; faceted surface, unperforated; (C)
J-II,4	--	7	19	--	white	*D (A1b?)*; inc; chipped edges; (C)
J-II,4	--	--	6	--	white	*D?*; inc; (C)
J-II,4	--	11	--	--	olive	*D*; inc; one edge bored; (C)
J-II,4	--	14	--	--	brown	*D*; inc; split, perforation botched; (C)

Context	Figure no.	Measurements			Mineral	Remarks
		L/gD (mm)	W/gD (mm)	Th/Wt (mm/gm)		
Beads—Continued						
J-II,4	--	34	6	--	gry/tan	*J2-362*; *A2b*; comp; unusual, longitudinal spiraliform groove; (B)
J-II,5	--	2	7	--	white	*A1b*; inc; (C)
J-II,5	--	3	9	--	black	*A1b*; comp; (C)
J-II,5	--	11	6	--	gray	*A2a*; comp; (C)
J-II,5	136:5; 142:3	8	11	6	brown	*J2-385*; *B1a*; comp; (C)
J-II,5	--	5	9	--	white	*B1b*; comp; (C)
J-II,5	--	11	6	--	black	*B2b*; comp; (C)
J-II,5	--	12	6	--	black	*B2b*; comp; (C)
J-II,5	--	15	--	--	green	*D?*; inc; irregular, ground; (C)
J-II,5	--	4	20	--	green	*D (A1b?)*; comp; (C)
J-II,6	--	1	5	--	white	*A1b*; comp; (C)
J-II,6	--	1	5	--	green	*A1b*; comp; (C)
J-II,6	--	5	14	--	white	*A1b*; comp; (C)
J-II,6	--	10	8	6	red/wh	*D (B2a?)*; comp; (C)
J-III,sf-1	--	15	12	--	black	*D (B2b?)*; inc; incomplete perforation; (C)
J-III,sf-1	--	11	6	--	dk gry	*J2-157*; *B2b*; comp; (B)
J-III,sf-1	--	15	11	--	tan	*J2-168*; *B2b?*; comp; (B)
J-III,1	--	20	--	--	tan	*A2a*; inc; (C)
J-III,1	--	6	11	--	red/orn	*D (A1b?)*; comp; (C)
J-A,3m	--	5	12	--	white	*A1b*; comp; (C)
J-A,3m	--	10	8	--	gray	*B2b*; comp; (C)
J-A,IV	136:15; 142:11	6	15	--	white	*D (A1b)*; inc; perforation incomplete; (C)
J-B,sf-1	--	26	--	--	white	*B2a*; inc; (C)
F19,sf-1	136:8	14	10	--	black	*B2b*; comp; (C)
F19,3	--	27	8	--	black	*D (B2b)*; comp; faceted surface; (C)
G13,3	--	5	7	--	aqua	*A1a*; comp; (C)
G17,2	136:9; 142:10	19	7	--	black	*B2b2*; comp; (C)
G17,2	--	--	--	--	gry/wh	*B2b2*; comp; (B)
G18,1	--	--	--	--	--	*B1b*; comp; (B)
G20,3	--	--	--	--	gry/grn	*A2b*; comp; (B)
GL1519,sf-1	--	16	7	--	pink	*B2b*; comp; (C)
GL1519,sf-1	--	2	3	--	aqua	*B1b*; comp; (C)
GL2024	--	17	14	12	white	*D (B2a?)*; comp; (C)
H13,1	--	10	7	--	olive	*B2a*; comp; (C)
H13,2	--	--	--	--	blk/wh	*B2b*; comp; rounded ends; (B)
H14,2	--	14	5	--	white	*A2b*; comp; (C)
H17,1	--	3	15	--	white	*D (A1b)*; comp; (C)
H19,3	--	--	--	--	gray	*B2b*; comp; rounded ends; (B)
K line,2	--	10	--	--	white	*A2b*; inc; (C)
L17,1	--	--	--	--	red	*B1a?*; comp; oval; (B)
L19,1	--	--	--	--	blue	*A1a*; comp; nonparallel ends; (B)
M18,1	--	--	--	--	blu/grn	*C1a?*; inc; (B)
M18,2	--	8	6	--	aqua	*B2b*; comp; (C)
MQ1014,2	--	--	--	--	white	*D (A1? B1?)*; comp; cylindrical; (B)
MQ1519,2	--	--	--	--	white	*D (A1? B1?)*; comp; cylindrical; (B)
MQ1519,3	--	--	--	--	--	*D?*; comp; disk; (B)
N17,5	--	--	--	--	blu/grn	*D?*; comp; slight grooving at 2 edges; (B)
N22,1	--	5	14	--	blu glass	comp; modern; (C)
P14,2	--	2	6	--	blu/grn	*A1b*; comp; (C)
PQ14,sf-1	--	1	5	--	white	*A1b*; comp; (C)
PQ14,sf-1	--	26	5	--	dk gry	*A2b*; comp; (C)
PQ14,sf-1	--	25	8	--	dk gry	*A2b*; comp; (C)
Q15,3	--	--	--	--	gray	*D (A2? B2?)*; comp; cylindrical; (B)
Q15,3?	--	--	--	--	gray	*D (A2? B2?)*; inc; roughly squared; (B)
R14,2	--	12	7	--	black	*B2b*; comp; (C)
RU1519,4	--	3	13	--	tan	*D (A1b?)*; comp; chipped edges; bowl sherd?; (C)
S15,1	136:4; 142:8	23	5	--	dk gry	*A2b*; comp; (C)
S15,4	--	18	--	--	brown	*B2a*; inc; (C)

Context	Figure no.	Measurements			Mineral	Remarks
		L/gD (mm)	W/gD (mm)	Th/Wt (mm/gm)		
Beads—Continued						
S17,2	--	19	4	--	dk gry	*A2b*; comp; (C)
T18,3	--	9	--	--	green	*B2a*; inc; (C)
T19,1	--	3	8	--	pink	*A1b*; comp; (C)
U15,3	--	--	--	--	--	*A1b?*; comp; (B)
W11,1	--	2	5	--	white	*A1b*; comp; (C)
W19,sf-1	--	16	--	--	pink	*J3-31*; *B2a2*; comp; (B)
X10,2	--	4	13	--	white	*A1b*; comp; (C)
X10,3	--	2	9	--	white	*A1b*; comp; (C)
Pendants (Note: The types *a-c* are described on p. 299.)						
J-I,6	--	(50)	28	13	lmst	*a*; inc; pebble?; overall polish; (C)
J-I,6	--	(19)	18	4	lmst	*a*; inc; rewkd stone bowl frag; (C)
J-I,6	136:21	(44)	20	7	low metam	*a*; inc; pebble; (C)
J-I,6	--	(29)	--	--	unident	*J-73*; *b?*; inc; scooplike, broken perforation; pendant?; (B)
J-I,7	136:25; 142:15	(28)	31	4	marble?	*J2-233*; *b*; inc; facelike decoration; (C)
J-I,8	--	(24)	10	--	tan	*J2-293*; *a*; inc; lentoid cross section, broken at perforation, sharp edges; (B)
J-I,8fl.	136:23; 142:16	26	15	4	lmst	*J2-316*; *a*; comp; fi; (C)
J-II,sf	--	15	--	--	--	*J2-5*; *a*; comp; crude oval pebble; (C)
J-II,1	--	(28)	17	4	lmst	*J2-118*; *a*; inc; stone bowl frag; (C)
J-II,1	--	46	19	4	marble?	*J2-95*; *a*; comp; long oval; (B)
J-II,2	--	25	8	7	marble?	*J2-251*; *a*; comp; rewkd bracelet frag?; (C)
J-II,2	136:22; 142:18	19	13	12	hemat?	*J2-271*; *a*; comp; pebble; (C)
J-II,2	--	(20)	(21)	6	obsid	*a*; inc; small frag; (C)
J-II,3	--	(15)	(23)	5	marble?	*a*; inc; stone bowl frag; (C)
J-II,3	--	(16)	(10)	6	marble?	*J2-309*; *b*; inc; foot-shaped; (C)
J-II,3	--	29	15	10	marble?	*c*; comp?; (C)
J-II,4	--	11	5	2	red	*a*; comp; stone bowl frag; (C)
J-II,4	--	14	13	5	red	*J2-361*; *a*; comp; short pebble; high polish; (B)
J-II,4	--	10	9	3	black	*J2-370*; *a*; comp; short pebble; high polish; (B)
J-II,6	136:27; 142:20	66	47	6	fossil?	*J2-408*; *a*; comp; 3 perforations; (C)
J-III,sf-1	--	--	(19)	3	obsid	*J2-172*; *a*; inc; long? oval; (B)
J-A,IV	136:29	27	26	6	lmst	*J2-313*; *b*; comp?; crosshatched incised design; (B)
K21,7	136:24	15	5	3	lmst?	*J3-32*; *a?*; comp; inverted teardrop shape (B)
L15,2	136:28; 142:17	21	10	6	lmst	*J3-36*; *b*; comp?; foot-shaped; ochre traces; (C)
L19,3	--	21	16	3	lmst?	*a*; comp; stone bowl frag; (C)
M18,2	136:26	31	39	6	lmst	*J3-16*; *a*; comp; stone bowl frag; (C)
MQ1519,2	--	--	--	--	hemat?	*c?*; comp; (B)
RU1014,1	--	(56)	45	15	unident	*a*; inc; long crude pebble; (B)
T16,4	--	22	17	8	cdy?	*a*; comp; (C)
W11,3	136:20	13	14	6	crystal	*J3-40*; *b*; inc; depression drilled into broken flat base; (B)
Broad, Flat Rings						
J-I,dmp	137:1	60	30	4	lmst sa/cl	inc; one end ground; (C)
J-I,3a	--	--	--	--	unident	inc; (B)
J-I,6	--	40	15	4	lmst sa/cl	inc; (C)
J-I,6	--	80	30	4	cal lmst	inc; 2 conical perforations; (C)
J-I,6	--	80	40	5	cal lmst	inc; (C)
J-I,8	--	--	30	4	marble?	inc; chipped perimeter; (C)
J-I,8fl.	--	70	40	3	serp?	inc; very high polish; (C)
J-II,1	--	30	7	4	lmst?	*J2-13*; inc; (C)

JARMO ARTIFACTS OF PECKED AND GROUND STONE AND OF SHELL

		Measurements				
Context	Figure no.	L/gD (mm)	W/gD (mm)	Th/Wt (mm/gm)	Mineral	Remarks
Ground Stone Balls*						
J-I,sf	--	--	--	19	11	grnst	comp; (C)
J-I,sf	--	--	--	40	--	marble?	comp; ca. ovate; 3 sides ground, ends battered; (C)
J-I,sf	--	--	--	(40)	--	marble?	inc; (C)
J-I,sf	--	--	--	(50)	--	lmst?	inc; weathered; (C)
J-I,sf	--	--	--	(53)	--	marble?	inc; (C)
J-I,1-2	--	--	--	25	18	marble	comp; (C)
J-I,1-2	--	--	--	50	--	lmst	comp; ground, one face rough; (C)
J-I,3	--	--	--	27	25.4	lmst	comp?; oblate; weathered; (C)
J-I,5	--	--	--	23	16.4	lmst	comp; (C)
J-II,sf	137:4	--	--	18	9	marble?	comp; incomplete perforation; (C)
J-II,1	--	--	--	20	10	marble?	J2-26; comp; (C)
J-II,1	--	--	--	20	11.4	marble?	J2-128; comp; (C)
J-II,1	--	--	--	21	13	marble	J2-38; comp; (C)
J-II,1	141:5	--	--	58	256	marble	J2-83; comp; (C)
J-II,1	--	--	--	50	--	marble	J2-34; comp; (B)
J-II,1	--	--	--	47	--	marble?	J2-49; comp; (B)
J-II,1	--	--	--	21	--	marble?	J2-50; comp; almost hemispherical; (B)
J-II,2	--	--	--	25	--	marble?	J2-248; comp; (B)
J-II,2	--	--	--	28	31	marble	comp; (C)
J-II,2	141:2	--	--	30	34.4	marble?	J2-232; comp; (C)
J-II,2	141:6	--	--	46	128.5	chl och	J2-255; comp; (C)
J-II,2fl.	--	--	--	22	--	orange	J2-281; comp; (B)
J-II,4	--	--	--	49	162	chl och	comp; (C)
J-II,4	--	--	--	60	277	lmst	comp; ochre traces; (C)
J-II,5	--	--	--	17	7.5	marble?	comp; (C)
J-II,5	137:2	--	--	38	79	black	comp; (C)
J-II,5	--	--	--	54	222	chl och	comp; ochre; (C)
J-A,3m	141:4	--	--	17	7	marble	comp; (C)
J-A,3m	--	--	--	19	10	marble	comp; a few peck marks, faceted, unfinished?; (C)
J-A,3m	--	--	--	39	--	marble	inc; rewkd; (C)
J-A,3m	--	--	--	41	--	marble	inc; (C)
J-A,3m	--	--	--	(50)	--	marble	inc; (C)
J-A,III	--	--	--	44	--	marble	inc; ochre traces on one side; light grinding of break; (C)
J-B,sf-1	--	--	--	18	8	marble?	comp; (C)
J-B,sf-1	--	--	--	(62)	--	gray	inc; (C)
J-B,1-2	--	--	--	15	5	gray	comp; weathered; (C)
J-B,1-2	--	--	--	18	9	marble?	comp; (C)
J-D,1fl.	--	--	--	22	15	marble?	comp; (C)
CF59,sf-1	--	--	--	(50)	--	marble	inc; (C)
GL1014,1	--	--	--	16	6.5	gray	comp; weathered; (C)
GL1519,sf-1	--	--	--	46	109	gry/wh	comp; (C)
GL1519,sf-1	--	--	--	24	18.5	red/wh	comp; (C)
GL1519,2	--	--	--	12.5	2.5	red	comp; (C)
GL2024,1	--	--	--	15.5	5	white	comp; (C)
HK15	--	--	--	49	161.6	white	comp; weathered; (C)
MQ1014,3	--	--	--	38	73	tan	comp; (C)
MQ1519,sf-1	137:3	--	--	43	117.6	blu/gry	comp; oblate; base very battered, then ground; ochre traces; (C)
MQ1519,sf-1	--	--	--	50?	--	black	inc; light grinding of break; (C)
MQ2024,1	--	--	--	20?	--	white	inc; (C)
VY1014,3	--	--	--	40?	38	ochre?	inc; (C)

---

*Our field notes also remark that there were 9 examples (none clearly complete), "ranging from 14 to 49 mm" in diameter, from various of the test squares.

Context	Figure no.	Measurements			Mineral	Remarks
		L/gD (mm)	W/gD (mm)	Th/Wt (mm/gm)		
Phallic Objects				(mm)		
J-I,3,pit 2	137:6; 140:20	(59)	(45)	31	marble?	J-75; inc; base and end battered; (B)
J-II,W,sf-3	137:7	(36)	(44)	--	marble?	inc; cup-on-stalk type; (C)
J-II,1	137:5; 140:18	(59)	(53)	27	marble?	J2-169; inc; base and end battered; (C)
J-II,2	142:32	--	--	--	marble?	J2-240; inc; cup-on-stalk type; height of vertical axis of bowl, 22 mm; bowl + stalk, 59 mm; width of bowl, 33 mm; (B)
J-II,5	--	(32)	(22)	(22)	marble?	inc; cup-on-stalk type; (C)
J-II,5	--	(35)	(26)	(30)	marble?	inc; cup-on-stalk type; (C)
J-II,6	--	(28)	(27)	(18)	marble?	inc; (C)
F17,1	137:8; 140:19	63	25	22	trav flnt?	comp; altered pebble?; (C)
Miscellaneous Stone Artifacts						
J-II,1	138:4; 142:27	49	26	11	calc?	J2-24; inc; braceletlike in section; (C)
J-II,2fl.	138:5	45	28	--	steat?	J2-278; comp; conical base; (B)
J-II,4	142:30	45	30	22	marble	J2-369; comp; pestlelike stump; (B)
G20,2	137:9; 142:26	57	29	--	marble?	J3-15; inc; fi; "spoon"; (B)
K16,1m	--	105	--	--	red	comp; large ball; (B)
L11,sf-1	140:10	132	--	--	lmst	comp; large ball; (B)
M21,sf-1	137:10; 142:31	71	14	--	marble	J3-30; comp; "nail"; (C)
S15,2	138:6	(27)	24	--	lmst	inc; pestlelike stump; (C)
V16,sf-1	137:11	--	28	13	marble	J3-24; almost comp; "stamp" or "labret"; (B)

SHELL ARTIFACTS

Context	Figure no.	Measurements			Type	Remarks
		L (mm)	W (mm)	Th (mm)		
J-I,sf-1	--	59	--	--	fossil	J-8; univalve shell cast; comp?; (B)
J-I,3	--	2	6	--	mussel?	bead, A1b type; comp; (C)
J-I,3,pit 2	--	--	--	--	fossil	bead, D? type; inc; (B)
J-I,6c	--	(20)	12	1	mussel	J2-166; pendant; inc; double perforation; triangular; (B); (cf. fig. 138:9)
J-I,7	--	(16)	--	--	mussel	J-72; pendant; inc; double perforation; round top; (B)
J-I,8	138:9; 142:19	18	11	2	mussel	J2-310; pendant; comp; red ochre traces; (C)
J-II,1	138:10	28	9	--	fossil	bead, A2b type; Dentalium?; (B)
J-II,1	--	2	5	--	mussel	J2-164; bead, A1b type; comp; (C)
J-II,1	--	(8)	7	--	fossil	bead, D type; Oliva?; inc, spire removed; (C)
J-II,3	--	(17)	--	--	marine	bead, D? type; Oliva?; inc, spire removed; (B)
J-II,3	--	(8)	--	--	fossil	bead, D type; Oliva?; inc, both ends gone; (B)
J-II,5	--	16	4	--	marine	J2-391; bead, A2b type; Dentalium?; comp?; (C)
J-II,5,W	--	(13)	--	--	marine	bead, A2b type; marine worm?; comp?; polished; (B)
J-A,1-2	138:13	10	4	--	marine	bead?; comp?; elliptical, unperforated; (C)
H14,2	--	15	5	--	marine	bead, A2b type; Dentalium?; comp?; (C)
L19,1	--	--	--	--	marine	bead, D type; Oliva?; comp?; (B)
L21,1	138:7; 142:14	15	9	--	fossil	J3-38; bead, D type; Oliva?; comp; (C)
N12,2	138:8	(16)	28	--	mussel	J3-1; pendant; owllike face; inc; (B)
P19,3	--	8	10	--	fossil	pendant, D type; snaillike; comp; one perforation; (C)

Context	Figure no.	Measurements			Type	Remarks
		L (mm)	W (mm)	Th (mm)		
T11,3	138:12	124	--	--	fossil	fossil cast; comp?; (C)
T18,5	138:11	(32)	--	--	mussel	pendant?; inc; 2 perforations, otherwise unaltered?; (C)
U15,1	--	10	7	--	marine	marine snail; comp?; one perforation; (C)
U15,4	--	(19)	(24)	2	mussel	pendant; inc; one perforation; (C)

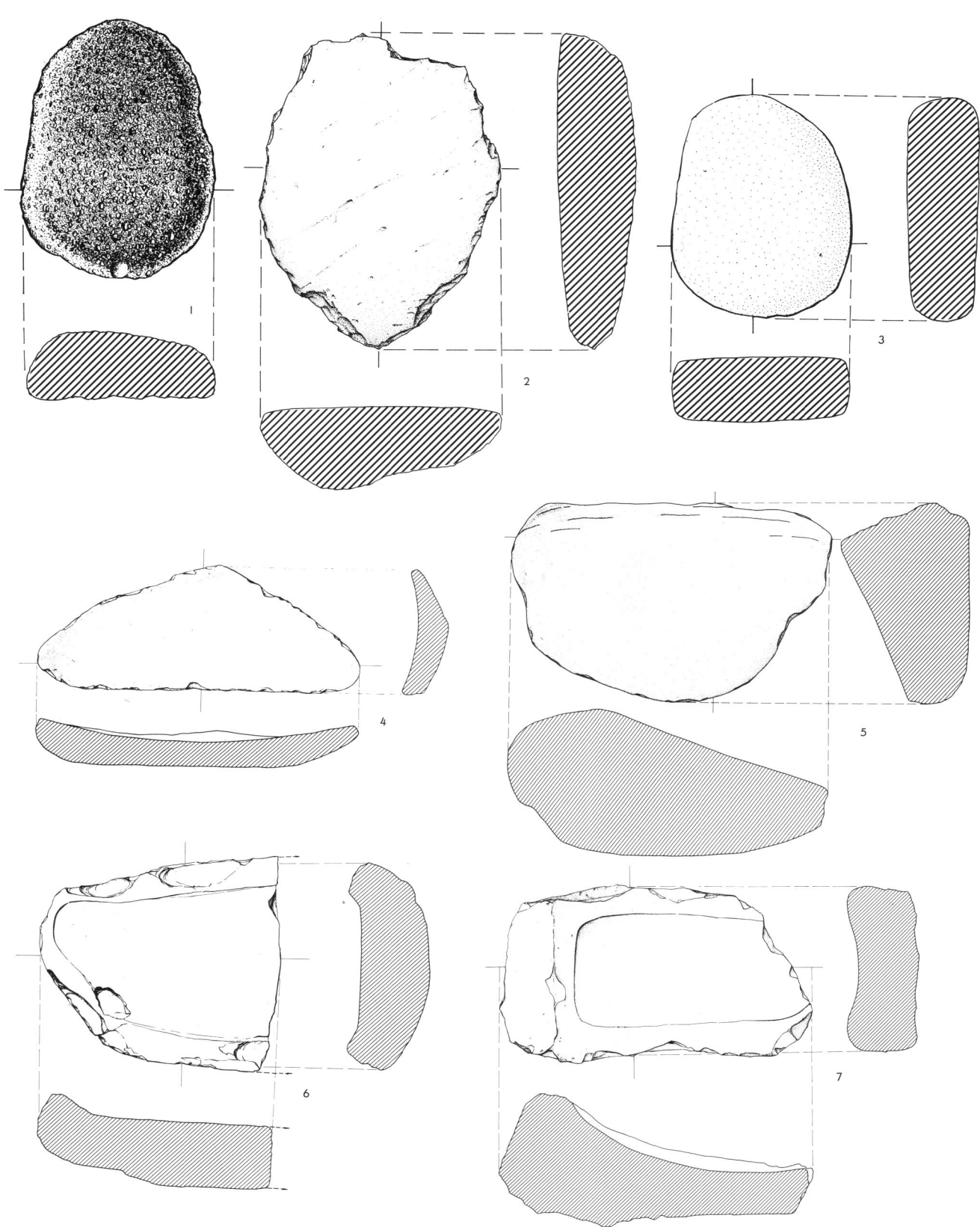

Fig. 127. Jarmo ground stone: mullers, *1* (from J-I,6), *2* (from J-I,5), *3* (from J-I,6); querns, *4* (from J-II,5), *5* (from J-II,2fl.), *6-7* (from J-I,3). Scales 1:3, *1-3*; 1:8, *4-6*; 1:9, *7*.

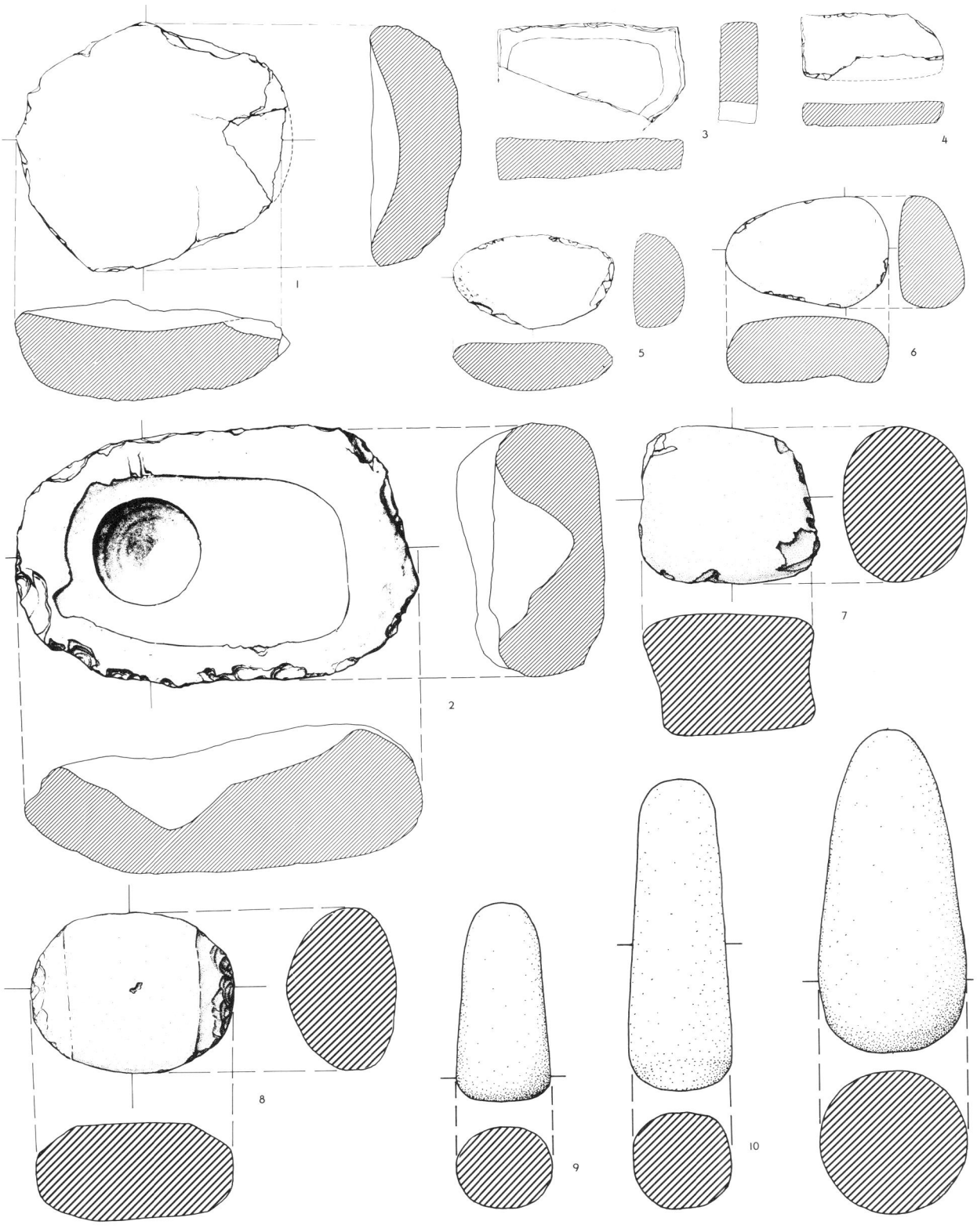

Fig. 128. Jarmo ground stone: querns, *1* (from J-I,3), *2* (from J-I,6); pecked and ground slabs, *3* (from J-I,5), *4* (from J-I,8), *5* (from J-I,5), *6* (from J-II,2fl.); utilized cobbles, *7* (from J-I,6), *8* (from J-I,5); pestles, *9* (from J-II,1), *10* (from J-II,6), *11* (from J-I,3-4). Scales 1:8, *1-6*; 1:3, *7-11*.

Fig. 129. Jarmo ground stone: pestles, *1* (from J-I,7), *2* (from J-II,2fl.); pestle-hammerstones, *3* (from J-I,6), *4* (from J-I,1-2), *5* (from J-I,3a), *6* (from J-II,1), *7* (from J-II,2fl.), *8* (from J-I,5), *9* (from J-I,8), *10* (from J-II,1); hammerstone, *11* (from J-I,3a); mortars, *12* (from J-II,1), *13* (from J-II,2), *14* (from J-II,2fl.), *15* (from HK16,sf-1), *16* (from J-II,2), *17* (from J-II,2fl.), *18* (from J-I,dmp). Scales 1:3, *1-11*; 1:8, *12-18*.

Fig. 130. Jarmo ground stone: mortar, *1* (from J-I,6); palettes, or pigment-grinding stones, *2* (from J-II,6), *3* (from J-II,3), *4* (from J-II,5), *5* (from J-I,6); disks with pecked depressions, *6* (from J-II,4), *7* (from J-II,1), *8* (from J-II,1E); rubbing and polishing stones and whetstones, *9* (from J-II,4), *10* (from J-I,1-2), *11* (from J-I,3,pit 2), *12* (from J-II,4); pecking and rubbing stones, *13-14* (from J-I,6). Scales 1:8, *1*; 1:3, *2-14*.

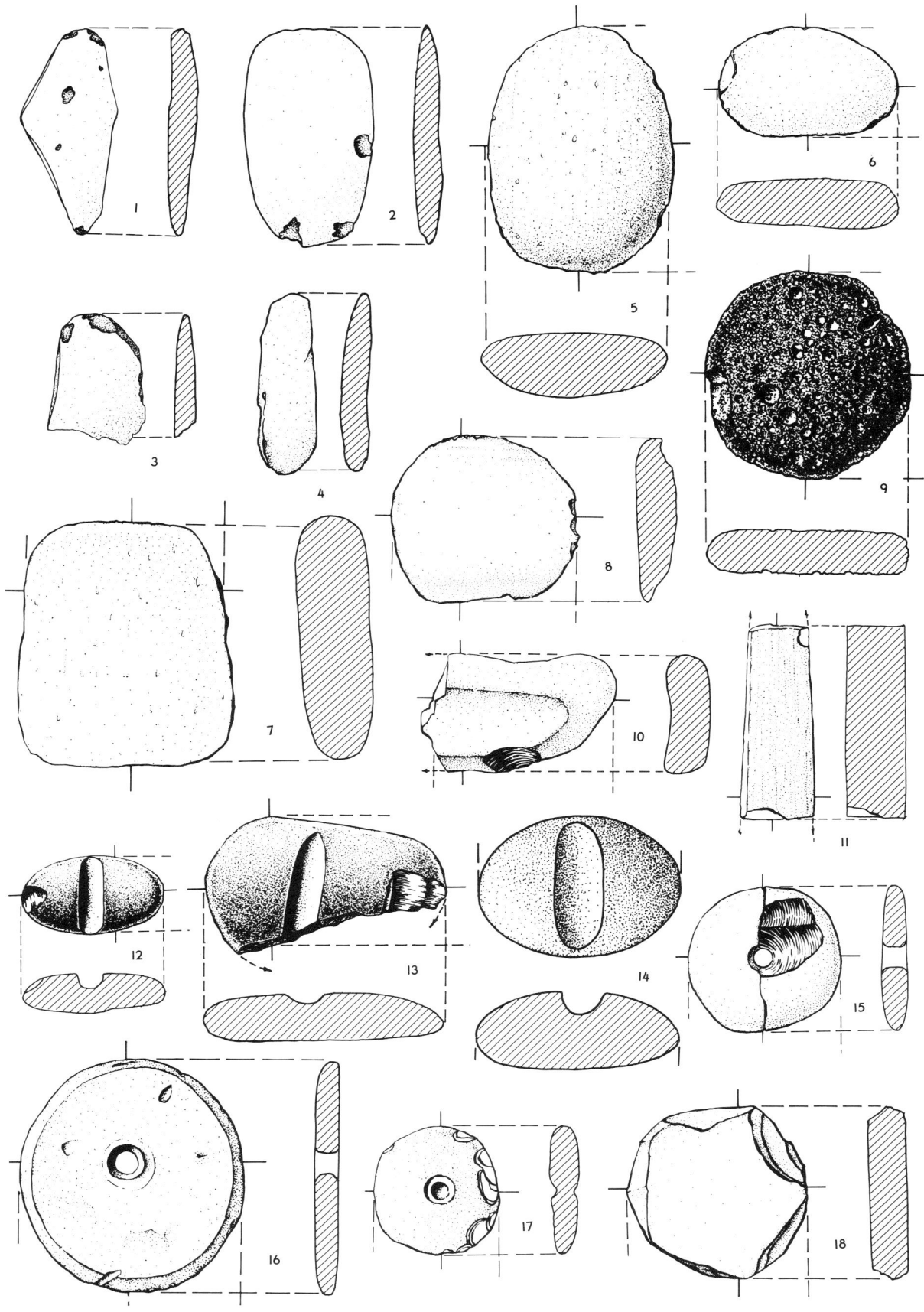

Fig. 131. Jarmo ground stone: retouchers, *1* (from J-I,8fl.), *2* (from RU1014,1), *3* (from J-I,8), *4* (from D19,5); rubbing and polishing stones and whetstones, *5* (from J-I,1-2), *6* (from J-I,3,pit 2), *7* (from J-II,3), *8* (from GL1519,2), *9* (from M17,2), *10* (from J-I,4-5), *11* (from G20,2); grooved stones, *12* (from PQ14,1), *13* (from J-II,1), *14* (from G20,2); whorls, *15* (from J-I,8-9), *16* (from J-A,IV), *17* (from J-I,6c), *18* (from J-I,8). Scale 1:2.

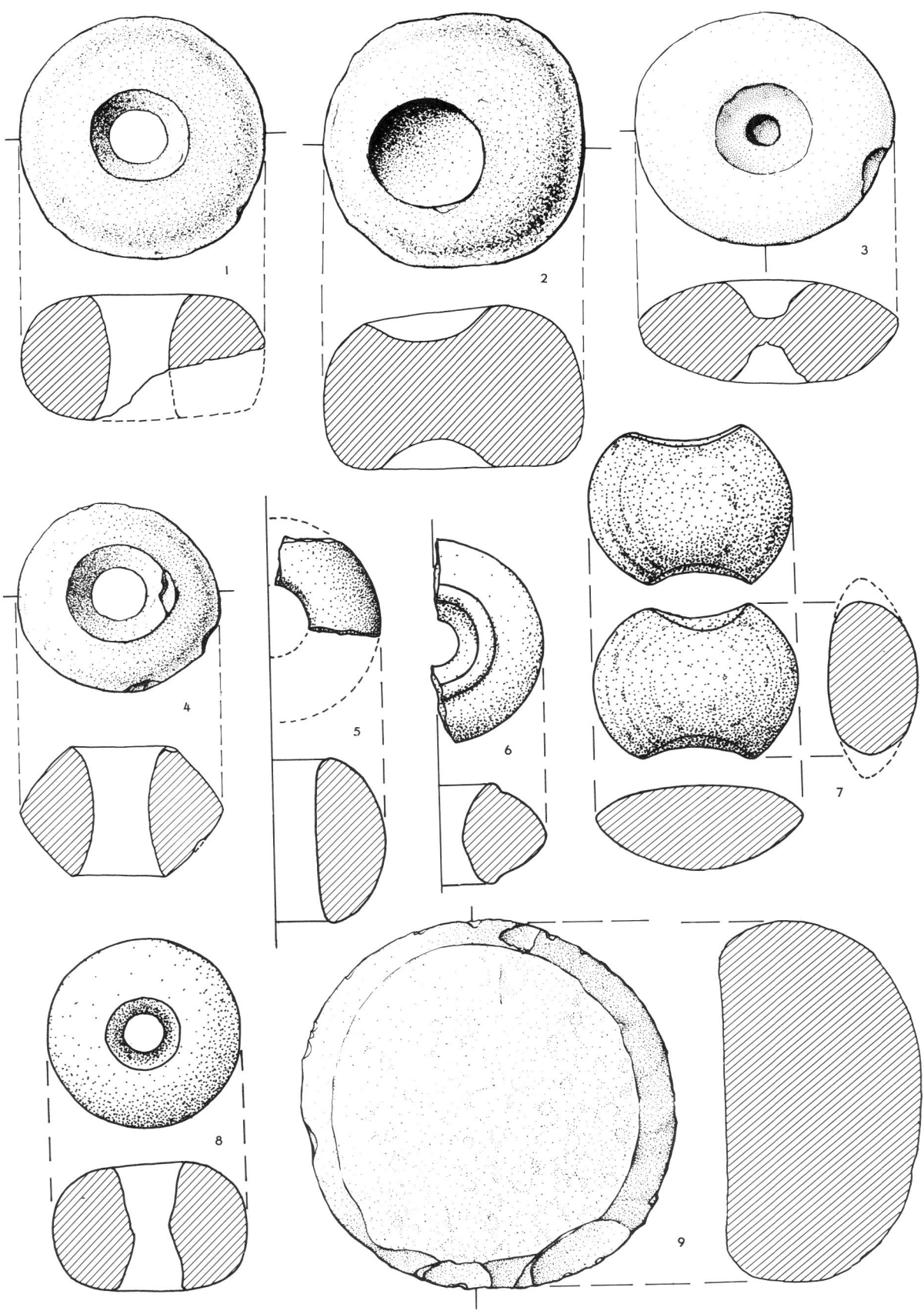

Fig. 132. Jarmo ground stone: digging-stick weights or maceheads, *1* (from J-II,6), *2* (from J-I,dmp), *3* (from J-I,6), *4-5* (from J-II,2), *6* (from J-II,5), *8* (from J-II,4); large drill bit, *7* (from MQ1519,sf-1); unfinished round stone blank, *9* (from GL1519,sf-1). Scale 1:2.

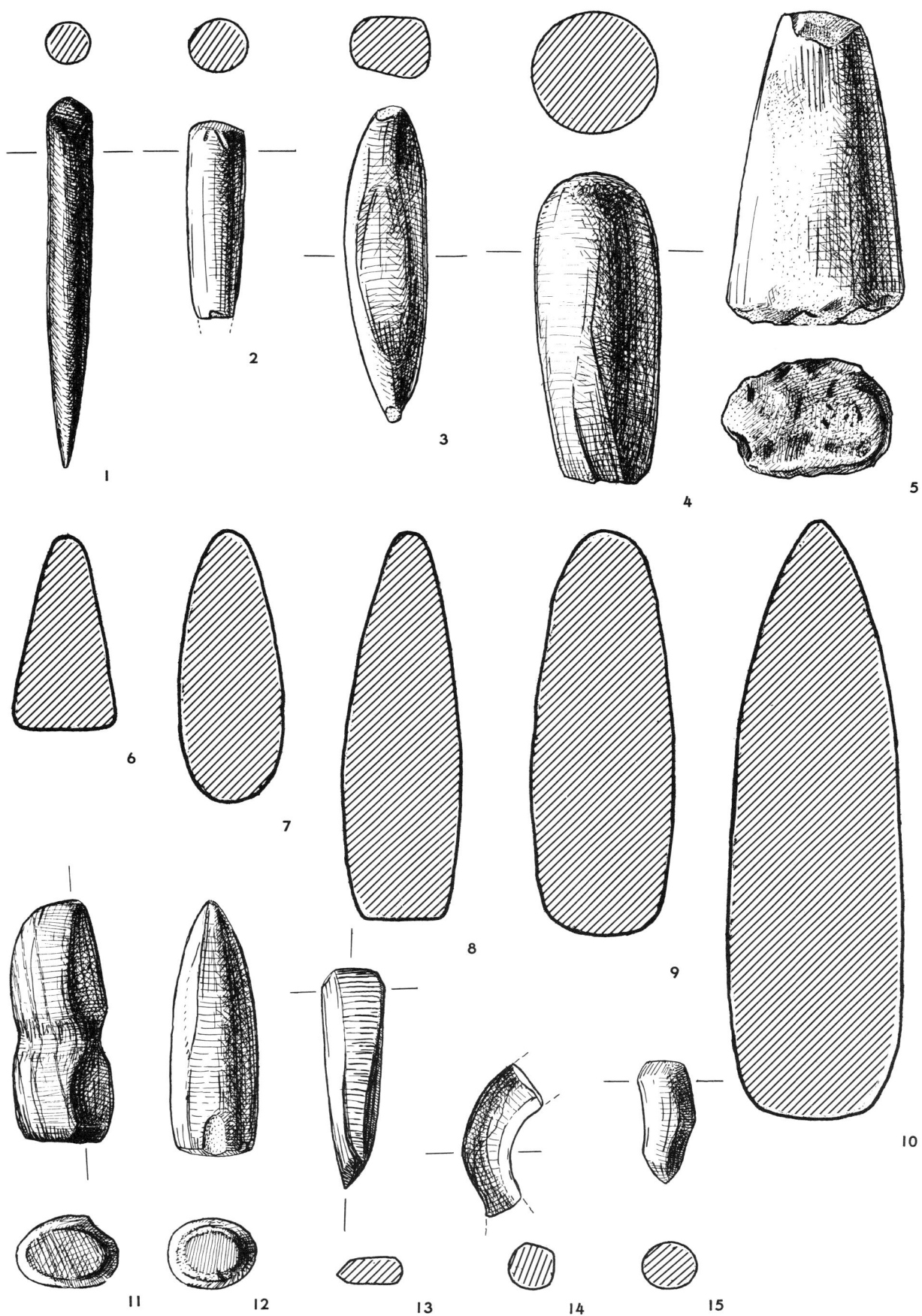

Fig. 133. Jarmo ground stone: small borers and/or small pestles, *1* (from J-I,dmp), *2* (from J-II,1), *3* (from J-II,3), *4* (from N18,4), *5* (from J-D,1fl.), *6* (from J-II,2fl.), *7* (from J-I,3), *8* (from J-II,2), *9* (from J-II,1), *10* (from J-I,3a), *11* (from J-II,1), *12* (from J-II,5), *13* (from J-I,8fl.); curved and humped objects, *14* (from J-I,8), *15* (from J-II,6). Scale 1:1.

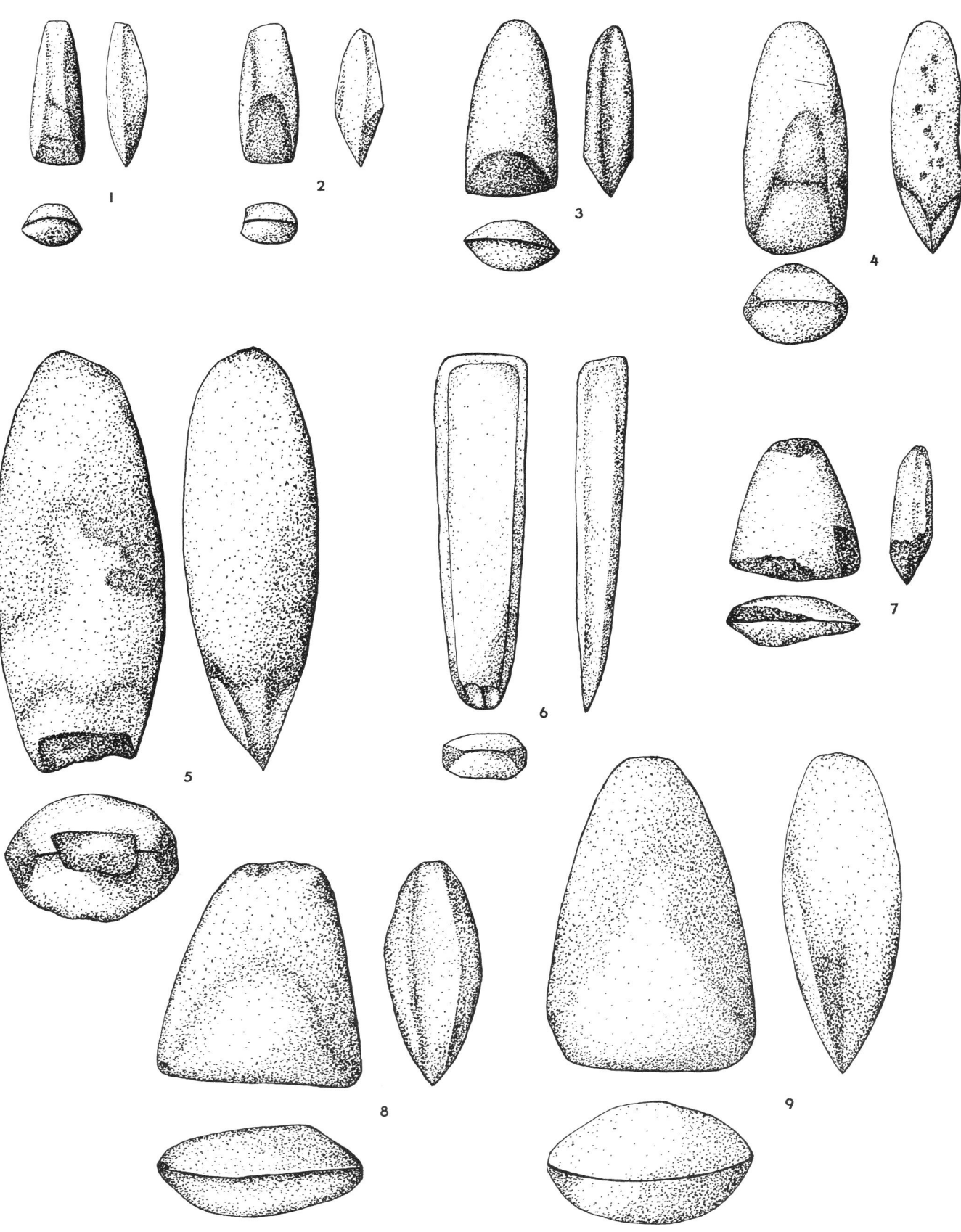

Fig. 134. Jarmo ground stone: celts and chisels, *1* (from J-II,2), *2* (from T16,4), *3* (from J-III,sf-1), *4* (from J-II,2fl.), *5* (from J-II,1), *6* (from J-I,8), *7* (from J-II,2), *8-9* (from J-II,1). Scale 1:1.

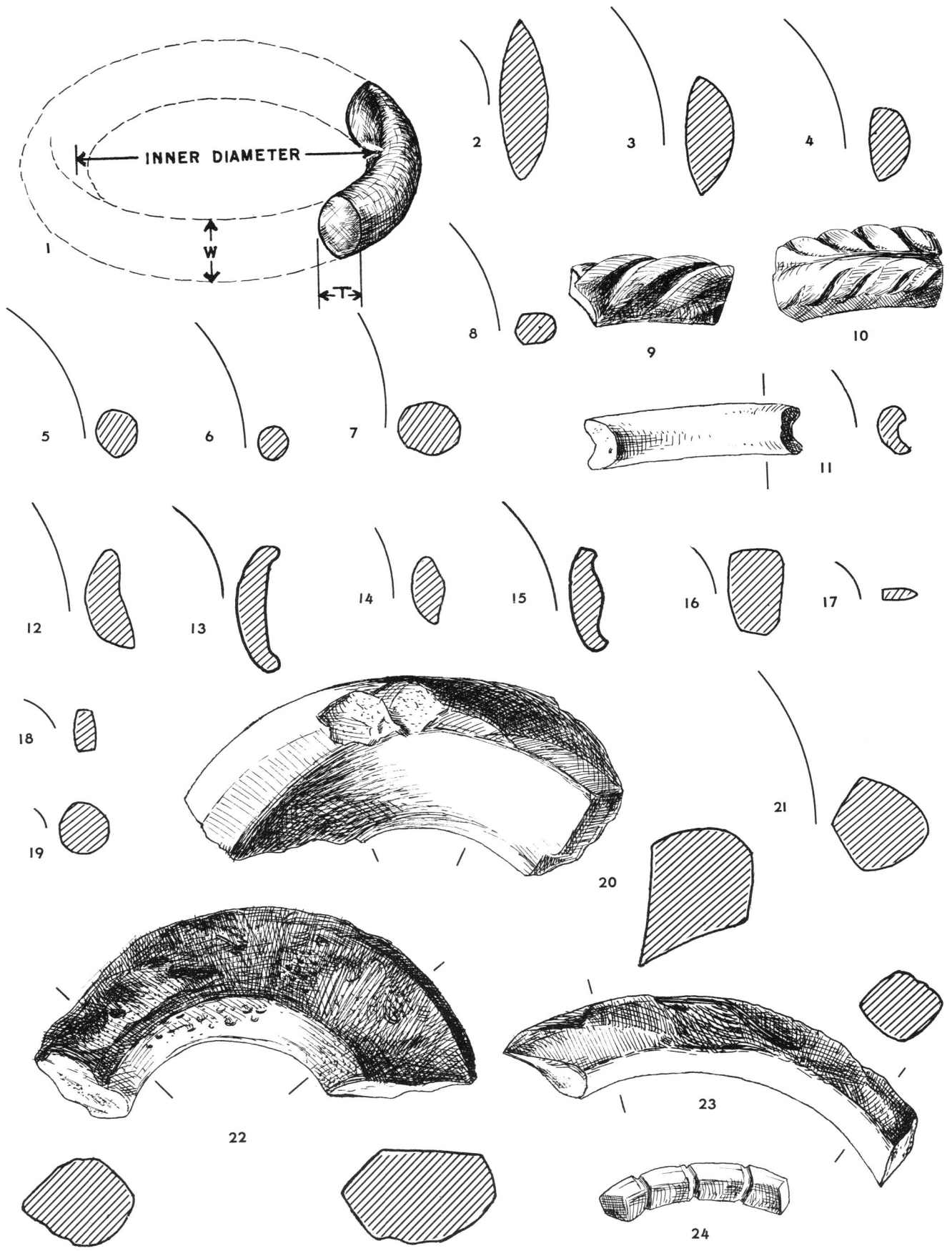

Fig. 135. Jarmo ground stone: indication of measurements for bracelets and rings, *1*; bracelets and rings, *2* (from F17,1), *3* (from J-II,2), *4* (from J-I,3), *5* (from GL1519,sf-1), *6* (from J-II,1), *7* (from J-II,5), *8* (from J-I,8), *9* (from J-II,1), *10* (from J-A,III-1), *11* (from J-II,2fl.), *12* (from J-II,1), *13* (from P19,3), *14* (from J-I,6), *15* (from J-I,8), *16* (from CF2529,1), *17-18* (from J-I,6), *19* (from N18,1), *20* (from J-I,sf), *21* (from RU1519,sf-1), *22* (from J-I,sf-1), *23* (from J-A,3m), *24* (from J-I,6). Scale 1:1.

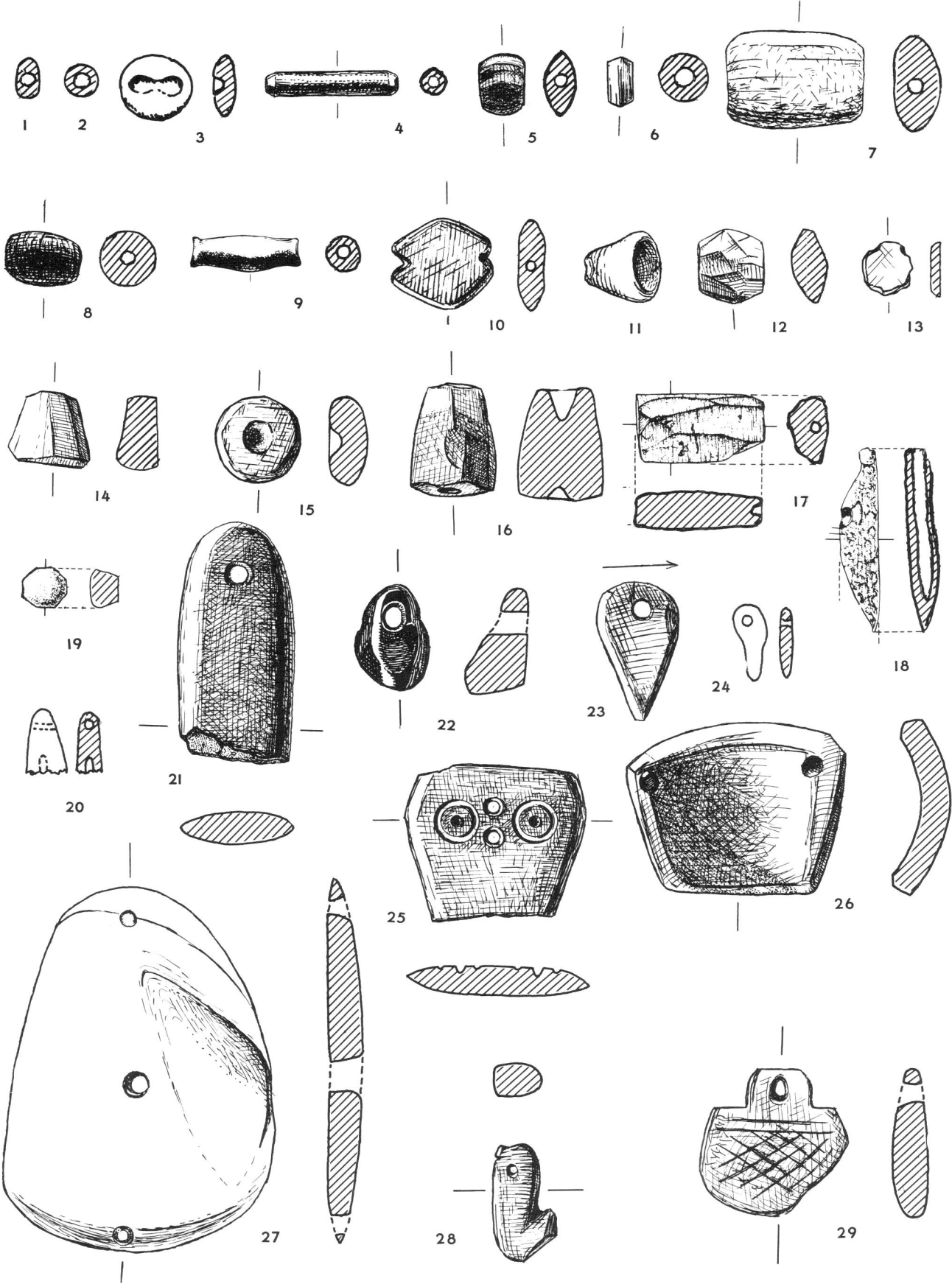

Fig. 136. Jarmo ground stone: beads, *1* (from J-I,7), *2* (from J-I,6c), *3* (from J-II,1), *4* (from S15,1), *5* (from J-II,5), *6-7* (from J-II,1), *8* (from F19,sf-1), *9* (from G17,2), *10* (from J-II,2), *11* (from J-II,1), *12* (from J-I,sf), *13* (from J-II,2), *14* (from J-II,4), *15* (from J-A,IV), *16-18* (from J-II,2); lead pellet, *19* (from GK59,4; see p. 000); pendants, *20* (from W11,3), *21* (from J-I,6), *22* (from J-II,2), *23* (from J-I,8fl.), *24* (from K21,7), *25* (from J-I,7), *26* (from M18,2), *27* (from J-II,6), *28* (from L15,2), *29* (from J-A,IV). Scale 1:1.

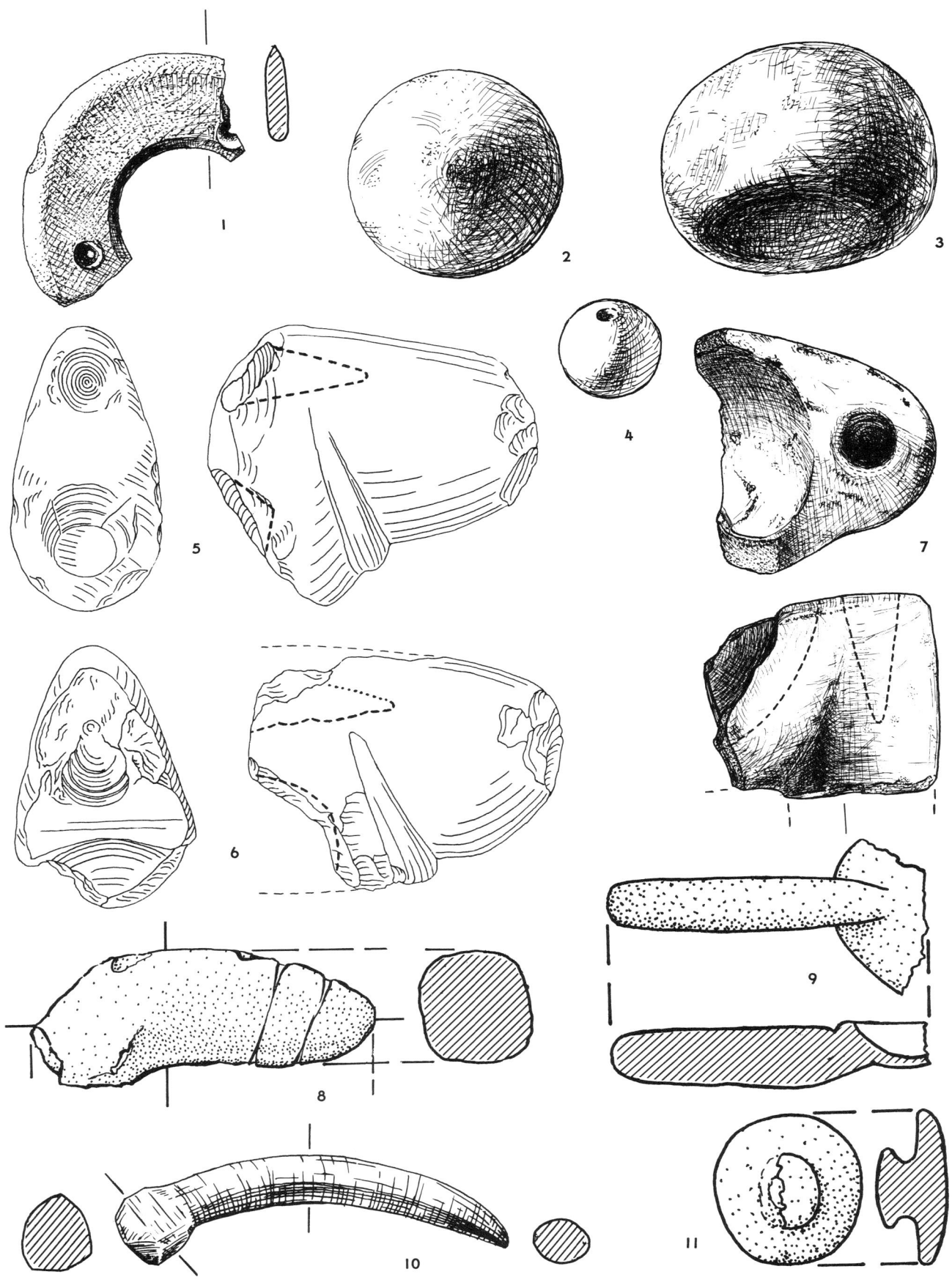

Fig. 137. Jarmo ground stone: broad flat ring, *1* (from J-I,dmp); ground stone balls, *2* (from J-II,5), *3* (from MQ1519,sf-1), *4* (from J-II,sf); phallic objects, *5* (from J-II,1), *6* (from J-I,3,pit 2), *7* (from J-II,W,sf-3), *8* (from F17,1); stone spoon, *9* (from G20,2); stone "nail," *10* (from M21,sf-1); stone "stud," *11* (from V16,sf-1). Scale 1:1.

Fig. 138. Jarmo ground stone: doorpost pivot stones, *1* (from J-II,4), *3* (from J-II,2fl.); unfinished round stone blank, *2* (from MQ1519,sf-1); miscellaneous, *4* (from J-II,1), *5* (from J-II,2fl.), *6* (from S15,2); shell objects, *7* (from L21,1), *8* (from N12,2), *9* (from J-I,8), *10* (from (J-II,1), *11* (from T18,5), *12* (from T11,3), *13* (from J-A,1-2). Scales 1:6, *1,3*; 1:2, *2,12*; 1:1, *4-11,13*.

Fig. 139. Jarmo ground stone: mullers, *1* (from J-I,dmp), *2* (from J-I,7); querns, *3* (from J-I,8fl.), *4* (from J-I,6), *5* (from J-I,1), *6* (from J-I,3); pestle, *7* (from J-I,3-4); mortars, *8* (from J-II,5), *9-10* (from J-II,2), *11* (from J-II,2fl.), *12* (from J-I,dmp). Scales ca. 1:3, *1-2*; 1:4, *7-8*; 1:5, *3,9-11*; 1:6, *6,12*; 1:7, *4-5*.

Fig. 140. Jarmo ground stone: palette, *1* (from J-II,3); rubbing stone, *2* (from R14,3); pecking and rubbing stone, *3* (from J-I, 3a); digging-stick weights or maceheads, *4* (from J-II,4), *5* (from J-II,5); whorl, *6* (from J-II,2); grooved stone, *7* (from G20,2); large drill bit, *8* (from MQ1519,sf-1); simulated drill showing how bit (no. *8*) could have been attached to a stick, *9*; quern and large ball, *10* (from J-II,W,sf-3 and L11,sf-1); doorpost pivot stones, *11* (from K16,1), *12* (from J-II,4), *13* (from J-II,2fl.); small borers and/or small pestles, *14* (from J-II,2fl.), *15* (from J-II,6), *16* (from J-II,2), *17* (from J-II,1); phallic objects, *18* (from J-II,1), *19* (from F17,1), *20* (from J-I,3). Scales ca. 1:3, *1*; 1:2, *2-8*; 1:8, *10-13*; 1:1, *14-20*.

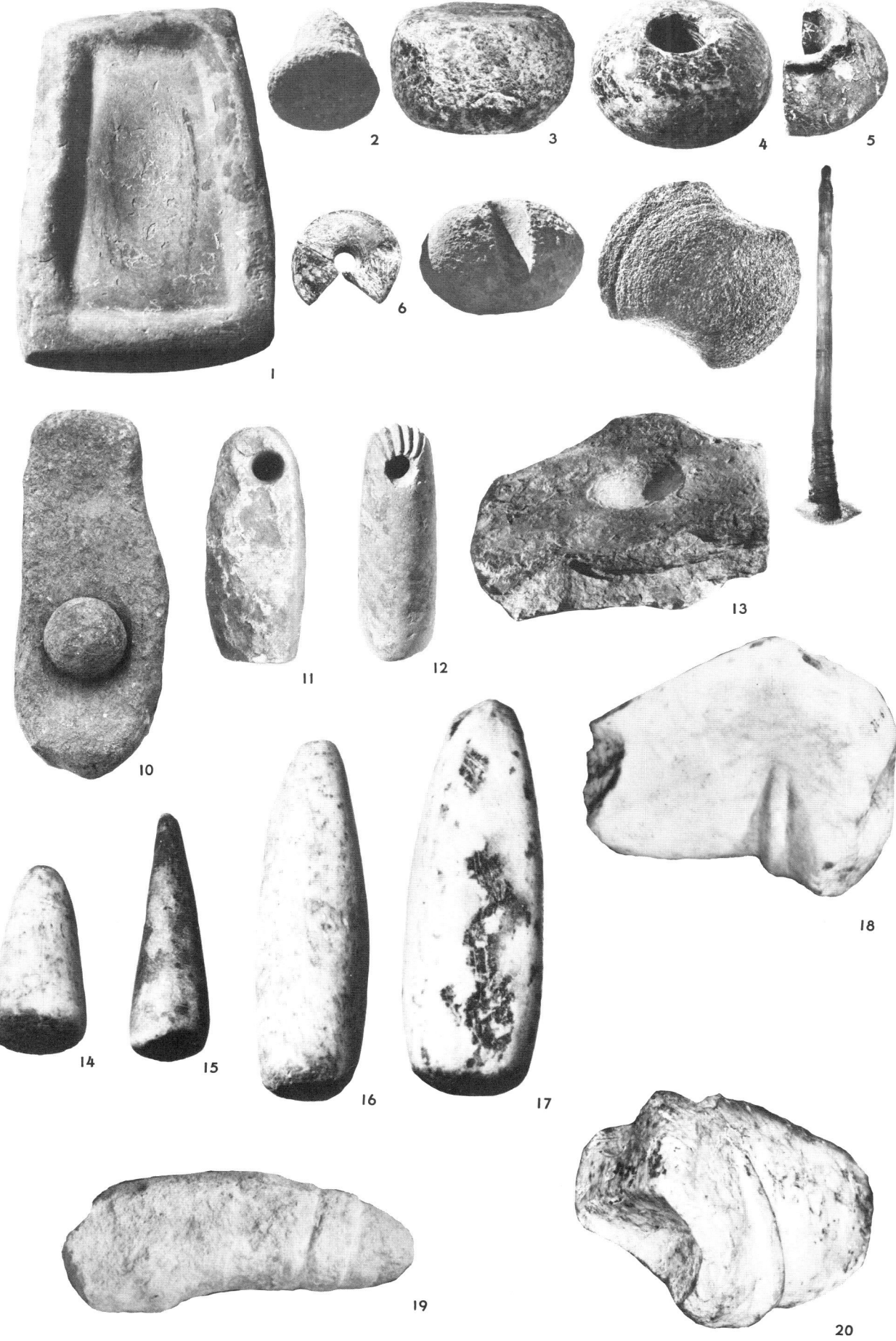

Fig. 141. Jarmo ground stone: hammerstone, *1* (from J-I,2-3); ground stone balls, *2* (from J-II,2), *4* (from J-A,3m), *5* (from J-II,1), *6* (from J-II,2); pecking and rubbing stone, *3* (from J-I,2-3); celts and chisels, *7* (from J-II,2), *8* (from J-II,6), *9* (from J-II,1), *10* (from Q14,4), *11* (from T16,4), *12* (from J-I,8), *13* (from J-II,3?), *14* (from RU1014,sf-1), *15* (from J-II,W,sf-3). Scale 1:1.

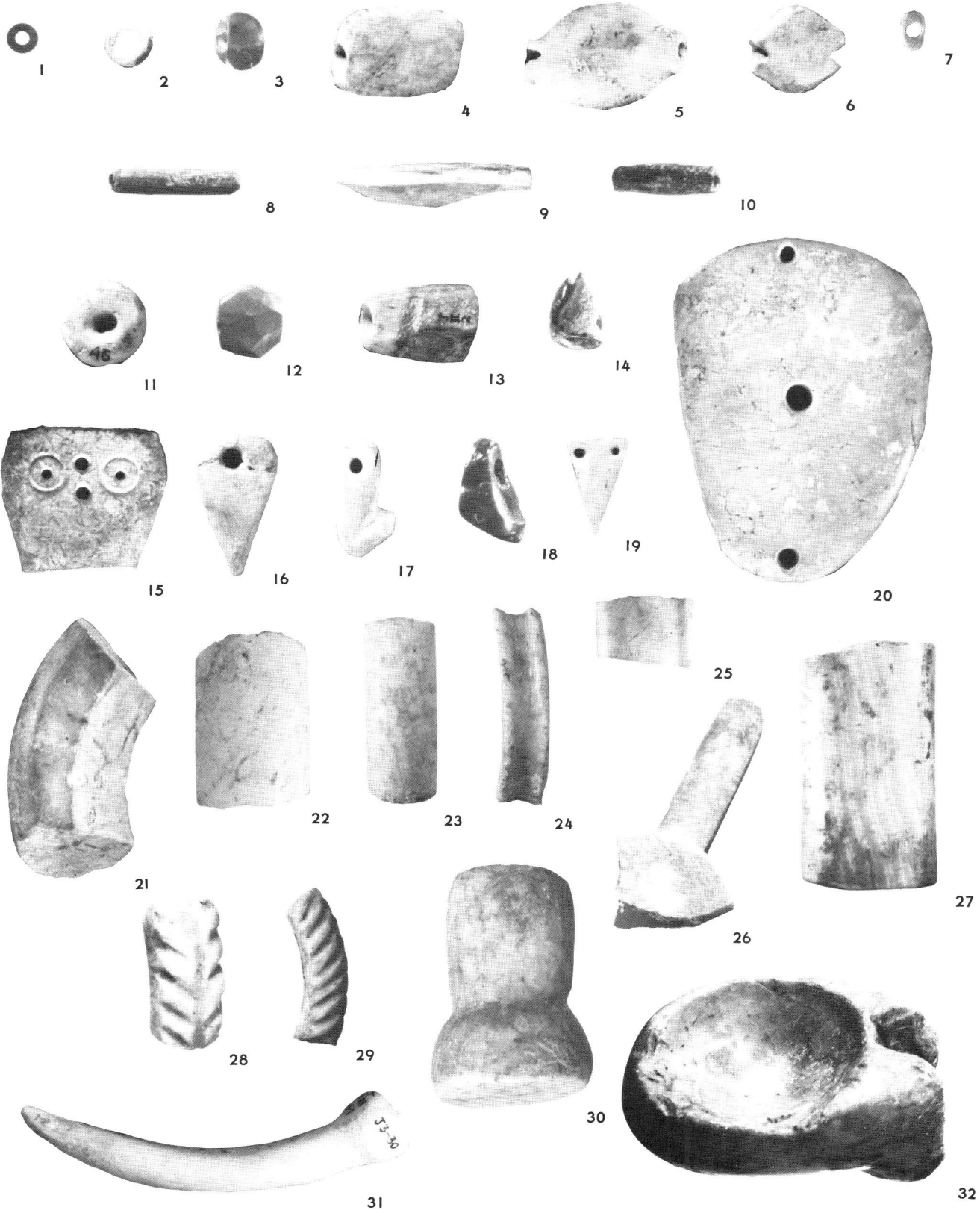

Fig. 142. Jarmo ground stone: beads, *1* (from J-I,6c), *2* (from J-II,1), *3* (from J-II,5), *4* (from J-II,1), *5* (from J-I,3,pit 2), *6* (from J-II,2), *7* (from J-I,7), *8* (from S15,1), *9* (from J-II,2), *10* (from G17,2), *11* (from J-A,IV), *12* (from J-I,sf), *13* (from J-II,2); shell, *14* (from L21,1), *19* (from J-I,8); pendants, *15* (from J-I,7), *16* (from J-I,8fl.), *17* (from L15,2), *18* (from J-II,2), *20* (from J-II,6); bracelets, *21* (from J-I,8), *22* (from J-II,2), *23* (from J-I,3), *24* (from J-II,2fl.), *25* (from J-I,8fl.), *27* (from J-II,1), *28* (from J-A,III-1), *29* (from J-II,1); stone spoon, *26* (from G20,2); stumplike object, *30* (from J-II,4); stone "nail," *31* (from M21,sf-1); phallic? object, *32* (from J-II,2). Scale 1:1.

REFERENCES

Bartlett, Katharine
    1933 *Pueblo milling stones of the Flagstaff region and their relation to others in the Southwest*. Museum of Northern Arizona, bull. 3. Flagstaff: Northern Arizona Society of Science and Art.

Beck, Horace C.
    1928 Classification and nomenclature of beads and pendants. *Archaeologia* 77:1-76.

Braidwood, Robert J., and Braidwood, Linda S.
    1960 *Excavations in the plain of Antioch I: the earlier assemblages, phases A-J*. Oriental Institute Publications, vol. 61. Chicago: University of Chicago Press.

Braidwood, Robert J.; Howe, Bruce; et al.
    1960 *Prehistoric investigations in Iraqi Kurdistan*. Studies in Ancient Oriental Civilization [SAOC], no. 31. Chicago: University of Chicago Press.

Garrod, D.A.E., and Bate, D.M.A.
    1937 *The Stone Age of Mount Carmel*. Vol. 1. Oxford: Clarendon Press.

Haury, Emil W.
    1931 Minute beads from prehistoric pueblos. *American Anthropologist*, n.s. 33:80-87.

Hayden, Julian D.
    1969 Gyratory crushers of the Sierra Pinacate, Sonora. *American Antiquity* 34:154-61.

Hole, Frank; Flannery, Kent V.; and Neely, James A.
    1969 *Prehistory and human ecology of the Deh Luran plain*. Memoirs of the Museum of Anthropology, University of Michigan, no. 1. Ann Arbor.

Korfmann, Manfred
    1973 The sling as a weapon. *Scientific American* 229 (4):34-42.

Petrie, W.M. Flinders
    1902 *Abydos*. Pt. 1. Egypt Exploration Fund, mem. 22. London.
    1917 *Tools and weapons*. Publications of the Egyptian Research Account and British School of Archaeology in Egypt, vol. 30. London.

SAOC 31
    1960 *Prehistoric investigations in Iraqi Kurdistan*. Robert J. Braidwood, Bruce Howe, et al. Studies in Ancient Oriental Civilization, no. 31. Chicago: University of Chicago Press.

Semenov, S.A.
    1964 *Prehistoric technology*. Trans. M.W. Thompson. London: Cory, Adams, and Mackay.

Solecki, Rose L., and Solecki, Ralph S.
    1970 Grooved stones from Zawi Chemi Shanidar, a protoneolithic site in northern Iraq. *American Anthropologist*, n.s. 72:831-41.

Sonnenfeld, J.
    1962 Interpreting the function of primitive implements. *American Antiquity* 28:56-65.

Wailly, Faisal el-, and Abu es-Soof, Behnam
    1965 The excavations at Tell es-Sawwan, first preliminary report (1964). *Sumer* 21:17-32.

Wright, Gary A.
    1969 *Obsidian analyses and prehistoric Near Eastern trade: 7500 to 3500 B.C.* Anthropological Papers of the Museum of Anthropology, University of Michigan, no. 37. Ann Arbor.

6

JARMO WORKED BONE

Patty Jo Watson

The Jarmo villagers do not seem to have been nearly so interested in the production of bone tools as they were in the chipping and grinding of stone and in the manufacture of clay figurines. The bone industry, to judge from the present sample, was not very large compared with either the flint and obsidian or the shaped clay industry, nor was there a great variety of items. (Possibly as much use was made of wood as of bone, but none of the wood was preserved.) The only worked bone category containing a really large number of items is that of awls, especially splinter awls. The majority of awls are medium to small, evidently meant for use with relatively lightweight materials (such as cloth, matting, and basketry, or thin animal skins). Heavy-duty awls are much less frequent at Jarmo. For purposes of general comparison, one may refer to the hundreds of awls found at Pecos, New Mexico (Kidder 1932). These are, on the average, considerably larger than the Jarmo awls. Most of the classes of Pecos awls, including splinter awls, were approximately 75-100 mm in length, at the top of the Jarmo range.

It is clear that the Jarmo villagers did possess rather finely woven cloth (chap. 7, Appendix) presumably manufactured from vegetable fibers (vegetable-fiber cloth was apparently present in some parts of Anatolia at least as early as the sixth millennium B.C. according to Burnham 1965 and Ryder 1965). They made slender bone needles with small eyes and probably used them to sew this cloth together for garments and other items. The awls might have been used with coarser cloth to make heavy bags and outer garments such as capes or cloaks and the like, and with hides to make water bags and other containers as well as footgear or other items of clothing.

The only particularly distinctive and characteristic type of bone implement from Jarmo is the haft (if that is what it is) made from a *Bos* or *Cervus* phalanx (large foot bone of cattle or red deer; fig. 143:2). Also noteworthy are the spoons, spirally ornamented rods, and the bone "points" (e.g., fig. 145:17,16, and 14, respectively), but objects of the latter two categories are quite rare.

The raw material for Jarmo bone tools seemingly came from both wild and domestic species: sheep/goat (some almost certainly from domestic animals), cattle, and red deer. Two items (possibly small awls; fig. 143:26-27) were made of hare metapodials.

The bone was worked by cutting or sawing and scraping (with flint or obsidian knives presumably), abrading (probably with fine-grained abrasive stone), polishing (perhaps with a piece of greasy hide or cloth), or some combination of these. The awls that are complete show traces of all these processes, as do some of the other items.

DESCRIPTION OF CATEGORIES

The present sample of worked bone from Jarmo includes 746 pieces (see table 23 for summary of worked bone by categories). The 521 recognizable objects were sorted into basic categories: hafts, awls, needles and pins, points, spoons, spirally ornamented rods, burnishers (*lissoirs*), worked horn-core tips, fleshers, and jewelry. The remaining 225 pieces were not clearly identifiable and were placed in various categories of miscellaneous items.

In the tabular material in this chapter the registration number of a specimen, if it has one, is given in italics. Objects in Chicago and Baghdad are indicated by (C) and (B), respectively. Numbers in parentheses indicate the greatest available measurement when an object is incomplete.

Hafts (figs. 143:1-3; 145:1-2)

This category comprises a series of phalangeal bones of large mammals, each with a hole bored longitudinally in the distal end. It has been suggested that these objects were used to haft flint blades. The blade would presumably have

---

The Jarmo worked bone from all three excavation seasons (1948, 1950-51, and 1955), with the exception of small decorative items such as beads and pendants, was sorted and classified by Perry Bialor, then a graduate student in the Department of Anthropology at the University of Chicago. The classification presented here is based on that used by Bialor with my revisions. The detailed descriptions and all tabulations are also mine, Bialor having supplied a catalogue of the objects but not a general description. I am indebted to Sandor Bökönyi, Hans Stampfli, and Mary Evins for the various specific identifications of bone.

The manuscript for this chapter was essentially completed by 1970. Very few additions and only minor revisions have been made since that date.

been inserted in the drilled shaft and held in place by bitumen or some other adhesive. Six of the 18 examples recovered do show traces of bitumen (one each from J-A,3m; J-I,3; J-II,3; and J-II,W,sf-3; and two examples from J-II,5), but it is usually on the lower surface. Only two have bitumen still adhering inside the perforation (both are from J-II,5). The borehole is nearly always very deep—usually within a centimeter or two of the end of the piece—but never completely perforates it. When the outer surface of the bone is free from weathering and limestone concretions, it is often shiny or polished looking, presumably from use, but it is not otherwise altered. On two specimens the drilling was badly placed and broke out through the dorsal surface of the piece; on one of these, a second correctly placed perforation was made. The drilling was probably done with a flint drill bit, perhaps mounted and used as a bow drill.

Hafts

Context	Measurements (mm)				Remarks
	L.	W.	Th.	Perf. Dia.	
J-A,3m	55	30	34	12-15	Red deer; (C)
J-A,3m	50	25	23	--	Red deer; (C)
J-I,3	65	30	32	13	*Bos*; (C)
J-II,1	55	20	25	10	*J2-141*; red deer; 1st phalanx; (C)
J-II,1	65	35	35	6-7	*Bos*; 1st phalanx; (C)
J-II,1	63	30	35	9	*Bos*; 1st phalanx; (C)
J-II,1	70	43	25	10	Onager; 1st phalanx; (C)
J-II,1	79	--	--	--	*J2-40*; onager?; (B); (fig. 145:1)
J-II,1	53	--	--	--	*J2-131*; red deer?; (B); (fig. 145:2)
J-II,2	68	32	30	12	*Bos*; 1st phalanx; (C)
J-II,2	55	22	25	10	Red deer; 1st phalanx; (C)
J-II,3	60	30	30	10	*Bos*; 1st phalanx; (C)
J-II,5	80	36	40	10, 10	*Bos*; 1st phalanx; 2 perforations; (C)
J-II,5	75	43	43	15-20	*Bos*; 1st phalanx; (C); (fig. 143:2)
J-II,W,sf-3	68	35	35	12	*Bos*; 1st phalanx; (C)
J-III,sf-1	(60)	43	45	12	*Bos*; 1st phalanx; (C)
K line,1	29	15	15	4	*J3-9*; pig; phalanx; (C); (fig. 143:1)
P16,3	71	40	33	--	*J3-3*; (B); (fig. 143:3)

All the hafts except one are large, within a range of 50-80 mm in length. The small one (fig. 141:1) could have been used only for a microblade less than 4 mm in width. Another possibility is that these hafts may have been used to mount splinter awls (see Tobler 1950, pl. XCIX*c*:1, where what appears to be a splinter awl is set in a clay haft).

Light-Duty Awls (figs. 143:4-11; 145:4-5)

Twenty-six of these awls were made by breaking a sheep/goat metapodial, then splitting one of the pieces lengthwise or cutting it obliquely some distance below the articulation. In either case, the articular end served as the butt of the tool, and the other end was sharpened with some abrasive object such as a piece of fine-grained sandstone. The split edges were apparently also smoothed by abrasion. Most of these awls are shiny and polished looking— presumably from use—on all outer surfaces, especially at the tip. Fine transverse striations resulting from the abrasion applied to the tip are usually visible at and near the pointed end. Occasionally, longitudinal scratches can be seen on the inner, concave surface of awls made on split shafts. These are probably traces of cutting and scraping with flint blades used in their manufacture.

Light-Duty Awls with Articular Butts

Context	Measurements (mm)			Remarks
	L.	W.	Th.	
J-I,3	88	--	--	*J-14*; (B)
J-I,7fl.	66	8	--	Artic. butt?; (B)
J-II,1	82	10	3	*J2-144*; (B)
J-II,1	33	9	4	Artic. butt, split; (C)
J-II,1	52	8	4	Split shaft; (C)
J-II,1	(77)	10	5	Butt broken; (C)

Light-Duty Awls with Articular Butts—*Continued*

Context	Measurements (mm)			Remarks
	L.	W.	Th.	
J-II,2	57	12	--	J2-264; (B); (fig. 145:4)
J-II,2	(37)	12	--	Butt broken; (C)
J-II,2	53	8	4	Metapodial butt; (C)
J-II,2	80	12	--	(B)
J-II,2fl.	64	9	10	Artic. butt, split; (C)
J-II,5	(11)	12	5	(C)
J-II,5	(75)	12	3	Artic. butt, split; (C)
J-II,5	89	10	5	(C); (fig. 143:4)
J-II,5	91	10	4.5	(C); (fig. 143:5)
J-II,6	112	10	3-4	(C); (fig. 143:6)
J-A,III	67	10	4	(C); (fig. 143:7)
D27,2	(61)	18	5	Butt broken; (C)
H24,3	83	13	5	Artic. butt, split; (C); (fig. 143:8)
L12,1	65	22	--	J3-12; (B)
M18,1	(40)	9	5	(C)
P16,3	(67)	10	6	Articular surface broken; (C)
P20,1	73	16	9	J3-10; (B)
S15,4	(45)	10	4	Butt broken; (C)
T18,3	68	15	4	J3-13; (C); (fig. 143:9)
X19,sf-1	(39)	9	4	Articular surface broken; (C)

NOTE: There were also 8 examples of ends of fragmented sheep/goat leg bones that were probably once the butts of light-duty awls: 1 proximal end (from J-I,2) and 7 distal ends (2 from J-II,1; 2 from J-II,2; and 1 each from J-II,4; J-II,5W; and J-III,1).

Nine light-duty awls consist of shaft fragments that lack an articular end and are simply split, then cut or broken off and smoothed at one end and left pointed at the other. In general, these awls are shorter than the awls with articular butts and are less common in the available sample of Jarmo worked bone. The butt ends of these light-duty awls made on shaft fragments are usually deliberately shaped (unlike those of splinter awls), and transverse striations—probably indicating shaping by abrasion—are frequently visible near the pointed ends. All high surfaces are usually well smoothed and shiny.

Light Duty Awls with Nonarticular Butts

Context	Measurements (mm)			Remarks
	L.	W.	Th.	
J-I,3a	35	9	3	(C); (fig. 143:10)
J-I,3-4	62	--	--	J-57; (B)
J-I,6	(48)	6	3	(C)
J-I,7	(61)	16	6	J2-59; (B)
J-I,8	(58)	10	10	(C); (fig. 145:5)
J-I,8fl.	102	8	--	Awl on fragment of long bone; (B)
J-II,1	43	9	3	(C); (fig. 143:11)
J-II,2	(22)	9	4	J2-265; (C)
J-II,2	41	7	2	(C)
K20,1	(27)	10	3	(C)

NOTE: The Chicago sample also includes 74 shaft fragments of what were presumably the light-duty awl type, with both their points and their butts gone. They were found throughout the various operations.

Heavy-Duty Awls (figs. 143:12-19,28; 145:3,6)

These awls range in size from 185 mm long and 35 mm wide (fig. 143:13) to a more slender specimen (figs. 143:16; 145:6) that is 110 mm long and 8-9 mm in diameter. The latter could be regarded as a particularly large light-duty awl.

The dividing line between light- and heavy-duty implements is not a distinct one, although the extremes are clear. The general method of manufacture for heavy-duty awls seems to have been the same as for light-duty ones: a bone shaft was split longitudinally or cut obliquely below the articulation, then the point was formed by abrasion (transverse striations are frequently visible at and near the tip). One example (fig. 143:14), however, looks as though it had been scraped and cut to a point rather than abraded.

Heavy-Duty Awls

Context	Measurements (mm)			Remarks
	L.	W.	Th.	
J-I,5	62	10	4	(C); (fig. 143:18)
J-I,6b	26	10	--	(B)
J-I,7	80	20	15	(C); (fig. 143:14)
J-I,7fl.	110	8	9	J2-276; (C); (figs. 143:16; 145:6)
J-I,8	46	5	--	(B)
J-I,8	53	7	--	(B)
J-II,1	50	8	--	(B)
J-II,2	140	28	12	Articular butt, split; (C); (fig. 143:12)
J-II,2	(86)	12	--	(B)
J-II,2	(90)	17	5	(C)
J-II,2	(30)	15	5	(C)
J-II,2	(50)	7	6	(C)
J-II,3	(90)	14	10	J2-311; (C); (fig. 143:17)
J-II,5	(40)	14	8	(C); (fig. 143:19)
J-II,5	41	10	8	(C)
J-II,5	133	25	--	(B); (fig. 145:3)
J-II,6	(40)	15	5	(C)
J-III,sf-1	(60)	15	9	(C)
GL1519,1	(82)	18	--	(B)
H24,3	36	8	3	(C)
L21,2	(40)	4	5	(C)
L22,2	75	17	14	(C); (fig. 143:15)
L24,sf-1	(12)	1	1	(C)
M20,sf-1	185	35	23	(C); (fig. 143:13)
MQ1519,2	88	15	--	(C)
N18,1	(55)	12	--	(B)
RU1519,2	(55)	12	5	(C)

NOTE: In the Chicago sample of Jarmo worked bone, there are also 15 miscellaneous shaft fragments with points that are probably pieces of heavy-duty awls. These were found in various contexts throughout the excavations; one from J-II,6 is illustrated (fig. 143:28).

Splinter Awls (fig. 143:20-23)

Splinter awls were by far the most common bone artifact produced at Jarmo, to judge from the present sample of the bone industry. They were made from slivers of bone (15-85 mm in length) and abraded at one end to form a point, although one was whittled into this shape (fig. 143:23) and one was double-pointed. Sometimes fortuitously pointed splinters were used as punches and awls. All 182 items in this category show definite use or wear at the tip, but only very rarely are there traces of shaping at the butt end or elsewhere. More than half of the group show striations at the tip. About 10% of the total are coarse or heavy in appearance and might be called "heavy-duty splinter awls." Nine somewhat dubious fragments that were probably splinter awls have not been included in the count.

There appears to be no particular significance in the different contexts from which splinter awls were recovered; their occurrence seems to be general throughout the operations and levels. These awls were presumably used for the same purposes as types previously described, but perhaps were more expendable.

The 123 complete examples of the light splinter awls range in length from 15 to 70 mm with a 37 mm average; the 19 complete heavy-duty awls range from 28 to 85 mm with an average of 36 mm. The Jarmo examples are definitely smaller than the 338 splinter awls found at Pecos, which ranged from 25 mm to somewhat over 150 mm in length with the average being about 95 mm.

Miscellaneous Awls (fig. 143:24-27)

Two tiny awls have been made on the split ends of two metapodials. One (fig. 143:24) has been deliberately shaped to a point by abrasion; transverse striations are visible on the cut edges and at the tip. The other (fig. 143:25) looks as though it had been broken—deliberately or fortuitously—and then used as an awl.

There are three other small awls of various kinds. They are made of hare leg bones. One of these (fig. 143:26) has a shiny shaft, a small articular butt, and a blunt point that looks smoothed and rounded from use. The specimen shown in figure 143:27 is more slender and pointed but in its present state shows no macroscopic signs of abrasion, only of use.

Miscellaneous Awls

Context	Measurements (mm)			Remarks
	L.	W.	Th.	
J-I,8	22	19	7	(C); (fig. 143:25)
L17,2	36	20	10	*J3-5*; (C); (fig. 143:24)
MQ1519,3	--	--	--	Hare metapodial; (C); (fig. 143:27)
R11,1	33.3	10	--	*J3-8*; hare metapodial; (B)
Z9,1	--	--	--	*J3-14*; hare metapodial; (C); (fig. 143:26)

There are 13 tip ends of awls, 8 with fresh breaks. The longest is 35 mm. Proveniences are as follows: J-I,sf-1; J-I,6; J-II,2; J-II,2fl. (3 examples); J-I,8; and J-B,2. The contexts of 5 are unknown.

Thirteen miscellaneous worked bone fragments, probably of awls, were also found. Proveniences are as follows: J-I,3; J-I,6c; J-II,1 (2 examples); J-II,2; J-II,2fl. (2 examples); J-II,3; J-III,sf-1; H17,2; H24,2; MQ1519,4; P16,6.

One object, found in J-I,8, looks as though it may have been an "awl blank" for the production of light-duty awls without articular butts, or of splinter awls. It is the proximal end of a cannon bone with deep, longitudinally scored grooves on two sides. It also has a transverse groove below the articulation and just above the break that may have been meant to break off the awl slivers outlined by the longitudinal grooves.

Needles (figs. 144:1-4; 145:7-11)

In 12 specimens the perforation or eye was produced by longitudinal scratching from both sides until the grooves met; this opening was then enlarged slightly (figs. 144:1-2; 145:9).

The only nearly complete needle of this type (*J2-236*)—from J-I,7—is 58 mm long and 2 mm in diameter. The top of the eye is broken off, but, when complete, the needle was probably not much over 60 mm long. All fragments in this class are about the same in diameter (2 mm) except one that is slightly larger (close to 3 mm). All are very shiny and polished looking; striations are not macroscopically visible. The only intact eye is about 1 mm in diameter. This type of needle was also found at Pecos (Kidder 1932, p. 22) but, just as the awls were, Pecos needles were apparently larger than their Jarmo counterparts. In a total of 15 such needles from Pecos, the range in length is from 2 inches to 4.5 inches (50 to 113 mm). Proveniences of the Jarmo needles with eyes made by scratching are as follows (unless otherwise indicated, one specimen was found in each level mentioned): J-I,6 (7 specimens, e.g., figs. 144:1 and 145:9); J-I,7 (*J2-236*); J-I,8; J-II,6; M18,2; and N17,4. All are in Chicago except the nearly complete specimen, which is in Baghdad.

In 10 other Jarmo specimens, the perforation is produced by drilling from both sides (e.g., figs. 144:3-4; 145:7-8,10-11). One complete example (*J2-269*, fig. 145:7) is from J-II,2; it is 67 mm long with a shaft diameter of 2.5 mm, a head diameter of 7 mm, and an eye diameter of 4 mm. The other fragments in this class had eyes of 2.0-2.5 mm except for one (from S17,4) with a 4-mm eye. The eye area of one needle—*J2-215* from J-II,2 (fig. 145:10)—had been flattened, probably to make perforation easier. One other fragment shows striations along the shaft, and another (from D19,4; fig. 144:4) shows both longitudinal and transverse striations. Two examples (from CF1519,2 and J-I,5) are gray in color, presumably from contact or near-contact with fire. The others are buff colored and are shiny and polished looking. Proveniences of the needles with drilled eyes are as follows (unless otherwise indicated, one specimen was found in each level mentioned): J-I,5; J-I,8 (*J2-282*); J-II,2 (4 specimens, including *J2-215* and *J2-263*); CF1519,2 (fig. 144:3); D19,2 (fig. 144:4); G15,2 (*J3-7*, fig. 144:2); and S17,4. The provenience for one specimen is lost. All needles of this type are in Chicago except *J2-215* and *J2-263*, which are in Baghdad.

There is one other needle in Baghdad (*J2-65* from J-I,6a), which has an eye diameter of 1.0 × 1.5 mm, but it is not possible to be certain from the drawing what type of head it has.

Pins (figs. 144:5-12; 145:12-13)

On 15 specimens the head is the enlarged butt end of the shaft (figs. 144:5-6; 145:12-13). None of these specimens is complete. The largest (fig. 144:5), found in PQ14,3-4, is 75 mm long and has a diameter of 9 mm. The others are all 4 mm or less in diameter, most being about 3-4 mm. All but two are quite shiny and polished. Proveniences are as follows:

J-I,3 (*J-26*)	J-II,3	MQ1519,sf-1
J-I,3,pit 2	J-II,5	P20,sf-1
J-II,1 (2 examples)	J-II,W,sf-3	PQ14,3-4 (fig. 144:5)
J-II,2 (*J2-218*; fig. 145:12)	J-A,III	T16,1
J-II,2fl. (figs. 144:6; 145:13)	M18,2	

All are in Chicago except *J-26*, which is in Baghdad.

On 22 specimens the head is tapered and rounded or squared-off with no particular demarcation of head from the rest of the shaft. None of these is complete; the longest (found in CF1519,2) is 65 mm long and 4 mm in diameter (fig. 144:7). Most are very well polished and buff in color, but one (from K19,1) is polished and black. Four have ends that appear to have been cut off square (see tabulation below). Proveniences are as follows:

J-I,3,pit 2	CF1519,2 (2 examples, 1 with squared end, fig. 144:7)	K19,1
J-II,1		K19,2 (2 examples)
J-II,2 (3 examples, including *J2-218* and *J2-243*)	GL1014,2	P16,3
	GL1519,3	R14,2
J-II,2fl. (2 examples, 1 with squared end, fig. 144:8)	H17,2 (squared end)	RU1519,sf-1
	H19,2	VY1519,sf-1
J-II,W,sf-3 (fig. 144:9)	K line,2 (squared end)	

All are in Chicago except *J2-218*, which is in Baghdad.

Three pins have decorated heads. One is a flattish gray fragment with an incised groove near the top (*J2-409* from J-II,6; fig. 144:10). Although the surface is polished, numerous transverse and horizontal striations are visible. A second example is from T18,sf-1 (fig. 144:11) and has a bell-shaped head; it is not possible to be certain whether the forked top was intentional or is the result of an old break. It is also quite well polished, as is the third example (*J3-98* from C22,2; fig. 144:12), which has a flattened perforated head. All three are in Chicago.

Shaft Fragments of Pins and Needles

Fifty-one pieces are portions of fine shafts, probably of needles or small pins. Fragments in this class with diameters of 2-3 mm are quite likely the shafts of needles; those with diameters of 3.5-4.0 mm are more likely to be the shafts of pins. The lengths of the fragments vary from 5 to 38 mm. Most pieces are buff to light brown in color and quite well polished, but 5 are gray and 6 are dark brown or black (all are polished).

There are 14 pieces of larger shafts, possibly fragments of pins. Lengths vary from 20 to 120 mm. Most are buff colored but only about half of them are polished; 4 show longitudinal striations (one of these also has transverse striations). Two are gray to black in color, indicating that the bone from which they were fashioned had been charred or burned.

Finally, there are 6 very large pieces, possible fragments of spoon handles or large pins. Lengths vary from 23 to 35 mm. All are polished and are buff to white in color.

Tips of Pins or Needles

Five of the tips show transverse striations (one has oblique transverse striations as well) and two (from J-I,3,pit 2 and J-I,6) show a series of intersecting planes that were formed by abrasion during the shaping of the tip. Two are brown in color, the rest are buff, and nearly all are polished.

Bevel-ended Shaft Fragments

Four shaft fragments are beveled at the ends. All have small diameters (ca. 2 mm) and may be reworked fragments of broken needles or the broken-off ends of bevel-ended needles. One fragment from J-I,6 (20 mm) has a bevel worked mostly from one side; a fragment from J-I,7 (10 mm) is beveled from one side at one end and apparently was worn smooth after beveling; another from J-I,7fl. (15 mm) has one end beveled from both sides, as does one from J-II,3 (32 mm). Three are light buff, but the specimen from J-I,7fl. is black to brown.

Bone "Points" or Gouges (figs. 144:13; 145:14)

Bone "points" or gouges are rare (6) and so far have been found only in the lower levels of J-I. They are fragments of hollow bone shaft cut transversely at one end and obliquely at the other. The oblique cut forms the point. The examples in Chicago are buff colored and polished and have signs of wear resembling that found on awls and hide smoothers. These points probably were not used as the heads of arrows but perhaps were just awls of a special kind or hafted in a special way. The examples in Chicago, however, show no evidence of hafting. Proveniences of bone points are as follows: J-I,6 (*J-44*); J-I,6a (*J2-67*, figs. 144:13 and 145:14); J-I,6-7; J-I,7 (*J2-275*); and J-I,8 (2 examples). *J-44* and *J2-275* are in Baghdad.

Pins or Needles

Context	No.	Diameter or range (mm)	Context	No.	Diameter or range (mm)	Context	No.	Diameter or range (mm)
Fine Shafts*			Medium Shafts			Large Shafts		
J-I,4	2	2-4	J-II,2	1	4	J-II,1	5	5-8
J-I,5	2	2-3	J-II,5	1	4	S17,4	1	4-7
J-I,6	16	2-4	GL1519,sf-1	1	4	Total	6	
J-I,7	7	2-3	GL1519,2	1	3.5-4			
J-II,1	3	3-4	H19,2	1	3	Tips of Pins or Needles		
J-II,2	2	3-4	K19,1	1	2.5	J-I,3,pit 2	1	3
J-II,2fl.	1	1.5	K19,2	2	3	J-I,4	1	2
J-II,3	4	1.5-3	N17,5	1	3-6	J-I,6	3	1.5-2
J-II,5	3	2-3.5	N18,2	1	4	J-II,2	1	2
J-III,sf-1	1	3.5	N18,4	1	3-6	E21,2	1	4
J-A,IV	1	2	P16,sf-1	1	3	N18,4	1	4
J-B,2	1	2.5	P20,sf-1	1	3	S15,3	1	2.5
K19,1	1	3	S17,4	1	7	sf	1	2
N12,sf-1	1	3	Total	14		Total	10	
P16,sf-1	1	2						
P17,3	1	3						
PQ14,4	1	2.5						
T16,1	1	3						
sf	2	3						
Total	51							

*Probably needles or small pins.

Spoons (figs. 144:14-20; 145:17-18)

Most of the spoons have round bowls, but 2 have oval, rather flat, bowls. There are 4 specimens that are relatively complete, and of these, 2 (*J-76*, fig. 144:14; and *J3-100*) have long handles and 2 (*J2-411*, fig. 145:17; and *J3-2*, fig. 144:15) have short handles. One short handle is perforated. A handle found in J-II,1 (fig. 144:20) was probably broken off a short spoon, although no fragment of the spoon bowl is attached. At the end of this detached handle is a perforation (4 mm in diameter) that was bored from both sides.

Nine of the preserved spoon bowls—from J-I,3,pit 2; J-II,1; J-II,3 (fig. 144:17); J-II,6; K line,1; N17,2 (fig. 144:15); PQ14,4; S15,4; and T11,3—are rather thin and delicate looking. The thickest example is no more than 3 mm at its

Spoons

Context	Description and measurements (mm)	Context	Description and measurements (mm)
J-I,3,pit 2	*J-76*; (L. 175); (B); (fig. 144:14)	N17,2	*J3-2*; round bowl (DIA. 36) with handle (L. 45+); (C); (fig. 144:15)
J-II,1	Handle (66 × 13 × 6) with perforation (DIA. 4); (C); (fig. 144:20)	N17,5	Handle fragment with very small part of bowl (MAX. 40 × 17 × 4); (C); (fig. 144:19)
J-II,1	Bowl fragment (DIA. ca. 40?); (C)	PQ14,4	Fragment of end of spatulate spoon (MAX. 28 × 22 × 2); (C)
J-II,3	*J2-303*; bowl fragment (MAX. W. now 10) with pieces of handle (L. 43); (C); (fig. 144:17)	Q15,2	*J3-100*; handle (95 × 6) with bowl (DIA. 23); (B)
J-II,5	*J2-404*; spatulate bowl (55 × 23 × 3); handle missing; (C); (figs. 144:18; 145:18)	S15,4	Bowl fragment (35 × 17 × 2); DIA. 35, probably close to original, but W. simply that of fragment; shiny black; (C)
J-II,6	*J2-411*; round bowl (DIA. 35) with short perforated handle (L. 14); (B); (fig. 145:17)	T11,3	Shallow round bowl fragment; original bowl TH. ca. 2 and DIA. ca. 55; (B); (fig. 144:16)
J-II,6	Bowl fragment, round and thin (DIA. 35, TH. 2); (C)		
K line,1	Round bowl fragment (DIA. 30, TH. 2) with small fragment of handle; (B)	Unknown	Handle fragment (L. 65, TH. 5) with stubs at former junction with bowl; (C)

maximum, and it thins to about 1.5 mm at the edges. This suggests that if these objects were eating utensils they were not used for spooning up large, heavy morsels. They are quite shallow also, and would not have been suitable for eating soup or other liquids. Foods like mush, porridge, or yogurt, however, could have been handled very efficiently with such spoons.

The spoons were apparently made by the same processes as the other bone objects: cutting and scraping with stone knives, abrading and shaping with coarse- to fine-grained stones, rubbing and polishing with a greasy hide. They are well made and in general very nicely finished, although on several of them the marks of the abrading or polishing tool are clearly visible as fine parallel striations.

Spirally Ornamented Rods

Five fragments of decoratively carved rods that may be portions of spoon handles or pins were found. Two are from J-II,1; one of these, *J2-204* (fig. 145:16), is in Baghdad and the other (fig. 144:21) is in Chicago. A third example, *J2-405* (fig. 145:15), is from J-II,5. The other two are from J-II,6 (fig. 144:22) and RU1519,1.

Burnishers (Lissoirs)

This category includes 43 fragments of worked bone, most of which are spatulate in shape and are probably burnishers (*lissoirs*) or hide smoothers (fig. 144:23-27; see also Semenov 1964, pp. 175-79). Included are 2 rectangular slips of bone, one from J-II,4 and the other from J-B,sf-1 (fig. 144:28), that might instead have been gaming pieces. A third fragment and possibly a fourth, both from J-B,2, may also fit into this group.

Burnishers (*Lissoirs*)

Context	Measurements (mm)			Remarks
	L.	W.	Th.	
J-I,W,sf	39	32	5.5	Probably rib fragment; both ends broken, longitudinal striations on one side, longitudinal and transverse striations on other side; (C)
J-I,3	65	--	--	*J-37*; rib fragment; (B)
J-I,3-4	45	26	3.5	Rib fragment?; all edges broken except one; a few longitudinal scratches; (C)
J-I,4	47	21	3	Rectangular, apparently complete; one end cut, other very shiny and smooth with mainly longitudinal but also some transverse striations; (C)
J-I,4	70	21	6	Fragment of split bone shaft?; one end broken, other well smoothed by use; inside edges showing transverse striations with longitudinal striations in center hollow and up to edges, longitudinal striations on outer surface; (C); (fig. 144:26)
J-I,5	45	17	3	Fragment, trough-shaped piece originally?; part of one rounded end intact; longitudinal striations inside and out; (C)
J-I,6	40	17	3	Fragment; part of one end ground flat, other end and one side broken off; numerous longitudinal striations on both surfaces; (C)
J-II,1	(see Remarks)			6 fragmentary pieces with part or all of only one working end preserved: 1 with both longitudinal and transverse striations; 2 with only longitudinal striations; 1 possibly a small hide smoother, with one end quite smooth and worn, the other end broken; 1 with one end squared by abrasion, other end broken off; 1 long narrow slip of bone, possibly part of awl shaft. Dimensions: 45 × 20 × 8 (fig. 144:27); 40 × 26 × 3 (fig. 144:25); 34 × 18 × 2; 38 × 7 × 2.5; 38 × 18 × 3; 57 × 15 × 5; all (C)
J-II,2	40	60	3	Large fragment, perhaps from wide burnisher; only one small piece of unbroken edge preserved but both inner and outer surfaces shiny from wear or polishing and showing longitudinal striations and various scratches; black flecks (bitumen?) adhering to one surface; (C)
J-II,2	35	18	5	Fragment with small groove cut across one end and six shallow cut marks along and at right angles to unbroken edge, other end and other edge broken, both surfaces with longitudinal striations; (C)
J-II,2	56	18	3.5	Piece of rib? with both ends broken; (C)
J-II,2	28	19	3	Specimen broken on both ends and one side, probably originally trough shaped, longitudinal striations both inside and out; (C)
J-II,2	(68)	23	--	Odd fragment; (C)
J-II,2fl.	50	13	3	Long narrow piece, perhaps once part of awl shaft; one end broken off, other end rounded and smooth with nearby traces of three cuts much smoothed over by wear; (C)

Burnishers (*Lissoirs*)—Continued

Context	Measurements (mm)			Remarks
	L.	W.	Th.	
J-II,3	29	14	5.5	Fragment, small piece of shiny smooth bone, probably once part of split shaft and hence trough shaped originally; all of one end and part of other end broken off; transverse striations on outside, longitudinal striations on inside; partially preserved end abraded flat; (C)
J-II,3	25	18	4.5	Small fragment, perhaps part of split rib; inner surface made up of cancellous tissue but well polished; one end broken, other end beveled to thin wedge; cf. Semenov's description of hide smoothers made of split rib, with cancellous tissue side used as main working surface (1964, p. 175); possibly from J-I,8 (label unclear); (C)
J-II,4	20	9	2	Very small fragment, perhaps from one end of hide smoother; longitudinal striations on both surfaces; (C)
J-II,5	32	16	3	Broken-off end; very shiny with longitudinal striations; tip especially smooth and worn; (C); (fig. 144:24)
J-II,6	118	28	2.5	Polished rib fragment; both ends broken off; a few transverse striations near end, longitudinal striations elsewhere; (C)
J-B,sf-1	64	26	3	Rectangular slip of bone, complete; probably made from rib fragment; one end cut, with transverse scratches nearby, longitudinal striations elsewhere; (C)
J-B,sf-1	40	16	2	End of spatulate object; rounded end especially worn and smooth; (C); (fig. 144:28)
J-B,2	50	25	3	Fragment, perhaps of rectangular piece like rectangular slip of bone from J-B,sf-1; transverse striations at one end, which has been cut or sawed, and longitudinal striations elsewhere; (C)
J-B,2	65	15	2	Fragment, perhaps of rectangular piece like rectangular slip of bone from J-B,sf-1; longitudinal striations; unbroken edge beveled off perhaps by wear; (C)
J-B,2	24	13	2	Fragment; both ends broken, one end possibly used as smoother; (C)
J-B,2	33	21	5	Fragment with only one side intact; longitudinal striations; (C)
E23,2	26	30	2.5	Broken-off end; (C)
E23,2	17	8	3	Very small fragment; all edges broken; (C)
E23,3	20	8	3	Both ends and one side broken; longitudinal striations on both surfaces; (C)
GL1519,1	19	20	2	Broken on three edges; longitudinal scratches; (C)
GL2024,sf-1	18	11	2	Small fragment; only one unbroken edge; (C)
M20,2	45	11	2	Incomplete piece; rough on one side, other side smoothed and shows transverse striations; one end rounded, other end broken off; (C)
MQ1519,3	25	11	1.5	Rib fragment?; both ends broken; longitudinal striations; gray, very shiny; (C)
MQ1519,3	16	10	2	Rib fragment?; both ends broken; longitudinal striations; gray, very shiny; (C)
RU1519,5	55	18	3	Rib fragment?; broken at both ends; longitudinal striations on both surfaces; (C)
RU1519,5	23	17	3	Rib fragment?; one end cut and smoothed, other broken; may have been rectangular object like first one mentioned from J-I,4; numerous longitudinal striations on both surfaces; (C)
T11,3	45	12	3	All edges but one broken; both surfaces very shiny with longitudinal striations; (C)
T16,4	16	15	2.5	Small fragment of one end of spatulate object; longitudinal striations; (C)
Z9,1	95	23	2	J3-6; one end broken off; intact end and edges very smooth, shiny, and well worn; (C); (fig. 144:23)

Worked Horn-Core Tips

A total of 22 worked fragments of horn-core points were found at Jarmo. This category can be divided into three groups as tabulated below.

Worked Horn-Core Tips

Description	No.	Provenience and remarks
Tips blunt and scarred or worn; may be flint-chipping implements or heavy-duty awls	13	J-II,1; J-II,2 (3 examples); J-II,2fl. (longitudinally grooved); J-II,4 (hole bored in proximal end); J-II,5 (2 examples); K line,1; MQ1519,sf-1; N17,1; RU1014,1 (proximal end cut off square and smoothed, fig. 144:30); X line,sf-1
Ground to rather sharp points, may be perforators	4	J-A,3m; J-I,6; J-I,8 (2 examples, e.g., fig. 144:29)
Tips broken off or gnawed off	5	G20,2 (cut off square and smoothed at proximal end); J-I,6; J-I,7; J-II,3; H16,sf-1 (two holes drilled longitudinally, one from each end)

Fleshers (figs. 144:31; 145:21)

Five objects that were possibly bone fleshers were found, but unfortunately not one of them has the working end intact. All were broken in antiquity at some point below the condylar surface, which probably served as the handle, but the resemblance is so close to fleshers identified elsewhere (see Steen 1966, p. 111; Kidder 1932, pp. 233ff., figs. 194-97) that it seems reasonable to suggest these objects were also used in hide preparation (see also Steinbring 1966). All the fragments come from J-I, levels 4, 5, or 8, except one which was found in J-D,sf-1 (this is the smallest fragment, however, and identification is not absolutely certain).

Fleshers

Context	Description and measurements (mm)
J-I,4	Fragment of left humerus of ungulate such as sheep/goat or gazelle; condyle partly trimmed or sawed off and very smooth and shiny as if from much use; 42 × 22 × 15; (C); (fig. 144:31)
J-I,4-5	Fragment of left humerus of sheep/goat or gazelle; part of condyle left on one end and trimmed like fragment from J-I,4; entire implement polished and smooth; 71 × 16; (C)
J-I,5	An articular end of sheep/goat or gazelle left humerus with small part of shaft preserved, much like fragment from J-I,4; whole object well polished; 45 × 26 × 15; (C)
J-I,8	Fragment of left humerus of pig; condyle and part of shaft present, both polished; 62 × 20 × 13; (C); (fig. 145:21)
J-D,sf-1	Small fragment of articular end, probably from humerus like those above?; 23 × 19; (C)

Jewelry (figs. 144:32-39; 145:19-20)

The jewelry or decorative objects made of bone include 15 beads, 18 rings, 17 ring or bead blanks, 1 bracelet fragment, and 2 pendants. All of the beads but one are tubular and seem to have been made from sections of hollow bone shafts; some are probably bird bone, one is a fragment of phalanx bone, probably of sheep/goat, and one looks like a hare or rodent bone. The technique used was probably much the same as that documented for the bone objects from Pecos (Kidder 1932, pp. 256ff., figs. 214, 217): a cut is made ringing the shaft just below the articular surface, which is then snapped off, and successive tubes are cut (or sawed) from the remaining shaft (fig. 144:32-33). The ends of the tubes may have been smoothed somewhat with a fine-grained abrasive stone, then the whole bead polished.

The bone rings are short, cylindrical objects of a general size and shape that would suggest they were used as finger rings. They were apparently made in the same way as the tubular beads—by cutting successive pieces from a hollow bone shaft. Three of the resulting rings are decorated with incised lines or grooves, but the majority are plain. Most are highly polished.

One exceptional ring (from T16,sf-1) is 30 mm wide and 5 mm thick and has an inner diameter of 30 mm (fig. 144:34); these dimensions indicate it was probably not a finger ring.

The blanks are bone shafts and shaft fragments that seem to have served as raw material for the manufacture of rings or beads. Some of the fragments contain part or all of the articular ends of the shafts. It is likely that these articular ends were cut or sawed off first, and then the remaining shaft was cut into beads or rings of the desired size as described above.

The bracelet fragment, found in J-II,1, is a small piece of what was apparently once a triangular-sectioned bone bracelet. The inner diameter was about 52 mm, the outer diameter 65 mm. No ornamentation is present on the preserved fragment.

One pendant, from J-II,1 (*J2-110*; figs. 144:39 and 145:19), is made from a worn canine tooth of a red deer (cf. the apparent imitation in stone in figs. 136:22 and 142:18). A hole about 3 mm in diameter has been bored through the root end and there are four small cuts, perhaps intended as decoration, near the lower end of the tooth.

The other complete pendant, found in J-II,2, is a perforated piece of polished bone 27 mm long. It is now in Baghdad.

Beads

Context	Measurements (mm)			Remarks
	L.	Dia.	Perf. dia.	
J-I,3	19	11	--	*J2-55*; (B)
J-I,7	25	4	--	*J2-206*; (B)
J-II,1	3	12	--	*J2-149*; disk bead; (B)
J-II,1	3	11	5	*J2-137*; disk bead; (C); (fig. 144:33)
J-II,1	11	5	--	Tubular bead; very small and thin walled; (C)
J-II,2	21	9	--	*J2-261*; (B); (fig. 144:32)
J-II,2	15	5	--	Gray, polished; both ends cut; (C)
J-II,2	15	6	--	Both ends broken; (C)
J-II,2fl.	30	10	--	(C)
J-II,3	30	14	--	*J2-304*; (B)
J-II,3	17	11	--	Made on 1st phalanx of sheep/goat; articular end trimmed off flush with rest of tube and abraded smooth; other end neatly cut and polished; shallow incision near nonarticular end (unsuccessful attempt to cut bead off here?); (C)
J-II,4	20	9	--	Probably bird bone; (C)
J-II,5	23	5	--	Probably bird bone; one end broken; (C)
J-II,5	22	7	--	Bird bone?; both ends cut and smoothed; all surfaces polished; (C)
J-B,sf-1	30	5	--	Hare or rabbit bone?; perforation very small and apparently completely natural channel, but ends neatly cut and smoothed; (C)

Rings

Context	Measurements (mm)			Remarks
	Inner dia.	W.	Th.	
J-I,dmp	12	7	2	*J2-58*; (C)
J-I,6	14	10	1	Incised lines or grooves around circumference; (C)
J-I,6	24	12	2	Incised lines or grooves around circumference giving fluted effect; (C)
J-I,6b	--	3	1.5	(C)
J-I,7	18-19	10	2	*J2-210*; three incised lines around circumference; (C); (fig. 145:20)
J-I,7	12	12	5	(C)
J-I,7	14	8	4	(C)
J-I,8	17-18	3	1	Fragment; (C)
J-II,1	19	3	1	Fragment; (C)
J-II,1	16	5	2.5	Fragment; (C)
J-II,6	22	4	2	Fragment; (C)
J-III,sf-1	16	4	2	Fragment; (C)
J-III,1	17-18	3	4	Fragment; polished, black; (C)
S15,sf-1	15	3	2	Fragment; brown; (C)
T16,sf-1	30	30	3	Broad, polished; (C); (fig. 144:34)
X10,2	19*	12	3	*J3-99*; (B)
Unknown	20-21	6	3	(C)
Unknown	--	3	1	(C)

*Probably outer diameter.

Ring and Bead Blanks

Context	Measurements (mm)			Remarks
	L.	Inner dia.	Th.	
J-I,3-4	14	--	--	*J-58*; fragment; incised groove at one end; (B)
J-I,5	27	10	--	Fragment of distal end of sheep/goat metapodial; marks of several attempts to cut through shaft just below condylar surface and traces of successful cut that allowed this surface to be snapped off; too small for adult's ring; (C)
J-I,6	85	11	4	Fragment of sheep/goat femur; most of condylar surface present at one end; traces of 2 or 3 unsuccessful attempts to cut or saw, plus successful cut that resulted in removal of fragment from rest of shaft; (C)
J-I,6a	31	15*	--	*J2-75*; fragment; polished, tubular; incised line at one end; (B)
J-I,6c	91	12	3	Probably distal end of sheep/goat humerus; shaft severed, and shallow cut made near end perhaps preparatory to removing a ring; (C); (fig. 144:36)
J-I,6c	37	5	4	Fragment of broken shaft; one end cut, second cut worked partly into shaft 20 mm from cut end; probably intended for tubular bead; (C)
J-I,7	19	8	2	Proximal end of sheep/goat metapodial; cut just below condylar surface; (C); (fig. 144:35)
J-I,7	48	13	4	Fragment of shaft of long bone; deep incision near one end indicating attempt to remove ring 7 mm wide; (C)
J-II,1	43	5	3	Sheep/goat metapodial from young animal, probably proximal end; (C); (fig. 144:37)
J-II,1E	45	13	5	Shaft fragment; 2 deep cuts at one end indicating attempt to make small ring ca. 10 × 10 × 2; (C)
J-II,2	37	10-11	4	Split half of distal end of sheep/goat metapodial; snapped off just below condylar surface; (C)
J-II,4	--	15	3	Shaft fragment; one end neatly cut, other end cut partly through and broken; dia. incomplete but probably inner dia. given; (C)
J-II,6	62	10	3	(C); (fig. 144:38)
J-III,sf-1	42	--	7-15	Shaft fragment of left humerus of pig; one end cut, other broken; (C)
J-III,sf-1	47	12 × 6†	4	Shaft fragment; one end cut, other broken; (C)
GF1519,1	25	4	2	Shaft fragment; one end cut, other broken; (C)
S15,sf-1	24	4	25	Shaft fragment; one end cut, other snapped off; (C)

*Probably outer diameter.
†Oval.

Miscellaneous Perforated Fragments

Three perforated pieces were found. They are described below.

Miscellaneous Perforated Fragments

Context	Description and measurements (mm)
J-II,4	Proximal end of sheep/goat cannon bone?; articular end trimmed flush with shaft, perforation (DIA. 4) drilled from end down into shaft; distal end broken off; part of small haft?; 30 × 10 × 12; (C); (fig. 144:40)
P16,sf-1	Fragment of sheep/goat phalanx; perforation (MAX. DIA. ca. 5) in center of one side at right angles to long axis of phalanx but reaching only central canal, not penetrating bone entirely; looks like a whistle but purpose impossible to define; L. ca. 22; (C)
MQ2024,sf-1	Fragment of calcined bone; broken or split longitudinally; split face smooth and polished from use; butt end perforated; perforation (DIA. 5) drilled from both sides; part of awl or bodkin, or pendant?; 40 × 12 × 7; (C)

Cut Ribs of Wild Bovid

Two fragments of worked *Bos* ribs were found. One, found in J-I,3a, is a long, rectangular-sectioned piece from a wild bovid. One end has been cut off neatly and there are several other cut marks near this end. The piece is 165 × 26 ×

16 mm. The other rib is a flat, platelike segment also neatly cut at one end and broken at the other and measuring 80 × 67 × 12 mm. Both rib fragments are in Chicago.

Miscellaneous Small Pieces of Worked Bone

There are 30 fragments that do not fit any of the major categories described above. Summary descriptions are given in the tabulation below.

Miscellaneous Worked Bone

Context	Measurements (mm)			Remarks
	L.	W.	Th. or dia.	
J-I,dmp	--	--	--	J2-45; tip end of small awl, pin, or needle?; (C)
J-I,sf-1	69	30	9	J-3; spatulate-ended fragment with perforation (15 × 6) worked into center; (B)
J-I,4	--	--	--	Same as item from J-I,dmp; (C)
J-I,5	57	17	8	Large, thick platelike piece; looks chipped or retouched on one edge; (C)
J-I,6	25	--	7	Incomplete tubular bead?; may be small phalanx but much altered by rodent chewing (probably mice); longitudinal hole from one end nearly to other; end from which hole made broken off; (C)
J-I,6a	98	20	15	Shaft fragment; both articular ends broken off; one end perhaps cut and broken off square; traces of battering at both ends; (C)
J-I,8	45	12	3	Tabular piece; well polished and beveled at preserved end; perforation (DIA. 3) drilled from both sides near bevel; (C)
J-II,1	138	27	5	Fragment; large, heavy piece of cannon bone shaft; both edges on interior surface scarred and battered as though object used as hammer; (C)
J-II,1	55	15	3	Part of shaft broken longitudinally; transverse striations on inside edges as though pieces rubbed on abrading surface; used as beamer?; (C)
J-II,1	35	--	5	J2-138; comblike fragment; incised and notched along edge to form rough teeth; (B)
J-II,1	23	19	3	Comblike fragment; 3 grooves worked in; (C); (fig. 144:42)
J-II,1	28	9	3	Groove worked into one end; cut marks or scratches visible on upper surface; (C)
J-II,1	16	16	--	Fragment; center perforation (DIA. 2.5); part of pendant?; (C)
J-II,1	38	15	10	J2-18; fragment; roughly cylindrical; one end smoothly cut off, the other snapped off; (C)
J-II,1	10	5	3*	Fragment; small section of burned tubular shaft; (C)
J-II,2	47	7	10	Rectangular piece of solid bone; one end with some cancellous tissue that has been cut and smoothed to present shape; other end sawed or cut off; 2 longitudinal striations worked into one side; (C)
J-II,2	112	10	4	Polished rodlike fragment; almost completely blackened; (C)
J-II,2	--	--	--	J2-299; shaped like small awl but several hollows or grooves worked into one surface, possibly as decoration; (B)
J-II,2fl.	65	17	8	Heavy shaft fragment; rounded, polished end; generally darkened in color, probably by fire; fine striations along one edge at right angles to shaft, elsewhere longitudinal striations; striations and cuts about rounded end, other broken off; (C)
J-III,sf-1	65	12	2	Fragment of cannon bone shaft; one end much smoothed (from use as hide scraper?); striations parallel to axis and especially apparent on outer surface; other end broken; (C)
J-III,sf-1	44	18	4	Solid, tabular bone fragment; one end cut and snapped, other abraded to sharp point; (C); (fig. 144:44)
G22,1	--	--	--	J3-11; looks somewhat like fishhook; (C); (fig. 144:41 and see Clark 1952, fig. 43)
G24,sf-1	--	--	--	Fragment; double-bored perforation; polished on one face; part of pendant?; (C)
GL1519,5	76	15	2	Fragment of split shaft; striations or scratches on inner surface; (C)
MQ2024,1	30	10	4	Fragment of calcined bone shaft; roughly diamond shaped; edges shaped by friction and showing numerous scratches; (C); (fig. 144:45)
N17,3	19	4	3	Fragment; one end pointed, other end broken; surfaces polished; fish gorge?, although very small; (C); (fig. 144:43)

Miscellaneous Worked Bone—Continued

Context	Measurements (mm)			Remarks
	L.	W.	Th. or dia.	
N18,4	25	3	2*	Fragment of shaft; bird bone?; highly polished; (C)
PQ14,4	89	16	11	Fragment of cannon bone shaft; both articular ends broken off; one end looks deliberately battered to blunt point; (C)
X12,2	15	10	5*	Calcined fragment of tubular bone; both ends snapped off; (C)
Y15,1	40	8	8	Cylindrically whittled fragment; outer surface cut away leaving core of cancellous tissue exposed in several places; (C)
Unknown	34	11	6	Fragment of polished gray bone; ridge carved in bas-relief at one end; (C)
Unknown	--	--	--	Tip end of small awl, pin, or large needle; (C)

*Inner diameter.

Fragments of Polished Bone

There are also 35 small fragments of miscellaneous polished bone; they are listed below.

Fragments of Polished Bone

Context	Measurements (mm)			Remarks
	L.	W.	Th.	
J-B,sf-1	27	9	4	Rib fragment?; transverse striations near one end on lower surface, longitudinal striations on upper surface; (C)
J-B,2	22	18	3	Fragment of tortoise carapace?; may have been cut on one edge; (C)
J-I,3	15	7	1	Shiny chip; (C)
J-I,3a	30	16	1	Shiny spall from shaft; (C)
J-I,5	26	14	4	Spall; worn and smooth on all surfaces as if weathered or waterworn; (C)
J-I,5	17	15	2	Same as above item; (C)
J-I,6	20	8	6	Thickish piece; looks weathered and smooth like spalls from J-I,5; (C)
J-I,6	26	7	1.5	Fragment; broken at both ends; part of small awl?; (C)
J-I,6a	16	5	3	Fragment; transverse cut on one end almost as for ring blank but perhaps part of pin or small awl; fresh break on end opposite cut; (C)
J-I,7	25	15	2	Fragment; worn or weathered; (C)
J-I,8	31	7	3	Splinter; shiny, black: from awl shaft?; (C)
J-II,1	--	--	--	Part of awl shaft?; marks of mouse-sized rodent teeth; (C)
J-II,1	55	17	5	Fragment of burnisher?; (maximum dimensions given); (C)
J-II,1	30	20	3	Same as above
J-II,1	35	25	2	Same as above
J-II,1	40	8	4	Same as above
J-II,1	23	11	2	Same as above
J-II,1	22	10	2	Same as above
J-II,2	57	20	4.5	Fragment of large, split shaft; much polished on inside edges where many longitudinal striations visible; outer surface also polished; (C)
J-II,2	56	9	6	Splinter; one naturally beveled end; polished on inner surface of bevel; (C)
J-II,2	29	7	2	Fragment; black, shiny; from burnisher?; (C)
J-II,3	30	10	3	Rib fragment?; used as hide smoother?; (C)
J-II,4	10	10	2	Chip; shiny and polished looking on both inner and outer surfaces; (C)
J-II,5	12	10	3	Flattened section of awl shaft from near tip?, but broken at both ends; very well polished, numerous transverse striations on edges and one surface; (C)
J-III,sf-1	38	16	5	Fragment; flat, tabletlike, gray; much polished on all surfaces, numerous longitudinal striations; (C)
J-III,1	35	15	2	Fragment of hollow shaft; much polished on outer surface; (C)

Fragments of Polished Bone—*Continued*

Context	Measurements (mm)			Remarks
	L.	W.	Th.	
GL2024,sf-1	30	10	3	Fragment; small, flat, shaped like asymmetrical teardrop; surface brown to black and nicked and battered but shiny where intact; transverse striations visible on edges—probably from the shaping abrader; some signs of wear on tip; (C); (fig. 144:45)
H20,2	25	18	5	Fragment; shiny, gray; longitudinal groove; (C)
RU1519,1	20	13	4	Fragment; small, gray; shiny outer surface with longitudinal scratches; cancellous tissue showing on inner surface; (C)
S17,2	22	15	5	Fragment of disk?; looks like part of rim with outer edge squared off neatly and all surfaces polished, striations in various directions; (C); (fig. 144:46)
T16,4	11	7	4	Fragment of shaft; gray; mirrorlike polish; (C)
T16,4	20	12	4	Black; (C)
Unknown	--	--	--	Small fragment of shaft; very shiny; (C)
Unknown	25	10	6	Fragment of rib; shiny, black; cut marks at one end, other end broken; (C)
Unknown	18	9	1.5	Fragment; very shiny, black, thin; numerous longitudinal striations; burnisher fragment?; (C)

DISCUSSION AND CONCLUSIONS

Stratigraphic Distribution of Categories

The bone artifacts from Jarmo are too small a sample to permit definite conclusions to be drawn concerning stratigraphic distributions. To the degree that the present sample may be representative, however, there do seem to be some trends (see table 23).

The hafts made of phalangeal bones are evidently characteristic of the later Jarmo levels. In addition, all spoons and spirally ornamented rod fragments (possible spoon handles) come from the later levels. Save for one example, all of the burnishers come from the later levels and this is also true for the bone beads. The only bone artifact found exclusively in the earlier levels is the point or gouge.

It is quite possible that these figures have little significance because the sample is so small that the distributions could be accidental, especially in view of the fact that the later levels involved many more cubic meters of excavated earth than did the earlier levels. For this reason, however, the distribution of bone points or gouges—restricted in the present sample to the earlier levels—quite likely reflects the true situation. This type of bone tool probably was made at Jarmo almost exclusively during the earlier occupation and had gone out of use by the time of the later levels. Distribution of phalangeal hafts is probably also representative of the real situation; these objects seem truly characteristic of later rather than earlier Jarmo.

Comparisons with Other Sites

There are few published comprehensive descriptions of bone industries from sites comparable with Jarmo.

The total of 83 bone artifacts from Ali Kosh (Hole, Flannery, and Neely 1969, pp. 214-19) includes both heavy- and light-duty metapodial and splinter awls, needles with drilled eyes, burnishers like the Jarmo ones (but called "spatulas"), and a few items not directly comparable with those from Jarmo (a chisel, a flaker or fabricator, long-bone hafts, a possible knife).

The range of bone tools from Hassuna includes a number of interesting pieces (Lloyd and Safar 1945, pl. X:2). There are many awls with articular butts and one with a bitumen haft (see also the one from Arpachiyah, Mallowan and Rose 1935, pl. XIIa, bottom row). One of the other Hassuna implements looks very much like a flesher (it is described as a chisel), and most of the pieces in the bottom row of plate X:2 in the Hassuna report (Lloyd and Safar 1945), some of them perforated, look like burnishers or smoothers comparable with those from Jarmo.

Similarly, from Matarrah there are a perforated burnisher and what looks like a flesher fragment (Braidwood, Braidwood, et al. 1952, fig. 21:9,14). There are also needles and tubular beads (Braidwood, Braidwood, et al. 1952, pl. XII:4 and probably 5, and pl. XII:10-11).

At Tepe Gawra, several awls with articular butts were found, as well as two bone tools that had apparently been hafted. One of them appears to be a splinter awl set in a clay haft, and the other is a spatulate object made on a split bone shaft that retains remnants of a bitumen haft (Tobler 1950, pls. XCIXc:1 and XCVIIIb:5).

The available sample of the Halafian bone industry from Banahilk is small (a total of 35 pieces) and only one type—cannon bone awls (7 examples)—is comparable with those of Jarmo. The worked bone from the Turkish

Halafian site of Girikihacıyan, although not abundant, shows somewhat closer similarities to some of the Jarmo pieces. Of the 52 identifiable bone tools found at Girikihacıyan, 19 were burnishers and 24 were awls. The burnishers were nearly all made of rib fragments and, like those from Jarmo, were probably hide-working tools. Most of the awls were made from ungulate metapodials and, again like the Jarmo specimens, consisted of light-duty and heavy-duty implements (long, slender points and short, blunt points).

FUNCTIONS OF THE JARMO BONE TOOLS

The sample of worked bone from Jarmo can be grouped according to labels that suggest possible functions. There are at least four such groups into which the available array of objects may be placed.

1. Hide-working tools: awls (possibly including the pointed horn-core tips and the points), fleshers, and burnishers. Hides were probably removed with sharp-edged flint or obsidian blades and flakes and were then soaked or allowed to decompose for a few days. Next, the flesh and hair were removed. The fragments here called fleshers were presumably used to clean excess tissue from the inside of the skin. The hair, if it could not be plucked off, was probably removed with stone scrapers. This could also have been done with a beaming tool or drawknife-like implement which could be made by removing part of one side of a bone shaft to produce two scraping edges. Such a tool would be used by grasping it in both hands, one on each end, and pulling it across the hide toward the body. (So far no beaming tool has been positively identified at Jarmo, although one fragment could have been part of one.) The hide might then have been treated by rubbing the entire outer surface with some substance such as animal fat. According to Semenov, this compresses the skin and makes it less permeable. The Jarmo burnishers look like fragments of the type of hide rubber and smoother illustrated in Semenov (1964, fig. 93).

Steinbring (1966) discusses bone hide-fleshers of the modern Ojibwa, but says nothing about rubbing or burnishing the hide. Driver (1969, p. 174), however, notes that North American Indian groups have various means of dressing hides, including rubbing them or pulling them back and forth over a hard surface (which would achieve the same result). At Hasanabad, a present-day village in western Iran, goat hides meant to serve as water containers are cured as follows: First, as much hair as possible is plucked from the skin. Next, the skin is put into a pot to soak in a mixture of flour and *dugh* (a kind of buttermilk made by churning yogurt) for one week, after which it is washed and placed for five to seven days in a liquid derived from soaking acorn hulls in water. The inside of the skin is thoroughly scraped with a knife, then the hide is stretched by two people pulling at it from opposite directions. It is then taken to a small sand pit near the village, packed tightly with sand, a little at a time, and beaten with a short wooden cylinder; this apparently stretches and shapes the skin. During this process the hide is frequently moistened with the acorn-hull solution. Finally, the skin is smoked over an oak fire.

The Jarmo bone awls were probably used in working up the hides to make garments, bedding, tents, and containers.

2. Cloth-working tools: needles and awls. The main identifiable cloth-working tool is the needle. All known examples are quite fine and slender, thus implying the presence of fine cloth. As mentioned earlier, awls might have been used for working coarse cloth such as burlap.

If tailored or even semitailored garments were worn, the cloth must have been cut with stone knives, or torn into pieces of the right size (a technique used in Hasanabad today where scissors are not ordinarily found in village homes). The tear could have been started and guided by cutting the edge of the cloth with a sharp-edged piece of flint or obsidian. The pieces may have been sewn together using fine vegetable fibers or possibly animal nerves or sinews as thread. Pieces of coarse cloth (to make a large bag, for instance) could have been fastened together just as pieces of leather can be by punching holes in the edges and lashing them together with heavy thread.

3. Decorative items: jewelry. The jewelry category is made up of items suggesting personal ornament, such as finger rings, beads, pendants, and a bracelet. Except for the rings, however, all of these items at Jarmo are more numerous and better made in ground stone.

4. Eating utensils: spoons, pins (if used as skewers). The group of eating utensils is made up largely of spoons, which are relatively common if one includes the handles that were probably from spoons. Some of the pins could have served as food skewers, somewhat as forks are used today.

There are a few other possible uses for some of the items in this category. Pins may have been used to fasten clothing or hair. Some awls may have been used in making matting or coiled basketry (see chap. 7, Appendix).

Heavy-duty awls, including some of the worked horn-core tips, could have served as weaving tools. Today, Hasanabad rug weavers use a blunt-pointed, wooden, awllike tool, which is periodically raked across the warp just above the advancing weft to keep the strands in order.

The pierced phalangeal bones may have been hafts for flint bladelets (or for splinter awls), but—as already noted—their function is not certain.

The overall impression given by the Jarmo bone industry, as we now know it, is that awls (especially light-duty awls) were by far the most important bone tools. Awls and awl fragments make up 50 percent of the total 746 fragments of worked bone. Splinter awls are much more common than any other single type of bone artifact. If these awls were indeed used in hide working and cloth working, then these must have been important activities.

Table 23.—Summary of Jarmo Worked Bone Artifacts by Categories

Category	Earlier levels (J-I,6-8; J-A,III, IV, and V)	Later levels (J-I,1-5; J-II,1-6; and all test squares)	Total
Hafts	--	18	18
Light-duty awls			
With articular butts	1	25	26
Without articular butts	3	6	9
Splinter awls	19	132	151
Shaft fragments, tips and butts missing	8	66	74
Heavy-duty awls	5	22	27
Splinter awls	3	19	22
Miscellaneous awls	1	4	5
Miscellaneous awl? fragments and awl tip ends	3	23	26
Needles			
With scratched eye	9	3	12
With drilled eye	2	8	10
Pins			
With enlarged head	1	14	15
With tapered and rounded head	--	22	22
With decorated head	--	3	3
Pin or needle shaft fragments			
Fine	24	27	51
Medium	--	14	14
Thick	--	6	6
Pin or needle tips	3	7	10
Points or gouges	6	--	6
Spoons	--	15	15
Spirally ornamented rod fragments	--	5	5
Burnishers	1	42	43
Worked horn cores			
With blunt tips	--	13	13
With sharp tips	--	4	4
Miscellaneous	2	3	5
Fleshers	1	4	5
Jewelry			
Beads	1	14	15
Rings	8	10	18
Ring and bead blanks	6	11	17
Bracelets	--	1	1
Pendants	--	2	2
Miscellaneous fragments			
Perforated	--	3	3
Worked bone	3	27	30
Polished bone	5	30	35
Total	115	603	718

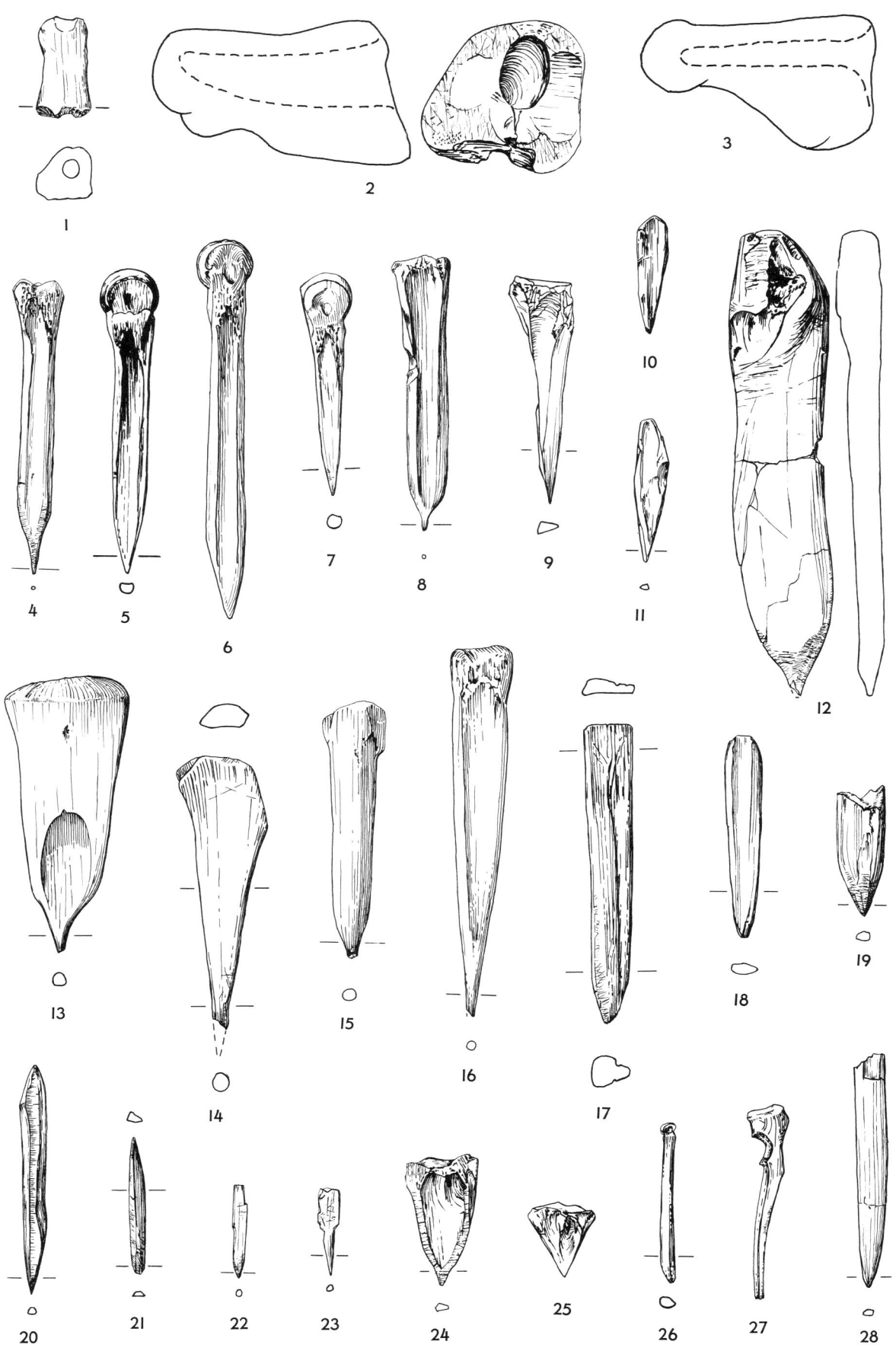

Fig. 143. Jarmo worked bone: hafts, *1* (from K line, 1), *2* (from J-II,5), *3* (from P16,3); light-duty awls, *4-5* (from J-II,5), *6* (from J-II,6), *7* (from J-A,III), *8* (from H24,3), *9* (from T18,3), *10* (from J-I,3a), *11* (from J-II,1); heavy-duty awls, *12* (from J-II,2), *13* (from M20,sf-1), *14* (from J-I,7), *15* (from L22,2), *16* (from J-I,7fl.), *17* (from J-II,3), *18* (from J-I,5), *19* (from J-II,5), *28* (from J-II,6); splinter awls, *20* (from P16,5), *21* (from S17,4), *22* (from J-II,3), *23* (from F25,2); miscellaneous awls, *24* (from L17,2), *25* (from J-I,8), *26* (from Z9,1), *27* (from MQ1519,3). Scale 3:5.

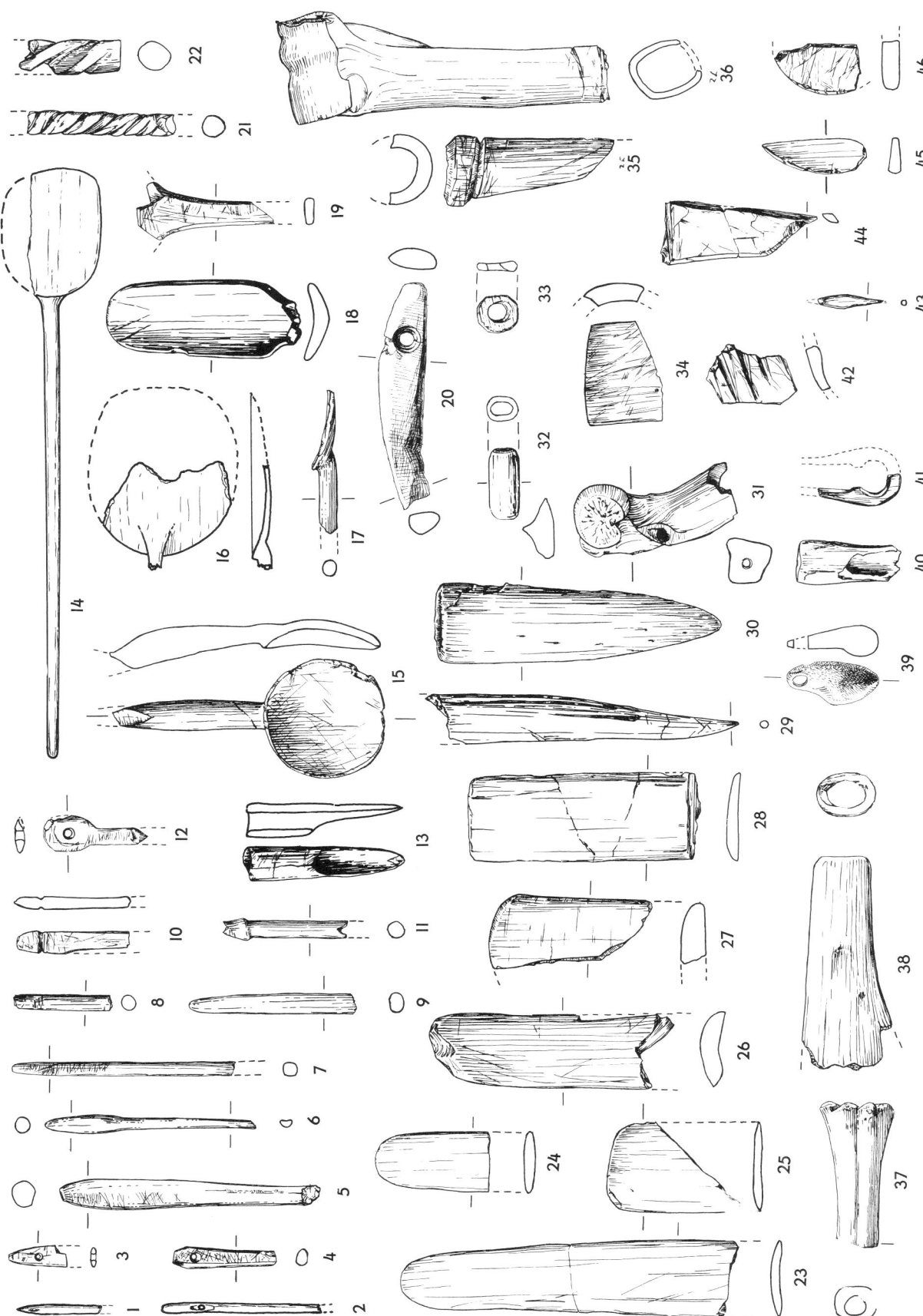

Fig. 144. Jarmo worked bone: needles, *1* (from J-I,6), *2* (from CF159,2), *3* (from G15,2), *3* (from J-I,4), *27* (from J-I,4), *28* (from J-B,sf-1); worked horn-core tips, *29* (from J-I,8), *30* (from RU1014,1); flesher, *31* (from J-I,4); jewelry, *4* (from D19,4); pins, *5* (from PQ14,3-4), *6* (from J-II,2fl.), *7* (from CF159,2), *8* (from J-II,2fl.), *9* (from J-II,W,sf-3), *10* (from T16,sf-1), *35* (from J-I,7), *36* (from T18,sf-1), *12* (from C22,2); bone point or gouge, *13* (from J-I,6a); spoons, *14* (from J-I,3,pit 2), *15* (from N17,2), *16* (from T11,3), *17* (from J-II,3), *18* (from J-II,5), *19* (from N17,5), *20* (from J-II,1); spirally ornamented rods, *21* (from J-II,1), *22* (from J-II,6); burnishers, or lissoirs, *23* (from Z9,1), *24* (from J-II,5), *25* (from J-I,6c), *37* (from J-II,1), *38* (from J-II,6), *39* (from J-II,1); miscellaneous perforated object, *40* (from J-II,4); miscellaneous small pieces, *41* (from G22,1), *42* (from J-II,1), *43* (from N17,3), *44* (from J-III,sf-1), *45* (from GL2024,sf-1); fragment of polished bone, *46* (from S17,2). Scale 3:5.

Fig. 145. Jarmo worked bone: hafts, *1-2* (from J-II,1); light-duty awls, *4* (from J-II,2), *5* (from J-I,8); heavy-duty awls, *3* (from J-II,5), *6* (from J-I,7fl.); needles, *7* (from J-II,2), *8* (from J-I,8), *9* (from J-I,6a), *10* from J-II,2), *11* (from J-II,3); pins, *12* (from J-II,2), *13* (from J-II,2fl.); bone point or gouge, *14* (from J-I,6a); spirally ornamented rods, *15* (from J-II,5), *16* (from J-II,1); spoons, *17* (from J-II,6), *18* (from J-II,5); jewelry, *19* (from J-II,1), *20* (from J-I,7); flesher, *21* (from J-I,8). Scale 1:1.

REFERENCES

Braidwood, Robert J.; Braidwood, Linda S.; Smith, James G.; and Leslie, Charles
    1952   Matarrah: a southern variant of the Hassunan assemblage, excavated in 1948. *Journal of Near Eastern Studies* 11:1-75.

Burnham, Harold B.
    1965   Çatal Hüyük—the textiles and twined fabrics. *Anatolian Studies* 15:169-74.

Clark, J.G.D.
    1952   *Prehistoric Europe: the economic basis.* New York: Philosophical Library.

Driver, Harold E.
    1969   *Indians of North America.* 2nd ed. rev. Chicago: University of Chicago Press.

Hole, Frank; Flannery, Kent V.; and Neely, James A.
    1969   *Prehistory and human ecology of the Deh Luran plain.* Memoirs of the Museum of Anthropology, University of Michigan, no. 1. Ann Arbor.

Kidder, Alfred Vincent
    1932   *The artifacts of Pecos.* Papers of the Southwestern Expedition, no. 6. New Haven: Yale University Press.

Lloyd, Seton, and Safar, Fuad
    1945   Tell Hassuna. *Journal of Near Eastern Studies* 4:255-89.

Mallowan, M.E.L., and Rose, J. Cruikshank
    1935   Excavations at Tall Arpachiyah, 1933. *Iraq* 2:1-178. (Reprint. *Prehistoric Assyria: excavations at Tall Arpachiyah, 1933.* London: Oxford University Press, Humphrey Milford.)

Ryder, M.L.
    1965   Report of textiles from Çatal Hüyük. *Anatolian Studies* 15:175-76.

Semenov, S.A.
    1964   *Prehistoric technology.* Trans. M.W. Thompson. London: Cory, Adams, and Mackay.

Steen, Charlie R.
    1966   *Excavations at Tse-ta'a, Canyon de Chelly National Monument, Arizona.* National Park Service Archeological Research Series, no. 9. Washington: National Park Service, U.S. Department of the Interior.

Steinbring, Jack
    1966   The manufacture and use of bone defleshing tools. *American Antiquity* 31:575-81.

Tobler, Arthur J.
    1950   *Excavations at Tepe Gawra.* Vol. 2. Museum Monographs. Philadelphia: University of Pennsylvania Press.

7

JARMO FIGURINES AND OTHER CLAY OBJECTS

Vivian Broman Morales

The material described in this chapter includes items from all three seasons at Jarmo. The finds of the first and second seasons fit together nicely to produce a stratigraphic sequence for each of three distinct and separate areas (J-I, J-II, and J-A), but there is not too much overlap from one operation to another. The earliest levels, represented in J-I, yielded a very small amount of figurine material. The test squares of the third season added mainly to the upper level material of J-II, with the exception of the ash area, which (with J-III) must be tentatively considered middle-upper rather than upper level only. Potsherds were found to cluster in certain areas (fig. 24) and did not seem to occur at more than 2.25 m below the surface. No pottery was found in the ash area.

All the figurine illustrations are reproduced at actual size, but the textile and basketry impressions are shown at a scale of 2:1. Cross sections of animal figurines were made at the center of the body whenever possible. Photographs and drawings of the same figurine are given the same number on the illustrations but are labeled *a* or *b*. Reconstruction drawings are based not only on evidence offered by the piece itself but also on similar examples in the same category. In addition, I made clay models of various key pieces to help determine the process of manufacture and to try to reproduce the objects plastically.

STUDY PROCEDURES

To date, about 5,500 pieces of shaped clay have been recovered at Jarmo. Clay pieces shaped into definite and recognizable forms occur in the earliest levels and persist throughout the site, whereas pottery was found only in certain areas of the upper third of the deposit. At Jarmo, then, there seems to be little correlation between clay used plastically for nonutilitarian objects and the development of pottery vessels.

The clay used for figurines at Jarmo appears to be very homogeneous. To the eye, the color and type of clay do not differ noticeably from the lower to upper levels, nor from one part of the mound to the other. Another factor in the homogeneous appearance of the clay objects is that they were at best only very lightly fired or baked, a technique that persisted throughout the occupation of the site. In water, the material turned into a fine colloidal suspension. This change was first observed when fragments of clay figurines accidentally got into the washing pan, a rare event as great care was taken to separate clay from stone before washing the day's finds. Figure 155:8 shows what happens to the lightly baked figurines when they get wet and why one could not expect much figurine material to be recovered from the surface levels. This animal figure was accidentally left out in a noon shower and was then preserved in its present state by a thin solution of Duco cement. The fact that the clay did not revert to plastic form indicates that the piece had been fired or baked, however slightly.[1]

Since the figurines could not be washed, they had to be cleaned with brushes and dental tools in order to reveal their original surface. Though some of the notches may result from excessive brushing or a slip of the dental pick, for the most part the figurines now show their true aspect, or what is left of it.

It is indeed remarkable how many were found, considering the fragility of the material and the possibility of weathering. Most, of course, are only fragmentary, some shattered by blows of the workmen's picks, others obviously broken in antiquity. As the workers became more proficient and learned to distinguish the figurines of clay from the soil of the same color they were more careful and saved all the fragments.

The clay was untempered, but there were occasional inclusions of small pebbles, plant fibers, and, more rarely, shell. Air holes were common, and we often probed them as possible perforations. Perforations in some of the beads, as observed in broken sections, suggest that they were perhaps formed over a straw or reed, which was then pulled out after drying or burned away in the firing, leaving the impressions of plant fiber in the hole.

This is a slightly revised version of a paper submitted in partial fulfillment of the requirements for the degree of Master of Arts in the Department of Anthropology, Radcliffe College, 1958.

[The manuscript for this chapter was essentially completed by 1971. Very few additions and only minor revisions have been made since that date.—EDS.]

Broken sections usually reveal a uniform color. Some cores are reddish but none are blackened. The clay ranges in color from very light pinkish beige through light reddish brown to darker gray. Some of the objects show burnish, though this is rare, and many bear the fingerprints of their creators. Some are nicely made and carefully finished, while others are crude and slipshod. There is no temporal division between careful and careless work; both are found in each level.

The clay used for modeling probably came from the wadi, where it was fine grained and relatively pure because of silting. Inclusions, as noted above, were rare and for the most part probably accidental, picked up when the clay was prepared for modeling. Later, when pottery was manufactured, figurines were occasionally fashioned from the chaff-tempered "pot clay," but these were very few in number compared with the greater numbers still made out of the unprepared modeling clay.

None of the clay figures were found in a context that could suggest ceremonial use or practice. There were no particular concentrations or groupings in the first and second seasons' material. Typological patterns appeared on the distribution sheets rather than being discernible in the field. The extensive testing of the third season, however, revealed a remarkable concentration in the large ashy area (p. 164), especially around the center, but no particular groupings were apparent and the fragments seemingly occurred at random.

Recognizable forms include animal figurines, human figurines, cones, beads, balls, and rods, as well as objects we refer to as "double-wing bases" and "stalk objects." In order to cope in an intelligent and intelligible way with thousands of fragments, one must order them in some fashion. My classification is arbitrary and may actually have little to do with what their makers, the Jarmo villagers, originally intended. That the makers themselves were numerous and variously skilled is evident, and in each category (though arbitrarily set up) there are crudely modeled examples as well as carefully and skillfully finished ones. It is most interesting to note that the majority of objects are small, even tiny; their size alone demands a great deal of skill and, one might add, practice. I feel that the modeling of clay, aside from any consideration of purpose and/or eventual use of the models as charms, "cult objects," or what not, was done with considerable verve: it seems that the people enjoyed making the objects, whatever their ultimate purpose was.

There are numerous lumps, blobs, and squeezed pieces, some of them bearing reed and mat impressions as though they had been pressed down beside the maker and then forgotten (later swept into the hearth to be hardened by the fire and thus preserved). Some recognizable forms (animals, humans, and others) were flattened or squashed while in a plastic state; others seem to have simply slumped under their own weight. This would seem to indicate a rather casual attitude toward the final product, no particular care being taken about keeping the objects in a safe place until thoroughly dry. This drying may have taken place beside the hearth, where accidents could easily befall the objects, or they may have been left outside in the sun.

If such a casual method of production can be postulated, it follows that one can imagine children producing models, most probably of animals, which are simple and uncomplicated forms and a subject that would be most familiar and interesting to them. The more sophisticated and composite forms of female figurines and the double-wing bases and stalk objects (there are numerous examples of these forms) may have been imitated by children, but more probably these were the "idea pieces" of adults, made solely by them.

Naturally each type designated is represented by a few good examples followed by a number of fragments whose classification is truly subjective. Therefore, single pieces should not be considered out of context without first making a careful assessment of the Jarmo material as a whole.[2]

Definite trends and patterns of manufacture that are very clear and important will be shown in the discussion of categories and the types therein. The figurines fell readily into a recognizable sequence with certain chains of relationship, the links of which are demonstrable. Partial order was established for the 3,000 pieces found in the first two seasons, and many more relationships became apparent with the addition of much new material from the third season, which fit into the typology quite naturally and vastly clarified the whole problem of classification. The total collection now consists of about 5,000 pieces, not including clay lumps.

CLASSIFICATION AND DESCRIPTION

Animal Figurines

In dividing the animal figurines into groups for study, I have relied on certain characteristics of manufacture, style, and posture of the various elements (head, ears, legs, tail). The more elements that appear in combination, the better defined the type. This system in general would apply to the consideration of any animal figurines, wherever numbers are sufficient to enable one to distinguish such combinations of features. Animals in other collections may suggest certain of the Jarmo types but should not be classified without an examination of all the animal figures and their elements separately. The animal form is a universal one where figurines are found, and too rigid a classification is not feasible.

In the present study I have given each type a letter as designation and have in most cases suggested what animal may have been represented. There are several individual figurines that seem easily identified—a pig, a bear, a dog. But if bear and pig are classified in the same group, it is because my classification is based on other than purely zoological factors. Although all such identifications and the reasons for them are included, the reader should not equate a type with one particular animal. The unknown factor always remains: What did the maker himself intend the figure to represent? If it looks just like a pig to us and he meant it to be a bear, who is right? The report on the animal bones recovered at Jarmo will allow us to speculate with some approach to the truth about what animals have been depicted. The figurines will in turn be of interest, but of little true value, to the zoologist, who must rely, after all, on bone identification.

The total number of figurines, whole and fragmentary, that have been judged to represent animals is about 1,100, or roughly 20% of all of the shaped clay material recovered from Jarmo at this present date. Less than a third of the animal figurines were unclassifiable by type, while still recognizable as animal forms. The distribution of these animal figures may be considered as general throughout the levels except for specific instances referred to in the discussion of each type. There are 14 types.

Type A (fig. 146:1-3)

Type A is a simplified form. The nose is short and rounded. Ears are indicated by a ridge pinched up over the top of the head. The forepart is massive, but the body tapers to narrow hindquarters so that there is no neck. The tail, usually found broken off, tends to be long and is extended straight out or turned up. Most of the examples have an accentuated spine, a pinched-up ridge down the center of the back (this is a feature common to most types). The legs are barely indicated, being very short and rounded. The form strongly resembles a pig and may well represent that animal. Though scattered through the levels, this type is concentrated in the lowest ones and would therefore seem to be an early version of the pig; type H, which is also piglike but confined to the upper levels, may be the later form for representing the same animal. There are 28 examples of type A, all found during the first two seasons. The size ranges from about 35 to 55 mm in length.

Type B (fig. 146:4-6)

The main characteristics of type B are shortness, stockiness, and a definite tendency toward fullness in the hindquarters. The head, when present, has a broad, pointed nose and generally hangs slightly downward. The neck is thick and short. The ears extend back and are short and rounded. The spine is usually accentuated, though some examples have smooth backs. The tail is short and turned down. Examples are found in all levels. There is little or no concern for detail in this type, and the figure is more or less carelessly made. The average length is about 42 mm. The animal is depicted standing still, in a placid attitude, which lends the impression that this may represent a domesticated form. There are, however, one beautifully modeled example that looks quite like a bear (fig. 146:4) and two others that are bearlike (fig. 146:5-6). This does not mean that all of the examples represent bears; in fact, the pig might again be suggested. The form is not well defined, although 26 figurines have been classified as this type.

Type C (figs. 147:1-7; 148:1-4; 149:1-8)

The head form of type C is the typological characteristic, but the general body form is also distinctive. The head bears indications of both ears and horns. The latter are broken off close to the head in most instances. The type is divided into three groups: C1 includes the more or less whole figurine, the head, and head-and-body fragments; C2 includes body and rear-end fragments only; C3 is horns.

The nose inclines and is sometimes vertically flattened and often finished at the tip with a horizontal pinch (one example has a vertically pinched tip; see fig. 147:1), which widens the end and gives the effect of a beard (fig. 147:2). Ears, indicated by slight projections on the sides of the head, are generally pinched out vertically and are never more than just slightly indicated (figs. 147:3; 148:3-4). The horns generally project from the top of the head and have broken off in all but one or two instances (fig. 148:1). One example that has a portion of the horn remaining shows that it curved forward (fig. 147:7), but it seems certain that most of the others had the horns curving back (fig. 148:4). These probably represent goats. There are a few examples with horns projecting laterally, which could mean that they were intended to represent sheep.

Two examples seem to be heads alone, fashioned as such without bodies. The base of one is round and flat (fig. 147:6) and that of the other is bulbous, preventing the object from standing upright (fig. 148:2).

Three examples have appliqué over the nose. On the two examples illustrated (fig. 147:4-5), the appliqué is incised, perhaps to indicate a forelock. Since, however, no other modification of the surface that suggests hair was attempted, the appliqué may have some other meaning.

The spine is usually pinched up, and the tail is short and rounded up, slightly extended, or down. The legs are more or less straight. The body form is further characterized by a fold between the front legs; this feature is sometimes very exaggerated. The rear end frequently has a similar fold between the hind legs. The rear-end fragments alone are classified as type C2, since they pertain almost exclusively to whole specimens of type C. In the "normal" condition, the fold is contained between the legs, which support the back end (fig. 149:1). A more exaggerated form has a very broad fold with the legs appearing as mere flaps that do not support the body but rest instead on the broad fold (fig. 149:2). Three examples show an even greater exaggeration of the fold, with the legs being barely indicated (fig. 149:3). Most of these fragments have the accentuated spine.

So far, no one has been able to suggest what this fold, at either end, represents. Considering the structure from a zoologist's point of view, Charles Reed says that it is most unrealistic, definitely not bone or flesh (pers. comm.). Neither is it convincing as a representation of hair, although the fore fold may represent a ruff of hair that would indicate the male of the wild sheep. Since the folds often occur at both ends on the same figurine, one would have to choose between sex symbols, as it were, if the rear fold were meant to represent an udder. We feel, however, that the rear fold is not a realistic representation of the udder and for the moment reject that interpretation.

Horns, type C3, indicate three different animals: the sheep, the domesticated goat, and the wild goat. Only three examples of wild goat horns were found (fig. 149:4-6), which, however, are too large to belong to any of the clay animal bodies recovered. These horns have a pinched edge that is modified by a series of flattened projections. The horns of the domestic goat have the pinched edge and are curved or curved and twisted in a very realistic manner (fig. 149:7). The sheep horns, which are round in section and curved (fig. 149:8), present a problem in classification, as they could be legs from animal figurines or arms or legs from human figurines. I have, therefore, been careful to choose only the most likely examples, all of which are about the size that the type C animals might have had.

Some of the goat horns are large and seem not to belong to the bodies that we have recovered so far; however, two of the heads are rather large, which suggests that there were indeed rather sizeable examples of this type. Four body fragments of light pinkish clay are close to the appropriate size, but they are too crude to have borne the more realistic horns.[3]

Technical difficulties seem to have imposed limits on size, a handicap that did not prevent the figurine makers from producing in quantity objects beautifully modeled in some detail on a scale that I found hard to duplicate. There are several type C figurines that are quite small but complete with all the attributes. Of all the animal figurine forms found at Jarmo, this type is the most detailed.

There are 101 examples of type C1, 69 of type C2, and 49 of type C3. So far no examples of type C have been classified from the lowest levels of J-I, but this does not mean that horned animals of the sheep and goat genera were unknown to the earliest inhabitants of Jarmo. Horn cores and bone fragments of sheep and goat have been found in the early levels, and further excavation could doubtless yield figurine examples of this type. It is certain that this form was meant to represent a horned animal of the sheep or goat variety, and wild goat is also suggested by three clay horn fragments. The large number of examples indicates that these animals were well known and played an important part in the economy of the Jarmo people. (I would say that most of these figurines look like goats, some look like sheep, but none are truly suggestive of *Bos* or of deer.)

Type D1 (fig. 150:4-7)

Type D1, which I have called "curly-tailed dogs," is represented by only 8 examples, 4 more or less whole and 4 fragmentary. Seven have a pinched-up spine. A whole animal with a smooth back has a long slightly arched neck (fig. 150:4). The remaining 3 more or less whole examples have short necks. The head of this type is small with a short, rounded nose; the ears are out and forward (fig. 150:5). The tail is up and curled around clockwise, resting on the right flank (fig. 150:4-6). On one back-end fragment, the tail rises straight up over the back and touches down on the spine, forming a sort of handle (fig. 150:7). The forelegs of all D1 examples (except, of course, the back-end fragments) are extended, suggesting a running or leaping posture. Reed says *only* dogs can have tails curled up; wolves definitely do not (pers. comm.).

Type D2 (fig. 150:1-3)

Type D2 is the figure of a small animal with a short body that is sometimes tapered. The head is erect, the forelegs are generally extended, and the tail is usually pointing up (fig. 150:1-2). The nose is generally short and blunt, the ears short and cocked up or forward. The effect of these characteristics is that of a very alert little animal, rather bouncy, almost prancing. There are 56 figurines in this group. Of the 27 fragments on which tail position can be judged, 19 have it pointing up, 7 have a "tab" tail pressed down, and one has the tail extending straight out behind. Twenty-four have the pinched-up spine and 19 have smooth backs.

The average length of these figures is about 40 mm, and many of the fragments appear to have been part of even smaller figurines. The modeling is usually crude, although the two best examples are carefully finished and well rounded with smooth backs.

It is very difficult to judge what sort of animal was meant to be represented by these forms; they lack sufficient anatomical detail for adequate classification, the best criterion being their appearance of jauntiness and alertness. The dog may be suggested, especially when one compares these forms with the dog figurines that are characterized by their curly tails (type D1). Type D2 needs better definition, however, before being identified with any specific animal. In view of the fairly uniform small size of this form, it may be suggested that it represents a relatively small animal, such as a fox. There is a single example, to be described later, that looks very foxlike, so that it is clear that the figurine makers could make foxes more realistic than these "dogs."

Type E (fig. 150:8-10)

Type E differs from type D in a tendency toward heaviness in the hindquarters, accented by a definite "rump hump" just over the hind legs and in front of the tail. The head is small, carried on a short, forward-pointing neck that is not raised as in type D. The nose is short and tapered. The ears are short and rounded and stand out but are not as cocked as those of type D.

The back is usually smooth rather than pinched up. The tail extends out behind or is carried slightly up. It is long and thick, and is round in section. It is sometimes further accentuated by an incision on either side which sets it off. All of the examples, with the exception of two back-end fragments that may be part of a different species, are small and might therefore be supposed to represent a small animal. In other words, there is not the size range here that is seen in types C and H, for example. Since there are only 22 examples, it seems likely that whatever animal this type represented, it was not a very important one in the Jarmo economy and may well be a small wild form. (Marten has been suggested.)

Although fewer examples were found, this type is better defined than type D and was clearly meant to portray a specific animal. A careful study of the animal bone material will doubtless reveal possibilities as to its identity.

Type F (fig. 151:1-5)

Type F is an even more specialized form and, in most cases, is more carefully made than either type D or type E. It is a form that clearly expresses movement: the forelegs are quite extended, and the back legs are extended back to a lesser degree. The head is carried on a somewhat arched neck so that it is held high and forward (fig. 151:2,5). A double incision on each side of the neck just behind the ears is a feature characteristic of this type, being found on 29 of the 76 examples (fig. 151:1,4). The ears are short and pointed up and forward; the nose is narrow and pointed forward. On some of the examples a mouth seems to be indicated by an incision. The spine is pinched up in most cases. In 5 of these figurines the genitals have been shown by an appliquéd pellet between the hind legs (fig. 151:1). This pellet is incised vertically. The tail can be depicted in various positions—up, out, or down.

The length ranges from about 35 to 45 mm. Most of the 76 examples are carefully made. The form most strongly suggests a horse, but the size range would seem to indicate that a small animal is being portrayed. If an animal as large as a horse were being depicted, one would expect at least as much variation in size as in the category of horned animals, but here the size is strikingly uniform and small. In addition, the position and treatment of the tail make it quite unlike a horse's tail; in fact, I believe that none of the Jarmo animal figurines represent the horse.

This type is quite clearly defined. As yet there is no indication of the meaning of the double incision behind the ears. More than half of the examples have this feature; those without it are obviously of the same group since the body form and treatment of other details are similar (fig. 151:3).

Although they are not demonstrably type F, 23 headless bodies may be mentioned here. All of them are small figurines in the same size range as types D, E, and F, but they lack the distinguishing features needed to classify them more specifically. Also included here are 5 headless front parts which may belong to type F or type H. These 28 examples figure in the total of 76 given above.

Type G (fig. 151:6-9)

Type G, consisting of 30 examples (including 8 in Baghdad awaiting reclassification), is very close to type F and may well be a form that represents the same animal. Nineteen are head fragments only. The rest are mainly front-end fragments that are very like type F but also suggest type H in that they are slightly more massive in the shoulders. The rounded ears point back and up and are set away from the head as are those of type F. Here, however, there are no double incisions. The nose is long and pointed, and the head, on examples with enough of the body present to show its position, is extended straight out on the neck, which is not arched as in type F (fig. 151:6,8). The muzzle may be round in section, square, or flattened vertically, and it may be turned up or down or be pointed straight out. In one instance eyes have been shown by round punctations (fig. 151:9). The spine is pinched up in all cases where this can be judged.

This form, as exemplified by 9 figurines, represents a small running animal, very like type F in size, style, and posture but lacking the complete set of features that characterize that type. Some of the heads may have belonged on type F rather than type G bodies, but since that cannot be judged, I include all of the separate heads here that do not have the double incision behind the ears.

Type H (figs. 152:1-7; 153:1-7)

Type H, another large animal category, with 283 examples, is rather hard to describe because of its tremendous variation. A few of the salient features are possessed by almost all examples. However, since so many features are present and since not all of these occur in the same combinations, there is much more variety within this type than in the other category that depicts a large animal, type C.

One of the most distinctive characteristics is a high crest at the neck (or even over the head), which is formed by the pinching up of the spine. If the back is smooth, this crest is a pronounced hump, giving the figure a hunched look (fig. 152:7). The bodies may have relatively straight backs or may taper toward the rear. Sometimes there is a hump at the rear, and a few examples have an even more exaggerated saddlebacked form.

The head bears a short to medium-length muzzle, rounded and tilted slightly up or squared off. Jowls are often suggested by the way in which the ears and muzzle were shaped; the ears are rounded and they also flare out and are sometimes pressed forward, while the muzzle is pressed down, creating a V underneath the chin and forming heavy "jowls" (fig. 152:1,6). The forelegs are generally extended, and the back legs are short and straight, so that this is another type that seems to represent a running animal, a wild rather than a domesticated one.

The position of the tail varies, being generally up or out or somewhere between. Length of the tail is hard to judge since most often it is broken off; some intact examples are short. Here again the incised pellet is used to indicate genitals and is sometimes found in conjunction with a pinched portion underneath the body near the hind legs, presumably the penis (fig. 152:6). (This representation of the penis would be realistic enough for pig, deer, and all other cloven-hoofed animals.) Some figurines have only the pellet, others only the pinched-up bit of clay, but it is clear that this type represents the male animal.

Type H figurines generally tend to be larger than any figurines previously discussed. There are no very small examples. Many of them are very carefully made and show considerable attention to detail. One example has diagonal incising, which may have been intended to represent hair (fig. 153:7). A few are burnished or partially burnished (fig. 153:5-6), and one can easily sense that greater care went into the making of figurines of type H than into those of type C.

It is quite evident that the wild pig is depicted by many of these figurines. One remarkable example is obviously a wild sow with a very long snout, high pinched-up spine and crest (the exaggerated crest is a characteristic of the wild pig, especially the male), and the teats clearly indicated by the pinching of a double line of points underneath (fig. 152:2). There is a male counterpart, complete with crest, forward-pointing ears, and incised pellet and pinched part underneath (fig. 152:3). The legs of these two examples are broken off, but otherwise they are complete.

Because the different combinations of type H features are so numerous (figs. 152 and 153), I would not care to say that only the pig is portrayed by this group. Other animals are probably represented, but I can state that certainly a great majority seem to be pigs, and this may indicate, therefore, that this animal played an important role in the economy of the Jarmo people.

The type H figurine is found throughout all levels of J-II and abundantly in the ash area, but only a few rare examples appeared in the upper levels of J-I. As I suggested in my discussion of type A, type H may be a later version, a new and more realistic way of portraying the pig. But such a suggestion cannot be substantiated until more excavation is done in the earliest levels and until we have a better understanding of the relationship of the ash area to the rest of the mound.

Type K (fig. 154:4-6)[4]

There are only 21 examples of type K, which is characterized by its sitting posture. The forelegs are short and straight or slightly extended. All but one (fig. 154:5), a very tiny figure, have the pinched-up spine. The body is tapered toward the rear, and the back legs are very short, practically nonexistent on some examples, thus giving the impression of a seated animal.

In 4 of these the back end is broken off, but in the examples that retain this portion the tail position varies: in 8 the tail is extended out and up and in 3 it is turned down. The largest of the figurines of this type (fig. 154:4) has a tail that is long and extended out and down. It is very definitely seated and alert. The other fragments may or may not be seated, but they certainly do not express any quick movement.

Again it is impossible to determine what animal or animals are being portrayed here. Dog or pig might be suggested, but I feel that this group should remain unidentified for the present as the examples are fragmentary and amorphous (fig. 154:6).

Type L (figs. 154:1-3; 155:7)

The least well defined of all the animal types is type L. Unlike type D, which has a characteristic posture, fragments of this type simply stand, with straight or slightly extended forelegs. The head is small with a short, round, pointed nose. The ears are short and held up (fig. 154:1-3). Type L figurines are medium to small in size, but a few heads that seem appropriate only to larger bodies are included here. One fragment, a head and forepart only, has tiny punctations at random over the surface (fig. 155:7).

Some of these fragments resemble type H examples but lack enough of the requisite features to be included in that type. Most of the others are amorphous, some being squashed, bloblike, or crudely made. It would be impossible to suggest an animal for this type. There are 43 examples, and their distribution is general throughout the mound.

Type M (fig. 154:7-8)

There are only 2 examples of type M, which is typified by a very swayed back. This effect is achieved by a hump at the shoulder and one at the rear end, with a "saddle" dip between. The back is rounded so that the humps are very prominent. The tail turns down. The legs are extended, forelegs forward and back legs slightly back. The neck is thick and looks arched because of the hump. Ears are indicated and were probably short. The head of one example is quite battered (fig. 154:8); the hump over the back of its neck is broken off and so was originally much more prominent. The other example has a short, blunt nose that points forward and short ears that point up and slightly out. One measures about 40 mm and the other 45 mm in length.

This form may be a variant of type H, a possibility that is suggested by the treatment of the back (though much more pronounced here) and by the posture, especially of the legs and neck. It may represent a humped ox, although there is certainly no definite evidence for the presence of this animal at Jarmo in the bone material that has been recovered.

Type N (fig. 154:9-13)

Animals with their legs in the form of a double-wing base constitute type N. (See also the category headed Double-Wing-based Objects, pp. 385f.). With the exception of a fragment of a small figurine (fig. 154:12), this type is crude and carelessly made. The bases are more or less flat. The forelegs are joined, as are the hind legs, to form a rounded, or sometimes a pointed, end to the base (fig. 154:9-10). Of those with heads remaining, none suggest any definite animal. The nose is short and pointed, ears are small and standing up, and the head is held up or out, rather like in type D. The head of one small figure resembles those in type C (fig. 154:11).

There are only 16 examples of this type. It represents a definite and special form, whose distribution so far parallels that of the double-wing-based objects, which are found in the upper levels only. I have placed this type N group in the animal category because the figures are demonstrably animal and I wish here to introduce a concept of "animalness" in connection with the double-wing-based figurines. As will be discussed and demonstrated presently, the figurine makers of Jarmo were capable of expressing thoughts in abstract forms. Just what was served, in this instance, by these expressions of animalness will be very hard to determine. Much may have been incorporated into a single form, and one would certainly hesitate to try to define any or all of its elements. I shall pursue this matter in my conclusions about animal figurines.

Miscellaneous and Special Forms (fig. 155:1-6)

In the group Miscellaneous and Special Forms are figurines that are of special interest either because the surface has been elaborated in some way or because the form suggests a definite animal but does not fit into any of the types already described.

One of these is a more or less whole figurine with a long, flat-ended muzzle, ears held up and forward, a pinched-up spine, and a bushy tail. The forelegs were extended but have been broken off. This particular example was probably intended to depict a fox (fig. 155:2b). It may be akin to type F or type G but seems to have enough of its own special character to warrant separate mention. Another fragment, a head and forepart only, closely resembles the "fox," and so it is paired with it (fig. 155:1).

There is also a rather crude and stumpy figurine with a short, rounded nose. The eyes are indicated by punctations and the mouth by an incision. A thick tail, round in section, apparently extended directly out behind but has been broken off. The whole figure is covered with small punctations (fig. 155:3). While at Jarmo, we gathered thorny spikes from the thistle that abounded near camp, and we set one in each hole. The effect was well worth it; the animal was unquestionably a porcupine!

Five other fragments with a punctated surface (one a very nice head) were found, but they cannot be classified by type or animal. One body fragment is covered with deep punctations ca. 3 mm in diameter. These are arranged in more or less diagonal rows and are flat on the bottom, showing that the punch used to make them was blunt (fig. 155:5). The punctations were made while the clay was still fairly plastic. It is difficult to say what was intended by this treatment. In the case of the porcupine we have a good explanation, but the other pieces—wherever enough of the figurine remains to judge—do not resemble porcupines.[5] One other example with punctation is already discussed under type L (fig. 155:7).

Another figure, nicely made but with the back end broken off, has extended forelegs. The neck and body are covered with fine parallel incised lines, and if these markings were intended to represent hair the method seems fairly successful. The form most closely resembles that of type H, in which most of the figures seem to represent the pig. However, wild pigs do not have very long or shaggy hair. The figure is certainly not goatlike. (One other body fragment that has less realistic incisions more widely spaced has been classed with the type H examples; see fig. 153:7.)

Considering the great number of animal figurines and fragments, the fact that less than a dozen show surface incision or punctation is truly remarkable. A few specimens show burnish, and two examples (types C1 and C2) bear traces of red ochre. No paint has been observed on any of the animal figurines. Evidently such detailing was not considered necessary; even eyes and mouths are only rarely shown. Attention was paid to certain details of manufacture, for example, ears and horns (type C), neck incisions in some cases (type F), and the V-muzzle and crest (type H), but further elaboration seems to have been considered superfluous. This is true for the other types as well. There are always a few examples in each type that are incised, but the use of that kind of decoration never became general at Jarmo. Therefore, it is very difficult to determine just what was meant by their use of incision.

Unclassifiable Figures and Fragments

As stated at the outset, less than one third (253) of the animal figures were unclassifiable by type. This number includes a few heads and various body parts, especially back ends, and many amorphous pieces which, although recognizable as animals, lack any distinguishing traits. Perhaps the most interesting in this sad heap of undefinable fragments are the squashed forms. Many of these forms bear the impression of a reed mat on the flattened surface. This would surely indicate a very casual treatment of the figurines (squashed forms occur in other categories, too) if such accidents could befall them even before they were baked. It strongly suggests that, whatever they were made for, the actual fashioning of the object—bringing the form into being, as it were—was the focal point of the whole procedure.

MEANING AND USE OF ANIMAL FIGURINES

The animal figurines represent about one fifth of the total number of shaped clay objects so far recovered from Jarmo. Since more of the upper-level areas have been exposed, it is natural that most of the specimens come from these levels. In judging the material from the lowermost levels of J-1, we can say that in the beginning the animal figurines were cruder and more generalized in shape, with fewer distinct types. Figurine-making, however, was practiced from the beginning, for there is ample figurine material in the earlier levels. Some of the early forms persist throughout but decline in frequency as newer, more specific, and more realistic forms are introduced, such as types C, F, and H. These three better-made types may yet be found in the lowest levels, but indications are that type H has its prototype in type A and, therefore, would not be likely to be found there. There may also be such prototypes for types C and F, but these have not yet been recognized.

One is at once struck by the fact that so much of the animal figurine material can be classified.[6] Not all types can be designated as representing one species of animal, but certain ones, especially types that were found in the greatest numbers, can be so identified.

There remain, then, the unclassifiable fragments, which do not constitute as large a proportion of the total number of animal figurines as one might have expected—a fact that immediately suggests several things. First, it seems that the makers meant to portray certain species, often designating even the sex. They also portrayed certain other aspects, and in a certain way, though individual variation in modeling is infinite. The figurines in any one level were obviously not all made by the same craftsman, which is also attested to by the considerable variation in quality of execution; the modeling ranges from indifferent to exquisite, and surface finishing varies from crude—with fingerprints and nail scoring—to carefully smoothed and burnished.

A further suggestion is that these animal figurines represent human wishes or desires aimed at a particular species or even an individual animal. (I have speculated that type N may represent "animalness," but so far this group is small and not very explicit.) Most of the figurines in the animal category might easily be viewed as a kind of wish inventory (large male about two years old, young female, etc.) or as charms to promote the well-being of a flock or of an individual animal. Figurines of game animals were probably made by the men who were most concerned with hunting. Whoever tended the domesticated flocks probably made the figurines of the domesticated animal types.

Since the animal figurines occur in great numbers and since some show carelessness in manufacture and/or drying practices (e.g., the squashed forms with mat impressions), one could conclude that the magic of the wish lay in the actual working of the clay. This procedure probably took place within the house; the maker, seated on a reed mat with the clay already prepared for use, could quickly and privately create his or her own personal magic. The figurine may then have been retained only until the wish concerning that animal was fulfilled. When it had served its purpose, it would have been discarded. One can imagine that the figurines, having served their magical function, passed directly into the hands of eager children who then used them as toys. And it is not unreasonable to speculate that the children may have created for themselves animal forms to act as imaginary flocks or to serve in an imaginary game of hunting.

Another factor that strengthens the notion of the transitory value placed on the figurines, not only animal but all others, is that none made of stone have as yet been found. The Jarmo people were skilled in the fashioning of decorative, nonutilitarian stone objects; this is amply demonstrated by the bracelet fragments, beads, pendants, and even stone spoons, as well as forms whose use is not clear (plugs, miniature pestles, etc.). If they had wished to make permanent figurines, it appears certain that they could have done so. That they did not, therefore, supports the idea that permanence was not necessary.

Reed has suggested several interesting points concerning his preliminary study of the animal bones. He has examined the animal figurine material with me on various occasions, and neither of us has been able to identify examples that suggest cervid or equid in the different groups of animal figures. Yet bones of both of these animal varieties occur at Jarmo. It is obvious that the villagers hunted the wild pig, and we have seen that both the pig and the bear were well represented in the figurine material.

Another interesting fact is that all of the animal figurines represent mammalian forms. There are no models of snakes, lizards, frogs, or turtles, either in realistic forms or, as far as I can discover, in abstract ones. This suggests to me that the children did not play at clay-modeling at all, at least as far as animal representation is concerned, or that they were supervised or circumscribed in their choice of subject matter. It is hard to imagine children playing creatively with clay and not making models of the smaller creatures with which they must have been thoroughly familiar. A frog or turtle would present a very attractive form to model, and lizards and snakes would be very simple and natural to do. While there may have been some feeling against these forms, it would almost seem that there was some sort of taboo restricting clay-modeling. There is, of course, nothing to preclude the modeling of clay figurines by the children out of doors, by any mud puddle; if only sun dried, products of this type would obviously not be expected to survive.

The type N abstract animal figurines are more than a little difficult to account for, given the explicitness of the other animal forms. They may have been true toys (a child's solution to the problem of modeling a four-legged creature), or initially perhaps they were the result of a top-heavy figure slumped under its own weight while drying. Or they may have been deliberate abstractions; this seems the more likely when one considers the probable animalness of some of the forms in the truly abstract categories of double-wing-based objects and stalk objects. Type N figurines, however, were not abstractions in the same sense as the double-wing bases or stalks. In this they are comparable to "lady stalks," which belong in the female figurine category, just as these type N objects belong in the animal figurine category. Here perhaps the wish was aimed at the welfare or increase of a herd of animals, wild or domesticated.

Type N is not a large one in the overall total of animal figurines and is so far associated only with the upper levels.

Human Figurines

Both male and female forms occur in the sample of human figurines from Jarmo. The female form shows many variations and was obviously of more interest as a subject to model. The male form is made in one type only and is far less numerous. Although all the female forms are seated and probably all have legs, the variations range from the most complex, composite, and realistic pregnant type to a very stylized type, almost unrecognizable as human. These variations do not represent a developmental sequence, for all of the forms occur together throughout the upper levels. In the lower levels, the type that I have called "early simple" is the only one known to occur, and a few examples of this form are also found in the upper levels. (Very few figurines made of "pot clay" have a definite, recognizable form. The examples that do occur will be described according to type. There are a few other pieces made of the pottery fabric, but the shapes are not classifiable.)

It is interesting to note that the female form is depicted in two ways—the pregnant, realistic type and the "lady stalk" type, the stylized expression of femaleness. The realistic figure gives the impression of a relaxed posture, the arms resting on the swollen stomach or on the upper legs or hanging at the sides. The "lady stalks" have few of the usual female attributes. They are composed of a stalk body, a small, sometimes barely indicated head or face, a coiled headdress, and legs fused together as one. The female form is *always* sitting, with the knees bent or with legs extended, never squatting or standing. There are no examples of mother and child combinations, nor are the females ever shown with the hands cupped under or holding the breasts, a position characteristic of female figurines in later periods.

The male form has no legs but, as represented by the torso, seems to indicate an attempt to portray a standing figure. One example has rounded shoulders and the arms pressed down at the sides, but in practically all other instances the arms are outstretched and the shoulders are massive. The base, in fact, is sometimes extremely small in proportion to the bulk above it, but the figurine stands well in spite of its top-heavy appearance.

The genitals are not delineated in the human forms (other attributes are sufficient to denote sex), although they are depicted on some of the animal figurines. The phallus is present as a separate form, but very few were found.

Female Forms

Early Simple Type (fig. 156:1-5)

The early simple type consists of a trunk and separate, extended legs. The figures are definitely in a sitting rather than squatting position. The form is a very simple one, usually rather crudely shaped. A few look as though a triangular piece of clay had been folded, forming the legs in a sitting position (fig. 156:1). The backs are rounded and buttocks are not indicated. These figurines are not represented as pregnant, nor do they seem to have had breasts. The top is usually broken off and no head remains. One exception is an example on which the stalklike body is bent; the resulting "chin" seems to indicate the beginning of a head, but the top is broken. No features are shown, either on this or on the one other whole example that has a head, where the head is formed by rounding and pinching the top of the trunk (fig. 156:4).

Arms are present on 4 examples and consist of mere stubs pinched out from the body. Three of these figurines are very small (ca. 20 mm high) and carefully made. The whole figurine described in the previous paragraph is one of these three. The fourth one is a large solid figure made of pot clay, complete but for the head and part of one leg. It is 56 mm high, and the base measures 50 mm from toe to back (fig. 156:5). The legs of another figure of pot clay indicate a slightly larger figurine. One of the small figures has an appliquéd strip over the ankle.

Further excavation in the earliest levels may well reveal more elaboration of the early simple type in the form of decoration by appliqué or incision. By definition, however, the shape is a simple one, and the usual female attributes are not indicated. The size range of the early simple type, except for the two pottery figurines, is medium to small (fig. 156:1-4), and most of the examples are crudely modeled. In addition, most of these figurines are quite fragmentary.

The simple type is, according to the evidence, definitely an early one. Of the 33 examples (5 doubtful), only 9 come from upper levels. None are recorded from J-III, and occurrences from the third season—when mainly middle and upper levels were exposed—are scattered; 3 of the 7 third-season examples may have come from the ash area (within which J-III lies), but this is questionable in each case.

Intermediate Type (fig. 156:6-9)

The intermediate type, with only 5 examples, is merely a modification and a slight elaboration of the simpler form. It is either simple or composite in structure. One example consists of a pair of legs, either crudely divided by modeling or, more likely, made separately and then pressed together. The stomach overlaps the legs, indicating a fat rather than a pregnant form. The body is broken off at the waist. The feet are modeled as one. This form, though modeled, is still rather crude and somewhat suggests a paleolithic figurine (fig. 156:6).

One even more fragmentary example has both legs broken off close to the body. Since they were set close together, it is hard to judge whether each was applied separately or both were made in a single piece, as in the simple type. The top part of the body is broken off above the protruding stomach.

Another example is close to the simple type in body shape, with legs and body seemingly modeled in one piece. One leg and the head are broken off. This figurine has pendulous breasts (or arms?) appliquéd on the body stalk below another appliquéd piece (a collar?). There are also two vertical rows of pin punctations between the "breasts" (fig. 156:7).

The fourth example consists of a long head with a pinched face but no features, and a back that is rounded and wrapped toward the front. Since the legs are broken off close to the body, it cannot be determined whether they were made separately or as one (fig. 156:8).

The last example was probably made in one piece; the legs were folded together over the body stalk, which is broken off just above the legs. Two small short flaps that were pinched out of the body stalk may represent arms. The back is very rounded and the figure suggests a fat female (fig. 156:9).

These forms are closely related to the early simple type in structure but may have been composite in manufacture; they certainly hint at the more detailed composite type. The figures seem to be fat rather than pregnant, all but the first having extremely fat legs and wide bottoms. The buttocks are not indicated except in the first one, where they result from the structure rather than from purposeful detailing. Four out of these five examples come from the earlier levels.

Composite Type—Pregnant (figs 156:10; 157:1-6; 158:1-3,7; 159:1-7)

In the composite, pregnant type we have examples of careful modeling and detail as well as larger figurines modeled around sticks or straws for reinforcement. The procedure seems to have been to model the parts separately, perhaps starting with the torso, but to assemble the other parts upward from the legs, which serve as the base. These legs were modeled separately, usually as rounded triangles, depicting a fat leg with the knee drawn up. Thinner extended legs were also found, but not often (the pair of legs that were found together, shown in fig. 159:1, is a unique example). The foot is indicated by pinching and turning up the tapered end of the leg or, more often, it is not differentiated at all.

The body, roughly conical in shape, was set over the legs so that the stomach protruded well onto the legs, and the back was shaped down over the legs behind. Buttocks were thus usually formed and modeled. The back was often simply rounded but could be nicely shaped, especially on the more carefully made figurines (fig. 157:6). Arms were then applied to the body either at the sides or well around to the back. These appendages were usually positioned straight down, then bent at the elbow so that the hands met high over the stomach, one on top of the other, where they were pressed down for a tight join. Hands were rarely detailed, but one has remained as a fragment where it was appliquéd on a thigh, which indicates an alternate placing of the arms, forward, with hands on top of the thighs (fig. 158:2). The breasts are small round pellets on the smaller figurines but are more substantial on the larger ones. Often the pellets have broken off, and it is difficult to determine if they even existed, especially on the small figures, where there was not much room between the arms.

One unique example has a single very pronounced and pointed projection on the chest, perhaps indicating the breast, but certainly not in a realistic fashion. The arms are pressed behind the back with the hands on the buttocks. The head is broken off. The base is slightly concave and rounded out in front, and it seems to have been finished without legs (fig. 156:10).

The umbilicus is often indicated, being punched well into the clay with a straw or small stick.

Heads have been lost from most of these figurines. Those that have survived have two shapes (with or without features): a simple, rounded knob (fig. 158:7) or a long, tapered form ending in a rounded point. Features were pinched (nose), or appliquéd (pellet eyes), or incised on the smooth surface. Too great elaboration of the head, however, would perhaps have spoiled the effect of the placid, pregnant female, with attention focused mainly on the fat legs, the rounded body, and the buttocks. Even the breasts were secondary, small and quickly applied, a factor that accounts for their absence on many of the fragments. Since they were not modeled from the body mass, they flaked off readily.

Individual variation in this group is remarkable. Few examples resemble each other to any great degree. Of course, the group is made up of fragments of the various parts, since whole figurines of the type are rare indeed. The method of manufacture makes this type susceptible to greater fragmentation than occurs in most other types.

Size range is another very interesting feature of this group. On the one hand, there are small forms that must have been very difficult to fashion and demonstrate the real skill of the Jarmo figurine makers. On the other hand, there are also quite large figurines that had to be reinforced with small sticks, since the untempered fabric did not lend itself to the manufacture of large forms without some support. One of these forms, deserving particular note, seems to have had no legs. The base was built up by pressing two roughly shaped conical pieces together; then a stick was set up as a backbone, around which the rest of the figure was modeled. The protruding stomach, with the umbilicus punched deep into the clay, was modeled out over the two basal cones, and the body rose above that, covering the stick. Large pendulous breasts, which come down to the stomach, were added. Unfortunately, this well-modeled figure seems to have been shattered in manufacture, probably while being fired. Since the fragments are somewhat warped, the problem of fitting the pieces together was even more difficult than usual. Enough remains, however, to suggest a reconstruction (fig. 158:3).

The head and arms of this specimen are missing. Indications are that the head was modeled over the top of the stick and that there was little or no neck. The arms seem to have hung straight down at the sides. Because of the way in which it has fragmented, it seems that the figure was built up in layers, the final one being carefully smoothed. (Or the layering may have been an aftereffect produced by the firing.) The whole was then covered with red ochre, which, although present when the fragments were found, rubbed off easily. It was therefore necessary to coat the figure with a thin wash of Duco cement, which imparts a gloss. This particular figure must have once been most impressive.

Another piece worthy of particular note is a body fragment with only one leg remaining. The legs were originally pressed together and held in place by a short straw or toothpick-sized stick (fig. 157:3). Up to the break, the body is tilted back alarmingly, almost parallel to the base. The buttock that remains is rounded and very prominent. The figure is covered with short parallel incisions and traces of a dark stain which might have been paint but whose precise character is almost impossible to determine since the presence of a hard crust formed by concretion makes it difficult to uncover the original surface. The incisions are haphazard and are presumably decorative. No umbilicus is indicated, but, uncharacteristically, a puncture in the anal region occurs. This is the only instance we have of such a detail, and it seems inappropriate when one considers that the genitals are never portrayed on any of the other human figures. Therefore, I conclude that the "anal" puncture on this female figurine is perhaps an accident.

One other fragment of this type is of special interest. The torso is broken off below the waist, but enough remains to indicate a pregnant form. The head is long and rounded, round in section, and completely featureless. However, a flattened strip of clay was joined to the back of the head and coiled around it clockwise, giving the effect of a tiara over the top of the head and ending in a long flap pressed down over the right side, behind where the ear might have been (ears are not generally depicted on human figurines). The coiled headdress or coil of hair is an interesting feature that is very important because it links the "lady stalks" (p. 381) with the more realistic female forms through this example and is again found in the double-wing-based objects (p. 385) and stalk objects (p. 386). The one breast remaining on this fragment is pendulous and overlaps the hand that rests on the upper abdomen, which shows unquestionably that the breasts were applied last but were fairly well pressed into the chest. Although this figurine is extremely fragmentary, it shows many interesting features and may be reconstructed fairly readily (fig. 157:5).

The legs of the composite, pregnant type are varied but are most artistically portrayed by a beautifully modeled pair found in J-III. They are well shaped and plump, and the feet are differentiated (fig. 157:2). It is this example that shows how the legs of this type can be paired in a realistic as well as artistic way. Many variations have been identified, many of them more stylized. Some were pressed together with a straw or twig between them for reinforcement. Instead of curving out, as does the pair described above, these examples seem to represent pairs with the knees drawn up against the stomach. In several instances there is a vertical incision on each side from the knee to the back of the leg, emphasizing the flexed posture (fig. 159:3).

One large, extended leg, 73 mm long × 33 mm high (anterior-posterior) × 25 mm wide, made of pot clay, has a flattened inner surface. On top, where the body of the figurine rested, the blackened core is visible. The piece was obviously fired whole and fell into fragments afterwards. This is the only example to date of a large composite form made of the pottery fabric.

Mentioned earlier on p. 378 (fig. 159:1) is a pair of extended legs that are definitely slim—a unique find. The more or less whole right leg has part of an appliquéd pellet at the ankle, which I assume is decorative. There is a heavier leg, belonging at one time to a hefty female (fig. 159:5), which is incised almost all the way around at the knee. There is still disagreement as to whether the pellet placed on the knee represents the patella or whether it is decorative. The pellet does not make a very convincing patella on a fat lady's leg, and it is used with an incision that I take to be the restriction of clothing. If a realistic kneecap had been desired, it could have been modeled, not just appliquéd as a mere pellet, since the leg itself is well made and nicely shaped. However, no particular costume can be inferred from this single example.

Other legs have appliquéd strips or pellets over the ankle (fig. 159:4,7), and one has a series of pin-sized punctations (fig. 159:6). Another has a series of fine-line horizontal incisions (fig. 159:2), which are presumably decorative and might be compared with others (fig. 157:3).

The distribution pattern of the composite, pregnant type allows us to draw only very general conclusions. The majority of fragments come from the upper levels (where pottery may occur), but there is one leg fragment from an early level which was paired and bears the perforation of such a pairing. Two of the intermediate type come from the same early level, thus indicating that further excavation of the earliest levels could presumably produce examples of the composite types. At present, however, the distribution pattern shows that the simple type was the major female form in the lowest levels and that the composite type, in all its variations, was the preponderant one in the upper levels. The few simple-type figurines found in the upper levels may represent the continuation of the earlier tradition. All of the variations of the composite types occur together; no developmental sequence from realistic to abstract is discernible. The total number of fragments of this type is 170 (49 bodies, 6 arms, 115 legs).

Composite Type—Nonpregnant (fig. 158:4-6)

Clearly, the stalklike bodies in the composite, nonpregnant type do not represent pregnant females. These figurines are more abstract and seem to depict, as the next group to be discussed (the composite, stylized type) surely does, femaleness alone. Just what this concept means, that is, how it should be understood in the light of what the Jarmo people were thinking in depicting it, is open to wide speculation.

The main insight to be gained from this particular type, and even more specifically from the next type, is that a more complex concept, or idea, governed the activity of fashioning such a form than just the simple, straightforward (to us) expression of fertility represented by the seated pregnant figure. Gender is not, after all, something to be acquired by any sort of magic. Pregnancy, however, is something that every female may aspire to, and rites and magic would be appropriate to it.

The earliest type of female figurine at Jarmo, as far as we understand it at the moment, is the simple type, definitely female but not pregnant or with breasts, attributes which are present in the later figures alone. This simple expression of femaleness may have represented fertility to its makers, but presently they became more specific and began creating more realistic forms. At the same time, however, they made other female forms that do not overtly (to us) indicate fertility but may, of course, have been intended to do so, perhaps being mere abstractions or symbols of that same concept.

But the evolution of the concept, whether of fertility or femaleness, does not stop there. The remarkable variation of these abstract forms continued into another series which represents "humanness," with no consideration of sex that we can see at present. These are the double-wing-based objects, which form a large and again varied category. The concept of humanness is developed further through the stalk objects, which seem to represent, as the forms become more abstract, a concept of life itself.

I introduce these matters now because of their great importance in understanding and evaluating this whole collection of human figurines. I certainly do not think that these are merely variations on the fertility theme; the material itself can clearly demonstrate that there is more than fertility involved, and I hope to be able to show this in the subsequent description of the related categories.

The composite, nonpregnant type is distinguished by its stalklike body; the top or head is broken off in every instance. One has had appliquéd arms broken off, and 3 others bear traces of appliqué that may have been arms. There are only 14 examples in this group, and they are all very fragmentary. It is not a type that can be too well defined, but it is very suggestive, if not altogether informative.

Five of the figures are interesting in that though they seem to have had no arms, all have appliquéd breasts (fig. 158:4-6). The breasts were applied separately on 4 of the figurines, but on the fifth only one lump of clay was appliquéd and then incised vertically to indicate a division (fig. 158:6). On 6 of the examples the stomach is rounded but is not intended to represent pregnancy. One might venture to guess that the fused legs of the composite, stylized type, rather than the more realistic paired legs of the composite, pregnant type, were characteristic of this composite, nonpregnant type, but there is no definite evidence one way or the other. The form definitely had legs rather than a round, concave base such as some of the stalk objects have.

Although the sample is admittedly very small, the distribution of this type parallels that of the pregnant type; there are no examples from the lowest levels. The implication is that this type is allied with the preceding one, though different from it and perhaps representing a different concept; a distinct type has here been introduced whose meaning is not yet clear.

Composite Type—Stylized (fig. 160:1-9)

The composite, stylized type is a truly abstract form composed of a stalk body with a small, sometimes barely indicated head or face, a coiled headdress, and the legs fused together as one. The face is sometimes indicated by a vertical pinch, but it is never further elaborated by features. The coil is generally wound clockwise and applied separately to the rounded tip of the stalk (fig. 160:3,5). The stalk body is tall and round in section and bears no trace of arms or breasts. Furthermore, this type is never shown as pregnant, although the stomach is occasionally represented as slightly overlapping the leg part.

The buttocks are sometimes indicated, but the legs are a single unit that looks very much like the previously discussed single leg of the other two composite types. This factor complicates sorting, for it is often difficult to determine if a leg is fused or one of a pair. (By "fused" I mean only one leg used to represent two; the legs are modeled as a single unit, but the viewer accepts this as representing two legs.)

Because the body was modeled separately and joined to the leg by pressing the two pieces together and smoothing the join, the figurines are prone to break at the juncture; no whole figurines of this type have yet been found. Before the key piece (fig. 160:1) was found, I classified the tops as stalk objects. Therefore, on recognizing the entire form, I called it a "lady stalk." This term is useful because it helps to distinguish this form from the other more realistic composite types and places it more in the realm of abstraction, like the stalk objects themselves and the double-wing-based objects.

All of the examples are small, and I found that it took some care and skill to reproduce these figures. It is a delicate form and therefore little wonder that no whole examples have as yet been recovered and that none of the fragments fit together to make a complete figure (one of the most frustrating aspects of Jarmo figurine material in general).

There are many variations of this type. In some cases the top of the stalk, instead of being coiled, is merely rounded over and the flap pressed down in back. As in the double-wing-based objects, this flap may be short, or long and tonguelike.

One very interesting form consists of a leg and head only, an odd-looking specimen that represents, perhaps, just "humanness" (fig. 160:8). There is another example very much like it, with the head broken off. Other variations are crude and depart rather drastically from the original lady stalk, but they are still recognizably related and portray the same idea of a seated figure, now less surely female, but still definitely human (fig. 160:7). This idea seems to degenerate all the way down to the form of a foot (or feet modeled as one) or a blobby leg (or legs). The blobby leg can be traced back to the original idea of a lady stalk but is now truly an abstraction understandable only in relation to all of the other examples and variations of the composite, stylized type. This type includes 59 examples that are represented by the stalk part, 37 that are legs, and 52 that are variations, making a total of 148 pieces for this group. Further study may increase the number of fragments that can be assigned to this type.

Now we are faced with the problem of what these lady stalks and their variations mean. In other categories one finds abstractions: double-wing-based animals, the double-wing-based figures themselves, stalk objects. Even the human male form is to a certain extent an abstraction. Since the Jarmo people were clearly adept at realistic representation, their manufacture of some of these abstractions must be considered as having symbolic meaning. Since the female figurines occur in many forms and varieties, one need not dismiss them all as fertility symbols. Certainly, during Jarmo times, there must have been a greater range of thought for the whole spectrum of figurines than we are able to suggest.

One figurine is extremely puzzling in that it combines both maleness and femaleness. The female shape as depicted in the Jarmo figurines is essentially a triangle with a broad base; shoulders are not prominent. The male shape, however, is basically an inverted triangle; the shoulders are massive, the arms are outstretched, and often there is no head. An attribute of the female form is the seated posture; that of the male is the upright stance. Now we have a figurine, very crude and of pot clay, with the torso of a male and the seated posture of a female. The whole has been jabbed with a small stick so that gashes cover the body and remaining arm, but the base is not punctured (fig. 160:9), and there is, therefore, no doubt about the orientation of the figure, nor about the combination of features. One thinks of models of human figures made by witch doctors or others desiring the death or discomfort of some individual. The object here, however, is very crude, has no head, and is not clearly either male or female and so is as unspecific as it could possibly be. This piece remains an enigma, but it definitely gives one the feeling that the meaning and purpose of the Jarmo figurines are as varied as the forms themselves and that one cannot classify them as merely "fertility symbols" or "cult objects."

Male Forms

Torso Type (figs. 161:1-9; 162:1)

As mentioned above, the shape of the male figurines is basically an inverted triangle, a torso with massive shoulders and outstretched arms curving forward at shoulder height. Often there is no head. The legs are not depicted. This combination of features gives the effect of a standing figure and eliminates the technical difficulty of trying to balance a heavy upper body on realistic legs. The base is round and usually flat or slightly concave. The torso is more or less round in section and may be slightly waisted before flaring out at the base. There are no variations within this type, although certain features differ in individual figurines. Most of these figures are crude and carelessly made. Sometimes the head is pinched to indicate a face, but generally the head is almost nonexistent, a mere stump. Of the 18 examples with the head more or less intact, 11 have the pinched face. In addition, several others seem to have had heads at one time. There are 100 examples (61 headless torsos) of the male form, but some of the bases included in this type are questionably classified.

One of the most interesting of these male forms has a massive head set well down on the shoulders (fig. 161:1). The face is roughly pinched, and the chin is long and narrow, perhaps indicating a beard. This figure is the best evidence to date that the torso type is intended to depict the human male. The top is more or less conical but flattened at the tip, suggesting a cap. There may have been pellet eyes, but this is by no means certain. Specks of a black stain or pigment on the head and body may have been bitumen or paint, as on an incised female figurine previously described (fig. 157:3). No pattern can be discerned in these specks, and it will probably be impossible ever to determine what they were.

A second figurine with an unusually long face may also represent a bearded man (fig. 161:4). The face is flattened as if it were appliquéd to the chest. The head slopes up to a low point at the top. The nose is barely indicated by a slight pinch, and the eyes and mouth are shown by punctations. There also seem to be punctations over the shoulders just where the arms are broken off. The base of the figure is decorated with short parallel incisions bordered by another incised line running horizontally slightly below the waist. Three other examples have similar incised decoration of the base. However, one of these lacks the encircling horizontal line (fig. 161:2) and is a truly curious figure, since it originally had three projections, two of which (broken off but probably not very substantial in any case) were surely arms. The third projection, whose tip is broken off, is on the back and seems to have been pinched out more or less horizontally. The head, badly battered but with evidence of a pinched face, terminates in a stubby point, much like the head of the second figurine described above. The projection on the back may indicate a hunchback or may be meant to represent a sack or other burden. A few other fragments in this group seem to have an incipient hump on the back between the shoulders, but this may be incidental to the modeling (more clay would have been added to the back to pull out for arms).

The rudimentary character of these stump-headed forms indicates that there was no wish or need to portray an individual but that here a universal form was being used to represent some fairly abstract concept. Two of the stump-headed forms resemble the tops of some of the human-headed double-wing-based objects in treatment. One is beveled above the vertical pinch; the bevel is divided vertically by incision, and horizontal parallel lines are incised on either side, like hair (fig. 161:5). Another is pinched with a more or less flat top (fig. 161:6).

Two figures have long heads tapered at the crown. The faces are pinched but there are no features (one example is shown on fig. 161:3). Two other figurines have small round heads. One of these figurines is flattened in front and back and is the only example with rounded shoulders and short arms held down at the sides instead of in the open embracing position. The head of the other is formed by a flap pressed down to the front. On this rather crude example the arms are slightly upraised, and one was pressed to the chest while the clay was still plastic, giving the effect of a declaiming orator (fig. 161:8).

One upper torso fragment is reminiscent of the Ubaid I and II figures in that the head is animallike (Wooley 1955, pl. 20: "lizard" goddesses). This Jarmo example is quite crude, the arms have been broken, and the head is twisted on the neck. The top comes to a rounded point, and the mouth is incised. Appliquéd pellet or strip eyes may have been present, but no trace of them remains (fig. 161:7).

There are four torso fragments that have a lump on the chest, suggesting that these figures may have been bearded. The head and arms are broken off. In general the male torso figurines and fragments are small to medium (30-40 mm), but one or two are fairly large (e.g., the piece shown in fig. 162:1 is 60 mm). As stated at the outset, all of these forms are crude, poorly modeled, and often twisted or otherwise distorted.

In addition to the 61 fairly identifiable torsos, about 30 round, concave-based fragments are within the size range of bases for male torso figures. Two of these are indented around or slightly below the waist, indicating perhaps that a strip of clay was once appliquéd there. Indentation of a different sort has been noted on stalk object bases (p. 387), with which these questionable torso bases might have been classed.[7]

A male torso figure of this same general type was found in level XIII at Tepe Gawra (Tobler 1950, p. 170 and pl. LXXXIII*b*,1). It has short, rounded arms, a stump head, and a broad appliquéd strip around the waist. The base is round and very concave. In size this figure is comparable to the Jarmo male figurines.

We now come to the problem of the purpose and meaning of the male figurines. Within the limits of this single form, a round-based torso with outstretched arms, there is still variety. From the evidence we have on the heads of these figures, the majority were very rudimentary and unrealistic. Therefore, the emphasis seems to be on the position of the arms—the all-embracing attitude. If this was meant to represent an all-powerful figure or a generative principle, it is much less well expressed than the pregnant female figurine. In its own way the male figure is certainly as abstract as the stylized type of female figurine; "torsoness," or the concept of a standing figure made without legs, is certainly an abstraction. In numbers the male figure, with only 100 examples, lags far behind the female, with a total of 370, including all of the variations. On this basis, it looks as if the male form had only secondary importance.

This form occurs in later periods at other sites in the Near East. Often it is just as crude or cruder in its simplest aspect; the arms occasionally become rounded stumps or are modeled as one with the body as if they were held down at the sides. These male figures from sites other than Jarmo are all torso forms, never modeled with legs.

Phallic Objects (fig. 162:2-5)

There are two phallic objects of marblelike stone that are very much alike (fig. 162:4-5; see p. 300 for discussion of these two artifacts). Both are pierced as if for hafting. Also found was one very crude, battered model of clay (fig. 162:3) which is obviously a version of the two stone examples. This piece has a shallow, more or less round depression on the surface that has the hafting perforation. There is also a fragment of a carefully made piece that has a depression and resembles this form, but it could be wrongly classified (fig. 162:2). Three other shapeless lumps of clay are considered to belong to this category only because they are pierced in the same fashion and have the shallow depression in conjunction.

A third object in marble (which may not even be a phallus; see p. 300) is more or less round and cuplike, and shallow, whereas the other marble examples are elongated and round or oval in section. This specimen has been broken through at the point of a perforation that may be analogous to the hafting perforation. A friable clay counterpart of this form has been found.

The above evidence is poor support indeed for phallic symbolism: 3 reliable examples (2 of stone and 1 of clay) and 5 others of highly questionable character. These objects may possibly have been connected with a fertility concept, which had its clearest expression in the pregnant female figurines. It is interesting to note that here for the first time we have objects of the same type depicted in both stone and clay. The bead and ball categories are the only other groups in which we find this dual expression. The presence of phallus-shaped objects carved of stone argues for some importance and emphasis on this organ, and the fact that so few have been found argues further that only a few people were allowed to concern themselves with its symbolism. If these objects were significant in the realm of personal sympathetic magic, as I believe many of the figurines were, there should be many more examples. Still, additional evidence would be required to carry speculation on this subject further.

HUMAN FIGURINE HEADS (figs. 163:1-14; 164:1-6)

Some examples of human figurine heads are remarkable for their careful modeling. This group, however, is one of the most frustrating in the inventory of Jarmo figurines since there are few clues, if any, to the type of body these heads once belonged to. None of the human heads were intended to stand alone, without a body, although there are two examples of animal heads that are complete as such. Only the recovery of more human figurines with heads intact will help to link the present examples with suitable body forms.

The total of 33 heads may be subdivided into four types. The first type is a broad, round head with a low, rounded top. The face may be flattened or the entire head may be quite cylindrical. There is little or no chin, and on only 2 of the 8 examples is the mouth shown. The nose is either pinched or appliquéd in the form of a strip. When the appliqué method is used for the nose, the eyebrows are generally applied in the same fashion. The eyes are usually appliquéd pellets, though on one example they are long incised slits (fig. 163:4) and on another, deep round punctations (fig. 163:3). One of these heads (fig. 163:1) is quite similar to the head on an almost complete figurine of the composite, pregnant type (fig. 157:4) and is therefore almost certainly from a female figurine. Another head, which incidentally has projections that may be ears, is enough like the above figurine also to be classed as female (fig. 163:2). An appliquéd pellet on the chest of one mentioned earlier may represent a breast (fig. 163:3); this figure is too fragmentary for us to be sure that it is female, but I would not be surprised to find that all the heads of this type belonged to female figurines.

Closely allied to these and a variant of the first type is a subgroup of 15 examples with long heads that taper to a rounded or coiled top. Only one has the mouth indicated. They have definite chins and appliquéd features; the nose and brows form a T or Y. Pellet eyes were appliquéd in all instances except 3 (the pellets are often missing, but the depressions indicate where they were originally pressed on). The first of these 3 exceptions has incised eyes and mouth (fig. 163:6), the second has deep incisions parallel to the underside of the eyebrows (fig. 163:5), and the last has no features whatever. Four additional examples have a coil (representing hair or a headdress) that winds clockwise around the head, high over the forehead, and terminates somewhere near the right ear (fig. 163:7-8,10). (The coil appears to be a female characteristic, and one of the heads bearing this feature is covered with red ochre [fig. 163:8], as is the large female figure described in the section on the composite, pregnant type [fig. 158:3].) Many of the lady stalk tops have such a coil or variation of it. Two of the heads of this type, but lacking the coil, have quite long, pointed chins, which seem to indicate beards (fig. 163:6,12). Because of the greater prominence of the brows of this variety, it is tempting to conclude that it belongs to the male form. These heads, however, show very fine, careful modeling, and the male forms are too crude to match. Yet there are no female forms that bear such well-modeled and realistic heads either.

Two examples are worthy of special note. These are long, tapered heads with the face squeezed down close to a very receding chin. They resemble markedly the head of the "lizard" goddess figures of the Ubaid period (fig.163:9,11).

The second type is extremely amorphous; the 4 examples are round, knoblike heads without features except that the nose is pinched on two of them (fig. 163:13-14). I could readily imagine these heads on female figurines of the composite, pregnant type; a fragment of one of these figurines does in fact bear such a head (fig. 158:7), though it had pellet eyes.

There are only 2 examples of the third type. One is a large and beautifully modeled specimen (fig. 164:1). The head is long with a very high, rounded forehead. The eyes are detailed in a different way, being incised ovals, not appliquéd pellets; the brows are modeled; the nose may have been an appliquéd strip, but it looks modeled (part of it is broken away); and the mouth is indicated by an incision. The other example is smaller and cruder. Again the head is long, with a high, rounded forehead. The eyes may have been appliquéd but there remain no traces of them, the nose is pinched out, and the mouth is not indicated. Three pellets around the back of the neck suggest a necklace, and other pellets presumably have broken off (fig. 164:2).

The 4 examples of the last type are small, flat-topped heads on long, cylindrical necks. Originally they may have been attached to stalk objects or double-wing bases rather than representational forms. The face is pinched in all cases. One has punctated eyes and an incised mouth (fig. 164:3); two have incised eyes and one of these also has an incised mouth and a line across the forehead (fig. 164:4-5). The fourth example has no facial features, but the flattened, somewhat concave top extends back to a short flap that is turned under in back (fig. 164:6).

There are also 3 crudely made fragments that are more or less cylindrical in section and have a pinched, featureless "face." These unclassifiable pieces do not constitute a type, nor are they included in the total of 33 given above.

Since there are many more female figurines than male, one might suppose that most of these heads were originally attached to female forms. The evidence for the coil as a feature of female figures has been demonstrated, but it could perhaps also be a feature of the male. Some of the heads with appliquéd features (which make up the first type) are probably male; those with very pointed chins undoubtedly are. Thus, there is probably not too much difference between male and female heads, and body form becomes the truly decisive factor. Only a larger sample of more or less whole figurines could solve this problem.

Meaning and Use of Human Figurines

It is indeed remarkable how few definite conclusions can be drawn from the study of the human figurine category. The meaning of the earliest form is not in the least clear; it may not even be female, but since the dichotomy—seated female vs. standing male—is evident in later forms, I have treated it as female. Although the meaning of the later and more realistic composite, pregnant type is quite understandable, there is little to indicate who made this type, or why. Generally of medium size, these figures could be individual charms used either to induce pregnancy or to sustain it and insure the birth of a healthy child. A state of personal health and well-being also may have been sought through charms. Could these charms have been used again and again by the original owner, or handed on to another, or was it necessary to make a new one for each occasion and each person?

The legless figure covered with red ochre seems to have been designed for greater permanence as well as importance, judging from its size and special coloring (fig. 158:3). There is also a leg made of pot clay that indicates another large figure but one that is cruder than the red-ochre lady. As far as I can tell from the available material, the large figurines are a late development, and the majority of the objects are medium to small throughout the occupation of the site. This element of size compels me to consider most of the Jarmo figurines in terms of individual and personal charms rather than cult objects in a broader sense. Clay figurine fragments were found everywhere, in rooms, outside houses, and in dump heaps. Thus, sympathetic magic is indicated on a popular basis, not yet formalized and ritualized to the extent that it was taken out of secular hands and away from the home.

The number and variety of human female forms lend weight to such an interpretation. The abstract forms may have been devised and accepted as having the same powers as the more realistic pregnant type and so served as fertility charms too, or they may have served other, unaccountable purposes. The fact that the realistic and abstract forms existed contemporaneously rules out any developmental sequence of abstraction with one form replacing another and makes it difficult to assess the meaning of the various forms. Each one may have been used for a distinct and separate purpose or wish, but the abstractions obviously derive from and are closely related to the more realistic forms. Therefore, the theory that all of them served the same basic function (to work magic) seems the most likely one at the moment. The fact that they are small and impermanent and were casually discarded is very significant, regardless of actual form.

The more carefully molded heads present a separate problem. Since the majority of male and female forms found with the head intact have either crude or rudimentary heads, it is hard to imagine just what figures the separate heads once belonged to, and since the emphasis seems to be placed on the posture and nature of the body, it is difficult to comprehend special modeling of the head. It may be just an indication of the maker's love of detail and perfection. These heads are definitely not yet in the realm of portrait heads, human or divine.

One final observation, suggested by Matson (pers. comm.), is that since women probably made the pottery we can assume that they also made what was modeled from pot clay. Upon examining the types of figurines made of pot clay, we find that most of them are female forms of the early simple type with the exception of a few legs of the composite type. This strengthens the notion that women made the other female figurines as well. There are also a few crude examples of animal figurines made of pot clay. Of these, type C is the only recognizable form to date, but none of the figures is modeled with anything like the skill seen in some of the wild forms, which, as I have indicated, were probably made by men who did the hunting. Thus it would seem that women may well have been in charge of domesticated flocks.

It is difficult, in considering the female figurine material on hand, to see a more generalized concept of "fertility" that might be applied to fields, flocks, and the like. The fertility and well-being of the flocks could be maintained by the use of animal figurine magic. As for the fertility of fields we have no way of knowing whether the pregnant female figurines were used as charms there. What we do know is that those considered here were found scattered haphazardly around the village. Undoubtedly, the pregnant female figurines were made by individual women in connection with a pregnancy, either desired or accomplished, for the purpose of assuring a successful conclusion.

These figures, both realistic and abstract, therefore represent the desires of the women of Jarmo and were made by them. The nature of these desires could have ranged far from human fertility and related matters.

There are no mother-and-child figurines or any realistic form that could be a baby or child figure, a fact that strongly suggests that children did not use the human figures as toys, at least not in a game of housekeeping with family figures. If the magic is indeed in the creation of the figures, figurine modeling would be definitely restricted to the adult population, especially the modeling of human forms. We can hardly judge whether, after they were created, they could be used again or handed on or had to be discarded each time, their magic being unrenewable. If the latter is true and they were in effect void after being used, the children might then safely handle them. Whether they actually did is open to speculation.

Double-Wing-based Objects

The double-wing-based objects and the next category, stalk objects, are the most interesting of the abstract forms. Whereas lady stalks (composite, stylized type) of the human figurine category are recognizably female, double-wing bases and stalk objects are recognizably human in some of their forms but are unassignable to either sex. This does not necessarily mean that for their makers they were neither male nor female, but only that they were not endowed with the usual attributes of sex that we have seen in the preceding category or any of those attributes that we associate with primitive art and sculpture. Even the base form of these figurines is unusual and distinct enough from that of the lady stalks not to be related, at least directly, to that abstraction. The base is usually long, rounded at the ends, flat on the bottom, and sometimes pinched in the middle. The body, squat or stalklike, rises from the center and faces one end of the base.

The total number of double-wing-based objects is 314, and the form has many variations. There are 108 fragments, mainly bases or parts of bases, that are unclassifiable but add to the very impressive total of this category. The base is stable and stylized, and the forms are medium to small with a few tiny ones (fig. 166:7-8). Base lengths range from about 16 mm to about 50 mm.

The distribution of finds is general over the mound but confined to the upper levels. So far no examples have been found in the earlier levels, but neither are any examples known to have been made of pot clay. There is the usual range from very careful workmanship to crude, twisted examples. Treatment of the top, or "head," varies and constitutes the basis on which the types are differentiated.

The key example of the human forms is unique in that the head may have been formed by appliquéing a flattened pellet to the rounded stalk. The nose has been pinched out and the eyes have been indicated by incision. The effect is a face more or less in the round rather than the pinched type that is usually seen on the lady stalks. The discovery of this more or less whole piece (fig. 164:7) clarified the classification of the human-headed forms, with features and without. These make up 50% of the 301 pieces classified as double-wing bases, as compared with 14% miscellaneous and 36% unclassifiable by type, mainly base fragments. (In addition, there are 13 examples in Baghdad from the first and second seasons that await reclassification.)

Human-headed Types (figs. 164:7-11; 165:1-12)

The 150 human-headed types seem to represent an abstract human form. All of them are pinched near the top to form a "face," and they can be subdivided according to the treatment of the top above the pinch. The 16 examples that make up the first group are definitely human. The pinch produces the nose, but other features are always incised; slanting incised lines mark the eyes, and the mouth is usually a thin incised line but may be a crude gash. One has a rounded top with a small knob pulled over to the left side (fig. 164:9). The knob, the sides, and the base are covered with thin, short incisions. Others have beveled tops, with or without a coil or flap down the back (fig. 164:8,10). Some tops are simply rounded. Beveled tops with a flap or coil are most common on the pieces with features (8 examples). The flap is not wound around the head, as it is on the lady stalks, but lies down the back, either straight or coiled. Often the flap or coil is broken off, but a depression sometimes remains where it was attached. Some of the examples are very neatly made, whereas others are carelessly done.

Closely related is a second group comprising 15 examples with the pinched face and the coiled flap but no features (fig. 165:1-2). Of these, 11 have beveled tops, 3 have rounded tops, and 1 has a flattened top. Again, the bevel is the prominent feature in conjunction with the coil, and in the third group there are 37 fragmentary examples of the beveled top with the flap down the back (fig. 165:3). Some of these flaps have broken off and so may have been coiled originally. As it is, these first three groups and a fourth group of 6 further examples, which again have the beveled tops but no flap (fig. 165:5-7), appear to be more or less the same form.

Next there are 7 variations with the flap but no bevel; these, too, have the pinched face (fig. 165:4,8). Then there are 27 examples with pointed tops and pinched faces (fig. 165:10-11), 11 with rounded tops and pinched faces (fig. 165:12), and 31 fragments with pinched faces but with tops broken off (fig. 165:9).

Using the pinch as the criterion for humanness, since it produces a face that in 16 of these 150 examples is adorned with features, we see that half of our total double-wing-base category seem to depict a human form. Just what this form represents is not known as yet. It certainly does show, as we have already seen in the category of lady stalks, the ability of the Jarmo figurine makers to produce remarkable abstract forms. Here again are demonstrated individuality and originality in producing small, even tiny, objects which have no evident meaning in present-day evaluation, though they obviously meant something very precise to the manufacturers. (Each piece is distinct in size, shape, and style; they were not being turned out as matched sets of gaming pieces, if such indeed was their use.)

Miscellaneous Forms (fig. 166:1-8)

Among the 43 examples in this group are some that may represent animals. There are 5 saddleback forms (fig. 166:1) and 4 eared forms (fig. 166:2-4). The tops of 4 other bases have been broken off, but they still retain strips or pellets of appliqué (fig. 166:5-6). The rest are more or less complete but are not suggestive of type (e.g., fig. 166:7-8).

DISCUSSION OF DOUBLE-WING-BASED OBJECTS

The double-wing-based objects are clearly no chance form. The treatment of the top part of some of these figures—the pinched face and coil—is obviously related to that of the lady stalks, but the beveled top, which is the most common type, appears only on this category.

Forms with double-wing bases have so far been found only in the upper levels at Jarmo, that is, in the top 2.0-2.5 m. None occurred in J-I below level 3. More digging in the lower levels, however, may reveal examples of this form. Furthermore, most of the examples were recovered in the top 1.0-1.5 m. Since this is a very specific and abstract form and since figurines from the lower levels have so far been generalized, nonspecialized forms for the most part, the double-wing bases could well be exclusively a later development.[8]

STALK OBJECTS

The composite, stylized type of the human figurines, the double-wing-based objects, and the stalk objects are all closely related categories. Stalk tops with the bases broken off could be either double-wing-based objects or the composite, stylized type, and I have already included in those categories a few tops that I am reasonably certain belong there. Some of the fragments now under discussion may have been legged (lady stalks), double-wing-based, or round based. Nevertheless, stalk objects seem to constitute a category of their own, regardless of their similarities to previously discussed forms.

Stalk objects, when more or less whole, are round at the base. There are about 15 intact examples with human heads whose bases are flat or concave on the underside. These are rather more like gaming pieces than the double-wing bases. In this category are 181 examples.

Coiled-Top Type (fig. 167:1-3)

Of the 18 pieces distinguished by a coiled top, only one, and that rather questionably classified as a true coil, is round at the base. However, this piece is the only one that has retained its base; all the others are top fragments only (fig. 167:1-3) and, therefore, may have been lady stalks. But since none of them has the pinch that forms the face, they have been grouped with stalk objects rather than with the composite, stylized type.

Human-headed Type (figs. 166:9-12; 167:4-14)

In the group of human-headed stalks, with features and without, there are 76 examples. The fragments could be lady stalks (p. 381) since many have the face pinch. I have grouped them in the rather catchall category of stalk objects so that the very important human figurine category would contain as few questionable fragments as possible, insofar as subjective sorting will allow.

The key example of the human-headed type is conical in shape and has a round, concave base (fig. 166:9). The nose is pinched out, and eyes and mouth are punctated. A flattened topknot crowns the head. Although its base is broken, the figurine is essentially complete and therefore has retained enough features to show that it represents a new form. Another conical piece (fig. 166:10), a top fragment only, has punctated eyes and a pinched nose but no mouth. Also related, though lacking features, is a more or less complete figurine (fig. 166:11) with a round, concave base, a pinched face, and a crest pinched up over the top, tiaralike, which is reminiscent of the coils on the lady stalks and some of the double-wing bases. It has one punctation in the center front of the stalk and several punctations behind at the "waist." These may be natural air holes, or they may have been manufactured. Another piece with the base broken off seems closely related, and, though the top is also broken, a crest effect rather than a coil seems to have been intended (fig. 166:12).

A tall, thin stalk with a round, slightly concave base (fig. 167:4) has a small pinch for the face placed well below the beveled, slightly concave top, which closely resembles that seen on many of the double-wing bases. Another complete example has a beveled top and coil behind and a round, slightly concave base (fig. 167:5). A few fingernail incisions occur on the front. With its pinched face, it is most comparable to one of the double-wing-based objects (fig. 164:9), except that the stalk object has no features.

Another complete example is tall and conical with a slightly concave base; it has a pinched face and coiled flap down the back (fig. 167:6). It, too, is comparable to the double-wing-based objects with coils and also suggests the lady stalks. Two others—also closely related, though without the pinch—have the top rounded over to form a short flap, which may be the back (uncompleted coil) or a face (fig. 167:7). Such a face is suggested by one unusual fragment; its top is rounded over and pinched to form a face, the eyes and mouth are incised (fig. 167:8), and a "necklace" of appliquéd pellets adorns the neck. This fragment (the base is broken off) is small and very nicely made; the stalk is tall and round and well formed. The impression is of a humanized serpent, but since there are no other examples of snakes or any other comparable pieces except the two featureless forms mentioned above, it is rather difficult to interpret this example.

Pellets appliquéd around the neck have until now been noted only on the composite type of female figurine, but three other stalk fragments with both tops and bases broken off have appliquéd pellets. Two have single pellets, and one has a ring of them (fig. 167:9-10).

Other fragments have coils, topknots, or bevels, and some of them may have been double-wing based. Some are eared and may represent animals rather than humans (fig. 167:11-14). There is considerable variety within the category, which is definitely concerned with a new form and not yet well defined.[9]

Conical Type (fig. 167:15-16)

There are 41 examples of tall, conical pieces that taper more or less uniformly upward. They have concave, slightly concave, or, more rarely, flat bases. All the tops are broken off. I have assumed that these objects are stalk-object bases. Their distribution is fairly general throughout the levels; examples also occur in the lower levels of J-I. This distribution corresponds, as one might expect, to that of the headed forms, that is, the upper half of the stalk object type.

In addition there are 7 squat forms (whose tops are broken off) with broad, very concave bases from which the stalk rises tall and thin, waisted above the base.

"Nails" (figs. 167:17-20; 168:1-2)

There are 39 examples that differ from the tall, conical pieces in that they rise almost straight, often with a slight waisting, from round, slightly concave bases (fig. 167:17-20). Fourteen of these are characterized by waisting near the base and a slight swelling of the stalk above; generally there seems to have been more shaping on these examples. Shallow indentations around the base suggest that appliquéd strips or pellets had been pressed on but have long since fallen off (fig. 167:19-20). Actual traces of them remain in only two cases: one where a single oval pellet is affixed to the stalk above the slight waisting, and one with two pellets side by side (fig. 168:1). All other indentations occur below the "waist." All the tops are broken off, but there is a strong suggestion of relationship to the male forms. The height and thinness of the stalk above the base, however, preclude their belonging to the male torso type, which is thick and supports massive shoulders and outstretched arms. These have a greater range in size than the other stalk objects. There are larger pieces (fig. 168:2) as well as a tiny one with a base diameter of about 6 mm.

DISCUSSION OF STALK OBJECTS

Although the numerous variations of stalk objects are due in part to the lack of definition of this category, it can readily be seen that true abstractions exist here, certainly of humanness and possibly, in a few examples, of animalness. In this, the category is akin to the double-wing bases, sharing several distinctive features with them. The stalk objects seemingly have a wider distribution in time, occurring also in the earlier levels, but the category must be better defined, again through more material, before this apparent distribution can have much weight and before their true relationship with the double-wing bases and other categories can be fully assessed.

CONES AND TETRAHEDRONS (fig. 168:3-7)

The predominant form in the cone category has an approximately ogival profile. The typical specimen measures about 12 mm in base diameter and about 10 mm in height (fig. 168:3). These examples are small, usually symmetrical, and carefully made and finished. There are 106 examples of this type, 93 of which occurred in J-I, especially in the lower levels, 6-8. Only 6 (one shown as fig. 168:4) were recovered during the third season, when excavation was confined mainly to the upper levels.

There are 35 examples that vary from the above type; they are squat, generally off-center and crude, and often have indentations made by finger pressure during the shaping of the clay. One whole, nicely executed example has a bulbous top (fig. 168:5) instead of the usual tapered tip. Other tips are blunt or battered or are broken off altogether.

In addition, 20 examples of tetrahedrons (fig. 168:6-7) were found. These, too, are small and are fairly well made. The sides, each about 20 mm in length, are slightly concave, and it is easy to see the way these forms were made: they were turned and pinched slightly between the fingers. Less skill was required in fashioning these than the ogival type of cones, which are rounded and smoothed. The tetrahedrons were recovered not only from the upper levels of J-II and from near the surface in two test squares but also from the gray-black ashy deposit in J-III and in test square P16.

There is a marked decline in the occurrence of ogival cones in the upper levels, and this scarcity is not well filled in by the tetrahedrons, as the totals show. The variations occur throughout with slightly greater concentration in the upper levels.

It is difficult to imagine what these cones were used for or what they were meant to represent. Counters or gaming pieces can be suggested. Or, if one considers them in the light of the other abstract forms already described, one might speculate that they are abstractions of the simple seated female form (the only human form yet known from the available early levels) and are therefore female symbols; alternatively, since there are no recognizable male forms, they might be abstractions representing the male. Aside from any consideration of sex, the very clear pattern of distribution is worthy of some note, and, because it parallels that of the simple seated female form, it is natural to link the two. Clearly a problem of this sort would be clarified by more figurine material from the earlier levels. The cones already recovered constitute an important category that can be viewed in a line with the other abstractions, perhaps even as forerunners of the double-wing bases, which so far are an exclusively later form.

BEADS (fig. 168:8-17)

There are 191 clay beads or bead fragments. The simplest form is a perforated ball, and most of the 23 examples of this type are crude, somewhat asymmetrical, and carelessly made. Two in this group are very small, 8 mm in diameter; one of these is very hard and smooth and may have been burnished. Others are as large as 20 mm in diameter. There are 38 disklike beads, which doubtless were first formed as balls and then flattened (fig. 168:8). They are fairly smooth, and some still bear fingerprints. These beads range from about 15 mm to 25 mm in diameter. The distribution of this circular, flattened type is general, as one would expect of such a simple form.

There are 71 barrel-shaped beads; 34 examples are round in cross section and 37 have been flattened. On the whole these were more carefully made than the disklike form, though some of them are also asymmetrical, but the ends are not carefully finished (fig. 168:8-10). Closely allied are 8 rounded rectangular beads, flattened or planoconvex in cross section.

There are 5 examples of a flattened, collared bead and 19 examples of a flattened, diamond-shaped bead (fig. 168:11; see also fig. 136:10, in stone). Some of the diamond-shaped type were better made than the simpler forms; this fact seems to indicate greater care in flattening the biconical ball, the initial step in the production of this shape. These diamond-shaped beads did not occur at all in J-I and were found only in the upper levels of the other operations or test squares.

Another specialized form, with only 5 examples, is the toggle bead (fig. 168:12). This fairly carefully made form is a rounded oval with two perforations. The greatest length is 25 mm, and the diameter ranges from 8 mm to 10 mm. Beads of this type were found only in the uppermost levels.

Three biconical beads with trimmed or flattened ends were carefully made (fig. 168:13). One was decorated with short fingernail incisions (fig. 168:14) and as such is unique since none of the other beads were embellished except for a few examples that were burnished.

There are 7 long cylinder beads that are perforated lengthwise, most of them well made, and 3 short cylinder beads that are flattened balls perforated through the short axis.

Nine beads have been classified as miscellaneous. Two look like seated figures. The body of one of these is rounded, is oval in cross section, and has the perforation lengthwise through the trunk (fig. 168:15). The head is broken off, and the short legs taper to rounded ends. Both these examples, fairly small and well made, came from the upper levels. Another bead, a disk with a double perforation like a button (fig. 168:16), was carefully made and came from the ash horizon. Also carefully made was an unusual spiked bead, its spikes being short with rounded tips (fig. 168:17). The other 5 miscellaneous beads are fragments only and represent various asymmetrical forms that do not fit into the preceding classification.

Some of the perforations seem to have been made by inserting a reed or straw into the wet clay, but the beads could just as well have been formed around the straw. The impression of plant fiber to be seen in some of the broken sections suggests that the straw may have been burned out in firing or removed prior to firing, after the bead had dried sufficiently.

The greatest number of beads came from the ash area. Since beads made of stone were also popular and more durable, it is not surprising that most of the clay beads are rather crude and that the shapes are relatively few and simple.

Unperforated Bead Shapes (fig. 168:18)

There are also 49 examples of what can be called bead shapes. These look very much like some of the forms discussed above, but they are not perforated. It is impossible to say whether they were ever intended to be beads. These objects may have dried too much before any perforation was attempted, or they may have been only an expression of plastic "doodling." Thirty of them are the flattened barrel shape; the remainder are either the rounded barrel, rounded rectangular, diamond, irregular, or planoconvex shape. One of the two planoconvex bead shapes is covered on the convex side with parallel incisions (fig. 168:18). There are a few unperforated beads in the lower levels, but like the perforated forms they occur mainly in the upper levels.

BALLS AND DISKS (fig. 169:1-10)

Many variations were found in the clay ball category. Balls range in diameter from 5 mm to 65 mm. Both crude and careful workmanship are exhibited. Many examples have a high proportion of plant inclusions, though perhaps the small pieces of chaff were deliberately mixed with the clay as a sort of temper. Such inclusions are found in balls even in the lowest levels and seem to be a trait that occurs throughout. The "tempered" balls are generally larger, in the 30-50 mm range, and are quite friable.

There are 1,153 more or less round clay balls, some of them fragmentary. Some are faceted as if by finger pressure; others are slightly biconical, indicating that they were shaped by being rolled between the palms. Some are rough surfaced, but most are smooth and rather carefully made, especially the smaller ones. Some (40 in number) are further modified by incision, usually a circle or spiral on opposing faces; 15 of this type are from 16 to 20 mm, and 24 are from 11 to 15 mm (fig. 169:1-4). One incised ball also has a fabric impression of what looks like two threads woven over two other threads (fig. 169:10). Another fabric impression occurs on a subhemispherical disk and covers the rounded surface (fig. 169:9). The fabric indicated on the clay balls is very fine, and there has been some discussion about the fibers used, with as yet no definite conclusions. These are the only fabric impressions so far noted at Jarmo, on clay or anything else. Numerous examples of reed basketry impressions have been found, however (fig. 169:13-14).[10]

Almost half of the balls are in the 11-15 mm size range, and about one fourth of the total is in the 16-20 mm range. One can only speculate on the use of these balls. Sling pellets might be suggested.[11] They may also have been used as counters; for instance, a shepherd counting his flock may have dropped a ball into a container to count off each sheep.[12] Incised balls may have represented a higher or multiple value. Alternatively they may all have been marbles and used only for play.

In addition to the regular, more or less round balls, there are 28 examples that have one flattened surface; they are planoconvex in section (fig. 169:5). Since these obviously do not roll, they could make good counters. Seventy-one examples are smooth but faceted, again perhaps to keep them from rolling. In addition, there are 12 biconvex balls and 10 disks that are flattened top and bottom (fig. 169:6), as well as 5 small oval balls.

Also found were 86 subhemispherical disks, 16 of which are incised (fig. 169:7-8). One of the 86 is the disk with the fabric impression mentioned above. These disks are planoconvex in cross section, and many have an impression of reed matting on the flattened surface. These, too, may have served as counters; they are often carefully made, and the convex surface is generally smoothed.

Flattened disks appeared in even greater numbers, with 206 examples. These are generally rougher and cruder than the subhemispherical disks and more frequently bear the impression of matting. They are also greater in diameter and often are only fragmentary because of their thinness.

A ball is one of the simplest forms that can be made from clay. Therefore, even when there is a large sample of balls, as in the Jarmo case, one cannot derive any startling conclusions from them. Clearly, the Jarmo people made them while sitting on reed mats. Most of the balls are small and round and were carefully shaped. Their surfaces were sometimes decorated; some had incisions, either short line or spiral.

MISCELLANEOUS

"Stamp Seal" (fig. 170:1)

A specimen that suggests a stamp seal appeared in J-II,2. Roughly conical in shape, it has a deeply incised spiral on the flat base. This object was fairly carefully made but, like most of the clay objects, only very lightly baked. It seems probable, therefore, that it was used for stamping decorations only on rather soft materials, such as fabrics or leather, or perhaps on the face or body. Naturally, no traces of such stamped designs were found. Pottery at Jarmo did not have stamped designs, but since it was sometimes decorated with red paint and since red ochre is to be seen on some of the figurines, we know that the color red was used to some extent. No trace of any color was discernible on the stamp.

Miniature Vessels (fig. 170:2-7)

Of the 89 examples of miniature vessels, only 19 are complete enough to be recognizable as true vessels. The rest only suggest small vessels and are much too fragmentary either to be used in reconstruction or to be perceived unquestionably as once actually part of a vessel. Of the 19 recognizable forms, 2 are almost spherical, ranging between 27 mm and 32 mm in diameter. The walls are thin, about 5-6 mm at the thickest. These little pots are very crude and have rough surfaces (fig. 170:2). Another small pot, with a diameter of 39 mm, is globular and has a restricted opening off center (ca. 18 mm); it, too, is crude and has a rough exterior (fig. 170:4). One more or less oval dish has a very shallow, smoothed-out depression, and as a result the base is quite thick. The sides and base are rounded, and the greatest diameter is about 40 mm (fig. 170:3). Another roughly oval form has a flat base with rounded, pinched-up sides. Two round vessels with diameters of 30 mm and 45 mm have flat bottoms and low, vertical sides. When the larger of the two was found, it contained a small obsidian bladelet section (fig. 170:7). In addition, there are fragments of 4 round, shallow, flat-bottomed dishes with low, pinched-up edges.

The most interesting fragments are 7 stemmed vessels made of the usual untempered clay (there are no examples whose fabric is pot clay). The most nearly complete example is 36 mm high and has a rim diameter of 32 mm (fig. 170:5). The base is flat. A round, shallow top piece, 70 mm in diameter, seems to have had its stem broken off. The other 5 examples are quite fragmentary and smaller than these two.

There is one small broken cuplike vessel 26 mm high (fig. 170:6).

The other fragments in this group are concavo-convex and some of them seem to be rim fragments, although no original form can be deduced from them. They are fairly thin, the average thickness being about 7 mm, and the exterior (convex) surface is generally smooth.

The distribution of the miniature vessels is general throughout all levels and is therefore apparently not related to the restricted distribution of normal pottery vessels. They are simple forms, rather crudely made, and probably were children's toys.

House Models? (fig. 170:9-11)

There are five fragments that were parts of what may have been house models.[13] They have flat bases with low sides forming square or rectangular chambers. The example from J-A has higher sides of more or less the same thickness rising to the rounded rim (fig. 170:9). The sides of the other examples are low, pinched up from the base so that the edges are thin and irregular (fig. 170:10-11). One of these fragments has a whole chamber that is more or less square.

Spindle Whorls (fig. 170:8)

There are 4 examples of spindle whorls from the uppermost levels of J-II. Of these, 3 specimens are pottery—2 complete (see fig. 170:8 for one example) and 1 broken in half. They are roughly circular, about 50 mm in diameter, with the perforation about 8 mm in diameter. They are flat with the edges somewhat smoothed and rounded and are probably worked sherds. The greatest thickness is 13 mm.

The fourth example is a clay fragment. It is slightly biconical in cross section. The surfaces are somewhat faceted, perhaps as a result of forming the disk, and the edges are nicely rounded. The perforation is small and was made by poking through from one side to the other while the clay was still soft. The reconstructed diameter is 45 mm and that of the perforation about 5 mm. The perforation is slightly off center.

So far these whorls (also rare stone whorls; see p. 294 and fig. 131:15-17) and the two fabric-impressed balls remain the only hints that there might have been textile manufacture at Jarmo. One would expect to find more spindle whorls, particularly in the upper levels, since knowledge of them is attested by the presence of at least three examples in clay. Although thread can be spun without the aid of spindle whorls, it is likely that they would have been used, certainly if much weaving were done. Spindles and spindle whorls made of wood are still very much in use in the area today, and it is entirely possible that the inhabitants of Jarmo also used wooden ones.

Clublike Forms (fig. 171:1-3)

There are 6 examples of clublike or pestlelike forms. An almost complete specimen, which comes from J-I,6, has a long, tapered handle that ends in a smooth, rounded, clublike base (fig. 171:1). The object is solid and seems to be chaff tempered, although this is unusual for such a large piece. It is 152 mm in length, and the greatest diameter of the head is 45 mm. End fragments of 2 quite similar examples were found in J-II,4. One of these fragments is larger and better shaped than the almost complete specimen already mentioned, and the other is smaller and cruder (fig. 171:2-3).

The head of the whole example is darkened by the stain of some material, but no other traces of the material remain. One of the other club-head fragments retains bits of what seems to be bitumen. It has been suggested that these clay implements were probably used as daubers to coat the insides of reed baskets with hot bitumen to make them waterproof. This seems very reasonable, since these "clubs" or "daubers" of clay could be shaped to the angle or width best suited to the particular job.[14] A broader surface could be manufactured with clay than would be possible with bone, and clay clubs would be easier to produce than wooden ones. (The fragment shown in figure 171:2 may have been formed around a stick.) They would also be lighter and easier to handle than stone, and indeed no stone forms of this type occurred.

Although it probably did not serve the same purpose, I have included here a pestlelike object of pottery, 102 mm long, which was found in J-II,2. The handle is thick, and both the top and base are a little larger than the shaft. Its top is flat. The base is so battered that there is no way of determining how or by what it was worn. It is hard to imagine what this object of fairly soft material was used for.

Two miniature forms that seem to be models of this type were found in J-II,1 and in J-II,5. The end of the handle of the smaller one is broken off; the preserved length is 22 mm and the greatest diameter of the head is only 10 mm. The other, slightly larger and more complete, measures 28 mm in length and 21 mm in greatest head diameter.

Spoons (fig. 171:7-10)

There are 5 fragments of spoons, of which the largest is the most questionable; it is lumpy and has a thick, rounded, triangular-sectioned handle and a thick, curved, slightly concave bowl (fig. 171:7). Three others have fragments of handles and portions of bowls (fig. 171:8-10). One of the handles seems to be complete, since the end is rounded off, making a very short handle (fig. 171:9). Another has a row of punctations on the handle, leading down to the bowl (fig. 171:8). The last, a fragment of a bowl only, is very thin and bears fingerprints. These objects are obviously quite fragile and useless for liquids.[15]

Miniature Stools (fig. 169:12,15)

There are 2 miniature stools, one of which consists of a pair of legs topped by an appliquéd ring of clay that forms a shallow cup. The legs are short and taper to a rounded tip (fig. 169:15). A fragment has been broken off below the cup; it seems to have been larger than the legs and set in a somewhat different plane from that of the legs. Therefore, it may be an unusual abstraction of a seated human form or may represent a stool (see Mallowan 1936, p. 19). The other example is whole; the slightly concave top is supported by four short legs (fig. 169:12).

Perforated Objects (fig. 171:4-6)

All 4 of these perforated objects are fragmentary and completely puzzling. Three are nicely shaped and well made. One of these has an end rounded over, and the resulting flap was pressed down to form a round hole. The combination of the shape and break indicates that it may have been paired (fig. 171:5). A tubular piece, broken in half lengthwise, seems to have been formed around a stick, which, when removed, left a long, smooth channel. This piece is tapered to a rounded tip, where a second hole was pushed through at a right angle to the channel. The third fragment is a flattened piece, planoconvex in cross section (fig. 171:4), whose perforation was forced through from the flattened surface (fig. 171:6). The last fragment is quite crude; it is a thick, rounded piece with a hole poked through it.

Stud or Plug (fig. 169:11)

There is one well-made stud or plug that is rounded and has somewhat battered ends. The form also suggests a spool but is very small.[16]

Rod Fragments

There are about 250 more or less cylindrical fragments, all with at least one end broken off. Of these, about 150 from the first and second seasons need reclassification in the light of amplified categories of lady stalks and stalk objects. Although a category of rods will always remain, these fragments are assumed to be mainly unidentifiable pieces of stalk objects. Some of these cylinders are very small and well made; others are rough and crudely fashioned. Distribution is general throughout, as it is for stalk objects.

Shaped Pieces

About 150 fragments of deliberately shaped forms are impossible to fit into any of the already established categories.

CLAY LUMPS

Among the total of 350 clay lumps are quite a few flattened pieces with grass or straw or mat impressions on one surface, as well as some with no impressions. There is also a large sampling of lumps which, though shaped in some fashion or other, are much less suggestive of forms than are the shaped pieces previously mentioned. They are an integral part of the whole picture presented by the clay figurine material, although they certainly do not have the immediate significance or appeal of the classifiable objects.

Clay, both shaped and unshaped, was found in large quantities throughout the excavated area, which was confined to the village site. The amount of this recovered material is remarkable, since the color of the clay objects did not differ greatly from that of the soil, and considerable skill was required to identify the fragments before they were smashed by the pick. This factor probably had much to do with the greater recovery rate of figurines in the soft, dark soil of the ash area, where objects of clay could be seen more easily.

At the end of the second season's testing, about one cubic foot of clay fragments was discarded from J-I and J-II and another from J-III. (Cubic-foot cartons were filled with the pieces to be discarded.) I estimate that a similar amount was discarded during the third season. Naturally, the lumps were carefully sorted before any were discarded.

The total of 5,500 clay pieces given at the beginning of this chapter includes the clay lumps that were saved and brought back from the field. These are all being kept, as are the shaped pieces, in the hope that one day they may reveal useful information about the grasses or reeds. Meanwhile they can be used for tests of clay composition and firing temperatures.

CONCLUSIONS

As presented here, the Jarmo figurines have simply been sorted into types, and these types have been described with reference to their possible use and meaning. There is no point at which one can say that such a classification is finished; new material from Jarmo or other sites in the same time range will always call for reassessment and reclassification of the older finds. Many questions can and should be put to this material. An investigation of a more technical nature can surely indicate many interesting facets and test some of the theories of manufacture.

The raw material in the untempered clay figurines appears to be homogeneous throughout the levels. Furthermore, the techniques used in the production of these small, lightly baked figurines do not change noticeably from the earlier to the later levels. Enough of the same forms continue from the earliest occupation to the latest to add to this impression of homogeneity. There is a proliferation of forms in the upper levels, which may be revealed in the lower levels as well when there are sufficient deeper exposures to permit valid comparison.

In the more fully documented upper levels we see that all forms occurred, realistic and abstract alike. Moreover, there seems to be no pattern with regard to time or area that would indicate that one form predated another or was restricted to any particular part of the mound. The ash area yielded figurines in greater concentration than other areas; moreover, it proved to be extensive, and preservation and recovery factors were more favorable there. Further excavation in the lowest levels may clarify the temporal distribution; examples of "later," more highly developed forms, or at least their prototypes, will probably be found down at the bottom of the mound. At present, the outstanding form from the available early levels that does not occur in the later levels is the cone. Balls in the 10-15 mm range also appear in large numbers in the early levels but occur rather prominently in some of the upper levels as well and thus do not indicate a significant pattern of distribution.

The remarkable thing about this collection from Jarmo is its size. That these fragile pieces, so like the soil in color, should have been found in such quantities is startling. And yet, during the autumn of 1954, in an area well north of the Chemchemal valley, similar clay objects were recovered wherever we tested. There were only a few, to be sure, since the soundings were never large, but more examples can be expected to turn up when more extensive excavations are carried out (Braidwood 1954, pp. 120-38). The workmen were familiar with the occurrence of clay figurines at Jarmo, and I am certain that a factor in the collection of such material is an acquaintance with the type of material to be found and a familiarity with the methods by which to recover it. The nature of the matrix being excavated is, of course, another factor. In the future we shall doubtless see the recovery of other collections of equal size and importance.

For the cultural level exhibited at Jarmo, clay figurines can give almost the only clue to the intellectual life of the inhabitants, above and beyond the material life to be seen in their tools and architecture. Until much more comparative material is available, further speculation on the meaning or purpose of the figurines is useless. For this reason I have given but scant attention to the clay figurine material from other sites, most of which is later in time and occurs in cultural settings well beyond early village life.[17]

The main point that we can conclude from the Jarmo figurine material at the present time is that realistic and abstract forms of both animals and humans occur. The more realistic forms appear to be "personal wishes," with the "desire" expressed in the *act* of modeling the form. The figure was then dried, fired, and kept until the wish was fulfilled, or it was discarded immediately after manufacture. Misshapen forms attest to this latter practice and denote perhaps failure, inadequacy, or else a short-term wish fulfillment, or at least insignificance of the final product.

The abstract forms are a bit more difficult to interpret. If the Jarmo inhabitants were in the habit of making "charms" to represent "desires," there is no limit to what they may have expressed in either realistic or abstract form. The forms that are definitely female include pregnant versions and ones that are not ostensibly pregnant.

Humanness and, even more abstractly, vitality may have been the expression intended in other "wishes" whose nature we cannot at present fathom. But in the abstract categories of double-wing bases and stalk objects we see the series beginning with demonstrably human forms and ending with forms that may represent animals, though not as clearly. Here humanness is clear in part, but the intent of the makers for the whole series is not.

What we certainly do not know is the extent to which these abstract forms represent concepts the same as, or different from, the realistic forms of animals and humans. The abstractions may be abbreviations, quick and easy references to the same "wish" as that expressed by the realistic forms, and if so are thus no more formal or complicated. Or they may refer to more complex "desires," which could not in any case be represented by a realistic form, and thus differ radically in underlying concept, though apparently not in manufacture, since careful and careless workmanship alike occur. Lastly, the abstract figures may represent incipient ritual forms to mask the true aspect of the "wish" out of respect, awe, or fright. None of them are durable or monumental enough to have been conceived with lasting value in mind, and they do not supersede the realistic forms.

Regardless of concepts and motives, the figurines were still made by different individuals, in and around their homes, and varying skill was displayed as well as variety of form, although certain general definable forms were well known and adhered to. This bespeaks a group activity that, while carried out by individuals in their own way, had cultural definition in both the realistic and abstract realms; forms fall into various categories not by chance but by tradition.

Children may have participated in the production of certain forms, perhaps the balls and the little clay vessels. They may also have been given any "wish" figures that had served their purpose and were no longer meaningful. It seems likely, however, that children's modeling in clay was restricted solely to the forms considered appropriate for them (balls, miniature vessels, possibly house models, and perhaps a few animals). The abstract and human forms were almost certainly taboo. Because the categories are so clearly definable, they could not have included many of the products of unrestricted childhood activity. The forms perhaps most natural for young clay modelers are noticeably absent: small forms such as frogs, lizards, and turtles, and family figures, including babies. The children of Jarmo doubtless had their own particular tasks, the boys herding and helping in the fields and the girls helping their mothers, tending babies, and preparing food. Toys were perhaps superfluous, although, of course, they could have been made of perishable materials. The clay figures recovered at Jarmo in all likelihood represent only in very small part the playthings of the junior members of this village society.

Since the figurine material, both realistic and abstract, seems to be mixed with the household debris in the same careless fashion as the everyday stone and bone implements and as yet has not been found at Jarmo in any ceremonial or architectural context, the figurines were probably used for daily or regular sympathetic magic of a more or less individual nature.

NOTES

1. During a visit with Dr. A.O. Shepard at her laboratory in Boulder, Colorado, in August 1958, we fired three small fragments of an animal figure in an electric kiln, recording time and temperature. I examined the pieces at 300°C, comparing them with the unfired parts of the same fragments kept out as controls, and found no change in color or hardness. Again, at 450°C the pieces under investigation showed no appreciable color change but seemed to be very slightly harder; I scratched them with a needle while examining the effect under a binocular microscope. At 550°C a small color change—a slight reddening—could be noted, and they also seemed slightly harder. Unfortunately, the thermocouple broke during the next test but I judged that the temperature reached about 600°-650°C. Again they were only slightly harder but had turned much redder. Further testing and experimenting can reveal a great deal about the actual firing of the figurines. A differential thermal analysis, for instance, could determine more precisely the temperature to which they were fired. However, since it is known that plasticity is lost in coarse clay at about 400°C and in kaolinite at about 450°C, and that clay will no longer slake at a temperature over 500°-600°C, it would seem from the interrupted test described above that the Jarmo clay figurines were fired to 400°-450°C and not much higher.

2. Ucko's reference (1968) to a portion of the Jarmo figurine material was based on his reading of this manuscript in its original form. His study, a broad one concerning the representation of the human figure in early Near Eastern context, led him to select only those human figurines from Jarmo which are naturalistic in form. This portion can be compared readily with material from the rest of the Near East. But since the presentation of the abstract human forms appeared not to be useful to his study, he simply ignored that portion of the Jarmo material.

3. Type C seems to be the only one, with the possible exception of type H, in which one finds a comparatively large animal form. The average size for all types and classes of Jarmo figurines is strikingly small and uniform within the categories. Only in the case of the human female figurines do some examples occasionally exceed the usual size—an important point that will be discussed at greater length in the section on the female figurines.

4. Letters I, J, and O have been omitted to avoid confusion with field numbers.

5. The hedgehog could be suggested, but that little animal has such a distinctive appearance that it is hard to imagine that its portrayal would not be clear. In the University Museum, Philadelphia, is a wonderful example of a hedgehog found at Tepe Gawra, level 5 (Speiser 1935, pl. XXXIVa). It is very realistic and has comb markings for the spines.

6. There is, of course, a compulsion to fit as many pieces as possible into groups. But colleagues who have examined the animal figurines have been able to see for themselves the criteria that were used for sorting into the various groups.

7. Unfortunately the torso bases cannot meaningfully be counted in the total of human figurines and so perhaps it is not useful to discuss them here.

8. Tobler (1950, p. 173 and pl. LXXXIIIe) describes 2 objects similar to double-wing bases as buffers or smoothers. In size they are comparable to the Jarmo examples, but not many forms of this type were recovered at Tepe Gawra.

9. Howe and I feel that the 2 clay figurines from Karim Shahir (see fig. 10:1a-b and p. 45) correspond most closely with these stalk objects from Jarmo.

10. See pp. 425f. for a report by Adovasio on the impressions of fabrics and basketry.

11. Sling pellets of the 11-15 mm range would be useful

only for hunting very small animals or birds. Since these creatures do not occur in the more realistic figurine categories, it seems unlikely that they played a part in the Jarmo economy.

12. According to Jacobsen (1946, p. 245), "The modern shepherd in Iraq will often make a number of pellets of clay and place them in a bag, one pellet for each of his animals, as he leaves with his flock in the morning. When he returns in the evening he will take out one pellet for each animal as it goes through the gate to the fold and he can thus see whether he has all his charges or whether some have strayed and must be sought for." See also Schmandt-Besserat 1977.

13. I am indebted to Jean Eckenfels for an alternative suggestion that they may have been counter boxes.

14. I am indebted to Linda Braidwood for this suggestion.

15. Very handsome counterparts to these spoons have been found—a few in bone, about the same size, and one nice example in stone, but fragmentary (fig. 137:9). A similar clay spoon has been reported from Ur (Woolley 1955, pl. 16).

16. Woolley (1955, pls. 15-16) illustrates both a clay spool and a clay plug from Ur.

17. There is always the possibility that in the course of earlier excavations at other sites, figurine material analogous to that of Jarmo may not have been observed or retained to the same degree as at Jarmo, and any comparisons with these other sites would, therefore, be inadequately based.

CATALOGUE OF ILLUSTRATED FIGURINES AND CLAY OBJECTS (figs. 146-71)

FIGURE 146. ANIMAL FIGURINES
1 Type A, from J-I,6 (in Baghdad)
2 Type A, from J-I,6c (J2-179, in Baghdad)
3 Type A, from J-I,8 (in Baghdad)
4 Type B, from J-II,1E (J2-184, in Baghdad)
5 Type B, from J-II,5 (in Chicago)
6 Type B, from J-II,1 (J2-162, in Chicago)

FIGURE 147. ANIMAL FIGURINES
1 Type C1, from J-II,5 (in Chicago)
2 Type C1, from P16,sf-1 (in Baghdad)
3 Type C1, from PQ14 (in Baghdad)
4 Type C1, from M19,3 (in Chicago)
5 Type C1, from M18,1 (in Baghdad)
6 Type C1, from J-III,sf-1 (J2-96, in Chicago)
7 Type C1, from J-III,sf-1 (in Chicago)

FIGURE 148. ANIMAL FIGURINES
1 Type C1, from PQ14,deep (in Chicago)
2 Type C1, from J-II,5 (J2-400, in Baghdad)
3 Type C1, from PQ14 (in Chicago)
4 Type C1, from S15,4 (J3-44, in Baghdad)

FIGURE 149. ANIMAL FIGURINES
1 Type C2, from J-III,1 (in Chicago)
2 Type C2, from J-III,sf-1 (in Baghdad)
3 Type C2, from J-III,sf-1 (in Baghdad)
4 Type C3, from S15,2 (in Chicago)
5 Type C3, from P16,5 (in Baghdad)
6 Type C3, from P16,5 (in Baghdad)
7 Type C3, from T12,2 (in Chicago)
8 Type C3, from R14,2 (in Chicago)

FIGURE 150. ANIMAL FIGURINES
1 Type D2, from P16,1 (in Chicago)
2 Type D2, from T19,1 (in Baghdad)
3 Type D2, from J-II,2 (in Chicago)
4 Type D1, from CF2529,sf-1 (in Chicago)
5 Type D1, from N18,4 (J3-57, in Baghdad)
6 Type D1, from Q15,3 (in Chicago)
7 Type D1, from U13,sf-1 (in Chicago)
8 Type E, from M18,1 (in Baghdad)
9 Type E, from N17,4 (in Chicago)
10 Type E, from J-II,3 (in Chicago)

FIGURE 151. ANIMAL FIGURINES
1 Type F, from J-II,4 (J2-307, in Baghdad)
2 Type F, from J-II,2 (J2-258, in Chicago)
3 Type F, from R11,1 (J3-66, in Baghdad)
4 Type F, from J-II,2fl. (J2-270, in Chicago)
5 Type F, from P16,3 (in Chicago)
6 Type G, from PQ14 (in Chicago)
7 Type G, from N17,2 (in Chicago)
8 Type G, from J-III,sf-1 (J2-97, in Chicago)
9 Type G, from T16,sf-1 (in Baghdad)

FIGURE 152. ANIMAL FIGURINES
1 Type H, from E21,4 (in Baghdad)
2 Type H, from P16,5 (J3-54, in Baghdad)
3 Type H, from J-II,6 (in Chicago)
4 Type H, from W11,4 (in Chicago)
5 Type H, from T16,2 (in Chicago)
6 Type H, from N18,4 (in Chicago)
7 Type H, from J-II,2 (J2-247, in Baghdad)

FIGURE 153. ANIMAL FIGURINES
1 Type H, from S15,3 (in Baghdad)
2 Type H, from N22,2 (in Chicago)
3 Type H, from J-II,3 (J2-302, in Chicago)
4 Type H, from J-II,5 (J2-397, in Baghdad)
5 Type H, from J-III,sf-1 (J2-174, in Chicago)
6 Type H, from W11,2 (J3-80, in Chicago)
7 Type H, from J-A,III-1 (in Chicago)

FIGURE 154. ANIMAL FIGURINES
1 Type L, from J-II,2fl. (in Chicago)
2 Type L, from J-II,6 (J2-412, in Chicago)
3 Type L, from S13,4 (in Baghdad)
4 Type K, from J-I,3-4 (J-49, in Baghdad)
5 Type K, from J-I,7 (in Baghdad)
6 Type K, from P16,sf-1 (in Baghdad)
7 Type M, from J-II,2 (J2-245, in Baghdad)
8 Type M, from J-I,8 (in Baghdad)
9 Type N, from J-III,1 (in Chicago)
10 Type N, from J-II,2 (in Baghdad)
11 Type N, from K18,1 (J3-50, in Chicago)
12 Type N, from K18,1 (J3-58, in Baghdad)
13 Type N, from J-III,sf-1 (J2-152, in Baghdad)

FIGURE 155. ANIMAL FIGURINES
1 Miscellaneous form, from Q15,1 (in Chicago)
2 Miscellaneous form, from PQ14 (in Baghdad)
3 Miscellaneous form, from S13,1 (J3-65, in Baghdad)
4 Miscellaneous form, from PQ14 (in Chicago)
5 Miscellaneous form, from J-II,4 (J2-371, in Chicago)
6 Miscellaneous form, from J-II,3 (J2-306, in Baghdad)
7 Type L, from J-III,sf-1 (in Chicago)
8 Disintegrated, from E21,4 (in Baghdad)

FIGURE 156. FEMALE FIGURINES
1 Early simple type, from J-I,6a (J2-63, in Chicago)
2 Early simple type, from J-I,8fl. (in Chicago)

3 Early simple type, from J-II,3 (*J2-364*, in Baghdad)
4 Early simple type, from J-I,8 (*J2-279*, in Baghdad)
5 Early simple type, from J-II,2fl. (*J2-305*, in Baghdad)
6 Intermediate type, from J-I,8 (*J2-291*, in Chicago)
7 Intermediate type, from J-I,7 (*J-68*, in Baghdad)
8 Intermediate type, from K21,7 (in Chicago)
9 Intermediate type, from S19,1 (in Baghdad)
10 Composite, pregnant type, from J-III,1 (in Chicago)

FIGURE 157. FEMALE FIGURINES
1 Composite, pregnant type (reconstruction)
2 Composite, pregnant type, from J-III,1 (*J2-185*, in Chicago)
3 Composite, pregnant type, from M16,1 (*J3-75*, in Chicago)
4 Composite, pregnant type, from P17,2 (*J3-70*, in Baghdad)
5 Composite, pregnant type (fragment and reconstruction), from X10,3 (in Chicago)
6 Composite, pregnant type, from J-II,2 (*J2-193*, in Baghdad)

FIGURE 158. FEMALE FIGURINES
1 Composite, pregnant type (fragment and reconstruction), from L23,2 (*J3-88*, in Chicago)
2 Composite, pregnant type (hand), from P18,2 (in Baghdad)
3 Composite, pregnant type (fragment and reconstruction), from N17,5 (*J3-41*, in Chicago)
4 Composite, *non*pregnant type, from P16,1 (in Baghdad)
5 Composite, *non*pregnant type, from P16,3 (in Chicago)
6 Composite, *non*pregnant type (head), from P16,4 (in Baghdad)
7 Composite, pregnant type, from W11,1 (*J3-76*, in Baghdad)

FIGURE 159. FEMALE FIGURINES
1 Composite, pregnant type, from MQ1519,3 (in Baghdad)
2 Composite, pregnant type, from P16,5 (in Baghdad)
3 Composite, pregnant type, from J-II,2fl. (in Chicago)
4 Composite, pregnant type, from N17,5 (in Chicago)
5 Composite, pregnant type, from GL2529,3 (in Chicago)
6 Composite, pregnant type, from P13,1 (in Baghdad)
7 Composite, pregnant type, from VY1014,2 (in Baghdad)

FIGURE 160. FEMALE FIGURINES
1 Composite, stylized type (fragment and reconstruction), from T12,2 (in Baghdad)
2 Composite, stylized type, from P16,3 (in Chicago)
3 Composite, stylized type, from S17,2 (in Baghdad)
4 Composite, stylized type, from Q18,1 (in Chicago)
5 Composite, stylized type, from RU1519,1 (in Baghdad)
6 Composite, stylized type, from P16,3 (in Chicago)
7 Composite, stylized type, from E21,2 (in Chicago)
8 Composite, stylized type, from P17,1 (in Chicago)
9 Composite, stylized type, from M16,sf-1 (in Baghdad)

FIGURE 161. MALE FIGURINES
1 Torso type, from M16,1 (*J3-63*, in Chicago)
2 Torso type, from PQ14,3-4 (in Chicago)
3 Torso type, from N18,3 (*J3-48*, in Chicago)
4 Torso type, from T14,sf-1 (*J3-85*, in Baghdad)
5 Torso type, from J-II,2 (*J2-254*, in Chicago)
6 Torso type, from C24,sf-1 (*J3-86*, in Baghdad)
7 Torso type, from P16,1 (in Baghdad)
8 Torso type, from N17,sf-1 (in Chicago)
9 Torso type, from P16,1 (in Chicago)

FIGURE 162. MALE FIGURINES
1 Torso type, from J-II,2 (*J2-228*, in Chicago)
2 Phallic object?, from M16,3 (in Chicago)
3 Phallic object, from J-II,2 (*J2-257*, in Chicago)
4 Phallic object (stone), from J-I,3,pit 2 (*J-75*, in Baghdad)
5 Phallic object (stone), from J-II,1 (*J2-169*, in Chicago)

FIGURE 163. HUMAN FIGURINES
1 Head, from S15,2 (*J3-77*, in Chicago)
2 Head, from T18,1 (in Chicago)
3 Head, from J-B,2 (*J-78*, in Baghdad)
4 Head, from T16,2 (in Baghdad)
5 Head, from L19,sf-1 (*J3-91*, in Chicago)
6 Head, from Q15,1 (*J3-64*, in Baghdad)
7 Head, from PQ14 (*J3-82*, in Baghdad)
8 Head, from N18,5 (in Baghdad)
9 Head, from S13,5 (in Chicago)
10 Head, from W11,4 (in Chicago)
11 Head, from S15,sf-1 (in Baghdad)
12 Head, from J-II,2 (in Chicago)
13 Head, from J-III,1 (in Chicago)
14 Head, from J-II,5 (in Baghdad)

FIGURE 164. HUMAN FIGURINES AND DOUBLE-WING-BASED OBJECTS
1 Human figurine, head, from J-I,3a (*J-61*, in Baghdad)
2 Human figurine, head, from J-I,8 (*J-77*, in Baghdad)
3 Human figurine, head, from J-III,sf-1 (*J2-100*, in Baghdad)
4 Human figurine, head, from J-II,2fl. (in Chicago)
5 Human figurine, head, from J-II,5 (*J2-380*, in Chicago)
6 Human figurine, head, from P16,5 (in Chicago)
7 Double-wing-based object, human-headed type, from T14,sf-1 (*J3-47*, in Chicago)
8 Double-wing-based object, human-headed type, from C24,sf-1 (in Baghdad)
9 Double-wing-based object, human-headed type, from K line,2 (in Chicago)
10 Double-wing-based object, human-headed type, from U15,3 (*J3-61*, in Baghdad)
11 Double-wing-based object, human-headed type, from Q14,2 (*J3-83*, in Baghdad)

FIGURE 165. DOUBLE-WING-BASED OBJECTS
1 Human-headed type, from T16,3 (in Baghdad)
2 Human-headed type, from Y11,sf-1 (in Chicago)
3 Human-headed type, from PQ14 (in Baghdad)
4 Human-headed type, from P16,1 (*J3-72*, in Chicago)
5 Human-headed type, from J-II,2 (*J2-252*, in Chicago)
6 Human-headed type, from J-II,2 (in Chicago)
7 Human-headed type, from U15,1 (in Baghdad)
8 Human-headed type, from S17,sf-1 (in Chicago)
9 Human-headed type, from K line,1 (in Chicago)
10 Human-headed type, from N17,2 (in Chicago)
11 Human-headed type, from P18,sf-1 (in Chicago)
12 Human-headed type, from Q15,1 (in Chicago)

FIGURE 166. DOUBLE-WING-BASED OBJECTS AND STALK OBJECTS
1 Double-wing-based object, misc. form, from S15,3 (in Baghdad)
2 Double-wing-based object, misc. form, from J-II,5 (in Chicago)
3 Double-wing-based object, misc. form, from X12,sf-1 (in Chicago)
4 Double-wing-based object, misc. form, from U11,2 (in Baghdad)

5 Double-wing-based object, misc. form, from M17,1 (in Baghdad)
6 Double-wing-based object, misc. form, from J-II,W,5 (in Chicago)
7 Double-wing-based object, misc. form, from J-II,2 (in Chicago)
8 Double-wing-based object, misc. form, from R18,1 (in Chicago)
9 Stalk object, human-headed type, from N18,5 (*J3-68*, in Chicago)
10 Stalk object, human-headed type, from H7,4 (in Chicago)
11 Stalk object, human-headed type, from T18,3 (in Baghdad)
12 Stalk object, human-headed type, from U15,3 (in Baghdad)

FIGURE 167. STALK OBJECTS
1 Coiled-top type, from J-II,2 (*J2-253*, in Chicago)
2 Coiled-top type, from J-III,sf-1 (in Baghdad)
3 Coiled-top type, from J-II,3 (in Chicago)
4 Human-headed type, from S13,5 (in Baghdad)
5 Human-headed type, from C22,1 (in Chicago)
6 Human-headed type, from S15,1 (in Baghdad)
7 Human-headed type, from J-II,5 (*J2-381*, in Chicago)
8 Human-headed type, from J-I,8 (*J2-287*, in Baghdad)
9 Human-headed type, from J-III,1 (in Chicago)
10 Human-headed type, from J-I,7 (in Chicago)
11 Human (or animal?), from J-III,sf-1 (in Baghdad)
12 Human (or animal?), from J-B,sf-1 (in Chicago)
13 Human (or animal?), from J-III,sf-1 (in Chicago)
14 Human (or animal?), from J-III,1 (in Chicago)
15 Conical type, from J-II,3 (in Chicago)
16 Conical type, from J-I,6 (in Chicago)
17 "Nail," from U11,2 (in Chicago)
18 "Nail," from Q15,3 (in Baghdad)
19 "Nail," from N18,5 (in Chicago)
20 "Nail," from T12,3 (in Chicago)

FIGURE 168. MISCELLANEOUS
1 Stalk object, "nail," from P18,1 (in Baghdad)
2 Stalk object, "nail," from U15,sf-1 (in Chicago)
3 Cone, from J-I,7fl. (in Chicago)
4 Cone, from P16,1 (in Baghdad)
5 Cone, from T18,3 (in Baghdad)
6 Tetrahedron, from J-II,1 (in Chicago)
7 Tetrahedron, from P16,5 (in Baghdad)
8 Bead, from PQ14 (*J3-69*, in Baghdad)
9 Bead, from T11,5 (in Chicago)
10 Bead, from P17,3 (in Baghdad)
11 Bead, from Q15,3 (*J3-56*, in Baghdad)
12 Bead, from W11,sf-1 (in Chicago)
13 Bead, from T11,4 (*J3-62*, in Chicago)
14 Bead, from T16,4 (*J3-43*, in Baghdad)
15 Bead, from J-III,sf-1 (*J2-171*, in Baghdad)
16 Bead, from K25,3 (*J3-97*, in Chicago)
17 Bead, from S13,3 (in Baghdad)
18 Bead shape, from M16,sf-1 (in Chicago)

FIGURE 169. MISCELLANEOUS
1 Ball, from W11,3 (in Chicago)
2 Ball, from T16,1 (in Baghdad)
3 Ball, from MQ1519,2 (in Baghdad)
4 Ball, from S15,sf-1 (in Chicago)
5 Ball, flattened, from RU1014,3 (in Baghdad)
6 Ball, disklike, from T16,4 (*J3-46*, in Chicago)
7 Disk, subhemispherical, from Q19,1 (in Baghdad)
8 Disk, subhemispherical, from MQ1014,1 (in Chicago)
9 Disk, fabric-impressed, from J-III,sf-1 (in Chicago)
10 Ball, fabric-impressed, from J-II,5 (in Chicago)
11 Stud or plug, from L21,2 (in Baghdad)
12 Miniature stool, from J-III,1 (in Chicago)
13 Reed matting impression, from X10,1 (in Chicago)
14 Coiled basketry impression, from J-I,6 (in Chicago)
15 Miniature stool, from J-II,2 (in Chicago)

FIGURE 170. MISCELLANEOUS
1 Stamp seal, from J-II,2 (*J2-200*, in Baghdad)
2 Miniature vessel fragment, from J-I,3a (in Chicago)
3 Miniature vessel fragment, from J-III,1 (in Chicago)
4 Miniature vessel fragment, from R11,14 (in Baghdad)
5 Miniature vessel fragment, from W11,4 (in Baghdad)
6 Miniature vessel fragment, from P16,2 (in Chicago)
7 Miniature vessel, from U17,sf-1 (in Chicago)
8 Spindle whorl, from J-II,2 (in Chicago)
9 House model?, from J-A,III (in Chicago)
10 House model?, from J-III,1 (in Chicago)
11 House model?, from Q14,4 (*J3-55*, in Baghdad)

FIGURE 171. MISCELLANEOUS
1 Clublike form, from J-I,6c (*J2-196*, in Chicago)
2 Clublike form, from J-II,4 (in Chicago)
3 Clublike form, from J-II,4 (in Chicago)
4 Perforated object, from L23,3 (in Chicago)
5 Perforated object, from X10,3 (in Chicago)
6 Perforated object, from VY1014,3 (in Baghdad)
7 Spoon, from T12,3 (in Chicago)
8 Spoon, from XL19,1 (in Chicago)
9 Spoon, from T11,4 (in Baghdad)
10 Spoon, from T11,4 (in Baghdad)

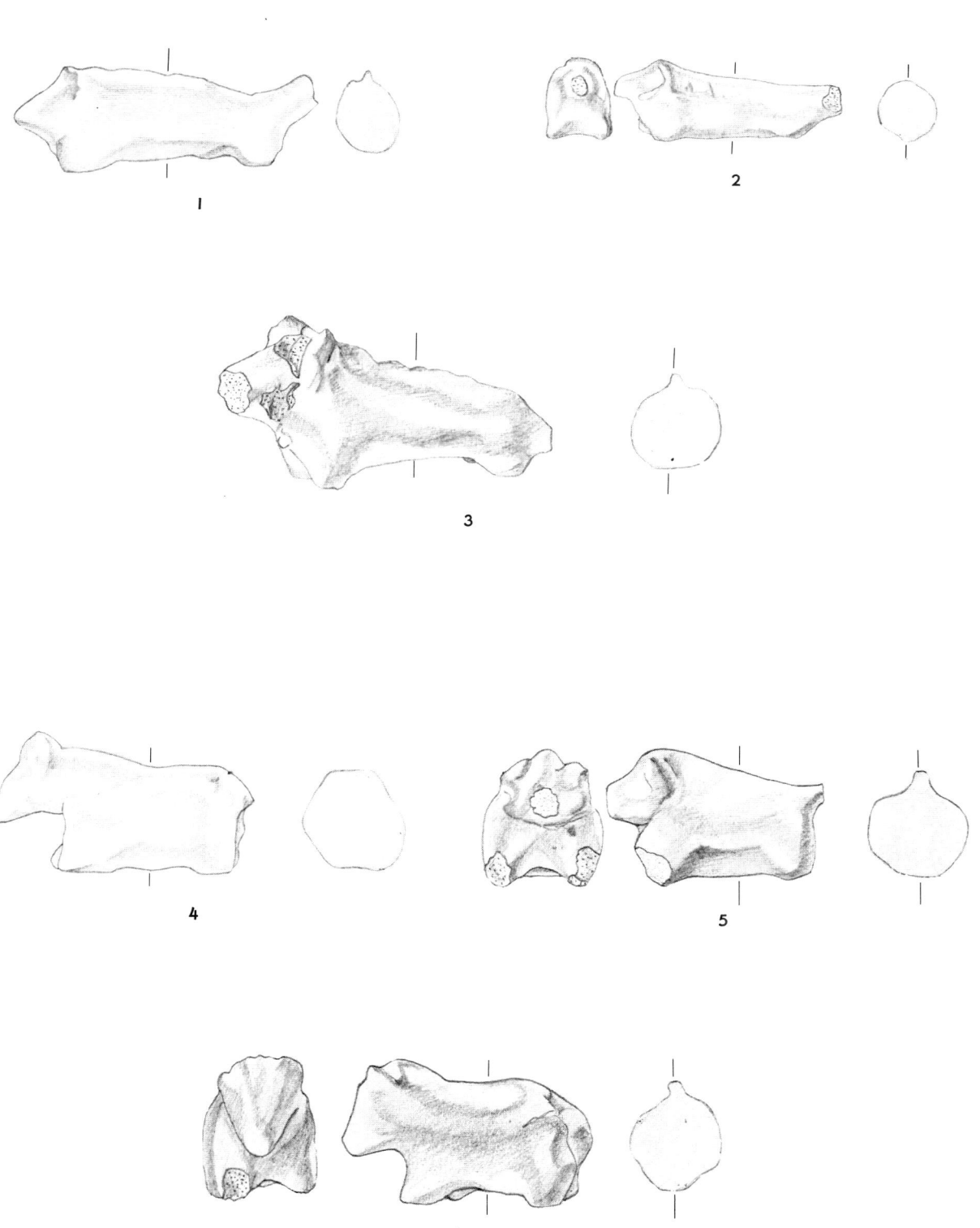

Fig. 146. Jarmo animal figurines: type A, *1-3*; type B, *4-6*. Scale 1:1.

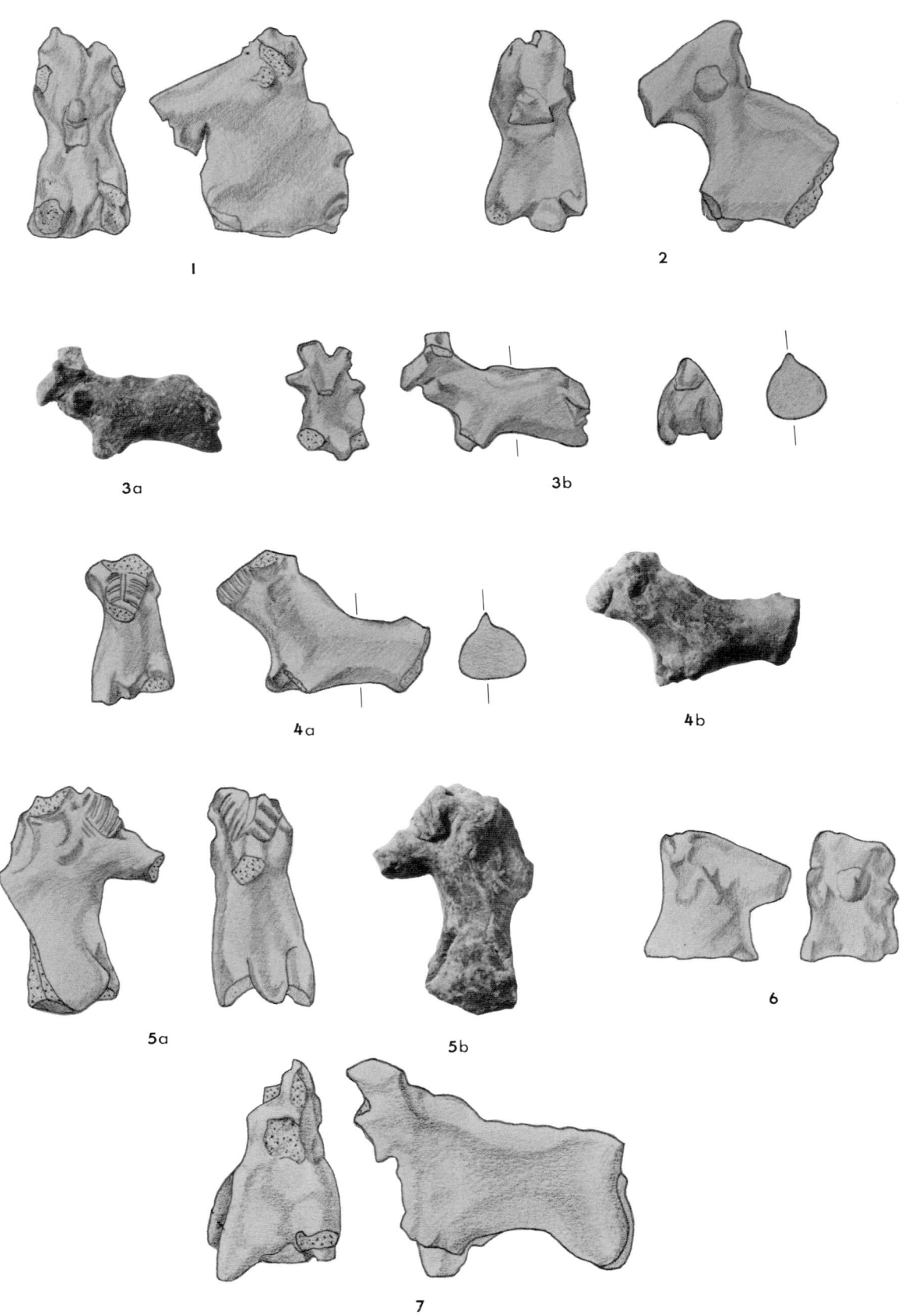

Fig. 147. Jarmo animal figurines: type C1, *1-7*. Scale 1:1.

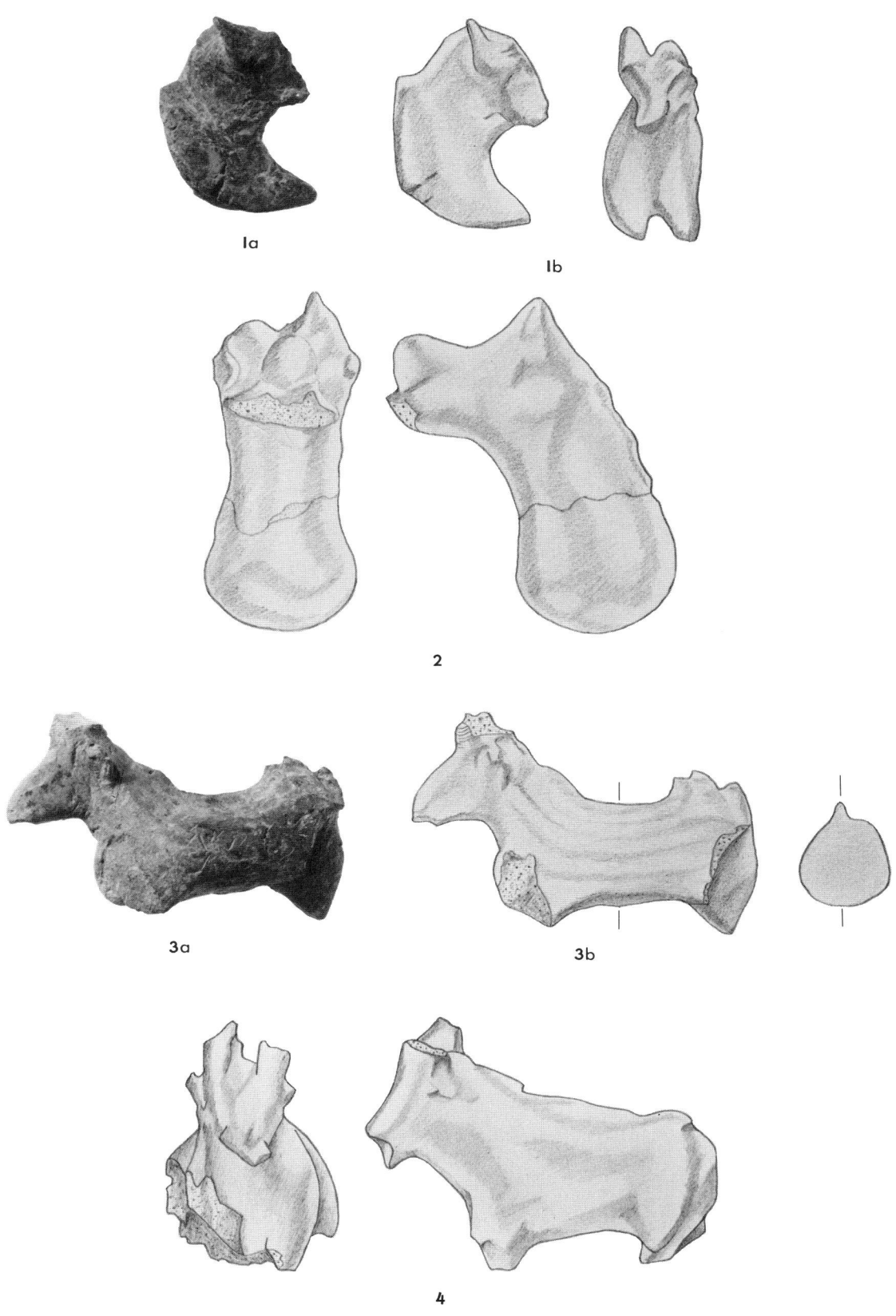

Fig. 148. Jarmo animal figurines: type C1, *1-4*. Scale 1:1.

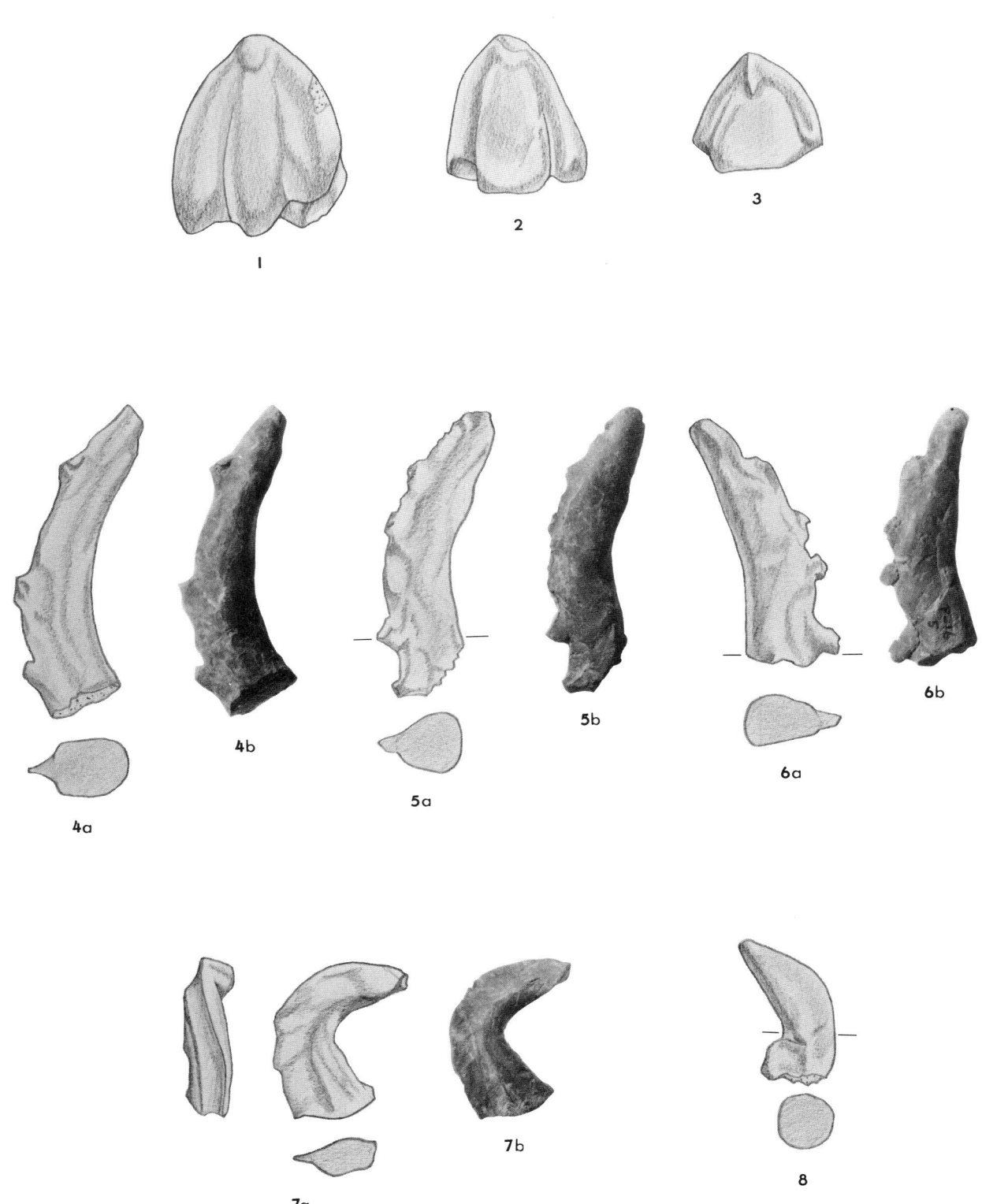

Fig. 149. Jarmo animal figurines: type C2, *1-3*; type C3, *4-8*. Scale 1:1.

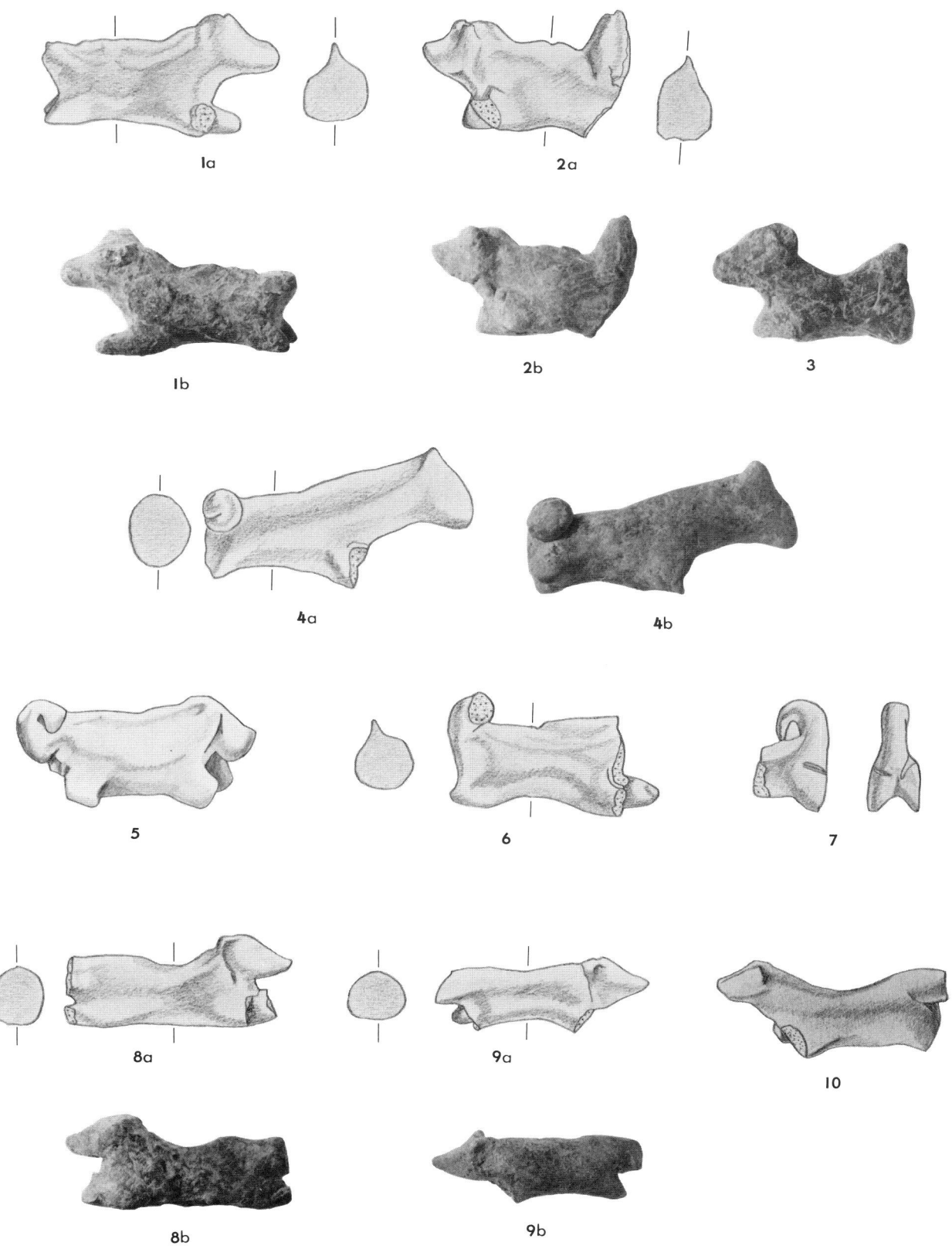

Fig. 150. Jarmo animal figurines: type D2, *1-3*; type D1, *4-7*; type E, *8-10*. Scale 1:1.

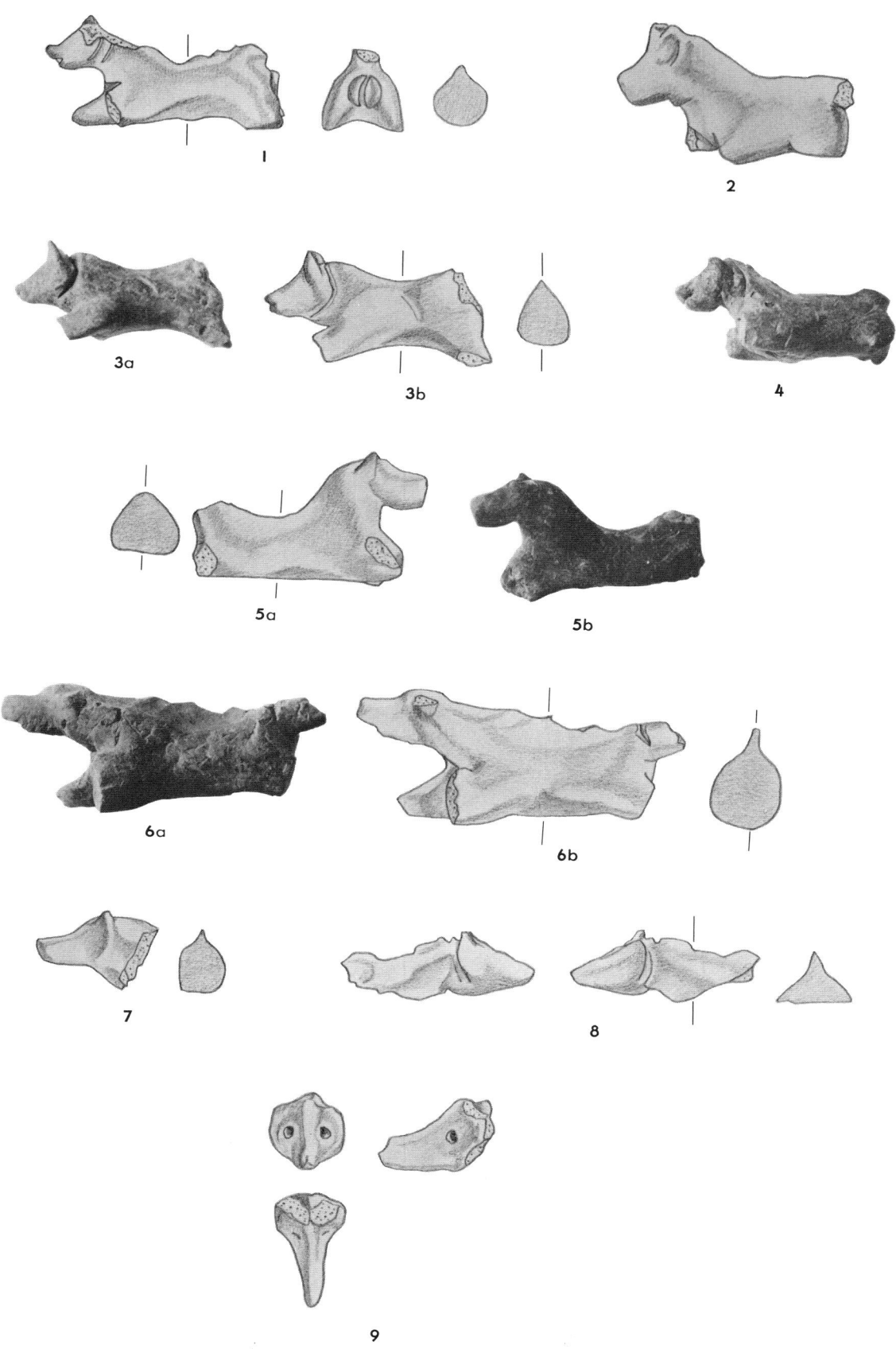

Fig. 151. Jarmo animal figurines: type F, *1-5*; type G, *6-9*. Scale 1:1.

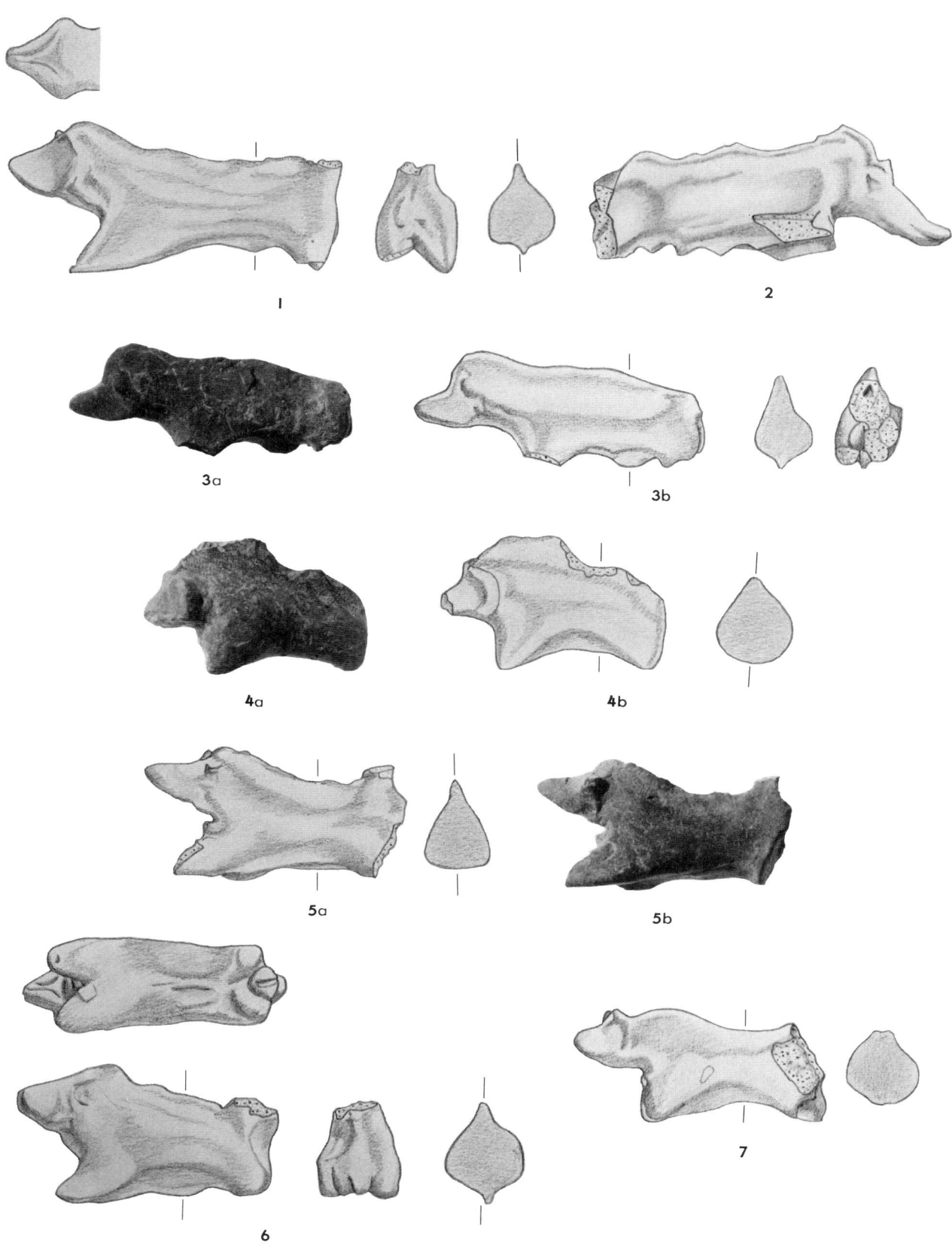

Fig. 152. Jarmo animal figurines: type H, *1-7*. Scale 1:1.

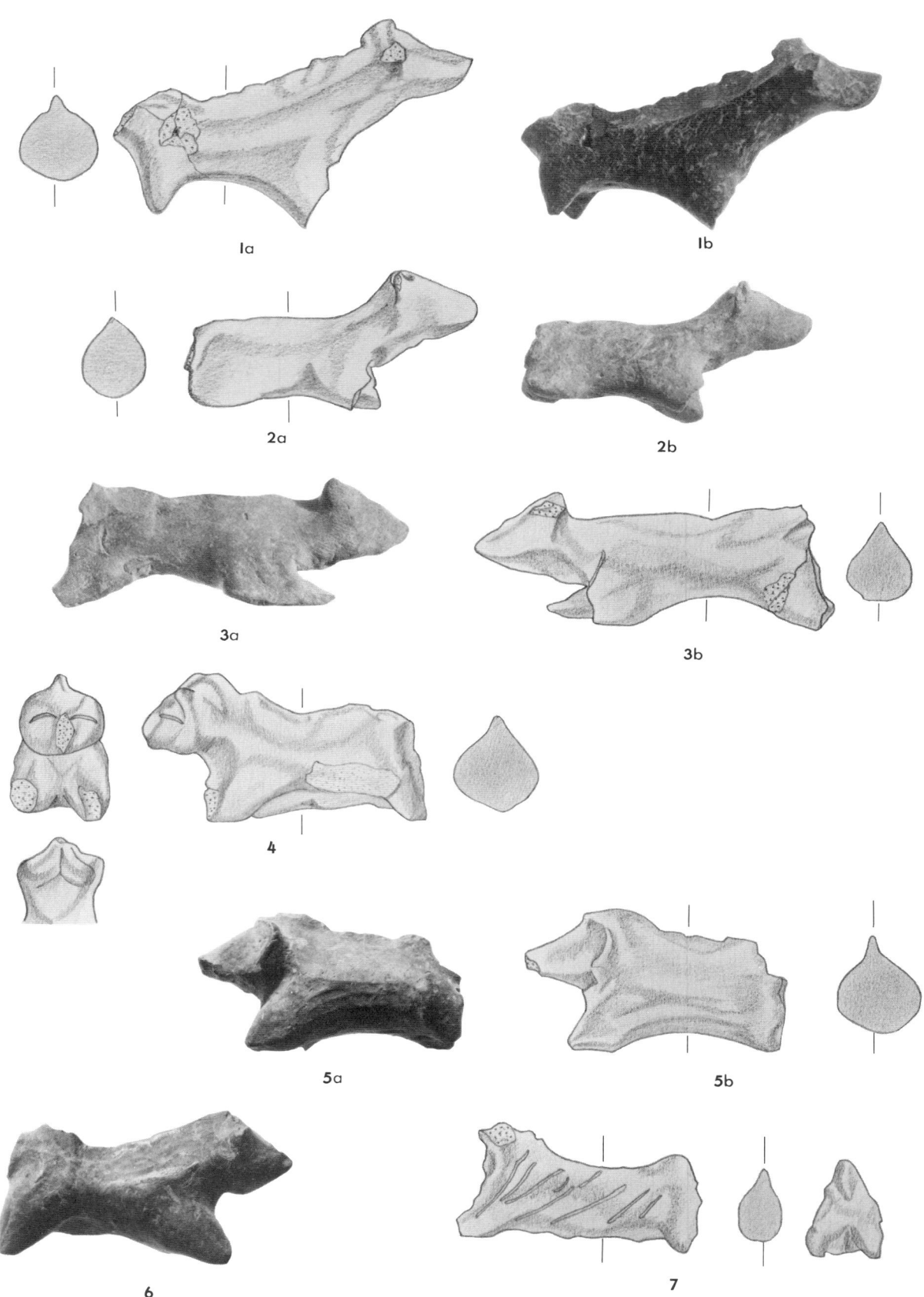

Fig. 153. Jarmo animal figurines: type H, *1-7*. Scale 1:1.

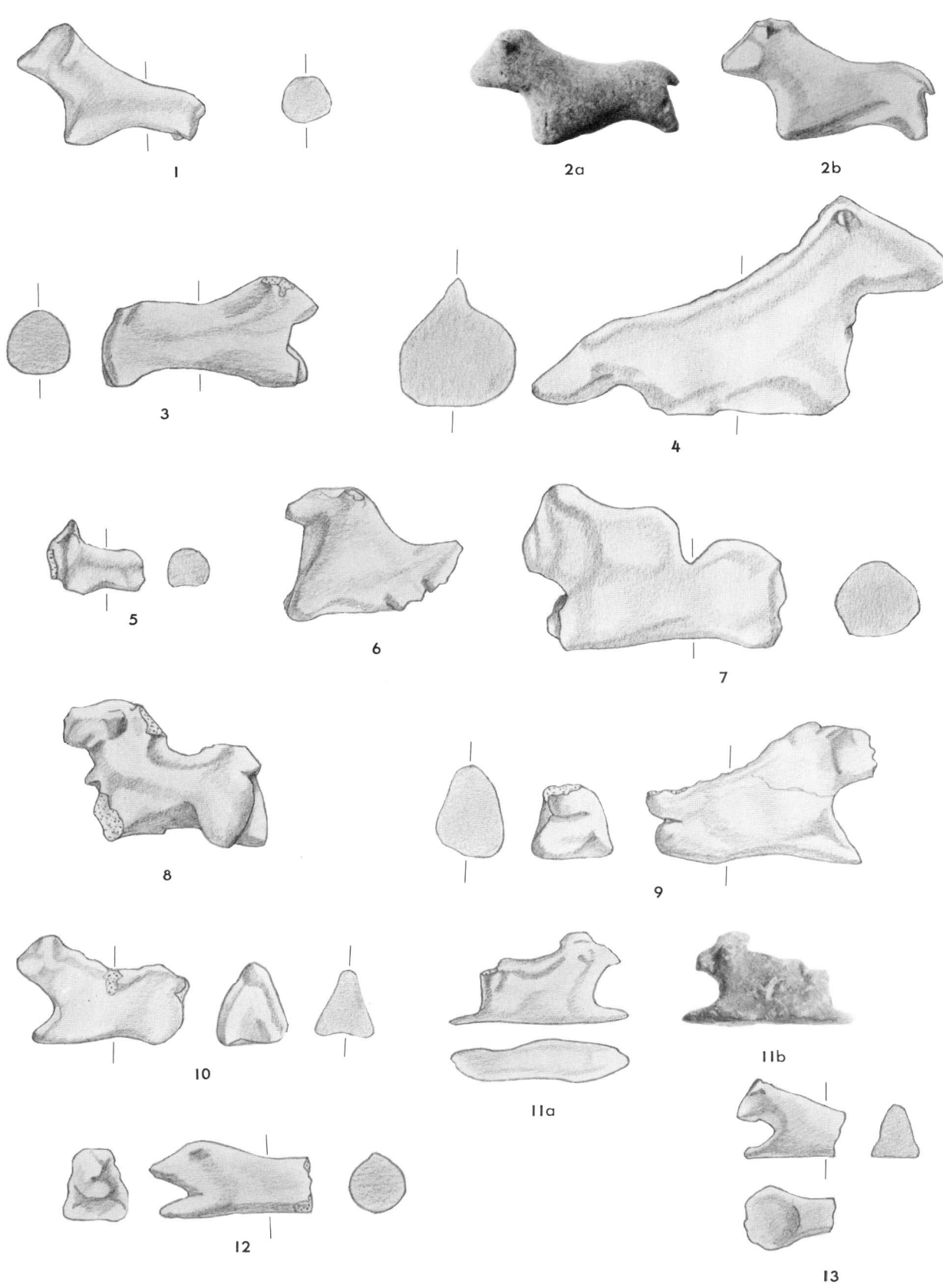

Fig. 154. Jarmo animal figurines: type K, *1-3*; type L, *4-6*; type M, *7-8*; type N, *9-13*. Scale 1:1.

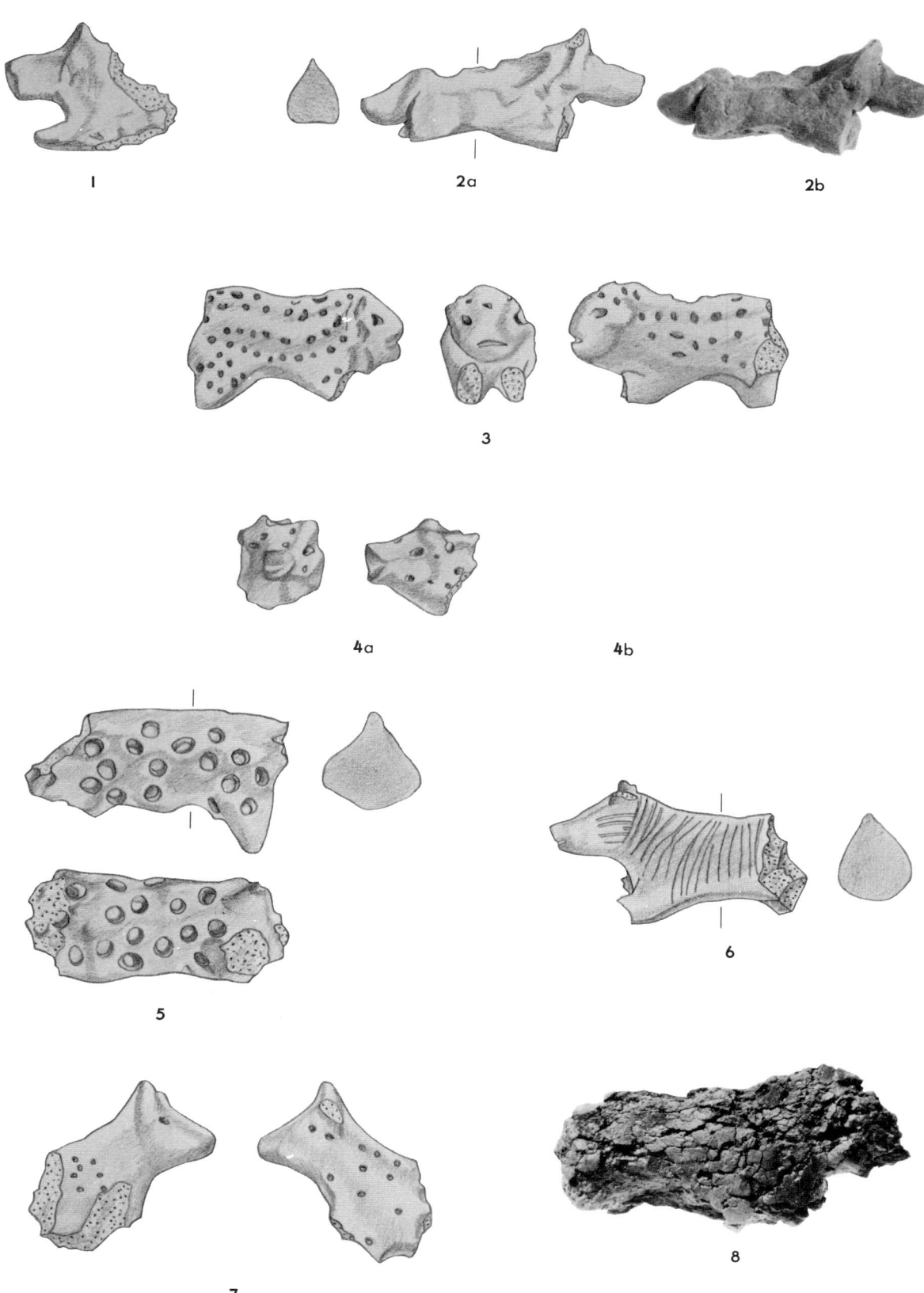

Fig. 155. Jarmo animal figurines: miscellaneous, *1-6*; type K, *7*; disintegrated, *8*. Scale 1:1.

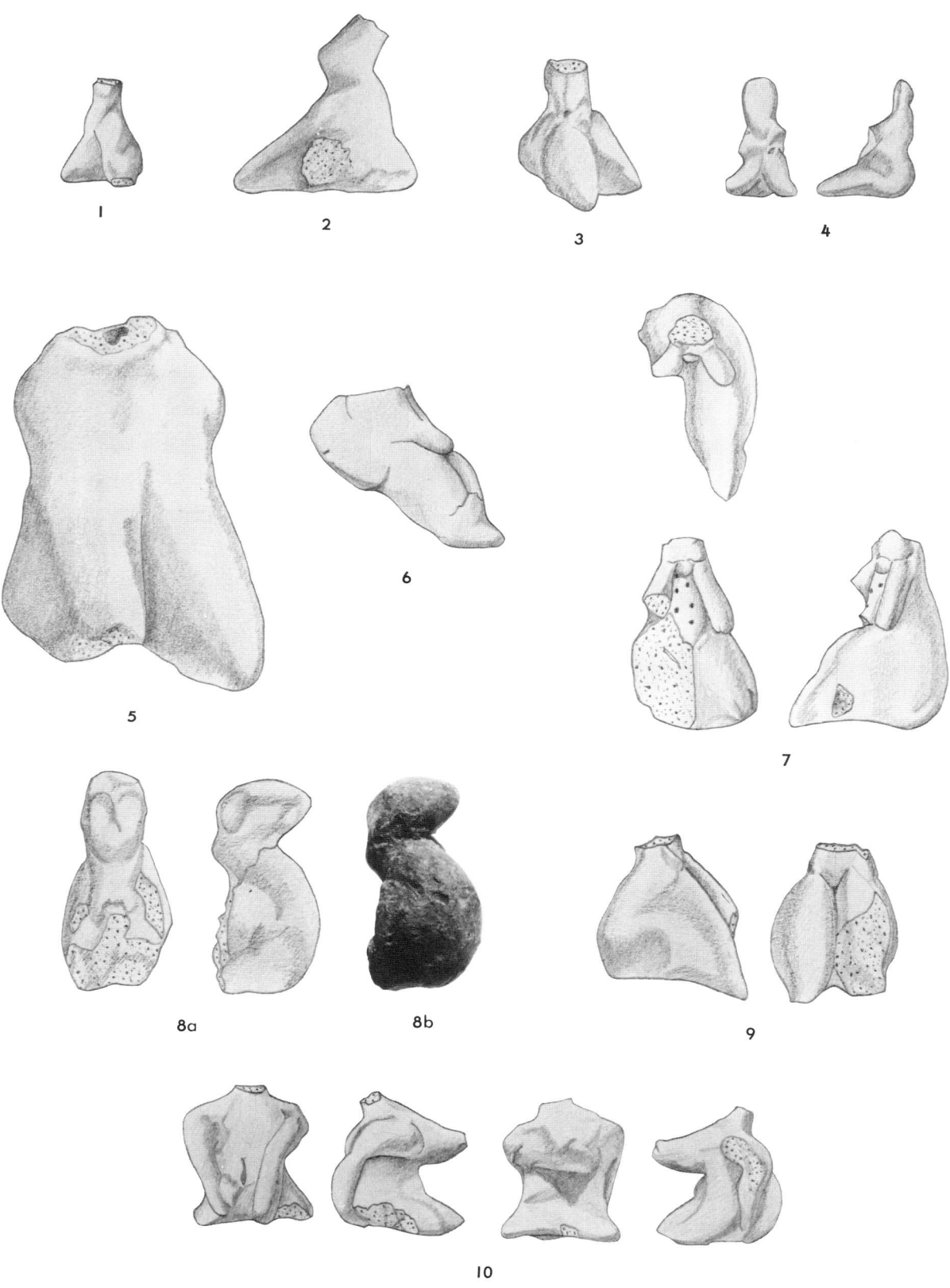

Fig. 156. Jarmo female figurines: early simple type, *1-5*; intermediate type, *6-9*; composite, pregnant type, *10*. Scale 1:1.

Fig. 157. Jarmo female figurines: composite, pregnant type, reconstruction, *1*; composite, pregnant type, *2-6* (reconstruction, *5c*). Scale 1:1.

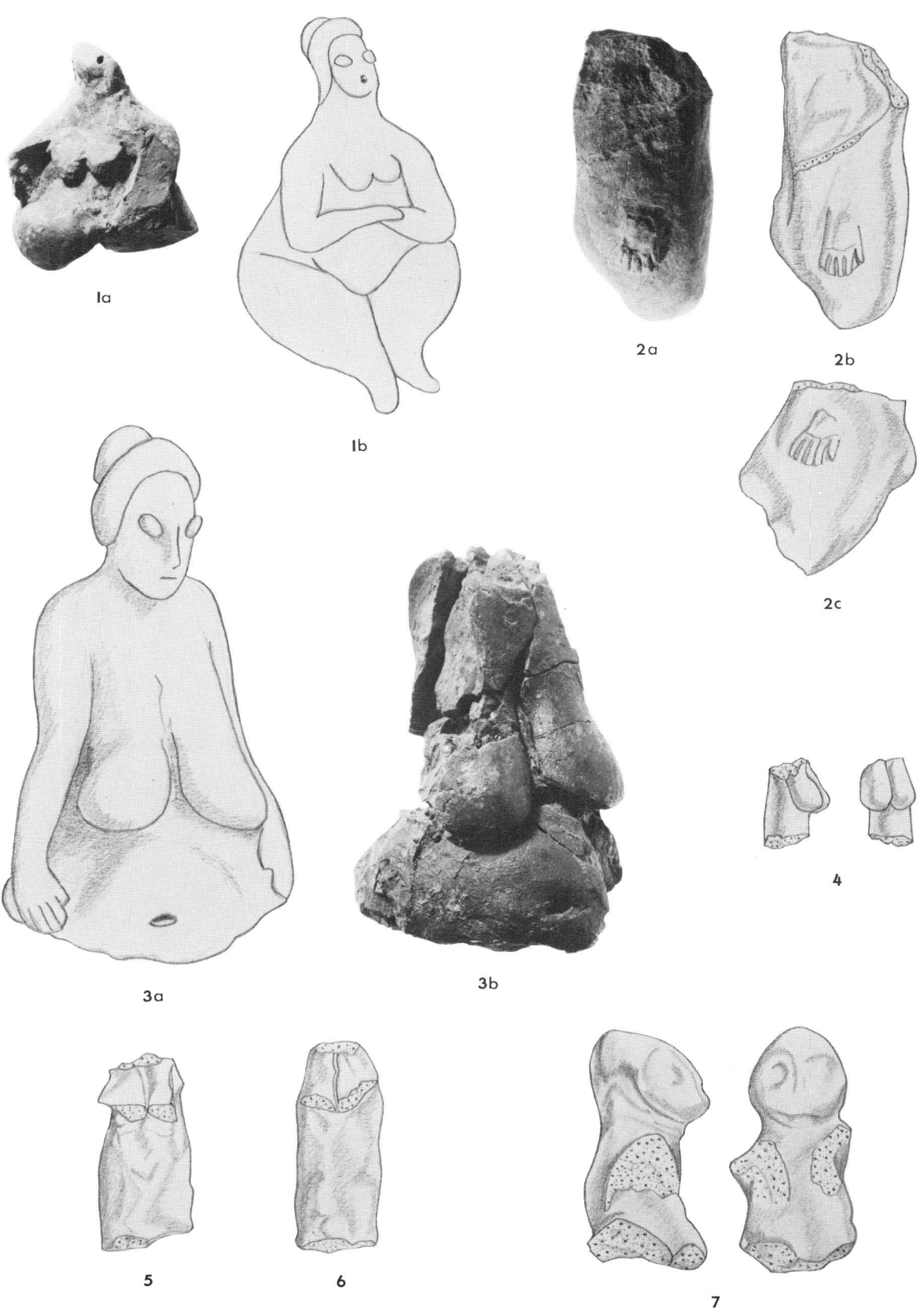

Fig. 158. Jarmo female figurines: composite, pregnant type, *1-3,7* (reconstructions, *1b* and *3a*); composite, *non*pregnant type, *4-6*. Scale 1:1.

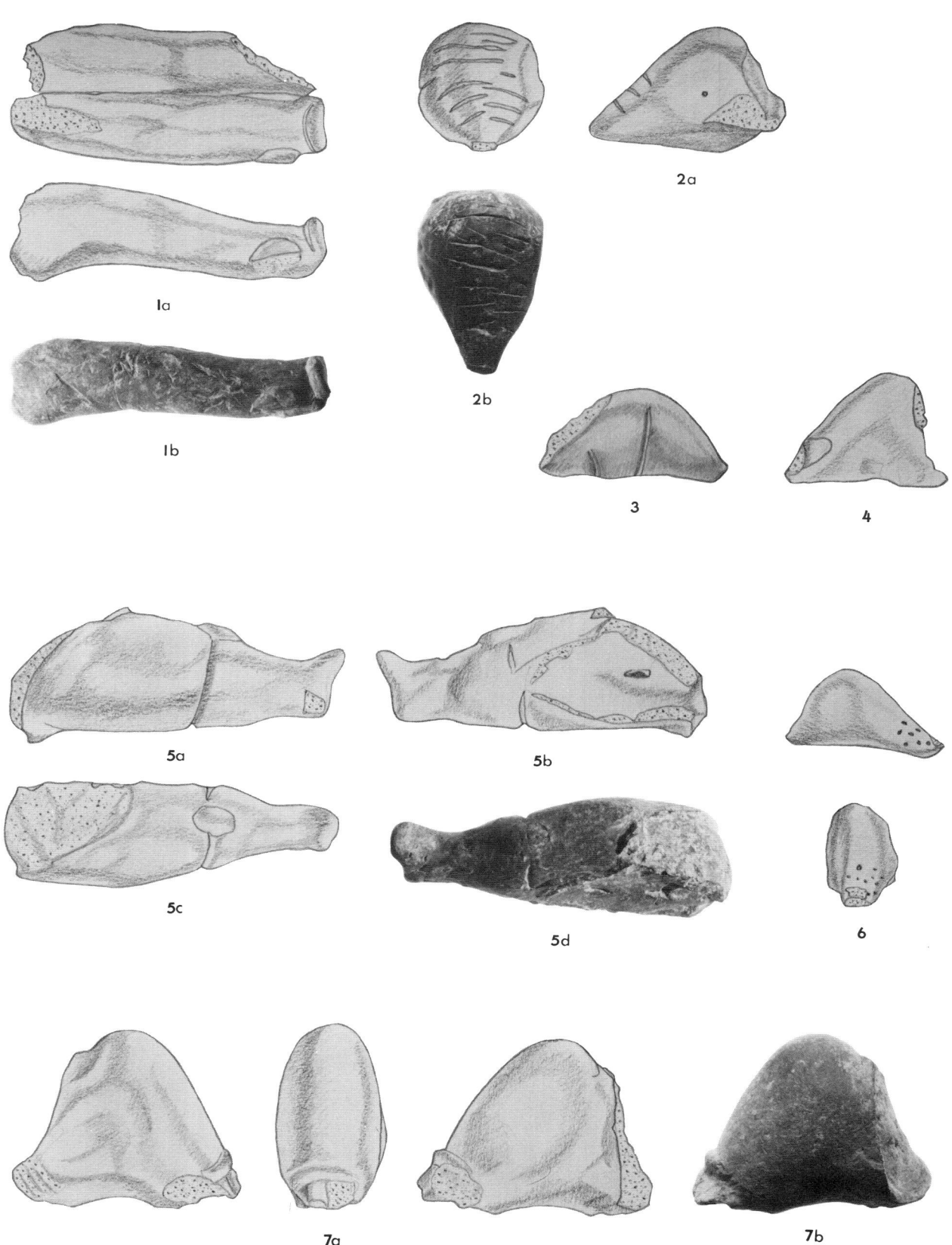

Fig. 159. Jarmo female figurines: composite, pregnant type, *1-7*. Scale 1:1.

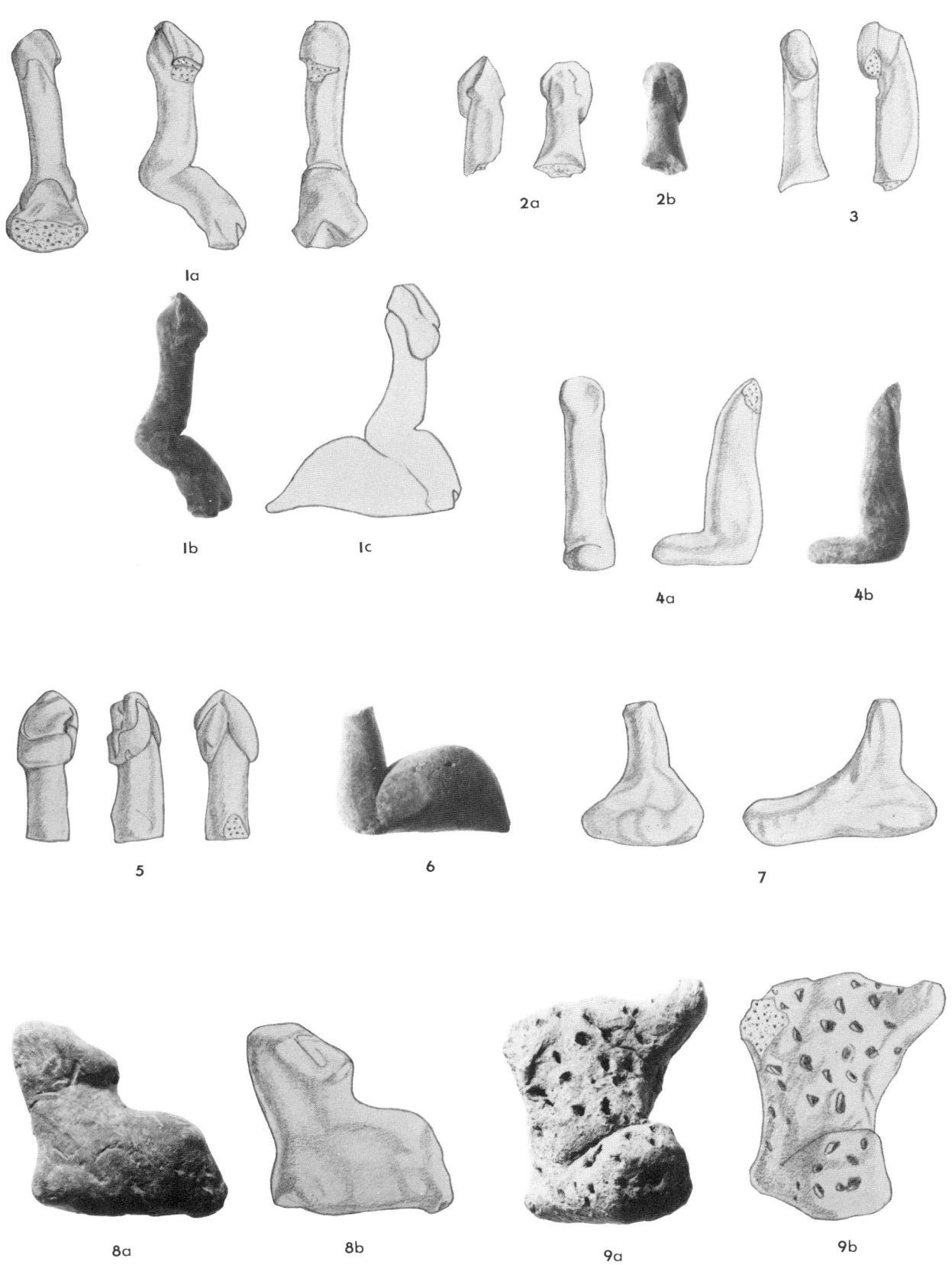

Fig. 160. Jarmo female figurines: composite, stylized type, *1-9* (reconstruction, *1c*). Scale 1:1.

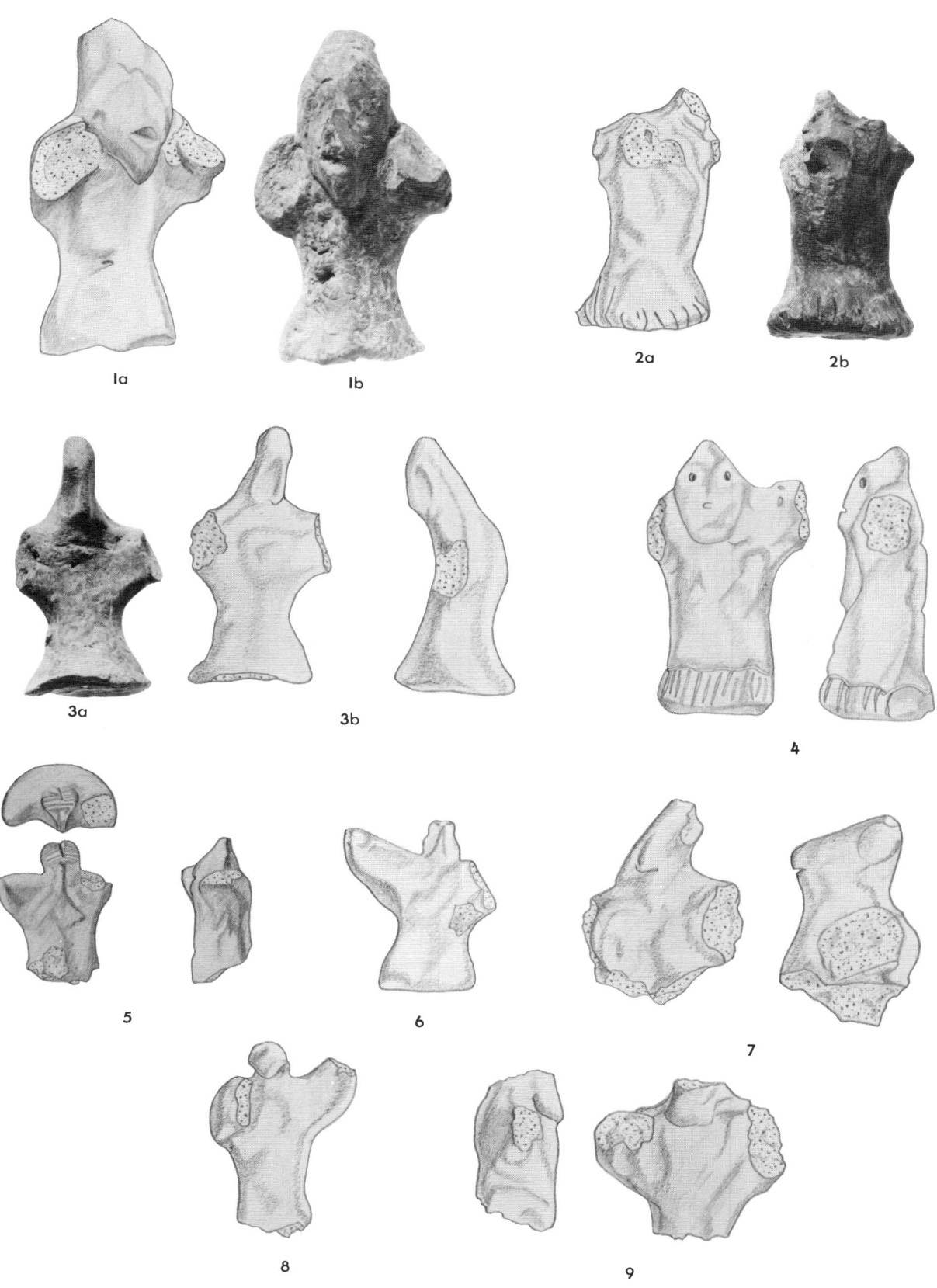

Fig. 161. Jarmo male figurines: torso type, *1-9*. Scale 1:1.

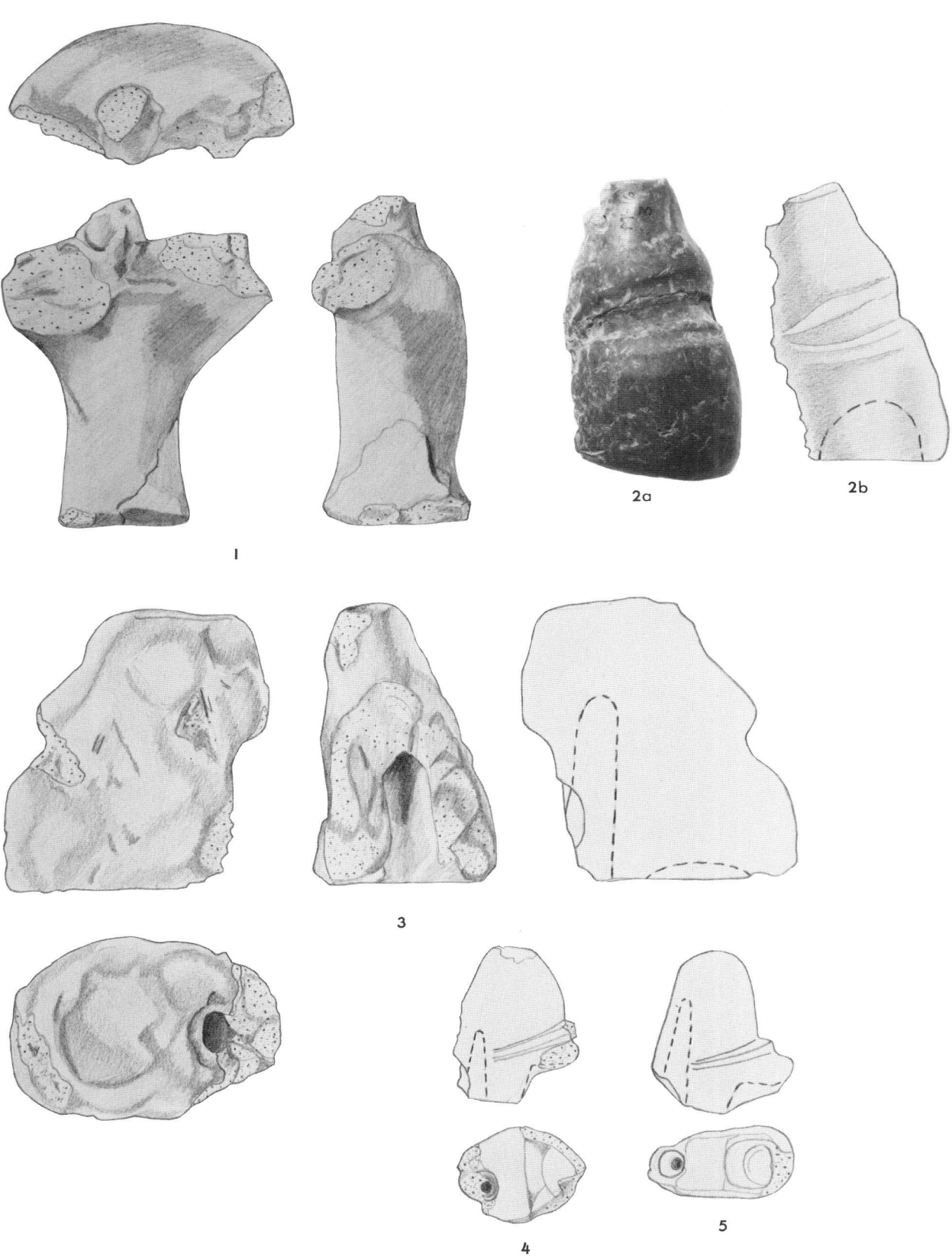

Fig. 162. Jarmo male figurines: torso type, *1*; phallic objects, *2-3* (*2* is questionable); phallic objects, stone, *4-5* (see figs. 137:5-6; 140:18,20). Scales 1:1, *1-3*; 1:2, *4-5*.

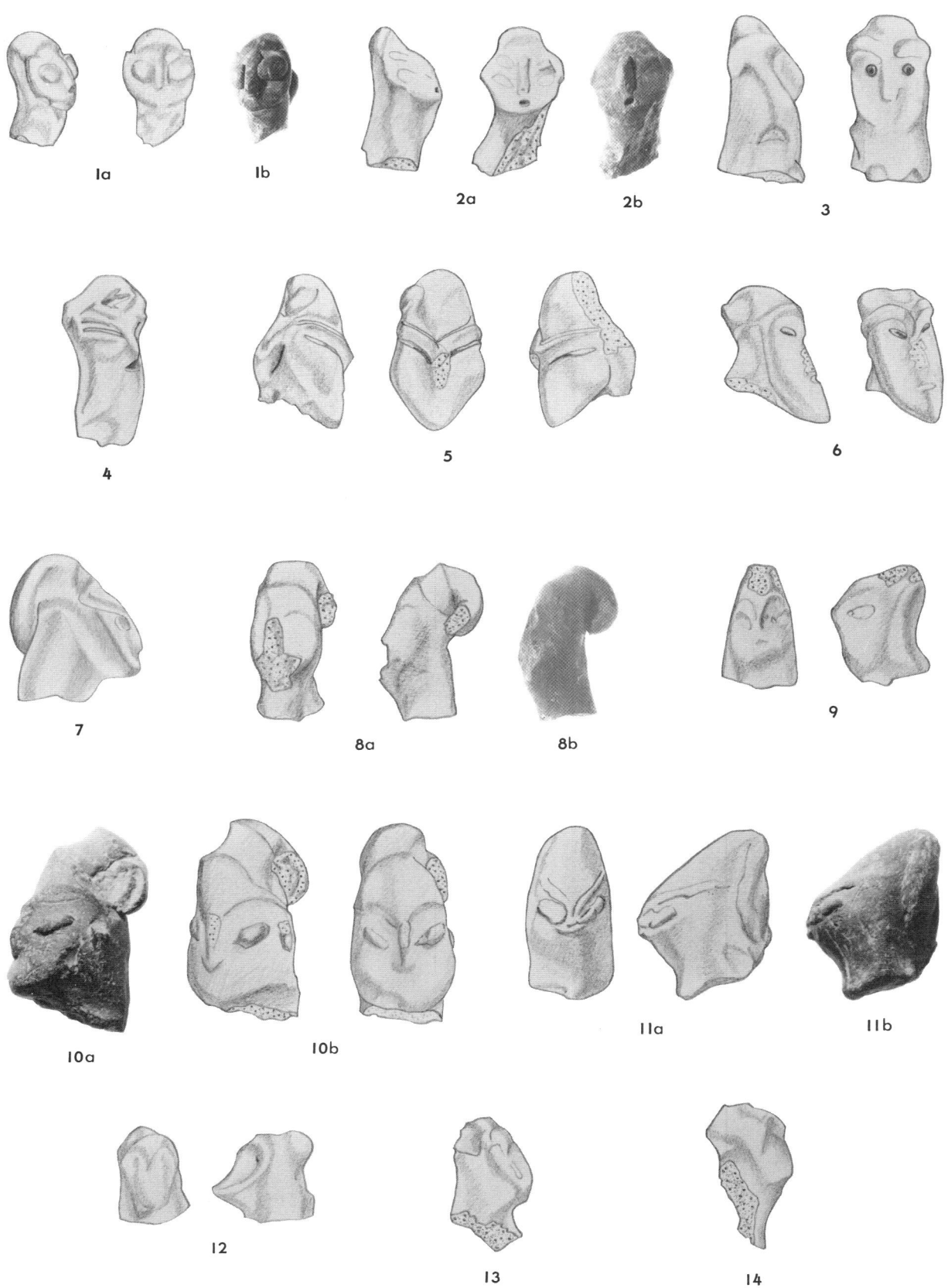

Fig. 163. Jarmo human figurines: heads, *1-14*. Scale 1:1.

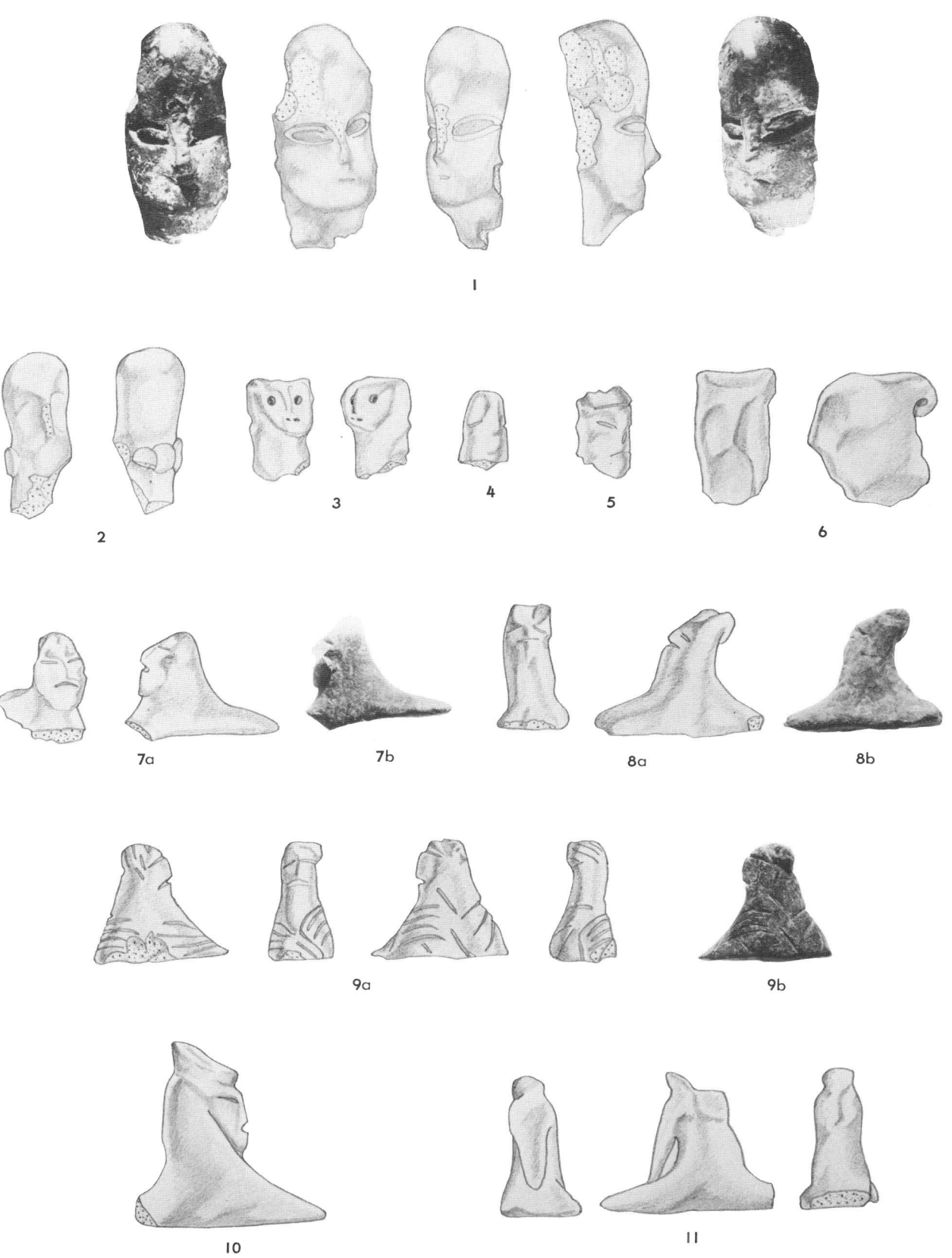

Fig. 164. Jarmo human figurines and double-wing-based objects: human figurines, heads, *1-6*; double-wing-based objects, human-headed type, *7-11*. Scale 1:1.

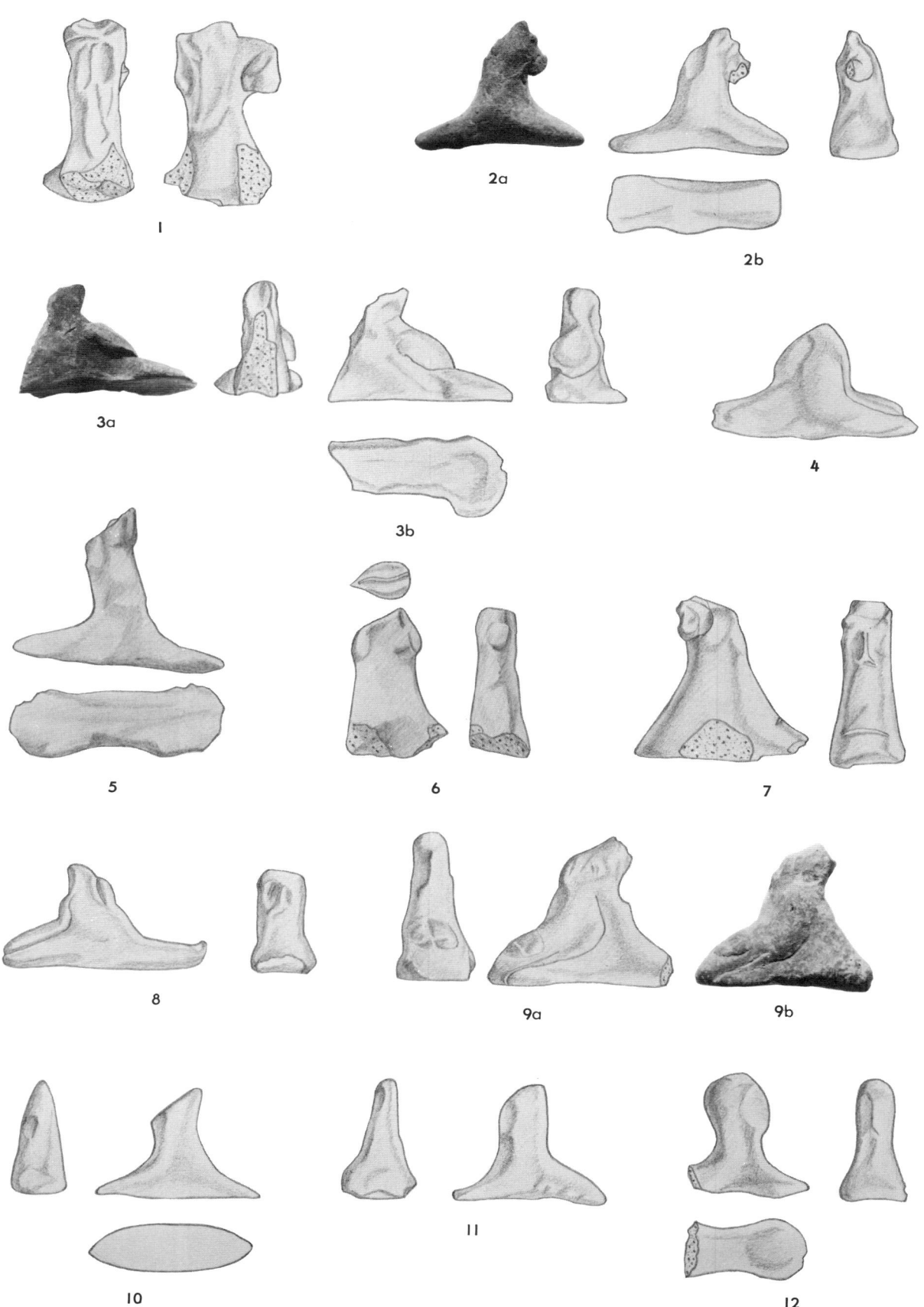

Fig. 165. Jarmo double-wing-based objects: human-headed type, *1-12*. Scale 1:1.

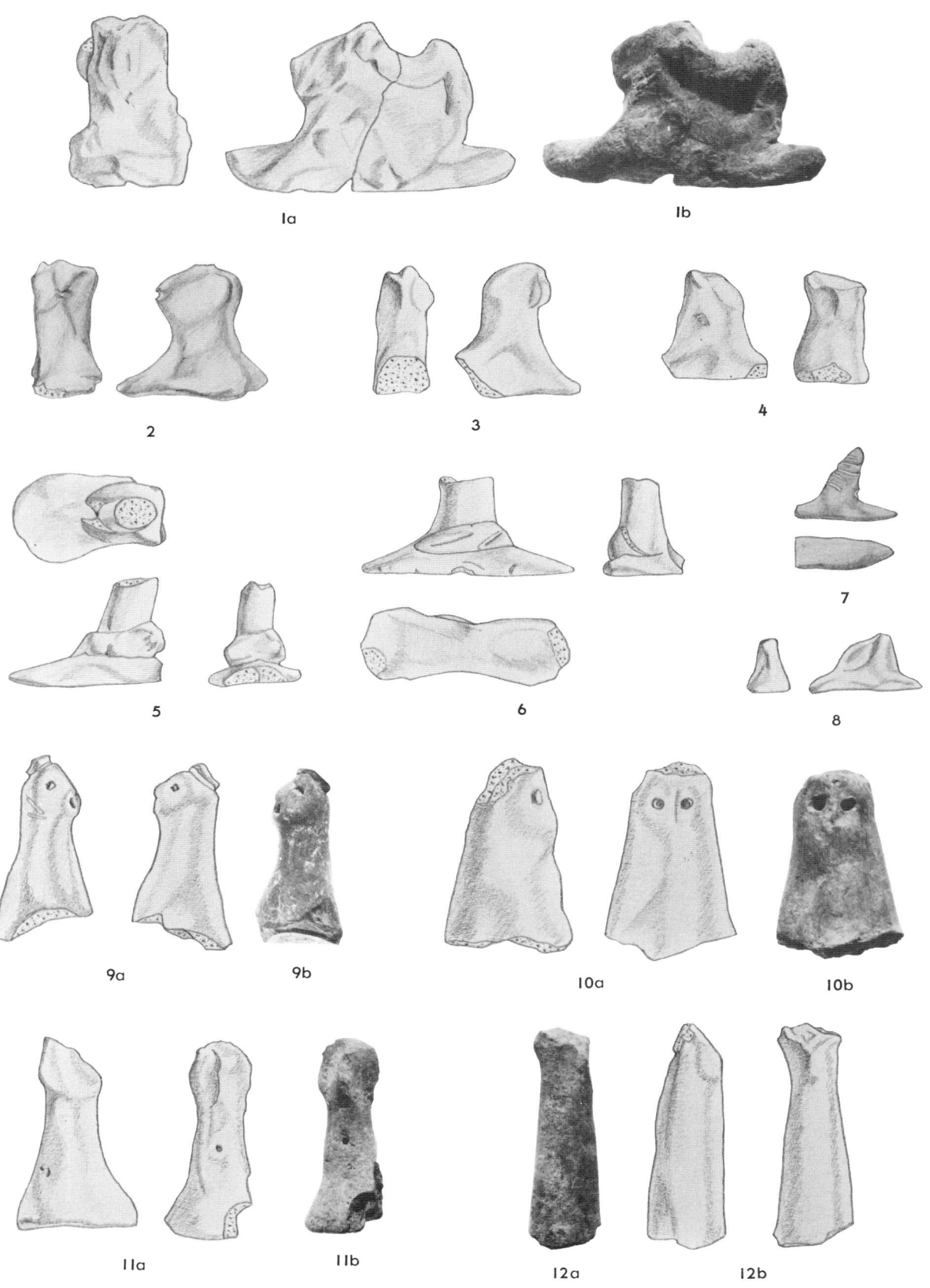

Fig. 166. Jarmo double-wing-based objects and stalk objects: double-wing-based objects, miscellaneous, *1-8*; stalk objects, human-headed type, *9-12*. Scale 1:1.

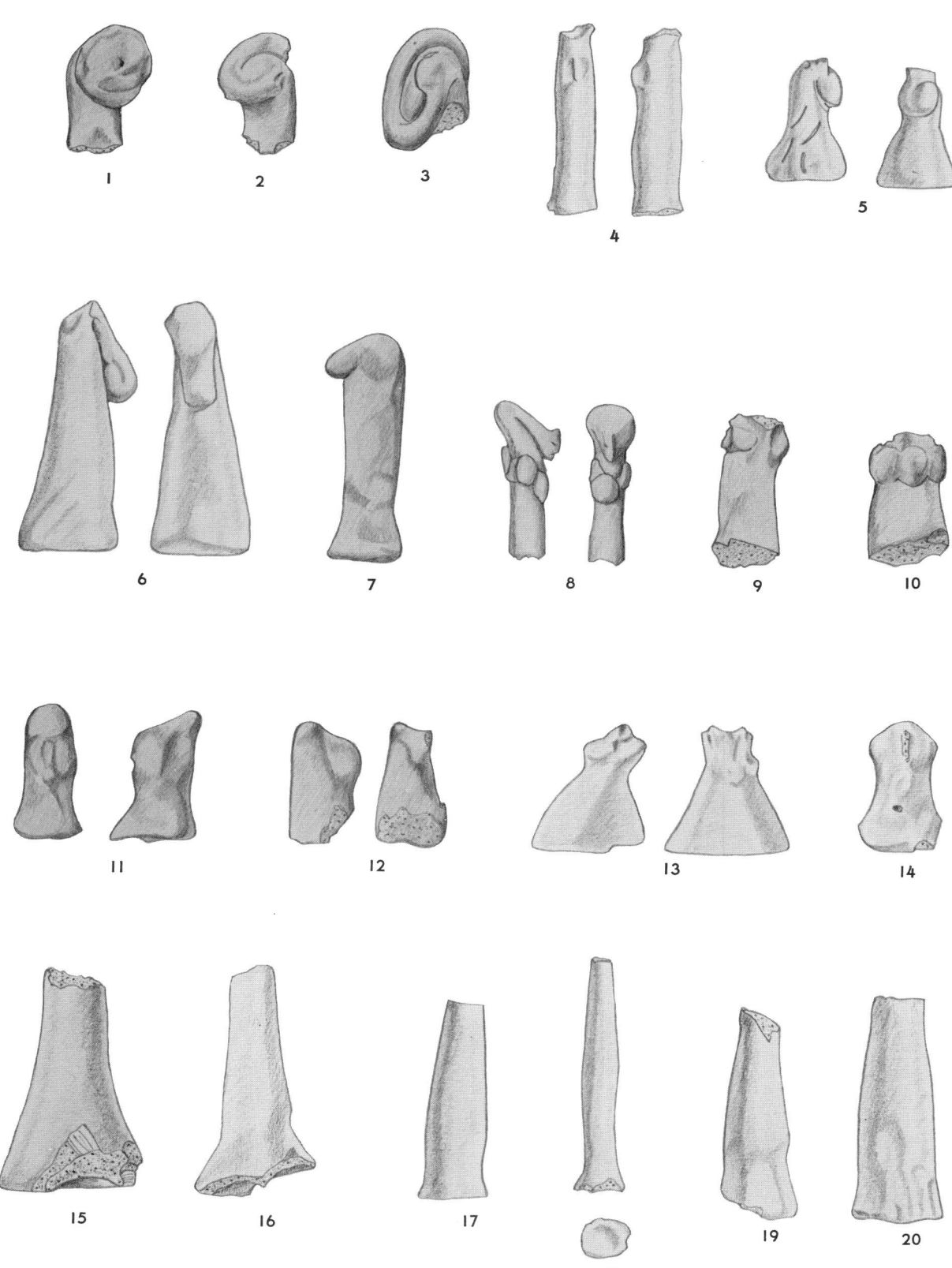

Fig. 167. Jarmo stalk objects: coiled-top type, *1-3*; human-headed type, *4-10*; human (or animal?), *11-14*; conical type, *15-16*; "nail," *17-20*. Scale 1:1.

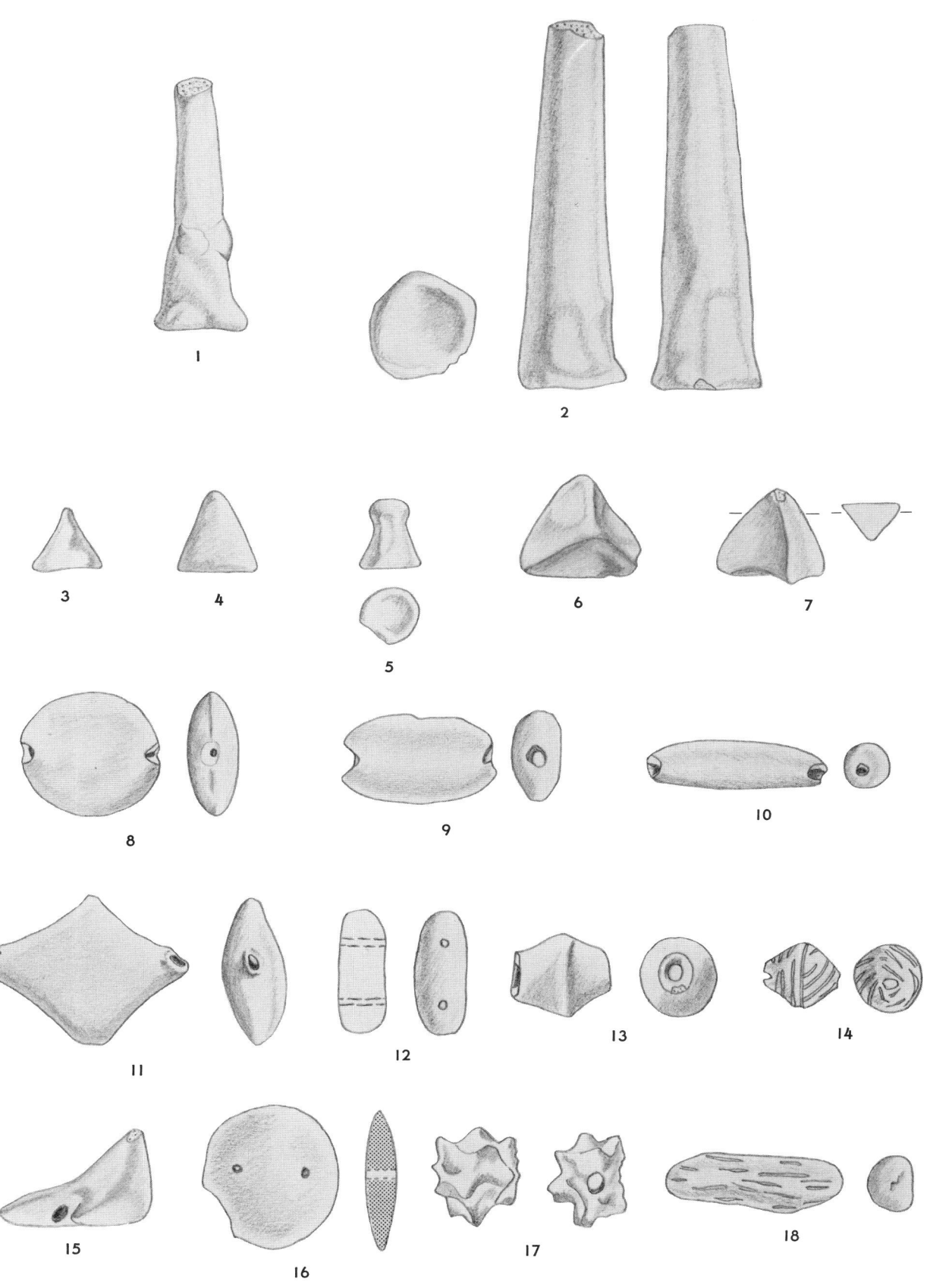

Fig. 168. Jarmo miscellaneous clay objects: stalk objects, "nails," *1-2*; cones, *3-5*; tetrahedrons, *6-7*; beads, *8-17*; bead shape, *18*. Scale 1:1.

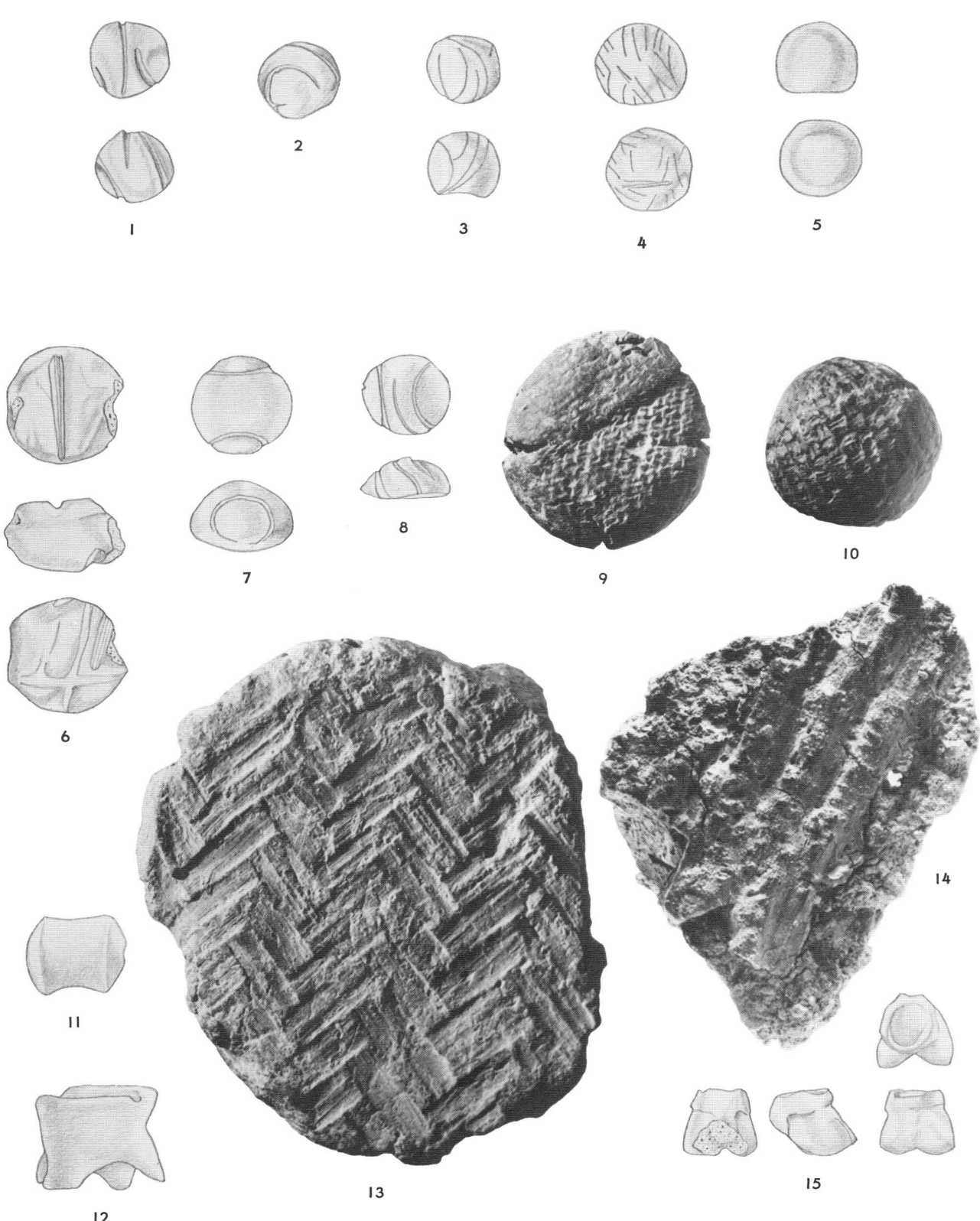

Fig. 169. Jarmo miscellaneous clay objects and impressed objects: balls, *1-4*; ball, flattened, *5*; ball, disklike, *6*; disks, subhemispherical, *7-8*; disk, fabric-impressed, *9*; ball, fabric-impressed, *10*; stud or plug, *11*; miniature stools, *12,15*; reed matting impression, *13*; coiled basketry impression, *14*. Scales 1:1, *1-8,11-12,15*; 2:1, *9-10,13-14*.

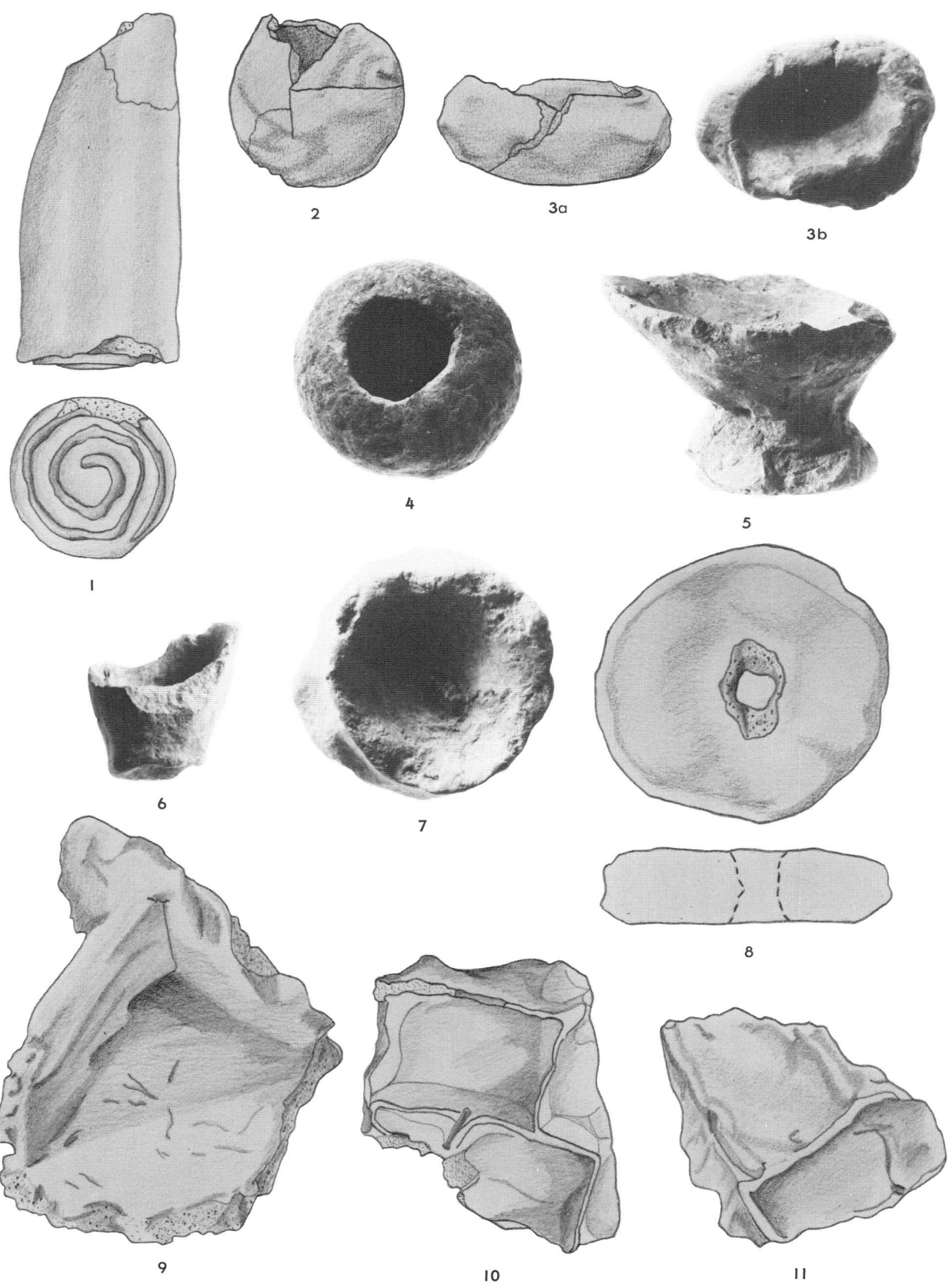

Fig. 170. Jarmo miscellaneous clay objects: stamp seal, *1*; miniature vessels, *2-7*; spindle whorl, *8*; house models, *9-11*. Scale 1:1.

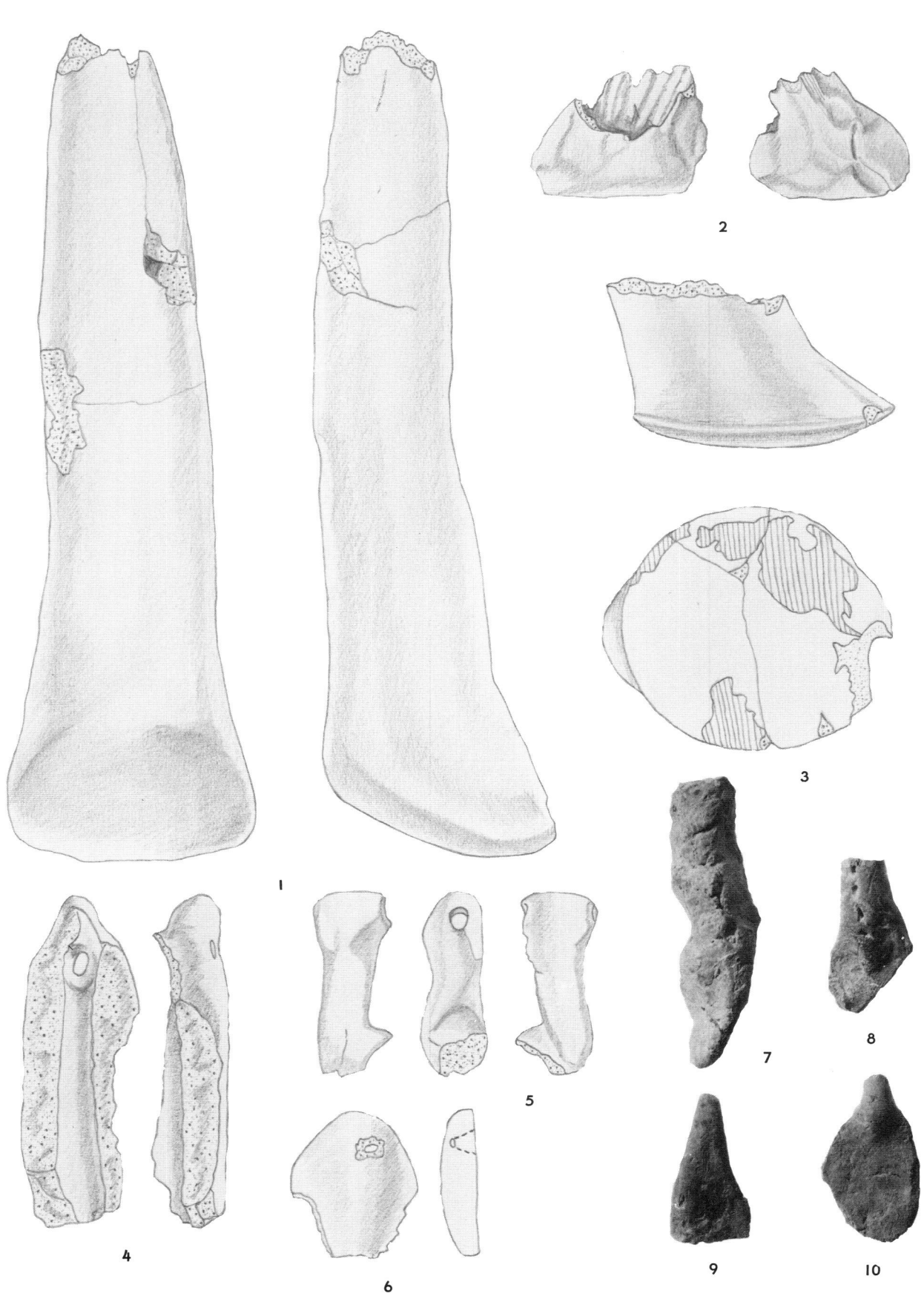

Fig. 171. Jarmo miscellaneous clay objects: clublike forms, *1-3*; perforated objects, *4-6*; spoons, *7-10*. Scale 1:1.

REFERENCES

Braidwood, Robert J.
1954 The Iraq-Jarmo Project of the Oriental Institute of the University of Chicago, season 1954-1955. *Sumer* 10:120-38.

Jacobsen, Thorkild
1946 The relative roles of technology and literacy in the development of Old World civilizations. In *Human origins: an introductory general course in anthropology, selected readings*, series 2, 2nd ed., pp. 241-49. Chicago: University of Chicago.

Mallowan, M.E.L.
1936 The excavations at Tall Chagar Bazar, and an archaeological survey of the Ḫabur region, 1934-5. *Iraq* 3:1-86.

Schmandt-Besserat, Denise
1977 An archaic recording system and the origin of writing. *Syro-Mesopotamian Studies* 1 (2):1-32.

Speiser, E.A.
1935 *Excavations at Tepe Gawra*. Vol. 1. Philadelphia: University of Pennsylvania Press.

Tobler, Arthur J.
1950 *Excavations at Tepe Gawra*. Vol. 2. Museum Monographs. Philadelphia: University of Pennsylvania Press.

Ucko, Peter J.
1968 *Anthropomorphic figurines of predynastic Egypt and neolithic Crete with comparative material from the prehistoric Near East and mainland Greece*. Royal Anthropological Institute Occasional Papers, no. 24. London: Andrew Szmidla.

Woolley, Sir Leonard
1955 *Ur excavations*. Vol. 4. *The early periods*. Publications of the Joint Expedition of the British Museum and of the Museum of the University of Pennsylvania to Mesopotamia. Philadelphia.

APPENDIX

NOTES ON THE TEXTILE AND BASKETRY IMPRESSIONS FROM JARMO

J. M. Adovasio

In May of 1969, this writer briefly examined a series of negative impressions in clay and bitumen recovered during the excavations at Jarmo. These impressions, which range in quality from excellent, with sharp definition of details, to poor, with near-total obliteration of all but the grossest technical attributes, appear to represent the imprints of several kinds of textiles and basketry. Two varieties of plain woven cloth—balanced plain weave with single warp and weft and balanced plain weave with double warp and weft—are represented. Of the three major subclasses of basketry, two—plaiting and coiling—were identified, each represented by a single type.

ANALYTICAL PROCEDURES

Each of the impressions, regardless of surface quality, was first dusted with fine white talc applied with a camel's hair brush. This dusting filled the minute cavities in the generally dark matrix of the impressions, allowing much sharper delineation of details even on the crudest specimens. Each specimen was then scrutinized with a seven-power hand lens or, in some cases, a variable-power stereoscopic microscope to insure recognition of the construction techniques employed.

CRITERIA OF CLASSIFICATION

The impressions representing identifiable basketry or textile techniques were allocated to four structural types according to the procedures and terminology outlined in Emery (1966) and Adovasio (1974, 1977a).

The four types established by the aforementioned procedures are presented below by major category (textiles or basketry) with numerical prefixes. Further details as well as comparative data on this material are available in Adovasio 1977b.

TEXTILES

Type I. Balanced Plain Weave with Single Warp and Weft (fig. 169:9)

Type I is the simplest of all textile techniques. Single-ply warps and wefts of generally equal size pass over and under each other in a 1:1 interval. ("Interval" denotes the number of elements or strips in each set that are crossed over by strips in the other sets. Intervals are usually designated numerically.) Each warp and weft passes over and under successive warp units, and each successive weft reverses the procedure of the one before it. All warps that lie above one passage of the weft lie below the next passage and so on. The number of warp and weft elements per centimeter is equal, hence the assignation of the term "balanced" to this type. No selvages are represented. The specimen is unmended and undecorated and appears to represent a portion of cloth fabric.

The source of the fiber used for the type I textile is unknown.

Type II. Balanced Plain Weave with Double Warps and Wefts (fig. 169:10)

Type II is identical to type I except that paired single-ply warp and weft elements are employed, resulting in an over-two, under-two interval of engagement (2:2). The number of warp and weft elements per centimeter is equal. The single specimen is unmended and undecorated and appears to represent a portion of cloth fabric.

The source of the fiber used for the type II textile is unknown.

BASKETRY

Type III. Twill Plaiting (fig. 169:13)

Technically, twill plaiting is the basketry equivalent of plain weaving in cloth fabrics. Plaiting is subdivided into two varieties, simple and twill, on the basis of interval. In simple plaiting, the interval is over one, under one (1:1). Twill plaiting is a variety of plaited basketry in which the weaving elements pass over each other in intervals of two or more. All specimens of twill plaiting found at Jarmo have a 2:2 interval. No selvages are represented nor are there any

---

The manuscript for this appendix was essentially completed by 1971. Very few additions and only minor revisions have been made since that date. An amplified version has been published (Adovasio 1977b).—EDS.

shifts. All specimens are unmended and appear to be portions of baskets, mats, or bags. Some type III impressions on bitumen may be the result of pitch that was applied to the inner surface of baskets to render them watertight.

All twill plaiting from Jarmo is made of longitudinally split reeds. Their genus and species are unknown.

Type IV. Close Coiling, Bundle Foundation, Noninterlocking Stitches (fig. 169:14)

A foundation consisting of a bundle of unsplit reeds is sewn with a noninterlocking stitch which pierces the bundle. Gapping is minimal, though the foundation is exposed. No accidental splitting of the stitch is apparent. The work direction is from left to right, although the work surface, for obvious reasons, is undetectable. No rims or centers are represented nor is the splice type discernible. The available specimens are unmended and undecorated and appear to be portions of large trays or bowls. Because all of these impressions are on bitumen, they may in fact represent remnants of pitch that was applied to the inner surface of the baskets to render them watertight.

Bundles are unsplit reeds whose genus and species are unknown. Stitches appear to be longitudinally split reeds of the same material.

REFERENCES

Adovasio, J.M.
    1974 Prehistoric North American basketry. In *Collected papers on aboriginal basketry*, ed. Donald R. Tuohy and Doris L. Rendall, pp. 98-148. Nevada State Museum, Anthropological Papers, no. 16. Carson City, Nev.
    1977a *Basketry technology*. Chicago: Aldine.
    1977b The textile and basketry impressions from Jarmo. *Paléorient* 3:223-30.

Emery, Irene
    1966 *The primary structures of fabrics*. Washington, D.C.: Textile Museum.

8

THE JARMO DEAD

Robert J. Braidwood

Only a small number of skeletons were encountered during our excavations. In the limited evidence we acquired, there was clearly a lack of uniformity in "burial" position as well as an apparent lack of attention to the preparation of graves or the deposition of goods with the dead. We are thus inclined to believe that the Jarmo people normally disposed of their dead outside the settlement proper and that most of the human skeletal remains encountered were hardly burials in the proper sense of the word.

In clearing the uppermost meter of deposit in J-I in 1948, a pair of infant skeletons (*J1-S1* and *J1-S2*)[1] in flexed positions and facing in opposite directions was exposed. They were assumed to be recent. As the exposure proceeded, a group of four skeletons (*J1-S3, S4, S5,* and *S6*) was found lying upon the third floor in one corner of a portion of *tauf* walling (figs. 44; 172:1,3). Although preservation of the bones was too poor to enable a positive determination, the group's disorder suggested that death came by accident, possibly a roof cave-in. No grave goods were noted, and neither the sex nor the age (beyond the fact that the individuals were adults) could be ascertained.

In our clearance to the first floor of J-II in 1950, a possibly recent skeleton (*J2-S1*) appeared at a depth too shallow for its pit to have been observed (fig. 56). The partial and very fragmentary remains of two youthful or young adult skeletons (*J2-S2* and *S3*) were found at the second floor of J-II. Both skeletons had been fragmented by the subsequent stone foundations of the first-level renovations. In fact, *J2-S3*, which consisted only of fragments of a right arm, some ribs, and a few bits of skull and jaw, lay somewhat lower, about a meter north of *J2-S1* and partly overlying *J2-S4*. This latter came as close to being a burial as anything we encountered; at least a partial outline of what seemed to be a pit was noted, and several halves of caprid lower jaws were scattered about the skeleton (fig. 172:2). The individual appeared to have been an adult male and was lying on his stomach, with his face turned toward the west, arms as if akimbo, and legs crossed. The vertebral column from sacrum to atlas was positioned in such a way that the atlas lay slightly east of north. The jaw and skull fragments were examined by Sherwood L. Washburn, who reported them to be "completely modern" with a "very high-bridged nose." In describing this same facial skeleton, J. Lawrence Angel observed that "the general impression is a face showing Iranian as well as Mediterranean traits" (Dahlberg 1960, p. 248). Dahlberg's study of the teeth (1960) supplemented the general observations he provided for the earlier Jarmo report (SAOC 31, p. 47). In brief, the teeth were small and completely modern in form. They show even milling and no marginal enamel fracture, suggesting a diet without coarse particles.

Skeleton *J2-S5* (like those of the *J1-S3* to *S6* group) appeared to be another example of the evidently typical position of a body due to accidental death. This skeleton, encountered in the clearing of the second floor in J-II, suggested a girl in her early teens (fig. 55). She lay on her back with arms out, hands up, and legs sharply flexed (fig. 172:4), perhaps crushed by a falling roof. There were no grave goods.

Very little information can be added for the operations in the spring of 1955. A single adult skeleton, lying in a flexed position, was encountered at about 0.75 m in depth, near one face of the two-meter square M20. The bones were in a very fragmentary condition, and the skeleton had not been completely cleared when it became obvious it would also yield little if any cultural information.

In sum, although far too little of the site is yet exposed to make the proposition a binding one, it does not appear that much cultural information is likely to come from on-site burials at Jarmo. Prospecting for an off-the-mound cemetery is one of the important aspects of unfinished business at the site.

NOTE

1. The code numbers for the skeletons generally follow the format established for identifying registered objects (see Introduction). Thus J1-S1 means the first skeleton encountered in the first season's work, etc.

The manuscript for this chapter was essentially completed in 1971. Very few additions and only minor revisions have been made since that date.

REFERENCES

Dahlberg, Albert A.
   1960 The dentition of the first agriculturalists (Jarmo, Iraq). *American Journal of Physical Anthropology*, n.s. 18:243-56.

SAOC 31
   1960 *Prehistoric investigations in Iraqi Kurdistan*. Robert J. Braidwood, Bruce Howe, et al. Studies in Ancient Oriental Civilization, no 31. Chicago: University of Chicago Press.

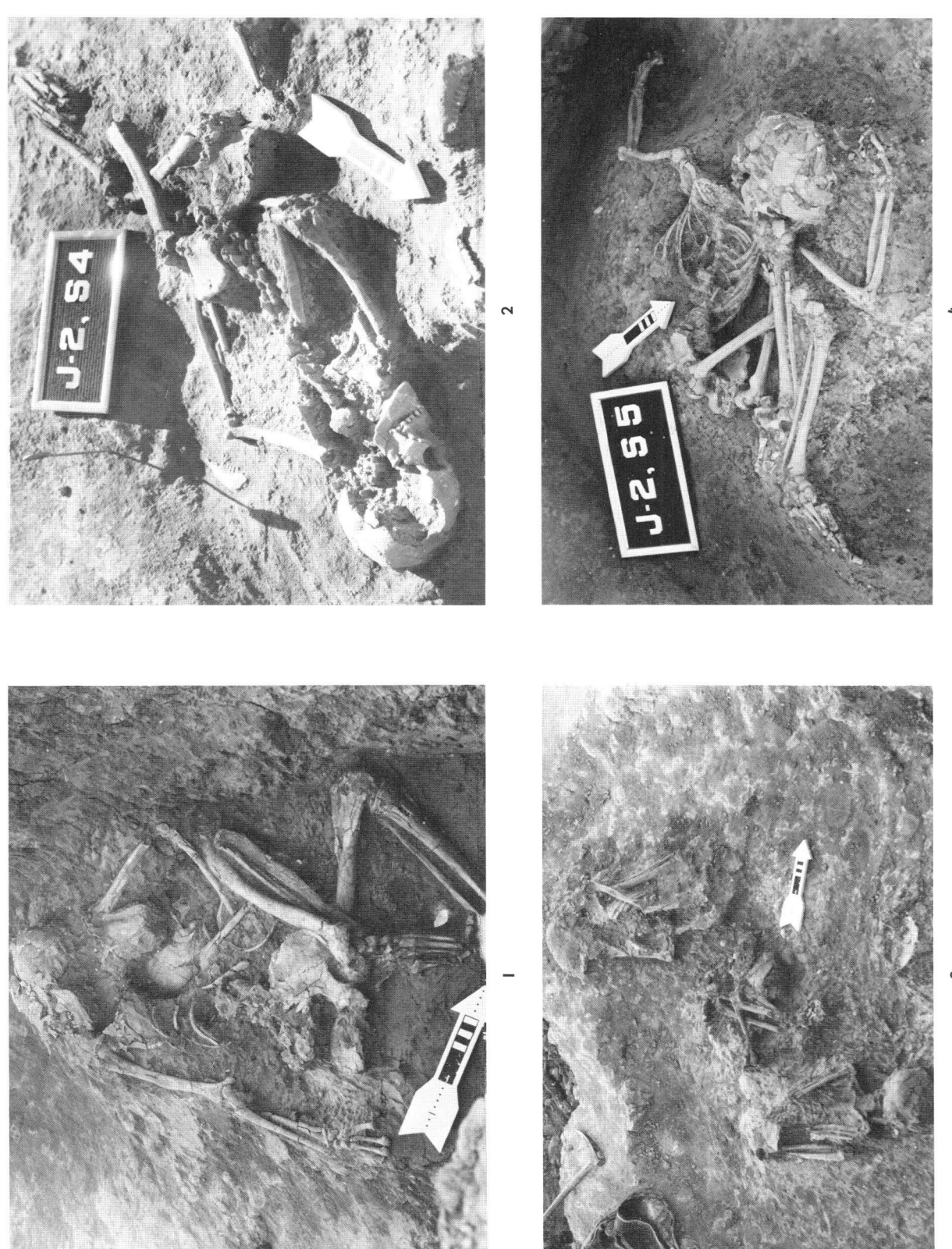

Fig. 172. The dead from Jarmo: *1*, skeleton *J1-S3* (from J-I,3); *2*, skeleton *J2-S4* (from J-II,2); *3* (*left to right*), skeletons *J1-S5*, *S6*, and *S4* (all from J-I,3); *4*, skeleton *J2-S5* (from J-II,2).

9

THE FAUNA OF JARMO
WITH NOTES ON ANIMAL BONES FROM
MATARRAH, THE ᶜAMUQ, AND KARIM SHAHIR

Hans R. Stampfli

GENERAL REMARKS

It has become usual for natural scientists to participate in archeological excavations, because the examination of the nonartifactual materials, particularly the remains of plants and animals, is of great importance for the clarification of ancient economic conditions. Every leader of an excavation knows this and excavates these items with as much care as he does the artifacts, and with equal zeal keeps them for further study. The remains of animals, mostly bones, may be fragile, however, and require considerable preparation. Further, they often are quite numerous and indeed may represent the bulk of the remains from an excavation.

Here, then, is the first problem: do all bones have to be collected, cleaned, numbered, packed, and sent away for examination in the laboratory? The answer is yes, if this is possible, for no adequate scientific analysis can be made if only a selection of the best-preserved pieces is available for study. This is as true for osteoarcheology as it is for other divisions of archeology. The ideal, of course, would be a completely excavated settlement, for a final definitive statement could be made only if all bones were present.

I realize perfectly that, because of technical and financial limitations, this ideal will be fulfilled only rarely. Few sites can be excavated completely, and often only some of the bones can be kept for laboratory examination. It must be stressed, however, that a layman's selection of bones not only is of little value to the osteologist but may also create a distorted, if not indeed false, image. From each excavation there must be at least some complete examples of specimens, and remaining material must be checked, counted, and selected by an expert.

Reed (1963) has recommended that the zoologist work with the archeologists at the place of excavation so that he can excavate and care for the bones and also study the fauna of the surrounding area. Of course, the zoologist must also have a good knowledge of osteoarcheology. Preliminary examination in the field is inadequate, and a careful, often tedious, examination in the laboratory must follow. Unfortunately, it may still happen that even if the bones have been collected properly, there is no qualified person to examine them.

Further difficulties arise from the fact that the osteoarcheologist must serve two masters. The archeologist wants a quick listing of the fauna and a summary of the relative frequencies of the wild and domestic animals and, if possible, of their origin, their importance, and use. The zoologist wants a more thorough examination, such as anatomical studies of the skeleton, in order to recognize changes resulting from domestication or those that led to the origin and evolution of species and races. If the study is published in an historical or anthropological periodical, zoological discussions may be incomprehensible to many readers, but a study in a professional zoological periodical may be even more technical and possibly not readily accessible to archeologists. However, short preliminary reports, published

---

I would first like to thank Charles A. Reed, without whose support this study could not have been made. He not only assisted me in getting the necessary funds but also conferred with me on some of the problems that arose as the study progressed.

The study was made possible by the Seessel and Anonymous Postdoctoral Fellowships of Yale University for 1965-66 and by a contribution, equally generous, from the Swiss National Fund for Scientific Research. The faunal material was lent by the Oriental Institute of the University of Chicago, and the study was made in the Peabody Museum of Natural History of Yale University in New Haven, Connecticut, where I was allowed to use the University's comparative osteological collection. Further comparative material was loaned by the Field Museum of Natural History in Chicago, the Museum of Comparative Zoology at Harvard University, and the American Museum of Natural History in New York. A list of the specimens referred to in these different collections and some of their measurements are given in tables 35-37. To all these institutions and to the people involved I owe many thanks. For the above outside loans I am indebted to Dr. Joseph C. Moore and Dr. Karel Liem at the Field Museum, Miss Barbara Lawrence at Harvard, and Dr. Richard Van Gelder at the American Museum.

Since my departure from the United States in 1966, I have not had access to the pertinent collections for updating and checking the information given here.

The translation into English was done by Miss E. Erni.

[The first draft of the manuscript for this chapter was finished by 1966. A reworking was essentially completed by 1971. Very few additions and only minor revisions have been made since that date.—EDS.]

without sufficient data and adequate analysis, may contain errors of interpretation often repeated in textbooks, from which they are often copied by later writers. The osteoarcheologist is mainly a zoologist, and his research must be accomplished with proper care if his discipline is not to slip from a science to a hobby.

It is to Reed's great credit that in his works he has criticized unsatisfactory osteological identifications and challenged the claims of some authors. Bones of wild animals have often been identified too carelessly as being those of domestic animals, mixed bones of sheep and goats have been separated and "identified" without skepticism, and important conclusions were too often published from inadequate samples. A study of the professional literature shows how little material on this subject there is from the Near East that can safely be used. Even the professional archeologist is only beginning to understand the early Near Eastern cultures. This problem is even more extreme for the osteoarcheologists. What we need are large samples of well-excavated bones, although, of course, the bones from smaller excavations are important, too. Study of the samples often takes months or even years in a well-equipped laboratory, but only such study can finally lead to a solution of these problems; certainly, preliminary reports alone on the discovery of a few bones, no matter how interesting the site may be archeologically, can never be sufficient.

Since I did not participate in the excavation of the material under examination, Reed, a member of the Iraq-Jarmo Project during 1954-55, acquainted me with it. Conclusions based on field identifications were published earlier (Reed 1960), but some of these have been changed by the present study. I was less interested in setting up new and revolutionary theories (more material is needed for that) than in giving a zoological documentation for some of the most important material. The discoveries from Jarmo, Matarrah, the Amuq, and Karim Shahir will be given in text, illustrations, and measurements, so that they can be referred to by later authors. The results are discussed and compared with those from other sites from the Near East for which the fauna have been reported; these sites do not otherwise form a unit. The sites and reports* in question are:

Ali Kosh (Flannery 1962)
Alishar Hüyük (Patterson 1937)
Anau (Duerst 1908)
Argissa-Magula (Boessneck 1962)
Beersheba (Bir es-Safadi and Bir Abou Matar) (Josien 1955, 1956)
Belt Cave (Coon 1951)
Boğazköy (Vogel 1952)
el Khiam (Vaufrey 1951)
Fikirtepe (Röhrs and Herre 1961)
Ḥorvat Beter (Beersheba) (Angress 1959)
Jericho (Zeuner 1955, 1958)
Shanidar Cave (Perkins 1964)
Shah Tepe (Amschler 1939)
Sialk (Vaufrey 1939)
Tell Asmar (Hilzheimer 1941)
Zawi Chemi Shanidar (Perkins 1964)

THE JARMO MATERIAL

The bone from Jarmo was collected during three seasons: in 1948 by Charlotte Otten, in 1950-51 by Fredrik Barth, and in 1954-55 by Charles Reed. The bones were in their original field sample packages, labeled as to operation, level, and date collected. Each field sample package of material was first examined separately; those field samples found near the surface were treated with particular caution in order to avoid possibly misleading influences due to plowing and other utilization of the site by later peoples. From the beginning, the bones of the various levels were examined by me with respect to their particular findspots so that any possible change in the composition of the fauna could be recognized.

Even throughout this stratigraphic sequence it appeared that no significant changes in the fauna had taken place (for exceptions see the sections on pig and onager). This conclusion may be due partly to the fact that most packages contained an unrepresentative distribution, since only those pieces were present which had been thought by the collector to be identifiable. A selection had, therefore, already been made, and the statistics were naturally slightly changed by this fact. However, a few of the field sample packages contained a representative distribution with various small sizes of splinters; one such package had material from the upper levels and two were of indeterminable stratigraphic context.

The measurements and census of kinds of bones were made in the usual way. Only bones of adult animals were measured; all measurements were made in millimeters, and questionable ones were put in parentheses. In the counting of the individuals, differences in size and age were also taken into account. The count of young animals was made according to the number of fourth lower deciduous premolars (dP_4) present; other deciduous teeth were taken into account as far as possible. A list of ages according to the fusion of epiphyses to diaphyses of the ends of different long bones was not made, because there were not enough of them to make such a census valid.

In the nonceramic level at Argissa-Magula, Thessaly, the bones were extremely splintered, and so a great many could not be identified (Boessneck 1962, p. 27). This was not true of the Jarmo material: even in the packages containing a complete sampling, conditions paralleled those of osteological materials from prehistoric and early historic archeological sites in Europe; the same bones were broken in the same way. Here, too, we are clearly dealing with refuse from meals, although from the evidence available no particular technique of slaughtering can be determined.

---

*Studies published after 1966, when Stampfli finished this manuscript, are not included.—EDS.

DISTINGUISHING THE SPECIES

It is not my intention to deal in this section with the skeletal differences between species, except for some preliminary considerations on bones of gazelles. Knowledge of the sometimes subtle differences in homologous bones of related species is, of course, absolutely necessary for the osteologist who deals with bones found in archeological excavations, for often there are only fragments which have to be identified anatomically as well as according to species. The difficulties of distinguishing the bones of sheep and goats are well known, and the presence of gazelles at many Near Eastern sites creates a further complication. Even the differentiation of bones of male deer from those of cattle can lead to difficulties, as is shown by a survey of the literature.

Normally it is not difficult to separate remains of cervids from those of bovids. In different sites of the Near East, however, bones of large stags have been found, which has led to some confusion. Thus, erroneous reports of a small type of cattle ("small *Bos*") are found in the literature (e.g., Reed in Braidwood 1954*a*, p. 135; Reed 1960, pp. 141, 165; Perkins 1960, p. 77), which have, however, been corrected by Reed (1961) and Perkins (1964, p. 1565). To complete the record, I would like to state again here that there is no evidence for the existence of small wild *Bos* in the area of northern Iraq, or probably anywhere else. All these remains of "small cattle" are bones of large male deer (*Cervus elaphus*). Such bones from the sites reported here are not only very big but also have a heaviness that is seldom observed in European stags.[1]

Sheep and Goat

The separation of bones of sheep from those of goats is still one of the most difficult tasks of the osteologist, although today we are well informed on the characteristics of some domestic breeds because of a thorough study by Boessneck, Müller, and Teichert (1964). But even when we take into account all of the known diagnostic characters, a great many excavated bones will always remain unidentifiable because of their fragmentary condition and heterogeneity (they naturally include bones from wild and domestic animals, juveniles and adults, males and females). Any identification of all bones of caprines (i.e., sheep and goats, sometimes termed "caprovines" in archeological literature) as one or the other of the two species, as has been done by some authors, is suspect.

Gazelle, Roe Deer, and Sheep and Goat

Remains of gazelles and roe deer have been found in many excavations. Separation of their remains—above all, distinguishing them from sheep and goats—is very important. If we look at modern skeletons, this distinction may seem easy, but the identification of the broken bones of excavated material is far more difficult.

No thorough study of the osteological characteristics of these species, particularly of the gazelle, has yet been done. Apart from some descriptions and illustrations of gazelles' horn cores (e.g., Hilzheimer 1941, p. 23; Duerst 1908, pl. 76), the only results I know of are in a study by Angress (1959, pp. 54ff.), and I can confirm these results. Unfortunately, my time was too limited and the material for comparison of the gazelle and roe deer too scarce to make a more exact study on distinguishing the osteological characteristics of these species. The identification of bones of gazelles is particularly important, since these animals seem to have been of great economic importance to the people of some settlements.

I shall try to show the most typical characteristics of the gazelle, roe deer, and caprines by short descriptions and illustrations in order to give later workers a basis for identifying these species. The bones of the different animals have been drawn at approximately the same size for easier comparison (fig. 173:1-10). Since the samples I had for comparison were inadequate for an exact study, the characteristics I mention will have to be reaffirmed in a larger series of skeletons.

Horn core.—Gazelles' horn cores can easily be separated from those of goats and sheep. Apart from differences in form and size, the internal compactness (no sinus spaces) and the external deep creases (particularly in the caudal part) make distinction easy. The horn cores of young gazelles are often goatlike, but they always have deeper creases and flatter lateral surfaces.

Scapula.—Two main characters make the identification of gazelles' scapulae possible: the curve in the caudal part (margo axillaris) of the collum scapulae is deep, and the edges, particularly the lateral one, are well marked (fig. 173:1*B*). The ASG distance (Boessneck, Müller, and Teichert 1964, p. 58) is smaller than in roe deer and caprines. It is possible to identify the scapula of the roe deer by the presence of a sharper brim in the caudal region of the facies costalis.

Humerus.—Since only the distal end of any humerus is usually found, only this part will be discussed here. As figure 173:2 indicates, the distal end of the humerus of the roe deer is quite different from that of the gazelle, so that differentiation is not difficult. The distinction between caprines and gazelles is also not too difficult to observe, since the trochlea of the gazelle shows a longer medial boundary in comparison to the width, and the "Führungskamm" (the sharp ridge on the medial aspect of the capitulum; fig. 173:2*B*) is more laterally situated.

Radius.—The separation of distal fragments of radii is difficult, if not impossible. Even those of roe deer cannot always be recognized, particularly as goats can also have strong ridges on the dorsal plane of distal radii. Remains of gazelles can perhaps be recognized by their small size and their more graceful shape. The identification of the proximal fragment of the radius (fig. 173:3) is simpler. The main characteristic of the gazelle's proximal radius, in contrast to that of the roe deer and that of caprines, is the lesser curve of the groove for the ulnar appendix on the volar brim (see *a* in fig. 173:3*B*); naturally, the different form of the humeral trochlea is reflected in the shape of the radius.

Ulna.—The ulna of the gazelle differs from that of each of the others by the less marked appendix (see *a* in fig. 173:4*B*), which fits into the curve of the radius mentioned above. The ulna of roe deer can be distinguished by the form of the olecranon.

Metacarpus.—The proximal end of the metacarpus (not illustrated) of the roe deer can easily be distinguished by the curve on the volar side, but fragments of a gazelle's metacarpus can hardly be separated from those of caprines. The best character for distinguishing a gazelle is the slenderness of the diaphysis. The trochleae at the distal end are so different in the three species that their identification is not difficult (fig. 173:5). Descriptions and indices are also given by Angress (1959, pp. 55ff.).

Pelvis.—The pelvis is somewhat differently constructed in the three groups. (A description will not be given here.) In excavations, however, often only parts of acetabula are found, making identification more difficult again. The roe deer has an acetabulum similar to that of the gazelle, having a bigger "lobate" in the caudal region (facies lunata; *a* in fig. 173:6*B*), unlike the acetabula of sheep and goats. A separation of bones of the gazelle and the roe deer is possible if there are other parts available, since the gazelle has an os ileum that is strikingly short in the medial part and a wider foramen obturatum.

Femur.—The main distinguishing features of the proximal part of the femur are the form of the caput femoris and the mode of attachment of this caput to the collum and to the trochanter major (fig. 173:7). In the gazelle and the roe deer the caput is longer than in the caprines; this length is even more marked in the gazelle than in the roe deer. Moreover, the depression between the caput and the trochanter major is more definite and has somewhat more angular corners than in sheep or goat. Differences can also be observed in the trochanter major, which is more curved, particularly in the gazelle. The distal end of a femur of a roe deer shows a typical cervid construction but may not always be easily distinguished from that of caprines. However, a distal fragment of a gazelle femur is easily recognized by the asymmetric form of the facies patellaris (fig. 173:8).

Tibia.—The tibia does not seem to have many characteristics that can be related to one species or another. The usefulness of the few that I could distinguish is not completely certain. Tibiae of roe deer can be recognized by their cervid-type form, particularly in the distal part of the diaphysis. In the gazelle the asymmetry of the astragalus (see below) is reflected in the facies, but it is not easily recognized.

Astragalus.—The astragalus of a roe deer is similar to that of a gazelle (fig. 173:9). Particularly striking are the more marked edges of the trochlea tali in the proximal part and the narrower facies of the calcaneus, compared with the caprines. The astragalus of a gazelle differs from that of a roe deer (and of course from that of a sheep or a goat) in the striking asymmetry of the edges of the trochlea tali: the lateral edge is elevated.

Calcaneus.—The calcaneus of a gazelle has a considerably smaller sustentaculum, which does not reach the plantar edge. This is not the case for the calcaneus of a roe deer or a caprine (fig. 173:10). Differences between the three groups are evident in the form of the facies of the os centrotarsale: in the gazelle it is long and flat; in the goat or sheep it is very curved and shows a more or less strong link to the sustentaculum. The calcaneus of the roe deer is intermediate between the other two animal groups in this respect.

Metatarsus.—All that has been said of the metacarpus is generally true also for the metatarsus. The form of the distal end typically shows the same differences. The identification of the metatarsus of the roe deer is simple because of a longitudinal indentation on its dorsal (anterior) surface. In the gazelle there is a hint of a crease right above the trochleae, as can also be observed in the metatarsus of *Bos*.

Phalanges.—The phalanges of the gazelle are easy to recognize because they are narrow and elegant (for description and proportions see Angress 1959, p. 55). The phalanges of a roe deer differ from those of the caprines mainly in the form of the proximal facies (shape, connection of the sesamoid bones).

DIFFERENCES BETWEEN DOMESTIC AND WILD ANIMALS

A modern domestic animal differs very much from its wild counterpart; one has only to think of the example of dog and wolf. In general, what are the most important marks of distinction?

The domestic animal's body usually has a different shape; it is usually smaller than that of its wild ancestor, and often also relatively stouter. The skull is usually shortened, although sometimes secondarily lengthened due to selective breeding. The sexual differences are less marked in domestic animals; there is, for example, a relative diminution of the horns of male bovids. The physiological capacity is changed; domestic animals are typically more fertile than wild animals and breed at a younger age. Selection has often been concentrated on the pelage, so that some breeds of domestic animal show less pigment or more pigment or variable patterns of spotting, or greater or denser growth of hair, etc., than other breeds of the same species. Even in their behavior the domestic animals differ from wild animals. For further study the summarizing works by Röhrs (1961) and Herre (1963) offer more complete data and discussion.

In the present study we have available only remains of bones and so must consider the general effects of domestication upon the skeletons of animals.

Great changes occur in the skull; mostly the facial part becomes shorter. However, the rate of decrease in size of the teeth is slower than that of the skull as a whole. Often one can recognize from the individual bones the smaller size and thus perhaps stouter shape of the whole body. The change in secondary sexual characters can be found first in the development of the horn cores, which are smaller and also often differently shaped.

Another factor that aids in detecting domestication developed through human cultural activities; at a certain season, usually before the onset of winter, a larger number of young animals, mostly males, were slaughtered, and the excavated bony remains of juvenile animals may therefore show an increase.

Although from the above statements the separation of the bones of domestic animals from those of related wild forms may appear to be relatively simple, the osteoarcheologist encounters other difficulties that often make separation impossible. In any case, clear differentiation is possible only if comparative skeletons are available of the species considered to have been the wild ancestor (and even here opinions of various scientists differ). Comparative collections do not always exist, however, or are sometimes impossible to find because the ancestor is extinct. As an instance, the skeleton of the wild ox (*Bos primigenius* Bojanus) has had to be reconstructed, for comparative purposes, from parts of several different finds. Skeletons of wild sheep and wild goats are rare and may well become even more difficult to collect, as only a relatively small number of these animals now exist in their original areas. Exact knowledge of the variability of the wild species is of course the prerequisite for the separation of domestic and wild populations according to form and size. We must not forget that the variability of the wild form itself could be rather large if the sample archeologically recovered covers a period of several thousand years. Still further variability would be involved if the population was living in a changing environment.

A fully complete skull, which would show the clear changes associated with domestication, is a rare find archeologically, and fragments are usually of little critical value in allowing positive identification. The horn cores, however, are genetically unstable and may change quickly under domestication, thus making them useful for the recognition of domestication. This instability, however, also has a negative side, for morphologic changes could also have occurred due to changing selective factors other than domestication (see the section on sheep and goats in the descriptions of species, pp. 442-45). Such "natural" changes occurred more slowly than those which appeared very soon after men started keeping and breeding wild animals. This circumstance is a favorable one for the archeo-osteologist, for already the earliest domestic animals can be recognized as such. Actually, breeding is the key to true domestication; herding of only semitamed animals would have produced few, if any, effects on the skeleton. However, I do not believe that such a form of keeping animals went on for a long time, if at all.

To summarize: what are the criteria to be used by the osteoarcheologist for distinguishing the broken bones of domestic animals from those of wild animals?

1. Domestic animals were at first smaller than their wild ancestors;[2] prehistoric remains of pigs and cattle that are smaller than those of the wild individuals are therefore evidence of domestic animals. Naturally, the range in size for either population cannot now be reckoned exactly, and in any case the two ranges would overlap. Unfortunately, the change in size in sheep and goat was very small or nonexistent, so that only extremes can be recognized through size differences.
2. Horn cores are well suited for the separation of wild from domestic animals, but variability of size and form of the wild species should necessarily be better known. Separation by sex has first to be made, after which one sometimes discovers that differentiation of the genera, as between sheep and goat, is difficult.
3. I think that the most certain sign of the keeping of domestic animals is the increase of remains of young animals in the material recovered. Here, intervention by man—the manipulation of propagation and the conscious choice of animals to be butchered (for example, the young males)—can be seen clearly. In addition, it is relatively simple to determine whether the remains are of young animals and to calculate the percentage these represent in the sample recovered. The age of an animal manifests itself in the whole skeleton and particularly in the teeth, which are among the hardest and most durable parts and are therefore more often found. At present, unfortunately, goats and sheep cannot be distinguished from one another by their teeth; also in these animals the identification of species on the basis of juvenile bones is questionable, so the differentiation of the two species must usually be based on the adult remains. The distinction between bones of pigs or cattle from those of the other species is usually obvious; also the differences between wild and domestic forms of pigs and cattle are clearer than with sheep and goat, since the diminution in size of domestic pigs and cattle was more rapid.

Many earlier authors attempted to distinguish domestic from wild animals by several characteristics of the bones, for example, hardness, color, and specific weight and density of the substantia compacta and substantia spongiosa. Bones of domestic animals not only are a different size and have a different exterior form but probably also have a different inner composition. A clear distinction based on such characters has not as yet been established, although several investigators are working on these problems. What will be required is an exact knowledge of the

STATISTICAL SUMMARY (see tables 24-37, pp. 456ff.)

Table 24 shows the number of identified bones for each part of the body of the more important of the nonhuman mammals, as found in selected upper-level contexts at Jarmo. Bones of the extremities and teeth are most numerous. Vertebrae and ribs are relatively rare; also, they are few compared with the number of bones found in settlements proved to have been excavated completely, for example, Burgäschisee-Süd in Switzerland (Boessneck, Jéquier, and Stampfli 1963), so that the present distribution is seemingly "unnatural." However, I still believe that the contents of the field sample packages on which table 24 is based represent the normal situation of recovery; had there been a sorting and differential selection at the site, *all* "unimportant" pieces such as fragments of vertebrae and ribs certainly would have been eliminated. Probably many small fragments were destroyed or lost during excavation. No particular butchering technique is noticeable—for example, one that would have involved bringing home only the extremities of wild prey; the remains of wild cattle, to mention one instance, show a normal distribution of skeletal parts.

The number of bones for each mammalian species is shown by tables 25 and 26; table 25 is more precise because it is based only on field sample packages with a normal distribution. Table 26 is included here to delineate possible differences between the upper and lower levels of operations I and II; it also contains the complete list of animals found.

The number of bones examined by me is 8,687 (tables 25 and 26). This number excludes the remains of rodents, birds, turtles, fish, and crabs, and a few unidentifiable fragments. Since most field sample packages contained a selection of well-preserved fragments, the number of unidentifiable pieces was small. The total number of bones excavated at Jarmo was considerably greater; Reed (1957, p. 43) mentioned that for the excavation of 1955 about 100,000 bones were sorted, of which only a small proportion were packed, the remainder being discarded at the site as unidentifiable fragments.

For a prehistoric site, Jarmo had a strong predominance of goats and sheep; their bones amounted to 73-91% of the counts, depending on the field sample packages selected. As a general rule, in Near East sites approximately 80% of the domestic animals are sheep and goats. Typically, the remaining 20% are important wild animals like gazelles, deer, wild cattle, and pigs; canids (dogs and wolves) are only sparsely represented. At Jarmo, there were more goats than sheep: according to the number of bones, goats were four times as numerous as sheep; according to the number of individuals, twice as numerous. Similar ratios are found by examination of the parts of the caprine skeleton: 23% of all horn cores, 35% of the humeri, 43% of the astragali, and 33% of the first phalanges are from sheep. We can assume that at Jarmo goats were three to four times more numerous than sheep.

The distribution of the species is not surprising, since, as mentioned above, for most sites of the Near East a strong predominance of sheep and/or goats has been shown. At Jarmo, however, the distribution of wild and domestic animals generally is not ordinary; the wild animals are considerably more strongly represented than anticipated, as can be seen in the percentages in tables 25 and 26. In the lower levels the proportion of wild individuals reaches nearly half the total. In one of the earliest summaries on Jarmo, Braidwood (1952, p. 30), on the basis of observations by Barth, suggested that only 5% of the fauna might have been wild. Unfortunately, when such erroneous preliminary judgments get into the general literature, they are difficult to eradicate.[3] Brentjes (1962*b*, p. 539) and Nagel (1961, p. 34), for instance, have quoted that figure of 5%; Nagel was even more explicit, stating that 80% of the fauna at Jarmo were domestic animals and that the remaining 15% were probably hunted animals. These errors of an earlier day should now be corrected.

As shown in the preceding section, distinguishing domestic from wild animals often is difficult, especially among the caprines. I separated them according to the male horn cores, the most prominent distinguishing feature (for details see the description of sheep and goats, pp. 443-44). It was evident that approximately two thirds of the horn cores came from males of domestic goats, and therefore I then arbitrarily separated the remaining bones of goats in a ratio of 2:1. An accurate separation of domestic and wild animals was not possible for sheep, but I believe that the sheep, too, belonged to the domesticated variety (see p. 444). As in the case of the goats, the bones of sheep were separated in a ratio of 2:1. More exact was the separation of domestic from wild pigs; the ratio of wild to domestic pigs was judged from measurements to be 6:1. Even if we assumed that all remains of sheep and goats come from domesticated animals, the total proportion of wild animals would nevertheless be more than 5%; calculated according to the *minimum* number of individuals (MNI) it would be approximately 20%. In summary, we may state that wild animals are considerably more strongly represented at Jarmo than was previously assumed.

How far can a difference between the lower and upper levels of the site be recognized in terms of osteological remains? Table 26 shows only small differences in the relative numbers of the species in the upper and lower levels. I consider the increase in the caprines from 73.3% in the lower levels to 81.4% in the upper levels to be insignificant as far as indicating any change in the economic life of the settlement is concerned. The decrease in the percentage of wild cattle from 8.9% to 3.0% is probably also meaningless. The remains of these animals were found accumulated as "bone nests" in a few spots and must therefore be considered rather accidental discoveries. The case of the onager is different; its bones and teeth were concentrated in the lower levels, but they appear in only a few of the intermediate to upper levels. (Surprisingly, most of the examples from the upper levels came from J-II,1.)[4] Presumably, hunting for onagers was practiced rarely or not at all in the terminal aspects of Jarmo's occupation.

The calculation of the percentage of the young animals leads to a result that is contrary to an earlier estimate. According to a statement by Braidwood (1952, p. 30), which was based only on a tentative field estimate by Barth, "an extremely high proportion of goat and sheep yearlings" should have been accounted for. My calculations, however, revealed that only 26% of the sheep and goats were young animals. The count was higher, 50%, for the pig, and, as based on a small sample of only eight individuals, the proportion of young gazelles reached 12.5% (table 25). The young of other species were not found in the samples in question. Although all the other packages of bones contained an unnatural selection, I still calculated the percentage of juvenile animals from the total available yields for J-I and J-II in order to find out whether there was any difference in the keeping of domestic animals between the lower and upper levels of Jarmo. I could do this easily because I could assume that all the teeth had been collected and kept and that, therefore, the result is of absolute validity. I found that the teeth also do not indicate that a particularly high percentage of juvenile animals can have been killed. For the lower levels only 20% of the sheep/goat remains were young animals and for the upper levels only 13%. I do not consider the difference of 7% to be significant.

As mentioned in the previous section an increased occurrence of young animals is to be taken as a sure sign of the keeping of domestic animals, but what does "increased occurrence" mean? Certainly, in material from a hunting economy, bones of young animals are extremely rare and reach only very low percentages of the total, but where do we draw the line? It is certain that the 50% count of young pig as recovered at Jarmo indicates domestication; this fact is also proved by the increasing numbers of smaller pigs in the upper levels (see also the section on pigs, pp. 445-47). However, the judgment becomes questionable in the case of the gazelles, of which only 12.5% are young animals. To judge from the horn cores, a certain number of domestic animals existed among the goats, and we must therefore consider that if 26% of the total are young, we have satisfactory evidence for the keeping of domestic animals. I believe that this is the lowest limit that should be considered.[5]

A comparison of the statistics of the faunal analysis for Jarmo with the corresponding statistics for other sites of the Near East cannot be easily made, either because no exact calculations were presented in the reports from other sites or because some statements seem doubtful. In table 27 the most important sites have been marked in a way similar to that used in the studies by Reed (1959, 1960). The disposition of the sites on this table approximates their geographical and chronological situation; their classification of species and counts, however, must remain rather vague. Since rather different methods of calculation were used for the different sites, I have not entered the exact numbers for the different species. It can thus be seen from this survey (table 27) that no clear picture emerges even if space and time are taken into account as important factors. Probably the economic conditions in the different settlements compared did not correspond. A predominance of sheep in one site and of goats in another, a stronger accent on the hunt in one place and a more intensive keeping of domestic animals in another must probably be regarded as part of a pattern of cultural variability in the early stage of the evolution of agriculture in the Near East.

From a comparative study of the *percentages* of wild and domestic animals one discovers rather different results from those gained from the study of young animals. The period of occupation of each settlement must, of course, always be considered. Jarmo shows a high percentage (40%) of wild animals as determined by the *total* count of identified bones; all the other sites compared here have lower percentages. Tell Asmar and Shah Tepe each have approximately 20%, Beersheba has 8%, and Horvat Beter, 16%. In Fikirtepe the proportion increases to 25%, and probably there were even more wild animals actually hunted there than assumed (see under Cattle, pp. 440ff.). The range of 0.9-2.4% of wild animals mentioned by Boessneck for Argissa-Magula (preceramic and "neolithic" levels) is probably somewhat low because some of the remains of big sheep may have to be assigned to the wild form (Boessneck 1962, p. 28, n. 7).

Unfortunately, most of the sources used for table 27 do not indicate how the relative number of young animals was calculated, so that the results of any comparison must leave some doubts as to their validity. For simplification, I shall here compare only the percentages of young sheep and goats from several Near Eastern sites.

A figure of 26%, approximately that available from Jarmo, was given by Boessneck (1962, p. 74) for the neolithic of Argissa-Magula in Thessaly; for all other sites the proportion of young animals is larger. For the two Palestinian sites, Bir es-Safadi and Bir Abou Matar, I reckon a figure of 40% for *Capra* and *Ovis* together (data from Josien 1955). In all levels of Belt Cave above layer 7, the young of sheep and goats made up 59% of these two species (Coon 1951). The figures presented in the well-known proposition made for the early domestication of sheep at Zawi Chemi Shanidar and Shanidar Cave (Perkins 1964, p. 1566) are strange: the values are generally rather varied, but the highest proportion is 57.9% for Shanidar Cave, level B-1. At the same time, for example, young sheep in layer D of Shanidar Cave reach the high figure of 42.9%. This, according to my opinion (see p. 435) would be considered proof of domestication. Such cannot, however, be the case for Shanidar D, a Mousterian level that is more than 46,000 years old. In levels B-1 and C, young animals also amounted to 42.9% and 21.9% of the count for goats, which should suggest domestication for that species. The identification of the bones as being of young animals was based on the degree of ossification of the distal epiphyses in the metapodials. A comparison with an age table based on the growth and eruption of the dP_4 of goats from this site would be very informative.

DESCRIPTION OF THE VARIOUS SPECIES

GAZELLE

Unfortunately, the importance of the gazelle in the era of the early village farming communities still cannot be defined, even with the material found at Jarmo (table 25). We can assume fairly definitely that in the paleolithic the gazelle played the same role in the Near East as did the reindeer in Europe in the same period, that is, it was the main animal of the hunt. This is apparent in statements by Coon which, however, are quite general and are of only slight value to the osteologist. The gazelle is particularly strongly represented in the so-called mesolithic levels of Belt Cave (61.5-88.9% of the faunal remains; Coon 1951, p. 46). In the "neolithic" levels at this site, the percentage of gazelles decreased to 3.0-5.6% at the same time as the percentage of sheep and goats increased. Unfortunately, Coon's text does not specify which bones were used for identification or in what proportion they appeared, nor was the method of distinguishing the young from the older animals stated. The decreasing importance of the gazelle in the early village era is also revealed by the percentage of its occurrence at Matarrah (1.4%; see p. 449) and at Ali Kosh (Flannery 1962, p. 130, fig. 12). In the ᶜAmuq the percentage of gazelles was not high either, but here the geographical position may have been an influence.

According to speculation by Brentjes (1962b, p. 539), gazelles were held in great herds by the early Near Eastern farmer and used as a living meat supply. Brentjes relied particularly on what he believed to be clearly proven maintenance of gazelles in Mesopotamia in the second and third millennia B.C. He also inferred from publications of osteological material in the Near East at sites such as Jericho, Karim Shahir, and possibly Jarmo that the keeping of gazelles had begun at the time of these settlements. Nevertheless, he himself mentioned the lack of exact reports on the zoological material.

Zeuner remarked that at Jericho "gazelle is frequent" (1955, p. 70) and wrote in a letter to Brentjes (see Brentjes 1962b, p. 538), "The normal meat supply for the town came from gazelle" (see also Zeuner 1963, p. 434). Unfortunately, we do not possess any exact statistics of the faunal remains from Jericho that would reveal how strongly the gazelle was actually represented, and a sentence such as "A very large number of bones come from animals of approximately sheep-size and of these many are gazelles" (Zeuner 1955, p. 70) prevents any possibility of certainty. I do believe that gazelles were present at Jericho, but without an exact count their full importance, particularly in comparison with sheep and goat, cannot be evaluated.

In any case, the percentage of gazelles in the fauna at Jarmo is smaller than previously assumed on the basis of preliminary reports; it was therefore not more important as a hunted animal than were wild cattle, deer, or onager (see, e.g., Brentjes 1962b, p. 539, and Narr 1961, p. 215). However, the effective percentage may be slightly higher than that given in table 25 (6.3%) since some bones among those listed as being from sheep and goat could possibly be bones of gazelle that could not be identified as such (for example, tibiae). If we compare the relative numbers of the three species (gazelle, sheep, and goat) according to the bones of highest frequency, we get the following result:

	Humerus (%)	Astragalus (%)
Gazelle	8	9
Sheep	30	41
Goat	62	50

Gazelles are absent today from Anatolia, Cyprus, and the Balkans, as they were in prehistoric times. However, where they do occur in other parts of the Near East, the frequency of their bones in prehistoric archaeological sites is usually low. Josien (1956, p. 725) found only 6% at Beersheba; Hilzheimer (1941, p. 47), 5.5% at Tell Asmar; and Angress (1959, p. 71), 15.6% at Horvat Beter. Amschler reported no bones of gazelles from Shah Tepe, but this conclusion may be due to an accident of sampling. The figures for Anau and Sialk cannot be calculated exactly.

No statement on the possibility that herds of more or less tamed gazelles might have been kept can be made based on my study of the faunal remains from Jarmo. There are a certain number of juvenile animals; in one field sample package from the middle portion of the upper levels the proportion of juvenile animals reached 20%, which may indicate either a factor of sampling or perhaps human intervention.

Generally it is assumed that all gazelle bones came from the Persian or "goitered" gazelle, *Gazella subgutturosa* (Güldenstädt),[6] but a positive identification by study of the bones is impossible. Most of the gazelle bones from Jarmo are the size of those in the modern skeletons (see also table 36), but some are a little bigger. This may be because the modern comparative material happens to come from small animals. It is striking that the bones of many species found at Jarmo exceed the modern ones in size.

The horn cores in the material from Jarmo show a greater variability than do those from other sites, but it should be noted that I had a greater amount of material at my disposal than was available in the case of earlier studies.

Comparative data on gazelle horn cores are (mm):

	Length	Circumference	Larger diameter	Smaller diameter
Tell Asmar	180	--	32-36	21-25
Sialk	200	--	33-38	20-26
Anau	145-210	89-105	30-38	21-27
Jarmo	140-190	87-120	28-42	22-31

DEER

Remains of deer have been reported from most of the early sites in the Near East; the only exceptions are Sialk, Beersheba, Jericho, and Horvat Beter. Three species have been distinguished: the Persian fallow deer, the European fallow deer, and the red deer.

Dama mesopotamica Brooke, the Persian fallow deer, survives today in only a few small spots of the Khuzistan plain of southern Iran and is certainly threatened by extinction there (for the latest report see Reed 1965). It formerly had a large range and was sometimes kept as a tame animal (Brentjes 1962a). Remains have been reported from Sotira (Zeuner and Ellis 1961), Khirokitia (King 1953), Shah Tepe (Amschler 1939), Oumm Qatafa (Vaufrey 1951, p. 201), and particularly from Mt. Carmel (Bate 1937, pp. 210ff.). The change in the relative number of bones of *Dama* and *Gazella* during successive periods of the late Pleistocene of Palestine was interpreted by Bate as evidence for a change of climate. Fritsch (1893, p. 18, cited by Bate 1937, p. 213) has reported *Dama mesopotamica* as having been probably present in Lebanon, and Lawrence (1956, p. 80) has reported the probable presence of this species in Mesopotamia.

The European fallow deer (*Dama dama* L.) has been reported from Tell Asmar in southern Iraq (Hilzheimer 1941) and was found in large numbers at Fikirtepe in northwestern Anatolia (Röhrs and Herre 1961), where it was the most important hunted animal. Fallow deer have also been reported at the late Pleistocene site of Ain Mallaha in Palestine (Perrot 1957, p. 109) and possibly from the site of Larissa in Thessaly (Boessneck 1965, p. 50).

Remains of red deer, *Cervus elaphus* L., excavated from sites in southwestern Asia, have often been referred to as the subspecies *C. e. maral* on the basis of the latter's geographical distribution in recent times, but no anatomical basis exists for such a subspecific designation. The proportion of bones of red deer in the faunal samples of several Near Eastern archeological sites runs as follows:

Site	Percentage of total sample of bone	Author and date of publication
Shanidar Cave	2.4-4.4	Perkins (1964, p. 1566)
Zawi Chemi Shanidar	8.9-24.5	Perkins (1964, p. 1566)
Belt Cave	ca. 1.3	Coon (1951, pp. 43ff.)
Bisitun	ca. 51.0	Coon (1951, pp. 43ff.)
Tamtama	ca. 66.0	Coon (1951, pp. 43ff.)
Hotu	ca. 8.0	Coon (1952, p. 243)
Shah Tepe	4.0	Amschler (1939, p. 81)
Argissa-Magula (preceramic and early ceramic)	ca. 1.0	Boessneck (1962, p. 81)
Matarrah	0.7	(p. 449)
Karim Shahir	7.1	(p. 451)
Jarmo	ca. 2.0	

Red deer have also been reported—but with no accompanying data—from Anau (Duerst 1908, p. 382), Alishar Hüyük (Patterson 1937, p. 296), Boğazköy (Vogel 1952, pp. 129f.), and Palegawra (Turnbull and Reed, pers. comm.).

At Jarmo, the only deer represented is *Cervus elaphus*; the fallow deer can be excluded on the basis of the smaller size of its bones, since nearly all the Jarmo remains come from very large animals. For comparison I had plaster casts taken of certain bones of a Persian fallow deer skeleton in Munich and made a series of measurements on them. Since the skeletal measurements of this species have not been published before, I give them in table 28 (see B, under *Cervus*). In particular, I compared the measurements of the Jarmo deer with those which Jéquier (Boessneck, Jéquier, and Stampfli 1963, pp. 74ff.) took on European deer of Bialowieza/Siebenbürgen and found that most of the bones from Jarmo reach at least the maxima as stated by Jéquier, and often exceed them.

The relative numbers of the deer at Jarmo correspond generally with those at the other sites listed above, with the exception of Bisitun and Tamtama.[7] Deer did not play an important role as a hunted animal in the early village-farming communities of the Near East; certainly it was not more important than the other hunted animals, such as wild cattle, wild pig, and onager.

I do not believe, from the sparse data presently available on deer, that conclusions can be drawn about vegetation—for example, that relative rarity of deer indicates a beginning or completion of deforestation or that any change in hunting behavior of the people concerned can be inferred.

ROE DEER

There are three antlers of roe deer which, judged by their basal circumference, must come from animals that are rather large for this species (cf. Boessneck, Jéquier, and Stampfli 1963, p. 104); in addition, one upper and one lower jaw were present.

Although roe deer are still present in northern Iraq (Hatt 1959, pp. 64ff.), their remains have rarely been reported from prehistoric archeological sites there or elsewhere in southwestern Asia. The bones of roe deer were, for instance, not found at Palegawra, although they were anticipated and carefully searched for (Turnbull and Reed, pers. comm.). Amschler's report (1939) of roe deer at Shah Tepe was based on only a few bones, as was the case with Jarmo. The possibility that this deer was not hunted, when other ungulates were, does not seem reasonable; it is true that the roe deer is small, but the meat is excellent, and one would expect that if this species had been present in any number, more of its bones would have been found in the excavations.

Measurements on such deer bones as were available are given in table 32 with the measurements of bones of various other animals.

CATTLE

The bones of cattle require special attention not only because the issue of whether wild or domestic forms were present is involved but also because they may be confused with the bones of large male red deer. Moreover, the possible presence of *Bison bonasus* L. has to be considered, since this animal was undoubtedly present in Iraq in the late prehistoric period (Hatt 1959, p. 67).

For the historian the proof of the first domestication of cattle is of great importance, since *Bos* was the first of the really large mammals to be domesticated. Apart from being important primarily as food animals, domestic cattle became the first common draught animals—a development that was a necessary cultural preadaptation for the spread of plough agriculture, with its accompanying economic and even political implications. Only the aurochs, *Bos primigenius* Bojanus, which lived in northern Africa and most of Eurasia, can be regarded as the ancestor of domestic cattle. In Assyrian times, as mentioned in the royal annals, the aurochs was still a common animal (Brentjes 1965, p. 33).

Any conclusion concerning the existence of domestic cattle at a prehistoric archeological site is based mainly on the size of the bones, the bones of small mature animals being regarded as those of the domesticated form. Nevertheless, differentiation between juvenile and mature animals tends to be difficult because, more than with many other populations of animals, the number of bones recovered is usually too small for reliable statistical calculations, a situation especially true for the earlier settlements. One reason for the dearth of cattle bones in these earlier archeological sites was the large size of the animals; wild cattle killed at any distance from a settlement would have had the meat stripped from the skeleton for easier carrying, and the bones would have been left at the kill site. In addition, wild cattle seem not to have been numerous in the Zagros region in the early post-Pleistocene and may not have been the prey of choice, considering their strength and fierceness and the abundance of other game. Even after domestication, cattle undoubtedly remained rather large for a somewhat longer time than did other animals upon being domesticated. The herds probably were small, and butchering was not frequent.

Since the distinction between domestic and wild animals in this early time range is dependent mainly on skeletal measurements, we require knowledge of the size variation of the bones of wild cattle. The normal ranges are given, especially in the studies by Bökönyi (1962) and by Boessneck, Jéquier, and Stampfli (1963). These figures refer to the European aurochs, but probably the Asian form (called *Bos namadicus* by Duerst and some other authors) differed very little from it.

The examination of remains of cattle is complicated by the fact that bison (*Bison bonasus* L.) and water buffalo (*Bubalus bubalus* L.) were both present in protoliterate Mesopotamia (Hatt 1959), and thus the possibility of their presence in earlier sites in southwestern Asia must always be considered.

The lack of reliability of some published claims of "domestic *Bos*" has already been discussed thoroughly by Reed (1960, pp. 141ff.). Often there were too few samples, or some of the bones were identified and published without explanations as to why they were considered to be those of domestic cattle (as in Vaufrey 1939, p. 197; Coon 1951, p. 44; Coon 1952, p. 243). Checking these data is now impossible in most cases, since the bones were usually not saved.

A survey of the literature reveals at once the degree of uncertainty in the identification of the remains of *Bos*. The normal ranges of size variations are unknown; often the animals are described simply as "small," "middle-sized," "medium-sized," or "large" *Bos*. However, efforts at overprecise systematics can also be found; remains of *Bos* from one or another particular area and time have been assigned to one or another race, a common tendency among earlier authors.[8] Today the trend is toward greater caution.

Bones definitely from domestic cattle can be found in most later sites, such as Alishar Hüyük (Patterson 1937, p. 307), Boğazköy (Vogel 1952, pp. 137ff.), Beersheba (Josien 1956, p. 725), Horvat Beter (Angress 1959, p. 68), Tell Asmar (Hilzheimer 1941, p. 46), Shah Tepe (Amschler 1939, pp. 91ff.), and Anau (Duerst 1908, pp. 359ff.). Bate (Mallowan 1946, pp. 124, 128; 1947, pp. 12f.) reported that cattle of different sizes were found at the sites of Tell Aswad, Tell Mefesh, and Brak.

A comparison of the measurements of domestic cattle, insofar as they have been published, shows that there is no uniform size and that most animals can be described as "medium-sized." Separation into two types, as was done for example by Angress (1959, p. 70), may sometimes be possible because of the great variability of domestic cattle. The uncertainty of such categorizations is evident in Duerst's work (1908). Amschler included male castrates as a distinct group in his discussion of bones of cattle from Shah Tepe. Such a group was probably to be found in all later settlements and it is one that presents further difficulties in exact identification. Röhrs and Herre (1961, pp. 114ff.) also reported domestic cattle from Fikirtepe, and there is no doubt that the bones of the smaller cattle they measured really were from domestic animals. But these authors themselves mentioned the continuous size range of the cattle bones recovered and remarked on the similarity in size of the larger specimens to those of wild cattle. Röhrs and Herre did not have available the studies of Bökönyi (1962) and Stampfli (Boessneck, Jéquier, and Stampfli 1963), whereby the normal range in size of wild cattle was established. Using these standards, I can state now that the largest bones previously assigned to domestic cattle from Fikirtepe were within the size range of the wild population. The percentage of the wild animals is thereby increased and accentuates the importance of the hunt for the supply of food of this settlement. If even a small part of the caprines at Fikirtepe were hunted, the proportion of wild animals could have been approximately 50%, similar to the situation at Jarmo.

The earliest available proof of domestic cattle comes from the preceramic level at Argissa-Magula, Greece (Boessneck 1962, p. 30); the level's radiocarbon determination is ca. 6500 B.C. (Watson 1965, p. 82).[9]

For the Near East, the publications on each of several sites present data on the percentage of the total number of cattle based on the recovered bones. Cattle were well represented at Fikirtepe and at Tell Asmar (20% and 19.7%, respectively) but accounted for less than 10% of the fauna at Tamtama, Bisitun, Ali Kosh, Karim Shahir, and in the preceramic levels of Argissa-Magula. All other sites reported show proportions between 10% and 20%, with most between 10% and 15%.

Jarmo belongs to the group in which cattle represented less than 10% of the total fauna; as a rough figure we can set 5%. It has to be taken into account, however, that the packages with remains of cattle do not represent a random distribution over the site. Hence the unrepresentative selection of the finds (see p. 432) has to be considered, especially since only a small part of the whole settlement was excavated.

It is absolutely clear, as matters stand, that at Jarmo no remains of domestic cattle have been found. All bones are clearly within the size range of those of *Bos primigenius*. Some are at or near the lower limit for known wild cattle, but this does not mean that they can be regarded as representing domestic animals. In contrast, an equal number of bones reach the upper limits in size; one distal fragment of a metatarsus sets a new record with its greatest width being 81.5 mm, which is 4.5 mm over the maximal value given by Bökönyi (1962, p. 202).

The bones of wild cattle from the upper levels at Jarmo have slightly smaller dimensions than do those from the lower levels. With considerable imagination one could claim that this indicates (or even proves) the beginning of a trend toward diminution in size and therefore the beginning of domestication. Such an interpretation, however, would be irresponsible in view of the small amount of material available for study.

The best proof that the aurochs existed at Jarmo is a horn core, probably of a female, which was salvaged in good condition (fig. 174:14). According to notes by Reed, made at the time of excavation, the external curve was 605 mm, but the tip of the core was broken after removal from the earth, so that the length of the outer curve of the remaining part is only 550 mm. The circumference at the base is ca. 300 mm. This horn core has a more pronounced twist than any other aurochs's horn core I have observed. Unfortunately, a fine specimen of an aurochs's skull from Jarmo has been lost (Reed, 1960, p. 142; see also Braidwood 1952, p. 30, fig. 21). I believe that it also was from a female.

Bison

Apart from Boessneck (1962, p. 31), no author has previously tried to distinguish the bones of bison from those of the aurochs in materials recovered from archeological sites in the Near East, although the possible presence of bison always has to be considered since in the protoliterate period this species was highly esteemed as an animal to be hunted (Hatt 1959, pp. 67ff.; Brentjes 1965, p. 34).[10] That bison was also hunted at Jarmo is shown by the presence of a few bones of this species at this site.

Ever since my study on the separation of *Bos* and *Bison* (Boessneck, Jéquier, and Stampfli 1963, pp. 117ff.), I have always been alert for possible remains of bison. There are, however, only a few fragments that can tentatively be identified as being from bison: a distal fragment of a humerus (fig. 174:13), an astragalus, and an os centrotarsale. The most important measurements (mm) and indices on the humerus fragment are as follows (the two indices cannot have absolute value for identification): greatest width, 100.0; greatest width of trochlea, 93.0; medial diameter of trochlea,

58.0; lateral diameter of trochlea, 38.0; *Verjüngungsindex* (index of diminution), 21.5; trochlear index (after Lehmann), 65.6.

SHEEP AND GOAT

The great importance of these small ruminants in the economy of the prehistoric as well as the early historic Near East has been illuminated mainly by Coon (1951), Zeuner (1955), and Reed (1959, 1960). Sheep and goats were also among the first animals to be domesticated, and their predominance is shown by the strong numerical representation of their remains in the following Near Eastern sites:

Site	Sheep and goat Approximate percentages	Site	Sheep and goat Approximate percentages
Tamtama	3	Fikirtepe	52
Bisitun	4	Ḥorvat Beter	85
Hotu	47	Beersheba	80
Belt Cave ("neolithic")	78	Shah Tepe	46
Shanidar Cave	97*	Tell Asmar	26
Zawi Chemi Shanidar	76*	Matarrah	60
Ali Kosh	41	Karim Shahir	56
Argissa-Magula (preceramic)	85	Jarmo	80

*These figures are based on the percentage of sheep and goats in a count which consisted *only* of bones of sheep, goats, and red deer—*not* considering any other fauna. Thus these figures cannot be directly compared with other figures in the table.

In the above list of sites, the bones of sheep and goats make up half or more of the total faunal list, save in the case of certain caves (Tamtama and Bisitun) and at the relatively late site of Tell Asmar. In the instance of Argissa-Magula in northern Greece, there is a high sheep/goat count in the preceramic level, but (based on smaller bone counts) the proportions of sheep/goat to cattle and pig bone counts vacillated as time went on (Boessneck 1962, p. 50 and table 1).

The bones of sheep and goat can in many cases be distinguished if they are well preserved. Even so, I consider both species together here because of the kinds of problems that arise, particularly in the examination of the horn cores. When examining bones recovered from early village-farming sites, osteoarcheologists have often concentrated on the horn cores; this emphasis is understandable since the rarity of intact skulls has usually made the characters of the horn cores the only clues available for determining race or discussing evolutionary changes as influenced by domestication. Earlier authors were often satisfied with one isolated unusual horn core upon which to establish a new subspecies or breed. It is true that transformations resulting from domestication show very quickly on the skull and maybe even sooner on the horns, so that perhaps such transformation can indeed actually be recognized by examination of the horn core. At the same time, however, the more unstable genetic structure of the domestic animal introduces a negative aspect in matters of identification, because changes in the shape of the horn and therefore of the horn core may result from relatively small changes of climate or food, or other environmental factors.

The research by Duerst (1926, p. 64) on environmental influences on the growth of horns is particularly well known; he discovered that size and shape of the horn depend directly upon the chemical composition of the animal's food and on the acidity of the soil. He stressed that the forming of the horns as a whole is undoubtedly a hereditary characteristic which can be a criterion of species, subspecies, and race, but that the final result depends very much on life-condition factors. What is important for this present study is his statement that the sinus structures in the horn cores (which, as we know, can be important aids in distinguishing sheep from goats) are dependent on the quality of the food. In a hot and dry climate, which has soil with a high pH value, an enlargement of the sinus spaces occurs, whereas under conditions of cold and damp the sinuses do not grow so large.

Duerst's investigations were made mostly on domestic animals; the results cannot be applied indiscriminately to wild animals, but the basic rules are probably similar. In a study like the present one, it must not be forgotten that in the course of several thousand years even the wild animals—in this particular case wild sheep and bezoar goats—could have undergone numerous changes, which might have been naturally induced by changes in climate and therefore also in vegetation. We have to consider possible changes in the structure of the skeleton and above all in the forming of the horn core. Unfortunately, we do not even know the variability of modern wild goats and wild sheep, but in my opinion such variability must be greater than expected, at least as far as the formation of the horn core is concerned. This variability can be seen by an examination of the three skulls of modern female wild sheep that were at my disposal as comparative material (fig. 175:6-8). All three came from the same area and all were fully adult, but their horn cores are of very different sizes and shapes. The comparative material available to me for the goat was more uniform, but this may be an accident of the sample.

There are a great many horn cores from Jarmo; most were collected by Reed in the third season, which shows clearly how much the presence of an expert at an excavation can enhance its results. Reed salvaged the cores by preserving them in papier-mâché jackets before removing them from the ground, or by gluing together some of the fragments that might otherwise have been scattered by the local workmen. These cores are important documents for the present work. Most of the horn cores recovered during the third season would have come from the upper-level test pits and hence cannot be related to a specific level in terms of the two major operations (I and II) of the earlier seasons. The horn cores recovered are extremely variable in size and shape, so that even assigning them to one or the other species—sheep or goat—often presents difficulties. A further problem is that most of the specimens are fragmentary, for example, the middle part of the horn core. However, even with the aid of cross sections of the cores one cannot in all cases definitely distinguish between the females of the two species (figs. 176-77). The structure of the surface and the size and extent of the sinuses may be aids in identification, but these characters are dependent on the age of the animal. An essentially sure determination is made possible by observing the angle between the base of the horn core and the midsagittal plane of the skull (fig. 179). However, a final identification will often be possible only after all available criteria have been taken into account. The difficulties are also increased by the presence of both domestic and wild animals and possibly transitory forms in the collection from any one site.

Although an identification of a "sheep" or "goat" may be possible in most cases, the separation of the domestic from the wild animal is unsatisfactory. Recently the horn cores of the goat have attracted added attention (Zeuner 1955). The changes in the appearance of the cross section and in the twist of the horn core have been cited particularly as criteria for domestication. Zeuner wrote (1955, p. 73) that the horn core of the male bezoar goat shows a more or less quadrangular cross section with sharp anterior keel and four surfaces (fig. 176). In the domesticated male the angularity of the external and internal surface disappears and is rounded so that the cross section assumes the form of an almond. In the female, however, domestic as well as wild goats have an almond-shaped cross section, and the anterior keel is often rounded.

The comparative material of modern goats available at Yale Peabody Museum was too limited for me to check all of these criteria. Two skulls of male goats were those of juveniles, but an adult male showed the characteristics described by Zeuner, and the horn cores of the skulls of females also corresponded to his descriptions. (Table 36 gives other measurements of the modern sheep and goat specimens available to me.)

There are no clear criteria in the literature for determining domestication in sheep, apart from the strongly curled horns that appear in male domestic sheep of later periods.

The Goat Horn Cores from Jarmo

Although there are many horn cores from Jarmo, not one corresponds to that of the modern male bezoar goat, *Capra hircus aegagrus* Erxleben, since none shows a clearly quadrangular cross section. In addition, only a few remains of female horn cores typical of *C. hircus aegagrus* can be found, so the suspicion may arise that there are no remains of wild goats, or only very few. This conclusion must be wrong, however, since there are remains which, because of their huge size, cannot belong to domestic animals. There are horn cores and parts of the skull with both horn bases (fig. 178:5-6) which must have belonged to extremely large and rugged male goats. In the best-preserved piece (fig. 178:3) the lower part of the right core has attached to it a part of the skull and a small remnant of the base of the left core. The bases of the horn cores may even touch anteriorly, and some skull fragments have a strong frontal part falling more or less vertically forward. No twisting can be observed, and the curvature seems to be less marked than in the modern bezoar goats.

These horn cores correspond in size and form to a male horn core from Jericho described and illustrated by Zeuner (1955, pl. VII, figs. 1a-b), which he declared to be the remnant of a domestic goat because it differed from the horn core of the normal male bezoar goat in having a large anterior diameter combined with an exceptionally small transverse diameter. He had not discovered any such cross section in any modern *C. hircus aegagrus*. But to me the size alone indicates the remains of a wild animal, and this particular Jericho horn core of Zeuner is absolutely the biggest horn core ever described. In addition, I do not believe that the flattening is necessarily a characteristic of domestication.

In the material from Jarmo there is a second group of horn cores of goats which are of considerable size (figs. 174:3,6; 178:4), but they are twisted and have a more rounded cross section. The anterior edge is sharp, the posterior edge more rounded. In the upper third they are two-edged and flat. Their cross sections therefore resemble those of wild bezoars but have less marked edges. The twisting, however, marks them as domestic animals. Judging by their size they must have belonged to males. The best-preserved piece (fig. 178:4) is an os parietale with the os occipitale partly preserved. However, the twisting is not so evident as it is in other pieces, but the angle between the two cores can be measured; it is approximately 18° (whereas that of a modern male bezoar is about 45°). The close positioning of the two horn cores is also striking in the skull fragments of the large male wild goats.

The other remains of goats' horn cores must have belonged to females, both wild and domestic individuals. A clear distinction cannot be made, but some few cores have the same cross section and are the same size as those of the modern female bezoar and are identified as such, although the possibility remains that they represent a variety of the female domestic goat. The greater number are cores with a clearly flat inner (medial) side, a form of cross section that has long been known. This form of core occurs in most European sites and has been mentioned previously for Jarmo by Reed (1959). However, the cores differ remarkably in size. Apart from many small and medium-sized examples (cf. figs. 175, modern; 178:7-10, Jarmo examples), there are a considerable number of larger ones that are too big for a bezoar but do have a flat inner side. I believe that they belong to the female of the large variety of wild goat mentioned above.

Even if we consider that a wild species—for example, the bezoar—can undergo changes in the course of thousands of years, we cannot assume such a strong change in the horns. Horns of sheep and goats change quickly under domestication but not in the wild, where size and form must be strongly hereditary, as Herre and Röhrs (1955) have stressed. The large, strong horn cores from Jarmo do not belong to *C. hircus aegagrus* Erxleben; instead they must belong to another wild subspecies. Nor, according to the illustrations in the study by Zeuner (1955, p. 79), do they belong to the male ibex of Sinai (*Capra nubiana* Cuvier), whose horn core has a rounded cross section. I cannot definitely identify this subspecies and so call it simply the "Jarmo wild goat."

As mentioned above, the appearance of flatness in a horn is not a definite mark of domestication. On the other hand, I believe that the twisted horns are excellent evidence for domestication, but one can never prove that such a twisting did not also occur in wild goats.

In the early stages of domestication, twisted horn cores can be observed only in the male. The identification of the female can be made only by size, but such identification is very uncertain if we consider that even wild goats may have rather small horns (see comparisons, fig. 180). Figure 180 shows the changes in the cross section of horn cores that result from domestication, depending on whether one takes the Jarmo wild goat or the bezoar goat as the ancestor.

In figure 181a, the female horn cores can be seen clustered in the lower left corner. The cores of the males show a greater scatter, correlated with the differences clearly apparent in the cross sections (figs. 176, 180). The chart is not uniform, because our base for comparison is small and pieces from different geographic regions and periods of time are being compared on the same diagram. The horn cores of the modern animals are noticeably among the smallest ones, or, in other words, the goats of Jarmo were much larger than goats are today. The biggest specimen is the horn core from Jericho described by Zeuner; the smallest is that of a modern wild goat. The limits of the areas that separate males from females and the domestic from the wild cannot be regarded as fixed.

Figure 181b shows, as well as the size (expressed by both the greater and lesser circumferences), the degree of flattening of the core; the flatter the cross section, the lower the specimen's position on the diagram. To the left at the top appear the few rounded horn cores of the females. Bad preservation may result in abnormal flatness, especially of the larger male horn cores which collapsed when buried under some depth of earth for several thousand years. These pieces have not been included in the diagram.

The Sheep Horn Cores from Jarmo

The variable forms of the horn cores in the modern comparative material have already been mentioned (p. 442). Cores of females are particularly variable and those of males change considerably with age.

The identification of the remains of female sheep in the material from Jarmo was difficult since the site yielded only a few fragments of frontal bones from which the angle of the horn on the skull could be determined. Of course, the more developed substantia spongiosa can be used to distinguish horn cores of sheep from those of goats, as can the flatter forms of the cross sections. On the other hand the structure of the horn-core surface in sheep is often rather like that of goats.

It is true that the horn sheath of the Field Museum's adult male sheep from Iran has a clearly triangular cross section, but that is not the inner, bony horn core (fig. 177), which is irregular in its cross section and shows a sharp posterior (caudal-lateral) angle. The juvenile animals have a much flatter horn core (fig. 175:3-4).

Fifteen pieces in the available Jarmo material could be identified as remains of male sheep; these differ in size and form and only four of them correspond to the comparative material. Most of them clearly show a cross section like a half circle; others are triangular, but there are also transitional forms and sizes (fig. 177).

Apart from the decrease in size and the strong twisting which appears later, I do not know of any characteristic typical of domestication in the sheep's horn core. The lack of any such characteristic, however, must not be used as a proof for nondomestication. The variability in the size and shape of the horn cores of these rams is too large for a wild population and would seem to indicate domestication. I believe that the smaller male cores come from domestic animals, although even in the males a clear separation cannot be made between domestic and wild, and in the females it is impossible to attempt to distinguish between the two.

Figure 182 shows the continuous transition from the smallest sheep horn cores (including those of the modern animal from Iran) to the largest representatives (including some from Jarmo). The separation of wild and domestic animals is naturally made more difficult by the possible appearance of castrated males. The broken lines in the chart indicating ranges in size are not meant to be exact.

The Other Sheep and Goat Bones from Jarmo

Here can be seen the same phenomenon as in the horn cores: most bones are larger than are those of the comparative skeletons. The biggest may well come from the male goats and sheep whose large size was indicated by their horn cores. However, we also have to include the possibility that remains of ibex may be present, since these animals may formerly have had a wider distribution in southwestern Asia than they do at present. For some bones such as the scapula, humerus, metacarpus, astragalus, and calcaneus a new maximum is reached (table 29). Otherwise there is a continuous scatter, as shown in figures 183 and 184. The continuous distribution is also visible in the diagram in figure 185 with regard to the lengths of the M_3's and the astragalus of sheep/goat.

A tabulation of the range in sizes of sheep and goat bones and horn cores is also provided (table 30).

Comparison of Sheep and Goat Bones from Jarmo with Those from Other Sites

Comparisons of the materials from Jarmo with those from other sites are possible only if previous publications have included measurements and pictures. Unfortunately, this has not always been the case.

The most interesting problem is whether the remains of the big wild goats with the flattened horn cores have been found in other excavations. The big horn core from Jericho, erroneously identified by Zeuner as that of a domestic goat, certainly belongs to the same type. I do not doubt that there were indeed domestic goats at Jericho, since the twisted horn cores, which Zeuner mentions and illustrates (1955, p. 77, fig. 4*a-b*), are definitive proofs of domestication. Another horn core of a large goat was found in Sotira (Zeuner and Ellis 1961, p. 235). How closely the remains of goats from Khirokitia (King 1953, p. 434) correspond to those of the wild goat of Jarmo cannot be decided positively, in spite of the description and the illustration. Certainly the Khirokitia cores form a wider angle—approximately 55° according to the illustration (King 1953, table CIV)—than do those of the present material, although King (1953, p. 434) also mentions "close" horn cores. I presume that the specimen from Khirokitia could be identical with the core from Jarmo, in spite of the larger angle. Aside from these large goats from Jarmo, the "normal" wild bezoar also existed in the Near East, as shown by study of the fauna at Sialk (Vaufrey 1939, pl. XXXII, fig. 6). However, the horn cores from Sialk are the only ones which correspond exactly to the available comparative material of male bezoars.

Medium-sized, twisted horn cores of goats have been mentioned more frequently, e.g., by Zeuner (1955, pp. 76f.), Vogel (1952, table 56, 19), Patterson (1937, fig. 249*E*), and Bate (Mallowan 1946, pp. 124, 128). One cannot doubt that such remains excavated at Boğazköy and Alishar Hüyük are from domestic animals, because of the relatively late date of these sites.

Smaller horn cores, clearly flat on the medial side, are mentioned equally often in the literature. These are usually attributed to female domestic goats. According to the measurements, examples as large as those of Jarmo were rare. Descriptions and illustrations can be found in Duerst (1908, pl. 76), Vogel (1952, table 56, 17), and Vaufrey (1939, pl. XXXII:5).

Discoveries of horn cores typical of female bezoars seem to be as rare as are those of the males. In the literature I could find only one clear example, namely no. 3 from Jericho (Zeuner 1955, p. 76), which Zeuner describes as "probably juvenile female."

Few reports have been made on the discoveries of horn cores of sheep that could be compared with our material, since drawings of the cross section are rarely included. There is a similarity between the large cores from Jarmo, the great horn core of Argissa-Magula (Boessneck 1962, p. 30), and the remains of wild sheep found in the cave "La Adam" in the Dobrogea (Rumania), which Radulesco and Samson (1962, pp. 292-95) illustrate. Otherwise, however, the available publications are not useful for comparisons.

Remains of a horizontal-horned breed at Tell Asmar are mentioned by Hilzheimer (1941, p. 37), at Ḥorvat Beter by Angress (1959, pl. IX), and at Toukh, Egypt, by Gaillard (1934, p. 84).

A comparison of the size of the bones shows that very big goats were both kept and hunted at Jarmo. Large caprines were also found at Fikirtepe, as were large wild cattle (p. 441); these finds strengthen the assumption that a greater percentage of wild animals were used at Fikirtepe than was originally published.

A comparison of the number of bones found does not lead to a satisfactory result even though the ages of the various sites noted above are taken into account. In some reports on settlement excavations, only the bones of goats are mentioned; in others, only sheep have been recorded. In addition, all combinations between these two extremes have been claimed.[11] In any case there is no proof of a predominance of the keeping of goats in the published statistics from the different sites. Probably, when domestication began, both the sheep and the goat were domesticated, one shortly after the other or perhaps both at the same time.

Claims for the presence of domesticated sheep or goats that predate such animals at Jarmo have been made for el-Khiam (Vaufrey 1951, pp. 215, 217) and for the late "mesolithic" of the Belt Cave (Coon 1951, p. 50) but with little supporting evidence. Similar reports from Zawi Chemi Shanidar (Perkins 1964) have greater credibility.

A final point, with regard to sheep at Jarmo: I must correct the report by Schachermeyer that mostly yearlings were found at this site (cited in Brentjes 1963, p. 8).

PIG

Until recently the small number of pig remains recovered and the uncertain proof of domestic pigs at prehistoric archeological sites in the Near East (Reed 1959, fig. 1) might have indicated that the meat of this animal was not favored or was even proscribed as food already in preliterate times. Brentjes's (1962*d*) study of sculptures and pictures, however, suggests that the pig played an important role in early oriental cults. Moreover, osteological evidence from recent excavations indicates that pig keeping was a part of the cultural patterns in the early Near East and the neighboring areas.

Although we have proof of the presence of domestic pigs as early as the seventh millennium B.C. (the "preceramic" of Argissa-Magula; Boessneck 1962), the fact remains that in all the known prehistoric sites in southwestern Asia and adjacent Europe pigs are rare. Although pigs may have been important for cults, they played a far less important role in the economy of ancient Near Eastern peoples than did sheep and goats, which were the main sources of meat and other animal products. This situation is in contrast to many European "neolithic" sites, where remains of pigs often far exceed those of the caprines. Flannery (1961b) identified domestic pigs at Banahilk, noting the existence of 14 domestic and 1 wild pig, as based on measurements of teeth. We can also asume that pigs had been domesticated by the time of phase B in the ᶜAmuq (p. 451).

In many sites, pig bones are only rarely found and some excavations yield examples that cannot be positively attributed to either wild or domestic pigs. Thus the domestication of the pig at el-Khiam (Vaufrey 1951, p. 217), at Sialk (Vaufrey 1939, p. 195), and at Tell Aswad (Bate in Mallowan 1946, p. 124) must be regarded as uncertain. Neither can I positively attest to the existence of a domestic pig in ᶜAmuq phase A, according to the present study (see p. 450). On the other hand there is clear proof of the remains of domestic pigs at the following sites: Shah Tepe (Amschler 1939, p. 73), Anau (Duerst 1908, p. 355), Beersheba (Josien 1956, p. 725), Tell Asmar (Hilzheimer 1941, p. 27), Boğazköy (Vogel 1952, p. 135), Alishar Hüyük (Patterson 1937, p. 302), Tepe Siahbid (Flannery 1961b), Fikirtepe (Röhrs and Herre 1961, p. 123). According to the results of my present examination of the bones, the pig can also be put on the list of domestic animals at Matarrah (contrary to the opinion of Flannery 1965, fig. 5). Discoveries of the wild pig are mentioned in the case of several other prehistoric and early historic sites. If a percentage is given or can be calculated, pigs are nearly always under 5% of the total count of fauna. The highest proportion of pigs in a Near Eastern faunal assemblage from an archeological site is 27% (all domestic) of the total bones recovered from Tell Asmar (Hilzheimer 1941, p. 27). Wild and domestic pigs together account for 25% at Matarrah, 14% at Fikirtepe, 10% at Argissa-Magula, and 5% at Shah Tepe. Distinguishing wild from domestic pigs is often possible only by the difference in their size. Such a decision cannot be based on the percentage of juvenile animals unless the sample includes a large number of bones.

In addition, distinguishing wild from domestic pigs on the basis of bone size is difficult since in most studies we deal only with the widths of parts of bones, which are often difficult to measure. Moreover, domestic pigs would often breed with wild ones, so that a population of prehistoric domestic pigs very often consisted of individuals of different forms and sizes. However, the decrease in size of pigs following domestication was rapid, a fact that makes differentiation easier. Also, rather early in the range of our interest here the percentage of juvenile bones increased, due to the higher fertility of the domestic sows, with the resulting possibility that there were many more piglets to be slaughtered.

Thanks to the studies of Opitz (1958) and Nanninga (1963), we are well informed on the variation in size of early historic European domestic pigs, and therefore on the lower size limit of European wild pigs. Unfortunately, there are fewer comparative measurements of wild and domestic pigs in the Near East. In his unpublished thesis for the M.A. degree, Flannery (1961b) recorded measurements of teeth of wild pigs, and these were published in part by Reed (1961, p. 32). In order to make Flannery's measurements generally available, I present here his list of the lengths of the upper and lower molars of 24 wild pigs from the Near East:

Lengths of M^3 and M_3 of Wild *Sus scrofa* from Southwestern Asia and Northern Africa (mm)

Catalogue no.	Provenience	M^3	M_3	Catalogue no.	Provenience	M^3	M_3
FMNH 92905	Iran	36.1	41.1	FMNH 84476	Iraq	35.5	37.6
FMNH 92906	Iran	33.2*	40.2	FMNH 44722	Syria	40.2	38.8
FMNH 92907	Iran	41.6	44.1	HUJ	Palestine	38.1	38.5
FMNH 92908	Iran	36.2	39.2	BPITA M681	Palestine	36.1	41.2
FMNH 92909	Iran	36.0	41.8	BPITA M683	Palestine	36.3	42.8
HBKW	Iran	37.3	40.8	BPITA M1346	Palestine	36.9	40.1
FMNH 42439	Iraq	38.8	40.2	BPITA M1849	Palestine	36.0	41.7
FMNH 42440	Iraq	37.3	41.9	BPITA M1928	Palestine	37.4	42.6
FMNH 43325	Iraq	35.5	41.2	BPITA MS/45	Palestine	34.1	39.4
FMNH 43327	Iraq	42.2	42.7	MNHNP 1880-608	Egypt	38.7	42.9
FMNH 46077	Iraq	42.8	49.3	MNHNP 1876-324	Algeria	36.6	35.0
FMNH 47417	Iraq	37.1	41.1	MNHNP 1912-542	Morocco	33.1	36.5

NOTE: Other measurements of modern pigs' teeth in the collections available to me are recorded in table 37. For abbreviations used, see p. 456.

*An original typographical error? Remeasurement showed this to be 36.2 mm.

I realize that Nanninga's measurements of domestic pigs in the middle European Iron Age cannot be applied directly to domestic pigs of the Near East. The diminution in size of domestic animals continued during much of the period in which animals were being domesticated; therefore the pigs of Manching on which Opitz and Nanninga base their studies may have been smaller than those of Jarmo. On the other hand these European studies were based on about 90,000 bones of pigs and are therefore very valuable comparative evidence.

A decrease in size of the wild form must have taken place too. This is evident in the measurements by Reed (1961, p. 31) and in those by Röhrs and Herre (1961, p. 113), which my own measurements confirm (table 28). The wild pigs of Jarmo were therefore somewhat larger than wild *Sus* living in southwestern Asia today. The maximal values by Nanninga on domestic pigs can therefore be used for establishing the boundaries of the ranges of the two forms.

Below I give the extremes of the ranges of measurements of some teeth and bones as published by the various authors mentioned and those from my own studies. These values illustrate the whole problem of distinguishing remains of domestic from those of wild animals according to their measurements.

Tooth/bone	Author	Measurement (mm)
M_3, length	Nanninga	39.0 (upper limit of domestic pig)
	Flannery	37.6 (lower limit of wild pig, not including specimens from northern Africa)
	Stampfli	37.0 (lower limit of wild pig)
M_3, length	Nanninga	36.5 (upper limit of domestic pig)
	Flannery	36.0 (lower limit of wild pig, not including specimens from northern Africa)
	Stampfli	34.5 (lower limit of wild pig)
Scapula, least width of collum	Nanninga	28.0 (upper limit of domestic pig)
	Stampfli	27.5 (lower limit of wild pig)
Humerus, distal width	Nanninga	44.0 (upper limit of domestic pig)
	Stampfli	47.7 (lower limit of wild pig)
Radius, proximal width	Nanninga	35.5 (upper limit of domestic pig)
	Stampfli	34.2 (lower limit of wild pig)
Astragalus, lateral length	Nanninga	42.0 (upper limit of domestic pig)
	Stampfli	47.0 (lower limit of wild pig)

Tables 24-26 show clearly that the percentage of pigs in the Jarmo fauna does not differ from that of other sites. From the lowest to the uppermost levels the pig (both domestic and wild) is poorly represented. We may calculate a rough average of 5%, which means a less strong representation of *Sus* than the first field examinations indicated.

Between the lower and the upper levels (table 26) there is a difference in that the later (upper) levels yielded seven times as many pigs as the earlier (lower) levels.[12] This difference is not accidental; it is due to domestication. The appearance of the domestic pig in the upper levels was already noted by Flannery (1961b) and Reed (1961, pp. 32f.), who based their opinion on examination of the teeth. However, a statement by Flannery (see Reed 1961, p. 32, fig. 1) must be corrected: the two M^3 specimens that were 40.5 mm and 43.2 mm long were found in the upper and not in the lower levels. The fact remains, however, that in the lower levels as exposed so far, only wild pigs have been found. On the other hand, the remains of a number of wild pigs also exist in the upper levels; these remains include other bones and not only the two teeth noted above. People were seemingly still hunting wild pigs as well as raising their own.

The transition from wild to domestic animal is as clear at Jarmo as at other archeological sites, and we do not necessarily have to consider the possibility of an importation of domestic pigs. However, the proof of domestication of the pig at Jarmo cannot be easily found in the table of measurements, since only the well-preserved (and thus only the adult) bones appear in it; these, naturally, are often the remains of wild pigs. Moreover, there are but few remains of really small animals; decrease in size following domestication had not yet progressed far. In addition, the value of the measurements of the size of the teeth often depends on the degree of interstitial wear between teeth; cheek teeth of older pigs hence become shorter. In table 31 only the measurements of teeth with slight or a moderate amount of interstitial wear are given; no teeth of very old animals are noted.

ONAGER

Eighty-five bones of equids were recovered, that is, 1.3% of the total number of bones from Jarmo; these do not provide sufficient data to solve the problem concerning the domestication of the onager. Opinions differ greatly as to whether domestication or the simple keeping of the species was involved. According to Hatt (1959, p. 34), the onager is very probably extinct in Iraq today. Herre (1958, p. 16) does not count it as among the domestic animals. Zeuner (1963, p. 367) reports that the ancient Sumerians domesticated it, but Brentjes (1965, p. 44) claims that it was never tamed in the Near East, only kept. According to Narr (1961, p. 284), it was probably already tamed in the fourth millennium.

In the sites being considered here, the greatest number of equid bones was found in Anau. Duerst (1908) attributes these remains to a new subspecies of the horse, but they are probably onagers. According to the most recent examination of the Palegawra bones, Turnbull and Reed (pers. comm.) think that all equid bones from that site belong to the onager, and none to horses or asses. The teeth from Sialk mentioned by Vaufrey (1939, p. 195) are also from onagers.

Equus sp., *Equus asinus*, or *Equus caballus* from prehistoric sites in the Near East have been identified by Coon (1951, p. 42), Amschler (1939, p. 54), Josien (1955, pp. 246ff.; 1956, p. 725), Boessneck (1962, p. 58), Patterson (1937, p. 309), Vogel (1952, pp. 133f.), Vaufrey (1951, pp. 198ff.), Angress (1959, p. 70), Reed (SAOC 31, p. 58), and Fraser (SAOC 31, p. 62). Distinguishing the ass, onager, and horse on the basis of bones and teeth is difficult. Some criteria of distinction have been proposed by Duerst (1908) and Hilzheimer (1941). According to Duerst the teeth of the asses have a different proportion of length to width than do those of onagers. But the ranges of the indices he gives (1908, p. 388) show strong similarities and often overlap. Even the total enamel pattern of the equid tooth is, according to Nobis (1954, p. 230), of small taxonomic value. I could not clearly recognize the metapodial characteristics observed by Hilzheimer (1941, pp. 9ff.) in a modern equid skeleton.

Of the 85 bones of onagers discovered at Jarmo, 53 come from one single findspot, J-I, 7fl. This is a striking example of how chance aggregations and accidental recoveries can influence the percentage representation of a species. A great part of this series is teeth whose proportions correspond to those of the onager.

The only well-preserved metatarsus and the remaining metapodial fragments of an equid tend to show the flattening of the lower end of the diaphysis and the backward curvature of the lower end of the metapodials, both characteristics being typical of this bone in the onager, according to Hilzheimer.

Measurements of the available bones of onager and of some of the less commonly encountered animals discussed below are given in table 32.[13]

FOX

Next to *Canis*, the fox is the most common carnivore at Jarmo. Most of the fox remains are upper and lower jaws, which allow some measurements. It is impossible for me to identify any subspecies. Hatt (1959, p. 38) assumed that the remains of fox at this site are to be assigned to *Vulpes vulpes flavescens* Gray. Table 32 gives measurements taken from foxes collected in the vicinity of Jarmo by Reed in 1955.

Foxes have been reported at several other excavations: Shanidar Cave, Hotu, Bisitun, Tamtama, Belt Cave, el-Khiam, Banahilk, Palegawra, and Argissa-Magula. Usually no measurements or descriptions have been given.

CAT

Discussion of the possibility of very early domestication of the cat in southwestern Asia was introduced by Zeuner (1958, pp. 54f.) following the discovery of an isolated lower carnassial tooth (M_1) of a small cat at Jericho. As Zeuner himself stressed, this discovery is no positive proof that cats were kept. Perhaps in the future the keeping or even domestication of the cat in prehistoric times will be inferred from the study of pictures and sculpture, but that possibility still remains unproved. For the present, therefore, we must continue to assume that cats first became domesticated in Dynastic Egypt.

The Jarmo excavations yielded four lower jaws and the proximal end of an ulna that could have been from domestic cat, but this judgment is based solely on size. Apart from size no distinctive characteristics can as yet be suggested. As long as there is no extensive comparative material on small wild cats, particularly on those still living in Iraq, a decision on whether these Jarmo examples were domestic or wild animals cannot be made. In my opinion the discoveries at Jarmo are remains of small wild cats (*Felis libyca*), which are to be found sparsely distributed in Iraq today (Hatt, 1959, p. 46).

LEOPARD

According to Reed's report (in Hatt 1959, p. 48), the leopard is rare in Iraq today; it is said to hunt wild sheep and wild goats. We may assume that it was more common in the past but had the same habits, so that it may have been killed occasionally by the people of Jarmo as an enemy of their herds.

The measurements for the Jarmo evidence are given in table 32. The identification of a distal fragment of a humerus, slightly too large for a leopard and too small for a lion, remains uncertain.

LION?

There is one piece of an epistropheus (axis) that could belong to a lion (table 32). The identification is not

LYNX

The lynx is said to exist today, its population greatly reduced, in the mountainous regions of Iraq (Reed in Hatt 1959, p. 47). In the Jarmo material one or two bones could be from this animal.

BADGER

The badger is still present in the foothills of Iraq (Hatt 1959, p. 43). The Jarmo bones include rather numerous fragments of the lower jaws of the badger, which correspond in size to those of the modern animal.

COMMON OTTER

One fragment of a lower jaw documents this species.

BEECH MARTEN

There is only one bone from this animal in the Jarmo collection: a fragment of a lower jaw.

POLECAT?

One lower jaw is very much like that of the modern polecat in size and form. Hatt did not mention this species in his monograph of the mammals of Iraq, but Turnbull and Reed (pers. comm.) found it at Palegawra.

HARE

Only a few fragments of bone testify to the presence of the hare, which is a very common animal today in the nonforested areas of northern Iraq.

NOTES ON OTHER SITES

MATARRAH

In contrast to Jarmo, Matarrah is not situated in the foothills but on the piedmont plain of north central Iraq. According to SAOC 31, p. 26, Matarrah represents "a somewhat impoverished southern variant of the Hassunan phase of culture." Since Hassuna was occupied soon after Jarmo, we can assume that the fauna would have been more or less the same, except for differences induced by environmental factors. Although only a few bones are reported from Hassuna, they confirm what was expected.

At Matarrah, as at Jarmo, bones of sheep and goats are present in great numbers. Probably most of these are of domestic animals; this assumption, however, cannot be proved osteologically. A huge molar is the only indication of a large and presumably wild caprine that was found at this site.

All the cattle remains, without exception, must be from the aurochs. In contrast, the bones of pigs are likely to be from domestic animals, a conclusion reached by means of their measurements and the percentage of juvenile animals. The pig at Matarrah represents 25% of the total fauna recovered. This large proportion perhaps shows an increasing importance of this animal in the local economy; the number of bones is, however, too small for statistical calculations. Information on the available Matarrah animal bones is given in the following two tabulations:

Counts and Proportions of the Matarrah Bones

Animals	Bones Count	%	Individuals Count	%
Gazelle	2	1.4	1	7.7
Deer	1	0.7	1	7.7
Wild cattle (aurochs)	15	10.0	1	7.7
Sheep	4	2.8	1	7.7
Goat	9	6.0	2	15.3
Sheep/goat	75	52.0	3	23.1
Pig	37	25.0	3	23.1
Fox	2	1.4	1	7.7
Total	146	100.0	13	100.0
Wild animals	20	13.5		
Domestic animals	126	86.5		

Measurements of the Matarrah Bones (mm)

	Gazelle	Wild cattle	Sheep	Goat	Sheep/goat	Pig
Humerus						
Distal width	23.0	--	--	24.0	32.0	39.0
Astragalus						
Lateral length	27.4	79.0	30.1	27.0	26.0, 28.9	40.0
Width of caput	16.0	52.0	18.4	16.0	16.0, 19.2	--
Metatarsus						
Distal width	--	70.0	--	--	--	--
Phalanx I						
Length	--	--	--	38.1	--	--
Proximal width	--	--	--	12.9	--	--
Phalanx II						
Length	--	52.0	--	--	--	30.0
Proximal width	--	35.0	--	--	--	--
M_3						
Length	--	--	--	--	23.5	--
Radius						
Proximal width	--	--	--	--	32.0	--
Tibia						
Distal width	--	--	--	--	26.0, 28.3, 28.4	29.0
Calcaneus						
Length	--	--	--	--	--	70.8
Ulna						
Least width of olecranon	--	--	--	--	--	24.2
Atlas						
Width of cranial facies	--	--	--	--	--	60.0

THE ᶜAMUQ

The ᶜAmuq is the area otherwise known as the plain of Antioch, which—when the Oriental Institute excavated there—was part of northwestern Syria. It is now politically a part of Turkey. Between 1932 and 1938, excavations were undertaken on several mounds, and a rather long overall sequence of assemblages extending from an early village-community phase (phase A) into the historical period was exposed. Description of the yields from several of the mounds that had earlier materials has been given by Braidwood and Braidwood (1960) and by Watson (1965). Certain bones saved from various levels were studied in part by J.W. Amschler of Vienna, who left an incomplete manuscript at the time of his death. (The ᶜAmuq selection had been sent to Vienna along with the 1948 Jarmo selection; see SAOC 31, p. 53, n. 6.) Reed (1959, p. 1631; 1960, p. 120) used Amschler's incomplete manuscript in his construction of chronological charts of the prehistory of Near Eastern domestication of mammals, and some data on pig teeth were incorporated into Flannery's unpublished M.A. thesis (1961b). What follows here is the first overall presentation of observations on the ᶜAmuq bones. The 349 bones available were distributed very unevenly throughout the different phases (table 33); unfortunately there are few remains from the early phases A, B, and C. Table 34 gives the measurements of the identified ᶜAmuq bones.

Phase A must date only slightly later than Jarmo, probably being contemporaneous with the occupation of Hassuna. Only 22 bones were available from the levels of phase A (table 33), and these represent cattle, goats, sheep, and pigs. Due to the small number of bones and uncertainty as to the basis for their selection,[14] no conclusions can be drawn concerning relative numbers of the original fauna. Cattle were represented by 9 bones; 8 of these were so large that they probably were from wild individuals, while one small astragalus may represent a young individual.

The bones of pigs, although not of large size, are still within the size range of wild individuals. One piece, a symphysis of a lower jaw, is of a size typical of the domestic pig, but I hestitate to certify domestication on the basis of a single piece of bone.

A fragment of a horn core of a goat has a flat internal side and the general size is considerable. It is of the same type as that already described as the remains of the female wild goat at Jarmo. Two horn cores, split longitudinally, belong to sheep. Whether they were from wild or domesticated animals cannot be determined.

According to the data by Amschler (see Reed 1959, 1960), the domestic goat was "probably present," but the domestic pig and cattle were only "possibly present." As indicated above, his statement may possibly be true for the pig, but in the sample available to me there are no certain remains of domestic goats or cattle in this level.

The general situation throughout the phase B range is similar; there are remains of cattle, pig, sheep, and goat, but here we can include the presence of domestic pig with greater certainty, for there are small bones and many remains of juvenile animals. According to Amschler the domestic sheep was "probably present" too, but the only two pieces that I can identify as being from that species could be from either domestic or wild individuals. Of the available remains of ᶜAmuq sheep from phases A to O, I cannot say positively that any were from domestic animals; of course, given the small sample available, this does not in any way prove that the sheep was not already domesticated.

In my opinion, the distal end of one phase B humerus of *Bos* is so small that it must be from a domestic animal. Similarly, two examples (a phalanx II and a phalanx III) are also small, as is an astragalus. However, with so few bones, and these probably dating from relatively near the time of the introduction of domestic cattle, one must be cautious in postulating domestication in the phase B levels. Thus, while I believe that at least a few of the bones mentioned above come from domestic cattle, final proof is still lacking.

The scarce material available from phase C makes definitive statements difficult. I presume that in this phase, in addition to the remains of domestic pig, there are also bones of domestic cattle; at least there is a metacarpus with a distal width of 66 mm that is too small for an aurochs.

From phase D up to the uppermost levels there is no doubt that domestic pigs as well as domestic cattle are present. Particularly in the case of cattle, the remains of the wild form become more and more rare in the later levels and finally disappear. Wild pigs seem to have been hunted throughout phase D, however, and also were crossed accidentally or intentionally with the domestic stock. In phases E and G, in addition to some bigger bones, there are bones of very small cattle, as small as those of the medieval cattle of Europe. This diminution in size is a very clear sign of continued domestication. In phase E, for the first time the existence of a domestic goat can be proved by a twisted horn core. As already mentioned, there is no proof of the domestication of the sheep. On the other hand, all of the remains of dogs from the ᶜAmuq are proof of the domestication of this species. Its bones are seen for the first time in phase D, a finding that corresponds to the data provided by Amschler (see Reed 1959, fig. 1). The dog is also represented in phases E, G, and N. In phase D there is a partial shaft of a femur from an animal about the size of a terrier, in phase E a fragment of jaw (length of M_1: 21.0 mm), and in phase G a humeral fragment (distal width: 32.1 mm).

For gazelle there are, among other remains, two horn cores (in phases M and N), each pierced at the base. These pieces may have served as ornaments or as tools. Because he found horn cores nearly exclusively, Hilzheimer (1941, p. 23) thinks that at Tell Asmar the gazelle was not a food animal but a cult animal.

The remains of fallow deer must have been trophies or material for tools since they are mostly antlers. Remains of red deer are also nearly exclusively antlers. The distal end of a metacarpus, very squat, may belong to the ibex, but I could not identify it definitively. Eight teeth (from phase G) belong to species of equid, perhaps onager. From a species of *Felis* (cf. *Felis pardus*, leopard) there are a fragment of a metatarsus and an upper canine of considerable size (phases G and O). An ulna is probably from a fox (phase H).

Karim Shahir

It is particularly unfortunate that the *whole* collection of animal bones recovered from the site of Karim Shahir (see p. 26) does not seem to have come finally to rest in the Field Museum of Natural History. SAOC 31, (p. 53, n. 6) suggests something of the circumstances involved. The Karim Shahir bones have been examined by several different scientists. The first examination was made by Barth, according to whom "the proportion of the bones of the potentially domesticable animals, especially sheep, goat and pig, was over 50%" (cited from Braidwood 1952, p. 26). Reed, after a brief examination of the collection in Vienna, agreed with Barth's identifications but questioned the proportions given. The material made available to me obviously does not contain all of the bones collected. I found none of the remains of the wolves, martens, and small mammals that Barth mentioned (SAOC 31, p. 53, n. 6). The major conclusion remains, however: there are no bones of domesticated animals. There are no remains of juvenile animals, and all the bones are of the size of the wild species. This is particularly evident in the remains of pigs, which all belong to large animals, and the bones of sheep and goats also belong mostly to large, powerful animals. Unfortunately there are no horn cores of goats, from which a better determination could be made concerning the wild or domestic state of this species. The sheep horn cores from this site come from wild sheep. While it is true that in the case of caprines it is not easy to distinguish wild from domestic animals by bone size alone, the complete absence of juvenile remains and the considerable size of the bones quite clearly indicate wild animals. Certainly there is no evidence of the existence of domestic goats or sheep in the collection I examined.

The remains of *Bos* are very fragmentary; this species is positively documented by only three bones. Two are from aurochs, while the third one must belong to a domestic animal, for it is of a slightly different color than the rest of the bones and I am convinced that it is intrusive and of modern origin—a distinct possibility in so shallow a deposit as Karim Shahir (p. 25). No domestic cattle were present at Karim Shahir. The bones of the caprines reach a proportion of approximately 47% of the total available to me, which is slightly lower than expected. This situation is due to the fact that the number of "unidentified bones" and the number of "various bones" is rather high.

Counts and Proportions of the Karim Shahir Bones

Animals	Bones Count	%	Individuals Count	%		Bones Count	%	Individuals Count	%
Gazelle	11	4.2	2	10.5	Boar	19	7.1	3	15.7
Deer	19	7.1	1	5.3	Fox	9	3.5	2	10.5
Wild cattle (aurochs)	9	3.5	1	5.3	Hare	2	0.7	1	5.3
Goat	3	1.3	1	5.3	Various (turtles, birds, etc.)	26	10.0		
Sheep	28	10.6	3	15.7	Unidentified	46	17.0		
Sheep/goat	93	35.0	5	26.4	Total	265	100.0	19	100.0

Measurements of the Karim Shahir Bones (mm)

	Gazelle	Deer	Wild cattle	Sheep	Goat	Sheep/goat	Wild pig
Horn core							
Circumference	--	--	--	195.0	--	--	--
Larger diameter	--	--	--	71.0	--	--	--
Smaller diameter	--	--	--	24.0	--	--	--
Scapula							
Least width of collum	14.5, 14.5, 16.0	--	--	24.0	--	23.0	--
Humerus							
Distal width	27.0, 27.3	--	--	32.0, 35.3, 37.0	--	34.5, 35.0, 36.5, 37.0	--
Radius							
Proximal width	--	66.5	--	--	--	41.5	--
Distal width	--	--	--	--	--	36.0	--
Femur							
Distal width	19.8, 27.0	--	--	--	--	--	50.0
Tibia							
Distal width	--	--	--	--	--	--	33.0
Astragalus							
Lateral length	28.7	--	--	35.5	--	32.2	46.0
Calcaneus							
Length	--	--	--	--	--	69.0, 74.0	--
Metacarpus							
Proximal width	19.8	--	--	--	--	--	--
Distal width	--	--	--	28.2	35.7	--	--
Metatarsus							
Distal width	--	--	--	30.0, 30.0	--	27.8	--
Centrotarsale							
Width	--	--	--	--	--	27.2	--
Phalanx I							
Length	--	--	--	43.0, 44.0, 46.5, 49.0	51.0	--	43.0, 44.0, 46.0
Phalanx II							
Length	--	45.5, 45.5, 46.5	39.0	--	32.0	--	--

According to the present material the people of Karim Shahir must have been only hunters and gatherers. The preferred animals for hunting were the caprines, followed by the deer, gazelle, and aurochs.

The information on the available Karim Shahir bones is tabulated on page 452.

DISCUSSION

The basic activity of the osteoarcheologist always remains the same: he seeks to identify the osteological materials anatomically and to determine the species to which they belong. He must approach his materials in different ways depending on the period from which the bones come. If the discoveries originated in the glacial or early postglacial era, that is, the time of hunters and food collectors, the problems of paleoenvironment (flora, fauna, climate) are the most important ones. The influence of man on other animals at that time must have been extremely small; at most, there was preference for hunting certain species.

The difficulties of evaluation become considerably greater when the discoveries come from the following period of early domestication. Now, interest focuses on the domestic animal as well. The osteoarcheologist's cooperation with the archeologist becomes more intensive and their joint conclusions are of particular importance in the field of cultural history.

Osteoarcheological studies of material from a third and last period, which continues to the present, shifts perhaps more into the field of pure zoology; animal domestication is completed, and the main focus is on the transformation of the domestic animal into new breeds.

The materials under discussion here come mainly from the second period. The main point of interest is domestic animals, particularly their importance and effect on the economy of early settlers. Naturally, at the same time, the problem of the transformation of the different species is involved. However, considerations of the natural environment and of changes in it are now more difficult to assess, because wild animals (which closely reflect the environment) have now lost their importance in the economy and are no longer so clearly evidenced in the bone samplings.

By providing objective assessment of the evidence for the existence of domestication the osteoarcheologist contributes to the reconstruction of the second period. His work has therefore a significance that far exceeds anatomical-zoological description alone. In the present study, I have shown how difficult objective assessment can be, for example, in the distinction between domestic or wild animal. The study is made even more difficult by further circumstances: all bones found (except those in graves or of sacrificed animals—not the case at our sites) are common food scraps. These do not necessarily reflect the natural milieu of the fauna of a site's immediate surroundings; they do not even show the real picture of the settlement's domestic world. The inhabitants' preference for or rejection of certain species as food means that the remains recovered from an archeological site may well present an incorrect picture of the biota at the time of occupation. Reed (1957) introduced the term "cultural filter" to cover all the human mechanisms that create bias in all studies of biological remains excavated from archeological sites. The rarity of remains of dogs discovered in sites occupied during the late prehistoric period in the Near East may be one result of such a cultural filter. From the paucity of evidence one must not necessarily conclude that there were only a few dogs. Dogs may even have had great importance as food animals, or their carcasses may have been discarded or buried outside the settlement.

Furthermore, it also has to be taken into account that only part of the potential remains has so far been recovered. Even when a settlement is completely excavated, which has not yet been done at any site in southwestern Asia, we possess only a fraction of the original garbage, the composition of which may have been subject to various circumstances producing bias. Some bones were eaten by dogs, and many decayed in a short time, particularly those of any juvenile animals or birds that might have been present. In the case of almost any animal, only certain resistant pieces are preserved, and then only under particular soil conditions.

Even were we to assume the existence of primitive hygienic practices we would still need to suppose that part of the settlement's trash was deposited in dumps or at least somewhere outside the settlement. How little of the original total may remain to be discovered is shown by reports from the site of Egolzwil 5 in Switzerland, where the excavators calculated that only 1% of the original bones had been preserved (Stampfli 1976). An even smaller number of bones, considering the duration of the settlement, appeared in a Roman villa (Stampfli 1968). We can conclude that the osteoarcheologist's material may be composed only of more or less carelessly discarded food waste that did not find its way to the regular dump.

The above statements show clearly that the collection of all bones is of great importance, so that we can exclude accidental situations insofar as is possible. We must not forget that different types of remains may have been deposited very randomly over the whole area of a site and that the area of excavation will generally be only a sample.

In spite of these limiting factors, however, it is possible to make important statements from a small number of bones. Thus a few bones of small cattle can demonstrate the domestication of this species, and the same would hold for the bones of small animals such as the dog and pig. To demonstrate sheep and goat domestication is more difficult, however; statistical calculations require a larger number of bones than are usually recovered.

The osteological remains from the excavations in the Near East are not uniform, even if place and time are taken into account as important factors. I think it is possible that settlements of the same period and situated in the same geographical area can show a different degree of husbandry. Also, at different sites the hunting of different animals may have been preferred. Such striking differences also occur in some European "neolithic" sites (Stampfli 1964). Therefore I do not believe that any *one* species was necessarily domesticated first. The goat certainly is one of the earliest domestic animals, at least in the Near East, but the sheep was probably domesticated at the same time. This should not surprise us, since Perkins (1964) has presented evidence at Zawi Chemi Shanidar that this species was an early domesticate.

Many of the caprines at Jarmo may have been wild animals, as the hunt appears to have been of greater importance to this settlement than heretofore assumed. This fact does not necessarily indicate a lower stage of cultural development than was previously assumed. Hunting and domestication certainly coexisted for a long time, since at first sufficient meat could not be supplied by domestic animals alone. At Jarmo, the hunt took place in the mountains as well as on the plains, in the woodlands as well as on the open steppe, and we assume that from time to time hunting expeditions were made into more distant regions. Of course, wild sheep and wild goat may at that time have lived near the settlement; if so, that circumstance probably contributed to an easier transition of the animals from wild to domestic. If one is attempting to reconstruct the environment from the osteological material, hunting techniques and hunting preferences must be taken into account, and these problems are not yet solved.

Undoubtedly, domestic animals were kept at Jarmo, but how intensive the domestication was cannot be concluded from the bones recovered. The horn cores of goats show considerable change from those of the wild species, and the first stage of domestication seems to have passed, but we must not forget that the identifying characteristics of domestication may have appeared very rapidly, possibly more so in one species than in another. The bones of pig and sheep indicate a rather early stage of domestication or perhaps a lack of human emphasis on manipulating these animals in favor of the goat. The fact that the available remains of domestic pig can be found only in the upper levels suggests that this species probably became domesticated at Jarmo during the life of the settlement.

Evidence for the domestication of cattle cannot be established at Jarmo. In the Near East this species was seemingly domesticated late; once cattle were domesticated, however, the diminution in size must have progressed quickly, as can be seen in the rather sparse material from the ᶜAmuq.

Although we do know something of the early development of the village-farming cultures in the Near East, any real synthesis of the development of animal domestication is still impossible. We cannot say today where in the Near East domestication first occurred or which species became the first domestic animal. Equally obscure are the motives or cultural happenstances that led to domestication. No one can deny that the Near East was an area of early animal domestication, but the discovery of domestic pigs and domestic cattle at an early date in Thessaly has raised anew the question of domestication of different species in different places. Discoveries in Anatolia could bring more surprises. In addition, we are still almost totally uninformed about the early domestic animals in southern and eastern Asia. The important discoveries in the Near East have been made only in the last two decades and are both too recent and too incomplete to allow us to definitely solve the problems of early domestication.

SUMMARY

General

1. This examination is based on the nonhuman bones excavated at the archeological sites of Jarmo, Matarrah, the ᶜAmuq sites, and Karim Shahir.
2. Some differences between the bones of gazelle, roe deer, and sheep/goat are discussed.
3. The distinguishing criteria of the bones of domestic mammals recovered from archeological excavations are discussed.
4. The results are compared with those of other sites of late prehistoric to early historic time in the Near East and neighboring regions.

Jarmo

1. The percentage of wild animals is larger than was previously assumed.
2. In the lower levels, and in the upper levels as well, goats and probably also sheep appear to have included domesticated as well as wild forms. Domestic pigs were found only in the upper levels. Cattle were not domesticated at this time.
3. The percentage of juvenile animals is not high at any level.
4. Between the lower and upper levels no significant differences in the fauna could be established except for the apparent decrease in frequency of the onager and the appearance of domestic pig.
5. The incidence of gazelle is less frequent than previously assumed. Keeping or herding of this species could neither be proved nor denied.
6. All remains of cervids belong to red deer and roe deer. Remains of the fallow deer (*Dama dama* or *Dama mesopotamica*) could not be found.

7. All remains of *Bos* are those of wild cattle.
8. The presence of remains of the typical modern male bezoar (*Capra hircus orientalis*) could not be proved; the remains of wild goat belong to another subspecies. Thus the origin of the domestic goat could not be clarified.
9. The variability of horn cores of male sheep indicates that this species was probably domesticated.
10. Sheep and goats were of considerable size.
11. The wild pig appears in the lower and upper levels, the domestic pig only in the upper levels. There is some overlap in size between wild and domestic individuals.
12. All equid bones probably belong to the onager.
13. The large canids at Jarmo have been shown to have been dogs, not wolves as was previously thought (chap. 10).
14. Domestication of the cat could neither be proved nor denied, but seems improbable.

MATARRAH

1. Probably all remains of sheep and goats are of domestic animals.
2. The bones of *Sus* are those of the domestic pig.
3. All bones of *Bos* belong to wild cattle.

THE ᶜAMUQ

1. In phase A the remains of goats, sheep, and cattle are all from wild populations. The existence of domestic pigs is very unlikely.
2. In phase B the pigs and the cattle were probably domesticated.
3. Definite statements on phase C are impossible due to the lack of material.
4. Phases D-O contain remains of domestic cattle, domestic pigs, domestic sheep, and domestic goats.
5. The domestic dog appears for the first time in phase D.

KARIM SHAHIR

There is no proof for domestication of any species; domestication of sheep and goat cannot be totally ruled out, but it is improbable.

NOTES

1. Although I have reasonable familiarity with the osteology of bovids, I, too, made a mistake early in the present study, identifying two first phalanges of deer as being from cattle.

2. Horses are one exception to this general rule, but they are not discussed here. There is another exception, of course: certain highly bred races of several domestic species that were developed only in the last century. Temporary increases in body sizes can also be observed from time to time in animals in other eras, as for example the Roman period in Europe.

3. [*Mea culpa!* However, a careful reading of my 1952 paper does show that my overly facile generalization was based solely on the *field* identifications made by Fredrik Barth during the 1950-51 season. Barth, then a young graduate student with some training in mammalian paleontology, has, since that time, gone on to a highly distinguished career in cultural anthropology. The facile generalization was mine, not his. —RJB]

4. [Stampfli's analysis of the relative absence of onager remains in the upper levels coincides with my own experience at Jarmo in the spring of 1955. I had seen the faunal collections of 1948 and 1950-51 in Amschler's laboratory in Vienna, and equid bones and teeth were definitely present although not numerous. When the excavation was renewed in 1955, however, we recovered no equid bones at all during the first several weeks.—CAR]

5. Contrary to the opinion of Flannery (1961a, p. 10), I consider 25% of yearlings for a completely hunting economy to be too high.

6. *Gazella gazella arabica* at Horvat Beter (Angress 1959, p. 58). Bate assumed that there were several kinds of gazelle in Wadi el-Mughara (1937, p. 216).

7. Coon (1951, p. 35) mentioned that the greater part of his sample consisted of fragments of shafts of long bones, which he at first believed were remains of equids. The identification of shaft fragments is known to be difficult.

8. See, for instance, articles by Duerst (1908) and Amschler (1939); the latter created a new subspecies—*Bos brachyceros arnei*—but these remains probably come from a female aurochs. See also Imhof (1964, p. 157).

9. The existence of domestic cattle at el-Khiam is not proved. Vaufrey (1951, p. 215) himself left the definition "domestic cattle" open.

10. According to Bate (1937, p. 216), Fritsch (1893, p. 37) proved *Bison* as well as *Bubalus* in Syrian cave deposits. *Bubalus* remains are mentioned by Lawrence (1956, p. 80).

11. Zeuner did not find any remains of sheep at Jericho and concluded that a minimum characteristic of the "neolithic" is the existence of only two domestic animals, namely the goat and the dog. I cannot agree with any such definition of the "neolithic" as based upon the presence of any two or more domestic animals.

12. [It is true that in the major exposures shown in table 26 (operations J-I and J-II) there were about seven times as many pig bones in the upper as in the lower levels. (Indeed, the overwhelming bulk came from the two uppermost levels of J-II.) At the same time it should be noted that about twice as large an area was exposed in the upper as in the lower levels in these two operations.—EDS.]

13. [Stampfli did not treat the evidence for the wolf and dog (see the Lawrence-Reed report, chap. 10) nor did he have all of the available evidence for the birds and smaller mammals (see Turnbull's report, chap. 11).—EDS.]

14. [Phase A and phase B materials came from a water-logged operation of very restricted size; phase C materials came from a still smaller area (Braidwood and Braidwood 1960, table 1).—EDS.]

ABBREVIATIONS FOR TABLES 24-37

AMNH	American Museum of Natural History, New York
BPITA	Biological-Pedagogical Institute, Tel Aviv
FMNH	Field Museum of Natural History, Chicago (for a short while called Chicago Natural History Museum)
HBKW	Hochschule für Bodenkultur, Vienna
HUJ	Hebrew University, Jerusalem
MCZ	Museum of Comparative Zoology, Harvard University, Cambridge, Mass.
MNHNP	Musée national d'histoire naturelle, Paris
YPM	Peabody Museum, Yale University, New Haven, Conn.
L	greatest length (if not otherwise noted)
W	greatest width (if not otherwise noted)
Lw	least width
C	circumference
Ø	diameter (if a horn core, at the base)
T	greatest thickness
H	height
Lr	larger
Sr	smaller
A	measurement on the alveolus
prox	proximal
dist	distal
lat	lateral
Ⓜ₃	M₃ not yet broken through
M₃↑	M₃ breaking through
w	wild
d	domestic
♂	male
♀	female
☿	castrate

All measurements are in millimeters.

Table 24.—Count of Identified Bones for Each Part of the Body of the More Important Nonhuman Mammals from Selected Upper Findspots at Jarmo

Bone	Cervus	Bos	Capra	Ovis	Capra/Ovis	Sus
Horn core, antler	7	4	28	2	8	--
Skull (part)	--	12	23	2	96	1
Upper tooth	--	1	--	--	256	7
Lower jaw	1	2	--	--	151	6
Lower tooth	--	4	--	--	170	6
Vertebra	--	5	1	2	111	--
Rib	--	2	--	--	46	--
Front leg	8	13	83	34	265	10
Hind leg	4	8	67	22	395	7
Phalanx	2	1	27	5	14	5
Miscellaneous	--	22	--	--	50	--
Total	22	74	231	67	1,562	42

Table 25.—Count and Percentages of Bones from Different Mammals from Various Upper Level Contexts in J-I,3 and from Several of the Test Squares at Jarmo

Species	Bone		Individuals			
			Total		Juvenile	
	Count	%	Count	%	Count	%
Gazelle	23	1.1	8	6.3	1	12.5
Red deer	22	1.1	4	3.1	--	--
Wild cattle	74	3.6	6	4.7	--	--
Goat (wild and domestic)	231	11.3	21	16.5	--	--
Sheep (wild and domestic)	67	3.2	10	7.9	--	--
Goat and/or sheep (wild and domestic)	1,562	76.6	62	48.8	16	26.0
Pig (wild and domestic)	42	2.1	8	6.3	4	50.0
Onager	1	0.1	1	0.8	--	--
Wolf and dog	11	0.5	3	2.4	--	--
Fox	3	0.2	2	1.6	--	--
Leopard	1	0.1	1	0.8	--	--
Hare	1	0.1	1	0.8	--	--
Total	2,038	100.0	127	100.0	--	--
Wild animals	761	38.0	58	46.0		
Domestic animals	1,277	62.0	69	54.0		

Table 26.—Count and Percentages of All of the Identified bones of Mammals (except Rodents) from Various Jarmo Findspots

Species	Operations I and II				Other Operations		Total	
	Lower levels		Upper levels					
	Count	%	Count	%	Count	%	Count	%
Gazelle (*Gazella subgutturosa* Güldenstädt)	83	5.9	136	4.0	49	2.7	268	4.0
Red deer (*Cervus elaphus* L.)	35	2.5	89	2.6	13	0.7	137	2.0
Roe deer (*Capreolus capreolus* L.)	--	--	2	0.1	3	0.2	5	0.1
Wild cattle (*Bos primigenius* Bojanus)	126	8.9	103	3.0	30	1.7	259	3.9
Wisent, bison (*Bison bonasus* L.)	--	--	1	--	5	0.3	6	0.1
Goat, wild and domestic (*Capra aegagrus* Erxleben? and *C. hircus* L.)	82	5.8	294	8.5	177	10.0	553	8.3
Sheep, wild and domestic (*Ovis orientalis* Gmelin and *Ovis aries* L.)	72	5.1	117	3.4	88	5.0	277	4.2
Goat and/or sheep (*Capra* and/or *Ovis*)	884	62.4	2,401	69.6	1,305	73.2	4,590	69.0
Pig, wild and domestic (*Sus scrofa* L. and *Sus domesticus* L.)	33	2.3	241	7.0	63	3.5	337	5.1
Syrian onager (*Equus hemionus* cfr. *hemippus* Geoffroy)	72	5.1	13	0.4	--	--	85	1.3
Wolf and dog (*Canis* sp.)	10	0.7	26	0.7	9	0.5	45	0.7
Fox (*Vulpes vulpes* L.)	12	0.8	8	0.2	23	1.3	43	0.6
Wild cat (*Felis libyca*)	2	0.1	2	0.1	3	0.2	7	0.1
Leopard (*Felis pardus* L.)	1	0.1	3	0.1	--	--	4	0.1
Lion? (*Felis leo* L.?)	--	--	1	--	--	--	1	--
Lynx (*Lynx lynx* L.)	1	0.1	1	--	--	--	2	--
Badger (*Meles meles* L.)	2	0.1	11	0.3	10	0.6	23	0.3
Common otter (*Lutra lutra* L.)	--	--	--	--	1	--	1	--
Beech marten (*Martes foina* Erxleben)	--	--	--	--	1	--	1	--
Polecat? (*Mustela putorius* L.?)	--	--	--	--	1	--	1	--
Hare (*Lepus* sp.)	1	0.1	1	--	2	0.1	4	0.1
Total	1,416	100.0	3,450	100.0	1,783	100.0	6,649	100.0
Wild animals	696	49.0	1,369	40.0				
Domestic animals	720	51.0	2,081	60.0				

Table 27.—Occurrences of Various Identified Mammals from a Variety of Sites in Southwestern Asia and from One Aegean Site, Arranged in *Very* Rough Chronological Order

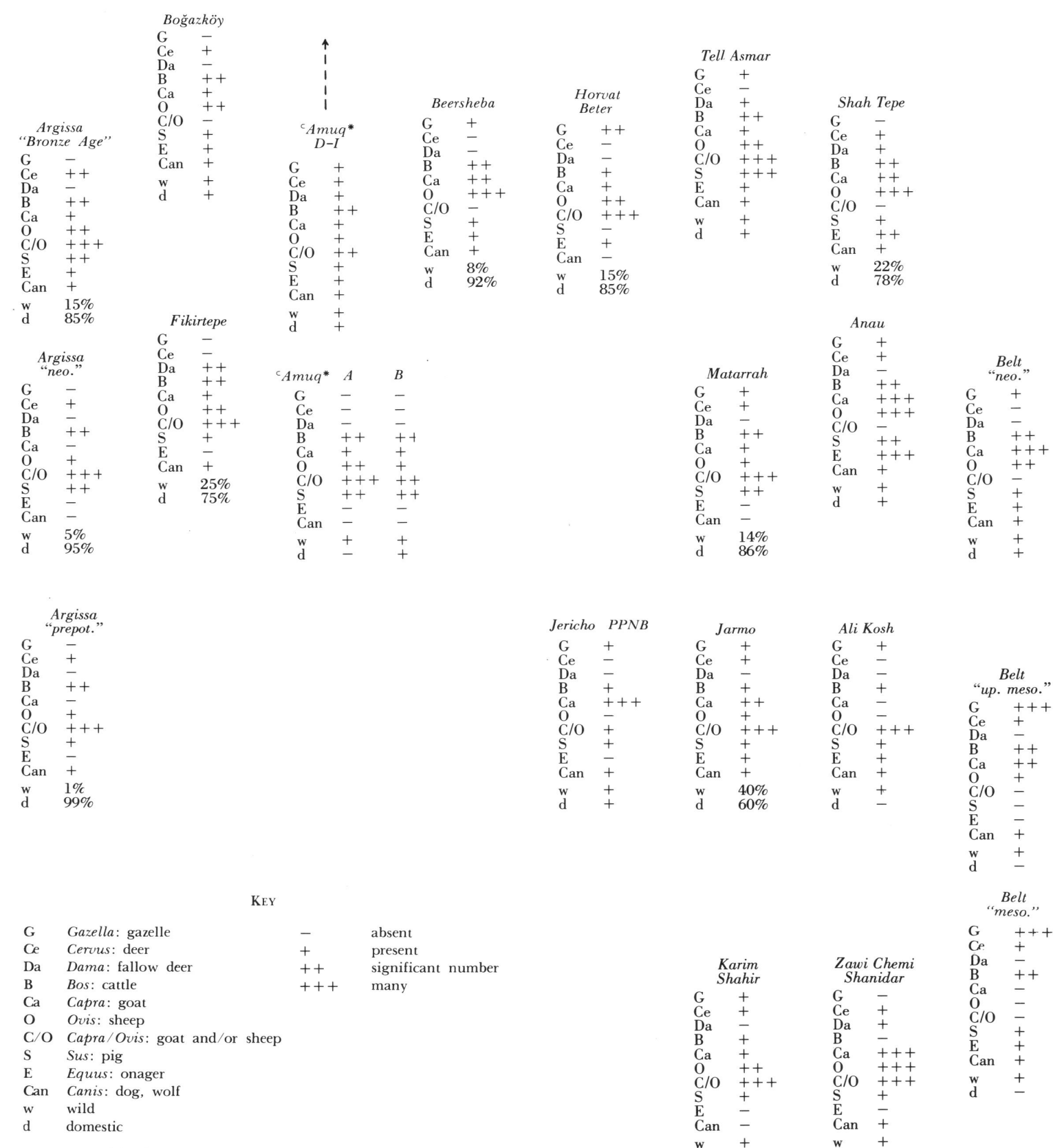

Table 28.—Measurements of Identified Bones of Gazelles, Deer, Bovines, Pigs, and Equids from Jarmo and Some Comparative Measurements

		Horn Core			M₃	Scapula	Humerus		Radius	Metacarpus		Pelvis	Femur	Patella	Tibia		Astragalus		Calcaneus	Centro-tarsale	Metatarsus		Phalanx I		Phalanx II	
Taxon	L	C base	Lr Ø	Sr Ø	L	Lw col	Dist W	Prox W	Dist W	Prox W	Dist W	Ø acet	Dist W	L	Prox W	Dist W	Lat L	W cap	L	W	Prox W	Dist W	L	Prox W	L	Prox W
Gazella																										
	--	87	28	23	17.0	15.8	25.5	25.9	--	19.2	23.0	20.5	--	--	--	21.5	25.0	13.9	--	21.2	19.2	21.5	36.6	10.6	--	--
	--	92	31	23	17.5	16.1	26.0	26.6	--	(21.0)	--	--	--	--	--	22.8	26.0	16.0	--	--	20.5	--	37.3	9.9	--	--
	--	95	32	22	17.9	16.2	26.8	--	--	--	--	--	--	--	--	23.2	26.4	16.0	--	--	--	--	38.8	10.2	--	--
	--	95	35	23	18.0	17.0	27.0	--	--	--	--	--	--	--	--	--	26.8	17.5	--	--	--	--	40.8	9.8	--	--
	--	95	33	23	18.2	--	27.0	--	--	--	--	--	--	--	--	23.5	26.8	15.5	--	--	--	--	--	--	--	--
	--	95	33	23	18.2	--	27.5	--	--	--	--	--	--	--	--	--	27.0	15.1	--	--	--	--	--	--	--	--
	190	95	34	22	18.2	--	27.8	--	--	--	--	--	--	--	--	24.0	27.4	17.8	--	--	--	--	--	--	--	--
	--	95	32	22	18.5	--	28.2	--	--	--	--	--	--	--	--	--	27.8	16.9	--	--	--	--	--	--	--	--
	--	95	33	24	18.5	--	28.2	--	--	--	--	--	--	--	--	25.1	27.8	17.2	--	--	--	--	--	--	--	--
	--	95	30	24	18.6	--	--	--	--	--	--	--	--	--	--	25.5	27.8	16.2	--	--	--	--	--	--	--	--
	--	95	33	23	19.0	--	--	--	--	--	--	--	--	--	--	--	--	--	--	--	--	--	--	--	--	--
	--	--	(35)	(24)	19.0	--	--	--	--	--	--	--	--	--	--	--	--	--	--	--	--	--	--	--	--	--
	--	100	33	23	19.1	--	--	--	--	--	--	--	--	--	--	--	--	--	--	--	--	--	--	--	--	--
	(155)	100	34	28	19.2	--	--	--	--	--	--	--	--	--	--	--	--	--	--	--	--	--	--	--	--	--
	150	100	34	25	19.2	--	--	--	--	--	--	--	--	--	--	--	--	--	--	--	--	--	--	--	--	--
	165	110	38	28	19.4	--	--	--	--	--	--	--	--	--	--	--	--	--	--	--	--	--	--	--	--	--
	140	100	35	25	19.5	--	--	--	--	--	--	--	--	--	--	--	--	--	--	--	--	--	--	--	--	--
	--	100	36	26	20.0	--	--	--	--	--	--	--	--	--	--	--	--	--	--	--	--	--	--	--	--	--
	--	100	37	25	--	--	--	--	--	--	--	--	--	--	--	--	--	--	--	--	--	--	--	--	--	--
	160	(100)	—	(23)	--	--	--	--	--	--	--	--	--	--	--	--	--	--	--	--	--	--	--	--	--	--
	140	100	34	24	--	--	--	--	--	--	--	--	--	--	--	--	--	--	--	--	--	--	--	--	--	--
	--	100	34	25	--	--	--	--	--	--	--	--	--	--	--	--	--	--	--	--	--	--	--	--	--	--
	--	100	38	25	--	--	--	--	--	--	--	--	--	--	--	--	--	--	--	--	--	--	--	--	--	--
	150	100	35	25	--	--	--	--	--	--	--	--	--	--	--	--	--	--	--	--	--	--	--	--	--	--
	165	105	38	25	--	--	--	--	--	--	--	--	--	--	--	--	--	--	--	--	--	--	--	--	--	--
	150	105	37	28	--	--	--	--	--	--	--	--	--	--	--	--	--	--	--	--	--	--	--	--	--	--
	--	105	35	26	--	--	--	--	--	--	--	--	--	--	--	--	--	--	--	--	--	--	--	--	--	--
	--	105	37	26	--	--	--	--	--	--	--	--	--	--	--	--	--	--	--	--	--	--	--	--	--	--
	--	105	36	25	--	--	--	--	--	--	--	--	--	--	--	--	--	--	--	--	--	--	--	--	--	--
	--	110	38	25	--	--	--	--	--	--	--	--	--	--	--	--	--	--	--	--	--	--	--	--	--	--
	165	110	38	28	--	--	--	--	--	--	--	--	--	--	--	--	--	--	--	--	--	--	--	--	--	--
	--	110	38	29	--	--	--	--	--	--	--	--	--	--	--	--	--	--	--	--	--	--	--	--	--	--
	--	(120)	(42)	31	--	--	--	--	--	--	--	--	--	--	--	--	--	--	--	--	--	--	--	--	--	--
A	175	90	31	22	18.5	14.2	24.2	23.0	21.6	19.2	18.8	23.8	29.4	24.2	32.4	20.0	25.0	14.8	53.4	19.3	18.2	19.1	33.5	9.8	17.6	8.2
Cervus																										
	--	--	--	--	--	(31.5)	58.0	64.0	60.0	49.5	(48)	(66)	(73)	(60)	(83)	52.0	57.0	38.0	--	44.8	--	--	60.5	26.0	41.0	21.0
	--	--	--	--	--	34.5	60.0	64.8	(62)	50.5	--	--	--	--	--	--	58.0	35.5	--	51.5	--	--	--	--	46.5	24.0
	--	--	--	--	--	42.0	60.0	--	(65)	--	--	--	--	--	--	--	61.5	35.5	--	--	--	--	--	--	48.0	24.0
	--	--	--	--	--	--	61.5	--	--	--	--	--	--	--	--	--	--	--	--	--	--	--	--	--	48.2	25.2
	--	--	--	--	--	--	68.2	--	--	--	--	--	--	--	--	--	--	--	--	--	--	--	--	--	--	--
	--	--	--	--	--	--	70.0	--	--	--	--	--	--	--	--	--	--	--	--	--	--	--	--	--	--	--
	--	--	--	--	--	--	72.0	--	--	--	--	--	--	--	--	--	--	--	--	--	--	--	--	--	--	--
B	--	--	--	--	--	36-40.5	58-65	55-62	49-59	40-47	40.5-47	45-56	73-79	58.5-60	79-87	49-54.5	57-58.5	36-37	118-133.5	44.5-47	37-43	40-48	57-63	20-24	43-44.5	19-20.5
B	--	--	--	--	--	27.3	48.0	--	--	34.8	33.4	46.5	--	--	65.0	40.9	--	--	--	--	32.1	36.0	--	--	--	--
Bos																										
	--	--	--	--	42.8	58.0	90.0	94.0	97.0	69.5	84.0	--	--	(75)	105	70.0	77.0	50.0	--	67.2	58.2	81.5	67.0	34.0	47.5	33.8
	--	--	--	--	46.5	(77)	92.0	(112)	98.0	74.0	--	--	--	(92)	--	75.0	81.0	47.3	--	--	--	--	72.0	—	49.5	37.0
	--	--	--	--	--	--	(100)	--	--	85.2	--	--	--	--	--	76.8	82.0	50.0	--	--	--	--	--	--	49.5	35.8
	--	--	--	--	--	--	108.0	--	--	--	--	--	--	--	--	--	82.5	--	--	--	--	--	--	--	49.7	32.0
	--	--	--	--	--	--	--	--	--	--	--	--	--	--	--	--	83.5	55.5	--	--	--	--	--	--	52.5	41.0
	--	--	--	--	--	--	--	--	--	--	--	--	--	--	--	--	85.0	58.5	--	--	--	--	--	--	53.5	42.0
	--	--	--	--	--	--	--	--	--	--	--	--	--	--	--	--	(87)	59.5	--	--	--	--	--	--	54.5	43.5
	--	--	--	--	--	--	--	--	--	--	--	--	--	--	--	--	90.0	59.5	--	--	--	--	--	--	--	--
C	--	--	--	--	--	51-82	90-118	91-120	81-108	66-88	68-88	--	--	--	--	68-90	77-95	--	--	--	55-69	62-77	--	--	--	--
D	--	--	--	--	40-46	--	--	--	--	--	--	--	75-95	105-123	--	--	45-60	--	60-73	--	--	61-80	—	42-52		
Sus																										
	--	--	--	--	--	33.8*	38.5	31.5	--	--	--	32.0*	(46)	--	--	30.2	40.5	--	--	--	--	--	43.0	16.5	23.5	16.8
	--	--	--	--	--	--	39.5	31.5	--	--	--	32.0	--	--	--	--	40.5	--	--	--	--	--	--	--	25.5*	17.5*
	--	--	--	--	--	--	41.2	--	--	--	--	33.0	--	--	--	--	42.5	--	--	--	--	--	--	--	25.8*	—
	--	--	--	--	--	--	48.0	--	--	--	--	--	--	--	--	--	42.5	--	--	--	--	--	--	--	--	--
	--	--	--	--	--	--	52.8*	--	--	--	--	--	--	--	--	--	44.2	--	--	--	--	--	--	--	--	--
	--	--	--	--	--	--	(58)	--	--	--	--	--	--	--	--	--	44.6	--	--	--	--	--	--	--	--	--
	--	--	--	--	--	--	--	--	--	--	--	--	--	--	--	--	44.6	--	--	--	--	--	--	--	--	--
	--	--	--	--	--	--	--	--	--	--	--	--	--	--	--	--	46.8*	--	--	--	--	--	--	--	--	--
	--	--	--	--	--	--	--	--	--	--	--	--	--	--	--	--	49.2	--	--	--	--	--	--	--	--	--
E	--	--	--	--	--	17.5-28	30.5-43.5	22-35.5	--	--	--	27-36	37.5-49	--	--	22.5-33.5	34.5-42	--	--	--	--	--	--	--	--	--
Equus																										
	--	--	--	--	--	--	69.0	71.0	--	--	40.8	--	--	--	--	61.0	50.5	—	--	--	--	38.1	79.5	40.8	38.5	39.0
	--	--	--	--	--	--	--	--	--	--	--	--	--	--	--	--	--	--	--	--	--	39.2	84.5	42.0	38.5	40.5
	--	--	--	--	--	--	--	--	--	--	--	--	--	--	--	--	--	--	--	--	--	--	--	--	39.5	39.8
	--	--	--	--	--	--	--	--	--	--	--	--	--	--	--	--	--	--	--	--	--	--	--	--	41.5	38.0
	--	--	--	--	--	--	--	--	--	--	--	--	--	--	--	--	--	--	--	--	--	--	--	--	41.5	39.0

NOTE: A = FMNH 84489, ♂; B = *Dama mesopotamica* (Jéquier 1963, from Munich casts); C = *Bos primigenius* (Bökönyi 1962); D = *Bos primigenius* (Stampfli 1963); E = *Sus domesticus* (Nanninga 1963).
*From one of the lower levels.

Table 29.—Measurements of Identified Bones of Goats and Sheep from Jarmo

Item no.	Sex	w/d	Horn core L	Horn core C base	Horn core Lr Ø	Horn core Sr Ø	Scapula Lw col	Humerus Dist W	Radius Prox W	Radius Dist W	Metacarpus Prox W	Metacarpus Dist W	Pelvis Ø acet	Femur Dist W	Patella L	Calcaneus L	Metatarsus Prox W	Metatarsus Dist W	Phalanx I L	Phalanx I Prox W	Phalanx II L	Phalanx II Prox W
Capra																						
316	♂	w	--	(210)	(75)	(45)	15.2	27.2	26.9	27.2	24.2	22.2	--	36.0	(28)	53.9	18.9	22.2	33.0	11.8	20.0	10.0
27	♂	w	--	(210)	(74)	(45)	16.2	27.3	27.0	28.5	24.2	23.1	--	36.5	(31)	54.0	19.1	23.5	33.0	11.5	21.5	12.5
52	♂	w	--	205	81	40	16.2	28.0	28.0	29.0	24.7	23.9	--	43.2	--	--	19.4	24.2	34.5	10.5	22.2	12.8
12	♂	w	(320)	(200)	(75)	—	17.8	28.0	28.2	29.2	25.2	23.9	--	--	--	--	19.4	24.4	34.5	11.5	22.8	10.5
13	♂	w	(260)	185	74	30	18.2	28.2	29.0	29.8	25.8	24.7	--	--	--	--	19.5	24.5	34.7	11.3	23.5	13.2
315	♂	w	--	(170)	68	(36)	18.2	28.8	29.0	30.5	26.0	26.2	--	--	--	--	19.5	24.8	34.8	11.5	23.8	14.1
18	♂	d	--	(165)	68	(35)	18.5	28.8	29.0	--	27.8	27.2	--	--	--	--	19.8	26.0	35.2	11.5	24.5	12.2
53	♂	d	(200)	165	60	40	19.0	28.9	29.5	--	--	27.3	--	--	--	--	19.8	--	35.5	11.0	24.5	11.8
126	♂	d	--	160	62	(38)	19.5	29.5	30.0	--	--	28.5	--	--	--	--	19.9	--	36.0	11.2	24.5	12.0
187A	♂	w	--	160	67	35	19.5	29.5	31.0	--	--	28.8	--	--	--	--	21.0	--	36.5	13.5	25.0	12.8
133	♂	d	250	(160)	55	37	19.6	29.5	31.0	--	--	29.0	--	--	--	--	21.0	--	37.2	11.8	26.0	17.0
137	♂	d	190	155	62	33	20.0	29.5	35.8	--	--	32.2	--	--	--	--	21.2	--	37.5	13.8	27.4	15.0
195	♂	d	(350)	155	59	36	20.5	29.7	--	--	--	34.2	--	--	--	--	21.5	--	38.0	13.0	27.8	15.9
174	♂	d	(250)	(150)	54	(38)	21.0	29.7	--	--	--	37.2	--	--	--	--	21.5	--	38.0	12.8	28.0	15.8
169A	♂	d	--	140	53	33	22.0	30.0	--	--	--	--	--	--	--	--	21.6	--	39.5	12.8	--	--
128	♂	d	(260)	(140)	--	--	23.5	30.0	--	--	--	--	--	--	--	--	21.8	--	40.1	12.8	--	--
191	♀	w?	(220)	110	37	26	26.0	30.0	--	--	--	--	--	--	--	--	22.2	--	--	--	--	--
324	♀	w?	--	110	35	27	26.0	30.2	--	--	--	--	--	--	--	--	22.6	--	--	--	--	--
321	♀	w?	--	110	40	27	28.2	30.2	--	--	--	--	--	--	--	--	23.6	--	--	--	--	--
221	♀	w?	--	110	(39)	27	--	30.2	--	--	--	--	--	--	--	--	--	--	--	--	--	--
118	♀	w?	--	(110)	40	24	--	30.3	--	--	--	--	--	--	--	--	--	--	--	--	--	--
87	♀	w?	(250)	110	(43)	21	--	30.3	--	--	--	--	--	--	--	--	--	--	--	--	--	--
15	♀	w?	--	110	38	26	--	30.5	--	--	--	--	--	--	--	--	--	--	--	--	--	--
4	♀	w?	--	110	36	27	--	30.8	--	--	--	--	--	--	--	--	--	--	--	--	--	--
2	♀	w?	--	105	38	25	--	31.0	--	--	--	--	--	--	--	--	--	--	--	--	--	--
102	♀	w?	--	105	37	26	--	31.0	--	--	--	--	--	--	--	--	--	--	--	--	--	--
130	♀	w?	--	105	39	26	--	31.0	--	--	--	--	--	--	--	--	--	--	--	--	--	--
183	♀	w?	--	100	37	24	--	31.3	--	--	--	--	--	--	--	--	--	--	--	--	--	--
389	♀	w?	--	100	38	24	--	31.4	--	--	--	--	--	--	--	--	--	--	--	--	--	--
54	♀	d?	--	100	36	24	--	32.0	--	--	--	--	--	--	--	--	--	--	--	--	--	--
105	♀	d?	--	100	35	22	--	--	--	--	--	--	--	--	--	--	--	--	--	--	--	--
86A	♀	d?	--	95	32	22	--	32.0	--	--	--	--	--	--	--	--	--	--	--	--	--	--
53A	♀	d?	--	95	33	22	--	32.0	--	--	--	--	--	--	--	--	--	--	--	--	--	--
138	♀	d?	--	95	33	21	--	32.0	--	--	--	--	--	--	--	--	--	--	--	--	--	--
107	♀	d?	--	95	33	21	--	32.2	--	--	--	--	--	--	--	--	--	--	--	--	--	--
1	♀	d?	--	95	35	22	--	32.2	--	--	--	--	--	--	--	--	--	--	--	--	--	--
328	♀	d?	--	95	34	22	--	32.5	--	--	--	--	--	--	--	--	--	--	--	--	--	--
68	♀	d	--	95	34	23	--	32.5	--	--	--	--	--	--	--	--	--	--	--	--	--	--
42	♀	d	--	(90)	33	22	--	32.8	--	--	--	--	--	--	--	--	--	--	--	--	--	--
71	♀	d	--	90	33	20	--	32.8	--	--	--	--	--	--	--	--	--	--	--	--	--	--
116	♀	d	(125)	90	33	20	--	33.8	--	--	--	--	--	--	--	--	--	--	--	--	--	--
117	♀	d	(110)	90	32	22	--	34.0	--	--	--	--	--	--	--	--	--	--	--	--	--	--
308	♀	d	--	90	31	24	--	34.4	--	--	--	--	--	--	--	--	--	--	--	--	--	--
186	♀	d	(190)	90	33	23	--	34.8	--	--	--	--	--	--	--	--	--	--	--	--	--	--
241	♀	d	--	90	32	22	--	34.8	--	--	--	--	--	--	--	--	--	--	--	--	--	--
469	♀	d	--	90	31	23	--	35.2	--	--	--	--	--	--	--	--	--	--	--	--	--	--

NOTE: For comparative measurements of modern bones, see table 36.

Table 29.—Continued

				Horn core			Scapula	Humerus	Radius		Metacarpus		Pelvis	Femur	Patella	Calcaneus	Metatarsus			Phalanx I		Phalanx II	
Item no.	Sex	w/d	L	C base	Lr ⌀	Sr ⌀	Lw col	Dist W	Prox W	Dist W	Prox W	Dist W	⌀ acet	Dist W	L	L	Prox W	Dist W	L	Prox W	L	Prox W
Capra—continued																							
498	♀	d	--	90	32	23	--	36.2	--	--	--	--	--	--	--	--	--	--	--	--	--	--
297	♀	--	--	90	30	21	--	--	--	--	--	--	--	--	--	--	--	--	--	--	--	--
428	♀	--	--	85	28	21	--	37.0	--	--	--	--	--	--	--	--	--	--	--	--	--	--
470	♀	d	--	85	31	22	--	37.0	--	--	--	--	--	--	--	--	--	--	--	--	--	--
70	♀	d	--	85	30	22	--	38.2	--	--	--	--	--	--	--	--	--	--	--	--	--	--
5	♀	d	--	85	31	29	--	39.0	--	--	--	--	--	--	--	--	--	--	--	--	--	--
461	♀	d	--	85	28	18	--	39.5	--	--	--	--	--	--	--	--	--	--	--	--	--	--
407	♀	d	--	75	26	19	--	39.5	--	--	--	--	--	--	--	--	--	--	--	--	--	--
300	♀	d	--	75	25	18	--	40.2	--	--	--	--	--	--	--	--	--	--	--	--	--	--
80	♀	d	--	75	28	19	--	45.0	--	--	--	--	--	--	--	--	--	--	--	--	--	--
135	♀	d	--	75	29	15	--	--	--	--	--	--	--	--	--	--	--	--	--	--	--	--
Ovis																							
50	?	?	47	60	21	14	21.5	26.0	27.5	22.7	22.6	21.8	30.0	34.8	--	61.2	20.5	22.5	36.0	12.8	27.0	14.2
132	♀	?	--	65	24	15	22.2	27.6	28.0	27.0	22.9	23.5	--	37.5	--	63.5	--	23.0	36.2	13.8	--	--
292	♀	?	--	(75)	(30)	(15)	--	28.3	28.2	30.3	23.2	23.8	--	39.2	--	63.5	--	23.8	36.8	11.8	--	--
82	♀	?	--	80	28	19	--	28.6	30.0	32.0	23.4	23.8	--	--	--	--	--	24.0	37.2	13.1	--	--
6	♀	?	--	85	30	19	--	29.0	30.5	--	23.5	25.2	--	--	--	--	--	24.0	37.9	13.9	--	--
139	♀	?	--	85	30	22	--	29.0	30.9	--	23.8	31.2	--	--	--	--	--	24.2	38.2	12.2	--	--
442	♂	d?	--	155	57	40	--	29.2	31.4	--	24.8	--	--	--	--	--	--	26.0	39.0	14.0	--	--
1	♂	d?	--	(160)	57	44	--	29.2	32.4	--	26.2	--	--	--	--	--	--	31.0	39.5	12.2	--	--
197	♂	d?	--	(160)	57	42	--	29.5	33.0	--	27.0	--	--	--	--	--	--	33.5	--	--	--	--
85A	♂	d?	(250)	160	56	42	--	29.5	33.2	--	27.2	--	--	--	--	--	--	--	--	--	--	--
136	♂	d?	(300)	165	58	45	--	30.6	35.5	--	--	--	--	--	--	--	--	--	--	--	--	--
52	♂	d?	(250)	165	58	41	--	30.8	--	--	--	--	--	--	--	--	--	--	--	--	--	--
97	♂	d?	--	(180)	63	(37)	--	30.8	--	--	--	--	--	--	--	--	--	--	--	--	--	--
17	♂	w	--	(185)	(70)	(50)	--	31.0	--	--	--	--	--	--	--	--	--	--	--	--	--	--
14	♂	?	(300)	185	64	43	--	31.2	--	--	--	--	--	--	--	--	--	--	--	--	--	--
124	♂	w	--	190	71	46	--	31.2	--	--	--	--	--	--	--	--	--	--	--	--	--	--
60	♂	w	(225)	190	70	48	--	31.5	--	--	--	--	--	--	--	--	--	--	--	--	--	--
76A	♂	w	--	200	71	48	--	31.8	--	--	--	--	--	--	--	--	--	--	--	--	--	--
Unnumbered specimens of *Ovis*																							
--	--	--	--	--	--	--	--	31.8	--	--	--	--	--	--	--	--	--	--	--	--	--	--
--	--	--	--	--	--	--	--	31.9	--	--	--	--	--	--	--	--	--	--	--	--	--	--
--	--	--	--	--	--	--	--	32.2	--	--	--	--	--	--	--	--	--	--	--	--	--	--
--	--	--	--	--	--	--	--	32.3	--	--	--	--	--	--	--	--	--	--	--	--	--	--
--	--	--	--	--	--	--	--	32.6	--	--	--	--	--	--	--	--	--	--	--	--	--	--
--	--	--	--	--	--	--	--	33.2	--	--	--	--	--	--	--	--	--	--	--	--	--	--
--	--	--	--	--	--	--	--	33.2	--	--	--	--	--	--	--	--	--	--	--	--	--	--
--	--	--	--	--	--	--	--	33.5	--	--	--	--	--	--	--	--	--	--	--	--	--	--
--	--	--	--	--	--	--	--	33.5	--	--	--	--	--	--	--	--	--	--	--	--	--	--
--	--	--	--	--	--	--	--	33.5	--	--	--	--	--	--	--	--	--	--	--	--	--	--
--	--	--	--	--	--	--	--	33.8	--	--	--	--	--	--	--	--	--	--	--	--	--	--
--	--	--	--	--	--	--	--	36.5	--	--	--	--	--	--	--	--	--	--	--	--	--	--
--	--	--	--	--	--	--	--	38.0	--	--	--	--	--	--	--	--	--	--	--	--	--	--

Table 30.—Counts and Size Ranges of the Identified Horn Cores, M_3's, and the Bones of Goats, Sheep, and Sheep/Goat from Jarmo

Bone and measurement taken	Capra		Ovis		Capra/Ovis	
	Count	Range	Count	Range	Count	Range
Horn core						
Length ♂	8	190-350	5	225-300	--	--
Length ♀	5	110-250	1	47(?)	--	--
Circumference ♂	16	140-210	12	160-200	--	--
Circumference ♀	41	75-110	8	60-85	--	--
Larger diameter ♂	15	53-81	12	56-71	--	--
Larger diameter ♀	41	25-43	8	21-30	--	--
Smaller diameter ♂	14	30-45	12	37-50	--	--
Smaller diameter ♀	41	15-27	8	14-22	--	--
M_3						
Length	--	--	--	--	142	21.0-30.8
Scapula						
Least width of collum	19	15.2-28.2	2	21.5-22.2	4	19.0-27.0
Humerus						
Distal width	55	27.2-45.0	30	26.0-38.0	22	24.5-38.4
Radius						
Proximal width	12	26.9-35.8	11	27.5-35.5	7	28.2-36.5
Distal width	6	27.2-30.5	4	22.7-32.0	1	28.0
Metacarpus						
Proximal width	7	24.2-27.8	10	22.6-27.2	4	22.4-30.6
Distal width	14	22.2-37.2	6	21.8-31.2	--	--
Pelvis						
Diameter of acetabulum	--	--	1	30.0	4	25.0-32.0
Femur						
Distal width	3	36.0-43.0	3	34.8-39.2	10	31.0-40.0
Patella						
Length	2	28.0-31.0	--	--	3	22.5-32.5
Tibia						
Proximal width	--	--	--	--	4	40.0-51.5
Distal width	--	--	--	--	40	22.0-30.0
Astragalus						
Lateral length	109	25.2-33.0	85	24.2-37.2	104	25.6-35.0
Width of caput	109	16.6-22.1	85	16.2-24.1	104	16.5-22.2
Calcaneus						
Length	2	53.9-54.0	3	61.2-63.5	6	57.2-(77)
Centrotarsale						
Width	--	--	--	--	15	21.2-29.0
Metatarsus						
Proximal width	19	18.9-23.6	1	20.5	--	--
Distal width	7	22.2-26.0	9	22.5-33.5	--	--
Phalanx I						
Peripheral length	16	33.0-40.1	8	36.0-39.5	--	--
Proximal width	16	11.8-12.8	8	12.2-12.8	--	--
Phalanx II						
Peripheral length	14	20.0-28.0	1	27.0	--	--
Proximal width	14	10.0-15.0	1	14.2	--	--

Table 31.—Length Measurements of Jarmo Pigs' Teeth Which Show Only Slight or Medium Interstitial Wear and of Wild and Domestic Comparative Instances

Upper jaw			Lower jaw			
M^3	M^2	M^1	M_3	M_2	M_1	Symphysis
Jarmo *Sus*						
33.3	22.2	15.3	--	--	--	35
34.5	22.3	--	--	--	--	53
--	--	--	--	--	--	65
--	18.0	15.5	--	21.2*	15.8*	71
--	18.4	15.0	--	25.5	18.8	74
--	18.5	15.0	--	--	--	76
--	18.8	14.5	--	--	--	85
--	20.2	16.9	--	--	--	92
--	20.8	15.3	--	--	--	--
--	21.0*	18.1*	--	--	--	--
--	21.2	16.9	--	--	--	--
--	21.9	17.8	--	--	--	--
--	23.2	16.7	--	--	--	--
28.5	19.2	16.0	36.0	21.0	18.0	--
30.5	21.4	16.2	36.2	22.7*	18.2	--
34.2	21.8	16.8	38.2	23.0*	18.5	--
34.4	22.1	16.8	40.5	23.6	18.6	--
40.5	22.2	17.3	47.1	24.1	19.6	--
42.2	22.5	17.4	--	24.3	--	--
43.2	24.0	17.9	--	--	--	--
43.2	24.8*	18.1	--	--	--	--
--	25.2	18.1	--	--	--	--
--	--	18.2	--	--	--	--
--	--	18.4	--	--	--	--
Sus scrofa from AMNH (2 ♂ and 3 ♀)						
34.5-39.0	22.2-24.2	15.9-17.5	37.0-41.4	21.4-23.6	15.5-17.5	--
Domestic *Sus* (Nanninga 1963)						
24.0-36.5	--	--	21.0-39.0	--	--	--

*Examples from lower levels.

Table 32.—Measurements of Various Animal Bones from Jarmo and Comparisons from Several Modern Sources

Species	Bone and measurement taken	Jarmo measurement	According to Jéquier 1963, p. 74	Species	Bone and measurement taken	Jarmo measurement	According to Jéquier 1963, p. 74
Cervus	Skull			Equus	Metatarsus (continued)		
	Least width behind orbits	130	122.5		Distal width	39.0	
	Width of brain case	115	109.5		P^2		
	Greatest width of occiput	150	109-131.5		Length	32.5	
	Height of occiput	95	80-87.5		Width	21.0	
	Width of condyli occipitalis	80	68-80		P_2		
Capreolus	Burr, circumference	80, 90, 100			Length	28.5, 25.6	
	Premolar, length	29.2			Width	15.5, 16.5	
Bos	Os intermedium				M_3		
	Width	32.2, 33.0, 31.8			Length	25.8	
	Height	41.5, 37.0, 36.2			Width	12.2	
	Os radiale			Felis sp.	Lower jaw		
	Length	60.5			P_3-M_1	20.8, 21.2	
	Height	39.0			P_4-M_1	16.0	
	Os ulnare				P_4-Alv. C	19.9	
	Length	52.8, 39.0			Ulna, least width of olecranon	10.0	
	Height	42.2, 31.8		Felis pardus	Metacarpus III, distal width	16.4	
	Os carpale 2+3				Metatarsus IV, distal width	11.7	
	Length	40.5, 45.5			Humerus, distal width	57.2	
	Width	43.0, 52.0		Felis leo?	Epistropheus, cranial part Width across proximal facets	55.8	
	Os tarsale 2+3						
	Length	46.5, 44.5			Width of dens (on the base)	17.0	
	Width	28.5, 30.7		Lynx	Lower jaw, P_3-P_4	19.2	
Capra	Epistropheus, width of cranial facets	54.5		Meles	M_1, length	16.2, 16.3, 16.5, 16.6, 17.5, 17.6	
Ovis	Epistropheus, width of cranial facets	47.0		Lutra	Lower jaw, C-M_2 (A)	33.4	
	Atlas, width of cranial facets	49.0, 53.0		Martes	Lower jaw, P_2-M_1	26.0	
Capra/Ovis	Atlas, width of cranial facets	44, 54, 56, 62, 62, 65		Putorius	Lower jaw, P_2-M_1 (A)	17.1	
	Epistropheus, width of cranial facets	39, 48, 49, 56		Lepus	Lower jaw, P+M	21.0	
Equus	Metatarsus				Radius, proximal width	8.0	
	Length	260			Femur, distal width	(13.5)	
	Proximal width	41.5			Tibia, distal width	13.4	

Table 32.—Continued

	Measurements									Measurements							
	Lower jaw				Upper jaw					Lower jaw				Upper jaw			
	Length				Length		Width			Length				Length		Width	
Species	P_1-M_3	P_{1-4}	M_{1-3}	M_1	P^4	M^1	P^4	M^1	Species	P_1-M_3	P_{1-4}	M_{1-3}	M_1	P^4	M^1	P^4	M^1
Vulpes																	
A. Excavated Jarmo specimens	57.2	33.2	24.5	15.2	15.0	10.8	7.0	12.5		--	--	--	15.1	--	--	--	--
	52.8	29.5	--	--	13.5	9.4	5.2	11.2		--	--	--	14.8	--	--	--	--
	--	--	24.2	14.2	14.2	10.0	5.8	11.5		--	--	--	15.2	--	--	--	--
	--	--	24.0	14.1	14.5	8.8	6.2	11.0		--	--	--	15.0	--	--	--	--
	50.5	--	--	--	--	9.1	--	11.2		--	--	--	14.4	--	--	--	--
	--	31.9	--	--	--	9.6	--	11.6		--	--	--	14.1	--	--	--	--
	--	29.8	--	--	--	--	--	--		--	--	--	16.8	--	--	--	--
	--	--	24.1	--	--	--	--	--	B. Modern northern Iraq specimens								
	--	--	25.2	--	--	--	--	--	FMNH 57256,* Spilik Pass	53.5	30.2	23.9	13.81	13.45	8.5	5.85	10.4
	--	--	24.4	--	--	--	--	--	FMNH 84472, ♂, Jarmo area (No M_3)	27.5	(No M_3)	14.4	13.28	9.0	6.5	10.2	
	--	--	--	16.0	--	--	--	--	FMNH 84473, ♂, Jarmo area	55.6	31.1	25.15	14.86	13.45	9.3	6.84	11.52
	--	--	--	14.3	--	--	--	--	FMNH 84474, ♀, Jarmo area	51.45	28.6	23.8	13.85	13.0	8.75	6.3	10.5
	--	--	--	14.5	--	--	--	--	FMNH 84475, ♂, Jarmo area	53.0	29.5	24.6	14.45	14.25	9.2	6.35	11.2
	--	--	--	15.5	--	--	--	--									

*Sex not recorded.

Table 33.—Identified Bones of Various Mammals from the Succession of Phases in the ᶜAmuq

Phase	Time (B.C.)	Bos d	Bos w	Sus d	Sus w	Capra	Ovis	Capra/Ovis	Gazella	Cervus	Dama	Misc.	Total
K-O	500	4	--	--	--	--	--	--	2	1	1	2	10
I-J	2000	--	--	--	--	--	--	2	--	1	--	3	6
H	2500	--	--	1	--	--	--	4	--	--	--	3	8
G	2900	34	2	8	--	4	6	13	--	4	22	9	102
F	3200	2	--	--	--	--	--	1	--	1	--	--	4
E	3600	56	--	19	4	5	11	22	1?	--	--	2	120
D	4250	15	--	5	1	--	2	11	2	--	--	2	38
C	4600	4	2	2	--	--	--	2	--	--	--	--	10
B	5000	4	8	7	2	1	2	5	--	--	--	--	29
A	5500 / 6000	--	9	1?	8	1	3	--	--	--	--	--	22
Total		119	21	43	15	11	24	60	5	7	23	21	349

Table 34.—Measurements of All Identified Mammalian Bones in the ᶜAmuq Sequence

	Horn cores				M₃	Scapula	Humerus	Radius		Metacarpus		Pelvis	Femur	Tibia		Astragalus		Calcaneus	Centrotarsale	Metatarsus		Phalanx I		Phalanx II	
Phase	L	C base	Lr Ø	Sr Ø	L	Lw col	Dist W	Prox W	Dist W	Prox W	Dist W	Ø acet	Dist W	Prox W	Dist W	Lat L	W cap	L	W	Prox W	Dist W	L	Prox W	L	Prox W
Gazella																									
D	--	--	--	--	--	13.5	--	--	--	--	--	--	--	--	--	--	--	--	--	--	--	--	--	--	--
D	--	--	--	--	--	14.5	--	--	--	--	--	--	--	--	--	--	--	--	--	--	--	--	--	--	--
M	160	95	33	23	--	--	--	--	--	--	--	--	--	--	--	--	--	--	--	--	--	--	--	--	--
N	(160)	(85)	(29)	(19)ᵃ	--	--	--	--	--	--	--	--	--	--	--	--	--	--	--	--	--	--	--	--	--
Cervus																									
G	--	--	--	--	--	--	--	--	--	--	--	--	--	--	--	--	--	--	--	--	--	52.0	18.6	--	--
Dama																									
G	--	--	--	--	--	--	--	--	--	--	33.3	--	--	--	--	--	--	--	38.0	--	37.5	--	--	--	--
Bos																									
A	--	--	--	--	--	--	--	--	--	--	--	--	--	--	--	73.0ᵇ	45.0ᵇ	--	--	53.0	--	--	--	46.0	33.5
A	--	--	--	--	--	--	--	--	--	--	--	--	--	--	--	--	--	--	--	--	--	--	--	(38)	29.2
A	--	--	--	--	--	--	--	--	--	--	--	--	--	--	--	--	--	--	--	--	--	--	--	47.0	33.4
B	--	--	--	--	--	--	78.0ᶜ	--	--	--	--	--	--	--	--	(70)ᵇ	42.0ᵇ	--	--	--	--	63.5	32.0	43.0	29.0
B	--	--	--	--	--	--	--	--	--	--	--	--	--	--	--	--	--	--	--	--	--	65.0	38.0	--	--
C	--	--	--	--	--	60.0	--	--	--	--	73.0	--	--	--	--	--	--	134.0	--	--	--	--	--	43.5	34.5
D	--	--	--	--	38.0	--	--	--	--	--	66.0	--	--	--	--	--	--	--	54.0	46.0	--	60.0	30.0	--	--
D	--	--	--	--	--	--	--	--	--	--	--	--	--	--	--	--	--	--	--	--	--	58.2	31.0	--	--
E	(170)	140	48	38	(37)	--	--	76.0	68.5	55.2	57.3	63.0	--	--	68.0	--	--	--	53.5	--	56.8	57.0	30.8	42.2	31.5
E	--	160	55	38	--	--	--	--	--	--	--	--	--	--	64.8	--	--	--	56.5	--	60.0	61.3	28.0	40.0	29.1
E	300	250	84	68	--	--	--	--	--	--	--	--	--	--	--	--	--	--	--	--	--	62.7	32.9	--	--
G	--	--	--	--	--	44.5	67.4	65.5	60.0	57.0	--	--	--	--	--	--	--	--	52.3	--	--	59.2	32.0	37.0	26.0
G	--	--	--	--	--	--	--	78.5	--	53.2	--	--	--	--	--	--	--	--	--	--	--	57.0	28.5	--	--
G	--	--	--	--	--	--	--	--	--	--	--	--	--	--	--	--	--	--	--	--	--	60.5	30.5	--	--
M	160	140	45	36	--	--	(92)	--	--	--	--	--	--	--	--	--	--	--	--	--	--	--	--	--	--
M	--	130	42	36	--	--	--	--	--	--	--	--	--	--	--	--	--	--	--	--	--	--	--	--	--
N	--	--	--	--	36.0	--	--	--	--	--	--	--	--	--	--	--	--	--	--	--	--	--	--	--	--
O	--	--	--	--	--	--	--	85.2ᵈ	79.0ᵈ	--	--	--	--	--	--	--	--	--	--	--	--	--	--	--	--
Capra																									
A	--	95	33	22	--	--	--	--	--	--	--	--	--	--	--	--	--	--	--	--	--	--	--	--	--
E	(160)	120	43	28	--	17.0	--	--	--	--	--	--	--	--	--	--	--	--	--	--	--	--	--	--	--
E	(180)	120	43	26	--	--	--	--	--	--	--	--	--	--	--	--	--	--	--	--	--	--	--	--	--
Ovis																									
A	--	--	--	--	--	--	--	--	--	--	23.0	--	--	--	--	29.4	18.3	--	--	--	23.6	--	--	--	--
D	--	--	--	--	--	--	--	--	--	--	23.4	--	--	--	--	--	--	--	--	--	--	--	--	--	--
E	--	--	--	--	--	--	37.0	30.5	--	--	--	--	--	--	--	--	--	--	--	--	--	38.3	13.0	--	--
E	--	--	--	--	--	--	31.4	--	--	--	--	--	--	--	--	--	--	--	--	--	--	--	--	--	--
G	--	--	--	--	--	--	31.2	--	--	--	--	--	--	--	--	38.5	27.3	--	--	--	--	39.3	13.4	--	--
G	--	--	--	--	--	--	--	--	--	--	--	--	--	--	--	--	--	--	--	--	--	37.0	13.3	--	--
Capra/Ovis																									
D	--	--	--	--	--	--	29.1	--	--	--	--	30.6	--	--	--	--	--	--	--	--	--	--	--	--	--
E	--	--	--	--	23.8	--	--	--	--	--	--	--	--	--	--	--	--	--	--	--	--	--	--	--	--
E	--	--	--	--	24.1	--	--	--	--	--	--	--	--	--	--	--	--	--	--	--	--	--	--	--	--
G	--	--	--	--	24.1	--	--	--	--	--	--	--	--	--	--	--	--	--	--	--	--	--	--	--	--
H	--	--	--	--	22.2	--	--	--	--	--	--	--	--	--	--	--	--	--	--	--	--	--	--	--	--
I	--	--	--	--	26.5	--	--	--	--	--	--	--	--	--	--	--	--	--	--	--	--	--	--	--	--
M	--	--	--	--	23.1	--	--	--	--	--	--	--	--	--	--	--	--	--	--	--	--	--	--	--	--
M	--	--	--	--	26.6	--	--	--	--	--	--	--	--	--	--	--	--	--	--	--	--	--	--	--	--
O	--	--	--	--	23.0	--	--	--	--	--	--	--	--	--	--	--	--	--	--	--	--	--	--	--	--
Sus																									
A	--	--	--	--	--	(27)	--	--	--	--	--	--	--	--	--	47.0	--	--	--	--	--	--	--	--	--
B	--	--	--	--	--	--	--	--	--	--	--	--	--	--	--	40.2	--	--	--	--	--	--	--	--	--
C	--	--	--	--	--	--	--	--	--	--	--	--	--	--	33.0	--	--	--	--	--	--	--	--	--	--
D	--	--	--	--	--	20.5	--	--	--	--	--	--	--	--	--	38.6	--	--	--	--	--	47.0	21.0	--	--
E	--	--	--	--	--	19.5	42.0	--	--	--	--	--	--	--	--	--	--	--	--	--	--	--	--	--	--

ᵃ Not quite on the base.
ᵇ Small, possibly juvenile.
ᶜ Width of trochlea.
ᵈ One piece: length, 290; width of olecranon, 60.2.

Table 35.—Skeletal Materials Used for Reference

Species	Museum	No.	Sex	Age	Locality
Ovis orientalis	FMNH	97983[a]	♂	adult	Iran, Kerman
		97945	♂	(M3)	Iran, Khorassan
		97946	♂	(M3)	Iran, Khorassan
		98123	♀	adult	Iran, Mazenderan
		97957	♀	adult	Iran, Isfahan
		97944	♀	adult	Iran, Mazenderan
		97948	♀	adult[b]	Iran, Khorassan
Capra aegagrus	FMNH	97913	♂	subadult	Iran, W. Azerbaijan
		97910	♂	M3 ↑	Iran, Mazenderan
		97917	♂	M3 ↑	Iran, Fars
		97925	♀	adult	Iran, Tehran
		97911	♀	M2 ↑	E-Varangarud
		97921	♀	subadult	Iran, Fars
		97919	♀	subadult	Iran, Isfahan
Gazella subgutturosa	FMNH	84489	♂	adult	Iraq, Kirkuk Liwa
		84491	♂	M3 ↑	Iraq, Kirkuk Liwa
		92917	♀	adult	Iran, Kermanshah
Sus scrofa	MCZ	51574	♂	adult[b]	Turkey
	AMNH	88690[c]	♂	adult	Iran, Turkman desert
	AMNH	88714[c]	♀	adult	Iran, Turkman desert
	AMNH	88724[c]	♀	adult	Iran, Turkman desert
	AMNH	97793[d]	♀	adult	Afghanistan, Mourghab valley
	MCZ	51621[e]	♀	adult	Near East

NOTE: See tables 36 and 37 for measurements taken from some of these skeletons.
[a] Subspecies *cyloceros*.
[b] Very old.
[c] Subspecies *attila*.
[d] Subspecies *nigripes*.
[e] Without statement of subspecies.

Table 36.—Measurements of Bones of Modern Gazelles, Sheep, and Goats

Bone and measurement taken	Gazella subgutterosa Güldenstädt ♂ 84489 adult	Gazella subgutterosa Güldenstädt ♀ 92917 adult	Ovis orientalis Gmelin ♂ 97983 adult	Ovis orientalis Gmelin ♂ 97945 (M3)	Ovis orientalis Gmelin ♂ 97946 (M3)	Ovis orientalis Gmelin ♀ 94948 adult	Ovis orientalis Gmelin ♀ 98123 adult	Ovis orientalis Gmelin ♀ 97957 adult	Ovis orientalis Gmelin ♀ 97944 adult	Capra aegragus Erxleben ♂ 97913 subadult	Capra aegragus Erxleben ♂ 97910 M3↑	Capra aegragus Erxleben ♂ 97917 M3↑	Capra aegragus Erxleben ♀ 97925 adult	Capra aegragus Erxleben ♀ 97911 (M3)	Capra aegragus Erxleben ♀ 97921 subadult	Capra aegragus Erxleben ♀ 97919 subadult
Skull																
W horn core bases	58.5	47.8*	95.5	89.0	82.2	--	78.0	72.0	74.0	98.0	91.0	81.0	62.0	67.0	--	--
W occip (mast)	62.2	57.2	91.5	74.2	64.0	--	69.2	61.0	64.0	86.0	74.0	66.0	61.0	64.0	--	--
W occip cond	37.0	36.0	45.6	49.3	47.0	--	44.8	42.5	46.0	52.0	51.0	51.0	44.0	47.5	--	--
H occip (bas-bre)	61.0	58.0	81.0	82.0	77.0	--	76.0	71.0	73.0	87.0	84.0	78.0	75.0	(64)	--	--
Horn core																
L front curve	175.0	--	295.0	160.0	70.0	--	90.0	60.0	40.0	320.0	215.0	185.0	130.0	60.0	--	--
C at base	90.0	--	150.0	135.0	105.0	--	85.0	75.0	55.0	150.0	135.0	105.0	65.0	65.0	--	--
Lr ∅	31.0	--	56.0	51.0	39.0	--	32.0	27.0	20.0	53.0	48.0	37.0	22.0	22.0	--	--
Sr ∅	22.0	--	41.0	33.0	25.0	--	19.0	17.0	15.0	38.0	37.0	27.0	16.0	17.0	--	--
Upper jaw																
L mol and premol	57.5	52.2	69.4	--	--	--	67.3	66.0	69.0	75.0	--	--	65.2	--	--	--
L molars	36.5	32.2	46.9	--	--	--	44.5	42.2	45.0	50.0	--	--	43.5	--	--	--
L premolars	22.0	20.5	23.9	--	--	--	24.5	25.8	25.0	28.5	--	--	23.5	--	--	--
L M^3	13.8	12.9	21.9	--	--	--	18.2	15.4	17.0	19.8	--	--	16.2	--	--	--
Lower jaw																
L mol and premol	61.2	55.0	72.2	--	--	--	71.5	69.2	71.5	79.5	--	--	66.2	--	--	--
L molars	41.8	38.2	50.2	--	--	--	50.8	48.2	50.4	55.0	--	--	39.1	--	--	--
L premolars	22.0	18.1	23.4	--	--	--	23.5	20.8	22.7	26.8	--	--	23.2	--	--	--
L M_3	18.5	17.4	25.0	--	--	--	23.9	21.0	23.0	25.0	--	--	19.2	--	--	--
Atlas																
L (cran-caud facets)	39.0	33.5	48.0	--	--	51.0	48.5	42.0	--	52.0	--	--	44.4	--	44.0	44.5
W cranial facets	37.8	34.5	46.0	--	--	54.6	47.7	43.8	--	60.5	--	--	47.1	--	45.2	46.5
W caudal facets	35.0	29.5	44.0	--	--	50.0	46.5	42.0	--	54.0	--	--	42.2	--	42.0	43.2
Epistropheus																
L epist body	49.0	--	50.0	--	--	59.0	51.3	43.4	--	--	--	--	46.0	--	43.2	44.0
W cranial facets	32.8	--	41.0	--	--	48.5	44.2	40.8	--	51.5	--	--	41.0	--	41.2	41.0
Scapula																
Lw col	14.2	--	18.3	--	--	23.5	18.9	16.6	18.6	22.0	--	--	17.5	--	16.5	17.5
Humerus																
L (cap-dist)	112.5	--	145.0	--	--	160.0	150.0	137.0	148.0	175.0	--	--	130.0	--	134.0	135.0
Prox ∅	34.0	--	43.5	--	--	52.0	45.5	42.0	48.5	55.0	--	--	40.3	--	41.0	43.0
Dist W	24.2	--	28.0	--	--	35.0	31.2	29.0	33.0	36.2	--	--	28.0	--	29.0	30.4
Ulna																
Lw olecranon	14.8	--	20.6	--	--	25.5	21.5	19.6	23.0	24.2	--	--	20.0	--	19.2	21.3
Radius																
L	145.0	--	175.0	--	--	200.0	180.0	173.0	175.0	190.0	--	--	150.0	--	148.0	151.0
Prox W	23.5	--	30.0	--	--	35.8	31.5	29.2	33.6	38.0	--	--	28.0	--	28.5	29.6
Dist W	21.5	--	26.5	--	--	32.3	28.6	26.2	30.7	34.5	--	--	25.6	--	27.2	28.8
Metacarpus																
L	155.0	--	155.0	--	--	170.0	165.0	152.0	156.0	132.0	--	--	108.0	--	106.6	108.1
Prox W	19.1	--	22.1	--	--	25.7	25.4	22.2	25.5	28.0	--	--	22.5	--	22.1	22.0
Dist W	18.8	--	23.8	--	--	27.4	25.7	24.2	27.2	34.0	--	--	24.9	--	24.8	25.4
Lw diaph	10.4	--	13.4	--	--	15.5	14.2	13.0	14.8	17.8	--	--	13.5	--	13.8	14.0
T diaph (dist)	--	--	10.0	--	--	11.6	10.1	10.1	10.1	12.0	--	--	8.4	--	8.8	9.5
Pelvis																
∅ acet	23.8	--	25.0	--	--	31.0	29.4	26.0	--	31.0	--	--	25.0	--	24.0	--
Ilium (acet-sacr artic)	--	--	56.0	--	--	64.0	53.0	57.0	--	54.0	--	--	63.0	--	58.3	66.0
T ilium	--	--	8.0	--	--	11.0	9.0	8.2	--	19.5	--	--	7.0	--	6.6	7.8
Femur																
L (cap-dist)	152.0	--	185.0	--	--	215.0	200.0	--	198.0	225.0	--	--	165.0	--	175.0	170.0
Prox W	42.2	--	44.2	--	--	54.0	49.4	46.2	52.0	--	--	--	40.3	--	41.2	40.5
Dist W	29.4	--	35.2	--	--	43.5	39.4	35.2	39.5	44.0	--	--	33.1	--	34.5	34.0
Patella																
L	--	--	--	--	--	38.6	34.2	27.3	33.2	33.0	--	--	--	--	27.0	29.0
Tibia																
L	199.0	--	240.0	--	--	265.0	250.0	230.0	245.0	265.0	--	--	200.0	--	200.0	205.0
Prox W	32.4	--	37.7	--	--	48.0	42.4	38.2	45.0	49.0	--	--	37.2	--	37.5	38.6
Dist W	20.0	--	23.2	--	--	29.8	27.0	24.2	28.2	30.0	--	--	22.4	--	24.5	24.7
Astragalus																
Lat L	25.5	--	26.0	--	--	31.0	29.6	27.4	30.8	30.9	--	--	26.2	--	27.6	27.8
W talus head	14.8	--	16.4	--	--	19.4	18.9	17.1	19.6	22.0	--	--	17.0	--	17.6	17.4
Calcaneus																
L	53.4	--	59.5	--	--	71.2	63.8	58.7	63.6	(68)	--	--	53.5	--	53.6	55.5
Centrotarsale																
W	19.3	--	21.3	--	--	25.3	23.4	21.6	24.4	28.0	--	--	21.8	--	22.1	21.4
Metatarsus																
L	168.0	--	170.0	--	--	190.0	175.0	167.0	168.0	143.5	--	--	119.0	--	116.6	116.2
Prox W	18.2	--	18.3	--	--	21.6	21.0	18.5	21.6	22.1	--	--	18.8	--	18.2	19.0
Dist W	19.1	--	23.4	--	--	26.0	24.8	23.2	27.1	29.6	--	--	22.4	--	22.4	23.2
W diaph	9.5	--	11.3	--	--	13.5	12.7	11.5	13.4	15.0	--	--	11.1	--	11.2	11.5
T diaph (dist)	--	--	9.4	--	--	11.5	10.7	9.5	10.0	12.0	--	--	8.6	--	8.8	8.8
Phalanx I																
L	35.5	--	39.0	--	--	44.2	40.8	39.0	40.8	43.2	--	--	35.2	--	34.2	36.6
Prox W	9.8	--	11.0	--	--	13.2	11.3	12.0	13.8	14.7	--	--	11.8	--	12.0	12.5
Phalanx II																
L	17.6	--	22.1	--	--	26.3	24.1	22.2	--	28.0	--	--	23.1	--	23.0	23.6
Prox W	8.2	--	10.3	--	--	12.9	12.5	11.8	--	13.0	--	--	10.2	--	10.1	11.2

NOTE: These specimens are in the collections of the Field Museum of Natural History, Chicago.
*Width behind the orbits.

Table 37.—Measurements of Teeth of Modern Wild Pigs on Skeletons in Two Museum Collections

Measurement taken	♂		♀			
	51574 MCZ	88690 AMNH	51621 MCZ	88714 AMNH	88724 AMNH	97793 AMNH
Upper jaw						
Length M^3-C (dist)	--	119.0	137.0	142.0	134.0	134.0
Length of P + M^1, P^1 incl.	--	125.3	123.0	--	122.0	120.0
Length of P + M^1, not P^1	--	117.0	114.0	--	112.0	109.0
Length of molars	76.0	79.5	73.0	76.0	74.0	74.5
Length of P^1-P^4	--	46.5	49.0	--	48.0	46.0
Length of P^2-P^4	--	38.4	41.0	--	38.6	35.4
Length of M^3	37.5	39.0	35.5	37.8	36.0	34.5
Width of M^3	21.5	22.0	21.5	22.0	20.5	19.5
Length of M^2	23.5	24.2	22.2	23.6	23.3	23.0
Width of M^2	19.0	21.4	20.0	19.3	18.8	18.8
Length of M^1	17.5	17.2	15.9	16.6	16.0	16.8
Width of M^1	15.5	15.5	16.0	15.8	15.5	15.4
Lower jaw						
Length M_3-C (dist)	160.0	158.0	150.5	151.0	148.0	148.0
Length of P + M, P_1 incl.	151.0	142.0	144.3	140.0	136.0	136.0
Length of P + M, not P_1	118.5	120.0	122.0	120.0	119.0	114.5
Length of molars	75.5	80.7	79.0	81.5	77.8	77.0
Length of P_2-P_4	43.7	41.3	43.1	42.3	42.5	39.4
Length of M_3	37.0	41.0	39.8	41.4	41.0	38.3
Width of M_3	17.4	19.0	17.6	18.5	17.0	18.0
Height of jaw behind M_3	57.0	57.5	53.0	56.0	53.0	53.0
Length of M_2	22.5	23.4	23.0	23.0	21.4	23.6
Width of M_2	15.5	17.0	15.9	16.0	15.3	15.8
Length of M_1	16.3	17.5	16.5	16.5	15.5	15.7
Width of M_1	11.5	12.5	12.0	12.0	11.8	12.3

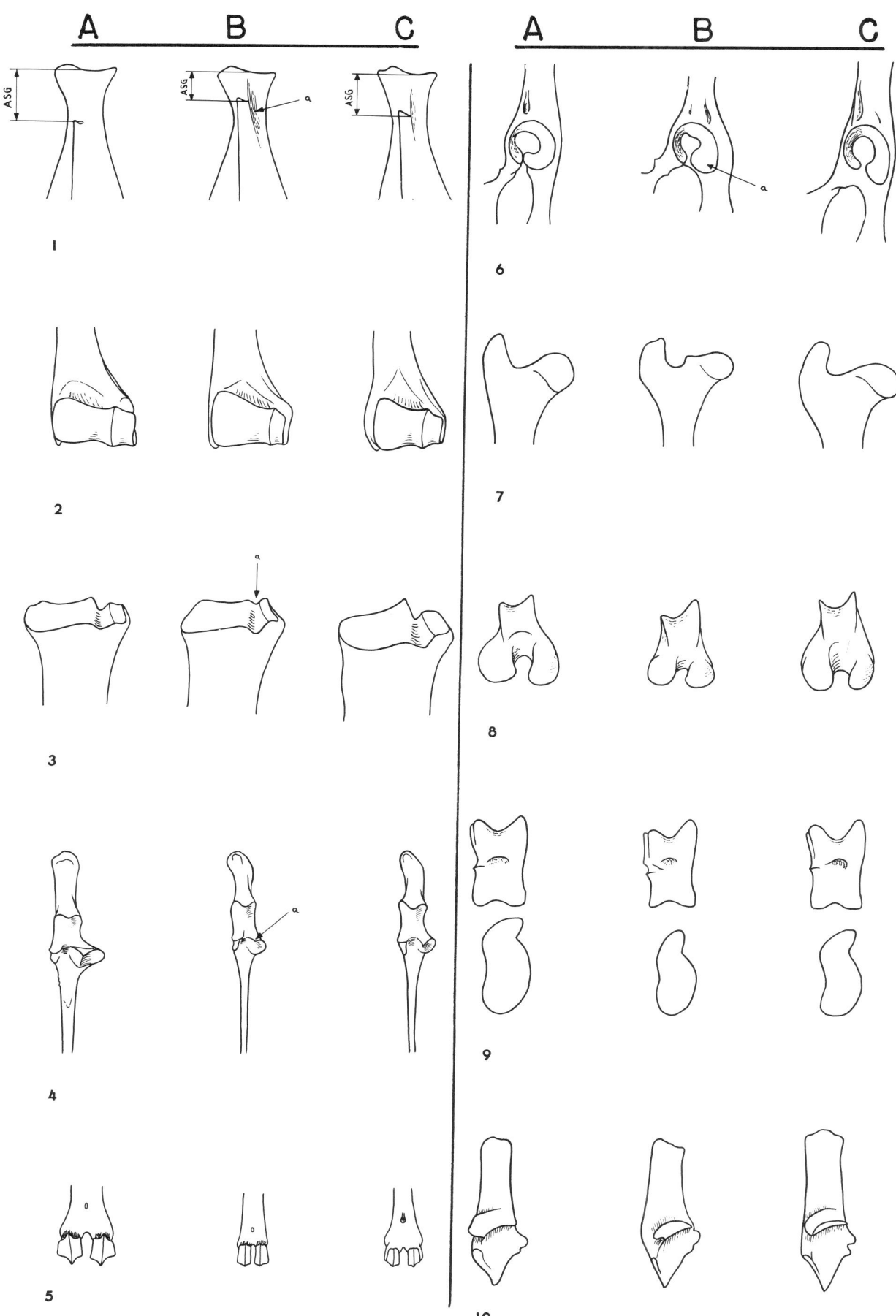

Fig. 173. Morphological characteristics useful in identification of bones of *A*, sheep/goat; *B*, gazelle; *C*, roe deer (see pp. 433ff.): *1*, scapula; *2*, distal humerus; *3*, proximal radius; *4*, proximal ulna; *5*, distal metacarpus; *6*, pelvis; *7*, proximal femur; *8*, distal femur; *9*, astragalus; *10*, calcaneus.

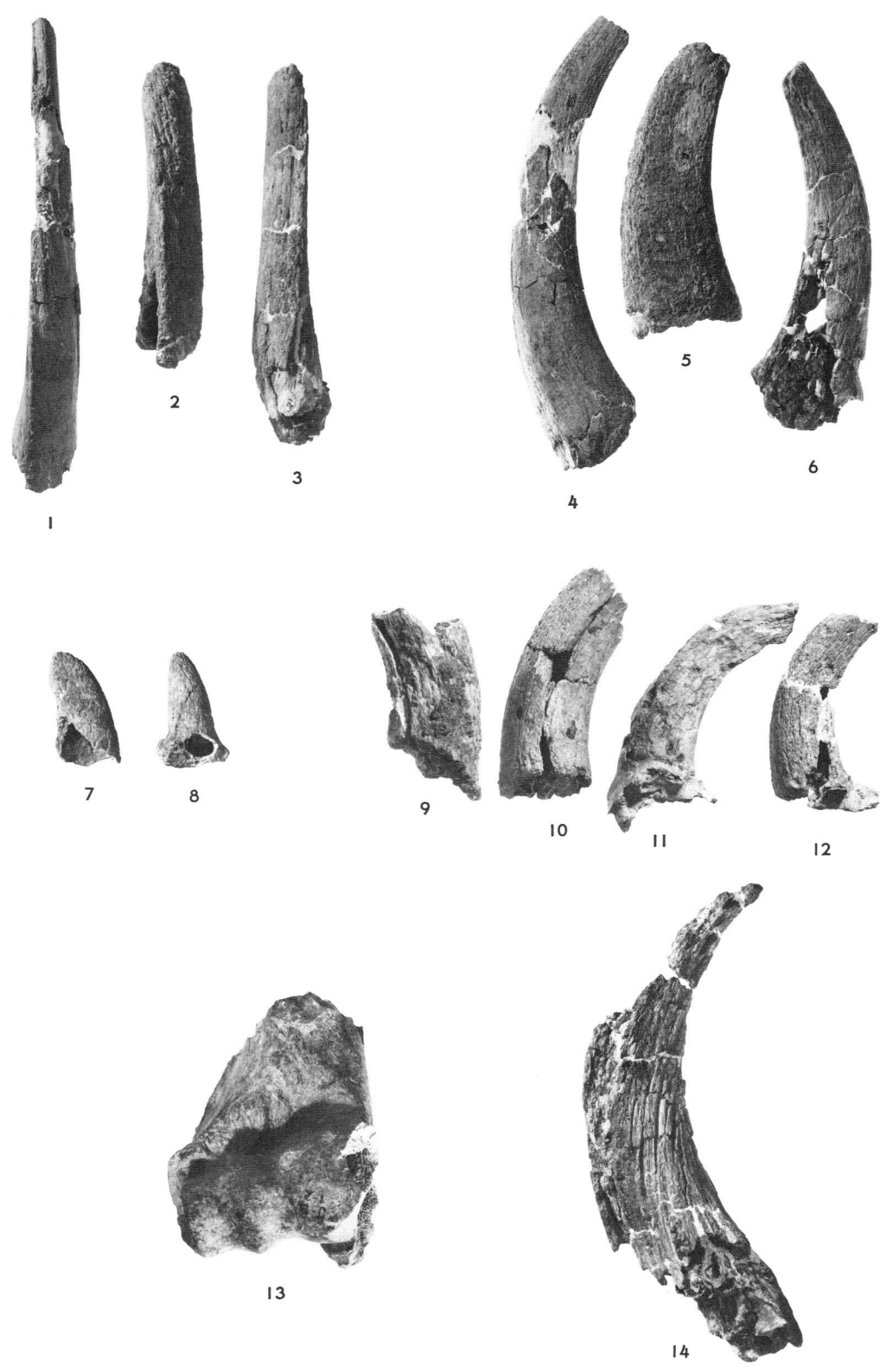

Fig. 174. Horn cores and humerus from Jarmo: *1* (no. 195), *2* (no. 18), *3* (no. 133), horn cores of domestic goat ♂♂, dorsal-frontal view; *4* (no. 195), *5* (no. 18), *6* (no. 133), horn cores of domestic goat ♂♂, lateral view; *7* (no. 292), *8* (no. 50, from J-II,2), horn cores of sheep ♀♀, lateral view; *9* (from J-I,3), *10* (no. 76A), *11* (no. 52), *12* (no. 85A), horn cores of sheep, ♂♂ frontal-lateral view; *13*, humerus of bison(?), dorsal view; *14*, horn core of *Bos primigenius*.

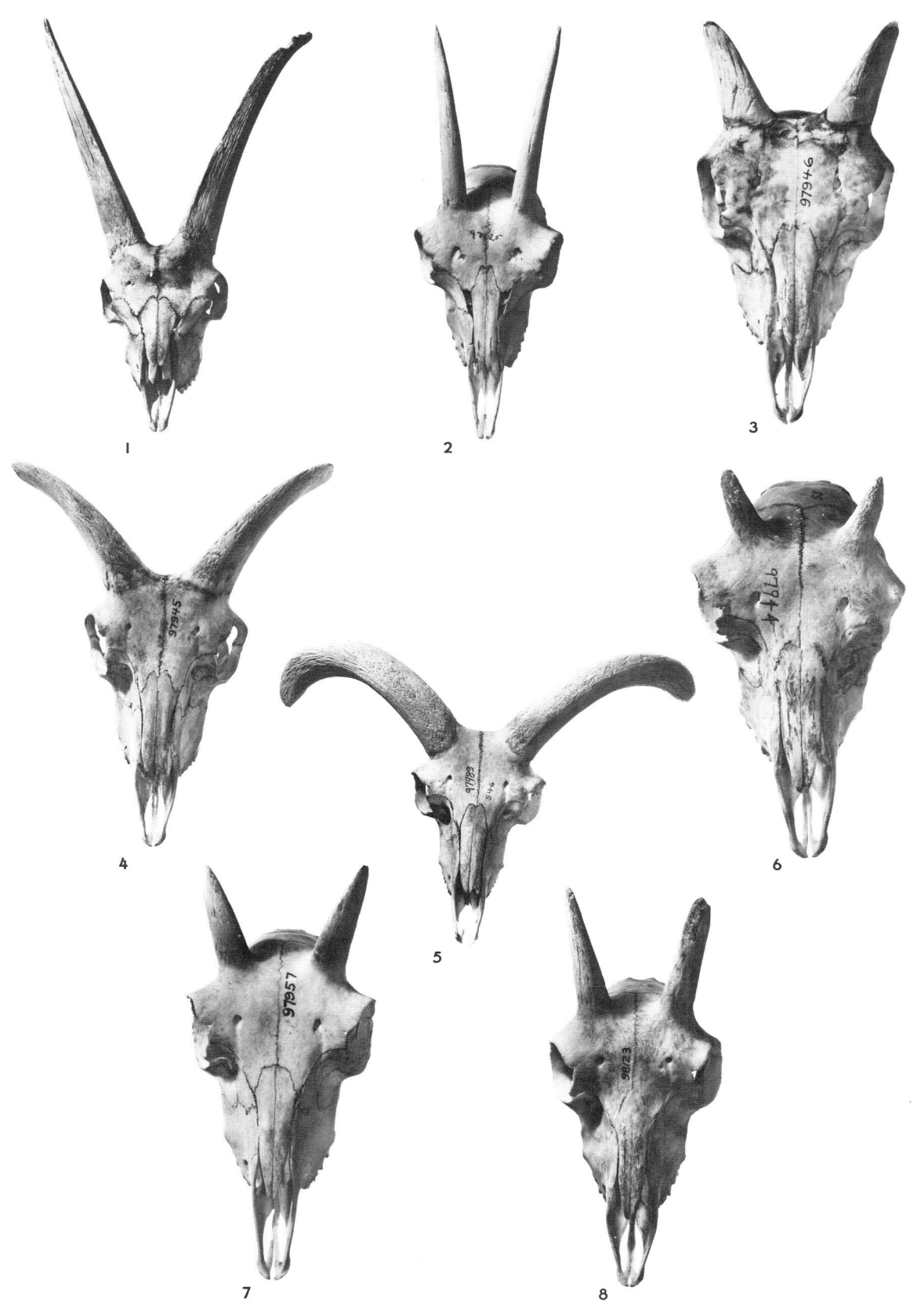

Fig. 175. Dorsal-frontal aspects of skulls of modern goats and sheep in the Field Museum of Natural History, Chicago: *1* (FMNH 97913), *Capra aegagrus* Erxl., bezoar goat ♂; *2* (FMNH 97925), *Capra aegagrus* Erxl., bezoar goat ♀; *3* (FMNH 97946), *4* (FMNH 97945), *Ovis orientalis* Gm., wild sheep ♂♂ juvenile; *5* (FMNH 97983/97946), *Ovis orientalis* Gm., wild sheep ♂; *6* (FMNH 97944), *7* (FMNH 97957), *8* (FMNH 98123), *Ovis orientalis* Gm., wild sheep ♀♀.

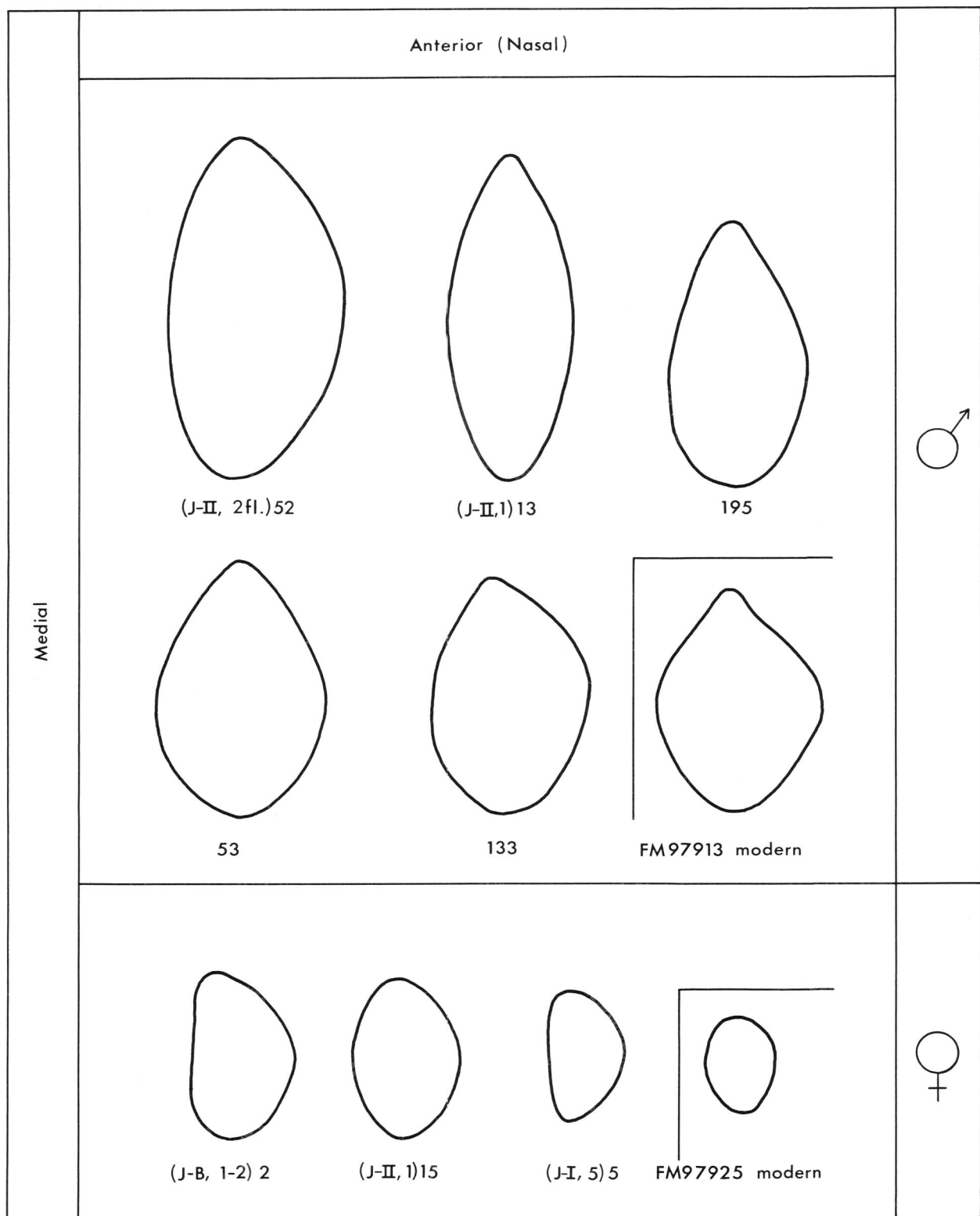

Fig. 176. Cross-section drawings of male and female goat horn cores from Jarmo, with FMNH comparisons.

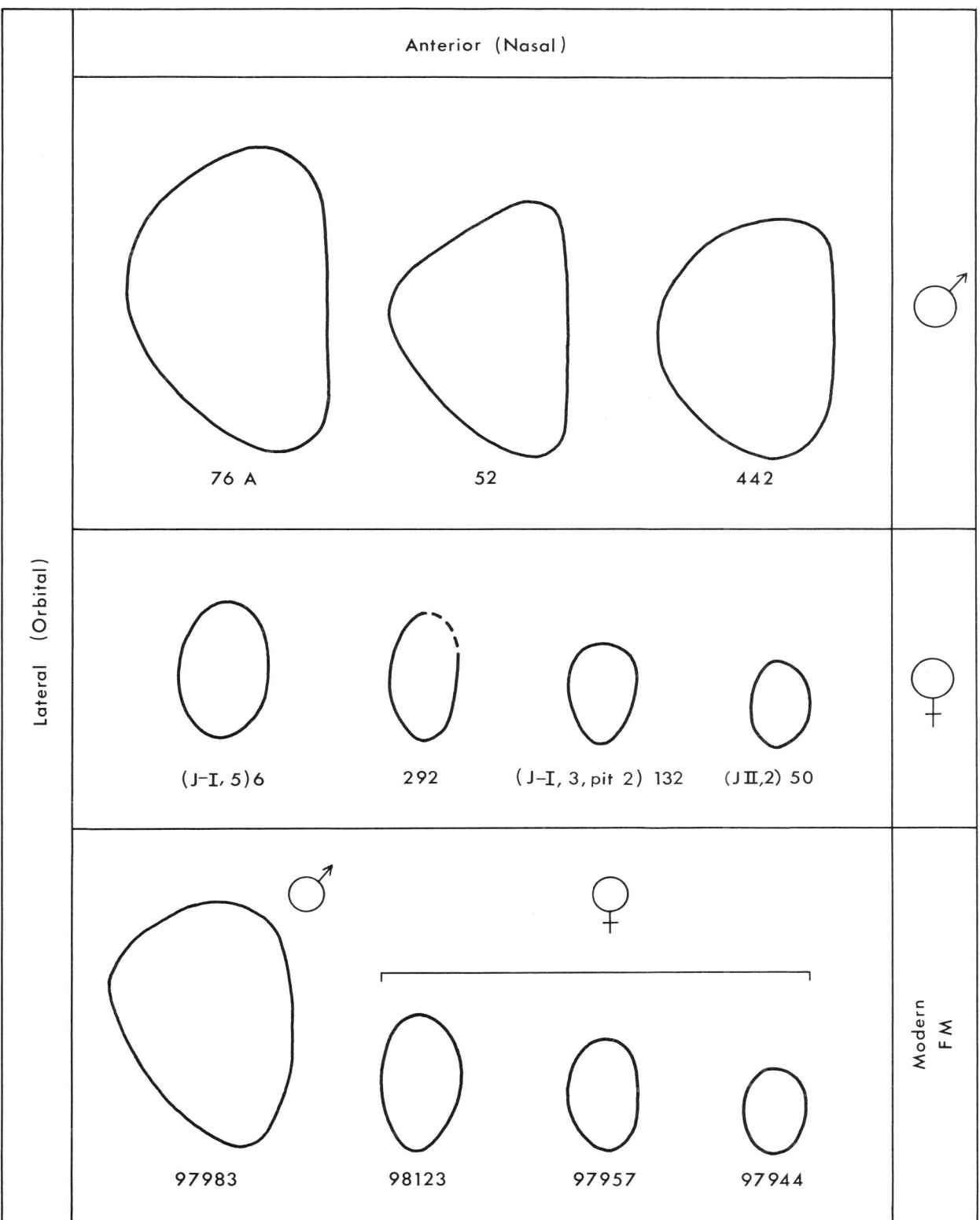

Fig. 177. Cross-section drawings of male and female sheep horn cores from Jarmo, with FMNH comparisons.

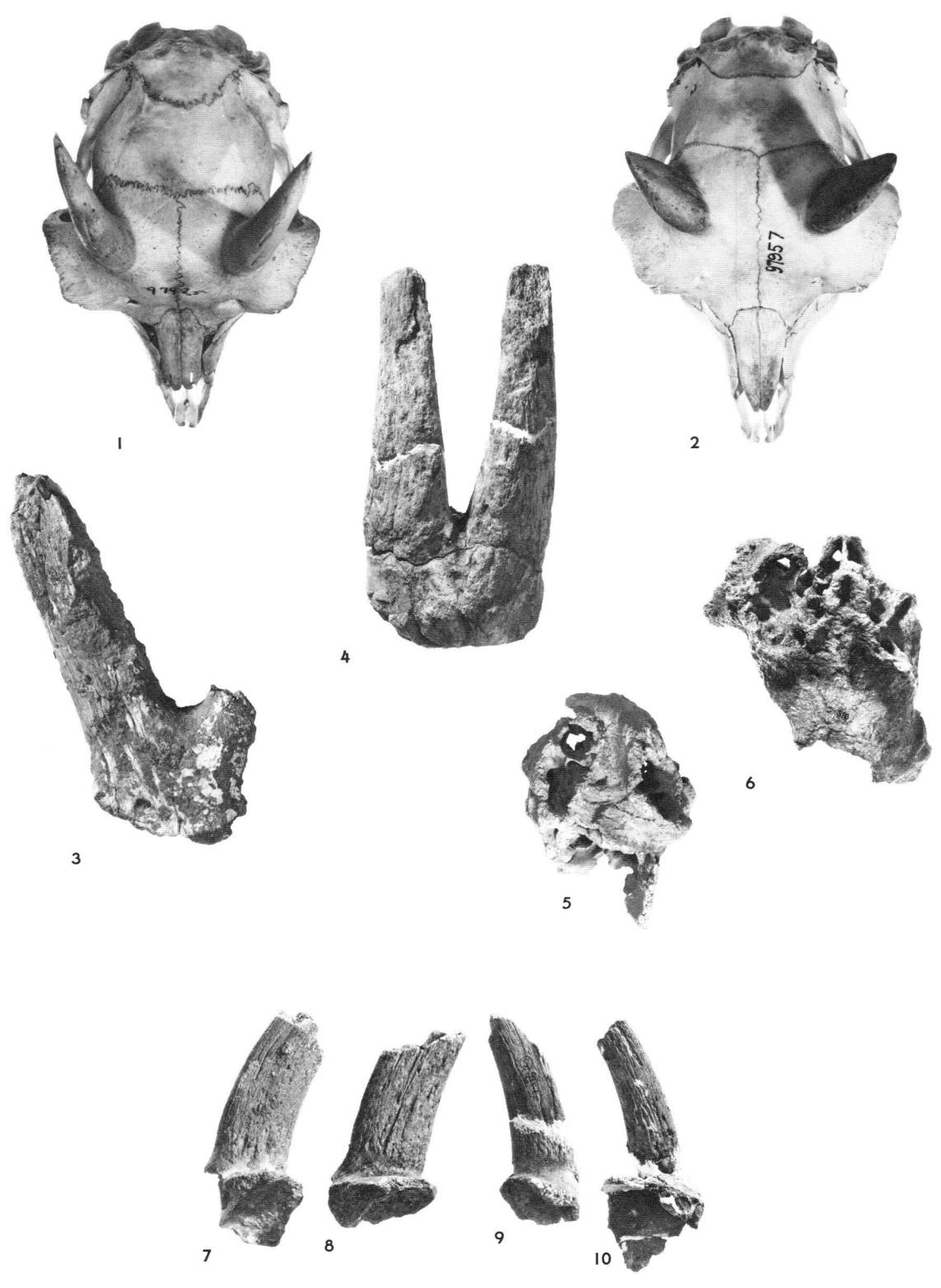

Fig. 178. Modern goat and sheep skulls (*1-2*) and a variety of Jarmo goat horn-core fragments (*3-10*): *1* (FMNH 97925), skull of *Capra aegagrus* Erxl., bezoar goat ♀; *2* (FMNH 97957), skull of *Ovis orientalis* Gm., wild sheep ♀; *3* (no. 52, from J-II,2fl.), horn core of wild goat ♂, frontal view; *4* (no. 53), horn cores of domestic goat ♂, frontal view; *5* (no. 187A), *6* (no. 316), skull fragments with bases of horn cores of wild goat ♂♂; *7* (no. 102, from J-A,III), *8* (no. 2, from J-B,1-2), horn cores of wild(?) goat, medial view; *9* (no. 5, from J-I,5), *10* (no. 300), horn cores of domestic goat, medial view.

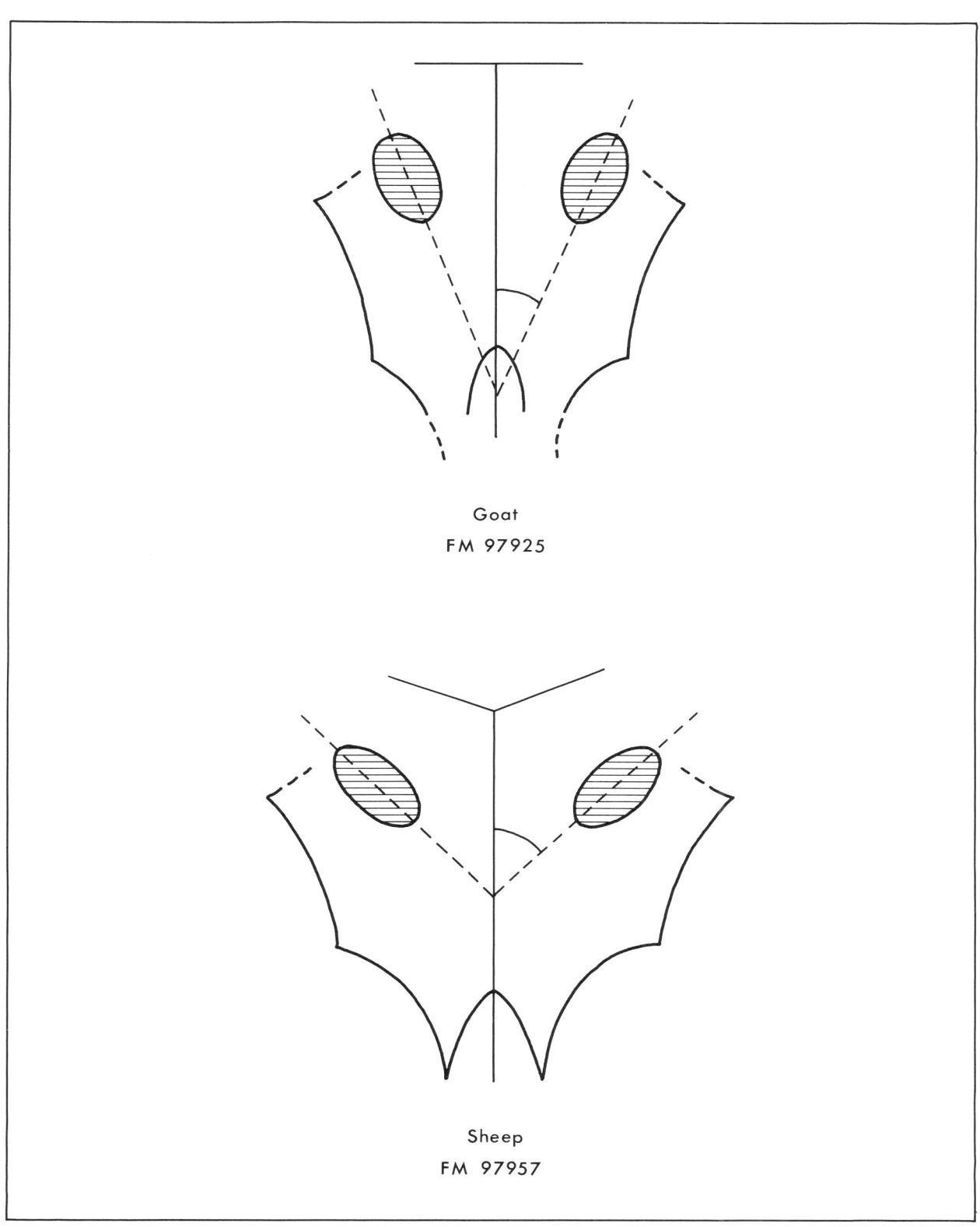

Fig. 179. Drawings showing the angle made by the base of the horn cores with the midsagittal plane of the skull in goat and sheep specimens from FMNH.

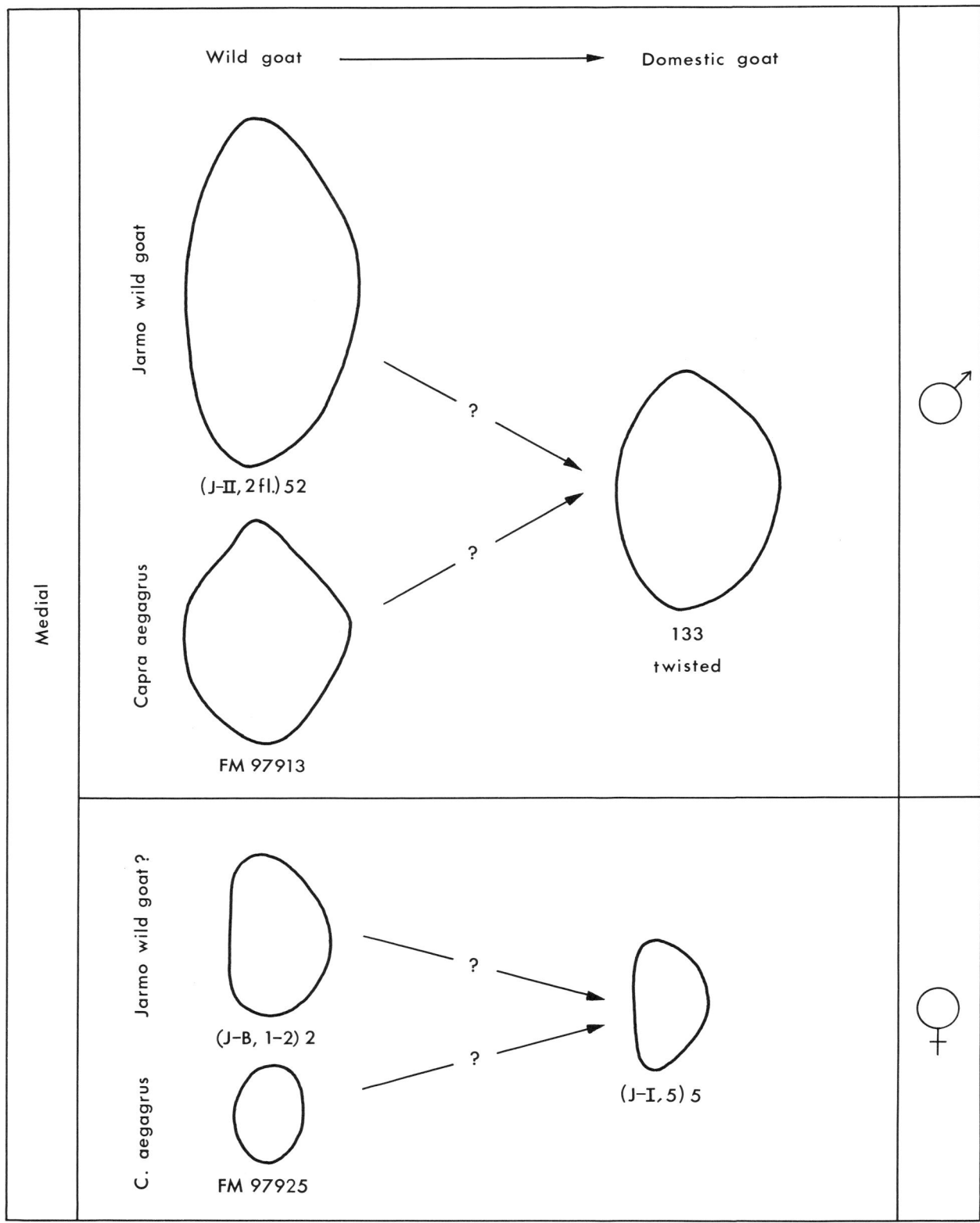

Fig. 180. Cross-section drawings of wild and domestic goat horn cores, male and female, from Jarmo, with FMNH comparisons.

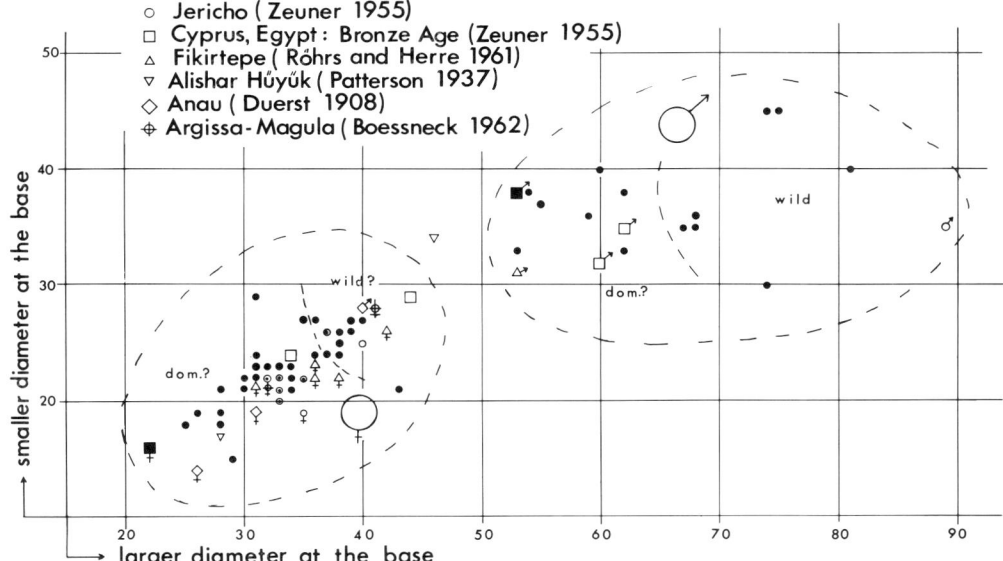
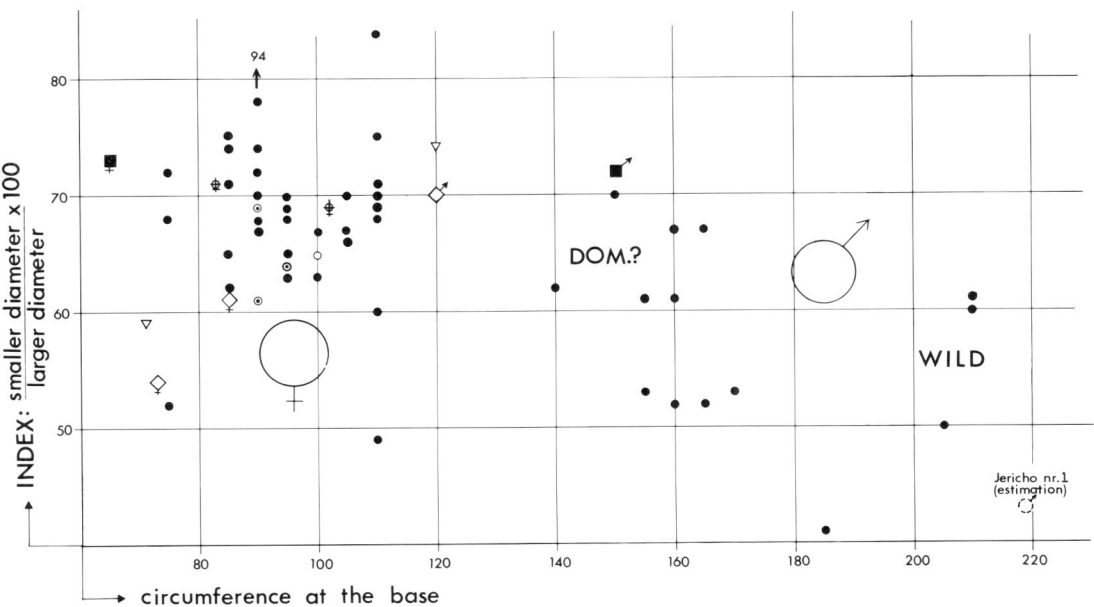

Fig. 181. Scatter diagrams of dimensions of goat horn cores from various sites: *a*, diameters of bases; *b*, basal circumferences and diameter indices. In *b*, the vertical column represents the ratio, expressed as percentages, between the smaller and larger diameters.

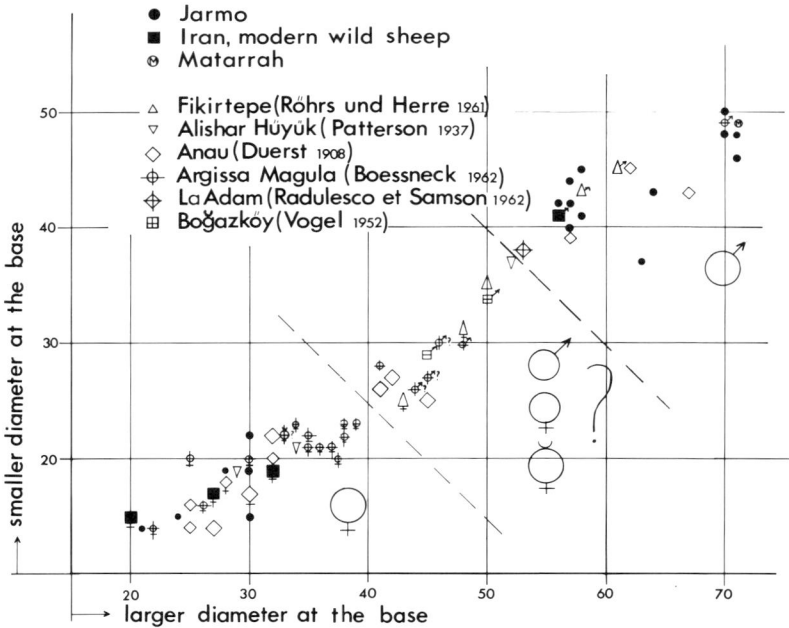

Fig. 182. Scatter diagram of dimensions of sheep horn cores from various sites.

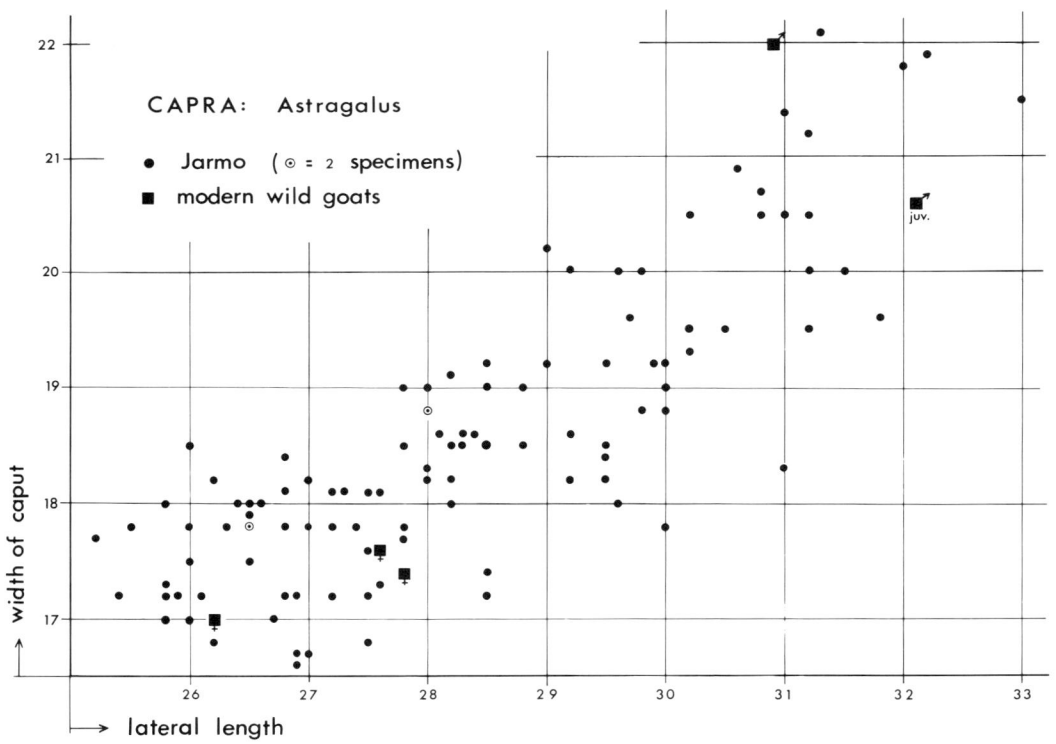

Fig. 183. Scatter diagram of dimensions of astragali of Jarmo goats and of modern goats.

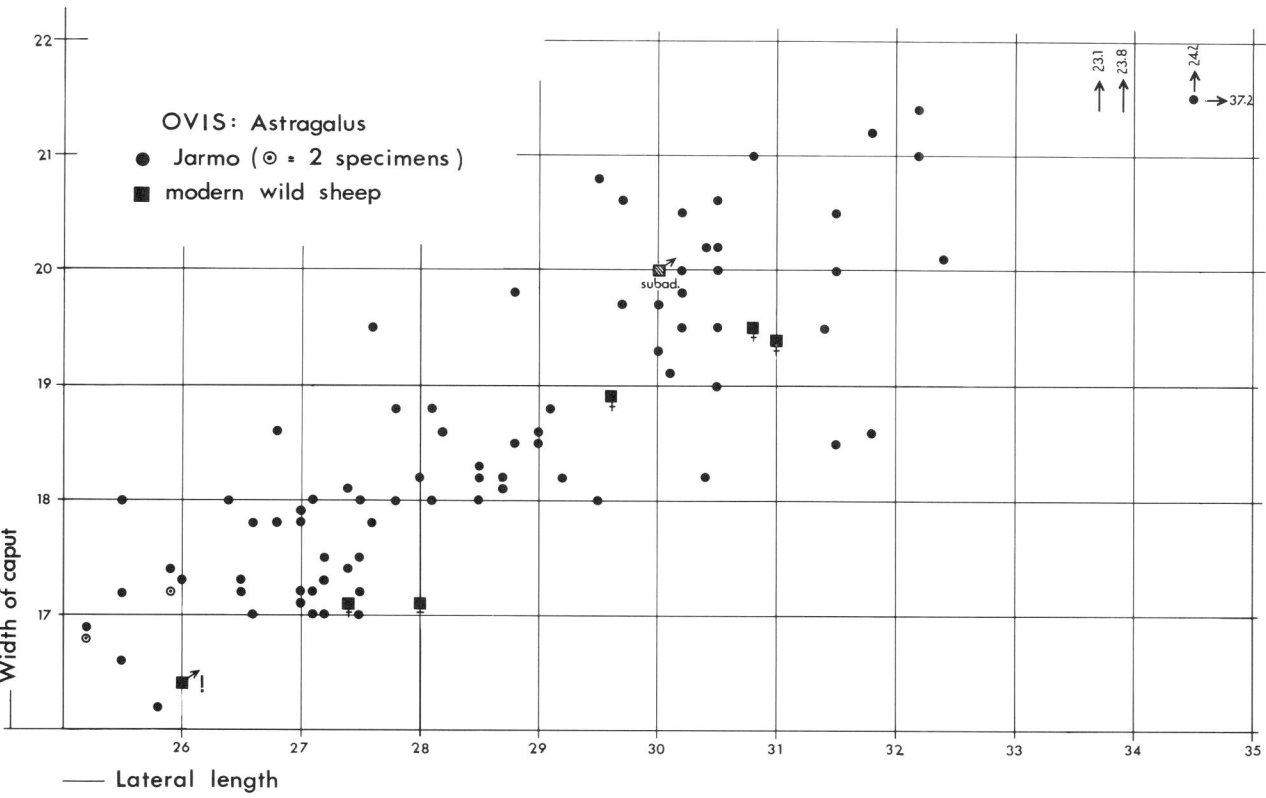

Fig. 184. Scatter diagram of dimensions of astragali of Jarmo sheep and of modern sheep.

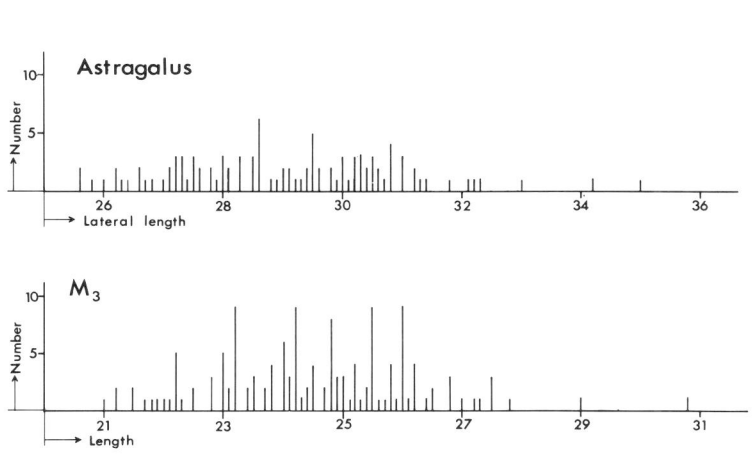

Fig. 185. Diagram showing the continuous distribution of the lengths of lower molars and astragali of sheep/goats.

REFERENCES

Amschler, J.W.
   1939 Tierreste der Ausgrabungen von dem "Grossen Königshügel" Shah Tepé, in Nord-Iran. *Reports from the Scientific Expedition to the North-Western Provinces of China under the Leadership of Dr. Sven Hedin: the Sino-Swedish Expedition*, publ. 9, vol. 7 (Archaeology), no. 4, pp. 35-129.

Angress, S.
   1959 Mammal remains from Horvat Beter (Beersheba). ʿ*Atiqot* 2:53-71.

Bate, D.M.A.
   1937 Palaeontology: the fossil fauna of the Wady el-Mughara caves. In *The Stone Age of Mount Carmel*, vol. 1, pt. 2, D.A.E. Garrod and D.M.A. Bate, pp. 135-233. Oxford: Clarendon Press.

Boessneck, Joachim
   1962 Die Tierreste aus der Argissa-Magula vom präkeramischen Neolithikum bis zur mittleren Bronzezeit. In *Die deutschen Ausgrabungen auf der Argissa-Magula in Thessalien*, vol. 1, V. Milojčić, J. Boessneck, and M. Hopf, pp. 27-99. Beiträge zur ur- und frühgeschichtlichen Archäologie des Mittelmeer-Kulturraumes, vol. 2. Bonn: Rudolf Habelt Verlag.
   1965 Die jungpleistozänen Tierknochenfunde aus dem Peneiostal bei Larissa in Thessalien. In *Paläolithikum um Larissa in Thessalien*, V. Milojčić, J. Boessneck, D. Jung, and H. Schneider, pp. 42-57. Ibid., vol. 1.

Boessneck, J.; Jéquier, J.-P.; and Stampfli, H.R.
   1963 Seeberg, Burgäschisee-Süd. Pt. 3. *Die Tierreste*. Acta Bernensia, vol. 2. Bern: Verlag Stämpfli.

Boessneck, Joachim; Müller, Hans-Hermann; and Teichert, Manfred
   1964 *Osteologische Unterscheidungsmerkmale zwischen Schaf* (Ovis aries Linné) *und Ziege* (Capra hircus Linné). Kühn-Archiv, vol. 78 (1-2). Berlin: Akademie-Verlag.

Bökönyi, S.
   1962 Zur Naturgeschichte des Ures in Ungarn und das Problem der Domestikation des Hausrindes. *Acta Archaeologica Academiae Scientiarum Hungaricae* 14:175-214.

Braidwood, Robert J.
   1952 *The Near East and the foundations for civilization*. Eugene, Oreg.: Condon Lectures, Oregon State System of Higher Education.
   1954a The Iraq-Jarmo Project of the Oriental Institute of the University of Chicago, season 1954-1955. *Sumer* 10:120-38.
   1954b A tentative relative chronology of Syria from the terminal food-gathering stage to ca. 2000 B.C. (based on the Amouq sequence). In *Relative chronologies in Old World archeology*, ed. Robert W. Ehrich, pp. 34-39. Chicago: University of Chicago Press.

Braidwood, Robert J., and Braidwood, Linda S.
   1953 The earliest village communities of southwestern Asia. *Journal of World History* 1:278-310.
   1960 Relative chronology and interpretation. In *Excavations in the plain of Antioch I: the earlier assemblages, phases A-J*, Robert J. Braidwood and Linda S. Braidwood, pp. 498-523. Oriental Institute Publications, vol. 61. Chicago: University of Chicago Press.

Braidwood, Robert J.; Braidwood, Linda S.; Smith, James G.; and Leslie, Charles
   1952 Matarrah: a southern variant of the Hassunan assemblage, excavated in 1948. *Journal of Near Eastern Studies* 11:1-75.

Braidwood, Robert J.; Howe, Bruce; et al.
   1960 *Prehistoric investigations in Iraqi Kurdistan*. Studies in Ancient Oriental Civilization [SAOC], no. 31. Chicago: University of Chicago Press.

Brentjes, Burchard
   1962a Cervinae. *Mitteilungen der anthropologischen Gesellschaft in Wien* 92:35-46.
   1962b Gazellen und Antilopen als Vorläufer der Haustiere im alten Orient. *Wissenschaftliche Zeitschrift der Martin-Luther-Universität Halle-Wittenberg, Gesellschafts- und Sprachwissenschaftliche Reihe*, Jahrgang 11 (6):537-48.
   1962c Mensch und Katze im alten Orient. Ibid., pp. 595-634.
   1962d Das Schwein als Haustier des alten Orients. *Ethnographisch-archäologische Zeitschrift* 3:125-38.
   1963 Die Schafzucht im alten Orient. Ibid. 4:1-22.
   1965 *Die Haustierwerdung im Orient*. Die Neue Brehm-Bücherei. Stuttgart: Franckh'sche Verlagshandlung, Kosmos-Verlag.

Coon, Carleton S.
   1951 *Cave explorations in Iran, 1949*. Museum Monographs. Philadelphia: University Museum, University of Pennsylvania.
   1952 Excavations in Hotu Cave, Iran, 1951, a preliminary report. *Proceedings of the American Philosophical Society* 96 (3):231-49.

Duerst, J. Ulrich
- 1908 Animal remains from the excavations at Anau and the horse of Anau in its relation to the races of domestic horses. In *Explorations in Turkestan: expedition of 1904, prehistoric civilizations of Anau*, vol. 2, ed. Raphael Pumpelly, pp. 339-442. Publications of the Carnegie Institution of Washington, no. 73. Washington, D.C.
- 1926 *Das Horn der Cavicornia*. Neue Denkschriften der Schweizerischen naturforschenden Gesellschaft, vol. 63. Zurich: Zürcher and Furrer.

Flannery, Kent V.
- 1961a Early village farming in southwestern Asia. In *Symposium: patterns of land utilization and other papers*, ed. Viola E. Garfield, pp. 7-17. Proceedings of the 1961 Annual Spring Meeting of the American Ethnological Society. Seattle: University of Washington Press.
- 1961b Skeletal and radiocarbon evidence for the origins of pig domestication. Master's thesis, University of Chicago.
- 1962 Faunal remains. In Excavations at Ali Kosh, Iran, 1961, Frank Hole and Kent V. Flannery, pp. 126-34. *Iranica Antiqua* 2:97-147.
- 1965 The ecology of early food production in Mesopotamia. *Science* 147:1247-56.

Fritsch, K.
- 1893 Die Funde des Herrn Pater Gottfried Zumoffen in den Höhlen am Fusse des Libanon. *Abhandlungen der naturforschenden Gesellschaft zu Halle* 19 (1):1-41.

Gaillard, Claude
- 1934 Contribution à l'étude de la faune préhistorique de l'Egypte. *Archives du Muséum d'histoire naturelle de Lyon* 14 (3):1-125.

Hatt, Robert T.
- 1959 *The mammals of Iraq*. Miscellaneous Publications of the Museum of Zoology, University of Michigan, no. 106. Ann Arbor.

Herre, Wolf
- 1958 *Abstammung und Domestikation der Haustiere*. Handbuch der Tierzüchtung, vol. 1.
- 1963 The science and history of domestic animals. In *Science in archaeology*, ed. Don Brothwell and Eric Higgs, pp. 235-49. New York: Basic Books.

Herre, Wolf, and Röhrs, Manfred
- 1955 Über die Formenmannigfaltigkeit des Gehörns der Caprini Simpson 1945. *Zoologische Garten*, n.s. 22:85-110.
- 1958 Die Tierreste aus den Hethitergräbern von Osmankayasi. In *Boğazköy-Ḫattuša*, vol. 2, *Die hethitischen Grabfunde von Osmankayasi*, Kurt Bittel, Wolf Herre, Heinrich Otten, Manfred Röhrs, and Johann Schaeuble, pp. 60-80. Wissenschaftliche Veröffentlichung der Deutschen Orient-Gesellschaft, vol. 71. Berlin: Verlag Gebr. Mann.

Hilzheimer, Max
- 1941 *Animal remains from Tell Asmar*. Trans. Adolph A. Brux. Studies in Ancient Oriental Civilization, no. 20. Chicago: University of Chicago Press.

Imhof, U.
- 1964 Osteometrische Untersuchungen an Rinderknochen aus Pfahlbauten des Bielersees. *Mitteilungen der Naturforschenden Gesellschaft in Bern*, n.s. 21:137-237.

Jéquier, J.-P.
- 1963 See Boessneck, Jéquier, and Stampfli 1963.

Josien, Thérèse
- 1955 La faune chalcolithique des gisements palestiniens de Bir es-Safadi et Bir Abou Matar. *Israel Exploration Journal* 5 (4):246-56.
- 1956 Faune chalcolithique du gisement de Bir es-Safadi à Beersheba (Israël). *Bulletin de la Société préhistorique française* 53:724-26.

King, Judith E.
- 1953 Mammal bones from Khirokitia and Erimi. In *Khirokitia: final report on the excavation of a neolithic settlement in Cyprus on behalf of the Department of Antiquities 1936-1946*, Porphyrios Dikaios, pp. 431-37. London: Oxford University Press.

Lawrence, Barbara
- 1956 Appendix E: cave fauna. In *An anthropological reconnaissance in the Near East, 1950*, Henry Field, pp. 80-81. Papers of the Peabody Museum of Archaeology and Ethnology, Harvard University, vol. 48 (2). Cambridge, Mass.

Mallowan, M.E.L.
- 1946 Excavations in the Baliḫ valley, 1938. *Iraq* 8:111-59.
- 1947 Excavations at Brak and Chagar Bazar. Ibid. 9:1-259.

Nagel, Wolfram
    1961   Zum neuen Bild des vordynastischen Keramikums in Vorderasien—I. *Berliner Jahrbuch für Vor- und Frühgeschichte* 1:1-125.

Nanninga, Onno
    1963   *Neue Funde des Schweines aus dem keltischen Oppidum von Manching.* Studien an vor- und frühgeschichtlichen Tierresten Bayerns aus dem Tieranatomischen Institut der Universität München, vol. 15. Munich: Verlag Kiefhaber, Kiefhaber, und Elbl.

Narr, Karl J.
    1961   *Urgeschichte der Kultur.* Stuttgart: Kröner Verlag.

Nobis, Günter
    1954   Beiträge zur Abstammung und Domestikation des Hauspferdes. *Zeitschrift für Tierzüchtung und Züchtungsbiologie* 64:210-46.
    1962   Zur Frühgeschichte der Pferdezucht. Ibid. 76 (2-3):125-85.

Opitz, G.
    1958   *Die Schweine des Latene-Oppidums Manching.* Studien an vor- und frühgeschichtlichen Tierresten Bayerns aus dem Tieranatomischen Institut der Universität München, vol. 3. Munich: Verlag Kiefhaber, Kiefhaber, und Elbl.

Patterson, Bryan
    1937   Animal remains. In *Researches in Anatolia,* vol. 9, *the Alishar Hüyük, seasons of 1930-32,* pt. 3, Hans Henning von der Osten, pp. 294-309. Oriental Institute Publications, vol. 30. Chicago: University of Chicago Press.

Perkins, Dexter, Jr.
    1960   The faunal remains of Shanidar Cave and Zawi Chemi Shanidar: 1960 season. *Sumer* 16:77-78.
    1964   Prehistoric fauna from Shanidar, Iraq. *Science* 144:1565-66.

Perrot, Jean
    1957   Le mésolithique de Palestine et les récentes découvertes à Eynan (Aïn Mallaha). *Antiquity and Survival* 2:91-111.

Radulesco, Costin, and Samson, Petre
    1962   Sur un centre de domestication du mouton dans le mésolithique de la grotte "La Adam" en Dobrogea. *Zeitschrift für Tierzüchtung und Züchtungsbiologie* 76 (2-3):282-320.

Reed, Charles A.
    1957   Zoology. In *The identification of non-artifactual archaeological materials,* ed. Walter W. Taylor, pp. 43-44. National Academy of Sciences–National Research Council, publ. 565. Washington, D.C.
    1959   Animal domestication in the prehistoric Near East. *Science* 130:1629-39.
    1960   A review of the archeological evidence on animal domestication in the prehistoric Near East. In SAOC 31, pp. 119-45.
    1961   Osteological evidences for prehistoric domestication in southwestern Asia. *Zeitschrift für Tierzüchtung und Züchtungsbiologie* 76 (1):31-38.
    1963   Osteo-archaeology. In *Science in archaeology,* ed. Don Brothwell and Eric Higgs, pp. 204-16. New York: Basic Books.
    1965   *Imperial Sassanian hunting of pig and fallow-deer, and problems of survival of these animals today in Iran.* Postilla, Peabody Museum of Natural History, Yale University, no. 92. New Haven, Conn.

Röhrs, Manfred
    1961   Biologische Anschauungen über Begriff und Wesen der Domestikation. *Zeitschrift für Tierzüchtung und Züchtungsbiologie* 76 (1):7-23.

Röhrs, Manfred, and Herre, Wolf
    1961   Zur Frühentwicklung der Haustiere: die Tierreste der neolithischen Siedlung Fikirtepe am kleinasiatischen Gestade des Bosporus. Ibid. 75:110-27.

SAOC 31
    1960   *Prehistoric investigations in Iraqi Kurdistan.* Robert J. Braidwood, Bruce Howe, et al. Studies in Ancient Oriental Civilization, no. 31. Chicago: University of Chicago Press.

Stampfli, Hans R.
    1964   Vergleichende Betrachtungen an Tierresten aus zwei neolithischen Siedlungen am Burgäschisee. *Mitteilungen der Naturforschenden Gesellschaft zu Bern,* n.s. 21:113-36.
    1968   Die Tierreste aus der römischen Villa Ersigen-Murain in Gegenüberstellung zu anderen zeitgleichen Funden aus der Schweiz und dem Ausland. *Jahrbuch des Bernischen historisches Museums in Bern* 45-46:449-69.
    1976   In *Das jungsteinzeitliche Jäger-Bauerndorf von Egolzwil 5 im Wauwilermoos,* René Wyss, pp. 125-40. Archaeologische Forschungen, naturwissenschaftliche Beiträge. Zurich: Schweizerischen Landesmuseum.

Turnbull, Priscilla F., and Reed, Charles A.
- 1974 *The fauna from the terminal Pleistocene of Palegawra Cave, a Zarzian occupation site in northeastern Iraq*. Fieldiana: Anthropology, vol. 63 (3). Chicago: Field Museum of Natural History.

Vaufrey, R.
- 1939 Faune de Sialk. In *Fouilles de Sialk près de Kashan, 1933, 1934, 1937*, vol. 2, R. Ghirshman, pp. 193-97. Musée du Louvre, Département des antiquités orientales, série archéologique, vol. 5. Paris: Librairie orientaliste Paul Geuthner.
- 1951 Etude paléontologique: I. Mammifères. In *Le paléolithique et le mésolithique du désert de Judée*, René Neuville, pp. 198-244. Archives de l'Institut de paléontologie humaine, mem. 24. Paris: Masson et Cie.

Vogel, Richard
- 1952 Reste von Jagd- und Haustieren. In *Boğazköy-Ḫattuša*, Kurt Bittel and Rudolf Naumann, pp. 128-53. Wissenschaftliche Veröffentlichung der Deutschen Orient-Gesellschaft, vol. 63. Stuttgart: Kohlhammer Verlag.

Watson, Patty Jo
- 1965 The chronology of north Syria and north Mesopotamia from 10,000 B.C. to 2000 B.C. In *Chronologies in Old World archaeology*, ed. Robert W. Ehrich, pp. 61-100. Chicago: University of Chicago Press.

Zeuner, Frederick E.
- 1955 The goats of early Jericho. *Palestine Exploration Quarterly* 87:70-86.
- 1958 Dog and cat in the Neolithic of Jericho. Ibid. 90:52-55.
- 1963 *A history of domesticated animals*. New York: Harper and Row.

Zeuner, Frederick E., and Ellis, A. Grosvenor
- 1961 Appendix 3: animal bones. In *Sotira*, Porphyrios Dikaios, pp. 235-36. Museum Monographs. Philadelphia: University Museum, University of Pennsylvania.

10

THE DOGS OF JARMO
Barbara Lawrence and Charles A. Reed

INTRODUCTION

The collection of the remains of larger canids from Jarmo, which had been reported briefly by Reed in 1961 and 1969, is here made a topic for special study. This is separate from Stampfli's more general report about the animals of this archeological site (chap. 9), in part because particular interest is attached to the early history of domestic dogs, and in part because Stampfli's time while in America was fully occupied with the remainder of the fauna from Jarmo. No account is presented here of Jarmo as an archeological site, as this information can be found elsewhere in this volume and in its predecessor (SAOC 31).

All archeological evidence indicates that Jarmo was occupied continuously for a period of only a few hundred years. Such being the situation, no effort has been made to separate individuals that were found in different parts of the mound, or at different depths within it. The population of dogs here studied is considered as a single gene pool, coming from one site within the chronological confines of those few hundred years, most probably between 9000 and 8500 B.P.

Some 53 cranial and mandibular fragments of *Canis* were collected, 18 of which are positively identifiable as *familiaris* (dog), while none are clearly *lupus* (wolf). In other words, of the unidentifiable remains, all could be dog. Dogs and wolves are so closely related that, unless one is dealing with extremes, identification depends on multiple characters. In the Near East, where the local species of wolf, *C. lupus pallipes*, is smaller than are members of more northern populations, this is particularly true. Teeth, being both conservative and individually variable, are undiagnostic over a wide range of size. Modifications in shape and proportion of the skull and mandible are more helpful in distinguishing dog. These, when combined with teeth of a particular size or spacing, may produce proportions that are quite unwolflike, even though particular measurements fall within the range for *pallipes*.

In the material at hand, only one cranial fragment is positively dog; the other 17 fragments of identifiable dog are all mandibular.

The series is of particular interest because the animals in question were in part as big toothed as the wolves of the area, and because the proportions of the posterior half of the jaw resemble very closely such massive breeds as the Eskimo dog.

THE EVIDENCE

MATERIAL EXAMINED

Thirty-six mandibular fragments (some may have been from the same animal)—17 cranial fragments, 40 isolated teeth or fragments of teeth, and 20 pieces of the postcranial skeleton—were examined.

COMPARATIVE SERIES

Canis lupus pallipes: British Museum of Natural History—13 from India, 1 from Iraq; Field Museum of Natural History—2 from Iraq (84468-9), 2 from Iran (99028 and 97778); Museum of Comparative Zoology—1 from Turkey (51602).

Canis familiaris: In particular, Museum of Comparative Zoology—7 Eskimo dogs (7406, 7407, 11176, 23713, 29800, 44469, 50502); Field Museum of Natural History—1 Kurdish dog (57252); as well as the series from Çayönü and Suberde (Lawrence 1980), and the prehistoric specimens from Jaguar Cave, Idaho (Lawrence 1967, 1968).

COMPARISONS

We emphasize that the diagnostic features that separate populations of ancient dogs from wild *Canis* differ from one region to the next, depending on the cranial characteristics of the locally occurring wild canids of the area in

---

The manuscript for this chapter was essentially completed by 1975. Very few additions and only minor revisions have been made since that date.—EDS.

question, as well as on the type of fragment recovered. Studies to date by Lawrence show a few characters that seem to have absolute diagnostic value for *familiaris* and none, except size, for *lupus*. However, since these characters are not universally present and often occur on less frequently preserved fragments, they are only of occasional use. Of these, some of the most typical for dog are flattening of the bullae; a more rounded, less posteriorly projecting, sagittal crest (fig. 190); and an elongated palate extending well beyond the level of the last molars.

Size, of course, may also be diagnostic, although the area of overlap is large, particularly in specimens from the Near East (table 38). While small size may often make jaws and cranial fragments of dog identifiable on this basis alone, this is less often true of teeth. Not infrequently, these are fully as large as those found in local wolves. Two examples are pertinent. The much-discussed Natufian *Canis* from Palestine has teeth that are within the range of size of *lupus pallipes* (Clutton-Brock 1962, p. 329). Yet, on the basis of a previously overlooked auditory bulla, Lawrence has been able to identify this specimen as *familiaris*. A small, typically *familiaris* jaw from Çayönü (Lawrence 1980) has the carnassial (26.3 mm) close to the mean for Near Eastern wolves. Similarly, many of the mandibular fragments from Jarmo, as far as teeth are concerned, could be wolf, and identification is possible only if other characters are considered as well.

As stated earlier, the fragments appear unusually massive. Comparison with a variety of dogs shows them to approach closely in size such big-toothed, massive-skulled breeds as the Eskimo dog. Jaws of seven of the latter were compared in detail with a series of five wolves from the Near East. Differences in proportion between these two series are best shown by means of ratio diagrams. Twelve measurements, selected from a sequentially numbered series of 71, are used. According to the type of difference they express, these measurements may be grouped in the following categories: (A) those expressing length (length of jaw, 34; alveolar length P_1-M_3, 17; alveolar length P_2-M_2, 70; and alveolar length P_2-P_4, 68); (B) those expressing lateromedial massiveness of jaw (maximum width ventral to M_1, 48; maximum width at base of ascending ramus, 51; and minimum width in region of premolars, 66); (C) size of teeth (crown length of M_1, 19; crown and alveolar lengths of P_4, 1 and 71; alveolar length of P_3, 67); (D) minimum height of jaw in region of premolars, 69.

These ratio diagrams, used also by Turnbull and Reed (1974, pp. 99-106) in their account of the Palegawra dog, are constructed as described by Simpson, Roe, and Lewontin (1960, pp. 356-58). The method is particularly well suited to comparing incomplete fragments in which relative rather than absolute dimensions need to be compared. Since the technique has not been much used by zooarcheologists, the following partial quote from Simpson, Roe, and Lewontin may be helpful in interpreting the diagrams presented here.

> The first step in constructing the diagram is to convert all the measurements into logarithms.... One specimen or group of specimens is then chosen as the standard of comparison. For each dimension the difference between the logarithmic value of the standard and each of the other specimens or groups is calculated. Each dimension, X, in each group is now represented by a new number: $d = \log^x - \log$ standard.... The values of d for the standard group itself are, of course, all zero. The horizontal scale in the diagram is marked off in units of d ... variates are placed ... along the vertical scale, and a line is drawn to connect the points for each group.... The values for d for each group or specimen are represented by points on the diagram at appropriate distances along the horizontal and vertical scales.... The horizontal distance between any two points is proportional to the ratio of the dimensions of the two animals.... Any specimen that has the same body proportions as the standard will be represented by a series of points falling on a straight line.... Any two specimens or groups which are proportioned alike will be represented by lines whose forms are alike even if neither is a straight line parallel to the standard.

Comparison of the five Near Eastern wolves and the Eskimo dogs, using logarithms of the means of the former as the standard (fig. 186), shows the Eskimo dogs to average smaller in categories A and C—length and size of teeth—but larger (more massive) in category B. Further, since the nature of the diagram is such that points equidistant from the standard have the same ratio to the standard, it is clear that the difference in proportions of jaw and teeth between dogs and wolves is largely in the region of P_1 and M_3, which were included in measurement 17. Characteristically, P_1 is more often reduced (or even lacking) in dogs than in wolves. Similarly, M_3 in dogs is often smaller relative to M_1 and M_2. This is reflected in the more wolflike proportions of length from P_2-M_2, measurement 70, and of P_2-P_4, measurement 68. The plot also shows that the increase in massiveness of the jaw anteriorly, measurement 66, is accompanied by a relative increase in height of the jaw in this region, measurement 69.

The comparative series of Near Eastern *Canis lupus pallipes* is a small one, so proportions of wolf as distinct from dog were further compared, insofar as possible, using six measurements only (nos. 34, 17, 48, 51, 19, and 1) of a larger series of *pallipes*, all from India (fig. 186). The other six measurements were not available for this series. In these more eastern *pallipes*, individual size averages smaller than in those from farther west, but proportions are much the same with the exception that there is a tendency for the jaw to be less massive, particularly at the base of the ascending ramus.

Apparently, then, at the westerly edge of the range of *pallipes*, the wolves tend to be more massive jawed than farther east, as well as slightly larger. Longer comparative series are essential before these preliminary conclusions can be categorically stated. While figure 186 is important in representing to what extent Eskimo dogs differ from such Near Eastern *pallipes* as are available, it masks the extent to which individual wolves in this area may resemble dogs.

For this reason, in analyzing the characteristics of the Jarmo population, the most massive of the series of *pallipes* (FMNH 84468, from the Zagros Mountains of northern Iraq) has been treated separately. Thus the standard used for comparison in figures 187-90 is based on the four remaining Near Eastern wolves. Although this distorts slightly the relationships shown in figure 186, it has the advantage of making possible a specimen-by-specimen comparison of the *Canis* from Jarmo with the most doglike of the wolves studied.

Of the Jarmo series, specimens PM30068, PM30075, and PM30077 (fig. 187), as well as PM30079, PM30080, PM30096, and PM30113 (fig. 188) are generally close to Eskimo dogs, in both size and proportions, lying near or above the upper limit for *pallipes* in massiveness, and near or below the lower limit in size of teeth and length of tooth row. Greatest variation occurs in size of P_3 and P_4, the former being noticeably large in PM30113 and the latter in PM30077.

The most massive specimen, PM30110, has large teeth and in these dimensions is not unlike FMNH 84468. An additional specimen, PM30033 (fig. 188), although less massive than the others, is still small toothed—in actuality and also in relation to massiveness of jaw—and is probably also *familiaris*.

In another series, PM30105, PM30029, PM30099, and PM30035 (fig. 189), the jaw is within the range of *lupus* for massiveness but the teeth are small, as is the length of the premolar series in the first three specimens, so that the proportions, though not as extreme as in the first series, are like *familiaris*. Finally, two anterior fragments of jaws, PM30015 and PM30104 (fig. 189), have the rami slim, but the length of P_2-P_4 of each is well below the limit for *lupus*.

Identification of the jaws of *Canis* from Jarmo is not based entirely on the quantitative characters discussed above. Certain qualitative characters, typical of Eskimo dogs, also set the Jarmo jaws apart. These characters are particularly helpful in separating them from the Zagros *lupus*, FMNH 84468. The most useful of these characters are the position of the last molar (embedded in the base of the ascending ramus), a strongly developed curvature of the lower tooth rows, a relatively more curving lower margin of the jaw, and small canines associated with thickening in the symphysial region. Details regarding the presence or absence of these features will not be given for all fragments but, where such confirming evidence is significant for purposes of identification, it is discussed below.

A number of specimens have M_3 set well back in the base of the ascending ramus. This is especially marked in PM30077, PM30110, and PM30113; PM30068 probably resembled these although the tooth is missing and the alveolus broken. Specimen PM30110, as well as PM30075 and PM30078, also resembles dog in the curvature of the tooth row and a thickening of the inner face of the jaw.

Curvature of the lower margin of the jaw has been helpful in confirming the identification of PM30033, PM30035, PM30079, and PM30113. Finally, in PM30079 the canine, although not precisely measurable, is smaller than in any wolf seen.

Specimen PM30027, an anterior mandibular fragment, as well as being massive, lacks P_1 and has the remaining premolar series short, as shown by the length from P_2 to mid P_4.

Specimen PM30031, a fragment of the posterior part of the jaw with the tooth row broken, when compared with *lupus* has the condyle and the angle of the jaw small, with the anterior border of the ascending ramus massive at its base. In all of these features it agrees with Eskimo dogs.

Finally, PM30044, a fragment of the posterior end of the tooth row of a small *Canis*, lacks M_3 and has the thickening at the base of the ascending ramus extending as far anteriorly as M_2, resembling in this, and in size, some of the dogs from Suberde.

Identification of skull fragments is more difficult and only one is positively dog. This specimen, PM30054, is part of the occipitoparietal region and has two typically doglike features. The sagittal and occipital crests have a pronounced downward curve and a posterior projection that is slight relative to the surface of the occipital bone (fig. 190). Further, this piece matches our series of Eskimo dogs in that the tip of the sagittal crest, in posterior view, is broadened and flattened.

Maxillary fragments are for the most part not positively diagnostic, although curvature of the tooth row in a number of these and the relatively small size of the teeth strongly suggest *familiaris*. Further, the size of the upper carnassials is within the range expected to match that of the lower carnassials (difference between the means for the lower and upper carnassial lengths in 13 *pallipes* is 1.9 mm, and between the means for 10 lower and 4 upper carnassial lengths in the Jarmo series is 2.1 mm), and curvature of the maxillary tooth rows matches well that of the series of Eskimo dogs, which have relatively broad palates. Two maxillary fragments, PM30014 and PM30076, which include part of the posterior end of the tooth row, strongly suggest dog. Both agree in being a little small for *pallipes* and in having the alveoli for M^1 and M^2 set medially. This condition results in the anteroexternal root socket for M^2 occupying the space between the external and internal roots of M^1. The same is apparently true of PM30083, where parts of both teeth remain. Four other specimens, PM30085, PM30086, PM30093, and PM30102, have somewhat larger teeth, at about the lower limit for *pallipes*. In all of these, M^2 is relatively larger and not so far set inward, so that the outer margin of the tooth row curves less. Another series, PM30097, PM30106, PM30107, and PM30109, includes P^3-M^2 and, in size of teeth, could be either Eskimo dogs or *pallipes*. The tooth rows, however, appear to curve more evenly and more pronouncedly than do those of *lupus*. Such a shape would match the more curved lower jaws, so it is presumed that these fragments of maxillae, too, are *familiaris* and reinforce the evidence of the lower jaws that this particular population had relatively wide palates.

Specimen PM30054, from the occipitoparietal region, has two characteristically doglike features. The sagittal and occipital crests have a pronounced downward curve and a posterior projection that is slight relative to the surface of the occipital bone (fig. 190). Further, this piece matches our series of Eskimo dogs in that the tip of the sagittal crest, in posterior view, is broadened and flattened.

DISCUSSION

Comparison of the Jarmo dogs with Eskimo dogs is not meant to imply a particularly close relationship with a breed so widely removed geographically. Massiveness is also characteristic of mastiffs and similar breeds. In this instance, the Eskimo dogs were considered to typify a particular assemblage of characters that is not uncommon in domestic dogs and were used because of their availability.

The occurrence at the present time, in the near vicinity of Jarmo, of a wolf that is typically wolflike in relative size of teeth and length of tooth row but has an unusually massive lower jaw can be variously interpreted. It might be evidence of some hybridization with dog or it might represent an extreme form of a distinct race of *lupus*, which typically resembles certain types of dogs in the proportions of the jaw. Such a race could be ancestral to the dogs of the area, a possibility that is strengthened by the differences between the dogs from Jarmo and those from two other sites in the Near East, Çayönü and Suberde (Lawrence 1980). However, until better comparative series of Near Eastern *Canis lupus* are available, any such suggestion is at best tentative. The last carefully detailed revision of Old World *lupus* was that of Pocock (1935) in which a single subspecies, *pallipes*, was recognized in the whole area from Turkey through India, most of the specimens coming from the latter place. Typically this is a small race, and for this reason, and because domestication in general was early in this area, it has often been cited as the ancestral form of *Canis familiaris*. To the south of the range of *pallipes*, Pocock recognized another even smaller race, *arabs*, occurring from Kuwait south and west into Arabia.

Nine specimens, primarily from eastern and southern Arabia, show that, on the basis of size, *arabs* cannot be distinguished from *familiaris*. As with the Indian *pallipes*, only six of the measurements used in identifying the Jarmo

Table 38.—Range in Certain Measurements of *Canis lupus pallipes* and *Canis familiaris*, Showing Overlap

	Canis lupus pallipes				*Canis familiaris*	
	Near Eastern		Indian		Eskimo	
	Min.	Max.	Min.	Max.	Min.	Max.
Length of jaw from middle of condyle to alveolus of I^1 (34)	158.3	179.6	154.1	173.2	152.2	167.1
Alveolar length, P_1-M_3 (17)	89.9	94.9	82.5	91.9	73.7	85.3
Crown length of P_4 (1)	13.6	16.5	13.1	14.9	12.1	14.7
Maximum width of P_4	7.0	8.3	6.4	7.3	6.5	8.0
Crown length of M_1 (19)	24.8	28.5	22.9	26.2	21.5	25.6
Maximum width of M_1	9.9	11.6	9.2	10.4	8.9	11.0
Crown length of P^4	--	--	21.1	23.9	19.1	23.0
Minimum width of P^4	--	--	8.2	9.1	7.5	9.5

NOTE: All measurements in mm.

Table 39.—Range and Mean of Four *Canis lupus pallipes* Used as the Standard in Figures 187-89

	Min.	Max.	Mean
Length of jaw from middle of condyle to alveolus of I^1 (34)	158.3	179.6	169.6
Alveolar length, P_1-M_3 (17)	89.9	94.9	91.8
Alveolar length, P_2-M_2 (70)	73.6	82.9	78.6
Alveolar length, P_2-P_4 (68)	39.0	44.5	41.7
Maximum width of jaw, ventral to M_1 (48)	12.1	13.2	12.7
Maximum width at base of ascending ramus (51)	10.7	12.8	11.5
Maximum width of jaw in region of premolars (66)	9.5	10.9	10.1
Crown length of M_1 (19)	24.8	28.5	26.7
Crown length of P_4 (1)	13.6	16.5	15.1
Alveolar length of P_4 (71)	12.6	16.0	14.3
Alveolar length of P_3 (67)	11.6	14.4	13.3
Minimum height of jaw in region of premolars (69)	20.6	24.7	22.9

NOTE: All measurements in mm.

dogs have been available for this series of *arabs*. These measurements (fig 186) show *arabs* to be very similar to the Indian *pallipes* in their proportions, to be smaller than the Jarmo dogs, and to differ from these and the Near Eastern *pallipes* in slimness of jaw.

If further collecting in the Near East confirms the apparent difference of Iranian-Iraqi wolves from the Indian *pallipes*, then the possibility that the Jarmo dogs are derived from a local race of wolves, which is like *familiaris* in certain proportions, will be strengthened. Such evidence will be important in furthering an understanding of the extent to which dogs are locally derived or have spread from a single center of domestication.

REFERENCES

Braidwood, Robert J.; Howe, Bruce; et al.
    1960 SAOC 31 (see below).

Clutton-Brock, Juliet
    1962 Near Eastern canids and the affinities of the Natufian dogs. *Zeitschrift für Tierzüchtung und Züchtungsbiologie* 76 (2-3):326-33.

Lawrence, Barbara
    1967 Early domestic dogs. *Zeitschrift für Säugetierkunde* 32 (1):44-59.
    1968 Antiquity of large dogs in North America. *Tebiwa, Journal of the Idaho State University Museum* 11 (2):43-49.
    1980 Evidences of animal domestication at Çayönü. In *The joint Istanbul-Chicago Universities' prehistoric research in southeastern Anatolia*, vol. 1, ed. Halet Çambel, pp. 257-308. İstanbul üniversitesi edebiyat fakültesi yayınları, no. 2589. Istanbul.

Pocock, R.I.
    1935 The races of *Canis lupus*. *Proceedings of the General Meetings for Scientific Business of the Zoological Society of London*, pp. 647-86.

Reed, Charles A.
    1961 Osteological evidences for prehistoric domestication in southwestern Asia. *Zeitschrift für Tierzüchtung und Züchtungsbiologie* 76 (1);31-38
    1969 The pattern of animal domestication in the prehistoric Near East. In *The domestication and exploitation of plants and animals*, ed. Peter J. Ucko and G.W. Dimbleby, pp. 361-80. Chicago: Aldine.

SAOC 31
    1960 *Prehistoric investigations in Iraqi Kurdistan*. Robert J. Braidwood, Bruce Howe, et al. Studies in Ancient Oriental Civilization, no. 31. Chicago: University of Chicago Press.

Simpson, George Gaylord; Roe, Anne; and Lewontin, Richard C.
    1960 *Quantitative zoology*. Rev. ed. New York: Harcourt, Brace.

Turnbull, Priscilla F., and Reed, Charles A.
    1974 *The fauna from the terminal Pleistocene of Palegawra Cave, a Zarzian occupation site in northeastern Iraq*. Fieldiana: Anthropology, vol. 63 (3). Chicago: Field Museum of Natural History.

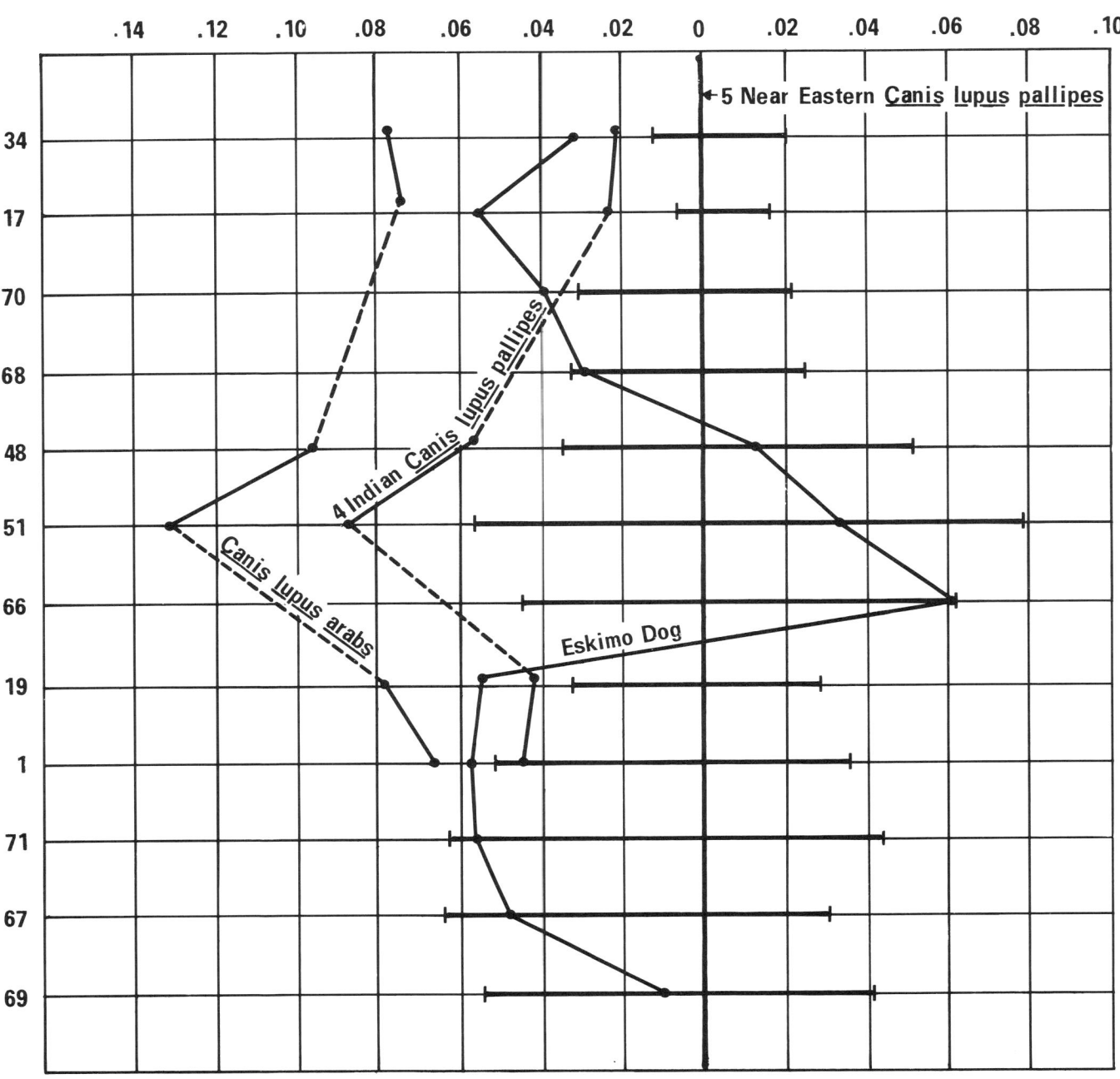

Fig. 186. Ratio diagram comparing a series of measurements of Eskimo *Canis familiaris*, Near Eastern *Canis lupus pallipes*, Indian *C. l. pallipes*, and *C. l. arabs*. The standard is the logarithm of the mean of each dimension of the five Near Eastern *pallipes*, and the horizontal scale represents the deviation from the standard of the means for the other three series. Six measurements each for Indian *pallipes* and for *arabs*, and twelve for *familiaris*, were used. The range of the five Near Eastern *pallipes* is also shown by plotting maximum deviation plus and minus from the standard.

In this and the following figures (figs. 187-89), solid lines connect points plotted in sequence; dashed lines are used when certain measurements are omitted. Measurements are as follows: crown length of P_4 (1); alveolar length P_1-M_3 (17); crown length M_1 parallel to inner margin (19); length of jaw from alveolus of I_1 to midpoint of condyle (34); maximum lateromedial width of jaw below M_1 (48); lateromedial width of jaw at anterior base of ascending ramus (51); minimum lateromedial width of jaw in region of premolars (66); alveolar length P_3 (67); alveolar length P_2-P_4 (68); minimum height of jaw in region of premolars (69); alveolar length P_2-M_2 (70); alveolar length P_4 (71).

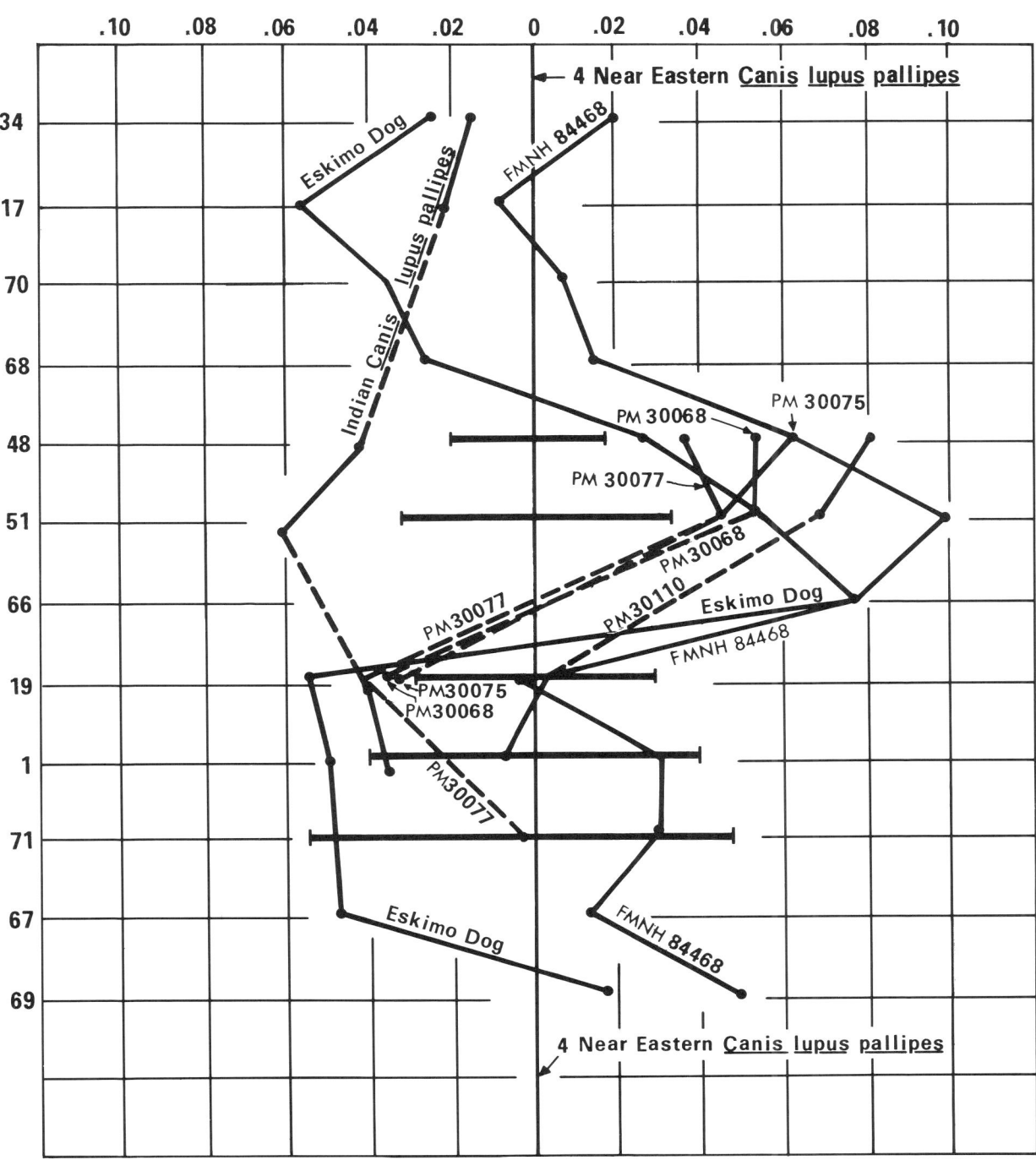

Fig. 187. Ratio diagram using four of the Near Eastern *pallipes* as the standard. The fifth specimen, FMNH 84468, is seen to resemble *familiaris* and to deviate more from the standard than does the Indian *pallipes*. Ranges for the standard and for *familiaris* are shown, as in fig. 186, by plotting, in each population, maximum deviations plus and minus from the standard for each dimension. Measurements as in fig. 186. Field Museum of Natural History numbers for the specimens from Jarmo: PM30068, PM30075, PM30077, PM30110.

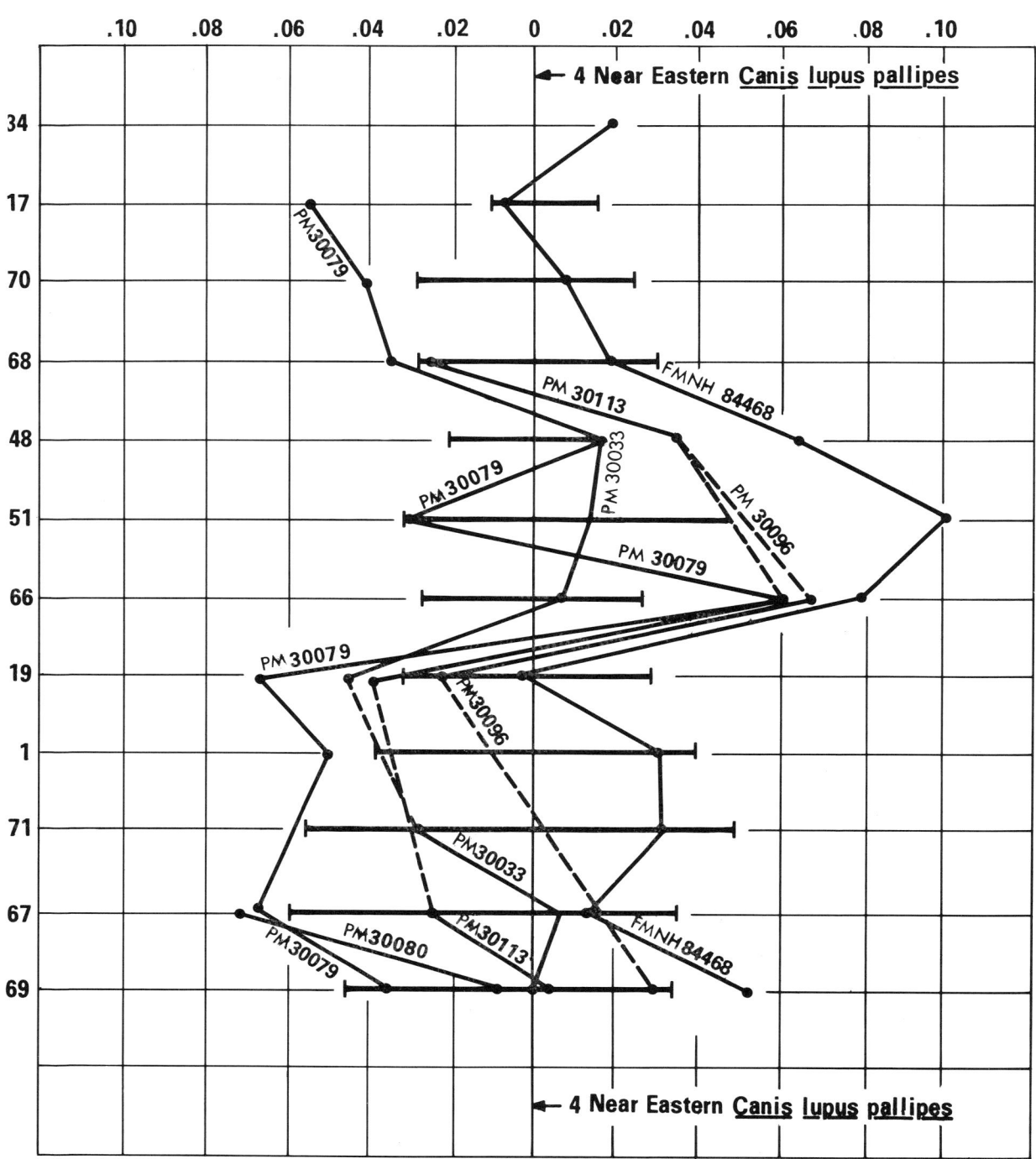

Fig. 188. Ratio diagram using same standard as fig. 187. Lines and measurements as in fig. 186. Field Museum of Natural History numbers for the specimens from Jarmo: PM30033, PM30079, PM30080, PM30096, PM30113.

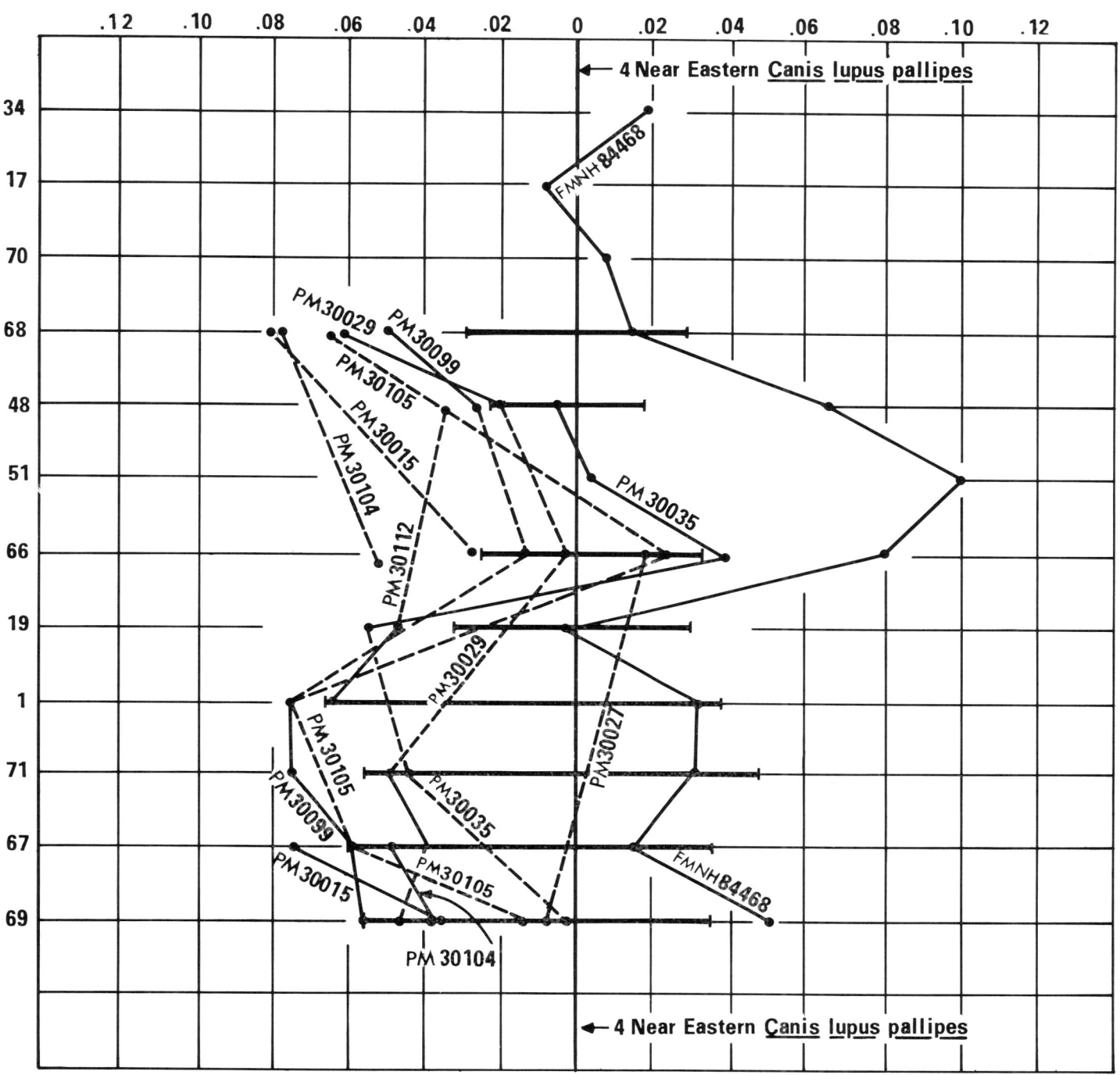

Fig. 189. Ratio diagrams using same standard as fig. 187. Lines and measurements as in fig. 186. Field Museum of Natural History numbers for the specimens from Jarmo: PM30015, PM30027, PM30029, PM30035, PM30099, PM30104, PM30105, PM30112.

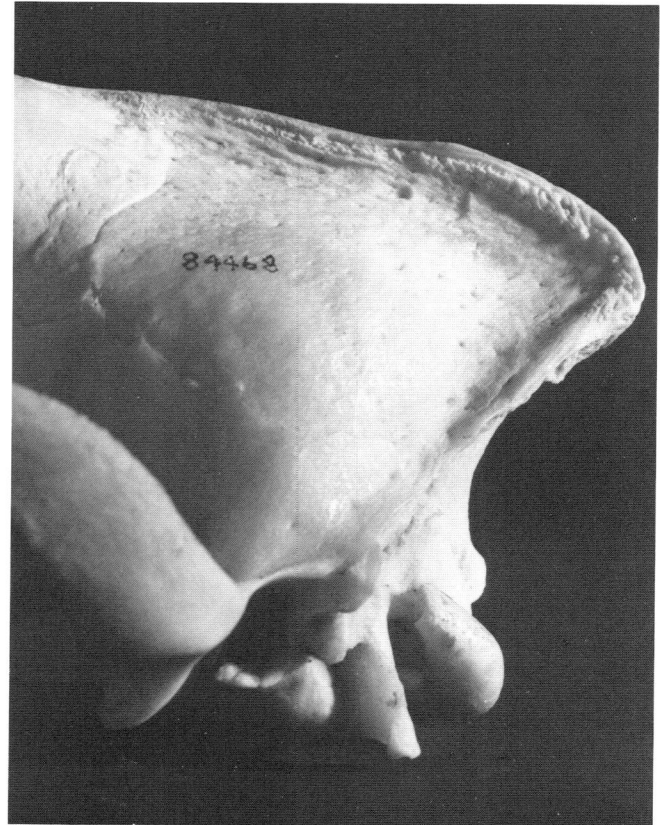

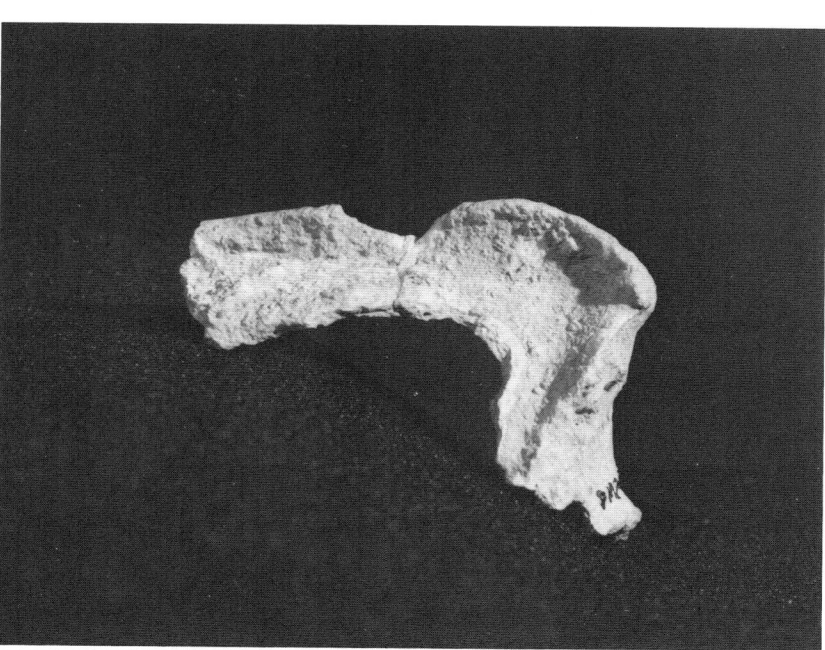

Fig. 190. *a*, Lateral view of the posterior part of the skull (FMNH 84468) of a modern wolf (*Canis lupus pallipes*) from northern Iraq; *b*, lateral view of the posterodorsal part of the skull (PM30054) of a dog (*Canis familiaris*) from Jarmo. Both are natural size, and the degree of development and the rugosity of the sagittal and lambdoidal crests indicate that both skulls are from adult animals. The smaller size of the skull and the lesser degree of posterior overhang of the sagittal crest of the prehistoric dog are apparent at a glance.

11

BIRDS AND SMALL MAMMALS FROM JARMO

Priscilla F. Turnbull

The bird and small mammal bones from the excavations at Jarmo were given to me for study by Dr. Charles A. Reed. The limited size of this collection is surprising, considering that many more bones of large mammals were found at the same site. Some 9,000 of the large bones have been studied by Dr. Hans Stampfli and described by him elsewhere in this volume (chap. 9). The bones included in the collection discussed here have been catalogued in the Division of Paleontology at the Field Museum of Natural History. PA and PM catalogue numbers refer to the archeological bird and mammal collections respectively.

Many reasons might be given for taking care to collect the microfauna at any archeological site. Foremost is the opportunity to gain more complete knowledge of the biotic environment existing at a particular place within particular time limits. No amount of care will ever result in a "complete" sampling, as we all know, but at least all possible avenues of collecting should be explored, even when interest is chiefly cultural. Furthermore, knowledge of the presence of these unobtrusive creatures may be important to a fuller understanding of man's movements and history. Small communities as well as large civilizations often come to mysterious ends; for example, the simple physical health of man and his important domesticates can be vastly affected by a few disease-carrying mice. Finally, study and recognition of the small elements in a collection of bones will surely teach us more of the details of post-Pleistocene climates, animal migrations, and food supplies. Some small animals are tied more closely to tolerable temperature and moisture zones than is man, who can and does go far afield to hunt or gather food. A changing rodent pattern might reflect significant environmental changes long before these are seen in man's changing habits.

Following is a discussion of the small vertebrates identified from Jarmo:

Class AVES
    Order Galliformes
        Family Phasianidae

Alectoris graeca, rock partridge. PA269, PA273-PA276: PA269 is a nearly complete skeleton of an immature specimen with unossified epiphyses, found in the blocking of the door below J-I,6. The bones are not mineralized and appear rather recent. The other catalogued specimens consist of isolated, mineralized limb bones from various levels.

Class MAMMALIA
    Order Insectivora
        Family Erinaceoidea

Erinaceus europaeus, European hedgehog. PM12882-PM12887: 5 mandibular fragments, several teeth, 1 proximal end of a femur. This hedgehog is a common inhabitant today in the area.

    Order Lagomorpha
        Family Leporidae

Lepus capensis, hare. PM12878-PM12881, PM12888-PM12889: 3 mandibular rami with teeth, several loose teeth, 2 humeri, 1 radius, 1 metatarsal.

    Order Rodentia
        Family Muridae

Tatera indica, antelope rat. PM12853-PM12860, PM12862-PM12864, PM12866-PM12870: 17 mandibular fragments, 12 with molar teeth. Numerous molar and incisor teeth and many limb bones refer to this murid. Various

---

I appreciate the privilege of working with the Field Museum's comparative zoological materials and the use of the library facilities; I thank Mr. E. Leland Webber, director, and Dr. Joseph C. Moore, former curator of mammals. I also thank Dr. Tibor Perenyi, staff artist, for technical advice in the preparation of the figures.

[The manuscript for this chapter was essentially completed by 1975. Very few additions and only minor revisions have been made since that date.—EDS.]

ages are represented by the jaws; some of the teeth retain the traces of original cusps on the transverse laminae of the molars, while others are so worn that the laminae are joined and no trace remains of the original cusps. (See fig. 191.)

Tatera and *Meriones* both live today (Hatt 1959, pp. 14-16) in Iraq in the alluvial plains habitat—in riverine thickets, in cultivated fields, and other well-drained den sites; in the southwestern desert where food and water are available and the soil permits burrowing; and in the Assyrian plains and foothills among the rocky hills and wadis. *Meriones* also lives today in the Kurdish mountains, especially in oak forests and in cultivated lands. Remains of *Meriones* were present at Palegawra cave, some 15 miles northeast of Jarmo, at an elevation of over 900 m (3,000+ ft), but no *Tatera* was recovered from that site (Turnbull and Reed 1974). The relatively small size of the cave may be said to account for the presence of only *Meriones* on the basis that it successfully kept out competitors such as *Tatera*, but *Cricetulus*, *Microtus*, and *Ellobius*, for example, are present in the Palegawra fauna as competing murids, though in smaller numbers. The high altitude is not a satisfactory explanation either, for the Warwasi shelter site in the Kermanshah valley, Iran, contained jaws of *Tatera* at an elevation of 1,330 m.

On the other hand, the reverse situation is even more difficult to understand, that is, at Jarmo (elevation ca. 800 m), where *Tatera* was found, *Meriones* and other murids would also be expected to be present. Reed collected live specimens of *Gerbillus*, *Cricetulus*, *Meriones*, *Microtus*, *Spalax*, and *Mus* from the area near Jarmo. Jarmo was a much larger operation (1,370 m^2) than Palegawra (30 m^2) (SAOC 31, pp. 38, 58), and it is strange that all rodent jaws are of a single species. Perhaps the sieving screens were too coarse to retain the bones of any rodents that were smaller than the relatively large *Tatera*.

Table 40 summarizes a series of measurements taken on the teeth in jaws of *Tatera* from Jarmo and on a series of modern specimens of *Tatera indica* from the vicinity of Kuh Hajeh, 15 miles southeast of Zabel, Kerman Province, eastern Iran, collected by the Field Museum Street Expedition of 1962.

Half of the *Tatera* jaws from Jarmo have relatively unworn molars and half have worn molars. (Figure 191 illustrates two of the *Tatera* jaws from Jarmo: in one, wear is just beginning to obliterate the original cusps; in the other, wear has progressed to the point that all trace of cusp pattern is gone and the lophs in each molar are joined together.) Lengths of M_1 from Jarmo vary, to some extent depending on the manner of abrasion, while the widths are quite constant. The lengths of M_1 in the modern specimens of *Tatera* vary through a range similar to that of the Jarmo specimens, while widths vary over three times as much as in the Jarmo collection.

Frequency histograms shown in figures 192 and 193 diagram these results. In figure 192, the maximum widths of M_1 in the modern *Tatera* population from Iran (*a*) are compared with the maximum widths of M_1 in the older prehistoric Jarmo population (*b*). In figure 193, the lengths of M_1 in the Iran population (*a*) are compared with those of the Jarmo specimens (*b*). The prehistoric specimens of these teeth are larger than the modern specimens as a whole, though overlapping occurs (50% in the case of the lengths, but only 17% in the widths).

Despite the variation, there is no doubt that the jaws of *Tatera* from Jarmo are of the species *indica*. As with some other elements of the late Pleistocene and early Recent faunas, the older forms were larger than modern representatives. The colder, moister climate of 8,500 years ago, more nutritious soil, and fuller growth development all may be causes. Furthermore, Kuh Hajeh in southwest Iran is drier and hotter than the Jarmo area in northeast Iraq, a fact that also contributes to the smaller size of the modern specimens.

Order Carnivora
Family Canidae

Vulpes vulpes, fox. PM12893-PM12900, PM12875: 6 mandibular rami with teeth, 2 metatarsals. Table 41 compares these specimens with those from Palegawra cave (Zarzian) and some Recent specimens. The specimens from Palegawra are larger than those from Jarmo in four of the six measurements. The modern fox teeth are the smallest of all except for the width of P_4, which is greater than in the compared archeological specimens.

Canis lupus, wolf. PM12901-PM12902: right ramus with P_{3-4}, right metatarsal II.

Family Ursidae

Ursus arctos, brown bear. PM12890: axis vertebra of a young individual. This is the first bear to be identified from either Jarmo or Palegawra, though it certainly is to be expected in the fauna of this time and place. In fact, Perkins reported bear from Shanidar Cave (1964). Not really from a small mammal, this small bone is included here to complete the list of known fauna from Jarmo.

Family Mustelidae

Martes sp., marten. PM12876: proximal half of a humerus. As Turnbull and Reed (1974) noted when describing the fossil mammals from Palegawra Cave, the presence of the stone marten does not indicate a forest environment; this animal lives easily in rocky hill country (Lay 1967).

Meles meles, badger. PM12903-PM12906: 4 mandibular rami (2 with teeth).

Family Felidae

Felis chaus, wildcat. PM12891: fragment of ramus with M_1.

Table 40.—Comparison of *Tatera indica* from Jarmo and Kuh Hajeh

	Jarmo	Kuh Hajeh
Length M_1	N = 12 OR = 3.1-3.4 mm M = 3.25 ± 0.03 s = 0.10 V = 3.0	N = 22 OR = 2.7-3.2 mm M = 3.05 ± 0.04 s = 0.19 V = 6.2
Width M_1	N = 12 OR = 2.5-2.6 mm M = 2.58 ± 0.01 s = 0.03 V = 1.15	N = 22 OR = 2.0-2.5 mm M = 2.30 ± 0.03 s = 0.12 V = 5.2

NOTE: N = number of specimens; OR = observed range; M = mean ± standard error; s = standard deviation; V = coefficient of variation.

Table 41.—Comparison of *Vulpes vulpes* from Jarmo, Palegawra, and Modern Collections from Iraq

	Jarmo	Palegawra	Modern Iraq
Length P_4	N = 3 OR = 8.7-9.4 mm M = 9.2	N = 2 OR = 9.2-9.6 mm M = 9.4	N = 6 OR = 8.15-9.05 mm M = 8.65 ± 0.13 s = 0.33 V = 3.9
Width P_4	N = 3 OR = 3.5-4.3 mm M = 4.0	N = 2 OR = 3.8-4.1 mm M = 3.95	N = 6 OR = 3.85-4.45 mm M = 4.1 ± 0.98 s = 0.24 V = 5.7
Length M_1	N = 5 OR = 13.6-15.2 mm M = 14.7 ± 0.03 s = 0.69 V = 4.7	N = 3 OR = 15.2-15.9 mm M = 15.6	N = 6 OR = 13.7-14.75 mm M = 14.2 ± 0.15 s = 0.37 V = 2.6
Width M_1	N = 5 OR = 5.6-6.3 mm M = 6.1 ± 0.12 s = 0.28 V = 4.6	N = 3 OR = 6.1-6.6 mm M = 6.3	N = 6 OR = 5.15-5.75 mm M = 5.5 ± 0.07 s = 0.03 V = 3.3
Length M_2	N = 2 OR = 6.9-7.8 mm M = 7.35	N = 5 OR = 6.8-7.4 mm M = 7.0 ± 0.12 s = 0.27 V = 3.8	N = 6 OR = 6.05-7.45 mm M = 6.8 ± 0.19 s = 0.49 V = 7.1
Width M_2	N = 2 OR = 5.2 mm M = 5.2	N = 5 OR = 5.3-5.8 mm M = 5.5 ± 0.08 s = 0.18 V = 3.2	N = 6 OR = 4.85-5.45 mm M = 4.25 ± 0.09 s = 0.22 V = 4.3

NOTE: N = number of specimens; OR = observed range; M = mean ± standard error; s = standard deviation; V = coefficient of variation. Five of the modern specimens from Iraq are from the Zagros area, and one is from the western part of Iraq.

CONCLUSIONS

Along with the important animals hunted for food at Jarmo, and described in this volume by Stampfli (chap 9), certain other wild inhabitants left their presence recorded in the horizons of that occupation site. Only one species of rodent was found preserved, but others must surely have lived there as well. In general, the more ancient jaws of *Tatera* from Jarmo are somewhat larger than the modern specimens from Kuh Hajeh. The fox (*Vulpes*) may have been an occasional food animal at Jarmo as it was elsewhere in southwestern Asia. The specimens of *Vulpes* from Jarmo possessed teeth that were somewhat smaller than the archeologically older specimens of *Vulpes* from Palegawra in all measured dimensions except width of P_4 and length of M_2 but larger than modern forms of the area. These observations add to the evidence that, in general, mammals living at a higher altitude (i.e., in colder habitats) and closer in time to the Pleistocene ice stages tended to be larger than equivalent groups living at lower altitudes and in more recent times.

REFERENCES

Hatt, Robert T.
    1959 *The mammals of Iraq*. Miscellaneous Publications of the Museum of Zoology, University of Michigan, no. 106. Ann Arbor.

Lay, Douglas M.
    1967 *A study of the mammals of Iran resulting from the Street Expedition of 1962-63*. Fieldiana: Zoology, vol. 54. Chicago: Field Museum of Natural History.

Perkins, Dexter, Jr.
    1964 Prehistoric fauna from Shanidar, Iraq. *Science* 144:1565-66.

SAOC 31
    1960 *Prehistoric investigations in Iraqi Kurdistan*. Robert J. Braidwood, Bruce Howe, et al. Studies in Ancient Oriental Civilization, no. 31. Chicago: University of Chicago Press.

Turnbull, Priscilla F., and Reed, Charles A.
    1974 *The fauna from the terminal Pleistocene of Palegawra Cave, a Zarzian occupation site in northeastern Iraq*. Fieldiana: Anthropology, vol. 63 (3). Chicago: Field Museum of Natural History.

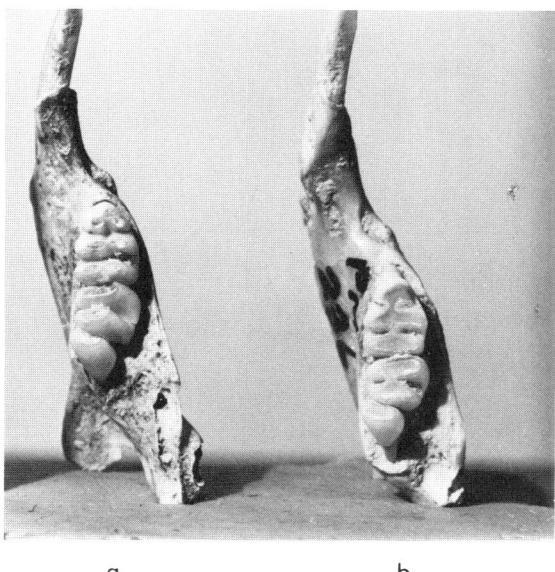

Fig. 191. Right mandibles with M_{1-3} of *Tatera indica* from Jarmo: *a*, PM12865, unworn specimen showing residual cusps on the teeth; *b*, PM12861, worn specimen showing lophs completely connected. Magnification ca. 3×.

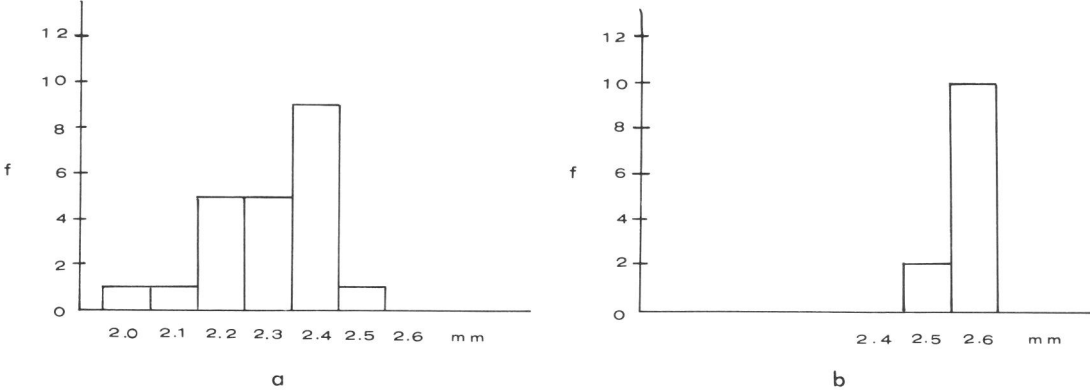

Fig. 192. Frequency histograms of *Tatera indica*, with maximum widths of M_1 measured in millimeters along the abscissa, and frequency along the ordinate: *a*, all right and left teeth (no. = 22) of 11 modern specimens from southeast Kerman Province, Iran; *b*, right and left teeth (no. = 12), indeterminate as to pairing, of specimens of early Recent age (ca. 8500 B.P.) from Jarmo.

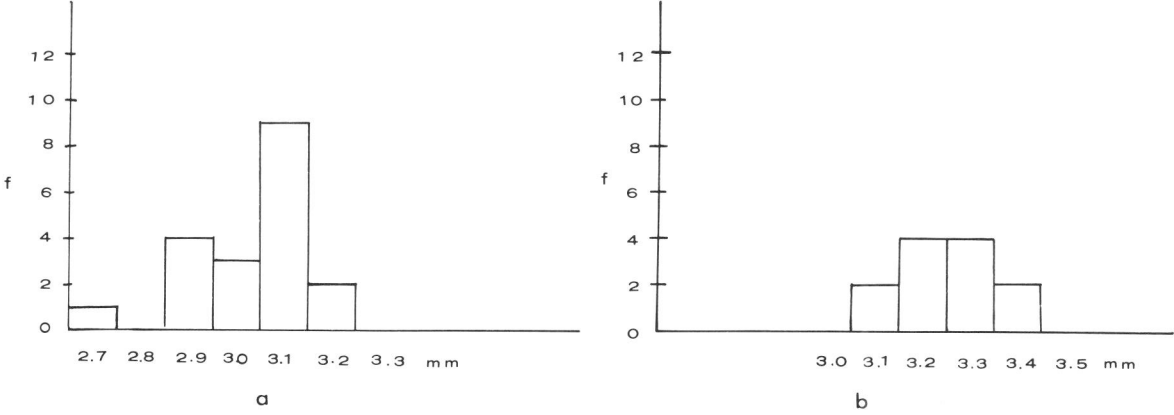

Fig. 193. Frequency histograms of *Tatera indica*, with lengths of M_1 measured in millimeters at the crown surface along the abscissa, and frequency along the ordinate: *a*, all right and left teeth (no. = 22) of 11 modern specimens from southeast Kerman Province, Iran; *b*, right and left teeth (no. = 12), indeterminate as to pairing, of specimens of early Recent age (ca. 8500 B.P.) from Jarmo.

12

A NOTE ON THE JARMO PLANT REMAINS

Patty Jo Watson

Since the publication of the preliminary report on the Iraq-Jarmo Project (SAOC 31), which included a chapter by Hans Helbaek on the Jarmo plant remains and their significance, a number of other sites have yielded botanical material relevant to this early village time range, and some detailed studies have been made of distributions of wild wheat and barley species (Harlan and Zohary 1966; van Zeist 1969; Zohary 1969). The most pertinent archeological sites include Ali Kosh, Beidha, Can Hasan, Çatal Hüyük, Çayönü, Choga Mami (Samarran levels), Hacılar, Jericho (Pre-Pottery Neolithic), Mersin, Mureybit, Ramad, Sawwan, Guran, Umm Dabaghiyah.

Earlier understandings concerning the origin and subsequent development of domestic wheat, barley, and other food plants have been expanded and revised in accord with the new evidence and have recently been clearly and carefully summarized in Jane Renfrew's general treatment of paleoethnobotany (1973), which has a full bibliography. The present account is a brief review of the new evidence as it pertains to the original finds from Jarmo.

The Jarmo plant material includes charred fragments and impressions of domesticated einkorn wheat (*Triticum monococcum*), domestic emmer wheat (*Triticum dicoccum*), wild two-row barley (*Hordeum spontaneum*), and a few two-row specimens that have a tough rachis and so are apparently domestic, lentils, blue vetchling, field peas, wild einkorn and emmer, *Aegilops* sp., *Prosopis* (*Lagonychium farctum*), and pistachio nuts (Helbaek 1960; 1966; pers. comm., February 5, 1972).

WHEAT

Carbonized grains of *T. monococcum* were found at Jarmo (Helbaek 1960, p. 107; 1966, p. 351). The same species also occurs at Ali Kosh (Bus Mordeh phase), Can Hasan III, Çatal Hüyük VI-II, Choga Mami, ceramic Hacılar, Jericho PPNB, Ramad, Sawwan, and possibly Umm Dabaghiyah. Helbaek (1972*b*) was unable to determine whether the single glume represented at Dabaghiyah is wild or domestic einkorn. Besides the carbonized grain fragments from Jericho PPNB that have been identified, there are apparently numerous impressions of plant parts in mud brick that have not been identified or described (Hopf 1969, p. 355).

Carbonized grains and impressions of *T. dicoccum* occurred at Jarmo (Helbaek 1960, pp. 102-3; 1966, p. 352). Remains of emmer wheat are also known from Ali Kosh (all three phases), ᶜAmuq A, Beidha, Can Hasan III, Çatal Hüyük VI-II, Çayönü, Choga Mami, aceramic and ceramic Hacılar, Jericho PPNA and PPNB, Matarrah, Ramad, Sawwan, and Umm Dabaghiyah.

Bread wheat is not known from Jarmo but has been found at Can Hasan III (also club wheat), Çatal Hüyük VI-II, Choga Mami, Hacılar, Ramad (also club wheat), and Sawwan.

Remains of wild einkorn (*Triticum boeoticum*), apparently carbonized, occur at Jarmo (Helbaek 1966, p. 351), and the species is also found at Ali Kosh (Bus Mordeh phase), Can Hasan III, Choga Mami, aceramic Hacılar, Mureybit, and possibly Umm Dabaghiyah (see note above concerning the single glume represented there).

Wild emmer (*T. dicoccoides*) has so far been reported only from Jarmo (both carbonized grains and imprints) by Helbaek (1966, p. 352) and from Çayönü by Stewart (Braidwood, Çambel, et al. 1974, p. 571).

BARLEY

Definitely wild two-row barley (*Hordeum spontaneum*) has been identified at Choga Mami (Helbaek 1972*a*) and at Mureybit (van Zeist and Casparie 1968), and Helbaek (1972*b*) found the imprint of one grain at Umm Dabaghiyah. Two-row barley that is apparently the cultivated species but closely resembles the wild form occurs at Jarmo, and also at Ali Kosh (Bus Mordeh phase), Beidha, Çatal Hüyük, and Guran (Renfrew 1969, p. 164).

With the possible exception of the Can Hasan III specimens, the earliest clear evidence for domesticated, hulled two-row barley comes from Jarmo in the form of a few carbonized fragments with undetached internodes: "The change from brittle to tough rachis in two-rowed barley is first demonstrated clearly in the material from . . . Jarmo. Here were found some spike sections with the lateral florets still held together. . . ." (Helbaek 1966, p. 358).

The manuscript for this paper was essentially completed by 1972. Very few additions and only minor revisions have been made since that date.

Definitely domesticated two-row barley (*Hordeum distichum*) occurs at Ali Kosh (Ali Kosh and Mohammad Jaffar phases), Can Hasan III, Choga Mami, Hacılar late neolithic, Matarrah, Sawwan, Guran, and Sabz.

Six-row barley is not known from Jarmo, but six-row hulled barley occurs at Ali Kosh (Bus Mordeh phase), Can Hasan late neolithic, Choga Mami (one example only), ceramic Hacılar, Mersin early neolithic, Sawwan, and Sabz. Six-row naked barley is reported from Çatal Hüyük VI-II, Choga Mami, aceramic and ceramic Hacılar, and Sawwan.

Finally, naked barley (not known to occur wild and hence assumed to be domestic) has been found at Ali Kosh (Bus Mordeh phase), Beidha, Can Hasan III, Choga Mami, aceramic Hacılar, and Umm Dabaghiyah (Helbaek 1966, pp. 356-57; 1972*a*, *b*; Hillman 1972). At Hacılar this barley is six-rowed, but at Can Hasan III it may be two-rowed.

LEGUMES

Although not so much attention is usually given to these species as to the small grains, they occur very early and very widely in the ancient Near East and were probably at least as important as wheat and barley (Zohary and Hopf 1973). Helbaek found field pea, lentil, and blue vetchling at Jarmo and also at Choga Mami. Pea is known from Çatal Hüyük VI-II, aceramic and ceramic Hacılar, and Jericho PPNB. Lentils are reported from Can Hasan III, aceramic and ceramic Hacılar, Jericho PPNB, Mureybit and Ramad; and vetch has been found at Ali Kosh (Mohammad Jaffar phase), Beidha, Can Hasan III, Çatal Hüyük VI-II, Çayönü, aceramic Hacılar, Jericho PPNB, and Mureybit. Chickpea has been identified at Çayönü, ceramic Hacılar, and Jericho PPNB.

DISCUSSION

Fieldwork and other research by various people have made possible the compilation of distribution maps for presumed wild ancestors of the major small grains: einkorn, emmer, and barley (Harlan and Zohary 1966; Harlan 1967; van Zeist 1969; Zohary 1969). It is not clear, however, how closely the distribution at the present time parallels the distribution during the period when these species were being utilized and domesticated by the prehistoric hunters and gatherers of southwestern Asia and southeastern Europe. This question is further complicated by the recent palynological findings of H.E. Wright, Jr., van Zeist, and their associates (summarized in Wright 1968; see also Wright 1976 and van Zeist 1976), which indicate that the vegetation patterns in the Zagros were very different 10,000 years ago from what they are now. Further work by these and other investigators will perhaps help clarify some aspects of the prehistoric distribution of the wild grain species. An equally important line of investigation centers on intensified recovery of plant remains (including pollen where possible) from archeological sites of the relevant time range. Techniques for concentrating and recovering carbonized plant fragments (Struever 1968; Watson 1976) are now being applied at various sites. As a result, our knowledge of prehistoric agricultural practices and of the histories of the various domestic plant species is increasing and changing rapidly. Yet it was Helbaek's painstaking pioneer work on the plant impressions and carbonized botanical remains from Jarmo and related sites that first demonstrated the great significance of this material and laid the foundation for all subsequent paleoethnobotanical research on early agriculture in southwestern Asia.

REFERENCES

Braidwood, Robert J.; Çambel, Halet; Lawrence, Barbara; Redman, Charles L.; and Stewart, Robert B.
    1974 Beginnings of village-farming communities in southeastern Turkey—1972. *Proceedings of the National Academy of Sciences of the United States of America* 71:568-72.

Braidwood, Robert J.; Howe, Bruce; et al.
    1960 SAOC 31 (see below).

Harlan, Jack R.
    1967 A wild wheat harvest in Turkey. *Archaeology* 20:197-201.

Harlan, Jack R., and Zohary, Daniel
    1966 Distribution of wild wheats and barley. *Science* 153:1074-80.

Helbaek, Hans
    1960 The paleoethnobotany of the Near East and Europe. In SAOC 31, pp. 99-118.
    1966 1966—Commentary on the phylogenesis of *Triticum* and *Hordeum*. *Economic Botany* 20:350-60.
    1972*a* Samarran irrigation agriculture at Choga Mami in Iraq. *Iraq* 34:35-48.
    1972*b* Traces of plants in the early ceramic site of Umm Dabaghiyah. Ibid.:17-19.

Hillman, G.C.
    1960 Plant remains. In Excavations at Can Hasan III 1969-1970, D.H. French, pp. 182, 185-88. In *Papers in economic prehistory*, ed. E.S. Higgs, pp. 181-90. Cambridge: At the University Press.

Hopf, Maria
    1969 Plant remains and early farming in Jericho. In *The domestication and exploitation of plants and animals*, ed. Peter J. Ucko and G.W. Dimbleby, pp. 355-59. Chicago: Aldine.

Renfrew, Jane M.
- 1969 The archaeological evidence for the domestication of plants: methods and problems. In ibid., pp. 149-72.
- 1973 *Palaeoethnobotany*. New York: Columbia University Press.

SAOC 31
- 1960 *Prehistoric investigations in Iraqi Kurdistan*. Robert J. Braidwood, Bruce Howe, et al. Studies in Ancient Oriental Civilization, no. 31. Chicago: University of Chicago Press.

Struever, Stuart
- 1968 Flotation techniques for the recovery of small-scale archaeological remains. *American Antiquity* 33:353-62.

Watson, Patty Jo
- 1976 In pursuit of prehistoric subsistence: a comparative account of some contemporary flotation techniques. *Mid-Continental Journal of Archaeology* 1:77-100.

Wright, H.E., Jr.
- 1968 Natural environment of early food production north of Mesopotamia. *Science* 161:334-39.
- 1976 The environmental setting for plant domestication in the Near East. Ibid. 194:385-89.

Zeist, Willem van
- 1969 Reflections on prehistoric environments in the Near East. In *The domestication and exploitation of plants and animals*, ed. Peter J. Ucko and G.W. Dimbleby, pp. 35-46. Chicago: Aldine.
- 1976 On macroscopic traces of food plants in southwestern Asia (with some reference to pollen data). *Philosophical Transactions of The Royal Society of London*, ser. B: *Biological Sciences* 275:27-41.

Zeist, Willem van, and Casparie, W.A.
- 1968 Wild einkorn wheat and barley from Tell Mureybit in northern Syria. *Acta Botanica Neerlandica* 17:44-53.

Zohary, Daniel
- 1969 The progenitors of wheat and barley in relation to domestication and agricultural dispersal in the Old World. In *The domestication and exploitation of plants and animals*, ed. Peter J. Ucko and G.W. Dimbleby, pp. 47-66. Chicago: Aldine.

Zohary, Daniel, and Hopf, Maria
- 1973 Domestication of pulses in the Old World. *Science* 182:887-94.

13

CLIMATIC CHANGE IN THE ZAGROS MOUNTAINS—REVISITED
H.E. Wright, Jr.

INTRODUCTION

In the many years that have passed since the preparation of initial reports on the late Pleistocene and early Holocene environmental setting for the Zagros Mountains and adjacent areas (Wright 1960, 1962), a few of the problems raised in those reports have been solved or at least more clearly defined. This has come about through further studies of the extent of glaciation in the mountains of the Mediterranean by various investigators, and particularly through the initiation of pollen studies in most of the regions north and east of the Mediterranean Sea. It is now feasible to examine this problem in a hemispheric context, especially now that ocean-core studies of all the oceans (including the Mediterranean Sea) have led to global numerical models of Ice Age climates (Gates 1976; Manabe and Hahn 1977).

PLEISTOCENE GLACIATION AND SNOW LINE

Determination of glaciation limits is one of the most useful ways of quantitatively estimating the nature of past climates. In a mountainous region snow usually accumulates preferentially in valley heads or on slopes sheltered from the wind and afternoon sun. If all the snow does not melt in the summer, then the snow of succeeding years increases the thickness of the snowpack. The lowest elevation above sea level for such patches of perennial snow is called the snow line. With continued accumulation the mass may become thick enough to flow as a glacier downhill from the snow line. Once glacier flow commences, erosion at the head of the glacier carves out a cirque in the valley floor. An ancient cirque can be identified by its steep headwall and relatively flat floor, contrasting with the V shape of unglaciated valley heads. The minimum elevation of small cirques provides an estimation of the ancient snow line. A large cirque is a less trustworthy indicator of the snow line than a small cirque, because its floor has usually been eroded below snow line by the more extensive glacial erosion characteristic of larger glaciers.

A second method of determining the ancient snow line is based on the observation that on modern mountain glaciers the equilibrium line (equivalent in elevation to the snow line on adjacent terrain) falls about midway in elevation between the terminal moraine of the glacier and the ridge crest above the glacier source.

A third method, also based on studies of modern glaciers, requires that the entire area covered by an ancient mountain-glacier system be mapped (Porter 1975). The equilibrium line is at an elevation above which lies 60% of the glacier area.

The distribution of cirques and of glaciers of different sizes in a particular mountain range depends not only on the mountain topography but also on the direction of exposure to sun and wind. The regional snow line can be estimated by averaging the calculations for local snow lines on north-facing and south-facing slopes.

Once the Pleistocene snow line has been determined, one can calculate the amount of snow-line depression (i.e., how much lower the snow line was in the Pleistocene than it is now), so long as the mountain range contains modern glaciers or at least perennial snow patches so that the modern snow line can be observed.

In the case of the Zagros Mountains, the investigations described in the initial report (Wright 1960) and then elaborated upon (Wright 1962) yielded evidence for Pleistocene cirques commonly at an elevation of about 2,100 m, with a few as low as 1,500 m, in the highest segment of the mountain range near where the borders of Iraq, Iran, and Turkey meet. On Cilo Dagh in this area a few modern cirque glaciers have an average basal elevation of 3,300 m. This means a depression of the Pleistocene snow line amounting to 1,200-1,800 m, by the first method of calculation described above. Moraines are present as low as 1,100 m, and calculation of Pleistocene snow line by the second method gives a figure close to 1,200 m, but the variability in the elevation of the crest line above the multiple cirques (2,700-3,700 m) makes this estimation relatively inaccurate.

The Pleistocene snow-line depression for the Zagros Mountains, estimated to be at least 1,200 m, is converted to temperature depression (the difference between modern and Pleistocene temperatures) on the basis of two assumptions. First, it is assumed that snow-line depression results solely from a reduction in mean annual temperature. This

---

The manuscript for this chapter was submitted in 1979.—EDS.

may be an oversimplification, for persistence of perennial snow depends also on the amount of winter snowfall, summer cloudiness (radiation melting), and other climatic factors. Second, it is assumed that the decrease in air temperature with increased altitude (lapse rate) was the same in the Pleistocene as it is today. For the Zagros Mountains, the lapse rate today is estimated as 0.7°C/100 m (Wright 1962); although this figure is based on admittedly poor local weather records, it is not unlike the figure for other semiarid areas.

On the basis of these two assumptions, a temperature decrease of 8°-12°C was estimated. Such a figure, however, seemed to be unreasonably large for an area lying at such a low latitude and so far from the margin of the continental ice sheet. Increased precipitation was therefore invoked to account for some of the glacial expansion. Such a hypothesis is consistent with the paleoclimatic conditions reconstructed in 1960, in which low-latitude desert regions were inferred to have pluvial climates during glacial episodes because the belt of prevailing winds would shift southward, bringing summer cloudiness to the Mediterranean as well as more snowfall.

The 1,200-1,800 m snow-line depression was challenged by Bobek (in Butzer 1971), who had previously estimated that the depression in the same area was 700 m (Bobek 1940) and had postulated that the climate during the glacial period was drier rather than wetter than it is today.

Messerli (1967) subsequently reviewed the subject of Pleistocene snow line for the entire Mediterranean region. He compiled figures on more than 200 mountain areas from Spain and Morocco to Iran, and he prepared maps showing elevations of Pleistocene snow line and, where possible, modern snow line. Although he shows that considerable variation exists in the elevations determined in different ways and by different investigators, the regional trends are clear. The Pleistocene snow line rises from west to east as precipitation declines along a uniform latitude in the north Mediterranean countries from Spain to Turkey, and it rises from north to south from less than 1,500 m in the Pyrenees to more than 3,500 m in the Atlas Mountains as the dry subtropical climatic belt is approached. On a local scale it rises from west to east across the Apennine Mountains in Italy and across the mountains of the Balkan peninsula. In Turkey it rises from 2,400 m on both the Mediterranean and Black Sea coasts to 2,900 m in the dry interior plateau; the few observations on the modern snow line in Turkey show the same trends, from 3,500 m on both coasts to 4,000 m in the interior.

According to Messerli's survey the depression of the Pleistocene snow line was generally greater than 1,200 m in the western Mediterranean and less than 1,200 m in the east. A key point in the east was Bobek's figure of 700 m for the Zagros Mountains. He postulates that this relation reflects a greater decrease in Pleistocene precipitation in the east than in the west, as well as increased summer temperatures in the east accompanying a more continental climate.

A recent study of the Kuh-i-Jupar in southeastern Iran, however, puts a different light on the snow-line relations for the east (Kuhle 1976). This mountain range is near Kerman, about 350 km southeast of the region in Kurdistan under consideration here, and it has the same climatic regime (although drier). Its crest exceeds 4,000 m; although no modern glaciers are present in the area today, another range 40-65 km to the south bears small glaciers or at least perennial snow patches at an elevation of 4,500 m. Kuhle identified landforms of two phases of Pleistocene glaciation throughout the area, and at the northeast base of the mountains he mapped a broad Pleistocene piedmont glacier that extends down to 1,900 m. He calculated the Pleistocene depression of the snow line as 1,650 m for the older phase and 1,550 m for the younger, using as a criterion the elevation midway between the terminal moraine and the mountain crest.

This conclusion supports the finding that the Pleistocene snow-line depression in the Zagros Mountains in Kurdistan exceeds 1,200 m. Thus it seems to have been greater in this part of the eastern Mediterranean than elsewhere, rather than less. The explanation previously presented (Wright 1960, 1962) is that the Pleistocene climate was marked not only by lower temperature but also by increased precipitation, especially on the windward (southwest) flank of the Zagros Mountains. Inference of increased precipitation would seem to be less justified, however, for the Kuh-i-Jupar, which is much farther east and is even drier than the Zagros Mountains. Furthermore, pollen studies of vegetation history show that the Mediterranean region was drier during the Pleistocene than it is now, not wetter.

Vegetation History

The pollen evidence for the Zagros Mountains comes principally from Lake Zeribar (van Zeist and Wright 1963; van Zeist 1967; van Zeist and Bottema 1977; Freitag 1977). This study, which is supported by analysis of surface pollen samples in transects from the Mesopotamian desert across the oak woodlands of the mountains to the steppe of the interior plateaus (Wright, McAndrews, and van Zeist 1967), indicates that before 11,000 years ago the Zeribar area had a steppe vegetation of *Artemisia* and chenopods like that of the cool, dry interior plateaus today, and that the oak woodland covering the hillsides today did not reach its present distribution until about 5,500 years ago.

Because the higher ridges of the Zagros Mountains have an upper tree line presumably controlled by temperature, it was first postulated that with Pleistocene temperature depression the woodland belt simply migrated to lower elevations, where it was warmer. To test this hypothesis, a second site near the present base of the woodland (700 m) was studied. This site, Lake Mirabad, has a pollen sequence essentially the same as that of Lake Zeribar, indicating that oak trees were nowhere in the Zagros foothills or piedmont before 11,000 years ago. Because oak woodland requires greater moisture than steppe, I proposed that the oaks took refuge in the mountains of the Levant, closer to the Mediterranean Sea (Wright 1968, 1970). Subsequent pollen studies by several workers show that during the Pleistocene the coastal mountains of Syria indeed had steppe vegetation with oak (Niklewski and van Zeist 1970) and that other areas in the north Mediterranean were dominated by steppe vegetation of *Artemisia*, chenopods, and grass, with some trees in the mountains, where moisture levels were higher (van Zeist, Woldring, and Stapert 1975; Wijmstra 1969; Bottema 1974; Frank 1969; Menéndez Amor and Florschütz 1963). Most of the pollen diagrams are sufficiently well dated to correlate the steppe phase firmly with the last glaciation, so the evidence is strong that the entire north Mediterranean region was dry during the glacial period. Apparently the Asiatic high-pressure area expanded to the south and west to cover not only this area but also Europe, which was characterized at the time by tundra vegetation with indications of dry conditions.

Although the eastern Mediterranean region is dry today, the dry climatic regime during the last glacial period was distinctly different from today's regime. Today the region has what is known as the Mediterranean climate, which owes its pattern to the northward expansion of the subtropical dry belt in the summer (causing the characteristic summer drought) and the southward expansion of the stormy westerlies in the winter. This pattern occurs today on the western side of all continents at latitude 30°-35°—South Africa, California, Chile, and southern Australia. During the Pleistocene, the pattern must have shifted to the south, that is, to Morocco, with deep eastward penetration of winter precipitation limited by the Atlas Mountains (Wright 1976, 1977). Support for this interpretation comes from the essential absence of pollen of evergreen oak, pistachio, and olive in the Pleistocene portions of the diagrams. These are trees whose distribution today is largely confined to the Mediterranean type of climate and which accordingly are highly adapted to summer droughts.

During the Pleistocene, the pattern of dry summers and wet winters in this region was replaced by a pattern of both summer and winter precipitation, but the total was insufficient to support the extensive growth of trees.

The pollen evidence thus supports Bobek's reconstruction of dry climatic conditions during the Pleistocene for Iran, but on the basis of pollen evidence rather than on the basis of glacial morphology. The hypothesis that attributes deep lowering of the Zagros snow line to greater snowfall is thus opposed by the pollen evidence, for there is no indication of tree growth on the windward side of the Zagros Mountains during the Pleistocene. Thus the deep depression of the snow line in the Zagros Mountains and Kuh-i-Jupar must be attributed primarily to depression of temperature, which in fact serves to increase the length of the winter snow season and thus the amount of snow accumulation. An ancillary climatic factor might be an increase in summer cloudiness, thus reducing radiational melting, although the cloudiness must not be so great as to bring enough rain to increase melting substantially beyond what would occur from the sun's radiation under clear skies.

Relation to Plant Domestication

When the problem of climatic change in the Zagros Mountains was initially considered, a central concern was the possible effects on cultural evolution. Although it was established by this time that plant domestication had occurred by 11,000-9,000 B.P., it was also assumed that the climatic change and glacial retreat had already been underway for several thousand years and that there was thus no compelling reason for supposing a causal relation between climatic change and plant domestication (Wright 1960).

This somewhat conservative conclusion was based on three circumstances or assumptions. First, the glacial studies included no radiocarbon dates, so there was no possibility of determining independently the chronology of ice retreat. It was thus assumed that the Zagros glaciers, like those in the Alps, had retreated well into the mountains by 11,000 years ago.

Second, it was reasoned that climatic change at the end of the Pleistocene would result in a simple altitudinal shift in vegetation zones and thus in a comparable shift in the human populations adapted to them.

Third, the faunal evidence from the late Paleolithic sites and the early cultivation sites showed no distinct differences so far as wild forms were concerned. If the wild fauna reflects the climate, then no significant climatic change is indicated.

Accordingly, the consensus in 1960 was that plant domestication and related cultural changes in the area were not precipitated by environmental change.

The pollen studies that were initiated soon thereafter failed to support any of these three assumptions. The organic content of the lake-sediment cores used for pollen analysis provided the materials necessary for radiocarbon dating, and the dated pollen profiles for Lake Zeribar indicate that after many thousand years of relatively stable steppe vegetation the transformation to woodland started very slowly about 14,000 years ago but then accelerated in a major way about 11,000 years ago. Thus the chronological coincidence of environmental change and plant domestication is close enough to suggest cause and effect.

As far as altitudinal shifts in vegetational zones are concerned, the pollen diagram from Lake Mirabad at the base of the oak woodland shows that during the Pleistocene the oak did not simply move from the Zeribar area down to the lower slopes but rather that it must have disappeared completely from the area.

The similarity in faunas is emphasized by Bökönyi (1977), who suggests that the large bone size for red deer from sites in the Kermanshah valley area implies large animals and thus a favorable habitat (presumably wooded), in contrast to the smaller bone size for the red deer of Scotland, which inhabits treeless terrain. But the red deer has a very wide distribution with many different ecotypes, and animal size may reflect a variety of environmental conditions, not just tree cover.

Bökönyi also suggests that the Kermanshah valley is wetter than the Zeribar area and would have more trees, but in fact today it is drier, being on the inner (northeast) edge of the belt of mountain woodland rather than in the heart of it, as is the case with Lake Zeribar.

In further defense of the faunal evidence for a Pleistocene forest cover, Turnbull and Reed (1974), in a faunal study of Palegawra, a cave site dated as 14,000 B.P., make a case for an earlier immigration of pistachio and oak trees as well as riverine trees to provide habitat for red deer and stone marten (although they do acknowledge that these animals can be found in treeless areas). They point out that Palegawra is at a lower elevation (990 m) than Lake Zeribar (1,360 m). With the assumption that temperature was the primary control on tree distribution, they reason that trees moved up the mountains as the climate began to warm 14,000 years ago. The pollen diagram from Lake Mirabad, however, which is at a still lower elevation (700 m) at the base of the modern oak woodland (van Zeist 1967), is so similar to the Zeribar diagram that such postulated upward movement of trees is unsupported, and a lateral movement from the west along the mountains as precipitation increased seems more likely. In any case, riverine trees can be expected in otherwise treeless vegetation, and the pollen record of such trees (or even a small number of upland trees) might be inconspicuous.

The question of the faunal similarities can be resolved by postulating that the mountain terrain is more critical than the vegetation or climate in the habitat requirements of red deer and the other mammals involved. Cliffs and alcoves may provide protection from the elements, and a variety of shrubs (as well as riverine trees) provide a food resource. Snow cover, although longer-lasting than today (to provide glaciers at high elevations), must have been less abundant in the foothills because of the drier climate, and in any case in mountain regions snow cover tends to be differential because of wind-drifting, solar heating on south-facing slopes, etc., thus exposing winter and spring forage for animals.

The general conclusion that climatic change about 11,000 years ago was roughly coincident with the first domestication of plants in the Zagros area has recently been rejected in toto by Pullar (1977), who proposes that the pollen surface-sample data on which the interpretation of the Lake Zeribar pollen diagram is based are misused, and that instead the diagram records an episode of vegetation clearance by slash-and-burn about 14,000 years ago for the purpose of plant cultivation. Independent evidence is said to come from charcoal layers in archeological sites—a notion she adopts from Lewis (1972). She proposes that grain cultivation itself is recorded by the increase in pollen of the *Cerealia* type. She further contends that the climatic change concerned involved a temperature increase of only a very few degrees, quoting Bobek's (1940) estimates for minimal snow-line depression as well as his statements (Bobek 1954) concerning the very minor changes in the level of Lake Rezaiyeh (Urmia). She concludes that if climatic change occurred at all it was not apparent until 8,000 years ago. She suggests that plant domestication was not recorded in the morphology of fossil seeds until 6,000 years after the first cultivation (3 mutations at 2,000 years each!).

Apart from the fact that no archeological evidence exists for plant domestication as early as 14,000 years ago, this reconstruction fails because all of the other points are either incorrect or have much more reasonable explanations (Wright 1980). For example, charcoal layers in cave earths or other archeological sites mean fires for cooking or heating rather than fly ash from fires on the landscape. *Cerealia*-type pollen doesn't necessarily come from cereal grains (wild or domestic), for certain other grass pollen grains have this type of pollen grain (van Zeist, Woldring, and Stapert 1975). Bobek's estimate of temperature depression on the basis of glaciation is incorrect, as discussed earlier, and his estimate on the basis of lake levels did not take into account the fact that decreased precipitation may cancel out the tendency for the lake level to rise when decreased temperature reduces evaporation. Any speculation on the length of time required for genetic changes to be recorded in cereal grain morphology has no basis.

Acceptance of the rough temporal coincidence of climatic change and plant domestication does not indicate cause and effect, of course. Nonetheless, an integrated hypothesis has been developed that postulates the following events (Wright 1976, 1977). The pollen diagrams from the north Mediterranean region indicate that the trees characterizing the modern Mediterranean climate with its summer drought—olive, pistachio, and evergreen oaks—were essentially absent before 11,000 years ago, implying that this type of climate existed to the south prior to this time, perhaps in western Morocco. If the Mediterranean-type trees were farther south, then perhaps the wild cereal grains (wheat and barley), as well as certain peas and beans that were domesticated at an early date, were also there, for these plants also occur today only in the Mediterranean climatic region of summer drought and thus must be adapted to it and not to a regime that includes summer rains. Thus the climatic change about 11,000 years ago may have resulted in the northward movement of the Mediterranean climatic zone to its present latitude and broad eastward extent. With the climatic change the diagnostic trees moved into the area, and the wild cereal grains and other herbs spread to the drier areas of the eastern Mediterranean (Iran to Greece). The stage was then set for the domestication of these plants by peoples who had previously depended on wild plant and animal foods.

This hypothesis may have a number of uncertain points related to the ecological and climatic factors in plant distribution, but certain elements of it are testable, for example the pollen and archeological record in Morocco for the time range in question. Undoubtedly the cultural developments leading to plant domestication were protracted and complex, but environmental change may have played a role.

REFERENCES

Bobek, Hans
  1940 Die gegenwärtige und eiszeitliche Vergletscherung im Zentralkurdischen Hochgebirge. *Zeitschrift für Gletscherkunde* 27:50-87.
  1955 Klima und Landschaft Irans in vor- und frühgeschichtlicher Zeit. *Geographischer Jahresbericht aus Österreich* 25 (1953-54):1-42.

Bökönyi, S.
  1977 *The animal remains from four sites in the Kermanshah valley, Iran—Asiab, Sarab, Dehsavar, and Siahbid: the faunal evolution, environmental changes and development of animal husbandry, VIII-III millennia B.C.* British Archaeological Reports, Supplementary Series, vol. 34. Oxford.

Bottema, S.
  1974 Late Quaternary vegetation history of north-western Greece. Ph.D. diss., University of Groningen. (See also Appendix: a late Quaternary pollen diagram from Ioannina, north-western Greece. In The climate, environment and industries of Stone Age Greece: part III, E.S. Higgs, C. Vita-Finzi, D.R. Harris, and A.E. Fagg, pp. 26-29. *Proceedings of the Prehistoric Society* 33 [1967]:1-29.)

Butzer, Karl W.
  1971 *Environment and archeology: an ecological approach to prehistory.* 2nd ed. Chicago: Aldine-Atherton.

Frank, A.H.E.
  1969 Pollen stratigraphy of the Lake of Vico (central Italy). *Palaeogeography, Palaeoclimatology, Palaeoecology* 6:67-85.

Freitag, H.
  1977 The Pleniglacial, Late Glacial and Early Postglacial vegetation of Zeribar and their present-day counterparts. *Palaeohistoria* 19:87-95.

Gates, W. Lawrence
  1976 Modeling the ice-age climate. *Science* 191:1138-44.

Kuhle, Matthias
  1976 *Beiträge zur Quartärmorphologie SE-iranischer Hochgebirge: die quartäre Vergletscherung des Kuh-i-Jupar.* Göttinger geographische Abhandlungen, vol. 67. Göttingen: Erich Goltze.

Lewis, Henry T.
  1972 The role of fire in the domestication of plants and animals in southwest Asia: a hypothesis. *Man*, n.s. 7:195-222.

Manabe, Syukuro, and Hahn, Douglas G.
  1977 Simulation of the tropical climate of an ice age. *Journal of Geophysical Research* 82:3889-911.

Menéndez Amor, Josefa, and Florschütz, F.
  1963 Sur les éléments steppiques dans la végétation quaternaire de l'Espagne. *Boletín de la Real Sociedad Española de Historia Natural, Sección Geológica* 61:121-33.

Messerli, Bruno
  1967 Die eiszeitliche und die gegenwärtige Vergletscherung im Mittelmeerraum. *Geographica Helvetica* 22:105-228.

Niklewski, J., and Zeist, Willem van
  1970 A late Quaternary pollen diagram from northwestern Syria. *Acta Botanica Neerlandica* 19:737-54.

Porter, Stephen C.
  1975 Equilibrium-line altitudes of late Quaternary glaciers in the southern Alps, New Zealand. *Quaternary Research* 5:27-47.

Pullar, Judith
  1977 Early cultivation in the Zagros. *Iran* 15:15-37.

Turnbull, Priscilla F., and Reed, Charles A.
  1974 *The fauna from the terminal Pleistocene of Palegawra Cave, a Zarzian occupation site in northeastern Iraq.* Fieldiana: Anthropology, vol. 63 (3). Chicago: Field Museum of Natural History.

Wijmstra, T.A.
  1969 Palynology of the first 30 metres of a 120 m deep section in northern Greece. *Acta Botanica Neerlandica* 18:511-27.

Wright, H.E., Jr.
  1960 Climate and prehistoric man in the eastern Mediterranean. In *Prehistoric investigations in Iraqi Kurdistan*, Robert J. Braidwood, Bruce Howe, et al., pp. 71-97. Studies in Ancient Oriental Civilization, no. 31. Chicago: University of Chicago Press.
  1962 Pleistocene glaciation in Kurdistan. *Eiszeitalter und Gegenwart* 12:131-64.
  1968 Natural environment of early food production north of Mesopotamia. *Science* 161:334-39.
  1970 Environmental changes and the origin of agriculture in the Near East. *BioScience* 20:210-12.

1976 The environmental setting for plant domestication in the Near East. *Science* 194:385-89.
1977 Environmental change and the origin of agriculture in the Old and New Worlds. In *The origins of agriculture*, ed. Charles A. Reed, pp. 281-318. The Hague: Mouton.
1980 Climatic change and plant domestication in the Zagros Mountains. *Iran* 18:145-48.

Wright, H.E., Jr.; McAndrews, J.H.; and Zeist, Willem van
1967 Modern pollen rain in western Iran, and its relation to plant geography and Quaternary vegetational history. *Journal of Ecology* 55:415-43.

Zeist, Willem van
1967 Late Quaternary vegetation history of western Iran. *Review of Palaeobotany and Palynology* 2:301-11.

Zeist, Willem van, and Bottema, S.
1977 Palynological investigations in Western Iran. *Palaeohistoria* 19:19-85.

Zeist, Willem van; Woldring, H.; and Stapert, D.
1975 Late Quaternary vegetation and climate of southwestern Turkey. *Palaeohistoria* 17:53-143.

Zeist, Willem van, and Wright, H.E., Jr.
1963 Preliminary pollen studies at Lake Zeribar, Zagros Mountains, southwestern Iran. *Science* 140:65-67.

14

ARCHEOZOOLOGICAL STUDIES IN THE NEAR EAST A SHORT HISTORY (1960-1980)

Charles A. Reed

INTRODUCTION

Twenty years ago I wrote a review (Reed 1960) of the history of our knowledge of the domestication of mammals in the Near East, which I define as that area which includes Egypt plus southwestern Asia west of the central deserts of Iran. At that time more supposition than fact existed on the topic, and I believe my article helped to give a firmer foundation to later studies. In the two decades between that writing and this, progress has indeed been admirable.

A second article of two decades ago (Reed and Braidwood 1960) attempted to reconstruct the environment of northeastern Iraq during the last glacial period, basing the conclusions primarily upon the supposed ecological requirements of the mammals, birds, reptiles, amphibians, and land snails recovered from archeological sites. That fauna, throughout the last glacial period and into the Recent, lacked the cold-tolerant populations (musk-oxen, reindeer, mammoths, woolly rhinoceroses, Arctic foxes, Arctic voles, etc.) one associates with an Eurasian boreal climate of the late Pleistocene. Instead, we found only the remains of animals that would be present in the area today if recent overhunting had not locally exterminated many of them. On these data we reconstructed an environment that included mountain glaciers but otherwise was not unlike that of northern Iraq before recent deforestation.

We did warn our readers in 1960 that macrofaunal data for paleoenvironmental reconstruction were not conclusive and that palynological evidence would provide a clearer picture. That evidence soon emerged for the late Quaternary of the Zagros Mountains and their foothills, as outlined by H.E. Wright (chap. 13). Thus Braidwood and I soon abandoned our concept of an environment relatively unchanged throughout the late Quaternary for our particular area of study. Necessarily in error, too, was our concept as of 1960 that, if the climate and biota remained generally stable, the cultural changes leading to the beginnings of agriculture must have been wholly induced by cultural evolution leading to a certain, but undetermined, level of social and technological complexity necessary for the practice of incipient agriculture. I continue to believe that a particular, but still unspecified, level of cultural complexity was necessary before agriculture could have occurred, but I believe as well that other factors (including environmental changes, in the case of the Near East at least) were also important (Reed 1969, 1977a, b; Braidwood 1979). But this topic is not one I can pursue here.

INNOVATIONS AND OTHER PROBLEMS (RETROSPECT SINCE 1960)

A. THE BRITISH ACADEMY MAJOR RESEARCH PROJECT IN THE EARLY HISTORY OF AGRICULTURE

The intellectual background of this project and its early history have been outlined and explained by Clark (1972). Basically, dissatisfaction had been mounting in Britain that the archeological contributions to solving the problems of the origins and early history of agriculture had been too narrowly based, too site-oriented, and too lacking in consideration of the totality of the environmental contributions to paleoeconomy in the particular time period involved. Funds were found, space was provided by the Department of Archaeology and Anthropology at Cambridge University, and a small but active staff began work in 1967 under the direction of Eric S. Higgs. The latter had had wide experience in engineering and farming before entering Cambridge as a "mature student" (Clark's description) to study prehistoric archeology. The essence of his thinking and mode of approach was published late in the history of the Project (Higgs and Jarman 1975); it is an essay worth reading.

Higgs was looking for people with imaginative approaches beyond the standard ones typically taught; such individuals were then attached alone or in small groups to existing archeological expeditions, particularly in southeastern Europe and southwestern Asia. Additionally, some other research was done in natural history, particularly with musk-oxen in northern North America and reindeer in western Greenland and from the late Paleolithic of central Europe. One intellectual aim was to question prior hypotheses and working assumptions related to the origins of the cultivation of plants and the domestication of animals, taking the point of view that these were probably gradual processes that covered a long range of prehistoric time during which hunters and gatherers were becoming more and more biologically informed, particularly about the environmental choices and the behavior of those social animals which were typically hunted. The idea, it seems to me, was that if hunters became sufficiently informed about social animals they would instigate closer contact with them, which would somehow lead to semitaming and thus to domestication.

This latter concept is as imprecise to me as was that of Zeuner (1963), who assumed that man would have become increasingly familiar with the social hoofed mammals which came to eat on growing crops and/or the stubble left after the harvest; I believe that such familiarity alone, no matter how achieved, would only add to the hunters' efficiency. Such hypotheses also discount the important factor of prestige accruing to the successful hunter in all hunting societies. The attitude of the hunter is the factor that must be changed if animals once hunted are to become kept and protected. Such a necessary change in attitude, in my opinion, cannot be brushed lightly aside, as has been discussed in more detail elsewhere (Reed 1977a, 1980).

When everything is rigorously scrutinized and questioned with the idea that the function of a new broom is to sweep clean, some mistakes will occur, but also much good may be accomplished. For instance, two chapters in *Papers in Economic Prehistory* (Higgs, ed., 1972), namely that of Payne (1972a), "On the Interpretation of Bone Samples from Archaeological Sites," and the one by Jarman and Wilkinson (1972), "Criteria of Animal Domestication," have served to clear away old cobwebs so that new directions for osteoarcheological research can be perceived.

At the same time, however, the considerable detailed research on the natural history of musk-oxen and on the preagricultural ecology of red deer and reindeer in Europe, while excellent studies in themselves, have added little to our understanding of the process of early domestication of dogs, sheep, goats, pigs, and cattle—the animals first domesticated.

Wilkinson's chapter (1972), "Current Experimental Domestication and its Relevance to Prehistory," in the same book, is of particular importance to zooarcheologists, but I find it less satisfactory than the two chapters by Payne and by Jarman and Wilkinson, mentioned above. The data are welcome, and the bibliography useful, but Wilkinson argued as if prehistoric man thought as would a modern scientist, with a library at his fingertips and the results of experiments in productivity, physiology, etc., known to him. Was prehistoric man a conservationist? (The behavior of nineteenth century Plains Indians and of twentieth century Eskimos, once they had acquired rifles, would argue the contrary.) If prehistoric man used his environment in a balanced way, he did so by necessity (as South African Bushmen do today; when the food supply diminishes, they move). Did man the hunter change to man the protector, to man the domesticator, so easily that the emotional and cultural aspects of this change are not worth consideration? I do not find in Wilkinson's report any hard data to convince me that my own concept of how domestication of animals occurred (Reed 1977a) is necessarily incorrect, as he would insist. Yet the chapter has much useful material and must be given due consideration in any attempted analysis of domestication of animals.

The clarification of the idea of the "site-catchment" (Vita-Finzi and Higgs 1970), a territorial approach to the interpretation of data from a prehistoric site (Higgs and Vita-Finzi 1972), has been useful in archeology. However, neither the idea nor its use is new, even if the phrase is; any competent archeozoologist has always carefully considered the various local environments in which animals might have been killed and from which they would have been taken to the site. The geographical attitude which pervades much of the research of the members of the British Academy Project was in part undoubtedly due to Higgs's original ideas and then to the influence of Vita-Finzi, a professional geographer. This geographical approach is obvious in many of the excellent publications which emerged from the work of the members of the Project; see the individual articles in the two books edited by Higgs (1972, 1975) and many of the articles in the bibliography (pp. 233-34) of the second volume.

Innovative projects, even if useful, may be short-lived, particularly if dependent upon the survival of a single individual. Thus it seems to have been with the British Academy Major Research Project in the Early History of Agriculture. Since the death of its director, Eric Higgs, in November 1976, the Project has been dissolved, most of the various members finding positions elsewhere. Yet it accomplished much good for the ten years it lasted, and it is obvious that the experiment of the new broom should be repeated occasionally.

B. TECHNIQUES

1. Palynology

While the recovery of pollen from a stratigraphic column as a tool for the reconstruction of environmental changes had its beginnings in Scandinavia in the late nineteenth century, the use of the technique in the Near East began more than sixty years later when H.E. Wright, as a member of the Oriental Institute's Prehistoric Project in 1960, collected hand-drilled cores from numerous lakes, ponds, and seeps in western Iran. From a study of the pollen of these cores emerged a completely new concept of the environment of the late Pleistocene and early Recent, as mentioned before and discussed elsewhere in this volume by Wright (chap. 13). The topic is introduced here again for zooarcheologists, to emphasize that we depend in large part upon the research of others to furnish us with the paleoenvironmental background for our studies, and to bring once again to the fore the picture of what to our human eyes was the generally bleak and adverse environment of a sagebrush-steppe for much of the Near East throughout the late Quaternary. However, a surprising richness of wild fauna occurred in the area during the late Pleistocene and into the Recent (Turnbull and Reed 1974; Bökönyi 1977; Stampfli, this volume, chap. 9).

2. Recovery of Osteological Specimens

In the recovery of bones of nonhuman animals from an archeological site, several factors exist which invariably skew the record, in comparison with what might be expected from consideration only of the remains of the actual carcasses carried to that site.

Bones of nonhuman animals found within an archeological living site represent either animals killed by humans or those which, like small burrowers, occupied the site after or even during the period of human occupation. For cave sites, further complexity may be added by the presence of skeletal parts of small birds and mammals derived from stomach pellets regurgitated by owls which perch inside the entrance to the cave. One job of the osteoarcheologist is to distinguish between these types of skeletal additions to a site's stratigraphy.

The bones of animals killed by humans, mostly for food but not necessarily always, may or may not have been taken to the site. In the case of large animals killed some distance away, the meat was probably cut from the skeleton and carried home, and the bones left in the field, or the skin may have been removed first, leaving the lower jaw and four feet still attached as handles, and then the meat would be cut off and piled on the skin to be carried or "schlepped" (dragged) away (Perkins and Daly 1968). In the latter case, the skeleton would be represented at the site only by those bones still attached to the skin.

The numbers of bones of large butchered animals that do reach a living site are, thus, not representative of the numbers of animals killed; only the bones of the feet and possibly lower jaws must be regarded as representative. To the degree, however, that some of these particular bones were chewed differentially by dogs (if present), the census will be further skewed. In contrast to the problem facing a single hunter after butchering a red deer, equid, or large wild bovid a considerable distance from camp, the situation facing a hunter after he had killed a wild goat, sheep, gazelle, or roe deer away from his home site was less difficult. He had only to eviscerate the animal, cut off and discard the top of the skull and the heavy horns (unless he had some particular use for them), then hoist the carcass onto his shoulders and carry it home. (I am not guessing; I have seen Kurdish hunters in northern Iraq today do as I have described.) Thus all the bones of such an individual kill, except possibly the horn cores, will reach the camp or village.

The nature and size of the settlement, the local customs relative to the dividing and sharing of a carcass, and the secondary uses of the bones (for tools, ornaments, soups, dog food, etc.) will all influence the number, kinds, amount of breakage, and distribution of the bones in the site. Actually, the pattern of hunting, butchering, and distribution of meat and bones can probably never be duplicated from a study of the broken bones remaining in an archeological site, unless an ethnological model is available for the particular area. For the prehistoric Near East no such model is available, and the butchering and distributional practices of present villagers probably provide too simplified a pattern to be useful (P.J. Watson 1979, p. 109). We can be sure, however, that the total process was more complex than we have typically imagined and may have changed seasonally in a standard cycle every year, a conclusion based on the model of the detailed study of the behavior of the Nunamiut Eskimo, caribou hunters of the northern side of the Brooks Range, Alaska, studied by Binford and Bertram (1977).

If flocks and herds of domestic animals such as sheep and/or goats, with perhaps fewer pigs and cattle, were kept, slaughtering and butchering might well have been done on the edge of the village or town, in which case we would expect that numerous bones of those animals would have been carried into the village or town. However, at the site of Dinka Tepe, a Bronze and Iron Age town in northwestern Iran, the large proximal limb bones were rare compared to the numbers of distal bones of the limbs (Gilbert and Steinfield 1977). Additionally, the size and plan of the settlement and the pattern of social complexity of the population will influence in various ways the flow of meat and bones throughout the settlement and result in different patterns of use and final deposition of bones (Gilbert 1978).

A number of excavators (Payne 1972b; Casteel 1972; Clason and Prummel 1977) have reported on experiments with the use of sieves of increasingly finer mesh. Obviously, finer screens catch smaller objects, until finally one may have to use a microscope to separate the wanted from the unwanted, as for example in a search for otoliths of fish (Casteel 1976, p. 37). Most other excavators will require less rigorous and less time-consuming techniques; each must make his own decisions but would be wise to check his results with experiments at screening occasionally.

3. Osteoarcheological Demography

(a) The excavated bones equal how many animals?—A major problem in the interpretation of osteoarcheological reports is that the data on numbers and kinds of bones of different animals have been published so variably that direct comparisons between sites have usually not been possible. The main problem was, and in part still is, the naïveté of most osteoarcheologists, including myself. Some people thought that a mere list of identified animals, with remarks such as "numerous" or "rare," was sufficient for a report; others published the totals of the identified pieces of bones (not realizing the factors that biased such counts). In the last decade or two, most osteoarcheological reports have given totals in terms of the Minimum Numbers of Individuals (MNI or MIND) for each kind of animal whose bones were present in the site.

White, who had first recommended the use of the MNI for archeological research, then offered a modification (White 1953) for improvement. He suggested matching right and left tibiae to determine which pairs were from the same individuals; each nonmatching tibia would then represent an additional individual. (Tibiae were presumably the bones he had in greatest abundance.) He did not himself try this process of matching, wondering if it would perhaps require an "expenditure of a great deal of time with small return" (1953, p. 397). Flannery (1967, p. 157), following White's suggestion, did expend the "great deal of time with small return," even though the results were occasionally improved. Krantz (1968), mentioning no prior investigators, suggested the same technique as had White, but proposed matching hemimandibles. Like White, he himself did not try the technique, nor did he seem to realize that mandibles of larger game are often left behind at the butchering site, so they cannot usually be useful indicators of the number of a particular species killed. Additionally, some mammals (equids and suids for example) have the hemimandibles fused at the symphysis, which fact would add complexities of which Krantz seemingly was not aware.

Bökönyi (1969a, 1970), evolving his own techniques as based on laboratory experience and on Russian publications back to 1948, increased the numerical count (sample size) of the MNI by dividing the bones of a given species found in a site into 12 groups according to age and size for each kind of bone of each group. (Actually, of course, the precise determination of such data for each bone is often not possible.) Summing up the results for each species, bone by bone, he achieved a "Minimum Number of Individuals" considerably higher than would have been arrived at by others who did not do the extra work.

Earlier, however, Perkins had realized that at best the MNI could represent only a relative measure of the numbers of individual, nonhuman animals originally killed for human use at an archeological site, and he produced a modification of the MNI which he called f (relative frequency); this relative frequency (f) is adjusted from the raw count of each kind of bone to correct for the number of kinds of bones which can be identified in one species as compared with another (Perkins 1964a). To the best of my knowledge, no one else has used Perkins's f, but he has continued to wrestle with the problem of finding the relationship between an original population of animals and the recovered populations of bones (Perkins 1973; Hesse and Perkins 1974). In the meantime, Higham (1968a, b), Thomas (1969), and Grayson (1978) had also been working on statistical approaches to osteoarcheological demography. Payne (1972a) wrote at some length on the problems of trying to deduce demographic and other conclusions from the raw data of osteological identifications and the numbers of parts of different bones of each species, and others since then (Grayson 1973, 1974, 1978; Casteel 1974, 1977) have added details and new approaches.

Gilbert and Steinfield (1977) have suggested that the use of the most frequent or the least frequent bone for any taxon is statistically misleading in determining an MNI useful for comparison with the MNI of other taxa, and Perkins (pers. comm.) additionally has suggested that each bone in a site could have come from a different animal; he has further recommended discarding both the most frequent and the least frequent quartile on the list of all the kinds of bones identified and counted for each taxon. The two central quartiles, Perkins believes, yield more valid proportions relative to the unknown total population of animals of the particular taxon which originally furnished bones to the archeological site. Obviously, the more valid one's estimates, the more useful will be the comparisons of relative populations of different taxa.

More recently, Grayson (1979) has reviewed and further analyzed this whole problem of quantification of faunal assemblages from archeological sites. He has concluded that most probably the use of the MNI can at best yield only a rough estimate of the relative order of frequency of different kinds of animals whose skeletal parts were brought originally to an archeological site. When the MNI for a particular species is very small or very large, the figure is probably useful in distinguishing the frequency for that species in the total population of hunted animals from the frequency of any other species which has quite a different MNI. However, if the several MNI's for different taxa are similar, then not even the relative order of frequency among them can be determined. In any case, "the relationship between minimum number of individuals and the actual number of individuals for any given faunal aggregate is usually unknown" (Grayson 1979, p. 230); the same conclusion was reached no matter what techniques were used to determine relative numbers of individuals which originally contributed their skeletal parts to any archeological fauna. As a result, estimates of weights of meat utilized by the human population of any given site cannot be determined quantitatively; as with the MNI, only the relative ordering of species contributing meat to the human population can be suggested.

Grayson's publication (1979) is much more thorough than this brief mention of it can indicate, and the original must be studied in detail by any students of archeological fauna who have hitherto had the belief that precise faunal quantification was possible. As an example, Grayson had earlier (1977) found, in the case of a rock shelter in eastern Oregon, that his faunal analyses by two different methods gave such divergent results as to produce different paleoenvironmental conclusions (neither of which was necessarily correct!). Another warning comes from the analysis by Guilday (1970) of the faunal remains recovered from the site of Fort Ligonier in western Pennsylvania. Historical records of this site, occupied by the British between 1758 and 1766, indicate how much food was supplied to the fort, and the extra meat derived from hunting can be estimated. However, the total amount of meat calculated in terms of the MNI of the bones recovered would have fed the garrison at full strength for only one day!

(b) *Available meat and osteoarcheology.*—Since any calculation of available meat must depend upon prior determination of absolute or relative numbers of animals of each species represented by the faunal sample, and since these figures are difficult to determine except for very large samples (Grayson 1979), the estimates of available meat cannot be dependably accurate. Attempts to use weights of identified pieces of bones from different species as a standard are automatically biased by the greater ease of identifying more pieces of bones from larger animals (Lyman

1979) plus all of the factors discussed above which are responsible for fewer bones of larger animals becoming included in a site than were bones of smaller animals.

Lyman (1979) has summarized the problems of determination of utilization of meat in some detail: different animals produce different ratios of "live weight" to "available meat" (this latter is the live weight less the weight of hide and skeleton). These ratios have been calculated for some species and, as would be expected, short-legged animals such as pigs have relatively more "available meat" than do long-legged ones such as deer. However, as would also be expected, individual wild animals vary considerably from domestic animals with respect to live weight and available meat, according to the figures in published tables based on domestic animals (Stewart and Stahl 1977). Thus the osteoarcheologist, particularly if dealing with sites containing bones of extinct animals (*Bos primigenius*) or those locally exterminated (such as *Cervus elaphus* in the Near East), has no available standard. Additionally, the proportion of waste between available meat and consumed meat will vary according to the human culture (is the marrow retrieved or not? are the bones pulverized and boiled for recovery of the contained fat or not?), human social status, amount of meat purposefully fed to dogs, age and condition of the animal being butchered, availability of other food, and numerous other factors. In his summary, Lyman wrote that there was "a myriad of factors."

To avoid in part some of the above-mentioned problems, Lyman recommended determination if possible of the number of each kind of "butchering units," the units being defined as the pieces into which people of a given group typically cut a carcass. However, if bones of different animals were differentially discarded at unknown butchering sites, such determination would seem to be impossible. Indeed, Lyman wrote that "each butchering unit must be skeletally defined for each different butchering pattern and therefore, very probably, for each site and component" (1979, p. 541). If the butchering unit can be determined, primarily from ethnological data, as with bison on the American high plains (Wheat 1972), the use of butchering units would be useful, but if the butchering practices of a prehistoric population are unknown and cannot be reconstructed, then "butchering units" are not useful.

(*c*) *Life tables, age groups, and human hunting preferences.*—The general assumption among zooarcheologists until a few years ago was that hunters' living sites would have a high proportion of bones of adult game animals, with young animals in a minority. This assumption was based on the general observation that, in the wild, the adult animals outnumbered the immature ones (the terms "young," "immature," and "mature" usually not being defined). A necessary corollary was the assumption that hunters' kills represented a random sample of the population from which it was taken. By contrast, so we believed, control of domestic herds meant that early villagers would slaughter other than at random, the choice being usually to kill a high percentage of the young males, particularly before the onset of winter. (This idea dates back to Coon [1951] if not earlier.) The location in time of that imaginary boundary between hunted and herded populations, as determined from study of the recovered bones from a site, was not a matter of agreement, but a vague feeling existed that one could have as much as 25% of hunters' kills be immature animals and still have the population of kills represent a random sample of the hunted population. A higher percentage of bones from immatures, particularly a *much* higher percentage, should therefore mean that such bones were from a domestic herd, certainly if a shift over a period of time to a higher percentage of immature animals killed can be demonstrated in the same site.

More than 10 years ago some archeozoologists began to question the validity of the concept of the random kill-pattern by hunters; thus Daly (1969, p. 152) wrote, "How does a group of people go about killing a perfect random sample of a wild population of animals?" and Higgs and Jarman (1969) commented that in some circumstances members of a hunting culture might by choice kill a high percentage of young animals. Payne (1972*a*) and Jarman and Wilkinson (1972) discussed at greater length this problem of comparing population structures of living animals as compared with age groupings of bones in archeological sites.

Jarman and Wilkinson did mention in passing that each species of animal would probably have a different natural demographic pattern, an important matter that Collier and White (1976) and G.A. Wright and Miller (1976) then considered independently. The former publication is the more general, being a survey of the literature on the structure of populations in the larger social wild mammals. The authors showed that, in general, the composition of herds changes—sometimes daily but particularly seasonally—with regard to ratios of sexes and ages, so that no standard population can be said to exist.

The publication by G.A. Wright and Miller was on the same topic but refers specifically to sheep. These authors analyzed the considerable data on life tables, survivorship curves, and cycle of annual behavior of different age groups of the American bighorn sheep (*Ovis canadensis*). They used this species, which has had no part in the history of domestication, because the data are available, whereas for most wild ungulates in the Near East they are not. However, such observations on the populations of *Ovis orientalis* as do exist (Decker and Kowalski 1972) agree with the pattern as seen in greater detail in *O. canadensis*. The essential fact is that a population of wild sheep has different subgroups at different times of the year; most of the males aged two years and older are usually in separate groups, but during the rutting season the individual males join the females and at that time small groups of mixed sexes form. In most years the ewes and young (lambs, yearlings, and some two-year-old males) form different groups, with different ranges and different patterns of seasonal movements from those of the rams. Within each of these groups, however, the structure of the population changes with the seasons. Particularly during the winter the lambs die at a high rate due to malnutrition and disease; at an average over the years, as many as 70% of each year's lambs may not survive the winter.

(Under particularly adverse conditions, such as occurred in northwestern Iran in 1971-1972, less than 1% of the annual production of lambs will live through their first winter [Valdez and Alamia 1977].) Other seasonal complexities also alter population ratios at different times of the year, and, for the whole area occupied by a population, some environmental differences also influence local situations.

Obviously a group of primitive hunters would have to do considerable calculating and planning to take a "random sample" of a population of wild sheep or other species back to their village. Indeed, in western North America, the Indians did not kill a random sample but preyed more heavily on the groups of ewes and young from late fall into early spring. Of the two groups, mature females were more often killed, at least judging by the faunal remains analyzed by G.A. Wright and Miller (1976).

The only herd ungulates widely hunted in southwestern Asia for which these variables of behavior and population structure have been studied are the gazelles *Gazella gazella* and *G. dorcas* in Palestine (Simmons and Ilany 1977). The annual cycle of behavior and the related demographic pattern are, of course, different from those of sheep, but the conclusions are the same: one has to know those annual cycles to be able to determine the meaning, in terms of human culture, of the nonhuman bones recovered from an archeological site.

After all of the above factors concerning populations of wild mammals have been considered, the assumption remains that if human hunters had a traditional pattern for hunting each species at each time of the year, and if each hunted species had a consistent cycle of annual behavior, the population of the bones of the hunted animals in the garbage of a site should remain fairly unchanged for a considerable period of time, perhaps centuries. Then, if a sudden change occurred in the kind and/or relative numbers of the bones of a hunted species, we should look for a reason. Some possible causes of a sudden change could be: environmental changes resulting in increase or decrease of the populations of hunted or hunters, new techniques of hunting or butchering by the humans, changes in human seasonal occupation of the site, or domestication of the hunted animals.

4. Determination of Domestic Status

In the Near East in 1954, when I first began excavating bones at archeological sites, the domestic or nondomestic status of the animals represented (the remains of which were not always accurately identified [Dyson 1960]) was almost always determined simply by the statement of the archeologist concerned. Such a statement was based either on identifications made by local laborers hired for digging or upon the archeologist's intuitive feeling as to where the site should be placed on a chronological chart, a chart that reflected the archeologist's own thinking as to when animals should have been domesticated. This was the pattern of thought, in spite of the fact that zooarcheology had had a long tradition in Europe—beginning with the pioneering work of Rütimeyer (1862)—that often had an emphasis on problems of domestication. How much had been accomplished in the century since Rütimeyer's early research can be seen by a survey of published studies on domestication (Angress and Reed 1962). On the eastern side of the Near East the faunal remains from Harappa had been studied in detail (Prashad 1936), and indeed in the Near East itself Dorothea M.A. Bate accomplished a long series of faunal studies in sites of late Pleistocene time (Bate 1927a, b, c, 1930a, b, 1932, 1937, 1938, 1941, 1942, 1947, 1954; Gardner and Bate 1937). However, excavators of Recent sites in southwestern Asia, with such rare exceptions as Duerst (1908), Amschler (1939), and Hilzheimer (1941), generally paid little attention to the wealth of available faunal remains until 1948, when Robert and Linda Braidwood took a zoologically oriented anthropologist, Charlotte Otten, into the field to study the excavated bones on the spot. In 1950-51 they repeated the experience with Fredrik Barth, and in 1954-55 I joined their group as osteoarcheologist.

In the meantime, Coon (1951) had published on the presence of early domesticated sheep and goats at Belt Cave, northern Iran, using the datum of a high proportion of immature animals as evidence for domestication. That same year, but independently, Barth was using this criterion in the field at Jarmo, and others have continued to use this technique when possible. This demographic approach to the determination of domestication has already been mentioned in some detail (p. 435) and will be discussed again in this chapter in the section on sheep.

My own approach, like that of many European investigators for more than a century, has been to place more emphasis on morphological changes as evidence for domestication (Reed 1959, 1961), but admittedly such changes did not occur in a population until after several or perhaps many generations had been reared under the protective hand of man and thus would not furnish evidence for antecedent events during the very earliest periods of domestication. We do not know how many generations of animals have to be protected from natural selection before changing gene frequencies produce recognizably different phenotypes in the skeleton, but presumably the rate of morphological variation would be different for different species and certainly would vary relative to the kind and degree of control exerted upon the domesticates by the domesticators.

The methods used to determine domestication are necessarily associated with each investigator's concept of how domestication began, but this latter side of the argument is rarely expressed, since data are so few and many scientists avoid unsupported speculation. In general, the members of the British Academy Major Research Project adopted the concept that increasing human association with hunted herd animals, beginning perhaps well back in the Pleistocene, led to such a degree of knowledge and understanding on the part of man and such tolerance on the part of certain species of hoofed mammals that the situation of husbandry would have developed automatically. (This concept, even if valid for hoofed mammals—and I think it not valid—does not explain the domestication of dogs, but neither does any other theory.) On the basis of their concept of the pattern of origins of domestication, the members of the British Academy Major Research Project published several articles and reviews on the topics of predomestic and early domestic mammals and on the differentiation of the osseous remains of wild from domestic animals of the same species (Higgs and Jarman 1969, 1972; Jarman 1970, 1971, 1972; Jarman and Wilkinson 1972; Wilkinson 1972). These reviews are useful in presenting new ideas, in clearing the intellectual underbrush, and in providing a wealth of examples and references on a variety of topics not often considered by osteoarchaeologists, but after reading them I still haven't been informed how the authors thought that men changed from hunters to herders or by what evidence we can follow the process.

In contrast to the ideas of the members of the British Academy Major Research Project, I have stressed (Reed 1977a, 1980) the importance to male hunters of the social values of success in the chase and the difficulty of changing such attitudes and social rewards so that such hunters would be satisfied to become protectors and often merely butchers of animals previously hunted. Hunters who no longer hunted would have lost prestige and power, and under those circumstances, so I have hypothesized, animal husbandry followed sedentarism, emerging at first as an innovative activity of mothers and daughters, with the latter more commonly involved. Under these conditions, if the hypothesis is valid, animal husbandry would not have had a long and gradual development, but a much more abrupt beginning that should have left a more definite record of change in population structure and in morphology (Reed 1977a).

Decrease in size of individual animals over time has been noted by many authors (see summary and discussion by Jarman and Wilkinson 1972; topics discussed by those authors will not be repeated here). Among early domesticates, such decrease in size has been noted particularly for cattle and pigs. Whatever the intertwining factors causing diminution may have been, the fact remains that, during historical periods for which some definite data are available, several kinds of domestic animals (particularly pigs, cattle, and horses, but others also) have become quite small under conditions of minimal care that included poor nutrition; examples are medieval European cattle and especially those taken to Greenland and reared there for several generations (Degerbøl 1936). We tend to assume that, because the individuals of some early domestic populations became smaller, they were receiving similar neglectful treatment, but Jarman and Wilkinson (1972) have pointed out some fallacies in this type of thinking.

A few additional words on the workings (or nonworkings) of Bergmann's Rule as possibly affecting our interpretations of size as a factor in early domestic mammals are offered here. Bergmann (1847) proposed the "rule" that for most warm-blooded (endothermal) animals that have a clinal distribution from warmer to colder regions, the size of the body will be smaller in the warmer part of the range and larger in the colder. The supporting physical principle for the supposed natural selection responsible for this result has been assumed to be the fact that a larger animal, having a lower surface-volume ratio than does a smaller one of the same species, will lose relatively less heat per unit volume. If one were to transplant this concept of a temperature-controlled cline on the present surface of the earth to a single area with rising temperatures over a continuous period of time, the animals would be expected to show a chronological cline from larger to smaller. The carnivores of Palestine (Kurtén 1965) and generally the wild cattle of Europe (Degerbøl and Fredskild 1970) and those of the Near East (Jarman 1969) seem to have satisfied those expectations during the period of increasing temperatures at the end of the Pleistocene and afterward.

As often true, however, things are not so simple as they seem at first, and while the carnivores and cattle of the Old World may conform to Bergmann's Rule the factors in some cases may be other than a simple correlation with temperature (McNab 1971). For instance, when two carnivores of somewhat similar size (foxes and jackals, for instance) eat similar food, the foxes will be disproportionately smaller in areas where the two species compete (northern Africa, Near East, Balkans) than where they do not (non-Balkan Europe, where the jackals don't occur). Since under these conditions foxes are smaller in the southern part of their range and larger to the north, they appear to be conforming to Bergmann's Rule, but ecologists regard this situation as one of character displacement. Other variables relative to size may also enter into any clinal pattern; for instance, in northeastern North America, wolves are smaller on the average than are those to the south (McNab 1971) because these more northern wolves are dependent on mice as a main item of diet for a part of each year.

All of these data and variables on size of body re Bergmann's Rule must be considered when one tries to evaluate the meaning of a change in size of any kind of animal for a given area over time. Thus the study of Davis (1977) on the correlation between size of foxes in Palestine (according to measurements of their teeth) and changes in temperature during the late Quaternary should, I believe, be regarded carefully before accepting as proved his conclusions that in Palestine since the end of the Pleistocene the rise in annual mean temperature has been 8°-9°C. Davis was well aware of the known variables and believed he had controlled them, but the tendency by nonbiologists will be to quote his conclusion as proved without consideration of other possibilities that could have affected the size of the foxes over time.

5. Possible Physical and Histological Differences between Some Bones of Wild and Domestic Mammals

A popular idea, often expressed in the earlier European literature on faunal studies, has been that bones, and weight-bearing bones particularly, of wild and domestic mammals could be distinguished by sight and feel; those of wild animals were supposedly more dense, heavier, and rougher on the external surfaces. I know of no study that validates this idea, and indeed one doesn't find it expressed anymore, but still the memory lingers. Indeed, one does wonder if bones of animals pampered in pens should not show differences from those of their wild relatives—other than the size of muscle scars, which one expects. One also wonders if animals fed by people untrained in nutrition should not have chemical and thus possibly physical differences from animals free on the hill, choosing their own diet. There are fallacies in all of this, of course, as many domestic animals are not now, and in former times were not, kept penned, except rarely, and some wild animals do suffer from malnutrition. Even so, I'm certain every faunal analyst involved in separating "wild" from "domestic" has thought that differences may occur in the internal microscopic structure of the bones of the two groups.

Investigating this problem, Drew, Perkins, and Daly (1971a) thought they found evidence of such differences. They used for primary comparison the same parts of homologous long bones of cattle, sheep, and goats from Suberde and Erbaba, sites several kilometers apart on the Anatolian plateau. Representative dates of the two sites are ca. 8520 bp and 7730 bp respectively;* all the bones from Suberde had been identified as coming from wild animals, those from Erbaba from domesticates (Perkins and Daly 1968). The general environment and the soils around the two sites are extremely similar.

At first the investigators looked for differences in trace elements, but found none. Thin sections of pieces of the bones were then prepared and subjected to the kinds of physical tests used by mineralogists to distinguish between rocks that are similar but slightly different. Without going into detail, I state here only that the investigators found consistent histological, colorimetric, and crystallographic differences (the last determined by use of the x-ray diffractometer) in the homologous bones from the two sites. They then applied the same tests to bones of sheep and goats from the level of 1.0-1.5 m at Zawi Chemi Shanidar (see table on p. 523) where Perkins (1964a) had determined that, by evidence then presented, the sheep were domesticated and the goats were not. Again, the histological and physical differences of the bones agreed with the prior determinations of domestic vs. nondomestic status.

Subsequently Drew, Perkins, and Daly (1971b) tried the same procedures on a goat's bone from the site of Ganj Dareh in Iran (age ca. 9000 bp) and on bones of a recently killed domestic sheep of the same area. The goat's bone in question was shown to have been domestic by the standards established in the previous experiments, and the bones of the domestic sheep also exhibited the proper characteristics as established by these experiments. The interesting aspect of the results of the tests on the specimen from Ganj Dareh is that in 1971 we did not know, as we do now (Hesse 1977), that the goats from that site were most probably domesticated.

The data and the conclusions reached by Drew, Perkins, and Daly (1971a) were immediately challenged by McConnell and Foreman (1971), who did not try the same experiments but argued by analogy with their own studies on the microscopic structure of human dental enamel (which is not bone) that Drew et al. must be incorrect. In my opinion and that of Drew, Perkins, and Daly (1971b) the argument of McConnell and Foreman as based on the microstructure of enamel should not be considered apropos of the situation in bone that was studied at much lower magnification. However, Drew et al. must have felt some pressure, possibly because Clason (1972) had questioned whether the mammals at Suberde were indeed wild and those at Erbaba domestic; whatever the reason, a summary of the procedures and results was presented anew in 1973 by the same authors (Daly, Perkins, and Drew 1973).

The techniques and/or conclusions of Drew et al. have been further criticized by J.P.N. Watson (1975) and by Zeder (1978); both tried in different ways to duplicate the results of Drew et al. Watson used bones from known examples of recent wild sheep and goats plus those of domestic sheep from the Iron Age of Italy, and Zeder used bones of recent wild and domestic sheep from Iran but from such different environments that some of the domestic sheep had had more exercise than others, indeed possibly more exercise than did some of the wild sheep.

Neither investigator could duplicate the results of Drew et al., and Watson suggested, on the basis of his own experiments, that their results were due to differential preservation of collagen in their samples of bones from different archeological sites. However, at Zawi Chemi Shanidar, Drew et al. had taken bones of sheep and goats from the same level of that one site, so the rate of disintegration of collagen in bones of the two species should have been identical.

Zeder's paper, a remarkable production for an undergraduate, is particularly valuable for its analysis of the changes that the microstructure of bones may undergo during the life of an animal due to differences in activity and diet. Her results often did not agree with her expectations, but they did not agree with the results of Drew et al. either. Some of her results were similar to some of those of Watson; others were not.

Most recently, Østergård (1980) repeated the crystallographic aspect of the research of Drew, Perkins, and Daly (1971a). With an x-ray diffractometer, he examined pieces taken from the epiphyses and diaphyses of long bones of wolf and dog, domestic ox and extinct *Bos primigenius*, and wild and domestic pigs. Østergård verified the observations of Drew, Perkins, and Daly (1971a) that the basal pinacoids of the hydroxyapatite crystals in the diaphyses

---

*In this article, bp is used instead of BC for all dates that have been determined radiometrically; the notation BC is used for all dates that have been determined in calendric years by historical data. The term BP, indicating that a radiometric date has been corrected for the bristlecone pine factor, is not used in this chapter. Radiometric dates expressed in bp are based on a half-life of C^{14} of 5,570 years and are not corrected for anything (Daniel 1972).

lie at right angles to the long axes of the bones but in certain areas of the epiphyses lie parallel to those long axes. However, the diffraction curves of his study exhibited no reproducible differences in the orientation of the apatite crystals of domestic and wild animals, thus differing from the results of Drew et al. The orientation of the hydroxyapatite crystals was not the only factor investigated by Drew, Perkins, and Daly (1971a), but the lack of duplication of those particular results by Østergård is perplexing.

Unfortunately, each investigator or group of investigators (except possibly Østergård in his crystallographic studies) was doing somewhat different things with bones of animals from different environments and doing those things in different ways. Until the techniques and the materials being investigated can be standardized, hopefully under Drew's direction, we can continue to expect divergent results, but here is certainly an area of research that should be continued.

6. Use of Computers in Faunal Analyses

During the last 20 years there has been an increase in the number of archeologists saving bones for study, a tremendous increase in the number of bones to be identified and studied, an increase in the number of faunal analysts, often an increase in the number of measurements taken on each piece of bone, and sometimes an increase in kinds of nonmetric observations recorded for each bone. On a site yielding numerous bones, the individual bits of data rapidly become unmanageable by any standards of 20 years ago. At first, most people resorted to various systems of punched cards from which individual categories of data could be retrieved by needle-sorting or other techniques. With continued excavation of ever more thousands (often tens of thousands) of bones, the number of punched cards in turn proved to be unmanageable, and individuals or small groups independently began to explore the possibilities of organizing their data for storage in, retrieval from, and manipulation by computers.

Insofar as I can determine, the first faunal analyst who began to record data with use of a computer in mind was Nils-Gustaf Gejvall, working on the bones from Lerna, a village site in the Peloponnesus occupied from the early Neolithic into Mycenean times. He had begun his work of identification in 1958 and, with other projects intervening, had carried it to completion by 1967, when he realized that a shorthand code he had been using for identification, description, and measurements could be converted into a computer code. This was done, the code was used, and the results of the study as well as the code and programs used were then published (Gejvall 1969; Bjälkefors 1969).

Gejvall's study of the faunal remains at Lerna was more thorough than most and has been quoted extensively, but insofar as I am aware, his use of a computer did not inspire anyone else to do the same.

The next individual who, faced with an overwhelming supply of broken bones from an archeological site, turned his mind to the use of a computer was Øystein LaBianca at Ḥesbân, a town in northwestern Jordan occupied from 1200 B.C. until the time of the occupation of the country by the Turks. Excavation there began in 1968 and continued intermittently for several years. During the second season (1971) the data on the hundreds of bones emerging daily from the site were being recorded by a system evolved in 1968, which formed the basis for a computer code developed in the autumn of 1971, after the return of the archeologists to the United States (LaBianca 1973). No code or program was published, however, and the journal was not one typically seen by prehistorians.

The third episode began in the late summer of 1970, when John McArdle and I stopped for some days at the Museum of Comparative Zoology, Harvard University, while on our way to work with Halet Çambel and Robert Braidwood at the prehistoric site of Çayönü, southeastern Anatolia. While we were at Harvard, Barbara Lawrence and Dexter Perkins showed us a form they had evolved for rapid recording of faunal data. We thought it excellent but changed it a bit to conform with some of our own ideas, and I then had several hundred such forms mimeographed for use at Çayönü, where they proved most efficient. A young archeologist at Çayönü, Steven LeBlanc, saw what we were doing and said that the categories on our form could be utilized to produce a computer code. He and McArdle pursued this project and soon organized the basis for such a code, although we continued to use the mimeographed forms throughout that season.

While still at Çayönü, we were visited by a group of American archeologists working in Iran, among whom was a young zoologist, Richard Redding, who was training himself to be a faunal analyst. He thought the idea of using a computer to be excellent and took both the idea and a copy of our code, as developed at the time, with him.

In April of the following year, 1971, when the Section on Animal Domestication of the Third International Congress of Museums of Agriculture met in Budapest, neither McArdle nor I could attend, but McArdle prepared a mimeographed outline of the technique, with discussions of the method and with forms attached (McArdle 1971). I wrote an introductory page, multiple copies were made and sent, and these were distributed at the meeting. By writing that introduction, I have been credited with an influence on the use of computers by faunal analysts that I don't deserve; such credit should go to LeBlanc and McArdle.

At least one European investigator, Hans-Peter Uerpmann, was stimulated by McArdle's handout in Budapest in 1971 to develop a similar code that met his special needs (Uerpmann 1978); he in turn has stimulated others, and so the ripples spread. Meanwhile, Juliet Clutton-Brock at the British Museum (Natural History) in London was trying to catch up on accumulations of bones from many sites dug during the last century or so in England, and independently she too turned to the computer for aid (Clutton-Brock 1975).

During this same period, McArdle tested his version of the code on a faunal collection from Girikihacıyan, a Halafian village near Çayönü, as a topic for his Master's thesis (McArdle 1974), and additionally prepared a manuscript on the code for publication. Redding had become a graduate student at the University of Michigan, where he was independently developing his own code and stimulating other students there to work with him. Redding and his coworkers also prepared a manuscript. The two manuscripts were sent independently to the journal *Paléorient*, arriving almost simultaneously on the editor's desk. He in turn chose me as one of the reviewers; I tried to get the two parties to settle upon a single version, but failed, so the manuscripts were published separately but in the same issue of the same journal (McArdle 1977; Redding, Pires-Ferreira, and Zeder 1977). Later, however, a unified version was achieved and published (Redding, Zeder, and McArdle 1978).

At Harvard, Richard Meadow, even though he knew of and was influenced by the work of Redding and McArdle, had somewhat different ideas and so has published another code (Meadow 1978). In California, Gifford and Crader (1977), although knowing of McArdle's work, independently published yet another code. There should be enough codes by now for all, and I suspect that we shall soon have a subset of computer specialists for faunal studies, with their own society.

Given the nature of the data of faunal studies and the pattern whereby a computer works, these various codes are necessarily similar but yet not interchangeable. Thus at present comparative analyses of data from different sites can be made only if the different investigators are using the same code, or if the data from one site is transposed into a different code—a somewhat laborious operation. Obviously benefits would accrue to all if those faunal analysts experienced in use of computers would agree on the same type of code so that the data from any site could be compared directly with those of another. That time has not yet arrived.

I see one danger from continuing intensification of use of computers. Like some ecologists and evolutionists who sit in offices and use computers to build models of what might be or might have been, some faunal analysts of the future may never dig a bone, never study a bone, not recognize a bone if they're shown one, and utterly forget that there was a time and place long ago inhabited by real people who hunted and/or kept real animals in a complex physical and cultural environment. People become fascinated by machines that produce make-believe models at the touch of a button.

7. Recovery of Entomological Remains

Pieces of the chitinous exoskeletons of insects and other anthropods can be recovered from fossil soils by flotation and can often be identified as to genus and species (Coope 1967). This information can then be used in the reconstruction of past climates and other environmental aspects of an area, as Coope and others have well demonstrated in a series of studies. Purely archeological use of such insects' parts has not been so common, but Costantini, Tosi, and Taglianti (1977) have shown that the remains of arthropods are often rather numerous in former living sites, and well worth salvaging. Working at several sites in Iran and Iraq, the authors have shown that the concentrated presence in former times of stored cereals or rotting meat within restricted areas of a settlement can sometimes be demonstrated by the presence of remains of insects highly diagnostic of particular conditions. Other kinds of insects can give detailed information on the surrounding microenvironment, such as salt marsh; some live as adults only briefly at a certain time of year, others occur only within particular limits of temperature or humidity. A new subdiscipline of archeology is being born.

8. Zooarcheology on the Assembly Line

LaBianca (1978) was faced with a situation in which some 1,200 fragmented bones of nonhuman animals were being excavated each day from the site of Tell Hesbân (twelfth century B.C. to fourteenth century A.D.), in Jordan. This embarrassment of riches, coupled with regulations against the removal of the bones from the country, necessitated the establishment of an assembly line, in which each bone was subjected to a precise sequence of procedures at the site as well as at an off-site laboratory. Not only were the bones cleaned, weighed, and labeled but also the data were then determined and recorded in a prearranged pattern that utilized to the best of their abilities unskilled, partially skilled, and skilled workers, in such a way that by the time a piece of bone had reached the end of the assembly line in the off-site laboratory the data on that piece of bone were ready for the computer. I have calculated that 1,200 bones each day, for four seasons of several weeks each, must have brought to that assembly line approximately 330,000 bones (maybe 300,000; I wouldn't quibble about a mere 30,000 bones).

DOMESTICATION

When I was writing more than 20 years ago, goats seemingly occupied the position of animals first domesticated in the Near East as known from the basal levels at Jarmo, ca. 8500 bp, and the presence of dogs in the Near East for that time was questionable except as suggested by figurines from Jarmo. For lack of evidence, domestication of several species was placed much later than we would place it today. Those conclusions of two decades ago are changed now, suggesting that these presented here will probably be changed in another two decades.

DOGS (*Canis familiaris*)

Lawrence (1967) found bones of early dogs at Çayönü, in southeastern Turkey, dated at about 9000 bp, and then specimens of the same species in far-away Idaho dated more than a thousand years earlier (Lawrence 1968). A few years later Turnbull and Reed (1974) announced the finding of what seems certainly to be the lower jaw of a dog from the shelter of Palegawra, in northern Iraq, dated between 14,000 and 12,000 bp. Not everyone agrees that the scraps of bone from Idaho, Turkey, and Iraq, upon which these determinations have been made, are really from domestic dogs and not merely from aberrant wolves (Herre and Röhrs 1977), so caution must be observed. However, the validity of the early date of domestic dogs is strengthened by finding the complete skeleton of a young *Canis* (not a jackal) buried beneath a human skeleton at Mallaha, northern Palestine (Valla 1977; Davis and Valla 1978). The date of death for the two so buried together was about 12,000 bp. Although proof of domestication is lacking, the close association in death indicates familiarity in life, so one can surmise the canid pup was either tamed wolf or domestic dog.

On the other hand, at Jericho, Clutton-Brock decided in 1969 that none of the canid remains could be identified definitely as dogs, thus denying the oft-quoted opinion of Zeuner (1958) that domestic dogs were present there already in the Pre-Pottery Neolithic A (PPNA), ca. 9700 bp. Later, Clutton-Brock (1979) had come to believe that inasmuch as dogs were known from elsewhere in the Near East by the eleventh millennium bp, they should have been present by then at Jericho, and presumably were. However, of the specimens of *Canis* available to her from the Proto-Neolithic (ca. 10,500 bp) and the Neolithic of Jericho, she has been unable to identify definitely any one as domestic dog without possible confusion with the small wolf, *Canis lupus arabs*, of the Arabian peninsula or with the large jackal, *Canis aureus lupaster*, present in Palestine in prehistoric times but now limited to Egypt and other parts of Africa. This problem of overlap in size and characters of certain dogs, wolves, and jackals from the Arabian peninsula has been a continuous one in the study of canids from archeological sites of the area and will obviously continue as such.

Fortunately for some Near Eastern zooarcheologists, the foothills of the Zagros Mountains, where Jarmo is situated, are beyond this area of difficulty; the wolves of the Zagros, *Canis lupus lupaster*, are larger than *C. l. arabs* from the Arabian peninsula, and the only jackal of the area is the small *C. a. aureus*. Even so, potential overlap in size between early dogs at Jarmo and wolves near the smaller end of their size range cannot be ignored (Reed 1961). However, elsewhere in this volume the fragments of the larger canids from Jarmo (ca. 8500 bp) have been determined by Lawrence and myself, at least to our own satisfaction, to have been the remains of dogs, not wolves. Yet dogs have been stated not to have been present in Khuzistan, southwestern Iran, until about 7500 bp (Hole, Flannery, and Neely 1969).

The above data present an enigmatic story. If domestic dogs were actually present in the Near East from 12,000 bp, or possibly earlier, their remains in archeological sites of the area between 12,000 and 7000 bp are curiously rare and often absent. Additionally, all of these early dogs are quite wolflike in size and general characters, often being identified as dogs only by slight morphological differences, determined statistically (chap. 10); only the oldest of the remains of dogs, the single mandible from Palegawra, really looks at first glance as if it had come from a dog.

Lastly, if dogs have been present in southwestern Asia since at least 12,000 bp, why do we find few or no dog-chewed bones in all the prehistoric sites that have been excavated there? By contrast, the bones in a Hittite site at which I once worked had often been chewed so thoroughly, presumably by dogs, as sometimes to be unrecognizable.

SHEEP (*Ovis aries*)

Present karyological and biochemical studies indicate that domestic sheep were derived from *Ovis orientalis*, the wild Asiatic sheep whose range is west of a line drawn from the Caspian Sea to the Strait of Hormuz (Bunch 1979); those sheep have 54 chromosomes as do domestic sheep, whereas native sheep to the east of that line have higher diploid numbers. West of the line mentioned above is the part of Asia where archeological research had already placed the early domestication of sheep, and the support of karyology to our archeology is indeed comforting.

When I wrote 20 years ago about the known sequence of domestication of hoofed food-animals in the prehistoric Near East, goats were earliest known—from Jarmo ca. 8500 bp. However, Perkins (1964*a*, *b*) has presented evidence that sheep were domestic earlier at Zawi Chemi Shanidar, a settlement on a narrow terrace near the river in the canyon of the Greater Zab River, northern Iraq; the radiocarbon determination is $10,870 \pm 300$ bp (Solecki and Rubin 1958). This date is almost 2,000 years earlier than any other known evidence for domestic sheep anywhere, and on this basis alone people have naturally been skeptical about Perkins's conclusion and have asked, "If domestic sheep were present in the mountains of northern Iraq by ca. 10,750 bp, why were they absent from all other sites in southwestern Asia until ca. 9000 bp?" To that query we have no answer.

Perkins's conclusion that domestic sheep, but not domestic goats, were present during the period of approximately 10,750-9,000 bp at Zawi Chemi Shanidar and at the same time were presumably being herded by the same people at the nearby Shanidar Cave (Solecki 1966) was based on two major assumptions, using his determinations of the relative frequencies (*f*; see p. 514) of sheep and goats at several periods throughout the prior 100,000 years. The first assumption was that the narrow canyon and precipitous mountains of the area were and are better habitat for wild goats than for wild sheep, so it would be expected that goats were more numerous and were hunted and killed more often and that therefore their bones would be more frequently represented in the successive layers of cultural debris of the two sites excavated (Shanidar Cave and Zawi Chemi Shanidar) than sheeps' bones. However, contrary to this expectation, the relative frequency of sheep at Zawi Chemi Shanidar increased considerably as compared with that of goats.

The second assumption was that wild populations of sheep and goats, maturing at approximately the same rate, would be expected to have the numbers of mature to immature bones preserved (and thus excavated) for each species relatively constant over time. As a diagnostic marker for testing this assumption, Perkins used the actual numbers of metapodials of the two caprine species, sheep and goats (see table on p. 523), and discovered that the proportion of immature sheep, but not of immature goats, increased markedly in the early Recent at Zawi Chemi Shanidar as compared with the late Pleistocene of Shanidar Cave (Perkins 1964a, table 1; reproduced here in expanded form as my table on p. 523).

Perkins interpreted the data he had accumulated on the basis of his ecological and ethological assumptions and concluded that sheep, but not goats, were domestic at Zawi Chemi Shanidar and at Shanidar Cave ca. 11,000-10,500 bp and subsequently. This conclusion has been widely quoted but has not been universally accepted; few of the doubters, however, have presented their reasons for doubt. Indeed, Brooke (1979), in a publication on the archeological evidence for early sheep, ignored Zawi Chemi Shanidar. One who has offered an explanation for the increased number of sheep in the early Recent of Zawi Chemi Shanidar is Dixon (1979); he has suggested that the well-known climatic changes at the end of the Pleistocene (including general warming, initiation of a Mediterranean type of climate, and increased growth of trees and grasses) might have been factors in the increased numbers of sheep available to the hunters who lived in the canyon of the Greater Zab, but such an increased population does not necessarily explain a simultaneous higher percent of bones of immature sheep recovered from Zawi Chemi Shanidar. Another possibility for an increase in the number of sheep (as well as of red deer) is that when people lived in a settlement closer to the Greater Zab they hunted more in the several small flatlands close to the river, where sheep and deer may well have been more numerous than goats. Possibly, in such an environment, a relatively larger number of immature sheep may have been killed as compared with the age groups killed by earlier people hunting sheep and goats in the mountains.

Primarily, I believe, some writers on the subject have thought intuitively that the time was too early (in comparison to the lack of evidence of any other known domestic sheep or other ungulates at the time), that numerous possible (but usually unnamed) variables were not and have not been considered, and that domestication of any species of social ungulates should have been accomplished by people who were settled into definite villages (a stage for which the excavations at Zawi Chemi Shanidar provided little evidence). Lastly, Perkins published only a preliminary table of his faunal results in an exceedingly short article, and then the whole collection of bones was unfortunately lost, so the data can never be reviewed.

The conclusions of one short statistical analysis (Hopkins 1967)[1] of Perkins's data were prepared but never published, but the manuscript came to the attention of Bökönyi, who referred to it in his own publication of 1977 (p. 9), stating that "after Hopkins's criticism serious doubts have arisen about the domesticated nature of the Zawi Chemi sheep." Since Hopkins did not include in his manuscript his statistical results, but only his conclusions derived therefrom, and additionally did not make as thorough an analysis as he should have, and since Bökönyi in turn stretched Hopkins's conclusions considerably, I have been forced here to review Perkins's data at more length than I had originally planned or desired.

Accordingly, I here republish (p. 523) Perkins's table of 1964a, with an additional two columns[2] of information: (1) the relative frequency (f) of sheep, goats, and red deer for each stratum of each site and (2) the number of immature metapodials recovered from each site.[3] Perkins determined his relative frequency (f) by dividing the total number of identified bones for each taxon by the number of bones identifiable as to genus in a skeleton of that taxon (22 for sheep or goat, 72 for red deer; see Perkins 1964a for additional explanation).

Perkins did not present a statistical evaluation of his data; presumably he regarded his conclusions as being so self-evident that no further analyses were necessary. Hopkins (1967) did do such analyses in part, but for sheep he omitted the statistical results from his manuscript and presented only his own conclusions. These latter almost entirely agreed with those of Perkins. The statistical test used by Hopkins was the determination of Z,[4] the standard normal deviation of the difference between two proportions (Appendix 1). The figures he tested were the proportion of immature sheep in one sample with the proportion of immature sheep in another sample. (The proportions of immature goats in the several samples have not been so analyzed; Perkins, Hopkins, and I seem to agree that this particular statistical nicety is unnecessary.)

The faunal samples from two layers have not here been considered; that from the deepest stratum (1.5-2.94 m) at Zawi Chemi Shanidar produced only four bones of sheep, all adult, and the sediments of layer B1 at Shanidar Cave are known to be mixed in part with materials from above and below. Of the other strata, the essential problem that emerged after some unnecessary statistical manipulations was the comparisons of populations of sheep from the Paleolithic (Late Pleistocene) layers with those of the early Recent (i.e., the comparison of the remains of sheep from the layers 0.5-1.5 m at Zawi Chemi Shanidar with those from layer C [Baradostian] plus layer D [Mousterian] in Shanidar Cave). The results are presented in my second table, part A, page 524; the Z of 1.68 can then be translated into

Perkins's Table of 1964a with Additional Calculations and Derived Data

Animal (genus)	Identified specimens (N)	Relative frequency (f)		Percentage of frequency (f) %	Total no. of distal ends of metapodials (N)	No. of distal ends of immature metapodials (N)	Percentage of immature animals in each genus %
Zawi Chemi Shanidar: 0.5-1.0 m in depth							
Ovis	63	63/22 =	2.86	81.0	48	26	54.2
Capra	8	8/22 =	.36	10.2	8	2	25.0
Cervus	22	22/72 =	.31	8.8			
			3.53	100.0			
Zawi Chemi Shanidar: 1.0-1.5 m in depth							
Ovis	473	473/22 =	21.50	65.0	176	78	44.3
Capra	79	79/22 =	3.59	10.9	72	18	25.0
Cervus	576	576/72 =	8.00	24.1			
			33.09	100.0			
Zawi Chemi Shanidar: 1.5-2.95 m in depth							
Ovis	4(adult)	4/22 =	.18	31.0			
Capra	0		.00	0.0			
Cervus	31	31/72 =	.40	69.0			
			0.58	100.0			
Shanidar Cave: layer B1 (Neolithic)							
Ovis	27	27/22 =	1.23	42.9	19	11	57.9
Capra	36	36/22 =	1.64	57.1	14	6	42.9
Cervus	0		.00	0.0			
			2.87	100.0			
Shanidar Cave: layer C (Baradostian)							
Ovis	17	17/22 =	.77	37.4	12	2	16.7
Capra	27	27/22 =	1.23	59.7	23	5	21.8
Cervus	4		.06	2.9			
			2.06	100.0			
Shanidar Cave: layer D (Mousterian)							
Ovis	8	8/22 =	.36	20.5	7	3	42.9
Capra	29	29/22 =	1.32	75.0	9	1	11.2
Cervus	6	6/72 =	.08	4.5			
			1.76	100.0			

an expression of statistical significance. This figure, .046, indicates that the difference between the proportions of the two populations of sheep is statistically significant at the level of .05 (i.e., there is less than one chance in 20 that the two sets of bones of sheep, as excavated, could have come from the same population).

When one compares the Baradostian population of sheep, alone, with that from Zawi Chemi Shanidar, the level of significance of difference is much greater; the figure of .022 means that there is only one chance in 45 that the two sets of bones, as excavated, could have come from the same population. In other words, the probability that the age composition of the populations of sheep at Zawi Chemi Shanidar was significantly different from that of the sheep of the Baradostian or of the Baradostian plus the Mousterian is high.

This latter fact was the one emphasized by Perkins, who did no statistics, and was also stated by Hopkins after he had done the statistics. This probability was ignored or not understood by Bökönyi, who concentrated instead on the similarity of the age grouping of the sheep from the Mousterian layer (42.9% immature) to that of the early Recent (46.9% immature). Perkins ignored this similarity, probably on the basis of the small sample from level D (only 7 metapodials of sheep), but Hopkins, after discussing the rather close similarity, wrote, "Clearly this is to a large extent a reflection of the small number of bones from which age can be determined in layer D...." Also, in an introductory note to Professor Braidwood, he wrote again of the impossibility of proving a significant difference in two percentages using the tiny sample of only seven bones from the Mousterian level. However, the actual sample of 7 metapodials recorded by Perkins does not indicate an unusual age distribution (Appendix 2).

By thus ignoring the sample of bones of sheep from the Mousterian as being too small for valid consideration, Hopkins agreed with Perkins that the sheep of the Baradostian and the sheep of the early Recent possessed two different life tables, with a significantly higher proportion of immature sheep in the Recent population. Even when we combine the sheep of the Baradostian and the Mousterian (my second table, part A, p. 524) we must reach the same

Analyses by Pairs of Pooled Samples of Perkins's Counts of All Distal Ends of Metapodials of Sheep from Several Strata at Shanidar Cave and Zawi Chemi Shanidar Compared with Distal Ends of Immature Metapodials of Sheep from the Same Samples

Provenience of samples compared	Distal ends of all metapodials	Distal ends of immature metapodials		Z^*	Statistical significance of difference
	Total number	Total number	Percentage		
A. Zawi Chemi: 0.5-1.5 m compared with	224	104	46.4	1.68	.046
Shanidar Cave: Pleistocene layers (Baradostian + Mousterian)	19	5	26.3		
B. Zawi Chemi: 0.5-1.5 m compared with	224	104	46.9	2.05	.022
Shanidar Cave: layer C (Baradostian)	12	2	16.7		
C. Zawi Chemi: 0.5-1.5 m compared with	224	104	46.9	0.21	.417
Shanidar Cave: layer D (Mousterian)	7	3	42.9		

SOURCE: Perkins 1964a.
*See Appendix 1 (p. 529).

conclusion. Bökönyi simply must not have understood the force of the argument and the finality of conclusions which emerge from the data, and I am sorry that, good friends as we have always been, I have had to emphasize that he has entered a statement into the literature which is contrary to the existing facts.

None of this dedication to statistics "proves" that the people at Zawi Chemi Shanidar had domestic sheep. What is obvious is that Perkins (1964a) was quite right in his statements that in the early Recent (1) sheep increased in actual numbers and the goats did not and (2) the proportion of immature sheep increased markedly, whereas in goats this pheomenon did not occur. Perkins attributed these changes to domestication of sheep, which is a logical conclusion, but other possible causative factors could have been environmental changes at the end of the Pleistocene favoring the increase of sheep over goats, changed hunting techniques of the human hunters, or a shift to areas for hunting that were ecologically different from those of the mountains. We cannot validly state, however, that the results of any statistical tests so far applied have cast doubts on Perkins's conclusions.

We must remember, too, that the physical tests of long bones of sheep from Zawi Chemi Shanidar (Drew, Perkins, and Daly 1971a) indicated that the sheep were domestic but that the goats were not. The validity of the techniques used, and of the conclusions derived, have been adversely criticized, as discussed elsewhere in this chapter, but no one has attempted duplication of the same techniques upon the same materials tested by Drew et al., so that validity of the criticisms has not been established.

Another unresolved problem is the definite increase in the relative frequency of red deer at Zawi Chemi as contrasted with their relative rarity in the Pleistocene levels in Shanidar Cave; in the Recent, the deer are roughly twice as numerous as goats and about one third as numerous as sheep, whereas in the Baradostian and Mousterian the deer were hardly represented. If we consider the increase in population of the sheep to be evidence of domestication, can we deny that, on the basis of the same type of evidence, the deer should be accorded the same status? If, on the other hand, we consider that the deer may have been more numerous amidst some of the flatter areas near the village than in the rugged hills where the cave is, could not the same argument be made for the sheep? One cannot at this time reach final conclusions.

Tentative evidence for possible early herding or other human control of sheep (and goats) has been presented by Moore (1979) for the site of Tell Abu Hureyra, on the right bank of the Euphrates River in north-central Syria. In a popular article, without supportive evidence, Moore mentioned that sheep, goats, and gazelles were being hunted during the Mesolithic phase (11,400-10,500 bp) of occupation of a fairly large village. Since little natural habitat for sheep and none for goats seemingly occur within 100 km of the site, I suggest that any bones of sheep or goats recovered from the lower (Mesolithic) levels of the tell were from animals maintained outside their natural habitat and thus under human control. The time would have been earlier than, but in part overlapping with, that of Zawi Chemi Shanidar, but I stress that the evidence for such possible human care of sheep and goats at Abu Hureyra is most indirect.

As now known, the presence of early domestic sheep subsequent to the time of occupation of Zawi Chemi is rather spotty, and we do not know whether this erratic pattern is actuality or only a reflection of our lack of knowledge. No domestic sheep are reported from quite a scatter of what seem to be permanently occupied sites later in time than Zawi Chemi Shanidar (but all dated probably earlier than 8500 bp): Mureybit on the Euphrates, Beidha in southwestern Jordan, Ganj Dareh in west-central Iran, and the lower levels at Çayönü. If the inhabitants of Abu Hureyra had herded sheep, one thinks that those of Mureybit should have done so too. Sheep should have been present at both places at the same time, or absent from both; this situation remains a problem at present. Beidha presumably was simply too far away from the center of domestication to have had sheep at such an early date. However, the "grill-plan subphase" of lower levels at Çayönü (Braidwood, Çambel, et al. 1974; Çambel and Braidwood 1980) can be dated to ca. 9500-9000 bp; wild sheep were present and the site is not far from Zawi Chemi Shanidar (a straight-line distance of only 470 km, or slightly less than 300 miles).

If domestic sheep had spread from Zawi Chemi Shanidar at a rate of approximately 300 m per year for 1,700 years, they should have reached Çayönü (and many other places) by 9000 bp. We have no record that such spread of domestic sheep happened, and indeed the relatively sudden appearance of domestic sheep about 9000 bp in the Ali Kosh phase of the cultural sequence on the Deh Luran plain, Iranian Khuzistan (Hole, Flannery, and Neely 1969), and toward the end of the main prehistoric phase at Çayönü (Çambel and Braidwood 1980) may have been due to domestication in situ of local wild sheep.

Early domestic sheep have also been found, ca. 8100 bp, in southeastern Europe, as at Nea Nikomedeia, Greek Macedonia (Higgs 1962). These sheep have often been considered to have been derived from wild sheep native to southeastern Europe, following the studies of Radulesco and Samson (1962) at the cave of "La Adam" in the Rumanian Dobrogea. Recently, however, Bökönyi (1978) has reviewed the literature on claims for the presence of wild sheep in the Holocene and Late Pleistocene of continental Europe and believes that no such claims are valid. Therefore, according to Bökönyi's interpretation, the supposedly wild sheep at "La Adam" must have been large domestic sheep newly moved into the area in the Neolithic. The strata in the cave had a steep gradient, and confusion of layers while excavating was unavoidable, according to Bökönyi. The gradient of the cave (Radulesco and Samson 1962, figs. 1-2) does not seem to me to have been as steep as Bökönyi indicated, but I do find more persuasive his argument that no other excavated site in the Balkans which has the same time sequence shows any evidence of wild sheep.

Until further evidence to the contrary appears, I am thus inclined to believe that the domestic sheep of Europe were derived entirely from sheep domesticated in southwestern Asia and moved to the Balkans. The further early history of such domesticated sheep in southeastern Europe has already been summarized by Bökönyi (1974).

GOATS (*Capra hircus*)

When excavating bones from Jarmo in the spring of 1955, I noted that the horn cores of many of the male goats were flattened on the medial sides, in contrast to the quadrangular shapes of the cores of wild goats collected at the time in the nearby mountains. Since the cores of the male domesticated goats living in the area at present are also medially flattened, I concluded that flattened horn cores were a sign of domestication (Reed 1959), although I did not then understand why.

These and other observations about the skulls of goats and sheep from Jarmo and other early agricultural sites in southwestern Asia led to the exploration of the coordinated evolution of behavior and cephalic anatomy in wild males of *Ovis* and *Capra* and the three other present genera in the Tribe Caprini (Schaffer and Reed 1972).

For males of both sheep and goats, selection for social dominance is exceedingly vigorous, involving horn-to-horn clashing and butting. Particularly in sheep and goats (less is known of the behavior in other Caprini) the loser of such a contest adopts a submissive role in the presence of male victors and essentially is excluded from the breeding population. Near-perfect horns of large size are thus a prerequisite for the transmission of a male's genes into the next generation, and selection for such horns is thereby rigid.

Under conditions of domestication, the natural structure of populations was disturbed artificially by selective killing. Effective breeding hierarchies would not then have become established, and natural selection for the wild type of horn would have been diminished, so that genes that allow the rounding of the medial and lateral angles of the horn cores would have accumulated.

The type of core so produced has been described in cross section as almond shaped, lens shaped, or lozenge shaped (different names for the same shape), and seemingly marks a primary stage in domestication, as described by Zeuner (1955) for a particularly large but slender horn core of a male goat from the Pre-Pottery Neolithic A (PPNA) at Jericho, by Reed (1959) for the remains of goats at Jarmo, and by Hole, Flannery, and Neely (1969, pp. 270-77) for the early goats from Tepe Ali Kosh, southwestern Iran. Perhaps the continued relaxation of selection for social dominance was then the factor that allowed the median side of males' horn cores to develop as a flat surface, a characteristic noticed first as a diagnostic feature of domestic goats at Jarmo in 1955 (Reed 1959). However, I do not understand why this particular shape has become universal or nearly so among male domestic goats.

Several complexities confuse our understanding of what was happening during the early history of domestic male goats (I omit the horn cores of females from this discussion only because their horn cores do not change as much as do those of males during the process of domestication): (1) the range of shapes of horn cores of wild goats has not been determined, and possibly some of the animals in any wild population may also have almond-shaped horn cores; (2) feral goats may sometimes interbreed with wild populations, diluting the natural gene pool; (3) perhaps because of such dilution, the males of some populations of wild goats, surviving peripherally under adverse environmental conditions, may have a high incidence of almond-shaped cores, a situation known to be true of the wild goats of the low, dry Jebel Hamrin on the southwestern border of the Deh Luran plain, Iranian Khuzistan (Hole, Flannery, and

Neely 1969, p. 270); (4) in the same population of male goats at some stage of early domestication may be found a full range of variation of horn cores from almond-shaped to medially flattened or slightly concave, a range of variation found at Jarmo (Reed 1960, p. 131); (5) Clutton-Brock (1979) has reported three bones of robust goats (listed by her as probably wild *Capra hircus aegagrus*) from the Proto-Neolithic layer at Jericho. I suggest that such bones, lacking published evidence to the contrary, could have been derived from *Capra ibex*. We have no evidence that ibex have ever been domesticated. The presence of domestic goats at Jericho has been stated by Clutton-Brock to be during the Pre-Pottery Neolithic B (PPNB), ca. 9000 bp; but the almond-shaped horn cores of a male wild goat (*C. h. aegagrus*) from the level of PPNA (Zeuner 1955, fig. 6) suggest incipient domestication, as Zeuner himself thought. These complexities mentioned above illustrate the principle that continuous morphological variations controlled by multiple genes in a single species, both throughout a population and over time, can result in microevolutionary morphologic changes between fully wild and fully domestic individuals; intermediate populations, due to chance genetic assortment, may be highly variable and the wild or domestic status of single horn cores from such a population may be difficult to determine.

A second tendency in the change in shape of horn cores, and thus of horns of goats under domestication, is for them to become twisted, as seen in most domestic goats of the world at present. Zeuner (1955) first noted that such twisting typically came later than the tendency toward rounding of the medial and lateral angles of the core; indeed, he placed the time of twisting in the eastern Mediterranean almost as late as the beginning of the Bronze Age. However, Bökönyi (1977) has noted such a tendency toward twisting in horn cores of male goats excavated at Asiab, western Iran, from levels nearly 10,000 years old, and such "incipient twisting" was one of the first characters of horn cores of male goats I noted when excavating at Jarmo in 1955.

In spite of such difficulties of interpretation, by 9000 bp or perhaps somewhat earlier, goats regarded as domestic were present at three corners of a triangle—Ganj Dareh (Hesse 1977), Ali Kosh (Hole, Flannery, and Neely 1969), and Çayönü (Braidwood, Çambel, et al. 1974; Çambel and Braidwood 1980)—that covered much of southwestern Asia. At the time, domestic goats may well have been at many if not most villages within the triangle and at many outside it. Indeed, domestic goats may have been present even earlier, as Bökönyi (1977) has identified as "domestic" a few horn cores of male goats from near the bottom of the excavation at Asiab, west-central Iran, on the basis of the cross-sectional shapes and the tendency to twisting of the cores. The date is reported as somewhat younger than 10,000 bp. (Having myself excavated the specimens and having again examined them more recently, I am not convinced of their domestic status.)

Anatomical evidence for domestic status of the goats at Ganj Dareh as based on the shapes of the horn cores is not definite, but strong evidence does exist for increased cultural control over goats at that site, beginning between levels E and D, or probably about 9000 bp (Hesse 1977). Additionally, caprine hoofprints in freshly made mud bricks in level D (Smith 1970) indicate close association between goats and humans, since sheep are not represented at the site and experiments have shown that only the freshly made brick, while still wet, will be indented by the hoof of a walking goat (Hesse 1977). Additionally, there is the identification as "domestic" of sections from weight-bearing surfaces of goats' limb bones from Ganj Dareh (Drew, Perkins, and Daly 1971a).

Perkins (1966) suggested in a preliminary note the probability of the presence of domestic goats in the early Neolithic of Beidha, southwestern Jordan, on the basis of the high proportion (54.5%) of preadult specimens of goats and ibexes combined in Neolithic levels there, as contrasted with the proportion (only 30.6%) of preadult specimens of gazelles in the same layers. The gazelles, supposedly not domesticated, were thus being used as a standard of a killed wild population against which to evaluate the presumed domestic population with selective killing of young.

Hecker (1975) has analyzed in detail the skeletal remains of goats and ibexes from Beidha (sheep were not present there) and concluded that no evidence for domestication could be found, but with the passing of time the goats and ibexes together did present a shift in the life table to a death rate higher than expected for the younger age groups. Hecker has interpreted these data as evidence for "cultural manipulation" of wild goats and ibexes by man, but not domestication; he suggested that at Beidha such cultural manipulation consisted of driving the animals into natural or artificial enclosures, followed by selective killing of some of the young and release of all those not killed. Such herding, penning, and selective killing might be considered a possible route toward domestication (Downs 1960) but, if it did occur, this type of human behavior is not known to me otherwise except with reindeer, which are already semidomesticates. Whatever the details, this cultural manipulation *sans* domestication at Beidha (if occurring) seemingly was functionally satisfactory, as the pattern continued there from ca. 8800 bp for 500 years, during which time domestic goats were already well known elsewhere in southwestern Asia. (Considering the data presented by G.A. Wright and Miller [1976] on age clusters of different population groups of wild sheep, one hesitates to accept Hecker's conclusions, lacking as we do any physical evidence of pens, etc., until we learn more about the age clusters of different population groups of wild goats and ibexes.)

CATTLE (*Bos taurus*)

The present opinion is that all domestic cattle, including the zebu, were domesticated from the wild long-horned ancestor, *Bos primigenius*. The concept of an ancestral population of wild short-horned cattle in the late Pleistocene and early Recent of the Eastern Hemisphere has not been verified paleontologically, so that remains of short-horned cattle when now found are assumed to be from domestic cattle.

Until recently, the available evidence indicated that cattle were domesticated at least 2,000 years later than sheep and 500-1,000 years later than goats. When domestic cattle were reported from undated sites in Egypt's Nubian Desert (Wendorf, 1977, p. 224) the record seemed unimportant, but several more such supposedly domestic cattle have since been found in the same area, dated to 9400-9000 bp (Wendorf, pers. comm.). Comment must be withheld until publication of the data, but if the cattle were indeed domestic the emphasis of our thinking on the beginnings of domestication of cattle must necessarily shift to the eastern Sahara under conditions of greater rainfall than at present. However, we can continue to regard cattle as relatively late domesticates in the Near East; if original domestication occurred in southwestern Asia or Greece, a human purposefulness may have been present which is not believed to have existed with the original domestication of sheep, goats, and pigs.

Wild cattle, particularly the males, were large, fast, and dangerous, as hunters knew; indeed, domestic bulls today can be dangerous, as many a farmer has proved by dying from an unexpected horn-thrust.

The obvious physical products to be gained from cattle, whether hunted or tame, were meat, bones, and hides, already available in some parts of the Near East by 8500 bp from domestic sheep, goats, and pigs. The possibility of humans thinking of cattle as potential producers of milk and/or power for draft must be discounted as of 8500 bp, several millennia in advance of long experience with cattle as domesticates. Instead, the pattern of thought and action leading toward the domestication of cattle may have been initiated by religion (Isaac 1962; 1963; 1970, pp. 105-7).

Many peoples have venerated cattle, and many peoples in many different ways still do. The earliest evidence presently found of such veneration is the burial of heads of wild bulls in the bases of clay house-walls at Mureybit, Syria, almost 10,000 bp (Stordeur 1979). This same pattern of association of heads of bulls and walls of buildings appears again at Çatal Hüyük, south-central Anatolia, ca. 7950-7000 bp, except that at Çatal Hüyük the heads of the bulls appeared as parts of shrines within the rooms. Too, at Çatal Hüyük the head was often modeled in clay and only the horns were real (Mellaart 1967). Additionally, paintings of bulls sometimes appeared on the walls of the same shrines, accompanied by painted diminutive figures of humans (Mellaart 1967, fig. 48). This is not the place to write a history of human veneration of cattle, but the pattern of such thought and action can be traced from ten millennia ago to the present, and I am supporting Isaac's suggestion (1970, p. 106) that possibly wild cattle were driven into pens, with the large bulls then being removed as needed for living sacrifices. The behavioral path from this situation to domestication is unknown, but with domestic sheep and goats present as a model of economic value, the thought could have occurred that the surviving cows and smaller bulls might be preserved alive for future meat and hides and perhaps even for an available population of sacrificial animals as needed.

Little evidence exists for this hypothetical ritualistic approach to the early domestication of cattle, but the continuing pattern of veneration of cattle for 10,000 years suggests to me that such an explanation merits serious consideration.

The earliest known domestic cattle, other than those possibly in Egypt's Nubian Desert, have been found not in southwestern Asia but in Greece at Argissa-Magula, Thessaly, ca. 8500 bp (Boessneck 1962) and at Nea Nikomedeia (Higgs 1962). The identifications as domestic have been based on small size in comparison with *Bos primigenius* and on the large numbers (50%) of immature specimens. At no time or place during this ninth millennium bp has any evidence for domestic cattle been found in southwestern Asia; well-excavated and well-studied sites such as Suberde, ca. 8500 bp (Perkins and Daly 1968), Jarmo, ca. 8500 bp (chap. 9), Jericho (both A and B levels of the Pre-Pottery Neolithic), ca. 10,000-8000 bp (Clutton-Brock 1979), and the basal levels (Ali Kosh) in the sequence at Deh Luran, Khuzistan, ca. 9500-7600 bp (Hole, Flannery, and Neely 1969), had no domestic cattle.

At present there is no evidence of domestic cattle in Asia prior to the middle of the eighth millennium bp, when they were present at both Çatal Hüyük, level VI (Perkins 1969), and in the Tepe Sabz levels at Deh Luran (Hole, Flannery, and Neely 1969). This near-simultaneous appearance in Asia of domestic cattle in Anatolia and southwestern Iran, with none being identified in the area in between at the same time, is an enigma. Were cattle first domesticated in Greece and then ferried to Anatolia, or were there two or possibly three separate centers of domestication, with or possibly without cultural contact?

One would logically expect domestic cattle to have been widespread throughout the Near East by 7500 bp, but many sites have no evidence of them during the next millennium, or even later. The Jordan valley, for instance, had no domestic cattle prior to 7000 bp (Ducos 1969), and Clutton-Brock (1979) does not list them in any number until the Early Bronze Age (6000 bp or later). In the ᶜAmuq sequence of northern Syria, definite evidence of domestic cattle did not appear before phase D, ca. 6250 bp (chap. 9). In northern Iraq, evidence of domestic cattle is, as mentioned before, absent not only from Jarmo ca. 8500 bp but also from Matarrah a thousand years later (chap. 9); they were, however, present at Banahilk by ca. 7000 bp (chap. 19).

These extremely spotty local primary appearances and the subsequent distribution of domestic cattle in southwestern Asia are most confusing, and at present we have no answer to this situation.

PIGS (*Sus scrofa*)

Our knowledge of the early history of domestication of pigs is weak. In nonagricultural human societies, humans and pigs compete for food, but domestic pigs could be fed in part on human excreta and agricultural waste low in calories while they were being kept away from growing crops. Thus humans restricted domestic pigs to a narrow ecologic niche, but the pattern obviously worked, as it works well for villagers in many parts of the world today.

The earliest domestic pigs, known from southwestern Asia about the middle of the ninth millennium bp, are distinguished from their wild contemporaries of the same local areas that were found in the same sites by the markedly reduced size of the jaws and dentitions; this reduction can be noted in the molars, particularly in the upper and lower third molars (Flannery 1961; Reed 1961). Such diminution of the jaws, indicating relatively small size of the whole head and probably also of the remainder of the body, would indicate that the domestic pigs were receiving a reduced diet, as compared with their wild contemporaries of the same area, and so probably were considerably restricted in their foraging. The continued reduction in size of domestic pigs throughout the history of the Near East is a topic deserving special study.

Stampfli (chap. 9) has presented a good résumé of the early history of domestic pigs in southwestern Asia; his studies indicate they were rare, if present at all, prior to ca. 8500 bp, when they appeared at Jarmo. In general, however, pigs were not a major economic factor in the life of prehistoric villages in the Near East, rarely being more than 5% of the domestic animals of a village.

As mentioned above, domestication of pigs earlier than 8500 bp has been suggested, but the evidence is as yet too meagre to accept. Thus the claim for domestication of pigs in the Crimea as early as in the Near East, or earlier, has been studied by Tringham (1969), who did not find the evidence convincing. Additionally, the presence of domestic pigs at Çayönü ca. 9000 bp is not as definite as I once thought (Reed 1969), on the basis of more recent excavations at the site (Braidwood, Çambel, et al. 1974; Çambel and Braidwood 1980).

For the middle of the ninth millennium bp, quite as early as at Jarmo, domestic pigs have been reported from various sites in the Balkans (Bökönyi 1974, p. 208), and those pigs may well have been domesticated independently from those of southwestern Asia. Certainly the domestic pigs found in northern China by 6000 bp (Ho 1977) were independently domesticated there, and domestic pigs may have been present, again probably independently domesticated, in southeastern Asia nearly as early (Higham 1977). In spite of many early opinions to the contrary, all of the wild pigs ancestral to the domestic ones belonged to the same species, *Sus scrofa* (Herre and Röhrs 1977).

EQUIDS

Bones of equids found in prehistoric sites in the late Quaternary of southwestern Asia have generally been assigned to the small Syrian onager (*Equus hemionus hemippus*) if west or south of the Zagros Mountains or to the larger *E. h. onager* if in the hills of those mountains or north of them. The small equids portrayed pulling carts or primitive war-chariots in the third millennium B.C. of Sumerian city-states have typically been considered to have been domesticated (or at least tamed) Syrian onagers (Zeuner 1963, pp. 367-73), whose use did not last later than the introduction of domestic horses from the Eurasiatic steppes early in the second millennium B.C.

Donkeys (*Equus africanus*) supposedly had been introduced from northern Africa into southwestern Asia about 3000 B.C. but were presumably used only as beasts of burden. However, Ducos (1970, 1975) decided that the remains of small and presumably wild equids from Mureybit, a village on the Euphrates dating from the tenth to ninth millennia bp, were from true donkeys and not from Syrian onagers, as would be expected on the basis of locality. Ducos's study was based on comparisons of teeth, occipital bones, and several bones of the limbs, and on the generally larger size of the ancient bones as compared with those from recent *E. hemionus hemippus*. This last criterion may not be valid, as individuals of a population of *hemippus* living in eastern Syria 9,000 years ago may well have been larger than their descendants of the nineteenth and twentieth centuries A.D. in the same area. Be that as it may, the differences of morphological detail remain; if Ducos's conclusions, as based on that morphology, are valid, then the small equids pictured by Sumerians during the third millennium B.C. may have been donkeys, not onagers, and the latter need not have had any history of domestication.

Some people have adopted Ducos's conclusions (Herre and Röhrs 1977) and some have not (Turnbull, pers. comm.; Perkins, pers. comm.), but the possibility of having had wild donkeys in southwestern Asia in the late Pleistocene and early Recent must be given careful consideration. One who failed to do so was Hecker (1975), who identified the remains of equids from Beidha as onagers without any comment that they might have been donkeys.

NOTES

1. Joseph Hopkins was at the time a student in the Department of Anthropology at the University of Chicago.

2. For the material in these two columns, I am indebted to Dexter Perkins and to Miss Mary Evins. Miss Evins is a graduate student in the Department of Anthropology at the University of Chicago who has studied a sample of nonhuman bones from Shanidar Cave that was not available to Perkins when he made the study he published in 1964a.

3. Unfortunately, Perkins did not determine the number of immature metapodials for the red deer, *Cervus elaphus*. Those data would have provided a useful control, since generally the deer are presumed not to have been domestic during the Pleistocene nor did they become domestic later, although note the arguments of Jarman (1970, 1971, 1972) that red deer, where their remains are numerous in archeological sites of the late Quaternary, had at least been herded as semidomesticates or had been even more firmly under human control.

4. I am indebted to Dr. Kathleen Crittenden, Department of Sociology, University of Illinois at Chicago Circle, for patiently leading me into the mysteries of Z, obviously made more mysterious by Hopkins's errors in writing his formulae.

APPENDIX 1*

Z (the standard normal deviation of the difference between two proportions) $= \dfrac{p_1 - p_2}{\sigma_{(p_1 - p_2)}}$, where

p_1 = the percentage of immature metapodials in the first of two samples being compared, and
p_2 = the percentage of immature metapodials in the second of two samples being compared, and

$\sigma_{(p_1 - p_2)} = \sqrt{\dfrac{\bar{p}(100 - \bar{p})}{m} + \dfrac{\bar{p}(100 - \bar{p})}{n}}$, where

$\bar{p} = \dfrac{np_1 + mp_2}{n + m}$,

n = total number of metapodials in sample 1, and
m = total number of metapodials in sample 2.

(Anyone possessing a copy of Hopkins's manuscript should be aware that in his formulae he erroneously wrote all plus [+] signs as negative [−]. Thus his formulae as written are unusable, although internal evidence indicates that he himself used the formulae correctly.)

APPENDIX 2

Let us assume that 25% of the animals killed of a wild-hunted population were immature, using for comparison the data for *Capra* at Zawi Chemi Shanidar. With regard to the sheep killed by Neanderthals living in Shanidar Cave during the Mousterian period, the question then becomes: What is the chance that, of 7 metapodials found, 3 of them would be of immature animals (= 42.9%)?

Nonmathematical logic dictates the thought that if 2 immature and 6 mature metapodials (8 total) equal 25% immature, then 3 immature and 4 mature metapodials (7 total) would not be a particularly rare combination.

To test this assumption, I proposed that
a = probability of retrieving an immature metapodial = 25% = ¼.
b = probability of retrieving a mature metapodial = 75% = ¾.
Then $a + b = 1$.

Expanding $a + b$ to the 7th power, $35 \cdot a^3 \cdot b^4$ yields the probability of finding 3 immature and 4 mature metapodials in a population of 7. The answer is 17.3%, which is close to 1 of every 6 trials—the same odds as attempting to roll any specified number from 1 to 6 with a single roll of a die.

Furthermore, the chances of getting less probable combinations can also be calculated:

4 immature metapodials to 3 mature	6.5%
5 immature metapodials to 2 mature	1.2%
6 immature metapodials to 1 mature	0.02%
7 immature metapodials to 0 mature	0.0006%
Subtotal	7.7206%

If, to the total of these possibilities, we add 17.3%, the previously calculated possibility of finding 3 immature to 4 mature metapodials, we get a total of 25.0206% (= ¼). Thus, in groups of 7 metapodials taken at random from a population of sheep which is 25% immature, we would *expect* to get a sample of metapodials of 3 immature to 4 mature, or less probable combinations, a quarter of the time. That Perkins actually did get such a combination of metapodials is, thus, not unexpected.

---

*For the discussion of, and formula for, Z (with somewhat different notation), see Hubert M. Blalock, *Social Statistics*, 2nd ed. (New York: McGraw Hill, 1979), pp. 232-34.

REFERENCES

Amschler, J.W.
- 1939 Tierreste der Ausgrabungen von dem "Grossen Königshügel" Shah Tepé, in Nord-Iran. *Reports from the Scientific Expedition to the North-Western Provinces of China under the Leadership of Dr. Sven Hedin: the Sino-Swedish Expedition*, publ. 9, vol. 7 (Archaeology), no. 4, pp. 35-129.

Angress, Shimon, and Reed, Charles A.
- 1962 *An annotated bibliography on the origin and descent of domestic mammals, 1900-1955*. Fieldiana: Anthropology, vol. 54. Chicago: Field Museum of Natural History.

Bate, Dorothea M.A.
- 1927a On the animal remains obtained from the Mugharet-el-Emireh in 1925. In *Researches in prehistoric Galilee, 1925-1926*, F. Turville-Petre, pp. 9-13. London: Council of the British School of Archaeology in Jerusalem.
- 1927b On the animal remains obtained from the Mugharet-el-Zuttiyeh in 1925. In ibid., pp. 27-34.
- 1927c On the animal remains obtained from the Mugharet-el-Zuttiyeh in 1926. In ibid., pp. 35-52.
- 1930a Animal remains from the Zarzi cave. In The palaeolithic of southern Kurdistan: excavations in the caves of Zarzi and Hazar Merd, D.A.E. Garrod, p. 23. *Bulletin of the American School of Prehistoric Research* 6:9-43.
- 1930b Animal remains from the Dark Cave, Hazar Merd. In ibid., pp. 38-39.
- 1932 A note on the fauna of the Athlit caves. *Journal of the Royal Anthropological Institute of Great Britain and Ireland* 62:277-79.
- 1937 Palaeontology: the fossil fauna of the Wady el-Mughara caves. In *The Stone Age of Mount Carmel*, vol. 1, pt. 2, D.A.E. Garrod and D.M.A. Bate, pp. 135-233. Oxford: Clarendon Press.
- 1938 Vertebrate remains from Wādi Dhobai, 1938. In The excavations at Wādi Dhobai, 1937-1938, and the Dhobaian industry, J. d'A. Waechter, V.M. Seton-Williams, Dorothea M.A. Bate, and L. Picard, pp. 292-96. *Journal of the Palestine Oriental Society* 18:172-86, 292-98.
- 1941 The bone-bearing beds of Bethlehem. *Nature* 147:783.
- 1942 The fossil mammals of Shukbah. *Proceedings of the Prehistoric Society* 8:15-20.
- 1947 Animal remains. In Excavations at Brak and Chagar Bazar, M.E.L. Mallowan, pp. 12-13. *Iraq* 9:1-259.
- 1954 Fauna. In Excavations at the Mugharet Kebara, Mount Carmel, 1931: the Aurignacian industries, Dorothy A.E. Garrod, p. 185. *Proceedings of the Prehistoric Society* 20:155-92.

Bergmann, Carl
- 1847 Über die Verhältnisse der Wärmeökonomie der Thiere zu ihrer Grösse. *Göttinger Studien* 3:595-708.

Binford, Lewis R., and Bertram, Jack B.
- 1977 Bone frequencies—and attritional processes. In *For theory building in archaeology*, ed. Lewis R. Binford, pp. 77-153. New York: Academic Press.

Bjälkefors, Ulf
- 1969 The programming. In Gejvall 1969, pp. 98-99, 109-12.

Boessneck, Joachim
- 1962 Die Tierreste aus der Argissa-Magula vom präkeramischen Neolithikum bis zur mittleren Bronzezeit. In *Die deutschen Ausgrabungen auf der Argissa-Magula in Thessalien*, vol. 1, V. Milojčić, J. Boessneck, and M. Hopf, pp. 27-99. Beiträge zur ur- und frühgeschichtlichen Archäologie des Mittelmeer-Kulturraumes, vol. 2. Bonn: Rudolf Habelt Verlag.

Bökönyi, Sándor
- 1969a [A new method for calculating the number of individual animals in osteological material from archaeological sites.] *Byulleten' Moskovskogo obshchestva ispitateleĭ prirody, otdel biologicheskiĭ* 74:69-71. (In Russian.)
- 1969b Archaeological problems and methods of recognizing animal domestication. In *The domestication and exploitation of plants and animals*, ed. Peter J. Ucko and G.W. Dimbleby, pp. 219-29. London: Gerald Duckworth.
- 1970 A new method for the determination of the number of individuals in animal bone material. *American Journal of Archaeology* 74:291-92.
- 1974 *History of domestic mammals in central and eastern Europe*. Budapest: Akadémiai Kiadó.
- 1977 *The animal remains from four sites in the Kermanshah valley, Iran—Asiab, Sarab, Dehsavar and Siahbid: the faunal evolution, environmental changes and development of animal husbandry, VIII-III millennia B.C.* British Archaeological Reports, Supplementary Series, vol. 34. Oxford.
- 1978 The introduction of sheep-breeding to Europe. *Ethnozootechnie* 21:65-70.

Braidwood, Robert J.
- 1979 Paleoenvironment and the appearance of village-farming communities in southwestern Asia. *Türk Tarih Kongresi* 8:37-45.

Braidwood, Robert J.; Çambel, Halet; Lawrence, Barbara; Redman, Charles L.; and Stewart, Robert B.
- 1974 Beginnings of village-farming communities in southeastern Turkey—1972. *Proceedings of the National Academy of Sciences of the United States of America* 71:568-72.

Braidwood, Robert J.; Howe, Bruce; et al.
  1960 *Prehistoric investigations in Iraqi Kurdistan.* Studies in Ancient Oriental Civilization [SAOC], no. 31. Chicago: University of Chicago Press.

Brooke, Clarke
  1979 The origin and the process of domestication. In *The domestication of sheep: their ancestors, geography, time period and people involved*, ed. Warren C. Foote and Thomas D. Bunch, pp. 18-23. Logan, Utah: Sheep and Goat Institute, Utah State University.

Bunch, Thomas D.
  1979 Cytological evidence on the ancestral stock of domestic sheep (*Ovis aries*). In ibid., pp. 14-17.

Çambel, Halet, and Braidwood, Robert J.
  1980 Comprehensive view: the work to date 1963-1972. In *The joint Istanbul-Chicago Universities' prehistoric research in southeastern Anatolia*, vol. 1, ed. Halet Çambel, pp. 1-64. İstanbul üniversitesi edebiyat fakültesi yayınları, no. 2589. Istanbul.

Casteel, Richard W.
  1972 Some biases in the recovery of archaeological faunal remains. *Proceedings of the Prehistoric Society* 38:382-88.
  1974 On the number and sizes of animals in archaeological faunal assemblages. *Archaeometry* 16:238-43.
  1976 *Fish remains in archaeology and paleo-environmental studies.* New York: Academic Press.
  1977 Characterization of faunal assemblages and the minimum number of individuals determined from paired elements: continuing problems in archaeology. *Journal of Archaeological Science* 4:125-34.

Clark, Grahame
  1972 Foreword. In Higgs, ed., 1972, pp. vii-x.

Clason, A.T.
  1972 Some remarks on the use and presentation of archaeozoological data. *Helinium* 12 (2):139-53.

Clason, A.T., and Prummel, W.
  1977 Collecting, sieving and archaeozoological research. *Journal of Archaeological Science* 4:171-75.

Clutton-Brock, Juliet
  1969 Carnivore remains from the excavations of the Jericho Tell. In *The domestication and exploitation of plants and animals*, ed. Peter J. Ucko and G.W. Dimbleby, pp. 337-45. London: Gerald Duckworth.
  1975 A system for the retrieval of data relating to animal remains from archaeological sites. In *Archaeozoological studies*, ed. A.T. Clason, pp. 21-34. Amsterdam: North-Holland.
  1979 The mammalian remains from the Jericho Tell. *Proceedings of the Prehistoric Society* 45:135-47.

Collier, Stephen, and White, J. Peter
  1976 Get them young? Age and sex inferences on animal domestication in archaeology. *American Antiquity* 41:96-102.

Coon, Carleton S.
  1951 *Cave explorations in Iran, 1949.* Museum Monographs. Philadelphia: University Museum. University of Pennsylvania.

Coope, G.R.
  1967 The value of Quaternary insect faunas in the interpretation of ancient ecology and climate. In *Proceedings of the VII Congress of the International Association for Quaternary Research* [Boulder, 1965], vol. 7: *Quaternary paleoecology*, ed. E.J. Cushing and H.E. Wright, Jr., pp. 359-80. New Haven, Conn., and London: Yale University Press.

Costantini, L.; Tosi, M.; and Taglianti, A. Vigna
  1977 Typology and socioeconomical implications of entomological finds from some ancient Near Eastern sites. *Paléorient* 3:247-58.

Daly, Patricia
  1969 Approaches to faunal analysis in archaeology. *American Antiquity* 34:146-53.

Daly, Patricia; Perkins, Dexter, Jr.; and Drew, Isabella Milling
  1973 The effects of domestication on the structure of animal bone. In *Domestikationsforschung und Geschichte der Haustiere*, ed. János Matolcsi, pp. 157-61. Budapest: Akadémiai Kiadó.

[Daniel, Glyn]
  1972 Editorial. *Antiquity* 46:265.

Davis, Simon
  1977 Size variation of the fox, *Vulpes vulpes*, in the palaearctic region today, and in Israel during the late Quaternary. *Journal of Zoology (London)* 182:343-51.

Davis, Simon J.M., and Valla, François R.
  1978 Evidence for domestication of the dog 12,000 years ago in the Natufian of Israel. *Nature* 276:608-10.

Decker, Eugene, and Kowalski, Gerald J.
    1972   *Iran wildlife investigations: the behavior and ecology of the urial sheep.* Fort Collins, Colo.: Department of Fishery and Wildlife Biology, Colorado State University, for the Iran Game and Fish Department, Tehran.

Degerbøl, Magnus
    1936   *Animal remains from the West Settlement in Greenland, with special reference to livestock.* Meddelelser om Grønland udgivne af Kommissionen for Videnskabelige Undersøgelser i Grønland, vol. 88, (3). Copenhagen: C.A. Reitzels.

Degerbøl, Magnus, and Fredskild, Bent
    1970   *The urus* (Bos primigenius *Bojanus*) *and Neolithic domesticated cattle* (Bos taurus domesticus *Linné*) *in Denmark, with a revision of* Bos-*remains from the kitchen middens: zoological and palynological investigations.* Kongelige danske videnskabernes selskab, biologiske skrifter, vol. 17 (1). Copenhagen: Munksgaard.

Dixon, Keith L.
    1979   The influence of Quaternary environments on the evolution and distribution of wild sheep (*Ovis* spp.). In *The domestication of sheep: their ancestors, geography, time period and people involved*, ed. Warren C. Foote and Thomas D. Bunch, pp. 1-13. Logan, Utah: Sheep and Goat Institute, Utah State University.

Downs, James F.
    1960   Domestication: an examination of the changing social relationships between man and animals. *Kroeber Anthropological Society Papers* 22:18-67.

Drew, Isabella Milling; Perkins, Dexter, Jr.; and Daly, Patricia
    1971a Prehistoric domestication of animals: effects on bone structure. *Science* 171:280-82.
    1971b Texture and composition of bone. Ibid. 172:972-73.

Ducos, Pierre
    1969   Methodology and results of the study of the earliest domesticated animals in the Near East (Palestine). In *The domestication and exploitation of plants and animals*, ed. Peter J. Ucko and G.W. Dimbleby, pp. 265-75. London: Gerald Duckworth.
    1970   The Oriental Institute excavations at Mureybiṭ, Syria: preliminary report on the 1965 campaign, part IV: les restes d'Equidés. *Journal of Near Eastern Studies* 29:273-89.
    1975   A new find of an equid metatarsal bone from Tell Mureibet in Syria and its relevance to the identification of equids from the early Holocene of the Levant. *Journal of Archaeological Science* 2:71-73.

Duerst, J. Ulrich
    1908   Animal remains from the excavations at Anau and the horse of Anau in its relation to the races of domestic horses. In *Explorations in Turkestan: expedition of 1904, prehistoric civilizations of Anau*, vol. 2, ed. Raphael Pumpelly, pp. 339-442. Publications of the Carnegie Institution of Washington, no. 73. Washington, D.C.

Dyson, Robert H., Jr.
    1960   A note on Queen Shub-ab's "onagers." *Iraq* 22:102-4.

Flannery, Kent V.
    1961   Skeletal and radiocarbon evidence for the origins of pig domestication. Master's thesis, University of Chicago.
    1967   Vertebrate fauna and hunting patterns. In *The prehistory of the Tehuacán Valley*, vol. 1: *environment and subsistence*, ed. Douglas S. Byers, pp. 132-77. Austin: University of Texas Press.

Gardner, Elinor W., and Bate, Dorothea M.A.
    1937   The bone-bearing beds of Bethlehem: their fauna and industry. *Nature* 140:431-33.

Gejvall, Nils-Gustaf
    1969   *Lerna: a preclassical site in the Argolid: results of excavations conducted by the American School of Classical Studies at Athens.* Vol. 1. *The fauna.* Princeton, N.J.: American School of Classical Studies at Athens.

Gifford, Diane P., and Crader, Diana C.
    1977   A computer coding system for archaeological faunal remains. *American Antiquity* 42:225-38.

Gilbert, Allan S.
    1978   Variables in the flow of meat and bones through Near Eastern prehistoric settlements. Seminar, Department of Anthropology, Columbia University, April 1978.

Gilbert, Allan S., and Steinfield, Paul
    1977   Faunal remains from Dinkha Tepe, northwestern Iran. *Journal of Field Archaeology* 4:329-51.

Grayson, Donald K.
    1973   On the methodology of faunal analysis. *American Antiquity* 38:432-39.
    1974   The Riverhaven no. 2 vertebrate fauna: comments on methods in faunal analysis and on aspects of the subsistence potential of prehistoric New York. *Man in the Northeast* 8:23-39.
    1977   *Paleoclimatic implications of the Dirty Shame Rockshelter mammalian fauna.* Tebiwa, Miscellaneous Papers of the Idaho State University Museum of Natural History, no. 9. Pocatello, Idaho.

1978 Minimum numbers and sample size in vertebrate faunal analysis. *American Antiquity* 43:53-65.
1979 On the quantification of vertebrate archaeofaunas. In *Advances in archaeological method and theory*, vol. 2, ed. M. Schiffer, pp. 199-237. New York: Academic Press.

Guilday, John E.
1970 Animal remains from archaeological excavations at Fort Ligonier. *Annals of the Carnegie Museum* 42:177-86.

Hecker, Howard M.
1975 The faunal analysis of the primary food animals from pre-pottery Neolithic Beidha (Jordan). Ph.D diss., Columbia University.

Herre, Wolf, and Röhrs, Manfred
1977 Zoological considerations on the origins of farming and domestication. In *Origins of agriculture*, ed. Charles A. Reed, pp. 245-79. The Hague: Mouton.

Hesse, Brian Carl
1977 Evidence for husbandry from the early Neolithic site of Ganj Dareh in western Iran. Ph.D. diss., Columbia University.

Hesse, Brian, and Perkins, Dexter, Jr.
1974 Faunal remains from Karataş-Semayük in southwest Anatolia: an interim report. *Journal of Field Archaeology* 1:149-60.

Higgs, Eric S.
1962 The biological data: fauna. In Excavations at the early Neolithic site at Nea Nikomedeia, Greek Macedonia (1961 season), Robert J. Rodden, pp. 271-74. *Proceedings of the Prehistoric Society* 28:267-88.
1972 Ed. *Papers in economic prehistory: studies by members and associates of the British Academy Major Research Project in the early history of agriculture.* Cambridge: At the University Press.
1975 Ed. *Palaeoeconomy: being the second volume of papers in economic prehistory by members and associates of the British Academy Major Research Project in the early history of agriculture.* Cambridge: At the University Press.

Higgs, Eric S., and Jarman, M.R.
1969 The origins of agriculture: a reconsideration. *Antiquity* 43:31-41.
1972 The origins of animal and plant husbandry. In Higgs, ed., 1972, pp. 3-13.
1975 Palaeoeconomy. In Higgs, ed., 1975, pp. 1-7.

Higgs, Eric S., and Vita-Finzi, C.
1972 Prehistoric economies: a territorial approach. In Higgs, ed., 1972, pp. 27-36.

Higham, Charles F.W.
1968a Patterns of prehistoric economic exploitation on the Alpine foreland: a statistical analysis of faunal remains in the Zoological Museum of Zürich University. *Vierteljahrsschrift der Naturforschenden Gesellschaft in Zürich* 113:41-92.
1968b Faunal sampling and economic prehistory. *Zeitschrift für Säugetierkunde* 33:297-305.
1977 Economic change in prehistoric Thailand. In *Origins of agriculture*, ed. Charles A. Reed, pp. 385-412. The Hague: Mouton.

Hilzheimer, Max
1941 *Animal remains from Tell Asmar.* Studies in Ancient Oriental Civilization, no. 20. Chicago: University of Chicago Press.

Ho, Ping-ti
1977 The indigenous origins of Chinese agriculture. In *Origins of agriculture*, ed. Charles A. Reed, pp. 413-84. The Hague: Mouton.

Hole, Frank; Flannery, Kent V.; and Neely, James A.
1969 *Prehistory and human ecology of the Deh Luran plain: an early village sequence from Khuzistan, Iran.* Memoirs of the Museum of Anthropology, University of Michigan, no. 1. Ann Arbor, Mich.

Hopkins, Joseph
1967 Identification of the domestication of animals without morphological change. Paper written for a graduate course in the Department of Anthropology, University of Chicago.

Isaac, Erich
1962 On the domestication of cattle. *Science* 137:195-204.
1963 Mythes, cultes et élevage. *Diogène* 41:72-95.
1970 *Geography of domestication.* Englewood Cliffs, N.J.: Prentice-Hall.

Jarman, M.R.
1969 The prehistory of Upper Pleistocene and Recent cattle, part I: east Mediterranean, with reference to north-west Europe. *Proceedings of the Prehistoric Society* 35:236-66.
1970 Isera, (Trentino) Cava Nord: fauna report. *Studi Trentini di scienze naturli* 47B:78-80.

1971 Culture and economy in the north Italian Neolithic. *World Archaeology* 2:255-65.
1972 European deer economies and the advent of the Neolithic. In Higgs, ed., 1972, pp. 125-47.

Jarman, M.R. and Wilkinson, P.F.
1972 Criteria of animal domestication. In ibid., pp. 83-96.

Krantz, Grover S.
1968 A new method of counting mammal bones. *American Journal of Archaeology* 72:286-88.

Kurtén, Björn
1965 *The Carnivora of the Palestine caves.* Acta Zoologica Fennica, vol. 107. Helsinki: Societas pro Fauna et Flora Fennica.

LaBianca, Øystein Sakala
1973 The zooarchaeological remains from Tell Hesbân. *Andrews University Seminary Studies* 11:133-44.
1978 The logistic and strategic aspects of faunal analysis in Palestine. In *Approaches to faunal analysis in the Middle East*, ed. Richard H. Meadow and Melinda A. Zeder, pp. 3-9. Peabody Museum of Archaeology and Ethnology, Harvard University, bull. 2. Cambridge, Mass.

Lawrence, Barbara
1967 Early domestic dogs. *Zeitschrift für Säugetierkunde* 32 (1):44-59.
1968 Antiquity of large dogs in North America. *Tebiwa, Journal of the Idaho State University Museum* 11 (2):43-49.

Lyman, R. Lee
1979 Available meat from faunal remains: a consideration of techniques. *American Antiquity* 44:536-46.

McArdle, John
1971 New method of recording and analyzing faunal material from archaeological sites. Paper prepared for the Section on Animal Domestication of the Third International Congress of the Museums of Agriculture, Budapest, 19-23 April 1971. Mimeographed. (With an introduction by Charles A. Reed.)
1974 A numerical (computerized) method for quantifying zooarchaeological comparisons. Master's thesis, University of Illinois at Chicago Circle.
1977 A numerical (computerized) method for quantifying zooarchaeological comparisons. *Paléorient* 3:181-90.

McConnell, Duncan, and Foreman, Dennis W., Jr.
1971 Texture and composition of bone. *Science* 172:971-72.

McNab, Brian K.
1971 On the ecological significance of Bergmann's Rule. *Ecology* 52:845-54.

Meadow, Richard H.
1978 "BONECODE"—a system of numerical coding for faunal data from Middle Eastern sites. In *Approaches to faunal analysis in the Middle East*, ed. Richard H. Meadow and Melinda A. Zeder, pp. 169-86. Peabody Museum of Archaeology and Ethnology, Harvard University, bull. 2. Cambridge, Mass.

Mellaart, James
1967 Çatal Hüyük: a Neolithic town in Anatolia. New York: McGraw-Hill.

Moore, Andrew M.T.
1979 A pre-Neolithic farmers' village on the Euphrates. *Scientific American* 241 (2):62-70.

Østergård, Morten
1980 X-ray diffractometer investigations of bones from domestic and wild animals. *American Antiquity* 45:59-63.

Payne, Sebastian
1972a On the interpretation of bone samples from archaeological sites. In Higgs, ed., 1972, pp. 65-81.
1972b Partial recovery and sample bias: the results of some sieving experiments. In ibid., pp. 49-64.

Perkins, Dexter, Jr.
1964a Prehistoric fauna from Shanidar, Iraq. *Science* 144:1565-66.
1964b The fauna from the prehistoric levels of Shanidar Cave and Zawi Chemi Shanidar. In *Report of the VIth International Congress on the Quaternary, Warsaw 1961*, vol. 2, International Association on Quaternary Research, pp. 565-72. Łódź: Państwowe Wydawnictwo Naukowe.
1966 Appendix B: the fauna from Madamagh and Beidha, a preliminary report. In Five seasons at the pre-pottery Neolithic village of Beidha in Jordan: a summary, Diana Kirkbride, pp. 66-67. *Palestine Exploration Quarterly* 98:8-72.
1969 Fauna of Çatal Hüyük: evidence for early cattle domestication in Anatolia. *Science* 164:177-79.
1973 A critique on the methods of quantifying faunal remains from archaeological sites. In *Domestikationsforschung und Geschichte der Haustiere*, ed. János Matolcsi, pp. 367-69. Budapest: Akadémiai Kiadó.
1978 Personal communication.

Perkins, Dexter, Jr., and Daly, Patricia
　1968　A hunters' village in Neolithic Turkey. *Scientific American* 219 (5):96-106.

Prashad, B.
　1936　*Animal remains from Harappa*. Memoirs of the Archaeological Survey of India, no. 51. Delhi: Manager of Publications.

Radulesco, Costin, and Samson, Petre
　1962　Sur un centre de domestication du mouton dans le Mésolithique de la grotte "La Adam" en Dobrogea. *Zeitschrift für Tierzüchtung und Züchtungsbiologie* 76 (2/3):282-320.

Redding, Richard W.; Pires-Ferreira, J. Wheeler; and Zeder, M.A.
　1977　A proposed system for computer analysis of identifiable faunal material from archaeological sites. *Paléorient* 3:191-205.

Redding, Richard W.; Zeder, Melinda A.; and McArdle, John
　1978　"BONESORT II"—a system for the computer processing of identifiable faunal material. In *Approaches to faunal analysis in the Middle East*, ed. Richard H. Meadow and Melinda A. Zeder, pp. 135-47. Peabody Museum of Archaeology and Ethnology, Harvard University, bull. 2. Cambridge, Mass.

Reed, Charles A.
　1959　Animal domestication in the prehistoric Near East. *Science* 130:1629-39.
　1960　A review of the archeological evidence on animal domestication in the prehistoric Near East. In SAOC 31, pp. 119-45.
　1961　Osteological evidences for prehistoric domestication in southwestern Asia. *Zeitschrift für Tierzüchtung und Züchtungsbiologie* 76 (1):31-38.
　1963　Osteo-archaeology. In *Science in archaeology*, ed. Don Brothwell and Eric Higgs, pp. 204-16. New York: Basic Books.
　1969　The pattern of animal domestication in the prehistoric Near East. In *The domestication and exploitation of plants and animals*, ed. Peter J. Ucko and G.W. Dimbleby, pp. 361-80. London: Gerald Duckworth.
　1977a　A model for the origin of agriculture in the Near East. In *Origins of agriculture*, ed. Charles A. Reed, pp. 543-67. The Hague: Mouton.
　1977b　Origins of agriculture: discussion and some conclusions. In ibid., pp. 879-953.
　1980　The beginnings of animal domestication. In *Animal agriculture: the biology, husbandry, and use of domestic animals*, 2nd ed., ed. H.H. Cole and W.N. Garrett, pp. 3-20. San Francisco: Freeman.

Reed, Charles A., and Braidwood, Robert J.
　1960　Toward the reconstruction of the environmental sequence of northeastern Iraq. In SAOC 31, pp. 163-73.

Rütimeyer, L.
　1862　The fauna of middle Europe during the Stone Age. *Annual Report of the Smithsonian Institution for 1861*, pp. 361-67.

SAOC 31
　1960　*Prehistoric investigations in Iraqi Kurdistan*. Robert J. Braidwood, Bruce Howe, et al. Studies in Ancient Oriental Civilization, no. 31. Chicago: University of Chicago Press.

Schaffer, William M., and Reed, Charles A.
　1972　*The co-evolution of social behavior and cranial morphology in sheep and goats (Bovidae, Caprini)*. Fieldiana: Zoology, vol. 61 (1). Chicago: Field Museum of Natural History.

Simmons, A.H., and Ilany, G.
　1977　What mean these bones? Behavioral implications of gazelles' remains from archaeological sites. *Paléorient* 3:269-74.

Smith, Philip E.L.
　1970　Ganj Dareh Tepe. *Iran* 8:178-80.

Solecki, Ralph S.
　1966　Prehistory in Shanidar Valley, northern Iraq. In *New roads to yesterday*, ed. Joseph R. Caldwell, pp. 96-125. New York: Basic Books.

Solecki, Ralph S., and Rubin, Meyer
　1958　Dating of Zawi Chemi, an early village site at Shanidar, northern Iraq. *Science* 127:1446.

Stewart, Frances L., and Stahl, Peter W.
　1977　Cautionary note on edible meat poundage figures. *American Antiquity* 42:267-70.

Stordeur, Danielle
　1979　Bone technology from the Epipaleolithic of Syria. Seminar, Department of Anthropology, University of Illinois at Chicago Circle, 15 May 1979.

Thomas, David H.
- 1969 Great Basin hunting patterns: a quantitative method for treating faunal remains. *American Antiquity* 34:392-401.
- 1971 On distinguishing natural from cultural bone in archaeological sites. Ibid. 36:366-71.

Tringham, Ruth
- 1969 Animal domestication in the Neolithic cultures of the south-west part of European U.S.S.R. In *The domestication and exploitation of plants and animals*, ed. Peter J. Ucko and G.W. Dimbleby, pp. 381-92. London: Gerald Duckworth.

Turnbull, Priscilla F., and Reed, Charles A.
- 1974 *The fauna from the terminal Pleistocene of Palegawra Cave, a Zarzian occupation site in the northeastern Iraq.* Fieldiana: Anthropology, vol. 63 (3). Chicago: Field Museum of Natural History.

Uerpmann, Hans-Peter
- 1973 Animal bone finds and economic archaeology: a critical study of 'osteo-archaeological' method. *World Archaeology* 4:307-22.
- 1978 The "KNOCOD" system for processing data on animal bones from archaeological sites. In *Approaches to faunal analysis in the Middle East*, ed. Richard H. Meadow and Melinda A. Zeder, pp. 149-67. Peabody Museum of Archaeology and Ethnology, Harvard University, bull. 2. Cambridge, Mass.

Valdez, Raul, and Alamia, Leticia V.
- 1977 Population decline of an insular population of Armenian wild sheep in Iran. *Journal of Wildlife Management* 41:720-25.

Valla, F.R.
- 1977 La sépulture H.104 de Mallaha (Eynan) et le problème de la domestication du chien en Palestine. *Paléorient* 3:287-92.

Vita-Finzi, C., and Higgs, E.S.
- 1970 Prehistoric economy in the Mount Carmel area of Palestine: site catchment analysis. *Proceedings of the Prehistoric Society* 36:1-37.

Watson, J.P.N.
- 1972 Fragmentation analysis of animal bone samples from archaeological sites. *Archaeometry* 14:221-27.
- 1975 Domestication and bone structure in sheep and goats. *Journal of Archaeological Science* 2:375-83.

Watson, Patty Jo
- 1979 *Archaeological ethnography in western Iran*. Viking Fund Publications in Anthropology, no. 57. Tucson, Ariz.: University of Arizona Press.

Wendorf, Fred
- 1977 Late Pleistocene and Recent climatic changes in the Egyptian Sahara. *Geographical Journal* 143:211-34.

Wheat, Joe Ben
- 1972 *The Olsen-Chubbuck site: a paleo-Indian bison kill.* Memoirs of the Society for American Archaeology, no. 26. Washington, D.C. (Issued as *American Antiquity* 37 [1/2].)

White, Theodore E.
- 1953 A method of calculating the dietary percentage of various food animals utilized by aboriginal peoples. *American Antiquity* 18:396-98.

Wilkinson, P.F.
- 1972 Current experimental domestication and its relevance to prehistory. In Higgs, ed., 1972, pp. 107-18.

Wright, Gary A., and Miller, Susanne J.
- 1976 Prehistoric hunting of New World wild sheep: implications for the study of sheep domestication. In *Cultural change and continuity: essays in honor of James Bennett Griffin*, ed. Charles E. Cleland, pp. 293-318. New York: Academic Press.

Zeder, Melinda A.
- 1978 Differentiation between the bones of caprines from different ecosystems in Iran by the analysis of osteological microstructure and chemical composition. In *Approaches to faunal analysis in the Middle East*, ed. Richard H. Meadow and Melinda A. Zeder, pp. 69-84. Peabody Museum of Archaeology and Ethnology, Harvard University, bull. 2. Cambridge, Mass.

Zeuner, Frederick E.
- 1955 The goats of early Jericho. *Palestine Exploration Quarterly* 87:70-86.
- 1958 Dog and cat in the Neolithic of Jericho. Ibid. 90:52-55.
- 1963 *A history of domesticated animals*. London: Hutchinson.

15

JARMO CHRONOLOGY

Robert J. Braidwood

Even with ample time for reflection on the available yields from each of the three field seasons at Jarmo, I maintain my original opinion that the site's inventory suggests only a single phase of occupation. There are, indeed, indications of technological and typological development and change within this phase, which of course implies cultural flux as well. Eventually, it may seem wise to divide the Jarmo phase into two or more subphases, but in my opinion this should remain a matter for future investigation, especially of the lower levels of the mound. My own assessment of the available evidence leads me to believe that the original Jarmo village lasted perhaps three (at the most, five) centuries.

At present, we can only attempt to reckon the site's approximate chronological position in two ways:

1. By one of the physical means of age determination. I myself remain persuaded that, for all its whimsies, the radioactive carbon method is the most hopeful. Assays on Jarmo samples have been made by only one of the other physical methods, archeomagnetism.

2. By means of "relative archeological chronology," i.e., an assessment of the apparent technological and typological comparability of all the artifacts in a given inventory or assemblage with those from other sites in the same general region. Certain factors are bound to bear on the general proposition. Consideration should be given to a combination of factors such as (1) the probable degree of paleoenvironmental similarity of the sites in question, (2) the availability of a stratigraphic succession of inventories on at least one or ideally more of the sites in the region, and finally (3) added substantiation through the availability of physically assayed age determinations, if such exist. Obviously, however, such a "relative archeological chronology" is heavily dependent on any given assessor's knowledge of the available comparative evidence (assuming it exists) and upon a fair degree of subjective good judgment.

At best, a combination of the above two approaches can provide us with only an approximate chronological scheme. Unfortunately, what follows is probably as far as we can go at the moment, but as more field research is done the scheme will become more realistic.

Radioactive Carbon Age Determination

No category of evidence from Jarmo has proved to yield more ambiguous and whimsical results than have the radiocarbon age determinations. Since W.F. Libby and his colleagues E.C. Anderson and J.R. Arnold were in the process of completing the pioneer steps in the development of the radioactive carbon method at the University of Chicago at the very time of our first two field seasons at Jarmo, it is not surprising that Jarmo provided some of the very first "unknown" samples to be assayed. To date, some eighteen Jarmo samples have received radiocarbon age determinations, and portions of several of these samples were given different preparation treatments before being assayed (e.g., GL-44, 48, and 49; W-607 and 608). The four determinations made in Libby's original Chicago laboratory and presumably those done in the Geochronology Laboratory in London were assayed by the old solid carbon counting method. (See Aitken 1974 and Ralph and Michael 1974 for general accounts of the radiocarbon age determination method.) The remaining determinations, all made later, were—as I understand it—assayed by one or another type of gas counting. The UCLA assays were made on collagen extracted from various splinters of animal bone. Following is the available Jarmo series:[1]

Sample	Description	Age BP	Age BC
C-113	Land snails, J-I,7 into 8	6707 ± 320[a]	4757 BC
C-742	Charcoal flecks, J-I,7 into 8	6606 ± 330[a]	4656 BC
C-743	Charcoal fragments, J-II,5	6695 ± 360[a]	4745 BC
C-744	Charcoal flecks, J-II,2 and 2fl.	5266 ± 450[a]	3316 BC
GL(=F)-44	Charcoal fragments, J-II,5	6650 ± 120[b]	4700 BC
GL(=F)-45	Charcoal fragments, J-I,8	6670 ± 120[b]	4720 BC

The manuscript for this chapter was essentially completed by 1975. Very few additions and only minor revisions have been made since that date.

GL(=F)-48	Same sample as GL-44, but with HCl and NaOH treatment	6930 ± 120[b]	4980 BC
GL(=F)-49	Same sample as GL-44, but filtrate alone assayed	6300 ± 180[b]	4350 BC
GL(=F)-50	Same sample as GL-45, but with HCl and NaOH treatment	6750 ± 120[b]	4800 BC
GrN-6353	Pottery, J-II,1	7655 ± 75[c]	5705 BC
H-551/491	Charcoal fragments, J-I,7	8520 ± 175[d]	6570 BC
W-607	Black ashy hearth material, PQ14 at 2.50 m. Sample no. 54	9040 ± 250[e]	7090 BC
W-608	Same sample as W-607. Humic fraction	7750 ± 250[e]	5800 BC
W-651	Charcoal fragments, J-II,4	8830 ± 200[e]	6880 BC
W-652	Charcoal fragments, J-I,7a	7950 ± 200[e]	6000 BC
W-657	Black ashy soil, PQ14 at 2.25 m. Sample no. 55	11,240 ± 300[e]	9290 BC
W-665	Black ashy soil, N18 at 2.00 m. Sample no. 53	11,200 ± 200[e]	9250 BC
UCLA-1714E	Collagen from animal bone splinters, J-I,7	7980 ± 140[f]	6030 BC
UCLA-1723A	Collagen from animal bone splinters, PQ14,5a	7800 ± 120[f]	5850 BC
UCLA-1723B	Collagen from animal bone splinters, PQ14,2	7270 ± 200[f]	5320 BC
UCLA-1723C	Collagen from animal bone splinters, K21,1	6180 ± 300[f]	4230 BC
UCLA-1723D	Collagen from animal bone splinters, K21,3	6550 ± 200[f]	4600 BC

It must be obvious, even to those with no particular sense of the relative archeological chronology of southwestern Asia, that the Jarmo determinations at the high and low extremes in this list suggest an impossible 6,000-year duration of occupation. We are left, then, with various options:

1. We could reject the radioactive carbon age determination method out of hand.

2. We could assume either that the site was completely and hopelessly disturbed (which we, who excavated it, certainly did not find to have been the case) or that some of the samples were contaminated in one way or another. A combination of these two options might also have been possible. Whatever the case here, we could then make what we took to be a realistic selection from among the available determinations. Our old friend and colleague Tjalling Waterbolk at Groningen tends to favor the latter of this pair of options and has made a selection of the determinations which seem most realistic from a radiocarbon laboratory point of view.[2] In doing so, he has concluded that Jarmo flourished about 8000 B.P. (Waterbolk 1971).

3. Finally, we could balance our assessment of the position of the site's "relative archeological chronology" within the fabric of the other available archeological inventories of approximately similar artifactual complexity in southwestern Asia and make a consequent selection of what seemed to be the most reasonable determinations. My own inclination would be to suggest that the village was occupied about three quarters to half a millennium earlier than the 8000 B.P. date proposed by Waterbolk.

ARCHEOMAGNETIC AGE DETERMINATION

Two sherds of the typical chaff-tempered later pottery from J-II,2 have been assayed by Dr. M.J. Aitken of the Research Laboratory for Archaeology and the History of Art at Oxford University. Aitken gives a general age for the sherds as of the sixth millennium B.C.[3]

RELATIVE ARCHEOLOGICAL CHRONOLOGY

A descriptive report on much of the Prehistoric Project's field-acquired material is hardly the place for a detailed comparison of items in the Jarmo assemblage with those of other now-excavated early village sites in the Zagros region, let alone with those of sites in other parts of southwestern Asia. Hence, I quite unashamedly set down my conclusions without elaborate documentation of my reasons.

First, I repeat my opinion that Jarmo itself did not have a very long duration. Also, again, I see no reason at present to believe that the site had a meaningful succession of two or more phases or "periods" simply because of the presence or absence of pottery in its available inventory. It would seem most likely that knowledge of pottery vessel making reached Jarmo from elsewhere, near the end of the site's occupation. (I would doubt that the appearance of pottery vessel making altered the general cultural milieu within the site any more than did the first appearance of the automobile in a rural American town about the year 1900.)

On the other hand, I do not suppose that the overall cultural level wherein Jarmo belongs—that of the primary village-farming communities—was of short duration. Indeed, the level may even have lasted well over a millennium. I now feel that Joan Oates's (1973) scheme of separating the Hassunan and related sites from the Jarmo-Ganj Dareh-Guran group has a validity which we did not see when our chart in SAOC 31 (fig. 8) was prepared. I would, however, now incline to refer to Oates's "Phase 2: Jarmo and Related Sites" as a *level* of primary village-farming communities and her "Phase 3: Hassuna and Related Sites" as a *level* of developed village-farming communities. Hence, to my present way of thinking, the Jarmo phase was one of no great duration within a putatively much longer general level of the primary village-farming communities of the region of the Zagros intermontane valleys and piedmonts.

One's thinking about chronological matters is bound to be affected by the fabric of radiocarbon age determinations which do exist, and I have acquired the habit of thinking in terms of radioactive carbon years (Libby half-life). In these terms, my guess for the span of the general level of the primary village-farming communities in the Zagros region would be from the last quarter of the eighth millennium into the first quarter of the sixth millennium. The inventories I have in mind as fitting within this time span would include those of Ganj Dareh, except its basal layers (Smith 1978), the Bus Mordeh and Ali Kosh phase materials (Hole, Flannery, and Neely 1969) of the site of Ali Kosh, whose radiocarbon determinations are as whimsical as those from Jarmo, the prehistoric yields from Guran (Mortensen 1963) and Sarab (Braidwood, Howe, and Reed 1961), and perhaps those of the several most basal layers of Shimshara (Mortensen 1970). Indeed, I still find the relative arrangement of these sites in Peder Mortensen's bar diagram (1963, fig. 22) quite satisfactory, although I expect some of his bars may be a bit too long.

In sum, my present inclination would be that (in terms of radiocarbon years) the primary village-farming community level in the Zagros slopes and piedmont region spanned the period between ca. 9,250 and 7,750 years ago. The Jarmo phase would have fallen somewhere in the middle of this time span. The preceding level of incipience must have obtained from ca. 9250 B.P. back to at least 11,000 B.P. or earlier (depending, of course, on the thorny problem of when "incipience" itself set in). The level of the developed village-farming communities, including the Hassunan and at least the earlier aspects of the Samarran and Halafian inventories doubtless fell within the general time range of 7,750 to 7,000 years ago or a bit later. Obviously, the time boundaries between the levels need not have been absolutely uniform over all of southwestern Asia. I would agree with Oates (1973, p. 175) that early aspects of the Hassunan and Samarran may well have overlapped later aspects of the primary village inventories of the Zagros flanks.

NOTES

1. In these lists, I adhere strictly to the most recent style used by the journal *Radiocarbon*, listing each determination in terms of the Libby half-life and with the following BC suggestion based simply on the subtraction of 1950 from the determination. Further, no attempt has been made to cope with the matter of calibration. In 1974, in her paper "Some Problems in Connection with the Evaluation of C^{14} Dates," Olsson discussed this very issue, stating that "it is evidently too early to decide on *one* calibration curve" (Olsson 1974, p. 317; her italics).

Each age determination in the list of Jarmo radiocarbon samples is followed by a superscript, a-f. The superscripts have been provided in order that the sources for the laboratory listings may be readily located. Those sources are as follows:

a. Libby 1955, pp. 79-81.
b. Deevey, Flint, and Rouse 1967, p. 31, and F.E. Zeuner, in a letter to RJB on June 26, 1957. The pertinent portion of the letter, containing the determinations originally presented by Zeuner, is quoted below:

> Here are some more Jarmo results:
> *Jarmo, 5th level*
> F.44 HCl treatment   6650 years ± 170
> (compare with C.743 HCl treatment   6695 ± 360)
> F.48 HCl and NaOH treatment   6930 ± 180
> F.49 Filtrate   6300 ± 160
>
> You will see from this what I mean. If treated with alkali you get an older date, whilst the filtrate that runs off provides a younger date. Hence C^{14} is selectively removed by this treatment. So this confirms my observations on Jericho material, and in the case of samples from alkali soils of arid type, I prefer to rely on HCl-treated specimens.
> *Jarmo, Basal layer, c. 5 m*
> F.45 HCl treated   6570 ± 165
> (compare with C.113 [shell]   6706 ± 330)
> F.50 HCl, NaOH   6750 ± 170
>
> In this case practically no alkali-soluble organic matter was present. This sample, therefore, appears to have been pure charcoal.
>
> I am letting you have these for your information and you see what I mean about the influence of alkali treatment. In my opinion it does not apply to all types of sample, but only those preserved in alkali-arid soils.

The 1950-65 comprehensive index of radiocarbon measurements (Deevey, Flint, and Rouse 1967) has published Zeuner's determinations but has provided some correction to those values. Our series (pp. 537-38) lists the updated determinations. Also note that in the comprehensive index, the laboratory code designation F (as given by Zeuner above) has been changed to GL.

c. H.T. Waterbolk, in a letter to RJB on July 4, 1972. The pottery assayed was a selection of normal Jarmo thick-bodied plant-tempered sherds with dark central cores, of the type Adams describes (p. 217) for the uppermost levels in the "midden" area of J-II. Publication of further Groningen determinations in *Radiocarbon* is anticipated soon.

d. K.O. Münnich, in a letter to RJB on May 10, 1977. It is noted that:

> This sample had been submitted to us by Prof. Schwabedissen, and the date probably was given to him in a handwritten date list, a copy of which I enclose together with the questionary we received from you via Schwabedissen.

e. Rubin and Alexander 1960, p. 182. However, through no fault of Rubin and Alexander, the contextual information on page 182 is confusing. Determinations W-607 and W-608 (Jarmo sample no. 54) came from PQ14 but at a depth of 2.50 m. The notation for J-II,7 means that the level at which sample no. 54 was found would have been at about the equivalent of J-II level 7 *had* the J-II operation been taken to such a depth. See figures 24 and 60.

f. Protsch and Berger 1973. See also sharp exception taken to this article (Bökönyi, Braidwood, and Reed 1973; Solecki and Solecki 1974).

2. Waterbolk considers the matter of the possible effect of bitumen contamination, and writes (1971, p. 27), "Our best estimation of the age of Jarmo is therefore c. 8000 B.P., which brings the site in the same chronological horizon as Ramad and Bouqras." Further, in a letter to RJB on February 9, 1971, Waterbolk also writes:

> As to the Jarmo dates, I tried once more, using the information you gave on the PQ14 samples.
> (1) H-491/551 and W-652 represent earlier levels than the other samples, yet they give late dates.
> (2) W-657, overlying W-607/608, is off by at least 2000 years, which must be due to contamination with 25% or more infinitely old carbon (probably bitumen).
> (3) I understand that the likewise too old W-665 is also from a relatively high level in the tell.
> (4) The alkali soluble fraction W-608 gives an age which is still within the general range of possibilities and agrees with W-652 (from insoluble material); the alkali insoluble

fraction W-607, however, is 1300 years older. The close proximity of W-657 is a reason for distrusting W-607.

The conclusion would then be that the best dates are W-652, H-491 and W-608, and a date of c. 8000 B.P. our best estimate for the basal levels of operation I. Are you shocked? An increase in use of bitumen in the course of the habitation could explain a great deal of the apparent anomalies. Is there any archeological evidence for such an increase?

In answer to Waterbolk's last point, there is no evidence we could use reliably in a quantitative sense to indicate such an increase in the use of bitumen. There appears to have been an adequate supply of bitumen at Jarmo from the start.

3. In a letter to RJB on July 14, 1975, Aitken states:

We have now made magnetic measurements on two of these sherds (both labelled 'S') and deduce that the ancient magnetic field in which they were baked was 0.44 ± 0.04 oersteds. This value (which incidentally is close to the present day field strength for the area) agrees well with the expected value for the period 5000-6000 b.c. (uncalibrated scale).

REFERENCES

Aitken, M.J.
1974 *Physics and archaeology*. 2nd ed. Oxford: Oxford University Press.

Bökönyi, Sandor; Braidwood, Robert J.; and Reed, Charles A.
1973 Earliest animal domestication dated? *Science* 182:1161.

Braidwood, Robert J.; Howe, Bruce; and Reed, Charles A.
1961 The Iranian Prehistoric Project. Ibid. 133:2008-10.

Braidwood, Robert J.; Howe, Bruce; et al.
1960 *Prehistoric investigations in Iraqi Kurdistan*. Studies in Ancient Oriental Civilization [SAOC], no. 31. Chicago: University of Chicago Press.

Deevey, Edward S.; Flint, Richard Foster; and Rouse, Irving
1967 *Radiocarbon measurements: comprehensive index, 1950-1965*. New Haven, Conn.: American Journal of Science.

Hole, Frank; Flannery, Kent V.; and Neely, James A.
1969 *Prehistory and human ecology of the Deh Luran plain*. Memoirs of the Museum of Anthropology, University of Michigan, no. 1. Ann Arbor.

Libby, Willard F.
1955 *Radiocarbon dating*. 2nd ed. Chicago: University of Chicago Press.

Mortensen, Peder
1963 Early village-farming occupation. In Excavations at Tepe Guran, Luristan, Jørgen Meldgaard, Peder Mortensen, and Henrik Thrane, pp. 110-21. *Acta Archaeologica* 34:97-133.
1970 *Tell Shimshara: the Hassuna period*. Kongelige danske videnskabernes selskab, historisk-filosofiske skrifter, vol. 5 (2). Copenhagen: Munksgaard.

Oates, Joan
1973 The background and development of early farming communities in Mespotamia and the Zagros. *Proceedings of the Prehistoric Society* 39:147-81.

Olsson, Ingrid U.
1974 Some problems in connection with the evaluation of C^{14} dates. *Geologiska föreningens i Stockholm förhandlingar* 96:311-20.

Protsch, Reiner, and Berger, Rainer
1973 Earliest radiocarbon dates for domesticated animals. *Science* 179:235-39.

Ralph, Elizabeth K., and Michael, Henry N.
1974 Twenty-five years of radiocarbon dating. *American Scientist* 62:553-60.

Rubin, Meyer, and Alexander, Corrinne
1960 U.S. Geological Survey radiocarbon dates V. *American Journal of Science Radiocarbon Supplement* 2:129-85.

SAOC 31
1960 *Prehistoric investigations in Iraqi Kurdistan*. Robert J. Braidwood, Bruce Howe, et al. Studies in Ancient Oriental Civilization, no. 31. Chicago: University of Chicago Press.

Smith, Philip E.L.
1978 An interim report on Ganj Dareh Tepe, Iran. *American Journal of Archaeology* 82:538-40.

Solecki, Rose L., and Solecki, Ralph S.
1974 Shanidar Cave. *Science* 184:937.

Waterbolk, H.T.
1971 Working with radiocarbon dates. *Proceedings of the Prehistoric Society* 37 (2):15-33.

16

MISCELLANEOUS ANALYSES OF MATERIALS FROM JARMO

Robert J. Braidwood

In retrospect, we freely admit that at Jarmo much more attention should have been given to the collection and analytical examination of materials, artifactual and nonartifactual. It may be recalled, however, that our excavations took place well before such reclamation processes as flotation and archeomagnetic assays were developed. Indeed, some of the whimsical quality of our radioactive carbon age determination series may be due to the then prevailing uncertainties as to how best to recover and package samples. In large part, what information we have was reported in SAOC 31 (esp. pp. 46-50).

BITUMEN

Of the small number of samples assayed in the Kirkuk laboratory of the Iraq Petroleum Company, Ltd., four contained bitumen. In two of these samples the bitumen had apparently been used as a cement in an earthy matrix—in one instance as an adhesive on a sickle blade (J-I,7) and in another as a coating over matting (J-II,5). In both these cases the low sulphur content of the bitumen suggests the seepages of the Kirkuk-Chemchemal valley region as sources but would exclude the sources of the Mosul region. The other two samples for which the I.P.C. analyses showed bitumen were of raw fragments encountered in the test squares. One of these could have come from almost any Iraqi seepage. The other could only have come from one of three (then identified) seepages, but one of these happens to be the Sagirma Dagh seepage on the Chemchemal valley flanks.

The use of bitumen as an adhesive (e.g., for hafting flint blades) and as a probable waterproofing (for mats and baskets) was evidently common at the time of Jarmo.

The I.P.C. report also included the remark "traces of oily matter—far too small for analysis" concerning the blackened end of a bone in J-II,1. Samples of the shiny blackened floors of the ovenlike features did not show traces of bitumen.

BOTANICAL MATERIALS

The résumé of Dr. Hans Helbaek's findings regarding the plant foods appears in chapter 12 of this volume.

Prof. Elso S. Barghoorn of the Biological Laboratories, Harvard University, examined a large number of samples of charcoal from Jarmo, Karim Shahir, and the Palegawra cave and was able to study about 150 of this series microscopically. About 60 specimens from Jarmo came through Barghoorn's demineralization treatment. Not all of these were examined by thin section, and oak, especially, was often identifiable by surface examination. Barghoorn's list of samples of the woody genera follows:

J-I,6a	3 oak (2 identified by sectioning)	J-II,3	1 oak
J-I,7	1 oak		1 unidentified tree
J-I,7a	5 oak (all surface identification)	J-II,4	3 oak (one sectioned), 1 quite large tree
	1 *Prosopis*, medium-sized tree, slow growing, narrow rings		1 *Tamarix*
J-I,8	3 oak (1 identified by sectioning)	J-II,5	7 oak, some large trees
J-I,8fl.	11 oak, some larger trees		1 *Prosopis*, fairly large tree, narrow rings
J-II,2	1 oak, badly charred		1 *Tamarix*
J-II,2fl.	3 oak, large trees	J-II,6	11 oak
		J-A,III	6 oak (2 identified by sectioning)

In his letters, Barghoorn, writing some time before the Wright-van Zeist palynological studies (see Introduction), was impressed by the quantity of oak samples from both Jarmo and Palegawra. The full implication of the woody flora evidence is not yet clear, and larger series as well as a greater number of occurrences of charcoal from the late Pleistocene-early Holocene of the region are badly needed.

The manuscript for this chapter was essentially completed by 1975.

METALS

Before examples of bona fide prehistoric native copper artifacts were recovered at Çayönü (Çambel and Braidwood 1970), it had not seemed very realistic to us that artifacts of metal might be recovered from the time range of sites such as Jarmo. However, with the Çayönü and various other recent instances (Wertime 1973, table 1) of the early appearance of copper in southwestern Asia, we went over our assortment of odd unanalyzed mineral fragments. Several bits of what we took to be possibly either malachite or copper oxide stain were found, but we have not yet been able to secure a proper identification of these fragments of unworked stone.

One other curious specimen that possibly indicates the use of metal at Jarmo appeared in one of the test squares of the GK59 group. Although it was found in the fourth level there (under the tough and blocky orange-buff silty clay; see pp. 155 and 164), we were not originally inclined to make much of it—possible intrusion being an issue—given its small size and the certainty that it was lead. We classified it as a bead, and its illustration (fig. 136:19) still remains in the bead category (p. 298). More recently, with the relatively early appearance of metal now more conceivable, we submitted this specimen to Prof. Norman Nachtrieb of the Department of Chemistry at the University of Chicago. Nachtrieb's letter of July 3, 1975, follows:

> I redetermined the density of your little lead specimen more carefully, and found $\rho = 10.95 \pm 0.09$ g/cm^3. More interesting are the results Dr. Jun Ito obtained by atomic absorption analysis and emission spectrographic analysis of small scrapings of the specimen and comparative analyses on 5 commercial sources of lead metal.
>
> You'll note that nickel is present in your specimen, but is absent or present only in trace amounts in the commercial specimens. Moreover, traces of cadmium and gallium are in your sample, but generally absent from the commercial samples. Antimony is present in your sample in significant concentration, but absent in all but one of the commercial specimens. Zinc and tin are much lower in your sample than in three of our commercial reference samples.
>
> I conclude that your sample is significantly different in composition than the average commercial grade of lead metal available in the U.S. Particularly noteworthy is the presence of nickel in your material, which is not common in commercial lead, and the relatively high concentration of antimony.

Dr. Ito's analyses of our sample and of commercial lead read as follows:

[Jarmo Lead Sample]

Element	Value	Method
Sb	0.42(2) wt%	Flameless AA
Ni	0.03 wt%	Flameless AA
Bi	0.01-0.05	Emission Spec. visual estimate (Bi lamp is not available)
Fe	0.005(1)	Flame AA
Cu	0.005-0.001	Emission Spec. visual estimate
Ag	0.005-0.002	Semiquantitative AA + Emission Spec.
Sn	0.005-0.002	Semiquantitative AA only
Tl	0.005-0.001	Semiquantitative AA + Emission Spec.
Ga	0.001	Emission Spec. visual estimate
Cd	0.001	Emission Spec. visual estimate
Zn	0.0002-0.0001	Semiquantitative AA

Soil elements found are Si,Al,Mg,Mn,Ca,Ba,Cr
Elements not detected are V,Zr,Be,Ge,In,Te,Mo,Pd,Rh,Pt,Au,Co,Li,Sc,Y,La,Yb

Commercial Lead

	Minor elements	Trace elements
Thick sheet metal	Bi,Zn,Sn	Tl,Fe,Cu
Thin sheet metal	Bi,Sn,Sb	Ag,Fe,Cu
Brick	Bi,Zn	Ag,Tl,Mn,Ni
Sink stopper	Bi,Zn,Sn	Ag,Cu,Fe
Baker chemical	--	Cu,Fe,Cd,Ga

Although the context seems reasonably certain, the size of this object still inclines us towards caution in asserting that lead was actually used by the people of Jarmo.

MOLLUSCA

Our estimate of the volume of unbroken snail shells found during our three seasons' work at Jarmo is over 2 m^3, but, given the fragility of these shells, the original bulk must have been very much greater. Following earlier identifications (SAOC 31, p. 48), Dr. Stuart Harris (then of Hunting Technical Services Limited) and the Rev. H.E.J. Biggs (attached to the British Museum of Natural History) undertook the study of the Jarmo mollusca. Biggs lists

Helix salomonica Naegele, *Helicella vestalis joppensis* Roth, *Jaminia septemdentata triticea* Rossm., and *Unio tigridis* Bourg. The last, freshwater clams, did not occur in great numbers; it was the *Helix salomonica* land snails which did so. Harris's letter of September 3, 1959, includes the following:

> Turning to the snails, you raise a number of points some of which I have been discussing with Biggs. First of these is the relative abundance of snails past and present. The relevant facts are these:
> 1. You have found a far greater abundance of snails at Jarmo than could reasonably be expected.
> 2. I have found quite a range of species in the bricks at Nimrod. Snails appear to have been abundant there in Assyrian times—but I could only find the occasional specimen of one species near there last spring.
> 3. Collections made by different people in the last 100 years show that:
>   a. Many species are extremely rare.
>   b. Some species have not been found alive since 1920 in spite of fairly detailed search.
>   c. About six species are still relatively abundant, though they, like the others, appear to be living under far from ideal conditions.
> 4. There has been a major change in the vegetation cover in Iraq in the last 300 years. The former climax floras have been destroyed and replaced by only a scanty steppe vegetation. The reason for this is the felling of trees for firewood and the ravages of goats.
>
> Now your difference in quantity of mollusca at Jarmo could well be due to collection of *Helix* for eating—though it would be interesting to know why they did not collect *Levantina* spp. which are bigger. I have never met any Arabs eating snails nor have I tried them myself, so I cannot answer your queries on the culinary uses of snails. Biggs suggests that possible factors are the availability of species and taste (toughness or sliminess). Thus in Spain and W. Africa men are selective in their snail eating.

Obviously, there was a good deal of protein available to the Jarmo people in these snails. While it does not pertain directly to Jarmo, Charles Reed's (1962) note *Snails on a Persian Hillside* is of interest here.

OBSIDIAN

In the middle 1960s, there was a momentary flurry of attention given both to prospecting for the possible sources of raw obsidian in the Near East and to the physical analysis of obsidian samples, whether from natural volcanic sources or in the form of artifacts recovered from various archeological excavations. Although this was far from the first concern with the analysis of Near Eastern obsidian (see, e.g., Frankfort 1927, pp. 190-92), the papers of Renfrew, Dixon, and Cann (1965, 1966) stimulated interest in the matter, while in 1964 the Joint Istanbul-Chicago Universities' Prehistoric Project had received a grant from the Wenner-Gren Foundation for Anthropological Research to allow for a preliminary prospecting survey for obsidian flows in Turkey (Benedict et al. 1980). In 1968, Richard A. Watson and Gary A. Wright resumed this survey and—pending their further reports—Wright's paper (1969) essentially summarizes what was accomplished. Unfortunately, travel restrictions in the northeastern frontier region and beyond the Turkey-U.S.S.R. boundary leave the survey for obsidian sources still quite incomplete at this time.

As for Jarmo, Gary A. Wright (1969, p. 22, table 5) lists some 14 samples, assayed as to elemental analysis, and gives the results in terms of the group designations of Renfrew: group 1g, 5 examples; group 4c, 8 examples; group ?, 1 example. Groups 1g and 4c were two of the three most utilized sources of supply so far identified in the analyses of southwest Asian obsidian artifacts. Group 4c, by far the most important one, is assigned to the Nemrut Dagh B flow, one of two sources on Nemrut Dagh near Van. Group 1g also "has its most probable source around Lake Van" (Wright 1969, p. 10). The third (group ?) has not yet been identified as to source. Contrary to our expectations (SAOC 31, p. 48), Wright's analyses of the Jarmo obsidian artifacts did not yield any samples derived from the Aksaray region.

Wright's study (1969) goes on to show that between them, groups 1g and 4c have been identified on artifacts coming from as far to the southeast of the Van sources as Ali Kosh and Eridu and as far to the southwest as Munhatta and Hazorea.

It is unfortunate that no other essentially precise physical analyses of Jarmo artifacts—petrographic, in particular—are available.

REFERENCES

Braidwood, Robert J.; Howe, Bruce; et al.
    1960 *Prehistoric investigations in Iraqi Kurdistan.* Studies in Ancient Oriental Civilization [SAOC], no. 31. Chicago: University of Chicago Press.

Benedict, Peter; Gordus, Adon A.; Özdoğan, Mehmet; and Wright, Gary A.
    1980 Location and chemical identification of some obsidian sources in the Aksaray-Nevşehir-Niğde region, central Anatolia. In *The joint Istanbul-Chicago Universities' prehistoric research in southeastern Anatolia,* vol. 1, ed. Halet Çambel, pp. 221-56. İstanbul üniversitesi edebiyat fakültesi yayınları, no. 2589. Istanbul.

Cambel, Halet, and Braidwood, Robert J.
    1970   An early farming village in Turkey. *Scientific American* 222 (3):50-56.

Frankfort, H.
    1927   *Studies in early pottery of the Near East II*. Royal Anthropological Institute Occasional Papers, no. 8. London.

Reed, Charles A.
    1962   *Snails on a Persian hillside*. Postilla, Peabody Museum of Natural History, Yale University, no. 66. New Haven, Conn.

Renfrew, Colin; Cann, J.R.; and Dixon, J.E.
    1965   Obsidian in the Aegean. *Annual of the British School at Athens* 60:225-47.

Renfrew, Colin; Dixon, J.E.; and Cann, J.R.
    1966   Obsidian and early cultural contact in the Near East. *Proceedings of the Prehistoric Society* 32:30-72.

SAOC 31
    1960   *Prehistoric investigations in Iraqi Kurdistan*. Robert J. Braidwood, Bruce Howe, et al. Studies in Ancient Oriental Civilization, no. 31. Chicago: University of Chicago Press.

Wertime, Theodore A.
    1973   The beginnings of metallurgy: a new look. *Science* 182:875-87.

Wright, Gary A.
    1969   *Obsidian analyses and prehistoric Near Eastern trade: 7500 to 3500 B.C*. Anthropological Papers of the Museum of Anthropology, University of Michigan, no. 37. Ann Arbor.

17

THE SOUNDINGS AT BANAHILK

Patty Jo Watson

Our reason for selecting Banahilk as one of the three soundings permitted the Iraq-Jarmo Project in 1954-55 was that it offered an excellent opportunity to recover and describe—at one site at least—the context of the well-known painted pottery first found at Tell Halaf early in this century. Hole, Flannery, and Neely (1969, p. 4) have remarked that in spite of 100 years of archeological research in southwestern Asia, no one can say just what "Halaf," "Ubaid," "Giyan V A," and the like mean in terms of whole artifact assemblages representing extinct cultures. Braidwood and Braidwood (1960) described the prehistoric materials of the ʿAmuq in terms of a succession of assemblages, but we do not have detailed knowledge of the context of the major horizon-marking ceramic styles of the post-Hassunan, pre-Sumerian Mesopotamian sequence, the first of which is the Halafian.

Thus, our orientation was toward Mesopotamian culture history. Within that framework, we were interested in beginning the task of defining a Halafian assemblage because the cultural context of this ware should include significant data on the development of food-producing communities in northern Mesopotamia and northern Syria. Because Banahilk is a small site and the majority of the occupation debris includes Halafian painted pottery, it seemed a good place to attempt to define a Halafian assemblage.

THE MOUND AND THE EXCAVATIONS

Banahilk is a small mound approximately oval in shape, about 100 m wide and 160 m long, with a maximum height somewhat more than 4 m. It is located 1 km southwest of the village of Diyana, in the plain north of Ruwanduz, at about 36°40′ N, 44°32′ E and approximately 674 m above sea level (SAOC 31, fig. 4). The plain is a small one, some 9 or 10 km in width and about twice that in length, and is surrounded by mountain peaks rising to 2,700-2,800 m above sea level. The Baradost range, with the cave of Shanidar and the nearby open-air site of Zawi Chemi Shanidar, lies 5 or 6 km to the west; the town of Ruwanduz is the same distance to the south across the asphalt highway that formerly ran to the Iranian border. The Ruwanduz River is joined by some tributary streams at the southwest corner of the plain and here enters the Guli Ali Beg Gorge. The Ruwanduz River is a tributary of the Greater Zab.

To the south of the mound of Banahilk is an aircraft landing field built by the British army and the Assyrian levies during the period of the Mandate. It was later used by the Iraqi army, as was Banahilk itself. On the summit of the mound are remains of a gun emplacement, and trenches have been dug into the slopes. There is also a large, recent cut on the east side of the site, from which earth has been removed.

The work at Banahilk consisted of a ten-day sounding made under my immediate supervision late in 1954. The sounding comprised four main operations: A, B, C, and D (fig. 194). Excavation of two other trenches was abandoned soon because their yield was found to be clearly disturbed. All excavation was carried out with small picks, the loose dirt being removed with shovels. No screens were used. The work team consisted of one Shergati Arab (Khalifa) and a small group of experienced local workmen from the Chemchemal area. The dig foreman—an extremely helpful, trustworthy, and reliable person—was Abdulla al-Masri as-Sudani who had worked with Braidwood at Jarmo and elsewhere over a period of some twenty years.

Because our tests were of such small size and short duration, due to the legal limits on soundings, not all the stratigraphic problems that arose could be satisfactorily resolved. Hence, careful attention to the findspot designations given in the following discussion is necessary.

This is a revised version of a paper submitted in 1956 to the Department of Anthropology, University of Chicago, in partial fulfillment of requirements for the Master of Arts degree (Watson 1956). Parts of the original text were subsequently reworked on several different occasions, but the most recent revision was completed in spring 1976. Very few additions and only minor revisions have been made since that date.

Drawings of the pottery and most of the other artifacts were made by Kari Roma and James Knudstad; Glen Cole did the chert and obsidian illustrations. Robert Braidwood, Linda Braidwood, and several members of the Oriental Institute editorial staff—Elizabeth Hauser, Jean Eckenfels, Heather Taylor, and Mary Evins—have all suggested numerous improvements in organization of the tables, catalogue, figures, and figure captions, for which I thank them. I am especially grateful to Heather Taylor for her painstaking labors on table 44.

Operation A (fig. 195:1) was begun as a 2 × 6 m trench on the west slope of the mound and was expanded on the north by an area 3 × 2 m. The operation was dug in four levels to a maximum depth of 1.25 m, where a segment of stone walling was uncovered. The context of the artifactual material here was unclear: a few sherds of Halaf-style painted pottery and also some of the plain ware that seems to belong with it at Banahilk were found in most levels, but with these were several metal objects and sherds from wheel-made vessels. Obsidian blade fragments were present, as well as some flint in the form of scrapers, utilized flakes, some flake cores, and a few blades. Larger stone objects included one complete pestle and a fragment of another. It is not clear what the admixture represents nor how the walling is related to what was found in other operations. The non-Halafian pottery found here is noted on page 567.

Operation B (fig. 195:2), also a 2 × 6 m trench, was placed on the east side of the mound, just south of the large cut mentioned above and parallel to it. Three levels were dug to a maximum depth of 0.75 m. Traces of two floors and of two stone walls were found; one of the floors was apparently associated with one of the walls, but the other two probably were not related. Lying only 20 cm below the surface was the first floor—a greenish clay surface with a short curbing of small limestone blocks at one end. The piece of floor that was found intact was at least as wide as the trench (2 m) but only 0.90 m long, although it could be traced somewhat farther than this along the trench wall profile.

The context of artifactual material from operation B was also unclear: no metal was found, but wheel-made pottery was present, even in the lowest level. However, there was a greater quantity of pottery of the Halafian painted style and also of the accompanying plain ware. Some interesting objects were found in this trench, notably five worked sheep/goat astragali ("knucklebone" gaming pieces) and a ground obsidian ornament.

Because of the disturbance found to characterize those parts of the mound, work in operations A and B was suspended, and two new operations were begun. One, operation W, was to be another 2 × 6 m trench southeast of the wall found in operation A; but at a depth of 0.30 m a scatter of rock was discovered, and excavation was discontinued here also. This rock may have been paving; it closely resembled the limestone scatters found at Karim Shahir and Jarmo (SAOC 31, pl. 22*A*). The other operation, TT, was to be a widening of an old army trench near the summit of the mound. A floor was found 0.55 m below the surface, but again the context proved unsatisfactory. It was decided to close the operation, because it was too near the gun emplacement.

Just before work in operation B was terminated, a 2 × 3 m area bordering on the recent cut on the eastern side of the site was laid out and designated operation C (fig. 196). This location was selected in order to get a good stratigraphic sequence as near the center of the mound as possible and also to reach the bottom of the deposit. Six floors, beginning at a depth of 0.80 m below the mound surface, had been found when the stone footing of a wall was exposed at a depth of 2.90 m. The trace of a floor probably associated with the wall was also found approximately level with the top of the foundation stones. The wall footing was left intact because the Directorate General of Antiquities had requested that no architecture be removed. Another pit, 2 × 2 m, was begun northeast of operation C in the bottom of still another army trench. This operation, C extension, was dug to a floor indicated by a narrow band of sherds and other debris, which marked the bottom of the deposit at nearly 3 m below the mound surface. The layer rested upon some 0.50 m of sterile red-brown earth that shaded to dark brown with white limestone specks—obviously the virgin soil underlying the mound.

Details on Levels of Operation C and C Extension (figs. 194, 196)

Level	Depth below surface (cm)
C,1	0-80 (to fl.1)
C,2	80-105 (to fl.2)
C,3	105-135 (to base of fl.3)
C,4	135-150 (to fl.4)
C,5	150-195 (to fl.5)
C,6	195-245 (to fl.6)
C,7	245-290 (limestone wall base and fl.7 at 270 cm)
C ext.,1	270-290
C ext.,2	290-370

The context of artifactual material from operation C seemed to be clear. The pottery was consistent, comprising Halafian-style painted ware and its associated plain ware. Other artifacts included clay rings, worked sherds (scrapers, perforated and unperforated disks, sherds with chipped edges), bone awls, one knucklebone gaming piece like those from operation B, a piece of a stamp seal, a fragment of a brown obsidian pendant, a few stone bowl fragments, and tools and flakes of chert and obsidian.

Operation D was laid out on the north slope of the mound (fig. 195:3), near an area where we had noted on the surface a concentration of Halafian-style painted sherds that had probably come from the digging of the cut on the eastern face. Operation D was begun as a 6 × 6 m square, but after the first 0.30 m the operation was reduced by half.

The 3 × 6 m trench to the northwest was called D*I*; a balk 1 m wide was left, and the 2 × 6 m trench southeast of that became D*II*. The material from level 1 (immediately beneath the plow zone) contained no painted sherds, very little plain ware, and only a few pieces of chipped stone. The sherds were not identifiable by form and were not saved. Sherds from all levels below this were saved and tabulated. At a depth of about 40 cm in D*I*, a deposit of trash, 0.50 m thick, yielded large numbers of painted sherds of the Halafian style. At the northern end of D*I* this deposit was found to rest upon 5-10 cm of clean, yellowish earth beneath which was a series of floor levels. In the southern end of D*I* the trash fill was 35-45 cm deeper than in the northern end and rested upon a floor. Beneath this were five more floors. In the southern end of D*I* there was also a shallow clay hearth (feature 1); a radiocarbon sample was taken from the charcoal and ash stratum immediately below it.

D*II* was excavated as a 2 × 6 m unit to a maximum depth of 1.20 m. Then, to speed up the excavation, a balk was left in the center and only the northern and southern 2 × 2 m squares were carried down as far as possible in the time remaining. A depth of 1.85 m was reached in the northern end and a depth of 2.00 m in the southern end. No floors were found; instead, trash fill like that of D*I*,2 continued to the limit of the excavation.

Details on Levels of Operation D (figs. 194; 195:3)

Level	Depth below surface (cm)
D,sf	0-15
D,1	15-35/20
D*I*,1-2*	35/20-50/30
D*I*,2 (north end)	20-90 (trash layer, removed to yellowish clay of fl.1)
D*I*,2 (south end)	50-95 (trash layer)
D*I*,fl.1	90-100
D*I*,fl.2	100-115
D*I*,fl.3	115-125
D*I*,fl.4†	195-210
D*I*,fl.5	125-145
D*I*,fl.6 (north end)	145-160
D*I*,fl.6 (south end)	210-225
D*I*,fl.7	160-175
D*II*,1-2	30/15-120/55 (to trash layer equivalent to D*I*,2)
D*II*,2	120/55-160/90 (trash layer)
D*II*N	90-185 (trash layer)
D*II*S	160-200 (trash layer)

NOTE: Operation D was laid out on the mound slope, and the natural strata were followed in excavating it. Because all depth measurements were made from the mound surface, the upslope end of a level was often farther below the surface than the downslope end. Accordingly, "35/20 to 50/30" means that the upslope end of the trench was dug from 35 to 50 cm below the surface, while the downslope end, in tracing the same level, was dug from 20 to 30 cm below the surface.

*At this point the operation was cut in half (see fig. 195 and p. 546), hence the designation "D*I*" and, below, "D*II*."

†This floor was found only in the south end of D*I*.

Thus, in terms of stratigraphic units, operation D comprises three main horizons (fig. 195:3), which may be described as follows: at bottom, a series of occupation levels with floors and Halafian painted pottery; next, fill (level 2) consisting of a trash deposit with much loose rock and much Halafian painted pottery; and at top, occupation debris (levels 1 and 1-2) with at least one floor and considerably less Halafian painted pottery. The same type of plain ware and the same chert and obsidian industry occur throughout, and all of these strata are considered to be Halafian.

ARCHITECTURAL TRACES AND STRATIGRAPHY IN OPERATION D

In level 1 a patch of ash was found about 0.20 m down in the southwestern part of the square, and beneath it was a patch of floor. East of this area near the southeast corner were two pestles lying side by side about 0.15 m apart. Nearby but slightly below them was an area of hardened earth or clay with part of a rim or curb. This fragmentary structure may have been similar to feature 1. In this same area and still in level 1 were three grinding stones. In the north end of the square another patch of floor was found 0.30 m below the surface in the northwest corner, and another hearth area appeared in the northeast corner. About 0.40 m down in the north end of D*I* was still another hearth area—a patch of fire-reddened and black earth with a plain ware pot set into it. Below this, appearing first in the northwest corner and then throughout the whole trench, were many unshaped limestone rocks. At first, an attempt was made to clear them in the hope that they represented some kind of architectural unit, but it soon became apparent that they were simply small, unworked rocks scattered through the deposit, perhaps marking the edge of a rock pile whose main body lay west of our opening. Besides limestone, there were some pieces of greenish sandstone. The deposit itself (level 2) was apparently a dump with much broken animal bone, sherds (both painted and plain), broken obsidian blades, and chert flakes and chips, but no floors or other architectural features. At the north end of the operation this trash rested on a layer of clean, yellow, clayey earth, about 5 cm thick. This, in turn, rested upon floor 1. Somewhat more to the south, the trash fill itself rested directly on floor 1. Beneath this floor, which slanted downward slightly to the south, was a series of other floors 10-15 cm apart. These floors were all of a clayey earth that was slightly greenish in color in floor 3 and all lower floors. Floors 1, 2, and 3 could be traced only in the north end of the trench and floor 4 only in the south end (fig. 195:3). Floors 6 and 7 were followed throughout. In the south end of the trench, the trash deposit rested on a thin layer of hard greenish earth, beneath which was floor 4. In the greenish layer (the color was probably derived from decomposed sandstone) was feature 1. Floor 4 could not be clearly traced beneath feature 1. When this feature was sectioned to enable us to take a radiocarbon sample, much charcoal and ash and a number of snail shells were found beneath it; the remains indicate that this was the hearth area for at least three floors (4, 6, and 7). The radiocarbon sample came from a concentration of charcoal and ash 0.15 m above floor 7, at about the level of floor 6. Above the radiocarbon sample area was a conspicuous layer of creamy-textured and light-colored ash, which may have resulted from the combustion of chaff-filled dung. This ash was also visible in the south wall of D*I* behind feature 1.

The peculiar arrangement of the floors found in operation D suggested that there should be a wall running east and west approximately in the middle of the trench, but no trace of such a wall was found. It may simply be that the south end of D*I* was disturbed before being filled with trash; that is, floors 1, 2, and 3 in the south end of the trench may have been destroyed before the area became a dump. Floor 4 in the south end of the trench would then be the same floor as floor 5 in the north end. However that may be, the yellowish clay at the north end of D*I* and the greenish layer at the south end to some extent sealed the floors beneath them. These layers may themselves be floors, more carefully made than the others.

The stratigraphy in D*I* can also be explained in another more complicated way: floors 6 and 7 may have belonged to a room that occupied the whole D*I* area and extended some unknown distance beyond on all four sides. A hearth area was established where feature 1 is situated. Soon after floor 6 developed, part of it was paved and a partition or screen wall without a stone footing was erected, creating a chamber directly north of the hearth area. This chamber may be referred to as D*I*a. The southern area may have been a little-used storage room or may not have been used at all. After floors 5, 3, and 2 had accumulated in D*I*a, the southern area was reoccupied and floor 4 developed there, settling slightly near the partition wall. By this time, floor 1 was in use in the northern chamber. Some time later, new floors (yellow clay in the northern chamber and greenish earth in the southern area) were laid in both rooms, and a clay basin (feature 1) was built as a proper hearth. Because this structure showed very little sign of having been used as a hearth, however, one must further suggest that the rooms were probably abandoned not long afterward, the partition removed, and trash subsequently dumped into the area from some point a little to the west and north. Besides the usual cultural debris, the trash contained many rocks, perhaps simply because a village midden was encroaching upon a rock heap accumulated for some other purpose, for example, a stone roadway such as Mallowan found at Arpachiyah (Mallowan and Rose 1935, p. 21, fig. 3, pl. I*b*). Apparently the area was later reoccupied, as shown by the patches of floor, the hearths, and the milling stone in level 1.

It is suggested that the time span represented by the floors of operation D was not a long one; not only had little debris accumulated between these floors but also two sets of sherds broken in antiquity and exposed in the context of two different floor levels (4 and 7) were found to fit together (as parts of a large painted jar similar to the one in fig. 200:2).

Because of lack of time, D*II* was not excavated beneath the trash deposit (D*I*,2), which was first encountered in D*II* at a depth of 0.55 m in the north end of the trench and 1.20 m in the south end. The trash fill in the southern corner of operation D is more than 0.50 m lower than the top of this deposit in the northern corner, where it first appeared; this difference indicates that the dump sloped off to the east and south. The maximum depth excavated was 1.85 m at the north end of D*II* and 2 m at the south end. At a depth of 1.30 m in the center of D*II* a concentration of charcoal and ash was found, from which a second radiocarbon sample was taken.

Virgin soil was not reached in operation D. The thickness of deposit was tested only in operation C, east of the mound's center, and was there found to be about 3 m.

The trash level of operation D was rich in small objects and pottery fragments. The plain ware from the floor levels (floors 1-7) was assumed to have been produced by the makers of the Halafian-style painted ware. A study of the plain ware from the trash fill indicates that this deposit represents activity of the same people who left the material associated with the floors; that is, the plain ware from the two contexts is very similar.

The assemblage in operation D, of which the Halafian-style painted pottery is a part, included quantities of well-preserved animal bone, stone bowl fragments, fully ground celts, bone awls or punches, milling stones, pestles, mortars, door pivot stones, stone beads, an incomplete seal pendant with incised decoration, a few other pendants or ornaments (including two of ground obsidian), chipped sherds and disks, pottery rings or beads, pottery spindle whorls, chert flakes and implements, and much obsidian in the form of blades.

SUMMARY OF ARTIFACT CATEGORIES

The Banahilk materials other than pottery include several items already well known from Arpachiyah (Mallowan and Rose 1935): carefully incised pendants and seals, perforated ground obsidian links, well-made stone vessels (mostly small bowls), fully ground celts, and obsidian blades. But two categories of Halafian pottery objects from Banahilk seem to be unique: a small round "sieve"—a disk 40-50 mm in diameter with many holes drilled in it (figs. 207:2; 208:10)—and a flat, oval, baked clay object with one or two holes punched through each end (figs. 207:6; 208:11).

Many sherds of painted vessels show definite chipping on one or more edges, that is, the pottery fragments are flaked as if they were chert. A few of these objects had apparently been used as scrapers, and they might well have served as clay-working tools for potters.

Female figurines attributed to the Halaf period are well known from Arpachiyah and Tell Halaf, but none were found at Banahilk.

The chert-obsidian industry at Banahilk is rather undistinguished. In general it resembles that of Hassuna and Matarrah, being quite different from the blade industry of Halafian levels in the ᶜAmuq. Chert and obsidian implements found at other Halafian sites have not been described in enough detail to permit significant comparisons to be made. Obsidian blades seem to occur at all the sites, however. The majority of Banahilk chert pieces were utilized flakes and waste flakes; there were a few scrapers and quite a few sickle teeth (usually nondescript bladelike flakes with no retouch except some occasional backing). Traces of a black substance, presumably bitumen used as an adhesive, are often present on these sickle teeth. There were also a few chert pieces that are probably fragments of drills. Besides these commonplace categories, there appeared a few microlithic tools, including nine *petits tranchets* (also called "trapezes" or "trapezoids," and often thought to have been used as transversely mounted projectile points) and one lunate. The obsidian implements were, for the most part, utilized and unutilized blades.

The Halafian-style painted ceramic at Banahilk falls within the range of pottery traditionally called Eastern Halaf (Perkins 1949, pp. 44-45; but see LeBlanc and Watson 1973). In texture it is more like the Arpachiyah and Tilkitepe wares[1] than those of Tell Halaf, Chagar Bazar, and Carchemish, but, unlike Arpachiyah, Banahilk yielded very few bichrome and no polychrome pieces. Moreover, there are no more than two vessels definitely identifiable as "cream bowls." Otherwise, shapes include simple bowls with rounded sides and flat rims that are square in section, shallower bowls with rims that are rounded or pointed in section, flare-sided bowls, "funnel-rim" bowls of a type common at Tell Halaf, rounded bowls with curved-in rims, large storage jars, smaller jars, and some very squat pots with bulging sides like those found at Tell Halaf and called *Büchsen* by Schmidt (Oppenheim and Schmidt 1943). A few miniature vessels of various kinds were also represented.

The design motifs of the Banahilk painted pottery add little to what is already known about Halafian motifs (the largest published repertoires are those of Tell Halaf, Arpachiyah, and Tepe Gawra; see LeBlanc and Watson 1973). The bucranium motif is rare at Banahilk, as it is at Tilkitepe (at least among the sherds I have seen). The few Banahilk examples resemble the so-called stylized bucranium (Mallowan and Rose 1935). The typical Halafian quatrefoil cross formée (usually referred to in the archeological literature as a Maltese cross) is fairly frequent, however.

The plain ware component of the Banahilk pottery industry is interesting, but so little information on plain wares from other Halafian sites has been published that few comparisons can be made. At Banahilk there are two basic textures: one is an orange-surfaced, chaff-tempered ware; the other is a heavier pottery containing little or no chaff, which has slipped brown surfaces that are sometimes lightly burnished on the outside. For a detailed description of some technological aspects of Banahilk plain ware, see pages 563-67. The shapes include sloping-shouldered jars and simple bowls in both wares, as well as lugged jars or pots (most of the lugs had broken off in antiquity and were found loose). These lugs sometimes project 50-60 mm from the body of the pot and are 30-50 mm in diameter.

In the present ceramic sample from Banahilk, plain ware is less common than painted ware. The total number of painted ware sherds recovered from all operations and levels (including surface sherds) is 3,230, whereas the total number of plain ware sherds is 1,762. This is a 65:35 ratio. In operation C, the ratio is 52:48 (412 painted, 360 plain); in operation D (floors only), it is 68:32 (1,064 painted, 519 plain).

PAINTED WARE (tables 42-44; figs. 197-201, 207:3-5)

The painted pottery sherd count at Banahilk was 3,230. Of this number, 737 sherds were from bowls, 906 sherds were from jars, and the bowl-jar ratio was thus ca. 4:5. The Halafian-style painted pottery at this site is generally well made and well fired, although some of the painted bowls have light gray cores. According to Matson's study of Banahilk ceramic technology (see chap. 18), visible inclusions in the clay are limestone grains up to 2 mm in diameter, fine specks of golden mica, and black grains of talc. Some sherds contain very fine chaff, although this does not seem to be characteristic of the majority of painted ware sherds. Some sherds contain so much limestone that they are grainy or gritty in appearance. Specimens made of this type of fabric are in the minority at Banahilk, but they are a definite component of the collection.

On a few sherds a whitish slip has been applied, but for the most part the vessels have slips of buff or pink like the fabric. The insides of most of the jars show clear traces of having been wiped or scraped with a finishing tool.

Three vitrified sherds were found; on one of them (a jar fragment) the painted design was still clear.

The paint on the Banahilk pottery varies from black to dark brown, light brown, red brown, orange, and red. It is frequently, but not always, lustrous.[2] Occasionally it was possible to observe areas of lustrous and of nonlustrous paint on the same sherds. On at least one sherd it was clear that the paint was lustrous where the fabric was thick and not lustrous where it was thin. There was one instance of lustrous paint on a sherd of quite poor fabric.

Matson's technological analyses have so far revealed no definite indication of trade wares among the Banahilk painted pottery. It seems to be a locally produced variant of the Halafian tradition.

The Banahilk painted pottery is decorated with the motifs familiar to us from Arpachiyah, Tell Halaf, Tepe Gawra, and other sites where the ware has been found (LeBlanc and Watson 1973). These Banahilk pottery designs are almost wholly nonrepresentational. The bird (fig. 198:5) and several stylized bucrania are the only representational motifs in the present sample, unless one considers the quatrefoil and rosette to be representations of flowers. The Banahilk bird may be compared to similar figures on Halafian painted ware at Tell Halaf (Oppenheim and Schmidt 1943, pls. LVII-LVIII) and Tepe Gawra (Tobler 1950, pls. CXVII-CXVIII).

The only complete vessel found at Banahilk was an unpainted miniature jar (fig. 203:32). The pottery classification is therefore based entirely on sherds and is necessarily inconclusive in some respects. Similarly, in the discussion of designs characteristic of the various form classes (see below), the zoned motifs noted as occurring on certain vessels may well have been combined with other motifs not preserved on the pieces found.

Many of the painted sherds have repair holes neatly drilled into them (fig. 197:4,9,11), and a few have traces of an adhesive (probably bitumen) as well (fig. 197:2).

A total of 23 such perforated sherds were found; of these all but 2 were bored from both sides. In only 6 do the perforations meet perfectly. Three perforations are not finished (two of these were started from both sides, the third from one side only); 2 sherds have one complete perforation and another hole started (from one side only) but not finished. One sherd has two complete perforations; 4 sherds have traces of black adhesive around the perforation and the broken edge. The repair holes are usually about 6-7 mm in diameter; the maximum diameter is 10 mm. The perforations are conical in longitudinal section, widest at the surface of the sherd, and narrow on the inside; this probably indicates that the drill was not parallel-sided but was winged or flanged, which increased the cross-sectional size above the tip. No such drills have been found in the Banahilk chert industry so far, although this could be an accident of sampling. Another possibility is that an initial perforation of very small diameter was made to guide the drilling of the actual repair hole, which, as noted above, was nearly always bored from both sides of the sherd. Such an initial perforation might have been made with a well-sharpened bone needle aided by an abrasive such as very fine sand. The repair hole could then be completed with an ordinary tapered chert drill (few undeniably clear examples of drills were found among the Banahilk chipped stone tools; for implements that might have been used for drilling, see fig. 213:10-11 and fig. 214:8). One sherd has an incomplete repair hole (begun from both sides) that must have been made by a winged drill or by the process just described—at any rate, a small drill hole was present inside a larger drilled depression.

The actual mending of a broken pot would have involved the following steps: drilling the repair holes on both sides of the break, applying adhesive along the edges of the break, fitting the pieces together, and tying them securely with cord. Of the 23 painted pottery sherds with repair holes, 15 were fragments of bowls and 8 were body sherds unidentifiable as to form.

Form Classes of the Painted Ware Vessels (table 42)

For a description and discussion of the painted pottery designs and the motif terminology used, see figures 205 and 206.

1. Bowls

IA. Round-sided bowls (fig. 197:1-6).—(1) Round-sided bowls with squared rims, decorated with bands and rim ticking;[3] (2) variants of subclass 1, i.e., round-sided bowls without squared rims, or very large heavy bowls otherwise of subclass 1, or bowls more or less of that shape but without the characteristic decoration (bands and rim ticking); (3) fragments of round-sided bowls but whether of subclass 1 or 2 undeterminable.

These simple hemispherical bowls with rounded sides vary slightly in profile from open (fig. 197:1) to more closed forms (fig. 197:4,6). One type (fig. 197:4), represented by a large group of bowls, always has the same characteristic squared rim and painted design, that is, rim ticking with a series of plain bands just under the rim both inside and out. As far as can be determined from the available Banahilk sherds, bowls of this type did not usually have a central design in the bottom of the vessel, but a similar bowl from Arpachiyah is decorated with a central cruciform bucranium (Mallowan and Rose 1935, p. 116), and a bowl from Tell Halaf that seems to be of this type has a central rosette design (Oppenheim and Schmidt 1943, pl. LXX:3).

There are variations of this type. On one example the band decoration outside is replaced by a cable motif, while inside there is a wavy line below a single rim band (fig. 197:3). The squared rim, whenever it occurs, usually has ticking. There are also extraordinarily large and heavy round-sided bowls (fig. 197:5-6). Other varieties of hemispherical bowls are shown in figure 197:1-2. The commonest variation in design is a combination of bands and wavy lines, either alternating with each other or zoned in a sequence of two or more bands followed by two or more wavy lines, all on the inside. The outside is painted with bands only. The rim may or may not be squared, but rim ticking appears only on the thick, heavy bowls (fig. 197:5-6).

IB. Shallow round-sided bowls (figs. 197:7-15; 198:1-7).—Open, round-sided, platelike bowls with elaboration of design on the interior in two areas—on the sides, and centrally in the bottom of the bowl; rims not squared.

The major painted decoration of these vessels is on the inside, and they resemble the polychrome bowls and plates of Arpachiyah (Mallowan and Rose 1935, pls. XVI-XVIII, fig. 55). The rims are not squared but taper to a rather thin edge, and the bases are flat. The pattern of decoration is often as follows: two or more plain bands outside at and below the rim and a zoned decoration of some sort inside that stops one half to two thirds of the way to the bottom. The commonest motifs used for the zoned area are chevrons, alternating opposed triangles, crosshatching, and banding (see figs. 205 and 206 and accompanying notes for illustrations and descriptions of these and other motifs). Whenever orientation of the sherds is certain, it has been noted that the chevrons point to the right and open to the left (fig. 198:2). Most of these motifs are combined with bands in some way. A few sherds also have a typically Halafian motif, the quatrefoil (fig. 198:3; also fig. 197:12, a very badly executed example). This figure looks like a four-petaled flower.

The inner decoration of the shallow bowls is often closed off by a band on the inside of the bowl (fig. 197:11). The only representational design, other than stylized bucrania, in the sample of painted pottery from Banahilk is on a bowl of this type (fig. 198:5). This design is a large bird of some sort (a stork?) with wings raised.

Bichrome designs (red and black paint deliberately contrasted), which are not very common at Banahilk, occur on several shallow bowls (figs. 197:7; 198:4-6).

The only complete profile of a shallow bowl (fig. 197:13) has on the inside what is apparently a very poorly executed cruciform double bucranium. Other bowls also have bucrania designs (figs. 197:7; 198:1).

One sherd (fig. 198:7) has a unique profile and is perhaps a fragment from a carinated bowl. Its orientation is unknown.

IC. Flare-rimmed bowls (figs. 198:8-12; 207:5).—(1) Rounded lower profile; (2) sharply angled lower profile ("cream bowl" and similar variants); (3) miscellaneous rims from flare-rimmed bowls with no indication of lower profile.

This group comprises rather special bowls of the same type as the so-called funnel-rimmed vessels (*Trichterrand-Becher, Trichterrand-Näpfe, Trichterrand-Schüsseln, Trichterrand-Teller*) of Tell Halaf (Oppenheim and Schmidt 1943, pl. VII). The Arpachiyah "cream bowl" is a spectacular variant; this type is very rare at Banahilk (figs. 198:9; 207:5).

Two main varieties of the flared profile were found at Banahilk. Figure 198:8 may represent a third form, similar to one from Tell Halaf (Oppenheim and Schmidt 1943, pl. LXXXII). In one of these two main variants—the cream bowl—the rim and side form a sharp angle with the base (fig. 198:9); in the other, the lower portion of the vessel is rounded rather than angled (fig. 198:10).

The major decoration of this group of bowls is on the inside, often on the inner face of the flaring rim. On the small cream bowls the outside is also decorated; one of these was apparently painted in bichrome (fig. 198:8).

ID. Flare-sided bowls (fig. 198:13-19).—Small cuplike or platelike bowls with flaring sides.

In this group are small vessels—cups and low bowls—with concave, flaring sides. The same profile occurs in the plain ware of Banahilk and of Tilkitepe. The majority of painted decoration was apparently confined to the outer surfaces, although the basal interior would have made a suitable field and was perhaps occasionally used, as was the case at Arpachiyah on at least one vessel (Mallowan and Rose 1935, fig. 56). Typically there is only a rim band inside, followed by one or more plain bands or by a wavy line (fig. 198:14,18-19). Outside, the whole surface of the sides down to the base is used to display a zoned or paneled or all-over design (fig. 198:14-15). One piece (fig. 198:13) is covered with a red wash inside and out.

Vessels comparable to these are found at many Halafian sites (e.g., see Mallowan and Rose 1935, figs. 56:1, 57:2, 58:4; and also figs. 69-72, in which several cuplike vessels are shown; see also the Tell Halaf material in Oppenheim and Schmidt 1943, pls. XXII:1,3-7,9-14; X:26-32; LXIX:7-9).

IE. Bowls with curved-in rims (holemouths) (figs. 198:20-22; 199:1-6).—Another group of rather small vessels is characterized by a very different shape. The rims are drawn in to make a closed bowl form, with carinated sides (fig. 199:1-2) or with a simple globular shape (figs. 198:21; 199:3). Two examples (figs. 198:22; 199:4) are almost miniatures, and two fragments (fig. 199:5-6) are from deeper vessels with straighter sides above the carination and with slightly out-turned rims.

Decoration on these vessels follows a characteristic pattern: an all-over design covers the outside of the bowl from the rim to just below the point of maximum diameter. The design is bounded at the bottom, and usually at the top as well, by a band. Inside, there is only a narrow rim band, or at most a rim band and wavy line combination. The commonest motif is an all-over crosshatch. Also common are zones of hatching between opposed wavy lines. One fragment has a bichrome checkered pattern on the outside (fig. 198:22).

This form occurs commonly at other Halafian sites such as Tell Halaf, Arpachiyah, and Tilkitepe (Mallowan and Rose 1935, figs. 60:1,3-6; 66:6; Oppenheim and Schmidt 1943, pls. LXV:9-11; LXVIII:7-10; LXIX:1,3-4; Watson, in prep.).

Table 42.—Banahilk

Form class	Surface	A	B	C,1	C,2	C,3	C,4	C,5	C,6	C,7	C ext.,1	C ext.,2	D*I*,1-2	D*I*,2	D*I*,fl.1	D*I*,fl.2
IA1	5	--	13	--	--	8	--	1(2)	3	6(18)	--	9	6(7)	94(99)	24	1
IA2	2	2	5	--	5(7)	4(13)	1	--	--	3(5)	1	6	5	16	2	1
IA3	--	--	--	--	--	--	--	--	--	--	--	--	--	--	--	--
Total IA	7	2	18	--	5	12	1	1	3	9	1	15	11	110	26	2
Total IB	3	2	15	6	3	8	2	1	--	7(9)	--	9	26(27)	67(71)	13	2?
IC1	--	--	3	--	--	--	--	--	--	2(4)	--	--	--	4	1	--
IC2	--	--	--	--	--	--	--	--	--	--	--	--	--	1	1	--
IC3	1	--	1	1	--	--	--	--	1?	--	--	--	5	1	2	--
Total IC	1	--	4	1	--	--	--	--	1	2	--	--	5	6	4	--
Total ID	1	3	5	4	1	--	--	--	--	1	--	2	10(11)	5	--	--
Total IE	5	3	10	--	--	3	--	--	--	10(12)	--	10	7(8)	48(49)	8	2(4)
Total I	17	10	52	11	9	23	3	2	4	29	1	36	59	236	51	6
Total II	1	1	7	1	1	3	--	2	1	1	--	5(6)	6	15	--	--
IIIA1	--	1	6	--	--	--	--	--	--	1	--	--	--	3	--	--
IIIA2	--	1	2	--	--	--	--	--	--	--	--	6	6	39(40)	9	--
IIIA3	--	--	1	--	--	1(3)	--	--	2	--	--	--	3	13(14)	1	--
IIIA4	1	--	1	2	--	--	--	1	1	--	1	--	5	19	1	--
Total IIIA	1	2	10	2	--	1	--	1	3	1	1	6	14	74	11	--
Total IIIB	--	2	13	--	--	5	--	--	1	1	--	7	10	28	10	--
Total IIIC	1	--	13	2	--	--	--	--	--	5(8)	--	3	9	47	23(26)	--
Total IIID	13	1	7	1	1	6	--	--	--	5	--	6	--	27	12(15)	--
Total IIIE	--	2	20	1	2(3)	4	2	--	2	5	--	4	2	34	7	1
Total III	15	7	63	6	3	16	2	1	6	17	1	26	35	210	63	1
Total IVA	--	1	3	--	2	1	--	--	--	--	--	1	1	3	--	1
Total IVB	--	--	3	--	--	1	--	--	--	1	--	1	1	5	1	2
Total IV	--	1	6	--	2	2	--	--	--	1	--	2	2	8	1	3
Total VA	3	12	72	9	13(18)	31	4	11	2	24	--	51	95	251	53	--
Total VB	--	2	28	5	7	24	--	2	1	5	--	6	17	56	14	2
Total V	3	14	100	14	20	55	4	13	3	29	--	57	112	307	67	2
Grand total	36	33	228	32	35	99	9	18	14	77	2	126	214	776	182	12
%	1.1	1.0	7.1	1.0	1.1	3.1	0.3	0.5	0.4	2.4	0.1	3.9	6.6	24.0	5.6	0.4

NOTE: When two or more sherds join they are counted as one, but the total number of fragments is given in parentheses.

II. Bowllike Jars (Büchsen) (fig. 199:7-11)

This group includes very squat, bulging-sided and large-mouthed, cuspidorlike pots, similar to some of those at Tell Halaf that Schmidt called *Büchsen* (Oppenheim and Schmidt 1943, pls. XII-XIII). None of the Banahilk sherds have the necks or rims preserved, but these pots must have had everted or very short straight rims like those from Tell Halaf. One (fig. 199:7) has a sharp carination unlike the usual rounded bulge (fig. 199:8). Most of these vessels were rather small.

Decoration is restricted to the outside upper two thirds of the vessel, covering the sides (usually with an all-over design) down to a point just below the bulge. One or more lines bound the decoration there. Similar examples from Tell Halaf often had broad flat rims with painted decoration.

Painted Ware Sherds

D*I*,fl.3	D*I*,fl.4	D*I*,fl.5	D*I*,feat.1	D*I*,fl.6	D*I*,fl.7	D*II*,1-2	D*II*,2	D*II*S	D*II*N	W 2x6	Total	%	Grand total	%
5	1	2	--	15(16)	4	10	10(12)	8	5	--	230	--	--	--
1	1	1	--	2	--	--	3	--	4	1	66	--	--	--
--	--	--	--	--	4	--	--	--	--	--	4	--	--	--
6	2	3	--	17	8	10	13	8	9	1	300	9.3	--	--
4(5)	1	8(9)	--	14	5	4	10	10(14)	6(7)	--	226	7.0	--	--
--	--	--	--	1	1	--	--	--	--	--	12	--	--	--
--	--	--	--	--	--	--	--	--	--	--	2	--	--	--
--	--	--	--	--	1	--	--	--	1	--	14	--	--	--
--	--	--	--	1	2	--	--	--	1	--	28	0.9	--	--
--	--	3	--	2	3	--	3	--	--	--	43	1.3	--	--
2	2	1	--	20(22)	2	--	2	3(4)	2	--	140	4.3	--	--
12	5	15	--	54	20	14	28	21	18	1	--	--	737	22.8
--	--	2	--	5	4	--	--	2(3)	--	--	--	--	57	1.8
--	--	--	--	1	2	--	--	2	1	--	17	--	--	--
2	4	2	--	9(11)	2	2	6(9)	--	7	--	97	--	--	--
2	4	--	--	5	2	--	2	--	2	--	38	--	--	--
1	--	--	--	5(6)	2	1	3	1	--	--	45	--	--	--
5	8	2	--	20	8	3	11	3	10	--	197	6.1	--	--
2	4	8	1	18	9	--	9	5	12	--	145	4.5	--	--
11	6	5	1	60(62)	13	--	3	2	12	--	216	6.7	--	--
4(5)	2	8(12)	2	55(57)	11	14(16)	19(20)	2	3	--	199	6.1	--	--
7	4	3	--	13	7	5	13	5	6	--	149	4.6	--	--
29	24	26	4	166	48	22	55	17	43	--	--	--	906	28.0
--	2	1	--	2	5	1	2	--	--	--	26	0.8	--	--
1	1	1	--	3	--	--	--	1	--	--	22	0.7	--	--
1	3	2	--	5	5	1	2	1	--	--	--	--	48	1.5
20	39	27	--	118	31	21	38	30	38	2	995	30.8	--	--
26	24	5	--	102	49	18	39	30	25	--	487	15.1	--	--
46	63	32	--	220	80	39	77	60	63	2	--	--	1,482	45.9
88	95	77	4	450	157	76	162	101	124	3	--	--	3,230	--
2.7	2.9	2.4	0.1	13.9	4.9	2.4	5.0	3.1	3.9	0.1	--	--	--	100.0

III. Jars

IIIA. Neck and rim fragments (figs. 199:12-21; 200:1).—(1) Vertical necks; (2) flaring necks; (3) short, straight necks with everted rims (some may be from vessels of type II); (4) neck fragments of indeterminable variety.

The three types of jar necks are illustrated. Unpainted vertical necks are rare; the tall neck was usually regarded as a suitable field for decoration, although some are simply painted all over on the outside or left with just a rim band inside and out.

The flaring necks are characteristically decorated as follows: on the inside, a rim band or a rim band with a wavy line below it; on the outside, several wide bands beginning with a rim band and culminating in a broad band at the junction of neck and shoulder. Smaller specimens are painted a solid color outside or are decorated with a rim band inside and out. One example has a solid zigzag cable just below the rim band outside.

Table 43.—Banahilk Painted Ware: Distribution of Diameters by Form Class

Diameter (mm)	IA1*	IA2*	IB*	IC*	ID*	IE*	II†	IIIA1*	IIIA2*	IIIA3*	IIIE‡	Total
40	--	--	--	--	--	--	--	--	--	--	5	5
50	--	--	--	--	--	--	--	--	--	--	3	3
60	--	--	--	--	--	--	--	--	1	--	13	14
70	--	--	--	--	1	--	1	1	--	--	6	9
80	--	--	--	--	1	--	--	--	--	--	6	7
90	--	--	--	--	--	2	1	1	--	--	4	8
100	--	--	--	--	1	10	1	2	2	--	8	24
110	--	--	--	--	--	12	3	1	1	1	3	21
120	--	--	1	--	3	6	--	--	6	1	5	22
130	--	1	2	--	3	3	2	--	2	--	3	16
140	--	--	2	--	1	7	1	1	3	1	4	20
150	--	--	--	--	1	2	--	--	--	--	1	4
160	2	--	9	--	--	7	5	1	3	2	--	29
170	--	--	--	--	--	--	1	--	1	--	--	2
180	2	--	10	--	--	1	2	--	3	3	--	21
190	1	1	5	--	--	--	--	--	1	--	--	8
200	6	7	8	1	2	1	1	--	1	--	--	27
210	4	--	1	--	--	--	--	--	--	--	--	5
220	8	3	1	--	1	--	1	--	--	2	--	16
230	4	2	--	--	--	--	--	--	--	--	--	6
240	12	4	2	1	--	--	--	--	--	--	--	19
250	7	1	--	--	--	--	--	--	--	--	--	8
260	11	4	--	--	--	--	--	--	--	--	--	15
270	1	3	--	--	--	--	--	--	--	--	--	4
280	3	--	1	1	--	--	--	--	--	--	--	5
290	4	--	--	--	--	--	--	--	--	--	--	4
300	2	--	--	--	--	--	--	--	--	1	--	3
310	--	--	--	--	--	--	--	1	--	--	--	1
320	2	1	--	--	--	--	--	--	--	--	--	3
Total (sherds)	69	27	42	3	14	51	19	8	24	11	61	329

*Rim diameter.
† Diameter at bulge (outside).
‡ Base diameter.

The vertical necks with everted flat rims seem always to have the flat top of the rim painted, with rim ticking if nothing else. The inside of the neck is usually plain, while the outside may display a solid coat of paint, or it may have bands if the neck is tall enough for these to be suitable.

IIIB. Neck/shoulder fragments.—This category consists of jar sherds from the junction of two different design fields—neck and body. The juncture is invariably marked with banding. A few of these sherds show part of the body design—for example, crosshatching, hatching between opposed wavy lines, crosshatched diamonds.

IIIC. Body sherds from large jars (fig. 200:2).—One group of fragments comes from large jars that apparently had flat bases and tall flaring necks. This form is represented by sherds only (but see the illustrated reconstruction). These sherds, usually from the body, are classified by their thickness and size and by the type of decoration. The designs are all-over or zoned and are usually executed rather boldly. The pattern of decoration on these jars (based on the illustrated jar and confirmed by sherds) was as follows: wide banding was applied to the outside of the neck from the rim to the neck/shoulder junction; another series of bands, two or three or more, was painted on the shoulder near the neck; the main design was applied over the bulge of the shoulder and down to a point about three fourths of the way to the base. This lower portion of the jar was left unpainted. The main design consisted of alternate zones of wavy lines and cables, or running crosshatched diamonds, or a bold all-over design of quatrefoils, hatched or solid checkerboard designs, solid right triangles, and the like. The illustrated vessel, for instance, has wavy lines alternating with bands. A splotchy asterisk occurred on one jar sherd, but the rest of the design was indeterminable.

IIID. Body sherds from small jars (fig. 201:1-2).—All sherds included here are from bodies of jars (perhaps of more than one type) that were apparently smaller than the vessels of the preceding group, and the sherds are thinner. Also, the decoration is much less bold. The commonest motifs are crosshatching (either all over, or in a wide zone), hatching between opposed wavy lines, and hatched cables. The area above the base was probably left unpainted.

IIIE. Bases (fig. 201:3-13).—Nearly all base fragments seem to be from jars. Large, thick sherds (e.g., fig. 201:4) may be from the large storage jars. Bases are usually flat, although there is a small ring base (fig. 201:13) and a few pedestal bases (fig. 201:14). A pedestal base occurs among the plain ware also (fig. 203:16), and pedestal bases are not unusual among Halafian vessels at other sites, for example at Arpachiyah and Tell Halaf (Mallowan and Rose 1935, fig. 65:4; Oppenheim and Schmidt 1943, pls. XXV:1,4 and XXIX:15).

IV. Miscellaneous Pieces (figs. 201:14-26; 207:3-4)

Miniature vessels (*IVA*) and lids, spouts, and other items (*IVB*) are grouped to make a miscellaneous category. As the illustrations show, miniature painted vessels were made in both bowl and jar shapes. Their functions are problematical, but at least some of them were probably toys.

One fragment of a small, platelike vessel was found in B*III*,2 (fig. 201:24). Another sherd (from D*I*,fl.6) has a small, vertically perforated lug (fig. 201:23). The illustrated spout (fig. 201:22) probably came from a rather large jar and has a clumsily painted red band around the base with another around the rim. Spouts also were found at Tell Halaf (Oppenheim and Schmidt 1943, pl. XXV:7-8,11).

There were 5 fragments of lids (fig. 201:25, an example from D*I*,2); one was apparently dome shaped (fig. 210:26, an example from B,1). Four other lid sherds were found, one each in C,3; C ext., 2; D*I*,fl.1; and D*I*,fl.6. Lids are well known from other Halafian sites such as Tell Halaf and Arpachiyah (Oppenheim and Schmidt 1943, pls. XXIII, XXIV; Mallowan and Rose 1935, fig. 58:1).

V. Body Sherds

This group comprises sherds whose form categories are indeterminable.

VA. Body sherds with paint.

VB. Body sherds without paint (i.e., unpainted parts of vessels that probably had some painted areas).

Table 44.—Distribution of Banahilk Painted Ware Designs by Form Class
(see figs. 205-6 and accompanying notes; also figs. 197-201)

Form class and design	No. of sherds
A1: ROUND-SIDED BOWLS WITH SQUARED RIMS, BANDS, AND RIM TICKING	
Bands	
Plain bands (fig. 197:1-2,4, etc.)	31
Bands alternating with wavy lines (fig. 197:3, inside)	15
Bands and rim ticking (fig. 197:1-4)	141
Bucrania (fig. 197:7)	1
Cables	
Cables with eye design and rim ticking (fig. 197:3)	1
Vertical bands and wavy lines	1
Total IA1	190
IA2. VARIANTS OF IA1	
Bands	
Plain bands	8
Bands alternating with wavy lines	13
Butterflies (figs. 197:5; 205:5a)	1
Cables (fig. 205:6)	
Cables with eye design (fig. 197:3)	1
Dotted cables (figs. 198:12; 199:5)	1
Hatched cables (fig. 205:6c)	1
Pierced cables (see note for fig. 205:6) and reserved hatched cable (fig. 205:6d), on single sherd	1
Zigzag cables (see note for fig. 205:6)	1
Checkerboard (fig. 205:7b)	1
Chevrons (figs. 198:2; 205:8)	1
Concentric designs	
Concentric arcs (fig. 205:9) (1 sherd with wavy lines also)	2
Concentric triangles (fig. 206:10)	1
Concentric zigzags (fig. 206:11)	1
Crosshatching (figs. 198:9,15,18; 199:1,4,9,12; 206:12)	1
Lines and dots (fig. 206:25)	1
Rim band inside and outside	3
Rim band and rim ticking (fig. 197:2-4)	3
Vertical lines	1
Wavy lines (figs. 198:15, inside; 200)	1
Total IA2	43

Table 44.—*Continued*

Form class and design	No. of sherds
IB. SHALLOW, ROUND-SIDED BOWLS WITH PAINTED INTERIORS	
Bands	
Plain bands	9
Bands alternating with wavy lines	7
Bands alternating with x's (fig. 205:2)	1
Bird with raised wings (fig. 198:5)	1*
Bucrania (fig. 205:4)	
Cruciform bucrania?	1
Cruciform double bucrania (figs. 197:13; 198:1)	1
Horizontal double bucrania	1*
Horizontal double pierced bucrania (fig. 197:7)	1
Horizontal single pierced bucrania	1
Butterflies (fig. 205:5c)	1
Cables (fig. 205:6)	
Open cables (fig. 205:6a) alternating with herringbone (fig. 206:20)	2
Red open cables (fig. 205:6a) alternating with black bands	1*
Red open cables (fig. 205:6a) alternating with black hatched bands (fig. 206:18)	1*
Solid cables (fig. 205:6b) alternating with hatched bands	1*
Zigzag cables (see note for fig. 205:6)	2
Checkerboard (fig. 205:7)	
Checkerboard inside, all-over spots outside	1
Checkerboard inside, lines and dots outside (see note for fig. 206:25)	1
Checkerboard of crosshatched squares alternating with xed squares (see fig. 205:7 and note)	1
Checkerboard of solid squares alternating with vertically hatched squares	1(*?)
Checkerboard of solid squares alternating with xed squares (fig. 205:7a)	1
Chevrons (figs. 198:2; 205:8)	22
Concentric designs	
Concentric arcs (fig. 205:9)	8
Concentric zigzags (fig. 206:11)	1
Crosshatching	
Plain crosshatching (figs. 198:15,18; 199:1,4,9,12; 206:12)	16
Crosshatching alternating with wavy lines	1
Diamonds (fig. 206:13)	
Running crosshatched diamonds	1
Running dotted diamonds	1
Running solid diamonds (fig. 199:8)	1
Dots	
Plain dots	3
Dots and wavy lines	1
Fish scales (fig. 206:17)	1
Hatched arcs (fig. 206:19)	1
Hatched bands (fig. 206:18)	1*
Hatching between opposed wavy lines (figs. 199:2; 206:21; 1 sherd with lines and dots outside, fig. 206:25)	2
Herringbone (figs. 197:8; 206:20)	3
Knotted lines (fig. 206:23) alternating with hatched bands (fig. 206:18)	1
Lattice	
Plain lattice (fig. 206:24)	2
Dotted lattice	1
xed lattice (fig. 206:33)	1
Quatrefoils (fig. 206:26)	
Plain quatrefoils	7
xed quatrefoils (1 sherd with crosshatching and alternating opposed triangles outside)	3
Reserved wavy lines (fig. 206:27)	14
Rings (fig. 206:29)	1
Rosettes (fig. 206:30)	9
Fringed spoke	1
Spots and dots (fig. 206:31)	1
Triangles	
Alternating opposed triangles (figs. 197:11; 206:32a)	13

Table 44.—*Continued*

Form class and design	No. of sherds
IB.—*Continued*	
Alternating opposed triangles (fig. 206:32*a*) alternating with chevrons (fig. 205:8)	1
Alternating opposed triangles (fig. 206:32*a*) alternating with hatched bands (fig. 206:18)	1
Right triangles (fig. 206:32*b*) in zones	1
Vertical bands	1
Wavy lines	6
Zigzags	
Plain zigzags (fig. 199:18)	2
Pierced zigzags (i.e., bisected by horizontal line)	1
Total IB	166
IC. FLARE-RIMMED BOWLS	
Bands	
Plain bands	1
Bands and spots (fig. 206:31)	1
Bucrania	
Horizontal bucrania	1
Vertical bucrania	1
Cables	
Dotted cables	1
Checkerboard	
Plain checkerboard (fig. 205:7*b*)	1
Checkerboard of solid squares alternating with xed squares (fig. 205:7*a*)	1*
Concentric designs	
Concentric arcs	1
Crosshatching	
Black crosshatching on all-over red paint	1*
Diamonds	
All-over crosshatched diamonds	1
Running crosshatched diamonds with solid triangle spacers (fig. 206:13*a*) (concentric arcs inside)	1
Running hatched diamonds with solid triangle spacers	1
Domes (fig. 206:14)	1*
Hatching between opposed wavy lines (fig. 206:21)	1
Herringbone	1
Quatrefoils	
xed quatrefoils (fig. 206:26)	3
Triangles	
Alternating opposed triangles (fig. 206:32*a*)	2
Vertical lines	
Short vertical lines and spots	1
Wavy lines	1
Zigzags	
Pierced zigzags	1
Total IC	23
ID. FLARE-SIDED BOWLS	
All-over paint outside (at least 2 also painted inside)	3
Checkerboard	1
Chevrons	1
Crosshatching	11
Diamonds	2
Dot circles (fig. 206:15)	1
Hatched bands	2
Reserved *x*'s (figs. 198:17; 206:28)	1
Spots and dashed lines (fig. 206:31)	1
Vertical lines	8
Wavy line at inside rim	1
Total ID	32

Table 44.—*Continued*

Form class and design	No. of sherds
IE. BOWLS WITH CURVED-IN RIMS (HOLEMOUTHS)	
All-over paint outside	2
Butterflies	
Plain butterflies (fig. 205:5*b*)	1
Alternating vertical and horizontal butterflies (fig. 205:5*c*)	1
Butterflies alternating with hatched squares	1
Cables	
Dotted cables alternating with bands and crosshatching	1*
Open cables	1
Checkerboard	
Plain checkerboard	1*
Checkerboard of crosshatched squares alternating with squares containing dotted arcs (fig. 198:20)	1
Checkerboard of diagonally hatched squares alternating with empty squares (fig. 205:7*d*)	1
Checkerboard of latticed squares alternating with squares containing butterflies	1
Checkerboard of solid squares alternating with xed squares	1
Chevrons	
Plain chevrons	10
Zones of chevrons alternating with zones of triangles	1
Concentric designs	
Concentric triangles	1
Concentric zigzags	1
Crosshatching	28
Diamonds	
Crosshatched diamonds	2
Hatching between opposed wavy lines (fig. 206:21)	14
Herringbone (fig. 206:20)	3
Lattice	
xed lattice (fig. 206:33)	1
Quatrefoils	
Plain quatrefoils	1
xed quatrefoils	1
Rim band and wavy line	1
Triangles	
Alternating opposed triangles	4
Right triangles	2
Rings (fig. 206:29)	1
Vertical lines	1
Total IE	84
II. BOWLLIKE JARS (*BÜCHSEN*)	
All-over paint inside and outside	1
Bands	1
Cables	
Solid cables alternating with hatched bands	1
Checkerboard	
Checkerboard of solid squares alternating with xed squares (fig. 205:7*a*)	1
Crosshatching	8
Diamonds	
Running dotted diamonds (figs. 198:12; 206:13*b*)	1
Running dotted diamonds alternating with zigzag or wavy line	1
Running solid diamonds (fig. 206:13*c*)	2
Hatching between opposed wavy lines	1
Herringbone (on everted rim)	1
Quatrefoils	
xed quatrefoils	2
Triangles	
Right triangles	3
Vertical bands	1
Wavy lines	1

Table 44.—Continued

Form class and design	No. of sherds

II.—*Continued*

  Zigzags
    Zigzags alternating with bands ... 1

                      Total II ... 26

IIIA1. FRAGMENTS OF VERTICAL JAR NECKS

  All-over paint outside ... 3
  Crosshatching ... 1
  Rim band ... 2
  Rim ticking ... 2

                      Total IIIA1 ... 8

IIIA2. FRAGMENTS OF FLARING JAR NECKS

  All-over paint outside (usually with rim band and wavy line inside) ... 17
  Bands
    Plain bands ... 47
    Bands and wavy lines ... 1
  Cables
    Solid zigzag cables alternating with bands ... 1
  Rim band inside and outside ... 11
  Zigzags ... 1

                      Total IIIA2 ... 78

IIIA3. FRAGMENTS OF SHORT, STRAIGHT JAR NECKS WITH EVERTED RIMS

  All-over paint outside with rim ticking ... 5
  Asterisks (fig. 205:1) ... 1
  Bands and rim ticking ... 8
  Rim design with band outside
    Alternating opposed triangles on rim ... 1
    Triangles on rim ... 4
    Zigzags on rim ... 1

                      Total IIIA3 ... 20

IIIA4. FRAGMENTS OF JAR NECKS OF INDETERMINABLE VARIETY

  All-over paint outside ... 11
  Bands
    Plain bands ... 18
    Bands and spots or dashes (fig. 206:31) ... 1
  Rings (fig. 206:29) ... 1
  Vertical lines and dots ... 1

                      Total IIIA4 ... 32

IIIB. JAR NECK/SHOULDER FRAGMENTS

  All-over paint on shoulder ... 8
  Bands
    Plain bands ... 88
    Bands and chevrons ... 1
  Crosshatching ... 6
  Diamonds
    Crosshatched diamonds ... 1
  Hatched bands (fig. 206:18) ... 1
  Hatching between opposed wavy lines (fig. 206:21) ... 1

                      Total IIIB ... 106

IIIC. BODY SHERDS FROM LARGE JARS

  Asterisks (fig. 205:1) ... 1
  Bands
    Plain bands ... 65
    Bands and wavy lines ... 7
  Boxes (fig. 205:3) ... 1

Table 44.—Continued

Form class and design	No. of sherds
IIIC.—Continued	
Butterflies	
Alternating vertical and horizontal butterflies (fig. 205:5c)	2
Cables	
Crosshatched cables	1
Fish-shaped cables (fig. 205:6e)	1
Hatched cables (fig. 205:6c)	2
Reserved hatched cables (fig. 205:6d)	1
Zigzag cables	1
Checkerboard	
Plain checkerboard	6
Plain checkerboard arranged in panels separated by wavy lines	1
Checkerboard of crosshatched squares alternating with empty squares (fig. 205:7c)	1
Checkerboard of crosshatched squares alternating with squares containing butterflies	2
Checkerboard of crosshatched squares alternating with squares containing rings	1
Checkerboard of crosshatched squares alternating with xed squares	1
Checkerboard of hatched squares alternating with xed squares	2
Checkerboard of solid squares alternating with dotted squares	1
Checkerboard of solid squares alternating with squares containing triangles	1
Checkerboard of solid squares alternating with xed squares	1
Chevrons	1
Crosshatching	5
Crosshatching between opposed wavy lines	1
Diagonal bands	1
Diamonds	
All-over dotted diamonds	1
All-over hatched diamonds	1
All-over solid diamonds (fig. 206:13d)	6
Running crosshatched diamonds	3
Running crosshatched diamonds alternating with hatched bands	1
Running hatched diamonds	2
Running solid diamonds (fig. 206:13c)	3
Hatched bands (fig. 206:18)	3
Hatching between opposed wavy lines (fig. 206:21)	1
Lattice	
xed lattice (fig. 206:33)	1
Quatrefoils	4
Triangles	
Alternating opposed triangles	4
Right triangles (about 18 sherds probably from one vessel)	33
Wavy lines	1
Total IIIC	171
IIID. BODY SHERDS FROM SMALL JARS	
Bands	
Plain bands	1
Bands and wavy lines	2
Butterflies	1
Cables	
Hatched cables	14
Pierced cables	1
Zigzag dotted cables	1
Checkerboard	
Plain checkerboard	2
Checkerboard of crosshatched squares alternating with empty squares (fig. 205:7c)	1
Checkerboard of diagonally hatched squares alternating with empty squares (fig. 205:7d)	1
Checkerboard of latticed squares alternating with xed squares	1
Checkerboard of solid squares alternating with xed squares (fig. 205:7a)	1
Chevrons	
Plain chevrons	4

Table 44.—Continued

Form class and design	No. of sherds
IIID.—Continued	
Chevrons alternating with bands	1
Chevrons alternating with zigzags	1
Concentric designs	
Concentric arcs	1
Concentric rings	3
Crosshatching	
Plain crosshatching	28
Crosshatching alternating with wavy lines	1
Dotted crosshatching	1
Zoned crosshatching	1
Crosshatching between opposed wavy lines	2
Diamonds	
All-over solid diamonds	4
Running crosshatched diamonds	3
Running crosshatched diamonds with solid triangle spacers (fig. 206:13a)	3
Running open dotted diamonds with dot spacers	3
Running solid diamonds alternating with open cable	1
Hatched bands	
Plain hatched bands	3
Hatched bands alternating with spots	1
Hatched bands alternating with x's	1
Hatching between opposed wavy lines	12
Herringbone	1
Lattice	
Crosshatched lattice	2
Dotted lattice	3
xed lattice	2
Quatrefoils	
Plain quatrefoils	6(1*)
Columns of xed quatrefoils separated by columns of alternating vertical and horizontal butterflies	1
Reserved wavy lines (1 also has crosshatched zone)	2
Reserved x's (fig. 206:28) in columns alternating with xed reserved x's	1
Rings and bands	1
Spots and bands	1
Triangles	
Alternating opposed triangles alternating with zones of crosshatching	7
Equilateral triangles	2
Right triangles	4
Zigzags	
Pierced zigzags	1
Total IIID	134
VA. BODY SHERDS	
Bands	
Plain bands	90
Bands and wavy lines	3
Butterflies	1
Cables	
Plain cables (fig. 205:6a)	5
Plain cables alternating with hatched bands	1
Fish-shaped cables (fig. 205:6e)	1
Hatched cables (fig. 205:6c)	8
Pierced cables	1
Reserved hatched cables (fig. 205:6d)	1
Zigzag cables	4
Checkerboard	
Plain checkerboard	9
Checkerboard of crosshatched squares alternating with xed squares	1

Table 44.—Continued

Form class and design	No. of sherds
VA.—Continued	
Checkerboard of solid squares alternating with xed squares	2
Chevrons	
Plain chevrons	23
Chevrons alternating with hatched bands	1
Concentric arcs	1
Crosshatching	79
Diamonds	
All-over solid diamonds	6
Crosshatched diamonds	26
Running dotted diamonds with solid triangle spacers	1
Running solid diamonds	2
Dots	
Plain dots	1
Lines and dots	2
Spots and dots (fig. 206:31)	1
Dotted rings (fig. 206:16)	1
Fish scales (fig. 206:17)	1
Hatched bands	
Plain hatched bands	4
Hatched bands alternating with dots	1
Hatched bands alternating with knotted lines	1
Hatching between opposed wavy lines	24
Herringbone	8
"Imitation *Wickelschnur*" (fig. 206:22)	2
Lattice	
xed lattice (1 with four squares per x [see design on fig. 210:1] rather than the usual one square per x [as in fig. 206:33])	2
Quatrefoils	
Plain quatrefoils	4
xed quatrefoils	4
Reserved wavy lines	2
Reserved x's (fig. 206:28)	1
Rings	2
Spots	1
Triangles	
Alternating opposed triangles	13
Right triangles	11
Wavy lines	23
Zigzags	
Plain zigzags	1
Plain zigzags alternating with crosshatching	1
Pierced zigzags	1
Zipper (fig. 206:34)	1
Total VA	379

NOTE: This table is based on a total of 1,491 sherds with classifiable designs from operations A, B, C, D, and the mound surface.
*Sherds with bichrome design.

TECHNIQUES OF MANUFACTURE AND USES OF THE PAINTED WARE VESSELS

All the painted pottery of Halafian style at Banahilk is handmade. To the naked eye, the fabric appears very similar to that found at Arpachiyah and Tilkitepe (see n. 1). The ware was made by people with excellent control over their materials; in general the vessels are well shaped, well painted, and well fired. There are certainly exceptions, however. The painted designs range from masterful to extremely poor in execution; the clay may have an excess of limestone, making it gritty, or the surface may even be marred by chaff impressions.

During the course of his studies of Banahilk pottery technology, Matson found some indication that both painted and plain wares were constructed by means of coils or slabs (see chap. 18). The sharp profiles of the flare-rimmed bowls could probably have been produced by careful work with a shaping tool similar to the potsherds and curved bits of gourd used by the Pueblo potters of the southwestern United States. The flaked sherds that are quite common at Banahilk (p. 569) might have been used for shaping pots or for scraping vessels during manufacture.

The large storage jars were apparently made in three sections: neck, body, and base. The base and body would probably have been joined first, and the neck later set into a hole of the proper diameter left for it. This latter technique is evident in several sherds, but the exact manner of joining body and base is not so obvious. Broken bases reveal a core inside—to all appearances a small inner base with a clay envelope smoothed around it. This may mean simply that this core base had been joined with the lower jar sides and the juncture made secure and invisible by smoothing clay over it, completely covering the original core base.

Spouts were inserted into holes left in the vessel walls. Clay was smoothed onto the outside at the base of the spout to hold it to the vessel.

Most of the painted pottery bowl forms were probably used in eating and drinking, the little cream bowls being perhaps an especially fancy, fragile kind of tableware. The jar forms must have been used for carrying and storing water, grain, wild seeds, fruits, and other foodstuffs. Some of these jars were equipped with lids; others intended for liquids had spouts.

PLAIN WARE (tables 45-46; figs. 202-3; 217:3-8)

The total count of prehistoric plain ware potsherds at Banahilk was 1,762; 369 sherds were from bowls, 555 were from jars, and the bowl-jar ratio was thus ca. 3:5.

The plain ware includes two basic varieties: one (type a) is chaff tempered, pale orange in color, and rough surfaced (fig. 217:4-5); the other (type b) lacks chaff and has well-smoothed (sometimes lightly burnished) brown surfaces (fig. 217:3,6-7). There are many sherds between these extremes, however. The plain ware sherds from the floor levels of operation D (a total of 361) were sorted into three fabric categories: 124 were chaff tempered (type a), 125 were not chaff tempered (type b), and 112 were indeterminate (type x). Thus, in this sample neither type a nor type b was preferred insofar as gross totals are concerned. The clay of both kinds is often dark at the center of the break, but pieces that are completely orange in section are not unusual for the chaff-filled variant.

These two plain ware varieties may perhaps be paralleled at other Halafian sites. Perkins, in referring to the results of a Harvard University survey of northern Iraq, mentions plain ware that is contemporary with Halafian painted pottery at Arpachiyah, Chagar Bazar, Tell Halaf, and other sites (Perkins 1949, p. 17). She also says that in her inspection of this plain ware she observed "numerous pieces of unpainted buff to brown pottery, sometimes quite fine in quality.... Likewise a fair amount of rough 'cooking pot' ware appears to coexist with the painted ware." Similarly, Schmidt refers to two groups of unpainted pottery at Tell Halaf: one reminiscent of the painted ware in technique and form, the other much cruder. The second or cruder type at Tell Halaf is apparently chaff filled and less well fired than the first type, "characteristisch ... ist ein mürber, etwas poröser Ton, der nicht so hart gebrannt ist ... und ist an der Oberfläche mit Strohspuren behaftet" (Oppenheim and Schmidt 1943, pp. 94-95).

Specks of lime and golden mica occur in sherds in both texture varieties at Banahilk. (See chap. 18 for a more detailed account of Banahilk plain ware technology.)

FORM CLASSES OF THE PLAIN WARE VESSELS (table 45)

The classification of forms of Banahilk plain ware pottery, like that of the painted pottery, was based almost completely on sherds because no whole vessels were found, except a miniature jar now in Baghdad (fig. 203:32). Nevertheless, a few of the vessels broken in antiquity were at least partially restorable.

I. Bowls

IA. Large, round-sided bowls (fig. 202:1-10).—(1) More open; (2) less open; (3) sides nearly vertical.
IB. Small bowls (figs. 202:11-17; 217:6-8).—(1) With flaring sides; (2) with rounded sides; (3) profile unknown.
IC. Sherds from bowls of indeterminable shape.—Probably IA or IB.
ID. Bowls and pots with curved-in rims (holemouths) (fig. 202:18-20).
IE. Deep, straight-sided bowls (fig. 202:21-24).—Bowl forms range from round-sided and flare-sided vessels to holemouth and deep, straight-sided pots (fig. 202:1-24). There are several examples of a definite ledge around the inside of a bowl just below the rim, probably to hold a lid (fig. 202:9). One bowl has an inside ledge so small that it scarcely seems functional (fig. 202:4). Ledges also occurred in some of the jar necks. Small vessels (fig. 202:11-13) were perhaps used as cups. The form of one small flared bowl (fig. 202:12) is interesting because the same profile has been found among the painted pottery (fig. 198:13). Another small vessel has a serviceable lug, perhaps indicating that something was heated in it (fig. 202:17).

There is a small group of deep, straight-sided bowls (IE) with lugs that appear to be similar to the "milk jars" at Hassuna, Matarrah, and al-Khan (Lloyd and Safar 1945, pl. XII:2 and fig. 3:7; Braidwood, Braidwood, et al. 1952, fig. 11:2; for al-Khan see this volume, chap. 20). It is impossible to determine from the Banahilk sherds whether these vessels were oval in plan as the Hassuna ones were. One example of the deep, straight-sided bowls has a squared rim (fig. 202:21).

Table 45.—Banahilk

Form class	Surface	A	B	C,1	C,2	C,3	C,4	C,5	C,6	C,7	C ext.,1	DI,1-2	DI,2	DI,fl.1	DI,fl.2
IA1	2	--	5	1	--	6	--	--	1	1	1	5	6	1	--
IA2	4	--	34(35)	2	2(3)	20(21)	1	--	1?	1(2)	2	13(24)	28(31)	3	--
IA3	1	--	13(17)	2	2	8(9)	1	--	1	1	6	--	11	1	--
Total IA	7	--	52	5	4	34	2	--	3	3	9	18	45	5	--
IB1	1	1	2	--	--	--	--	--	1	--	--	--	2	--	--
IB2	1	--	3	--	1	3	--	--	--	--	--	4	1	--	--
IB3	--	--	1	--	--	2	--	--	--	--	--	1	--	--	--
Total IB	2	1	6	--	1	5	--	--	1	--	--	5	3	--	--
Total IC	--	--	2	--	3	3	--	--	--	--	--	--	--	--	--
Total ID	--	--	17	1?	1	15	2	--	2	--	1	5	3	--	1
Total IE	1	--	--	2	--	--	--	--	--	--	--	--	--	--	--
Total I	10	1	77	8	9	57	4	--	6	3	10	28	51	5	1
Total IIA	5	--	29(33)	3	2	9	1	1	2	1	4	17	24(25)	6	1
Total IIB	1	--	3	--	2	16	1	--	--	--	1	7(59)	10(17)	1	--
Total IIC	--	--	16(18)	4	6(7)	22(23)	4	--	1	--	1	6	10	7	--
Total IID	2	--	31	11	4	32	2	3(5)	1	1	6	4	30(59)	--	2
Total II	8	--	79	18	14	79	8	4	4	2	12	34	74	14	3
Total III	1	--	2	--	--	1	--	1(2)	--	--	--	1	1	--	--
Total IVA	--	--	2	1	2	3	--	--	1	--	--	--	--	--	--
Total IVB	4	1	7	--	2	7	--	--	1	1	1	5	9	1	--
Total IV	4	1	9	1	4	10	--	--	2	1	1	5	9	1	--
Total V	4	--	55(56)	24	15	53(55)	--	1	4	2	3	18	51(52)	7	1
Grand total	27	2	222	51	42	200	12	6	16	8	26	86	186	27	5
%	1.5	0.1	12.6	2.9	2.4	11.3	0.7	0.3	0.9	0.4	1.5	4.9	10.6	1.5	0.3

NOTE: When two or more sherds join they are counted as one, but the total number of fragments is given in parentheses.

II. Jars

IIA. Wide-mouthed, short-necked jars (fig. 202:25-32).—This group comprises sloping-shouldered jars that often have sturdy lugs just below the neck. No whole vessel exists in this group, but there are enough pieces of two or three examples to indicate the sloping-shouldered profile, quite unlike the sharply defined shoulders of the painted jars. It is probable that the profiles of this category differed from those of the plain ware category IIB (see below), although there are no pieces large enough to demonstrate this conclusively. The ledge in one jar neck seems to have been continuous around the inside and was perforated, presumably to permit tying on a lid (fig. 202:26). The squared rims on several examples (fig. 202:30,32) may be compared with the squared rims characteristic of round-sided painted ware bowls.

IIB. Jars with flaring necks (fig. 203:1-7).—This category is represented in the present Banahilk sherd collection by rim fragments only. The necks are taller than those of wide-mouthed jars. The necks may also be proportionately narrower than those of the wide-mouthed jars at the point where the profile draws in near the shoulder junction.

IIC. Neck/shoulder fragments (whether from jar form IIA or IIB cannot be determined).

IID. Bases (fig. 203:8-16).—These examples simply illustrate the range of variation in base profile. No *certain* correlation between any of these profiles and the two jar classes (IIA and IIB) can be established because no whole vessels were found. However, in a few cases several pieces of smashed pots were found in a single provenience unit, and the following relationships were noted: one reconstructed wide-mouthed jar with rounded base was found in DI,fl.7; and 2 reconstructed examples of a flaring-necked jar with a sharper profile at the base were found in DI,2.

Because jar bases often seem to have been made separately from jar bodies, one cannot say for certain that a base

Plain Ware Sherds

DI,fl.3	DI,fl.4	DI,fl.5	DI,feat.1	DI,fl.6	DI,fl.7	DII,1-2	DII,2	DIIS	DIIN	Total	%	Grand total	%
--	--	--	--	4	3	2	--	--	--	38	--	--	--
1	2	2	1(2)	18	10	4	3	3	3	158	--	--	--
--	--	1	--	1	1	--	--	2	1	53	--	--	--
1	2	3	1(2)	23	14	6	3	5	4	249	14.1	--	--
--	--	--	--	1	--	1	--	--	--	9	--	--	--
--	--	--	--	2	--	1	--	--	1	17	--	--	--
--	--	--	--	1	--	--	--	--	2	7	--	--	--
--	--	--	--	4	--	2	--	--	3	33	1.9	--	--
--	--	--	--	--	--	--	3	1	--	12	0.7	--	--
--	--	--	--	4	1	4	4	1	3	65	3.7	--	--
1	1	1	--	4	--	--	--	--	--	10	0.6	--	--
2	3	4	1	35	15	12	10	7	10	--	--	369	21.0
5	2	3	--	11	13	1	6(7)	3	7(32)	156	8.9	--	--
3	--	3	--	9	1	--	2	--	2	62	3.5	--	--
6	1	--	--	16	7	8	3	6	3	127	7.2	--	--
4	2	5	--	25	14	2	20(21)	5(7)	4	210	11.9	--	--
18	5	11	--	61	35	11	31	14	16	--	--	555	31.5
--	--	1?	--	2	--	--	2(14)	--	1	--	--	13	0.7
--	--	--	--	1	--	--	--	--	--	10	0.6	--	--
--	--	2	--	4	2	2	5	2	--	56	3.2	--	--
--	--	2	--	5	2	2	5	2	--	--	--	66	3.7
62	25	--	--	150	48	42	137(138)	48(50)	9(10)	--	--	759	43.1
82	33	18	1	253	100	67	185	71	36	--	--	1,762	
4.7	1.9	1.0	0.1	14.4	5.7	3.8	10.5	4.0	2.0	--	--	--	100.0

that is well smoothed inside belonged to a bowl. The jar base could have been smoothed before it was joined with the jar body.

The heeled base (fig. 203:11-12) occurs at Matarrah (Braidwood, Braidwood, et al. 1952, p. 12, fig. 10:21), probably at Hassuna (Lloyd and Safar 1945, fig. 6:7, and see mention of ogee curves to the base, p. 277), and at Ali Agha (see chap. 20).

There is one complete example of a high pedestal base (fig. 203:16). Such a base, higher than this one, occurred at Matarrah (Braidwood, Braidwood, et al. 1952, fig. 16:5), and pedestals are not uncommon in Halafian painted pottery.

III. Trays (fig. 203:17-18)

The Banahilk trays are large, low-walled, oval vessels, quite plain inside (i.e., definitely not of the husking-tray type). One nearly completely restorable example was found (fig. 203:18); this tray measured 260 × 180 mm.

Trays also occur at Jarmo, Ali Agha, al-Khan, Matarrah (Braidwood, Braidwood, et al. 1952, p. 11, fig. 9:11-13), and Hassuna (Lloyd and Safar 1945, pl. XIV, bottom right). Painted as well as plain ware trays were found at Arpachiyah (Mallowan and Rose 1935, figs. 69:2; 79:6).

IV. Miscellaneous Pieces (figs. 203:19-34; 217:3)

Miscellaneous pieces include such items as miniature vessels (IVA) and a variety of other objects (IVB) including lugs and spouts broken from their vessels in antiquity and lids. Most of the lugs probably belonged to wide-mouthed jars (several such vessels had lugs or stumps of lugs still in place). No sherd identified as a flaring-necked jar has been found with a lug. Another type of vessel that may have had lugs is the bowl with curved-in rim. Whenever the orientation of the lugs could be determined, they pointed nearly straight out or slightly upward.

The miniatures (fig. 203:25-27,32) are not very common, but the category includes one complete small jar (fig. 203:32). There is a small heeled bowl (fig. 203:25) that is paralleled rather closely by one from Ali Agha.

There are 21 lids. Those illustrated represent three different varieties, but the forms shown in figure 203:29-30 are unusual, whereas the one in figure 203:28 is the common type. It is possible that a few lids might have been classified as bowls if only a small part of the rim had been present. The object depicted in figure 203:30 was probably originally intended to be completely perforated, perhaps so that it could be tied on, but the perforation as found was incomplete. Plain ware lids also occurred at Tell Halaf (Oppenheim and Schmidt 1943, pl. XXXIII:11-12).

Figure 203:33 shows a sherd with several small holes punched partially through it. The holes are arranged in a circular scatter. Figure 203:31, from C,3, shows a fragmentary spout.

Figure 203:34 depicts a sherd with a vertical lug so small that it would hardly have been very useful. Such a lug is unusual because most of the other Banahilk examples are sturdy and were apparently quite functional (fig. 203:19-24). A total of 25 plain ware lugs was recorded.

Techniques of Manufacture and Uses of the Plain Ware Vessels

The Banahilk plain ware is all handmade. The wide-mouthed jars (IIA) seem to have been made in two sections, body and base. The base disk was perhaps joined to the body in the same manner as for the painted jars. The large lugs were apparently attached as follows: a round hole was left in the side of the jar, a cylindrical core was inserted there, and its juncture on the inside of the vessel smoothed down; then, outside, a lump of clay was molded over the projecting core and smoothed into the sides of the jar, forming the completed lug (fig. 217:3).

Plain ware jars with flaring necks seem to have been made in three sections—neck, body, and base—as were the painted jars also. There are indications, however, that the neck-shoulder junction was made in a different way from that used for the square-shouldered painted jars. With the less sharply shouldered plain ware jars, the potter seems to have simply joined the neck and shoulder pieces somewhere below the base of the neck proper. Two or three examples of sherds from the shoulder region of plain ware jars show grooves, which may indicate a tongue-and-groove type of juncture, over which clay from the neck portion was smoothed both inside and outside the body portion.

The plain ware bowls were doubtless all-purpose dipping, serving, eating, and drinking vessels. Wide-mouthed jars probably represent cooking and storage vessels. They seem often to have had lids, whereas there is no evidence that lids were ever used on flaring-necked jars. The sturdy lugs characteristic of wide-mouthed jars would also be useful on cooking pots for lifting them when hot. Flaring-necked jars were probably used for storage, and perhaps for cooking or for holding water as well. The jar bases found are not charred or scorched on the outside but are often well blackened on the inside.

The trays might have been useful for serving large amounts of meat and vegetables, as trays are used in the Near East today for carrying rice and meat to diners.

The miniatures were probably toys.

Interrelations of the Plain and Painted Wares

Both the main forms of plain ware—bowls and jars—often have squared rims, a feature characteristic of some of the round-sided painted bowls. Such rims are seen more frequently in the latter type of vessel.

The flare-sided, cuplike vessel profile (fig. 202:12) appears in both plain and painted ware at Banahilk. Some of the small plain ware bowls with curved-in rims parallel in profile some examples of the painted ware (fig. 199:1,3).

Functions of plain and painted ware vessels at this site probably overlapped to some extent. Jars of both wares must have been used for storage and for carrying water, and bowls of both wares must have been used in serving and eating of food. However, probably only plain ware pots were used for cooking food.

External Relations of the Plain Ware

The chaff-filled variant of Banahilk plain ware looks, macroscopically, very similar to the Ali Agha and al-Khan plain ware. That the relationship is more than just a superficial resemblance due to both wares being coarse and chaff filled is perhaps indicated by a few parallels in forms, which have been mentioned above (pp. 563, 565): the heeled bases and the miniature heeled vessel, the tray form, and probably the "milk jar." These parallels from Ali Agha and al-Khan forms tie the Banahilk plain ware into the complex of coarse wares from Hassuna, Matarrah, and Jarmo and substantiate Caldwell's suggestion (cf. fig. 106) of a continuity of this tradition from Jarmo to Hassuna and later.

The plain ware from the Halafian levels at Arpachiyah is not described in detail (Mallowan and Rose 1935, p. 172, fig. 79), but there are certainly parallels in form with the Banahilk plain ware. Small, cuplike bowls, the jars, and the trays from Banahilk resemble vessels from Arpachiyah (Mallowan and Rose 1935, fig. 79:1,4-6).

The forms of the illustrated examples of plain ware (*unbemalte Keramik*) from Tell Halaf (Oppenheim and Schmidt 1945, pls. XXXIII, CIII-CIV) do not parallel those of Banahilk closely, but simple collared jars like some from Tell Halaf (Oppenheim and Schmidt 1943, pl. XXXIII:8,10) do occur at Banahilk, as do round-sided bowls (Oppenheim and Schmidt 1943, pl. XXXIII:16).

Table 46.—Banahilk Plain Ware: Distribution of Diameters by Form Class

Diameter (mm)	IA1*	IA2*	IA3*	IB1*	IB2*	ID*	IE*	IIA*	IIB*	IID†	Total
50	--	--	--	--	--	--	--	1	--	4	5
70	--	--	--	--	--	--	--	--	--	--	0
80	--	--	--	--	1	3	--	6	--	8	18
90	--	--	--	2	--	--	--	--	--	4	6
100	--	--	--	2	--	2	--	3	1	10	18
110	--	--	--	--	--	3	--	2	--	9	14
120	1	1	1	2	1	4	--	4	2	4	20
130	--	1	--	--	--	3	--	2	2	3	11
140	1	2	6	--	--	2	--	14	7	2	34
150	1	2	--	--	--	2	--	5	--	1	11
160	--	3	6	--	--	2	--	5	2	1	19
170	--	4	1	--	--	--	--	3	1	2	11
180	1	4	2	--	--	1	--	4	2	--	14
190	--	6	1	--	--	1	--	3	1	--	12
200	--	7	2	--	--	1	--	7	2	2	21
210	1	5	3	--	--	1	--	2	--	--	12
220	2	7	3	--	--	1	--	1	2	2	18
230	--	6	1	--	--	--	1	2	--	2	12
240	2	4	2	--	--	1	--	--	3	1	13
250	--	5	2	--	--	--	--	1	--	--	8
260	1	2	--	--	--	--	--	--	1	--	4
270	--	2	--	--	--	1	--	1	--	--	4
280	1	3	--	--	--	--	--	1	--	--	5
290	--	2	--	--	--	--	--	--	1	--	3
300	1	--	--	--	--	--	--	--	--	--	1
310	2	1	--	--	--	--	--	--	--	--	3
320	1	1	--	--	--	--	--	--	--	--	2
330	1	2	--	--	--	--	--	--	--	--	3
340	1	--	--	--	--	--	--	--	--	--	1
350	--	2	--	--	--	--	--	--	--	--	2
360	--	--	--	--	--	--	--	--	--	--	0
370	--	--	--	--	--	--	--	--	--	--	0
380	--	--	--	--	--	--	--	--	--	--	0
390	--	--	--	--	--	--	--	--	--	--	0
400	--	1	--	--	--	--	--	--	--	--	1
410	--	1	--	--	--	--	--	--	--	--	1
Total (sherds)	17	74	30	6	2	28	1	67	27	55	307

*Rim diameter.
†Base diameter.

NON-HALAFIAN POTTERY (figs. 204, 216)

In operations A, B, TT, and W, we found 567 sherds of non-Halafian wheel-made fine ware and handmade coarse ware. Because the great majority of pottery found with and near the stone walls of operation A was non-Halafian, it seems likely that these architectural remains are also non-Halafian. But this non-Halafian pottery is by no means a homogeneous lot. A few of the pieces represent types distinctive enough that Rudolph Dornemann, curator of Old World Archaeology, Milwaukee Public Museum, was able to give them at least approximate time ranges (pers. comm.), and these ranges are rather widely separated. Dornemann assigns a few pieces to the early Hellenistic period (figs. 204:13,16-17; 216:1,11), some to the Iron Age (figs. 204:2-4,6,10-11,19-20; 216:2,4,6,8-9), and others to the early second millennium B.C. (figs. 204:5,7,9,14-15; 216:5,7,10). Thus, this material represents a considerable mixture of chronological periods.

POTTERY OBJECTS (table 47; figs. 207:1-2,6; 208:1-11; 217:1-2)

This artifact grouping includes worked sherds of various kinds, spindle whorls, and sieves or strainers, as well as a series of miscellaneous terra-cotta items. The most numerous objects are worked sherds. Halafian painted pottery lends itself admirably to reworking, and many sherds are chipped, ground, or perforated. (Findspots not mentioned in the text are given in table 47.)

Table 47.—Banahilk Pottery Objects

	Surface A	B	C,1	C,3	C,4	C,5	CI	DI,sf	DI,1-2	DI,2	DI,fl.1	DI,fl.2	DI,fl.3	DI,fl.4	DI,fl.6	DII,1-2	DII,2	DII,N	DII,S	TT	Total
Chipped bowl sherds	--	1	--	--	--	1	--	--	--	4	1	--	2	--	1	--	--	--	1	--	10
Chipped jar sherds	--	--	--	--	--	--	--	--	2	7	2	1	--	--	2	1	2	1	--	--	18
Chipped and ground sherds	--	--	--	--	--	--	--	--	--	--	--	--	1	1	--	--	--	--	1	--	3
Ground sherds	--	2	--	--	--	--	--	--	--	1	1	--	--	--	--	--	--	--	--	--	4
Unperforated plain ware disks	1 (40)	4 (40-95)	--	1 (45)	--	--	1 (45)	--	--	2 (45-50)	--	--	--	--	1 (45)	--	--	--	--	--	10
Unperforated painted ware disks	1 (25)	--	1 (40)	--	--	--	--	--	3 (20-40)	7 (20-100)	3 (25)	3 (20-60)	--	--	--	--	2 (40-50)	--	--	--	20
Perforated plain ware disks	--	--	--	--	--	--	--	--	--	--	--	--	--	--	--	--	--	--	1 (20)	--	1
Perforated painted ware disks	--	1 (20)	--	--	--	--	1 (30)	1 (15)	5 (15-25)	2 (15-30)	3 (15-25)	1 (15)	1 (25)	--	--	--	--	--	1 (20)	--	16
Pottery disks, large central perforation	1	2	1	1	--	--	--	--	3	1	--	--	--	1	--	--	1	1	1	1	13
Biconical whorls	--	--	--	--	--	--	--	--	1	1	--	--	--	--	--	--	--	--	--	1	3
Concave-based whorls	--	--	--	--	--	--	--	--	--	2	--	--	--	--	--	--	--	--	1	--	3
Sievelike objects	--	1	--	--	1	--	--	--	2	1	1	1	--	--	--	1	--	--	--	--	7
Baked clay ovals	--	--	--	--	--	--	--	--	1	--	--	--	--	--	1	1	--	--	--	--	5
Total	2	11	2	2	1	1	2	1	17	28	11	7	4	2	5	3	5	2	5	1	113

NOTE: Figures alone = no. of examples; figures in parentheses = dimensions in mm.

Worked Sherds (figs. 208:1-3; 217:1-2)

There are 29 pottery fragments that have been flaked to an edge, much as though they were flint (figs. 208:1; 217:1-2). The majority show no drastic edge wear, although all show wear to some degree. They may have been potters' implements for working clay (see Guthe 1925, p. 27, pl. 11). Some examples seem to have been present at Tell Halaf (Oppenheim and Schmidt 1943, pls. LV:6; LIX:7). Ten of the Banahilk chipped sherds are fragments of round-sided bowls and 18 are jar body sherds.

Seven body sherds show grinding on one or more edges. One of these sherds was ground on all surfaces so that most of the paint was removed. Another has one edge ground to a neat bevel.

There are 32 pottery fragments that have been chipped or ground to discoid shapes (fig. 208:2-3) and range from 23 to 95 mm in diameter. Both plain and painted sherds were used. What these objects may have been is not clear, but very similar disks are often found in prehistoric sites in the southwestern United States (e.g., Kidder 1932, p. 146, fig. 128). Both the plain ware and painted ware disks have been chipped into shape.

Also found were 2 unperforated disks of non-Halafian ware, both ground into shape. One (70 mm in diameter) is from the surface of operation A and is a portion of a wheel-made vessel. The other (25 mm in diameter) is from A*II*,3. It is chipped into shape and has an incomplete perforation.

One incompletely perforated plain ware disk, chipped into shape, was found.

There are 16 perforated or semiperforated painted ware disks that range in size from 15 to 30 mm. In all but 4 examples the perforations are complete. The majority of the edges are ground and the rest are chipped.

The final group comprises 13 small disks in which the central perforation is large in proportion to the disk as a whole. Most of these are reworked bits of potsherd, but a few were modeled in wet clay and then fired (fig. 208:6).

Other Pottery Objects (figs. 207:1-2,6; 208:4-11)

Besides the worked sherds of various categories discussed above, several other kinds of pottery objects occurred. Three biconical spindle whorls were found (fig. 208:7-8), as well as 7 fragments of sievelike objects (figs. 207:2; 208:10). The latter are small disks, perhaps 40-50 mm in diameter, judging from the only nearly complete one. They were perforated several times with holes bored from both sides. On one specimen the holes were punched in the wet clay before firing rather than being drilled after firing. Whether these were really sieves is not known.

Fragments of 5 very thin baked clay ovals (figs. 207:6; 208:11) make up another rather problematic group. They are no more than 3-4 mm thick and are 50-60 mm in length and breadth. All but one have four small punched perforations each, two at each end. The exception has one perforation at each end. All but one of these objects have impressions on the surfaces, apparently of the palms of the hands that molded them.

Three funnellike objects (fig. 208:9), probably concave-based spindle whorls, were found.

Among the miscellaneous pottery and clay objects recovered is a pottery cylinder (fig. 207:1) of hard orange clay, which is like the clay of the painted pottery. It is broken, and the maximum length now is about 35 mm, the diameter about 15 mm. Its provenience is mound surface. A baked clay ball about 35 mm in diameter was found in TT. There are 3 pieces of unbaked clay: 1 small amorphous lump from D*I*,fl.2; 1 triangular-sectioned piece from operation B about 25 mm long by 88 mm wide with several impressions, perhaps of straws or small reeds, on two surfaces; and 1 broken cylinder from D*I*,1-2 about 30 mm in diameter and 20 mm long. A small unbaked clay barrel bead was found in C,4, and 1 short cylindrical bead of vitrified clay occurred in D*I*,fl.6.

Eighteen irregular pieces of fired clay containing chaff occurred in A*I*,2. Two unfired clay feet or supports were also found in operation A (A*I*,3 and A*I*,4). These look very much like the feet of the mud flour bins used in some local villages today and may be quite recent in origin. Also from A*I*,4 are 7 pieces of unfired clay, each about 50 mm thick. One surface of each piece is fairly smooth and shows marks from having been wiped. The other surface is not smoothed. These pieces may have been part of a clay flooring or the plaster of a storage pit. On the surface of the mound was found a broken pottery shovel or scoop, which is 160 mm long and 140 mm wide at the widest point; the handle, 40 mm thick, was broken off.

Some of the pottery objects from Banahilk are paralleled rather closely by examples from Tell Halaf, such as the chipped sherds (Oppenheim and Schmidt 1943, pls. LV:6; LIX:7), perforated disks with ground edges (Oppenheim and Schmidt 1943, pl. CXIII:27-28 [29 is apparently both chipped and ground]), rings (Oppenheim and Schmidt 1943, pls. LXIII:13-21; XXXVII:12-22 [12-14 are painted, unlike any of this type from Banahilk]) and funnellike objects (Oppenheim and Schmidt 1943, pl. XXXVIII:23). Schmidt suggests that these funnellike objects may be spindle whorls (Oppenheim and Schmidt 1943, p. 134). Spindle whorls of baked clay are known from several Halafian sites and some are comparable to those from Banahilk (Mallowan and Rose 1935, fig. 49:15; Mallowan 1933, pl. LXIX:8-10; and see Tobler 1950, p. 168).

Chipped Stone Industry (table 48; figs. 212-15)

Of the total of 1,896 pieces of chert and obsidian recovered from Banahilk, only 730, or 39%, including cores and core fragments, are clearly utilized, definitely retouched, or made into recognizable tools. The definitely retouched and recognizable tool categories are only one half of the 730 total (about 377 pieces, or 20% of the 1,896 total). These figures may be compared with those for Matarrah, where, in a similar type of chipped stone industry, recognizable tools and pieces with definite retouch made up slightly less than 5% of the total Chicago sample, but 80% of the total showed signs of use (Braidwood, Braidwood, et al. 1952, p. 19). In the small sample from Ali Agha (approximately 500 flint and obsidian pieces), roughly 50% were unused and unrecognizable as tools (see chap. 20).

Chert

Cores (figs. 212; 213:1).—Except for one bladelet core (fig. 213:1), the cores are all flake cores with one or two main striking platforms (fig. 212). A few have more than two platforms, and on such cores flakes seem to have been taken off all around the core perimeter wherever possible. The platforms seem not to have been prepared prior to striking off the flakes; instead, use was made of fortuitous platforms that were sometimes a part of the original pebble surface or were formed during the flaking process.

Table 48.—Banahilk

Type of specimen	Surface	TT	A	B	C,1	C,2	C,3	C,4	C,5	C,6	C,7	C ext.,1	D*I*	D*I*,1-2
CHERT														
Flake cores	3	--	5	2	3	--	5	1	2	--	--	--	9	4
Bladelet core fragments	--	--	--	--	--	--	--	--	--	--	--	--	--	--
Core fragments	--	--	1	--	--	--	--	--	--	--	--	--	--	1
Utilized flakes	13	2	8	6	7	2	20	--	3	--	2	1	8	10
Scrapers	4	--	--	1	--	--	--	--	--	--	--	--	--	--
Blade fragments	4^a	--	1^b	2^c 1^d	--	1^e	3^f	--	--	--	--	--	2^g	--
Bladelike flakes	1^b	--	--	--	--	--	--	--	1^c	--	--	--	4^i	3^c
Sickle flints	--	--	5	6	1	1	4	--	--	--	--	1	3	3
Unutilized flakes and chips	26	3	75	58	19	12	85	22	6	2	8	4	70	84
Microflints*	--	--	1	1	--	--	2	--	--	--	--	--	3	3
Miscellaneous†	--	--	--	4	1	--	1	--	--	--	--	1	6	2
Total chert	51	5	96	81	31	16	120	23	12	2	10	7	105	110
OBSIDIAN														
Utilized blades														
Chipping on bulbar face	6	--	3	2	--	--	--	--	1	2	--	--	1	2
Chipping on upper face	5^k	2^m	7^m	1	--	1	--	--	--	1	--	--	--	5
Chipping on both faces on one or both edges	6^l	--	1	1	--	2	--	--	--	1	--	--	6	--
Alternate-opposite chipping	2	--	1	--	2	--	1	--	--	1	--	--	3	1
End chipping	1	--	--	1	--	--	--	--	--	--	--	1°	1	1
Only slightly utilized	--	--	--	--	2	--	5	1	1^n	1	--	--	--	--
Unutilized blades	--	--	1	1	1	--	1	--	--	--	--	--	3	6
Utilized bladelets	--	--	--	--	--	--	--	--	--	--	--	--	--	--
Unutilized bladelets	--	--	1	1	--	--	--	--	--	--	--	--	--	--
Utilized flakes	15	--	2	--	--	1	4	3	1	--	--	--	3	3
Unutilized flakes	9	--	18	10	3	4	23	3	--	5	1	5	23	23
Miscellaneous‡	2	--	--	--	--	--	1	--	--	1	--	--	--	--
Total obsidian	46	2	35	16	8	8	35	7	3	12	1	6	40	41
Grand total	97	7	131	97	39	24	155	30	15	14	11	13	145	151

NOTES

*Microliths: A*III*,3—drill; B,1—lunate; C,3—1 *petit tranchet*, 1 doubly-pointed piece (fig. 213:9); D,1—1 drill, 2 possible scrapers; D*I*,1-2—all *petits tranchets*; D*I*,2—3 *petits tranchets*, 1 stubby micropoint, 1 broken drill?; D*I*,fl.7—1 *petit tranchet*, 1 drill fragment?: D*I*/N—*petit tranchet*.

†Miscellaneous Chert: B,1—flake with notch worked into end opposite bulb; B*I*-*II*,2—bladelike flake with traces of adhesive over most of surface; B*I*-*II*,3—pebble fragment with two or three flakes knocked off it, possibly core; B*III*,2—core revival flake?; C,1—drill (fig. 213:10); C,3—rodlike piece of chipped chert; C ext.,1—fabricator?; D*I*—3 large flakes and 1 smaller flake that may be core trimming debris, 1 utilized flake with notch on one edge, 1 possible burin; D*I*,1-2—1 possible drill, 1 burin?; D*I*,2—1 flake with "nose" produced by notching, 1 small chert point, 1 small flake with oblique retouch producing two shallow notches near one end; D*I*,1-2—3 flakes with traces of adhesive but no sheen, 1 tip end of possible blade, 1 possible burin, 1 flake with long shallow notch worked into one side; D*II*,2—1 drill (fig. 213:11), 1 flake with much adhesive but no sheen, 4 retouched flakes (1 possibly broken drill, 1 possibly fragment of *petit tranchet*, 1 with alternate-opposite edge chipping, 1 partially backed).

‡Miscellaneous Obsidian: sf—2 unutilized bladelike spalls; C,3—drill; C,6—point?; D*I*,2—1 brown and black retouched blade fragment, 1 notched blade, 1 serrated blade, 1 steeply retouched blade.

The source of raw material was probably the wadi bed, where there are chert pebbles that have washed down from the mountains. The chert ranges in color from green to bluish gray, gray black, white, red, or brown. The flakes were taken off with no great care, the only necessity apparently being the need for a sharp edge. Hinge fractures are frequently seen.

Utilized and retouched flakes (figs. 213:10-12; 214:1-3).—The flakes all show some degree of chipping on one or more edges, indicating that they had probably been used in some way, perhaps once or a few times as a cutting tool, and then discarded. The amount of edge wear is often very slight, and no example is really heavily chipped. There are, however, a few flakes besides those discussed below that were retouched to serve specific functions (fig. 213:10-11).

Sickle flints (fig. 213:2-6).—The criterion for calling a piece of flint or chert a sickle flint was the presence of sheen on both faces of an edge. In many cases the pieces with sheen also showed traces of a black substance, which was probably a hafting adhesive of some sort, most likely bitumen. Sickle flints were made on ordinary flakes or on

Chipped Stone

DI,2	DI,fl.1	DI,fl.2	DI,fl.3	DI,fl.4	DI,fl.5	DI,fl.6	DI,fl.7	DII,1-2	DII,2	DIIS	DIIN	W 2x6	Total	% chert or % obsidian
6	1	--	1	--	--	--	1	5	2	--	2	1	53	3.95
1	--	--	--	--	--	--	--	--	--	--	--	--	1	0.07
5	--	--	--	--	2	--	--	3	1	--	--	--	13	0.97
65	6	--	3	--	1	2	1	8	9	2	10	14	203	15.13
6	--	--	--	--	--	--	--	--	--	--	--	--	11	0.82
12[h]	--	--	--	--	--	--	2[b]	--	--	--	--	--	28	2.09
26[j]	1[c]	1[b]	--	--	1[b]	--	--	--	1[b]	--	--	--	39	2.91
21	1	1	1	1	--	--	1	8	1	1	2	1	63	4.69
158	22	5	5	4	7	4	6	96	57	10	14	20	882	65.72
5	--	--	--	--	--	--	2	--	--	--	1	--	18	1.34
3	--	--	--	--	--	--	--	6	7	--	--	--	31	2.31
308	31	7	10	5	11	6	13	126	78	13	29	36	1,342	100.00
19	2	1	--	--	--	--	--	--	--	--	--	--	39	
34	4	4	--	--	--	--	3	2	3	1	2	1	76	
24	2	2	--	--	--	--	--	6	4	--	--	1	56	38.40
4	--	1	1	--	--	--	--	1	1	--	--	--	19	
--	2	--	--	--	--	--	--	--	1[p]	--	--	--	8	
--	--	--	--	1	1	--	--	--	2	--	1	--	15	
22	4	2	1	1	2	--	2	--	5	1	--	--	53	9.60
--	--	--	--	--	--	2	--	--	--	--	--	--	2	1.10
--	--	--	--	--	--	2	--	--	--	--	--	--	4	
20	--	1	--	--	2	--	3	5	5	--	2	3	73	13.20
41	2	4	--	1	3	--	1	14	5	--	--	3	201	36.30
4	--	--	--	--	--	--	--	--	--	--	--	--	8	1.40
168	16	15	2	3	8	4	9	28	26	2	5	8	554	100.00
476	47	22	12	8	19	10	22	154	104	15	34	44	1,896	

KEY

[a] All utilized, 1 possibly a sickle flint (traces of adhesive but no sheen)
[b] Utilized
[c] Unutilized
[d] See fig. 215:4
[e] Backed (see fig. 214:7)
[f] Poor ones
[g] 1 utilized, 1 with nibbled retouch around two sides and one end
[h] 5 utilized, 4 unutilized, 3 indeterminate
[i] 2 utilized, 2 unutilized
[j] 11 utilized, 12 unutilized, 3 indeterminate
[k] 1 brown and black
[l] 1 transparent
[m] 1 with end chipping also
[n] Transparent
[o] Notched
[p] On both ends

bladelike flakes (fig. 213:2-3,5). Occasionally a true blade (fig. 213:4,6) was used. No flint or chert blade cores were found, however, and fragments that can be attributed to blades are rare. Nevertheless, there is one fragment of what seems to be a bladelet core (fig. 213:1), and fragments of obsidian blades occur frequently.

The sickle flakes are sometimes backed in a casual way, presumably to make them fit more firmly into the haft. The backing is not precise or particularly neat, but does serve to position the hafted edge at more of a right angle to the long axis of the flake. Some of the sickle armatures were apparently selected from flakes with naturally steep backs. To judge from the pattern of adhesive traces on some of them, these flakes were embedded quite deeply in the haft so that only half or less of the flake was free.

We do not know whether the Banahilk implements were curved sickles as some of the Jarmo and Hassuna ones apparently were (fig. 123; Lloyd and Safar 1945, fig. 37) or whether they were straight harvesting knives like the early Egyptian and Palestinian examples (Caton-Thompson and Gardner 1934, pls. XXVIII:1-2 and XXX:1; Garrod and Bate 1937, pl. XIII:1).

Bladelike flakes (fig. 214:5-6).—These relatively long and narrow flakes are too irregular in shape or dimensions to fit the definition of blades.

Blades (figs. 213:4,6; 214:4,7).—Undeniable examples of true chert blades are not common at Banahilk. "True blade" is used here to indicate a neat, straight-edged, parallel-sided flint that is at least twice as long as it is wide and has a small bulb of percussion at one end.

Microliths (fig. 213:7-9).—Microliths make up a small but very interesting group. The characteristic example is a small triangular or trapezoidal point with retouched tang and sharp transverse cutting edge (fig. 213:7). These are similar in appearance to the trapezoids or microtransverse arrowheads (*petits tranchets*) of the European mesolithic (Clark 1936, fig. 51), and an unretouched variant is also known from early dynastic Egypt. (Large metal chisel-ended arrow tips were apparently used in Europe until a few hundred years ago; at any rate one is depicted by the sixteenth-century painter Hieronymus Bosch in *The Crowning with Thorns*.) The European and Egyptian ones were used to tip arrows and were apparently very efficient for killing large mammals, including human beings (Clark 1952, pp. 35-36, pl. Ia). The microliths from Banahilk were probably made to serve the same function; they were probably projectile tips. Similar implements were found at Mersin (Garstang 1953, fig. 29).

Only one microlithic lunate (fig. 213:8) is present among the Banahilk flints. Because it comes from level 1 of operation B, it could be post-Halafian. Like the trapezoid, this form is typical of certain mesolithic industries in Europe and is also found in the Near East in assemblages of the terminal food-gathering era and later. Both trapezoids and lunates were unearthed at Palegawra and Jarmo (SAOC 31, pls. 24, 2nd row; 18B).

More extensive excavation at Banahilk would doubtless yield more microliths and possibly reveal a greater variety, although they probably formed a minor part of the flint-obsidian industry as a whole. The finding of these microliths at a Halafian site is not surprising if one recalls the occurrence of microliths in late prehistoric to early historic contexts in southern Iraq (Adams 1960, p. 26, n. 2). For instance, microliths are reported at both Choga Mami (Mortensen 1973) and Tell es-Sawwan (al-Tekriti 1968).

Unutilized flakes and chips.—Those pieces of chert that have no edge chipping or wear visible to the naked eye make up by far the largest of the chipped stone categories. They probably represent manufacturing and trimming debris.

Obsidian (figs. 214:8; 215:1-8)

When the Banahilk obsidian is translucent, it is usually olive green, but frequently pieces are opaque black, some are brown or brown and black, and a few are smoky gray. A very few fragments are almost as transparent as modern window glass. Several specimens were sent to the University of Michigan for neutron activation elemental analysis to determine their source. The results indicate that four of the specimens are from a source that may be in the Beyazid area about 310 km northwest of Lake Van. Obsidian from the same source has been found in the Halafian levels at Arpachiyah and apparently at Tilkitepe as well. The other Banahilk specimens (a total of seven) are from Nemrut Dagh, which also furnished obsidian to Arpachiyah and Tilkitepe (G. Wright 1969, pp. 22-23).

Utilized and unutilized flakes and blades.—This category represents manufacturing and trimming debris for the most part, with some of the pieces showing enough edge wear to be classed as utilized (fig. 215:3-7) and a few pieces fairly carefully retouched (figs. 214:8; 215:1-2,8).

Discussion

The Banahilk chert industry—one of flakes rather than blades—is very similar to that of Hassuna, Matarrah, and Ali Agha. This kind of flake industry is quite different from the neat blade industry of Jarmo.

The chipped stone from Girikihacıyan generally resembles that of Banahilk in that it is a chert flake industry combined with quantities of obsidian blades (LeBlanc 1971, p. 65; Watson and LeBlanc, in prep.). The proportion of chert to obsidian is also similar: 71% chert to 29% obsidian at Banahilk, and 76% chert to 24% obsidian at Girikihacıyan.

At Tell Halaf, a number of chert (or flint) and obsidian implements were recovered (Oppenheim and Schmidt 1943, pls. XXIV, XXXV, CX-CXI). Flint and obsidian blades were found there as well as good blade cores in both kinds of material. In flint there were also drills, burins, a hammerstone, and two or three pieces of retouched tabular flint (Oppenheim and Schmidt 1943, pls. XXXV:23,25, and probably 22; CXIII:6-7). Objects made of obsidian included a possible drill, one or two pieces that may be end scrapers on blades, a concave-based arrowhead, and a hammerstone. There were miscellaneous utilized blades and pieces in both flint and obsidian. Schmidt says that the flint is less common than obsidian, but he attributes this to the fact that obsidian is easier for the workmen at the site to see. Although there is no detailed treatment of chipped stone in the Tell Halaf report, at least it is clear that it differed from the Banahilk industry in including good blades and blade cores.

The flint blade industry of phase C of the ʿAmuq (the phase in which the Halafian pottery first appears in that area) is not comparable to that of Banahilk (Braidwood and Braidwood 1960, pp. 150-54).

At Tell Aswad in northern Syria several projectile points occurred in levels attributed to the Halafian (Mallowan 1946, fig. 13:9-11,17).

Some pieces of flint and obsidian were found at Arpachiyah (Mallowan and Rose 1935, fig. 52:13-25, pls. XI*c*, XII*b*), including some obsidian bladelet cores. There were also a few flint blades. Blades also occurred at Yunus (Woolley 1934). At Tepe Gawra, blades in flint and obsidian appeared in the lowest levels, which may be partially late Halafian debris (Tobler 1950, pls. XCIII*a*:1-4 [no. 2 is flint, but the others are obsidian]; CLXXVI:1 [obsidian]).

At the present time, the chipped stone industry of Banahilk is the only one known in any detail in the eastern part of the area where Halafian painted ware is distributed. If this Banahilk stone industry and that of ʿAmuq phase C, on the western end of the Halafian area, prove to be representative of their respective regions, then the striking homogeneity of the painted pottery that has been noted from northern Iraq across northern Syria does not reflect similarity in all aspects of the technology throughout the area.

GROUND STONE OBJECTS (figs. 209:1-4,12; 210)

Ground stone objects from Banahilk include several celts, a number of small items that are presumably ornamental, and portions of stone vessels.

Celts (fig. 209:1-2)

Five celts were found, and their distribution was as follows: D*I*,1-2 (2 examples); D*I*,2; D*I*,fl.4; D*II*,1-2 (in Baghdad). Four are complete or nearly so, and 1 is a small fragment of the bit. All are fully ground, and most show fine striations from the grinding process. Of the complete specimens, 3 are apparently normal in size, that is, 60-80 mm in length, but the fourth (possibly a chisel) is a miniature example only 35 mm long. All 4 broaden at the bit and narrow to the butt, and all have "axe-type" rather than "adze-type" sections. One of the larger ones shows marks of hammering on the butt and on the sides as well. The butt end of another may also have been used as a hammer, but it is so badly broken that one cannot be certain.

The fifth piece in this group, the fragment of a celt bit, has been reworked somewhat, for one of the broken edges has been ground smooth.

Fully ground celts are reported from Tell Halaf (Oppenheim and Schmidt 1943, pls. XXXVI:1-11; CXII:1-15), from Arpachiyah (Mallowan and Rose 1935, fig. 52; the impression of the wooden haft of one of these was still discernible), from level VI at Hassuna where Halafian pottery occurs (Lloyd and Safar 1945, fig. 21:11), from Tepe Gawra (Tobler 1950, p. 202), and from Tilkitepe (Korfmann 1982).

Ornamental Objects (fig. 210)

Four of the ground stone items found at Banahilk were made of obsidian. One, from D*I*,fl.5, is an oval object about 40 mm long and 20 mm wide, with a perforation at each end that was bored from both sides and measures 10-15 mm in diameter. This object was first shaped by chipping and then was ground and polished on both surfaces and around the edges. There is some chipping on the lower surface that perhaps occurred accidentally during use. It is planoconvex in section and, although worn and less shiny, is exactly paralleled by finds from Arpachiyah TT6 (Mallowan and Rose 1935, pl. XI*a*) and from level XVIII and the northeast base cut at Tepe Gawra (Tobler 1950, pls. XCII*c*:2; CLXXV:70). The Arpachiyah obsidian ovals were used in a necklace alternately with cowries that had been cut open and filled with red pigment (Mallowan and Rose 1935, p. 97).

A second obsidian ornament, from D*I*,fl.6 (fig. 210:4), which is also paralleled at Arpachiyah (Mallowan and Rose 1935, pl. XI*b*), is apparently a fragment of a necklace or belt. This rectangular piece probably had two perforations, one at each end, but only one perforation (bored from both sides) is preserved. The Banahilk specimen is ground and polished on the upper surface and chipped on the lower.

A third ground obsidian ornament is a thin isosceles triangle (fig. 210:5) from B*I-II*,3. It also has a perforation at each end that was bored from both sides. This triangular ornament is not paralleled in the published objects at Arpachiyah but is similar to one from the northeast base cut at Tepe Gawra (Tobler 1950, pls. XCII*a*:9; CLXXV:69).

The last object is a small fragment of ground obsidian, probably a piece of one of the oval necklace links. This planoconvex piece was found in operation TT and is polished on both faces.

The tools with which such tiny perforations were made in the ornamental objects just described have not been found. There is nothing in the chipped stone industry as we know it that would serve; the borer for such a purpose would have to be very slender and sharp.

One other artifact that may be obsidian, a bracelet fragment some 40 mm long and 5 mm in cross-sectional diameter, was found in A*I*,1.

Three incised stone objects were found at Banahilk—2 pendants and 1 stamp seal. One of the pendants has a latticed design carefully incised on the flat upper surface (fig. 210:2). The object is broken at the perforation, which is a transverse one. The design consists of two lattices, the second superimposed at a 45° angle to the first. The result is a series of boxes with a neat X in each one (this same design appears on the painted pottery). The actual construction of such a complicated-looking design would not be difficult, although it would have to be done very carefully. The Banahilk specimen also has incised nicks along the lower edge.

The pendant from D*I*,2 (fig. 210:1) is a worked red-orange chert pebble. A transverse perforation was made through a projection at one end, and the flat upper surface was covered with a linear design basically quite similar to that already discussed. Here, however, the first lattice is smaller than the second so that the second grid forms one X for every four squares of the first grid, not simply an X in each square. There are tiny pockmarks (possibly the beginnings of drill holes) on the pendant—four on the edge of the design surface itself and two or three on the perforated projection. None is more than 1 mm in diameter. Though these seem to be haphazardly placed, they call to mind the seals from Tepe Gawra that were decorated with figures produced by juxtaposed drill holes (Tobler 1950, pl. CLXXIII:32-37). A polished but undecorated pebble of the same size and shape as this incised one was found in D*I*,1-2 and was perhaps intended to be worked into a pendant also.

The third incised object (fig. 210:3), from C,4, is apparently the fragment of a circular stamp seal made of a greenish black rock, probably diorite. It is decorated like the first pendant described above and has nicks all around the edge as well. Part of a knob or handle may be seen on the lower surface.

These incised objects from Banahilk are closely paralleled by several examples from Arpachiyah (Mallowan and Rose 1935, e.g., pls. VIII*a* and VII*a*:561) and by one from level XX at Tepe Gawra (Tobler 1950, pl. XCII*a*:1).

Two other pendants were found. One, from A*III*,3, was made from an oblong reddish brown slate pebble that has been broken and split, probably since manufacture, and it is now 55 mm in length. The pebble was not worked except for being pierced. A number of these long slate pebbles were found at Banahilk but none had been worked except this one and two others that were from D*I*,2.

The second pendant is a miniature celt from D*I*,1. It is made from a black rock resembling diorite and is perforated in the center and polished. The dimensions of the object are 40 × 30 × 20 mm and the perforation is 5 mm in diameter. The bit was either not carefully finished or else it had been broken and then smoothed.

Nine beads were found at Banahilk (fig. 210:6-8). One, from D*I*,fl.6, is a simple, short cylinder bead made of vitrified gray-black clay. One other bead, from B*I*,1, is approximately the same shape, although cruder, and it was made of a soft gritty white substance that looks like frit. Mallowan reports that frit was found in the Halafian strata at Arpachiyah (Mallowan and Rose 1935, pp. 91, 97).

Half of another very small, short cylinder bead made of a blue stone, possibly turquoise, was recovered in D*I*,2. One bead (fig. 210:6) is a small perforated lump of red orange rock very similar to the chert of the incised pendant described above. A small, perforated, flat greenish bit of rock from D*I*,fl.1 may also be chert. A bead of white flint was found in D*I*,2 (fig. 210:8); it is flat on one surface but ridged on the other, and thus it has a triangular cross section. Two disk-shaped beads were made of small, flat, approximately round pieces of rock—one of green slate (D*I*,2) and the other of black rock (D*I*,fl.1). The latter (fig. 210:7) has, in addition to the central perforation, three drill holes around the periphery that may have been made to aid in cutting the small disk out of a large piece of stone. All four holes were bored from both sides.

Finally, there is a small unbaked clay barrel bead about 10 mm long (from C,4).

Miscellaneous (fig. 209:3-4,12)

A small fragment of a macehead was found in D*I*;2 (fig. 209:4). It was bored from both sides and the complete original object was probably a flattened sphere. The material used was white marble or very hard limestone. Several maceheads were found at Tell Halaf (Oppenheim and Schmidt 1943, pls. XXXVI:13-25; CXII:18-21) and one at Arpachiyah (Mallowan and Rose 1935, pl. X*c*).

A fragment of a stone lid of pink and white marble occurred in D*I*,2 (fig. 209:12). The diameter is 140 mm, so the lid could have served to cover collared or flaring-necked plain ware or painted ware jars, for instance. The remains of a black substance, probably an adhesive such as bitumen, are present on it. At Arpachiyah a pottery lid was found stuck to a jar mouth by means of bitumen (Mallowan and Rose 1935, fig. 49:23).

Two worked slate pebbles came from D*I*,2. A third, from A*III*,3, has already been described in the discussion of ornamental objects. One of those from D*I*,2 has a groove incised near one end (fig. 209:3); the other has been ground to a chisellike edge at one end, but the opposite end is now broken.

Four pieces of stone (from D*I*,2 and D*II*,2) that showed traces of grinding or polishing were found; in no case could the form of the original complete object be determined. One (from D*I*,2) is a small oblong piece of obsidian about 15 mm long with the beginning of a perforation at one end. It is ground smooth on both surfaces and on one edge and is perhaps a small fragment from an obsidian ornament like those described earlier. A fifth piece of black rock with a double-bored perforation was found in D*I*,1; it is difficult to say what the original object was—perhaps a pendant.

A stone disk about 60 mm thick and 80 mm in diameter, with a slight depression surrounded by a rim on one face, was found in D*I*,fl.6. This object may represent a stage in the manufacture of a stone vessel. The outer surface is shaped and smoothed; if this disk was intended to be a bowl, the next step would have been to drill out the interior (see SAOC 31, p. 45). A technique similar to that suggested by Moholy-Nagy (p. 294) for the manufacture of stone bracelets at Jarmo could have been used for the Banahilk bowls.

An extremely interesting surface find was made near the airfield. It is a black hemispherical seal with a transverse perforation. Carved into the surface is a representation of an animal with branching horns, probably a roe deer. The representation is paralleled by that in a seal impression from Tepe Gawra, level IX (Tobler 1950, pl. CLXVI:118).

Stone Vessels (table 49; fig. 209:5-11)

The Banahilk stone vessels were made of hard limestone, soft marble, diorite, and obsidian. They were manufactured carefully, probably by a combination of pecking, drilling, grinding, and polishing the stone. An early stage in the process seems to be illustrated by the worked piece of limestone described above.

Well-made stone bowls are present at Arpachiyah (Mallowan and Rose 1935, fig. 44) and at Tepe Gawra (Tobler 1950, pp. 208-9), but at Tell Halaf only one ground stone vessel was found (Oppenheim and Schmidt 1943, p. 120, pl. XXXVII:24). In general, the stone bowls from Banahilk are similar to those from Jarmo, Arpachiyah, and Tepe Gawra.

No complete stone vessels and few complete profiles were found at Banahilk. The following classification was based on fragments (a total of 38).

I. Round-sided Bowls

IA. Very open and shallow round-sided bowls (fig. 209:5,7).—The open round-sided bowls in the present sample are all small vessels, except one that is 220 mm in diameter at the rim (fig. 209:7). This interesting fragment is made of marble, and the iron minerals in the rock stand out from the surface on the inside of the bowl, making it very rough to the touch. H.E. Wright, who detected this while examining the bowl fragments to determine the type of material used, suggested that this is perhaps due to the dissolving action of whatever the bowl may have contained in the past. The marble was gradually eaten away from around the more resistant iron inclusions. As would be expected, the effect becomes more pronounced farther down the side of the vessel, whereas it is not so noticeable near the lip.

The complete profiles of only two of the open round-sided bowls were found, and their flat bases are not especially sharply set off from the sides.

IB. Less open round-sided bowls (fig. 209:6).—The less open bowls are also small forms but deeper in proportion to their diameters than those of the preceding type. The one complete profile has a flat base distinctly set off from the side.

IC. Bowls with sides vertical or slightly drawn in at lip (fig. 209:8-9).—The two vessels with nearly vertical sides are again small forms; both are rim fragments.

II. Flare-sided Bowls

A fragment of one vessel with flaring sides was found. It was probably a small bowl also, although its diameter is uncertain.

III. Bowls with Everted or Profiled Rims (fig. 209:10-11)

Of the fragments of bowls with everted rims, only one has a complete profile (fig. 209:11), but the other two vessels seem to have had upper walls that curved out to a flattened rim. The complete profile fragment is different from the other two in that the latter do not have the extraordinary thickening of the body wall and are not so squat in general profile. In profile, the more complete fragment is much like one from Arpachiyah that has a sharply marked shoulder under the rim (Mallowan and Rose 1935, fig. 44:9), but the Banahilk example is less open.

IV. Miscellaneous Fragments

Three of the six classifiable miscellaneous fragments (table 49) are parts of bases and three are parts of rims. One of the rim fragments seems to be from a small shallow vessel (with a rim diameter about 100 mm), although the orientation is not certain. It is not so round sided as the open, shallow bowls discussed above. The second rim fragment appears to be from a small, thin-walled square or rectangular vessel, possibly a miniature. The third piece may be from the body of a bowl with an everted rim or perhaps from a holemouth vessel.

The remaining 15 pieces are small body fragments from vessels whose form cannot be determined. In some of these pieces there is some indication of profile or a definite curvature. Other fragments are so small that it is impossible to tell anything about the form of the original vessel. One thin piece (from D*I*,fl.7) had been perforated in two places approximately a centimeter apart, presumably for mending. The diameter of each of the tiny perforations is about 2 mm.

Table 49 summarizes the data regarding the distribution of the Banahilk stone vessels and indicates the raw materials of which they were made. The material identifications were made by H.E. Wright, Jr.

Table 49.—Banahilk Stone Vessels

Form class	Provenience	No. fragments	Rim diameter (mm)	Material	Remarks
IA. Very open, round-sided bowls	C ext.,2	1	120?	Light gray limestone	Bh-15; (B)
	DI,2	3	100	Gray limestone	
			100	Gray limestone	
			160	Yellow white limestone	
	DI,fl.2	1	220	White marble with red and black veining	(fig. 209:7)
	DI,fl.4	1	120?	Yellow limestone	
	DIIN	2	60	Gray limestone	Bh-14; (B); (fig. 209:5)
			100	Yellow white marble with blue veining	
IB. Less open, round-sided bowls	BIII,2	1	100	Yellow limestone	
	DI,fl.3	1	140	Yellow limestone	(fig. 209:6)
	DI,fl.6	1	120-140	White marble with black veining	
IC. Round-sided, nearly holemouthed bowls	DI,2	1	80	Diorite?	(fig. 209:8)
	DI,fl.2	1	100	Pink white limestone	(fig. 209:9)
II. Flare-sided bowls	DI,2	1	140?	Yellow limestone	
III. Bowls with everted rims	DI,2	2	--	Diorite?	(fig. 209:10)
			--	Yellow limestone	Max. body diameter, 180 mm
	DIIN	1	100	Yellow gray limestone	Bh-13; (B); (fig. 209:11)
IV. Miscellaneous fragments with profile or definite curvature	Surface	1	--	Yellow white limestone	Base diameter, 40 mm
	DI,fl.5	2	100	Green gray stone	
			--	Yellow white limestone	Fragment of small square or rectangular vessel
	DI,fl.6	2	--	Gray marble with black veining	Base diameter, 60 mm
			--	Obsidian	Max. body diameter, 180+ mm
	DIIN	1	--	Yellow white limestone	Base diameter, 90-100 mm

NOTE: (B) = vessel now in Baghdad.

MILLING STONES AND OTHER LARGE STONE OBJECTS (figs. 211, 218)

The only large stone objects recovered at Banahilk are grinding stones, including mortars, pestles, querns, and rubbing stones.

Mortars and Pestles (fig. 218:1-4)

There are five mortar fragments, each consisting of a circular depression worked into a suitable rock. The rock itself is not modified. The mortars, if complete, would have ranged from 150 to 200 mm in maximum diameter. The depressions all measure about 100 mm in diameter at their greatest extent, narrowing to 40 or 50 mm at the bottom. The depressions are 40-60 mm deep, except for one from DI,fl.5 that is barely 10 mm deep (fig. 218:1). The latter may have been a doorpost pivot rather than a mortar; the depression is shallow and more or less even in depth, that is, not deeply indented in the center. The other four mortar fragments came from the mound surface (1 specimen), DI,fl.6 (2 specimens, 1 of which is shown in fig. 218:3), and DII,1-2 (1 specimen).

In DII,1-2 was found a complete cylindrical pestle, about 170 mm in length and 45-50 mm in diameter. Near it was a very similar pestle, broken at one end, that probably once had about the same dimensions. Two pestles found in

A*I*,1 and A*I*,4 are not cylindrical but are enlarged at one end; on both of these the smaller end is broken. The better preserved of the two (from A*I*,1) is 150 mm long and 60-70 mm in diameter. The other is 40-50 mm in diameter (fig. 218:2).

Querns and Handstones (figs. 211; 218:4)

Because of their size and weight, none of the querns found at Banahilk were brought back. Unfortunately, records are available for only 12 of the querns found; drawings were made of 5 examples (e.g., fig. 211:2). Lengths, widths, and thicknesses of the 5 recorded querns are 330 × 230-240 × 60 mm, 420 × 190 × 60 mm, 290 × 110 × 70 mm (all 3 from D*I*); 300 × 150 × 50 mm, 300 × 180 × 50 mm (both from D*II*,1-2). The other 7 quern fragments were found in D*I* (3 specimens), D*II*,1-2 (2 specimens), B*II*,3 (1 specimen), and C,3 (1 specimen).

Distributional data on handstones (figs. 211:1; 218:4) are also incomplete. (The specimen shown in fig. 218:4 could have been a large pestle.) A total of 5 were recovered. Measurements have been recorded for 2 handstones that are not illustrated: 180 × 100 × 40-50 mm and 80 × 65 × 30 mm.

Pot Lids

Two specimens that appear to have been pot lids were found (see also p. 574). One is greenish slate, found in D*I*,2, and the other is green sandstone, found in D*II*,2. The slate piece was apparently once octagonal in shape, but about one fifth of it is broken away so that it now measures 110 × 90 × 10-15 mm. All the edges are smooth and were apparently ground into shape. The sandstone specimen is round, but it has rough edges; shaping was done by percussion. Neither has traces of adhesive.

Miscellaneous

A green sandstone fragment (approximately a quarter of the size of the original), which could perhaps have been a macehead or digging stick weight, was found in A*I*,4. It was more or less square and measured 65 × 60 × 30 mm. Its perforation was bored from both sides.

Two stones were found that may have been used for polishing. One of these (from C,6) is a fine-grained, smooth-surfaced gray rock, pear-shaped in plan. It measures 100 × 65 × 45 mm. All surfaces bear very fine striations running for the most part horizontally around the rock, not longitudinally up and down it. There are also pockmarks on the ends suggesting that it was used occasionally as a pestle or hammer. The other piece (from D*I*,fl.7) is a roughly spherical unworked black stone, 90 × 80 × 70 mm in size, with small depressions or pockmarks in the otherwise smooth surface that do not look man-made. The smoothness of the rest of the surface suggests that the object might have been used for polishing (walls or floors perhaps), although it is quite heavy.

BONE OBJECTS (figs. 208:12-15; 219)

The bone objects found at Banahilk consist largely of implements usually called awls or punches. They are manufactured from the leg bones of sheep and goats. There are 16 awls and awl fragments, 11 being broken-off tips of awls. Awls of sheep/goat long bones with articular butts (identified by C.A. Reed) were found in C,2 (fig. 219:4), C,3 (fig. 208:14), C,4 (figs. 208:12,15; 219:2-3), D*I*,2 (fig. 208:130), and D*II*N. The broken-off tips occurred in the following proveniences: C,1, C,2, C,3, C,5 (2 examples), D*I*,1-2, D*I*,2 (2 examples), D*I*,fl.1, D*I*,fl.6, D*II*,2.

The awls invariably show definite working at the tip: the bone has been abraded to a point, and the resultant horizontal striations at and near the tip end are usually clearly visible. In addition, the point is often polished, either from use or from the process of manufacture. Most of the awl fragments have quite slender points, but one heavier and well-worn fragment was found that has apparently been blunted from use. These tools probably had a number of uses, among which is usually suggested the working of leather and cloth. A bone awl or punch with a lump of bitumen serving as a haft was found at Arpachiyah (Mallowan and Rose 1935, pl. XII*a*, bottom row) and another at Hassuna (Lloyd and Safar 1945, pl. X:2, no. 23). An example from Tepe Gawra had a clay haft (Tobler 1950, pl. XCIX*c*:1).

One of the most interesting finds in the worked bone category was a group of 5 knucklebone (sheep/goat astragali) gaming pieces (fig. 219:1). These 5 bones occurred together in B*III*,2, and all have the sides ground smooth in a similar fashion, probably by having been rubbed against an abrasive surface. Two of them are completely flattened by abrasion, but the rest have some traces of the articular surfaces left. Such knucklebone gaming pieces are still used in Europe and the Near East[4] (fig. 220; and see Schaeffer's discussion of those found at Ras Shamra [Schaeffer 1962, pp. 102, 105]).

Two other knucklebone gaming pieces were found, one in D*II*,1-2 and the other in trench W. The latter specimen is not abraded as all the others are but only gouged in a few places.

Another interesting object (from D*I*,2) is a fragment of what looks like a bone hammer head. This is a short cylinder with a perforation, presumably for a haft. It was probably manufactured from the end of a bovid long bone (C.A. Reed, pers. comm.).

A slender, flat, double-pointed bone object was found in B,1. It is very thin and flat in section and was probably made from a split rib fragment.

Miscellaneous worked bone includes the following pieces: a two-pronged antler (B*III*,2) with the prong tips worn, presumably from use; a sheep/goat horn core with the outer rough surface cut or ground off, leaving a cylindrical rod of bone (D*I*,fl.6); a piece of what was probably sheep/goat femur (C,3) with one end cut off and the other broken away so that part of a hollow cylinder is left; a piece of sheep/goat ilium (C,2) with a long narrow piece cut out of one side of it; 5 bits of bone showing polishing, from either manufacture or use, but too small to be classifiable (3 specimens were from D*I*,2, while D*I*,feat.1 and C,3 each yielded 1 specimen); a small, highly polished, hollow section of bone shaft with four cut marks near one of the ends (from TT).

Miscellaneous Materials

Two bits of a blue substance, perhaps azurite, were found in D*II*,fl.2, as well as two small pieces of yellow ochre, one in D*II* on the surface and one in A*I*. Lumps of black, red, and yellow pigment were reported at Arpachiyah (Mallowan and Rose 1935, p. 100).

In D*I*,2 a piece of damp earth was found that contained faint white traces or what may have been ghosts of reeds. These traces were similar to the remains of reed flooring at Jarmo (p. 156).

SUBSISTENCE INFORMATION

Animal bone recovered from Banahilk is described in detail by Laffer (chap. 19). As she notes, most of this bone came from domesticated sheep, goat, cattle, and pig. There are only two bone fragments that might be dog (or wolf). The wild species represented include sheep, goat, cattle, deer (red and roe), fox, bear, leopard, hedgehog, birds, fish, and snail. The one equid bone found came from A*I*,3 where there is wheel-made pottery as well as Halafian ware; hence it may belong to a post-Halafian period.

The present faunal sample indicates that Halafian pastoralism at Banahilk was based largely on domesticated goats, sheep, pigs, and cattle, in order of decreasing importance. Some hunting or trapping was apparently also done, however, to judge from the number of wild animals represented. The big land snails may also have been a fairly common diet item. Their shells occurred in definite concentrations as well as scattered finds. Near the north end of D,1 was a thick deposit of shells about 0.5 m in diameter, while in D*II* at a depth of approximately 0.9 m another concentration was uncovered. Abundant snail shells were also present in the charcoal and ash deposits beneath the hearth floor (feature 1), discovered when Matson was taking a radiocarbon sample in D*I* (fig. 195:3).

No plant remains were recovered at Banahilk. In other Halafian contexts, there is poplar at Tell Aswad and emmer wheat and barley at Arpachiyah. Helbaek mentions six-row barley in Halafian context and states that flax occurred at Arpachiyah and Brak (Helbaek 1960*a*, pp. 190, 192-93; 1960*b*, pp. 110, 115).

For the Turkish Halafian site of Girikihacıyan, van Zeist has identified domestic emmer, einkorn, and barley, as well as flax, lentils, and vetch (van Zeist 1979-80). At Yarim Tepe II, carbonized grain has been found, but detailed identification is not yet available (Merpert and Munchaev 1973, p. 112).

DISCUSSION AND CONCLUSIONS

The Banahilk sondage was not extensive enough to permit an estimate of the village population, although the community could not have been very large if the mound limits (100 × 160 m) mark its approximate extent (16,000 m^2 or 1.6 ha). Total population at any one time was probably less than 200 people. Architecture probably consisted of *tauf* and mud-brick dwellings with stone-footed walls. In our trenches no remains were found of the round structures known from Arpachiyah, Yarim Tepe II, Girikihacıyan, and elsewhere, but it is likely that some would have been exposed by more extensive excavation.

The wadi, in combination with one or more springs, would have served as the water supply of the village, and subsistence must have been based on cereal cultivation as well as the tending of domestic goats, sheep, cattle, and pigs. Various wild fruits and nuts (e.g., pears, apricots, plums, cherries, walnuts, and acorns) would have been seasonally available in this area, as well as wild legumes and seeds of wild grasses. As already noted, the Banahilk villagers must have done some hunting. The trapezoids are the only type of possible projectile point yet found at Banahilk, although there are several arrowheads from the Halafian levels at Tell Aswad (Mallowan 1946, fig. 13:9-11,17), and a concave-based obsidian arrowhead at Tell Halaf is said to have come from the Halafian levels (Oppenheim and Schmidt 1943, pl. XXXIV:21).

The large land snails could have been a fairly steady item of diet during the favorable season of the year. They must have been boiled in their shells, because the shells are nearly always found complete and uncharred (see Reed 1962 for a detailed discussion of these snails in prehistoric times and today).

Present evidence suggests use of the following domestic tools and weapons: hatchets with fully ground stone heads, obsidian knives (i.e., obsidian blades—perhaps hafted, although there is no pattern of backing the blades), flint drills, bone awls, sickles set with flint flakes, and possibly arrows tipped with trapezoidal flints.

Analysis of a few samples of obsidian from Banahilk indicates that it was imported from at least two different source areas in Turkey—Nemrut Dagh on Lake Van and perhaps the Beyazid region several hundred kilometers northwest of Lake Van. Bitumen also may have been traded into the Banahilk area, in this case probably from the general region of Kirkuk (a number of bitumen seeps are known in the Jarmo-Chemchemal vicinity, for instance).

There is no evidence for the style of clothing or material used for it at Banahilk. Impressions of fine cloth were found at Jarmo (SAOC 31, p. 46; also this volume, chap. 7, appendix to chap. 7, and fig. 169:9-10), and flax seeds have been identified at Girikihacıyan, Tell es-Sawwan, Choga Mami, Brak, and Arpachiyah (van Zeist 1979-80; Helbaek 1959, 1960a, 1972). As Helbaek notes, however, the *Linum* may have been collected for the oil its seeds yielded as well as for the fibrous possibilities of the rest of the plant. In any case, cloth made of flax fiber has been recovered from Çatal Hüyük (Ryder 1965).

Personal ornament apparently included incised pendants, stone beads, and perhaps obsidian necklaces.

Household equipment would have included, for each family, several plain ware pottery vessels: cups and small bowls for individual use and large jars and pots for food and grain storage, for cooking, and perhaps for water carrying, although skins could also have served this last purpose. The painted pottery probably functioned largely as vessels for serving food and also as cups, plates, and small bowls for individual use in eating and drinking. The large flare-necked painted jars may have been utilized for storage or for holding water.

There are not many stone bowls in the present sample of artifacts from Banahilk, and all those represented are small. Perhaps they had some special function (cf. Mallowan and Rose 1935, pp. 76, 100). The size of several of the stone bowls overlaps with the cup/small bowl category of both painted and plain ware, but the series of stone bowl fragments with identifiable shapes and diameters is too small to permit definite conclusions to be drawn.

There are three radiocarbon determinations for Banahilk (Lawn 1973, p. 373):

P-1501 ... 4359 ± 78 BC ... D*II*, 1.3 m below surface
P-1502 ... 4801 ± 85 BC ... D*I*,fl.6, beneath feature 1, 2.2 m below surface
P-1504 ... 4904 ± 72 BC ... D*I*,fl.6, beneath feature 1, 2.2 m below surface

Determinations for related sites are:

Tell Halaf (Vogel and Waterbolk 1964, p. 355)
  GrN-2660 ... 5620 ± 35 BC
Arpachiyah (Stuckenrath and Ralph 1965, p. 188)
  P-584 ... 5077 ± 83 BC
  P-585 ... 6114 ± 78 BC
Girikihacıyan (van Zeist, in letters to RJB on 9-5-74 and 4-21-80)
  GrN-5882 ... 4515 ± 100 BC
  GrN-6245 ... 4855 ± 45 BC
  GrN-6246 ... 5000 ± 45 BC
Yarim Tepe II (Merpert and Munchaev 1973)
  Lab. no. unknown ... 3210 ± 130 B.C. (This date seems much too late.)

With the possible exception of the above Yarim Tepe date, all the dates given are based on the 5568 half-life and 1950 base date; no corrections or calibrations have been made.

It can be seen that most of the presently available radiocarbon dates suggest a late sixth to early fifth millennium placement for the Halafian culture.

Recent excavation (since World War II) of other Halafian material has included the work of Perrot at Turlu in southern Turkey (Mellink 1964, p. 156; Mellaart 1970; LeBlanc and Watson 1973), that of Merpert and Munchaev at Yarim Tepe II in northern Iraq (Merpert and Munchaev 1969, 1971, 1973), Davidson at Tell Agab (Davidson and McKerrell, 1976), and Hijara at Arpachiyah (Hijara 1978), as well as the work at Girikihacıyan near Diyarbakır, Turkey, undertaken by the Joint Prehistoric Project of the University of Istanbul and the Oriental Institute, University of Chicago.

Girikihacıyan was located in 1963 by members of the Joint Istanbul-Chicago Prehistoric Project. In 1968, a controlled surface collection and a brief excavation were carried out there under my direction (Braidwood, Çambel, and Watson 1969; Redman and Watson 1970), and in 1970 excavation was continued (Braidwood, Çambel, et al. 1971; LeBlanc 1971; LeBlanc and Watson 1973; Watson and LeBlanc 1973; Watson and LeBlanc, in prep.). Insofar as we now know this Turkish Halafian assemblage, the percentage of painted ware is considerably smaller than it was at Banahilk. Statistical comparison of motifs on the painted pottery of Banahilk, Girikihacıyan, and five other sites indicates that the Girikihacıyan painted pottery design repertoire most resembles that of Tell Halaf and Arpachiyah, whereas Banahilk painted pottery is more like that of Arpachiyah than any of the other sites in the sample (LeBlanc and Watson 1973).

As the Braidwoods noted repeatedly (Braidwood and Braidwood 1953; 1960, p. 508), no Halafian assemblage has yet been adequately defined, although the distinctive Halafian painted pottery has been well known since the excavations at Tell Halaf early in this century. This is, to a considerable extent, still true: no definition of a complete Halafian assemblage based on secure stratigraphic relationships has yet been published (see Braidwood and Braidwood 1953 for details on the stratigraphic problems at each of the Halafian sites then known). The data from Banahilk, however, mark a beginning, and comparative information will be available in the near future from Agab (Davidson and McKerrell 1976), Arpachiyah (Hijara 1978), Girikihacıyan, and Yarim Tepe II. Descriptions of plain ware and chipped stone industries for five Halafian sites will then be at hand, as well as quantitative information on both painted pottery and plain ware.

The Banahilk material comes from a limited sounding only and the data base is small; architectural remains are very sparse, artifacts other than pottery are not abundant and do not include certain important categories such as figurines. There is one female figurine in undeniable Halafian context in level TT6 at Arpachiyah and apparently at least one from Yarim Tepe II (Merpert and Munchaev 1973, pl. XLIII:12). Tell Halaf has yielded several, but although Schmidt states that the paint on the Tell Halaf figurines is like that on the Tell Halaf pottery (Oppenheim and Schmidt 1943, p. 100), there are no published data on findspots for the figurines.

It has been suggested that the cream bowl form of painted pottery would probably be characteristic of Halafian assemblages, but although there are numerous sherds of flare-rimmed bowls at Girikihacıyan none is of the cream bowl variety, and these are very rare at Banahilk (only two vessels are definitely represented in the present sample of 3,230 sherds). Portions of the foundations of at least seven round buildings were found at Girikihacıyan (at least one with a rectangular antechamber), but no trace occurred in the admittedly limited soundings at Banahilk of this tholos form of architecture which is quite well expressed in other Halafian sites in northern Iraq and Syria. These may be genuine distributional differences or they may be accidents of sampling, or it may be that Banahilk was a somewhat backward or provincial community lacking such refinements as cream bowls and tholoi. Moreover, it is not clear how representative the Banahilk type of chipped stone industry is, particularly since a blade industry has been found to be associated with Hassunan and Samarran pottery at Tell Shimshara (Mortensen 1970), and since there are not only blades and burins but also javelin points at the Hassunan site of Umm Dabaghiyah (Kirkbride 1972, pls. XVII-XVIII). Such an unprepossessing flake industry as that recovered at Banahilk may be only a local phenomenon, although the chipped stone of Girikihacıyan is similar.

So far there is very little detail available on Yarim Tepe II,[5] but it is clear that when the findings regarding this site are published it will be the best known of any Halafian community yet excavated. Several round mud-brick houses, varying in diameter from 2.75 to 5.60 m, and some rectangular buildings (one of them apparently quite large) have been found. Pottery kilns are also noted at that site. Bones of domestic sheep, goat, cattle, and pig,are reported, as well as considerable quantities of carbonized grain.

With respect to the objectives stated at the beginning of this report, one can say that the Banahilk sondage did mark a beginning in the recovery, description, and quantification of Halafian painted pottery and associated materials from at least one site. Because of the political situation it is unlikely that further work can be undertaken at Banahilk in the near future. Nevertheless, the Banahilk material, when combined with that from the more recently excavated sites noted above, provides the basis for a much clearer understanding of the Halafian manifestation than has previously been attainable.

NOTES

1. Tilkitepe is an Urartian site on Lake Van. Halafian material is present in the pre-Urartian basal levels (Belck 1899; 1900, pp. 54-55; Pfeiffer 1940; King 1912; Reilly 1940; Korfmann 1982). In July 1955, I waś able to examine 139 of the Halafian sherds from Tilkitepe. My notes on this collection have been included in Korfmann's synthesis (Watson 1982; see also LeBlanc and Watson 1973).

2. To investigate this question of paint luster, I examined 1,082 sherds from all levels and operations. Of the total, 610 (56.4%) had lustrous paint, 235 (21.7%) had slightly lustrous paint, and 237 (21.9%) had matte paint.

3. *Rim ticking* refers to short painted lines actually on top of the rim; hence a squared rim makes a good field. A *rim band* is a painted band encircling the vessel at and just below the rim.

4. One of the workmen at the Salahedin rest house, where we stayed during part of the winter of 1954-55, demonstrated how the knucklebones are manipulated in playing. One of the bones is propelled by snapping it forward with the second finger, which is released more or less forcibly from behind the first finger. In a village in western Iran, I was given two knucklebone gaming pieces that were artificially smoothed or ground on two faces exactly as the prehistoric ones from Banahilk had been (fig. 219:1). When asked how the smoothing was accomplished, my informant picked up a piece of local fired brick (made in Kermanshah) and demonstrated by rubbing the bone briskly up and down against the rough brick surface.

5. Preliminary reports and notes on Yarim Tepe II are provided by Merpert and Munchaev (1969, 1971, 1973) and by Postgate et al. (1972, 1973).

CATALOGUE OF ILLUSTRATIONS (figs. 194-200)

FIGURE 194. PLOT PLAN

FIGURE 195. OPERATIONS A, B, AND D

FIGURE 196. OPERATION C AND C EXTENSION

FIGURE 197. PAINTED WARE

1 Form class IA2, from D*I*,1-2: hard buff paste with chaff impressions in surface; matte red brown paint

2 Form class IA2, from C,2: limy, light buff paste; matte red brown paint; remains of adhesive (bitumen?) visible along all three edges outside and around mend holes

3 Form class IA2, from mound surface: hard pinkish buff paste, not much lime visible; fairly lustrous red to black paint

4 Form class IA1, from D*II*N: well-surfaced pinkish buff paste; lustrous black paint; mend hole

5 Form class IA2, from D*I*,fl.1: very hard pinkish buff paste; lustrous brown paint

6 Form class IA2, from D*I*,fl.3: hard orange paste, lime specks visible; lustrous black to brown paint

7 Form class IB, from mound surface: hard pinkish buff paste; lustrous red brown paint contrasting with deep wine red of triangle zones
8 Form class IB, from D*I*,2: pinkish buff paste; lustrous red brown paint
9 Form class IB, from D*I*,2: well-surfaced, hard pinkish buff paste; maroon to brown paint—blistered, flaked off, only slightly lustrous; mend hole
10 Form class IB, from D*II*N: hard pinkish buff paste; lustrous red to black paint; traces of adhesive along broken edges
11 Form class IB, from D*II*,1-2: paste surfaces darkened, apparently from overfiring; paint blistered and cracked in several places; mend hole
12 Form class IB, from D*I*,7: pinkish buff paste, somewhat limy; lustrous red brown paint; inside design meant to be quatrefoil, but very poorly done
13 Form class IB, from D*I*,fl.6: soft paste with tiny chaff impressions in surface, pale buff on surface, light brown inside; lustrous red paint
14 Form class IB, from D*I*,2: hard pinkish buff paste; matte brick red paint
15 Form class IB, from D*I*,fl.5: limy pinkish buff paste; matte red to black paint

FIGURE 198. PAINTED WARE

1 Form class IB, from B*I-II*,3: brownish buff paste, not especially limy; brown paint, slightly lustrous
2 Form class IB, from D*I*,2: buff paste; lustrous red brown paint
3 Form class IB, from D*I*,2: pinkish buff paste; matte brown paint
4 Form class IB, from D*I*,2: pinkish buff paste, slightly limy; bichrome dark brown and maroon paint, not especially lustrous
5 Form class IB, from C,1: orange to buff paste, somewhat limy; bichrome red and black design outside; red design of bird with upraised wing inside, not especially lustrous
6 Form class IB, from D*I*,1-2: dirty buff paste, rather limy; matte bichrome maroon and black paint inside
7 Form class IB, from C,1: pale buff paste, slightly limy; matte rusty orange paint
8 Form class IC, from D*I*,fl.6: limy grainy paste; bichrome red and black checkerboard design inside, not especially lustrous
9 Form class IC, from C,1 (see fig. 207:5): smooth, hard pinkish buff paste; lustrous black paint
10 Form class IC, from D*I*,2: hard orange paste; lustrous red brown to dark brown paint
11 Form class IC, from D*I*,fl.3: very smooth, hard orange buff paste; lustrous red brown paint
12 Form class IC, from D*I*,1-2: hard pale pinkish buff paste; slightly lustrous brown paint
13 Form class ID, from D*I*,2: dark buffish orange paste; originally red paint all over, inside and out, now almost completely worn off
14 Form class ID, from mound surface: smooth, hard pinkish buff paste; lustrous dark brown paint
15 Form class ID, from D*I*,2: smooth, hard pinkish buff paste; lustrous brown paint
16 Form class ID, from D*I*,fl.7 and fl.6 (2 sherds glued together): smooth, hard pale buff paste; matte black to brown paint
17 Form class ID, from C,2: smooth, hard pinkish buff paste; lustrous red brown paint, design apparently meant to be reserved x
18 Form class ID, from D*I*,1-2: smooth, hard pinkish buff paste; very lustrous red brown paint
19 Form class ID, from C ext.: limy paste; matte brown paint; sherd very worn
20 Form class IE, from D*II*N: smooth, hard orange buff paste; rather lustrous brown paint
21 Form class IE, from mound surface: pale buff paste, slightly limy; slightly lustrous black to brown paint
22 Form class IE, from D*I*,2: pale buff paste, rather limy; bichrome brown and maroon paint outside

FIGURE 199. PAINTED WARE

1 Form class IE, from D*I*,fl.6 and D*I*,2 (2 sherds fitted together): hard orange paste; slightly lustrous dark brown paint
2 Form class IE, from C,7: hard orangeish buff paste; lustrous red brown to dark brown paint
3 Form class IE, from D*I*,fl.6: pinkish buff paste, very slightly limy; lustrous dark brown paint
4 Form class IE, from D*I*,fl.6: pinkish buff paste, rather limy; matte red paint, badly worn
5 Form class IE, from B,1: orange to brown limy paste; matte bichrome maroon and black paint, both outside and inside
6 Form class IE, from mound surface: pinkish buff paste, slightly limy; lustrous brown paint
7 Form class II, from B*I-II*,2: very smooth, hard light orange buff paste; lustrous brown paint
8 Form class II, from D*I*,1-2: smooth, hard pinkish buff paste; lustrous brown paint
9 Form class II, from C,6: buff paste with a fair amount of lime; matte red brown paint
10 Form class II, from D*I*,2: buff paste, not especially limy; slightly lustrous black to brown paint
11 Form class II, from D*I*,fl.6: hard pinkish buff paste; highly lustrous black to red paint; beginning of a perforation visible in section on one broken edge, bored from outside
12 Form class IIIA1, from D*I*,fl.7: smooth, hard light pink buff paste; matte dark brown to black paint
13 Form class IIIA1, from D*I*,2: hard pink paste; lustrous red brown paint inside, matte brown to red paint outside
14 Form class IIIA2, from D*I*,2: hard pinkish buff paste; matte maroon paint; adhesive (presumably bitumen) visible along part of one of the breaks, on outside surface
15 Form class IIIA2, from C ext.,2: smooth, hard buff paste; lustrous dark brown paint
16 Form class IIIA2, from C ext.,1: orange buff paste, slightly limy; lustrous red brown paint
17 Form class IIIA2, from D*I*,2: light orange buff paste; fairly lustrous black paint
18 Form class IIIA2, from D*I*,fl.1: smooth, hard pink to orange buff paste; matte brown paint
19 Form class IIIA3, from D*I*,2: fine, smooth buff paste; lustrous black paint
20 Form class IIIA3, from D*I*,4: orange buff paste, slightly limy; red black paint, slightly lustrous
21 Form class IIIA3, from D*I*,1-2: orange buff paste, with impressions of very fine plant fibers(?); matte black paint

FIGURE 200. PAINTED WARE

1 Form class IIIA3, from D*I*,fl.6: limy buff paste; black to brown paint, very worn
2 Form class IIIC, from D*I*,fl.4: hard pink to buff paste, some lime visible; red to black paint, not especially lustrous

FIGURE 201. PAINTED WARE
1. Form class IIID, from D*II*,2: hard orange paste; slightly lustrous red brown paint
2. Form class IIID, from D*I*,2: hard orange paste; fairly lustrous dark brown to red paint
3. Form class IIIE, from D*I*,fl.1: hard orange buff paste
4. Form class IIIE, from D*I*,fl.2: orange paste, slightly limy
5. Form class IIIE, from D*I*,2: hard buff paste
6. Form class IIIE, from D*II*,2: well-surfaced, hard tan paste; lustrous dark brown paint
7. Form class IIIE, from D*I*,2: hard buff paste
8. Form class IIIE, from D*I*,fl.3: pink to cream buff paste; slightly lustrous red brown paint
9. Form class IIIE, from D*I*,2: buff paste, slightly limy
10. Form class IIIE, from D*I*,4: smooth, hard pinkish buff paste; lustrous dark brown paint
11. Form class IIIE, from D*I*,2: hard orange paste, very slightly limy
12. Form class IIIE, from D*I*,2: buff paste
13. Form class IIIE, from C,7: rather soft pale paste, worn on surfaces
14. Form class IV, from D*I*,1-2: hard reddish paste
15. Form class IV, from D*I*,fl.7: hard pinkish buff paste; slightly lustrous red brown paint
16. Form class IV, from D*II*,2: well-surfaced, hard pinkish buff paste; lustrous brown paint
17. Form class IV, from D*II*,2 (*Bh-20*) (see also fig. 207:4): miniature spouted vessel; a few traces of black paint outside, remains of narrow black rim band inside; orientation unclear
18. Form class IV, from C ext.,2: greenish paste, rather limy
19. Form class IV, from D*I*,fl.7: somewhat grainy pinkish buff paste; slightly lustrous black paint
20. Form class IV, from D*I*,fl.7: pinkish buff paste; slightly lustrous black paint
21. Form class IV, from D*I*,fl.6: orange paste; lustrous red brown paint
22. Form class IV, from D*I*,fl.6: buff paste, slightly limy; trace of reddish brown band at base of spout, paint very worn
23. Form class IV, from D*I*,fl.6: slightly grainy, hard orange paste; matte red paint
24. Form class IV, from B*III*,2: hard buff paste with little lime; lustrous brown paint
25. Form class IV, from D*I*,2 (*Bh-29*) (see also fig. 207:3): small lid with rosette design on top, wavy lines around sides
26. Form class IV, from B,1: limy buff paste; blistered-looking black paint, slightly lustrous

FIGURE 202. PLAIN WARE (see footnote for fabric types)
1. Form class IA, from D*I*,fl.7 (see also fig. 217:4): fabric type a; brittle, hard red orange paste
2. Form class IA, from B*III*,2: fabric type x; red orange paste
3. Form class IA, from D*II*,2: fabric type b; hard orange tan paste
4. Form class IA, from D*I*,fl.6: fabric type x; orange paste
5. Form class IA, from D*I*,1-2: fabric type x; orange surfaces, gray core
6. Form class IA, from D*I*,2: fabric type b; orange paste, lightly burnished on outside surface
7. Form class IA, from D*I*,2: fabric type b; orange to gray paste
8. Form class IA, from C ext.: fabric type a; light tan surfaces, gray core
9. Form class IA, from D*I*,fl.6: fabric type b; brown paste
10. Form class IA, from D*I*,2 (see also fig. 217:5): fabric type x; brittle, hard orange paste with some chaff
11. Form class IB, from A*I*,3: fabric type b; brown surfaces and core
12. Form class IB, from D*II*N (see also fig. 217:7): fabric type b; brown surfaces, dark gray core
13. Form class IB, from D*I*,1-2: fabric type b; brown surfaces, dark gray core
14. Form class IB, from D*II*N: fabric type b; brown surfaces, gray core
15. Form class IB, from D*II*,1-2 (see also fig. 217:8): fabric type x; hard orange paste with chaff and lime, red brown surfaces
16. Form class IB, from C,2 (see also fig. 217:6): fabric type b; brown surfaces, dark gray core
17. Form class IB, from D*I*,fl.6: fabric type b; gray surfaces, dark gray core
18. Form class ID, from B,1: fabric type b; tan surfaces, gray core
19. Form class ID, from D*I*,1-2: fabric type b; orange surfaces, gray core
20. Form class ID, from C,3: fabric type b; gray surfaces and core
21. Form class IE, from mound surface: fabric type b; orange tan surfaces, gray core
22. Form class IE, from C,1: fabric type x; orange paste with lime
23. Form class IE, from C,1: fabric type b; brown surfaces, orange brown core
24. Form class IE, from D*I*,fl.7: fabric type a; tan surfaces, gray core
25. Form class IIA, from D*I*,2: nipple lug; fabric type b; brown surfaces, gray core
26. Form class IIA, from D*I*,fl.7: fabric type a; light, soft, very chaffy yellow paste; ledge apparently ran all the way around inside of neck
27. Form class IIA, from D*I*,fl.1: fabric type b; brown and gray surfaces, dark gray core
28. Form class IIA, from B*I-II*,2: fabric type b; brown to gray paste
29. Form class IIA, from D*II*S: fabric type b; brown surfaces, brown to gray core
30. Form class IIA, from D*II*N: fabric type b; brown surfaces, gray core
31. Form class IIA, from D*I*,fl.7: fabric type a; buff-colored soft surfaces, gray core
32. Form class IIA, from D*I*,fl.3: flattened nipple lug; fabric type b; gray paste

FIGURE 203. PLAIN WARE (see footnote for fabric types)
1. Form class IIB, from C,3: fabric type x; hard orange paste with lime
2. Form class IIB, from D*I*,fl.6: fabric type b; orange brown paste with lime
3. Form class IIB, from B,1: fabric type a; red orange paste
4. Form class IIB, from B,1: fabric type a; orange surfaces, gray core
5. Form class IIB, from D*I*,2: fabric type b; brown paste
6. Form class IIB, from C,3: fabric type x; orange paste

NOTE: Fabric type a is chaff-tempered paste. Fabric type b is not chaff tempered. Fabric type x is neither type a nor b but has some characteristics of each. See discussion of fabric types on p. 563.

7 Form class IIB, from D*I*,1-2: fabric type b; lightly burnished surfaces, brown to gray core
8 Form class IID, from C,3: fabric type a; orange surfaces, dark gray core
9 Form class IID, from D*I*,fl.3: fabric type b; buff surfaces, gray core
10 Form class IID, from D*I*,fl.6: fabric type a; soft whitish paste with lots of chaff
11 Form class IID, from D*I*,fl.7: fabric type a; soft surfaces, orange to brown core
12 Form class IID, from D*I*,1-2: fabric type a; brown paste
13 Form class IID, from D*I*,2: fabric type b; brown surfaces, gray core
14 Form class IID, from D*I*,2: fabric type b; smooth, hard tan surface outside, much blackened inside
15 Form class IID, from D*I*,2: fabric type b; brown to gray paste
16 Form class IID, from D*II*,2: fabric type x; buff surfaces, orange core
17 Form class III, from B*I-II*,2: fabric type b; tan to gray paste, smooth, hard surfaces
18 Form class III, from D*II*,2, D*II*S, and D*II*N (several sherds fitted together): fabric type x; rather brittle orange paste; a white deposit adheres to the walls and bottom inside to a height of 3 cm above the bottom of the vessel; vessel is oval in plan, 260 × 180 mm
19 Form class IV, from D*I*,fl.6: detached lug; fabric type x; orange tan to gray paste
20 Form class IV, from C,2: detached lug; fabric type x; tan to gray paste
21 Form class IV, from D*I*,2: detached lug; fabric type x; orange paste
22 Form class IV, from B,1: detached lug; fabric type b; lightly burnished brown surfaces, black core
23 Form class IV, from B,1: detached lug; fabric type b; lightly burnished brown surfaces, black core
24 Form class IV, from D*I*,1-2: detached lug; fabric type b; dark gray paste
25 Form class IV, from C,2: fabric type a; dark gray paste
26 Form class IV, from C,3: fabric type b; orangeish surfaces, brown core
27 Form class IV, from D*I*,fl.6: fabric type b; orangeish surfaces, dark gray core; traces of adhesive along break on one side
28 Form class IV, from C,3: fabric type x; orange tan surfaces; orange to brown core
29 Form class IV, from A*III*,2: fabric type b; tan surfaces, dark gray core
30 Form class IV, from D*I*,fl.6: fabric type b; brown to gray paste
31 Form class IV, from C,3: fabric type x; orange paste
32 Form class IV, from C,6: miniature jar
33 Form class IV, from C,7: fabric type b; brown surfaces, dark gray core
34 Form class IV, from D*II*,2: fabric type a; orange paste

FIGURE 204. NON-HALAFIAN POTTERY*

1 Sherd, from A*I*,3, nondiagnostic: chaff-tempered paste, soft surfaces buff to gray in color, gray core
2 Sherd, from A*I*,3, probably Iron Age (see also fig. 216:4): grit-tempered paste, lightly burnished brown to black surfaces, orange brown core
3 Sherd, from A*I*,3, probably Iron Age (see also fig. 216:6): grit-tempered paste, orange core, buff surfaces; buff slip

*Age estimates by Rudolph Dornemann, p. 567.

4 Sherd, from A*I*,3, probably Iron Age (see also fig. 216:2): grit-tempered paste, buff surfaces, bright orange core
5 Sherd, from A*I*,3, probably early second millennium (see also fig. 216:7): grit-tempered paste, brown surfaces, light brown core
6 Sherd, from A*I*,3, probably Iron Age: grit-tempered paste, brown surfaces and core
7 Sherd, from A*I*,3, probably early second millennium: grit-tempered paste, buff surfaces
8 Sherd, from A*I*,3, nondiagnostic: very fine-grained paste, very little chaff or grit
9 Sherd, from A*I*,3, probably early second millennium: grit-tempered paste, light brown surfaces and core
10 Sherd, from A*I*,3, probably Iron Age: grit-tempered paste, brown surfaces, brown to gray core
11 Sherd, from A*I*,3, probably Iron Age: blocky brown grit-tempered paste, smooth brown surfaces
12 Sherd, from A*I*,3, nondiagnostic: paste with very little grit, orange brown surfaces, orange core
13 Sherd, from A*I*,3, early Hellenistic: rather grainy light brown paste, surfaces also rather grainy; sherd shows three shallow grooves
14 Sherd, from B*I-II*,2, probably early second millennium (see also fig. 216:5): limy, grit-tempered buff paste
15 Sherd, from A*I*,3, probably early second millennium (see also fig. 216:10): brittle, grainy orange paste, some grit present
16 Sherd, from A*I*,3, early Hellenistic (see also fig. 216:11): grit-tempered paste, brown surfaces and core
17 Sherd, from A*I*,4, early Hellenistic (see also fig. 216:1): grit-tempered paste, light buff surfaces, brown core
18 Sherd, from TT, nondiagnostic: paste brown at the edges, dark at the core, some chaff present and also grit; inner surface is orange, outer surface has red slip with pattern burnishing beginning about 6-7 cm below the lip and forming an open crosshatch
19 Sherd, from B,1, probably Iron Age (see also fig. 216:8): gritty black paste with a soft white mineral as temper (calcite?), dark brown to black surfaces
20 Sherd, from A*III*,1, probably Iron Age (see also fig. 216:9): grit-tempered brown to orange paste, light brown surfaces

FIGURE 205. PAINTED WARE MOTIFS

FIGURE 206. PAINTED WARE MOTIFS

FIGURE 207. POTTERY OBJECTS

1 Figurine leg?, from mound surface (*Bh-31*)
2 Sievelike object, from B*III*,2 (*Bh-22*)
3 Lid fragment, from D*I*,2 (*Bh-29*) (see also fig. 201:25)
4 Spouted miniature vessel fragment, from D*II*,2 (*Bh-20*) (see also fig. 201:17)
5 Painted "cream bowl" fragment, from D*I*,1-2 (*Bh-30*)
6 Perforated oval ornament, from D*I*,fl.6 (*Bh-21*)

FIGURE 208. POTTERY AND BONE OBJECTS

1 Chipped sherd from vessel of form class IIIC, from D*I*,fl.1 (see also fig. 217:2): hard buff paste, lustrous dark brown paint; design perhaps all-over crosshatched diamonds constructed on a lattice
2 Disk-shaped chipped sherd, from D*I*,1-2: hard buff paste, lustrous dark brown paint
3 Plain ware sherd ground into thick disk, from D*I*,fl.6: fabric type a; paste orange at surfaces, gray at core
4 Pottery bead, from D*II*S: probably made by perforating a small sherd from both sides, then grinding it to a small disk

5 Small perforated pottery disk, perhaps a bead, from D*I*,1-2: probably a painted ware sherd, bored from both sides, then edges ground
6 Pottery ring, from D*I*,2: hard pink buff paste; like painted ware, but not modeled from a sherd
7 Spindle whorl, from D*I*,1-2: orange paste, somewhat like plain ware fabric type a
8 Incompletely perforated spindle whorl; from D*I*,2: heavy dark gray paste
9 Funnel-shaped whorl, from D*I*,2: fine-grained, very dark gray paste
10 Fragment of sievelike pottery object, from D*I*,1-2: paste is like that of the painted ware; holes are bored from both sides
11 Perforated oval pottery object with possible palm prints on surfaces, from D*I*,1-2: light brown paste
12 Bone awl, from C,4 (see also fig. 219:2): made on sheep/goat distal tibia, articular end complete, epiphysis not fully fused; shaft broken off, then ground to point (grinding evidenced by striations visible all around pointed end—most at right angles to long axis)
13 Bone awl, from D*I*,2: made on split long-bone shaft too worn for species to be identified
14 Socket-headed bone awl, from C,3: made on medial half of left proximal radius, possibly of *Dama*; striations visible around point at right angles to long axis
15 Bone awl, from C,4 (*Bh-2*) (see also fig. 219:3): made on distal tibia of sheep/goat, epiphysis missing; striations visible around point at right angles to long axis

FIGURE 209. GROUND STONE
1 Celt, from D*I*,fl.4 (*Bh-16*): black rock, possibly diorite; fully ground; bit nicked and worn; butt apparently used as hammer, and hammering marks also exist elsewhere on surface
2 Celt, from D*I*,1-2: black rock, possibly diorite; apparently made by smoothing and grinding a pebble of approximately right size and shape; numerous planes and facets on surface, probably from the shaping process; pebble cortex remaining in some places
3 Pebble with narrow groove incised around one end, from D*I*,2: dark green slate
4 Macehead fragment, from D*I*,2: yellowish white marble or hard limestone
5 Stone bowl, form class IA, from D*II*N (*Bh-14*): gray limestone
6 Stone bowl, form class IB, from D*I*,fl.3: limestone, gray at surface but yellow in break
7 Stone bowl, form class IA, from D*I*,fl.2: marble, white with black and red veining; the iron minerals which cause the veining stand out from the surface on the inside of the bowl, this effect being more pronounced on the lower parts of the sides but not so noticeable near the rim (Wright suggests this might be due to whatever substance the bowl habitually held, which dissolved the marble around the more resistant iron minerals)
8 Stone bowl, form class IC, from D*I*,2: black rock, possibly diorite; horizontal polishing striations visible both inside and out
9 Stone bowl, form class IC, from D*I*,fl. 2: pinkish white limestone
10 Stone bowl, form class III, from D*I*,2: black rock, possibly diorite or a rock metamorphosed from it; exact orientation of profile uncertain
11 Stone bowl, form class III, from D*II*N (*Bh-13*): yellow to gray limestone
12 Lid, from D*I*,2: pink and white marble; lower surface blackened (by fire?); traces of adhesive (bitumen?) on lower surface and along one broken edge

FIGURE 210. GROUND STONE
1 Pendant neatly incised with intersecting lattice pattern, from D*I*,2 (*Bh-7*); red orange chert; made from a natural pebble by smoothing one face flat
2 Incised pendant, from TT,1 (*Bh-8*): black stone, possibly diorite; the projection for the perforation is broken
3 Incised stamp seal fragment, from C,4 (*Bh-9*): greenish black rock
4 Ground obsidian ornament, from D*I*,fl.6: broken at both ends
5 Triangular ornament, from B*I-II*,3: obsidian; one perforation at each end
6 Bead, from B,1: red chert; probably bored from one side only
7 Bead?, from D*I*,fl.1: black rock; central perforation and three peripheral ones all bored from both sides
8 Bead, from D*I*,2 (*Bh-12*): white chert; triangular-sectioned

FIGURE 211. MILLING STONES
1 Handstone, from A*III*,1 (left at site)
2 Quern, from D,1 (left at site)

FIGURE 212. CHIPPED STONE
1 Flake core, from D*I*,2: gray and tan chert; flakes taken off all around circumference on face shown; part of original pebble cortex remaining on face not shown; note large cone of percussion on upper part of illustrated face
2 Flake core, from D*I*,1-2: gray and tan chert; flakes taken off in at least two directions; much cortex remaining on face not shown
3 Discoidal flake core, from D*I*,fl.1 (*Bh-24*): red brown chert; flakes struck off all around circumference of both faces
4 Flake core, from D*I*,2: gray chert; flakes struck off from both ends on both faces and from one side

FIGURE 213. CHIPPED STONE
1 Bladelet core fragment, from D*I*,2: gray chert; lower end apparently reused as scraper after core broke
2 Sickle flake, from D*I*,2: gray chert; edge at left reworked to some extent (flakes struck from direction of bulbar face toward upper surface) to produce steep back; sheen covering edge at right in illustration and overlying secondary chipping; stippling indicates traces of adhesive (bitumen?)
3 Sickle flake, in D*I*,2: dark gray chert; not backed, but pronounced longitudinal ridge present (see cross section) which could have aided hafting; sheen present on edge at right overlying chipped surfaces, more noticeable on upper surface than on bulbar surface
4 Sickle blade, from D*I*,fl.3: gray chert; no backing; sheen on edge at right, noticeably less sheen on small flake scars along same edge
5 Sickle flake, from D*I*,2: dark gray chert; no secondary chipping and no backing, but pronounced median ridge which might have facilitated hafting; sheen covering edge at right and as far back as ridge on upper face, but present only on one corner of bulbar face; bulbar face probably once almost completely embedded in adhesive; on upper face, traces of adhesive (which apparently once covered left half of flint to ridge) represented by stippling
6 Sickle blade, D*I*,2: dark gray chert; sheen on edge at right; no backing, but ridge down center which might

have facilitated hafting; a few traces of adhesive near edge at left

7 *Petit tranchet* projectile tip, from D*I*,2: gray chert; very fine neat retouch down both sides converging opposite cutting edge
8 Lunate, from B,1: brown chert; carefully backed
9 Double-pointed piece, from C,3: gray chert; points produced by retouch from bulbar face
10 Flake, probable drill, from C,1: gray chert; steep retouch on both edges converging toward broken tip
11 Flake, probable small drill, from D*II*,2: gray chert; alternate-opposite retouch converging on tip
12 Utilized flake, scraper?, from B*III*,2: red brown chert

FIGURE 214. CHIPPED STONE

1 Flake, scraper?, from D*I*,2: gray chert; reworked on right edge of upper face
2 Flake, from D*I*,1-2: gray chert; "nose" produced by use and/or retouch from bulbar face
3 Flake, from D*I*,2: gray chert; both edges utilized
4 Blade fragment?, from B*III*,2: gray chert; retouched steeply from bulbar face on both edges
5 Heavily utilized bladelike flake, from D*I*,2: brown chert; natural cortex "backing"
6 Bladelike flake, from D*I*,2: tan chert; slightly utilized on both edges
7 Backed blade, from C,2: brown chert
8 Drill, from C,3 (*Bh-26*): obsidian; neat backing along both edges

FIGURE 215. CHIPPED STONE

1 Blade, from D*I*,fl.2: translucent greenish black obsidian; retouch from upper surface along left edge and angling toward bulb, retouch and use on right edge largely from upper face but some also from bulbar face
2 Blade fragment, from D*I*,fl.2: opaque black obsidian; steep retouch (alternate-opposite) and signs of use on both edges
3 Blade fragment, from D*I*,2: translucent olive green obsidian; left edge heavily utilized, right edge slightly utilized
4 Blade fragment, from D*I*,fl.2: olive green obsidian, translucent where thin; secondary flaking over upper face, much secondary chipping from upper face on both edges of bulbar face
5 Blade fragment, from D*I*,2: opaque black obsidian; both edges used and/or retouched on both faces, especially along right edge of upper face
6 Blade fragment, from D*I*,2: greenish black obsidian; some use and retouch on both edges
7 Blade fragment, from D*II*,2: translucent gray obsidian; some use and retouch on both edges

8 Flake, from D*II*,fl.2: opaque black obsidian; two shallow notches worked into one edge from upper face

FIGURE 216. NON-HALAFIAN POTTERY*

1 Sherd, from A*I*,4, early Hellenistic (see also fig. 204:17)
2 Sherd, from A*I*,3, probably Iron Age (see also fig. 204:4)
3 Sherd, from A*II*,4, nondiagnostic
4 Sherd, from A*I*,3, probably Iron Age (see also fig. 204:2)
5 Sherd, from B*I-II*,2, probably early second millennium (see also fig. 204:14)
6 Sherd, from A*I*,3, probably Iron Age (see also fig. 204:3)
7 Sherd, from A*I*,3, probably early second millennium (see also fig. 204:5)
8 Sherd, from B,1, probably Iron Age (see also fig. 204:19)
9 Sherd, from A*III*,1, probably Iron Age (see also fig. 204:20)
10 Sherd, from A*I*,3, probably early second millennium (see also fig. 204:15)
11 Sherd, from A*I*,3, early Hellenistic (see also fig. 204:16)

FIGURE 217. WORKED PAINTED-WARE SHERDS AND PLAIN WARE (see footnote, p. 582, for plain-ware fabric types)

1 From D*I*,2: chipped sherd, painted ware
2 From D*I*,fl.1 (see also fig. 208:1): chipped sherd, painted ware
3 Form class IVB, from C,5: detached lug, showing construction details; plain ware, fabric type b
4 Form class IA, from D*I*,fl.7 (see also fig. 202:1): plain ware, fabric type a
5 Form class IA, from D*I*,2 (see also fig. 202:10): plain ware, fabric type a
6 Form class IB2, from C,2: (see also fig. 202:16): plain ware, fabric type b
7 Form class IB1, from D*II*N (see also fig. 202:12): plain ware, fabric type b
8 Form class IB2, from D*II*,1-2 (see also fig. 202:15): plain ware, fabric type x

FIGURE 218. GROUND STONE

1 Fragment of grinding stone or door pivot stone, from D*I*,fl.5: gray green rock
2 Pestle fragment, from A*I*,4: fine-grained green rock
3 Mortar fragment, from D*I*,fl.6: gray and white limestone
4 Handstone or large pestle, from D*I*,fl.3: coarse-grained green black rock

FIGURE 219. BONE OBJECTS

1 Knucklebone gaming pieces, from B*III*,2 (*Bh-4*)
2 Long-bone awl, from C,4 (see also fig. 208:12)
3 Long-bone awl, from C,4 (*Bh-2*) (see also fig. 208:15)
4 Long-bone awl, from C,2 (*Bh-1*)

---

*Age estimates by Rudolph Dornemann, see p. 567.

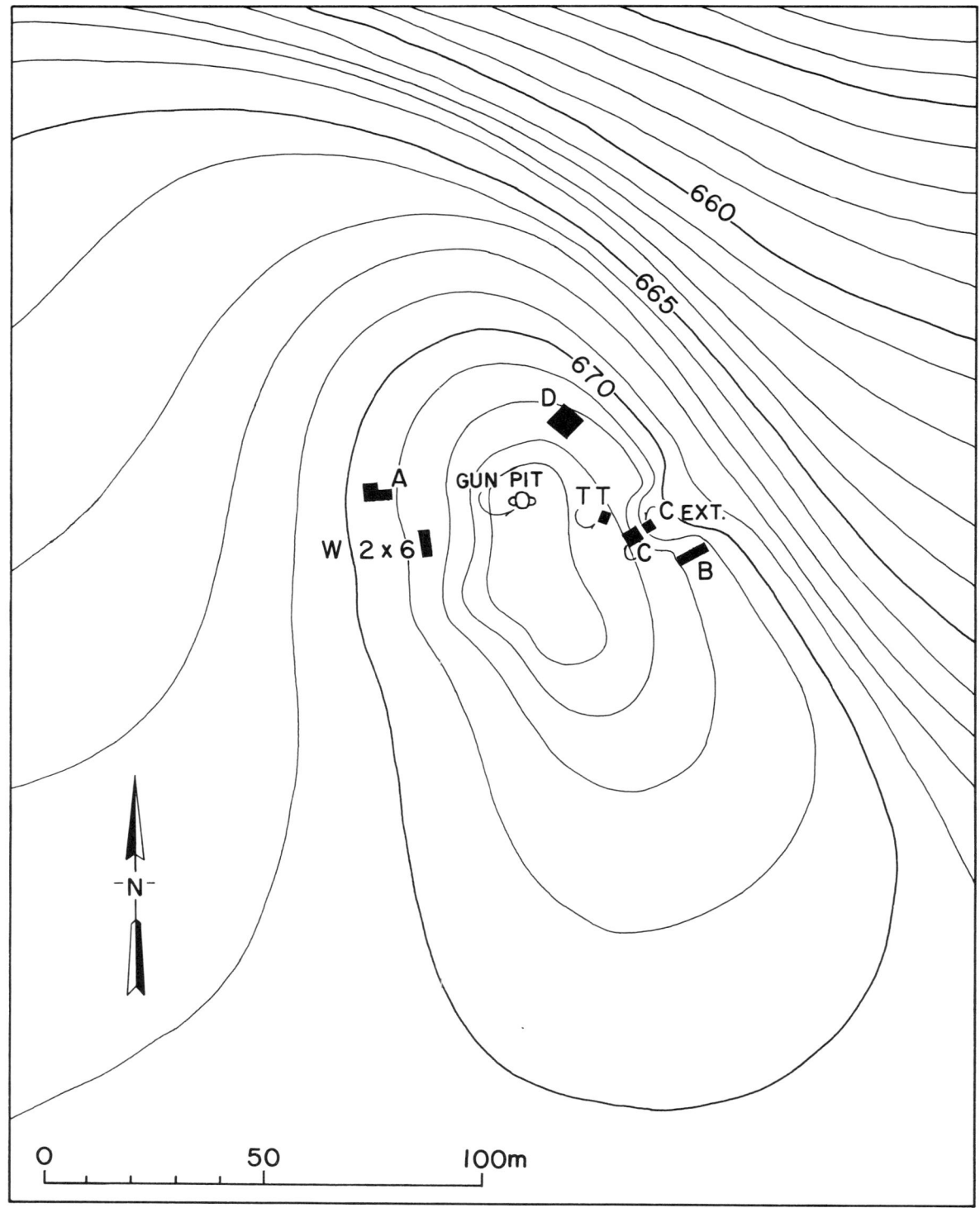

Fig. 194. Plot plan of Gird Banahilk.

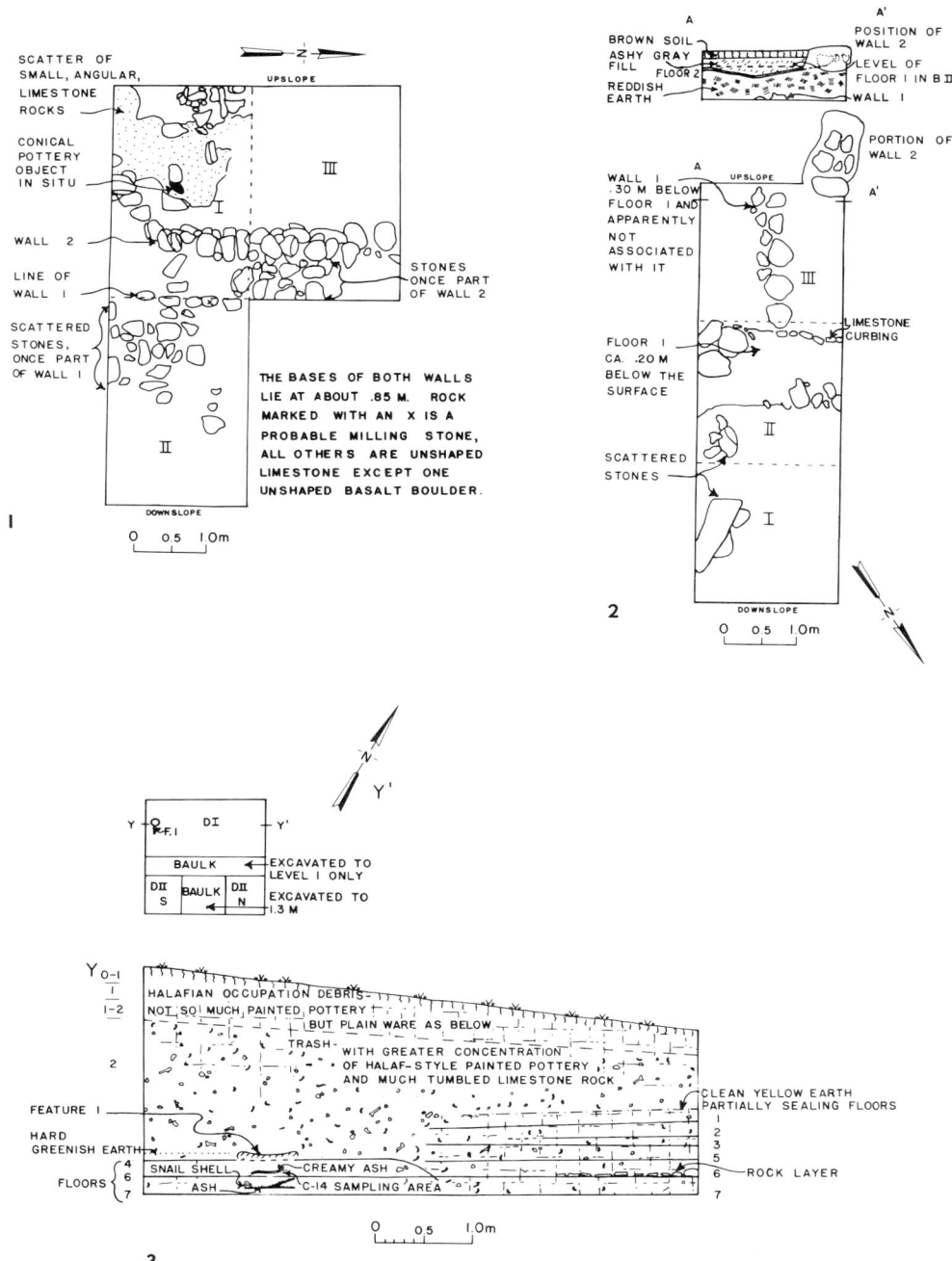

Fig. 195. Banahilk: *1*, operation A, plan; *2*, operation B, section and plan; *3*, operation D, schematic plan and section.

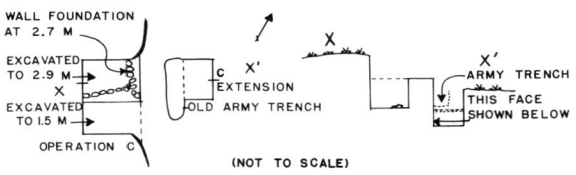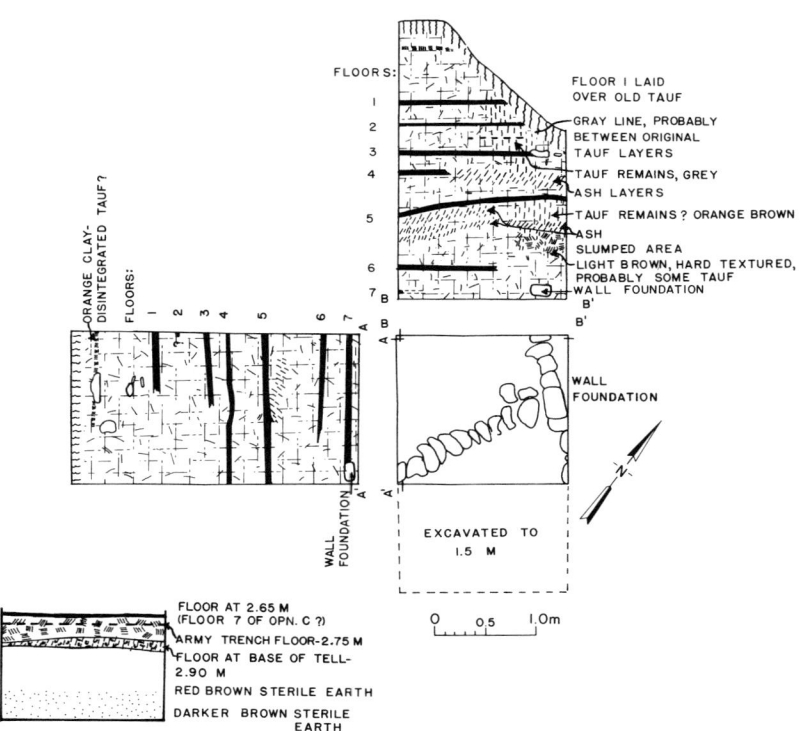

Fig. 196. Banahilk: *1*, operation C and C extension, plan and section; *2*, operation C, sections and plan; *3*, C extension, section.

Fig. 197. Banahilk painted ware: bowls, form class IA, *1-6* (all are form IA2 except no. *4*, which is IA1); bowls, form class IB, *7-15*. Scale 1:3. (Rim and base diameters given in mm.)

Fig. 198. Banahilk painted ware: bowls, form class IB, *1-7*; bowls, form class IC, *8-12*; bowls, form class ID, *13-19*; bowls, form class IE, *20-22*. Nos. *9* and *16* are artist's reconstructions from sherds. Scale 1:3.

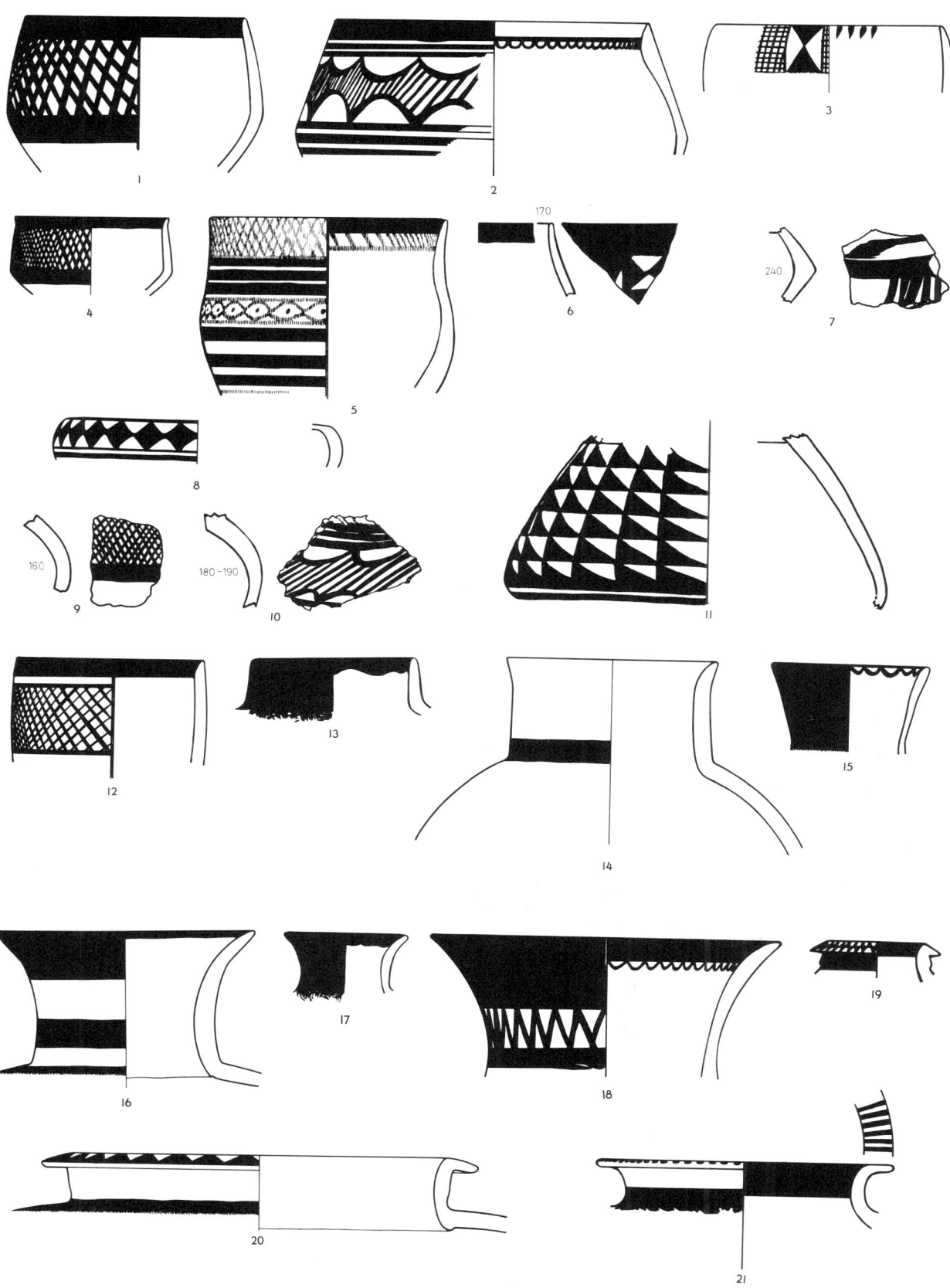

Fig. 199. Banahilk painted ware: bowls, form class IE, *1-6*; jars, form class II, *7-11*; jar necks, form class IIIA1, *12-13*; jar necks, form class IIIA2, *14-18*; jar necks, form class IIIA3, *19-21*. Scale 1:3.

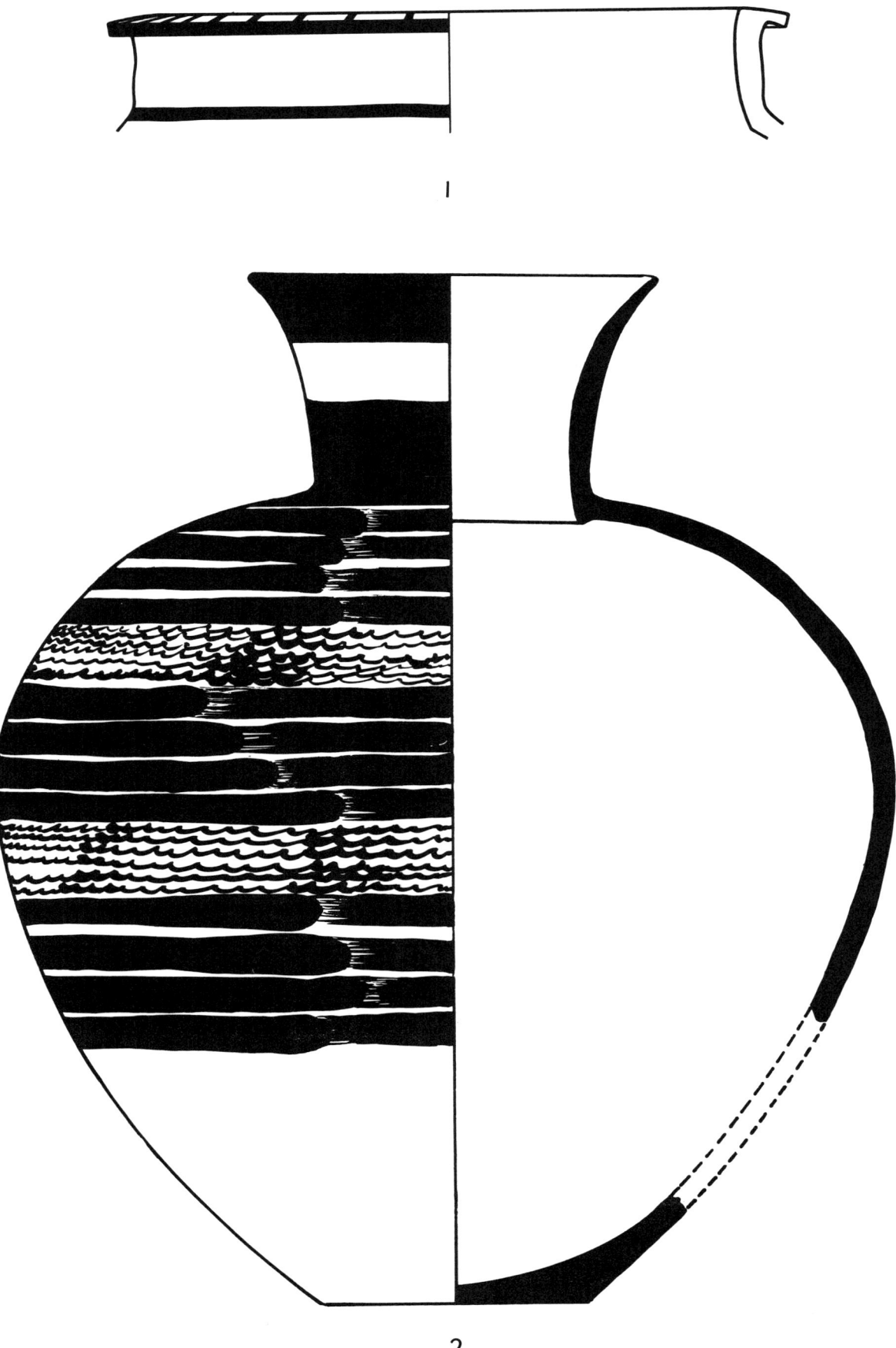

Fig. 200. Banahilk painted ware: jar neck, form class IIIA3, *1*; jar, form class IIIC, *2* (artist's reconstruction from sherds). Scale 1:4.

Fig. 201. Banahilk painted ware: jars, form class IIID, *1-2*; bases, form class IIIE, *3-13*; miscellaneous, form class IV, *14-26*. Scale 1:3.

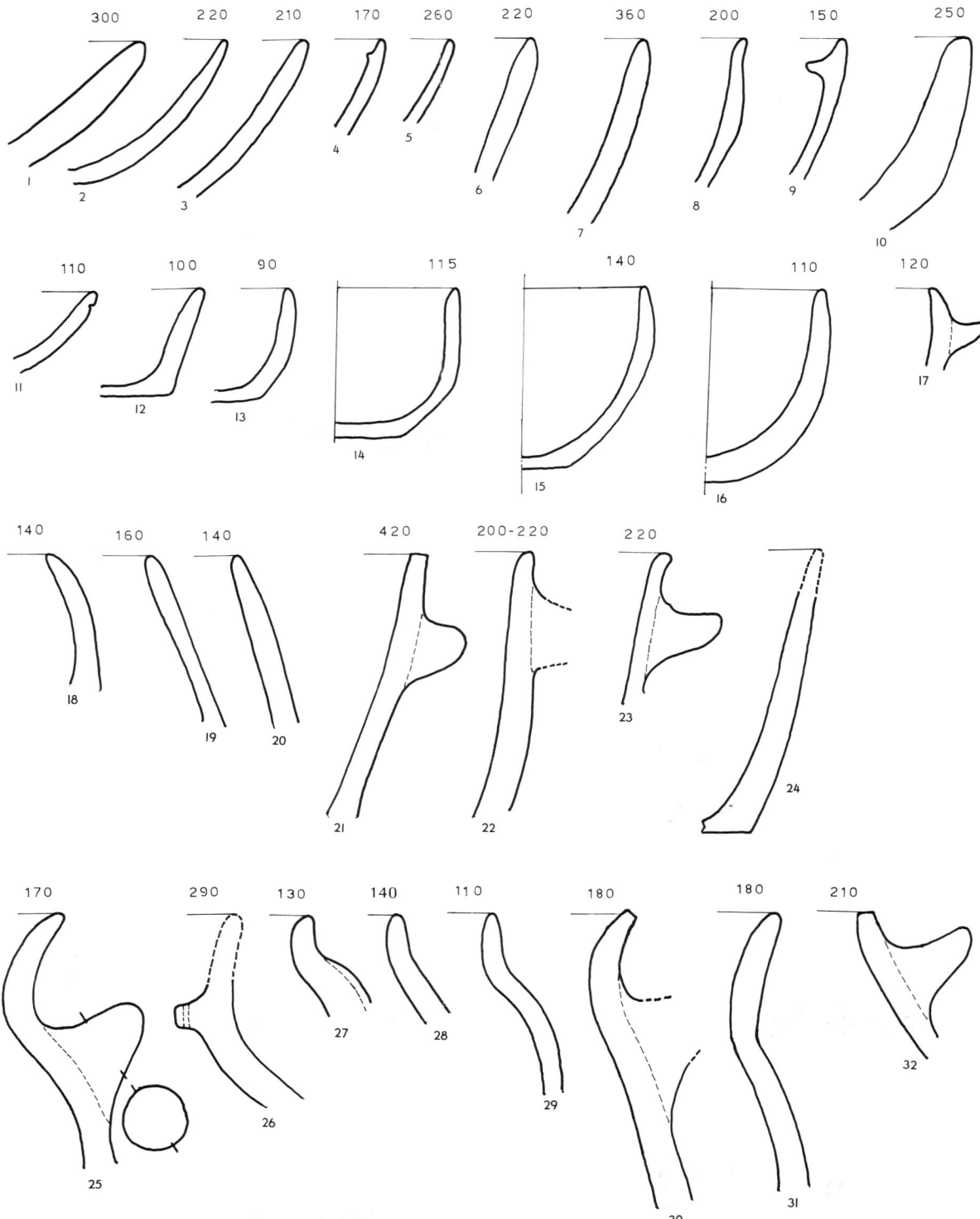

Fig. 202. Banahilk plain ware: bowls, form class IA, *1-10*; bowls, form class IB, *11-17*; bowls, form class ID, *18-20*; bowls, form class IE, *21-24*; jars, form class IIA, *25-32*. Scale 1:3.

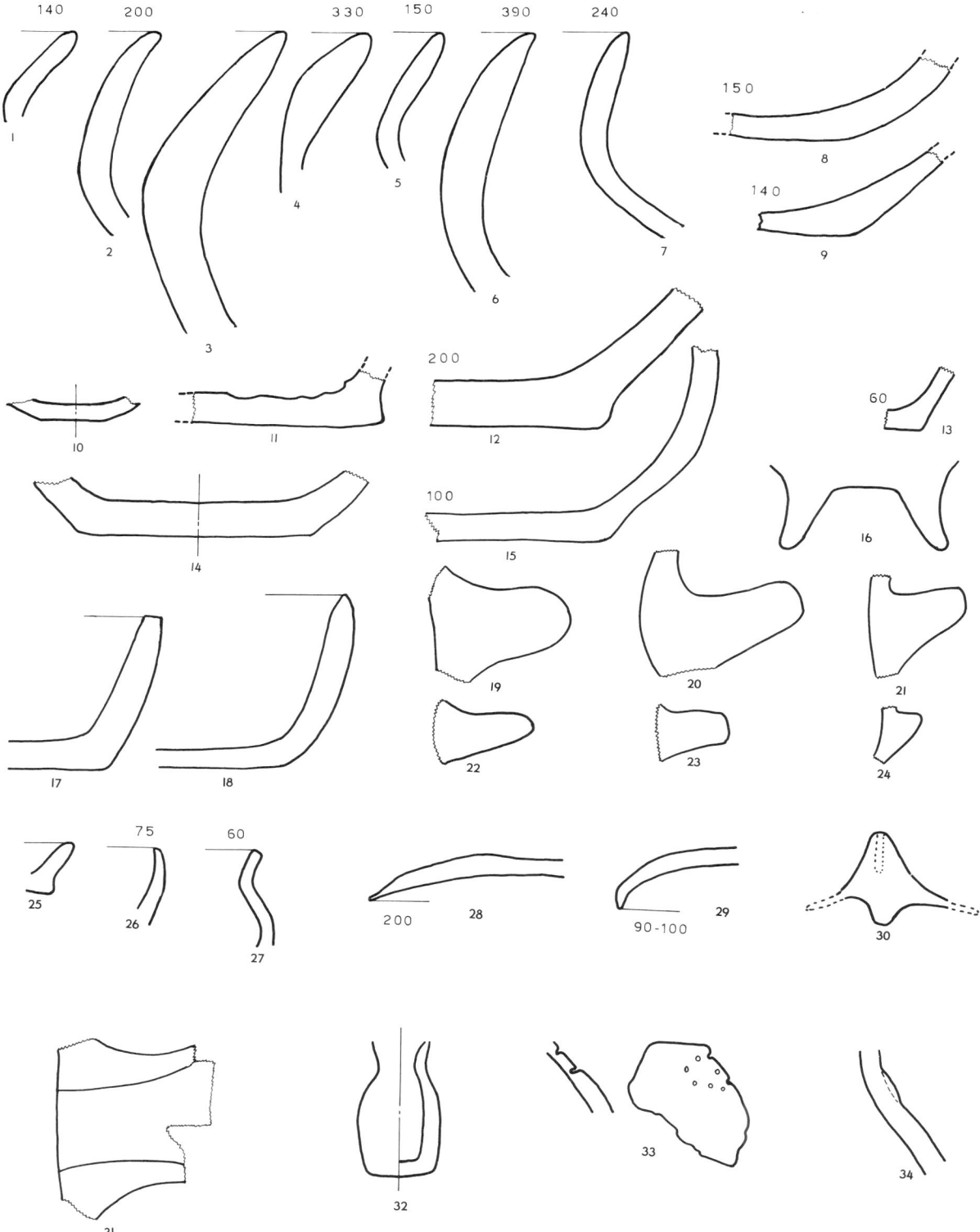

Fig. 203. Banahilk plain ware: jars, form class IIB, *1-7*; bases, form class IID, *8-16*; trays, form class III, *17-18*; miscellaneous, form class IV, *19-34*. Scale 1:3.

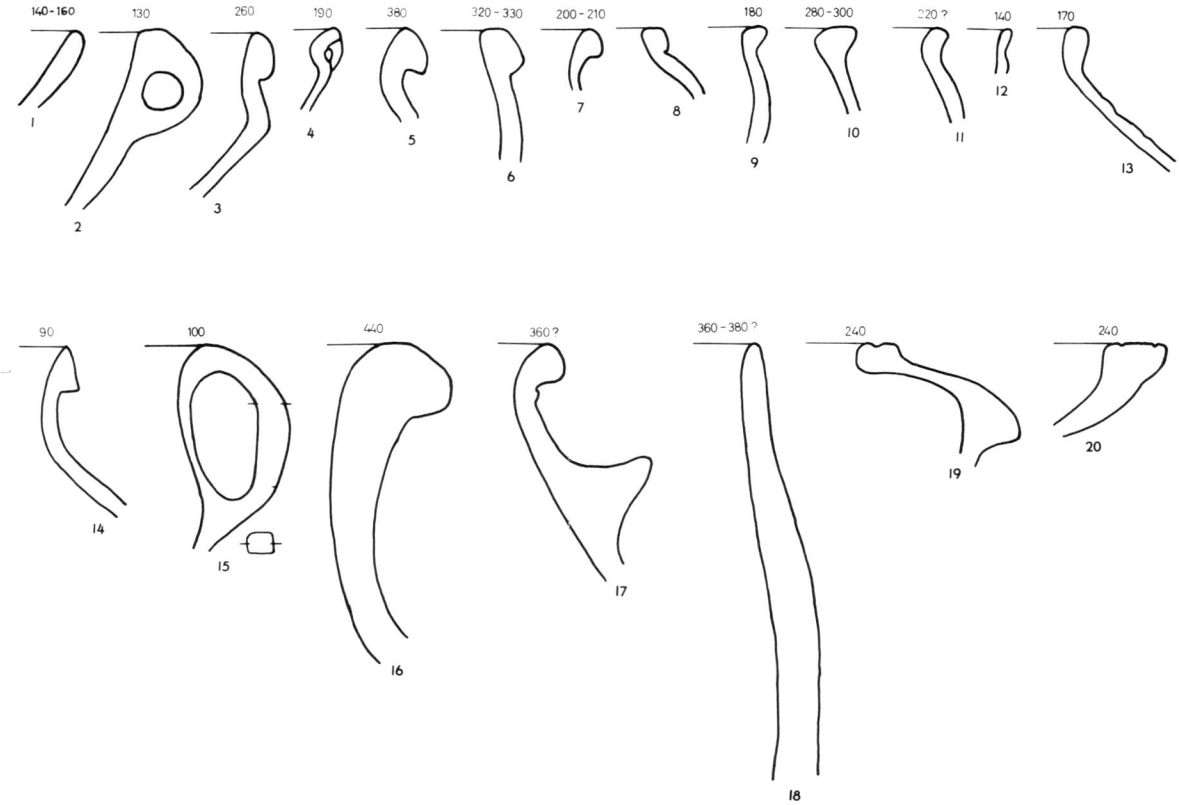

Fig. 204. Banahilk non-Halafian pottery (sherds that postdate the Halafian-period occupation of Banahilk [Rudolph Dornemann, pers. comm., p. 567]): probably early second millennium, *5,7,9,14-15*; probably Iron Age, *2-4,6,10-11,19-20*; early Hellenistic, *13,16-17*; nondiagnostic or unknown sherds, *1,8,12,18*. See also fig. 216. Scale 1:3.

Fig. 205. Banahilk painted ware designs.

Notes on Fig. 205

No.	Design	Description and remarks
1	Asterisk	Rare; star made by three painted lines intersecting.
2	Band(s) alternating with x's	One or more bands above and below a zone of repeated x's.
	Bird	Not shown here. See p. 550 and fig. 198:5.
3	Boxes	One of the many all-over designs constructed on a background lattice. However, in this motif, lattice is formed by double lines, then alternate boxes of inner lattice are filled in with paint. Compare fig. 205:7 below.
4	Bucranium	Based on representation of a bull's head, usually with special emphasis on S-curved horns. Banahilk variants all stylized: horizontal (double and/or pierced) (figs. 205:4a; 197:7), cruciform (figs. 197:13; 198:1), and elongated vertical bucrania (figs. 205:4b; 198:9). (See Mallowan and Rose 1935, pp. 154-63, for discussion and illustration of large series of bucranium motifs at Arpachiyah; see also Oppenheim and Schmidt 1943, pl. LIII:3-6,8,12,14, and pls. LIX, LXII.)
5	Butterfly	Actually two solid triangles opposed at their apices; motif oriented vertically or horizontally, or composed of alternating vertical and horizontal butterflies.
6	Cable	This motif frequently zoned; cable may be open (formed by two interweaving or opposed wavy lines, see fig. 205:6a), solid (rare, formed by filling in openings with paint, see fig. 205:6b), hatched (very common, see fig. 205:6c), dotted (formed by placing one dot in each opening), pierced (bisected), reserved (hatching made outside cable openings only, see fig. 205:6d), zigzag (formed by two intersecting zigzags instead of two wavy lines); fish-shaped (with intersecting zigzag lines that are extended so whole motif resembles row of stylized fish swimming nose to tail, see fig. 205:6e). Also 2 examples of an eye design (fig. 197:3).
7	Checkerboard	Lattice drawn over surface to be decorated, alternate squares then filled in with paint (solid squares) or hatched, crosshatched, or latticed; unfilled squares left without decoration (empty squares) or containing a single x, dot, ring (1 example), triangle, or butterfly, or dotted arcs. Compare fig. 205:3 above.
8	Chevrons	Small V-shaped elements that always point to the right (whenever orientation of sherd is known); a common zoned motif.
9	Concentric arcs	Series of nested arcs often pendent from a band or sometimes overlapping another such series.

Notes on Fig. 206

No.	Design	Description and remarks
10	Concentric triangles	Series of two or more nested triangles all formed on common base line (i.e., small triangle in center with successively larger ones built up around it).
11	Concentric zigzags	Zoned series of nested horizontal zigzags, closely spaced and neatly in phase.
12	Crosshatching	Two sets of straight lines that intersect at any angle except a right angle or that are oriented diagonally whenever they do intersect at a right angle.
13	Diamonds	Several variants: commonest, running crosshatched diamonds in zone set off by bands, occasionally combined with triangles as spacers (fig. 206:13a); all-over netlike design produced by covering vessel with broad open crosshatching, then filling in with paint the alternate rows of diamonds formed by the intersecting lines (fig. 206:13d); less common, single or multiple dots inside open diamonds in zones (figs. 206:13b and 198:12; on 1 example dots are also in the butterfly-shaped spaces between diamonds); running solid diamonds (fig. 206:13c). A zone of running open diamonds superficially resembles a zigzag cable (fig. 205:6), but the techniques used to produce the two designs differ: running diamonds are created in a modular fashion as linked but separable entities, whereas a zigzag cable is produced by constructing two horizontal zigzags that intersect each other to form a design that resembles a series of running diamonds.
14	Domes	Half an ellipsis cut at shortest diameter, resembling in outline old-fashioned domed beehive (1 example only—a series of domes in a zone on inside of flare-rimmed bowl).
15	Dot circles	Circles formed by small dots; zoned in both Banahilk examples.
16	Dotted rings	Evenly spaced circles with one dot in center of each.
17	Fish scales	Several curved lines overlapped, resembling fish scales; uncommon.
18	Hatched bands	Two or three bands with short, narrow, diagonal, or vertical lines drawn between them.
19	Hatched arcs	Vertically hatched arcs (1 example only—sherd from shallow round-sided bowl with two such zones).
20	Herringbone	Oblique hatching alternating in direction from zone to zone with horizontal lines between. See also fig. 197:8.
21	Hatching between opposed wavy lines	Set of two opposing scallops painted so that crest and trough are out of phase, then diagonal hatching in space between the two.
22	"Imitation Wickelschnur"	Based on use of lines and dots: two rows of dots placed along one line, one row above line and one below it, so that individual dots are opposite each other. Found by Schmidt at Tell Halaf (Oppenheim and Schmidt 1943, p. 35, pl. XLVII:2-3).
23	Knotted line	Line with solid circles spaced along it.
24	Lattice	(To be distinguished from crosshatching.) Two sets of evenly spaced straight lines that intersect at right angles; not so much a decorative motif itself as a basis for construction of more complex designs (checkerboards, quatrefoils, all-over right triangles, xed lattices, etc.).
25	Lines and dots	Horizontal lines or narrow bands alternating with horizontal rows of dots.
26	Quatrefoil	Common motif constructed on a lattice, occurring in both zoned and all-over designs. It resembles a four-petaled flower and is very striking if neatly done. The method of construction seems to have been as follows: a lattice was painted over the surface to be decorated and four lattice squares formed the design unit; two curved lines were drawn diagonally across each square of the design unit to form a petal (or leaf); these four petals were joined at the center point of the four-square unit, thus forming a quatrefoil in outline; next, the background of the petals was filled in with paint in each four-square unit. The result is a series of reserved (unpainted) quatrefoils; the color of the pot's surface (buff or pink) contrasts with the painted areas (black or red) that outline them. If one ignores the petals when viewing the design, the painted area stands out as a cross formée. Often there are also diagonal lines bisecting the petals; they were probably added to the original lattice before the quatrefoils were made (i.e., a pattern of crisscrossed squares was drawn first; see fig. 206:33 below).
27	Reserved (unpainted) wavy line	Paint used as background color; wavy line appears where pot's surface has been left unpainted.
28	Reserved (unpainted) x's	All-over design based on lattice. It is formed by filling in four more or less equilateral triangles, one based on each side of a lattice square. Sufficient space is left between triangles to form an x (which is centered in the square) in the background color of the pot. If one concentrates on the painted background rather than the x, one can discern a disarticulated cross formée.
29	Rings	Uncommon motif consisting of small circles painted in a zone.
30	Rosette	Occurs within shallow round-sided bowls as a central design in bottom; usually a whorl of painted petals dominating interior of vessel. In 1 example, rosette is surrounded by a painted background with only a narrow line of the unpainted pot surface left to outline the petals. On another example the petals have been formed in reserve by a spokelike radiation of lines, each of which broadens at outer end to enclose tip of reserved petal. There is a spokelike variant in which the spoke lines are fringed.
31	Spot (i.e., large dot), dot, dashed lines, and band combinations	Several variants.
32	Triangles	Motif used in a number of designs: alternating opposed triangles (formed by imposing bold zigzag on single horizontal line, thus forming triangles above and below line, then filling them with paint; typically, there are bands above and below the triangle zone); right triangles, common motif used as all-over design on jars (series of lines drawn diagonally over a lattice pattern and bisecting each lattice square; the right triangles thus formed in the squares are filled with paint); triangle motif that seems to occur as a spacer with zones of running diamonds (zone boundary lines above and below serve as one side of the triangles that partially fill the spaces between individual diamonds; see fig. 206:13a).
33	xed lattice square	Rare motif making use of two all-over lattices, one painted at 45° angle to the other, so that each square of the base lattice contains an x. This same design was engraved on many of the Halafian seals and pendants at Arpachiyah (Mallowan and Rose 1935, fig. 50, pl. VIIa) and on 3 at Banahilk (fig. 210:1-3). Compare also fig. 205:7a.
34	Zipper	Pair of narrow parallel lines with spaced series of opposed dots on inner side of each line, closely resembling an open zipper (1 example only).

Fig. 206. Banahilk painted ware designs. (See notes on opposite page.)

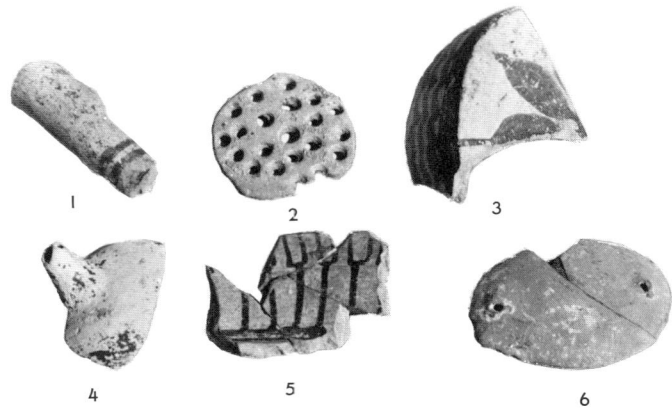

Fig. 207. Banahilk pottery objects now in Baghdad: broken cylinder, possibly a figurine leg, *1*; sievelike object, *2*; lid fragment, *3*; spouted miniature vessel fragment, *4*; painted "cream bowl" fragment, *5*; perforated oval ornament, *6*. Scale 1:2.

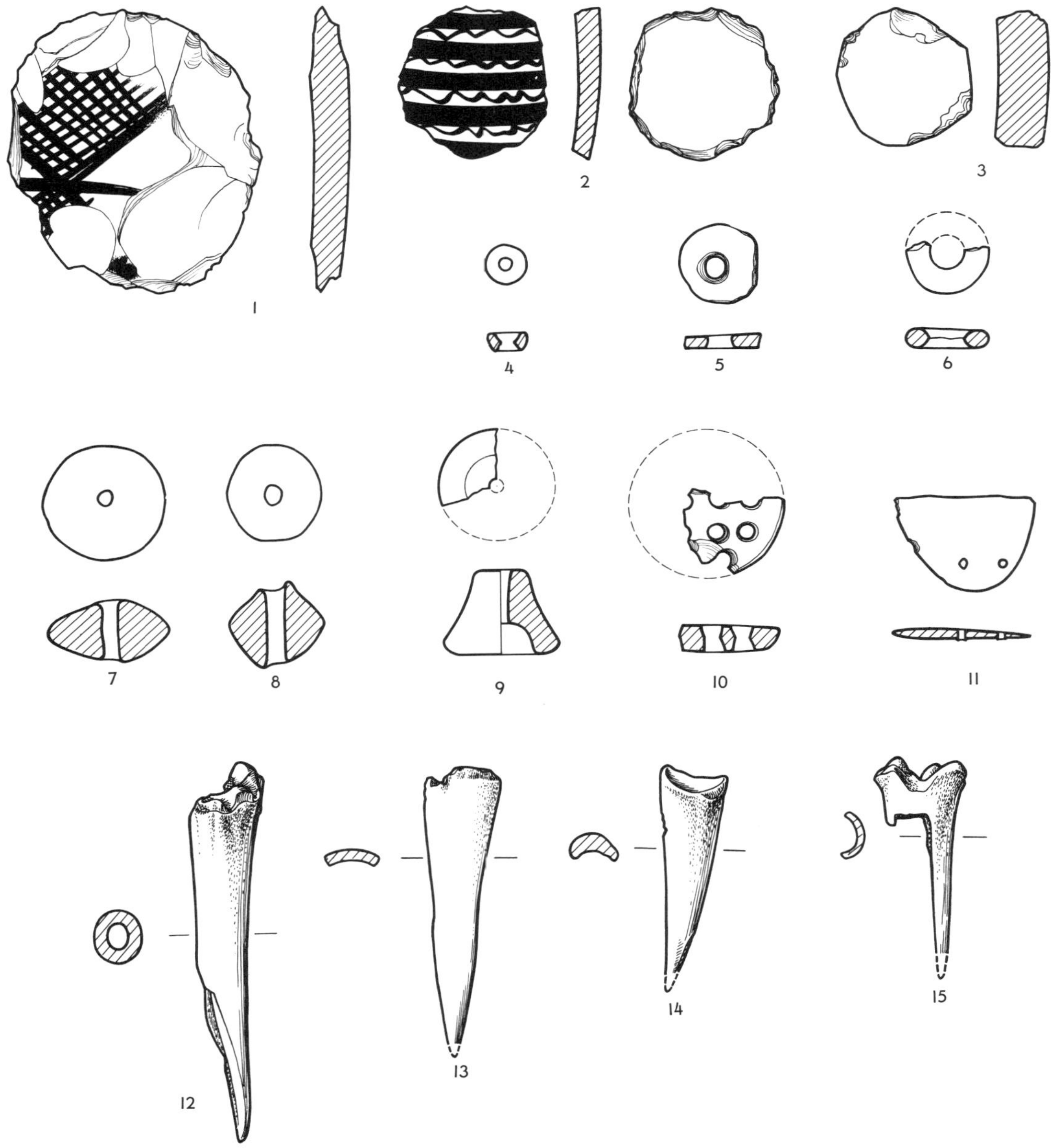

Fig. 208. Banahilk pottery and bone objects: worked sherds, *1-3*; pottery rings or beads, *4-6*; pottery whorls, *7-9*; sievelike pottery object, *10*; perforated flattened pottery oval, *11*; bone awls, *12-15*. Scale 1:2.

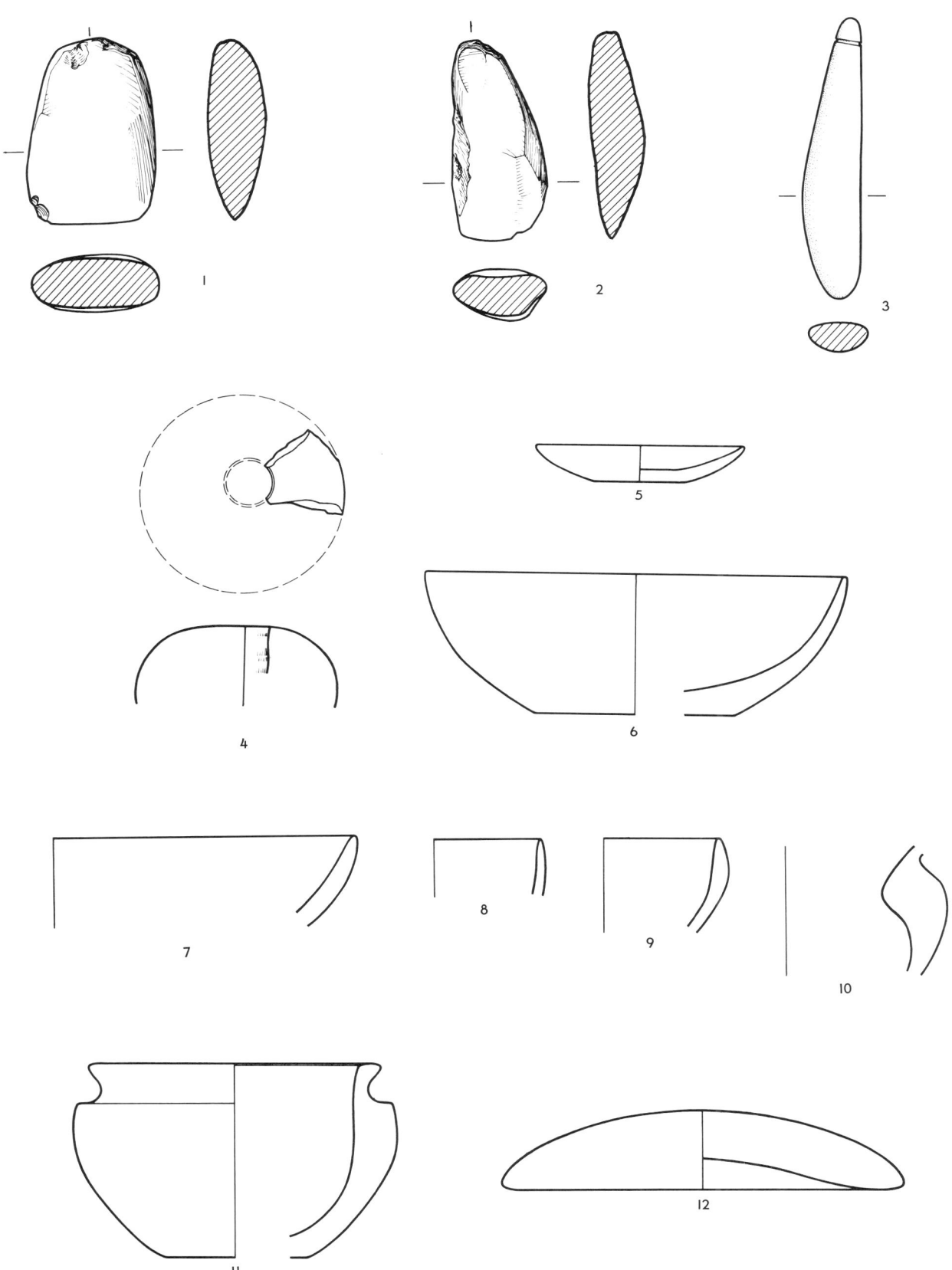

Fig. 209. Banahilk ground stone: celts, *1-2*; grooved pebble, *3*; macehead fragment, *4*; vessels, *5-11*; lid, *12*. Scale 1:2.

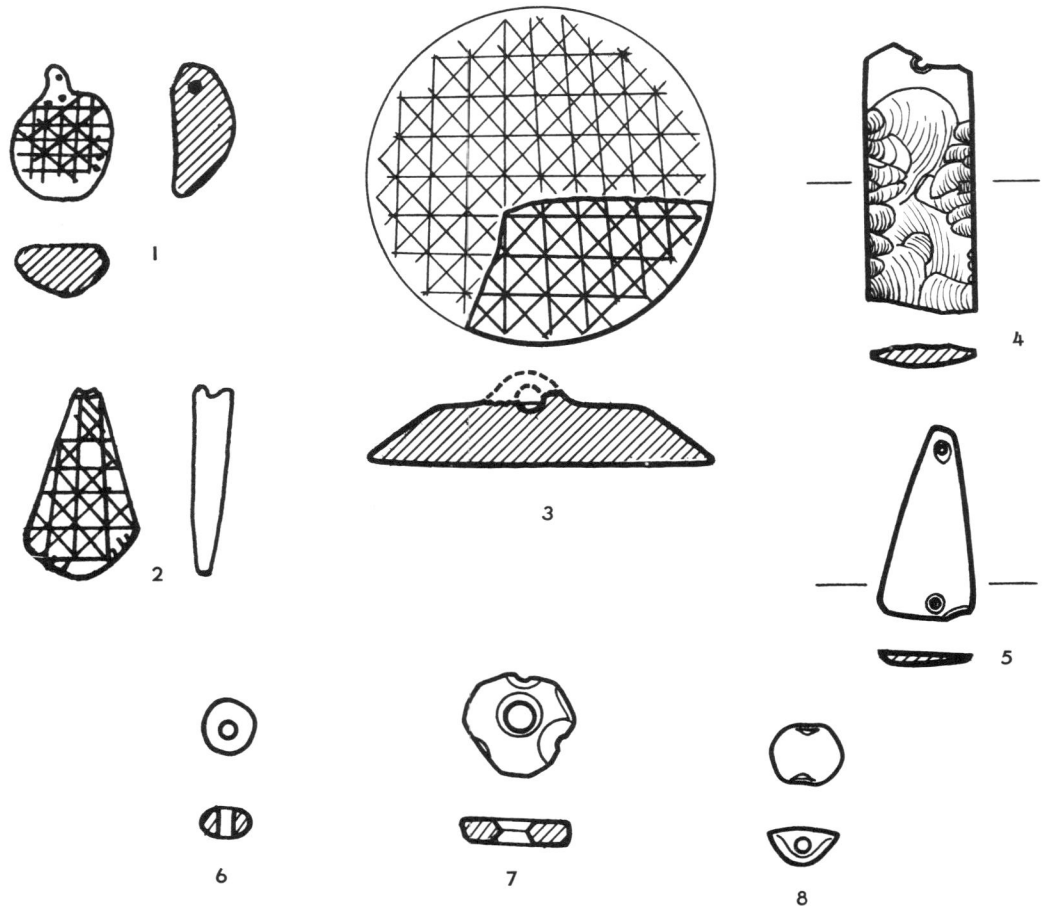

Fig. 210. Banahilk ground stone: incised pendants and seal, *1-3*; ground and perforated obsidian ornaments, *4-5*; beads, *6-8*. Scale 1:1.

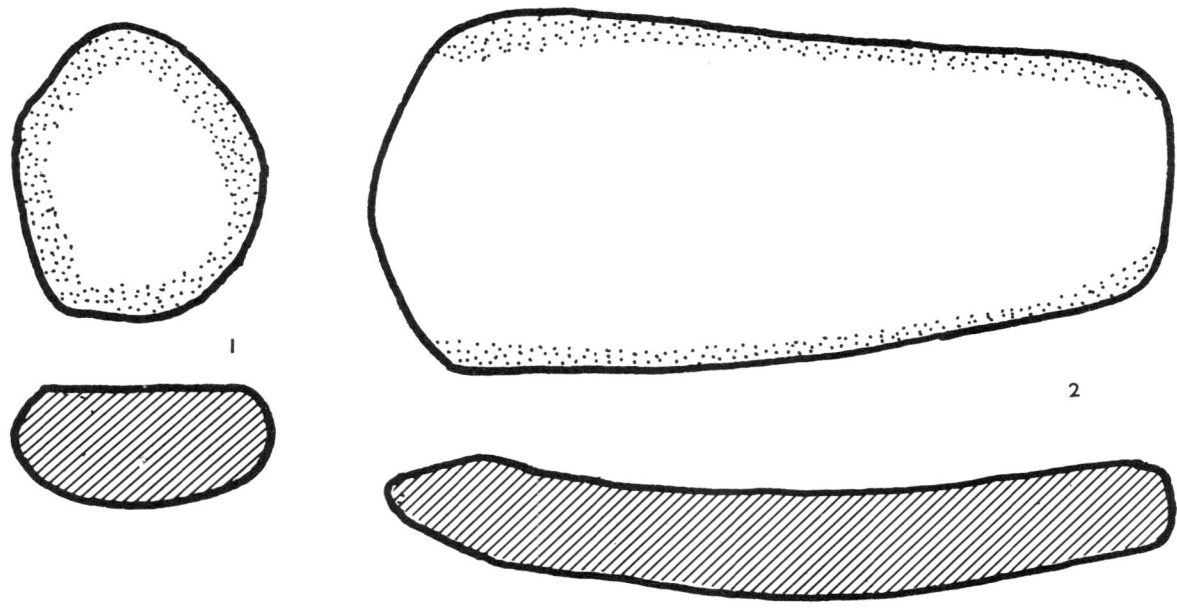

Fig. 211. Banahilk milling stones: handstone, *1*; quern, *2*. Scales 1:2, *1*; 1:4, *2*.

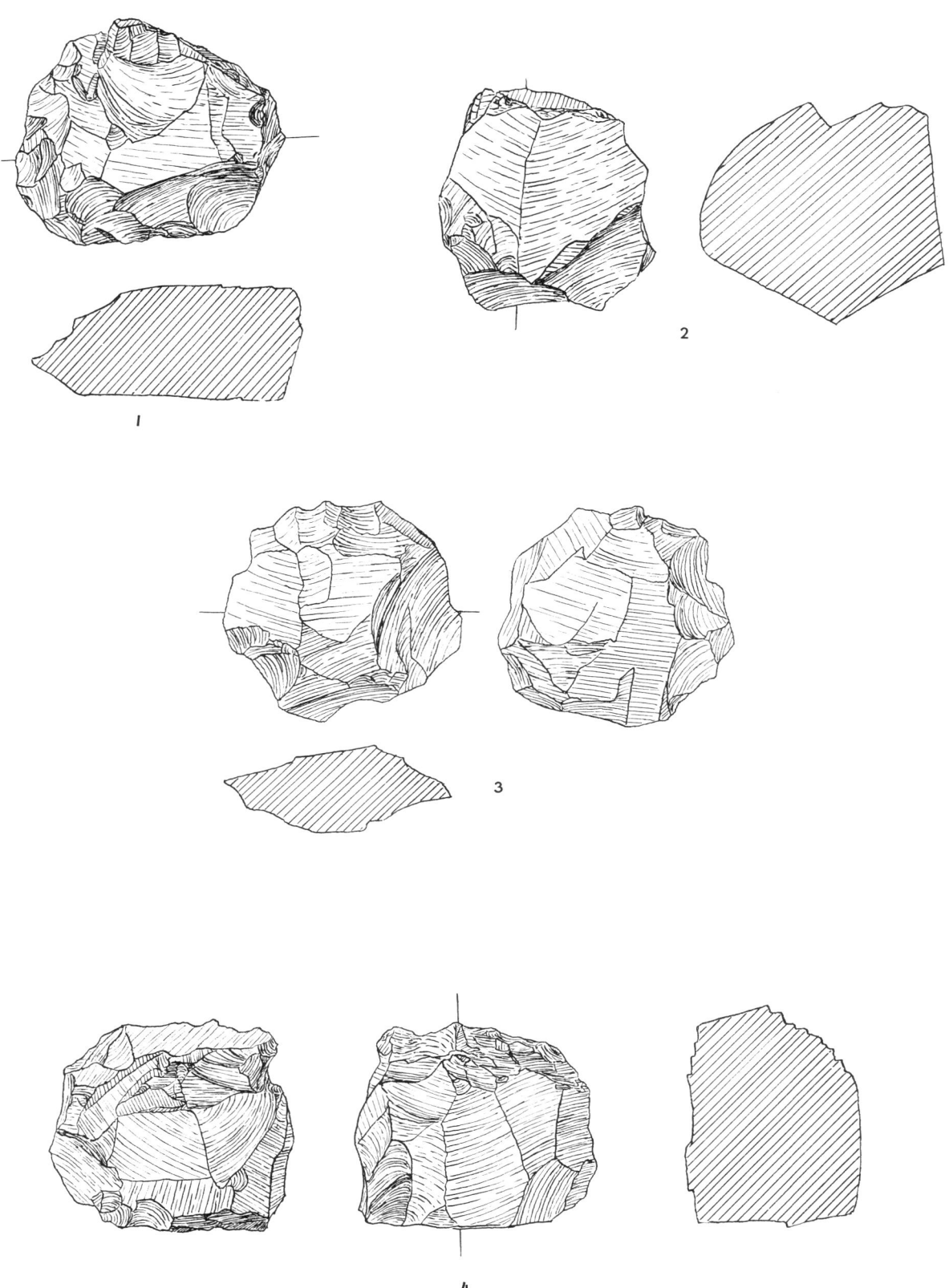

Fig. 212. Banahilk chipped stone: flake cores, *1-4*. All chert. Scale 1:1.

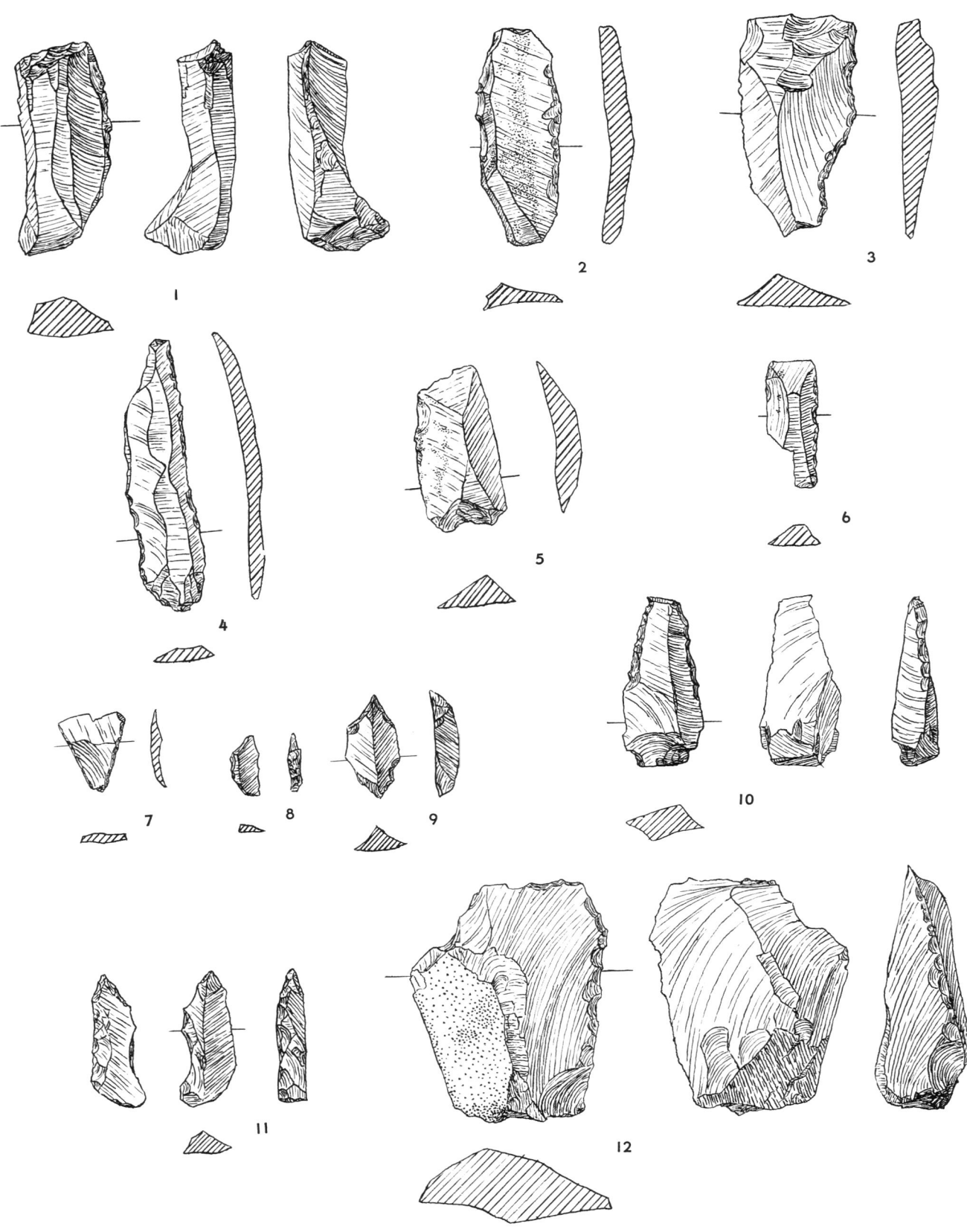

Fig. 213. Banahilk chipped stone: bladelet core, *1*; sickle flints, *2-6*; *petit tranchet* projectile tip, *7*; lunate, *8*; double-pointed piece, *9*; drills, *10-11*; utilized flake, *12*. All chert. Scale 1:1.

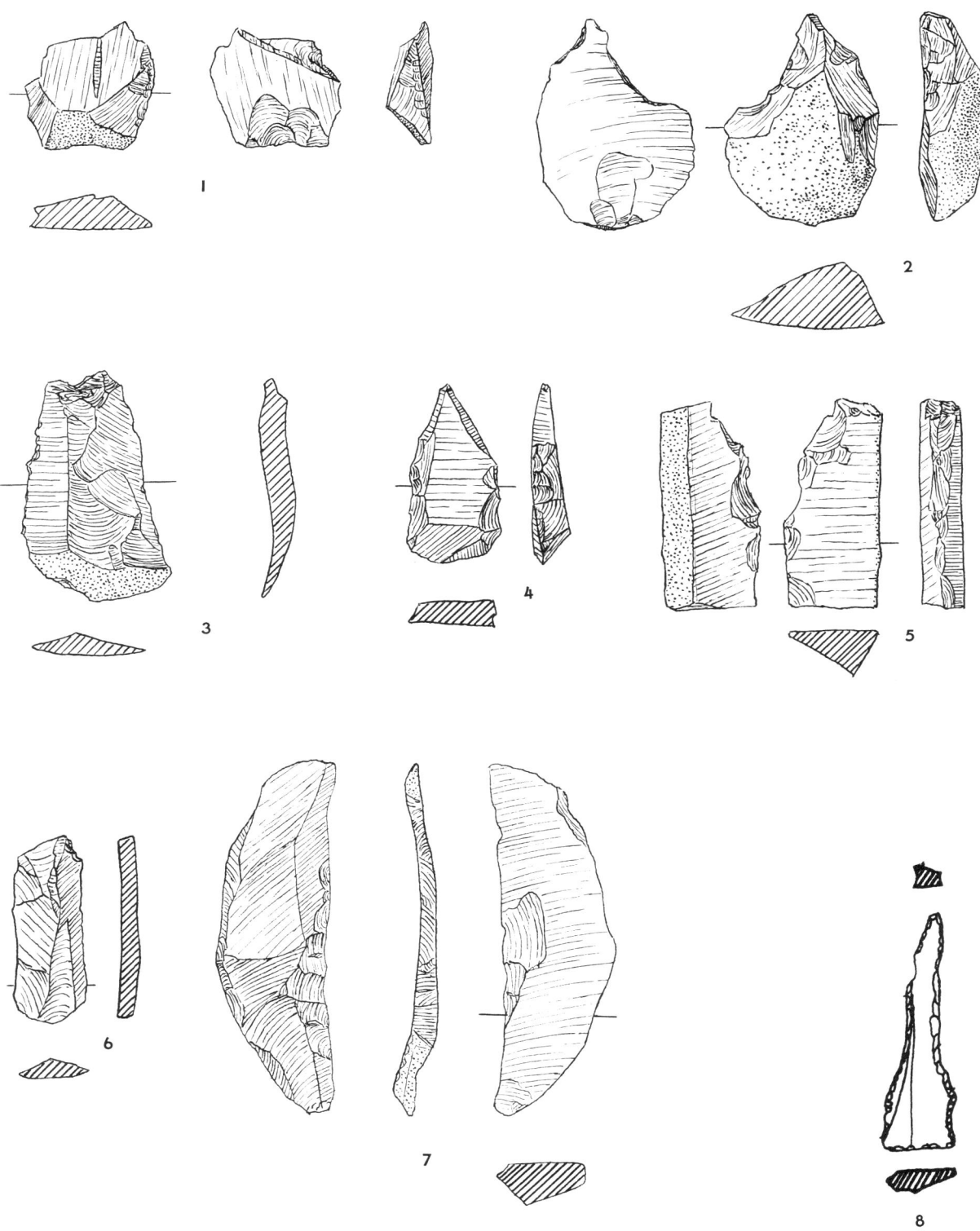

Fig. 214. Banahilk chipped stone: utilized flakes, *1-3*; fragments of blades or blakelike flakes, *4-6*; backed blade, *7*; drill, *8*. No. *8* is obsidian; remainder are chert. Scale 1:1.

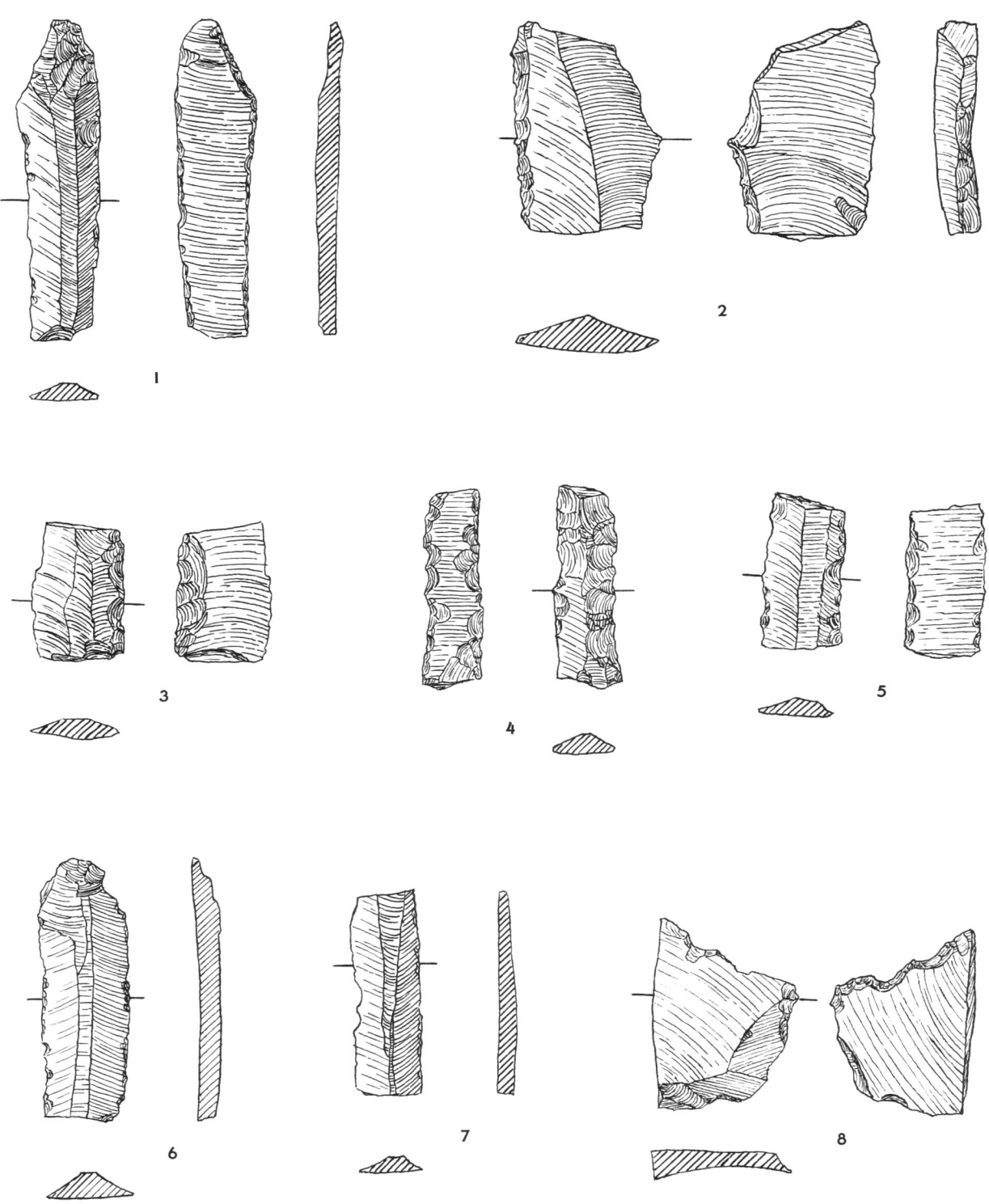

Fig. 215. Banahilk chipped stone: blades and blade fragments, *1-7*; utilized or retouched flake, *8*. All obsidian. Scale 1:1.

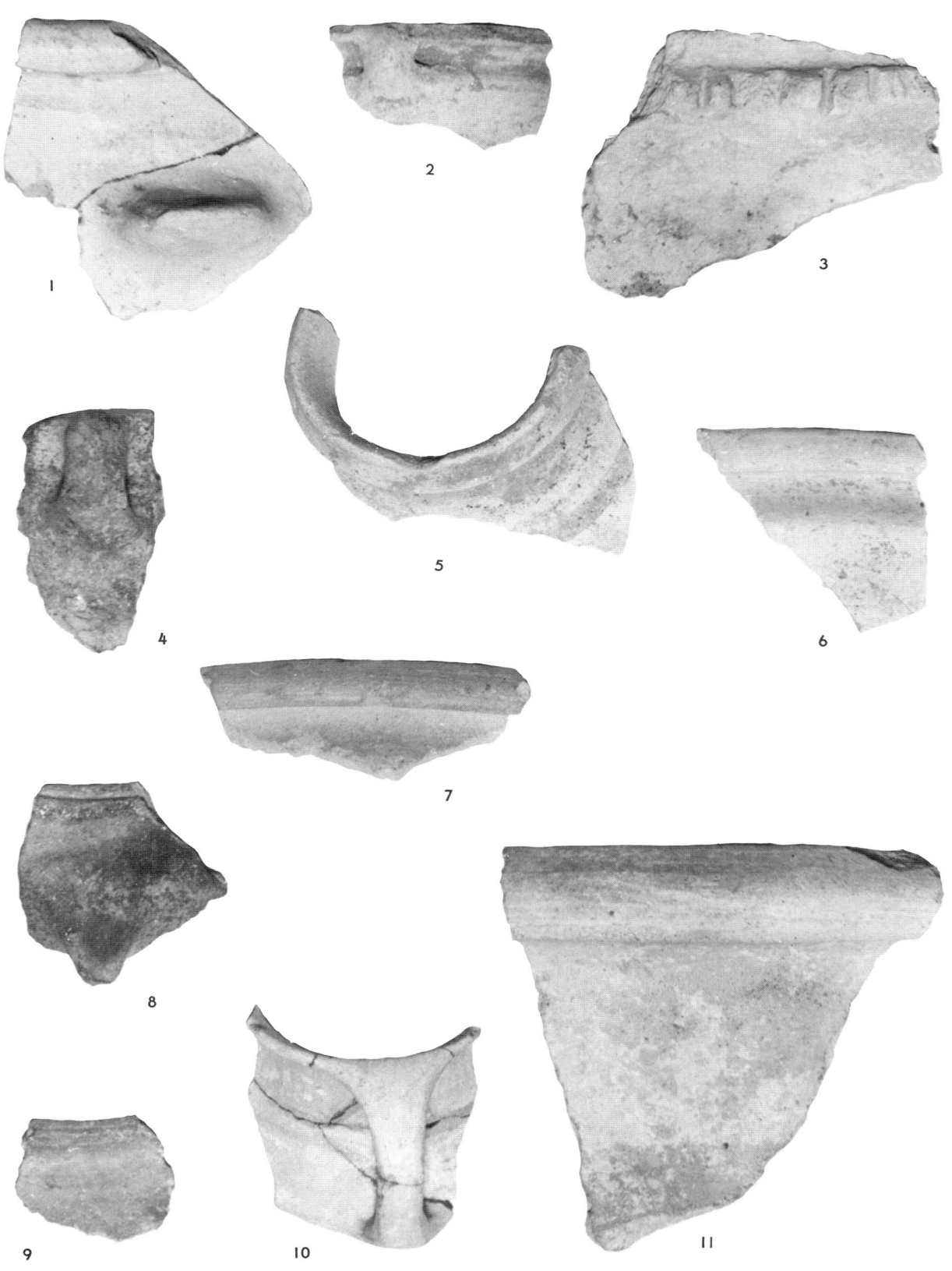

Fig. 216. Banahilk non-Halafian pottery: probably early second millennium, *5,7,10*; probably Iron Age, *2,4,6,8-9*; early Hellenistic, *1,11*; nondiagnostic or unknown sherd, *3*. See also fig. 204. Scale 1:2.

Fig. 217. Banahilk worked painted-ware sherds and Banahilk plain ware: painted-ware chipped sherds, *1-2*; detached lug, showing details of construction, form class IVB, non-chaff-tempered plain ware, *3*; chaff-tempered plain ware, form class IA, *4-5*; non-chaff-tempered plain ware vessels, form class IB, *6-7*, and indeterminate fabric type, *8*. Scale 1:2.

Fig. 218. Banahilk ground stone: fragment of grinding stone or door pivot stone, *1*; pestle fragment, *2*; mortar fragment, *3*; handstone or large pestle, *4*. Scale 1:2.

Fig. 219. Banahilk bone objects: sheep/goat knucklebone gaming pieces, *1*; bone awls, *2-4*. Scale 1:2.

Fig. 220. Game of knucklebones as played in a contemporary Iranian village.

LIST OF REGISTERED OBJECTS

Register number	Description	Material	Provenience	Disposition
Bh-1	Awl, incompletely joined epiphysis	Bone	C,2	Baghdad
Bh-2	Awl, hollowed shaft, notched articular end	Bone	C,4	Chicago
Bh-3	Beater, inc.	Bone	D*I*,2	Baghdad
Bh-4	5 astragalus gaming pieces	Bone	B*III*,2	Baghdad
Bh-5	Double-pointed object	Bone	B,1	Baghdad
Bh-6	Stamp seal	Black stone	Surface	Baghdad
Bh-7	Incised pendant	Red orange chert	D*I*,2	Baghdad
Bh-8	Incised pendant, inc.	Black stone	TT,1	Baghdad
Bh-9	Incised stamp seal, inc.	Black stone	C,4	Chicago
Bh-10	Ground oval ornament	Black obsidian	D*I*,fl.5	Baghdad
Bh-11	Pendant, inc.	Brown obsidian	C,3	Baghdad
Bh-12	Bead	White chert	D*I*,2	Chicago
Bh-13	Carinated bowl, inc.	Yellow gray limestone	D*II*N	Baghdad
Bh-14	Bowl, inc.	Gray limestone	D*II*N	Baghdad
Bh-15	Bowl, inc.	Light gray limestone	C ext.,2	Baghdad
Bh-16	Celt	Black stone	D*I*,fl.4	Chicago
Bh-17	Small celt	Green stone	D*II*,1-2	Baghdad
Bh-18	Small perforated celt	Black stone	D,1	Baghdad
Bh-19	Bead	Baked clay	D*I*,fl.6	Baghdad
Bh-20	Spouted miniature vessel, inc.	Pottery	D*II*,2	Baghdad
Bh-21	Perforated oval ornament	Baked clay	D*I*,fl.6	Baghdad
Bh-22	Sievelike object	Baked clay	B*III*,2	Baghdad
Bh-23	Barrel bead	Unbaked clay	C,4	Chicago
Bh-24	Discoidal flake core	Red brown chert	D*I*,fl.1	Baghdad
Bh-25	Projectile point (*petit tranchet*)	Chert	D*I*,2	Baghdad
Bh-26	Drill	Obsidian	C,3	Baghdad
Bh-27	Spindle whorl	Baked clay	TT,1	Chicago
Bh-28	Funnellike object (whorl?), inc.	Baked clay	D*II*N	Baghdad
Bh-29	Lid, inc.	Painted pottery	D*I*,2	Baghdad
Bh-30	Cream bowl, inc.	Painted pottery	D*I*,1-2	Baghdad
Bh-31	Cylinder (figurine leg?), inc.	Pottery	Surface	Baghdad

NOTE: inc. = incomplete.

REFERENCES

Adams, Robert McC.
1960 Factors influencing the rise of civilization in the alluvium: illustrated by Mesopotamia. In *City invincible*, ed. Carl H. Kraeling and Robert M. Adams, pp. 24-46. Chicago: University of Chicago Press.

Belck, W.
1899 Excerpt from a letter to Rudolf Virchow in *Verhandlungen der Berliner Gesellschaft für Anthropologie, Ethnologie, und Urgeschichte* 1899, p. 580.
1900 Bericht über die armenische Forschungsreise der HHrn. W. Belck und C.F. Lehmann. Ibid. 1900, pp. 44-66.

Braidwood, Robert J., and Braidwood, Linda S.
1953 The earliest village communities of southwestern Asia. *Journal of World History* 1:278-310.
1960 *Excavations in the plain of Antioch I: the earlier assemblages, phases A-J*. Oriental Institute Publications, vol. 61. Chicago: University of Chicago Press.

Braidwood, Robert J.; Braidwood, Linda S.; Smith, James G.; and Leslie, Charles
1952 Matarrah: a southern variant of the Hassunan assemblage, excavated in 1948. *Journal of Near Eastern Studies* 11:1-75.

Braidwood, Robert J.; Çambel, Halet; and Watson, Patty Jo
1969 Prehistoric investigations in southeastern Turkey. *Science* 164:1275-76.

Braidwood, Robert J.; Çambel, Halet; Redman, Charles L.; and Watson, Patty Jo
1971 Beginnings of village-farming communities in southeastern Turkey. *Proceedings of the National Academy of Sciences of the United States of America* 68:1236-40.

Braidwood, Robert J.; Howe, Bruce; et al.
1960 *Prehistoric investigations in Iraqi Kurdistan*. Studies in Ancient Oriental Civilization [SAOC], no. 31. Chicago: University of Chicago Press.

Caton-Thompson, G., and Gardner, E.W.
1934 *The desert Fayum*. London: Royal Anthropological Institute of Great Britain and Ireland.

Clark, J.G.D
 1936 *The mesolithic settlement of northern Europe.* Cambridge: Cambridge University Press.
 1952 *Prehistoric Europe: the economic basis.* New York: Philosophical Library.

Davidson, T.E., and McKerrell, Hugh
 1976 Pottery analysis and Halaf period trade in the Khabur headwaters region. *Iraq* 38:45-56.

Garrod, D.A.E., and Bate, D.M.A.
 1937 *The Stone Age of Mount Carmel.* Vol. 1. Oxford: Clarendon Press.

Garstang, John
 1953 *Prehistoric Mersin: Yümük Tepe in southern Turkey.* Oxford: Clarendon Press.

Guthe, Carl E.
 1925 *Pueblo pottery making.* Papers of the Southwestern Expedition, no. 2. New Haven: Yale University Press.

Helbaek, Hans
 1959 Notes on the evolution and history of *Linum. Kuml* 1959, pp. 103-29.
 1960a Ecological effects of irrigation in ancient Mesopotamia. *Iraq* 22:186-96.
 1960b The paleoethnobotany of the Near East and Europe. In SAOC 31, pp. 99-118.
 1963 Textiles from Çatal Hüyük. *Archaeology* 16:39-46.
 1972 Samarran irrigation agriculture at Choga Mami in Iraq. *Iraq* 34:35-48.

Hijara, Ismail
 1978 Three new graves at Arpachiyah. *World Archaeology* 10:125-28.

Hole, Frank; Flannery, Kent V.; and Neely, James A.
 1969 *Prehistory and human ecology of the Deh Luran plain.* Memoirs of the Museum of Anthropology, University of Michigan, no. 1. Ann Arbor.

Kidder, Alfred Vincent
 1932 *The artifacts of Pecos.* Papers of the Southwestern Expedition, no. 6. New Haven: Yale University Press.

King, L.W.
 1912 The prehistoric cemetery at Shamiram-alti. *Proceedings of the Society of Biblical Archaeology* 34:198-204.

Kirkbride, Diana
 1972 Umm Dabaghiyah 1971, a preliminary report: an early ceramic farming settlement in marginal north central Jazira, Iraq. *Iraq* 34:3-15.

Korfmann, Manfred
 1982 *Tilkitepe: Die ersten Ansätze prähistorischer Forschung in der östlichen Türkei.* Istanbuler Mitteilungen, Beiheft 26. Tübingen: Ernst Wasmuth.

Lawn, Barbara
 1973 University of Pennsylvania radiocarbon dates XV. *Radiocarbon* 15:367-81.

LeBlanc, Steven A.
 1971 Computerized, conjunctive archeology and the Near Eastern Halaf. Ph.D. diss., Washington University.

LeBlanc, Steven A., and Watson, Patty Jo
 1973 A comparative statistical analysis of painted pottery from seven Halafian sites. *Paléorient* 1:117-33.

Lloyd, Seton, and Safar, Fuad
 1945 Tell Hassuna. *Journal of Near Eastern Studies* 4:255-89.

Mallowan, M.E.L.
 1933 The prehistoric sondage of Nineveh, 1931-1932. *Annals of Archaeology and Anthropology of the University of Liverpool* 20:128-79.
 1946 Excavations in the Balih valley, 1938. *Iraq* 8:111-59.

Mallowan, M.E.L., and Rose, J. Cruikshank
 1935 Excavations at Tall Arpachiyah, 1933. Ibid. 2:1-178. (Reprint. *Prehistoric Assyria: excavations at Tall Arpachiyah, 1933.* London: Oxford University Press, Humphrey Milford.)

Mellaart, J.
 1970 The earliest settlements in western Asia. In *The Cambridge ancient history,* 3rd ed., pp. 248-326. Cambridge: Cambridge University Press.

Mellink, Machteld J.
 1964 Archaeology in Asia Minor. *American Journal of Archaeology* 68:149-66.

Merpert, Nicolai Ia., and Munchaev, Rauf M.
 1969 The investigation of the Soviet Archaeological Expedition in Iraq in the spring 1969. *Sumer* 25:125-31.
 1971 Rannezemledel'cheskie poseleniya severnoĭ Mesopotamii (po materialam raskopok Sovetskoĭ ekspeditsii). *Sovetskaja arkheologija* 1971, no. 3:141-69. (Early agricultural settlements in northern Mesopotamia [based on data from the excavations of the Soviet Expedition]. *Soviet Anthropology and Archeology* 10:203-52.)
 1973 Early agricultural settlements in the Sinjar plain, northern Iraq. *Iraq* 35:93-113.

Mortensen, Peder
 1970 *Tell Shimshara: the Hassuna period.* Kongelige danske videnskabernes selskab, historisk-filosofiske skrifter, vol. 5 (2). Copenhagen: Munksgaard.

1973 A sequence of Samarran flint and obsidian tools from Choga Mami. *Iraq* 35:37-55.

Oppenheim, Max Freiherr von, and Schmidt, Hubert
1943 *Tell Halaf*. Vol. 1: *die prähistorischen Funde*. Berlin: Walter de Gruyter.

Perkins, Ann Louise
1949 *The comparative archeology of early Mesopotamia*. Studies in Ancient Oriental Civilization, no. 25. Chicago: University of Chicago Press.

Pfeiffer, Robert H.
1940 The excavations at Van in 1939. *Bulletin of the American Schools of Oriental Research* 78:31-32.

Postgate, J.N., and the editors of *Iraq* [D.J. Wiseman and J.D. Hawkins]
1972 Excavations in Iraq 1971-72. *Iraq* 34:139-50.
1973 Excavations in Iraq 1972-73. Ibid. 35:189-204.

Redman, Charles L., and Watson, Patty Jo
1970 Systematic, intensive surface collection. *American Antiquity* 35:279-91.

Reed, Charles A.
1962 *Snails on a Persian hillside*. Postilla, Peabody Museum of Natural History, Yale University, no. 66. New Haven.

Reilly, Edward Bowen
1940 Tilkitepedeki ilk kazılar (1937). [Test excavations at Tilkitepe (1937).] *Türk tarih, arkeologya ve etnografya dergisi* 4:145-65.

Ryder, M.L.
1965 Report of textiles from Çatal Hüyük. *Anatolian Studies* 15:175-76.

SAOC 31
1960 *Prehistoric investigations in Iraqi Kurdistan*. Robert J. Braidwood, Bruce Howe, et al. Studies in Ancient Oriental Civilization, no. 31. Chicago: University of Chicago Press.

Schaeffer, Claude F.A.
1962 *Ugaritica IV*. Mission de Ras Shamra, vol. 15. Institut français d'archéologie de Beyrouth, Bibliothèque archéologique et historique, vol. 74. Paris: Librairie orientaliste Paul Geuthner.

Stuckenrath, Robert, Jr., and Ralph, Elizabeth K.
1965 University of Pennsylvania radiocarbon dates VIII. *Radiocarbon* 7:187-99.

Tekriti, Abdul Qadir al-
1968 The flint and obsidian implements of Tell es-Sawwan. *Sumer* 24:53-55.

Tobler, Arthur J.
1950 *Excavations at Tepe Gawra*. Vol. 2. Museum Monographs. Philadelphia: University of Pennsylvania Press.

Vogel, J.C., and Waterbolk, H.T.
1964 Groningen radiocarbon dates V. *Radiocarbon* 6:349-69.

Watson, Patty Jo
1956 New Halafian material from northern Iraq: the Halaf "Period" reconsidered. Master's thesis, University of Chicago.
1982 The Halafian pottery of Tilkitepe, seen in the Hittite Museum, Ankara (Citadel), 1955. In *Tilkitepe: Die ersten Ansätze prähistorischer Forschung in der östlichen Türkei*, Manfred Korfmann, pp. 203-12. Istanbuler Mitteilungen, Beiheft 26, Tübingen: Ernst Wasmuth.

Watson, Patty Jo, and LeBlanc, Steven A.
1973 Excavation and analysis of Halafian materials from southeastern Turkey: the Halafian period reexamined. Paper read at the symposium Recent Research in Anatolian Prehistory. 72nd Annual Meeting of the American Anthropological Association, 28 November-2 December 1973, New Orleans.
in prep. Girikihacıyan: an Halafian site in southeastern Turkey.

Woolley, C. Leonard
1934 The prehistoric pottery of Carchemish. *Iraq* 1:146-62.

Wright, Gary A.
1969 *Obsidian analyses and prehistoric Near Eastern trade: 7500 to 3500 B.C.* Anthropological Papers of the Museum of Anthropology, University of Michigan, no. 37. Ann Arbor.

Zeist, Willem van
1979-80 Plant remains from Girikihacıyan, Turkey, *Anatolica* 7:75-89.

18

THE BANAHILK POTTER
Frederick R. Matson

During the excavations at Banahilk, it was my privilege to spend seven days at the site getting acquainted with its ceramic problems. A sample of the local clay was collected and given preliminary tests in the field. At the request of the excavator, Patty Jo Watson, I sorted the daily accumulation of sherds after they had been washed and then selected the materials to be sent back to the base camp for more detailed study and ultimate division with the Directorate General of Antiquities of Iraq. A group of sherds showing evidence of methods of manufacture, overfiring, or other clues of technological interest were set aside for laboratory examination. Of the sherd materials returned to the United States, approximately 140 pieces have been examined in detail in my laboratory, and the physical properties of the raw clay brought back have been studied in terms of its mineralogical constituents, its working properties that would be of concern to a village potter, and its firing behavior. On the basis of the information thus obtained, supplementing Watson's detailed analysis of the shapes and decorations of the Banahilk wares, interpretative comments are offered on the Banahilk potters' techniques and their products.

When sherds were being selected for further study while all of the materials were still laid out on the air strip adjacent to the site, small chips were broken off many of them so that freshly fractured surfaces could be observed and a more effective sorting made in terms of fabric and color. The approximately 140 sherds chosen for laboratory study were sorted into painted and plain wares. All of the pieces eventually had a slice removed from an edge by means of a diamond-impregnated copper lapidary wheel so that a smooth, fresh surface one to three inches in length along the edge of each sherd could be studied.

The surfaces and the edges of the sherds were examined under a binocular microscope at a magnification of nine times and the pieces classified according to texture. A low-power reading glass was also useful with the more coarsely textured sherds. This sorting was done in a darkened room using raking light from a small tensor lamp which accentuated any surface irregularities that might be clues as to method of construction and which cast shadows in the small surface holes that had originally contained fine bits of chaff. A separate card was prepared for each sherd studied; on it were recorded the sherd's laboratory number, provenience, texture, percent absorption, percent porosity, surface decoration, and color, as well as details about its manufacture and any organic inclusions found. Thus organized, the data could be quickly summarized.

THE BANAHILK CLAY

During the course of the excavations a sample of clay was taken from a culturally sterile area (4 × 11.55 cm) in the bottom of the C extension trench, which had been dug down ca. 80 cm past the bottom of the deepest cultural deposit, well into sterile soil. This sample was dried and shipped to my laboratory.

This clay is light brownish gray (Munsell 10YR 6/2). To prepare it for testing, a portion was washed through a series of increasingly finer standard-mesh sieves. The mineral grains and calcified aggregates remaining on each sieve were dried and weighed. The weight of each of the sieved fractions expressed as a percentage of the total weight of the inclusions (40 gm) is reported in the tabulation at the top of page 616.

The fraction coarser than 20 mesh contained many calcareous aggregates as well as lime tubes about 1 mm in diameter that appeared to be casts of rootlets. Dark angular to rounded granules—largely of talc and a few of serpentine and quartz—and fragments of shell constituted the collection. The 20-40 mesh fraction contained proportionately more of the talc granules and the shell fragments. A sample was washed in dilute HCl to remove the calcite so that the other grains could be

---

I should like to acknowledge the assistance I have received in the study of the Banahilk clay and sherds from the following graduate students: Nanna Bolling, Lynn A. Brant, James Dutt, Robert H. Johnston, Prudence Rice, and John A. Senulis. Working with them was one of the pleasures of this study. The Central Fund for Research of The Pennsylvania State University has provided welcome and needed annual support for the laboratory studies. Grant no. GS-357 of the National Science Foundation supplied stipends for some of the graduate assistants mentioned above. Grateful acknowledgment is made of this support.

[The manuscript for this chapter was essentially completed by 1972. Very few additions and only minor revisions have been made since that date.—EDS.]

Weight Percentage Distribution of Banahilk Mineral Grains

Sieve mesh designation	Percent inclusions
Coarser than 20	15
20-40	35
40-60	30
60-80	15
80-100	5

better studied. In the 40-60 mesh fraction the dark talc granules constituted more than half of the sample, and this ratio continued in the finer fractions. These mineral collections were studied in conjunction with the thin section of the raw clay that was prepared, and grain identifications were checked in powder mounts with a set of index of refraction liquids. X-ray diffraction analysis showed that illite is the predominant clay mineral present. Study of the thin section provided little additional mineralogical information; it only served to emphasize that the clay was fine in texture except for the presence of much calcite and talc. The other minerals present, such as quartz, limonite, black iron-rich flecks, and possibly tremolite, were usually in grains no larger than 0.06 mm.

This clay, rich in talc (which expands very little when heated) and in related ferromagnesian minerals, should have good thermal shock resistance and therefore should be an excellent material from which to make pottery. In Greece on the island of Siphnos a similar talc-rich clay is used to make casseroles that are distributed throughout the country both to the islands and the mainland because they do not crack readily on the cooking hearths.

Three of the physical properties of clays that provide useful information about their working characteristics are the percentage of water of plasticity, the percentage of linear drying shrinkage, and the slaking time. There are standard ways of determining these properties in commercial ceramic laboratories, but these methods have been followed only approximately by Robert H. Johnston, who conducted our tests. He prepared 1-inch cubes of five clays, including that from Banahilk. Normally, larger test bars are made, preferably $1 \times 1 \times 7$ inches, but the size of the clay samples available did not permit the preparation of large bars nor an extensive series of bars. Therefore these figures are of value only in a comparative sense within our small series. The properties of the five clays are reported in table 50. When comparing them, since the samples are small, the range of values must be kept in mind as well as the average figure.

Table 50.—Working Properties of Five Clays from Northern Iraq

	Provenience of clay*	Water of plasticity†			Linear drying shrinkage†			Average slaking time†		
		Mean (%)	Range (%)	No. tests	Mean (%)	Range (%)	No. tests	Minutes	Seconds	No. tests
C-1	Banahilk	37.8	36.4-39.7	3	9.4	8.5-10.4	5	6	15	5
C-2	Ali Agha	37.2	30.4-41.0	3	5.5	5.0-6.4	5	2	38	5
C-4	Mosul	33.5	33.2-34.2	5	10.7	10.4-10.8	5	8	58	5
C-7	Salahedin	25.8	25.3-26.0	5	7.8	7.7-7.8	5	5	46	5
C-8	Hassuna	30.7	29.9-31.4	5	8.3	7.8-8.8	5	22	49	5

*The samples from the five sites are further identified as follows: Banahilk—clay from the excavation on the Diyana plain; Ali Agha—clay from the excavation; Mosul—red clay from a road cut enroute to Arpachiyah; Salahedin—red clay from a road cut between Erbil and Salahedin; Hassuna—clay from level Ia.

†The formulas by which the values were calculated may be expressed as follows:

$$\% \text{ water of plasticity} = \frac{\text{weight plastic} - \text{weight dry}}{\text{weight dry}} \times 100$$

$$\% \text{ linear drying shrinkage} = \frac{\text{length plastic} - \text{length dry}}{\text{length dry}} \times 100$$

Slaking time = length of time (measured with a stop watch) that it takes a 1-inch cube of clay to disintegrate when submerged on a coarse screen in water

It is unnecessary to make detailed comments on the data in table 50, as the results are self-evident. It can be said that the Banahilk and Ali Agha clays require the most water to make them plastic. The Banahilk clay is a high-shrinkage variety compared to the others, and it slakes down rapidly in water. The water of plasticity and linear drying shrinkage values for the Banahilk clay are quite normal, but the very short slaking time suggests that the clay has poor bonding strength, and this may account for the use of dung in the clay for the utilitarian vessels. It is probable that clay from a different source was used for the manufacture of the jars.

To study the color development, briquettes formed from the Banahilk clay were fired at successively higher temperatures up to 1000°C. Special series of firings were also conducted under reducing conditions, with varying amounts of salt added to the clay. Much data was accumulated, but only the colors developed in the normal firing sequence will be reported here, for the other results belong to specialized studies.

Table 51A.—Color Changes in the Banahilk Clay When Fired

Temperature (°C held for 30 minutes)	Munsell color notation	Munsell soil color names
Unfired	10YR 6/2	Light brownish gray
600°	10YR 7/6	Yellow
700°	5YR 7/6	Reddish yellow
900°	5YR 7/6	Reddish yellow
1,000°	2.5YR 8/4	Pale yellow

The colors found on the surface and in the oxidized core of the Banahilk pottery rarely exceed the 900° test color. Yellow sherds are indeed a rarity. This suggests that mounded brush and dung fires, not kilns, were used for the firing of the pottery. In a kiln hot spots would develop, thus exposing the contents to higher temperatures. Table 51A should be used in conjunction with Table 51B, in which the color results of some refiring experiments are shown.

Table 51B.—Color Changes After Refiring of Banahilk Sherds

Sherd	Feature	Munsell color notation		
		Original	After refiring at 800°C	After refiring at 900°C
Plain Ware				
A	Surface	2.5Y 8/4	10YR 8/3	10YR 8/4
	Core	2.5Y 7/0	5YR 7.5/6	7.5YR 7.5/6
C	Surface	10YR 8/3	7.5YR 9/6	7.5YR 9/6
	Core	2.5Y 7/0	7.5YR 8/6	10YR 8/4
D	Surface	7.5YR 7/5	5YR 8/6	2.5Y 8/3
	Core	2.5Y 5/0	5YR 7/6	2.5YR 6/6
E	Surface	10YR 8/3	10YR 9/3	10YR 9/3
	Core	2.5Y 5/0	5YR 7/6	2.5YR 6/7
J	Surface	2.5YR 6/7	2.5YR 6/8	2.5YR 6/8
	Core	2.5Y 7/0	5YR 7/6	2.5YR 7/6
Painted Ware				
G	Paint	2.5YR 6/8	2.5YR 6/8	2.5YR 6/8
	Surface	7.5YR 8/4	7.5YR 8/6	2.5YR 6/8
	Core	7.5YR 5/0	5YR 7/8	2.5YR 7/8
L	Paint	10R 4/6 to 2/2	10R 4/6 to 2/2	2.5YR 5/8 to 4/8
	Surface	7.5YR 8/4	7.5YR 8/6	7.5YR 8/6
	Core	10R 7/8	5YR 7.5/8	2.5YR 6/7
M	Paint	5YR 3/4	5YR 5/4	2.5YR 4/5
	Surface	10YR 8/4	10YR 8/4	10YR 8/4
	Core	2.5YR 6/6	2.5YR 6/6	2.5YR 6/6
N	Paint	2.5YR 4/6 to 5/8	2.5YR 4/6 to 5/8	2.5YR 4/6 to 5/8
	Surface	10YR 8/4	7.5YR 8/4	7.5YR 8/4
	Core	5YR 7/6	5YR 7/6	5YR 7/6
O	Paint	2.5YR 4/6 to 5/8	2.5YR 4/6 to 5/8	2.5YR 4/6 to 5/8
	Surface	2.5Y 8/4	10YR 8/4	10YR 8/4
	Core	5YR 7/6	5YR 7/6	5YR 7/6
Painted Ware (Dark Sherds Originally Overfired in a Reducing Atmosphere)				
P	Paint	2.5YR 5/4	10YR 5/4	10R 5/4
	Surface	10YR 5/3	10YR 5/3	2.5YR 6/4
	Core	2.5Y 6/0	10YR 5/3	10YR 5/3
Q	Paint	10YR 4/1	10YR 4/1	10YR 4/1
	Surface	10YR 6/2	5YR 5/3	2.5YR 4/4
	Core	2.5Y 6/0	10YR 5/2	10YR 5/2
R	Surface	10YR 5/3	5YR 6/3	2.5YR 5/2
	Core	2.5Y 6/0	10YR 5/3	10YR 5/3

Table 51B.—*Continued*

Sherd	Feature	Munsell color notation		
		Original	After refiring at 800°C	After refiring at 900°C
Diyana Ware				
B	Surface	10YR 8/3	2.5YR 6/8	2.5YR 5/8
	Core	2.5Y 5/0	2.5YR 6/7	2.5YR 4/4
F	Surface	2.5YR 7/6	5YR 6/6	2.5YR 5/6
	Core	2.5YR 5/0	5YR 6/6	10R 5/4
H	Surface (slip)	10R 4/4	10R 4/4	10R 4/4
	Core	2.5YR 6/6	2.5YR 6/8	10R 5/4
I	Surface (slip)	10R 4/4	10R 4/4	10R 4/4
	Core	2.5YR 6/8	2.5YR 6/8	10R 5/6
K	Surface	7.5YR 6/4	5YR 6/6	2.5YR 5/6
	Core	7.5YR 7/4	5YR 7/8	2.5YR 6/6

SHERD REFIRING TESTS

More than one clay may have been used by the Banahilk potters for the production of the plain, painted, and Diyana wares. The pottery could possibly have been made in nearby villages with differing clay resources. To check on this, slices cut from selected sherds were refired to moderately high temperatures. The colors thus developed in the slices from originally low-fired utilitarian ware could then be compared with the better-fired ceramic products from the site. It was realized that the duration of the original firing, as well as the temperature reached, the hearth atmosphere, and possible changes caused by ground water penetration during the millennia of burial in the soil, could affect the degree of color development in refiring. It was hoped that an approximately common ceramic color denominator might thus be attained. Eighteen sherds, labeled A through R, from Banahilk were selected for such testing, and two slices, each about 0.25 in. wide, were cut from the sherds. One slice from each sherd was fired to 800°C in an electric furnace in an oxidizing atmosphere, and the temperature was maintained for 30 minutes. The other set of slices was then fired to 900°C for 30 minutes. The results in terms of color changes are tabulated in Table 51B. These refiring tests helped to establish the groupings upon which the ware classification was eventually based. The results of the refiring study are discussed in each of the characterizations of the wares, so they need not be repeated here. The chief conclusions of this test were:

1. The painted pottery had seldom been fired above 900°C.
2. Much of the utilitarian ware was made from a calcareous pale-yellow-burning clay.
3. A red-burning clay was used in the Diyana plain for the production of some ware—at least pottery made from such clay was used there, but it could have been produced in a village in the adjacent mountain region.

An interesting sidelight of this test is the demonstration of the stability of the ware and possibly of the bond strength of the clay. The lime in the refired samples was calcined to some degree, particularly in the 900°C firing. In the four years since the time of the test the lime has rehydrated and again become calcium carbonate. Volume expansion is involved, yet none of the sherds has disintegrated. Test briquettes of clays containing much lime frequently crumble into a mound of grains within one or two years after the firings take place. It is probable that the lime had been calcined at the time of the original firing, so space for volume expansion was developed at that time. However, several of these sherds had originally not been fired much over 600° or 700°C. Doubtless the weaker pottery disintegrated within a few years after it had been fired.

ABSORPTION AND POROSITY STUDIES

The amount of water absorbed by pottery vessels is of importance in evaluating the effectiveness of their use as water jars. Enough water must seep through the vessel walls so that the exterior remains damp enough to undergo the cooling effect of evaporation. On the other hand, the pots must not be too porous if they are to be of practical use. A simple test that can be carried out on sherds is to gently boil them in water under controlled conditions and determine how much water has penetrated them. The percent absorption is calculated as

$$\% \text{ absorption} = \frac{\text{weight of wet sherd} - \text{weight of dried sherd}}{\text{weight of dried sherd}} \times 100$$

This method, however, tests only the approximate permeability of the sherds; it does not provide an exact measurement. The results can be misleading if materials of different specific gravities are being tested. A better measure, although more time-consuming to determine, is the percentage of porosity. The formula for this is given below.

$$\% \text{ porosity} = \frac{\text{weight of wet sherd} - \text{weight of dry sherd}}{\text{volume of sherd}} \times 100$$

Thus absorption is a measure of the amount of penetrable pore space per unit of dry sherd weight, while porosity is a measure of the penetrable pore space per unit of sherd volume. Many sherd measurements have been made in the past (Matson 1941), but it was thought worth running a series of tests on the Banahilk sherds because there were observable variations in the wares in terms of appearance, texture, etc. The results ranged from 22% to 54% absorption in the 77 sherds tested. Since the data are discussed in each of the ware sections of this report, no further comment is needed here. When the absorption was plotted against the porosity, it was found that the values for all of the sherds, except those that were badly overfired and scoriaceous, fell close to a straight line on the graph. Thus all the clays used for the wares had about the same specific gravity.

THE WARES

Plain Ware

This ware, which has vessel walls 10-22 mm thick, is abundantly tempered with fine chaff. The chaff impressions remaining in the sherds show that the individual particles had the striated surface structure of grasses and that the pieces were seldom over 5 mm in length. When the chaff was added to the clay and water, it was flexible or again became so, for the impressions in the clay are often curved as a result of the wedging of the clay or from the preparation of the coils of which the walls were built. Dried grasses or reeds would be difficult to crush to this small size. Sherds in which the abundant chaff impressions appear usually have black cores, which may indicate not only that the paste had a low firing temperature but also that it had a rich organic content. It is probable that the potter added dung to the clay to make it more plastic. This view has been supported by experiments in which dung was added to clay, which was formed into bowls and then fired. The identification of the Banahilk ware as dung tempered has also been supported by the fact that chaff impressions appeared on the walls of the experimentally fired pieces and by studies of the short pieces of chaff washed from the dung of sheep/goat, cattle, donkey, camel, yak, and horse.[1]

The local calcareous clay used at Banahilk to form the mud walls of the houses was rather mealy. A mud plaster smeared on the surfaces of such walls to fill in the cracks and smooth the surfaces would have been more plastic if tempered with dung, if it were available. Such a paste could also have been used to form the very porous household vessels. Wall building and pot making are daily occupations at some seasons of the year for the residents of many Near Eastern villages.

The dung-tempered pottery absorbs more water into its walls than do the other Banahilk wares. The water absorption of this pottery is 36-54%, while that of the painted jars is 22-38%. It would be instructive to try correlating the shapes of the vessels made of this porous ware with the household uses to which they could have been put, by observing present-day local village households.

The refiring experiments of the plain ware produced interesting results. This ware is low-fired and usually has black or gray cores and gray to tan surfaces. Six of these refired sherds developed colors characteristic of high-lime clays (using the Munsell color terminology)—reddish yellow to light red. They often had a pale yellow thin surface layer caused by the concentration there of soluble salts. The seventh sherd was light red at 800°C and pale red to red at 900°. Two additional dung-tempered sherds classed with the red ware in the group studied were made of this red-firing clay. It is interesting to observe that this red clay, which was characteristically used to produce the Banahilk burnished ware, was occasionally employed for the manufacture of domestic ware. One may speculate that the women making the burnished pottery also made their own porous household ware from the same red clay and when doing so added some dung to the clay in accordance with standard village practice.

Chaff cannot be readily seen on the exterior surfaces of the sherds, for they have often been wet-smoothed by the potters when the vessels were partly dry, and the embedded chaff has been covered by a thin layer of clay. This is less true of the interior surfaces. Chaff holes can, of course, be seen in saw-cut sections of sherds, but they can best be studied in freshly fractured edges.

There is varied distribution of the chaff in the vessel walls. Some cores are rich in chaff; others have little, the chaff being concentrated near the surfaces. Occasionally the curving alignment of the chaff impressions suggests the boundary zone between coils or slab edges. Thus the clay-dung-water paste often was not carefully wedged to produce a uniform body, and at times a dung-rich clay was smeared on the surfaces of the almost completed vessels to reduce surface cracking or granulation and to produce a smooth finish. Dents on a few surfaces indicate the use of the paddle and anvil in the final shaping of the pots.

As might be expected, the amount of chaff present varies in the 23 sherds studied and does not correlate with the thickness of the vessel walls nor with the abundance of the limestone granules in the paste. While the availability of dung at the time of year that the vessels were made might be a factor, as might the number of grazing animals near the settlement whose dung could be collected by the children (a chore that is still carried out by small village children today), it is more likely that the variability indicates the degree of experience or skill developed by the potters. This dung-tempered plain ware is low-fired and would probably have been made by women as one of their household chores. It represents the least craft-oriented pottery produced in the Banahilk community. A few of the sherds are badly overfired, scoriaceous, warped, and blistered and have a cracked exterior surface skin. Excess dung in the clay, unskilled firing of the ware, or gusty winds causing very hot flames to impinge on the ware during firing could produce such defects. These bloated and very porous vessels would not have been rejected but would have been used if at all possible, judging by what one observes in Near Eastern villages today.

The texture and mineral inclusions of this ware have been studied under the binocular microscope and in six petrographic thin sections prepared from slices taken from sherds. The range in grain size and the frequency of the minerals in the clay (which of course is itself a complex mineral) varied greatly among the individual sherds. Limestone granules were usually less than 1 mm in diameter, but were occasionally as coarse as 4 mm. The amount present in the thin sections ranged from sparse to moderate. There was much secondary deposition of fine calcite and possibly gypsum in the chaff holes. The other minerals were the same as those reported for the painted ware; in fact, both wares are made of the same general type of clay, but the plain ware contains more limestone granules. The minerals other than calcite range in grain size from 0.01 to 0.5 mm. Some subangular to subround pebbles of talc or talc aggregates occur in sizes up to 2 mm.

A photomicrograph of thin section P-158 seen with transmitted light is reproduced in figure 221.

Painted Ware

A group of 46 Halaf-style painted sherds from 41 collared jars and 5 bowls was studied in detail. It was a pleasure to examine the jar sherds, for they come from vessels that were skillfully made. The interior surfaces show parallel series of finger striations from the final wet-smoothing of the walls. The exterior surfaces are polished, and they often do not show striations or polishing scratches, nor do most of them show surface deformations due to paddle-and-anvil compression. It would be tempting to suggest that the perfection of the exterior surfaces could indicate the forming of these vessels in molds, were it not for the fact that similar well-made jars are well known as a classical product of the American Indians of New Mexico, who achieve the perfection of the jar surfaces by repeated polishing over a period of several days as the vessels gradually dry. The few Banahilk painted sherds examined that retain polishing striations show that the surfaces were finished before the painted decoration was applied. It is only on sherds that have a red slip covering large body areas that burnishing marks (broader and more indented than polishing scratches) can be seen on the slipped surfaces.

None of the painted sherds studied show evidence of coil or slab building on their fractured edges, doubtless because of the paddle-and-anvil compaction of the walls. Some sherds do show clearly that the collar was added to the jars as a separate and final unit. At least three of the sherds examined received secondary use as scrapers, judging from the stepped fracturing of both the interior and exterior surfaces along one edge of each sherd. The relatively dense body of sherds of this ware would provide a useful material for scrapers. Secondary use of sherds was doubtless quite common, yet seldom are items that were treated in this manner identified in archeological studies. Herzfeld (1932, pl. XXVII) illustrates a series of such sherds.

The bowls are less well made than the jars. Fine chaff marks show that some dung was included in the paste, suggesting a different technique of vessel forming that required a more plastic clay. The surfaces are smoothed and scraped, but not polished. Many of the bowl sherd cores are gray, indicating a relatively low firing temperature and an organic enrichment (dung) of the paste. Possibly the bowls and jars were made by different groups of potters. It would be interesting to know if the design repertoires differed according to the shape of the vessel.

The texture of each of the painted sherds was studied under a binocular microscope; both a freshly fractured edge and an edge cut with a diamond-impregnated saw and then ground smooth with abrasives were examined. Most of the sherds were consistently very fine textured and contained occasional grains of limestone that ranged in size from mere flecks to pieces about 2 mm in diameter. In the sherds fired at the higher temperature the limestone grains were white (probably because they had been calcined) while those in the lower-fired pieces were gray. Lime "pops"—expansion spalling caused by the swelling when the calcined lime rehydrated—were particularly visible on the surfaces where a thin wash of fine clay had covered the lime granules. Flecks of mica and fine black inclusions (talc) were seen in about one third of the sherds.

Some of the painted sherds differ in that they have some fine chaff marks on the sherd surfaces, indicating that the potter had added a small amount of dung to the clay when preparing it. The most interesting point in this connection is that the five bowl sherds in the sampling are all in this second group. In addition, there are six sherds from globular jars and one from a small jar. A possible difference in craft tradition in the manufacture of the bowls and most of the jars has already been mentioned. Study of the data on relative frequency and distribution of the bowls and jars from the Banahilk excavations may help in understanding these differences.

The painted jars, presumably containers for water and other liquids, have a uniform wall thickness and a smooth surface free of imperfections. Their decoration aside, their functional perfection reminds one of the wheel-made water jars still in use in some Spanish villages today. The water absorption of the jar sherds was 22-38%, while that of the dung-tempered painted sherds was 33-43%. Thus there is some overlap between the two groups. Average figures are not presented, because the samples are too small.

The paint used to decorate the ware is undoubtedly an iron-rich red mountain clay that has been washed to remove the sand grains and other impurities. Judging from similar clay paints that I have seen in use in Lebanese villages today, it would have been sticky, would have adhered well to the surface of the unfired vessel, and would probably have had a high shrinkage during drying which would result in cracks if too thick a layer of paint were applied. A thick paint would be like a slip such as that used to cover large areas of some vessels, while too thin a paint would be so watery that the design would appear very pale on the fired pot. The degree of control shown in the application of a paint slip can give one an estimate of the potter's skill.

In general, when vessels are fired, the painted decoration retains a red color at temperatures up to about 800°C if the atmosphere is oxidizing during the final stages of firing. Higher temperatures, however, cause a brown color to develop, and slightly higher ones produce a black color. This is largely due to vitrification of the paint, for a glassy coating on the surface of the pigment particles prevents air from reaching the iron in the clay paint (which is black at the higher temperatures) and oxidizing it to red as the ware cools. The above is a very general statement, far from complete, of an involved reaction. For studying pottery in terms of the colors developed in the paint, however, it will suffice. On a far simpler level, these color differences are similar in principle to those one sees on the classical Greek Black Figure and Red Figure wares.

To determine the uniformity of the firing practices at Banahilk, two color sortings of the painted ware were made at the time of the excavations when the sherds were being processed. In a series of 196 sherds from operation DI,2, trash level, two thirds had red brown paint (including many sherds whose painted surfaces varied in color from red brown toward dark brown or black), while one third were painted black. In a group of 175 sherds from operation DII,1-2 (not under the floor), the sherds were equally divided between the two color categories. It would therefore appear that there was considerable variation in the firing control. Since the color often varied markedly on the surface of a single sherd, it is likely that kilns were not used but that the vessels were fired in a mound of dung cakes and brush in the manner still used at Diyana today, in central Africa, and in the American Southwest where not dissimilar painted jars are made by the Hopi Indians.

The paint on the Banahilk sherds tends to flake or abrade off the vessels if they are not fired to a high enough temperature. If the paint is too thick, especially when the firing temperature has been high, it shrinks and therefore cracks, and then flakes off the sherds (at least after long burial in the ground where they have been subject to dampness and to the action of frost and salts). Half of the painted sherds studied had imperfect paints that were either crazed or flaked. It is interesting to examine the surface of the paint with a raking light in a room in which the main lights have been turned off. One can then see dull, pebbled, bubbly, ash-encrusted, cracked, satiny, or vitreous surfaces and form an opinion as to the success of the potters in firing their wares.

The red clay paint was applied to the vessels when they were still moist. This can readily be established by examining sherds, usually those with red or brown decoration, from which part of the paint has disappeared. It can be seen that the vessel surface areas originally covered with paint had fired to a light brown color, whereas the parts of the designs that were never covered with paint—the zones within the diamonds or between parallel bandings—have a pale yellow, almost white, surface that some archeologists have mistakenly termed a slip. This light color develops during firing because of the concentration of soluble salts on the surface of the ware as the vessels dry. The surface is far less porous immediately under the paint, so those places not thus covered provide the areas for the evaporation of the water from the drying vessels and for the resulting concentration of soluble salts on the surface. These salts react with the clay during firing, especially in reducing atmospheres, to cause a bleaching effect. I have discussed this phenomenon several times (Matson 1955, p. 37; 1969, p. 594; 1971, pp. 66-68) and have been able to produce it in laboratory experiments. This light color is the same as the scum on the surface of brick, a development that brick manufacturers try to avoid. Bricks made today near Tehran, for example, show such markings because they have been stacked diagonally—lattice fashion—while being dried. Where the bricks were in contact with one another, the surface is brown to red; where the intermediate zone in the stacking permitted the surface to be directly exposed to the air, the fired color is white to yellow. This alteration in surface color is particularly characteristic of iron-bearing clays rich in lime if soluble salts are present in them.

Firing under completely reducing conditions (possibly with the ware buried in fuel and ash so that air could not reach it) occurred occasionally. Four of the painted sherds are almost vitrified, a condition that could have developed at the firing temperatures available only if reducing conditions existed. They have retained their shape, but they are medium gray in color throughout the body, the lime granules have interacted with the clay, and the body is dense and hard, giving a distinctive sharp sound when struck. The absorption of these sherds is very low, 1-17%. Such overfiring could result if it was very windy at the time of firing; a glowing hot area well banked with ash and fuel would have developed because of the exceptionally good draft created by the wind.

Thin sections, 0.03 mm in thickness, were prepared from slices taken from 11 of the 46 painted sherds selected for detailed study. The mineralogical constituents of these sections were all similar, but the texture varied from exceptionally fine grained to moderate. Voluminous notes have been accumulated from the study of the Banahilk pottery thin sections over the past several years, but a presentation of the detailed data would not further the understanding of the cultural significance of the pottery. Instead, a general summary discussion will be given.

The clays used by the Banahilk potters come from a region where there are basic rocks as well as limestones. The clays on the several sides of the Diyana plain may well vary somewhat in physical properties and mineralogical composition because of the mountain-ringed nature of the plain. Calcite (occasionally some in crystalline form), chrysotile, quartzite, quartz, very fine sandstone, feldspar, biotite, muscovite, possibly tremolite, and occasional grains of pyroxene and amphibole minerals occur in the thin sections. Their color and pleochroism may have been altered due to the firing of the pottery and the resulting oxidation of some of the iron present in the minerals. It would seem that the mineral and rock fragments present in the clay are largely derived from a metamorphic zone, possibly one in which the ferromagnesium minerals are the result of the metamorphism of dolomite. Since more than one type of talc-chrysotile-serpentine pebble occurs together with mineral clusters in tiny rock fragments in the clay, and since the aggregates are not sufficiently rounded to have been transported very far by water action, it is likely that they come from a nearby gneissic structure and are included as detritus in the clay deposits.

In terms of the potters on the Diyana plain, the clays available would seem to vary from high limestone marls to which dung must be added to make them sufficiently plastic to red-burning clays that can be burnished. In between are the clays used for most of the painted ware; they are good plastic clays from which jars can be made.

The thickness of the painted decoration can easily be measured in the thin sections at high magnification. It is usually about 0.015 mm thick, and in the lower-fired specimens shows some optical orientation of the particles, for sections of the paint band in the thin section extinguish when viewed with crossed Nicol prisms when the microscope stage is rotated. Figure 222 is a photomicrograph of thin section P-151.

The mineral grains in the painted ware do not tend to be oriented parallel to the surfaces of the vessels. This would suggest that there was a minimum of wet working and that the paddle and anvil were used to refine the forms and compact the walls of the vessels after they had been built up from slabs and coils and partly dried. The relative thinness of the walls of the large jars (7-12 mm), the fairly low percentage of absorption, and the fact that the larger pores, rather flattened, occur in the central part of the sherd core would also suggest wall compaction by paddle and anvil.

Textural variation among the sherds is largely due to the size and number of the limestone granules present. These granules rarely exceed 2 mm in diameter, and usually 0.5-1.0 mm is the maximum size. Variation in size and frequency is not unusual in clay beds deposited by water action in valleys near weathering limestone outcrops. The mineral grains in the thin sections are rarely over 0.5 mm in size; occasionally they are as large as 1 mm. The frequency of these larger grains, however, is low, which suggests that the Banahilk potters making the painted ware were careful in selecting their clay. Without field observations and samplings of the available clay sources, it is useless to speculate as to whether they powdered and winnowed the clay to remove the coarser particles. Judging by the textural variability between sherds, it is unlikely that they levigated the clay. Given the geological setting of the Diyana plain, procurement of the fine textured clays would not be difficult.

Diyana Ware

A very different clay was used for the manufacture of some of the pottery found at Banahilk. It develops a good red color when refired to 800° and 900°C, but may be gray, tan, or brown in the low-fired pottery. The exterior of some of the sherds is burnished, but others have a red-slipped surface that was burnished after the slip was applied. Of the small group of 11 sherds that were examined, nine contained some chaff markings ranging from sparse to abundant. All of the sherds had subangular talc or talc aggregates; these inclusions occurred in sparse to moderate amounts.

It is possible that this is a mountain clay that was also used for the preparation of the red paint and for the slip used by the potters. It could also be the lateralized surface clay at the site itself. This possibility is suggested because many of the plain ware sherds that were refired developed a bright red color in splotches on the surfaces and along the old fractured edges of the sherds where the soil was in contact with the ware for a long period of time.

As has been noted, this clay burnishes readily. It also produces a less porous pottery than that made from the calcareous clay of the plain ware; the absorption for the 8 sherds tested was 29-34%, which is like that of the painted ware. (The 3 heavily chaff-marked sherds were not included, as they behave like the plain ware in terms of water absorption, ranging from 44% to 47%.)

The 3 thin sections prepared from slices of sherds of this group provided interesting information. Talc and chrysotile are important ingredients in the form of mineral grains and also as finely disseminated particles and aggregates in the clay. Other items appearing in the thin sections are small lumps of very fine-textured sandstone (the source of the angular quartz particles), serpentine (chrysotile grains that are just beginning to alter), quartzite, and shattered quartz.

The photomicrograph seen in figure 223 is that of thin section P-155 prepared from a burnished sherd that contained a small quantity of chaff impressions.

This ware, rich in talc, is clearly related to the modern Diyana ware, which will be discussed next, and its place of manufacture, one might guess, should be sought along the western edge of the Diyana plain.

MODERN DIYANA WARE

Three surface sherds picked up in or near the village of Diyana are quite different in appearance from the ancient ware. They are of brown clay with a dark gray core (hence low-fired), have a burnished surface, and are abundantly tempered with talc grains usually less than 1 mm in diameter. The black surface decoration is produced by using a lump of bitumen as a crayon and drawing the design on the vessel while it is still hot, just after it has been removed from the ashes of the hearth on which it was fired. A plain body sherd from the Banahilk excavations (BI) is also of this ware. The 4 sherds are shown in figure 224. We were told that this pottery is made at the village of Havdian, which is at the western edge of the Diyana plain just south of a spur of the Baradost mountain range.

The thin sections of these 4 sherds show that talc is the dominant inclusion, but some lumps of fine-grained sandstone and a little feldspar also appear. These sections are not dissimilar, save for the size of the talc grains, to those of the Diyana ware. The water absorption of the 4 sherds varied from 23% to 32%, which is in the same range as the painted ware and the Diyana ware.

I have seen ware similar to this in decoration made in the village of Diyana. However, the local calcareous clay that was used fires to a reddish yellow color. Dung cakes served as the fuel. The woman firing the pottery decorated it with bitumen in the manner described above, just after removing it from the hearth at the end of the brief firing. The bitumen melted readily on the still hot vessel. Two figurines of goats that were acquired from this potter show the very fine chaff markings that suggest the use of dung in tempering the clay. Unfortunately, there was no opportunity to question her, but a photographic record was made of her firing and decorating techniques (figs. 225-26). It was the visit to this woman's courtyard that aroused my interest in the ceramic ecology of contemporary village potters.[2]

NOTES

1. I have mentioned the possibility of dung tempering in the Banahilk clay before (Matson 1956, p. 355; 1960, p. 68; 1969, p. 596). A detailed report on the experimental studies of the use of dung in pottery manufacture will be published elsewhere in association with Dr. Robert H. Johnston.

2. There are two other brief records of modern village pottery manufacture in this area: Macfadyen visited the village of Bedyal, about 50 miles northwest of Diyana near Barzan, in 1936. Dönmez and Brice reported in 1953 that straw-tempered storage jars are made at Dara, about 16 miles southeast of Mardin in southeastern Turkey. Galloway (1958, p. 366) reports that the Oxford University expedition to northeastern Iraq in 1956 "brought back specimens of pottery made by Assyrians in the village of Diyana. The pottery is of interest because of its primitive design and the fact that it is built up by the coil process, and no wheel is used. The specimens are now in the possession of the Pitt-Rivers Museum, Oxford."

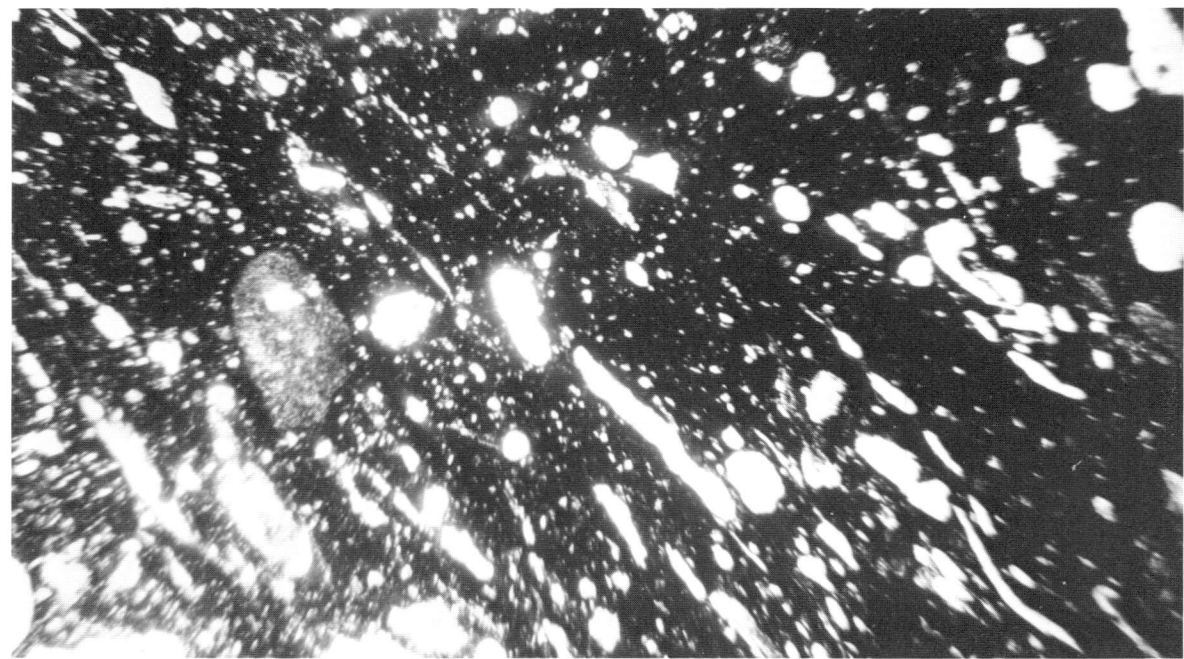

Fig. 221. Photomicrograph of Banahilk plain ware sherd P-158. Photographed with transmitted light. The width of the area seen in the illustration is 3 mm. Most of the larger white areas are the holes left when the chaff was burned out in the firing of the pottery. A few are air pockets. Note the tendency toward parallel alignment of the chaff in the worked clay, as well as a flexed stem, and the round to oval cross sections of some chaff particles, as well as the presence of a pebble of the talc aggregate (light gray). The black background is the carbon-black core of this low fired sherd, and the very fine angular white specks are the grains of quartz.

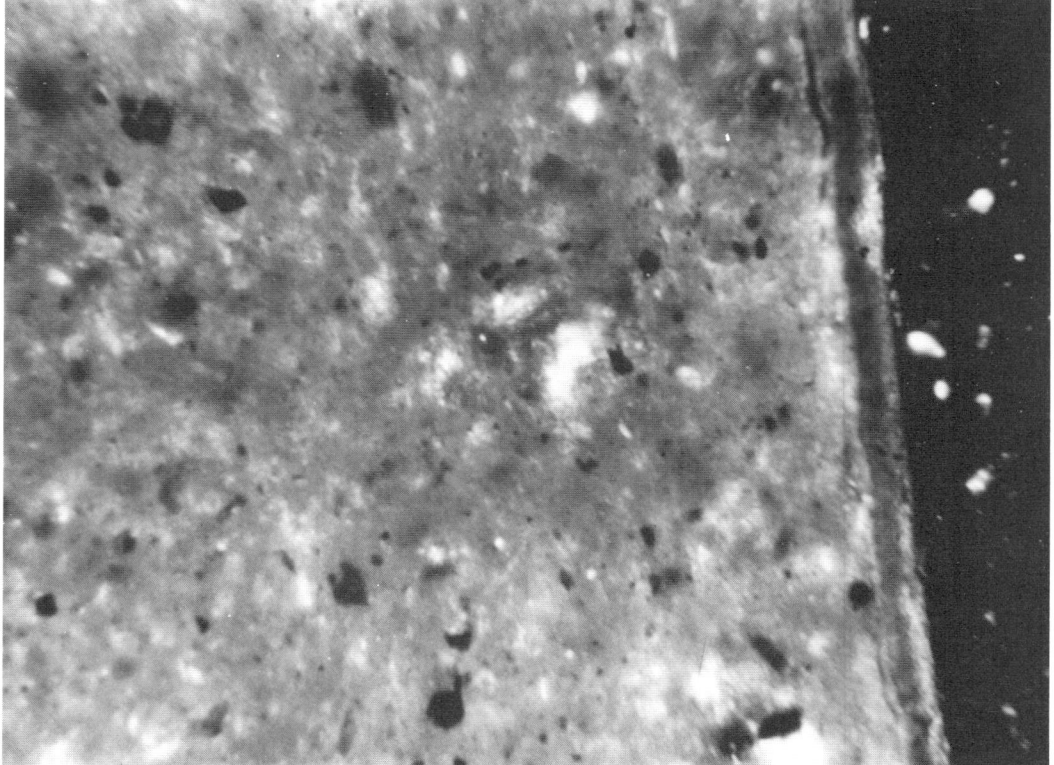

Fig. 222. Photomicrograph of Banahilk painted-ware sherd P-151 with paint on the surface of the thin section. Photographed with crossed Nicol prisms. The width of the area shown is 0.3 mm. The birefringence of the paint layer can be clearly seen, as can the separation of the paint from the body of the sherd.

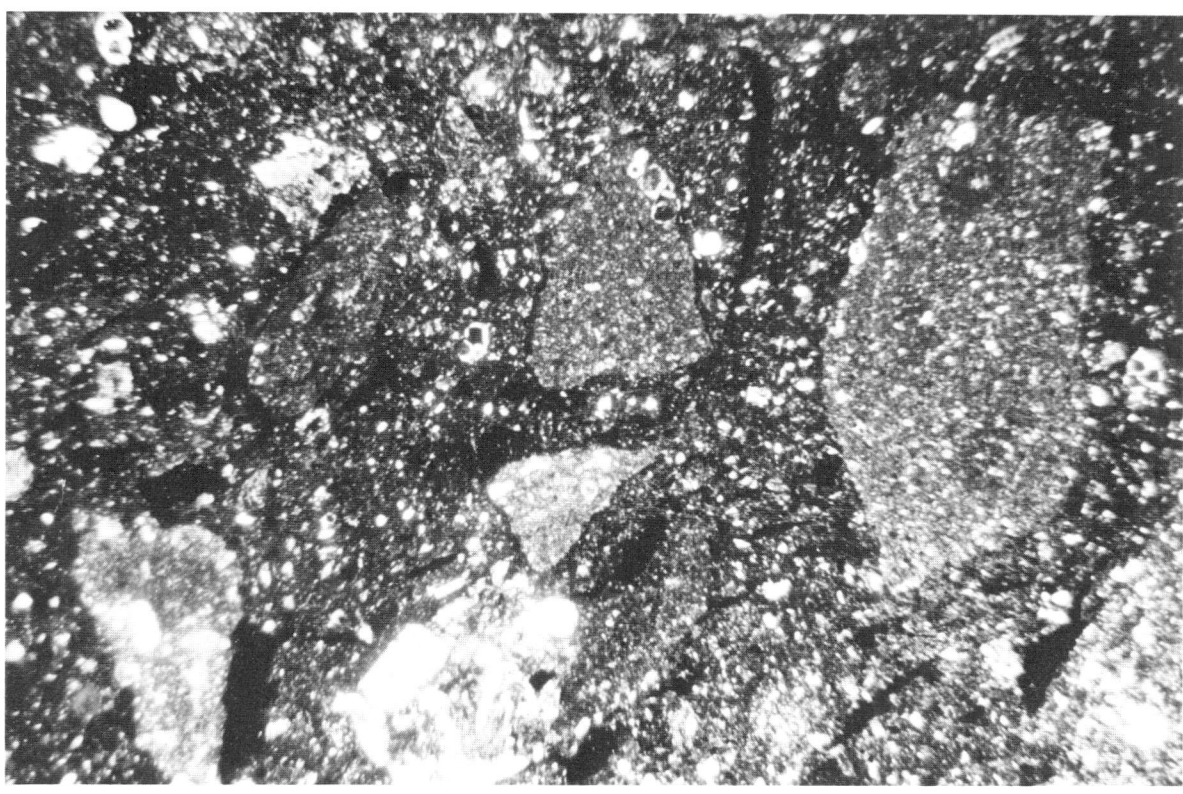

Fig. 223. Photomicrograph of Banahilk Diyana ware sherd P-155. Photographed with crossed Nicol prisms. The area shown is 3.5 mm wide and 2.3 mm high. Visible are several of the angular grains of talc aggregate, white grains of calcite and quartz, a cluster of feldspar and mafic minerals, and pore holes (black) that preserve the longitudinal and cross-sectional traces of the chaff.

Fig. 224. Modern Diyana ware: *1-2,4*, bitumen-decorated sherds, surface collected in or near the village of Diyana; *3*, plain body sherd from the Banahilk excavations (B,*I*). Scale 1:1.

Fig. 225. Diyana village woman decorating spouted vessel with pitch immediately after it was removed from the hearth.

Fig. 226. Two goat figurines made by Diyana village women. The height of the figurines is 13 cm.

REFERENCES

Dönmez, Ahmet, and Brice, W.C.
    1953   A water jar, built without a wheel, in the Kurdish village of Dara. *Man* 53 (article no. 131):90.

Galloway, J.P.N.
    1958   A Kurdish village of north-east Iraq. *Geographical Journal* 124:361-66.

Herzfeld, Ernst
    1932   *Iranische Denkmäler*. Reihe 1: *Vorgeschichtliche Denkmäler*. Lieferung 2: *Steinzeitlicher Hügel bei Persepolis*. Berlin: Reimer and Vohsen.

Macfadyen, W.A.
    1947   Bedyal pottery: a painted ware made in Iraqi Kurdistan. *Man* 47 (article no. 43):47-48.

Matson, Frederick R.
    1941   Porosity studies of ancient pottery. *Papers of the Michigan Academy of Science, Arts, and Letters* 26 (1940 meeting): 469-77.
    1955   Ceramic archaeology. *American Ceramic Society, Bulletin* 34:33-44.
    1956   Techniques of the Early Bronze potters at Tarsus. In *Excavations at Gözlü Kule, Tarsus*, vol. 2, Hetty Goldman, pp. 352-61. Princeton, N.J.: Princeton University Press.
    1960   Specialized ceramic studies and radioactive-carbon techniques. In *Prehistoric investigations in Iraqi Kurdistan*, Robert J. Braidwood, Bruce Howe, et al., pp. 63-70. Studies in Ancient Oriental Civilization, no. 31. Chicago: University of Chicago Press.
    1969   Some aspects of ceramic technology. In *Science in archaeology: a survey of progress and research*, rev. and enl., ed. Don Brothwell and Eric Higgs, pp. 592-602. New York and Washington: Praeger.
    1971   A study of temperatures used in firing ancient Mesopotamian pottery. In *Science and archaeology*, ed. Robert H. Brill, pp. 65-79. Cambridge, Mass.: MIT Press.

Munsell Color Company
    1975   *Munsell Soil Color Charts*. Baltimore.

19

THE FAUNAL REMAINS FROM BANAHILK
Joanne P. Laffer

The osteological remains collected at Gird Banahilk during the 1954-55 field season of the Iraq-Jarmo Project were sorted according to level and excavation square at the site. After Charles A. Reed made a preliminary study of the bones, they were sent to the Peabody Museum of Natural History, Yale University. There, further and somewhat more complete identification of some of the bones was made by Emily Oaks in 1963, after which the collection was moved to the Field Museum of Natural History, Chicago, where it is now stored. The remains consist of 962 pieces of bone, of which 152 (15.8% of the total) are unidentifiable. Of the identified fragments, 95.9% are from sheep, goat, pig, and cattle, and 4.1% are from other species. The identified species are listed below.

Ovis aries (domestic sheep)
Ovis orientalis (wild sheep)
Capra hircus hircus (domestic goat)
Capra hircus aegagrus (wild goat)
Bos taurus (domestic cattle)
Bos primigenius? (wild cattle)

Cervus elaphus (red deer)
Capreolus capreolus (roe deer)
Vulpes vulpes (red fox)
Ursus arctos (brown bear)
Felis pardus (leopard)
Canis sp. (dog or wolf)

Erinaceus sp. (hedgehog)
Equus sp.? (onager?)
bird
fish
Helix salomonica (snail)

The bones available for study are generally in an excellent state of preservation. Few show evidence of having been burned or gnawed. Domestic dog is apparently not present in the sample, and if this species was absent at Banahilk it would account for the lack of any gnawing or splintering of the bones found in the sounding. Only two pieces in the total sample—one a mandibular fragment from the posterior part of the ascending ramus and one piece of shaft of a distal humerus—have been tentatively assigned to either dog or wolf. The humerus, which lacks the distal epiphysis, may have belonged to a young dog, although the identification is by no means positive. Because of the evident absence of gnawed bones and the absence of remains that were positively dog, I suggest that the Halafian people of Banahilk probably did not keep domestic dogs.

Large concentrations of shells of the land snail *Helix salomonica* were found in different parts of the soundings, and there was also a random scatter of shells throughout the excavation. The snails, along with the meat available from the domestic animals, appear to have been a significant part of the diet (Reed 1962).

Only one bone of an equid—a first phalanx—was found. It appeared in the third level of the A trench (70/25 to 70/70 cm deep). According to Watson (p. 546), there is an admixture of wheel-made pottery and metal objects in the A trench, which makes the contexts of the finds there unclear. Quite possibly this one equid phalanx is intrusive. It probably does not belong with the Halafian occupation of the site. The location of Banahilk on a plain to which access was available only through narrow gorges or over high mountains would have made it an unlikely area in which to find wild equids, whose natural habitat is more open country.

The status of potentially domesticable species is an important problem facing the analyst of faunal remains from archeological sites that date to the time period between about 7,000 and 12,000 years ago. For the Halafian sites, the question of the status of cattle is particularly pressing, for these are some of the earliest sites from which domestic cattle are known at present. Domestication may possibly be indicated by distinct morphological changes that have taken place in the bones, by metrical data indicating a reduction in size of the domesticated species as compared to their wild counterparts, or by a different survivorship pattern, indicated by age at death, than would be expected in a wild population.

Perkins (1964a, b) and Hole, Flannery, and Neely (1969) have stated that a high incidence of young animals, particularly those under about three years of age, is an indication that an animal population is domestic. At Shanidar

---

This paper was originally prepared as a thesis for the Master of Arts degree, which was granted in 1973 by the Department of Anthropology, University of Illinois at Chicago Circle. I wish to acknowledge the help of Professors Charles A. Reed, James Philips, and Robert J. Braidwood in the preparation of this manuscript, and the assistance of Christine T. Laffer, who skillfully made the original drawings from which those in figure 227 were made.

[The manuscript for this chapter was essentially completed by 1977. Very few additions and only minor revisions have been made since that date.—EDS.]

Cave (layer B1) and at Zawi Chemi Shanidar, both dated to ca. 10,870 ± 300 B.P., Perkins found that immature sheep represented 44-57% of the remains of *Ovis*. Although the sheep showed no morphological changes that indicated domestication, Perkins concluded that the age structure of the population was one factor that would indicate such status. Hole, Flannery, and Neely have presented a more complete discussion of the use of data on age groups as an aid in determining domestication but also have warned against uncritical use of this sort of information, which is tentative at best. One problem with this type of comparison is that the animal populations used for compiling the patterns of survival are always modern, living populations. There is, of course, no guarantee that populations of animals in the past had the same patterns. Nevertheless, analysis of populations of wild sheep in the Deh Luran plain, southwestern Iran, indicated that about 63% of the animals survived beyond their third year. Only about 42% of the individuals in a domestic population survived beyond this age. In a study of North American bighorn sheep, Geist (1971) found that 95% of the rams in a wild population would have a life expectancy of over 3.7 years. A similar pattern was projected for the ewes, and Geist concluded that wild populations showed a low incidence of mortality for young and subadult individuals. McArdle (1974), after discussing the use of such survivorship data, applied them to the analysis of the osteological remains from the Halafian site of Girikihacıyan. He found different patterns of survival for sheep/goat and for pig, compared to the pattern indicated for the cattle. McArdle reported that 46.5% of the sheep and goat remains for which the age could be determined and 68.3% of the ageable pig remains were from young animals in which the M_3 or P_4 had only just begun to wear. Only 37.1% of the bovine remains were from young animals, however (McArdle 1974, table I). He concluded that while most of the remains of caprines, suids, and bovids were from domestic animals, the people of Girikihacıyan were exploiting the cattle in a way that was different from the exploitation of the caprines and suids. The differential uses of bovids by the Halafians that were suggested by McArdle included eating cattle only when they died naturally, maintaining more adult herds for use as traction or dairy animals, and possibly (to judge by the frequency of the bucranium as a design element on the pottery) assigning cattle an important role in the ideological system.

The faunal remains from Banahilk were aged on the basis of the relative times of eruption of the teeth, and four age groups were constructed. A young animal was indicated by the presence of a deciduous P_4 in a mandible, by an unerupted M_3 in a mandible or maxilla, or by a loose M_2 that showed very little wear and no sign that the M_3 had erupted as yet. A subadult animal was indicated by an M_3 that showed only slight wear (i.e., the appearance of the tooth indicated that it had erupted but had not had much opportunity to wear). A mature animal was considered to be one in which the M_3 showed extreme wear, including a considerable amount on the posterior cusp. Presented below are two tabulations—the first summarizing data on the age groups of the different genera from Banahilk and the second providing comparative data from Silver (1963) that can be used to assign an approximate age to the various age groups in each genus. The subadult group will always contain relatively few individuals, as this category probably represents in the total life-span a period of less than a year and perhaps not more than six months, during which the M_3 will be erupted but will show only very slight wear. Because the teeth of sheep and goats are indistinguishable in archeological contexts, the data for these two genera are combined in both tabulations. Thus, in my summary of Silver's data, I give the age range as the minimum necessary to encompass both genera, which are separated in Silver's original publication.

Percentage of Specimens of Domesticated Animals from Banahilk in Each Age Category

Genus	Number of specimens	% Young	% Subadult	% Adult	% Mature
Ovis/Capra	80	46.3	6.3	42.5	5.0
Sus	28	64.3	21.4	14.3	0
Bos	8	50.0	25.0	12.5	12.5

Relative Age When Teeth Erupt Based on "Older Data" of Silver

Tooth	Ovis/Capra	Sus	Bos
dP_4	6 weeks	2-7 weeks	birth to 3 weeks
P_4	17-30 months	2 years	18-30 months
M_2	12-18 months	18-24 months	15-18 months
M_3	2-4 years	3 years	24-30 months

SOURCE: Silver 1963, pp. 262-65.

Silver's older data were gathered from nineteenth century authors and were compared with data from modern breeds kept on a highly nutritional diet. It was found that in almost all cases modern breeds were younger when their teeth erupted than their nineteenth century counterparts. Silver commented that it seemed wise to use the older data for comparison with data from archeological sites where the plane of nutrition of the animals is unknown. However, the information tabulated above, which is derived from his data, yields only roughly comparative figures, and it should be used with caution. The figures do indicate that, given the best comparative data available, the domesticated animals were less than 2½ years old if the dP_4 has been retained and that cattle and pigs were close to 3 years old if the M_3 has erupted but shows very little wear. Caprines were around 4 years of age or perhaps younger if the M_3 shows very little wear.

If this information is applied in a very general way to the Banahilk data, it can be estimated that about 47.5% of the caprines at Banahilk survived beyond about 4 years of age. About 14.3% of the pigs survived for some time after about 3 years of age, but none achieved any great age. Similarly, although the bovine sample is admittedly very small, only about 25% survived much beyond 3 years of age. Thus, the age data obtained from the Banahilk fauna lend support to other data indicating that the sheep, goats, pigs, and cattle at this site were domestic. Moreover, the cattle here have the same sort of pattern of survival as the other domesticates, in contrast to the cattle from Girikihacıyan (McArdle 1974).

Although a pattern of early age of animals at death such as this one at Banahilk might possibly suggest a seasonal hunting pattern, it can also suggest selective culling of herds (Perkins and Daly 1968; Bökönyi 1972). There does not seem to be any particular indication of seasonal occupation at Banahilk, however, and a village such as this, small though it may have been, was probably permanent, as were other Halafian sites. A more likely explanation for the youthfulness of the various domestic animals whose bones were found in archeological contexts is that the optimal age for slaughter is at the beginning of the subadult stage when the growth curve has begun to level off. For central and western European animals this age is about 1½ years for pigs, 2½-3½ years for cattle, and about 1-2 years for sheep and goats (Uerpmann 1973, p. 316).

SHEEP/GOATS (*Ovis/Capra*)

The remains of sheep and goats constituted by far the largest part of the bones from Banahilk. A total of 492 bone fragments were identified as belonging to *Ovis/Capra*. This represented 60.7% of the bones whose genus could be identified and 41.1% of the total number of bones from Banahilk. Probably the figure of 60.7% is a better representation of the actual frequency of the caprines in the faunal sample, since many of the unidentified bones were found to be very similar to each of the three groups of domestic animals. Therefore, had these unidentified bones been somewhat more complete they would probably have been distributed among the identified bones in such a way as to change the relative proportions of these bones by very little.

The bones of sheep and goats are extremely difficult to tell apart, as has been noted by various authors (Perkins 1959; Reed 1961; Higham 1968*b*). In all cases the teeth of sheep and goats are completely indistinguishable and must simply be identified as belonging to caprines. The horn cores and complete metapodial bones are generally distinguishable and have distinct morphological characteristics for each genus.

In 1953, Gramova published an index that aids in determining whether a distal metacarpal bone belongs to *Capra* or *Ovis*. Since then Boessneck, Müller, and Teichert (1964) and Hole, Flannery, and Neely (1969) have applied the index to metatarsal bones and found that it reliably separates the genera, although there is some overlap of the indices for the metatarsal. Using this index, I separated the metapodial bones from Banahilk into two distinct groups (table 52) with 4 being placed in *Ovis* and 6 in *Capra*.

Boessneck, Müller, and Teichert (1964) made one of the most complete studies of the postcranial skeletons of sheep and goats that had yet been undertaken. They were able to find morphological criteria that separated almost all of the postcranial elements of the skeleton of the two genera, the distal tibia being an exception that no amount of study would separate. Problems, however, arose with their work; the application of purely visual criteria lacked precision (Higham 1968*b*, p. 64), and their study was based completely on caprines that were domestic and European. There is, therefore, no assurance that their criteria will hold either for wild caprines or for domestic caprines in the Near East.

In an attempt to fill this gap and to find criteria useful for her own work, Barbara Lawrence (1980) studied 13 wild goats and 15 wild sheep from Iran. After finding apparent differences and comparing them with those of Boessneck, Müller, and Teichert (1964), Lawrence applied her data to 13 domestic sheep and 5 domestic goats. She thus found reliable differences in the bones involved—in the elbow joint, the distal parts of the scapula, the ilium in combination with the acetabulum, the distal metapodial bones, the astragalus, and the calcaneus.

Higham (1968*b*) also found a difference in the metacarpal bones of sheep and goats—namely, the ratio of the minimum anterior-posterior diaphysial width to the minimum transverse diaphysial width. Again, the problem with this ratio is that it was computed on a sample of European domestic caprines. In addition, given the kind of fragments usually found in Near Eastern archeological sites, the analyst may not be certain that the necessary part of the shaft is present. Only two metacarpal bones from Banahilk seemed to have the part of the shaft that would yield the appropriate measurements for the index, and the results of the computation confirmed the identification of one goat and one sheep made previously on the basis of morphological criteria. There is, therefore, a strong possibility that the index will be accurate for Near Eastern caprines, although it needs to be checked against a large sample of metacarpal bones from that area.

Using the work of the above authors, and also skeletons of Near Eastern Caprini available at the Field Museum of Natural History, I was able to classify about 34.1% of the 492 caprine fragments from Banahilk as either *Ovis* or *Capra*. Of these separated fragments, 72, or 42.9%, were found to be *Capra*, and 96, or 51.1%, were *Ovis*. This would indicate that the flocks of the people of Banahilk were almost equally divided between sheep and goats, with a slight preponderance of sheep.

The character of the area around Banahilk is such that the availability of wild sheep and goats to the people living in the village can be assumed. However, the occupation of Banahilk occurred at a time when one expects to find domestic sheep and goats at sites in the Near East. Perkins (1964*a, b*) has argued for the presence of domestic sheep at Zawi Chemi Shanidar at a date more than 10,000 years ago, and Shanidar is only a few kilometers west of Banahilk. Further, at the site of Jarmo (ca. 8500 B.P.) Reed (1959) found evidence for the presence of domestic goats, a conclusion that was supported by the studies of Stampfli (chap. 9).

Reed (1959) discussed the changes that occurred in the horn cores of goats under domestication. The horn cores became flattened on the medial side and some developed a slight twist. They changed from a generally quadrilateral shape in cross section to a lozenge shape and finally became quite flat medially. Hole, Flannery, and Neely (1969) discussed the changes in horn cores of sheep under domestication and concluded that they tended to become more goatlike. While the horn cores of wild sheep were almond shaped in cross section, with the point aimed posteriorly, those of domestic sheep had the point aimed anteriorly and tended to become medially flattened. While the criteria for horn cores of sheep, as described in Hole, Flannery, and Neely, proved more difficult to apply than the criteria for horn cores of goats, it was possible to identify both wild and domestic sheep as well as goats among the fauna of Banahilk, as summarized in the following tabulation:

Caprine Horn Cores from Banahilk

Genus	Wild	Domestic	Indeterminate	Total
Ovis	1	2	4	7
Capra	4	10	2	16
Indeterminate	--	--	2	2

The apparent paradox of finding more than twice as many horn cores of goats as of sheep can be resolved by suggesting the possibility of the existence of hornless sheep. Hole, Flannery, and Neely (1969) found a skull of a hornless sheep in the Bus Mordeh phase at Ali Kosh (ca. 9000 B.P.), McArdle (1974) found a fragment of a hornless or dehorned caprine at Girikihacıyan, and Lawrence (1980) found two cranial fragments of hornless sheep and a third with a much smaller horn core at Çayönü (9000 B.P. or older). If some early domestic sheep were either hornless or dehorned, sheep would have contributed far fewer horn cores to the archeological record than would goats.

Various measurements were taken of the caprine bones at Banahilk. In general, the results tended to confirm the difficulty of distinguishing *Ovis* and *Capra* on the basis of metrical analysis. In particular, the fragments of scapulae, most of which were pieces of the neck and glenoid fossa, were most difficult to distinguish. An index of neck length to minimum neck width was computed for all caprine distal scapular fragments by Boessneck, Müller, and Teichert (1964). Their work established an index value of 1.2 as the breakpoint and assigned scapulae with an index value less than this figure to sheep and those with a greater index value to goats. However, there is considerable overlap between the indices of sheep and goats (Boessneck, Müller, and Teichert 1964, diagram I), which gives a limited value to the use of the index alone. The index in combination with the shape of the coracoid region does, however, frequently allow a distinction to be made. Similarly, the morphological criteria for distinguishing the distal humeri (Boessneck, Müller, and Teichert 1964; Lawrence 1980) were not clearly applicable in all cases, although with the comparative material available at the Field Museum of Natural History many of the humeri were separated as to genus with considerable assurance. Other postcranial elements that were found to be separable were the proximal radius, ulna, distal femur, patella, calcaneus, astragalus, distal metapodials, first and third phalanges, and in some cases the second phalanx. An interesting insight into separating the metapodial bones came when Gramova's index and Boessneck, Müller, and Teichert's morphological criteria were applied separately. In all cases the separate analyses resulted in the same conclusions as to the proper identification of the bones. The metrical data are summarized in table 52.

So that there can be no confusion as to how measurements were taken on the osteological material from Banahilk, drawings and descriptions of each class of measurement are given in figure 227. Throughout this study the words *width*, *depth*, and *length* are used to mean measurements taken in a particular plane and direction. Width is a lateral

Table 52.—Summary Data on Caprini from Banahilk

Measurement	No.	$\bar{X}$	Range (cm)	s	V
Ovis/Capra					
M^1					
Midlength	9	1.33	1.09-1.55	0.1834	13.8
M^2					
Midlength	24	1.59	1.34-1.70	0.1017	6.4
M^3					
Midlength	12	1.57	1.37-1.77	0.1032	6.6
M_1					
Midlength	26	1.35	1.04-1.80	0.1740	12.9
M_2					
Midlength	32	1.58	1.36-1.90	0.1376	8.7
Scapula					
Index: $\frac{\text{neck length}}{\text{min. neck width}}$	13	1.22	1.07-1.44	0.1153	9.5
Same index as above, split into two populations: Capra?*	6	1.34	1.27-1.44	0.0689	5.2
Ovis?*	7	1.12	1.07-1.19	0.0482	4.3
Index of glenoid fossa: $\frac{\text{max. width} \times 100}{\text{max. depth}}$	10	65.90	57.70-71.50	4.4790	6.8
Pelvis					
Acetabulum: max. height	7	2.45	2.12-2.82	0.2768	11.3
Tibia					
Max. distal width	16	2.75	2.15-3.36	0.3431	12.5
Second phalanx					
Midlength	11	2.07	1.89-2.31	0.1230	6.0
Ovis					
Humerus					
Distal epiphysis: max. width	15	3.24	2.66-3.89	0.3721	11.5
max. depth	15	2.92	2.42-3.64	0.3444	11.8
Radius					
Max. proximal width	4	3.21	2.01-3.40	0.1916	6.0
Max. distal width	2	3.15	3.14, 3.16	--	--
Max. distal depth	2	2.08	2.03, 2.12	--	--
Ulna					
Radioulnar joint: max. width	5	1.84	1.71-2.01	0.1100	6.0
Ilium					
Lateral length	4	5.77	5.43-6.58	0.2977	3.0
Min. depth	4	1.71	1.69-1.89	0.1285	7.5
Patella					
Max. length	2	3.17	2.76, 3.58	--	--
Max. depth	4	1.66	1.48-1.83	0.1432	8.7
Max. width	3	2.29	2.18-2.47	0.1597	7.0
Astragalus					
Min. length	18	2.36	2.15-2.59	0.1328	5.6
First phalanx					
Min. length	3	3.86	3.42-4.55	0.6050	15.6
Distal metapodial bones					
Epiphysial index: $\frac{\text{outer diameter} \times 100}{\text{inner diameter}}$	4	70.30	64.00-76.00	5.6480	8.0
Capra					
Humerus					
Distal epiphysis: max. width	11	3.33	2.85-4.30	0.5380	15.2
max. depth	11	2.94	2.47-3.74	0.4887	16.6
Ulna					
Radioulnar joint: max. width	2	2.37	2.24, 2.49	--	--
Radius					
Max. proximal width	5	3.11	2.32-4.05	0.5808	18.6
Max. distal width	1	2.45	--	--	--
Max. distal depth	1	1.90	--	--	--
Distal metapodial bones					
Epiphysial index: $\frac{\text{outer diameter} \times 100}{\text{inner diameter}}$	6	59.00	58.00-61.00	1.2650	2.1
Astragalus					
Min. length	7	2.19	2.07-2.35	0.1106	5.0
Third Phalanx					
Max. length	1	2.81	--	--	--

NOTE: In the data above, the symbols $\bar{X}$, s, and V stand for mean, standard deviation, and coefficient of variation, respectively. Standard deviation is a measure of how far each individual measurement in a group of measurements varies, on the average, from the mean of the whole group. It is a measure of the dispersion or variability within a sample. The coefficient of variation is a normalizing statistic that is found by dividing the standard deviation by the mean of the sample and multiplying the result by 100. This statistic allows the investigator to compare the variability of two samples that differ in absolute size. Coefficients of variation have been compared for linear dimensions on numerous relatively homogeneous groups of mammals, and they tend to run between 4 and 10, with 5 or 6 being an average figure (Simpson, Roe, and Lewontin 1960). If the sample contains an admixture of remains of different sexes and ages or of remains of both wild and domestic animals the coefficient of variation will be higher. The high coefficients of variation in the above table may be the result of any one of these three sources of heterogeneity.

*The index for the neck of the scapula split naturally into two subgroups at the median of the range for the single population. Boessneck, Müller, and Teichert (1964) used 1.20 as the maximum for sheep but cautioned about an overlap between Capra and Ovis for this index. Here the index is split only tentatively, because the morphological criteria did not always agree with the assignment according to the index.

measurement taken from one side of a bone to the other, or from the lateral to the medial side of the bone. Depth is a measurement taken in the same plane as the width but in an anterior-posterior direction. Length is taken in a plane perpendicular to the width and depth, and measures the proximodistal distance. The two exceptions to this rule are the teeth and the innominate. The length of teeth is traditionally measured in the anterior-posterior direction for molars. That tradition is followed in this study. The innominate does not lie in the same plane as the rest of the bones of the body, and the terms as used elsewhere seemed inappropriate. The drawings in figure 227 should clarify the meanings of the terms.

Data from age groups and from horn cores confirm that the people of Banahilk kept domestic sheep and goats. While they also hunted wild caprines, the evidence from the horn cores would seem to indicate that about 70% of the remains were from the domestic species. Although this figure fails to take the indeterminate horn cores into consideration, it also fails to allow for the fact that relatively few ovine horn cores were found. Thus, the people of Banahilk depended on domestic sheep and goats for a significant proportion of their diet.

PIGS (*Sus scrofa*)

Remains of pigs constituted 122 identified fragments—15.1% of all identified fragments and 12.6% of the total remains. These fragments, however, show a different distribution from those of the other domestic animals, as can be seen most readily below.

Remains of Domestic Animals from Banahilk as Percentages of the Total Identified Remains

Genus	Teeth and fragments of jaws and teeth (%)	Other skeletal fragments (%)
Sus	56.6	43.4
Capra/Ovis	37.4	62.6
Bos	18.4	81.6

The fact that the remains of teeth constitute such a large proportion of all the suid remains may be accounted for in two ways. As was indicated by the age data (p. 630), pigs tended to be slaughtered while quite young. There is a possibility that the bones of very young animals, being quite fragile, are not preserved as readily as those of older animals, while the teeth of such young animals are less readily destroyed. The bones of suids, moreover, having a rather high fat content, may possibly tend to decay more readily than the bones of other animals. Again, the teeth as the hardest parts of the skeleton would tend to be preserved.

In 1961, Flannery did an extensive study of *Sus scrofa* from archeological sites and established criteria, based on dental measurements, for the size range of teeth of domestic pigs. On the basis of his study, he concluded that the upper limit for the length of an M^3 in domestic *Sus* of the Near East was 3.20 cm and that any specimen falling in the range from 3.20 to 3.40 cm should not be considered clearly domestic. He further set lower limits for length of M^3's of wild pigs as 3.76 cm for M_3 and 3.31 cm for M^3. Data for the length of molar teeth from the pigs of Banahilk are tabulated below and also compared with data from seven wild *Sus scrofa* recorded by Flannery (1961).

Flannery, who included the suid teeth from Banahilk in his study, suggested that only two teeth, the largest M^1 and the largest M^2, were suggestive of wild animals. The measurements from Banahilk given below were checked against Flannery's measurements on the same teeth and found to be comparable. The data indicate that the *Sus scrofa* at Banahilk were domestic.

Midlengths of Molars of *Sus scrofa* from Banahilk Compared with Ranges Given by Flannery for Same Measurements on Teeth from Seven Wild Iraqi Pigs

Tooth	No.	Range (cm)	$\bar{X}$	s	V	Range (cm) for seven wild Iraqi pigs
M^1	8	1.31-1.93	1.60	0.193	12.04	1.51-1.88
M^2	8	1.47-2.32	1.87	.262	14.01	2.07-2.63
M^3	1	2.75	--	--	--	3.55-4.28
M_1	5	1.36-1.66	1.56	.120	7.97	1.60-1.85
M_2	3	1.74-1.95	1.86	.109	5.81	2.18-2.47
M_3	4	2.86-3.40	3.15	0.224	10.40	3.76-4.93

SOURCE OF COMPARATIVE DATA: Flannery 1961, fig. 12.

Further study of the postcranial skeletons of pigs was reported by Barbara Lawrence in her preliminary analysis of the fauna from Çayönü. The suid remains at Çayönü were studied by Hans Stampfli, and his comparative material was included in Lawrence (1980). Summarized below are the metrical data for the postcranial suid remains from Banahilk with comparative data from Stampfli (Lawrence 1980), where applicable.

Measurements of Postcranial Bones of *Sus scrofa* from Banahilk
Compared with Çayönü Data of Lawrence

Specimen	No.	Range (cm)	$\bar{X}$	s	V	Range (cm) for wild pigs from Çayönü
Scapula						
Glenoid fossa: max. width	4	2.04-2.62	2.25	0.255	11.3	--
max. depth	4	2.71-3.36	3.09	.275	9.0	--
Neck: min. width	6	1.06-2.04	1.70	.336	19.7	--
Distal humerus						
Epiphysis: max. width	5	3.42-4.08	3.74	.314	8.67	4.30-4.50
max. depth	3	2.70-4.19	3.57	.774	21.7	--
Distal tibia						
Max. width	3	2.55-3.73	3.03	.454	15.0	3.25-3.45
Max. depth	2	2.27, 3.37	--	--	--	--
Astragalus						
Min. length	6	3.20-4.02	3.52	0.348	9.89	--

SOURCE OF COMPARATIVE DATA: Lawrence 1980, table 4.

Again, the problem of using comparative data from other sites revolves around the question of comparability of measurements. For the maximum width of the distal epiphysis of the humerus and the maximum width of the distal tibia, the measurements seem to be comparable, and the results indicate that the suid sample from Banahilk, while very small, is within the domestic range. Of the three distal tibiae measured from Banahilk, one, the largest, was within the range for wild pigs reported by Stampfli (Lawrence 1980). This one measurement may well represent an unusually large individual within the domestic population. Jarman (1971) has argued that when defining domestic populations on the basis of metrical data alone, the decreasing mean of the population over time is especially important because the total range of individual variation within local wild and domestic populations is usually not well defined. Therefore, larger measurements from a local population could represent the upper end of the range of individual variation—"feral individuals, or wild-domestic crosses" (Jarman 1971, p. 257).

The information on age categories (p. 630), derived from determination of age at death, and measurements of teeth and of postcranial remains all tend to confirm that the people at Banahilk kept domestic pigs.

CATTLE (*Bos*)

Cattle were represented at Banahilk by a total of 163 identified fragments—16.9% of the total remains and 20.1% of the identified remains. The percentage of teeth and jaws was unusually low, while that of other skeletal elements was high (p. 634). The age data for *Bos*, however, were very similar to the same data for sheep and goats (p. 630), 75% of the teeth for which age could be determined being from young and subadult animals.

The problem of separating the bones of *Bos* and *Bison* can be as difficult to solve as that of separating those of the Caprini. In addition, some of the bones of cattle can be confused with those of red deer (*Cervus elaphus*). This confusion was so likely, in fact, that two investigators first identified a race of small *Bos* for the late Pleistocene in the Near East (Reed 1959; Perkins 1960) and then after more careful analysis removed the remains of "small *Bos*" from the record and placed the finds in *Cervus elaphus* (Reed 1961, p. 34; Perkins 1964a, p. 566). The bovine remains from Banahilk have been carefully studied with this possible confusion in mind and the remains of *C. elaphus* separated from those of *Bos*.

Olsen (1960) has written a field manual directed at the problem of distinguishing the bones of *Bos taurus* and *Bison bison*. Although his researches were done on Old World domestic *Bos* and North American *Bison*, the manual was used in searching for the presence of remains of *Bison* among the bovine remains at Banahilk because it was available to me and because of its completeness. Olsen's distinguishing characteristics for the bones of *Bos taurus* seemed, in general, to hold for the bones of these Near Eastern cattle, and no certain remains of *Bison* were identified. In addition, Flannery has stated that no certain remains of *Bison* have been found in Mesopotamia, the southern Zagros, or Khuzistan (Hole, Flannery, and Neely 1969, p. 302). Hatt has suggested the possibility of *Bison* in the Near East, mainly on the basis of extremely accurate representations of such animals on cylinder seals and pottery, but he noted that in historic times there were no records of *Bison* nearer than the Caucasus Mountains (Hatt 1959, p. 22). On the other hand the remains of *Bos* are commonly found at sites in the Near East. In consideration of all these observations, I believe I am justified in placing the bovine remains from Banahilk in *Bos*.

The question of the domestic status of bovine remains has always been handled by referring to comparative metrical data, the assumption being that domestic cattle were considerably smaller than their wild counterparts. Although various authors (e.g., Jarman 1969, 1971) have criticized the way in which conclusions have been drawn from these data, the best currently available criteria for deciding whether cattle are domestic continue to be based on comparative measurements of size. Jarman did, however, have an excellent argument when he commented that using comparative data from widely separated geographical areas was of questionable value (Jarman 1971, p. 239). Here, therefore, I have used mostly comparative data from sites that are geographically close to Iraq. In his comprehensive study of remains of *Bos primigenius* and early neolithic *Bos taurus* in Denmark, Degerbøl (Degerbøl and Fredskild 1970) found that wild *B. primigenius* displayed a considerable amount of sexual dimorphism. Size differences were so great that measurements on female bones frequently lay outside the range of the same measurements taken on males. Furthermore, the measurements of the bones of female *B. primigenius* and those of the male *B. taurus* tended to overlap. Because a similar sexual dimorphism would be expected among *B. primigenius* in other areas of the Eurasian landmass and because the study is so complete, Denmark is the one area of northwestern Europe that is included in the tables of comparative measurements. All other sites are geographically closer to Banahilk. Listed below are the sites and references from which comparative data were taken.

Sites from Which Data Were Taken for the Construction of Comparative Measurements of *Bos*

Site	Approximate date (B.P.)	Reference	Bos primigenius	Bos taurus
Danish sites	Neolithic and earlier	Degerbøl and Fredskild 1970	X	X
Palestinian sites	"Mesolithic": 15,000-10,000	Jarman 1969	X	--
Mureybit, Syria	10,000	Ducos 1972	X	--
Argissa-Magula, Greece	8500	Boessneck 1962	X	X
Itzaki and Arapi, Greece	8500	Boessneck 1956	--	X
Nea Nikomedeia, Greece	8100	Higgs 1962	--	X
Çatal Hüyük, Turkey:				
layer VI	7650	Perkins 1969	X	X
layer XII	8050			
Tepe Sabz, Deh Luran plain, Iran	7410-6000	Hole, Flannery, and Neely 1969	X	X
Girikihacıyan, Iraq	6800	McArdle 1974	--	X
Anau, Turkmen, S.S.R.	6200	Duerst 1908	X	X
Tel Aviv, Israel	6000	Ducos 1968	--	X
Shah Tepe, Iran	6000-5000	Amschler 1939	--	X
Fikirtepe, Turkey	5500	Röhrs and Herre 1961	--	X

Table 53 gives the data on bovine remains from the above-mentioned sites as compared with data from Banahilk. The comparative data in this table have been grouped into roughly geographical regions designated as area 1, Danish sites; area 2, Greek sites; area 3, two sites in Turkey and one in northern Greece, all of which yielded remains of rather large domestic cattle; area 4, several sites in the Near East from Palestine to the Zagros Mountains; and area 5, two sites farther to the east. In the case of Banahilk, the data include the number of specimens and the means of measurements. For the other sites, since some of the comparative data combine data from several sites, only the ranges of measurements are given. Table 54 gives the complete measurements with mean, range, standard deviation, and coefficient of variation for all of the bovine remains from Banahilk (for explanation of Banahilk measurements, see p. 644 and fig. 227).

In analyzing the data presented in table 53 the problem of comparability of measurements again presents itself. Many authors publish measurements without saying how they are taken. A width on the distal humerus or metapodial bones may be taken either at the end of the shaft or across the distal epiphysis, and the maxima thus obtained will be different. Measurements defined as being the distal width of one of these bones are, therefore, next to useless if the author does not say at what point the width was estimated (e.g., Röhrs and Herre 1961, p. 117; Perkins 1969). The problem becomes particularly acute with the first and second phalanges, for which measurements are frequently published. The lateral length of these bones (fig. 227:18) will vary considerably, depending on how the bone is held when measured. If it is laid flat on the table and a measurement taken, a truly maximum measurement (lateral length, posterior) will be obtained. If, however, the phalanx is held so that the proximal surface lies evenly on the measuring arm of the caliper, and a lateral length taken, a measurement closer to the physiological length of the bone (lateral length) is obtained. Both measurements are equally valid, but only Ducos (1968) and Degerbøl (Degerbøl and Fredskild 1970) indicate clearly just how this length was taken. For purposes of table 53 all lengths of phalanges I and II were assumed to have been taken as if they were lateral lengths, except those for Denmark (Degerbøl and Fredskild 1970) and those for Tel Aviv (Ducos 1968) and Mureybit (Ducos 1972).

Because some authors have criticized the use of metrical data from widely separated geographical regions as a standard of comparison by which to judge whether cattle from a particular site are wild or domestic, in table 53 the sites were grouped into as closely contiguous geographical regions as possible. Study of this table, however, yields the interesting conclusion that the data reported from Denmark by Degerbøl provide an excellent standard of comparison for almost all sites in the Near East and Greece, with the exception of the three sites in area 3 of the table (Nea Nikomedeia, Çatal Hüyük, and Fikirtepe). In only two measurements does there seem to be much discrepancy between the ranges established by the Danish study and those established by studies in Greece and southwestern Asia. The maximum width of the distal radius is larger in domestic cattle of Denmark than in those of the other sites and shows a considerable amount of overlap with *B. primigenius* from that area, and the maximum width of the distal articular surface of the metacarpal bones is noticeably smaller in domestic cattle from Denmark, with, again, considerable overlap with the same measurement on wild cattle. Because Degerbøl's study was made on fairly complete skeletons of *B. primigenius*, there can be little doubt that the skeletons were identified correctly, and his study can, therefore, provide a valuable standard for the size ranges of *Bos primigenius* throughout the Near East.

Three sites have yielded very large measurements for domestic cattle. They were grouped together (area 3) because whenever the data were included with either the Greek sites (area 2) or the sites in the region of Palestine and the Zagros Mountains (area 4) they significantly extended the ranges of the measurements from these areas. In the case of Fikirtepe, Röhrs and Herre (1961) stated that some of their cattle were quite large and were possibly transitional between wild and domestic cattle. For Nea Nikomedeia, Higgs (1962) determined the domestic status of the cattle by comparison with British Ayrshire cattle and with the skeletal collections of cattle in the British Museum of Natural History. For Catal Hüyük, Perkins has published only the measurement of the width of the distal humerus, so there are few data to use by way of comparison. Although these all seem to be rather large cattle and may not yield particularly useful comparative data, the investigators each had their reasons for considering them domestic. Again, Jarman (1971) was probably correct in commenting that it is the decreasing means of the measurements that are indicative of domestication.

Viewed in this light, the cattle at Banahilk were probably domestic. There are some large measurements that may indicate either unusually large individuals within the domestic population or the successful hunting of wild cattle by the people of Banahilk. The maximum width of the distal articular surface of the humerus contains one measurement from Banahilk (9.37 cm) that is well within the range of wild cattle from Denmark, and this bone may be from a wild animal. The same can be said for the largest cubonaviculars, the two largest distal metacarpal bones, and the largest metatarsal bone. Comparing the measurements of the phalanges becomes more difficult. Of the 8 first phalanges of *Bos* from Banahilk, 4 have a greater lateral length posterior and a greater maximum proximal depth than any first phalanges of domestic cattle from Denmark. All 8 of these Banahilk bones, however, have a shorter lateral length posterior than any first phalanges of wild cattle from Palestine and the Zagros Mountains (table 53, area 4). If Boessneck (1956, 1962) had only stated how he measured the lateral length of the first phalanx, his data from Greece would provide a very useful comparison. If his maximum lateral length of 6.80 cm for first phalanges of domestic cattle from Greece was actually a lateral length, posterior measurement, then just two of these bones from Banahilk are above the range of the Greek domestic cattle.

The site of Tel Aviv has yielded rather small specimens of domestic cattle bones (Ducos 1968). In a comparison of measurements, it has been found that the posterior lateral length of 5 first phalanges and 5 second phalanges from Banahilk are above the size range reported for such bones from Tel Aviv (table 53, area 4). The material from Tel Aviv, however, was dated at about 6000 B.P., approximately 1,000 years later than the Banahilk material, and although domestication of animals (with the possible exception of the dog) tended to be later in Palestine than in the region of the Zagros Mountains, the time difference could still be an important factor when trying to explain the small size of the cattle from Tel Aviv.

Bos primigenius remains from Mureybit in Syria (Ducos 1972) have probably provided the best data for comparison with Banahilk. As mentioned before, all of the first phalanges from Banahilk are smaller than the phalanges from Mureybit when measured for posterior lateral length. Similarly, the second phalanges from Banahilk all fall below the second phalanges reported from Mureybit in posterior lateral length (Ducos 1972). In summary, the measurements on bovine bones from Banahilk tend to indicate that the animals they represent were mostly domestic, although some bones were large and may be from wild animals.

Like the remains of *Sus scrofa*, the bovine remains from Banahilk constitute quite a small sample. The coefficients of variation of all the measurements, except those of the second phalanx and the astragalus, are rather high. The same is true of both the caprine and suid remains. This high indication of variation may be a reflection of

Table 53.—Range of Measurements (cm) of Bovine Remains from Banahilk Compared with Those from Other Areas

	M^3	M_3	Distal humerus		Distal radius	Astragalus		Cubonavicular		Metacarpus		
	Length	Length	Maximum width	Maximum width of articular surface	Maximum width	Lateral length	Medial length	Maximum width	Maximum depth	Maximum proximal width	Maximum width of distal shaft	Maximum width of distal articular surface
Banahilk	(2) 2.98, 3.14	(1) 3.84	(3) 5.77-7.96 $\bar{X}=6.99$	(2) 7.68, 9.37	(2) 7.50, 8.63	(4) 6.62-7.12 $\bar{X}=6.94$	(5) 6.16-6.87 $\bar{X}=6.54$	(5) 5.54-6.82 $\bar{X}=6.39$	(5) 4.76-5.58 $\bar{X}=5.25$	(2) 6.44, 6.95	(5) 5.29-6.78 $\bar{X}=5.98$	(5) 6.02-7.54 $\bar{X}=6.61$
Area 1 Danish sites		(d) 3.73-4.15 (w) 4.25-5.23	(d) 7.60-9.10 (w) 8.50-11.60	(d) 7.50-9.00 (w) 8.10-10.80	(d) 7.20-8.70 (w) 7.80-11.40	(d) 6.00-7.50 (w) 7.60-9.70		(d) 5.70-6.20 (w) 6.10-8.20	(d) 5.00-6.20 (w) 5.80-7.90	(d) 6.10-7.20 (w) 6.30-9.00		(d) 5.90-7.30 (w) 6.60-8.80
Area 2 Argissa-Magula Itzaki & Arapi		(d) 3.20-3.85	(d) 7.10-9.10 (w) 10.00	(d) 6.00-8.45 (w) 9.00, 9.10	(d) 6.00-7.20	(d) 5.50-7.00 (w) 8.15	(d) 5.10-6.75 (w) 7.55	(d) 4.80-5.90		(d) 5.00-6.35 (w) 6.40-7.20		(d) 5.10-6.45 (w) 6.60
Area 3 Fikirtepe Çatal Hüyük Nea Nikomedeia		(d) 4.30	(d) 6.30-10.50	(d) 7.50-9.80		(d) 5.60-7.90	(d) 5.20-7.30			(d) 5.60-8.30		(d) 6.50-7.80
Area 4 Palestinian sites (Mesolithic) Mureybit Tepe Sabz Girikihaciyan Tel Aviv	(d) 2.60-3.04 (w) 3.00-3.20	(d) 3.30-4.30 (w) 3.94-4.90		(d) 6.40-8.00 (w) 9.00	(d) 6.18-7.40 (w) 8.61-11.38	(d) 5.56-7.10 (w) 7.32-8.92		(d) 4.54-5.20 (w) 6.50-8.20	(d) 3.80-4.70 (w) 5.74-6.74	(d) 4.90-5.54	(d) 4.50-5.30 (w) 5.72-7.06	(d) 4.80-5.70 (w) 7.00-9.27
Area 5 Anau Shah Tepe		(d) 3.70, 3.90	(d) 6.40-6.90 (w) 9.40	(d) 6.10-8.10	(d) 8.20 (w) 9.10	(d) 6.90				(d) 5.80-7.10		(d) 5.80-7.30

Table 53.—Continued

	Metatarsus				First phalanx				Second phalanx				Third phalanx
	Maximum proximal width	Maximum proximal depth	Maximum width of distal shaft	Maximum width of distal articular surface	Lateral length	Posterior lateral length	Maximum proximal depth	Maximum proximal width	Lateral length	Posterior lateral length	Maximum proximal depth	Maximum proximal width	Maximum length
Banahilk	(3) 4.76-5.89 $\bar{X}=5.17$	(3) 4.63-5.61 $\bar{X}=4.99$	(2) 5.08, 5.87	(2) 5.50, 6.69	(8) 4.83-6.91 $\bar{X}=6.11$	(8) 5.13-7.21 $\bar{X}=6.35$	(8) 2.88-4.15 $\bar{X}=3.61$	(8) 2.37-3.75 $\bar{X}=3.23$	(8) 3.65-4.49 $\bar{X}=4.16$	(7) 4.00-4.82 $\bar{X}=4.51$	(7) 2.88-3.70 $\bar{X}=3.30$	(9) 2.89-3.81 $\bar{X}=3.32$	(5) 5.69-8.20 $\bar{X}=6.57$
Area 1	(d) 5.80-7.10 (w) 6.20-8.20			(d) 4.90-5.90 (w) 5.00-7.30		(d) 5.90-6.60 (w) 6.30-8.40	(d) 3.10-3.60 (w) 3.40-4.50	(d) 3.00-3.90 (w) 3.40-4.50		(d) 4.00-4.40 (w) 4.40-5.60	(d) 3.30-3.80 (w) 3.60-4.60	(d) 2.70-3.35 (w) 3.30-4.30	(d) 7.30-8.50 (w) 8.60-10.40
Area 2	(d) 3.60-5.90 (w) 6.85	(d) 4.60-5.60		(d) 4.75-6.40	(d) 5.10-6.80 (w) 7.00-7.55			(d) 2.35-4.00 (w) 3.45-4.25	(d) 3.20-4.40 (w) 4.60-5.20		(d) 3.20-3.45	(d) 2.45-3.40 (w) 3.50-3.70	(d) 6.70-7.80 (w) 9.05
Area 3	(d) 5.00, 5.10				(d) 6.10-7.40				(d) 3.80-5.60				(d) 6.60-9.90
Area 4	(d) 3.86-5.06	(d) 3.70-4.40	(d) 4.60-5.02	(d) 4.80-6.32 (w) 6.54-8.50	(d) 5.90-6.80 (w) 7.00-7.70	(d) 5.10-6.12 (w) 7.22-8.48	(d) 2.56-3.56 (w) 3.26-4.90	(d) 2.18-3.36 (w) 3.10-4.56	(d) 4.20-4.90 (w) 4.50-5.70	(d) 3.30-4.20 (w) 4.62-6.02	(d) 2.30-3.66 (w) 3.10-4.42	(d) 2.32-3.20 (w) 3.10-4.50	(d) 5.30-7.90 (w) 6.80-10.90
Area 5	(d) 4.10-5.20	(d) 4.00, 4.30		(d) 4.90-6.70	(d) 5.50-7.10 (w) 6.60, 7.10		(d) 2.50-4.10	(d) 2.10-3.40 (w) 3.60, 3.90	(d) 3.70-4.30 (w) 4.10, 4.40		(d) 2.60-3.80	(d) 2.60-3.40 (w) 3.60, 3.80	(d) 6.50-8.00

NOTE: Numbers in parentheses = total number of specimens; (d) = domestic (*Bos taurus*); (w) = wild (*Bos primigenius*).

Table 54.—Measurements of Five Bovines from Banahilk

Measurements of remains of *Bos* from Banahilk are presented in detail and then summarized. Each horizontal row, below, presents the data for the measurement indicated at the beginning of the row. Where more than one measurement of a tooth or a bone is given, the data for each specimen are kept together, and thus the figures grouped vertically in each column represent all the data from one specimen. One fragment of a left astragalus, one first phalanx, and two second phalanges have been omitted as belonging to modern cattle. They came from the mixed trenches, were all of a different color and less mineralized than the Halafian remains from Banahilk, and were as small as modern Near Eastern cattle.

	Measurements (cm)					$\bar{X}$	s	V
M^1								
Midlength	2.24	2.47	2.56	--	--	2.42	--	--
M^2								
Midlength	3.33	2.99	2.72	--	--	3.01	--	--
Width, base of enamel	1.89	2.34	2.05	--	--	2.09	--	--
Max. width	--	2.36	2.35	--	--	2.36	--	--
M^3								
Midlength	2.71	2.71	--	--	--	--	--	--
Max. length	2.98	3.14	--	--	--	3.06	--	--
Max. width	2.56	2.31	--	--	--	2.44	--	--
M_1								
Midlength	2.58	--	--	--	--	--	--	--
Max. width	1.64	1.69	--	--	--	1.67	--	--
M_2								
Midlength	3.25	2.91	2.75	2.38	--	2.82	0.2619	12.8
Max. width	1.81	1.79	1.64	1.44	--	1.67	.1712	10.3
M_3								
Midlength	3.78	--	--	--	--	--	--	--
Max. length	3.84	--	--	--	--	--	--	--
Max. width	1.81	--	--	--	--	--	--	--
Scapula (glenoid fossa)								
Max. width	5.25	--	--	--	--	--	--	--
Max. depth	6.55	--	--	--	--	--	--	--
Distal humerus								
Max. width	--	7.96	7.25	5.77	--	6.99	--	--
Max. width, articular surface	9.37*	7.68	--	--	--	8.53	--	--
Max. depth, articular surface	9.87*	8.22	--	--	--	9.05	--	--
Proximal radius								
Max. width	7.92	--	--	--	--	--	--	--
Max. depth	3.85	4.21	4.41	--	--	4.16	--	--
Ulna								
Max. width at radioulnar joint	5.16	4.69	3.55	--	--	4.47	--	--
Distal tibia								
Max. width	7.29	6.41	--	--	--	6.85	--	--
Max. depth	5.40	4.52	--	--	--	4.96	--	--
Proximal metatarsal								
Max. width	5.89	4.87	4.76	--	--	5.17	--	--
Max. depth	5.61	4.72	4.63	--	--	4.99	--	--
Distal metatarsal								
Max. shaft width	5.87	5.08	--	--	--	5.48	--	--
Max. shaft depth	3.30	3.00	--	--	--	3.15	--	--
Max. width, articular surface	6.69	5.50	--	--	--	6.10	--	--
Proximal metacarpal								
Max. width	6.95	6.44	--	--	--	6.65	--	--
Max. depth	3.89	3.58	--	--	--	3.74	--	--
Distal metacarpal								
Max. shaft width	6.78*	6.71*	5.58	5.52	5.29	5.98	.7107	11.9
Max. shaft depth	3.54*	3.48*	2.84	3.14	2.99	3.20	.3044	9.5
Max. width, articular surface	7.54*	7.40*	6.10	6.08	6.02	6.61	.9271	14.0
Cubonavicular								
Max. width	6.71	6.24	6.21	6.03	5.51	6.14	.4324	7.0
Max. depth	5.23	5.49	5.18	5.58	4.76	5.25	.3290	6.1
Astragalus								
Lateral length	7.12	7.10	6.91	6.62	--	6.94	.2319	3.34
Medial length	6.64	6.50	6.54	6.16	6.87	6.54	.2478	3.94
Min. length	5.54	5.42	5.51	5.19	--	5.42	0.1585	2.93

*Possibly wild.

the difficulty of working with small samples, or it may be a reflection of the increased variability permitted within domestic populations by the decreased selective pressures favoring large size (Herre 1963; Jarman 1971). The high coefficients of variation may also be the result of heterogeneous samples, as discussed earlier. Whatever the reason, the coefficient of variation for different measurements frequently lies above 10% for bovine, suid, and caprine remains from Banahilk.

The small sample of bovine bones also makes working with special statistical techniques difficult. For example, if the relative importance of number of foot bones to leg bones is calculated, an argument in favor of a "schlepp effect" could be made (Perkins and Daly 1968). At the site of Suberde in south central Turkey, dated at about 8450 B.P., Perkins and Daly found that their bovine sample contained a disproportionately large number of foot bones (83%) compared to leg bones (17%). These proportions contrasted with another site in southern Turkey, Can Hasan, where the cattle were known to be domestic, and where the ratio of the number of foot bones to leg bones was 62-38% (Perkins and Daly 1968, p. 104). The authors concluded that the cattle found at Suberde were wild and were slaughtered at some distance from the home settlement. The hunters would then butcher the meat at the kill site and return home with the meat, hide, and foot bones, the last probably still attached to the hide. Perkins and Daly coined the term "schlepp effect" to describe the disparity between the number of different kinds of limb bones that resulted from this treatment of the cattle.

At Banahilk, foot bones make up 87.8% of the sample of limb bones, and long bones make up only 12.2%—an even lower proportion than was found at Suberde. At the same time there is little evidence of gnawing by carnivores that might have selectively destroyed long bones. In view of the metrical data that indicate that the population was mainly a domestic one, the low incidence of bovine foot bones may perhaps be explained by the small size of the sample and the fact that only a small part of the site was excavated. The cattle may have been slaughtered in a part of the site that has not been excavated, and the meat may then have been distributed in a way that would account for the distribution of the bones. On the other hand, the discovery of the marked schlepp effect should, perhaps, cause us to modify any decision favoring the domestic status of the bovines that is based on metrical analysis and to consider the larger bones, then, as having come from wild cattle. Still, many of the bones are so small that at least some of them must have come from domestic animals.

Similarly, the bovine sample is both too small and too fragmentary for us to attempt to separate either the phalanges or metacarpals by sex on the basis of such ratios as maximum proximal width to width of articulating surface of fore-phalanges, or distal width to distal diaphysial width of metacarpals and metatarsals (Higham 1967a, 1967b, 1969). Higham studied the limb bones of Aberdeen Angus and Red Danish cattle of known sex and age and found that certain bones and certain measurements displayed a high degree of sexual dimorphism. Measurements of the length of the astragalus showed little sexual dimorphism, while the maximum distal width of the metacarpal bone and the width of the proximal articulating surface and the maximum proximal width of the first phalanx of the forelimb showed a high degree of sexual dimorphism. The maximum distal width of the metatarsal and the proximal width of the first phalanx of the hind limb showed more overlap between the sexes but were still quite sexually dimorphic. In all cases males tended to be larger than females (Higham 1969).

Five distal metacarpal bones from Banahilk were measured, and although the sample is extremely small they do seem to form two groups similar to those found by Higham. For example,

Maximum distal diaphysial width (cm)	6.02	6.08	6.10	7.40	7.54
Maximum distal width (cm)	5.29	5.52	5.58	6.71	6.78

The existence of two groups is obvious. They could represent males and females or wild and domestic cattle. With such a small sample they could also be one population from which only rather extreme members have been drawn as a result of sampling error. The coefficients of variation for the measurements plotted above are given in table 54. If the metacarpal bones are considered as one population, the coefficients of variation for the two measurements are both above 11%. If the two groups are considered separately, however, the coefficients of variation are all below 3%: the coefficient of variation of the maximum distal shaft width for the large group is 0.73, for the small group 2.8. The coefficient of variation of the maximum width of distal epiphyses for the large group is 2.3, for the small group 0.67.

Although we have concluded that the five distal metacarpal bones do seem to form two distinct groups, the coefficients of variation in the separate groups are so small that they simply may indicate that the groups are too small to reveal the variability that should be expected in any population of animals. Since the groups are so small, I applied the non-parametric Fisher Exact Probability Test (Siegel 1956) to the data and found that there is a 10% probability that the remains came from animals of a single population. This is a rather low probability, and it is more likely that they belonged to separate populations of either males and females or wild and domestic animals.

As stated before, the metrical data indicate that most of the bovine remains from Banahilk were from domestic animals, a conclusion that is supported by the age data presented on p. 630. Judging by their larger size, a few remains (indicated by an asterisk in table 54) are possibly from wild animals, and if these larger measurements are excluded from the Banahilk data, the information obtained from the other bones should contribute to our knowledge of the range of variation of domestic cattle in the Near East.

Minimum Number of Individuals

The Halafian people of Banahilk kept domestic sheep, goats, pigs, and cattle. From the frequencies of identified bones, the conclusion may be drawn that sheep and goats were by far the most important of their domestic animals and that pigs and cattle were relatively minor elements in the faunal spectrum. Cattle, however, would appear to have been somewhat more important than pigs. A calculation of the minimum number of individuals in each domestic species is another indication of the relative importance of each of these species. The number thus calculated cannot in any way be considered to represent the actual numbers of individuals present; rather, an estimation of the minimum number gives an indication of relative importance, which can then be used to estimate the relative amount of meat contributed by each species to the people's diet.

The calculation of the minimum number of individuals is usually based on the single most frequently occurring bone of a species in the remains. Higham (1968a) recommended using remains of teeth and jaws for this purpose and stated that the minimum number of individuals probably more accurately represented the relative importance of the species at a site than did raw frequencies of bones. Perkins (1964a, b) and Daly (1969) have recommended calculating relative frequencies of individuals of various species in a sample by dividing the total number of identified bones per species by the number of diagnostic bones in one skeleton of an animal of each of the species in question. All that this calculation tells the investigator, however, is that out of all the bones of a particular species that he has identified, he could construct that many whole individuals. This calculation would, therefore, tend to yield a smaller number of individuals than a careful consideration of a frequently occurring element such as jaws and teeth, where rights and lefts are first separated and then studied for possible matches. When pairs are found they are considered to represent one individual, and they, together with the unmatched remains, are used to indicate the minimum number of individuals. Both methods, however, are probably equally valid, provided they are applied uniformly throughout the site, since the conclusions sought are the relative importance of the various species, not actual herd sizes. The method of Perkins and Daly, however, might be much more practical when studying the remains from a very large site where a careful matching of the most frequently occurring element would be too cumbersome a procedure.

Banahilk, however, has yielded a very small sample. Therefore, the minimum number of individuals has been calculated for each of the domestic species at Banahilk, based on the most frequently occurring element that has been identified in the remains. Relative frequencies have been calculated for each species, based on the minimum number of individuals, and these frequencies compared with frequencies based on bone counts. The results are as follows:

	Individual animals		Bone fragments
	Min. no.	%	%
Bos	9	15.8	21.0
Sus	12	21.1	15.7
Caprines	36	63.2	63.3

Here, the frequencies based on counts of bones represent the proportion of each domestic species compared to all the fragments of domestic animals found and therefore differ from those frequencies given at the beginning of each section earlier in this report. Because using the teeth as a basis for calculation results in the largest number of individuals, sheep and goats were lumped together under caprines. The relative frequency of sheep and goat, as based on two frequently occurring bones that are identifiable as to species, are as follows:

	Astragalus		Humerus	
	Min. no. of individuals	%	Min. no. of individuals	%
Ovis	14	56	12	44.4
Capra	6	24	9	33.3
Undetermined	5	20	6	22.2

Although in terms of percentages cattle appear to represent a small fraction of the domestic animal population at Banahilk, each animal of this species yields a considerably larger amount of meat than do pigs, sheep, or goats. A calculation of meat yield based on the minimum number of individuals tends to establish the bovines as an important dietary element for the people of Banahilk. For purposes of estimating the amount of usable meat obtainable from the animals found in archeological sites, White (1953) estimated that long-legged animals such as cattle, sheep, and goats would yield about 50% of their live weight as usable meat and that short-legged animals such as pigs would yield about 70%. For purposes of the comparison, caprines were assumed to yield approximately 34.65 kg of usable meat apiece and bovines 360 kg. Since about 64% of the pigs were slaughtered when very young, two thirds of the pigs were assumed to be young animals and were calculated to have yielded about 33.75 kg of usable meat apiece. The other third were calculated at the young-adult weight of 78.75 kg each (Reed, pers. comm.). The bovines, therefore, represented 63.9% of the meat contributed by domestic animals, while caprines contributed 24.6% and pigs 11.5%.

Other animals such as *Capreolus capreolus*, *Cervus elaphus*, and *Helix salomonica* would have contributed an undetermined amount to the villagers' diet, but with the possible exception of the snails it would have been a relatively small proportion compared with the domestic animals.

Notes on Fig. 227

1 Molar
L = midlength
WB = width at base of enamel
W = max. width
2 Distal scapula
L = neck length
W = min. neck width
WG = width of glenoid fossa
DG = max. depth of glenoid fossa
3 Distal humerus
W = max. width of articular surface
MW = max. width
D = max. depth of articular surface
4 Ulna
W = max. width of radioulnar joint
5 Proximal radius
W = max. width
D = max. depth
6 Innominate
L = lateral length
H = max. height of acetabulum
D = min. depth of ilium
7 Patella
L = max. length
W = max. width
D = max. depth
8 Distal tibia
W = max. width
D = max. depth
9 Cubonavicular
W = max. width
D = max. mid-depth
10 Astragalus
L = min. length
ML = medial length
LL = lateral length
11 Proximal metacarpal
W = max. width
D = max. depth
12 Proximal metatarsal
W = max. width
D = max. depth
13 Proximal first phalanx
W = max. width
D = max. depth
(Second phalanx measured similarly)
14 Distal first phalanx
W = max. width
D = max. depth
(Second phalanx measured similarly)
15 First phalanx, anterior surface
W = min. width
(Second phalanx measured similarly)
16 Third phalanx
L = max. length
17 Distal metapodial
W = max. distal shaft width
WA = max. width of articular surface
D = max. distal shaft depth
I = inner diameter of trochlea
O = outer diameter of trochlea
18 First phalanx
LL = lateral length
(Min. length is taken in the same plane as LL but is the minimum such measurement for the phalanx.)
LP = lateral length, posterior
D = min. depth
(Second phalanx measured similarly)

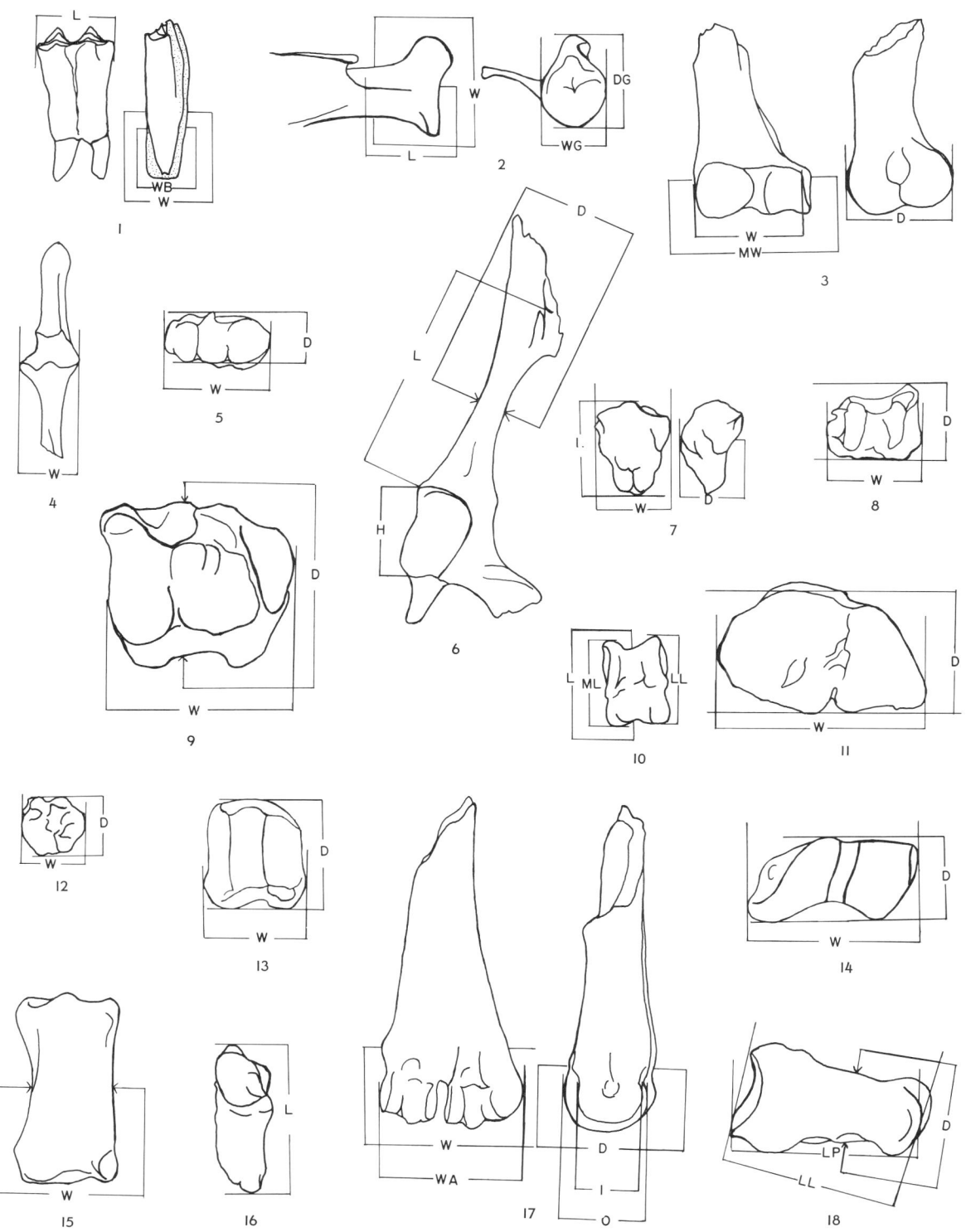

Fig. 227. Guide to measurements taken on Banahilk fauna. (See notes on opposite page.)

REFERENCES

Amschler, J.W.
 1939 Tierreste der Ausgrabungen von dem "Grossen Königshügel" Shah Tepé, in Nord-Iran. *Reports from the Scientific Expedition to the North-Western Provinces of China under the Leadership of Dr. Sven Hedin, the Sino-Swedish Expedition*, publ. 9, vol. 7 (Archaeology), no. 4, pp. 35-129.

Boessneck, Joachim
 1956 Zu den Tierknocken aus neolithischen Siedlungen Thessaliens. *Bericht der römisch-germanischen Kommission 1955*, vol. 36:1-51.
 1962 Die Tierreste aus der Argissa-Magula vom präkeramischen Neolithikum bis zur mittleren Bronzezeit. In *Die deutschen Ausgrabungen auf der Argissa-Magula in Thessalien*, vol. 1, V. Milojčić, J. Boessneck, and M. Hopf, pp. 27-99. Beiträge zur ur-und frühgeschichtlichen Archäologie des Mittelmeer-Kulturraumes, vol. 2. Bonn: Rudolf Habelt Verlag.

Boessneck, Joachim; Müller, Hans-Hermann; and Teichert, Manfred
 1964 *Osteologische Unterscheidungsmerkmale zwischen Schaf* (Ovis aries Linné) *und Ziege* (Capra hircus Linné). Kühn-Archiv, vol. 78 (1-2). Berlin: Akademie-Verlag.

Bökönyi, S.
 1972 Zoological evidence for seasonal or permanent occupation of prehistoric settlements. In *Man, settlement and urbanism*, ed. Peter J. Ucko, Ruth Tringham, and G.W. Dimbleby, pp. 121-26. London: Gerald Duckworth.

Daly, Patricia
 1969 Approaches to faunal analysis in archaeology. *American Antiquity* 34:146-53.

Degerbøl, Magnus, and Fredskild, Bent
 1970 *The urus* (Bos primigenius Bojanus) *and neolithic domesticated cattle* (Bos taurus domesticus Linné) *in Denmark*. Kongelige danske videnskabernes selskab, biologiske skrifter, vol. 17 (1). Copenhagen: Munksgaard.

Ducos, Pierre
 1968 *L'origine des animaux domestiques en Palestine*. Publications de l'Institut de préhistoire de l'Université de Bordeaux, mem. 6. Bordeaux: Imprimeries Delmas.
 1972 The Oriental Institute excavations at Mureybiṭ, Syria: preliminary report on the 1965 campaign, part V: les restes des Bovidés. *Journal of Near Eastern Studies* 31:295-301.

Duerst, J. Ulrich
 1908 Animal remains from the excavations at Anau and the horse of Anau in its relation to the races of domestic horses. In *Explorations in Turkestan: expedition of 1904, prehistoric civilizations of Anau*, vol. 2, ed. Raphael Pumpelly, pp. 339-442. Publications of the Carnegie Institution of Washington, no. 73. Washington, D.C.

Flannery, Kent V.
 1961 Skeletal and radiocarbon evidence for the origins of pig domestication. Master's thesis, University of Chicago.

Geist, Valerius
 1971 *Mountain sheep: a study in behavior and evolution*. Chicago: University of Chicago Press.

Gramova, V.
 1953 [Osteological characters of the genera *Capra* and *Ovis*: manual for distinguishing excavated remains]. *Trudy Komissii po Izucheniju Chetvertichnogo Perioda* 10 (1):1-123.

Hatt, Robert T.
 1959 *The mammals of Iraq*. Miscellaneous Publications of the Museum of Zoology, University of Michigan, no. 106. Ann Arbor.

Herre, Wolf
 1963 The science and history of domestic animals. In *Science in archaeology*, ed. Don Brothwell and Eric Higgs, pp. 235-49. New York: Basic Books.

Higgs, E.S.
 1962 The biological data: fauna. In Excavations at the early Neolithic site at Nea Nikomedeia, Greek Macedonia (1961 season), Robert J. Rodden, pp. 271-74. *Proceedings of the Prehistoric Society* 28:267-88.

Higham, C.F.W.
 1967a The economy of Iron Age Veileby (Denmark). *Acta Archaeologica* 38:222-41.
 1967b Stock rearing as a cultural factor in prehistoric Europe. *Proceedings of the Prehistoric Society* 33:84-106.
 1968a Faunal sampling and economic prehistory. *Zeitschrift für Säugetierkunde* 33:297-305.
 1968b Trends in prehistoric European caprovine husbandry. *Man*, n.s. 3:64-75.
 1969 The metrical attributes of two samples of bovine limb bones. *Journal of Zoology* 157:63-74.

Hole, Frank; Flannery, Kent V.; and Neely, James A.
 1969 *Prehistory and human ecology of the Deh Luran plain*. Memoirs of the Museum of Anthropology, University of Michigan, no. 1. Ann Arbor.

Jarman, Michael R.
 1969 The prehistory of Upper Pleistocene and Recent cattle, pt. 1: east Mediterranean, with references to north-west Europe. *Proceedings of the Prehistoric Society* 35:236-66.
 1971 Culture and economy in the north Italian Neolithic. *World Archaeology* 2:255-65.

Lawrence, Barbara
 1980 Evidences of animal domestication at Çayönü. In *The joint Istanbul-Chicago Universities' prehistoric research in southeastern Anatolia*, vol. 1, ed. Halet Çambel, pp. 257-308. Istanbul üniversitesi edebiyat fakültesi yayınları, no. 2589. Istanbul.

McArdle, John Edward
 1974 A numerical (computerized) method for quantifying zooarcheological comparisons. Master's thesis, University of Illinois at Chicago Circle.

Olsen, Stanley J.
 1960 *Post-cranial skeletal characters of* Bison *and* Bos. Papers of the Peabody Museum of Archaeology and Ethnology, Harvard University, vol. 35 (4). Cambridge, Mass.

Perkins, Dexter, Jr.
 1959 The post-cranial skeleton of the Caprinae: comparative anatomy and changes under domestication. Ph.D. diss., Harvard University.
 1960 The faunal remains of Shanidar Cave and Zawi Chemi Shanidar: 1960 season. *Sumer* 16:77-78.
 1964a The fauna from the prehistoric levels of Shanidar Cave and Zawi Chemi Shanidar. In *Report of the VIth International Congress on the Quaternary, Warsaw 1961*, vol. 2, International Association on Quaternary Research, pp. 565-72. Lódź: Państwowe Wydawnictwo Naukowe.
 1964b Prehistoric fauna from Shanidar, Iraq. *Science* 144:1565-66.
 1969 Fauna of Catal Hüyük: evidence for early cattle domestication in Anatolia. *Science* 164:177-79.

Perkins, Dexter, Jr., and Daly, Patricia
 1968 A hunters' village in Neolithic Turkey. *Scientific American* 219 (5):96-106.

Reed, Charles A.
 1959 Animal domestication in the prehistoric Near East. *Science* 130:1629-39.
 1961 Osteological evidences for prehistoric domestication in southwestern Asia. *Zeitschrift für Tierzüchtung und Züchtungsbiologie* 76 (1):31-38.
 1962 *Snails on a Persian hillside*. Postilla, Peabody Museum of Natural History, Yale University, no. 66. New Haven, Conn.

Röhrs, Manfred, and Herre, Wolf
 1961 Zur Frühentwicklung der Haustiere: die Tierreste der neolithischen Siedlung Fikirtepe am kleinasiatischen Gestade des Bosporus. *Zeitschrift für Tierzüchtung und Züchtungsbiologie* 75:110-27.

Siegel, Sidney
 1956 *Nonparametric statistics for the behavioral sciences*. New York: McGraw-Hill.

Silver, I.A.
 1963 The ageing of domestic animals. In *Science in archaeology*, ed. Don Brothwell and Eric Higgs, pp. 250-68. New York: Basic Books.

Simpson, George Gaylord; Roe, Anne; and Lewontin, Richard C.
 1960 *Quantitative zoology*. Rev. ed. New York: Harcourt, Brace.

Uerpmann, Hans-Peter
 1973 Animal bone finds and economic archaeology: a critical study of 'osteo-archaeological' method. *World Archaeology* 4:307-22.

White, Theodore E.
 1953 A method of calculating the dietary percentage of various food animals utilized by aboriginal peoples. *American Antiquity* 18:396-98.

20

THE POTTERY FROM THE SOUNDINGS AT GIRD ALI AGHA AND AL-KHAN

Joseph R. Caldwell†

Gird Ali Agha is a low mound lying on a natural hill above the left bank of the Greater Zab (figs. 2 and 228). The mound covers an area of about 80 × 100 m and has a probable depth of deposit of about 2 m. The top of the mound is an old Kurdish cemetery; hence the test trenches were laid out below this on the western slope, overlooking the river. Two main trenches, operations A and B, were each begun as 2 × 6 m rectangles, laid out on an east-west axis.

Operation A was found to contain a great deal of coarse, plain pottery (many of the sherds in quite large pieces) and a very poor flint industry consisting mostly of chips and irregular flakes. There was evidence of two pits, but both were fairly shallow and no other features could be determined. Limestone concretions began to appear in the reddish earth about 35 cm below the surface. This zone continued to a depth of about 90 cm. A 2 × 2 m portion at the upper (east) end of the trench was slightly expanded and dug to a depth of 1.35 m. Pottery ceased to appear toward the base of the concretion zone, and a sterile zone of reddish silt lay beneath. Work in A was then abandoned in favor of the more productive operation B, which lay some 6 m east and higher on the slope (fig. 229).

The original 2 × 6 m trench of operation B was enlarged in order to follow floors or levels of compacted earth. Three such floorlike horizons were observed, at depths of about 40, 55, and 70 cm. A large pit (feature 4), which seems to have been dug into the third floor, was traced but proved to be highly irregular and fairly shallow. A hearth area connected with the second floor yielded a somewhat questionable sample for radiocarbon dating, but it has not yet been assayed.[1] There were also two pits, one within the other (fig. 229), which seemed to be associated with the second floor. No other evidence even approaching architecture was found, and it was thought that the base of the deposit was reached in the bottom of the large pit (feature 4) at approximately 1.25 m below the surface. The occupational features in both A and B are complex and somewhat enigmatic, but all are taken to represent the same cultural horizon, since the same type of coarse plain ware was found throughout.

At the geologist's request a 1-m² pit was excavated to a depth of 1.2 m at the northwest base of Ali Agha. It yielded no artifactual material beyond random and enigmatic bits of pottery.

Tell al-Khan, the second site of interest in this chapter, lies just south of M'lefaat and the Erbil-Mosul road (figs. 1 and 236) on the west bank of the Khazir River. An account of this site was given in SAOC 31 (pp. 25, 35, and 66) and no further description need be added here.

During a postgraduate residence in Chicago in 1956, I was invited to make a study of the pottery fragments recovered from Ali Agha and al-Khan. Considering the restricted exposures made on the two sites, the amounts of prehistoric pottery that they yielded were relatively large. It seemed to us that this material might, for the first time, afford a link between the sequences of Jarmo and Hassuna. Assuming that such a comparative stratigraphy approaches completeness, we would have, in effect, a continuous ceramic sequence for the Mosul-Kirkuk region, a useful check and reference for radiocarbon age determinations, and a body of ceramic material changing through time. From this, in turn, certain inferences might be drawn about the historical conditions that can account for the kinds of cultural change observed. The sequence of the pottery industries that would result from this link would permit tentative conclusions about the regional continuity of cultural change. Here, however, we are concerned only with what is to be learned by analysis of ceramic forms and decoration through comparison of the assemblages from level to level and from site to site.

Ali Agha and al-Khan were selected for investigation precisely because the surface collections from these sites showed them to be close to the Jarmo-Hassuna range of time. As a result of the test excavations, the excavators first proposed a sequence of Jarmo, Ali Agha, Hassuna, and al-Khan. This sequence was based on several observations. First, the coarse pottery that is characteristic of certain of the later Jarmo levels bore some resemblance to the coarse

---

This account is based upon the field notes of Vivian Broman Morales, who supervised the soundings of both Ali Agha and al-Khan. See also SAOC 31, pages 26, 37-38, 66. The soundings at Ali Agha were conducted from November 15 to 23, 1954, and those at al-Khan from December 8 to 15, 1954.

[The manuscript for this chapter was essentially completed by 1957. Very few additions and only minor revisions have been made since that date. Caldwell died in 1973.—EDS.]

ware in the earliest assemblage at Hassuna. Also, the material from Ali Agha was nearly all a fairly similar coarse ware. Finally, the assemblage at al-Khan comprised Hassuna "standard" wares in addition to some coarse ware. Thus, whether the Ali Agha ceramics were more like later Jarmo or earlier Hassuna and hence more nearly contemporary with one or the other or whether Ali Agha was intermediate between the two and consequently intermediate in time could not be decided without further study, but in any case Ali Agha must certainly have been occupied during the range of time bracketed by Jarmo and Hassuna. Al-Khan, on the other hand, must have been closer in time to Hassuna than to Jarmo or Ali Agha.

My study of the Chicago samples of potsherds does not alter this proposed sequence but indeed documents it in greater detail. As a result it has been possible to place Ali Agha and al-Khan more precisely, in a relative chronological sense. Matarrah, near Kirkuk, may also be brought into the picture (Braidwood, Braidwood, et al. 1952), and a cursory inspection of the literature suggests that the same could be done for the deep levels at Nineveh.[2] The results may be summarized as follows:

The relative position of Ali Agha.—The pottery from Ali Agha has features that first appeared in those upper levels of Jarmo where pottery occurs: the ware is coarse, painting is rare, and shouldered jars are predominant in the assemblage. If we discount the possibility of cultural lag at Jarmo, Ali Agha cannot be earlier than the time represented by J-II,2 of Jarmo. But Ali Agha yields some new features, which are also found in the lowest level of Hassuna: shouldered bowls were less common, collared jars and ogival bases appeared, shouldered jars were larger, and vessel lugs became hemispherical instead of elongated like those at Jarmo. On this basis, it may be inferred that Ali Agha is later than upper Jarmo. But is it as late as lower Hassuna? Here we note that there are differences between the pottery industries encountered in the two excavated areas at Ali Agha, A and B. Operation B contained fragments of collared jars and ogival bases—vessel features characteristic of lowest Hassuna—but none of these occurred in Ali Agha A. If this difference is not due to sampling error, we might infer that the yield of A is earlier than that of Hassuna. But we have already said that it is later than the Jarmo material. Therefore the materials from A at Ali Agha must have been made at a time intermediate between the occupation of Jarmo and the occupation of Hassuna. On the other hand, the sherds found in B, also later than Jarmo, may be earlier than or contemporary with the pottery from basal Hassuna, but they are probably later than the pottery of Ali Agha A.

The relative position of al-Khan.—The greater part of the pottery of al-Khan resembles Hassuna standard wares. Coarse ware is in the minority in our sample and the Samarran style is rare or absent. Therefore, it would appear that al-Khan was temporally equivalent to the Hassuna levels that show the dominance of the standard wares and the decline of the coarse ware but are prior to the appearance of the Samarran style.

The relative position of Matarrah.—Similarly, the lowest levels of Matarrah (which were occupied before the appearance of the Samarran style) can be seen as having been temporally equivalent to the Hassuna levels during the dominance of the standard wares and prior to the appearance of the Samarran style. The upper levels of Matarrah, with Samarran pottery, were, then, equivalent to those levels at Hassuna in which the Samarran style was dominant.

Regional ceramic differences between the Mosul and Kirkuk areas.—There are, however, features of the Matarrah pottery sequence (near Kirkuk) that do not accord with or are not represented at Hassuna and al-Khan (near Mosul). At Matarrah the Hassuna variety called "standard painted" ware was absent, the "standard incised" type was more carefully decorated, and the coarse ware continued in quantity long after the appearance of the Samarran style.

Essential continuity in the lower Zagros valleys and piedmont.—Despite the differences noted between the Mosul and Kirkuk areas, the sites of the lower montane valleys and piedmont have features that are not shared with the riverine sites of the adjoining Tigris-Euphrates plain. At all the more northerly lower Zagros valley and piedmont sites examined so far, the Samarran style appears as an *addition* to the continuing ceramic complex typified by the Hassuna standard ware and its cognates. At Samarra and Baghouz on the plain, on the other hand, the equivalent painted pottery industries are entirely in the Samarran style (Herzfeld 1930; du Mesnil du Buisson 1948; Leslie in Braidwood, Braidwood, et al. 1952; Braidwood 1954).

Observations concerning the origin of the Samarran style.—There is no clear evidence that the Samarran painted pottery style developed out of the Hassuna standard style. Moreover, it would seem reasonable to believe that the Samarran style reached the Zagros piedmont and lower valleys from the plain where it apparently constituted the total painted pottery production of such sites as Samarra and Baghouz. It is not very likely that the Hassuna standard painted style has any relevance to the origin of the earliest of the painted pottery styles of the southern Mesopotamian alluvium (e.g., Eridu ware and Hajji Mohammad ware). With the Samarran style, the question of interconnections with the origin of the southern painted styles is perhaps more relevant.

In sum, the evidence suggests that there were strong regional and local continuities in the lower valleys and piedmont of the Zagros from the end of the Jarmo occupation through the interval when the Samarran style became part of the pottery industries of these upland regions. The ceramic inventories appear to have been essentially similar and will doubtless show essentially the same changes from site to site. In culture-historical terms this may represent a high degree of residential stability. In this region the picture suggested by the available ceramic evidence is one of gradual change, undisturbed by any major event that might have created a cultural discontinuity. The local continuities themselves suggest the same interpretation. A continuity is manifested in all levels of Matarrah (absence of the standard painted ware, careful execution of standard incised ware), which can be contrasted with another local continuity at Hassuna itself, again suggesting that the region was culturally stable during this range of time. It is possible that these sites continued to be occupied by descendants of their original settlers.

During the time that the Samarran painted style flourished, the interaction area may have become larger than previously. It is not simply trade or more occasional varieties of communication that we consider here (although there is, indeed, modest evidence at Hassuna for some form of contact with the Syro-Cilician communities of the northwest), but rather some closer kind of interaction that could account for the detailed ceramic connections between such riverine plain sites as Baghouz and Samarra and the Samarran levels of the sites in the lower Zagros valleys and piedmont. As more sites are excavated and greater understanding of the time factor is achieved, it will probably be possible, by determining the limits of local variation, to learn which communities were in closest contact with each other.

The following chart gives a summary of the ceramic sequence.

CERAMIC FEATURES	JARMO	ALI AGHA	HASSUNA	MATARRAH	AL-KHAN
Ubaidian sherds in small numbers near surface at Hassuna; Ubaidian surface scatter at Matarrah			XII XI		
General sequence of Halafian wares			X IX		
Halafian wares in quantity; Samarran and Hassunan wares now scarce			VIII VII		
Halafian sherds appear in small numbers at Hassuna; still coarse ware at Matarrah			VI V	IX-1 IX-2	
Samarran ware increases in quantity as "archaic" wares disappear; "milk jars"; Samarran ware appears			IV III	VI-3 VI-4	▮
"Husking trays" follow Hassuna "standard painted" and "standard painted and incised" wares			II Ic	VI-5	
"Archaic painted" and "standard incised" wares at Hassuna; "archaic coarse" ware, burnished wares, collared jars, ogee bases, chaff tempers at Ali Agha		B	Ib Ia		
Shouldered bowls rare, but large shouldered jars with round lugs at Ali Agha; coarse wares, shouldered jars with vertical lugs, large trays at Jarmo	I* II*-1 2	A			
Pottery vessels appear in Zagros valleys and piedmont: fine-chaff-tempered, some painted wares, shouldered bowls common	1 3 2 4 3 5				
Pottery vessels not found in any of the lower levels so far exposed at Jarmo	4 6 5 6 7 8				

*Only operations I and II are accounted for here, and the *suggested* equivalences are *not* demonstrable.

DESCRIPTION OF WARES

Following the usage of Lloyd and Safar (1945, pp. 276-78), we distinguish a coarse ware that is generally thick in cross section, fired at a low temperature, and invariably tempered with chaff or straw. Fine ware, for us, is a term used in a generic sense for the fabrics of the Samarran style and the Hassuna standard types, all of which have a relatively thin vessel wall. Fine ware was often slipped and incised and/or painted, fired at higher temperatures than was coarse ware, and apparently tempered with grit. These two wares are quite dissimilar, and for each there is a series of characteristic vessel forms. One can see in the forms a strong tendency for the vessels of one ware to be used in ways not intended for the other. For the purpose of this study, then, each ware can be regarded as having a distinct historical continuity in time and space.[3]

FORM CATEGORIES OF THE COARSE WARE

Vessels as wide as or wider than they are deep are called bowls; vessels of greater height than width are called jars. Among the bowls, I distinguish those that do not have an angled shoulder as bowls with rounded sides. Bowls with flaring sides are those with straight or slightly concave (flaring) walls projecting outward to a wide mouth. This distinction between bowls and jars does not provide a satisfactory means of classifying vessels with angled or carinated sides, however, and the category of shouldered jars and bowls subsumes a continuous range of variation between tall and shallow vessels with angled sides.

Another form category is the "milk jar," a term suggested by Lloyd and Safar (1945, p. 278);[4] the vessel has a distinctive down-turned lug and an oval plan view, which is usually reflected in the curvature of the sherds. Still another form category can be readily distinguished, because it is oval in plan and its wall height is only about a quarter of the minimum diameter; this category comprises large trays, small trays, and Lloyd and Safar's "husking trays" (1945, pp. 277-78).

The continuous range of variation within the category of shouldered jars and bowls has been mentioned. This range is also strikingly exhibited in most other coarse ware categories at Ali Agha, with the probable exception of the trays. Comparison of vessel profiles shows that the category of bowls with rounded sides merges at one end of its spectrum with the bowls with flaring sides and at the other end merges with the shouldered jars and bowls themselves.

Bowls with Rounded Sides (fig. 230:1-11)

Inasmuch as there are no rounded bottoms in our coarse ware sampling from either Ali Agha or al-Khan, the bases of bowls with rounded sides are all likely to have been flat, and perhaps most commonly had a distinct "heel" projecting beyond the side (e.g., fig. 231:14). Vessel profiles that can be classed in this group occur at all the sites referred to above, including Jarmo. Indeed, some of the Jarmo stone vessels have profiles that could be included here. These usually lack the heel probably once present on the Ali Agha vessels, but it is interesting to note that a heel does also occur on some Jarmo stone bowls (e.g., fig. 102:9).

The examples from Ali Agha A show a great range in rim diameter size, from 70 to 440 mm. In Ali Agha B the size range is from 90 to perhaps 600 mm with a mode between 200 and 300 mm.

As a class, bowls with rounded sides seem relatively more important at Ali Agha than at Jarmo. At the latter site, bowls are more frequently shouldered. At al-Khan, rounded bowls were evidently less common; only two appeared in the sample of 38 coarse ware sherds brought back to Chicago. We may note here Lloyd and Safar's observation that in the later levels of coarse ware occurrence at Hassuna, husking trays and milk jars become more numerous than other forms. These varieties are also more abundant in the al-Khan sample.

Bowls with Flaring Sides (fig. 230:14-18)

The examples illustrated appear to have come from bowls with flaring sides. Again, bases must have been flat and probably had a heel. There are four such rims from Ali Agha A samples and eight more from Ali Agha B samples, but none in the al-Khan sample brought back to Chicago. Some flaring rims from al-Khan are regarded as having belonged to milk jars. A similar bowl form evidently occurred at Matarrah (Braidwood, Braidwood, et al. 1952, p. 11, fig. 9:10). The tall, flat-based bowl form with flaring rim from Jarmo may be related to that from Ali Agha (fig. 105:1,3-4,12). A possible link to the Jarmo stone bowl profiles may also be seen (e.g., fig. 101:1-3).

Shouldered Jars and Bowls (fig. 230:12-13,19-34)

Adams notes (p. 218) that a "flat-based, shouldered pot or deep bowl" is unquestionably the predominant form of the Jarmo later pottery manifestation. It apparently has no certain precursor in the stone bowl industry. These vessels were of different sizes and proportions, with rim diameters from less than 70 mm to more than 300 mm and heights from 40 mm to more than 200 mm. At one end of this range were vessels with more constricted rims and the portion of the wall above the shoulder higher than the portion of the vessel below the shoulder. At the other end of the distribution were vessels with the sides above the shoulder (either flaring or rising vertically) about the same height as the walls below the shoulder. The former could be distinguished as shouldered jars and the latter as shouldered bowls, but it is important to note that Adams's study of the distribution of the diameters of rims, shoulders, and bases shows no bimodality; the range of variability is continuous. The differences between jars and bowls, at least in the shouldered vessel category, were originally not as distinct at Jarmo as the differences we find later at Ali Agha. Indeed, Adams concludes that in the earlier pottery the emphasis had been on the manufacture of vessels of general utility rather than on the specialized production of large and small pots for different uses.

Sherds of comparable coarse-ware shouldered vessels are the most characteristic single form in the sample from operations A and B at Ali Agha. The profiles were evidently similar to those of Jarmo, but the vessels at Ali Agha appear to have been somewhat larger. One important difference is that the lugs usually found in this form are of the round, nodal variety at Ali Agha but are pierced and vertical at Jarmo. In the uppermost pottery samplings at Jarmo, however, a few examples of the nodal lugs did occur. Moreover, with the increase in size of shouldered vessels at Ali Agha it becomes easier to see the small shouldered bowls as forming a somewhat differentiated group. At the same time, small shouldered bowls are less common at Ali Agha and are still less common in the coarse ware at the later sites of Hassuna and Matarrah.

At the lowest level at Hassuna, Ia (Lloyd and Safar 1945, pp. 276-77), and in the lower phase at Matarrah (Braidwood, Braidwood, et al. 1952, pp. 11-12, pl. V:1-3,5), more divergent but still basically similar shouldered forms are again most representative of the coarse ware. At Hassuna and Matarrah, vessels are usually narrower at the rim than those at Jarmo and often are furnished with low or high collars. At Hassuna and Matarrah, vessel bases are clearly distinguishable from the lower walls, and often they protrude slightly to form a heel. The lower walls in many cases are nearly horizontal; others have a distinctive ogee curve. At Jarmo, on the other hand, as the lower vessel walls narrow toward the small undifferentiated base they are straight or slightly rounded but never have the ogee curve. At Hassuna and Matarrah the nodal lug that appears rarely in the upper levels at Jarmo and becomes characteristic at Ali Agha is still the predominant apppendage on shouldered vessels. These characteristics are sometimes paired, and an illustration of a sherd from Hassuna suggests that the upper wall of at least this vessel was entirely covered with nodes (Lloyd and Safar 1945, fig. 6:15). At these later sites we also find appendages in the forms of horizontal bars and T and inverted U shapes, all of which occur rarely at Jarmo and Ali Agha. Vessels at Hassuna and Matarrah are somewhat larger than those at Ali Agha, which in turn are larger than those at Jarmo. A few shouldered bowls are to be found at the later sites but, in contrast to those from Jarmo, are readily distinguishable from the shouldered jars and are not important numerically.

In the above comparisons it appears that the shouldered vessels at Ali Agha possess characteristics that are found at Jarmo only, or at both Hassuna and Matarrah, or at all three of these other sites. In their gross features the Ali Agha vessels are intermediate in form in a continuum of coarse ware shouldered vessels that extends from the Jarmo pottery-bearing levels well into the time of the Hassuna standard wares.

At Ali Agha, moreover, we may suspect that there is some time difference between the yields from A and B. The entire Ali Agha pottery industry is comparatively homogeneous, but variations in A are more like the pottery of the upper Jarmo levels, while variations in B tend in the direction of the Hassuna and Matarrah pottery. In Ali Agha A as at Jarmo, none of the rims of the shouldered jars have a definite collar. In B, on the other hand, about one third (eight specimens) of our small collection of jar rims have a bend that could be considered a collar. The bend, however, does not become as acute, nor does the collar reach the height sometimes attained at Hassuna and Matarrah. At Jarmo and in Ali Agha A no sherds were found showing the ogival curve of the lower wall, but at Ali Agha B there are a few showing this feature so characteristic of the Hassuna and Matarrah manifestations.

There are two examples at Ali Agha B of the miniature shouldered bowl (fig. 230:33-34), which appears to be a distinctive form of the larger shouldered bowls.

Trays

Included here are flat-bottomed vessels with wall height about a quarter or less of the minimum diameter. Vessel profiles are similar regardless of size. The walls join the base at an angle that is usually distinguished by an exterior heel, and these sides may be vertical or somewhat convex (e.g., fig. 213:2) but are more often slightly flaring. Most vessels seem to be oval in plan. It will be useful to consider three kinds of trays: (1) the large "husking trays," named and described by Lloyd and Safar (1945, pp. 277-78), which are distinguished by incising or by stick or finger impressions on the interior; (2) similar large trays that lack the interior treatment; and (3) some very small trays of nearly identical form.

"Husking trays" (fig. 231:1-4).—So-called husking trays represent one of the later developments within the coarse ware series. None were found at Jarmo or Ali Agha. The appearance of this variety at Hassuna seems to be delayed until level II, where it begins at the time Hassuna standard painted ware comes into general use. Smith reports husking trays from all levels at Matarrah (Braidwood, Braidwood, et al. 1952, pp. 9-10), an observation that has been confirmed by reexamination of the Matarrah specimens in Chicago; they are present even in the basal level 5 of operation VI. In the Matarrah sequence, however, husking trays evidently increase in number toward the top and finally comprise about one third of the coarse ware complement. Fifteen fragments of husking trays from al-Khan, which is believed to be later than Ali Agha, make up nearly 50% of the coarse ware sherds brought to Chicago.

The al-Khan specimens resemble those from Hassuna and Matarrah. Since the plan of this kind of vessel is generally oval, precise length-breadth measurements are impossible to obtain from sherds. I was able to project two curves that yielded diameters of approximately 500 and 540 mm, a size conforming to the Hassuna and Matarrah range. The Hassuna average is 600 mm long and 400 mm wide, and a vessel from Matarrah (Braidwood, Braidwood, et al. 1952, pl. V:4) is nearly this large. Vessel heights obtained for three al-Khan specimens are from 76 to 105 mm and again approximate the Hassuna and Matarrah examples.

Interior treatment consists of pitting in the bottom and rough incising on the walls. The pitting was done by pressing the clay while soft with a round-ended or, less frequently, a sharper instrument. The resulting impressions are regular and closely spaced, about 20 mm across and 10 mm deep. Our small sample shows none of the triangular punctated or parallel-grooved bottoms illustrated from Hassuna and Matarrah, nor does it show any of the perforated bottoms found in the Matarrah upper phase (Braidwood, Braidwood, et al. 1952, p. 11). The incised lines on the interior walls are widely spaced and vertical, diagonal, or crosshatched.

As is true for the rest of the coarse ware series, the fabric of the husking trays is extremely soft. It may be significant that the edges of the interior punctation and incising show not the slightest sign of having been rubbed or worn after firing.

Large trays (fig. 231:5-6,9).—As a category, the large trays differ from the husking trays only in lacking the interior treatment. The size, plan, and profiles are about the same. Height again ranges from about 70 to 100 mm, and two rim curves projected from al-Khan specimens suggest diameters of 280 and 520 mm. The vessels are again oval in plan, and the measurements are thus only approximate, but they suffice to indicate that the large trays and husking trays were about the same size.

We have already suggested that the husking tray was a relatively late development within the coarse ware series. Evidently this was simply an innovation in the large tray form. The large tray as a type is clearly the older of the two, occurring in the upper pottery levels at Jarmo (p. 220, figs. 108:13; 109:18). The husking tray, on the other hand, does not appear at Jarmo or Ali Agha and is not yet known to be present at Hassuna before level II.

The temporal distribution of the large tray, with its distinctive profile and oval plan, seems to be additional evidence of a ceramic continuity extending from the time range of upper Jarmo well into Hassuna times. There are two specimens from Ali Agha A in Chicago, six from Ali Agha B, and two from al-Khan. The al-Khan examples are somewhat aberrant and have more convex (incurving) walls than the others. Fourteen specimens are reported from Matarrah (where they were termed "large flat-bottomed bowls" [Braidwood, Braidwood, et al. 1952, p. 11]). The oval bowls from Hassuna level Ic appear to be a similar if not identical form (Lloyd and Safar 1945, pl. XIV:1).

Small trays (fig. 231:7-8,10).—Small trays were represented by three examples, one each from operations A and B at Ali Agha, and one from al-Khan. Profiles are similar to those of the large trays and husking trays, but these vessels are much smaller. The specimens from Ali Agha are oblong like the larger trays, and the same may be true of the al-Khan example. In all three cases, the smallest curves would have projected to a minimum diameter of about 100 mm, and if we can assume that these little vessels had the same proportions as large trays, the greater diameter would then have been about 130 mm.

Although small trays are rare, the similarity in size, profile, and plan can be seen as additional evidence of continuity between Ali Agha and al-Khan. This thread might possibly extend back to the lower pottery manifestation at Jarmo, where a painted fragment of a slightly larger tray is also oval in plan (fig. 105:10). In the same level the stone vessel complement shows a circular tray or dish that is 70 mm in diameter and has a similar profile.

"Milk Jars" (fig. 231:11-14)

At Hassuna, Lloyd and Safar found that, following the occurrence of husking trays in level II, "in the later levels . . . coarse ware was confined mainly to large, almost vertical-sided oval vessels with lug handles to which we gave the name 'milk jars'" (1945, p. 278, fig. 3:7, pl. XII:2, right). One of the specimens is from level III; the other appears in a figure entitled "levels II-VI," although coarse ware does not appear in the sherd tabulation above level II. Evidently the milk jar follows the husking tray at Hassuna and from that time on most of the coarse ware was made in that form.

There are some milk jar fragments in the small sample of coarse ware at al-Khan. Since they do not occur at Jarmo or Ali Agha, sites regarded as earlier than al-Khan, we can indirectly confirm Lloyd and Safar's assignment of this form to "later levels." Of 37 coarse ware sherds at al-Khan, possible milk jar fragments are represented by 6 specimens: 2 lugs, 2 rims, and 2 oval bases.

ASSIMILATIONS

The fine and coarse wares were apparently made side by side during part of the occupation at Hassuna as well as at Matarrah and al-Khan. It is therefore not surprising to find the characteristics of one ware occasionally copied in the other. At Matarrah, Smith notes about 20 coarse ware sherds decorated in the style of Hassuna standard incised ware (Braidwood, Braidwood, et al. 1952, pp. 12-13, fig. 11). Examples are present in both the upper and lower phases. Matarrah also yielded a few examples of pedestal or ring bases and the rim of a globular vessel, all made in the coarse ware (Braidwood, Braidwood, et al. 1952, p. 12, fig. 10:16-18 and fig. 10:9). At al-Khan also, a similar rim of a globular vessel (fig. 231:15) and 3 coarse sherds from ring bases (fig. 231:17-18) were found. The coarse globular vessels at Matarrah and al-Khan were probably copied from fine ware vessels, of which this is a characteristic form. The ring bases were possibly also derived from the fine ware, although at al-Khan only one example—on a sherd of a vessel with a very high pedestal—is present in the fine ware itself. It should be noted that at Ali Agha, believed to have been occupied before the fine ware came into existence, there are none of these transfers of profile type from one ware to the other.

Transfer seems to have been clearly in the other direction, that is, from coarse to fine ware, in the single instance of what in the Matarrah report is called a nipple lug (Braidwood, Braidwood, et al. 1952, p. 14, fig. 7:8). This is not the nipple lug that occurs on the shouldered jars at Ali Agha but is the variety with down-turned tip found on the later milk jars at Hassuna.

Less certainly suggesting transfer in the same direction were two Matarrah fine ware sherds with clay shaped up to represent in one case a face and in the other an eye and eyebrow (Braidwood, Braidwood, et al. 1952, fig. 6:30-31). Similar instances that are less complete occur earlier at Ali Agha and include one horizontal incised lug eye that is similar to the specimens from Matarrah and resembles the eyes of the painted and modeled Samarran face jar at Hassuna (Lloyd and Safar 1945, p. XVII:2).

Fine-Chaff-Tempered and Smoothed Sherds (figs. 231:19-55; 235:2)

Most sherds from the deeper pottery-bearing levels of Jarmo are tempered with relatively small fragments of chaff and are generally well smoothed or burnished. A considerable proportion (65 of 204) show traces of paint (p. 216). In contrast, the shallow pottery-bearing levels yielded few sherds with any evidence of paint or burnish. Of 832 specimens, only 28 had special surface treatment of any kind. Such treatment was apparently confined to the smaller vessels, for it does not appear on sherds that exceed 10 mm in thickness.

In this respect the pottery from Ali Agha A resembles the later Jarmo pottery. Only four sherds showed the tiny lacunae indicative of fine chaff; these are from small vessels, as each specimen measured only 7 mm in thickness. One of these (figs. 235:2) appears to have come from a small spouted vessel. There are no sherds sufficiently smoothed to be considered burnished, and only one example shows a trace of red paint.

From Ali Agha B, 17 sherds could be considered as having been tempered with fine chaff (fig. 231:19-25). These, too, are from smaller vessels, with walls averaging 7 mm in thickness. Seven of these sherds were carefully smoothed, including five rims of small bowls ranging from 140 to 260 mm in diameter. Three specimens of the fine-chaff-tempered pottery (fig. 231:19,24-25) are similar to coarse ware forms, but one is somewhat smaller. The forms of the other bear a striking resemblance to the Hassuna standard fine ware bowls: hemispherical profile, slightly thinned and everted lips, and rounded or flattened bottoms.

Some of the Matarrah sherds in Chicago were reexamined in connection with this study. I did not take time to see if a distinction between fine and coarse chaff tempering would be useful but simply picked out all those that seemed most highly smoothed and in some cases had been highly burnished. Of some 17 sherds that could be selected on this basis, all turned out to be from the lower levels of Matarrah. Thus, a small but consistent group of carefully smoothed or burnished sherds can be said to be characteristic of earlier Matarrah, but highly smoothed or burnished chaff-tempered vessels apparently did not continue to be made during the time range of the later (Samarran) levels there. Of the 17 well-smoothed sherds, about two thirds are tempered with fine chaff. These sherds are from vessels that are somewhat smaller than most, their rim diameters ranging from 120 to 260 mm.

Thus, in the lower level at Matarrah, as in Ali Agha B, there is a connection between fine chaff tempering, careful smoothing, and smaller vessels. Whereas the vessels at Ali Agha usually approximate forms that were later to become prevalent in the Hassuna standard fine ware, those at Matarrah continued to be made in shapes characteristic of the coarse ware.

Summarizing so far, it may be said that the well-made fine-chaff-tempered pottery, which occurs first at Jarmo, was later replaced there and at Ali Agha by coarse ware. Somewhat later, we believe, there appeared in Ali Agha B a small number of fine-chaff-tempered sherds presaging some of the vessel forms of the Hassuna standard series. The transitional nature of these smoothed and fine-chaff-tempered sherds may also be reflected at Matarrah, where similar pottery continued to be made in forms corresponding to the coarse ware.

A connection between this fine-chaff-tempered pottey and a burnished type distinguished by Lloyd and Safar at Hassuna may now be suggested (1945, p. 278, fig. 7). Like the fine ware, this pottery is grit tempered, but some of the profiles are reminiscent of coarse ware forms as well as fine ware forms. Not only does it have features intermediate between the coarse and fine wares but there is a strong hint in the Hassuna sherd counts that it may be chronologically intermediate as well (Lloyd and Safar 1945, fig. 5). This burnished pottery occurs infrequently in level Ia at the base of Hassuna, where nearly all sherds are of coarse ware and only 8 of the burnished examples were counted. Then, in the next levels, Ib and Ic, while the count of coarse ware is diminishing and sherds of the Hassuna standard varieties of fine ware appear and increase, the burnished pottery reaches its highest frequency—53 and 51 sherds in the two levels, respectively. After that, it disappears with the coarse ware. Subsequent levels yield, in what is essentially an overlapping continuum of styles, the maximum of Hassuna standard varieties (levels Ic through V) being followed shortly by the maximum of Samarran (levels IV through VI).

FORM CATEGORIES OF THE FINE WARE

The fine ware from al-Khan includes the same series of standard types as that of Hassuna, but here the Samarran style is virtually absent. Again, as at Hassuna the fine ware is divisible into two form categories, jars and bowls.

Jars (fig. 231:26-31)

The fine ware jars are all globular or spheroidal, with vertical necks and narrow openings. Although al-Khan yielded no complete examples, we may suppose that vessel size was within the range of those from Hassuna, or 210 to

250 mm in height and maximum diameter (Lloyd and Safar 1945, fig. 4; although they also mention storage jars nearly 1 m high at Hassuna, p. 279). Measurable rim diameters are from 65 to 125 mm, with a mode between 95 and 125 mm. At both Hassuna and al-Khan the globular portions of the vessels are usually decorated by incising, sometimes combined with painting. Necks are usually painted or plain. The small sample of rims recovered does suggest a tendency for the shorter necks to be decorated, whereas at least some of the taller ones were plain.

The Samarran style at Hassuna includes a few rather similar jars. On these, however, the necks are slightly outturned rather than nearly vertical as in the Hassuna standard varieties.

Bowls (fig. 231:32-55)

In the other main category of fine ware at al-Khan, bowls, the vessels have sides that are more or less rounded up to the rim and have bottoms that continue the curve. In exception to this, a few shallow bowls have slightly concave or flaring sides (fig. 231:32), half a dozen are flattened at the base, another half dozen have distinguishable shoulders, and one sherd is a sharp or carinated shoulder.

It may be important to note that the bowl forms at al-Khan intergrade imperceptibly. Despite this it is possible to distinguish several general shapes, which show some correlation with vessel size, as tabulated below.

Rim Diameters of al-Khan Fine Ware Associated with Vessel Forms

Vessel form	Range of rim diameters (mm)	Modal range of rim diameters (mm)
Collared jars	65-125	95-125
Bowls with incurved rims	95-215	155-185
Spherical bowls	95-215	155-185
Bowls with outturned rims	95-375	155-185
Bowls with vertical rims	95-305	215-245
Shallow bowls	95-445	215-245

Two of these forms—shallow bowls and bowls with vertical rims—are usually larger than the others, with diameters in the modal range of 215-245 mm. The other three forms, bowls with incurved rims, spherical bowls, and bowls with outturned rims, are smaller (155-185 mm). A few bowls with distinct shoulders, not included in the above tabulation, are also smaller.

Decoration of the Fine Ware

Usually, but not invariably, the smaller vessels are decorated by painting and/or incising. All sherds representing bowls with distinct shoulders are decorated.

The division of the pottery according to forms, as given above, cuts across the division according to the types of decorations, given below. The type names are those proposed by Lloyd and Safar. Each kind of decoration may be found on both jars and bowls, although jars tend more often to be incised, or incised and painted. Similarly, the various types of decoration, with the exception of "archaic painted," were made together during most of their history. Standard incised begins earlier, however, and the proportions of the others vary somewhat by level at Hassuna.

Hassuna "Standard Incised" (fig. 234:1-7)

This variety at al-Khan, as at Hassuna, comprises vessels usually covered on the exterior by a thin slip and fired to a creamy, sometimes pinkish, color. The designs were drawn over the greater part of the exterior with a fine-pointed instrument while the slip was still wet. The decoration has a cursive quality, especially on the jars. Jars are more numerous than bowls.

In the use of chevrons, polygonal areas with crosshatching or line filling, and a few minor motifs, the standard incised designs resemble the painted designs of the Hassuna standard painted series. There are, however, many paired slash and slash-and-line incised designs which have no painted counterparts. We may say that the standard incised pottery of al-Khan is nearly like that of Hassuna. A possible local difference at al-Khan may be the infrequency of the pine-tree motif and of chevrons in narrow vertical bands.

No class of vessels similar in decoration to standard incised is reported from Samarra or Baghouz. R.J. Braidwood cited Lloyd and Safar's observation that the fine incised ware from Matarrah flourished more there than at Hassuna (Braidwood, Braidwood, et al. 1952, p. 4). Reexamination of the Matarrah sherds in Chicago shows that the excellence of the incised decoration is characteristic throughout the levels, which suggests a persisting local tradition. One difference was noted between the incised pottery of the upper and lower Matarrah levels, however: bowls from the lower levels are decorated predominantly by incising and those from the upper levels by a combination of incising and punctation or simply by punctation. This parallels a difference that we shall see when we come to consider the standard incised and painted type. In the pre-Samarran levels at Hassuna such decoration shows more incising than punctation. In the Samarran levels at Hassuna as well as in some instances at Samarra and Baghouz it is punctation that is emphasized. Incising, when it does occur, is in short strokes.

Hassuna "Standard Painted and Incised" (fig. 234:8-15)

With one exception the standard painted and incised sherds at al-Khan conform to the type described at Hassuna. The incised motifs may also be compared with standard incised motifs, which are present in the same proportions; most common is the paired slash motif, then the chevron, then the slash-and-line. Some of the less common standard incised designs are not found, perhaps because the sample is small.

The painting on the painted and incised sherds shows one notable difference from the standard painted type described in the next section: painting is in solid areas, bands, and broad lines—a treatment featured on only a few of the standard painted sherds. The reason for the absence of painted chevrons, zigzags, and filled polygonal areas is simply that on this type these are executed by incising.

At Hassuna, Lloyd and Safar (1945, p. 280) see within this standard painted and incised type a development that begins in Hassuna level Ib, with ordinary incised ware showing occasional painted additions. By the time of level III it shows "a fully developed combination of shapes and designs." They also distinguish a later Samarran variant of the earlier Hassunan type of painted and incised pottery. The Samarran painted and incised pottery does not replace its Hassuna counterpart but is an addition to the continuing pottery complex.

At al-Khan, painted and incised decoration appears more frequently on the bowl form that has a distinct shoulder. The tall-sided shouldered bowls found at Hassuna seem to be absent. This may be a local difference, but judging from the Hassuna illustration, one may suspect that the tall bowls are Samarran rather than Hassunan. In the al-Khan sample there is only one painted and incised sherd that could conceivably be classified as Samarran (fig. 234:11). The sherd is from a jar that had a zone of short slashed lines under the neck, below which were four horizontal painted lines. Such treatment is characteristic of incised and painted sherds at Samarra and Baghouz as well as of the Samarran style at Hassuna.

Although vessels decorated by incising alone seem to have been absent from Samarra, there are some specimens in which painting is combined with incising, and this is also perhaps Lloyd and Safar's later Samarran variant at Hassuna. At Samarra the incising is in short strokes, and we have already seen that at Matarrah the incised pottery in the upper (Samarran) levels emphasizes short strokes and punctation. At Matarrah there are only six examples of painted and incised sherds, four of these from jars.

More frequent than incising at Samarra are combinations of painting and punctation, the latter confined to a band below the necks of jars and high-necked jars—the *Töpfe mit kurzem Hals* and *Flaschen mit hohen Hals* (Herzfeld 1930).

Hassuna "Standard Painted" (fig. 235:1,3-26)

Lloyd and Safar compare the Hassuna standard painted type to an earlier variety at Hassuna, "archaic painted," from which they believe it to have been derived (1945, p. 279). In their view, the standard painted ware showed signs of a slight change in tempering and an increase in firing temperature. Painting was no longer almost red but came to vary from red brown to almost black, and the ware showed a greater variety of motifs and some interior decoration. Jars became a little squatter and had shorter necks.

The painted pottery from al-Khan is essentially similar to the standard painted variety at Hassuna. The main design categories include polygonal areas filled with crosshatching, parallel lines, polygonal areas filled with parallel lines, repeated chevrons usually joined to form a horizontal band of zigzags around the vessel, the solid area and broad-line painting previously described for the incised and painted type, and miscellaneous infrequent motifs. The polygonal areas filled with crosshatching or parallel lines are generally pendant from the rims of bowls (e.g., fig. 235:10) or from the neck juncture in the case of jars (e.g., fig. 235:15). At Hassuna, crosshatching and parallel lines are used in the archaic painted and standard painted types very much as at al-Khan, but in the standard painted series at Hassuna a tendency toward more variation and the use of frets, complex designs, and background filling is seen.

At Samarra and Baghouz, crosshatching is frequently a part of more complicated designs, appearing within bands, triangles, and long rectangular areas, and as filling within frets or as the background for frets. This kind of treatment can also be noted on sherds from the Samarran levels of Hassuna and Matarrah. These levels also yield crosshatching that is formed by the intersection of sheaves of parallel lines; such crosshatching is sometimes used as fill within "out of phase" zigzag motifs. The chevron design that occurs on archaic painted and standard painted wares both at Hassuna and al-Khan may or may not be repeated to form a zigzag. In the Samarran levels of Hassuna and Matarrah, and perhaps less frequently at Samarra and Baghouz, the chevrons are better executed than in the standard painted series.

658 PREHISTORIC ARCHEOLOGY ALONG THE ZAGROS FLANKS

CONCLUSIONS

Continuity and Change

The present study has been primarily concerned with ceramic continuity and change within a portion of the Zagros intermontane valleys and piedmont region. I have attempted to establish as precisely as possible the temporal relationship between the stratigraphic sequences of Jarmo and Hassuna and to show connections between these and other sites examined by the Iraq-Jarmo Project. In the course of the study it became necessary to distinguish two slightly variant ceramic traditions in the area, one in the region of Mosul, where Ali Agha, al-Khan, Hassuna, and Nineveh are located, and the other near Kirkuk, where Jarmo and Matarrah were found. The later appearance of Samarran pottery in the piedmont and lower montane valley sites, however, required comparisons with the classic Samarran occurrences at Samarra and Baghouz on the Tigris-Euphrates plain. In view of the stated objectives it seemed unnecessary to consider the manifest connections of the Hassuna assemblages with the Syro-Cilician communities of the west and northwest, or with the Halafian assemblages that immediately follow the range of time with which we are concerned. Moreover, anything that might—in the present state of knowledge—be said concerning western or later Halafian linkages would be a repetition of accounts already published (Lloyd and Safar 1945, pp. 263-66; Perkins 1949, p. 15; Braidwood and Braidwood 1960, pp. 507-9).

We turn now to the beginning of our ceramic history. After the disappearance of the initial painted chaff-tempered ware at Jarmo, an unpainted, coarser, and heavily chaff-tempered ceramic became characteristic of the entire Kirkuk-Mosul portion of the lower Zagros valleys and piedmont. The pottery industries of the uppermost Jarmo levels (J-II,1-2), the lowest level at Hassuna (Ia), and the entire and evidently(?) briefer occupation at Ali Agha consist almost entirely of coarse ware. Furthermore, the vessel forms in these same horizons of the three sites show general similarities. In this range of time these three sites have more ceramic features in common than they have with the pottery of any later phase. Unlike the earlier painted pottery from Jarmo or the much later Hassuna standard pottery, the later Jarmo, the Ali Agha, and the basal Hassuna coarse ware pottery suggest one continuing ceramic tradition. Then, as time went on and the Hassuna archaic and the fine wares made their appearance, the proportion of coarse ware decreased. Eventually, within the full Hassuna range, coarse ware seems to have been restricted to particular vessel forms, such as husking trays and milk jars, forms that evidently served uses that had not been superseded by the predominant standard types. Thus change came within the separate histories of the coarse and fine wares. Changes also took place within given form categories of each of the wares.

An example of such change in the coarse ware can be seen in what we call the shouldered jars and bowls (fig. 232). Shouldered jars and bowls are the predominant shape in the uppermost levels of Jarmo. Although the silhouettes of some earlier painted bowls and even of still earlier Jarmo stone vessels may presage this form, its full development clearly came with the advent of undecorated coarse ware at the end of the Jarmo occupation. This general shouldered form continues as the most numerous one at Ali Agha and basal Hassuna. The shouldered coarse ware vessels at Ali Agha, moreover, have no features that are not also found at Jarmo and Hassuna, and indeed the Ali Agha examples appear to be intermediate in form between those of the other two sites, presumably because they are intermediate in time. The average vessel at Ali Agha is larger than the Jarmo specimens but not quite so large as those at Hassuna. The peculiar nodal variety of lug that begins to appear in upper Jarmo is predominant at Ali Agha and also at Hassuna. The rims of shouldered jars are least constricted at Jarmo, slightly more so at Ali Agha, and most constricted at Hassuna. Some Jarmo rims are slightly flared, but none apparently have the vertical high or low "collar" found on many of the Hassuna specimens. Ali Agha is again intermediate, with a few sherds approaching the low collar form. At Jarmo the lower body profile of shouldered jars narrows smoothly to a flat base, while at Hassuna the lower body often forms an ogival curve between base and shoulder. At Ali Agha a few sherds already show the ogival curve.

A slight time difference probably exists between the materials from operations A and B at Ali Agha if our small samples can be trusted. B exposure was situated higher on the mound, and the ceramic features most closely resembling basal Hassuna—low collars, the ogival curve, and even a few fine-chaff-tempered and grit-tempered sherds—come from B. The specimens from A are more like upper Jarmo in these respects and hence are probably slightly earlier than those of B.

Turning to other coarse ware forms, we note that bowls with rounded sides, evidently with a flat base and heel, are present in the coarse ware at each site, including basal Hassuna and Matarrah. There may be a thread of continuity back to the somewhat similar bases on some Jarmo stone vessels. Some Jarmo stone bowl bases are flat, and the distinctive heel itself occurs on other contemporary forms. At Ali Agha, bowls with rounded sides are relatively more important than at Jarmo, where a high proportion of bowls are shouldered. At al-Khan, the number of round-sided bowls is negligible. Since most of the al-Khan coarse ware consists of husking trays and milk jars, one may suppose that the uses to which the round-sided coarse ware bowls were put had been taken over by the numerous fine ware forms.

Bowls with flaring sides seem to have had a similar history. Stone specimens were present before pottery appeared at Jarmo. Pottery examples occurred at Jarmo and Ali Agha but were rare or absent at al-Khan, again presumably because fine ware vessels were being used for the same purposes that coarse ware had been used for previously.

The evidence from Hassuna suggests that husking trays were a relatively late development within the coarse ware series, and this possibility is confirmed to some degree by their frequent occurrence in the al-Khan sample. Presumably the appearance of these distinctive vessels in basal Matarrah means that the Matarran lower levels were indeed equivalent to the levels of Hassuna before the appearance of the Samarran ware there, and hence of the same time range as al-Khan. From this point of view, the absence of Hassuna standard painted from all Matarran levels, the strong continuance of coarse ware into the Samarran levels, and the peculiar flourishing of Hassuna standard incised throughout the occupation of Matarrah may be taken as hints of a regional difference that distinguishes the Kirkuk from the Mosul area.

The husking trays seem to be similar, in all respects save interior treatment, to the category of large trays that occurred earlier in the uppermost Jarmo exposures and in the Ali Agha samples. It would doubtless follow that it was from this class that the husking tray was derived. Eventually these became a hallmark of this coarse ware vessel tradition.

Turning now to the other wares, we note that in level Ib at Hassuna the coarse ware—which in Ia constituted nearly the entire pottery industry—was accompanied by a strain of burnished ware, a significant amount of Hassuna standard incised ware, and some archaic painted ware. Hassuna standard painted had not yet appeared, however. The burnished pottery has some features that may suggest it was transitional between the coarse and fine wares, but like the latter it is grit tempered.

A few well-smoothed sherds occurred at Ali Agha. These are all from operation B, which, as has been noted, yielded materials probably a little later than those of the deposits investigated in A. Unlike the burnished pottery at Hassuna, the smoothed pottery from Ali Agha is tempered with fine chaff. The vessel forms of this type resemble forms that later became prevalent in the Hassuna standard types. Again, one has the impression of a transition to the fine ware, but along somewhat different lines than at Hassuna. At Matarrah, burnished and well-smoothed sherds, again usually tempered with fine chaff, were in a definite minority in the lower levels.

In summary, the evidence from Hassuna, Ali Agha, and Matarrah is that well-smoothed and/or burnished pottery is found at about the time of transition from coarse to fine ware. It is interesting to see how this supposed transition is differently represented at each of the three sites. At Hassuna, vessels are grit tempered and made in fine and coarse ware forms. At Ali Agha they are fine-chaff-tempered and made in fine ware forms. At Matarrah they are mostly fine-chaff-tempered and made in coarse ware forms.

There is as yet no evidence of any specific antecedent for the standard incised ware. This suggests that the earlier development of this type was not represented at any of the sites that have been examined, although it was the first of the Hassuna standard wares to be adopted by the contemporary pottery makers at all the sites so far excavated. The trend we have described in connection with the burnished ware probably took place over the entire area and provided the context out of which the various standard types were developed.

It is possible, however, that we are close to the main line of the development of the Hassunan standard painted series, which began its vogue a little later than did Hassuna standard incised. Lloyd and Safar regard their archaic painted ware as a transitional variety. It reached its culmination at Hassuna in levels Ic and II, the time when standard painted first appeared in small amounts. Subsequently, archaic painted ware disappeared at about the time the coarse ware was becoming less frequent.

We have some difficulty in understanding the tabulation of the Hassuna sherd count (Lloyd and Safar 1945, fig. 5) that suggests that the coarse ware was no longer being made by the time the first Samarran sherds appeared, i.e., in level III. It seems, however, that at least the milk jars continued to be made and became what is said to be the main coarse ware form. Curiously, however, Lloyd and Safar's tabulation does not mention coarse ware sherds from levels higher than III. We are loath to suppose that this variety was no longer present as a regular component of the Hassuna pottery industry. Certainly the use of coarse ware persisted throughout the whole range at Matarrah.

Such a site as al-Khan fits neatly into the Hassuna sequence. There is a high proportion of the Hassunan standard varieties and some coarse ware as well. The latter includes both husking trays and milk jars, as we noted, both of which are late in the coarse ware continuum. Thus, it may be proposed that al-Khan has approximate chronological equivalence to Hassuna level III. There is even a handful of Samarran sherds at al-Khan; these are just beginning to appear in level III in Hassuna. The only difference one finds between the two samplings is that there were still a few archaic painted sherds in this level III of Hassuna. Only one doubtful specimen of this variety was found at al-Khan, but the sampling was very restricted.

LOCAL CONTINUITY AT MATARRAH

At Matarrah, in the Kirkuk piedmont plain and about 150 km southeast of Hassuna, the details of the ceramic sequence are somewhat different. In the earliest level, operation VI-5, coarse ware was already associated with a small amount of Hassuna standard incised. These two varieties continued throughout the lower levels, with the coarse ware overwhelmingly predominant, until in the upper levels we see the addition of pottery of the Samarran style. The curious feature of the Matarran sequence, as compared with those of Hassuna and al-Khan, is the complete absence of

Hassuna standard painted ware—an absence that can hardly represent an important chronological difference, because this ware was also absent from the levels of Matarrah that had Samarran pottery while it continued to be associated with Samarran at Hassuna. Thus, the absence of this variety at Matarrah seems to represent a local situation. Further, as we noted above, coarse ware including husking trays continued to appear in quantity throughout the entire Matarran sequence, long after the appearance of the Samarran sherds which marked the beginning of the later phase. The proportion of coarse ware sherds in the later levels varies from 55% to 15% (see Braidwood, Braidwood, et al. 1952). What appears to be another local variation is the excellence of the decoration of the Hassuna standard incised ware at Matarrah—a tradition that was maintained during both the lower and upper levels at the site. In the uppermost levels the use of punctation predominated.

Variance between the Classic Samarran and the More Northerly Samarran Occurrences

We still know relatively little about the nature of the relationship between the Hassunan standard painted and the Samarran painted styles, but hypotheses have been proposed by Lloyd and Safar and by R.J. Braidwood and Leslie. The important fact that these authors take into account is that the upper levels of Hassuna yield quantities of both Hassuna standard painted and Samarran sherds. At Hassuna, the standard painted variety continued strongly after the Samarran style had appeared. As noted above, such was not the case at Matarrah, where Hassuna standard painted ware did not appear either in the pre-Samarran lower levels or when Samarran pottery appeared. The stratigraphy of these two sites suggests, however, that in the Zagros intermontane valleys and piedmont region generally, as opposed to the Samarra and Baghouz riverbank areas, the Samarran style was added to the continuing pottery industries.

The majority of design motifs and variations that characterize the busy, lineal, and neat Samarran style probably have no real prototypes in the Hassunan standard painted style. Nevertheless, there are other design elements that have, and these shared elements are more frequent in the Samarran levels at Hassuna and probably at al-Khan than at Samarra and Baghouz. In other words, as more excavation is done, we may expect Hassuna-Samarra correspondences in painted designs to be least frequent in those Samarran sites par excellence of the middle reaches of the Euphrates-Tigris riverbanks and most frequent in the Samarran-yielding levels of sites such as Hassuna that lie in the more northerly regions. Variation again is underlined by the absence of incised pottery (as against painted and incised) at Baghouz and Samarra, as contrasted to Hassuna and Matarrah. The Samarran style in the intermontane Zagros valleys and piedmont region, as we know it so far, is less homogeneous than the Samarran of the riverbank sites. The more upland style represents a blend of design elements that are in part classic Samarran and in part a derivation of the Hassunan standard painted style tradition.

NOTES

1. [The assay was published late in 1973 (*Radiocarbon* 15:372). The laboratory sample number is P-1499; the age determination is 6927 ± 63 (4977 B.C.). The contextual information given in *Radiocarbon* is certainly garbled. Since the floor of reference for the hearth area (feature 6) from which the sample was taken was not clear (fig. 229), it is questionable how meaningful this single determination may be.—EDS.]

2. [When Caldwell wrote this, such sites as Sawwan, Umm Dabaghiyah and Yarim Tepe I were, of course, not yet excavated (cf. Oates 1973).—EDS.]

3. [A separate study of the fabrics of the Ali Agha and al-Khan pottery has been undertaken by Matson. However, his photographs of typical Ali Agha coarse ware sherds are included here in figure 233.—EDS.]

4. The term "milk jar" as used throughout the Matarrah report (Smith in Braidwood, Braidwood, et al. 1952, pl. V) refers to shouldered jars, not to the form for which the name was originally proposed by Lloyd and Safar (cf. Lloyd and Safar 1945, fig. 3:7, pl. XII:2, right). In the present report I use the term as Lloyd and Safar originally proposed it.

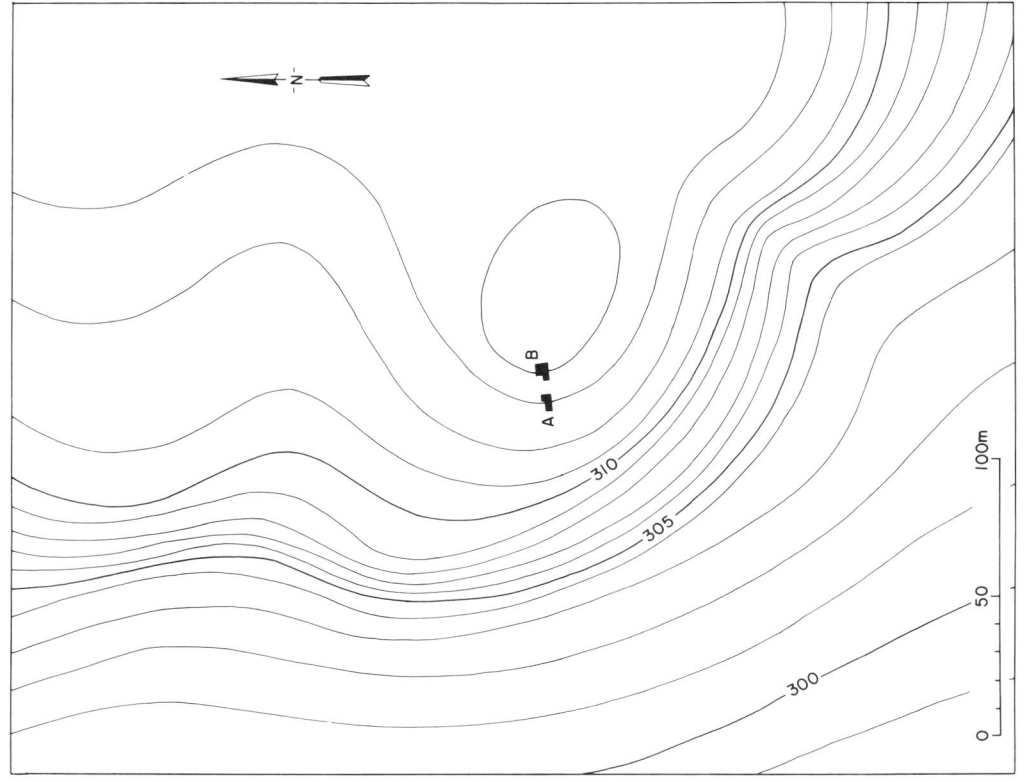

Fig. 229. Plan and section of operation B at Ali Agha.

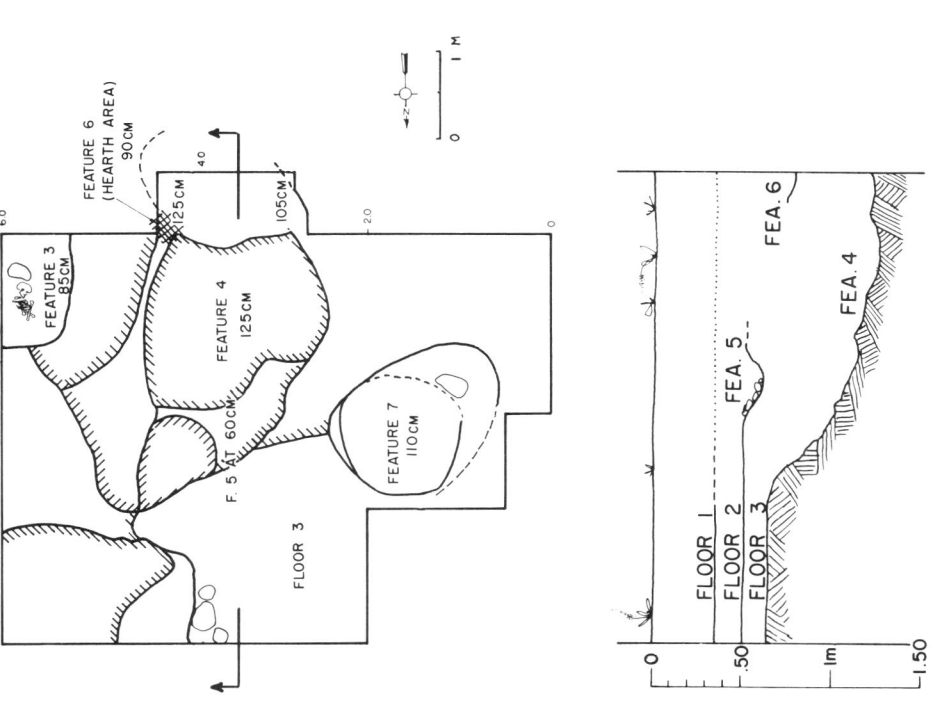

Fig. 228. Plot plan of Gird Ali Agha.

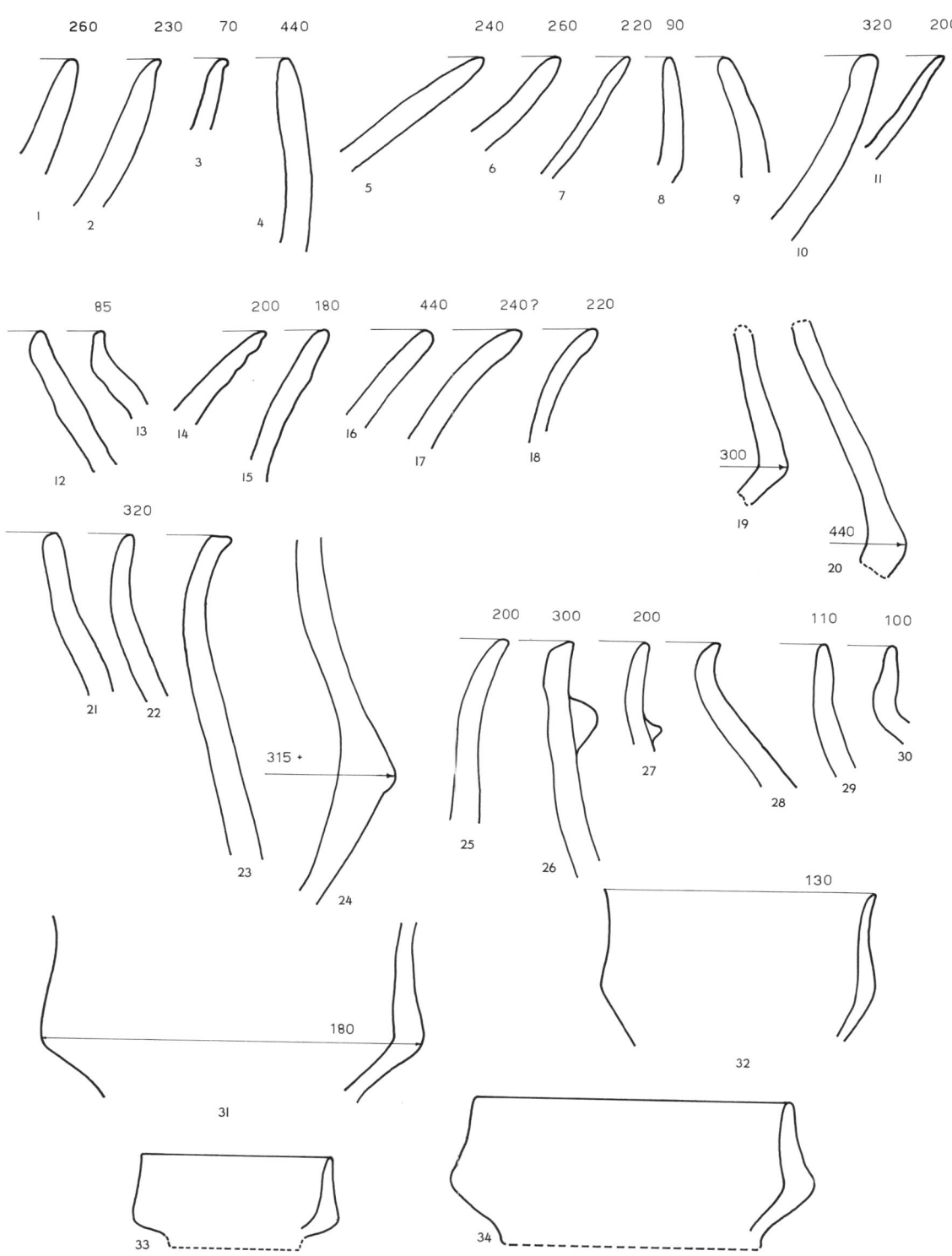

Fig. 230. Ali Agha pottery: coarse ware. *1-34*. Scale 1:3. (Diameters given in mm.)

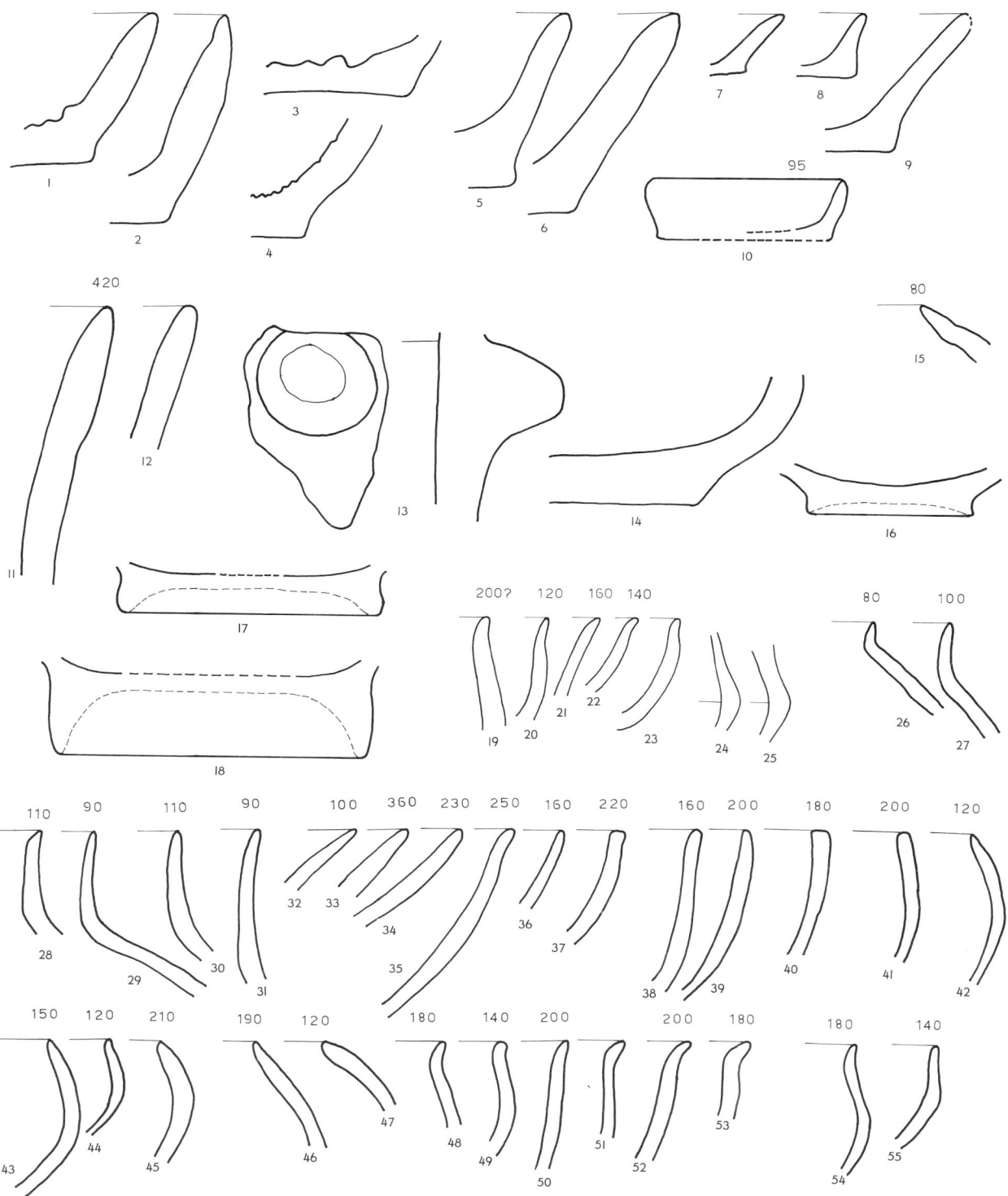

Fig. 231. Al-Khan and Ali-Agha pottery: al-Khan coarse ware, *1-4,10-18*; al-Khan fine ware, *26-55*; Ali Agha coarse ware, *5-9*; Ali Agha fine ware, *19-25*. Scale 1:3.

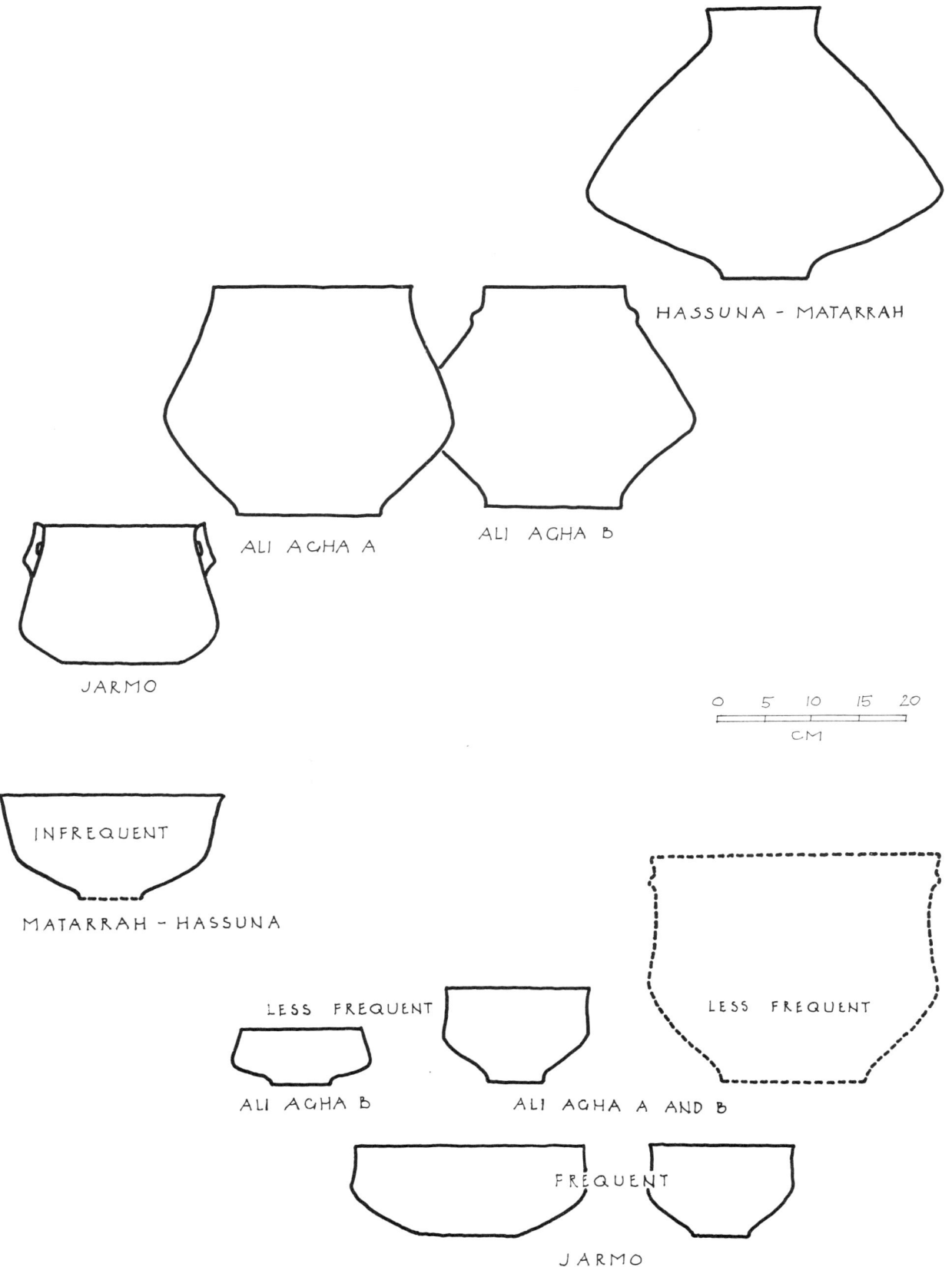

Fig. 232. Suggested sequence or relationships of shouldered pottery profiles.

Fig. 233. Ali Agha pottery: coarse ware, *1-9*. Scale ca. 3:4.

Fig. 234. Al-Khan pottery: standard incised ware, *1-7*; painted and incised ware, *8-15*. Scale 1:2.

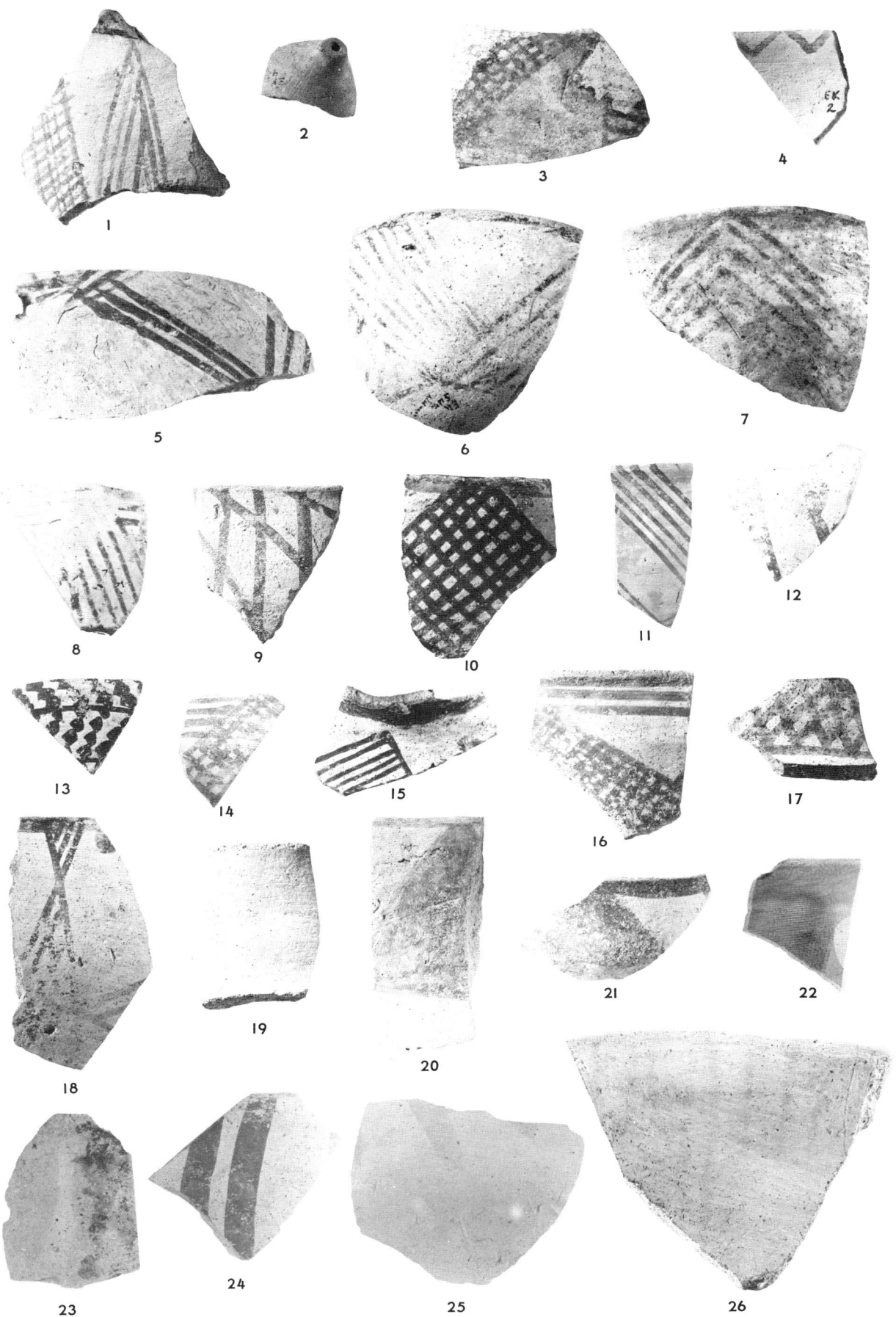

Fig. 235. Al-Khan pottery: painted ware, *1-26*. Scale 1:2.

REFERENCES

Braidwood, Robert J.
- 1954 The Iraq-Jarmo Project of the Oriental Institute of the University of Chicago, seasons 1954-55. *Sumer* 10:120-38.

Braidwood, Robert J., and Braidwood, Linda S.
- 1960 *Excavations in the plain of Antioch I: the earlier assemblages, phases A-J*. Oriental Institute Publications, vol. 61. Chicago: University of Chicago Press.

Braidwood, Robert J.; Braidwood, Linda S.; Smith, James G.; and Leslie, Charles
- 1952 Matarrah: a southern variant of the Hassunan assemblage, excavated in 1948. *Journal of Near Eastern Studies* 11:1-75.

Braidwood, Robert J.; Howe, Bruce; et al.
- 1960 SAOC 31 (see below).

du Mesnil du Buisson, [Robert].
- 1948 *Baghouz, l'ancienne corsôtê: le tell archaïque et la nécropole de l'Age du Bronze*. Leiden: E.J. Brill.

Herzfeld, Ernst E.
- 1930 *Die vorgeschichtlichen Töpfereien von Samarra*. Forschungen zur islamischen Kunst II, vol. V. Berlin: Reimer and Vohsen.

Lloyd, Seton, and Safar, Fuad.
- 1945 Tell Hassuna. *Journal of Near Eastern Studies* 4:255-89

Oates, Joan
- 1973 The background and development of early farming communities in Mesopotamia and the Zagros. *Proceedings of the Prehistoric Society* 39:147-81.

Perkins, Ann Louise
- 1949 *The comparative archeology of early Mesopotamia*. Studies in Ancient Oriental Civilization, no. 25. Chicago: University of Chicago Press.

SAOC 31
- 1960 *Prehistoric investigations in Iraqi Kurdistan*. Robert J. Braidwood, Bruce Howe, et al. Studies in Ancient Oriental Civilization, no. 31. Chicago: University of Chicago Press.

APPENDIX

THE NONCERAMIC YIELD FROM ALI AGHA AND AL-KHAN

Editors

Since Caldwell's treatment of the Ali Agha and al-Khan finds (chap. 20) deals only with pottery, we supply the following observations, taken mainly from Vivian Broman Morales's field notes. Like the potsherds (the Chicago portion of which is temporarily in Matson's laboratory at Pennsylvania State University), the nonceramic materials from the two sites were divided and a substantial share is in the Iraq Museum, Baghdad.

ALI AGHA

Even considering the brief time spent on the Ali Agha soundings (nine days), with a small crew of workmen, the nonceramic inventory was incredibly small. For example, the worked flint (whether utilized pieces or debitage) amounted to only about 375 pieces and the obsidian to about 150 pieces. Of the obsidian, however, about 50 examples were of the tool type known as side-blow flakes (see Hole's "thin sections," p. 247). No flint sickle blades were noted in the field, but two examples were later identified upon restudy of the Chicago sample. Broman Morales's field summary of the nonceramic yield from Ali Agha runs as follows:

> The total assemblage of worked stone at this site is very meagre and the flint tools are nondescript, the best pieces being scrapers of various types. There are many primary flakes, some showing signs of use or wear. The obsidian industry seems to be better defined, though microlithic. It includes many chips and flakes, in addition to the characteristic side-blow flakes which are occasionally retouched on the bulbar surface at the point of percussion. There are also used blades and bladelets (a few used as end scrapers) and utilized chips. In the category of larger stone objects, which are also rare, there are celt-like pebble tools and flaked pebbles (used as choppers?) and some boulder mortar and possible pestle fragments.
>
> Worked bone is also scarce, there being a few (6) splinter awls and 2 bone beads.
>
> Clay objects are scarce, too, and fragmentary, but the female figurine (simple seated form) is the most numerous. There are also 2 clay beads and various other small bits which are unidentifiable.
>
> Save for the pottery, which occurred in overwhelming quantities, the other industries are poor indeed and poorly defined.
>
> Of the material selected for the Baghdad Museum, the bulk came from feature 4 in operation B, located near the crest of the mound. This feature consisted of a large, irregular "pit" or shallow depression filled with fine black dirt and containing pottery, flint, obsidian, a few bone tools and a few fragments of clay objects. This deposit of black dirt occurred first at 60 cm below the surface and continued to 1.25 m at the deepest point. It cut into hard red soil and probably at that depth represents the base of the occupational deposit. The museum has been given the total assemblage of material coming from this feature, which represents also the lowest level of the site. A few other pieces were added to round out the picture, but the assemblage from feature 4 in itself is typical and a good example of the quality and quantity of the stone industry at Gird Ali Agha.

The feature 4 material in the Iraq Museum is marked $\frac{AA}{F\text{-}4}$ and consists of the following:
$\quad\quad B$

Large stone
- 1 celtlike pebble tool with oblique chipped and battered cutting edge, pebble butt
- 1 smaller chipped pebble tool, similar to above but with blunter chopping edge
- 1 ±round flint flake tool (planoconvex) with alternate-opposite edge flaking and wear

Flint
- 4 pebble cores (fragments) with random flaking
- 2 small flakes used as thumbnail scrapers
- 1 bladelike flake end-and-side scraper
- 1 small flake used as side scraper
- 14 primary flakes showing no signs of use

Obsidian
- 14 side-blow flakes, 2 retouched at point of percussion
- 1 blade end scraper
- 4 utilized blades
- 3 bladelet fragments
- 1 utilized chip
- 12 primary chips

Bone
- 4 splinter awls
- 1 fragment of polished bone

Clay
- 1 small barrel bead
- 1 flattened clay "arm"
- 1 rod section
- 1 bent rodlike "arm"

Shell
- 1 fragment of a dentalium bead

In addition to the material from feature 4, the following items were added to the Baghdad sample:

Larger stone and flint from operation A, 0-30 cm
- 1 shallow boulder mortar fragment
- 1 smooth, flat irregular pebble with smooth edges
- 1 flat pebble fragment with chipped edges
- 1 pyriform flat pebble—used as smoother or grinder?
- ½ flattened disk of yellow ochre
- 4 amorphous flake cores
- 1 flake with nibbled retouch or wear on one edge
- 1 flake used as a scraper
- 2 irregular chipped pebbles
- 43 unused flakes and chips
- 3 chipped pebble flakes

Bone
- 2 bone splinter awls, $\frac{AA3}{B}$ and $\frac{AA\ 30\text{-}60}{B}$
- 1 bone bead, $\frac{AA3}{B}$

Clay
- 2 seated female figurines (fragmentary), $\frac{AA\ \approx\text{-}30}{A}$ and $\frac{AA3}{B}$
- 4 perforated sherd fragments

Larger stone and flint from the surface
- 1 small chipped celt fragment—butt end only
- 1 planoconvex pebble flake, unifacially flaked on three sides
- 3 flat river pebbles with chipped edges
- 2 amorphous cores
- 3 chipped pebbles (corelike)
- 2 chipped pebble flakes
- 4 miscellaneous chipped flakes
- 4 fragments with ground surfaces

The artifacts in the above listings may be taken as typical of the Ali Agha inventory insofar as the yield from our small soundings represents it.

AL-KHAN

The stepped clearance on the east face of the old British tank-trap trench at al-Khan (SAOC 31, pp. 25, 35) was done with six to eight workmen, coincident with our exposures on M'lefaat. The work lasted for less than six full days. Broman Morales's field notes follow.

> A 2 × 8 m trench was cut into the north face of the old army trench exposing a section of about 3 m of deposit before sterile red silt was encountered. There was much Islamic pottery in the top half to three quarters of a meter, after which a wide band of silt yielded only a few bits of Hassuna ware until a level of compacted silt was reached at about 2.20 m below the surface. Five steps were cut, the first two at about 1.80 m and 2.0 m, still in the silt, and the third at the first level that seemed compacted. There was no evidence of architecture nor of true floors, or other signs of actual occupation. Hassuna painted, Hassuna incised, and some painted and incised sherds were present all the way to sterile soil, along with various forms of coarse ware and "husking trays." There were practically no Samarran painted sherds.
>
> The stone industry associated with the Hassuna pottery is a poor one indeed. A single short, truncated, conical bead of ground and polished black stone was found. Some few fragments of larger worked stone, mostly pestles and grinding stones, and one or two fragments of polished stone are about the extent of the finds, save for a few flint chips and flakes, all irregular and fragmentary. No obsidian was noted here. . . . The flints excavated at al-Khan are mainly crude flakes showing signs of use. They are of interest because of their negative character—a quality shared with the flint industry of Matarrah and with much of the flint work of Hassuna. The flints were divided equally between the Directorate General of Antiquities [Iraq Museum] and Chicago.

An actual count of the flint does not appear in the field notes. However, the Chicago half of the chipped stone material amounted to only 58 pieces, plus two bits of obsidian (one evidently a fragment of a side-blow flake).

It seems quite clear that our sounding at al-Khan did not expose an actual living area within the settlement itself.

REFERENCE

SAOC 31
    1960 *Prehistoric investigations in Iraqi Kurdistan.* Robert J. Braidwood, Bruce Howe, et al. Studies in Ancient Oriental Civilization, no. 31. Chicago: University of Chicago Press.

21

THE SOUNDINGS AT M'LEFAAT

Margaret Dittemore

INTRODUCTION

This paper is a descriptive analysis of the artifactual material recovered from M'lefaat, a small mound in northeastern Iraq, excavated by the the Prehistoric Project of the Oriental Institute, University of Chicago, under the direction of Robert J. Braidwood in the fall of 1954. The limited testing of Tell M'lefaat was supervised by Vivian Broman Morales, a grantee of the Department of Anthropology, University of Chicago. The excavation lasted four and a half days.

The present writer did not have firsthand experience with the excavation but has prepared this report with the aid of Broman Morales's field notes, the two published preliminary accounts of the excavation (Braidwood 1954; SAOC 31), and a revised version of a paper prepared in 1963 by Peter Benedict, then a graduate student in the Department of Anthropology, University of Chicago. With the exception of a representative sample left in Baghdad, Iraq, most of the artifactual material recovered from the site is now a part of the collections of the Oriental Institute, University of Chicago.

THE SITE

The mound of M'lefaat lies near the junction of two very different ecological zones—the foothills of the Zagros Mountains and the Assyrian piedmont. It is at approximately 36°18′ N and 43°33′ E and at an elevation of ca. 290 m above sea level. The mound measures 125 × 75 m. When examined by its excavators the site had a concrete-faced World War II machine gun emplacement on it. A tank-trap trench flanked it on the southwest, and the ruins of a small barracks were situated between the mound and the river bank to the east. To the north of the site are the gravel hills and the rising limestone system of the Jebel Maghreb and the Jebel Ain al-Sufra; to its south and west are the rolling grassy plains of the Assyrian steppe. M'lefaat lies northeast of the Tigris-Greater Zab confluence on the west bank of the Khazir River, a small perennial river draining that part of the plain (fig. 1 and SAOC 31, pl. 6*B*). To the west of M'lefaat and the Khazir River is the plain of Mosul. The granary of the Assyrian empire, it has been one of the richest and most heavily occupied areas of the piedmont.

Immediately to the south and east of M'lefaat is the plain of Keramlais, which has been identified as the battlefield of Gaugamela or Arbela (331 B.C.).

THE EXCAVATION AND THE ARCHITECTURAL REMAINS

Three trenches, operations I, II, and III, were put into the mound (fig. 236), testing from its crest down to a depth of 2.15 m below the surface. This depth was reached in the south end of operation I at a point slightly off the crest of the mound.

Approximately 20 m² were exposed by operation I (fig. 239). The operation was started as a 2 × 8 m trench oriented almost north-south at 20° east of north and later partially enlarged on its east face to uncover the entire outline of a circular depression called feature 1. The excavator subdivided operation I into five arbitrary levels as follows: level 1 extending from the surface to a depth of 0.50 m, level 2 from 0.50 to 0.75 m, level 3 from 0.75 to 0.85 m, level 4 from 0.85 to 0.90 m, and level 5 from 0.90 to 2.15 m. The operation was subsequently enlarged, and levels 1–3 in this enlargement were extended from the surface to 0.70 m. Virgin soil was reached at ca. 1.90 m below the surface.

In the original trench, at ca. 0.10 m below the surface, a band of limestone concretions—small white granules set in alternating matrices of red clayey soil and fine grayish brown soil—was identified. It persisted down to a depth of ca. 0.90 m. Much small bone and chipped and ground stone were recovered from this limestone concretion zone. Some clay objects, wheel-made plain ware, and a tiny blue stone bead(?) fragment were also found at this level.

This chapter is a slightly revised version of the descriptive section of a paper submitted in 1978 in partial fulfillment of the requirements for the Master of Arts degree in the Department of Anthropology, University of Chicago.

Two pits in operation I (features 1 and 1A, also noted as I/1 and I/1A), one partially overriding the other and together somewhat ovoid in plan (ca. 3.55 × 2.70 m), were traced from their initial exposure at ca. 0.70 m to their base at 1.55 m below the surface. The lower portion of feature 1A, an earlier, smaller pit, appears to have been partially filled in at a depth of 1.25 m and covered over with cracked and broken stone, perhaps to form a level surface for the living floor above it. This floor appears to have extended to the north and east, covering an area almost 4 × 3 m. A hearth depression was identified at the southern end of the floor. The sides of feature 1, the later, larger pit, were first encountered at 0.70 m below the surface. No details of this feature could be traced in the band of limestone concretions that occurred above this level.

Features 1 and 1A contained a sizeable quantity of worked stone including a celt fragment, a ground sphere, a boulder mortar, and a variety of bladelets, flakes, scrapers, and other tools. A number of clay fragments, a stone bead, and two pieces of worked bone were also recovered. The appearance here of sherds of a late wheel-made plain ware was attributed by the excavator to rodent activity. These features are believed to represent two phases of what was probably a small pit house, whose original depth and roofing arrangement could not be determined.

To the west of features 1 and 1A in operation I, a relatively sterile area of compact red soil with no limestone concretions was encountered and followed from ca. 0.90 m below the surface (the base of the occupation level associated with feature 1, the later pit) down to a depth of ca. 1.90 m. A fine zone of limestone concretions of a more crystalline form occurred again and was followed to the base of operation I at 2.15 m below the surface in its southern portion. The entire operation was disturbed by rodent activity.

Operation II was a step trench 2 m wide, dug into the inner face of the tank-trap trench on the southwestern side of the mound (see figs. 236-37). An earlier survey party had discovered a whole pot in the wall of the trench and a quantity of chipped stone on its slope. It was hoped that a stratigraphic sequence of occupation might be readily obtained in this area; however, a large pit of a much later date that encompassed most of the operation was encountered, upsetting the area's stratigraphy. Clay fragments showing impressions of matting, a small clay figure, and a number of flakes, scrapers, and bladelets of chipped stone were recovered. The extremely disturbed character of the fill caused the excavator to abandon operation II, and the material is treated here as if it were from a single unstratified context.

Operation III (fig. 238), located slightly to the southwest of operation I, was begun as a 2 × 3 m trench laid out on an east-west line at 60° west of north. It was later extended on its north, east, and south faces, making a 4 × 4 m square. A total of 16 m² was thus exposed. Level 1 extended from the surface to a depth of 0.40 m, level 2 from 0.40 to 0.85 m, and level 3 from 0.85 to 0.90 m below the surface. These levels were distinguished on the basis of the architectural activity identified.

A quantity of cracked and broken stone, much of it worked, occurred in operation III, level 1. An intrusive burial was encountered and removed at ca. 0.40 m below the surface. At about this same depth in the east end of the trench a number of small rough stones believed to form about one third of a circumference of a circle (ca. 0.40 m in diameter) appeared. As this line of stone was only ca. 0.15 m thick, however, the excavator doubts that it served as the foundation for a wall of room height. Beneath this semicircle of stone a pebble layer identified as a floor appeared at a depth of 0.60 m. Two discontinuous concentrations of pebbles occurred in the south and middle sections of the trench. The cultural material recovered from this level included large worked stone, used bladelets, flakes, and scrapers, and debitage. A number of sherds, a shell fragment, and a small white bead preform(?) were also recovered. A second floor was identified at ca. 0.75 to 0.90 m below the surface in the southwest corner. A scatter of large stones at this level of the second floor was uncovered. Its purpose was unclear unless it, together with an assortment of other stones recovered at the same relative depth, was associated with an earlier occupation level.

Between these two floors, alternating layers of red and black fill were encountered. It is believed that these, in conjunction with the pebble scatter, were purposefully laid and that the whole may represent an attempt at architectural renovation. However, the evidence for architectural activity here is certainly more ambiguous than in operation I.

Broman Morales estimates that the average depth of the deposit at the site was 1.5 m. This fact, together with the architectural remains, indicates an occupation of some permanence. It is interesting to note that, aside from some pottery and an intrusive burial, no later material was recovered from the mound. Although radiocarbon samples were taken, the disturbed character of the fill from which they were recovered has discouraged their submission for radiocarbon age determination. It follows that the placement of M'lefaat within the chronological framework which resulted from the Prehistoric Project's work is largely dependent upon available typological comparisons of the artifacts.

INTRUSIVE MATERIALS

Aside from an intrusive surface burial and a tiny (7 × 5 mm) blue frit barrel bead, the only type of artifact found that could not be associated with the M'lefaat assemblage was pottery.

Slightly over 100 potsherds were found at the site. Twenty-six are identified as having been recovered from within the mound: 18 from I,5, 5 from II, and 3 from III. The excavator believes that these potsherds are intrusive and attributes their occurrence to rodent activity, both in ancient and in modern times. RJB comments on the entire sample:

> Most of these are small, worn, and without known diagnostic features save that they tend to have been wheel-made. Most of these sherds came from the surface, although a few were from within the uppermost half meter's depth. Some hints of Hassunan, Gawran, and Ninevite V types exist in the general collection but—given M'lefaat's situation adjacent to a fordable stretch of the Khazir—it would be strange not to anticipate traces of passersby over a long range of northern Mesopotamian history.

THE ARTIFACTUAL MATERIALS
The Chipped Stone Industry

TYPOLOGY

The technological and functional character of the assemblage was of primary concern in the organization of these materials. Attributes have been chosen in an attempt to reveal processes of raw material selection and use, manufacturing techniques, and functional and stylistic elements of the assemblage. The types express a primary concern with function. This has been approached with some caution, recognizing the problems in attempting to discern tool use largely through an examination of morphological and macrowear traits. The multiple uses to which many of these tools have been put (particularly flakes and bladelets, which make up a large part of the M'lefaat assemblage) make their categorization even more difficult. This problem is also stressed in various ethnographic accounts (Gould, Koster, and Sontz 1971, pp. 160-63). The association of tools recovered from within the site and experimental studies conducted both on manufacture and use lend support to these conclusions. Only with a more comprehensive analysis combining both macromorphological and microwear studies, however, will a more complete understanding of the range of activities in which the people of M'lefaat participated be possible.

A second concern here is with the technological processes evident in the manufacture of these tools. Too often, typologies concerned only with retouched tools neglect or treat incorrectly the unretouched chipped stone as well as the chipping debris resulting from tool production. These materials are valuable sources of information that can contribute toward our understanding of the different manufacturing techniques used at a site.

TERMINOLOGY

Terms used in this analysis are primarily those defined by Crabtree (1972). The rock color chart of the Geological Society of America was used in color identification of the stone artifactual materials.

No attempt has been made to separate the blades into groups on the basis of their physical measurements. This decision was made after a review of the archeological literature in which blades have been variously subcategorized according to a variety of indices and after a study of the M'lefaat examples themselves. Correlations of the length, width, and thickness of complete unretouched blades were not particularly high. However, 95% of this sample appeared to be between 5 and 10 mm in width. Likewise, almost 84% (683) of the used blades and blade fragments in the "used bladelet" category were between 5 and 10 mm in width, and 97% (736) were less than 10 mm in width. Thus the term "bladelet" is used throughout this report to represent the very small, uniform size of blade that the people of M'lefaat produced.

METHODS OF MEASUREMENT

Measurements were taken in the following manner: *length* was measured as the longitudinal dimension along the medial axis from the bulb of force to the distal edge; *width* was measured as the maximum lateral dimension perpendicular to the medial axis; *thickness* was measured as the maximum transverse dimension below the bulb of force; *edge angle* was measured as the angle between the dorsal and ventral surfaces at the edge(s) of the specimen believed to be the working edge (Wilmsen 1974, pp. 65-66). The instruments used were a vernier caliper to measure length, width, and thickness, a protractor to determine edge angles, and a 10× hand lens to study the flakes and bladelets for evidence of use-wear or retouch.

TECHNIQUES OF TOOL PRODUCTION

Several different manufacturing techniques may be inferred through an examination of the chipped stone materials recovered from M'lefaat. The largest component of the assemblage is the prismatic bladelets and bladelet fragments whose shared attributes suggest the utilization of a pressure technique in their production. These bladelets are small, each having a fairly uniform width and parallel sides or margins. Generally, they have small platforms and diffuse bulbs of force. Parallel bladelet scars appear on their ventral surfaces. Those bladelet cores recovered also support the conclusion that a pressure technique was involved.

A very low percentage of utilized bladelets actually have cortex, suggesting that the core was prepared before the bladelet removal was begun. This preparation was probably accomplished by reducing the cobble to a roughly pyramidal form by percussion. Most platforms exhibit multiple flake scarring. No grinding or scoring as methods of platform preparation have been detected. The large number of "platform tablet" flakes and "bladelet core wall" flakes recovered—types usually understood to reflect attempts at rejuvenating the core—suggests the importance of a carefully prepared platform. The larger dimensions of the platform tablet flakes suggest the core may have been rejuvenated several times before being discarded. The tool used in the removal of bladelets from these cores may have been an antler or wood tang, but there is no direct evidence of either.

A number of the M'lefaat examples were produced by percussion and are characterized by expanded distal ends or by irregular flake scars on their dorsal faces. A number of cores exhibiting somewhat irregular bladelet removal scars also suggest this technique, although several of these (from II) may have resulted from a breakdown in the pressure removal series. The very conical outline of one core (from I,1) makes it difficult to conceive how it could have been held in a vise. The majority of the cores are more elongated, however, and have some sort of "backing." Unfortunately, I have not been able to detect statistically significant differences in bladelet or core attributes that would indicate the use of different techniques in their production.

The percussion technique was certainly used at M'lefaat for the manufacture of flakes. This is evident in a number of attributes common to the tools made on flakes (e.g., used flakes and scrapers) as well as in much of the chipping debris. These attributes include prominent bulbs of force, large striking platforms, well-defined and rather erratic rings of percussion on the ventral face, and flake scars on the dorsal surface. The cores recovered appear as the products of rather random multidirectional flake removal. The high percentage of utilized flakes with cortex (91%) and the lack of alteration in these flakes except for their working edge suggest they were either the by-products of this reduction process or of the initial preparation of bladelet cores. It is not certain which percussion technique was used in the production of these materials, although the direct hand-held technique is suggested. A large number of the flakes are characterized by pronounced bulbs of force and the absence of lips. The limited production and utilization of flakes indicate that flakes were definitely of secondary importance to the industry.

The majority of freshly struck bladelets and flakes appear to have been sufficient for most tasks, as only a small number have been intentionally altered. They were sometimes retouched, occasionally to produce other tools but more often to thin, straighten, or sharpen a working edge or to blunt an unused one. Different forms of retouch were probably used for adapting the bladelets or flakes to different functions.

Aside from the tool-specific techniques used in the production of implements such as burins, several other techniques were used to modify bladelets and flakes at M'lefaat. A simple form of retouch restricted to the margins of the implement and resulting in the appearance of a series of small, shallow, round or ovate contiguous flake scars perpendicular to the edges is most often represented. The regularity of the scarring and the differential patination where it occurs suggest that these examples have been deliberately altered. This was probably accomplished through the direct application of a pressure tool to the stone with a minimum of edge preparation. (The removal of long lamellar flakes requiring platform preparation was not seen in the M'lefaat industry.) Simple shallow retouch as described above appears on a variety of bladelets as well as on reamers, perforators, and some scrapers, suggesting a uniformity of technique. Some notching also resulted from the unifacial removal by pressure of round microflakes. Steep marginal retouch, usually on bladelet ends rather than lateral edges (e.g., scrapers), was accomplished either through pressure or percussion.

Edge dulling that produced crushed or very steep edges (too abrupt to be cutting edges) may have been to facilitate hafting or the use of an implement without hafting it. This was accomplished either through percussion or pressure. Although burins were found, the use of the burin technique to blunt or back an edge of other bladelets has not been identified. It is likely that a large number of the tools recovered were hafted, although there is no direct evidence of this procedure.

General Description (tables 55-56; figs. 240-42)

The analysis of the chipped stone industry of M'lefaat is based on a collection of 1,687 pieces, of which 221 have been classified as chipping debris. Approximately 78% (1,313) of these are from I, 11% (186) from II, and 11% (189) from III. The collection appears primarily as a small bladelet industry, with the majority of the bladelets produced by the pressure technique. The industry is technologically homogeneous throughout the excavation, though there do seem to be some differences in function or utilization of the tools from one operation to another.

Bladelets used as tools or modified to make other tools constitute approximately 80% (1,182) of the industry. Very few bladelets or flakes, however, have been extensively altered before use. Unmodified or only minimally modified pieces seem to have been sufficient for most of the tasks performed. Most of the tools are made of flint ranging in color from a yellowish gray to an olive black. Only 9 obsidian examples were recovered—3 from I,1, 4 from II, and 2 from III,1.

Chipping Debris

Material exhibiting discernible characteristics of flaking but no signs of use or retouch that would put it into another category is included here. Largely the by-product of the reduction process, this material is of particular value for technological reconstruction. It has been subdivided into classes on the basis of shared attributes that broadly represent various stages in the manufacturing process. With the exception of one small blade core of obsidian (from II), all pieces of chipping debris are of flint.

Bladelet cores (fig. 240:1-3).—Thirty-two bladelet cores were found in the excavation. These cores are circular to oval in cross section and have an elongated, sometimes conical, outline. Their platforms are flat, or in several instances (from I,1 and I/1) slightly concave, occurring at right angles to the long axis of the piece. The platform may appear as a single flake scar but usually exhibits multiple flake scarring. None show evidence of grinding or abrasion.

The majority of the cores (22) show that thin symmetrical bladelets (ranging from 2 to 9 mm in width) have been removed in a unidirectional fashion from the platform toward the tip. There are two cases from I,1 that show multidirectional bladelet removal. On only two cores (from I,1 and I/1) do the thin bladelet scars extend entirely around the circumference of the core, resulting in an oval to round cross section. The others exhibit a "backing," usually a broad single or multiflaked facet and/or a cortex remnant. This frequently represents one third of the circumference of the core and results in a more rectangular core cross section.

Ten cores (4 from I,1, 3 from II, and 1 each from I/1, I,1-3, and III,2) exhibit irregular bladelet scarring around their periphery, with pronounced erratic compression rings and frequent step and hinge fractures. These attributes suggest the use of the percussion technique in bladelet production. Several of these (from II) may have resulted from a breakdown in the pressure removal series, however. One core from I,1 and 1 from I/1 show multidirectional bladelet removal.

All 32 cores range from 11 to 35 mm in height and average 25 mm. Their platforms average 15 × 21 mm. All are of a fairly hard (ca. 7-8) cherty flint, and range in color from a light olive gray to an olive black. One small obsidian core (from II; fig. 240:3) was recovered.

Flake cores (fig. 240:4-6).—Fourteen cores exhibit the multidirectional removal of flakes of various shapes and sizes. These cores are roughly spheroid to cuboid in appearance and have irregular broad flake scarring over much of their surfaces. None of them can be specifically referred to as a prepared core. All seem to have resulted largely from a more or less random reduction of river cobbles. It appears that either the natural cortex surface or a flake scar was used as a platform. There is no evidence of grinding or abrasion in the making of platforms. One example (from I,1) has only a few flakes removed and may have been the result of material testing. These cores range from 18 to 36 mm in diameter, averaging 24 mm. They range in color from a very pale orange to grayish red. All but two examples (1 from I/1 and 1 from I,5) have cortex.

Core portions (fig. 240:7-8).—Ten core fragments preserve the majority of the core's circumference and a part of the flaking surface, exhibiting relatively uniform bladelet scars. Eight of the 10 examples are the heels of cores (fig. 240:7-8). One of the examples (from I,1) includes its original striking platform. All range in length from 13 to 22 mm and average 16.6 mm. They vary in color from very light gray to dark gray. Six have some cortex.

Core tablet flakes (fig. 240:9-10).—Eight roughly discoidal flakes exhibit what appears to be a core's striking platform on their dorsal face. Around the edges of these flakes can be seen the truncated top ends of flake or bladelet scars from the striking platform's periphery. The more complete examples are oval in outline and show evidence of flake or bladelet removal around one half to three quarters of their perimeter (fig. 240:9). The remaining edge may be absent, or it may have cortex or multiflake scarring. Five of the 8 examples have bulbs of force on their ventral surfaces, implying that they were removed from the core by a horizontal blow. Crushing and battering marks around the platform edges suggest that these flakes were removed to revive the striking platform. The majority of the platforms show multiscarring. The 8 flakes average 18.25 × 23.87 mm in size. They range in color from light olive gray to brownish gray.

Platform section flakes.—Two other examples (from I,1 and I,3) include part of the flaking surface, exhibiting blade scars and a much smaller portion of the working platform than the core tablet flakes do. These are slightly crescent shaped. Neither has any cortex.

Bladelet core wall flakes (fig. 240:13).—Seventeen more or less rectangular flakes and flake fragments exhibit relatively uniform bladelet scars that cover their dorsal face parallel to the longitudinal axis. Several (from II and III,1) exhibit what appears to be a crushed or receding platform at the proximal end. In addition, 7 bladelet core wall flakes have been used as side scrapers (see p. 678) and 2 as end scrapers (see p. 677).

Primary cortex flakes.—The dorsal surfaces of 17 flakes and flake fragments were entirely covered by cortex.

Unused flakes.—Twenty-nine flakes and flake fragments exhibit no evidence of use-wear or retouch. Fifteen of them have cortex and are between 10 and 20 mm in width. Five more without cortex are of equal width. They vary in color from light olive gray to dark reddish brown.

Crested bladelet (fig. 240:11).—One long, rather thin bladelet (30 × 7 mm) of triangular section has flakes at right angles to the midrib.

Secondary crested bladelets.—Eleven elongated bladelike flakes bearing multiple flake scars at right angles to their longitudinal axis over approximately one half of the dorsal face were identified. They are triangular in cross section. They range in length from 17 to 51 mm; the mean length is 31 mm. They range in width from 10-17 mm; the mean width is 13.63 mm. They vary in color from yellowish brown to brownish gray.

Miscellaneous (fig. 240:12).—Eighty unspecialized flakes, flakelike bladelets, and angular chunky fragments with limited flaking over some of their surfaces may be by-products of the reduction process. Some exhibit parallel bladelet scars and may be the by-products of bladelet making. Five flakes (2 from I,1, 2 from I,4, and 1 from III,1) end in hinge fracture, and 1 (from I,1) suggests an attempt to remove a large number of step fractures. Many of these pieces have a large bulb of force, erratic percussion rings, and other features suggesting the use of the percussion technique. A large number of flakes and chips that exhibit one or more negative flake scars from previous flake removals have cortex covering part of their dorsal surfaces. Some of this debris may have resulted from natural flaking.

Cutting and Scraping Tools—Bladelets

Nibbled bladelets (fig. 241:3-5).—One hundred and fifty-seven bladelets and bladelet fragments are marked along one or more of their lateral edges by a regular pattern of small squamous flake scars resulting from use. (There are approximately 8 scars per 10 mm.) A number also exhibit light polish, although little abrasion was noted. Where nibbling occurs on only one edge, light to moderate wear—usually crushing and small-scale flake scarring—may appear on other parts of the bladelets. No pattern in its occurrence was noted, however.

Most of these bladelets and bladelet fragments were recovered from operation I, although 12 were found in II and 12 in III. Approximately 56% of them (86) are between 5 and 10 mm in width. Four obsidian bladelets (1 from I,1 and 3 from II) were recovered. These are all less than 10 mm in width. The remaining examples are all of flint varying in color from yellowish gray to olive black. Approximately 9% (14) exhibit cortex.

Notched bladelets (fig. 241:6-9).—Seventy-five bladelets and bladelet fragments are marked by a distinct notch or notches on one or more edges. Twenty-two of the bladelets exhibit unifacial notching accomplished through the removal of multiple small flakes by pressure. The remainder appear to have been notched through edge use; in a small number this may have occurred accidentally. Six bladelets and bladelet fragments exhibit multiple notches (fig. 241:6). All notches occur on the bladelets' lateral edges. Other forms of wear, including dulling and chipping, also occur on these implements.

These examples were recovered from all three operations. Approximately 71% (50) of them are between 5 and 10 mm in width. All are made of flint and range in color from a yellowish gray to an olive black. Seven examples have cortex.

Backed bladelets (fig. 241:15-17).—There are 16 bladelet fragments with backing in the form of steep retouch along one edge. All have been broken or snapped transversely at one or both ends. Ten midsections, 3 distal sections, and 3 proximal sections are represented. Wear in the form of crushing and small-scale flake scarring, suggesting light to moderate use, occurs on the unbacked edges. All examples are less than 10 mm wide, their average width being 5.9 mm. All are made of flint varying in color from light brownish gray to black. None of the examples have any cortex.

Miscellaneous retouched bladelets (fig. 241:10-12).—On 35 bladelets and bladelet fragments, regular flake scarring resembling retouch is seen along one or more edges. Although the distinction between intentional retouch and retouch obtained through use is a difficult one to make, a particular regularity in scarring and differential patination where it occurs on the bladelets suggest that these examples have been deliberately altered. Twelve examples exhibit zones of retouch unifacially along one edge only and show evidence of some wear on the other margin. Alternate-opposite retouch is evident on 10 examples. One proximal fragment (from II) has steep, broad retouch around its entire tip. The other examples have been partially retouched along their edges.

All but two bladelets (1 from II and 1 from III,1) were recovered from I. Seventy-one percent (25) of them are between 5 and 10 mm in width. All are of flint and vary in color from pale brown to olive black. None have any cortex.

Used bladelets (fig. 241:13-14).—A total of 815 bladelets and bladelet fragments exhibit wear that occurs mainly as nicking, crushing, or small-scale flake scarring in irregular zones or concentrated in recesses along the edge. Limited abrasion and polish were also noted. Preliminary analysis of a number of these bladelets suggests their use in various activities such as cutting, whittling, etc. This was determined on the basis of differences noted in a number of studies (e.g., Semenov 1964; Frison 1968; Tringham et al. 1974) that have analyzed the effects of both natural and intentional agents on various types of stone. A more systematic appraisal (particularly of patterns of microflaking) would no doubt result in the subdivision of the used bladelet category into several categories representing differences in primary use.

These examples were recovered from all levels with over one half coming from operation I,1. Ninety percent (736) of all examples are less than 10 mm in width. Approximately 64% (525) of them exhibit light to moderate wear as described above and are between 5 and 10 mm in width. There are 3 obsidian examples (1 from I,1 and 2 from III,1). All 3 are less than 10 mm in width. The rest of these bladelets and bladelet fragments are of flint varying in color from yellowish gray to black. Nearly 16% (126) have some cortex.

Unused bladelets.—Twenty-three bladelets and bladelet fragments have no evidence of use-wear or retouch. Of these, 15 are between 5 and 10 mm in width and exhibit no cortex. All are of flint varying from yellowish to brownish gray in color.

Cutting and Scraping Tools—Flakes

Nibbled flakes (fig. 242:13).—There are 19 flakes and flake fragments that are marked by a regular pattern of small squamous flake scarring (approximately 6-7 scars per 10 mm) along one or more edges. Usually this occurs on their longer edges. Slight polish is evident along these edges also, but very little abrasion has been noted. Other wear in the form of light to moderate dulling and chipping does appear elsewhere on the flakes but no particular pattern in its occurrence has been noted.

The size and shape of the flakes are varied; seemingly no attention was given to their overall form. All are of flint varying in color from yellowish gray to reddish brown. Six examples (3 from I,1-3, 2 from II, and 1 from III,1) have cortex.

Notched flakes (fig. 242:14-15).—Fourteen flakes and flake fragments exhibiting distinct notching on one or more of their edges were recovered. Four (2 from I,1 and 2 from I/1) exhibit unifacial notching accomplished through the removal of multiple small flakes—no doubt by pressure. The remainder of the notches appear to have been formed through edge wear, which may be either natural or the result of use. Multinotching occurs on 3 flakes (1 from I,1, 1 from I,1-3, and 1 from III,1). Most notches occur on a flake's longer edge. On 8 of the 14 flakes, the edge opposite the notched edge shows signs of wear.

The size and type of flakes are varied; no attention seems to have been given to their overall form. Two flakes exhibiting hinge fractures (from I,1 and I,1-3) are represented. All are of flint and vary in color from light bluish gray to grayish brown. Five examples (1 from II and 4 from III,1) exhibit cortex.

Used flakes (fig. 242:16).—There are 197 flakes and flake fragments that show wear—mainly nicking, crushing, or small-scale flake scarring—in irregular zones or concentrated in recesses along their edges. Limited abrasion and polish were also noted. Preliminary analysis of a number of these flakes suggests their use in a variety of actions such as cutting, sawing, scraping, whittling, etc. This usage was determined on the basis of differences noted in a number of studies (e.g., Semenov 1964; Frison 1968; Tringham et al. 1974) which have analyzed the effects of both natural and human agents on various types of stone. A more systematic appraisal would no doubt result in the division of the used flake category into several subcategories representing differences in primary use.

These flakes and flake fragments are highly variable in shape and size, being largely the by-products of the reduction process or, in a few cases, of the rejuvenation of blade cores. Faces of blade cores and a number of flakes that exhibit hinge fracture and step flaking are represented. Slightly over one half (83) of these flakes are between 10 and 20 mm in width and show light to moderate wear as described above. All are of flint and range in color from bluish white to grayish black. Approximately 42% (83) show cortex.

Cutting and Scraping Tools—Scrapers (fig. 242:1-12)

Used bladelets, flakes, and their fragments exhibiting a distinctive concentrated edge wear or retouch along one or more margins were recovered. A total of 61 such implements were identified, the majority coming from I,1 (including I/1 and I/1A). Differences in these scrapers, particularly with regard to edge angle (see Wilmsen 1968) and the thickness or breadth of their working edge, may be largely attributed to function. It is notable that retouch occurs only with scrapers made on bladelets, creating a semisteep to steep edge. The remaining scraper edges exhibit use-wear. Most of these scrapers are very small.

End scrapers on bladelets (fig. 242:2-3).—Eight bladelet fragments exhibit semisteep to steep unifacial retouch along one of their transverse edges. The retouch occurs along both proximal and distal bladelet ends—ends that vary from straight to oblique. One example (from II) has been notched on one margin near its working end. Crushing and small-scale flake scarring occur along the lateral margins of several bladelet fragments.

All but one example (from II) were recovered from operation I. All are of flint varying in color from dark yellowish brown to dark reddish brown. None have any cortex.

Side scrapers on bladelets (fig. 242:1).—Eight bladelets and bladelet fragments have concentrated wear or retouch along one or both of their lateral margins. On 2 examples (1 from I,4 and 1 from I/1) this appears as semisteep retouch along the lateral margins. A third example (from I/1) has alternate-opposite wear along its lateral margins and steep unifacial retouch across its proximal end. Various sorts of wear occur unifacially on the other examples. The removal of small flakes from both surfaces on 1 bladelet fragment (from I,1) suggests that it was used in some sort of cutting or sawing action as well as for scraping. The converging edges of a triangular-shaped bladelet fragment (from I,1) are marked by a fine squamous scarring, possibly from use on a soft material. Crushing and small-scale flake scarring appear elsewhere on these bladelets and bladelet fragments, but no pattern in occurrence has been noted.

All 8 examples are from I. All are of flint and vary in color from dark yellowish brown to olive black. One complete bladelet (from I,1; fig. 242:1) has cortex, which serves as a backing, along one lateral edge.

End scrapers on flakes (fig. 242:7-10).—Fourteen flakes and flake fragments are distinguished by a zone of concentrated edge wear (either natural or from use) along one of the transverse edges. This zone is usually opposite the bulb of force and on all but one example is unifacial. This example, a moderate-size chip (from I,1), has a fine pattern of squamous scarring on one end and on one side of its dorsal surface, with crushing and irregular flake scarring occurring on the ventral surface of its opposite lateral margin. Another flake (from I,1) exhibits squamous flake scarring and associated polish as well. A large chunky rectangular-shaped scraper (from I,1) has wear on one end and also along one side (fig. 242:9), but the heaviest wear occurs on the end. A notch appears on the side. Wear along the lateral margins of these scrapers is usually in the form of crushing and small-scale flake scarring and probably cannot be considered part of the working edge of the implements considered here.

The overall shape of the flake received only minimum attention. However, there does seem to have been some selection for chunky angular chips with more mass. All examples are of flint ranging in color from pale yellowish orange to brownish black. Three exhibit cortex. Two are bladelet core wall flakes.

Side scrapers on flakes (fig. 242:4-6).—On 26 flakes and flake fragments there is a zone of concentrated edge wear along one or both of their lateral margins. In no case does this appear as deliberate retouch but instead resembles wear (usually unifacial) that may have resulted from either natural or artificial pressure. In addition, 3 flake fragments (1 from I/1 and 2 from II) show the removal of small flakes from both surfaces, creating a pattern of wear that suggests their use in activities such as cutting or sawing. On 2 examples (1 from II and 1 from III,1) a combination of microflaking and heavy diagonal striations also suggests a cutting action. In these 5 cases the edge angles vary between 30° and 55°. Four examples are marked by a regular small squamous flake-scarring and associated polish, suggesting their use in scraping a soft material. One diamond-shaped flake (from I,1; fig. 242:5) with alternate-opposite retouch along its two converging lateral margins terminates in a sharp, pointed tip. Wear in the form of crushing and small-scale flake scarring appears elsewhere on the flakes and flake fragments, but no pattern in its occurrence was noted.

The overall shape of the flakes received minimum attention, but there does seem to be some selection for more bladelike flakes that have a long lateral margin. A cortex backing is to be seen on 10 flakes, along one of their lateral margins. Operation I yielded 7 bladelet core wall flakes. All are of flint varying in color from pale yellowish brown to brownish gray.

Rounded scrapers (fig. 242:11-12).—Concentrations of steep retouch or wear around the semicircular to circular margins of the dorsal surface were found on 5 rather chunky discoid flakes. Three flint flakes (from I/1, I,2, and II) exhibit wear around approximately one half of their periphery (fig. 242:11). A blade core flake (from III,1), also of flint with a cortex backing, has crushing and step-scarring along part of its cortex edge. An obsidian oval-shaped flake (from I,1; fig. 242:12) has been retouched around most of its edges and has a large notch on one side.

Piercing and Reaming Tools

Perforators (fig. 241:18-22).—A total of 24 bladelets and bladelet fragments have been modified by steep marginal retouch concentrated near one of the ends, resulting in very thin pointed tips of triangular to quadrilateral cross section. Of these, 16 examples display alternate-opposite retouch, with that on the ventral side occurring near the end forming the point or tip (fig. 241:19,21). Bilateral retouch that is limited to the working area is characteristic of 8 examples (7 from I,1 and 1 from I/1). Two fragments (both from I,1) have a retouched notch on one edge; on 1 of these fragments the retouching has left a barblike projection (fig. 241:22).

All 24 examples were recovered from I. Three are complete bladelets (1 from I,3, 1 from I,2, and 1 from I,1; fig. 241:19-21). They are 38 mm, 40 mm, and 21 mm in length, respectively. The first 2 of these bladelets have been altered on both ends. One end has been retouched to a point and the other to a diagonal truncation. The remaining 21 examples are all tip fragments varying in length from 11 to 30 mm, with a mean of 18.62 mm. All 24 examples range from 3 to 9 mm in width, averaging 5.6 mm. All are of flint varying from light olive gray to black in color. None have cortex.

Reamers (fig. 241:24-25).—Five bladelets, quadrilateral in cross section and terminating through retouch in slightly narrowed blunted tips, were identified. One bladelet (from I/1) exhibits alternate-opposite retouch, with the ventral face retouch occurring mainly near the tip (fig. 241:25). Only the dorsal surfaces of the remaining 4 have been modified. One example (from I/1; fig. 241:24) has limited bilateral retouch at one end, forming a blunted tip. Use-wear appears elsewhere along its edges. Two bladelets (both from I,1-3) show retouch along one edge and light to moderate dulling and flake scarring on the other. The working ends of all 4 of these examples are their proximal ends. The fifth bladelet (from I/1A) has been retouched bilaterally, forming working tips at both ends of the bladelet.

All 5 examples are from operation I. They range in length from 33 to 43 mm, averaging 37.4 mm. Their mean width is 10 mm, and the width ranges from 9 to 11 mm. All are of flint varying in color from moderate yellowish brown to dusky yellowish brown. None have cortex.

Concave-ended bladelets (fig. 241:26-29).—Sixteen bladelets and bladelet fragments have been retouched along one of the short axes to produce a concave-shaped end. All come from operation I. One bladelet (from I,1-3; fig. 241:27) has two opposing notches near its base. It has been tapered to a point on one end through alternate-opposite retouch. The second complete bladelet (from I,1; fig. 241:26) has been tapered at one end and given a concave base by steep marginal retouch on its ventral face. Its unretouched edges extend as shoulders, and its other end is blunted by heavy wear. These bladelets are 20 mm and 26 mm in length. The remaining 14 fragments (all from I,1) have several combinations of retouch and wear along their edges. Eleven have steep retouch along one margin and have light to moderate wear (in the form of crushing and small flake scarring) along the other. One has alternate-opposite retouch along its edges, and another example has heavy wear (including crushing and abrasion) along both margins of its ventral face. A final example exhibits slight nibbling. These fragments are between 7 and 29 mm in length and average 15.4 mm. The average width of all 16 examples is 7 mm, and the range is from 5 to 9 mm. All are of flint varying in color from pale yellowish brown to grayish brown. None have any cortex.

Table 55.—Chipped Stone Tools

	Operation, level or operation/feature												No. tools	% tools
	I,1	I/1	I/1A	I,2	I,3	I,1-3	I,4	I,5	II	III,1	III,2	III,3		
CHIPPING DEBRIS														
Bladelet cores	11	3	1	--	1	1	--	2	6*	5	2	--	32	14.5
Flake cores	3	2	--	3	--	--	--	2	2	2	--	--	14	6.3
Core portions	8	--	--	--	--	--	--	--	2	--	--	--	10	4.5
Core tablet flakes	4	--	--	--	--	1	--	--	2	1	--	--	8	3.6
Platform section flakes	1	--	--	--	1	--	--	--	--	--	--	--	2	0.9
Bladelet core wall flakes	3	--	2	--	--	--	--	2	4	4	--	2	17	7.7
Primary cortex flakes	2	3	--	--	--	1	--	--	6	4	1	--	17	7.7
Unused flakes	9	8	--	--	1	1	2	--	5	2	1	--	29	13.1
Crested bladelet	--	--	--	--	--	--	--	--	--	1	--	--	1	0.5
Secondary crested bladelets	2	2	--	2	1	--	--	1	--	2	1	--	11	5.0
Miscellaneous	25	13	1	5	--	3	3	3	16	10	1	--	80	36.2
Total	68	31	4	10	4	7	5	10	43	31	6	2	221	--
Percentage	30.8	14.0	1.8	4.5	1.8	3.2	2.3	4.5	19.5	14.0	2.7	0.9	--	100.0
CUTTING AND SCRAPING TOOLS														
Bladelets														
Nibbled	77*	27	4	10	1	11	--	3	12*	12	--	--	157	10.7
Notched	40	13	2	7	1	--	--	--	9	3	--	--	75	5.1
Backed	12	1	--	1	--	1	--	--	--	1	--	--	16	1.1
Miscellaneous retouched	25	3	1	3	1	--	--	--	1	1	--	--	35	2.4
Used	426*	102	19	39	24	34	1	9	77	72*	7	5	815	55.6
Unused	9	6	--	--	--	--	--	--	8	--	--	--	23	1.6
Flakes														
Nibbled	3	4	--	--	--	4	--	--	7	1	--	--	19	1.3
Notched	5	2	--	--	--	2	--	--	1	4	--	--	14	1.0
Used	78	22	5	4	4	13	3	3	24	26	8	7	197	13.5
Scrapers														
End, on bladelets	5	2	--	--	--	--	--	--	1	--	--	--	8	0.5
Side, on bladelets	4	2	--	--	1	--	1	--	--	--	--	--	8	0.5
End, on flakes	10	2	--	2	--	--	--	--	--	--	--	--	14	1.0
Side, on flakes	8	4	1	2	1	3	--	2	3	1	1	--	26	1.8
Rounded	2*	1	--	1	--	--	--	--	--	1	--	--	5	0.3
PIERCING AND REAMING TOOLS														
Perforators	18	2	1	2	1	--	--	--	--	--	--	--	24	1.6
Reamers	2	--	1	--	--	2	--	--	--	--	--	--	5	0.3
Concave-ended bladelets	14	--	--	--	--	2	--	--	--	--	--	--	16	1.1
Shouldered blade	1	--	--	--	--	--	--	--	--	--	--	--	1	0.1
MISCELLANEOUS TOOLS														
Burins	2	--	--	--	--	--	--	--	--	--	--	--	2	0.1
Burin spalls	5	--	--	--	--	1	--	--	--	--	--	--	6	0.4
Total	746	193	34	71	34	73	5	17	143	122	16	12	1,466	--
Percentage	50.9	13.2	2.3	4.8	2.3	5.0	0.3	1.2	9.8	8.3	1.1	0.8	--	100.0

*Indicates the occurrence of obsidian.

Shouldered blade (fig. 241:23).—One bladelet fragment (from I,1) is shouldered by steep marginal retouch confined to its distal end. Its tip has been broken, obscuring any signs of wear suggesting use that might appear there. Light to moderate wear in the form of dulling and flake scarring appears elsewhere on its edges. Its end has been diagonally retouched. It is 25 × 12 mm and is a grayish flint.

Burins (fig. 241:1-2).—One bladelet fragment and one bladelike flake may have served as burins. Each exhibits one or more facets parallel to its long axis or at an oblique angle to it. No other attention seems to have been given to the shaping of the implements, although they undoubtedly did serve a chisellike function. Both artifacts are made of flint, light gray and reddish brown in color. Both are from I,1.

The bladelet fragment (fig. 241:1) has a single facet along one edge where a flake has been removed. Its diagonal end is roughly worn. The opposite edge shows moderate to heavy wear. This example measures 31 × 14 mm. The bladelike flake (fig. 241:2) is thick, and multiple facets appear at both ends. The notch on one edge of this example

Table 56.—Cutting and Scraping Tools

BLADELETS

	Nibbled	Notched	Backed	Miscellaneous retouched	Used
Length* (mm)					
Number	19	9	--	--	110
Mean	33.60	29.71	--	--	29.14
Range	22	34	--	--	31
Length† (mm)					
Number	138	66	16	35	705
Mean	19.50	19.32	16.13	17.44	18.95
Range	33	26	24	30	23
Width (mm)					
Number	157	75	16	35	815
Mean	9.40	9.62	5.87	8.47	9.07
Range	15	18	4	12	10
Thickness (mm)					
Number	157	75	16	35	815
Mean	2.74	2.49	2.00	2.35	2.51
Range	5	5	2	4	4

*Whole bladelets.
†Bladelet fragments.

FLAKES

	Nibbled	Notched	Used
Length (mm)			
Number	19	14	197
Mean	23.77	21.08	29.88
Range	21	16	58
Width (mm)			
Number	19	14	197
Mean	16.16	18.33	19.42
Range	21	15	42
Thickness (mm)			
Number	19	14	197
Mean	5.83	6.42	7.35
Range	11	12	15

SCRAPERS

	End, on bladelet	Side, on bladelet	End, on flake	Side, on flake	Rounded
Length (mm)					
Number	8	8	14	26	--
Mean	15.88	21.13	29.00	33.04	--
Range	27	31	34	36	--
Width (mm)					
Number	8	8	14	26	5
Mean	9.50	9.87	20.93	21.56	23.00
Range	3	6	17	20	15
Thickness (mm)					
Number	8	8	14	26	5
Mean	3.13	3.00	8.85	10.36	11.66
Range	4	3	24	12	3
Edge Angle (°)					
Number	8	8	14	26	5
Mean	67.50	56.87	56.57	49.56	64.00
Range	17	20	22	48	7

does not appear to be a stop notch, since the facet extends the entire length of the edge. The size of this implement is 27 × 17 mm.

Burin spalls.—Six small bladelets resembling burin spalls were recovered (5 from I,1 and 1 from I,1-3). They are long, bladelike, and slightly semicircular in outline and have a triangular to quadrilateral cross section. All are made of flint varying in color from a pale pink to a medium dark gray. The average length for 5 of the 6 is 26 mm.

Ground Stone Tools

An assortment of ground stone materials was recovered from M'lefaat through surface survey and excavation. A combination of flaking, pecking, and grinding was used in the manufacture of these tools. Several of the examples were made of stones or river cobbles that were selected because relatively little alteration of them was needed in order to produce the desired artifact. A perforated oblate spheroid (from II,2; fig. 243:5) is a good example. All of the celts and celt fragments (except for one example from I,2) appear to have first been flaked to obtain the desired shape, particularly the butt and bit ends. Further modification was accomplished through pecking and grinding, largely limited to the bit end. Alterations through manufacture on all of these examples appear to be primarily utilitarian.

The individual ground stone objects recovered during the excavation are described below by category. All ground stone objects recovered from the surface of the site, whether they are now in Chicago or in Iraq, are listed separately under the heading Surface Materials.

Excavated Materials

Perforated oblate spheroids.—One complete example (from III,2; fig. 243:5) and one fragment (from I,1) were found. Both have smoothly ground surfaces and holes drilled through them near their centers. The hole of the complete example was drilled from both sides. This example measures 97 × 36 mm and weighs 486 gm. Both examples are made of limestone.

Rod fragments.—Three rodlike fragments with rounded to oval cross sections and ground and polished surfaces were recovered. All three are broken transversely, and both ends of one example (from III,3) are missing. This fragment is made of metamorphosed limestone and measures 34 mm in diameter. The unbroken end of the second fragment (from I,1-3; fig. 243:4) is flattened and has evidence of heavy pecking and dulling. It measures 27 mm in diameter. The third fragment (from III,1) may have been naturally formed. It measures 11 mm in diameter and is round and polished on its unbroken end.

Ground spheres.—One gray limestone sphere (from I/1) with a smoothly ground surface was found. A large chip has been removed from the surface. The sphere measures 55 mm in diameter and weighs 170 gm.

Beads and bead fragments.—Three examples of possible beads or bead fragments were recovered. One small barrel bead (from I/1) of blue frit or faience is intrusive. It measures 7 × 5 mm. A possible bead fragment of blue stone (malachite?) was recovered from I,2. It measures 4 × 5 mm. A white cylindrical pebble (from III,1) that is rounded in cross section and has truncated ends appears to be a bead blank. It measures 8 × 10 mm.

Celts and celt fragments (fig. 243:1-3).—Both fully ground and chipped and ground stone celts and celt fragments of hard fine-grained material were recovered. A large complete pebblelike celt (from III,1; fig. 243:1) is roughly triangular in outline and has a slightly planoconvex cross section. Its butt is rounded, and the sides are roughly flaked and pecked, diverging toward a ground and polished spatulate bit. Minor chipping and striations occur along the working edge. The celt measures 88 × 42 × 16 mm and weighs 83 gm. Two other possible examples (1 from I,1 and 1 from III,1) have celtlike forms but are incompletely shaped.

Five celt fragments are represented. Two are of bit ends (1 from I,1 and 1 from I/1) and have finely ground and polished surfaces. The latter example has a planoconvex cross section. Three butt fragments (1 from I,1, 1 from I,2, and 1 from I,3) have ground and polished faces and pecked sides. Two roughly rounded butt ends have been chipped and blunted. The butt of the third example (from I,3) is flat and smooth from grinding.

Grinding stones.—According to Broman Morales's field notes, boulder mortars, pestles, and milling stones occurred "in quantity" within the excavation, including one boulder mortar found in III,2. Under it, on the floor below, was a mat impression (fig. 243:6-9). However, there is no additional information on these other artifacts.

Ground stone fragments.—Three unidentifiable fragments with ground stone surfaces were found (1 from I,5 and 2 from III,2).

Surface Materials

Mention should be made of some of the ground stone objects recovered from the surface. Although their provenience is uncertain they may indeed complement the excavated material in giving us some notion of the range of activities pursued by the people of M'lefaat. (As noted on p. 672, very little material from any time later than the occupation period was recovered from the site.) The ground stone surface materials in the Chicago sample consist of a "waisted" pebble disk (82 mm), two celts of naturally worn pebbles with only minor pecking and grinding at their butt and bit ends, and two limestone grinding stones. One of the grinding stones is a large boulder quern, measuring 300 × 160 × 110 mm (fig. 244:3), its broken surface originally pecked and then worn smooth—through grinding—into an oval-shaped depression. The other, a much smaller oval-shaped stone, 145 × 105 × 35 mm (fig. 244:5), has a slightly concave working surface. A combination of pecking and grinding was used in making these grinding stones. Neither has associated plant remains. Among the surface materials in the Baghdad sample are one hammerstone, a pestle fragment, and a quantity of chipped and ground celts and celt fragments. Other items left in Iraq include nine boulder mortars and querns, three more or less complete (two are shown in fig. 244:1-2) and six fragments, a mortarlike bowl (fig. 244:4), and four pebble grinders or milling stones.

Table 57.—Ground Stone Tools

	Operation, level or operation/feature												
	I,1	I/1	I/1A	I,2	I,3	I,1-3	I,4	I,5	II	III,1	III,2	III,3	No. tools
Perforated disks	1	--	--	--	--	--	--	--	--	--	1	--	2
Rod fragments	--	--	--	--	--	1	--	--	-	1	--	1	3
Ground spheres	--	1	--	--	--	--	--	--	--	--	--	--	1
Beads and bead fragments	--	1	--	1	--	--	--	--	--	1	--	--	3
Ground stone fragments	--	--	--	--	--	--	--	1	--	--	2	--	3
Celts and celt fragments	3	1	--	1	1	--	--	--	--	2	--	--	8
Boulder mortars	--	1	--	--	--	--	--	--	--	--	--	--	1
Total	4	4	0	2	1	1	0	1	0	4	3	1	21

Clay Objects

Approximately 40 pieces of shaped clay were recovered; they come mainly from I. Objects lacking any definite characteristics that would facilitate classification by form are referred to here as clay lumps. The remainder—fragments of figurines, rods, balls, simple clay beads, and other deliberately shaped pieces—have been noted. These categories were initially used by Broman Morales in her classification of the Jarmo clay objects. It should be noted that within the Jarmo classification rod fragments are assumed to be largely unidentifiable pieces of "stalk objects."

The clay used in the shaped pieces at M'lefaat ranges from a light brown to a dark yellowish brown. It is relatively homogeneous in color and texture within each piece. As at both Jarmo and Karim Shahir, it was not tempered. Some of the objects appear to have been lightly fired or baked.

The 31 individual objects in Chicago are described below according to their provenience:

Context	Description and measurements
I,1	5 rod fragments: 2 are flattened, oval in cross section, and 13 and 22 mm long; the others are 9, 11, and 14 mm long
	3 round ball fragments: 2 have groovelike depressions on their broken surfaces, indicating that the balls may have been perforated; 10, 12, and 18 mm in diameter
	2 disk or flattened ball fragments: 1 is ca. ½ of a thin planoconvex disk, 21 mm in diameter; the other is ca. ½ of a biconical flattened disk, 26 mm in diameter
	1 rodlike "eared" piece; triangular in cross section due to its pinched back; 32 mm long
	1 clay lump; faint striations on one side that excavator suggests are reed impressions
	1 "collared" rodlike piece; oval in cross section, appliquéd clay forming "collar" at one end; 24 mm long
I/1	3 rod fragments: 1 is more conical in shape, measuring 15 mm in diameter and 27 mm long; other 2 are 18 and 23 mm long
	1 "lipped" clay piece; lipping perhaps caused by thick reed impression
	2 shaped pieces
I/IA	1 flattened rodlike fragment; 19 mm long
	1 planoconvex oval disk; reedlike impressions on its flat side; 16 mm in diameter
	1 clay lump with a deep reedlike impression, 2-3 mm deep and 6 mm wide
	1 shaped piece
I,3	3 shaped pieces
I,1-3	1 rodlike fragment with a "coiled top" at one end tapering toward a round pointed base at the other, suggested by the excavator to be either an arm or leg; 24 mm long
I,5	2 shaped pieces
II	1 human figurine fragment, described by excavator as "small simple seated form," resembling Early Simple Type at Jarmo (fig. 156:1-5); a trunk in a sitting position with one separate extended leg and the other leg chipped away
	1 drop-shaped piece with a sharp projecting point suggested by the excavator to be either an arm or leg

Table 58.—Miscellaneous Materials

	Operation, level or operation/feature												No. objects
	I,1	I/1	I/1A	I,2	I,3	I,1-3	I,4	I,5	II	III,1	III,2	III,3	
Clay objects	13	6	4	--	3	1	--	2	2	--	--	--	31
Worked bone	1	1	1	--	1	--	--	--	--	--	--	--	4
Mat impressions	--	--	--	--	--	--	--	--	3	--	1	--	4
Pigment	--	--	--	--	1	--	--	--	--	--	--	--	1
Worked shell	--	--	--	--	--	1	--	--	--	--	--	--	1
Total	14	7	5	0	5	2	0	2	5	0	1	0	41

WORKED BONE

Four pieces of worked bone were recovered in the excavation. Weathering could be responsible for this small number, although none of these pieces are badly weathered.

One possible haft fragment was found in operation I/1. It was made on the proximal end and part of the shaft of the right humerus of *Ovis*. An oval-shaped hole (8 mm in diameter) was bored under the condyle. The fragment measures 48 × 40 × 33 mm.

Two awls and one awl fragment were also found. One example (from I,3) is described in Broman Morales's field notes as a "small complete awl—bird bone." It is missing from the Chicago collection. The other two examples are an almost intact splinter awl (from I,1) and a splinter awl fragment (from I/1A). Both are of unidentifiable bone. The tip has been broken off the otherwise intact awl. Irregular transverse scratches around the tip end suggest the awl was used in a rotating fashion. The example measures 52 × 15 × 5 mm. The fragment is of the smoothed and polished tip end of a splinter awl. It measures 45 × 7 × 4 mm.

NOTE: The faunal material recovered at M'lefaat has been identified by Priscilla Turnbull and is discussed by her in chapter 22.

MAT IMPRESSIONS (fig. 243:6-9)

Impressions of matting were identified in two operations. Several fragments were recovered from II. The excavator identified another fragment, from III,2, as "on the floor" below a boulder mortar, approximately 0.65 m beneath the surface. Preliminary study by Dr. Jack Harlan, University of Illinois, Champaign-Urbana, indicated that the impressions of long interwoven strips (5-10 mm in width) of material were impressions of wood. Examination of the sections of thicker fragments revealed several layers of these interwoven strips held together by bitumen. It was suggested that this coating and the dryness of the soil were responsible for the preservation of the mat impressions.

PIGMENT

One small lump of red ochre measuring 10 mm in diameter was recovered from operation I,3 at a depth of 0.8-0.9 m.

WORKED SHELL

A pendant of clam shell was recovered from I,1-3. It is rectangular in shape, measuring 24 × 17 mm. A hole (ca. 3 mm in diameter) has been drilled through it about 4 mm from one edge.

CATALOGUE OF ILLUSTRATIONS (figs. 236-44)

FIGURE 236. PLOT PLAN

FIGURE 237. TRENCH SECTIONS

FIGURE 238. OPERATION III

FIGURE 239. OPERATION I

FIGURE 240. CHIPPED STONE
 1 Pyramidal blade core (flint), from I/1
 2 Pyramidal blade core (flint), from I,1
 3 Pyramidal blade core (obsidian), from II
 4 Polyhedral flake core (flint), from I,2
 5 Polyhedral flake core (flint), from I,5
 6 Amorphous flake core (flint), from I,5
 7 Blade core fragment (flint), from I,1
 8 Blade core fragment (flint), from I,1
 9 Blade core fragment, core tablet (flint), from I,1
 10 Blade core fragment, core tablet (flint), from I,1
 11 Blade core fragment, crested blade (flint), from III,1
 12 Flake core fragment (flint), from III,1
 13 Blade core fragment, core wall (flint), from I,5

FIGURE 241. CHIPPED STONE
 1 Burin (flint), from I,1
 2 Burin (flint), from I,1
 3 Nibbled blade fragment (flint), from I,1
 4 Nibbled bladelet fragment (flint), from I,1
 5 Nibbled bladelet fragment (flint), from I,1
 6 Notched blade fragment (flint), from I,1
 7 Notched blade fragment (flint), from I,1
 8 Notched bladelet (flint), from I/1
 9 Notched bladelet fragment (flint), from I,1
 10 Retouched blade (flint), from III,1

11 Retouched blade fragment (flint), from I,1
12 Retouched bladelet fragment (flint), from I,1
13 Used blade fragment (flint), from I/1
14 Used bladelet fragment (flint), from I,1
15 Backed bladelet fragment (flint), from I,1
16 Backed bladelet fragment (flint), from III,1
17 Backed bladelet fragment (flint), from I,1
18 Perforator (flint), from I/1A
19 Perforator (flint), from I,3
20 Perforator (flint), from I,2
21 Perforator (flint), from I,1
22 Perforator (flint), from I,1
23 Shouldered blade fragment (flint), from I,1
24 Reamer (flint), from I/1
25 Reamer (flint), from I/1
26 Concave-ended bladelet (flint), from I,1
27 Concave-ended bladelet (flint), from I,1-3
28 Concave-ended bladelet fragment (flint), from I,1
29 Concave-ended bladelet fragment (flint), from I,1

FIGURE 242. CHIPPED STONE
1 Side scraper on blade (flint), from I,1
2 End scraper on blade fragment (flint), from I,1
3 End scraper on blade (flint), from I/1
4 Side scraper on flake (flint), from I,5
5 Side scraper on flake (flint), from I,1
6 Side scraper on flake (flint), from I,1-3
7 Side scraper on flake (flint), from I,2
8 End scraper on flake (flint), from I,1
9 End scraper on flake (flint), from I,1
10 End scraper on flake (flint), from I,1
11 Rounded flake scraper (flint), from I/1
12 Rounded flake scraper (obsidian), from I,1
13 Nibbled flake (flint), from I,1-3
14 Notched flake (flint), from I,1
15 Notched flake (flint), from I,1-3
16 Used flake (flint), from I/1A

FIGURE 243. GROUND STONE AND MAT IMPRESSIONS
1 Celt, from III,1
2 Celt, from I,3
3 Celt, from I/1
4 Rod fragment, from I,1-3
5 Perforated oblate spheroid, from III,2
6 Mat impression, from III,2
7 Mat impression, from III,2
8 Mat impression, from III,2
9 Mat impression, from III,2

FIGURE 244. GROUND STONE
1 Boulder mortar, from sf
2 Boulder mortar, from sf
3 Boulder quern, from sf
4 Mortarlike bowl, from sf
5 Grinding stone, showing concave surface, from sf

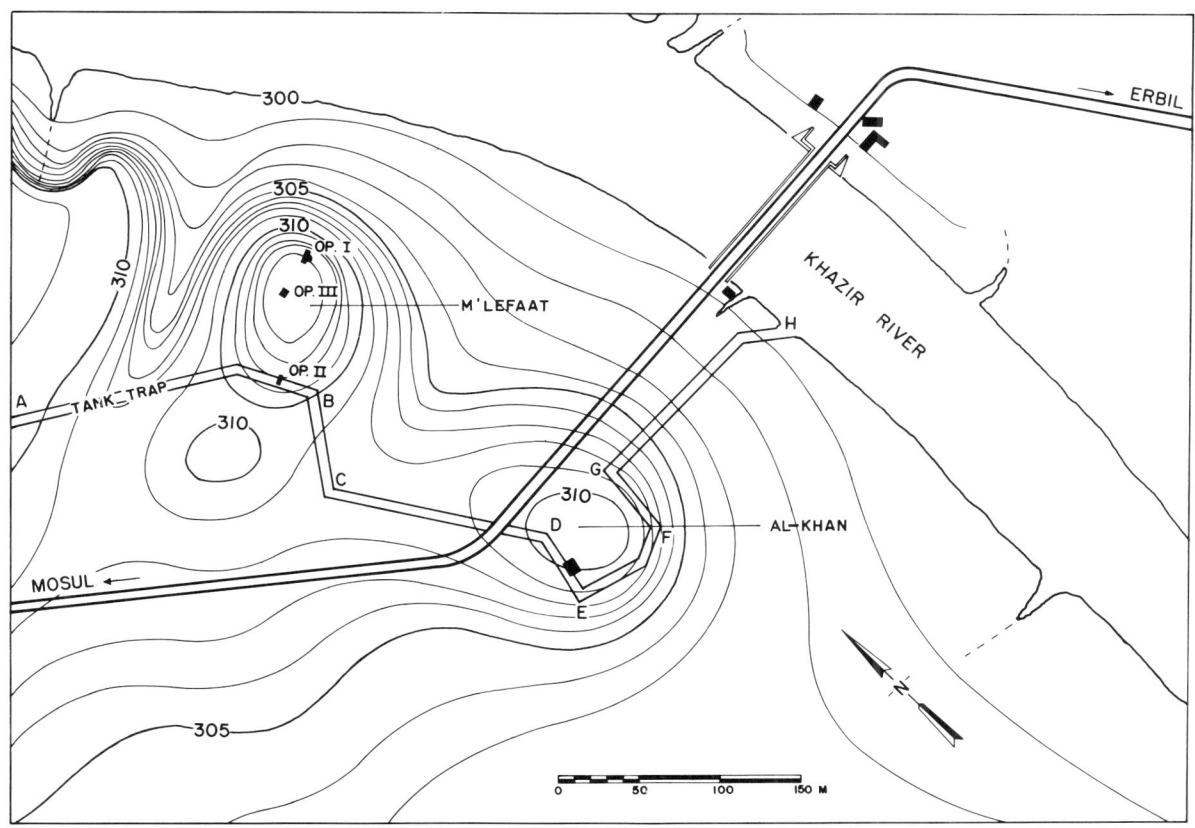

Fig. 236. Plot plan of M'lefaat and al-Khan.

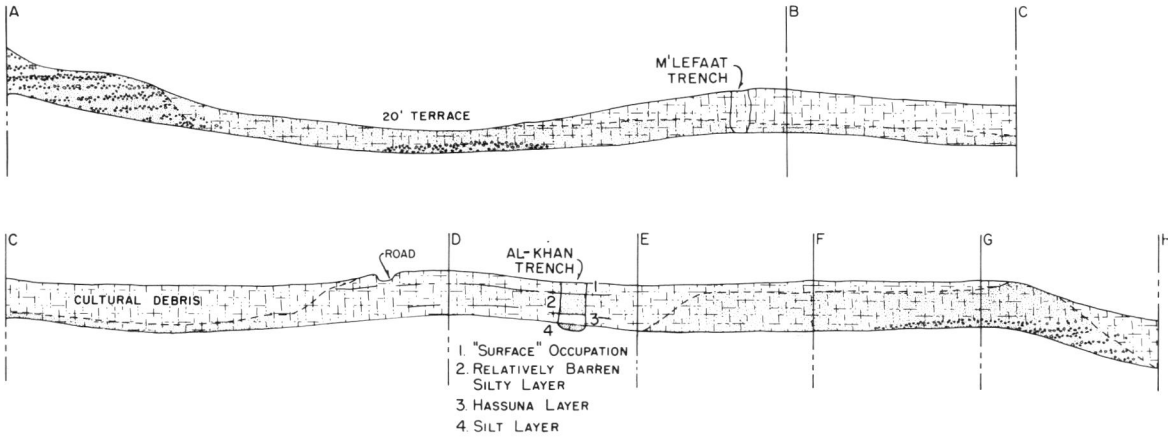

Fig. 237. Diagrammatic section of M'lefaat and al-Khan as it appears on the more northerly face of the tank-trap trench. (From a sketch, not to scale, by H.E. Wright, Jr.)

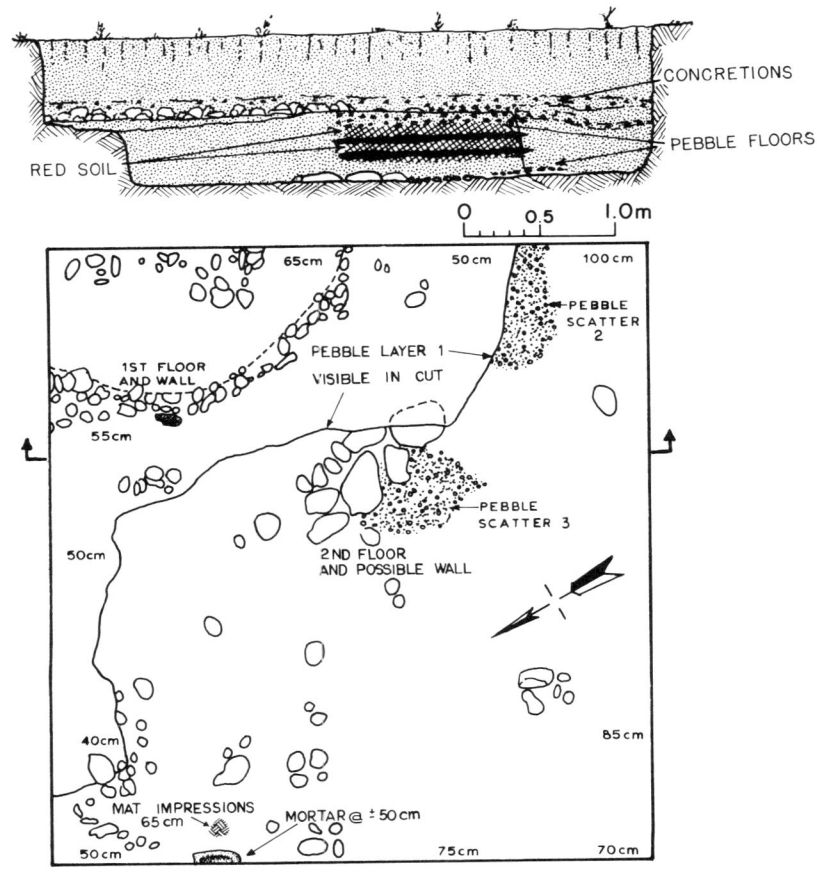

Fig. 238. Section and plan of operation III at M'lefaat.

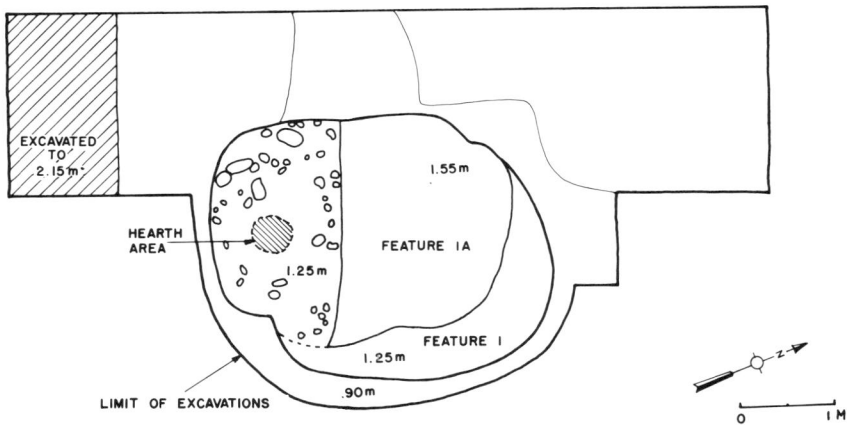

Fig. 239. Plan of operation I at M'lefaat, showing features 1 and 1A.

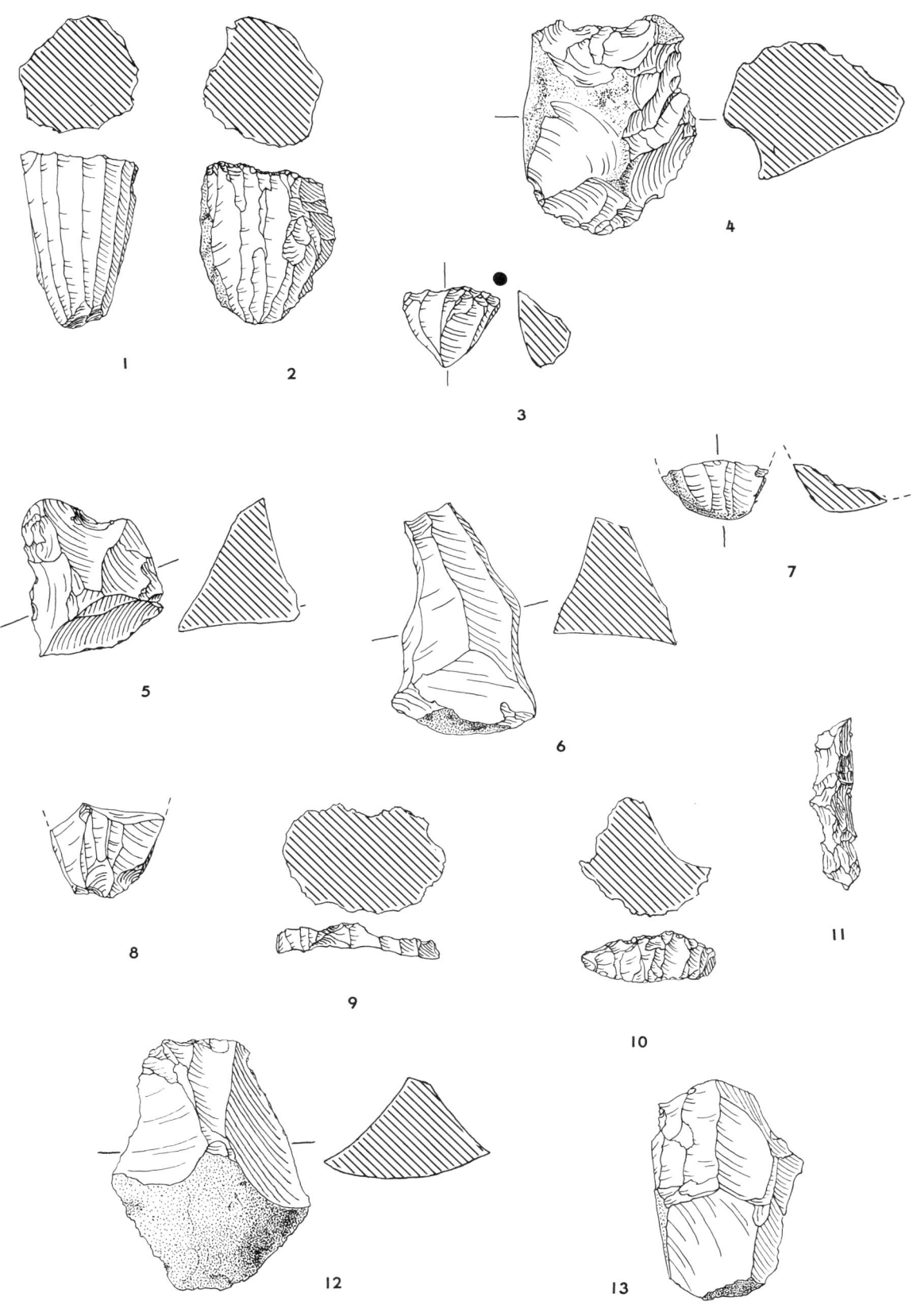

Fig. 240. M'lefaat chipped stone: blade cores, *1-3*; flake cores, *4-6*; blade core fragments, *7-11,13*; flake core fragment, *12*. No. *3* is obsidian; remainder are flint. Scale 1:1.

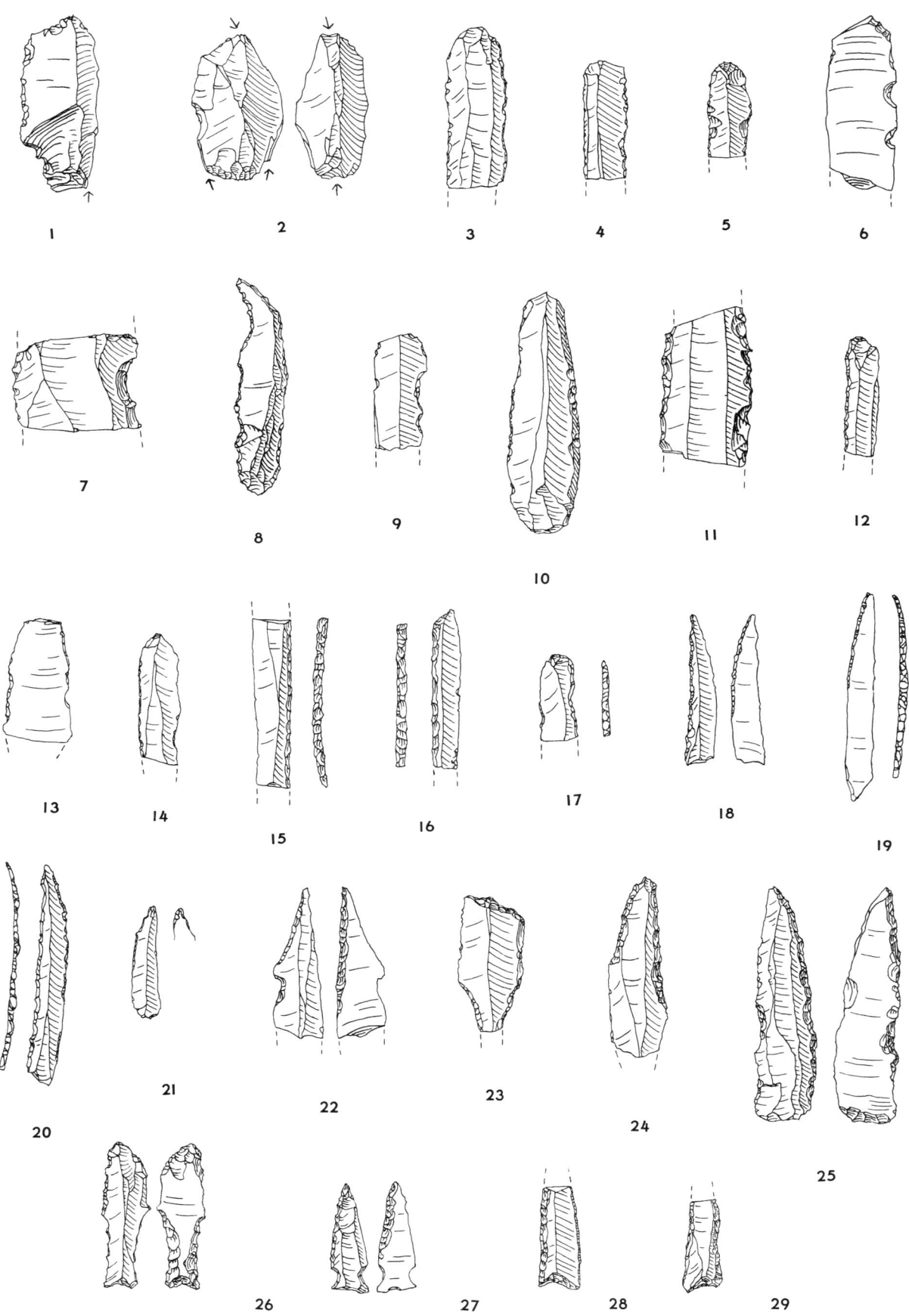

Fig. 241. M'lefaat chipped stone: burins, *1-2*; nibbled blade fragments, *3-5*; notched blade and fragments, *6-9*; retouched blade and fragments, *10-12*; used blade fragments, *13-14*; backed bladelet fragments, *15-17*; perforators, *18-22*; shouldered blade fragment, *23*; reamers, *24-25*; concave-ended bladelets and fragments, *26-29*. All flint. Scale 1:1.

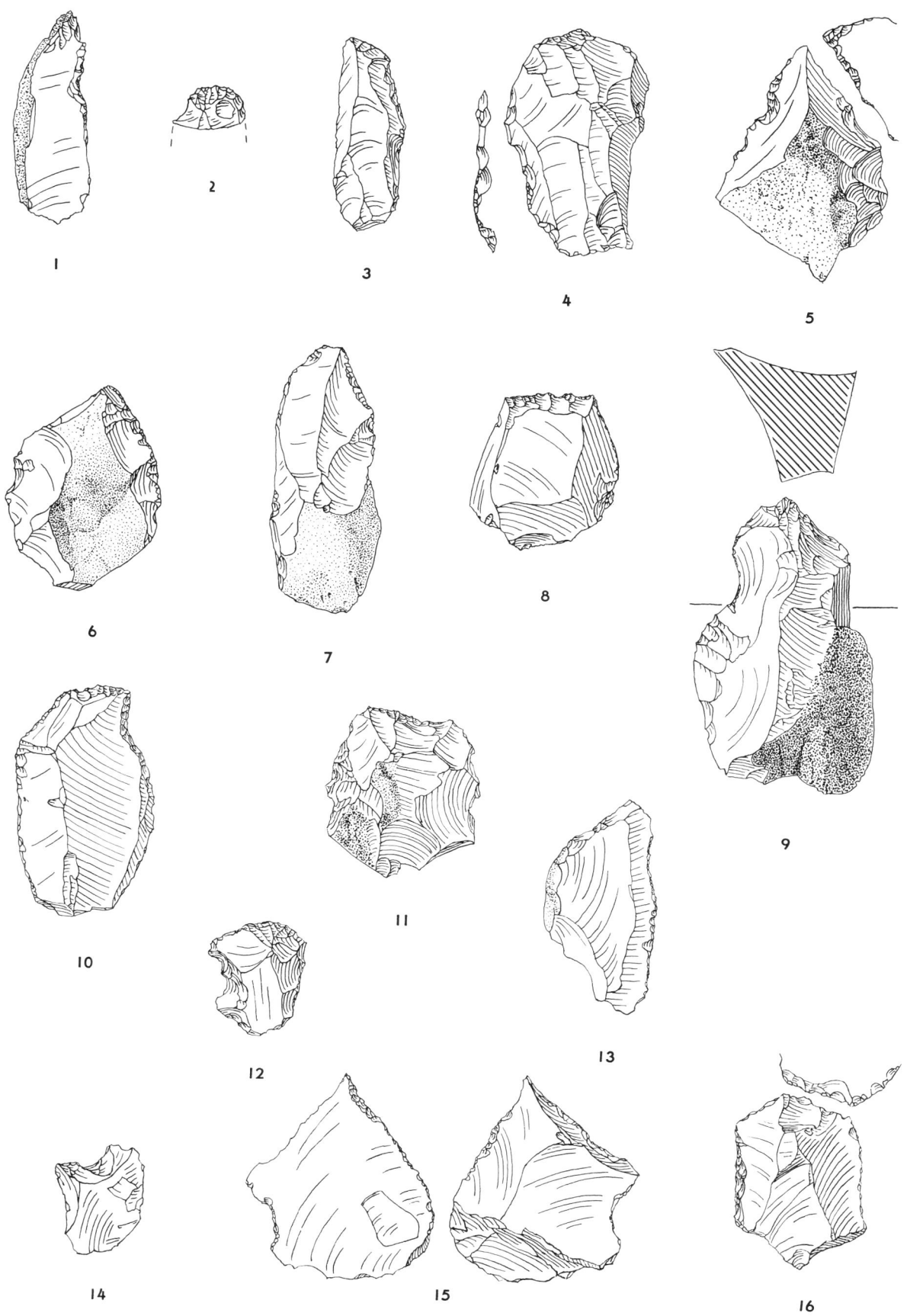

Fig. 242. M'lefaat chipped stone: side scraper on blade, *1*; end scraper on blade and fragment, *2-3*; side scrapers on flakes, *4-7*; end scrapers on flakes, *8-10*; rounded flake scrapers, *11-12*; nibbled flake, *13*; notched flakes, *14-15*; used flake, *16*. No. *12* is obsidian; remainder are flint. Scale 1:1.

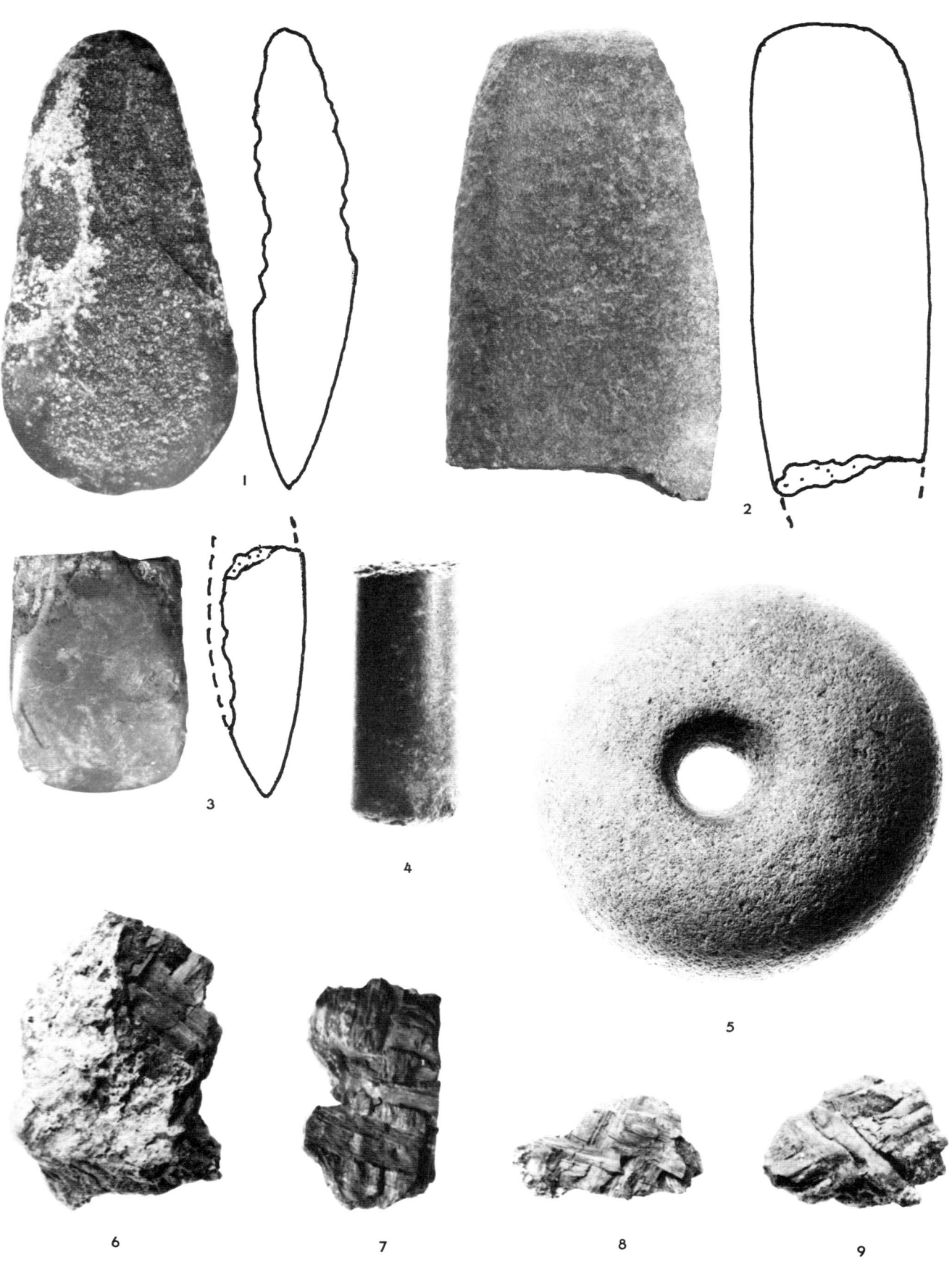

Fig. 243. M'lefaat ground stone and mat impressions: celts, *1-3*; rod fragment, *4*; perforated oblate spheroid, *5*; clay mat impressions, *6-9*. Scales ca. 1:1, *1-3*; ca. 4:5, *4-5*; ca. 6:5, *6-9*.

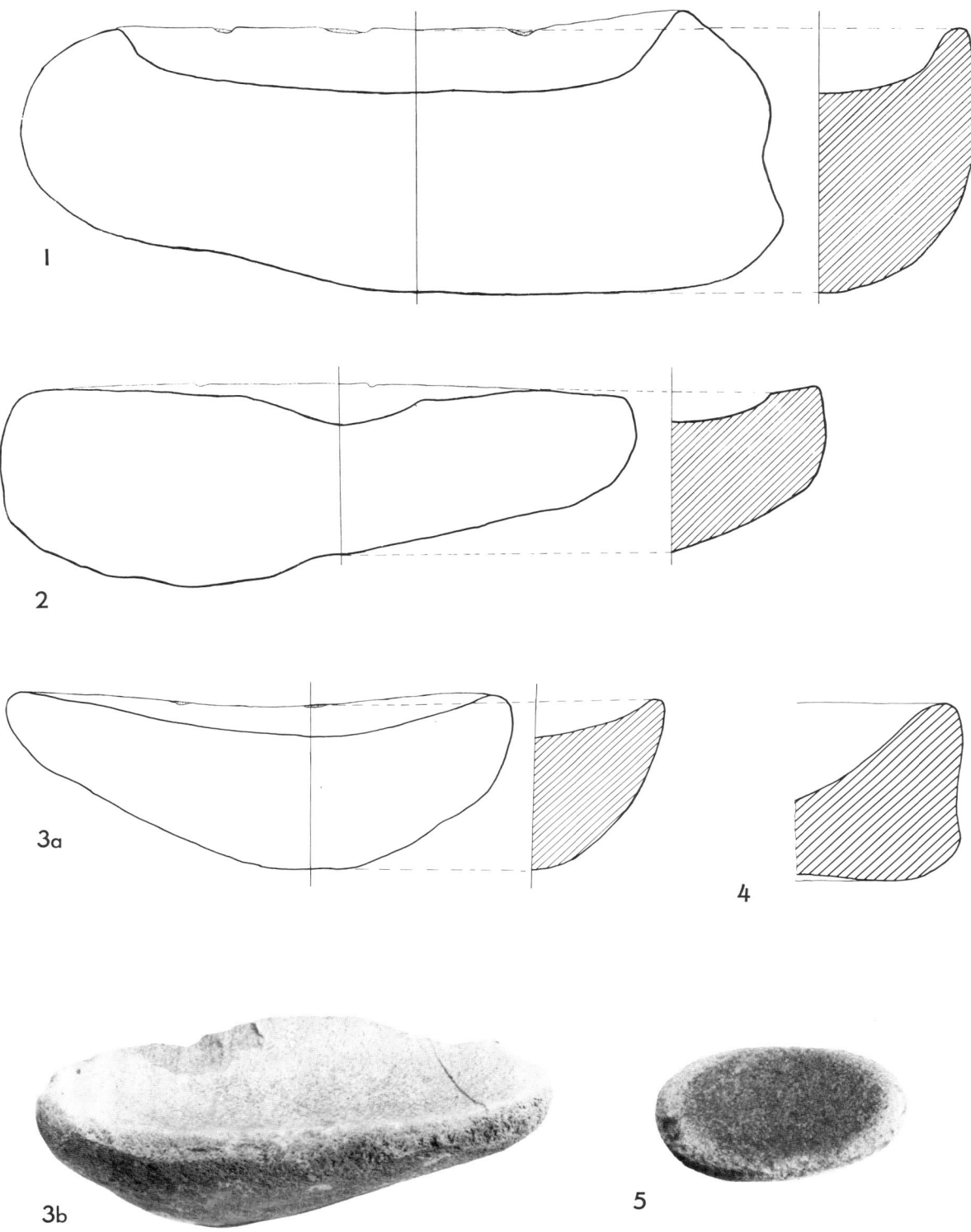

Fig. 244. M'lefaat large ground stone: boulder mortars, *1-2*; boulder quern, *3*; mortarlike bowl, *4*; grinding stone showing concave surface, *5*. Scale ca. 1:4.

REFERENCES

Benedict, Peter
    1963   The assemblage of small objects from Tell M'lefaat. Unpublished manuscript, Department of Anthropology, University of Chicago.

Braidwood, Robert J.
    1954   The Iraq-Jarmo Project of the Oriental Institute of the University of Chicago, season 1954-55. *Sumer* 10:120-38.

Braidwood, Robert J.; Howe, Bruce; et al.
    1960   SAOC 31 (see below).

Crabtree, Don E.
    1972   *An introduction to flintworking.* Occasional Papers of the Idaho State University Museum, no. 28. Pocatello, Idaho.

Frison, George C.
    1968   A functional analysis of certain chipped stone tools. *American Antiquity* 33:149-55.

Gould, Richard A.; Koster, Dorothy A.; and Sontz, Ann H.L.
    1971   The lithic assemblage of the western desert aborigines of Australia. *American Antiquity* 36:149-69.

Great Britain, Naval Intelligence Division
    1944   *Iraq and the Persian Gulf.* Geographical Handbook Series, B.R. 524. London.

Harrison, David L.
    1968   *The mammals of Arabia.* Vol. 2. *Carnivora, Artiodactyla, Hyracoidea.* London: Ernest Benn.

SAOC 31
    1960   *Prehistoric investigations in Iraqi Kurdistan.* Robert J. Braidwood, Bruce Howe, et al. Studies in Ancient Oriental Civilization, no. 31. Chicago: University of Chicago Press.

Semenov, S.A.
    1964   *Prehistoric technology.* Trans. M.W. Thompson. London: Cory, Adams, and Mackay.

Tringham, Ruth; Cooper, Glenn; Odell, George; Voytek, Barbara; and Whitman, Anne
    1974   Experimentation in the formation of edge damage: a new approach to lithic analysis. *Journal of Field Archaeology* 1:171-96.

Wilmsen, Edwin N.
    1968   Functional analysis of flaked stone artifacts. *American Antiquity* 33:156-61.
    1974   *Lindenmeier: a Pleistocene hunting society.* New York: Harper and Row.

22

THE FAUNAL REMAINS FROM M'LEFAAT

Priscilla F. Turnbull

Considering that only four and a half days were spent digging the test trenches at M'lefaat, it is hardly surprising that relatively few bones were recovered. Of the 150 individual bones, virtually every piece has been identified as to species except for some splinters of long bones and rib fragments.

If it is assumed that M'lefaat was either a seasonally occupied or sedentary site adjacent to plots of wild or primitively cultivated grain, a picture emerges of a well-situated homesite, near a wide variety of foods obtainable by both hunting and gathering/cultivating. The fossil record has preserved only part of the available faunal elements and it is necessary to consider the absence of some expected forms.

SUMMARY OF THE FAUNA

A list of the faunal species found at M'lefaat follows:

MAMMALIA	*Canis* ?*lupus* (wolf), *Vulpes vulpes* (red fox), *Felis catus* (wild cat), *Sus scrofa* (wild pig), *Bos primigenius* (wild cattle), *Ovis orientalis* (wild sheep), *Gazella subgutturosa* (gazelle), *Spalax leucodon* (lesser mole rat), Rodentia indet., and *Lepus* sp. (hare)
AVES	*Anas platyrhynchos* (mallard duck), *Anser anser* (gray lag goose) or *A. fabalis* (bean goose), *Accipiter* cf. *gentilis* (northern goshawk), *Tyto alba* (barn owl), and *Corvus corone* (hooded crow)
PISCES	*Heteropneustes fossilis* or *Mysteus pelusius* or *M. colvilli* (catfish)
MOLLUSCA	*Unio tigridis* (freshwater clam) and *Helix salomonica* (land snail)
CRUSTACEA	*Potamon potamios* (freshwater crab)

The bones in this collection have been catalogued in the Division of Paleontology at the Field Museum of Natural History.

The largest number of bones came from operation I, feature 1, a small pit house between levels 1 and 3. The trench called operation II produced a smaller number, and very few came from operation III. Dittemore's report (chap. 21, esp. table 55) shows that the largest concentration of artifactual material also comes from within or is closely associated with the two phases of the pit house in operation I, levels 1-3. Also, although the concentration of artifacts differs in the various tested areas of the mound, consistency of type appears to hold true. SAOC 31 (pp. 50-51) states that "the general run of surface material and the artifacts from our soundings give every appearance of making up a consistent assemblage." Therefore I have treated the fauna as a single entity.

Table 59 is a summary of the kinds of bone of the major game animals present at M'lefaat. Sheep and gazelle together comprise 86% of the total bone and 50% of the minimum number of individuals (MNI has been computed by the same method as that described in Turnbull and Reed 1974, p. 93). No bones of goat could be positively identified in this collection, although a few specimens (e.g., a charred vertebra) may be either sheep or goat. The presence of sheep reflects the terrain; on the flat grassy plain, sheep better withstand hotter summer temperatures than do goats, which also require rougher, rockier terrain. Of course, a larger sample may well have contained significant amounts of goat bones; nevertheless, one has the feeling that had goat been an important food item at M'lefaat, some identifiable remains would have turned up in the test trenches.

Although juvenile sheep bones are present, it is not possible with so small a sample to state that these sheep were domestic; as many bones of juvenile gazelle occur as bones of juvenile sheep.

The proportions of domestic sheep and goat, when present in a fauna, exaggerate the proportions of small bovids present. But the wild fauna, which is expected to reflect quite precisely the site conditions, is often distorted by the "cultural filter" (Reed 1963, p. 210). Of the faunal bones recovered from M'lefaat, on the Khazir River at the border of

---

I am indebted to Dr. Eitan Tchernov, Hebrew University, Jerusalem, for identifying the bird bones for which no comparative osteological collections exist at the Field Museum of Natural History. Loren Woods, formerly curator of fishes at the Field Museum, has helped me with the fish identifications. Professor Charles A. Reed, University of Illinois at Chicago Circle, has made numerous suggestions and comments.

[The manuscript for this chapter was essentially completed by 1977. Very few additions and only minor revisions have been made since that date.—EDS.]

Table 59.—The Bones of Game Animals from M'lefaat

Element	Sus	Bos	Ovis	Gazella	Lepus	Vulpes	Total
Horn cores	--	--	--	1	--	--	
Skull fragments	--	1	--	--	--	--	
Mandibular fragment	--	--	--	1(J)	--	--	
Loose teeth	--	--	1	--	--	--	
Vertebrae	--	--	6	--	--	--	
Scapulae	--	--	4	6	--	1	
Humeri	--	--	1	4	--	2	
Radii/ulnae	1	1	8	6	--	--	
Carpals	--	--	1	2	--	--	
Metacarpals	2	--	4(2J)	2(1J)	--	--	
Pelvic fragments	3	--	--	2	--	--	
Femora	--	--	1	2	--	--	
Tibiae/fibulae	--	--	1	5	2	--	
Tarsals	--	--	5	11	1	--	
Metatarsals	--	--	4(1J)	9	--	--	
Metapodials indet.	--	--	--	5(2J)	2	2	
Phalanges I	--	--	8(1J)	8(2J)	1	1	
Phalanges II	1	--	3	2	--	--	
Phalanges III	--	--	3	7	--	--	
Total no. bones	7	2	50	73	4	6	142
MNI	3	2	4	6	2	2	
% of juvenile bones			8	8			
% of total bones	5	1.5	35	51	2.9	4	
% of MNI	15.5	10.5	21	32	10.5	10.5	

NOTE: J = juvenile.

the piedmont and lower Zagros foothills, 32% are gazelle; these animals were abundant on the plain, within easy reach of the people living at the mound. Of the bones at Karim Shahir and Jarmo (chap. 9) and at Palegawra (Turnbull and Reed 1974)—all in the intermontane valleys—between 6% and 10% are gazelle. Perhaps not quite as optimal a habitat as the open plain, the valleys are still good gazelle country. By the time of Jarmo, there were domestic sheep to replace gazelle. But early, at Palegawra, the percentage of MNI for equids was more than for sheep, goat, and gazelle together! Warwasi, higher up on the Kermanshah plain in Iran, contained no gazelle; the hunters there were concerned almost exclusively with onagers (Turnbull 1975, p. 152). Since the equids normally thrive in the very environment that is favorable for gazelle, choice and convenience rather than strict availability must explain why the faunal list from M'lefaat contains no equids. In other words, the cultural filter was in operation.

Returning to table 59, it is evident that remains of *Bos* are present at M'lefaat, as they are at nearly all the prehistoric sites in the area of southwestern Asia. This genus is present always as a small percentage of the fauna, but it undoubtedly represents a desirable game animal and a ubiquitous one since it is found from the piedmont plain to the foothills and open forests. Specimen P27753, part of the proximal end of a left radius, is so large that it must be considered *Bos primigenius*.

Cervus elaphus, red deer, is a large game animal that is important at many sites but does not appear in the inventory at M'lefaat. Possibly the environment was inimical to deer, or again chance may have excluded it from this small collection. The smaller fallow deer, *Dama mesopotamicus*, is another cervid that might be expected in this fauna, as might also the little roe deer, *Capreolus capreolus*. Cervids were evidently absent or rarely available in the area, or else the cultural choice of the hunters was to disregard them.

The bones of pig, *Sus scrofa*, at M'lefaat are large, particularly the two metacarpals that are probably from the same individual and are certainly from wild stock. Measurements are as follows:

	Maximum length (mm)	Distal width (mm)
L. metacarpal III	96.2	25.0
L. metacarpal IV	94.2	22.4

Wild equids (hemiones, onagers, or wild half-asses all applicable names) are animals of the grassland-steppe, yet are absent from Matarrah (chap. 9) as well as from M'lefaat. It is doubtful that their absence from the archeological sites just mentioned should be interpreted as absence from the area. Killing these large, fleet animals may well have been beyond the capabilities of these hunters, though not of the more ancient hunters who occupied Palegawra and Warwasi shelters some thousands of years earlier. The easy availability of medium-sized sheep and gazelles made it unnecessary for hunters to tackle these much larger equids. If more grain was being consumed by the time of M'lefaat, there was less dependence on large animals.

Hares, *Lepus ?capensis*, were ubiquitous in southwestern Asia and probably were often trapped by women and children. The mole rat, *Spalax leucodon*, may have been present in the vicinity of the mound. Many other rodents were found represented in the bone inventory from Jarmo, Palegawra, and Warwasi.

The small number of bones of fox, *Vulpes vulpes*; wild cat, *Felis catus* (distal end of a left tibia, P27840, smaller than that of *F. chaus* in FMNH); and possibly wolf, *Canis lupus* (distal end of a metatarsal, P27739; this specimen might possibly be identified as dog, *C. familiaris*) from M'lefaat may also represent food animals that were rather rare.

For so small a collection, identifications of bones of birds from M'lefaat are especially welcome. The skill of these hunters at birding is attested by the presence of bones of duck, goose, owl, hawk, and crow. The ducks were hunted on the river, and the geese would often be found in the area during migration or wintering.

Catfish spines, possibly of the genera and species *Heteropneustes fossilis*, *Mysteus pelusius*, and/or *M. colvilli* were identified. The several vertebrae and a hyomandibular fragment are not identifiable.

The presence of shells of the pelecypod *Unio tigridis* indicates that the meat of freshwater clams was eaten at the site. The claw of a crab, probably *Potamon potamios*, is further evidence that the river was exploited by the people of M'lefaat. The edible land snail, *Helix salomonica*, was present as well. More extensive excavation would surely produce many more remains of invertebrates, birds, fishes, and small mammals.

CONCLUSIONS

It is risky to draw many firm conclusions about a fauna when the sample is as small as this one. All indications are that these late hunting-gathering people were utilizing the food animals (and plants as well, of course) from the immediate vicinity, which differed to a greater or lesser degree from the other sites in northern Iraq-Iran. The bone from this piedmont site consists mainly of remains of desert gazelle and grassland sheep. East of this area, at sites in the intermontane valley zone of the Zagros chain, remains of goats are more numerous, as well as bones of equids and large cervids, none of which were found in the small sample excavated at M'lefaat. Absence from the mound, however, does not imply total absence from the vicinity in the case of the equids and perhaps the cervids as well. Undoubtedly, herds of onager swept over the piedmont, but these animals may have been very difficult for hunters to kill. The local environment perhaps put limits on the hunters.

M'lefaat exemplifies a living site to which hunters brought the game that was the most easily found, killed, and butchered. Large, fleet hemiones, running in herds, perhaps could not be caught easily by small hunting parties in the open. It is also probable that preference for meat of sheep and gazelle played a significant part in explaining the absence of the bones of large and medium-sized cervids. Thus the environment may have contained more available game than could or would always be exploited.

From the list of bones in table 59 it is apparent that whole carcasses were not brought back to M'lefaat. Since practically no fragments of skull, jaws, or even teeth occur and most of the bones are those of legs or feet, it seems evident that these hunters carried back only the meatiest portions of the kill to their living site.

Hunting occurred out in the piedmont-steppe, home of the gazelle, fox, and hare, or in the grassy hills where sheep abounded, or along the river where cattle and pigs found water and shelter in the trees and shrubs that grew beside it. Butchering was done at the site of the kill, where much of the bone was discarded. By the time M'lefaat and other open-air sites were being occupied, it may not have been necessary to be as dependent on large game if cereals were being exploited.

REFERENCES

Braidwood, Robert J.; Howe, Bruce; et al.
   1960   SAOC 31 (see below).

Reed, Charles A.
   1963   Osteo-archaeology. In *Science in Archaeology*, ed. Don Brothwell and Eric Higgs, pp. 204-16. New York: Basic Books.

SAOC 31
   1960   *Prehistoric investigations in Iraqi Kurdistan*. Robert J. Braidwood, Bruce Howe, et al. Studies in Ancient Oriental Civilization, no. 31. Chicago: University of Chicago Press.

Turnbull, Priscilla F.
   1975   *The mammalian fauna of Warwasi rock shelter, west-central Iran*. Fieldiana: Geology, vol. 33. Chicago: Field Museum of Natural History.

Turnbull, Priscilla F., and Reed, Charles A.
   1974   *The fauna from the terminal Pleistocene of Palegawra Cave, a Zarzian occupation site in northeastern Iraq*. Fieldiana: Anthropology, vol. 63 (3). Chicago: Field Museum of Natural History.